Acclaim for Jung Chang and Jon Halliday's

MAO

THE UNKNOWN STORY

"Provocative. . . . It moves at a brisk pace and is filled with evocative descriptions of dramatic events." —*Chicago Tribune*

"Amazing. . . . It is hard to imagine a more thoroughly researched biography. . . . Powerful and absorbing." —*The New York Sun*

"If any single book in our own time has the capacity to change the course of history, this is it. The story is so shocking that reading it literally takes your breath away." —*The New Criterion*

"No reader can be unmoved by this book's passion, or unimpressed by the mountain of evidence upon which it rests. . . . This is the book that will wreck Mao's reputation beyond salvage." —*Commentary*

"Groundbreaking. . . . Meticulous and comprehensive. . . . An excoriating portrait." —*Vogue*

"An entertaining and, for the big picture, an ultimately informative book about a figure ever ready for reexamination." —*Time*

"Mind-boggling. . . . Copiously researched . . . brimming with interviews and facts. . . . This astonishing book is a must-read." —*USA Today*

ALSO BY THE AUTHORS

BY JUNG CHANG

Wild Swans

BY JON HALLIDAY

Sirk on Sirk

The Psychology of Gambling
(coeditor Peter Fuller)

The Artful Albanian

JUNG CHANG

JON HALLIDAY

M·A·O

THE UNKNOWN STORY

Jung Chang was born in Yibin, Sichuan Province, China, in 1952. During the Cultural Revolution (1966–1976) she worked as a peasant, a "barefoot doctor," a steelworker, and an electrician before becoming an English-language student and, later, an assistant lecturer at Sichuan University. She left China for Britain in 1978 and was subsequently awarded a scholarship by the University of York, where she obtained a Ph.D. in linguistics in 1982, the first person from the People's Republic of China to receive a doctorate from a British university. Her award-winning book, *Wild Swans*, was published in 1991, and has sold more than 10 million copies in thirty languages.

Jon Halliday is a former Senior Visiting Research Fellow at King's College, University of London. He has written or edited eight previous books.

M·A·O

THE UNKNOWN STORY

JUNG CHANG

JON HALLIDAY

ANCHOR BOOKS

A DIVISION OF RANDOM HOUSE, INC.

NEW YORK

FIRST ANCHOR BOOKS EDITION, NOVEMBER 2006

The Library of Congress has cataloged the Knopf edition as follows:
Chang, Jung.
Mao : the unknown story / Jung Chang and Jon Halliday.—1st ed.
p. cm.
Includes bibliographical references and index.
1. Mao, Zedong, 1893–1976. 2. Heads of state—China—Biography.
I. Title: Unknown Story. II. Halliday, Jon. III. Title.
DS778.M3C38 2005
951.05'092—dc22
[b] 2004063826

Anchor ISBN-10: 0-679-74632-3
Anchor ISBN-13: 978-0-679-74632-4

Author photograph © Lisa Weiss
Book design by Pamela G. Parker

www.anchorbooks.com

Printed in the United States of America
10 9 8

CONTENTS

PART SIX —*Unsweet Revenge*

LIST OF ILLUSTRATIONS

Photograph no. 10, by Auguste François, is reproduced by permission of Réunion des Musées Nationaux; no. 14, by Cecil Beaton, by permission of the Beaton Estate; no.16, by permission of Getty Images; no. 19, by permission of Wang Dan-zhi; nos. 29 and 39, by permission of the Rossiiskii Gosudarstvennyi Arkhiv Kinofotodokumentov (the Russian State Archive of Cine-photo Documents); nos. 34 and 49, by Henri Cartier-Bresson, by permission of Magnum Photos; no. 45, by Du Xiu-xian; no. 53, by Lu Hou-min; nos. 61, 63, 64 and 65, by Li Zhen-sheng; nos. 67, 72, 76 and 77, by Du Xiu-xian.

LIST OF MAPS

Maps by ML Design, London

LIST OF ABBREVIATIONS IN TEXT

CCP	Chinese Communist Party
Cominform	Communist Information Bureau
Comintern	Communist International
CP	Communist Party
8RA	Eighth Route Army
GRU	Glavnoye Razvedyivatelnoye Upravleniye (Chief Intelligence Directorate), Soviet Military Intelligence
N4A	New Fourth Army
ZZZ	Zhang Zhi-zhong

NOTE ABOUT SPELLING IN TEXT

Chinese personal names are given surname first. In some cases, where people have a very common surname, we refer to them by their given names after first mention. We have spelled the names so as to make them as distinctive and easily recognizable as possible. For those not in *pinyin* (the official Mainland system), the *pinyin* version is given in the index.

For place names, we have used *pinyin*, except for Peking (Beijing), Yenan (Yan'an), Canton (Guangzhou), and the islands of Quemoy (Jinmen) and Matsu (Mazu).

China

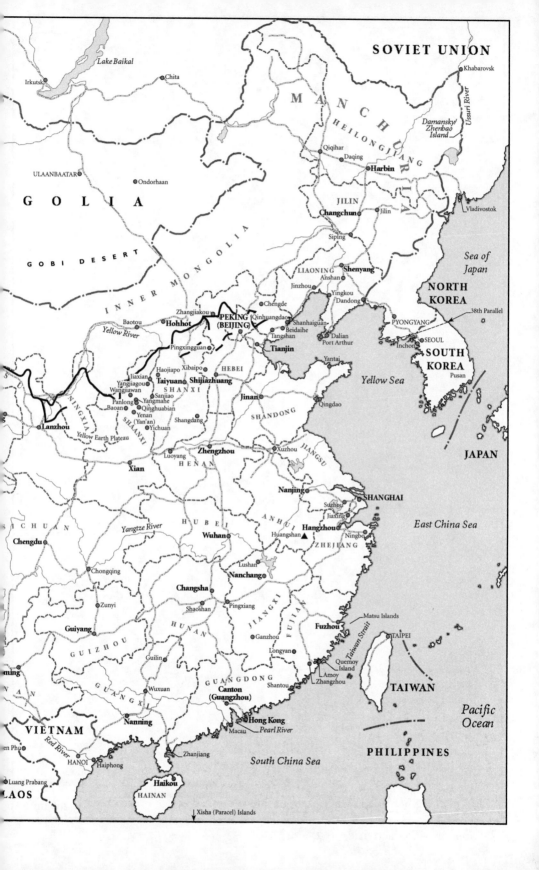

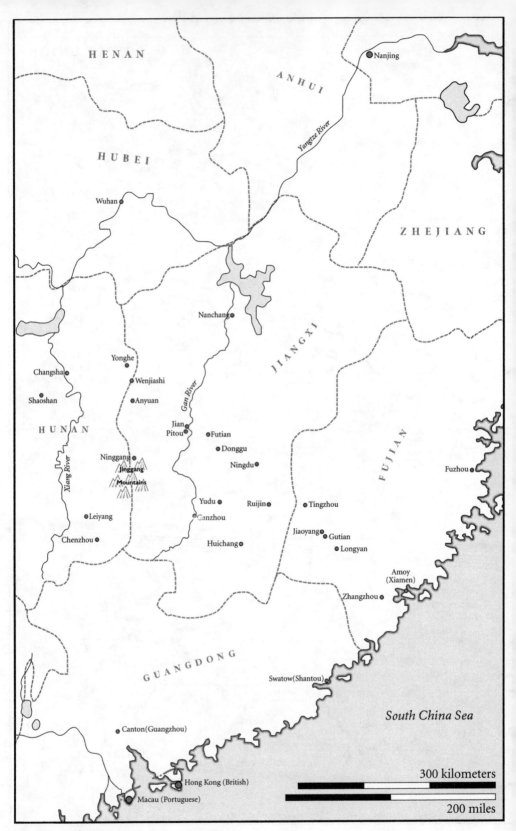

The area of Mao's activities, 1927–34

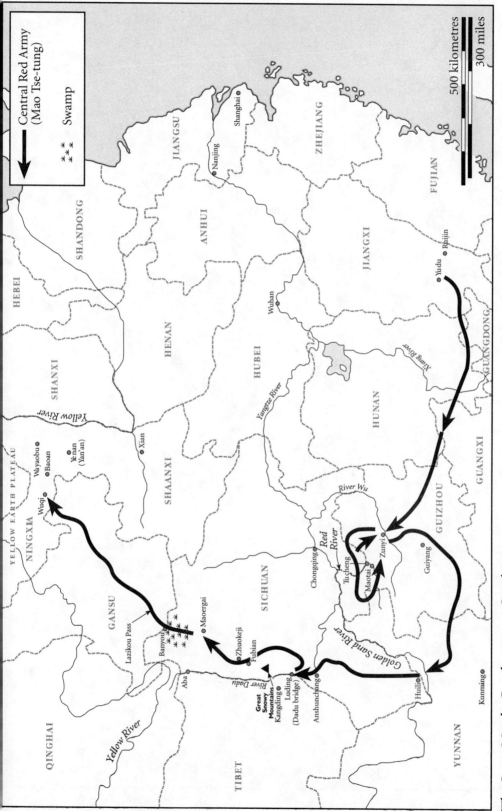

The Long March, October 1934–October 1935

PART ONE

LUKEWARM
BELIEVER

ON THE CUSP FROM
ANCIENT TO MODERN

(1893–1911 ∗ AGE 1–17)

MAO TSE-TUNG, who for decades held absolute power over the lives of one-quarter of the world's population, was responsible for well over 70 million deaths in peacetime, more than any other twentieth-century leader. He was born into a peasant family in a valley called Shaoshan, in the province of Hunan, in the heartland of China. The date was 26 December 1893. His ancestors had lived in the valley for five hundred years.

This was a world of ancient beauty, a temperate, humid region whose misty, undulating hills had been populated ever since the Neolithic age. Buddhist temples dating from the Tang dynasty (AD 618–906), when Buddhism first came here, were still in use. Forests where nearly 300 species of trees grew, including maples, camphor, metasequoia and the rare ginkgo, covered the area and sheltered the tigers, leopards and boar that still roamed the hills. (The last tiger was killed in 1957.) These hills, with neither roads nor navigable rivers, detached the village from the world at large. Even as late as the early twentieth century an event as momentous as the death of the emperor in 1908 did not percolate this far, and Mao found out only two years afterwards when he left Shaoshan.

The valley of Shaoshan measures about 5 by 3.5 km. The 600-odd families who lived there grew rice, tea and bamboo, harnessing buffalo to plough the rice paddies. Daily life revolved round these age-old activities. Mao's father, Yi-chang, was born in 1870. At the age of ten he was engaged to a girl of thirteen from a village about ten kilometers away, beyond a pass called Tiger Resting Pass, where tigers used to sun themselves. This short distance was long enough in those years for the two villages to speak dialects that were almost mutually unintelligible. Being merely a girl, Mao's mother did not receive a name; as the seventh girl born in the Wen clan, she was just Seventh Sister Wen. In accordance with centuries of custom, her feet had been crushed and bound to produce the so-called "three-inch golden lilies" that epitomized beauty at the time.

Her engagement to Mao's father followed time-honored customs. It

was arranged by their parents and was based on a practical consideration: the tomb of one of her grandfathers was in Shaoshan, and it had
to be tended regularly with elaborate rituals, so having a relative there
would prove useful. Seventh Sister Wen moved in with the Maos upon
betrothal, and was married at the age of eighteen, in 1885, when Yi-chang
was fifteen.

Shortly after the wedding, Yi-chang went off to be a soldier to earn
money to pay off family debts, which he was able to do after several years.
Chinese peasants were not serfs but free farmers, and joining the army
for purely financial reasons was an established practice. Luckily he was
not involved in any wars; instead he caught a glimpse of the world and
picked up some business ideas. Unlike most of the villagers, Yi-chang
could read and write, well enough to keep accounts. After his return, he
raised pigs, and processed grain into top-quality rice to sell at a nearby
market town. He bought back the land his father had pawned, then bought
more land, and became one of the richest men in the village.

Though relatively well off, Yi-chang remained extremely hard-
working and thrifty all his life. The family house consisted of half a dozen
rooms, which occupied one wing of a large thatched property. Eventually
Yi-chang replaced the thatch with tiles, a major improvement, but left
the mud floor and mud walls. The windows had no glass—still a rare
luxury—and were just square openings with wooden bars, blocked off at
night by wooden boards (the temperature hardly ever fell below freezing). The furniture was simple: wooden beds, bare wooden tables and
benches. It was in one of these rather spartan rooms, under a pale blue
homespun cotton quilt, inside a blue mosquito net, that Mao was born.

MAO WAS THE third son, but the first to survive beyond infancy. His
Buddhist mother became even more devout to encourage Buddha to
protect him. Mao was given the two-part name Tse-tung. *Tse*, which means
"to shine on," was the name given to all his generation, as preordained
when the clan chronicle was first written in the eighteenth century; *tung*
means "the East." So his full given name meant "to shine on the East."
When two more boys were born, in 1896 and 1905, they were given the
names Tse-min (*min* means "the people") and Tse-tan (*tan* possibly
referred to the local region, Xiang*tan*).

These names reflected the inveterate aspiration of Chinese peasants
for their sons to do well—and the expectation that they could. High positions were open to all through education, which for centuries meant
studying Confucian classics. Excellence would enable young men of any
background to pass imperial examinations and become mandarins—all
the way up to becoming prime minister. Officialdom was the definition

of achievement, and the names given to Mao and his brothers expressed the hopes placed on them.

But a grand name was also onerous and potentially tempted fate, so most children were given a pet name that was either lowly or tough, or both. Mao's was "the Boy of Stone"—*Shi san ya-zi*. For this second "baptism" his mother took him to a rock about eight feet high, which was reputed to be enchanted, as there was a spring underneath. After Mao performed obeisance and kowtows, he was considered adopted by the rock. Mao was very fond of this name, and continued to use it as an adult. In 1959, when he returned to Shaoshan and met the villagers for the first—and only—time as supreme leader of China, he began the dinner for them with a quip: "So everyone is here, except my Stone Mother. Shall we wait for her?"

Mao loved his real mother, with an intensity he showed towards no one else. She was a gentle and tolerant person, who, as he remembered, never raised her voice to him. From her came his full face, sensual lips, and a calm self-possession in the eyes. Mao would talk about his mother with emotion all his life. It was in her footsteps that he became a Buddhist as a child. Years later he told his staff: "I worshipped my mother . . . Wherever my mother went, I would follow . . . going to temple fairs, burning incense and paper money, doing obeisance to Buddha . . . Because my mother believed in Buddha, so did I." But he gave up Buddhism in his mid-teens.

Mao had a carefree childhood. Until he was eight he lived with his mother's family, the Wens, in their village, as his mother preferred to live with her own family. There his maternal grandmother doted on him. His two uncles and their wives treated him like their own son, and one of them became his Adopted Father, the Chinese equivalent to godfather. Mao did a little light farm work, gathering fodder for pigs and taking the buffalo out for a stroll in the tea-oil camellia groves by a pond shaded by banana leaves. In later years he would reminisce with fondness about this idyllic time. He started learning to read, while his aunts spun and sewed under an oil lamp.

MAO ONLY CAME back to live in Shaoshan in spring 1902, at the age of eight, to receive an education, which took the form of study in a tutor's home. Confucian classics, which made up most of the curriculum, were beyond the understanding of children and had to be learned by heart. Mao was blessed with an exceptional memory, and did well. His fellow pupils remembered a diligent boy who managed not only to recite but also to write by rote these difficult texts. He also gained a foundation in Chinese language and history, and began to learn to write good prose, calligraphy and poetry, as writing poems was an essential part of

Confucian education. Reading became a passion. Peasants generally turned in at sunset, to save on oil for lamps, but Mao would read deep into the night, with an oil lamp standing on a bench outside his mosquito net. Years later, when he was supreme ruler of China, half of his huge bed would be piled a foot high with Chinese classics, and he littered his speeches and writings with historical references. But his poems lost flair.

Mao clashed frequently with his tutors. He ran away from his first school at the age of ten, claiming that the teacher was a martinet. He was expelled from, or was "asked to leave," at least three schools for being headstrong and disobedient. His mother indulged him but his father was not pleased, and Mao's hopping from tutor to tutor was just one source of tension between father and son. Yi-chang paid for Mao's education, hoping that his son could at least help keep the family accounts, but Mao disliked the task. All his life, he was vague about figures, and hopeless at economics. Nor did he take kindly to hard physical labor. He shunned it as soon as his peasant days were over.

Yi-chang could not stand Mao being idle. Having spent every minute of his waking hours working, he expected his son to do the same, and would strike him when he did not comply. Mao hated his father. In 1968, when he was taking revenge on his political foes on a vast scale, he told their tormentors that he would have liked his father to be treated just as brutally: "My father was bad. If he were alive today, he should be 'jet-planed.'" This was an agonizing position where the subject's arms were wrenched behind his back and his head forced down.

Mao was not a mere victim of his father. He fought back, and was often the victor. He would tell his father that the father, being older, should do more manual labor than he, the younger—which was an unthinkably insolent argument by Chinese standards. One day, according to Mao, father and son had a row in front of guests. "My father scolded me before them, calling me lazy and useless. This infuriated me. I called him names and left the house... My father... pursued me, cursing as well as commanding me to come back. I reached the edge of a pond and threatened to jump in if he came any nearer... My father backed down." Once, as Mao was retelling the story, he laughed and added an observation: "Old men like him didn't want to lose their sons. This is their weakness. I attacked at their weak point, and I won!"

Money was the only weapon Mao's father possessed. After Mao was expelled by tutor no. 4, in 1907, his father stopped paying for his son's tuition fees and the thirteen-year-old boy had to become a full-time peasant. But he soon found a way to get himself out of farm work and back into the world of books. Yi-chang was keen for his son to get married, so that he would be tied down and behave responsibly. His niece was at just the right age for a wife, four years older than Mao, who agreed to his father's plan and resumed schooling after the marriage.

The marriage took place in 1908, when Mao was fourteen and his bride eighteen. Her family name was Luo. She herself had no proper name, and was just called "Woman Luo." The only time Mao is known to have mentioned her was to the American journalist Edgar Snow in 1936, when Mao was strikingly dismissive, exaggerating the difference in their ages: "When I was 14, my parents married me to a girl of 20. But I never lived with her . . . I do not consider her my wife . . . and have given little thought to her." He gave no hint that she was not still alive; in fact, Woman Luo had died in 1910, just over a year into their marriage.

Mao's early marriage turned him into a fierce opponent of arranged marriages. Nine years later he wrote a seething article against the practice: "In families in the West, parents acknowledge the free will of their children. But in China, orders from the parents are not at all compatible with the will of the children . . . This is a kind of 'indirect rape.' Chinese parents are all the time indirectly raping their children . . ."

As soon as his wife died, the sixteen-year-old widower demanded to leave Shaoshan. His father wanted to apprentice him to a rice store in the county town, but Mao had set his eye on a modern school about 25 kilometers away. He had learned that the imperial examinations had been abolished. Instead there were modern schools now, teaching subjects like science, world history and geography, and foreign languages. It was these schools that would open the door out of a peasant's life for many like him.

IN THE LATER NINETEENTH CENTURY, China had embarked on a dramatic social transformation. The Manchu dynasty that had ruled since 1644 was moving from the ancient to the modern. The shift was prompted by a series of abysmal defeats at the hands of European powers and Japan, beginning with the loss to Britain in the Opium War of 1839–42, as the powers came knocking on China's closed door. From the Manchu court to intellectuals, nearly everyone agreed that the country must change if it wanted to survive. A host of fundamental reforms was introduced, one of which was to install an entirely new educational system. Railways began to be built. Modern industries and commerce were given top priority. Political organizations were permitted. Newspapers were published for the first time. Students were sent abroad to study science, mandarins dispatched to learn democracy and parliamentary systems. In 1908, the court announced a program to become a constitutional monarchy in nine years' time.

Mao's province, Hunan, which had some 30 million inhabitants, became one of the most liberal and exciting places in China. Though landlocked, it was linked by navigable rivers to the coast, and in 1904 its capital, Changsha, became an "open" trading port. Large numbers of foreign traders and missionaries arrived, bringing Western ways and institutions. By the time Mao heard about modern schools, there were over a hundred of them, more than in any other part of China, and including many for women.

One was located near Mao: Eastern Hill, in the county of the Wens, his mother's family. The fees and accommodation were quite high, but Mao got the Wens and other relatives to lobby his father, who stumped up the cost for five months. The wife of one of his Wen cousins replaced Mao's old blue homespun mosquito net with a white machine-made muslin one in keeping with the school's modernity.

The school was an eye-opener for Mao. Lessons included physical training, music and English, and among the reading materials were potted biographies of Napoleon, Wellington, Peter the Great, Rousseau and Lincoln. Mao heard about America and Europe for the first time, and laid eyes on a man who had been abroad—a teacher who had studied in Japan, who was given the nickname "the False Foreign Devil" by his pupils. Decades later Mao could still remember a Japanese song he taught them, celebrating Japan's stunning military victory over Russia in 1905.

Mao was only in Eastern Hill for a few months, but this was enough for him to find a new opening. In the provincial capital, Changsha, there was a school specially set up for young people from the Wens' county, and Mao persuaded a teacher to enroll him, even though he was strictly speaking not from the county. In spring 1911 he arrived at Changsha, feeling, in his own words, "exceedingly excited." At seventeen, he said goodbye forever to the life of a peasant.

MAO CLAIMED LATER THAT when he was a boy in Shaoshan he had been stirred by concern for poor peasants. There is no evidence for this. He said he had been influenced while still in Shaoshan by a certain P'ang the Millstone Maker, who had been arrested and beheaded after leading a local peasant revolt, but an exhaustive search by Party historians for this hero has failed to turn up any trace of him.

There is no sign that Mao derived from his peasant roots any social concerns, much less that he was motivated by a sense of injustice. In a contemporary document, the diary of Mao's teacher, Professor Yang Chang-chi, on 5 April 1915 the professor wrote: "My student Mao Tse-tung said that . . . his clan . . . are mostly peasants, and *it is easy for them to get rich*" (our italics). Mao evinced no particular sympathy for peasants.

Up to the end of 1925, when he was in his early thirties, and five years after he had become a Communist, Mao made only a few references to peasants in all his known writings and conversations. They did crop up in a letter of August 1917, but far from expressing sympathy, Mao said he was "bowled over" by the way a commander called Tseng Kuo-fan had "finished off" the biggest peasant uprising in Chinese history, the Taiping Rebellion of 1850–64. Two years later, in July 1919, Mao wrote an essay about people from different walks of life—so peasants were inevitably mentioned—but his list of questions was very general, and his tone unmistakably neutral. There was a remarkable absence of emotion when he mentioned peasants, compared with the passion he voiced about students, whose life he described as "a sea of bitterness." In a comprehensive list for research he drew up in September that year, containing no fewer than 71 items, only one heading (the tenth) was about labor; the single one out of its 15 sub-heads that mentioned peasants did so only as "the question of laboring farmers intervening in politics." From late 1920, when he entered the Communist orbit, Mao began to use expressions like "workers and peasants" and "proletariat." But they remained mere phrases, part of an obligatory vocabulary.

Decades later, Mao talked about how, as a young man in Shaoshan, he cared about people starving. The record shows no such concern. In 1921 Mao was in Changsha during a famine. A friend of his wrote in his diary: "There are many beggars—must be over 100 a day . . . Most . . . look like skeletons wrapped in yellow skin, as if they could be blown over by a whiff of wind." "I heard that so many people who had come here . . . to escape famine in their own regions had died—that those who had been giving away planks of wood [to make coffins] . . . can no longer afford to do so." There is no mention of this event in Mao's writings of the time, and no sign that he gave any thought to this issue at all.

Mao's peasant background did not imbue him with idealism about improving the lot of Chinese peasants.

BECOMING A COMMUNIST

(1911–20 ★ AGE 17–26)

MAO ARRIVED IN CHANGSHA in spring 1911, on the eve of the Republican Revolution that was to end over two thousand years of imperial rule. Though Changsha seemed "just like a mediaeval town" to the British philosopher Bertrand Russell a decade later, with "narrow streets . . . no traffic possible except sedan chairs and rickshaws," it was not merely in touch with new ideas and trends, it seethed with Republican activity.

The Manchu court had promised a constitutional monarchy, but the Republicans were dedicated to getting rid of the Manchus entirely. To them Manchu rule was "foreign" domination, as the Manchus were not Han Chinese, the ethnic group that formed the bulk—about 94 percent—of the population. The Republicans lit sparks through newspapers and magazines that had sprung up all over China in the previous decade, and through the entirely new practice of public debates, in what had hitherto been an almost totally private society. They formed organizations, and launched several—unsuccessful—armed uprisings.

Mao quickly caught up on the issues through newspapers, which he read for the first time now, at the age of seventeen—the start of a life-long addiction. He wrote his first, rather confused, political essay expressing Republican views, and pasted it up on a wall at his school, in line with the latest trend. Like many other students in the school, he cut off his pigtail, which, as a Manchu custom, was the most obvious symbol of imperial rule. With a friend, he then ambushed a dozen others and forcibly removed their queues with scissors.

That summer, extremely hot and humid as usual in Changsha, students debated feverishly about how to overthrow the emperor. One day, in the middle of an impassioned discussion, a young man suddenly tore off his long scholar's gown, threw it on the ground and yelled: "Let's do some martial exercises and be prepared for war [against the emperor]!"

In October an armed uprising in neighboring Hubei province heralded the Republican Revolution. The Manchu dynasty that had ruled China for over 260 years crumbled, and a republic was declared on 1 January 1912. The child emperor, Pu Yi, abdicated the following month.

Yuan Shih-kai, military chief of the country, became the president, succeeding the interim provisional president, Sun Yat-sen. The provinces were controlled by army strongmen with allegiance to Yuan. When Yuan died in 1916, the central government in Peking weakened, and power fragmented to the provincial chiefs, who became semi-independent warlords. Over the following decade, they fought spasmodic wars, which disrupted civilian life in combat zones. But otherwise the warlords left most people relatively unaffected. Indeed, the rather loosely governed fledgling republic opened up all sorts of career opportunities. The young Mao faced a dazzling range of choices—industry, commerce, law, administration, education, journalism, culture, the military. He first enlisted in one of the Republican armies, but left within months, as he did not like the drilling, or chores like carrying water for cooking, which he hired a water vendor to do for him. He decided to go back to school, and scanned the array of advertisements in the papers (the ads, colorful and rather sophisticated, were also a new thing in China). Six institutions drew his attention, including a police college, a law college—and a school that specialized in making soap. He picked a general high school and stayed for six months before boredom drove him out to study by himself in the provincial library.

At last Mao found something he loved doing. He spent all day there, devouring new books, including translations of Western writings. He said later that he was like a buffalo charging into a vegetable garden and just gobbling down everything that grew. This reading helped free his mind of traditional constraints.

But his father threatened to cut him off unless he got into a proper school, so Mao entered a teacher-training college. It required no tuition fees and offered cheap board and lodging—like other such colleges in those days, as part of China's efforts to promote education.

This was spring 1913, and Mao was nineteen. The college embodied the open-mindedness of the time. Even its building was European style, with romanesque arches and a wide columned porch, and was suitably called *yang-lou*—"Foreign Building." The classrooms had smart wooden floors and glass windows. The students were exposed to all sorts of new ideas and encouraged to think freely and organize study groups. They turned out publications about anarchism, nationalism and Marxism, and for a while a portrait of Marx hung in the auditorium. Mao had earlier come across the word "socialism" in a newspaper. Now he encountered "communism" for the first time. It was a period of real "Let a Hundred Flowers Bloom"—a phrase Mao invoked for a moment under his own rule later, but without allowing a tiny fraction of the freedom he himself had enjoyed as a young man.

Mao was not a loner, and, like students the world over, he and his friends talked long and hard. The college was situated near the Xiang River, the biggest river in Hunan. Swimming in the Xiang inspired Mao to write a rather flamboyant poem in 1917. In the evenings the friends would go for long walks along its banks, enjoying the sight of junks gliding by the Island of Oranges which was covered with orchards of orange trees. On summer evenings they climbed the hill behind the school and sat arguing deep into the night on the grass where crickets crooned and glow-worms twinkled, ignoring the summons of the bugle to bed.

Mao and his friends also traveled. There was complete freedom of movement, and no need for identity papers. During the summer vacation of 1917, Mao and a friend wandered round the countryside for a month, earning food and shelter from peasants by doing calligraphy to decorate their front doors. On another occasion, Mao and two fellow students walked along a newly built railway, and when dusk descended, knocked on the door of a hilltop monastery overlooking the Xiang River. The monks allowed them to stay the night. After dinner the friends followed the stone steps down to the river for a swim, and then sat on the sandy bank and expounded their views, to the lapping of the waves. The guest room had a veranda, and the friends went on talking in the quiet of the night. One was moved by the loveliness of the still night, and said he wanted to become a monk.

In this and other conversations, Mao poured scorn on his fellow Chinese. "The nature of the people of the country is inertia," he said. "They worship hypocrisy, are content with being slaves, and narrow-minded." This was a common enough sentiment among the educated at the time, when people were casting around for explanations for why China had been so easily defeated by foreign powers and was trailing so badly in the modern world. But what Mao said next was uncommon extremism. "Mr. Mao also proposed burning all the collections of prose and poetry after the Tang and Sung dynasties in one go," a friend wrote in his diary.

This is the first known occasion when Mao mentioned one theme that was to typify his rule—the destruction of Chinese culture. When he first said it in that moonlit monastery, it had not sounded totally outlandish. At that time of unprecedented personal and intellectual freedom, the freest moment in Chinese history, everything that had been taken for granted was questioned, and what had been viewed as wrong proclaimed as right. Should there be countries? Families? Marriage? Private property? Nothing was too outrageous, too shocking, or unsayable.

IT WAS IN THIS ENVIRONMENT that Mao's views on morals took shape. In the winter of 1917–18, still a student as he turned twenty-four, he wrote extensive commentaries on a book called *A System of Ethics*, by a minor late-nineteenth-century German philosopher, Friedrich Paulsen. In these notes, Mao expressed the central elements in his own character, which stayed consistent for the remaining six decades of his life and defined his rule.

Mao's attitude to morality consisted of one core, the self, "I," above everything else: "I do not agree with the view that to be moral, the motive of one's action has to be benefiting others. Morality does not have to be defined in relation to others . . . People like me want to . . . satisfy our hearts to the full, and in doing so we automatically have the most valuable moral codes. Of course there are people and objects in the world, but they are all there only for me."

Mao shunned all constraints of responsibility and duty. "People like me only have a duty to ourselves; we have no duty to other people." "I am responsible only for the reality that I know," he wrote, "and absolutely not responsible for anything else. I don't know about the past, I don't know about the future. They have nothing to do with the reality of my own self." He explicitly rejected any responsibility towards future generations. "Some say one has a responsibility for history. I don't believe it. I am only concerned about developing myself . . . I have my desire and act on it. I am responsible to no one."

Mao did not believe in anything unless he could benefit from it personally. A good name after death, he said, "cannot bring me any joy, because it belongs to the future and not to my own reality." "People like me are not building achievements to leave for future generations." Mao did not care what he left behind.

He argued that conscience could go to hell if it was in conflict with his impulses:

> These two should be one and the same. All our actions . . . are driven by impulse, and the conscience that is wise goes along with this in every instance. Sometimes . . . conscience restrains impulses such as over-eating or over-indulgence in sex. But conscience is only there to restrain, not oppose. And the restraint is for better completion of the impulse.

As conscience always implies some concern for other people, and is not a corollary of hedonism, Mao was rejecting the concept. His view was: "I do not think these [commands like 'do not kill,' 'do not steal,' and 'do not slander'] have to do with conscience. I think they are only out of self-interest for self-preservation." All considerations must "be purely calculation for oneself, and absolutely not for obeying external ethical codes, or for so-called feelings of responsibility . . ."

Absolute selfishness and irresponsibility lay at the heart of Mao's outlook.

These attributes he held to be reserved for "Great Heroes"—a group to which he appointed himself. For this elite, he said:

> Everything outside their nature, such as restrictions and constraints, must be swept away by the great strength in their nature . . . When Great Heroes give full play to their impulses, they are magnificently powerful, stormy and invincible. Their power is like a hurricane arising from a deep gorge, and like a sex-maniac on heat and prowling for a lover . . . there is no way to stop them.

The other central element in his character which Mao spelled out now was the joy he took in upheaval and destruction. "Giant wars," he wrote, "will last as long as heaven and earth and will never become extinct . . . The ideal of a world of Great Equality and Harmony [*da tong*, Confucian ideal society] is mistaken." This was not just the prediction that a pessimist might make; it was Mao's desideratum, which he asserted was what the population at large wished. "Long-lasting peace," he claimed:

> is unendurable to human beings, and tidal waves of disturbance have to be created in this state of peace . . . When we look at history, we adore the times of [war] when dramas happened one after another . . . which make reading about them great fun. When we get to the periods of peace and prosperity, we are bored . . . Human nature loves sudden swift changes.

MAO SIMPLY COLLAPSED the distinction between reading about stirring events and actually living through cataclysm. He ignored the fact that, for the overwhelming majority, war meant misery.

He even articulated a cavalier attitude towards death:

> Human beings are endowed with the sense of curiosity. Why should we treat death differently? Don't we want to experience strange things? Death is the strangest thing, which you will never experience if you go on living . . . Some are afraid of it because the change comes too drastically. But I think this is the most wonderful thing: where else in this world can we find such a fantastic and drastic change?

Using a very royal "we," Mao went on: "We love sailing on a sea of upheavals. To go from life to death is to experience the greatest upheaval. Isn't it magnificent!" This might at first seem surreal, but when later tens of millions of Chinese were starved to death under his rule, Mao told his inner ruling circle it did not matter if people died—and even that death was to be celebrated. As so often, he applied his attitude only to other people, not to himself. Throughout his own life he was obsessed with finding ways to thwart death, doing everything he could to perfect his security and enhance his medical care.

When he came to the question "How do we change [China]?" Mao laid the utmost emphasis on destruction: "the country must be . . . destroyed and then re-formed." He extended this line not just to China but to the whole world—and even the universe: "This applies to the country, to the nation, and to mankind . . . The destruction of the universe is the same . . . People like me long for its destruction, because when the old universe is destroyed, a new universe will be formed. Isn't that better!"

These views, worded so clearly at the age of twenty-four, remained at the core of Mao's thinking throughout his life. In 1918, he had little prospect of putting them into practice and they had no impact, though he seems to have been someone who made an impression. His teacher Yang Chang-chi wrote of him in his diary of 5 April 1915: "My student Mao Tse-tung said that . . . his . . . father was a peasant and is now turning into a merchant . . . And yet, he [Mao] is so fine and outstanding. Really hard to come by . . . As peasant stock often produces extraordinary talents, I encouraged him . . ." But Mao did not appear to have leadership qualities. Another teacher of his said later that he showed "no special talent for leadership" at school. When he tried to form a sort of club and put up notices, only a few people turned up and it did not come to anything. When a dozen friends formed a New People's Study Society in April 1918, Mao was not elected its leader.

HE EVEN FOUND IT HARD to get a job after he graduated from the teacher-training college in June 1918. At the time, it was common for young graduates to aspire to go abroad to study. For those whose families could not afford to support them, as in Mao's case, there was a scheme to go to France on a work-and-study program. France needed manpower after losing so many young men in the First World War (one of the jobs Chinese laborers had been brought in to do was to remove corpses from the battlefields).

Some of Mao's friends went to France. Mao did not. The prospect of physical labor put him off. And another factor seems to have played a part—the requirement to learn French. Mao was no good at languages, and all his life spoke only his own local dialect and not even the *putonghua*— "common speech"—that his own regime made its official language. In 1920, when going to Russia was in vogue, and Mao fancied going (he told a girlfriend "my mind is filled with happiness and hope" at the thought), he was deterred by having to learn Russian. He made a stab at it, taking lessons from a Russian émigré (and agent), Sergei Polevoy. But according to Polevoy the other students teased Mao when he could not even master the alphabet, and he left in a huff. Unlike many of his radical contemporaries, including most of the future Chinese Communist leaders, Mao went to neither France nor Russia.

Instead, after leaving the college, Mao borrowed some money and set out for Peking, the capital, to try his luck. Peking in 1918 was one of the most beautiful cities in the world, where in front of magnificent palaces camels strolled in the streets. The imperial gardens near where Mao took lodgings had just been opened to the public. When winter came, he and his friends—all southerners who had seldom seen snow or ice—would marvel at the frozen lakes, encircled by drooping willows heavy with icicles and wide-open winter plums.

But life in the capital was harsh. The great freedom and opportunities that modernization had introduced to China had brought little material advantage, and much of the country was still extremely poor. Mao stayed with seven other friends in three tiny rooms. Four of them squeezed onto one *kang*, a heated brick bed, under a single quilt, packed so tight that when one of them needed to turn, he had to warn the men on either side. Between the eight of them, they had only two coats, and had to take turns going out. As there was heating in the library, Mao went there to read in the evenings.

Mao got nowhere in Peking. For a while he found work as a junior librarian, earning 8 yuan a month—a living wage. One of his jobs was to record the names of people who came to read the newspapers, many of whom he recognized as leading intellectuals, but he made no great impression, and they paid him no attention. Mao felt snubbed, and he bore his grudges hard. He claimed later that "most of them did not treat me like a human being." Less than six months after arriving, he left, so broke that he had to borrow money to travel home in stages. He returned to Changsha in April 1919, via Shanghai, where he saw his friends off to France. He had looked in from the outside at the intellectual and political life of cosmopolitan big cities, and now had to settle for a lowly job as a part-time history teacher in a primary school back in his home province.

Mao did not present himself as a model teacher. He was unkempt, and never seemed to change his clothes. His pupils remembered him disheveled, with holes in his socks, wearing home-made cotton shoes ready to fall apart. But at least he observed basic proprieties. Two years later, when he was teaching in another establishment, people complained about him being naked from the waist up. When asked to dress more decently, Mao retorted: "There wouldn't be anything scandalous if I was stark naked. Consider yourself lucky I'm not completely naked."

MAO HAD RETURNED to Changsha at a pivotal historical moment. At the time, there were a number of enclaves in China leased by foreign powers. These operated outside Chinese jurisdiction, with foreign gunboats often nearby to protect expatriates. Newly awakened public opinion in China demanded that these virtual mini-colonies be handed back. And yet, the Paris Peace Conference of 1919, which drew up the post–First World War settlement, and in which a Chinese delegation took part, allowed Japan to stay on in territory in Shandong which Japan had seized from Germany during the war. This infuriated nationalist sentiment. On 4 May 1919, for the first time in history, a big street demonstration took place in Peking, denouncing the government for "selling out," and protesting against the Japanese holding on to Chinese territory. The movement ripped across China. Japanese goods were burned in cities and towns, and shops that sold them were attacked. Many Chinese were disappointed that a Republican government had not managed to obtain a better deal from foreign powers than its Manchu predecessor. The sentiment grew that something more radical must be done.

In Changsha, where there were now so many foreign interests that Japan, the US and Britain had opened consulates there, a militant student union was formed, which included teachers. Mao was actively involved as the editor of its magazine, the *Xiang River Review*. In the first number, he declared his radical views: "We must now doubt what we dared not doubt, employ methods we dared not employ." It was a shoestring operation: Mao not only had to write most of the articles himself, in stifling heat, while bedbugs raced over the pile of soft-bound Chinese classics that formed his pillow, he had to sell the *Review* at street corners. Only five issues were published.

Mao continued to write occasional pieces in other journals. Among his output were ten articles dealing with women and the family. Mao was an advocate of women's independence, free choice in marriage, and equality with men—views not uncommon among the radicals. These outpourings seem to have been inspired by the death on 5 October 1919 of his mother, whom he loved. He had been sending her prescriptions for her ailments, diphtheria and a lymph node condition, and had arranged for her to be brought to Changsha for treatment. There, in spring that year, she had her first and only photograph taken at the age of fifty-two, with her three sons, an image of inner peace. Mao wears an expression of quiet determination and aloofness. Unlike his two brothers, who are clad in farmers' garments and look like gauche peasants, he has an air of grace in his long gown, the traditional attire for scholars and gentry.

In Mao's relationship with his mother, while she seems to have shown unconditional love and indulgence for him, his treatment of her combined strong feelings with selfishness. In later life, he told one of his closest staff a revealing story: "When my mother was dying, I told her I could not bear to see her looking in agony. I wanted to keep a beautiful image of her, and told her I wanted to stay away for a while. My mother was a very understanding person, and she agreed. So the image of my mother in my mind has always been and still is today a healthy and beautiful one." On her deathbed, the person who took priority in Mao's consideration was himself, not his mother, nor did he hesitate to say so.

Less surprisingly, Mao treated his dying father coldly. Yi-chang died from typhoid on 23 January 1920, and before his death he longed to see his eldest son, but Mao stayed away, and showed no feeling of sadness for him.

In an article written on 21 November 1919, shortly after his mother's death, and entitled "On Women's Independence," Mao claimed that "Women can do as much physical labour as men. It's just that they can't do such work during childbirth." So his answer to "women's independence" was that "women should prepare enough … before they marry so as to support themselves," and even that "women should stockpile necessities for the period of childbirth themselves." Evidently, as a man, Mao did not want to have to look after women. He wanted no responsibility towards them. Moreover, his insistence that women could manage the same kind of manual labor as men, which went against obvious reality, showed he felt little tenderness towards them. When he came to power, the core of his approach to women was to put them to heavy manual labor. In 1951 he penned his first inscription for Women's Day, which went: "Unite to take part in production …"

AT THE END OF 1919, radical students and teachers in Hunan started a drive to oust the provincial warlord governor, whose name was Chang Ching-yao. Mao went with a delegation to lobby the central government in Peking, writing petitions and pamphlets on an altar in a Tibetan temple where he was staying. Although the delegation failed to achieve its goal, Mao was able as a leading Hunan radical to meet some famous personalities, including Hu Shih, a brilliant liberal figure, and Li Ta-chao, a prominent Marxist.

But it was on his way back via Shanghai that Mao had the crucial encounter that was to change his life. In June 1920 he called on a Professor Chen Tu-hsiu, at the time China's foremost Marxist intellectual, who was in the midst of forming a Chinese Communist Party (CCP). Mao had written a long article calling him "a bright star in the world of thought." Aged forty, Chen was the undisputed leader of Chinese Marxists, a true believer, charismatic, with a volatile temper.

The idea of forming this Communist Party did not stem from the professor, nor from any other Chinese. It originated in Moscow. In 1919 the new Soviet government had set up the Communist International, the Comintern, to foment revolution and influence policy in Moscow's interest around the world. In August, Moscow launched a huge secret program of action and subversion for China, starting a commitment of money, men and arms three decades long, which culminated in bringing the Communists under Mao to power in 1949—Soviet Russia's most lasting triumph in foreign policy.

In January 1920 the Bolsheviks took Central Siberia and established an overland link with China. The Comintern sent a representative, Grigori Voitinsky, to China in April. In May it established a center in Shanghai, with a view, as another agent reported to Moscow, to "constructing a Chinese Party." Voitinsky then proposed to Professor Chen that a Communist Party be set up. By June Voitinsky was reporting home that Chen was to be made Party Secretary (i.e., the head) and was contacting "revolutionaries in various cities."

This was exactly when Mao showed up on Chen's doorstep. He had chanced upon the emergence of the CCP. Mao was not invited to be one of the founders. Nor, it seems, was he told it was about to be formed. The eight or so founding members were all eminent Marxists, and Mao had not yet even said that he believed in Marxism. The Party was founded in August, after Mao had left Shanghai.*

But although not one of the founders, Mao was in the immediate outer ring. Professor Chen gave him the assignment of opening a bookshop in Changsha to sell Party literature. The professor was in the middle of making his influential monthly, *New Youth*, the voice of the Party. The July issue carried write-ups about Lenin and the Soviet government. From that autumn the magazine was subsidized by the Comintern.

Mao's job was to distribute *New Youth* and other Communist publications (as well as selling other books and journals). Though not a committed Communist, Mao was a radical. He also loved books and welcomed a job. Soon after he returned to Changsha, an advertisement issued about the bookshop contained the bizarre declaration, penned by himself that: "There is no new culture in the entire world. Only a little flower of new culture has been discovered in Russia on the shores of the Arctic Ocean." The bookshop immediately placed an order for 165 copies of the July issue of *New Youth*, by far its biggest order. Another large order, 130 copies, was for *Labour World*, a new Party journal for workers. Most other journals the bookshop ordered were radical and pro-Russia.

---

* This has been a delicate point for Mao and his successors, and as a result official history dates the founding of the Party to 1921, as that was the first time Mao could verifiably be located at a Party conclave, the 1st Congress. This is duly commemorated with a museum in Shanghai which enshrines the myth that Mao was a founding member of the Party. That the Party was founded in 1920, not 1921, is confirmed both by the official magazine of the Comintern and by one of the Moscow emissaries who organized the 1st Congress.

Mao was not risking his neck by undertaking pro-Communist activities, which were not a crime. For now, Communist Russia was actually in vogue. In Changsha, a Russia Study Society was being founded, with no less a personage than the county chief as its head. Russia's popularity was in large part due to a fraud perpetrated by the new Bolshevik government—the claim that it was renouncing the old Tsarist privileges and territory in China, when in fact it retained them. Russian-controlled territory covered over a quarter of a million acres, and constituted the largest foreign concession in the country.

Mao was in charge of the bookshop, but he got a friend to run it. An important trait emerged at this time—he had a gift for delegating chores, and spotting the people to perform them. Mao gave himself the title of "special liaison man," soliciting donations from the wealthy, and dealing with publishers, libraries, universities and leading intellectuals all over the country. Professor Chen and a number of luminaries were listed as guarantors for the bookshop, which hugely boosted Mao's status, and helped him to win a creditable post as headmaster of the primary school attached to his old college.

There is no evidence that Mao formally joined the Party now, although by November, thanks to the bookshop, he counted as "one of us." When Moscow decided to set up an organization in Hunan called the Socialist Youth League, to create a pool of potential Party members, Mao was contacted to do the job. The following month, in a letter to friends in France, he declared that he "deeply agreed" with the idea of "using the Russian model to reform China and the world." This was his first expression of Communist belief.

APPROACHING TWENTY-SEVEN, Mao had become a Communist—not after an idealistic journey, or driven by passionate belief, but by being at the right place at the right time, and being given a job that was highly congenial to him. He had effectively been incorporated into an expanding organization.

His best friend at the time, Siao-yu, thought the cost of the Russian way was too high and wrote to Mao from France saying what he and some others felt:

> We don't think some human beings should be sacrificed for the welfare of the majority. We are in favor of a moderate revolution, through education, and seeking the welfare of all ... We regard Russian-style—Marxist—revolutions as ethically wrong...

Mao summed up their approach as "using peaceful means to seek the happiness of all." He argued against it not on idealistic grounds but invoking sheer realism: "I have two comments . . . : All very well in theory; but can't be done in practice." "Ideals are important," said Mao, "but reality is even more important."

Mao was no fervent believer. This absence of heartfelt commitment would result in a most unconventional and unusual relationship with his Party throughout his life, even when he was the head of that Party.

LUKEWARM BELIEVER

(1920–25 ★ AGE 26–31)

A T T H E S A M E T I M E as Mao became involved with the Communist Party, he developed a relationship with the daughter of his former teacher Yang Chang-chi. Yang Kai-hui, eight years Mao's junior, was to become his second wife.

She was born in 1901 in an idyllic spot outside Changsha. A delicate and sensitive child, she was brought up by her mother, who came from a scholar's family, while her father spent eleven years abroad, in Japan, Britain and Germany, studying ethics, logic and philosophy. When he returned to Changsha, in spring 1913, he brought back European ways, and encouraged his daughter to join him and his male students at meals, which was unheard-of in those days. Beautiful, elegant, wistful and articulate, she bowled over all the young men.

Her father was impressed with Mao's brains, and gave him high recommendations to influential people. "I am telling you seriously," he wrote to one of them, "these two people [Mao and another student, Cai He-sen] are rare talents in China, and will have a great future ... you cannot but pay serious attention to them." When he became a professor of ethics at Peking University in 1918, he welcomed Mao to stay with his family during Mao's first—and fruitless—venture to Peking. Kai-hui was then seventeen, and Mao was very keen on her, but she did not respond. She wrote years later:

> When I was about seventeen or eighteen, I began to have my own views about marriage. I was against any marriage that involved rituals. I also thought that to seek love deliberately would easily and inevitably lose true, sacred, incredible, the highest, the most beautiful and unsurpassable love! ... There is an expression which best expressed my thoughts: "Not to have if not perfect."

In January 1920, her father died. Mao was in Peking on his second trip, and spent a lot of time with the family. It was then that she fell in love with Mao. She was to write:

Father died! My beloved father died! Of course I was very sad. But I felt death was also a relief for Father, and so I was not too sad.

But I did not expect to be so lucky. I had a man I loved. I really loved him so much. I had been in love with him after I had heard a lot about him, and had read many of his articles and diaries... Although I loved him, I would not show it. I was convinced that love was in the hands of nature, and I must not presumptuously demand or pursue it...

So she still held back. Then they were parted when Kai-hui escorted her father's coffin back to Changsha, where she entered a missionary school. The distance only heightened her feelings. She later recalled:

He wrote me many letters, expressing his love. Still I did not dare to believe I had such luck. If it had not been for a friend who knew his [Mao's] feelings and told me about them—saying that he was very miserable because of me—I believe I would have remained single all my life. Ever since I came to know his true feelings towards me completely, from that day on, I had a new sense. I felt that apart from living for my mother, I was also living for him... I was imagining that if there were a day when he died, and when my mother was also no longer with me, I would definitely follow him and die with him!

When Mao returned to Changsha later that year, they became lovers. Mao was living in the school where he was the headmaster, and Kai-hui would visit him there. But she would not stay the night. They were not married, and the year was 1920, when living together outside marriage was unthinkable for a lady. Nor did Mao want to be tied down. In a letter to a friend on 26 November, he inveighed: "I think that all men and women in the marriage system are in nothing but a 'rape league'... I refuse to join this rape league." He broached the idea of forming a "Resisting Marriage Alliance," saying: "Even if no one else agrees with me, I am my own 'one-man alliance.'"

One night, after she was gone, Mao was unable to sleep, and wrote a poem that opened with these lines:

> *Sorrow, piled on my pillow, what is your shape?*
> *Like waves in rivers and seas, you endlessly churn.*
> *How long the night, how dark the sky, when will it be light?*
> *Restless, I sat up, gown thrown over my shoulders, in the cold.*
> *When dawn came at last, only ashes remained of my hundred thoughts...*

Helped by this poem, Mao managed to persuade Kai-hui to stay overnight. The walls were just thin boards, and some of the residents complained when the pair made passionate love. One neighbor cited a rule saying that teachers' wives were forbidden to sleep in the school, but Mao was the headmaster: he changed the rule, and started a precedent that teachers' wives could stay in schools.

For Kai-hui, staying the night meant giving the whole of herself. "My willpower had long given way," she was to write, "and I had allowed myself to live in romance. I had come to the conclusion: 'Let Heaven collapse and Earth sink down! Let this be the end!' What meaning would my life have if I didn't live for my mother and for him? So I lived in a life of love . . ."

Mao's feelings were no match for Kai-hui's, and he continued to see other girlfriends, in particular a widowed teacher called Si-yung, who was three years his junior. She helped a lot with raising funds for the book-shop, as some of her pupils came from rich families. She and Mao trav-eled as a couple.

When Kai-hui found out, she was shattered: "Then suddenly one day, a bomb fell on my head. My feeble life was devastatingly hit, and was almost destroyed by this blow!" But she forgave Mao. "However, this was only how I felt when I first heard the news. After all, he is not an ordi-nary man. She [Si-yung] loved him so passionately she would give every-thing for him. He also loved her, but he would not betray me, and he did not betray me in the end." Mao seems to have explained away his affair by claiming he felt unsure of Kai-hui's love. She chose to believe him:

> . . . now the lid on his heart, and on my heart, were both lifted. I saw his heart, and he saw mine completely. (We both have proud tempera-ments, me more so at the time. I was doing everything to stop him from seeing my heart—my heart of love for him—so that he came to doubt me, and thought I didn't love him. And because of his pride, he wouldn't let any feelings show. Only now did we truly understand each other.) As a result, we were closer than ever.

Kai-hui moved in with Mao, and they got married at the end of 1920. At the time, radicals shunned the old family rituals that cemented marriage, and a new registration system had yet to be adopted, so there was not even a formal certificate.

On account of her marriage, Kai-hui was expelled from her mission-ary school. Mao's affairs continued, and he actually started two new rela-tionships soon after his marriage. A close friend of his at the time told us this, writing the characters bu-zhen, "unfaithful," on the table with his finger. One of these liaisons was with a cousin of Kai-hui's. When Kai-hui found out, she was so distraught that she hit her cousin, but she rarely made scenes, and stayed faithful to Mao. She was later to write with resignation:

> I learnt many more things, and gradually I came to understand him. Not just him, but human nature in all people. Anyone who has no

physical handicap must have two attributes. One is sex drive, and the other is the emotional need for love. My attitude was to let him be, and let it be.

Kai-hui was by no means a conventional Chinese wife bound by tradition to endure her husband's misconduct. In fact she was a feminist, and later wrote an essay on women's rights: "Women are human beings, just as men are . . . Sisters! We must fight for the equality of men and women, and must absolutely not allow people to treat us as an accessory."

AT THE TIME OF Mao's second marriage, Moscow was stepping up its efforts to foment subversion in China. It began secretly training a Chinese army in Siberia, and explored armed intervention in China, as it had just attempted, unsuccessfully, in Poland. Simultaneously, it was building up one of its largest intelligence networks anywhere in the world, with a KGB station already established in Shanghai, and numerous agents, both civilian and military (GRU), in other key cities, including Canton, and, of course, Peking.

On 3 June 1921, new top-level Moscow representatives arrived, both under pseudonyms—a Russian military intelligence man called Nikolsky and a Dutchman called Maring, who had been an agitator in the Dutch East Indies. These two agents told the CCP members in Shanghai to call a congress to formalize the Party. Letters went out to seven regions where contacts had been established, asking each to send two delegates and enclosing 200 yuan to each place to cover travel to Shanghai. One lot of invitations and money came to Mao in Changsha. Two hundred yuan was the equivalent of nearly two years' salary from his teaching job, and far more than the trip could require. It was Mao's first known cash payment from Moscow.

He chose as his co-delegate a 45-year-old friend called Ho Shu-heng. They left quite secretively on the evening of 29 June in a small steamboat, under a stormy sky, declining the offers of friends to see them off. Although there was no law against Communist activities, they had reason to keep their heads down, as what they were engaged in was a conspiracy—collusion to establish an organization set up with foreign funding, with the aim of seizing power by illegal means.

The CCP's 1st Congress opened in Shanghai on 23 July 1921, attended by 13 people—all journalists, students or teachers—representing a total of 57 Communists, mostly in similar occupations. Not one was a worker. Neither of the Party's two most prestigious members, Professors Li Ta-chao and Chen Tu-hsiu, was present, even though the latter had been designated the Party chief. The two Moscow emissaries ran the show.

Maring, tall and mustachioed, made the opening speech in English, translated by one of the delegates. Participants seemed to recall its length—several hours—more than its content. Long speeches were rare in China at the time. Nikolsky was remembered as the one who made the short speech.

The presence of the foreigners, and the control they exercised, at once became an issue. The chair was allotted to one Chang Kuo-tao (later Mao's major challenger), because he had been to Russia and had links with the foreigners. One delegate recalled that Kuo-tao at one point proposed canceling the resolution of the previous evening. "I confronted him: how is it that a resolution passed by the meeting could be canceled just like that? He said it was the view of the Russian representatives. I was extremely angry . . . 'So we don't need to have meetings, we just have orders from the Russians.' " The protest was in vain. Another delegate suggested that before they went along with the Russian plans they should investigate whether Bolshevism actually worked, and proposed sending one mission to Russia and one to Germany—a proposal that alarmed Moscow's men, and was duly rejected.

Mao spoke little and made little impact. Compared with delegates from the larger cities, he was something of a provincial, clad in a traditional cotton gown and black cotton shoes, rather than a European-style suit, the attire of many young progressives. He did not strive to impress, and was content mainly to listen.

The meeting had started in a house in the French Settlement, and the police in these enclaves, known as "Concessions," were vigilant about Communist activities. On the evening of 30 July a stranger barged in, and Maring, smelling a police spy, ordered the delegates to leave. The Chinese participants adjourned to a small town outside Shanghai called Jiaxing, on a lake strewn with water chestnuts. Moscow's men stayed away from this final session for fear of attracting attention.

The wife of a Shanghai delegate hailed from the lakeside town, and she rented a pleasure boat, in which the delegates sat at a polished table where food, drinks and mahjong sets had been laid. A thick carved wooden screen separated this inner chamber from the open, but sheltered, front of the boat, where the delegate's wife sat with her back against the screen. She told us how, when other boats passed, she would tap on the screen with her fan, and inside the mahjong tiles would click loudly as they were shuffled. Soon it started to pour, and the boat was enveloped in rain. In this dramatic setting, the Chinese Communist Party was proclaimed—somewhat inconclusively, as without Moscow's men present no program could be finalized. The congress did not even issue a manifesto or charter.

The delegates were given another 50 yuan each as return fare. This enabled Mao to go off and do some sightseeing, in comfort, in Hangzhou and Nanjing, where he saw his girlfriend Si-yung again.*

DEPENDENCE ON MOSCOW and Moscow's money remained a sore point for many in the Party. Professor Chen, who came to Shanghai in late August to take up the post of Secretary, informed his comrades: "If we take their money, we have to take their orders." He proposed, in vain, that none of them should be full-time professional revolutionaries, but instead should have independent jobs, and use them to spread the ideas of revolution.

Chen argued vehemently with Maring about the latter's insistence that the CCP was automatically a branch of the Comintern, and particularly over the notion that Nikolsky had to supervise all their meetings. "Do we have to be controlled like this?" he would shout. "It simply isn't worth it!" Often he would refuse to see Maring for weeks running. Chen would yell, bang his palm on the table, and even throw teacups around. Maring's nickname for him was "the volcano." On the frequent occasions when Chen exploded, Maring would go next door to have a smoke while Chen tried to simmer down.

But without Moscow's funding the CCP could not even begin to carry out any activities such as publishing Communist literature and organizing a labor movement. Over a nine-month period (October 1921–June 1922), out of its expenditure of 17,655 yuan, less than 6 percent was raised inside China, while over 94 percent came from the Russians, as Chen himself reported to Moscow. Indeed, there were many other Communist groups in China at the time—at least seven between 1920 and 1922, one claiming as many as 11,000 members. But without Russian funds, they all collapsed.

Unlike Chen, Mao showed no qualms about taking Moscow's money. He was a realist. Russian funding also transformed his life. After the congress he began to receive 60–70 yuan a month from the Party for the Hunan branch, soon increased to 100, and then 160–170. This large and regular income made a tremendous difference. Mao had always been short of money. He had two jobs, headmaster and small-time journalist, and he dreaded having to depend on these two occupations to make his living. In two letters written in late November 1920 to a friend, he had complained bitterly, saying: "a life just using the mouth and brain is misery to the extreme . . . I often go without a rest for 3 or 4 hours [*sic*], even working into the night . . . My life is really too hard."

Then he had told some friends: "In the future, I most likely will have to live on the salaries of these two jobs. I feel that jobs that use only the

* Si-yung was to die of illness in 1931.

brain are very hard, so I am thinking of learning something that uses manual labour, like darning socks or baking bread." As Mao had no fondness whatever for manual labor, to volunteer such an idea showed he had reached a dead end.

But now he had a comfortable berth as a subsidized professional revolutionary. He gave up journalism, and even resigned his job as headmaster, able at last to enjoy the kind of existence he could hitherto only dream about. It seems to be now that he developed his lifelong habit of sleeping late into the day and staying up reading at night. In a letter to his old best friend Siao-yu written two months after the 1st Congress, he was almost ecstatic:

I am now spending most of my time nursing my health, and have become much fitter. Now I feel extremely happy, because, apart from getting healthier, I don't have any burden of work or responsibility. I am busy having good food every day, both indulging my stomach and improving my health. I also can read whatever books I want to read. It is really "Wow, what fun."

To be able to eat his fill and read to his heart's content was Mao's idea of the good life.

In October 1921 he was able to set up house with Kai-hui, in a place called Clear Water Pond, and had enough money to afford servants. It was a lovely spot, where water flowed into a large pond and changed from muddy to clear, giving the place its name. The house was a traditional building, with black wooden beams and motley brick walls, overlooking fields of vegetables and backing on to low hills.

In theory, the house was the office of the Hunan Party branch. As the provincial Party leader, one of Mao's main tasks was to recruit members, but he did not throw much zeal into the cause. When he had first been asked to recruit for the Youth League in November 1920, he had delegated the job to someone else and gone off on holiday with his girlfriend Si-yung, claiming that he was off "to research education."

Unlike most founding dictators—Lenin, Mussolini, Hitler—Mao did not inspire a passionate following through his oratory, or ideological appeal. He simply sought willing recruits among his immediate circle, people who would take his orders. His first recruit, his friend and bookshop manager Yi Li-rong, described how, soon after Mao came back from the 1st Congress, he called Yi out of the bookshop. Leaning against a bamboo fence in the yard, he told Yi that he ought to join the Party. Yi muttered some reservations about having heard that millions had died in the Russian Revolution; but, as he said, Mao "asked me to join and so I joined." This was how Mao set up his first Party branch in Changsha. It consisted of just three men: himself, Yi, and the friend he had taken to the 1st Congress.

The next to join were members of Mao's family—his wife and his brothers, whom he had sent for from the village. Tse-min had been running the family business and was smart with money. He took charge of Mao's finances. Mao summoned more relatives from their village to Changsha, and doled out various jobs. Some entered the Party. Outside his circle of family and friends, his recruiting was sparse. Mainly, he trawled very close to home.

Actually, at the time, quite a lot of young people in Hunan were attracted to communism, including the man who was to become Mao's No. 2 and president of China, Liu Shao-chi, and a number of other future Party leaders. But they were introduced to the Party not by Mao but by a Marxist in his fifties called Ho Min-fan, who had been county chief of Changsha. Min-fan sponsored Liu and others for membership in the Socialist Youth League in late 1920, and made the introductions for them to go to Russia. He himself did not get to go to the Party's 1st Congress because the invitation was sent to Mao, who was extremely jealous of Min-fan, especially of his success at recruiting. When Liu Shao-chi returned from Moscow in 1922, Mao grilled him about how Min-fan had achieved this.

Once Mao became official CCP branch boss, he schemed to oust his unwitting rival. Min-fan ran a public lecture center which occupied a fine property, a grand clan temple called Boat Mountain. Claiming to need it for Party purposes, Mao moved in, together with his group, and made life so impossible for Min-fan that he ended up leaving both the premises and the Party milieu. Mao told Liu Shao-chi a year later that Min-fan, Liu's mentor, had been "disobedient. So we drove him out of Boat Mountain." By using the word "disobedient," especially about some-one much older, Mao was revealing his thuggish side. He had not behaved this way in his earlier persona. When he first met his friend, the liberal Siao-yu, Mao had bowed to show respect. He had been cour-teous to his peers and superiors alike. A taste of power had altered his behavior.* From this time on, Mao's friendships were only with people who would not challenge him, and these were largely apolitical. He was not friends with any of his political colleagues, and hardly ever social-ized with them.

Removing Min-fan was Mao's first power struggle. And he won. Under Mao, there was no Party committee. Meetings were rare. There was just

---

* Siao-yu parted company with Mao around now, and later became a Nationalist govern-ment official. He died in Uruguay in 1976.

Mao giving orders, though he took care to report regularly to Shanghai, as required.

MAO WAS DOING NOTHING about another major task, which was to organize labor unions. He felt no more sympathy for workers than he did for peasants. Writing to a friend in November 1920, in which he complained about his own conditions as an intellectual, he remarked: "I think labourers in China do not really suffer poor physical conditions. Only scholars suffer."

In December 1921, workers in Anyuan, an important mining center straddling the Hunan–Jiangxi border, wrote asking the Communists for help, and Mao went up to the mine—the first time on record that he went near any workers. He stayed a few days and then left, delegating the practical work to someone else. After this brief dip in the grimy world of the coal miners, he told Shanghai that he had come "to his wits' end" with "the workers organisation."

There were effective labor organizers around, though, especially two non-Communists who founded a Hunan Labor Union and recruited more than 3,000 of the approximately 7,000 workers in Changsha. The two were arrested in January 1922 while leading a big strike. In the small hours, they were executed—hacked to death in the traditional manner, an event that gave rise to a storm of protest nationwide. When the governor who killed them was later asked why he did not target Mao, his answer was that he had not seen Mao as a threat.

IT WAS THANKS TO HIS ineffectiveness at organizing labor and recruiting that Mao was dropped from the Party's 2nd Congress in July 1922. This was a most important occasion, as it passed a charter and endorsed joining the Comintern, thus formally accepting outright Moscow control. Later, Mao tried to explain away his absence by claiming that he "intended to attend" but "forgot the name of the place where it was to be held, could not find any comrades, and missed it." In fact, Mao knew plenty of Party people in Shanghai, including some of the delegates, and there was no chance that he could have accidentally missed what was a very formal occasion. His absence from the congress meant that he might lose his position as the Party boss in Hunan. Russian funds would no longer come through him, and he would have to take orders from someone else. This prospect spurred him to act: first he visited a lead and zinc mine in April 1922, and in May he went back to Anyuan, the coal-mining center. He also led a number of demonstrations and strikes. On 24 October, when Kai-hui gave birth to their first child, a son, Mao was not with her, as he was away negotiating on behalf of the

builders' union. He gave their son the name An-ying: *An* was a generation name; *ying* meant "an outstanding person."

Mao also finally set up a Hunan Party committee at the end of May,
a year after being made Hunan boss. It had thirty members, most of them
not recruited by himself.* The future president, Liu Shao-chi, described
on his deathbed how the committee worked under Mao. "I had many
meetings at Chairman Mao's house," he wrote, "and apart from asking
questions, I had no chance to speak at all. In the end, it was always what
Chairman Mao said that went . . . the Party in Hunan already had its own
leader and its own distinctive style—different from the Party in Shanghai."
Liu was putting on record as explicitly as he could that Mao had already
started behaving dictatorially in the earliest days of the Party.

Meanwhile, as Mao worked to mend fences with the center of power,
he had a lucky break. In January 1923 most of the CCP cadres working
in Shanghai found themselves at odds with an order from Moscow to do
something seemingly bizarre, and arbitrary: to join another political party,
the Nationalists (also known as the Kuomintang, or KMT). Moscow
needed provincial Communists who would support its position—and
found Mao.

THE NATIONALIST PARTY had been founded in 1912 by the merger
of a number of Republican groups. Its leader was Sun Yat-sen, who had
briefly been the first provisional president of the Republic, before losing
power to the army chief Yuan Shih-kai. Since then, Sun had been trying
to form his own army and overthrow the Peking government.

This objective led Sun to embrace Moscow. The Russians shared his
goal of subverting the Peking government, as it was refusing its consent
to their occupation of Outer Mongolia, which was then Chinese territory. The CCP was far too small to topple the Peking government, so
Moscow's envoys looked round among various provincial potentates, and
found that the only one willing to accept the Soviet presence was Sun.

Sun was based in Canton, the capital of the southern coastal province
of Guangdong. He asked the Russians to help him build a force strong
enough to conquer China. In September 1922 he told a Russian envoy
that he wanted to establish "an army with arms and military matériel
supplies from Russia." In return, as well as endorsing the Soviet occupation of Outer Mongolia, Sun proposed that Russia occupy the huge
mineral-rich province of Xinjiang in the northwest. Russia's chief envoy,
Adolf Joffe, reported in November that Sun "asks that one of our divisions should take Xinjiang . . . where there are only 4,000 Chinese troops

---

* Total Party membership nationwide was 195 as of the end of June 1922.

and there cannot be any resistance." He suggested to the Russians that they invade from Xinjiang deep into the heartland of China, as far as Chengdu in Sichuan, on his behalf.

Not only did Sun have big ambitions and few scruples, he had a sizable party with thousands of registered members, and a territorial base with a major seaport at Canton. So in early January 1923 the Soviet Politburo decided: "Give full backing to the Nationalists," with "money [from] the reserve funds of the Comintern." The decision was signed by the up-and-coming Stalin, who had begun to take a close interest in China. Sun had thus become, as Joffe told Lenin, "*our* man" (italics in original). His price was "2 million Mexican dollars maximum," roughly 2 million gold rubles. "Isn't all this worth 2 million roubles?" Joffe asked.

Moscow knew that Sun had his own agenda, and was trying to use Russia, just as Russia was trying to use him. It wanted its local client, the CCP, to be right there on the spot to ensure that Sun toed Moscow's line and served Moscow's interest. So it ordered the Chinese Communists to join the Nationalist Party. In a secret session, Stalin spelled out: "we cannot give directives out of here, Moscow, openly. We do this through the Communist Party of China and other comrades in camera, confidentially . . ."

Moscow wanted to use the CCP as a Trojan horse to manipulate the much bigger Nationalist Party; but all CCP leaders, starting from Professor Chen, opposed joining Sun's party, on the grounds that it rejected communism and that Sun was just another "lying," "unscrupulous" politician out for power. Moscow was told that sponsoring Sun was "wasting the blood and sweat of Russia, and perhaps the blood and sweat of the world proletariat."

Maring, the Comintern envoy, faced a revolt. This is almost certainly why Mao was brought to Party HQ. The pragmatic Mao embraced Moscow's strategy. He promptly joined the Nationalist Party himself. A more fervent Communist, actually an old friend of Mao's, Cai He-sen, told the Comintern that when Maring put forward the slogan "All work for the Nationalists," "its [only] supporter was Mao."

Mao did not believe in his tiny Party's prospects, or that communism had any broad appeal. He made this crystal-clear at the CCP's 3rd Congress in June 1923. The only hope of creating a Communist China, he said, was by means of a Russian invasion. Mao "was so pessimistic," Maring (who chaired the congress) reported, "that he saw the only salvation of China in the intervention by Russia," telling the congress "that the revolution had to be brought into China from the north by the Russian army." This was in essence what happened two decades later.

His enthusiasm for the Moscow line shot Mao into the core of the Party, under Maring. There he exerted himself as never before, now that he could see hope in what he was doing. Moscow's chief bagman in China, Vilde, who doubled as the Soviet vice-consul in Shanghai, singled out Mao and one other person in a report to Moscow as "most definitely, good cadres." Mao was appointed the assistant to Party chief Professor Chen, with responsibility for correspondence, documents, and taking the minutes at meetings. All Party letters had to be co-signed by him and Chen. In imitation of Chen, Mao signed with an English signature: T. T. Mao. One of the first things Chen and he did was to write to Moscow for more money—"now that our work front is expanding."

HAVING SHEPHERDED its local Communist clients into the Nationalists, Moscow now sent a higher-level operator to control both the CCP and the Nationalists and to coordinate their actions. Mikhail Borodin, a charismatic agitator, was appointed Sun Yat-sen's political adviser at Stalin's recommendation in August 1923. A veteran of revolutionary activities in America, Mexico and Britain, he was a good orator, with a powerful voice, a dynamic organizer and a shrewd strategist (he was the first person to recommend that the Chinese Communists should move to northwest China to get near the Russian border, which they did a decade later). He inspired descriptions like "majestic," and radiated energy even when ill.

Borodin reorganized the Nationalists on the Russian model, dubbing their institutions with Communist names, such as Propaganda Department. At the Nationalists' First Congress in Canton, in January 1924, Mao and many other Chinese Communists took part, and the tiny CCP secured a disproportionate number of posts. Moscow now started to bankroll the Nationalists in a big way. Most importantly, it funded and trained an army, and established a military academy. Set on a picturesque island in the Pearl River some ten kilometers from Canton, the Whampoa Academy was modeled on Soviet institutions, with Russian advisers and many Communist teachers and students. Planes and artillery were shipped in from Soviet Russia, and it was thanks to Russian-trained troops, backed in the field by cohorts of Soviet advisers, that the Nationalists were able to expand their base substantially.

Mao was very active in the Nationalist Party, and became one of sixteen alternate members to its top body, the Central Executive Committee. For the rest of the year, he did most of his work in the Nationalist office in Shanghai. It was Mao who helped form the Hunan Nationalist branch, which became one of the biggest.

Mao even went as far as seldom attending meetings of his own Party. His keenness about working with the Nationalists drew fire from his fellow Communists. His old—and more ideological—friend Cai later complained to the Comintern that in Hunan "our organisation lost almost all political significance. All political questions were decided in the Nationalist provincial committee, not in the Communist Party Provincial Committee." Another dedicated labor organizer concurred: "Mao at that time was against an independent trade union movement for workers."

Moreover, Mao suddenly found himself cold-shouldered by some of Moscow's envoys, as his patron Maring had left China the previous October. Although Mao got on well with Borodin, he struggled to defend himself against the ideological purists. Moscow had ordered the Chinese Communists to keep their separate identity and independence, while infiltrating the Nationalists, but the ideologically woolly Mao could not draw the line between the parties. On 30 March 1924, one of these ideologue envoys, Sergei Dalin, wrote to Voitinsky:

> What you would hear from CC [Central Committee] Secretary Mao (undoubtedly a placeman of Maring's) would make your hair stand on end—for instance, that the [Nationalist Party] was and is a proletarian party and must be recognised by the Communist International as one of its sections ... This character represented the Party in the Socialist Youth League ... I have written to the Party's CC and asked it to appoint another representative.

Mao was duly fired from this position. Criticized as "opportunistic" and "right-wing," he found himself kicked out of the Central Committee, and was not even invited to attend the next CCP congress scheduled for January 1925.* His health now took a downturn, and he grew thin and ill. A then house-mate and colleague told us that Mao had "problems in his head ... he was preoccupied with his affairs." His nervous condition was reflected in his bowels, which sometimes moved only once a week. He was to be plagued by constipation—and obsessed by defecation—all his life.

Mao was edged out of Shanghai at the end of 1924. He returned to Hunan, but not to any Party position, and the only place to go was his home village of Shaoshan, where he arrived on 6 February 1925 with over 50 kg of books, claiming he was "convalescing." He had been with the Communist Party for over four years—years full of ups and downs. At the age of thirty-one, his lack of ideological clarity and fervor had landed him back in his family property. Mao's setbacks during these initial years of the CCP are still kept tightly covered up. Mao did not want it known that he had been ineffectual at Party work, or extremely keen on the Nationalist Party (which became the main enemy for the Communists in the years to come)—or that he was ideologically rather vague.

---

* The CCP at that point had 994 members.

RISE AND DEMISE IN
THE NATIONALIST PARTY

(1925–27 ★ AGE 31–33)

FOR EIGHT MONTHS MAO LIVED in the family house in Shaoshan. He and his two brothers had inherited the house and a fair amount of land from their parents, and the property had been looked after by relatives. The two brothers had been working in Changsha for the Party, having been recruited by Mao. Now they both came home with him. In Changsha, only 50 km away, the Hunan Communists were organizing strikes, demonstrations and rallies, but Mao was not involved. He stayed at home, playing cards a lot of the time.

But he was watching out for a chance to return to politics—at a high level. In March 1925, Sun Yat-sen, the Nationalist leader, died. His successor was a man whom Mao knew, and who was favorably disposed towards him—Wang Ching-wei. Wang had worked with Mao in Shanghai the year before, and the two had got along very well.

Born in 1883, Wang was ten years Mao's senior. Charismatic, and an eloquent orator, he also had film-star good looks. He had played an active part in Republican activities against the Manchus, and when the Revolution broke out in October 1911 was in prison under a life sentence for his repeated attempts to assassinate high officials of the Manchu court, including the regent. Released as the dynasty collapsed, he became one of the leaders of the Nationalist Party. He was with Sun Yat-sen in Sun's last days, and was a witness to his will, which was a strong credential to succeed him. Most important, he had the blessing of Borodin, the top Russian adviser. With about 1,000 agents in the Nationalist base, Moscow was now the master of Canton, which had taken on the air of a Soviet city, decked out with red flags and slogans. Cars raced by with Russian faces inside and Chinese bodyguards on the running-boards. Soviet cargo ships dotted the Pearl River. Behind closed doors, commissars sat around red-cloth-covered tables under the gaze of Lenin, interrogating "trouble-makers" and conducting trials.

The moment Sun died, Mao dispatched his brother Tse-min to Canton to reconnoiter his chances. Tse-tan, his other brother, followed. By June it was clear that Wang was the new Nationalist chief, and Mao began to spruce up his credentials by establishing grassroots Party branches in his area. Most were for the Nationalists, not the Communists. Having been shunted out of the CCP leadership, Mao was now trying his luck with the Nationalists.

At the top of the Nationalists' program was "anti-imperialism." The Party had made its main task the defense of China's interests against foreign powers, so this became the theme of Mao's activity, even though it was far removed from peasants' lives. Not surprisingly, the reaction was indifference. One of his co-workers recorded in his diary of 29 July: "Only one comrade turned up, and the others didn't come. So the meeting didn't happen." A few days later: "The meeting failed to take place because few comrades came." One night, he and Mao had to walk from place to place to get people together, so the meeting started very late, and did not finish until 1:15 AM. Mao said he was going home, "as he was suffering from neurasthenia, and had talked too much today. He said he wouldn't be able to sleep here . . . We walked for about 2 or 3 *li* [1–1.5 km] and just couldn't walk further. We were absolutely exhausted, and so spent the night at Tang Brook."

Mao did not organisze any peasant action in the style of poor versus rich. This was partly because he thought it was pointless. He had told Borodin and some other Communists before, on 18 January 1924:

> If we carry out struggles against big landlords, we are bound to fail. [In some areas, some Communists] organised the illiterate peasants first, then led them in struggles against relatively rich and big land-lords. What was the result? Our organisations were immediately broken, banned, and these peasants not only did not regard us as fighting for their interests, they hated us, saying that if we hadn't organised them, there would not have been disasters, or misfortune.
>
> Therefore, until we are confident that our grassroots branches in the countryside are strong . . . we cannot adopt the policy of taking drastic steps against relatively rich landowners.

Mao was being pragmatic. A Communist called Wang Hsien-tsung in Mao's area was organizing poor peasants to improve their lot at the time when Mao was in Shaoshan. He was accused of being a bandit, and was arrested, tortured and beheaded by the local police.

Mao prudently decided to steer clear of any such dangerous and futile activities, but the Hunan authorities still viewed him with suspicion, as he had the reputation of being a major radical. That summer there was a drought and, as had often happened in the past, poor peasants used force to stop the rich shipping grain out for sale in the towns and cities. Mao was suspected of stirring things up. In the provincial capital there had also been large "anti-imperialist" demonstrations, following an incident in Shanghai on 30 May when British police killed ten protesters in the British Settlement. Although Mao played no role in the Changsha demonstrations, and was living quietly at home, miles away, he was still assumed to be an instigator, and this notion crops up in an early appearance in US government records. The US consulate in Changsha forwarded to Washington a report by the president of Yale-in-China about "Bolshevistic disturbances" in Changsha on 15 June, saying that the Hunan governor had "received a list of twenty leaders of agitation, including Mao Tse-tung, known to be the leading Communist propagandist here." Mao was a name, even to an (unusually well-informed) American.

So an arrest warrant was issued in late August. Mao, who was leaving for Canton in any case, decided it was time to decamp. He did so in a sedan chair, heading first to Changsha and telling the bearers that if asked who their passenger was, they should say they were carrying a doctor. Some days later a few militiamen turned up in Shaoshan in search of Mao. Finding him absent, they took some money and left, but did not otherwise disturb Mao's family.

On the eve of his departure from Changsha, Mao took a stroll along the Xiang River, and wrote a poem in which he looked to the future:

> *Eagles soar up the long vault,*
> *Fish fly down the shallow riverbed,*
> *Under a sky of frost, ten thousand creatures vie to impose their will.*
> *Touched by this vastness,*
> *I ask the boundless earth:*
> *Who after all will be your master?*

Mao's nose did not fail him. Within two weeks of arriving in Canton, in September 1925, he was given a clutch of key jobs by the Nationalist chief. Mao was to be Wang Ching-wei's stand-in, running the Propaganda Department, as well as editor of the Nationalists' new journal, *Politics Weekly*. And to underline his prominence, he also sat on the five-man committee vetting delegates for the Nationalists' second congress the following January, at which he delivered one of the major reports. Wang's role in Mao's rise is something which has been sedulously obscured by Peking, all the more so because Wang became the head of the Japanese puppet government in the 1940s.

Mao's ability to work at full pitch in Canton was due in no small part to his discovery of sleeping pills at this time. He had previously suffered from acute insomnia, which left him in a state of permanent nervous exhaustion. Now he was liberated. Later he was to rank the inventor alongside Marx.

In November 1925, while working for the Nationalists, Mao voiced an interest in the question of the Chinese peasantry for the first time. On a form he filled out, he said that he was "currently paying special attention" to these many tens of millions. On 1 December he published a long article on peasants in a Nationalist journal, and he wrote another a month later for the opening issue of the Nationalist magazine *Chinese Peasants*. Mao's new interest did not stem from any personal inspiration or inclination; it came on the heels of an urgent order from Moscow in October, instructing both the Nationalists and Communists to give the issue priority. The Nationalists heeded this call at once.

It was the Russians who first ordered the CCP to pay attention to the peasantry. Back in May 1923 Moscow had already referred to "the issue of peasants" as "the centre of all our policies," and had ordered the Chinese revolutionaries to "carry out peasant land revolution against the remnants of feudalism." This meant aiming to divide the Chinese peasants into different classes on the basis of wealth, and to stir up the poor against the better-off. At that time, Mao had been cool towards this approach, and when his reservations were reported to Moscow he had been stripped of one of his posts. Mao's position, as Dalin wrote to Voitinsky in March 1924, was that: "On the peasant question, the class line must be abandoned, there is nothing to be done among the poor peasants and it is necessary to establish ties with landowners and *shenshih* [gentry] . . ."

But now Mao shifted with the prevailing wind, though he got into trouble with the Russians over ideological phraseology. In his articles, Mao had attempted to apply Communist "class analysis" to the peasantry by categorizing those who owned their small plot of land as "petty bourgeoisie" and farmhands as "proletariat." A blistering critique appeared in the Soviet advisers' magazine, *Kanton*, which reached a high-grade readership in Russia, where the first personal name on its distribution list of about forty was Stalin's. The critic, Volin, a Russian expert on the peasantry, accused Mao of arguing as though the peasants were living in a *capitalist* society, when China was only at the *feudal* stage: "one very important error leaps sharply to the eye: . . . that Chinese society, according to Mao, is one with a developed capitalist structure." Mao's article was said to be "unscientific," "indiscriminate" and "exceptionally schematic." Even his basic figures were way out, according to Volin: he gave the population as 400 million, when the 1922 census showed it was actually 463 million.

Luckily for Mao, the Nationalist Party did not require such high standards of theoretical correctness. In February 1926 his patron Wang Ching-wei appointed him a founding member of the Nationalists' Peasant Movement Committee, as well as the head of the Peasant Movement Training Institute, set up two years before with Russian funds.

It was only now, when he was thirty-two, that Mao—assumed by many to this day to have been the champion of the poor peasants—took any interest in their affairs. Under Mao, the Peasant Institute churned out agitators who went into the villages, roused the poor against the rich, and organized them into "peasant associations." In Hunan they were particularly successful after July, when the Nationalist army occupied the province. The Nationalists had just begun a march north from Canton (known as "the Northern Expedition") to overthrow the Peking government. Hunan was the first place on the 2,000-kilometer route.

The Nationalist army was accompanied by Russian advisers. The Russians had also just opened a consulate in Changsha, and the KGB station there had the second-largest budget of any of the fourteen stations in China after Shanghai. An American missionary wrote home later that year from Changsha: "We have a Russian Consul [now]. No Russian interests here at all to represent . . . it is plain . . . what he is up to . . . China may pay high for his genial presence . . ." With close Russian supervision, the new Nationalist authorities in Hunan gave peasant associations their blessing—and funding—and by the end of the year the associations had sprung up in much of the countryside in this province of 30 million people. The social order was turned upside down.

At this time, warlords had been fighting sporadic wars for ten years, and there had been more than forty changes of the central government since the country had become a republic in 1912. But the warlords had always made sure that the social structure was preserved, and life went on as usual for civilians, as long as they were not caught in the crossfire. Now, because the Nationalists were following Russian instructions aimed at bringing about a Soviet-style revolution, social order broke down for the first time.

Violence erupted as poor peasants helped themselves to the food and money of the relatively rich, and took revenge. Thugs and sadists also indulged themselves. By December there was mayhem in the Hunan countryside. In his capacity as a leader of the peasant movement, Mao was invited back to his home province to give guidance.

CHANGSHA, WHEN MAO returned, was a changed city, with victims being paraded around in dunce's hats (a European invention) as a sign of humiliation. Children scampered around singing "Down with the [imperialist] powers and eliminate the warlords," the anthem of the Nationalist Revolution, sung to the tune of "Frère Jacques."

On 20 December 1926 about 300 people crowded the Changsha slideshow theater to listen to Mao, who shared the stage with a Russian agitator called Boris Freyer. (Like virtually every Russian agent in China at this time, he later disappeared in Stalin's purges.) Mao was no orator; his speech was two hours long, and flat. But it was moderate. "It is not the

time yet to overthrow landlords," he said. "We must make some concessions to them." At the present stage, "we should only reduce rents and
interest rates, and increase the wages of hired hands." Quoting Mao as
saying "we are not preparing to take the land immediately," Freyer told
the Russians' control body, the Far Eastern Bureau, that Mao's speech
was basically "fine," but inclined towards being too moderate.

Though Mao did not address the issue of violence, his general
approach was not militant. Shortly afterwards he went off on an inspection tour of the Hunan countryside. By the end of the tour, which lasted
thirty-two days, he had undergone a dramatic change. Mao himself was
to say that before this trip he had been taking a moderate line, and "not
until I stayed in Hunan for over thirty days did I completely change my
attitude." What really happened was that Mao discovered in himself a
love for bloodthirsty thuggery. This gut enjoyment, which verged on
sadism, meshed with, but preceded, his affinity for Leninist violence.
Mao did not come to violence via theory. The propensity sprang from
his character, and was to have a profound impact on his future methods
of rule.

As he wrote in his report about his tour, Mao saw that grassroots peasant association bosses were mostly "ruffians," activists who were the poorest and roughest, and who had been the most despised. Now they had
power in their hands. They "have become lords and masters, and have
turned the peasant associations into something quite terrifying in their
hands," he wrote. They chose their victims arbitrarily. "They coined the
phrase: 'Anyone who has land is a tyrant, and all gentry are bad.' " They
"strike down the landlords to the ground, and stamp on them with their
feet . . . they trample and romp on the ivory beds of the misses and
madames. They seize people whenever they feel like it, put a high dunce's
hat on them, and parade them round. All in all, they thoroughly indulge
every whim . . . and really have created terror in the countryside."

Mao saw that the thugs loved to toy with victims and break down
their dignity, as he described with approval:

> A tall paper hat is put on [the victim], and on the hat is written landed
> tyrant so-and-so or bad gentry so-and-so. Then the person is pulled
> by a rope [like pulling an animal], followed by a big crowd . . . This
> punishment makes [victims] tremble most. After one such treatment,
> these people are forever broken . . .

The threat of uncertainty, and anguish, particularly appealed to him:

> The peasant association is most clever. They seized a bad gentleman
> and declared that they were going to [do the above to] him . . . But
> then they decided not to do it that day . . . That bad gentleman did

not know when he would be given this treatment, so every day he lived in anguish and never knew a moment's peace.

Mao was very taken with one weapon, the *suo-biao*, a sharp, twin-edged knife with a long handle like a lance: "it . . . makes all landed tyrants and bad gentry tremble at the sight of it. The Hunan revolutionary authorities should . . . make sure every young and middle-aged male has one. There should be no limit put on [the use of] it."

Mao saw and heard much about brutality, and he liked it. In the report he wrote afterwards, in March 1927, he said he felt "a kind of ecstasy never experienced before." His descriptions of the brutality oozed excitement, and flowed with an adrenalin rush. "It is wonderful! It is wonderful!" he exulted.

Mao was told that people had been beaten to death. When asked what to do—and for the first time the life and death of people hung on one word of his—he said: "One or two beaten to death, no big deal." Immediately after his visit, a rally was held in the village, at which another man, who was accused of opposing the peasant association, was savagely killed.

Before Mao arrived, there had been attempts by the leaders of the peasant movement in Hunan to bring down the level of violence, and they had detained some of those who had perpetrated atrocities. Now Mao ordered the detainees to be released. A revolution was not like a dinner party, he admonished the locals; it needed violence. "It is necessary to bring about a . . . reign of terror in every county." Hunan's peasant leaders obeyed.

Mao did not once address the issue that concerned peasants most, which was land redistribution. There was actually an urgent need for leadership, as some peasant associations had already begun doing their own redistribution, by moving boundary markers and burning land leases. People put forward various specific proposals. Not Mao. All he said at a Nationalist land committee meeting discussing this issue on 12 April was: "Confiscation of land boils down to not paying rent. There is no need for anything else."

What fascinated Mao was violence that smashed the social order. And it was this propensity that caught Moscow's eye, as it fitted into the Soviet model of a social revolution. Mao was now published for the first time in the Comintern journal, which ran his Hunan report (though without his name on it, and in a shortened version). He had shown that although he was ideologically shaky, his instincts were those of a Leninist. Some other Communists—especially the Party leader Professor Chen, who flew into a rage when he heard about mob atrocities and insisted that they had to be reined in—were ultimately not Communists of the Soviet type. Now, more than two years after casting him out, the CCP readmitted Mao into the leading circle. In April 1927 he was restored to the Central

Committee, though only into the second tier without a vote (called an alternate member).

Mao was based at this time in the city of Wuhan, on the Yangtze, some 300 km northeast of Changsha, where he had moved from Canton with the Nationalist headquarters as the Nationalist army pushed north. Now even more prominent among the Nationalists as an overseer of the peasant movement, he stepped up the training of rural agitators so that they spread his violent line to new areas taken by the army. One text that Mao selected to guide his trainees described peasant association activists discussing ways to deal with their victims. If they were "stubborn," "we'll slit their ankle tendons and cut off their ears." The author greeted the punishments, in particular this gruesome one, with rapture: "I had been listening so absorbedly as if in a drunken stupor or trance. Now I was suddenly woken up by the yelling of 'Wonderful,' and I too couldn't help bursting out 'Wonderful!' " This account was extraordinarily similar to Mao's own report, both in style and language, and was most likely written by Mao himself.

AS VIOLENCE ACCELERATED under Mao's tutelage, the Nationalist army turned against the Soviet model their party was following. A large part of the army was from Hunan, and the officers, who came from relatively prosperous families, found that their parents and relatives were being arrested and abused. But it was not just the better-off who suffered; the rank-and-file were also being hit. Professor Chen reported to the Comintern in June: "even the little money sent home by ordinary soldiers was confiscated," and the troops were "repelled by the excesses," seeing that the outcome of their fighting was to bring disaster to their own families.

Many in the Nationalist Party had been unhappy about their leaders adopting Moscow's line right from the start, when Sun Yat-sen embraced the Russians in the early 1920s. Their anger had reached the boiling point after the Nationalists' second congress in January 1926, when the much smaller CCP (with far fewer than 10,000 members) seemed to have hijacked the Nationalists, who had several hundred thousand members. Under Wang Ching-wei, one-third of the 256 delegates were Communists. Another third were "on the left," among whom was a large contingent of secret Communists. Not only had Moscow planted its Trojan horse, the CCP itself, inside the Nationalists, it had also infiltrated a large number of moles. Now, over a year later, the mob violence condoned by their party led many prominent Nationalists to call for a break with Moscow's control, and with the Chinese Communists.

The crisis quickly came to a head. One thousand kilometers to the north, on 6 April 1927 the Peking authorities raided Russian premises and seized a large cache of documents which revealed that Moscow was engaged in extensive subversion aimed at overthrowing the Peking government and replacing it with a client. The documents also showed secret Soviet links with the Chinese Communists. In fact, one important CCP leader, Li Ta-chao, and some sixty other Chinese Communists were arrested in the Russian compound, where they had been living. Li was soon executed by strangulation.

The raids received wide publicity, as did the documents. The proof of Soviet subversion on a massive scale outraged Chinese public opinion and alarmed Western powers. Unless the Nationalists took decisive action to dissociate themselves from the Russians and the CCP, they risked being seen as part of the conspiracy to turn China into a Soviet satellite. Many Nationalists might leave the party, the general public would be repelled, and the Western powers stiffened in their resolve to give full backing to the Peking regime. It was at this point that the commander-in-chief of the Nationalist army, Chiang Kai-shek, took action. On 12 April he gave orders to "cleanse" the Nationalist Party of Communist influence. He issued a wanted list of 197 Communists, headed by Borodin and including Mao Tse-tung.

CHIANG KAI-SHEK HAD been born into a salt merchant family in the east coast province of Zhejiang in 1887, six years before Mao. Later familiar abroad as "the Generalissimo," he was a professional military man, and in public presented a stolid, rather remote and humorless appearance. He had trained in Japan, and in 1923, as Nationalist chief of staff, had headed a mission to Soviet Russia. At the time he was regarded by the Russians as on the "left wing of the Nationalists" and "very close to us," but his three-month visit turned him profoundly anti-Soviet, particularly on the issue of class struggle: he was deeply averse to Moscow's insistence on dividing Chinese society into classes and making them fight each other.

But Chiang did not breathe a word in public about his real views when he returned to China. On the contrary, he gave Borodin the impression that he was "extremely friendly to us, and full of enthusiasm." He concealed his true colors for one simple reason—the Nationalists were dependent on Soviet military assistance for their goal of conquering China. Chiang, who meanwhile had risen to No. 2 in the Nationalist Party, had, however, been quietly preparing the ground for a split, and had already removed some Communists from key positions in March 1926. This caused the Russians to start plotting ways to get rid of him. According to one of their agents in Canton, their idea was "to play for time and prepare the liquidation of this general [Chiang]." A year later, in early 1927, Borodin had issued a secret order to have Chiang arrested, though the plan did not materialize.

The moment the Peking government published documents about Russian subversion, Chiang acted. On 12 April, he issued a notice which said, in essence: arrest Communists. He moved first in Shanghai, which had been the HQ of the CCP, and where he himself was. The Communists had armed pickets there. Chiang took steps to disarm them. Towards this end he enlisted gangsters to pick a fight with the pickets, to create an excuse for his army to descend and confiscate the arms. Communist strongholds were assaulted, many trade union leaders arrested, and some shot. Chiang's troops opened fire with machine-guns on a subsequent protest march. In the space of a few days, there were probably more than 300 deaths on the Communist side. Chiang had broken the Communists as an organized force able to operate in public in Shanghai, though the CCP leadership remained largely intact—and, amazingly, Shanghai continued to be where the Party Center resided and operated, clandestinely, even in the middle of the purge. For the following five or six years, "Shanghai" was synonymous with the CCP leadership (and we use it in this sense).

After Chiang Kai-shek started killing Communists in Shanghai, Nationalist chief Wang Ching-wei, who was in Wuhan, some 600 km inland, broke with the CCP and submitted to Chiang. From now on, Chiang Kai-shek became the head of the Nationalist Party. He went on to build a regime that lasted twenty-two years on the mainland, until he was driven to Taiwan by Mao in 1949.

IN THE LEAD-UP TO Wang's split, Mao faced a choice. He had been much more appreciated by Wang than by his fellow Communists and most Russians, and he had risen much higher among the Nationalists than in the CCP. Should he now go with Wang? He was later to say of this time: "I felt desolate, and for a while, didn't know what to do." It was in this rather torn state of mind that one day he ascended a beautiful pavilion on the bank of the Yangtze in Wuhan. Originally built in AD 223 the Yellow Crane Pavilion was a landmark. Legend had it that here a man had once beckoned to a yellow crane flying along the Yangtze, rode on its back to the Celestial Palace—and never returned. The Yellow Crane thus came to mean something gone forever. Now it seemed an apt metaphor for everything Mao had built up for himself in the Nationalist Party. It was a day darkened with heavy rain. As he stood by the carved balustrade of the pavilion, looking across the vastness of the Yangtze, "locked in," as he wrote in a poem, between Mount Snake and Mount Tortoise on either side, but extended to the infinite by the deluge from the sky, Mao pondered his alternatives. In a traditional libation, he poured his drink into the torrent below, and finished his poem with the line: "The tide of my heart soars with the mighty waves!"

Mao made a bid to keep Wang on the Communists' side by disowning the peasant association thugs whom he had previously hailed as wonderful, and casting them as scapegoats. On 13 June, Wang Ching-wei told other Wuhan leaders: "Only after Comrade Mao Tse-tung's report did we realise that peasant associations are controlled by gangsters. They don't know anything about the Nationalists or the Communists, they only know the business of killing and arson." Mao's attempt to pass the buck was futile. His Nationalist mentor was already planning to break with the Communists, and blame them for all the rural atrocities. As the most vocal promoter of this violence, Mao had to say goodbye to Wang and the Nationalists. He was already on the wanted list. But quite apart from this, to stay with Wang would mean having to become a moderate, and respect social order. Mao was not prepared to do this, not after he had discovered his fondness for brutality in rural Hunan. Nearly a decade before, as a 24-year-old, he had expressed his craving for violent and drastic social change: "the country must be . . . destroyed and then re-formed . . . People like me long for its destruction . . ." The Soviet model suited his impulse.

For the first time, Mao had to risk his neck. During the arrest scare two years before, he had had time to summon a sedan chair and make off in leisurely fashion to Changsha. But now escape was not so simple. There was no obvious safe haven and the killing of Communists had started. Professor Chen's eldest son was arrested and beheaded on 4 July. By the end of the year, after the Communists had launched violent uprisings of their own and taken many lives, tens of thousands of Communists and suspects were slaughtered. Anyone could be arrested, and killed, simply on the charge of being a Communist. Many died proclaiming their faith, some shouting slogans, others singing the "Internationale." Newspapers hailed executions with pitiless headlines.

Mao first had to ensure his personal safety. Then he decided to use the CCP and the Russians for his own ends. This decision, taken in summer 1927, when he was thirty-three, marked Mao's political coming of age.

LONG MARCH TO SUPREMACY IN THE PARTY

HIJACKING A RED FORCE AND TAKING OVER BANDIT LAND

(1927–28 ∗ AGE 33–34)

AT THE TIME Chiang Kai-shek broke with the Communists in April 1927, Stalin had emerged as the No. 1 in the Kremlin and was personally dictating policy on China. His reaction to Chiang's split was to order the CCP to form its own army without delay and occupy territory, with the long-term aim of conquering China with the gun.

The military option—the use of force to bring the Chinese Communists to power—had been Moscow's favored approach ever since the Comintern was founded in 1919. As long as the Nationalists were in play, Moscow's strategy had been for CCP members to infiltrate and subvert the Nationalist armed forces. Once the break came, Stalin ordered the Communists to pull out those units they were able to control, and "form some new corps."

Stalin sent a trusted fellow Georgian, Beso Lominadze, to China. Jan Berzin, the head of Russian military intelligence, the GRU, wrote to the commissar for war, Kliment Voroshilov, who chaired the China Commission in Moscow, that Russia's top priority in China now was to establish a Red army. A huge secret military advice and support system for the Chinese Communists was set up in Russia. The GRU had men in all the main Chinese cities, providing arms, funds and medicine, in addition to intelligence that was often critical to the CCP's survival. Moscow also sent top-level advisers to China to guide the Party's military operations, while greatly expanding military training for CCP cadres in Russia.

The immediate plan, devised in Moscow, was for the Communist units pulled out of the Nationalist army to move to the south coast to collect arms shipped in from Russia, and set up a base. At the same time, peasant uprisings were ordered in Hunan and three adjacent provinces where there had been militant peasant organizations, with the goal of taking power in these regions.

Mao agreed with the military approach. On 7 August 1927 he told an emergency Party meeting presided over by Lominadze: "power comes out of the barrel of the gun" (a saying that later acquired international fame). But within this broad design, Mao harbored his own agenda—to command both the gun and the Party. His plan was to build his own army, carve out his own territory, and deal with Moscow and Shanghai from a position of strength. To have his own fiefdom would safeguard his physical survival. He would of course remain in the Party, as its association with Russia was his only chance of achieving anything more than being a mere bandit.

At this time, Professor Chen had just been dismissed as Party chief by Lominadze, and made the scapegoat for the Nationalist split. His replacement was a younger man called Chu Chiu-pai, whose main qualification was his closeness to the Russians. Mao was now promoted, from the Central Committee to the Politburo, though still as a second-level member.

It was now that Mao embarked on a series of steps that would take him to the top of the Communist ladder in the space of four years. As of summer 1927, he had no armed men at his service, and held no military command, so he set out to acquire an armed force by taking over troops that other Communists had built up.

AT THE TIME, the main force the Reds were able to pull out of the Nationalist army consisted of 20,000 troops stationed in and around Nanchang, the capital of Jiangxi province, about 250 km southeast of Wuhan and 300 km east of Changsha. These troops had nothing to do with Mao. On 1 August they mutinied, on Moscow's instructions. The main organizer of the mutiny was Chou En-lai, the Party man designated to run the military, with immediate supervision from a Russian military adviser, Kumanin.* They then headed straight for Swatow (Shantou) on the coast, 600 km to the south, where the Russians were supposed to ship in arms.

Mao set out to lay his hands on some of these men. On their way to the coast they were scheduled to pass near South Hunan. In early August he proposed to the CCP leadership that he launch a peasant uprising in South Hunan, to establish what he called a big Red base, covering "at least five counties." In fact, Mao had no intention of trying to start such a rising. He had never organized one, nor did he think it could be done. (The earlier peasant violence in Hunan had been carried out under the

---

* This mutiny entered myth as a purely Chinese operation under the misleading name of "the Nanchang Uprising," and 1 August was later designated the founding day of the Chinese Communist Army. But, as Stalin bluntly put it, the operation was "on the initiative of the Comintern, and only on its initiative." These words were deleted from the published version of Stalin's speech. The man in charge of delivering arms to the mutineers was Anastas Mikoyan.

protection of the then radical government.) The sole purpose of the proposal was to set up his next request, which was for a large contingent of the mutineers to come to his aid on their way to the coast. Failing to realize that this Hunan initiative was only a ruse to angle for the troops, Shanghai approved Mao's plan.

The leaders of the Hunan "uprising" were scheduled to meet on 15 August at the Russian consulate in Changsha, to launch the action. But Mao did not turn up, although he was on the outskirts of the city. As he was in charge of the mission, the meeting had to be postponed to the following day, when again he failed to show up. He only finally appeared on the 18th, when he moved into the consulate, for the sake of security. To his angry and frustrated comrades, he offered the excuse that he had been conducting "investigations into the peasantry."

Mao concealed the true reason for his four-day absence—which was to give himself time to see how the mutineers were faring, and whether they would still be passing South Hunan and thus be available to him. If not, he had no intention of going to South Hunan.

The mutineers had got off to a bad start. Within three days of leaving Nanchang, one-third of them had deserted; many others had died drinking dirty water from rice paddies in humid 30-plus centigrade temperatures. The survivors had already lost nearly half their ammunition. The dwindling ranks were struggling just to survive and make it to the coast, and the chances of any making a detour to help him were nil.

So when Mao finally joined his comrades at the Russian consulate, he demanded that the plans for an uprising in South Hunan be canceled, even though it had been his proposal in the first place. Instead, he insisted on attacking just Changsha, the provincial capital, arguing that they should "narrow down the uprising plan."

The aim of this new plan was exactly the same as before—to lay his hands on some armed men. At this point the only Red forces anywhere near him were outside Changsha. They consisted of three groups: peasant activists with weapons seized from the police; unemployed miners and mine guards from the mine at Anyuan, which had closed down; and one army unit that had been stranded en route to join the Nanchang mutineers. Altogether, the force totaled several thousand. Mao's point in advocating an attack on Changsha was that these forces would be deployed for action, and he could maneuver to become their boss.

The ploy was successful. Mao's proposal to go for Changsha was adopted, and he was put in control by being made head of a "Front Committee." This made him the Party representative on the spot and thus the man with the final say, in the absence of higher authority. Mao had no military training, but he pitched hard for this job by staging a show of enthusiasm for Moscow's orders in front of the two Russians at the meeting, who called the shots. "The latest Comintern order" about uprisings was so brilliant, Mao said, "it made me jump for joy three hundred times."

Mao's next move was to *prevent* the troops actually going to Changsha, and instead have them muster at a place where he could abduct them. This place had to be far enough away from Changsha that other Party or Russian representatives could not easily reach it. There was no telephone or radio communication with these forces.

On 31 August, Mao left the Russian consulate, saying that he was going to join the troops. But he did not do this. Instead, he made his way to a town called Wenjiashi, 100 km east of Changsha, and there he stayed. On the launch day set for 11 September, Mao was not with any of the troops, but lying low in Wenjiashi. By the 14th, before the troops had got anywhere near Changsha or suffered serious defeats, he had ordered them to abandon the march on Changsha and converge on his location. As a result, the Party organization in Changsha had to abort the whole design on the 15th. The secretary of the Soviet consulate, Maier, referred to the retreat as "most despicable treachery and cowardice." Moscow called the affair "a joke of an uprising." It does not seem to have realized that Mao had set the whole thing up solely in order to snare the armed units.

The operation appears in history books as "the Autumn Harvest Uprising," portrayed as a peasant uprising led by Mao. It is the founding moment of the international myth about Mao as a peasant leader, and one of the great deceptions of Mao's career (to cover it up he was to spin an elaborate yarn to his American spokesman, Edgar Snow). Not only was the "uprising" not an authentic peasant undertaking, but Mao was not involved in any action*—and actually sabotaged it.

But he got what he was after—control of an armed force, of some 1,500 men. Due south about 170 kilometers from Wenjiashi lay the Jinggang Mountain range, traditional bandit country. Mao had decided to make this his base of operations. The lack of proper roads meant that many of China's mountain areas were largely out of reach of the authorities. This particular place had an added advantage: it straddled the border of two provinces, and so was on the very outer edge of both provinces' control.

Mao had a link with a successful outlaw in the area, Yuan Wen-cai. Yuan and his partner Wang Zuo had an army of 500 men and controlled most of one county, Ninggang, which had a population of 130,000. They lived by collecting rents and taxes from the local population.

Mao anticipated problems getting the commanders of the force he had hijacked to go to the bandit country without explicit Party orders, so at Wenjiashi he first sought out a few men he knew already and secured

---

* One of Mao's closest subordinates confirmed that by the time Mao turned up, "the Autumn Harvest Uprising had failed."

their support, before he called a meeting of the commanders on 19 September. He arranged for his supporters to serve tea and cigarettes so that they could come into the room and keep an eye on things. The argument was fierce—the main commander demanded that they proceed with the old plan and go for Changsha. But Mao was the only Party leader present (the others and the Russians were 100 km away in Changsha), and he prevailed. The force set off for Jinggang Mountain. At first, Mao was such a stranger to the troops that some thought he was a local and tried to grab him to carry guns.

Mao was dressed like a country schoolteacher, in a long blue gown, with a homespun cotton scarf around his neck. Along the way, he talked to soldiers, assessing their condition and gauging their strength—"as if counting family treasure," one soldier recalled.

When Mao first told the troops that they were about to become "Mountain Lords"—bandits—they were dumbfounded. This was not why they had joined a Communist revolution. But, speaking in the name of the Party, he assured them that they would be special bandits—part of an international revolution. Banditry was also their best chance, he argued: "Mountain Lords have never been wiped out, let alone us."

Still, many were depressed. They were exhausted, and malaria, suppurating legs and dysentery were rife. Whenever they stopped, they were swamped by their own thick stench, so foul it could be smelled a couple of kilometers away. Sick and wounded would lie down in the grass, and often never get up again. Many deserted. Knowing that he could not force his men to stay, Mao allowed those who wanted to leave to do so, without their guns. Two of the top commanders opted to leave, and went to Shanghai. Both of them later went over to the Nationalists. By the time he reached the outlaw land, Mao had only about 600 men left, having lost well over half his force in a couple of weeks. Most of those who stayed did so because they had no alternative. They became the nucleus from which Mao's force grew—what he later called the "single spark that started a prairie fire."

ARRIVING IN BANDIT COUNTRY at the beginning of October Mao's first step was to visit Yuan, accompanied by only a few men, so as to reassure the bandit chief. Yuan had some armed men hidden nearby in case Mao brought troops. Finding Mao apparently no threat, Yuan had a pig slaughtered for a banquet, and they sat drinking tea and nibbling peanuts and melon seeds.

Mao got his foot in the door by pretending he was only pausing en route to the coast to join the Nanchang mutineers. A deal was struck. Mao could stay temporarily, and would feed his own troops by staging looting expeditions. But to start with, they would be looked after by the outlaws.

By February 1928, four months later, Mao had become the master of his hosts. The finale of this takeover took place after Mao's men captured the capital of Ninggang county from the government on 18 February, in what was, by the bandits' standards, a sizable military victory. This was also the first battle that Mao was involved in commanding—watching through binoculars from a mountain opposite.

Three days later, on the 21st, Mao held a public rally of an organized crowd of thousands of people to celebrate the victory. The climax was the killing of the county chief, who had just been captured. An eyewitness described the scene (in cautious language, as he was telling the story under Communist rule): "A fork-shaped wooden frame was driven into the ground . . . onto which Chang Kai-yang [the county chief] was tied. The whole place was ringed with ropes from one wooden pole to another for hanging slogans. People thrust their spears, *suo-biao*, into him and killed him that way . . . Commissar Mao spoke at the rally." Mao had earlier expressed a special fondness for this weapon, *suo-biao*. Now, under his very eyes, it pierced the life out of the county chief.

Public execution rallies had become a feature of local life since Mao's arrival, and he had demonstrated a penchant for slow killing. At one rally, staged to celebrate a looting expedition at the time of the Chinese New Year 1928, he had written couplets on sheets of red paper, which were pasted onto wooden pillars on both sides of the stage. They read:

> *Watch us kill the bad landlords today.*
> *Aren't you afraid?*
> *It's knife slicing upon knife.*

Mao addressed the rally, and a local landlord, Kuo Wei-chien, was then put to death in line with the prescriptions of Mao's poetry.

Mao did not invent public execution, but he added to this ghastly tradition a modern dimension, organized rallies, and in this way made killing compulsory viewing for a large part of the population. To be dragooned into a crowd, powerless to walk away, forced to watch people put to death in this bloody and agonizing way, hearing their screams, struck fear deep into those present.

The traditional bandits could not match Mao and his orchestrated terror, which frightened even them. Yuan and Zuo submitted to Mao's authority; soon after this they allowed themselves and their men to be formed into a regiment under him. Mao had out-bandited the bandits.

AS SOON AS he had reached the bandit land, Mao had sent a messenger to Party headquarters in Changsha. Contact was established within days, in October 1927, by which time Shanghai had received reports about the events surrounding the Autumn Harvest Uprising. What could not have failed to emerge was that Mao had aborted the venture, and had then made off with the troops without authorization. Shanghai sent for Mao (along with others) to discuss the fiasco. Mao ignored the summons, and on 14 November he was expelled from his Party posts.

The Party made a determined effort to get rid of him. On 31 December, Shanghai told Hunan that "the Centre" considered that "the . . . army led by comrade Mao Tse-tung . . . has committed extremely serious errors politically. The Centre orders [you] to dispatch a senior comrade there, with the Resolutions [expelling Mao] . . . to call a congress for army comrades . . . to reform the Party organization there." Clearly anticipating trouble from Mao, the message added: "assign a brave and smart worker comrade to be the Party representative."

The banner of the Party was critical to Mao, as he had little personal magnetism. His solution to the Party order was simple: prevent the news of his expulsion from ever reaching his men.

A week after Shanghai issued its order, the entire Hunan committee was conveniently—some might say suspiciously—arrested by the Nationalists. Mao's troops never learned that the Party had withdrawn its mandate from him. It was not until March 1928 that the first Party envoy was allowed to appear in Mao's base, bringing the message that expelled him. But Mao outsmarted the Party by ensuring that the envoy could only deliver the message to a few hand-picked lackeys, and then pretending to submit by resigning his Party post, which he passed on to a stooge. He awarded himself a new title, Division Commander, and continued to control the army.

THIS BANDIT COUNTRY made an ideal base, well supplied with food. The mountains, though rising to only 995 meters, were steep, and gave excellent security, being ringed by precipices, with dense forests of fir and bamboo that were permanently shrouded in mist, and teemed with monkeys, wild boar, tigers and all sorts of poisonous snakes. It was easy to defend, and to get out of in an emergency, as there were hidden byways leading out to two provinces—narrow mud paths buried under masses of vegetation, impossible for strangers to spot. For outlaws, it was a safe haven.

Mao and his troops lived by staging looting sorties to neighboring counties, and sometimes farther afield. These forays were grandly called *da tu-hao*—literally, "smash landed tyrants." In fact they were indiscriminate, classic bandit raids. Mao told his troops: "If the masses don't understand what 'landed tyrants' means, you can tell them it means the moneyed, or 'the rich.'" The term "the rich" was highly relative, and could mean a family with a couple of dozen liters of cooking oil, or a few hens. "Smash" covered a range of activities from plain robbery and ransom to killing.

These raids made frequent headlines in the press, and greatly raised Mao's profile. It was now that he gained notoriety as a major bandit chief.

But his bandit activities garnered little support from the locals. One Red soldier recalled how hard it was to persuade the population to help them identify the rich, or to join in a raid, or even share the loot. Another described one night's experience:

> We usually surrounded the house of the landed tyrant, seizing him first and then starting to confiscate things. But this time as soon as we broke in, gongs sounded all of a sudden . . . and several hundred enemies [villagers] emerged . . . They seized over forty of our men, locked them up in the clan temple . . . beat them and trussed them up, the women stamping on them with their feet. Then grain barrels were put over them, with big stones on top. They were so badly tortured . . .

Although Mao claimed an ideological rationale—fighting the exploiting classes—the fact that his incursions were virtually indistinguishable from traditional bandit behavior remained a permanent source of discontent in his own ranks, particularly among the military commanders. In December 1927 the chief commander, Chen Hao, tried to take the troops away while on a looting expedition. Mao rushed to the scene with a posse of supporters, and had Chen arrested, and later executed in front of the entire force. Mao almost lost his army. In the space of the few months since he had snatched the force away, all its main officers had deserted him.

As a means to curry favor with the troops, Mao set up "soldiers' committees" to satisfy their wish for a say in the proceeds of looting. At the same time, secret Party cells were formed, answering only to Mao as the Party boss. Even ranking military superiors did not know who was a member of the Party, which amounted to a secret organization. In this way Mao used the control mechanism of communism, as well as its name, to maintain his grip on the army.

But as his grip remained far from iron-clad, and he himself was certainly not popular, Mao could never relax his vigilance about his personal safety, and it was from now that he began to perfect the security measures that developed in later life into a truly awesome—if largely invisible—system. To begin with, he had about a hundred guards, and the number grew. He picked several houses in different places in bandit country, and had them fully rigged for security. The houses invariably had escape exits such as a hole in the wall, usually at the back, leading into the mountains. Later, on the Long March, even when he was on the move, most of his houses had one notable characteristic: a special exit leading to an emergency escape route.

Mao lived in style. One residence, called the Octagonal Pavilion, was of great architectural distinction. The spacious main part, opening onto a large courtyard set beside a river, had a ceiling consisting of three layers of octagonal wooden panels that spiraled into a little glass roof, like a glass-topped pagoda. It had belonged to a local doctor, who was now moved to a corner of the courtyard but continued to practice—most convenient for Mao, as he was never quite free of some ailment or other.

Another house that Mao occupied, in the big town of Longshi, was also a doctor's, and also magnificent. It had a strange beauty that bespoke the former prosperity of the town. The enormous house was half a European masonry villa, with an elegant loggia above a row of Romanesque arches, and half a brick-and-timber Chinese mansion, with layers of upturned eaves and delicate latticed windows. The two parts were grafted together by an exquisite octagonal doorway.

Mao's actual HQ in Longshi was a splendid two-story mansion set in 2,000 square meters of ground, once the best school for young men from three counties—until Mao came. The whole top floor was open on three sides and looked out onto a vista of rivers and clouds. It had been designed for the pupils to enjoy the breeze in the stifling days of summer. Mao's occupation of this building was to set a pattern. Wherever he went, schools, clan temples and Catholic churches (often the sturdiest buildings in many parts of remote rural China) were commandeered. These were the only buildings large enough for meetings, apart from being the best. School classes, naturally, were shut down.

During his entire stay in the outlaw land, which lasted fifteen months, Mao ventured into the mountains only three times, for a total period of less than a month. And when he did go, he was not exactly traveling rough. When he went to call on bandit chief Zuo, he stayed in a brilliantly white mansion known as the White House, formerly owned by a Cantonese timber merchant. He was entertained lavishly, with pigs and sheep slaughtered in his honor.

The contours of Mao's future lifestyle in power were already emerging. He had acquired a sizable personal staff, which included a manager, a cook, a cook's help with the special duty of carrying water for Mao, a groom who looked after a small horse for his master, and secretaries. One errand boy's "special task" was to keep him supplied with the right brand of cigarettes from Longshi. Another orderly collected newspapers and books whenever they took a town or looted a rich house.

MAO ALSO ACQUIRED a wife—his third—almost as soon as he settled in outlaw country. A pretty young woman with large eyes, high cheekbones, an almond-shaped face and a willowy figure, Gui-yuan was just turning eighteen when she met Mao. She came from the rich county of Yongxin at the foot of the mountain, and her parents, who owned a teahouse, had given her the name Gui-yuan (*Gui*: osmanthus, and *yuan*: round) because she was born on an autumn evening when a round moon shone above a blossoming osmanthus tree. She had attended a mission- ary school run by two Finnish ladies, but was not content with being brought up as a lady. Her restless, fiery temperament rejected the tradi- tional claustrophobic life prescribed for women, and made her yearn for a wider world, enjoyment, and some action. So, in the stirring atmosphere of the Northern Expedition army's entry into her town in summer 1926, she joined the Communist Party. Soon she was making speeches in public, as a cheerleader welcoming the troops. At the age of only sixteen, she was appointed head of the Women's Department in the new government for the whole county, starting her job by cutting off her own long hair, an act that was still revolutionary and eyebrow-raising.

A year later, after Chiang Kai-shek's split, Communists and activists were on the run, including her parents and younger sister, who had also joined the Party. Her elder brother, also a Communist, was thrown into prison, along with many others, but the outlaw Yuan was a friend of his, and helped to break him out of jail. Gui-yuan and her brother escaped with the outlaws, and she became best friends with Mrs. Yuan. Zuo, the other outlaw, who had three wives, gave her a Mauser pistol.

When Mao came, Yuan assigned her to act as his interpreter. Mao did not speak the local dialect, and he never learned it. Here, as in his later peregrinations, he had to communicate with the locals through an interpreter.

Mao at once began to court her, and by the beginning of 1928 they were "married"—with no binding ceremony but a sumptuous banquet prepared by Mrs. Yuan. This was barely four months after Mao had left Kai-hui, the mother of his three sons, the previous August. He had writ- ten to her just once, mentioning that he had foot trouble. From the time of his new marriage, he abandoned his family.

Unlike Kai-hui, who was madly in love with him, Gui-yuan married Mao with reluctance. A beautiful woman in a crowd of men, she had many suitors and considered Mao, at thirty-four, "too old" and "not worthy" of her, as she told a close friend. Mao's youngest brother, Tse- tan, handsome and lively, also fancied Gui-yuan. "My brother has a wife," he said. "Better to be with me." She chose the elder Mao because she felt the "need for protection politically in that environment," as she later conceded.

In a world of few women and a lot of sexually frustrated men, Mao's relationship with Gui-yuan caused gossip. Mao was careful: he and Gui- yuan avoided appearing in public together. When the couple walked past the building that housed wounded soldiers, he would ask Gui-yuan to go separately.

By the end of a year of marriage, Gui-yuan had resolved to leave Mao. She confided to a friend that she was unlucky to have married him and felt she had "made a big sacrifice" by doing so. When Mao decided to leave the outlaw land, in January 1929, she tried desperately to stay behind. Gui-yuan may well have been thinking about more than just leaving Mao. She had been swept into a maelstrom while still only in her teens, and now her desire to quit was so strong that she was prepared to risk capture by the Reds' enemies. However, Mao ordered her to be taken along "at any cost." She cried all the way, repeatedly falling behind, only to be fetched by Mao's guards with his horse.

MAO'S STANDING WITH the Party began to change in April 1928, when a large Red unit of thousands of men, the surviving Nanchang mutineers, the troops he had angled for right from the start, sought refuge in his base. They came to Mao as a defeated force whose much-depleted ranks had been routed on the south coast the previous October, when the Russians failed to deliver the promised arms. The remnants of the force had been rallied by a 41-year-old officer called Zhu De, a former professional soldier with the rank of brigadier, and something of a veteran among the mainly twentyish Reds. He had gone to Germany in his mid-thirties, and joined the Party before moving on to Russia for special military training. He was a cheerful man, and a soldier's soldier, who mingled easily with the rank and file, eating and marching with them, carrying guns and backpacks like the rest, wearing straw sandals, a bamboo hat on his back. He was constantly to be found at the front.

Mao had always coveted the Nanchang mutineers, and when he first arrived in outlaw territory had sent a message urging Zhu to join him, but Zhu had declined. Shanghai's orders had been to launch uprisings in the southeast corner of Hunan around New Year 1928, and Zhu, as a loyal Party man, had followed orders. The uprisings failed abysmally, thanks to the sheer absurdity and brutality of Moscow's tactics. According to a report at the time, the policy was to "kill every single one of the class enemies and burn and destroy their homes." The slogan was "Burn, burn, burn! Kill, kill, kill!" Anyone unwilling to kill and burn was termed "running dog of the gentry [who] deserves to be killed."

In line with this policy, Zhu's men razed two whole towns, Chenzhou and Leiyang, to the ground.* The result was to foment a real uprising— against the Communists. One day, at a rally held to try to force peasants to do more burning and killing, the peasants revolted and killed the attending Communists. In village after village and town after town where

---

* One of the Russians in Shanghai told Moscow that "everything has been given over to fire and the sword and people were shot right and left."

Zhu's men were active, rebellions sprang up against the Reds. Peasants slaughtered grassroots Party members, tore off the red neckerchiefs they had been ordered to wear, and donned white ones to demonstrate their allegiance to the Nationalists.

Once Nationalist troops began to apply pressure, Zhu had to run, and thousands of civilians went with him: the families of the activists who had done the burning and killing, who had nowhere else to go. This was what Moscow had intended: peasants must be coerced into doing things that left no way back into normal life. To "get them to join the revolution," the Party had decreed, "there is only one way: use Red terror to prod them into doing things that leave them with no chance to make compromises later with the gentry and bourgeoisie." One man from Leiyang recounted: "I had suppressed [i.e., killed] counter-revolutionaries, so I could not live peacefully now. I had to go all the way . . . So I burned my own house with my own hands . . . and left [with Zhu]."

After these people left, the cycle of revenge and retribution brought more casualties, among them a young woman who had been adopted by Mao's mother, called Chrysanthemum Sister. She had followed Mao into the Party and married a Communist, and they had a young child. Although it seems she and her husband did not support the killings by the Reds, nevertheless her husband was executed after Zhu's army left Leiyang, and his head exhibited in a wooden cage on the city wall. Chrysanthemum Sister was imprisoned. She wanted to recant, but her captors refused permission. She wrote to a relative that she was made to "suffer all the pains I had never imagined existed" and yearned for death: "I long to die and not go on being tortured . . . It would be such relief to leave this world. But my poor [baby], it's so painful to think of him. I had so many plans about bringing him up. Never did I dream all this was going to happen . . . My baby must not blame me . . ." Chrysanthemum Sister was later executed.

Zhu came to Mao as a defeated man, while Mao could represent himself as the person who had in effect saved what was the largest detachment of Communist troops still functioning, at a time when other Red bases were crumbling. All the uprisings the Russians had ordered in the past months had ended in failure. The most famous Red base, Hailufeng, on the south coast, collapsed in late February 1928. During its two-month existence, the area, called "Little Moscow"—there was even a "Red Square," with a gateway copied from the Kremlin—became a carnage ground under its leader Peng Pai, a man with a thirst for blood.* Over 10,000 people were butchered; "reactionary villages were razed wholesale to the ground."

* He praised Lenin, not inappositely, with these words: "His law has no detail. It just kills all opposition. His workers and peasants can just kill off all the landed tyrants, bad gentry,

These failed areas had carried out killing and burning on a much larger scale than Mao's. Mao was not a fanatic. He would stop his men from burning down Catholic churches (which were often the best buildings in rural areas) and fine houses, telling them to keep them for their own use. Killing served its purposes, but it should not jeopardize his broader political interests.

By the time Zhu De came to Mao, Moscow had begun to stop the "aimless and disorderly pogroms and killings" which it termed, with the Communist penchant for jargon, "blind-action-ism" and "killing-and-burning-ism." Shanghai ordered killing to be more targeted. This was exactly what Mao had been doing. He emerged as shrewd and far-sighted, and this dealt him back into the game—and into the Party's good graces. And Stalin's too. Even Mao's disobedience vis-à-vis the Party now had a plus side, as Stalin badly needed a winner—someone with initiative, not just a blind subordinate. Moscow's ability to operate in China, already weakened by Chiang Kai-shek's policy switch in spring 1927, had been further impaired after Russian diplomats were caught red-handed in an attempted putsch in Canton (known as "the Canton Commune") in December 1927. Some missions, including the one in Changsha, were shut down, and Moscow lost diplomatic cover for many of its operatives.

As soon as Zhu De arrived, Mao acted to retrieve his Party mandate, writing to Shanghai on 2 May demanding to form a Special Committee headed by himself. Without waiting for a reply, he had it announced at a rally to celebrate the Mao–Zhu link-up that Mao *was* the Party commissar—and Zhu the commander—of what was to become known as "the Zhu–Mao Red Army." Mao then held a "Party congress" with delegates appointed by himself, and just set up the Special Committee, with himself as its head.

There was an extra reason why Mao required an urgent Party mandate. The contingent Zhu commanded was 4,000 strong, and far outnumbered Mao's, which counted just over 1,000; moreover, half of Zhu's men were proper soldiers, with battle experience. So Mao needed a Party mandate to secure his authority. To establish some martial credentials in the presence of Zhu's army, Mao sported a pistol when he met them, one of the few times he was ever seen carrying one. He soon gave it back to a bodyguard. Mao believed in the gun, but he was not a battlefield man.

While waiting for endorsement from Shanghai, Mao began to behave like a good Party member, accepting Party orders and regular inspectors,

landlords, capitalists, with no need to report to anyone ..." The regime called on people to "disembowel and slice off heads ... slaughter on the spot with no hesitation. Have absolutely not a shred of feeling ...," "kill, kill freely. To kill is the topmost important work in an uprising." Children were praised for "automatically killing reactionaries."

and filing long reports. Till now he had not bothered to find out how many Party members there were in his territory, and had given vague— and exaggerated—answers to an inspector: this county had "over 100," that one "over 1,000." Now Party committees started to function.

He also began to carry out land redistribution, central to the Communist program. He had not bothered to do this before, as it was irrelevant to how he ruled, which was simply by looting.

MEANWHILE, MAO'S LETTER demanding a Party post, which, like all other correspondence, was carried by special messenger, was sent on by Shanghai to Moscow. It reached Stalin on 26 June 1928, right in the middle of the CCP's 6th Congress, then meeting in secret just outside Moscow. That this was the only time any foreign party held a congress in Russia speaks for the exceptional importance Stalin ascribed to China, as does the fact that the Russians arranged and paid for over 100 delegates to travel clandestinely from China.

Stalin's line was delivered by Comintern chief Nikolai Bukharin in an address that spanned nine buttock-numbing hours. Mao was not among those present. He had already adopted a tyrant's golden rule, one to which he stuck for the rest of his life: not to step out of his lair unless he absolutely had to.

Moscow had reservations about Mao. Chou En-lai, the key figure at the Congress, said in his military report that Mao's troops had "a partly bandit character," meaning that Mao did not always toe the line. Yet, fundamentally, Mao was in favor with Moscow, and was cited at the Congress as a key fighting leader. The fact was that he was the most effective man in applying the Kremlin's policy which, as Stalin reiterated to the Chinese Party leaders in person on 9 June, was to establish a Red Army. While in Russia, every delegate to the Congress received army training, and detailed military plans were drawn up. Stalin, the old bank-robber, got personally involved in the financing via a huge counterfeiting operation.

Mao fitted Stalin's bill. He had an army—and a base—and was an old Party member. Moreover, he now had the highest profile, even if of a notorious kind, among all Chinese Communists. He was, as Stalin was later to say to the Yugoslavs, insubordinate, but a winner. And however disobedient he might be, Mao clearly needed the Party, and needed Moscow, and this made him essentially subject to control.

Mao's demands were met in full. By November he had been told that he was in charge of the Zhu–Mao Red Army and its territory around the outlaw land. This was a key moment in his rise. He had faced down the Party—and Moscow itself.

SUBJUGATING THE
RED ARMY SUPREMO
(1928–30 ★ AGE 34–36)

MAO RECEIVED Shanghai's endorsement as head of the Zhu–Mao Army in November 1928, and at once began planning to leave the outlaw land with the army, to take over new domains and new armed forces. He was also leaving because the region was about to be attacked. In June that year, Chiang Kai-shek had defeated the Peking government and brought much of China under his control, setting up his capital in Nanjing. Chiang's troops were on their way to Mao's territory. Mao set off on 14 January 1929. The bulk of the Zhu–Mao Army, now some 3,000 strong, left with him, as did Zhu De, whom Shanghai had appointed military supremo of the army.

Fifteen months after his arrival, Mao left behind a depleted land. In his first experience of running a base he had shown that he had no economic strategy but looting, tantamount to "slash and burn." A Party inspector wrote to Shanghai:

> Before the Red Army came . . . there was quite an atmosphere of peaceful and happy existence . . . the peasants . . . had quite enough to live on . . . Since the Red Army came, things were totally changed. Because the Red Army's sole income was robbing the rich . . . because even petty bourgeois, rich peasants and small pedlars were all treated as enemies, and because after great destruction, no attention was paid to construction or to the economic crisis, the countryside is totally bankrupt, and is collapsing by the day.

Mao's men had bled the place dry, and the locals loathed them. When he departed, he left behind his wounded and the civilian Communists. Those captured by the regular government army were lucky—they were merely machine-gunned to death. Those who fell into the hands of local forces were disemboweled, burned alive, or slashed slowly to death. Many hundreds were killed.

A report to Shanghai by the stay-behind Party committee revealed that the bitterness bequeathed by Mao's regime was so intense that even

the Nationalists "burning houses and killing ring-leaders did not generate hatred from the average masses for the reactionaries." People were
defecting when they could: those "under our Red power naturally do not
dare to act reactionary," the report stated. "But the masses outside [our
control] are crossing over to the Nationalists en masse." The report
blamed the locals, saying that they "have always been no good."

The original outlaws, who were mostly locals and stayed behind, fared
much better. Most of them survived—including the two chiefs, Yuan
and Zuo. However, these two met their deaths a year later, in March
1930—at the hands of Communists who returned to the area. Moscow
had ordered the CCP to double-cross those it termed "bandits"—in
effect, to use them and then kill them. "Alliance with bandits and other
similar groups is only applicable before an uprising," stated one resolution. "Afterwards you must disarm them and severely suppress them . . .
Their leaders must be regarded as leaders of counter-revolutionaries,
even if they helped uprisings. And these leaders must all be completely
eliminated."

Yuan and Zuo's followers fled back into the depths of the mountains
and became fiercely anti-Communist. A Red search unit reported that
"the local population resented us, and did everything to protect the
[outlaws]." Having lived under both the bandits and the Communists,
the locals knew which they preferred.

ON THE JOURNEY out of the outlaw land, Mao loped along, crack-
ing jokes to his entourage. He had cause to be cheerful. Shanghai and
Moscow's acceptance of his demands showed that he could get his way.
Indeed, at that very moment, January 1929, in Moscow, GRU chief Jan
Berzin and Stalin's China apparatchik, Pavel Mif, were meeting to dis-
cuss how the Soviet army could give "practical help to Zhu–Mao," whom
Moscow was tracking closely. This is the first known occasion when
Moscow was arranging military aid specifically for the Mao–Zhu force,
now publicly described as "the most formidable among the Communists."

Government forces were in hot pursuit, and Mao's army had to fight
pitched battles, in one of which Zhu De's wife was captured. Later she
was executed and her head stuck on a pole in Changsha. It was during
this low point in Zhu's fortunes that Mao mounted a power grab against
him. Within two weeks of leaving the outlaw land, Mao had abolished
Zhu De's post as military supremo, awarded by Shanghai, and concentrated all power in his own hands. As the Red force was being attacked
by the Nationalists, Zhu did not retaliate. He was no match for Mao in
exploiting a crisis.

Mao did not inform Shanghai about his seizure of power. Instead he
wrote to tell Shanghai how glad he was to submit to Party orders. "How

should the Red Army proceed?" he wrote. "We particularly thirst for instructions. Please could you send them winging my way?" "The resolutions of the 6th Congress are extremely correct. We accept them jumping for joy." "In the future, we hope the Centre gives us a letter every month." Mao was currying favor with Shanghai hoping that when they got wind of his coup against Zhu De, they would be better disposed towards him.

Still, Zhu De refrained from exposing Mao. Zhu had no craving for power, nor any gift for intrigue. And since reporting to Shanghai was the job of the chief, to write himself would amount to declaring war on Mao.

In March, Mao had another lucky break, this time involving the Nationalists. Although a central government had been in place for nearly a year, Chiang Kai-shek faced powerful opponents, some of whom now started a war against him. Troops who were hot on Mao's trail were pulled back to deal with the rebels. A delighted Mao informed Shanghai that the enemy, who had come within half a kilometer of his rearguard, had "suddenly turned back" and let him go.

By this time Mao had entered the southeast coastal province of Fujian, where he managed to capture Tingzhou—a sizable city, but weakly defended. Located on a navigable river teeming with cargo boats, it was a wealthy place, with strong overseas links. Grand European buildings stood next door to ornate bazaars selling wares from all over Southeast Asia. Mao filled his coffers by robbing the rich. "Our supply is no problem," he told Shanghai, "and morale is extremely high."

The army acquired a uniform for the first time, from a factory that had been making them for the Nationalists. Up till then Red soldiers had been wearing clothes of all kinds and colors, sometimes even women's dresses and Catholic priests' vestments. (One Italian priest was particularly worried about the Reds taking his fascist shirt.) The Communists' new uniform, gray, was like the Nationalist one, but had a red star on the cap, and red insignia.

The city's defender, Brigadier Kuo, had been captured alive on Mao's specific orders, and then killed. A rally was held at which his corpse was hung upside down from a chestnut tree by the dais where Mao made a speech, and the corpse was then paraded through the streets. To show that the old order had been supplanted, Mao also had the city hall razed to the ground.

He set up headquarters in a magnificent old-style villa overlooking the river. But in May his new haven was disturbed when a man called Liu An-gong arrived, sent by Shanghai to take up the No. 3 position in the Zhu–Mao Army. An-gong was fresh from Russia, where he had received military training. He was appalled by what Mao had done to Zhu De, and the way he was running the army. Mao, he charged, was "power-grabbing," "dictatorial"—and was "forming his own system and disobeying the leadership."

Mao could no longer conceal his coup. On 1 June 1929, nearly four months after he had pushed Zhu De out, Mao wrote to Shanghai saying that "the Army" had "decided temporarily to suspend" Zhu's post because "it found itself in a special situation." He did his best to minimize the impact by tucking the information away as item 10 in his long 14-item report. The rest of the report was couched in a very obedient, even ingratiating tone, larded with professions of eagerness to receive Party instructions: "please . . . set up a special communications office," he wrote, to make it possible to communicate directly with Shanghai, adding: "Here is opium worth 10,000 yuan as start-up funds for the office." Mao was trying everything, even drug money, to coax Shanghai to endorse his seizure of power.

With An-gong on his side—and the Red Army no longer being pursued by the Nationalists—Zhu De now stood up to Mao. And he had most of the troops behind him. Mao was extremely unpopular, as an official report later told Shanghai: "the mass as a whole was discontented with Mao." "Many comrades felt really bitter about him" and "regarded him as dictatorial." "He has a foul temper and likes to abuse people." For the sake of balance, Zhu was also criticized, but for trivial things like "bragging," and lacking decorum—"when he was in full flow, he would unconsciously roll his trousers up to his thighs, looking like a hooligan, with no dignity."

There was still a degree of democratic procedure among the Communists, and issues were frequently debated and voted on. Party representatives in the army met on 22 June and voted to dismiss Mao as Party boss of the army and reinstate Zhu as military supremo. Mao later described himself as having been "very isolated." Before the vote he had threatened: "I have a squad, and I will fight!" But there was nothing he could do, as his followers were disarmed before the meeting.

Having lost control of his own force, Mao started jockeying to recover power. His plan was to take control of the region where he was, a newly occupied territory in Fujian near the southeast coast, complete with its own Red force. It was also the richest area the Communists had ever held, with a population of some 1.25 million. Mao told the new leadership of the army that now that he had been voted out, he wanted to go and "do some work with local civilians." Nobody seems to have realized that this request was a cover to enable Mao to gatecrash on the local Reds and commandeer their Party organization.

Mao left HQ on a litter, with his wife and a few faithful followers. One of them remembered: "When we left . . . our horses were confiscated from us, so our entourage really looked rather crestfallen." This bedraggled group headed for Jiaoyang, where Mao had got a local crony to call a congress. The Zhu–Mao Army had helped create the base, so Mao had clout, even though Shanghai had not assigned it to Mao, but to the Fujian Committee. Mao's plan was to manipulate the congress and insert the followers who had left the army with him into the leading posts.

By 10 July some fifty local delegates had gathered in Jiaoyang, having been notified that the congress was to open next day. Instead, Mao sent them away for a whole week to conduct "all sorts of investigations," in the words of a report written immediately afterwards. When the conclave finally opened, Mao feigned illness, and further delayed the meeting. In fact he was not ill, his secretary later disclosed. The report complained that the congress "lasted too long" and operated in a "slack" style, being strung out for "as long as twenty days"—by which time government forces were closing in. At this point, the report continued, "news came that [Nationalist] troops were coming . . . so the Front Committee . . . changed the plan . . . and the congress . . . was closed . . ."

The delegates left without voting for the key posts. As soon as their backs were turned, Mao assigned these posts to his cronies, passing off his action as the decision of the congress. One of his men was made de facto head of the regional Red Army force. Mao's followers were all from Hunan, and could not even speak the local dialect.

When the local Reds discovered that Mao had deprived them of control of their own region, they were outraged. In the following year they were to rebel against Mao, which led him to unleash a bloody purge.

While the congress was still going on, the delegates had already shown that they feared and disliked Mao. The report said that when he was present "the delegates rarely spoke," whereas in his absence "they began to debate passionately, and things improved tremendously." Mao had no mandate over this civilian Party branch. That authority belonged to the Fujian Provincial Committee. The delegates had wanted this body to be represented at the congress, to protect them from Mao. However, the post-mortem noted, "our messenger was arrested, and our report was lost, so there was no one from the Provincial Committee to . . . guide the congress." The post-mortem did not say whether anyone suspected foul play, but there was already a pattern of communications being suddenly broken at critical junctures for Mao.

Once he had seized control of this new territory, Mao set out to undermine Zhu De. An ally in this scheme was a man from Zhu's staff called Lin Biao, a loner and a maverick in his early twenties, whom Mao had been cultivating ever since Lin had come to the outlaw land the year before.

Lin Biao had three qualities that caught Mao's eye. One was military talent. Lin had wanted to be an army man ever since childhood, and had relished life at the Nationalists' Military Academy at Whampoa. He was well versed in military strategy, and had proved his flair in battle. His second quality was that he was unconventional. Unlike many other senior military men in the CCP, he had not been trained in the Soviet Union and was not steeped in Communist discipline. It was widely known in Zhu De's ranks that Lin had kept loot, including gold rings, for himself, and had contracted gonorrhea. The third quality, and the one most welcome to Mao, was that Lin bore a grudge against Zhu, his superior, for having reprimanded him; this was something that Lin's extreme sense of pride could not take.

As soon as Lin appeared, Mao sought him out and befriended him, winning his favor by inviting him to lecture to his own (Mao's) troops, an honor he accorded no one else. From here on, Mao built a special relationship with Lin. Decades later he was to make him his defense minister and second in command. In this long-lasting crony relationship, Mao took great care to massage Lin's vanity and to let him act above the rules, in return for which Mao was able to call repeatedly on Lin's complicity.

Their first collaboration occurred at the end of July 1929, when the Nationalists attacked. As the military supremo, Zhu drew up the battle plan, which called for all units to rendezvous on 2 August. But come the day, the unit Lin commanded was nowhere to be seen. He had stayed behind, together with Mao and the Fujian unit that Mao had just collected. Together, the two of them had control over about half of the Red forces, then totalling upwards of 6,000, and Zhu had to fight with only half the men he expected. Nonetheless, his under-strength force acquitted itself well.

But if half the army refused to obey his orders, Zhu could not command it effectively. With the army gridlocked, loyal Party members and Red Army men looked to Shanghai to sort the problem out.

AT THIS TIME, the mainstay of the Party leadership in Shanghai was Chou En-lai. The man who held the formal top post as general secretary, Hsiang Chung-fa, a sailor-dockworker, was a figurehead, appointed solely because of his proletarian background. But the real decision-makers were operatives sent by Moscow, who in those days were mainly non-Russians, mostly European Communists. The immediate bosses were a German called Gerhart Eisler (later Moscow's intelligence chief in the US) and a Pole known as Rylsky. These agents controlled the Party budget, down to the slightest detail, as well as communications with Moscow. They made all policy decisions, and monitored their outcome. Moscow's advisers supervised military activities. Their Chinese colleagues referred to them as *mao-zi*, "Hairy Ones," as they had more body hair than the Chinese. "German Hairy," "Polish Hairy," "American Hairy," etc., frequently cropped up in conversations among the Chinese. One probably stooped agent was known as "Hunchback Hairy." The "Hairies" gave orders through Chou En-lai, who later won international fame as prime minister for a quarter of a century under Mao. But the real Chou was not the suave diplomat foreigners saw, but a ruthless apparatchik, in thrall to his Communist faith. Throughout his life he served his Party with a dauntless lack of personal integrity.

Chou first encountered communism in Japan, where he arrived in 1917 as a nineteen-year-old student just as the Bolshevik Revolution broke out. He made his choice while studying in Western Europe, joining the Chinese Communist Party branch in France in 1921. There he became a fervent believer, and his dedication was reflected in his asceticism. Good-looking and attractive to women, he was far from indifferent to beauty himself. When he first arrived in France, he was constantly heard admiring its women. "What beautiful girls! . . . The women here [in Paris] are so attractive," he wrote to a friend back home. Soon he acquired a sexy girlfriend, with whom he was very much in love, but once he converted to the Red faith he did what many missionaries had done: he chose a wife not based on love but on whether she could be a partner in the mission.

Many years later, in a rare moment of candor, Chou revealed to a niece how he had picked his wife. He mentioned the woman with whom he had been in love, and said: "When I decided to give my whole life to the revolution, I felt that she was not suited to be a lifelong partner." He needed a spouse who would be as devoted as he was. "And so I chose your aunt," he said, "and started writing to her. We established our relationship through correspondence." He entered a loveless marriage at the age of twenty-seven, with a 21-year-old zealot called Deng Ying-chao, who was noticeably plain and ungainly.

Tenacious and indefatigable, even impervious to cold, Chou was a good administrator and a brilliant organizer. Moscow spotted him, and gave him the crucial task of creating the Chinese Communist army. In 1924 he was sent back to China, where he soon became director of the Political Department of the Whampoa Military Academy, the Nationalists' officer-training base founded by the Russians. Chou's secret responsibility was to plant Communist agents among the higher ranks, with a view to taking over part of the Nationalist army when the time came—which he did in the form of organizing the Nanchang Mutiny in August 1927, after Chiang broke with the CCP. By the time the mutineers were defeated on the south coast, Chou was delirious with malaria and kept yelling "Charge! Charge!" He was carried onto a small boat by colleagues, and escaped to Hong Kong through seas so violent they had to tie themselves to the mast to keep from being swept overboard.

After that, he proceeded to Shanghai, where he ran the Party's daily business from the beginning of 1928. He proved to be a genius at operating in clandestine conditions, as people who worked with him testify. That summer he went to Russia, where he met Stalin before the 6th CCP Congress convened there. He was the dominant figure at the congress, delivering no fewer than three key reports, as well as serving as the congress secretary. His domain was vast: he set up the Chinese KGB,[*] under Moscow's guidance, and ran its assassination squad. But organizing the Chinese Red Army was his main job.

Among the qualities that made Chou an ideal apparatchik were discipline and unswerving obedience to Moscow's line, as well as slavishness. He could absorb any amount of caning from his masters. In future years, as prime minister under Mao, he was willing to abase himself repeatedly, using such toe-curling language that his audiences would cringe with embarrassment. He had already begun producing humiliating self-criticisms decades earlier. "I . . . would like the whole Party to see and condemn my errors," he said in 1930, and pledged to criticize his "serious systematic errors" himself in the Party press. Once, at a meeting he attended, one of Moscow's German envoys, perhaps spotting a streak of masochism in Chou, said: "As for Comrade En-lai, we of course should smack him on the bottom. But we don't want to kick him out. We must reform him . . . and see if he corrects his mistakes." Chou just sat there and took it.

Chou does not seem to have aspired to be No. 1; he was not a program-setter, and seems to have needed orders from above. He could also be long-winded. One of his subordinates in the 1920s remembered: "Once he started talking, he could not stop. What he said was clear, but not punchy . . . he would talk as if teaching elementary school children." He could talk for seven or eight hours non-stop, boring his listeners so thoroughly that they would doze off.

Chou's loyalty, combined with undoubted ability, was the main reason Moscow picked him to be chief Party leader from 1928, so it fell to him to deal with the dispute in the Zhu–Mao Army. On Moscow's instructions, he wrote to the army on 21 August 1929, giving Mao full backing and rejecting all the criticisms. Mao, he insisted, was "absolutely not patriarchal." Mao's abolition of Zhu De's post was judged correct. An-gong, the Party envoy who had spoken up against Mao, was recalled. He was soon killed in battle.

Even though Mao had broken all the rules, Shanghai endorsed him.

---

[*] Like its Russian counterpart, it changed names many times, and we shall call this apparatus "the Chinese KGB."

Mao was insubordinate, but a winner. His ambition demonstrated the kind of lust for power essential to conquer China, especially when the Communist forces numbered mere thousands, up against millions on the Nationalist side.

There were two added factors that came into play in Mao's favor at this moment. Two thousand kilometers north of his location the Russians controlled the Chinese Eastern Railway in Manchuria, which cut 1,500 km through northeast China from Siberia to Vladivostok. Along with this, Moscow had inherited from the Tsars by far the largest foreign concession in China, occupying well over 1,000 square kilometers. Communist Russia had initially promised to give up its extraterritorial privileges, but it never kept its promise,* and the Chinese seized the railway in summer 1929.

Moscow formed a Special Far East Army, headed by its former chief military adviser to Chiang Kai-shek, Marshal Blyukher, and prepared to invade Manchuria. Stalin also mooted organizing an uprising in Manchuria to occupy Harbin, the major city in northern Manchuria, "and establish a revolutionary government." With characteristic brutality, Stalin listed one aim, almost casually, in brackets, as: "(massacre the landowners . . .)." In November Russian troops invaded, moving 125 km into Manchuria.

Moscow wanted the Chinese Communists to create some diversionary military pressure. It ordered the CCP to "mobilise the whole Party and the population to be ready to defend the Soviet Union with arms." It was in this context of protecting Russia's state interests that Mao's drive assumed urgent importance. Chou's letter reinstating Mao enjoined: "your first and foremost task is to develop your guerrilla area . . . and expand the Red Army . . ." On 9 October the Soviet Politburo, with Stalin present, named "the regions of Mao Tse-tung" (no mention of Zhu) as the key area for expanding partisan warfare in connection with the Manchuria railway crisis.

Moscow had another pressing reason to single out Mao, and this was to do with Trotsky, Stalin's *bête noire*, whom he had just exiled. Trotsky had a small, but dedicated, following in China, and Professor Chen Tu-hsiu, the former head of the CCP, cast as the scapegoat by Moscow two years before, was showing signs of tilting towards Trotskyism. Chen also spoke out against the CCP supporting Russia over the railway—a stance, he said, that "only makes people assume that we dance to the tune of roubles."

---

* Comintern chief Bukharin called the railway zone "our revolutionary forefinger pointed into China," and it was serving as a major base for Russian funding and sponsorship of Chinese Communists.

Stalin was worried that Chen might throw his considerable prestige behind the Trotskyists. Moscow's agents in Shanghai were concerned that Mao, to whom Chen had once been a mentor, might side with him.

For all these reasons, the Russians backed Mao, and promoted him with zeal in their media. During the critical months of the Manchuria crisis there were no fewer than four items about Mao in the Soviet Party's key organ, *Pravda*, which was soon describing him as the "leader" (*vozhd*—the same word as used for Stalin). No other Chinese Communist was ever so lavishly acclaimed—not even Mao's nominal superiors, like the Party general secretary.

When Chou's instructions to reinstate Mao reached them, Zhu De and his colleagues bowed to Shanghai's edict, and forwarded the letter to Mao. At the time, Mao was staying in a picturesque village some distance away, in an elegant two-story villa with a palm tree in the courtyard. He had been taking his ease, consuming plenty of milk (a rarity for the Chinese), as well as a kilo of beef stewed into soup every day, with a whole chicken on top. He would describe how fit he was, applying his characteristic yardstick: "I can eat a lot and shit a lot."

The letter elated Mao. Far from earning him a reprimand, his violation of Party rules and sabotage of his colleagues had brought him only reward. In triumph, he lingered in the village for over a month, waiting for the pressure from Shanghai to pile on Zhu De to kowtow.

At the time, Mao had his wife, Gui-yuan, staying with him, as well as a couple of acolytes. He did not talk politics with the women, preferring to relax with them. After dinner the two couples would walk to a little bridge to enjoy the twilight over a brook lush with water-grass. When darkness fell, peasants would light pine torches at the water's edge. Shoals of fish would converge on the beacons, and the peasants would catch them with nets, or even bare-handed. Fish heads were Mao's favorite morsel, and were said to enhance the brain. During the day he sat by his window reading English out loud in his heavy Hunan accent, to the amusement of his friends. This stumbling performance, without really striving to progress, was a kind of relaxation for Mao.

Zhu De and his colleagues "wrote again and again urging comrade Mao to return," as they reported to an obviously anxious Shanghai. But Mao stayed put until late November, when Zhu sent troops to escort him back formally, as a show of submission.

On 28 November Mao wrote Shanghai a letter that delighted Chou En-lai with its "very positive" spirit and declaration that Mao "completely accepts the Centre's instructions." But Mao's main act of deference was reserved for Moscow. He condemned his old mentor Professor Chen as "anti-revolution," and proposed a "propaganda drive" against him. A point was made of denouncing Trotsky by name. The troops were given daily pep talks on "armed support for the Soviet Union."

Having subjugated Zhu, Mao kept him on as a figurehead, and let the army continue to be called the Zhu–Mao Army. This way, Mao both satisfied Moscow and Shanghai, which specifically ordered "unity," and exploited Zhu's high prestige among the troops. Zhu went on performing as a front-man for Mao for almost half a century until the two men died within weeks of each other in 1976.

Yet sometimes Zhu gave vent to his anger and frustration. In February 1931 he grumbled to military leaders that he was "just a plaything in Mao's hands, he had no power, Mao just toyed with him." This was reported to Moscow, but the Russians did not lift a finger to restrain Mao.

MAO'S RETURN TO COMMAND was announced to a big meeting of army delegates gathered in the town of Gutian in December 1929. To forestall dissent, he employed a ruse. He knew that what the soldiers hated most was the practice of executing deserters. According to a contemporary report to Shanghai, "every time before setting off, a few deserters would be executed and placed along the road as a warning to others." Incidentally, this demonstrates how hard it was to keep people in the Red Army, contrary to oft-recycled claims. The fact was that even executions did not always work, as the report continued: "But we still can't stop deserters."

At Gutian, Mao made much of introducing a resolution to abolish the practice. This move was tremendously popular with the soldiers. But a few months later, when the Gutian resolutions were circulated, this item was not among them. Once Mao had established himself, it disappeared. Deserters continued to be executed.

Having inveigled the delegates at Gutian into looking more favorably on him by showing specious tolerance towards the issue of desertion, Mao was able to get what he really wanted: resolutions to condemn whatever stood between him and absolute power, notably the authority of the professional military. Mao was not a professional army man. Zhu was. So Mao invented a Soviet-style pejorative tag, "purely military viewpoint," to lay down the line that it was wrong to place too high a value on military professionalism. He loathed the convention of voting even more, as it was a free vote that had turfed him out of office. So he labeled holding a vote as "ultra-democracy," and abolished the practice.

Mao was addicted to comfort, while Zhu lived like an ordinary soldier. Aversion to privilege was particularly strong in the army because many had originally been attracted to join by the lure of equality, which was the Party's main appeal. To quell any protests about privilege, Mao now invented the term "absolute egalitarianism" to designate an offense, adding the word "absolute" to make it harder for opponents to disagree. It was from this time on that privilege was formally endorsed as an inalienable part of Chinese communism.

As 1930 dawned, Mao, having just turned thirty-six, could look back on the previous year with considerable satisfaction. The Party had handed him the biggest Red Army outside the Soviet bloc after he had broken all the rules. Moscow and Shanghai were palpably bribing him, which meant they needed him. Now he could further exploit the leverage this gave him.

"Where do I go now?" asked Mao, as he set off on horseback humming a poem along mossy woodland paths. Mao knew exactly where he was going: to carry out more takeovers.

TAKEOVER LEADS TO DEATH
OF SECOND WIFE

(1927–30 ∗ AGE 33–36)

AFTER CHIANG KAI-SHEK established a Nationalist government based at Nanjing in 1928, with nominal authority over the whole of China, he launched a drive to weld the many different armies controlled by provincial potentates into a unified national army under his control. This met ferocious resistance from an alliance of warlords, and by the beginning of 1930 each side had deployed hundreds of thousands of troops. The resulting internecine fighting presented the CCP with a chance to expand its own army and bases.

Moscow began to consider forming a Communist state in China. Chou En-lai set off for the Soviet Union in March 1930, bringing with him a detailed report on the Chinese Red Army, saying it had some 62,700 men, made up of 13 armed groups (called "armies") spread over 8 provinces. The Zhu–Mao Army was the best-known of these, and accounted for almost one-quarter of the total, having expanded to nearly 15,000 men, thanks to its control of a large base. Bases were the key to expanding the army, as possession of a base enabled the Reds to acquire conscripts.

While Chou En-lai was away, the man in charge in Shanghai was Mao's fellow Hunanese and former subordinate, Li Li-san. Li-san, who had made his name as a labor organizer, was an impulsive activist and passionate advocate of further expansion. Under him, a highly ambitious plan was devised to seize a large chunk of the interior, including big cities like Nanchang and Changsha, and form a Red government in the heart of China, at Wuhan, on the Yangtze. Mao was assigned to take Nanchang, the capital of Jiangxi.

Mao was a realist. He knew that even given the infighting among the Nationalists, the Red Army had no hope of seizing and holding major cities. At first he expressed reluctance to carry out the plan, but within days of voicing doubts he was bursting with zeal. He still had no faith in the project, but he realized that he could exploit Shanghai's fantasy for his own purpose, which was to take over the second biggest Red Army branch, run by Peng De-huai.

PENG, WHO WAS five years Mao's junior, was born in a village in Mao's own district in Hunan. He was to rise to be Communist China's first defense minister, and also Mao's fiercest and bravest critic within the regime—for which he would pay with a long-drawn-out and agonizing death.

Peng had a highly expressive mouth and eyes, which seemed to show a permanent sadness. He cared about the poor and the downtrodden. Unlike most Communist leaders, he had had a poverty-stricken childhood, which scarred him profoundly. When his mother died, his youngest brother, who was six months old, had starved to death. Decades later, Peng wrote of his childhood:

> In bitter winter, when other people were wearing padded clothes and shoes, my brothers and I wore straw sandals on bare feet, and clothes made of palm leaves, like primitive men . . . When I was ten, there was nothing at all to live on. On New Year's Day, when rich people's homes let off firecrackers, my family had not a grain of rice. So I took my second brother to go begging, for the first time.

He described how he fainted from hunger after they got home. Out of pride, he refused to go begging next day, so his grandmother, who was over seventy, went hobbling on bound feet, pulling along his younger brothers, one of them only three years old. Watching them disappear into the snow, Peng said later that he felt sharp knives were cutting at his heart, and he went into the mountains and chopped some firewood which he sold for a small packet of salt. That evening he would not eat the rice his grandmother's begging had brought home, and the whole family wept.

When he was fifteen, his village was hit by drought, which brought starvation for many. Peng became involved in an attempt to force a wealthy landlord to hand out some rice, by climbing onto the roof of the landlord's granary and removing the tiles to reveal the grain the man had denied having stored. Peng was placed on a wanted list, and had to flee. In 1916 he joined the Hunan army and became an officer. He was sometimes invited by local dignitaries to banquets where young girls barely in their teens were available for their pleasure. One girl of thirteen told Peng she had been badly beaten by a pimp because she declined to sleep with officers. Peng bought her freedom, and thereafter turned down all invitations to banquets. He became attracted to communism "to find a way out for the poor," as he put it.

Peng secretly joined the CCP just after New Year 1928. That July he mutinied against the Nationalists, taking 800 men with him. The Party told him to make contact with Mao, who was in the outlaw land nearby at the time. Peng arrived in December, just as Mao was making ready to quit the base. Mao needed someone to stay behind to hold the fort, as possession of a base was his main asset.

So Mao grabbed Peng and told him to stay and defend the territory— a doomed task. After Mao was gone, government troops came in force. Peng's men had to break out through deep snow, climbing over precipices and inching along tiny tracks normally used only by wild animals.

From then on, Mao continued to treat Peng as his subordinate, and Peng made no objection. But Shanghai did not formally endorse this arrangement, and Mao's mandate did not, officially, extend beyond the Zhu–Mao Army. In early 1930, when Moscow and Shanghai reorganized all Red Army forces nationwide in preparation for establishing a Communist state, Peng's army, which had grown at an extraordinary rate to 15,000—the same number of troops as Mao's—was made independent of Mao. Peng's men were excellent soldiers, with a strong esprit de corps. A Party inspector told Shanghai that Peng's army "has the highest morale. The troops obey orders, have strong discipline and a great spirit of camaraderie, and are brave soldiers . . . They are very loyal to Peng De-huai personally. The wounded in the rear hospitals, once recovered, absolutely insist on returning to [Peng's] army . . . It has very few deserters."

Mao was determined to control Peng and his crack force. This was why he suddenly expressed an eagerness to attack Nanchang. If he was there, rather than down south on the Jiangxi–Fujian border, this would bring him hundreds of kilometers closer to Peng, who was nearby. Mao's secret plan was to go and physically join forces with Peng, as this was the only way he could exert control over Peng and his army.

Mao set off north, saying he was going for Nanchang, as the Party had ordered. But when he reached the outskirts of Nanchang, at the end of July, he fired only a few shots and then moved his army towards Changsha, which Peng had just captured on 25 July.

Changsha was the only provincial capital the Reds took, and Peng held it for eleven days, proclaiming a Communist government, with his HQ in the American Bible Institute. His success rang alarm bells in Western capitals, especially Washington, which now, for the first time, registered the Chinese Communists as a serious force. One reason was the death in combat of Seaman 1st Class Samuel Elkin, the first US serviceman to die fighting Chinese Communists, killed on the USS *Guam* on the Xiang River by shelling from Peng's forces en route to Changsha—on the Fourth of July. Gunboats of four foreign powers, particularly the USS *Palos*, played a critical role in driving Peng out of the city on 6 August.

In mid-August, Peng received a message out of the blue saying that Mao was coming to "help" him. Mao wrote simultaneously to Shanghai, on 19 August, to say that he had abandoned his assignment to attack Nanchang in order to go to Peng's rescue, claiming that Peng was in deep trouble—"suffering considerable deaths and losses." Peng told Mao flatly that he was not in trouble and did not need help, but this was not enough to shake off Mao, who cunningly countered by telling Peng to come and help *him*, as he was about to attack a town called Yonghe, located in between them, about 100 km east of Changsha.

When Peng joined up with him, on 23 August, Mao announced that Peng's corps was now merged with his own, under his own command, leaving Peng as mere deputy military commander, under Zhu De. Mao tried to blow smoke at Shanghai (and Moscow) by claiming that the goal in merging the armies was to attack Changsha a second time—a move opposed by both Peng and Zhu De, who argued that it had no prospect of succeeding, as the element of surprise, essential to Peng's capture of the city, had been lost.

But Mao insisted, and assured Shanghai that together the two corps could easily "occupy Changsha ... then attack Wuhan ... to trigger a general uprising in the whole of China." Mao stoked Shanghai's delusions by suggesting that the occupation of Wuhan was imminent, and with it the establishment of a Red government: "Please could the Centre instruct on taking Wuhan," he wrote in his most ingratiating style, "and start preparations for organising a government ..." In fact, Mao had no intention of going anywhere near Wuhan.

Nor did he really think he could seize Changsha. Still, to cement his absorption of Peng, he ordered Changsha to be attacked. The result was "huge human losses," Moscow was told. These were much greater for Peng's units than for Mao's, as Mao had avoided a genuine strike at Changsha, whereas Peng had faithfully carried out orders and attacked the city directly The GRU chief in China, Gailis, told Moscow that "Mao just looked on."

At the end of three weeks, Mao called off the siege, insisting that Peng's army should move off with him. This met with resistance from Peng's officers, and some even tried to break away. (The Chinese Red Army, like Chinese forces in general at this point, was not like a modern army where orders were obeyed unconditionally and unquestioningly.) Mao soon launched a bloody purge against them.

Mao also used the siege of Changsha, which made headlines, to promote himself to the top job, and raise his profile further. When he started the siege, on 23 August, he proclaimed an All-China Revolutionary Committee, put it in command of all Red Armies, governments and Party branches, with himself as chairman, and sent an announcement to this effect to the press.

Two months before, on 25 June, Mao had already issued two press releases giving himself this title. No newspapers seem to have carried these, but Mao pasted them up as notices. Shanghai's reaction had been to announce on 1 August that the post of chairman belonged to the Party's (nominal) general secretary, Hsiang Chung-fa. Mao was now reiterating his self-appointment over Hsiang's head, in defiance of Shanghai.

But Mao received no punishment. The new Red state that Moscow had decided to install in China needed power-hungry leaders, and Mao was the hungriest around. On 20 September his second-level membership of the Politburo was restored, paving the way to top jobs in the coming Red state. Moscow had rejected Wuhan as the location, ordering the state to be established in "the Red Army's largest secure region"— which was Red Jiangxi.*

The defeat and heavy casualties inflicted by Mao's siege of Changsha were blamed on the impulsive Li Li-san. Li-san had told the Russians it was their "internationalist duty" to send in troops to help the Chinese Reds in their fight. During the Russian invasion of Manchuria the year before, he had gladly called for the Chinese Reds to "defend the Soviet Union with arms." Now he proposed that Moscow should reciprocate, and this riled Stalin, who suspected Li-san of trying to drag him into war with Japan. Li-san had also incurred Stalin's ire by saying that Mongolia, which Soviet Russia had annexed from China, should become part of Red China. The Comintern condemned Li-san on 25 August for being "hostile to Bolshevism, and hostile to the Comintern," and in October a letter arrived ordering him to Moscow. There Stalin turned him into a kind of all-purpose scapegoat, and he was repeatedly called on to stand up and denounce himself.† Li-san entered history books as the man responsible for all the Red losses in the early 1930s. High on the list of losses were those suffered during the siege of Changsha, which were in fact entirely Mao's responsibility, incurred for his own personal power.

MAO'S QUEST FOR POWER also brought tragedy to his family. In 1930 his ex-wife Kai-hui and their three young sons, the youngest three years old, were still living in her family home on the outskirts of Changsha when Mao laid siege to the city.

Mao had left them exactly three years before, when he set off, osten-

---

* What we call "Red Jiangxi" does not include the base in northeast Jiangxi under Fang Zhi-min.
† One day, a Chinese was present at a talk in Moscow by a man who denounced Li Li-san ferociously. Afterwards he asked the speaker who he was, and was astonished to get the answer, "I am Li Li-san." In February 1938 Li-san was arrested, and he spent nearly two years in prison.

sibly to take part in an "Autumn Harvest Uprising," but actually to poach his first armed force. Barely four months after his departure, he had married somebody else.

Although Changsha was ruled by a fiercely anti-Communist general, Ho Chien, Kai-hui had been left alone, as she was not engaged in Communist activities. Even after Peng De-huai had taken Changsha and nearly killed him, Ho Chien took no reprisals against her. But after Mao turned up and subjected the city to a second lengthy assault, the Nationalist general decided to take revenge. Kai-hui was arrested together with her eldest son, An-ying, on An-ying's eighth birthday, 24 October. She was offered a deal: her freedom if she would make a public announcement divorcing Mao and denouncing him. She refused, and was executed on the cloudy morning of 14 November 1930. Next day the Hunan *Republican Daily* reported her death under the headline "Wife of Mao Tse-tung executed yesterday—everyone claps and shouts with satisfaction." This undoubtedly reflected more loathing of Mao than of Kai-hui.

When Kai-hui was brought into the "court" in army HQ, wearing a long dark blue gown, she showed no sign of fear. There on a desk were placed a brush, some red ink, and a sticker with her name on it. After asking a few questions, the judge ticked the sticker with the brush dipped in the red ink, and threw it on the floor. This was the traditional equivalent of signing a death warrant. At this, two executioners peeled off her gown as spoils. Another found a bonus—2.5 yuan wrapped in a handkerchief in one of the pockets.

And so she went to her death, on a winter day, wearing a thin blouse, at the age of twenty-nine. As she was taken through the streets, tied up with ropes, which was the normal treatment for someone about to be executed, an officer hailed a rickshaw for her, while soldiers ran along on both sides. The execution ground lay just beyond one of the city gates, among the graves of the people executed who had no one to take their bodies home. After they shot her, some of the firing squad took off her shoes and threw them as far as they could: otherwise, legend went, they would be followed home and haunted by the ghost of the dead.

As the executioners were having lunch afterwards at their barracks, they were told that Kai-hui was not dead, so seven of them went back and finished her off. In her agony her fingers had dug deep into the earth.

Her body was taken back to her village by relatives, and buried in the grounds of her family home. Her son was released, and early in 1931 Mao's brother Tse-min arranged for the three boys to travel to Shanghai, where they entered a secret CCP kindergarten.

When Mao learned of Kai-hui's death, he wrote in what seems to have been genuine grief: "The death of Kai-hui cannot be redeemed by a hundred deaths of mine!" He spoke of her often, especially in his old age, as the love of his life. What he never knew is that although Kai-hui did love him, she had also rejected his ideology and his killings.

IN THE YEARS between Mao deserting her and her death, Kai-hui wrote reflections on communism, and on her love for Mao, in eight intense, forgiving and occasionally reproachful pieces, which she concealed in her house. Seven were discovered in cracks in the walls in 1982, during some renovation work. The eighth came to light under a beam just outside her bedroom during repairs in 1990. She had wrapped them up in wax paper to protect them from damp. Mao never saw them, and most are still kept secret—so secret that even Mao's surviving family were barred from seeing the most devastating passages.

The writings show the pain Kai-hui suffered from Mao's desertion, her disappointment and bitterness at his heartlessness towards her and their sons—and, perhaps more damning, her loss of faith in communism.

The earliest piece is a poem, "Thoughts," dated October 1928. Mao had been gone for a year, and had only written once. He had mentioned having trouble with his feet. In June, when a CCP inspector she referred to as "First Cousin" went off to Mao's area, she gave him a jug of chili with fermented beans, Mao's favorite dish, to take to her husband. But there was no reply. On a cold day, Kai-hui missed Mao:

> *Downcast day a north wind starts,*
> *Thick chill seeps through flesh and bones.*
> *Thinking of this Far-away Man,*
> *Suddenly waves churn out of calm.*
> *Is the foot trouble healed?*
> *Is the winter clothing ready?*
> *Who cares for you while you sleep alone?*
> *Are you as lonely and sad as I am?*
> *No letters are coming through,*
> *I ask, but no one answers.*
> *How I wish I had wings,*
> *Fly to see this man.*
> *Unable to see him,*
> *Sorrow, it has no end . . .*

The next piece, written to First Cousin in March 1929, and marked "not sent," talks about her loneliness and her yearning for support:

I cower in a corner of the world. I am frightened and lonely. In this situation, I search every minute for something to lean on. So you take a place in my heart, and so does Ren-xiu who is staying here—you both stand side by side in my heart! I often pray: "Please don't let these few people be scattered!" I seem to have seen the God of Death—ah, its cruel and severe face! Talking of death, I do not really fear it, and I can say that I welcome it. But my mother, and my children! I feel pity for them! This feeling haunts me so badly—the night before last it kept me half awake all night long.

Worrying about her children, and clearly feeling she could not count on Mao, Kai-hui wrote to her First Cousin:

I decided to entrust them—my children—to you. Financially, as long as their uncle [probably Mao's brother Tse-min] lives, he will not abandon them; and their uncle really loves them deeply. But if they lose their mother, and a father, then just the love of an uncle is not enough. They need you and many others' love for them to grow naturally as if in a warm spring, and not be destroyed by violent storms. This letter is like a will now, and you must think I am mad. But I don't know why, I just can't shake off the feeling over my head of a rope like a poisonous snake, that seems to have flown in from Death, and that binds me tightly. So I cannot but prepare! . . .

Kai-hui had this premonition because on the 7th of that month the Hunan *Republican Daily* reported that Zhu De's wife had been killed and her head exposed in a street in Changsha. The paper carried two articles in which the writers said how much they enjoyed seeing the severed head. In April, Kai-hui wrote down some thoughts which she wanted to send to a newspaper but did not, entitled: "Feeling of Sadness on Reading about the Enjoyment of a Human Head":

Zhu De's wife I think most likely was a Communist. [words missing from original] Or even an important figure. If so, her execution is perhaps not to be criticised. [words crossed out] And yet her killing was not due to her own crime. Those who enjoyed her head and thought it was a pleasurable sight also did so not because of her own crime. So I remember the stories of killing relatives to the ninth clan for one man's crime in the early Manchu period. My idea that killers are forced into killing turns out not to make sense here. There are so many people so exultantly enjoying it that we can see glad articles representing them in newspapers and journals. So my idea that only a small number of cruel people kills turns out not to be true here. So I have found the spirit of our times . . .

Yet I am weak, I am afraid of being killed, and so afraid of killing. I am not in tune with the times. I can't look at that head, and my breast is filled with misery . . . I had thought that today's mankind, and part of mankind, the Chinese, were civilized enough to have almost abolished the death penalty! I did not expect to see with my own eyes the killing of relatives to the ninth clan for one man's crime . . . (To kill the wife of Zhu De, although not quite the ninth clan, basically comes to this.) . . . and the human head is becoming a work of art needed by many!

The abolition of the death penalty, and of torture, had been a very popular aim earlier in the century, and the Chinese Communist Party's charter of 1923 had included these among its goals.

Kai-hui had naturally been reading about Mao's own killings in the newspapers. He and his troops were always called "bandits," who "burned and killed and kidnapped* and looted." Newspapers had also reported that Mao had been driven out of the outlaw land and "surrounded on three sides, Zhu–Mao will have no chance whatever to survive."

Kai-hui still loved Mao, and above all wanted him to give up what he was doing and come back. On 16 May 1929, in a poem marked "To First Cousin—not sent," she wrote eight agonized lines imploring Mao's return:

> *You are now the beloved sweetheart!*
> *Please tell him: Return, return.*
> *I can see the heart of the old [probably referring to her*
> *mother] is being burnt by fire,*
> *Please return! Return!*
> *Sad separation, its crystallisation, chilling misery and*
> *loneliness are looming ever larger,*
> *How I wish you would bring home some news!*
> *This heart, [unclear in original], how does it compare with*
> *burning by fire?*
> *Please return! Return!*

Soon after this, a letter came from her First Cousin, saying that Mao was going to Shanghai (the Party had ordered him there on 7 February 1929). This meant she might be able to see him, and Kai-hui was rapturous. She opened her next letter, "to First Cousin," with: "Received your letter. How happy and relieved I am!" She dreamed:

> If the financial situation allows, I must get out of here to do a few years' study . . . I want to get out, and find a job . . . I'm really in a great hurry to do some studies . . . Otherwise I can only feel the pains of emptiness, and feel I have nothing to lean on.
> That letter like a will, I didn't send. If you can come home once, that would be all I dare to hope.

Her thoughts then reverted to Mao, the possibility that he might not go to Shanghai, and his safety if he did:

* One of the people kidnapped by Mao's force was an American Catholic priest, Father Edward Young, whom the Reds tried to ransom for $20,000. Young escaped. His Chinese fellow hostages and prisoners were killed.

Probably he wouldn't be able to go to Shanghai? I'd rather he didn't go. I'm worried for him again now. Oh, heaven! I'll stop here . . .

She started to write to Mao, but changed her mind. There was a heading "To my beloved—not sent," and the rest was torn out. Instead, she wrote down the story of her life, which she finished on 20 June 1929. Clearly, this was her way of telling Mao about herself, her thoughts and feelings. The memoir told two things: how passionately she loved him, and how utterly unable she was to tolerate violence and cruelty. The latter theme seems to have assumed an even larger place in her mind, as she began and ended her narrative with it.

She recalled that at the age of six, she began to see the world as a sad place:

I was born extremely weak, and would faint when I started crying . . . At the time, I sympathised with animals . . . Every night going to bed, horrible shadows such as the killing of chickens, of pigs, people dying, churned up and down in my head. That was so painful! I can still remember that taste vividly. My brother, not only my brother but many other children, I just couldn't understand them at all. How was it they could bring themselves to catch little mice, or dragonflies, and play with them, treating them entirely as creatures foreign to pain?

If it were not to spare my mother the pain—the pain of seeing me die—if it were not for this powerful hold, then I simply would not have lived on.

I really wanted to have a faith! . . .

I sympathized with people in the lower ranks of life. I hated those who wore luxurious clothes, who only thought of their own pleasure. In summer I looked just like people from lower ranks, wearing a baggy rough cotton top. This was me at about seventeen or eighteen . . .

She wrote about how she fell in love with Mao, how totally she loved him, how she learned about his infidelities, and how she forgave him (these pages are in chapter 3). But at the end she showed that she was thinking of breaking away from him and the ideology to which he had introduced her:

Now my inclination has shifted into a new phase. I want to get some nourishment by seeking knowledge, to water and give sustenance to my dried-up life . . . Perhaps one day I will cry out: my ideas in the past were wrong!

She ended her memoir with:

Ah! Kill, kill, kill! All I hear is this sound in my ears! Why are human beings so evil? Why so cruel? Why?! I cannot think on! [words brushed out by her] I must have a faith! I must have a faith! Let me have a faith!!

Kai-hui had been drawn to communism out of sympathy for the deprived. Her crying out for "a faith" says unmistakably that she was losing her existing faith, communism. She did not condemn Mao, whom she still deeply loved. But she was letting him know how strongly she felt about the killing, something she had hated since childhood.

She wrote this piece primarily for Mao, thinking she might be able to see him in Shanghai. But as time wore on, it became clear that she would not, and in fact he was studiously avoiding the city. Kai-hui hid what she had written so far, twelve pages, between bricks in a wall.

It was in a mood of despair that she wrote her last piece on 28 January 1930, two days before the Chinese New Year, traditionally the time for family reunion. Four pages long, it described what she had been through in the past two and a half years since Mao left. She began by recalling her feelings in the days just after he went:*

For days I've been unable to sleep.

I just can't sleep. I'm going mad.

So many days now, he hasn't written. I'm waiting day after day. Tears . . .

I mustn't be so miserable. The children are miserable with me, and Mother is miserable with me.

I think I may be pregnant again.

Really so wretched, so lonely, so much anguish.

I want to flee. But I have these children, how can I?

On the morning of the fiftieth day, I received the priceless letter.

Even if he dies, my tears are going to shroud his corpse.

A month, another month, half a year, a year, and three years. He has abandoned me. The past churns up in my mind scene after scene. The future I envisage also churns in my mind scene after scene. He must have abandoned me.

He is very lucky, to have my love. I truly love him so very much!

He can't have abandoned me. He must have his reasons not to write . . .

Father love is really a riddle. Does he not miss his children? I can't understand him.

This is a sad thing, but also a good thing, because I can now be an independent person.

I want to kiss him a hundred times, his eyes, his mouth, his cheeks, his neck, his head. He is my man. He belongs to me.

Only Mother Love can be relied on. I'm thinking about my mother . . .

* The following words were mostly recalled from memory after reading this document in an archive, and some may therefore not be exact. Ellipses represent parts that cannot be recalled; most other punctuation has been added for clarity.

Yesterday, I mentioned him to my brother. I tried to look normal, but tears fell, I don't know how.

If only I can forget him. But his beautiful image, his beautiful image.

Dimly I seem to see him standing there, gazing at me with melancholy.

I have written to First Cousin, saying this: "Whoever takes my letter to him, and brings his letter to me, is my Saviour."

Heaven, I can't help worrying about him.

As long as he is well, whether or not he belongs to me is secondary. May heaven protect him.

Today is his birthday. I can't forget him. So I quietly had some food bought, and made bowls of noodles [a special birthday meal, since long noodles symbolise long life]. Mother remembers this date, too. At night in bed, I think sad thoughts to myself.

I hear he has been ill, and it comes from overwork . . . Without me beside him, he will not be careful. He will simply tire himself to death.

His health is really such that he can't work. He racks his brains too much. Heaven protect me. I must work hard, hard. If I can make 60 yuan a month, I can call him back, and ask him not to work any more. In that case, with his ability, his intelligence, he may even achieve immortal success.

Another sleepless night.

I can't endure this now. I am going to him.

My children, my poor children hold me back.

A heavy load hangs on my heart, one side is him, the other is my children. I can't leave either.

I want to cry. I really want to cry.

No matter how hard I try, I just can't stop loving him. I just can't . . .

A person's feeling is really strange. San Chun-he loves me so much, and yet I don't even look at him.

How I love him [Mao]! Heaven, give me a perfect answer!

Shortly after these heart-rending words were written, her First Cousin was arrested and executed. He was buried behind her house.

Months later, she herself was dead. During his assault on Changsha, Mao made no effort to extricate her and their sons, or even to warn her. And he could easily have saved her: her house was on his route to the city, and Mao was there for three weeks. Yet he did not lift a finger.

BLOODY PURGE PAVES THE
WAY FOR "CHAIRMAN MAO"

(1929–31 ★ AGE 35–37)

IN THE YEAR and a half since leaving the outlaw land at the beginning of 1929, Mao had seized total control over two major Red Armies, the Zhu–Mao Army and Peng De-huai's, as well as one significant Red base, in Fujian. All along, he had also had another sizeable Red Army in his sights, this one in Jiangxi, the province between Fujian and Hunan.

Under a charismatic and relatively moderate leader called Lee Wen-lin, the Jiangxi Reds had carved out some quite secure pockets. They had been warm hosts to Mao when he had first descended on them straight from the outlaw land in February 1929. That stay had been brief, with Nationalist troops hot on Mao's heels, but he had nonetheless promptly declared himself their boss, and when he departed had left behind his youngest brother, Tse-tan, as chief of Donggu District, the Jiangxi Reds' center. Neither move was authorized by Shanghai, and the locals were not happy. But they did not resist Mao, as he was leaving.

Mao expected his brother to seize control for him, but Tse-tan lacked Mao's aggressiveness and lust for power. A Party inspector described him as "working like someone suffering from malaria, suddenly hot and suddenly cold . . . rather childish, and afraid of making decisions." So three months later Mao sent over a Hunanese crony, Lieu Shi-qi, with authority over his brother.

Lieu took away from Tse-tan not just his position but also his girlfriend, whom he himself married. The woman in question, Ho Yi, was the sister of Mao's wife, Gui-yuan, so Lieu became Mao's brother-in-law. Like Mao he was "foul-tempered and foul-mouthed," according to his comrades, with as much elbow, and as few scruples, as Mao. By the time Mao returned to Red Jiangxi to try to consolidate his hold on it, in February 1930, Lieu had strong-armed himself into several leading posts.

Mao returned because he now had the military force to make a grab for power in Jiangxi, but once again he did so by chicanery. A grandly termed "joint conference," supposedly comprising representatives of all the Reds in Jiangxi, was convened at a place called Pitou. Then at the last minute Mao juggled the timetable. Having announced that the conference was to open on the 10th of February, he suddenly advanced it to the 6th, so by the time key delegates arrived, including many locals who had been resisting Lieu's power-grab, the conference was over.

The Pitou "joint conference" was in fact little more than a family affair between the two brothers-in-law, and it duly gave Mao the endorsement to be the overlord of Red Jiangxi, with Lieu as his man on the spot. The leader of the Jiangxi Reds, Lee Wen-lin, was demoted to a lowly office job.

Most Jiangxi Reds opposed these decisions, and Mao had to resort to terror to silence them. At Pitou he ordered the public execution of four well-known local Communists who were charged with being "counter-revolutionaries." These were the first Communists murdered by Mao whose names are known.

Mao and Brother-in-law Lieu used executions to scare off potential dissenters. One Party inspector reported at the time that Lieu constantly "burst out with wild abuse . . . saying things like 'I'll have you executed!' " One particular charge used to send victims to their death was a phrase in vogue in Stalin's Russia—that the subject was a "rich peasant," or "kulak." Mao claimed that in Jiangxi, "Party organisations on all levels are filled with landlords and kulaks," on the sole ground that most Jiangxi Red leaders came from affluent families. In fact, Mao himself belonged to a "kulak" family.

The Chinese Communists had killed one another before, but hitherto most killings seem to have been settling clan or personal scores, using ideological labels.* Mao's killings were in order to further grander ambitions.

WHILE MAO WAS muscling in on Jiangxi, he did his utmost not to alert Shanghai, which had granted him no mandate to take over the Jiangxi Reds. On the contrary, it gave the Jiangxi Red Army the status of a separate army, on a par with the Zhu–Mao Army, and appointed a man called Cai Shen-xi as its commander.

When Cai arrived in Jiangxi, Mao refused to let him take up his post, and simply appointed his own brother-in-law Lieu to head the Jiangxi Army. Mao was able to conceal this from Shanghai because there was no telephone, radio or telegraph communication at the time. The only links

---

* In the outlaw land, the first Communist county chief of Ninggang was killed, in September 1928, by his fellow-Communists, seven months after he had been installed at a rally where his Nationalist predecessor was speared to death. The man Mao left in charge of the area was also killed in a bloody vendetta nine months after Mao's departure. He had apparently had the beautiful young wife of a Party official tortured and executed on the charge of being an enemy agent. He was then killed on the same charge.

were couriers, who took several weeks each way between Shanghai and the base. We have reason to believe that he and his brother-in-law Lieu murdered one uncooperative Party inspector called Jiang Han-bo, and then faked a report to Shanghai in Jiang's name spouting Mao's line.

Mao's plan was to create a fait accompli. Till now he had been writing regular servile letters to Shanghai. Now he stopped completely, and he ignored repeated summonses to go to Shanghai. To get Shanghai off his back it seems he even went so far as to spread a rumor that he had died of an illness. As Mao was a famous "bandit chief," the news received wide coverage in the Nationalist press, which was a convenient way to float a story for which he could plausibly disown responsibility.

The ploy was a success, in the short term. On 20 March an obituary framed in black appeared in Moscow in the Comintern magazine *International Press Correspondence*: "News has arrived from China that Comrade Mau Tze Dung ... the founder of the Red Army, has died at the front in Fukien as a result of long-standing disease of the lungs."

But within a fortnight, Moscow and Shanghai discovered that Mao was alive and kicking, and furthermore had seized control of the Jiangxi Army. On 3 April, Shanghai issued a sharp circular to all Red Armies telling them that they must obey no one but Shanghai. The circular made a point of criticizing Mao (without naming him) for taking over the Jiangxi Red Army without authorization.

When Shanghai's document reached Jiangxi, the local Reds rose up against Mao in May. In some areas, cadres encouraged revolts by the peasants against the Mao–Lieu regime. Before Mao came, the Jiangxi Reds had paid attention to issues such as welfare and production, building a factory to make farm implements and household utensils. Mao and Lieu condemned these programs as "constructionism." Lieu wrote that: "for the need of struggle, reducing production is unavoidable." Deprived of the chance to raise output, and squeezed dry by taxes (which Lieu claimed they "jumped up with joy to pay"), the peasants rebelled in district after district, raising slogans like "Give us a quiet life and quiet work!" Lieu crushed the revolts mercilessly: "As soon as anyone is spotted wavering or misbehaving, they are to be arrested," he ordered. "There must be no feelings for relatives or friends. Anyone who comes to your home or anywhere else who does not behave correctly ... you must report ... to the authorities so they can be seized and punished ..."

Lieu claimed that the revolts were led by "AB elements [who] have become Party branch secretaries." "AB," standing for Anti-Bolshevik, was the name of a defunct Nationalist group, which Lieu spuriously resuscitated to condemn local dissenters. Within a month, thousands of peasants and Communists had been killed.

At this moment, an opportunity opened up for the Jiangxi Reds. At the beginning of August 1930, Mao and his army were hundreds of kilometers away, near Changsha, trying to take over Peng De-huai's army. The Jiangxi Reds, led by their old chief Lee Wen-lin, seized the chance, convened a meeting and fired Lieu. A boisterous audience booed and barracked Lieu—and through him Mao—for "only thinking about power," as Lieu later admitted to Shanghai, "becoming warlords" and "putting the Party in great danger." Lieu was denounced for executing "too many" of their comrades, and for creating "an immense Red terror."

The locals called on Shanghai to expel Lieu from the Party. But, lacking killer instinct, they let him go to Shanghai, which gave him a post in another Red base. There he met his match. The boss there, Chang Kuo-tao, was as baleful as Mao himself, and did his own slaughtering, during which Lieu was killed. After Lieu left, his wife, Mao's sister-in-law Ho Yi, went back to Mao's brother Tse-tan.

With the sacking of Lieu, Mao had lost his man in Jiangxi. After he wound up the siege of Changsha, he returned to Jiangxi to reassert control—and take revenge. En route, on 14 October, he denounced the Jiangxi Reds to Shanghai: "The entire Party [there] is under the leadership of kulaks . . . filled with AB . . . Without a thorough purge of the kulak leaders and of AB . . . there is no way the Party can be saved . . ."

It was just at this time that Mao learned that Moscow had given him the ultimate promotion—making him head of the future state. His aggressive pursuit of power had won him appreciation. Now that he had Moscow's blessing, Mao decided to embark on a large-scale purge, get rid of all who had opposed him, and in the process generate such terror that no one would dare disobey him from now on. Shanghai was in no position to restrain him, as in mid-November a fierce power struggle broke out there among the leadership, brought about by a relative unknown called Wang Ming, who in future years would be a major challenger of Mao's.

IN LATE NOVEMBER, Mao started his slaughter. He ordered all the troops to gather in the center of the Red territory, where it was hard to escape. There, he claimed that an AB League had been uncovered in the branch under Peng De-huai—which in fact contained people who had resisted being taken over by Mao. Arrests and executions began. One interrogator wrote in his unpublished memoirs how an officer who had led an attempt to leave Mao's fold was tortured: "the wounds on his back were like scales on a fish."

Mao had a score to settle with the Zhu–Mao Army too, since it had voted him out as its chief the year before. Quite a lot of Red Army officers had reservations about Mao, evinced in what an officer called Liou

Di wrote to Shanghai on 11 January 1931: "I never trusted Mao," he wrote. After one battle, "I met many officers in different army units . . . They were all very uneasy, and looked dejected. They said they did not know working in the Communist Party required them to learn sycophancy, and that it was really not worth it. I felt the same, and considered that the Bolshevik spirit of the Party was being sapped day by day . . ." Mao was accused of "the crime of framing and persecuting comrades," and of "being a wicked schemer," as he admitted to Shanghai on 20 December 1930.

To run the purge, Mao used a crony called Lie Shau-joe, deemed by his comrades to be "vicious and dirty." "Lie is disliked by most of the troops," one Party inspector had written, "because he is all bravado haranguing the men before a battle, but cowardly in battle." People working under him had been begging the Party to "fire him and punish him."

Lie proceeded by first arresting a few people, and then using torture to get them to name others; then came more arrests, more torture, and more of Mao's foes scooped up. According to a senior officer, Lie and his men would "simply announce 'You have AB among you,' and would name people . . . no other evidence at all; these people . . . were tortured and forced to admit [they were AB], and also to give the names of a dozen or so other people. So those other people were arrested and tortured and they gave scores more names . . ."

Mao wrote to Shanghai himself on 20 December that in the space of one month "over 4,400 AB have been uncovered in the Red Army." Most were killed—and all were tortured, Mao acknowledged. He argued that if victims were unable to stand torture and made false confessions, that itself proved they were guilty. "How could loyal revolutionaries possibly make false confessions to incriminate other comrades?" he asked.

Once he had tightened his grip on the army, Mao turned his attention to the Jiangxi Communists. On 3 December he sent Lie with a list of his foes to the town of Futian, where the Jiangxi leaders were living. Mao condemned the meeting in August which had expelled his ally Lieu as an "AB meeting" which "opposed Mao Tse-tung." "Put them all down," he ordered, and then "slaughter en masse in all counties and all districts." "Any place that does not arrest and slaughter, members of the Party and government of that area must be AB, and you can simply seize and deal with them [*xun-ban*, implying torture and/or liquidation]."

Lie arrived at Futian on 7 December, arrested the men on Mao's list and tortured them through the night. One method was called "striking landmines," which slowly broke the thumb with excruciating pain. Another technique, also slow, so as to maximize the pain, was to burn victims with flaming wicks. Lie was particularly vicious towards the wives of the Jiangxi leaders. They were stripped naked and, according to a protest written immediately afterwards, "their bodies, particularly their vaginas, were burned with flaming wicks, and their breasts were cut with small knives."

These atrocities ignited a mutiny, the first ever openly to challenge Mao. It was led by the above-mentioned senior officer, Liou Di, who actually came from Hunan and had known Mao for some years. Because of his Hunan origins, Mao had earlier wanted to enlist him on his side to help control part of the Jiangxi Army. Mao's man Lie summoned Liou Di on 9 December, first claiming that he had been identified as AB, then promising to let him off the hook if he would collaborate.

In a letter to Shanghai after the revolt, Liou Di described what happened. He saw the torturers tucking in at a banquet of "drinks, meats and hams," with their victims laid out at their feet, and heard Lie brag about his torturing "cheerfully, in high spirits," to flattering noises from the others. Carried away, Lie let slip that the whole thing "was not a question of AB, but all politics." "I arrived at the firm conclusion that all this had nothing to do with AB," Liou wrote. "It must be Mao Tse-tung playing base tricks and sending his running dog Lie Shau-joe here to slaughter the Jiangxi comrades."

Liou Di decided to try to stop Mao, but he had to employ subterfuge: "if I were to act as a Communist and deal with them honestly, only death would await me. So I shed my integrity . . . and switched to a Changsha accent [to assert his non-Jiangxi identity], and told Lie: 'I'm an old subordinate of Your Honor . . . I will do my best to obey your political instructions.'" He also pledged allegiance to Mao. "After I said this," he wrote, "their attitude changed straight away . . . They told me to wait in a small room next door . . ." Lying there in bed that night, with the screams of a tortured comrade coming through the wall, Liou Di planned his moves.

Next morning, he stepped up his flattery of Lie, and managed to gain his freedom. Lie told him to go back and "eliminate all the AB in your regiment at once." When he got back, Liou Di told his fellow officers what he had seen and heard, and obtained their support. On the morning of the 12th, he gathered his troops, raided the prison at Futian and released the victims. Not being a killer, he did not pursue Mao's cronies, all of whom, including Lie, got away. Lie, though, was later killed by an avenger.

That night, posters went up in Futian saying "Down with Mao Tse-tung!," and the next morning an anti-Mao rally was held. In the afternoon the Jiangxi men left town and moved across the River Gan to put themselves out of Mao's reach. They sent out a circular with this description of Mao:

He is extremely devious and sly, selfish, and full of megalomania. To his comrades, he orders them around, frightens them with charges of crimes, and victimises them. He rarely holds discussions about Party matters . . . Whenever he expresses a view, everyone must agree, otherwise he uses the Party organisation to clamp down on you, or invents some trumped-up theories to make life absolutely dreadful for you . . . Mao always uses political accusations to strike at comrades. His customary method regarding cadres is to . . . use them as his personal tools. To sum up . . . not only is he not a revolutionary leader, he is not a . . . Bolshevik.

Mao's goal, they said, was to "become Party Emperor."

However, an envoy from Shanghai happened to be present, and told them to stop denouncing Mao in public, on the grounds that Mao had "an international reputation." They obeyed at once, and entrusted their fate to Shanghai: "We must report Mao Tse-tung's evil designs and his slaughter of the Jiangxi Party to the Centre, for the Centre to resolve it," they told their troops.

The delegates they sent to Shanghai were all people who had been tortured by Mao's men. There they presented the Party leadership with evidence hard to impugn—their torture scars. Moreover, they said, Mao "did not carry out the [leadership's repeated] instructions. He . . . has ignored comrades sent by the Centre and deliberately created problems for them . . . The Centre wrote several times to try to transfer Mao Tse-tung, but he simply ignored the letters."

But Moscow's envoys and the Shanghai leadership, headed by Chou En-lai, backed Mao, even though they knew the charges against him were true, and had seen the marks of torture at first hand. Chou himself told Moscow's man, the Pole Rylsky, that "the arrests and torture of members of our Party . . . did in fact take place." But in the Stalinist world, a purger was always the victor,* as Moscow was looking out for the hardest people. The Jiangxi Reds, though loyal to the Party, were labeled "counterrevolutionaries" and ordered to submit to Mao or face "ruthless armed struggle," i.e., annihilation. Mao was "fundamentally correct," Moscow said, adding that "this line of ruthless struggle against the enemies of the revolution must [be continued]." This was another milestone for Mao: he had won backing from Moscow for murdering his fellow Party members, who had done absolutely nothing wrong vis-à-vis their Party. They had not killed or wounded a single Party member, while Mao had trampled all over the Party's rules.

Shanghai even sent the victims' appeals against Mao back to him—a signal to Mao that he was at liberty to punish them in whatever way he

---

* Even when the purge had counterproductive effects. A 1932 report by the (Communist) Federation of Labor said workers were "simply scared" to join Communist unions: "They have seen that the majority [*sic*] of the workers [who were] members of the trade union were executed [i.e., by their own comrades] on the charge of belonging to 'AB.' "

desired. On these heart-rending reports, a spidery hand minuted the words: "After translation [into Russian], return to Mao." Or, simply: "To Mao." These words were in the hand of the head of the Organization Department, Kang Sheng. A lean, mustachioed man with gold-rimmed spectacles, a connoisseur of Chinese art and erotica, with an equally discerning eye for the range of pain produced by torture and torment, Kang was later to achieve infamy as Mao's persecutor designate. Now, with these indifferent yet sinister words, he consigned the victims to Mao—and certain death.

With this encouragement from Shanghai, Mao had Liou Di and his fellow mutineers "tried" and executed. Before they died, they were paraded round the Red area as a deterrent to the locals. Representatives from all over the base were brought to watch the executions as a lesson.

Red Jiangxi was ravaged, as a later secret report revealed: "All work was stopped in order to slaughter AB." "Everyone lived in fear . . . At the fiercest, two people talking together would be suspected of being AB . . . All those who were not demonic in striking AB were treated as AB . . ." Appalling torture was commonplace: "There were so many kinds . . . with strange names like . . . 'sitting in a pleasure chair,' 'toads drinking,' 'monkeys holding a rope.' Some had a red-hot gun-rod rammed into the anus . . . In Victory County alone, there were 120 kinds of torture." In one, termed with sick inventiveness "angel plucking zither," a wire was run through the penis and hung on the ear of the victim, and the torturer then plucked at the wire. There were also horrible forms of killing. "In all counties," the report said, "there were cases of cutting open the stomach and scooping out the heart."

Altogether, tens of thousands died in Jiangxi. In the army alone, there were about 10,000 deaths—about a quarter of the entire Red Army under Mao at the time—as revealed by the secret report immediately afterwards. It was the first large-scale purge in the Party, and took place well before Stalin's Great Purge. This critical episode—in many ways the formative moment of Maoism—is still covered up to this day. Mao's personal responsibility and motives, and his extreme brutality, remain a taboo.

Next door in Fujian, the local Reds had also rebelled against Mao, voting out his followers in July 1930 while he and his army were away. Many thousands were now executed; the figure, just taking those whose names are known and who were later officially cleared, is 6,352. In one county the victims were hauled through the streets to their execution with rusty wires through their testicles. Frightened and thoroughly disillusioned, the head of Red Fujian fled at the first opportunity, when he was sent to Hong Kong to buy medicine. He was only one of many senior Communists who deserted. Another was Peng De-huai's de facto adopted son.

★

JUST AFTER THE mutiny against Mao, the Jiangxi Communists had appealed for support to Zhu De and Peng. "Comrades," they pleaded, "is our Party going to be for ever so black and lightless?" These two had no love for Mao. One night after a good deal of rice wine, Zhu remarked to an old friend: "Many old comrades . . . have been killed in the purge. The man behind their killing is you know who." The friend knew he meant Mao and said so in his memoirs. Then he quoted Zhu saying: "The Futian incident was also entirely caused by old Mao slaughtering AB. So many comrades have been killed . . ." Zhu "looked immensely sad." However, he and Peng stuck with Mao. Shanghai and Moscow were behind Mao, and siding with the Jiangxi Reds would mean cutting themselves off from the Party. Mao had laid the groundwork for framing Zhu and Peng. He had been purging Zhu De's staff, and had had two of Zhu's five aides-de-camp executed. Nor would it be difficult for Mao to coerce some torture victim to make accusations against Zhu—and Peng. One message had reached Russia's military intelligence chief in China suggesting that "Peng might be mixed up" in AB.

Not only did Mao blackmail the military commanders, he made sure they had the blood of their comrades on their hands. He ordered Zhu to sit on the panel that sentenced Liou Di to death.

Zhu and Peng did not stand up to Mao for another reason. At this time, in December 1930, Chiang Kai-shek had just won the war against his Nationalist rivals, and was launching an "annihilation expedition" against the Communists. Zhu and Peng cared about the Red Army, and feared that a split would doom it. Their attitude differed from Mao's. During this and subsequent attacks by Chiang in 1931, Mao never halted the purge, and when the Generalissimo paused, Mao redoubled his internecine killings—even though the people he was killing had just been fighting Chiang at the front.

MAO'S RUTHLESSNESS PRODUCED an effective policy against Chiang. This was to "lure the enemy deep into the Red area and strike when it is exhausted." Mao argued that as the Nationalists were not familiar with the terrain, the conditions must favor the Reds. Because there were so few roads, Nationalist troops would have to rely on local supplies, and since the Reds could control the population they could deprive the enemy of food and water. Mao's plan was to force the entire population to bury their food and household goods, block every well with huge stones, and evacuate to the mountains so that Chiang's army could not find water or food, or laborers and guides. The strategy turned the Reds' base into a battlefield, imposing colossal hardships on the entire population, whom Mao forced into harm's way.

Few Red leaders agreed with Mao, but his strategy worked. A Nationalist commander later lamented that everywhere "we saw no people, the houses were cleaned out as if by floods, there was no food, no woks, no pots... We couldn't get any military information." Chiang reflected in his diary: "The difficulty of annihilating the [Communist] bandits is greater than a big war, because they fight in their territory and can get the population to do what they want."

Yet it was not Mao's brutal strategy that clinched the Reds' victory. What really tipped the scale was Russian assistance—though this remains virtually unknown. Moscow set up a top-level Military Advisory Group in the Soviet Union to plan strategy, and a military committee in Shanghai, staffed by Russian and other (especially German) advisers. The critical help came from Soviet military intelligence, the GRU, which had a network of more than 100 agents in China, mostly Chinese operating in Nationalist offices near the Red Army, whose main job was to provide information to the Chinese Communists. In early 1930, Moscow had dispatched a star officer, the half-German, half-Russian Richard Sorge,* to Shanghai. Sorge's main coup was to infiltrate the German military advisers' group at Chiang's forward intelligence HQ, where he worked on the disgruntled wife of one of the advisers, Stölzner, to steal the Nationalist codes, including those used for communications between the General Staff and units in the field. This information from Russian spies gave Mao an incalculable advantage. The CCP also had its own agents working in the heart of Nationalist intelligence. One, Qian Zhuang-fei, became the confidential secretary of the Nationalist intelligence chief U. T. Hsu, and played a big role in Mao's success.

These intelligence networks provided Mao with precise information about the movements of Chiang's army. Two weeks into the expedition, on 30 December 1930, Mao used 40,000 troops and civilians to lay an ambush against 9,000 Nationalist troops. The previous day he had learned exactly which units were coming, and when. Mao waited from dawn on a distant peak, while fog and mist shrouded the mountains, and then watched the action amidst maple leaves, some still blazing red on the trees and others fallen on the frosty ground. In the afternoon sunshine, excited cries from below announced victory. Most of the Nationalist troops had simply put up their hands, and the Nationalist commander was captured. The general was exhibited at a mass rally, which Mao addressed, and at which, under guidance, the crowd yelled: "Chop his head off! Eat his

---

* Subsequently famous as the spy who in 1941 provided Stalin with the vital intelligence that Japan was not going to attack the Soviet Far East when Hitler invaded European Russia. One of Sorge's assistants was a woman called Zhang Wen-qiu, whose two daughters later married Mao's two surviving sons. She had come to Sorge's attention through Agnes Smedley, an American agent for the Comintern.

flesh!" His head was then sliced off, and sent down the river attached to a door, with a little white flag saying it was "a gift" for his superiors.

This ambush ended Chiang's first expedition, from which the Red Army gained both arms and prisoners, as well as radios and radio operators. Mao's prestige rose. Few had any idea about the critical role played by Russian intelligence, as well as by Russian money, medicine and arms. Mao had even asked for poison gas.

In April 1931, Nationalist troops came back for a second "annihilation expedition." Again they were thwarted by the tactic of "luring the enemy deep into the Red area," and again Moscow provided critical aid and intelligence, this time including a high-powered two-way radio acquired from Hong Kong, and Russian-trained radio technicians. For this campaign, Mao was able to intercept enemy communications.

But at the beginning of July Chiang Kai-shek himself led a vastly expanded force of 300,000 men for a third expedition, and modified his tactics so that it was much harder for Mao to use his intelligence advantage to lay ambushes. Moreover, this time the Generalissimo's forces were ten times the size of Mao's, and were able to stay and occupy the areas they were "lured" into. The Red Army found itself unable to return. Within two months the Red base had been reduced to a mere several dozen square kilometers, and Mao's men were on the verge of collapse.

But Chiang did not press on. Mao was saved by the most unlikely actor—fascist Japan.

IN 1931, Japan stepped up its encroachment on Manchuria in northeast China. Faced with threats at opposite ends of his vast country, Chiang decided on a policy of "Domestic Stability First"—sort out the Reds before tackling Japan. But Tokyo torpedoed his timing. On 18 September Chiang boarded a ship from Nanjing to Jiangxi to give a big push to his drive against Mao's shrunken base. That very night, at 10:00 PM, Japan invaded Manchuria, in effect starting the Pacific—and Second World—War. The Nationalist commander in Manchuria, Chang Hsueh-liang, known as the Young Marshal, did not fight back. Over sixty years later, he told us why: resistance would have been futile. "There was no way we could win," he said. "We could only fight a guerrilla war, or have a shambolic go at it . . . The quality of the Chinese army could not compare with the Japanese . . . The Japanese army was really brilliant . . . 'Non-resistance' . . . was the only feasible policy."

By the time Chiang Kai-shek arrived in Jiangxi next day, 19 September, Japan had already occupied the capital of Manchuria, Shenyang (aka Mukden), and other major cities, and he had to rush back to Nanjing on the 20th to cope with the crisis. He did not declare war on Japan, reasoning, like the Young Marshal, that armed resistance would be futile, given

Japan's overwhelming military power. Chiang's tactic was to use China's huge space, manpower and daunting terrain to buy time, knowing that it was virtually impossible for Japan to occupy and garrison the whole of China. For now, he sought intervention from the League of Nations. His long-term plan was to modernize his army, build up the economy, and fight Japan when there was some chance of winning.

"This misfortune might even turn out to be a blessing in disguise," Chiang wrote in his diary, "if it gets the country united." Nanjing immediately decided to "suspend the plan of . . . annihilating the Communists," and proposed a United Front against Japan. The CCP spurned the idea, saying that any suggestion that it was willing to join a United Front was "ridiculous in the extreme." The Communists' attitude was that the Nationalists, not the Japanese, were their chief enemy, and their slogans made this pointedly clear, ordaining "*Down with* the Nationalists," but merely "*Oppose* Japanese imperialists." The Party's "central task" was described as "defending the Soviet Union with arms" (following Moscow's line that the Japanese invasion of Manchuria was a prelude to attacking the Soviet Union).

Since then, history has been completely rewritten, and the world has come to believe that the CCP was more patriotic and keener to fight Japan than the Nationalists were—and that the CCP, not the Nationalists, was the party that proposed the United Front. All this is untrue.

When he came up with the idea of a United Front against Japan, Chiang pulled his troops out of the war zone in Jiangxi. The Reds at once exploited this opportunity to recover lost territory, expand, and establish their own state.

On 7 November 1931, the fourteenth anniversary of the Russian Revolution, this state was proclaimed. Although it was not recognized by any other country, not even its sponsor, the Soviet Union, it was the only Communist regime in the world outside the Communist bloc, which then consisted only of Russia and Mongolia.

This state was made up of several Red regions dotted around the heartland of the country, in the provinces of Jiangxi, Fujian, Hunan, Hubei, Henan, Anhui and Zhejiang. At its maximum, the total territory covered some 150,000–160,000 square km, with a population of over 10 million.* At the time of its founding the largest enclave was the "Central Base Area," the region where Mao was operating, which consisted of Red Jiangxi and Red Fujian, covering some 50,000 sq. km, with a population of 3.5 million. Moscow had designated it as the seat of the Red government over a year before, with the town of Ruijin as its capital.

---

* Thanks to the control of the Red territories, Party membership rose to 120,000 in 1931, from 18,000 at the end of 1926.

Moscow also appointed Mao head of the state, with the very un-Chinese title of chairman of the Central Executive Committee. He was "prime minister" as well, being chairman of the body called the People's Committee. On the evening the posts were announced, a crony came to see Mao. This man had personally tortured Lee Wen-lin, the Jiangxi Red leader Mao most hated, and afterwards had reported the details to Mao. He now came to offer congratulations. "Mao *Zhu-xi*—Chairman Mao!" he called out. "You learn really fast," Mao replied. "You are the first person." This torturer was the first person to use the title that was to become part of the world's vocabulary: "Chairman Mao."

MAO AND THE FIRST
RED STATE

(1931–34 ★ AGE 37–40)

RUIJIN, THE CAPITAL of the new Red state, was situated in southeast Jiangxi, in the middle of a red-earth basin cradled by hills on three sides. It was 300 roadless km from the Nationalist-controlled provincial capital, Nanchang, but only about 40 km from the large Red-held city of Tingzhou over the border in Fujian, which was linked to the outside world by river. Semi-tropical, the area was blessed with rich agricultural products, and endowed with unusual giant trees like camphor and the banyan, whose old tough roots rose overground, while new roots cascaded from the crown.

The headquarters of the Red government lay outside the town, at the site of a large clan temple 500 years old, with a hall spacious enough to hold hundreds of people for the inevitable meetings. Where the clan altar had stood, a stage was built in the Soviet Russian fashion. On it hung red woodcut portraits of Marx and Lenin, and between them a red flag with a gold star and a hammer and sickle. A red cloth above it was stitched in gold thread with the slogan: "Proletariat of all the world, unite!" Next to it, in silver, was the slogan: "Class Struggle." Down both sides of the hall, makeshift partitions demarcated fifteen offices as the new state administration. They had names that were direct translations from Russian, and were a mouthful in Chinese, like "People's Commissariat for Internal Affairs."

Behind the clan temple, a large square was cleared of trees and farm-land to make room for the Communists' staple activity: mass rallies. Later on, various monuments were built on this square. At one end was a timber-and-brick dais for holding Soviet-style military reviews. At the other was a tower to commemorate Red Army dead (called "martyrs"), shaped like a giant bullet, with numerous bullet-like stones sticking out of it. Flanking this were two memorials, one a pavilion, the other a fortress, named after two dead Red commanders. The whole set-up anticipated Tiananmen Square in Communist Peking, though the monuments were much more imaginative and colorful than the leaden architecture later to disfigure Tiananmen.

Nearby, deep in a wood, the Communists built a camouflaged auditorium with a capacity of 2,000, whose excellent acoustics were designed to make up for the absence of microphones. It was octagonal, shaped like the Red Army cap of the day. The façade was reminiscent of a European cathedral, only with shuttered windows, through which people could look out, but not in. Above the central gate was an enormous red star with a globe bulging out in the middle, firmly locked in by a hammer and sickle. Next to the auditorium was an air-raid shelter capable of holding over 1,000 people, with two access doors located just behind the stage, so that the leaders could reach it first.

The leaders lived in a mansion which had belonged to the richest person in the village, situated to one side of the clan temple now turned government office. Here Mao chose the best accommodation, a corner suite at the back with a window looking out onto the temple. This window was specially made for him, as the previous owner, out of deference for the temple, would not have any windows overlooking it. Mao also had a brick floor laid over the timber to keep out rats.

The land abutting the leaders' residence was taken over to house guards and orderlies, as well as high-security installations like the gold store, the switchboard and the radio station. Apart from some villagers kept on to work as servants, the rest were evicted en masse, and the whole area was barricaded off from the outside. None of the Party bosses was able to speak the local dialect, and most made no effort to learn, so they needed interpreters to communicate with the locals, with whom they had little contact anyway. Cadres from the region acted as their links. It was the style and pattern of an occupying army.

ON 7 NOVEMBER 1931, Ruijin held a grand celebration to mark the founding of the Red state. That evening, tens of thousands of locals were organized to put on a parade, holding bamboo torches and lanterns in the shape of stars or hammers and sickles. The streams of lights simmered against the darkness of the night, producing quite a spectacle. There were drums and firecrackers and skits, one with a "British imperialist" driving before him prisoners in chains labeled "India" and "Ireland." A generator, roaring in an air-raid shelter by the side of the temple, produced electricity, which shone in the numerous small bulbs arrayed along wires slung from pillar to pillar. They illuminated the endless banners and slogans of different colors that also hung from the wires—as well as giant red, white and black posters on the walls. Mao and the other leaders stood on the presidium, clapping and shouting slogans, as the procession passed below them. This was Mao's first taste of future glories when up to a million people would hail him on Tiananmen.

But here there was one vital difference: Mao in Ruijin was not the supreme leader. Although Moscow made him the "president" and the "prime minister," it did not make him the dictator. Instead it surrounded him with other men whom it could trust to obey its orders. At the top of the army was Zhu De, who was appointed chief of the Military Council. Zhu had been trained in Russia, and the Russians knew him—and knew that he was loyal. Moscow had earlier considered Mao for the post, but had changed its mind. He ended up as only one of the Council's fifteen ordinary members.

Most importantly, Mao had a direct, on-the-spot Chinese boss: Chou En-lai, who was to arrive from Shanghai in December 1931, the month after the regime was established, and take up the post of Party chief. In the Communist system, Party boss was the highest authority, above the head of state. With Chou's arrival, the center of the Party itself shifted to Ruijin, and Shanghai became little more than a liaison office with the Russians. Reliable radio communication was established between Ruijin and Moscow, via Shanghai, where a young man called Po Ku* was in charge. The person controlling communication with Moscow was not Mao but Chou En-lai. It was Chou who built Ruijin into a Stalinist state. Mao was not the main person responsible for the foundation and operation of Red Ruijin.

Chou was a master of organization, and under him the whole society was dragooned into an all-encompassing, interlocking machine. He was instrumental in building a huge bureaucracy, whose job was not only to run the base, but also to coerce the population into executing Party orders. In any one village, the state set up dozens of committees—"recruitment committee," "land committee," "confiscation committee," "registration committee," "red curfew committee," to name but a few. People first got enmeshed in an organization from the age of six, when they had to join the Children's Corps. At the age of fifteen, they were automatically enrolled in the Youth Brigade. All adults except the very old and crip-

---

* The nominal Party No. 1, Hsiang Chung-fa, had been executed by the Nationalists that June, after a tip-off which the Nationalist intelligence chief U. T. Hsu strongly suggested had come from the Communists themselves. At first Hsiang refused to admit he was the CCP No. 1. "And, seeing this rather stupid-looking man," Hsu wrote, "we felt we could well be mistaken. But a colleague said that . . . when Hsiang was a sailor, he had been addicted to gambling, and once when he had lost every penny, he vowed to kick the addiction, and chopped off the tip of the little finger of his left hand . . . The man's left little finger did indeed have a chunk missing . . ." After Hsiang was identified, he went down on his knees to beg for his life, "and at once gave us four top addresses." Chou En-lai later remarked that Hsiang's fidelity to communism could not be compared even to the chastity of a prostitute.

pled were put into the Red Defense Army. In this way, the entire population was regimented, and a web of control was formed.

This machine was an eye-opener to Mao. Before Chou arrived, Mao
had ruled the Red land in bandit style, with less regimentation of the
population as a whole; but it did not take long for him to appreciate the
advantages and potential of the new way. When he eventually took power
nationwide, he inherited this totalitarian machine and made it even more
seamless and intrusive than Ruijin—or Stalin's Russia. And he retained
Chou's services till Chou's last breath.

Chou had also founded the Chinese KGB, then called the Political
Security Bureau, under Moscow's supervision, in 1928. He and his assistants brought the system into Ruijin, and kept the state alive via terror.
Whereas Mao had been using terror for personal power, Chou employed
it to bolster Communist rule. The henchmen Mao used for his purges
had been cynical and corrupt, and out for personal gain. Chou employed
Soviet-trained professionals.

When Chou first arrived in Ruijin at the end of 1931, he had adjudged
Mao's purge methods as not altogether correct. Mao had "relied entirely
on confessions and torture," and "caused terror in the masses." Chou
rehabilitated some victims. One man recalled the process. An official

> took out a notebook and began to read out names. Those whose names
> were read out were ordered to go and stand in the inner courtyard
> under armed guards. There were scores of names . . . Mine was called,
> too. I was so frightened I sweated all over. Then we were questioned
> one by one, and cleared one by one. In no time, all the detainees were
> released. And all the incriminating confessions were burned on the
> spot . . .

But within a matter of months Chou had brought this respite to an
end. Even so short a period of rehabilitation and easing up had released
a groundswell of dissidence. "Relaxing about purges caused counter-
revolutionaries . . . to raise their heads again," Chou's security men noted
aghast. And as people thought, wishfully, that there would be "no more
killings," "no more arrests," they started to band together to defy
Communist orders. It rapidly became clear that the regime could not
survive without constant killings, and killing soon restarted.

THE RED STATE regarded its population as a source of four main
assets: money, food, labor and soldiers, first for its war, and ultimately to
conquer China.

There was a big money-spinner in the region—the largest deposit in
the world of tungsten, an extremely valuable strategic mineral that had
previously been mined by a consortium of foreign capital. The Red regime

resumed mining at the beginning of 1932. With soldiers and slave laborers as miners, the tungsten was exported across the Reds' southern border
to the Cantonese warlords who, though White, were anti-Chiang, and
eager to make money. The Red area was in theory under blockade, yet
trade with the Cantonese boomed, even when they and the Red Army
were sometimes fighting each other. Salt, cotton, medicine and even arms,
were openly trucked in, in exchange for tungsten. The operation was run
by Mao's brother Tse-min, who was head of the state bank.

In spite of the vast profits it was making from tungsten and other
exports, the regime never relaxed its schemes to extract the maximum
from the local population. Although peasants now got their own land,
and ground rent was abolished, they were in general worse off than before.
Prior to this, most people had some possessions beyond those needed for
sheer survival; now these extras were taken away, under various ruses.
One was to coerce people to buy "revolutionary war bonds." To pay for
these, women were made to cut their hair so that they would hand over
their silver hairpins, together with their last bit of jewelry—traditionally
their life savings. The fact that people had such jewelry in pre-Communist
days was a telling indication that their standard of living had been higher
then. After people bought the war bonds, there would be "return bonds
campaigns," to browbeat purchasers to give back the bonds for nothing.
The upshot was, as some daring inhabitants bemoaned, that "the
Communists' bonds are worse than the Nationalists' taxes."

The method was the same with food. After paying grain tax, peasants
were pressured to *lend* more grain to the state, in drives with slogans like
"Revolutionary masses, lend grain to the Red Army!" But the food "lent"
was never returned. It was in fact food on which peasants depended for
survival. Mao simply ordered them to cut down on their already meager
consumption.

Most men of working age were drafted into the army or as conscript
labor. After three years of Communist rule, there were hardly any men
left in the villages aged between their early teens and fifty.

Women became the main labor force. Traditionally, women had done
only fairly light work in the fields, as their bound and crippled feet meant
that heavy manual labor caused great pain. Now they had to do most of
the farm work, as well as other chores for the Red Army, like carrying
loads, looking after the wounded, washing and mending clothes, and
making shoes, for which they had to pay for the material themselves—
no small extra burden. Mao, who had thought since his youth that women
were capable of doing as much heavy labor as men, was the strongest
advocate of this policy. He decreed: "Rely overwhelmingly on women to
do farm work."

The welfare of the locals was simply not on the agenda (contrary to the myth Mao fed to his American spokesman Edgar Snow). In some villages, peasants were not allowed any days off at all. Instead they got meetings, the Communists' great control mechanism. "The average person has the equivalent of five whole days of meetings per month," Mao observed, "and these are very good rest time for them."

Standards of health did not improve either. There was a former British missionary hospital in Tingzhou which treated ordinary people. After Mao stayed there and liked it, he had it dismantled and relocated in Ruijin, and reserved it for the Communist elite. Mao himself was very careful about his health, always traveling with his own mug, which he used whenever he was offered a cup of tea. At one point he stayed in a village called Sand Islet, where the only drinking water came from a stagnant pond. To make sure he did not catch anything, he ordered a well to be dug. As a result, the villagers had clean drinking water for the first time. After this, Communist offices began to have wells dug where they were billeted, but there was no effort to provide the locals with clean water.

Education, Mao claimed via Snow, had brought about higher literacy rates in some counties "than had been achieved anywhere else in rural China after centuries." In fact, education under the Reds was reduced to primary schools, called "Lenin schools," where children were taught to read and write to a level at which they could take in basic propaganda. Secondary schools were mostly closed down, and commandeered as quarters for the leaders and venues for meetings. Children were used as sentries, and formed into harassment squads, called "humiliation teams," to hound people into joining the army and to pressure deserters to return. Teenagers were sometimes encouraged to serve as executioners of "class enemies."

ONE OF MAO'S main contributions to the running of the Red state was to start a campaign in February 1933 to squeeze out more from the population. He told grassroots cadres to uncover "hidden landlords and kulaks." As the Reds had been targeting these "class enemies" for years, it was inconceivable that any such species could have remained undetected.

Mao was not a fanatic, searching for more enemies out of ideological fervor. His was a practical operation whose goal was to designate targets to be shaken down, and to create enemies who could be "legitimately," according to Communist doctrine, dispossessed and worked to death— what Mao himself termed "to do limitless forced labour." The other point was to scare the rest of the population into coughing up whatever the regime demanded.

Mao's order to cadres was to "confiscate every last single thing" from those picked out as victims. Often whole families were turned out of their homes, and had to go and live in buffalo sheds, *niu-peng*. It was during this era that the miserable dwellings into which outcasts were suddenly pitched came to receive this name. Over thirty years later, in the Cultural Revolution, the term was widely used for detention, even though at that time people were not usually detained in rural outhouses, but in places like toilets, classrooms and cinemas.

Mao's campaign produced many tens of thousands of slave laborers, but it turned up little for the state coffers, as peasants genuinely had nothing left to disgorge. The authorities reported that only two out of twelve counties in Jiangxi were able to produce any "fines" and "donations" at all, and the total amount was a fraction of the target set by Mao.

The plight of the victims was vividly portrayed by a Red Army officer called Gong Chu, who described passing by a place called Gong Mill near Ruijin, inhabited by people with the same family name as his, which meant they might share ancestors with him.

> I went into a big black-tiled bungalow... I was struck by a tremendous air of sadness and desolation. There was no furniture at all, only one broken table and a bench. There were two middle-aged women and an old woman, plus three young children, all in rags, and looking famished. When they saw me come in with four bodyguards wearing pistols, they went into a tremendous panic...

Then they heard Gong Chu's name, and they "went down on their knees in front of me, and begged me to save their lives."

> Between sobs the old woman said: "My old man had read some books [which meant the family had been relatively well off], and so had my two sons. We had over ten *mu* of land and my two sons tilled it... my old man and two sons were all arrested... and were beaten and hung up, and 250 yuan was demanded from us. We did all we could to make up 120 yuan, and also gave them all the women's jewelery... But... my old man was still left there hanging till he died, and my two sons were killed as well. Now they are forcing us to pay another 500 yuan, otherwise all six of us will be imprisoned. Commander! We hardly have anything to eat, where can we find the 500 yuan? Please, think of our common ancestry and put in a fair word for us."

The woman told Gong Chu her husband had wanted to go and look for him. But the authorities

> "forbade us from setting one step outside the village. Today Heaven really opened its eyes, that you should have come into our family. Please Commander, save us!" After these words, she banged her head on the ground non-stop. Her two daughters-in-law and the children were all kowtowing and crying.

Gong Chu promised to help, but ultimately did nothing—as he knew that intervening could easily make things worse. Some months before, when he had tried to help a doctor in a similar situation, vengeful grass-roots cadres had waited till he left and then "killed the doctor and confiscated his medicine shop. His widow and children became beggars." It was events like these that drove Gong Chu to reject communism and flee at the first opportunity.*

Mao was also resourceful in making people "volunteer" to join the Red Army. When one cadre had difficulty getting people to enlist, Mao told her to "find counter-revolutionaries within three days." She did, and those scared of falling foul of the regime joined up. In one district, the man in charge of conscription failed to produce enough conscripts. Mao had this man, Cai Dun-song, brought to him, and had him worked over, most likely tortured, as Cai "confessed" to having formed an "anti-Communist brigade." A mass rally was held at which Mao announced the confession, and Cai and a number of others were executed on the spot. A cadre who had worked with Cai said that afterwards "in less than half a month, I enrolled more than 150 people."

CHINA'S FIRST RED STATE was run by terror and guarded like a prison. A pass was needed to leave one's village, and sentries were ubiquitous round the clock. One person who did have a chance of getting away was the manager of state monument-building who had access to cash. He took 246.7 yuan—enough to buy a pass and pay contacts. But before he could make his getaway, he was arrested. He then managed to break out of jail, with the collusion of two senior cadres, one of them a man who had seen his brother killed as AB. The manager was caught and brought before a kangaroo court attended by hundreds of people, then executed. Old-timers recalled that not only was anyone "trying to flee to the White area" killed, but sometimes "if a prisoner escaped, the jailer was executed."

In this prison-like universe, suicide was common—an early wave of what was later to grow to a flood throughout Mao's reign. The number of suicides was so staggering, even among officials, that the regime had to tackle it publicly, as proclaimed by a slogan: "Suicides are the most shameful elements in the revolutionary ranks."

Even a very high-ranking officer, Yang Yue-bin, a favorite of Mao's, was desperate enough to flee and defect to the Nationalists. He gave away

---

* Gong's devastating memoir was published in Hong Kong in 1954. The post-Mao president of China, Yang Shang-kun, himself a witness to the Ruijin time, acknowledged to a small circle that the memoir was true, though it was banned in China. However, Gong was allowed to go back and live in the Mainland in 1991, age ninety.

the location of Party leaders' houses. The Nationalists bombed the site, and the leaders had to decamp wholesale.

Ordinary people had more chance to escape if they lived on the edge of the Red region, and some grassroots cadres who hated the regime organized mass escapes. Any cadre under the slightest suspicion of being unreliable would be transferred away from the outlying districts at once. Many waited until the Nationalists attacked and then tried to go over. In the last days of the Red state, when the Nationalists were closing in, whole villages rebelled, and started to attack the Red Army as it retreated, wielding the only weapons they had, knives and spears, as all firearms had been rounded up by the regime.

The state's response was to be merciless and not to take the slightest chance. At its nadir, even everyday social intercourse and hospitality could bring death. "No family was allowed to have visitors to stay overnight," veterans recalled. "Any family found to have done so was killed together with the visitor."

The Ruijin base, the seat of the first Red state, consisted of large parts of the provinces of Jiangxi and Fujian. These two provinces suffered the greatest population decrease in the whole of China from the year when the Communist state was founded, 1931, to the year after the Reds left, 1935. The population of Red Jiangxi fell by more than half a million— a drop of 20 percent. The fall in Red Fujian was comparable. Given that escapes were few, this means that altogether some 700,000 people died in the Ruijin base. A large part of these were murdered as "class enemies," or were worked to death, or committed suicide, or died other premature deaths attributable to the regime.* The figure of 700,000 does not include the many deaths in the large areas the Reds occupied for inter-mittent periods, or the huge number of deaths in the five Red bases in other parts of China that came under Ruijin.

Years later, locals would point out to travelers mass graves and derelict villages. People who lived under China's first Communist regime rejected it. When the first Russian intelligence officer visited the area immedi-ately after the Communists took it in late 1949 the newly arrived Party chief told him that in all Jiangxi "there was not one member of the CCP."

---

* In 1983, after Mao was dead, 238,844 people in Jiangxi were counted as "revolutionary martyrs," i.e., people who had been killed in wars *and* intra-Party purges.

TROUBLEMAKER TO FIGUREHEAD

(1931–34 ★ AGE 37–40)

WHEN MAO WAS inaugurated as president of the Red state, he had in fact lost his former absolute control over the area, and especially over the Red Army. Moscow had appointed Zhu De the army chief. Moreover, as Party secretary, Chou En-lai was the No. 1. Mao refused to fit into a collective leadership and tried intimidation. His colleagues fought back and accused him of a multitude of sins, even of adopting a "kulak line," an accusation Mao himself had used to send many Jiangxi Reds to their deaths. Now he was up against a steel wall. At a meeting after Chou arrived, Mao took the chair and started behaving as though he were still in charge. The others intervened to unseat him, and put Chou in the chair. Very soon Mao asked for "sick leave," which was happily granted, and he left Ruijin in a sulk at the end of January 1932.

He went off to a commandeered Buddhist temple called Donghua Hill, one of many giant rocks rising out of the plain round Ruijin. Covered with metasequoias, cypresses and pines, and dotted with smooth black stones, the hill sheltered the ancient temple in its luxuriant midst. Here Mao spent the days with his wife, Gui-yuan, and a detachment of guards. It was large and rang with echoes. Moss grew on the damp earthen floor. Outside Mao's monastery room, leaves fell in the winter wind and rain sank into the cracks of the stone courtyard, bringing out more chill. It was a mournful scene.

Mao had brought with him two iron-clad cases filled with documents, newspaper cuttings, notes, and poems he had composed over the years. When it was sunny, the bodyguards would set out these cases in the courtyard, one on top of the other, and Mao would sit on a makeshift stool reading and rereading the contents, pondering how to reclaim his lost power.

He still received top-level documents daily, along with his beloved newspapers, both Nationalist and Communist. It was from these newspapers that he spotted a golden opportunity—which he may in fact have created himself. Between 16 and 21 February, a "recantation notice" appeared in major Nationalist newspapers, bearing Chou En-lai's then pseudonym, renouncing communism and condemning the Communist Party, especially for its subservience to Moscow. The CCP office in Shanghai went to considerable lengths to counter the impact, and put it about that the notice was a fake, circulating leaflets to this effect and trying to place statements in the newspapers.

Although there is no doubt that the notice was a plant, Chou's name and authority were undermined. Mao was thus able to exploit this vulnerability. His strategy was not to try to unseat Chou, which would have been unrealistic, but to get Chou to back him to sideline Zhu De and regain control of the army.

In early March, Mao was invited to a crisis meeting 125 km west of Ruijin, outside the city of Ganzhou, which the Red Army had been trying in vain to capture. The minute the invitation arrived Mao hurried off, even though it was raining hard. Gui-yuan tried to get him to wait until it stopped, but he insisted on leaving at once, and was drenched in an instant. He raced on horseback through the night, and when he got to the meeting weighed straight in to criticize the military command. Most other leaders were in no mood to listen to a lecture from him, and no one suggested he should be reinstated as head of the army.

But now that Mao was back with the army, he hung on there, and started to put his scheme into action. The Reds soon had to call off the siege of Ganzhou, and the majority agreed they should fight their way westwards to link up with another Red pocket on the Jiangxi–Hunan border. Mao, however, insisted they should go in the opposite direction. As he dug his heels in, it fell to Chou En-lai, as Party chief, to make a decision. Chou opted to endorse both plans, but to send only one-third of the army in the direction favored by the majority, while dispatching the greater part of the army with Mao in the direction Mao wanted. Chou thus allowed Mao to snatch back control of two-thirds of the army, against the wishes of most of the leadership.

The most likely explanation for this extraordinary decision is that Chou felt it was better, probably vital, to placate Mao. He knew that Mao had threatened to frame both Peng De-huai and Zhu De (plus another Party leader who had opposed Mao, Xiang Ying) with accusations of being "AB." Mao had not batted an eyelid about slaughtering tens of thousands of loyal Reds who had stood in his way. Mao, in fact, was quite capable of having planted the recantation notice himself. He had displayed a penchant for manipulating the press; for example, creating the rumor of his own death. And why did the fake recantation come right at the time when Chou had just supplanted Mao as the No. 1 in the Red state? Chou could not afford to make an enemy out of Mao.

Chou's fear of Mao dated from now and was never to leave him. Mao was repeatedly to dangle the planted recantation over Chou, right up to Chou's death more than four decades later.

Mao had told Chou and the military leadership that he wanted to go northeast. After he set off, he suddenly changed route and led his two-thirds of the army to the *southeast* coast, only informing Chou when he was well on the way, making it impossible for Chou to say no. Later Mao's colleagues condemned the excursion as an interruption that had "delayed our plans."

In making this detour, Mao had the collaboration of his old accomplice Lin Biao, the man who had ganged up with him before to sabotage Zhu De. Lin was the core commander of the force assigned to Mao. On 20 April this force took the prosperous city of Zhangzhou, very near the coast, which was feebly defended and which Mao had targeted for personal reasons.

One was to gain prestige in the wider world, as Zhangzhou was well connected internationally. Very much with newspaper coverage in mind, Mao entered the city on a white horse, looking uncharacteristically smart in a Sun Yat-sen suit and topee. The army marched in four columns, with bugles blowing. Mao sent his colleagues press cuttings that he collected about himself, reporting his exploits in terms like: "Red Army in Zhangzhou; whole coast shaken; over 100,000 flee"; "28 foreign gunboats gathering in Amoy." Mao was well aware that the higher his profile, the more obliging Moscow would be. Indeed, when his exasperated colleagues moved to oust him later that year, Moscow restrained them, citing this very reason. As their representative in Shanghai, the German Arthur Ewert, reassured the Russians, he had immediately stressed to Ruijin that "Mao Tse-tung is already a high-profile leader ... And so ... we have protested against Mao's removal ..."

But the key reason for Mao to go to Zhangzhou was to amass a private fortune. A large number of crates marked with huge characters, "To be delivered to Mao Tse-tung personally," went back to Jiangxi. They filled a whole truck, and when the road ran out they were carried by porters. They were said to contain books Mao had bought or looted, and some did. But many contained gold, silver and jewels. They were secretly carried to the top of a mountain by porters, and stored inside a cave by two trusted bodyguards, supervised by Mao's brother Tse-min. The entrance was sealed, and only these few knew about the haul. The Party leadership was kept in the dark. Mao had bought himself insurance in case he fell out with the Party—and with Moscow.

WHILE MAO HAD been lingering in Zhangzhou, in May 1932 Chiang Kai-shek was gearing up for another "annihilation expedition," his fourth, deploying half a million troops. The setting up of the Red state had convinced him that the Communists were not going to unite with him against Japan. On 28 January that year, Japan had attacked Shanghai, China's key commercial and industrial city, 1,000 km from Manchuria. This time, Chinese troops fought back, taking tremendous casualties. As Japan's military objectives in the Shanghai area at this stage were limited, the League of Nations was able to broker a ceasefire. Throughout the crisis, which lasted till late April, the Reds worked single-mindedly to expand their own territory.* After the crisis subsided, Chiang resuscitated his policy of "Domestic Stability First," and geared up to attack the Red bases again.

When they received this intelligence, the CCP leadership cabled Mao to bring the army back to the Red base without delay. Mao replied that he did not believe Chiang would "launch an offensive like the third expedition last year," and told the Party its "assessment and military strategy are utterly wrong." He refused to leave Zhangzhou until nearly a month had elapsed and Chiang's intention was made public—and Mao proven wrong.

On 29 May he had to return to Red Jiangxi. Thanks to Mao having led them into an isolated cul-de-sac, the tens of thousands of troops with him had to march back over 300 km, in searing heat, and a large number fell ill and died. En route, they had to fight an extra enemy—the Cantonese, who had previously avoided fighting the Reds. The Cantonese had adopted an independent position vis-à-vis Chiang—indeed, had been hatching a plot against him. But Mao's foray into Zhangzhou had alarmed them: it was only about 80 km from their own province, and the proximity of the danger goaded them into action. Near a town called Water Mouth, the Red Army had to fight one of its few really tough battles, suffering unusually high casualties. The Red soldiers who fought most impressively were some recent mutineers from the Nationalist army, who went into battle stripped to the waist and brandishing giant knives.†

---

* On 15 April the Communists issued a "declaration of war on Japan." This was a pure propaganda stunt, and it was more than five years before the Red Army fired a shot at the Japanese (except in Manchuria, where the Party organization came under the control of Moscow, not Ruijin)—making this one of the longest "phoney wars" in history. In fact, the CCP's proclamation was more a declaration of war on Chiang Kai-shek than on Japan, as it asserted that "in order to . . . fight the Japanese imperialists, it is necessary first of all to overthrow the rule of the Nationalists." In secret intra-CCP communications, there was not a single reference to Japan as the enemy.

† The mutineers belonged to a unit of 17,000 men whose commander had brought them over to the Reds from Ningdu in December 1931. This was the only mutiny in the Communists' favor since Nanchang in 1927—and for many years to come. These newcomers increased the Red Army's strength in the Fujian–Jiangxi theater by one-third, to over 50,000 men. Their commander, Ji Zhen-tong, quickly realized what he had let himself and his army in for, and asked "to go to the Soviet Union for studies"— the only pretext he could give to get away. He was soon arrested, and later executed.

In spite of causing all these unnecessary casualties and hardships for the Red Army, not only was Mao not reprimanded, he went on the offensive by demanding that he be given the highest post in the army, that of chief political commissar. Mao can only have been encouraged by Moscow's unbelievably indulgent attitude towards him. While Mao was dallying in Zhangzhou, the Party leadership, Chou included, had collectively cabled Moscow, calling Mao's actions "hundred percentage right opportunism" and "absolutely contrary to instructions of the C.I. [Comintern]." But Moscow's response was that they must at all costs keep Mao on board, and maintain his profile and status. It was clear that Moscow regarded Mao as indispensable, and the Kremlin consistently showed a regard for him that it did not bestow on any other leader. If it came to a showdown, Moscow would most likely take Mao's side.

On 25 July, Chou recommended meeting Mao's demands, "in order to facilitate battle command at the front." His colleagues wanted to give the job to Chou, but Chou pleaded: "If you insist that Chou is to be the chief political commissar, this would . . . leave the government Chairman [Mao] with nothing to do . . . It is awkward in the extreme . . ." On 8 August, Mao was appointed chief political commissar of the army.

MAO HAD REGAINED control of the army, but differences with his colleagues only deepened. In summer 1932, Chiang was focusing his attacks on two Red territories north of Jiangxi; on Moscow's instructions the Party ordered all its armies to coordinate their movements to help these areas. Mao's assignment was to lead his army closer to the two bases under assault and draw off enemy forces by attacking towns. He did this for a while, then when the going got tough simply refused to fight anymore. In spite of urgent cables asking for help, he basically sat by for a month while Chiang drove the Reds out of these other two bases.

Chiang's next target was Jiangxi. Moscow had decided that the best strategy here was to meet Chiang's attack head-on, but once again Mao just withheld his consent, insisting that it would be much better to disperse the Communist forces and wait and see. Mao did not believe that the hugely outnumbered Red Army could defeat Chiang, and seems to have set his hopes on Moscow bailing out the Chinese Reds. At the time, Moscow and Nanjing were negotiating to restore diplomatic relations, which Moscow had severed in 1929 over China's attempt to take control of the Chinese Eastern Railway in Manchuria. Mao's calculation seems to have been that Chiang would have to allow the Chinese Reds to survive as a gesture to Moscow.

Mao's colleagues regarded his passive delaying tactics as "extremely dangerous." Mao would not budge. "Sometimes arguments became endless, endless," as Chou put it; "it is impossible to know what to do."

An emergency meeting had to be convened at the beginning of October, which turned into a showdown with Mao. All the eight top men in the Red base gathered in the town of Ningdu for a meeting chaired by Chou. The anger that flared against Mao can be felt through the jargon the participants used to describe the scene, where, as they put it, they "engaged in unprecedented two-line struggle ["two-line" means as if against an enemy], and broke the previous pattern of yielding to and placating" Mao, which was a reference to Chou's kid-glove treatment of Mao.

Mao was denounced for "disrespect for Party leadership, and lacking the concept of the Organization"—in other words, insubordination. The tone would have been harsher still if it had not been for Chou, who, as some of his colleagues reported, "did not criticise Tse-tung's mistakes unambiguously, but rather, in some places, tried to gloss over and explain away" his actions. The top cadres still in Shanghai, especially Po Ku, were so infuriated with Mao that they wired their colleagues in Ningdu without consulting Moscow's representatives (which was most unusual, and a sign of how angry they were), calling his actions "intolerable" and saying he must be removed from the army. There was even a suggestion that he should be expelled from the Party.

Giving Moscow no time to intervene, the leaders in Ningdu dismissed Mao on the spot from his army post, although in deference to Moscow's orders not to impair Mao's public image, the troops were told that he was "temporarily returning to the central government to chair everything." Moscow was told that Mao had gone to the rear "owing to sickness."

During the conference, Mao cabled Shanghai twice from Ningdu, which was clearly an attempt to enlist Moscow's help. But Ewert, Moscow's man in Shanghai, who had also lost patience with Mao, chose to report to Moscow by courier, not cable, so the news of Mao's dismissal did not reach Moscow until the conference was over. Ewert found himself having to explain his failure to save Mao to Moscow. The "decision ... to remove and criticise" Mao had been taken "without prior agreement with us" and Ewert said he disagreed with it: "a decision like this [should not] be taken without exhausting all other possibilities ..." Although "there is no doubt whatever that ... Mao Tse-tung is wrong ... friendly persuasion must be used with Mao."

Moscow ordered the CCP: "Regarding your differences with comrade Mao Tse-tung, we repeat: Try to win him for the line of active struggle in a comradely way. We are against recalling Mao Tse-tung from the army at the present time if he submits to discipline." On 2 November, Stalin was asked "urgently" for his opinion. Mao's colleagues were then told to explain why they had pushed Mao out of the army. Moscow criticized Mao's critics, and praised Chou's gentle handling.

Russian backing came too late for Mao, who had left Ningdu on 12 October, his post as army commissar taken by Chou. Mao never forgave his opponents at Ningdu, and they were later made to pay, some of them dearly. The main butt of Mao's resentment was Chou, even though he had tried to safeguard Mao, the reason being that he ended up with Mao's job. In later life, Chou made more than 100 self-denunciations, and the fiercest self-flagellation was reserved for Ningdu. Forty years later, as prime minister, in spring 1972, right after being diagnosed with cancer of the bladder and in the middle of extremely demanding negotiations with the US, Japan and many other countries (at which he greatly impressed his foreign interlocutors), Chou was made to perform one groveling apology after another to groups of high officials. One topic that kept recurring was Ningdu.

CONFIDENT THAT HE mattered to Moscow, Mao adamantly refused to go and do his job in Ruijin, and went instead to "convalesce" in Tingzhou, where the former missionary Hospital of the Gospel provided the best medical care in the Red area (before Mao had it moved to Ruijin). He stayed in a sumptuous two-story villa which had formerly belonged to a rich Christian and had been commandeered for the Red elite. Cradled in a wooded hill and encircled on both levels by spacious loggias carved in dark wood, the villa afforded shade and breeze ideal for the southern heat, as well as scent and beauty from the orange trees and banana leaves in the subtropical garden.

From this elegant villa, Mao ran a competing HQ. He summoned various followers, and told them not to stand and fight when they came under attack from the Nationalists, but to evacuate front-line areas. The attitude he encouraged his coterie to adopt towards Party orders was: "carry them out if they suit you, and ignore them if they don't."

In January 1933, Po Ku, the 25-year-old who had been running the Party office in Shanghai (and who had just urged his colleagues at Ningdu to dump Mao), arrived in the Ruijin base.* Po Ku was fourteen years Mao's junior, and had only been in the Party seven years. He was extremely bright, and impressed Edgar Snow as having a mind "very quick and as subtle as, and perhaps more supple than Chou En-lai's." He spoke good Russian and English, and knew Moscow's ways, having trained there for three and a half years (1926–30). Above all, he was exceptionally decisive, a quality much appreciated by his comrades, most of whom were exasperated by Chou, who was seen as far too accommodating towards

---

* The Party was no longer able to operate underground in any city in the White areas, as a result of effective Nationalist policing plus massive defections. In history books this failure is blamed, unfairly, on Li Li-san, the all-purpose scapegoat.

Mao. Even though Po Ku was much younger and less experienced, the majority voted for him to take over the Party chair from Chou, who retained command of the military. Chou let this happen, as he had no thirst for personal power, nor did he yearn to be No. 1. In fact, he rather seems to have welcomed there being somebody above him.

Po was incensed by what Mao had been doing, and decided to act at once, as Ruijin faced an imminent onslaught from Chiang. In addition, Po was receiving a lot of other complaints about Mao. Peng De-huai described Mao as "a nasty character" who "had insulted" Zhu De. He "likes to stir up squabbles," Peng said. "Mao's methods are very brutal. If you do not submit to him, he will without fail find ways to make you submit. He does not know how to unite the cadres."

Po's hands, however, were tied. When he left Shanghai, Moscow's agent Ewert had told him bluntly that he absolutely had to work with Mao. But this injunction did not extend to Mao's followers, and here Po took action. From February 1933 on, a string of Mao's acolytes—all low-level, including Mao's brother Tse-tan—was criticized in the press, though only the top few knew that Mao was the real target, and his reputation among the rank and file was carefully preserved. Moreover, Po did not use Mao's killer methods. Although the language was high-decibel ("smash into smithereens," "cruelly struggle"), Mao's followers were treated as comrades who had erred, not as "enemies," and some were allowed to retain important posts.

Po Ku was able to dismantle Mao's separate chain of command, and unite the Party to fight Chiang, with great success. For the first time, the Red Army defeated the Generalissimo's crack troops in battles involving tens of thousands of men. Chiang's latest annihilation expedition folded in March 1933.

DURING THIS FOURTH campaign, Chiang had to fight the Reds against the background of a deepening national crisis. In February 1933 the Japanese had thrust out of Manchuria across the Great Wall into north China proper, threatening Peking. That same month the Japanese set up a puppet state called Manchukuo in the northeast.*

Ruijin also won this fourth campaign thanks to great help from the Soviet Union, which had just restored diplomatic relations with Chiang, in December 1932. Restoring formal ties allowed Russia to get more intel-

---

* Apart from Japan, the only states that recognized it were El Salvador, the Vatican and the Soviet Union, where the Manchukuo flag flew over consulates at Chita and Vladivostok. This was part of an attempt by Stalin to appease Tokyo, to try to prevent it turning north to attack the Soviet Union.

ligence officers back into China under diplomatic and press cover, to help the Chinese Communists. The Russian military attaché, GRU Major-General Eduard Lepin, played a central role, as he regularly saw Chiang and top Nationalist officers, and could pass high-level up-to-date information to the Chinese Red Army, also acting as liaison between it and the military advisory group for the CCP in Moscow. Moscow's secret military advisers in China also had a big hand in the war. When Mao later met one of them, the German Communist Otto Braun (the only one who got through to Ruijin), Mao paid him a compliment. After Mao greeted him "with stiff formality," Braun recorded, "Mao acknowledg[ed] the successful counter-offensive . . . in the winter of 1932–33. He said he knew that the impetus for it came from me . . ."

The main military figure on the Chinese Red side during this fourth campaign was Chou En-lai, and the fact that the Reds were winning unprecedented victories under his leadership greatly boosted Chou's status and confidence. Mao knew that Moscow recognized winners, and Chou's military triumph could well tip Moscow in Chou's favor—especially as Mao had opposed Moscow's war strategy in the first place. So in February 1933 Mao moved back to Ruijin from his "convalescence," and started to be cooperative. Moscow continued to accord him unique care and attention, repeatedly admonishing his colleagues that they "must incorporate Mao in work at all cost . . . Regarding Mao Tse-tung, you must try your utmost to adopt an attitude of tolerance and conciliation . . ."

Mao went on taking part in top meetings and chairing those to which his post entitled him. He was kept fully briefed and retained his elite privileges. But he knew that Moscow had reservations about him—not least from the way that his acolytes were denounced in the Red newspapers. He could also read the strength of the wind that was blowing against him in the startling degree of his own isolation. Hardly anyone came to visit him. His followers avoided him. Sometimes, his wife recalled, he did not exchange a word with anyone outside his family for days. Mao was to say decades later that it was as if he had been "soaked in a piss barrel, and been sloshed up and down several times, so I really stank."

A further indication of the way he had slipped in Moscow's favor came early in 1934, when he lost his position as "premier"—while retaining the grander one of "president." The main duty of the premier was to run the administration, which Mao could not be bothered to do; and the Party wanted someone in the post who would actually do the job. An ambitious thirty-four-year-old called Lo Fu, who had been trained in Russia, took his place. Mao was compensated by being made a full member of the Politburo for the first time since 1923, but he did not get into the inner core of the Party, the Secretariat. He was not on the list approved by Moscow. Mao boycotted the Party plenum that implemented these decisions, claiming illness. Another "diplomatic disorder," Po Ku remarked, but let him be.

Mao was still given a high profile and maximum exposure in CCP and Moscow publications. To the population in the Red area—and to the outside world, including the Nationalists—Mao was still "the Chairman." But in private, Po Ku compared him to Russia's figurehead president. "Old Mao is going to be just a Kalinin now," he told a friend. "Ha, ha!"

HOW MAO GOT ONTO
THE LONG MARCH
(1933–34 ★ AGE 39–40)

IN SEPTEMBER 1933, Chiang Kai-shek mobilized half a million troops for yet another "annihilation expedition"—his fifth—against the Ruijin base. In May he had agreed to a truce with the Japanese, acquiescing to their seizure of parts of north China, in addition to Manchuria, and this freed him to concentrate in strength against the Reds.

Over the previous months Chiang had been building solid roads that enabled his troops to mass in the area and bring up supplies. With this logistic preparation, Chiang was now able to close in on the Red area. The armies then pushed into the Red base slowly, pausing every couple of kilometers to construct small forts that stood so close together they could virtually be connected by machine-gun fire. The Reds were tightly encircled by these blockhouses. As their commander, Peng De-huai, described it, Chiang was forcing the Red area "to shrink gradually: the tactics of drying the pond and then getting the fish."

The Red Army had only one-tenth of Chiang's strength, and was far less well armed. Chiang's army, moreover, was now much better trained, thanks to the work of a large group of German military advisers. In particular, the Generalissimo had obtained the services of the man who had played the key role in reconstituting the German army in secret after the First World War, General Hans von Seeckt. So Moscow built up a "German" network of its own to help the Chinese Reds to counter Chiang's advisers. It dispatched a German-speaking military expert, Manfred Stern (later famous as General Kléber in the Spanish Civil War), to be the chief military adviser, based in Shanghai. And the German Otto Braun was sent to Ruijin in September, as de facto army commander on the spot.

In Ruijin, Braun settled in the barricaded area reserved for Party leaders, in a thatched house in the middle of rice paddies. He was asked to "stay inside my house as much as possible for my safety as a 'foreign devil,' and in view of the constant [Nationalist] clamour about 'Russian agents.'" He was given a Chinese name, Li De—"Li the German"—and provided with a "wife," whose one vital qualification was that "she had to be big," and "of very strong physique," the assumption being that foreigners needed strong women to cope with their sexual demands.

According to Mrs. Zhu De (successor to the one executed by the Nationalists), whose information reflected the gossip of the day, "no women comrades wanted to marry a foreigner who could not speak Chinese. So for a while they [the Party] could not find a suitable partner." Eventually they lit on a good-looking country girl who had been a child bride and had escaped to join the revolution. However, in spite of high-level pressure, she refused. "A few days later, she received an order: 'Li De is a leading comrade sent to help the Chinese revolution. To be his wife is the need of the revolution. The Organization has decided that you marry him.' She obeyed, with great reluctance . . . they did not get on."

In this, her second arranged marriage, this woman bore Braun a son. The boy had dark skin—closer in color to that of a Chinese than a white person's, which prompted Mao to crack a joke: "Well, this defeats the theory of the superiority of the Germanic race."

The man closest to Braun was Po Ku, the Party No. 1, who had worked with him in Shanghai, and could talk to him in Russian. They played cards with the interpreters and went horse-riding together. Chou En-lai, as the No. 2 and the senior military man, also saw Braun a lot. But Braun had little to do with Mao, whom he met only at official functions. On such occasions, Braun wrote, Mao "maintained a solemn reserve." Mao spoke no Russian, and kept his guard up with Braun, regarding him as a threat.

BY SPRING 1934, Chiang's expedition had been pressing in on the base for about six months. Neither Moscow's advisers nor any of the CCP leaders had a solution for countering Chiang's blockhouse war and overwhelming military superiority. Red leaders in Ruijin knew the base's days were numbered, and began to plan a pull-out. On 25 March, Moscow sent Ruijin a cable which was intercepted by British intelligence, saying that the prospects for the base were dire—even more dire, it said, than the CCP itself seemed to appreciate. As soon as Po Ku received this message, he started trying to get Mao out of the way. On 27 March, Shanghai wired Moscow to say that Ruijin "communicates that Mao has been ill for a long time and [it] requests that he be sent to Moscow." But Mao was not ill at all. Po Ku and his colleagues did not want him around, in case he made trouble again.

Ruijin's request to evacuate Mao was rejected. On 9 April Moscow cabled that it was "against visit of Mao" because the journey, which would involve passing through White areas, would be too risky. "He absolutely must be treated in the soviet region [i.e. Red area in China], even if that necessitates large costs. Only in the case of total impossibility of treating him on the spot and of danger of fatal outcome of illness can we agree to him coming to Moscow."

Mao had no wish to be evicted. "My health is good. I'm not going anywhere," he rejoined to Po Ku, who controlled communications with Moscow. But Po soon came up with another solution—to leave Mao behind to hold the fort. Keeping the head of state in situ would be a perfect way of proclaiming that the Red state lived on.

No one wanted to be left behind. Many who stayed lost their lives, either in battle, or captured and executed. Mao's youngest brother Tse-tan was one of them. Another was the friend Mao had brought to the CCP's 1st Congress, Ho Shu-heng. Yet another was the former Party No. 1, Chu Chiu-pai. And resentment was strong among those who survived. The No. 2 stay-behind, Chen Yi, had a serious shrapnel wound in the hip. He had himself carried on a stretcher to Zhu De, and pleaded, in vain, to be taken along. Two decades later he recalled with anger how the decision was broken to him (incidentally giving a rare insight into how CCP leaders viewed their colleagues' sophistry): "I was given hot air: 'You are a senior official, so we ought to carry you along on a stretcher. But because you have been working in Jiangxi for well over ten years [*sic*], you have influence and prestige . . . Now that the Centre is going, we can't face the masses if we don't leave you behind.'" The man spouting this hot air was Chou En-lai.

Mao knew that if he were left behind he would be far removed from the Party's center and from the army—even if he happened to survive. He did not intend to be got rid of so easily. At this point, having been deprived of military command, Mao was not with any army. But as government chairman he was his own master and could choose what he wanted to do and where he wanted to be. Over the next half a year, he devoted himself to making sure that Po Ku and Co. could not leave him marooned when they left.

So he staked out a position on the escape route. The first place he camped out was the southern front, which at the time was the envisaged exit point. Here the Communists faced the Cantonese warlord who had been doing a lucrative trade with them in tungsten, and who hated Chiang. Unlike other fronts, where the Nationalists were pressing in deeper and deeper, here there was not much fighting. In late April, the Cantonese warlord began talking to the Reds about providing a corridor through which they could move out, and then on. As soon as Mao learned this, he descended on the HQ of the southern front in Huichang, right on the main road out of the Red area.

It was clear to local leaders that Mao had no official business to explain his presence, and moreover that he had time on his hands. He went hill-climbing for leisure, and would drop in on commanders, settling himself comfortably on their beds and chatting on and on. He even did things like correcting training programs for local units, sometimes taking hours to correct one document.

In July, he left as abruptly as he had descended. He had learned that the exit point had been shifted to the west. That month, a unit 8,000-plus strong was dispatched to scout the route. Mao returned to Ruijin. A month later, as soon as the new exit point was confirmed—Yudu, a town 60 km west of Ruijin—Mao turned up at local Party HQ with an entourage of some two dozen, including a secretary, a medic, a cook, a groom, and a squadron of guards. The HQ lay a stone's throw across the street from a river crossing which was just beyond a Sung-dynasty archway in the city wall, and this was the chosen breakout point. Mao squatted here to make sure he was taken along with the main force when the leadership left.

Before he left Ruijin, Mao decided to hand over to the Party his treasure hoard, the gold, silver and jewelry he had kept hidden in a cave for the past two years. He told his bank-manager brother Tse-min to give it to Po Ku. By concealing his haul until the eleventh hour, Mao had displayed a major lack of commitment to the Party, and to Moscow, and this level of disloyalty might be held against him by the Kremlin. Mao had broken many rules, including all three of the cardinal principles he himself had codified: always obey orders, do not take a needle or thread from the masses (i.e., no unauthorized looting), and, particularly, hand in all captured goods. But "privatizing" loot was uniquely unacceptable, as it showed that he had contemplated splitting from Moscow.

As the Nationalists were coming, it made no sense to leave the haul buried in a cave. Now was the time to cash it in—for a ticket on the evacuation. The Party was desperate for funds for the journey, and had been begging Moscow to send more money.* Mao delivered his cache and also promised Po Ku that he would behave. Po agreed to take him along. He may not have had much choice, as Mao had physically planted himself astride the departure point.

At the last minute Xiang Ying, the relatively moderate "vice-president" of the Red state, was designated to head the stay-behinds. Xiang was the only person in the leadership from a working-class background, and he accepted the job without demur, demonstrating a spirit of self-sacrifice rare among his peers. He did, however, express grave concern about Mao

---

* Moscow's monthly subsidy to the CCP for 1934 was 7,418 "gold dollars." The Russians tried to send in arms direct, but the Chinese Red Army was unable to fulfill Moscow's recommendation to establish a foothold at a port, where "contraband munitions and medicine could be transported."

going with the leadership. Xiang had had ample experience of Mao's character in the Red base, where he had arrived in 1931 at the height of Mao's slaughter of the Jiangxi Communists, and was convinced that Mao would stop at nothing in his pursuit of personal power. Xiang had tried, unsuccessfully, to protect the Jiangxi Reds. Mao loathed him, and had forced torture victims to denounce him. Chou En-lai told the Comintern that "people arrested testified that [Xiang Ying] . . . belonged to AB." Aleksandr Panyushkin, later the Russian ambassador to China, said straight out that Mao had tried to get rid of Xiang Ying by labeling him "AB": "Only the intervention of the Politburo prevented Mao from doing away with Xiang Ying." At Ningdu in 1932, Xiang had been one of those most insistent on having Mao sacked from his army command. Mao's intense hatred was to lead to Xiang's death ten years later.

Xiang argued strongly against taking Mao along. Otto Braun recalled that Xiang "made distinct allusions to the terrorist line of Mao Tse-tung and his persecution of loyal Party cadres in about 1930. He warned against underestimating the seriousness of Mao's partisan struggle against the Party leadership. His [Mao's] temporary restraint was due only to tactical considerations. He . . . would avail himself of the first opportunity to seize exclusive control of Army and Party." But Po Ku, according to Braun, seemed optimistic: "He said . . . [he] had talked this over with Mao and was positive that he would not consider provoking a crisis of leadership . . ."

Mao had indeed begun to behave. Until July, when he was camping at the southern front, he had carped at the leadership's instructions at every turn, telling officers to disobey orders and issuing his own, countermanding the Party's. When one of Mao's acolytes told him that he had been appointed land minister in one place, Mao told him to go to a quite different place and do a different job: "You are not going to be the land minister there. Go to Huichang County to be government chairman there."

But, come September, everything changed. When Lin Biao, who had been used to Mao running down the leadership, paid him a visit, Lin's companion noticed that far from "being engaged in factional activities on the sly," Mao was "very disciplined."

WHEN THE NEWS reached him in Yudu that he was definitely going to be taken along, Mao sent for his wife. No children could go, so their two-year-old son, Little Mao, had to be left behind. Mao never saw him again.

Little Mao had been born in November 1932, and was Mao's second child with Gui-yuan. Their first child, a daughter, had been lost. She had been born in June 1929, in the city of Longyan in Fujian, in a particularly lovely house. When the baby was shown to him, Mao had produced one of his characteristic cracks: "Hey, this girl knows how to pick a good date: she wouldn't come out till she found a nice place!" Less than a month after she was born, Gui-yuan had to leave the town with Mao, and the baby was left with a local wet nurse. Mao's path then took the couple away from the city for nearly three years. When Gui-yuan finally returned, she was told the girl had died, but she could not bring herself to believe this, and after the Communists took power two decades later she began to look for her. The quest went on obsessively for decades until near the end of her life in 1984.

As Gui-yuan could not bring Little Mao along on the evacuation, she entrusted the boy to her sister, who was married to Mao's brother Tse-tan. The couple, as well as her brother and parents, were left behind. Gui-yuan wept bitterly at being parted from her son. (Her third child, a son, had died a few months earlier within days of being born.) Little Mao stayed with his wet nurse for a while. After the Nationalists took the Red territory, Tse-tan moved him secretly. But Tse-tan was killed in battle in April 1935 before he could tell his wife where.

Once Mao came to power, Gui-yuan, who had by then long ceased to be Mao's wife, tried desperately to find Little Mao, with tragic results. Her sister, who felt guilty about Little Mao being lost while in her care, was killed in a car accident in November 1949 as she set off one night to chase a lead, within days of the Reds taking the area. In 1952 a young man was found who might possibly have been Little Mao. Gui-yuan's brother recalled that Gui-yuan "rushed to identify him. She mainly checked two things, whether the boy had oily ears, and whether he had armpit odour [uncommon for Chinese]. She was convinced her children all inherited these characteristics of Mao Tse-tung's. After inspecting him, she was convinced it was her Little Mao."

But many other Communist women who had had to abandon their children had embarked on the same kind of quest, and one Red Army widow had already identified the boy as her son. The Party adjudicated that the boy belonged to this other woman. Gui-yuan's brother went to see Mao, who had not been involved up to now, and showed him a photograph of the teenage boy, hinting that Gui-yuan would like Mao to intervene. But Mao declined, saying: "It's awkward for me to interfere." Mao told him to do what the Party decreed. Gui-yuan did not give up, and fought a painful—and tragic—battle for years. She and her brother kept in touch with the young man until his death from liver cancer in the 1970s, even taking care of his wedding arrangements.*

---

* This sort of tragedy was by no means uncommon. The revolution brought much heartache to its adherents. Before they took power, Communists were expected not just to make sacrifices vis-à-vis their children, but literally *to sacrifice them*, and selling one's

★

MAO SHOWED NO particular sadness about leaving Little Mao behind, and did not even say goodbye to his son. His sorrow was reserved for himself. Gong Chu, the commander of the Red Army at Yudu, left a telling account of the last weeks before Mao departed, when Mao was staked out in his HQ. In early September Gong was studying a map when

> suddenly my bodyguard came in and announced: "Chairman Mao is here!" I ... ran to the front gate, and saw Mao Tse-tung with two body-guards dismounting ... He looked yellow and drained. I asked him: "Is the Chairman not well?" He answered: "You are right. I have recently been suffering from ill health, but more of a pain is that I feel extremely down ..."
>
> After he washed his face, he lit a cigarette and said: "... I'll be here for quite a while."

Mao said to Gong that as they were old friends from the outlaw land, " 'I hope you can come and have a chat whenever you have the time in the evenings.' ... Mao Tse-tung liked talking." Gong took Mao up on his invitation, and after Gui-yuan joined Mao, she would "prepare delicious suppers. And the three of us would chat and drink and smoke, often ... till midnight ... From my observation, Mao's place was not visited by other people except me ... It really felt as if he was isolated and miserable."

One day Gong bought a hen and some pigs' trotters for dinner. Mao was "cheerful, and drank a lot." He complained about the leadership, but more as a heart-to-heart between old friends than as sabotage. When Gong mentioned he had been given a reprimand for something, Mao "said he had not been in agreement with the reprimand. It was all because Chou En-lai was too harsh ... Also, he said, [his Party foes] wanted all power in their hands ... He seemed deeply resentful of them."

Mao became doleful from drink, and recounted the various punishments visited on him. At one point, lamenting that he was no longer the

---

children—or having them sold—to raise funds for the Party was not uncommon. The Party cell of Gui-yuan's friend Zeng Zhi in Amoy sold her baby son for 100 yuan; the buyer paid in advance and the Party spent the money before presenting her with a fait accompli. More than half a century later, she said: "Of course, it was extremely painful. Before my son was delivered to [the buyer's] house, my husband and I carried him to Sun Yat-sen Park to play. He was such a cute baby, over 40 days, he smiled all the time. We gave him the name *Tie-niu* (Iron Ox). He never cried without a good reason, and rarely passed stool or water on himself. So we carried him there to play. He was really really happy. Then he was gone. And it was just unbearable. I managed to overcome the hurt. But my baby died 26 days later... Our Party Secretary didn't dare to tell me, although I had heard. He kept quiet as I didn't say anything. Sometimes at night, it hurt so much I wept, but quietly, because it was embarrassing to let others know [that she was crying for her child]. Then one day, he saw I had been crying, and he guessed I knew, and he apologised to me."

big boss, "tears ran down his cheeks. He was coughing from time to time, and his face looked drawn and dried and sallow. Under the flicker of a tiny oil lamp, he was quite a picture of dejection."

Neither the collapse of the Communist state nor the separation from his son could wound Mao like his loss of personal power.

Then, just when everything seemed set, Mao's plans nearly fell apart. Days before the planned departure, his temperature shot up to 105.8°F and he grew delirious with malaria. It was the malaria season, and the mosquitoes in Yudu were so thick in the air that they flew right into people's nostrils. Even quinine failed to do the trick. It was vital for him to recover—and recover fast, so that he could leave with the others. The best doctor in the Red area, Nelson Fu, who had looked after Mao in the missionary hospital in winter 1932–33, raced over from Ruijin and got him into good enough shape to travel. Patient and doctor both knew Fu had saved Mao's life—and his political fortunes.

Dr Fu became the overseer of Mao's physicians for decades. In 1966, in Mao's Great Purge, he wrote to Mao and brought up this episode in Yudu. "I saved your life," he said, "I hope you can save mine now." The then 72-year-old had been savagely beaten, his ribs broken and his skull fractured. Mao did lift a finger, but not very forcefully, by minuting on Fu's letter: "This man . . . has not committed big crimes, perhaps he should be spared." But then he heard that Fu had allegedly talked to other Party leaders about his (Mao's) health, which was a big taboo for Mao. Mao let Fu be thrown into prison. The septuagenarian doctor did not last two weeks, and died on the floor of his cell.

MEANWHILE THE RED ARMY kept up a fighting retreat as Chiang's army advanced, while preparations for the evacuation went on in secret. The move was forced, but it enabled the Reds to carry out a strategic shift towards the northwest, with the ultimate goal of reaching Russian-controlled borders, in order to receive arms—an operation later known as "to link up with the Soviet Union." It had been planned for years. Back in 1929 GRU chief Berzin had briefed Sorge that his mission was to try to get the Chinese Red Army to the Soviet border.

In July, one unit of 6,000 men was sent out in the opposite direction as a decoy. It carried 1.6 million leaflets, which filled 300 shoulder-pole loads, and adopted the grandiose name of "Red Army Vanguard Northbound to Fight the Japanese."* Its movements were given maximum publicity, and the unit came to realize that it was a decoy, something that even its leaders had not been told. The men felt bitter, and doubly

---

* Red leaders acknowledged later that the name was only for propaganda. "No one dreamed of a march north to fight the Japanese," Braun observed.

so because the task assigned was pointless: a small unit like theirs could not possibly fool the enemy or draw them away from Ruijin. Instead, they found themselves being relentlessly pursued by other Nationalist forces. Within a few months, virtually the entire decoy force was wiped out.

Part of the preparation for the evacuation was screening all proposed evacuees, a process run by Chou En-lai. Those rated unreliable were executed. They totaled thousands. Among those killed were most of the teachers in army schools, who were often captured former Nationalist officers. The executions took place in a sealed-off mountain valley, where a huge pit was dug. The victims were hacked to death with knives, and their bodies kicked down into the pit. When this pit was full, the rest were made to dig their own holes in the ground, and were then hacked to death, or buried alive.

The massacre was carried out by the state security system—although many security men had themselves by now lost faith in the regime and were being killed in their turn. One of those who had lost faith was the head of the team guarding the Military Council. In the confusion of leaving, he slipped away and hid in the hills. But the authorities found his hiding-place by arresting his girlfriend, a local peasant. After a gun battle, this expert marksman shot himself.

IN OCTOBER 1934, the rule of this brutal regime came to an end. At Yudu, pontoon bridges were set up across the river. At the prow and stem of each boat hung a barn lantern, and more lanterns and torches shone on both banks, glowing in the water's reflection. Families of the soldiers and organized peasants lined the banks to say goodbye. The badly wounded had been billeted on local families. As troops padded past on the cobblestone path underneath the city wall, down to the crossing point, in a corner house near the wall a twelve-year-old boy had his eyes glued to a crack in the door, holding his breath. His father, a small shopkeeper, had been killed four years before, at the height of Mao's AB slaughter, when people were being executed even for being "active shop-assistants." Like many others, he was glad to see the back of the Reds, as he made abundantly clear when we met him sixty years later.

At about 6:00 PM on 18 October, looking gaunt but composed, with his long hair combed back, Mao left the local Party HQ surrounded by bodyguards, crossed the street, passed the Sung-dynasty archway and stepped onto the pontoon bridge.

This rickety bridge did not just carry Mao across the water, it bore him into legend. His murderous past and that of the CCP regime were about to be left behind. And Mao himself was about to create the most enduring myth in modern Chinese history, and one of the biggest myths of the twentieth century—"the Long March."

LONG MARCH I:
CHIANG LETS THE REDS GO
(1934 ★ AGE 40)

SOME 80,000 PEOPLE set off on the Long March in October 1934. The procession moved out over a ten-day period in three columns, with the two oldest and core units, under Lin Biao and Peng De-huai respectively, on each side of the HQ. The 5,000-strong HQ consisted of the handful of leaders and their staff, servants and guards. Mao was with the HQ.

They moved slowly due west, burdened by heavy loads. Arsenal machinery, printing machines and Mao's treasure were carried on shoulder-poles by thousands of porters, most of them recently press-ganged conscripts, watched over by security men. The chief of the administrators revealed that the heaviest burdens were carried by people "who had just been released from the hard labour teams, and they were very weak physically . . . some just collapsed and died while walking." Numerous marchers fell sick. One remembered:

> The autumn rain went on and on, making our paths nothing but mud . . . and there was nowhere to escape the rain, and no good sleep to be had . . . some sick and weak fell asleep and never woke up. Many suffered infected feet, which had to be wrapped in rotten cloth and produced unbearable pain when stepping on the ground . . . As we left the base area further and further behind, some labourers deserted. The more obedient ones begged in tears to be let go . . .

The bolder ones simply dropped their loads and fled when their minders were distracted. Soldiers, too, deserted in droves, as the vigilance of their increasingly exhausted bosses wavered.

The marchers faced the daunting prospect of four lines of block-houses—the same blockhouses that had doomed their Red base. Yet these turned out to be no obstacle at all—seemingly inexplicably.

The first line was manned by Cantonese troops, whose warlord chief had been doing profitable business with the Reds and had promised to let them through. Which he did. This combat-free breakout, however, was not due just to the anti-Chiang Cantonese. The Generalissimo was well aware that the Reds intended to pull out by way of the Cantonese front, and moreover he knew that they were going to be let through. On 3 October, shortly before the breakout began, he had told his prime minister that the Cantonese were going to "open up one side of the net" to the Reds. And yet Chiang explicitly rejected the idea of sending forces loyal to himself to the breakout sector. A close aide argued with him that to get Canton "to carry out orders, we have to have our men on the spot." Chiang told him not to worry.

The marchers reached the second line of blockhouses at the beginning of November. Although the columns offered an easy target, extending over tens of kilometers, they were not attacked. The Cantonese again made no trouble. And neither did the other force defending part of this second line, which was under General Ho Chien, the fiercely anti-Communist Hunanese who had executed Mao's ex-wife Kai-hui.

It was the same story at the third fortified line; yet Chiang not only did not reprimand Ho Chien for his apparent dereliction, on 12 November he promoted him to commander-in-chief of operations against the marchers. So it was this fierce anti-Communist who manned the fourth fortification line, situated at an ideal place to wipe out the Reds, on the west bank of the Xiang, the largest river in Hunan (which had inspired Mao's poetry in his youth). There were no bridges, and the Reds, who had no anti-aircraft guns, had to wade across the wide river, easy targets from land and air. But again they went completely unmolested while they took four days to trudge across, spread along a stretch of river 30 km long. The commanding points on the banks were unmanned, and the troops under Ho Chien just looked on. Chiang's planes circled overhead, but only to reconnoiter, and there was no aerial bombing or even strafing. Mao and the HQ forded the river undisturbed on 30 November, and by the next day, 1 December, the 40,000-strong main Red force was over.

Only now did Chiang, who had been monitoring the crossing "with total concentration," his aides observed, seal off the river and order heavy bombing. Part of the Red rear guard was cut off on the east bank. The marchers who got across were down to half their original number,* but included the main combat troops and the HQ. Chiang knew this. His commander Ho Chien wrote the following day: "The main force of the bandits have all [crossed the river], and are fleeing to the west."

---

* Of the other half (amounting to some 40,000), who did not make it past the river, "over 3,000" were killed at the Xiang. The rest were either scattered at the Xiang, or had perished during the preceding six weeks' trek from illness or exhaustion, or had been casualties of small skirmishes, or had deserted.

There can be no doubt that Chiang let the CCP leadership and the main force of the Red Army escape.

WHY SHOULD CHIANG have done this? Part of the reason soon emerged when, after the crossing of the Xiang, Chiang's army drove the marchers farther westward towards the province of Guizhou, and then Sichuan. Chiang's plan was to use the Red force for his own purposes. These two provinces, together with neighboring Yunnan, formed a vast southwestern region covering well over 1 million sq km, with a population of about 100 million; they were virtually independent of the central government, as they kept their own armies and paid little tax to Nanjing. Sichuan was particularly important, being the largest, richest and most populous, with some 50 million people. It was shielded on all sides by almost inaccessible mountains, which made access "more difficult than ascending to the blue sky," in the words of the poet Li Po. Chiang envisaged it as "the base for national revival," i.e., a safe rear for an eventual war against Japan.

Chiang could effect control only if he had his own army actually in the provinces, but they had rejected his army, and if he were to try to force his way in, there would be war. Chiang did not want to have to declare war openly on the warlords. His nation-building design was more Machiavellian—and cost-effective. He wanted to drive the Red Army into these hold-out provinces, so that their warlords would be so frightened of the Reds settling in their territory that they would allow Chiang's army in to drive the Reds out. This way, Chiang figured, his army could march in and he could impose central government control. He wanted to preserve the main body of the Red Army so that it would still pose enough of a threat to the warlords.

Chiang spelled out his plan to his closest secretary: "Now when the Communist army go into Guizhou, we can follow in. It is better than us starting a war to conquer Guizhou. Sichuan and Yunnan will have to welcome us, to save themselves . . . From now on, if we play our cards right . . . we can create a unified country." On 27 November, the very day the Reds started crossing the Xiang River and headed for Guizhou, Chiang issued his blueprint for nation-building, a "Declaration on the division of powers between the central government and the provinces."

This agenda remained secret throughout Chiang's life, and is still concealed by both Nationalist and Communist official histories. Both attribute the Communists' escape to regional warlords, with Chiang blaming the warlords, and the Communists praising them. Both share the same concern: not to reveal that it was the Generalissimo himself who let the Reds go. For the Nationalists, Chiang's methods for establishing his sway over the wayward provinces were too devious, and his miscalculation about using the Reds—which ultimately led to their triumph—too humiliating. For the Communists, it is embarrassing to acknowledge that the famed Long March was to a large extent steered by Chiang Kai-shek.

LETTING THE REDS go was also a goodwill gesture on Chiang's part towards Russia. He needed a harmonious relationship with the Kremlin because he was under threat from Japan. And the CCP was Moscow's baby.

But there was another, more secret and totally private reason. Chiang's son Ching-kuo had been a hostage in Russia for nine years. Ching-kuo was Chiang Kai-shek's sole blood descendant, not by the famous Mme Chiang, but by his first wife. After Ching-kuo was born, Chiang seems to have become sterile through contracting venereal disease several times, and he adopted another son, Weigo. But Ching-kuo, as the only blood heir, remained the closest to his heart. Chiang was steeped in Chinese tradition, in which the central concern was to have an heir. To fail to carry on the family line was regarded as *the* disgrace, the greatest hurt one could inflict on one's parents and ancestors, whose dead souls could then never rest in peace. One of the worst curses in China was: "May you have no heir!" And respect for one's parents and ancestors, filial piety, was the primary moral injunction dictated by tradition.

In 1925, Chiang had sent Ching-kuo, then fifteen years old, to a school in Peking. This was a time when Chiang's star was ascending in a Nationalist Party that was sponsored by Moscow. In no time, the Russians were on to Ching-kuo, and invited him to study in Russia. The young man was very keen. A few months after he arrived in Peking, Ching-kuo was taken to Moscow by a little-known but pivotal figure called Shao Li-tzu, who was a key Red mole inside the Nationalist Party.

Planting moles was one of the most priceless gifts that Moscow bequeathed to the CCP. Mostly these moles joined the Nationalists in the first half of the 1920s, when Sun Yat-sen, who was courting the Russians, opened his party to the Communists. Infiltration worked on several levels. As well as overt Communists working inside the Nationalist movement, as Mao did, there were also secret Communists, and then a third group, those who had staged fake defections from the CCP. When Chiang split from the Communists in 1927, a large number of these secret agents stayed as "sleepers," to be activated at the appropriate time. For the next twenty years and more, they were not only able to give the Reds crucial intelligence, they were often in a position to have a substantial influence on policy, as many had meanwhile risen very high in the Nationalist system. Ultimately, the agents played a gigantic role in help-ing deliver China to Mao—probably a greater role in high-level politics than in any other country in the world. Many remain unexposed even today.

Shao Li-tzu was one of them. He was actually a founding member of the CCP, but on Moscow's orders he stayed away from Party activities, and his identity was kept secret even from most Party leaders. When Chiang turned against the Communists in Shanghai in April 1927, Shao wrote the Russians a telegram that was instantly forwarded to Stalin, asking for instructions: "Shanghai disturbs me very much. I cannot be the weapon of counter-revolution. I ask for advice how to fight."

For the next twenty-two years, Shao stayed with the Nationalists, occupying many key posts—until the Communist victory in 1949, when he went over to Mao. He died in Peking in 1967. Even under Communist rule, his true face was never revealed, and he is still presented today as an honest sympathizer, not a long-term sleeper.

It was undoubtedly on Moscow's instructions that Shao had brought Chiang's son to Russia in November 1925. When Ching-kuo completed his studies there, in 1927, he was not allowed to leave, and was forced to denounce his father publicly. Stalin was keeping him hostage while telling the world that he had volunteered to stay. Stalin liked to hold hostages. Peggy Dennis, the wife of the US Communist leader Eugene Dennis, described a visit from the Comintern éminence grise Dmitri Manuilsky as she and her husband were about to leave Russia to return to America in 1935: "The bombshell was dropped quietly ... Almost casually, Manuilsky informed us that we could not take Tim [their son] back, '... We will send him at some other time, under other circumstances.'" The Russians never did.

The fact that Ching-kuo was a hostage was spelled out to his father in late 1931—by none other than his own sister-in-law, Mme Sun Yat-sen (née Soong Ching-ling), who was another Soviet agent.* Speaking for Moscow, she proposed swapping Ching-kuo for two top Russian agents who had recently been arrested in Shanghai. Chiang turned the swap down. The arrest of the two agents was a public affair, and they had been openly tried and imprisoned. But Moscow's offer unleashed a

---

* She was the sister of Mme Chiang Kai-shek. The fact that she was a Russian agent remained a secret throughout her long life, and remains little-known to this day. But a secret letter she wrote on 26 January 1937 to Wang Ming, the head of the CCP delegation in Moscow, and her controller, shows her role beyond any doubt. The letter opens: "To Comrade Wang Ming. Dear Comrade: It is necessary for me to inform you the following facts since they may endanger my activities ... in China in the near future. I place them before your consideration in the hope that you will advise me as to what course to pursue ..." One of the points in her letter was complaints about the American Comintern agent Agnes Smedley who, Mme Sun said, brought "foreign sympathizers home, with the result that this special house which has been used for important purposes now has been ruined ... I forwarded your instructions to isolate her" to the CCP.

torrent of anguish in Chiang, who thought his son might now be "cruelly put to death by Soviet Russians." On 3 December 1931 the Generalissimo wrote in his diary: "In the past few days, I have been yearning for my son even more. How can I face my parents when I die [if Ching-kuo is killed]?" On the 14th: "I have committed a great crime by being unfilial [by risking the death of his heir] . . ."

Chiang continued to be consumed by anxiety about what might happen to his son, and his anguish and bitterness almost certainly explain an event that happened thousands of kilometers away. At exactly this time, December 1931, Shao Li-tzu's son was found shot dead in Rome. This son had been taken by Shao to Russia in 1925 as Ching-kuo's traveling companion. But, unlike Ching-kuo, Shao junior was later allowed to return to China. The Italian press covered this death as a lovers' tragedy, one paper running the story under the headline "The tragic end of a Chinese who had wounded his lover"—a woman reported as Czech. But Shao and his family were convinced that the murder of his son, which has been covered up by both Nationalist and Communist parties, was carried out by Nationalist agents, and this could only have been done with Chiang's authorization, as personal vengeance: a son for a son.

By the time the Long March began, Chiang had devised a carefully crafted swap: the survival of the CCP for Ching-kuo. It was not an offer that could be spelled out. He executed his plan in subtle ways. His scheme was to keep the Reds temporarily confined, and then use the Japanese to break them. Chiang regarded war with Japan as inevitable, and was well aware that Russia wanted this war. Stalin's most dreaded scenario was that Japan would conquer China, and then, with China's resources and a porous 7,000-kilometer border, would attack the Soviet Union. Chiang reckoned that once the Sino-Japanese war started, Moscow would be bound to order its Chinese clients to get active against Japan. Until that day, Chiang would allow the Reds to survive, which he hoped would be a big enough quid pro quo to get his son back.

Chiang did not want the Reds to cling on in the rich heartland of China. His aim was to drive them into a more barren and sparsely popu-lated corner, where he could box them in. The prison he had in mind was the Yellow Earth Plateau in northwest China, mainly the northern part of Shaanxi province. To make absolutely sure that the Reds would walk into his fold, Chiang allowed a Communist base to flourish there, while vigorously stamping out the others elsewhere in China.

The main person Chiang used to implement this scheme was none other than Shao Li-tzu, the man who had taken Chiang's son to Russia. Shao was appointed governor of Shaanxi in April 1933. Though Chiang certainly knew Shao's true colors, he never exposed him, and continued to use him as if he were a bona fide Nationalist. Chiang's relationship with Shao, as with many other key moles, was an almost unbelievably complex web of intrigue, deceit, bluff and double-bluff that eventually was to spin out of his control and contribute to his downfall.

Chiang's calculation was that only a mole could foster a Red pocket, as any authentic Nationalist would destroy it. And, indeed, it was only after Shao was appointed to the area that what had hitherto been a tiny Red guerrilla operation began to grow in Shaanxi (and the edge of Gansu immediately to the west).* At the exact moment the Long March began, in mid-October 1934, Chiang came to Shaanxi province for a visit. While publicly calling for the Red "bandits" to be "wiped out," he allowed the Red base to expand in an unprecedented manner; inside a few months, it had grown to cover 30,000 sq km, with a population of 900,000.

What Chiang had created was a corral into which he would herd all the different detachments of the Red Army as he drove them out of their various pockets in the heartland of China. His plan was to weaken them significantly along the way, but not kill them off entirely. Chiang later told an American emissary: "I drove the Communists from Jiangxi to . . . northern Shaanxi, where their number was reduced to a few thousands and they were left unpursued."

The way he steered them was by communicating his own deployments by radio, which he knew would be intercepted. The Reds found that "enemy telegrams were constantly intercepted and decoded by us, and our army knew the intentions and movements of the enemy like the back of our hand." But Chiang declined to change his codes. And the Reds went where there were no enemy troops, or very few.

In order to make sure that the Reds followed the route he had mapped out, and to rule out any change in their instructions, Chiang decided the eve of the Reds' departure was the moment to cash in a huge intelligence coup. In June the Nationalists had covertly raided the CCP's Shanghai radio station, which had been the link between Ruijin and Moscow. For several months, the Nationalists kept the station operating under their control, and then in October they shut it down altogether. The CCP tried to re-establish a link by sending a top radio operator to Shanghai, but he defected as soon as he arrived. Assassins were sent after him. They missed the first time, but managed to kill him in his bed in a German hospital at the second attempt. From now on, Shanghai became largely irrelevant to the CCP, although it remained an important base for Moscow's secret services.

---

* The Nationalist army commander in Shaanxi was a fellow traveler called General Yang Hu-cheng, who had earlier asked to join the Communist Party, and whose relationship to the Reds was known to Chiang. He collaborated well with Shao.

★

THE LONG MARCH was used by Chiang to initiate his Reds-for-son swap. Just before the breakout from the Ruijin base, he sent a request through diplomatic channels asking for his son to be returned. On 2 September 1934 he recorded in his diary that "a formal representation has been made about getting Ching-kuo home." During the crucial period of the breakout in October–November, Chiang found a way of emphatically telling the Russians he was closing his eyes and letting the Reds go, by not merely absenting himself from the front line, but heading off a thousand kilometers in the opposite direction for a very long forty-day public tour of North China.

Moscow understood the message. During the precise period between Chiang requesting his son's release and the day Mao and Co. crossed the Xiang River and were free of Chiang's blockhouses, Moscow dramatically increased surveillance of its hostage. Ching-kuo, who had previously worked in a village and a Siberian gold mine, was now working in a machinery plant in the Urals. Then, as he later recounted, "from August to November 1934, I was suddenly . . . placed under the close surveillance of the Russian NKVD [KGB]. Every day I was shadowed by two men."

At the beginning of December, just after the Chinese Reds walked past the last blockhouses, Chiang asked for his son again (as the KGB informed Ching-kuo). But the Russians told Chiang that his son did not wish to return. "There is no end to the Russian enemy's revolting deceit," Chiang wrote in his diary, although he said he could "cope with it calmly." "I feel I have indeed made progress since I can even shrug off this family calamity." Chiang knew his son would be safe—if he did more for the Reds.

LONG MARCH II: THE POWER BEHIND THE THRONE

(1934–35 ∗ AGE 40–41)

B Y MID-DECEMBER, Chiang had steered the Long March into Guizhou, the first province he wanted to bring under control. As he had foreseen, the arrival of a Red Army 40,000 strong threw the local warlord into a panic. Chiang "has long wanted to take over Guizhou," the warlord recalled feeling at the time. "Now, the Central Government Army is coming hot on the heels of the Red Army, and I could not possibly turn him down . . . I was really in turmoil. Under the circumstances, I decided to place myself under Chiang's command." On 19 December, eight divisions of the Central Government Army marched into the provincial capital and at once started building an airport and roads. Soon afterwards, they took over key positions and, as the warlord put it, "turned themselves from guests into masters."

Chiang then funneled the Red Army northward to his next target, Sichuan, by blocking off other routes while leaving this passage wide open. Chiang's plan was to repeat his Guizhou takeover here, and then propel the Reds farther north into Shaanxi. But here things began to deviate from the planned scenario, as Mao started to behave in ways Chiang could not have predicted. Mao was determined not to move into Sichuan. His motive, however, had nothing to do with Chiang, but with his struggle for power within his own Party.

Mao had started taking active steps to seize the leadership of his Party once the marchers entered Guizhou. This required splitting his Party foes from within. In particular, he had been cultivating two key men with whom he had not previously been on the best of terms: Wang Jia-xiang, nicknamed the "Red Prof," and Lo Fu, the man who had taken away his job as "prime minister." Mao had crossed swords with them in the past, but now he buttered them up, as they both had grudges against Party No. 1 Po Ku.

The two had been students in Moscow with Po, who was the younger man but had leapfrogged over both of them to become their boss, and had sometimes excluded them from decision-making. Po "sidelined me,"

Lo Fu said years later, and this drove Lo into Mao's arms. "I felt I was put in a position completely without power, which I resented bitterly," Lo recalled. "I remember one day before the departure, comrade Tse-tung had a chat with me, and I told him all my resentment without reserve. From then on, I became close to comrade Tse-tung. He asked me to stick together with him and comrade Wang Jia-xiang—so that way a trio was formed, headed by comrade Mao."

The trio traveled together, usually reclining on litters. Bamboo litters were authorized for a few leaders, each of whom was also entitled to a horse, and porters to carry their belongings. For much of the Long March, including the most grueling part of the trek, most of them were carried. Mao had even designed his own transportation. Mrs. Lo Fu recalled him making preparations with the Red Prof, and showing off his ingenuity. "He said: 'Look, we have designed our own litters . . . we will be carried.' He and Jia-xiang looked rather pleased with themselves showing me their 'works of art': their kind of litter had very long bamboo poles so it would be easier and lighter to carry climbing mountains. It had a tarpaulin awning . . . so [the passenger] would be shielded from the sun and the rain."

Mao himself told his staff decades later: "On the March, I was lying in a litter. So what did I do? I read. I read a lot." It was not so easy for the carriers. Marchers remembered: "When climbing mountains, the litter-bearers sometimes could only move forward on their knees, and the skin and flesh on their knees were rubbed raw before they got to the top. Each mountain climbed left a trail of their sweat and blood."

Wafted on other men's shoulders, Mao plotted a coup with Po Ku's two jealous colleagues. When the road was wide enough, they talked side by side; and on narrow paths, when they had to go in single file, they arranged their litters so that their heads were together. One meeting was held in an orange grove, golden with ripe fruit hanging among bright green leaves. The litter-bearers were taking a break, and had laid down their burdens next to each other. The trio decided to work together to "throw out" Po, along with Braun, the German adviser, and give Mao control of the army. As Mao was still very unpopular, and was not even a member of the Secretariat, the core body, he did not shoot for the top Party slot at this stage. That position was earmarked for Lo Fu, the only member of the trio who was in the Secretariat. The Red Prof's reward would be full Politburo membership. The trio started to lobby for a meeting to discuss how the Reds had lost their state.

Po Ku consented to a post-mortem. In fact, he had been feeling so bad about the Reds' failure that his colleagues thought he might commit suicide, after seeing him repeatedly pointing a pistol at himself.

So a gathering of twenty men, the Politburo and selected military commanders, convened on 15–17 January 1935 in the city of Zunyi in north Guizhou. Much of the meeting was taken up with rehashing the question of responsibility for the collapse of the Red state. Mao's trio blamed everything on the key pre–Long March leaders, especially Po and Braun.

It is commonly claimed that Mao became the leader of the Party and the army at the Zunyi meeting—and by majority mandate. In fact, Mao was not made chief of either the Party or the army at Zunyi. Po Ku remained Party No. 1, endorsed by the majority; the consensus was that losing Ruijin could not be blamed on him. Braun, as the only foreigner, provided a convenient scapegoat and was removed from military command. But although Mao's two co-conspirators proposed that Mao take over, no one else seems to have supported this, and Chou En-lai was reconfirmed as military boss, with "responsibility for final decision-making in military matters."*

However, Mao did achieve one critical breakthrough at Zunyi: he became a member of the Secretariat, the decision-making core. The previous make-up of this group had been established by Moscow in January 1934. It had seven members, of whom four were on the March: Po Ku, Chou En-lai, Lo Fu, and a man called Chen Yun. The other three were Xiang Ying, Wang Ming, the CCP's representative in Moscow, and Chang Kuo-tao, leader of what was then the second-largest Red base. At Zunyi, the Red Prof proposed that Mao be brought into the Secretariat. Actually, the Red Prof had no right to make this nomination, as he was not a full Politburo member. But Po Ku was too guilt-ridden and demoralized to oppose Mao's promotion, and it went through. Moscow was not consulted, as radio contact had been severed.

Once inside the Secretariat, Mao was in a position to manipulate it. Of the four other members on the March, Lo Fu was already an ally, and Chen Yun took no interest in power, and was often physically absent, coping with logistics. That left Chou and Po. Mao's strategy towards Chou was to split him off from Po with a combination of carrots and sticks, of which the foremost was blackmail, by threatening to make him co-responsible for past failures. At Zunyi it was decided that a resolution should be produced about how the Red state had been lost, and Mao's co-conspirator Lo Fu contrived to get himself the job of drafting it, which would normally be done by the Party No. 1.

This document would be the verdict. It would be conveyed to the Party, and reported to Moscow. Lo Fu first produced a draft with the

---

* Lack of majority support for Mao is also clear from the fact that when he later referred to those who had supported him at Zunyi, he never produced more than two names—those of his two co-conspirators.

subtitle "Review of military policy errors of Comrades Po Ku, Chou En-lai and Otto Braun" and naming Chou as a co-culprit in the loss of the Red state. After Chou agreed to cooperate, his name was dropped and the blame deleted.

As Braun drily put it, Chou "subtly distanced himself from Po Ku and me, thus providing Mao with the desired pretext to focus his attack on us while sparing him." That left Po as the only problem, and Mao could always put him in the minority. Indeed, as soon as the Zunyi meeting was over and most of the participants had rejoined their units, Mao secured from this new core group the unheard-of and decidedly odd-sounding title of "helper to comrade En-lai in conducting military affairs." Mao had shoved a foot back inside the door of the military leadership.

This new core then elevated the Red Prof to full Politburo member-ship, and before long awarded him a high military post, even though he knew nothing about military matters. Most importantly, three weeks after Zunyi, on 5 February, in a village where three provinces met called "A Cock Crows Over Three Provinces," Lo Fu was catapulted into the No. 1 Party post in place of Po Ku. Mao and Lo Fu first got Chou to capitulate and then confronted Po Ku with a "majority" in the core. Po agreed to surrender his post "only as the result of numerous discussions and pressure," as he described it.

Lo Fu's rise to Party No. 1 was an underhand coup, and so it was kept secret from both Party members and the army for weeks. The change at the apex was only revealed when a military victory put the plotters in a stronger position. Po was now excluded from decision-making, and as Lo Fu was a rather feeble character, Mao called the shots.

THE ZUNYI MEETING decided to move into Sichuan. Sichuan lay just north of Zunyi, and was the obvious place to head for, being large, rich and populous—and long since recommended by the Russians to the force from Ruijin. It was much closer to Soviet-controlled Mongolia, and to Xinjiang (which had by now become a virtual Soviet colony, garrisoned by Russian forces), two places to which Moscow had been preparing to ship arms for the CCP. The former chief Soviet military adviser in China, Stern, had been investigating ways to link Sichuan with locations where the Russians could even supply "aeroplanes and artillery... and enough weapons to arm 50,000 people."*

---

* Soviet military attaché Lepin secretly advised on the best supply routes. The former CCP leader Li Li-san was sent from Moscow to a secret GRU base on the Chinese border, to try to establish radio contact. The US vice-consul in Yunnan, Arthur Ringwalt, spotted the danger, and warned Washington in early January 1935: "The situation appears to be increasingly serious for China. Unless a miracle happens, the Communists will force an entry into Szechwan [Sichuan] by one route or another. [Then] it will be only

But Mao did not want to go to Sichuan. To do so would mean join-ing up with Chang Kuo-tao, a veteran who headed a much stronger force numbering 80,000-plus. Once they linked up with this powerful army, there would be no hope of Lo Fu becoming Party leader—or of Mao becoming the power behind the throne.

Chang Kuo-tao had chaired the Party's 1st Congress in 1921, when Mao was a marginal participant and Lo Fu not even a Party member (Lo joined in 1925). He was a bona fide member of the Secretariat—unlike Mao, who had just squeezed his way in against the rules. In addition, Kuo-tao was a full member of the Comintern Executive Committee, which gave him considerable prestige, and he had influence in Russia, where he had lived for years, and met Stalin. After he returned from Moscow to China in January 1931, he was sent by Shanghai to head a Red enclave called Eyuwan, on the borders of the provinces of Hubei, Henan and Anhui in east-central China. There he built up a base compa-rable to Ruijin, which by summer 1932 had an area of over 40,000 sq km and a population of 3.5 million, with an army of 45,000 men. After he was driven out that autumn by Chiang Kai-shek, he moved to north-ern Sichuan, where he built a new and bigger base within a year, and expanded his army to over 80,000.* Kuo-tao was undoubtedly the most successful of all the Communists. Once he joined the rest of the leader-ship, it seemed inevitable that he would be elected the new boss.

Nor could Mao expect to turn him into a puppet. Kuo-tao had no compunction about killing for power. In his bases he had carried out bloody purges of the original local commanders, who had opposed him. Like Mao, he personally chaired interrogations involving torture. His victims were usually bayoneted or strangled to death; some were buried alive. As his military commander Xu put it, he would readily "get rid of people who stood in his way, to establish his personal rule."

With this daunting figure to contend with, Mao's prospects of coming out on top would be dim. Moreover, if he waged a power struggle against

---

a matter of time before the well-known plan . . . to establish communications with Soviet Russia will have been carried out. Then it will be useless to talk further about commu-nist suppression."

Another person who made the point was, surprisingly, a very important British spy for Russia, Kim Philby. In an article about Tibet published in Nazi Germany in 1936, Philby emphasized the strategic significance of the Chinese Reds linking up with the Russians in the northwest.

* Chang Kuo-tao was so successful mainly because the part of Sichuan he entered was in the grip of some exceptionally heartless warlords who squeezed the population so hard that even in towns there were many people who could not afford clothing, and were walking round completely naked. There had been several peasant uprisings just before Kuo-tao's army arrived, and his forces had been able to enlist recruits en masse. He also had a military chief, Xu Xiang-qian, who was arguably the most talented of the Chinese Communist commanders.

Kuo-tao, he might well be risking his own life. So far, Mao had been dealing with Party leaders whose devotion to the Party meant they would kill on its behalf but not for personal power. He had been perfectly safe with Po Ku or Chou En-lai even if he made trouble for them. He could not count on that much forbearance from Kuo-tao, so his overriding goal was to delay any move into Sichuan until he had an unbreakable grip on the Party leadership.

But Mao could not spell out this goal. He had to go along with the plan to head for Sichuan. On 19 January 1935 the force with him set off from Zunyi, and on the 22nd they cabled Chang Kuo-tao, who was in north Sichuan, announcing they were coming and telling him to move south to link up with them. But Mao had a trick up his sleeve. Four days later he insisted that the Red Army should ambush an enemy force that was tailing their group. This force was from Sichuan, and had a tough reputation. Mao's unspoken private calculation was that the Red Army might well suffer a defeat, in which case he could argue that the Sichuan enemy was too fierce, and then demand to stay in Guizhou.

The idea of the ambush was absurd, as the enemy unit Mao picked to attack was not barring the way into Sichuan, but was *behind* the Reds, and was not even harassing them. In fact the original plan which had designated Sichuan as their destination had specifically ordered: "keep well away from" pursuers, and "not to tangle" with them. But Mao managed to win consent from Chou En-lai, who had the final say in military decisions, most probably by threatening Chou that if he failed to go along he would be named as co-responsible for losing the Red state in the "resolution" Lo Fu was writing. It seems Chou had a mortal fear of disgrace—a weakness that Mao was to exploit repeatedly in the decades to come.

ON 28 JANUARY, Mao ordered his ambush set up to the east of a place called Tucheng, with a devastating outcome for the Reds. The enemy lived up to its fearsome reputation, and quickly seized the advantage, shattering the force that Mao had stationed with their backs against the turbulent Red River where it rushed between steep cliffs. Mao stood on a peak in the distance watching his troops being decimated, and only at the end of a whole day's bloody battle did he permit a withdrawal. It was raining hard and the retreating troops panicked, jostling to get ahead on the slippery mountain paths. The women and wounded were pushed to the back. The enemy was so close behind that one pursuer grabbed Mrs. Zhu De's backpack with one hand, while pulling at her gun with the other. She let go her backpack and ran. It was the only battle on the March when people in the HQ had had such a close brush with the enemy.

Four thousand Red Army men were killed or wounded—10 percent of the total. Tucheng was the biggest defeat on the Long March, and was remembered as such in private, while being completely suppressed in public—because Mao was responsible, having picked both the ground and the moment. In one day he brought about far greater casualties than had been incurred in the previous biggest loss, at the Xiang River (just over 3,000). The myth is that Mao saved the Red Army after Zunyi. The truth is the exact reverse.

The Communists crossed the Red River to the west in disarray over hastily constructed pontoons, abandoning heavy artillery and equipment like the X-ray machine. Zhu De personally covered the retreat, Mauser in hand. Normally calm, this day he lost his temper and yelled at his officers in frustration. The exhausted men had to carry or pull their wounded comrades along winding paths above vertiginous cliffs. Heavy snowfalls blanketed the dense forests and the valleys. The bitter cold, hunger, exhaustion, and the cries of pain from the wounded haunted many survivors for decades to come.

THIS TRAGIC SCENE was exactly what Mao wanted in order to argue that the Sichuan army was too grim to tangle with, and that therefore the Reds should not make for Sichuan as the original plan had laid down. But they were already inside the southeast corner of Sichuan, and many felt they had to push on northward.

The main military commanders, even Mao's old crony Lin Biao, supported pressing deeper into Sichuan. Furthermore, they all felt very unhappy about having let Mao dictate the Tucheng ambush. When Mao turned up at Lin Biao's to justify himself (and lay the blame on others), Braun noticed that Lin looked "decidedly sour." But Mao prevailed, with the backing of Lo Fu. Lo shared an interest with Mao in avoiding—or postponing—joining up with Chang Kuo-tao, as his own newly acquired position as Party No. 1 would be seriously endangered if they linked up with Kuo-tao this soon. On 7 February 1935 the new Lo Fu leadership announced that the original plan—to go into Sichuan—was scrapped, in favor of Mao's proposal to stay put in Guizhou.

The Communists turned around and crossed the Red River again. The thousands of wounded were dumped in the wintry wilderness, with little food and medicine. Within a few months most were dead.*

---

* Normal procedure on the March was to leave the wounded with local families, with some money. The fate of those left behind was a matter of luck. Chang Kuo-tao's branch left behind some women soldiers who were too ill and weak to go on. When Party historians went looking for them half a century later, they found they had endured atrocious experiences. The locals, whose families had suffered at the hands of the Reds, took it out on them, and tortured some of the women to death by driving wooden stakes into their vaginas and cutting off their breasts. To survive, some women married more affluent peasants. But when their own Party came to power they were designated as "landlords," and denounced, humiliated and discriminated against for life. In 1985, in bitter

Mao's force reoccupied Zunyi on 27 February. Chiang wanted to harry the Reds into Sichuan, so he sent a feisty general with two divisions to retake the city, which he also bombed. The Reds managed to fend these troops off. Mao was hugely delighted, especially as these were crack troops, and this meant he might be able to stay—at least for time enough to enable him and his puppet Lo Fu to consolidate their power. He penned a poem to voice his satisfaction:

> *Idle claim that the strong pass is a wall of iron,*
> *Today I crest the summit with one stride.*
> *Crest the summit,*
> *The rolling mountains sea-blue,*
> *The dying sun blood-red.*

It was only now that Mao and Lo Fu informed the army, including Chang Kuo-tao, that Lo Fu was the new No. 1, and that Mao had joined the Secretariat. There was nothing Kuo-tao could do. Mao and Lo Fu had deliberately waited until they had a "victory" under their belts before disclosing the changes. Once these were announced, and there was no open protest, Lo Fu appointed Mao as "General Front Commander," a new post created specially for him, and his first formal military position for two and a half years.

The "win" was in fact a Pyrrhic victory. Peng De-huai recorded "great losses" in his corps. "Only one regiment can maintain . . . 50 to 60 men per company . . . Now all the regiment headquarters and the corps HQ were empty as if they had been cleaned out by floods." Another "deeply worried" senior officer counseled: "We have not many troops left; we should avoid having tough battles . . . the Red Army can no longer stand such cost."

Mao, however, was bent on taking on more of Chiang's forces. They now controlled Guizhou, and he needed to tackle them if he was to stand a chance of establishing a base in the province—essential for his plan to stay out of Sichuan. On 5 March he issued an order to "eliminate two Central Government divisions." This touched off a barrage of protest from the field commanders who had been infuriated by the way Mao had been squandering their troops. Lin Biao cabled "most urgently" on the 10th against taking on these hard-bitten enemies.

At dawn that day Lo Fu called some twenty people to a council of war, with the field commanders present. Mao found himself completely isolated on the issue of attacking Chiang's crack forces. Even his ally Lo

---

November cold, the few seen by Party historians, by then in their sixties and seventies, were so poor that they did not wear shoes to the encounter, as these were considered too valuable to endanger for such a non-essential occasion.

Fu disagreed. When Mao misplayed his hand and threatened to resign as Front Commander, the majority jumped at the offer. Peng De-huai was appointed in his place, and the council voted to steer clear of Chiang's forces.

This time it seemed that Mao was really out. But he lost no time in plotting to reverse the decisions. That night, kerosene lamp in hand, he walked over to see Chou En-lai, who theoretically still had the final say in military matters, and talked him into holding another meeting in the morning—crucially, without the field commanders, who had returned to their units.

Mao offered Chou an inducement. With the creation of the post of General Front Commander, Chou had become somewhat redundant. Mao now suggested scrapping the post of Front Commander and setting up a new body to be called the Triumvirate, consisting of Chou, himself and the Red Prof.

With the field commanders absent, Mao was able to manipulate the second meeting. The decisions to appoint Peng in Mao's place and to avoid Chiang's forces were both annulled. A clear ruling by a quorum was thus overturned by a rump, with the crucial complicity of Chou. Moreover, as a result of these underhand changes, from 11 March 1935 on, the top army command did not contain a single genuine officer.

The new Triumvirate immediately ordered an attack on Chiang's forces near Maotai, the home of the most famous Chinese liquor, where the enemy was well dug in. "Disengage fast," Peng pleaded. "Enemy fortifications are solid, and geography is bad for us. There is no possibility of breaking [this Chiang unit]." But the Triumvirs insisted: "Throw in all our forces tomorrow . . . absolutely no wavering."

When the Reds launched a frontal offensive, Chiang's army was ready with heavy machine-guns, and routed the attackers, who suffered well over a thousand casualties. The routed Communists crossed the Red River once again and were forced into Sichuan.

Having got them where he wanted, Chiang blocked their way back into Guizhou. But Mao still spurned the obvious best option—to go on north—and ordered the Red Army to turn around and cross the river again and force its way back into Guizhou. This was so unreasonable and so unpopular that an unusual order was issued, for the eyes of the top commanders only, specially enjoining: "This crossing to the east must not be announced and must be kept secret."

For two months, the Red Army had been "circling in an ever-contracting area, so that it passed through some districts two or three times," in "exhausting and fruitless wandering," a perplexed Braun observed, taking the whole thing to be "erratic." It had fought seemingly gratuitous battles, at horrendous cost. Moreover, Mao had not just brought disasters on the army under him, he was also placing Chang Kuo-tao's army in jeopardy, by obliging it to hang around and wait for him. Mao later shamelessly called this fiasco his "tour de force." The fact that these huge losses were due to his jockeying for personal power remains unknown to this day.

CHIANG KAI-SHEK, TOO, was baffled to see the enemy "wandering in circles in this utterly futile place." Unaware of Mao's private agenda, Chiang had expected the Reds to go to Sichuan. Assuming that his own army would be following them in, on 2 March he had flown to Chongqing, the largest city in the province, to enforce central government rule. Chiang tried to terminate the quasi-independent fiefs, but the warlords put up dogged, though non-martial, resistance. He found himself powerless to subdue them, as his army was not on hand.

Chiang now redoubled his efforts to drive the Reds into Sichuan, subjecting them to heavy aerial bombardment, making it impossible for Mao to establish a foothold in Guizhou. At the same time Chiang very publicly transferred army units away from the Sichuan border as a way of signaling: There are no troops on that border. Go to Sichuan! But Mao determinedly led the exhausted Red Army in the opposite direction, southward.*

Under non-stop aerial attack, "forced marches of 40 to 50 km were the rule," Braun wrote.

> The troops were showing increasing symptoms of fatigue . . . When planes buzzed over us, we simply threw ourselves down on the side of the road without looking for cover as we used to do. If bombs began falling in a village or farm where we slept, I no longer woke up. If one landed close to me, I just turned over . . .
> The number of deaths, more from disease and exhaustion than battle wounds, increased daily. Although several thousand volunteers had been enlisted since the beginning of the year,† the ranks had visibly dwindled.

During this headlong rush, the Reds had to abandon more of their medical equipment and disband the medical corps. Henceforth the wounded got virtually no treatment. As well as bullet and shrapnel wounds, many suffered severe and agonizingly painful foot infections.

The folly of Mao's maneuvers is brought into focus by the experience

---

* Chiang and his officers were so mystified that they thought Mao wanted to attack the capital of Guizhou, where Chiang was, to try to get Chiang himself. But the Reds sped past without stopping.
† In Guizhou, where the population was dirt-poor, the Reds had recruited many thousands of young men.

of one unit, the 9th Corps, that got cut off at the River Wu, leaving its 2,000 men stranded north of the river. As a result, they were forced to move on into Sichuan. And, lo and behold, except for one or two skirmishes, they were totally unmolested. Unlike Mao's contingent, who had to go through weeks of depleting forced marches and bombing, these men strolled in broad daylight on main roads, and could even take days off to rest.

ONE VICTIM OF Mao's scheming was his wife. She had been traveling with the privileged wounded and sick in a special unit called the Cadres' Convalescent Company, which included thirty women, mainly top leaders' wives. After the battle at Tucheng, the Red Army had marched all day, about 30 km, in a downpour. At a place called White Sand, Gui-yuan left the litter which had been allocated to her two months before when she was too heavily pregnant to get on a horse, and lay down in a thatched hut. Several hours later she gave birth to a baby girl, her fourth child with Mao, on 15 February 1935. She was shown the baby, wrapped in a jacket, by her sister-in-law, Tse-min's wife. The army spent only one day in White Sand. As she had done twice before, Gui-yuan had to leave her baby behind. She wept when the litter carried her away and Mrs. Tse-min took the baby, with a handful of silver dollars and some opium, which was used as currency, to find a family to take it in. Mrs. Tse-min had asked Gui-yuan to give the girl a name. Gui-yuan shook her head: she did not think she would ever see the girl again. Her instinct was right. The old lady to whom the baby was entrusted had no milk. Three months later, boils erupted all over the baby's body, and it died.

In later life, when Gui-yuan spent a great deal of time looking for the babies she had been forced to abandon, she never seriously tried to look for this daughter. She would say to people close to her: "The girl born on the Long March, I didn't even get a good look at her. I wasn't even clear where exactly she was born, and who we gave her to..." But the child stayed on her mind. In 1984, the year of Gui-yuan's death, her former chief on the March visited her in hospital. He told us that while they were talking about something else, she suddenly asked him, out of the blue: "Where, but where was it that I had that baby, do you remember?"

Mao did not come to see Gui-yuan, although they were in the same town. It was not till later, when their paths happened to cross, that she told him she had left the baby behind. Mao said blandly: "You were right. We had to do this."

Deep down, Gui-yuan was wounded by Mao's indifference. She would tell friends that the remark of his that pained her most was when he would say to other women with a grin: "Why are you women so afraid of giving birth? Look at [Gui-yuan], giving birth for her is as easy as a hen dropping an egg."* Two months after giving birth, while Mao led the Red Army on the hellish march southward away from Sichuan, Gui-yuan was hit by a bomb and nearly died. Early one evening in mid-April, three planes appeared between terraced rice paddies on mountain slopes, flying so low that people on the ground could make out the pilots' faces. Machine-guns rattled, and bombs dropped along the path where Gui-yuan and her comrades were catching their breath. Limbs flew into trees, and blood and brains puddled the ground in crimson.

More than a dozen shrapnel splinters sliced into Gui-yuan's skull and back, one ripping the right side of her back wide open. She was soaked in blood. A doctor picked out shrapnel splinters with tweezers and applied the wound-salve *baiyao* to stem the bleeding. Gui-yuan lay unconscious, with blood pouring out of her nose and mouth. The doctor who gave her an injection of cardiotonic thought that she might have two hours to live. Her company leaders decided to leave her behind with a local family. Mao, who was in the next village, was informed about her condition. He did not come to see her—he was "tired." He just said he did not want her left behind, and sent over a doctor and two of his own litter-bearers. Mao did not come to see her until the third day. By then she had recovered consciousness, but was still unable to speak, or even cry. Continuing the journey was agony; Gui-yuan kept on fainting, only to be woken up by stabs of excruciating pain. She begged her comrades to shoot her.

AFTER TWO MONTHS of rushing farther and farther south with no end in view, everybody was asking: "Where are we going?" Among the top echelon who knew about the plan to link up with the Red Army branch in Sichuan, and the long-term strategy of getting closer to Russia, a deep resentment grew towards Mao. Lin Biao clamored: "This way, the troops will be dragged to ruination! We absolutely cannot have him in command like this!" Lin wrote to the Triumvirate in April, calling on Mao to hand over command to Peng De-huai, and for the whole force to go straight to Sichuan. Everyone was furious with Mao, even Lo Fu, who had at first acquiesced in his scheme. The sacrifices were just too horrendous. Braun recalled: "One day Lo Fu, with whom I normally had little contact . . . began talking of what he termed the catastrophic mili-

---

* Giving birth on the March was a nightmare. One woman who had gone into labor had to walk to the night's destination with the baby's head dangling out. Next day before dawn, weeping at leaving her baby in a bundle of straw in the empty hut, she had to walk on, and fainted wading through an icy river. Her women comrades found a table to carry her on. The wife of Teng Fa, the then head of the Chinese KGB, had a most painful delivery. Writhing in agony, she cursed her husband for making her pregnant. Teng Fa was fetched, and stood uncomfortably in the little hut, hanging his head. Mrs. Po Ku would say half jokingly: "On the march, I prefer a donkey or a horse to an old Male!"

tary predicament engendered by Mao's reckless strategy and tactics ever since Tsunyi [Zunyi]." Lo argued that if they were to avoid annihilation, the Triumvirate "had to be replaced by competent military leaders."

Mao was livid about the change in Lo Fu. Braun noticed that when Mao once struck up a conversation with him, "the name of Lo Fu brought a sharper tone to his voice. Lo Fu, he said, had panicked and was intriguing against him." But Lo was no real threat, as he had laid himself open to blackmail by Mao from the moment he agreed to delay meeting up with Chang Kuo-tao to preserve his own position as Party No. 1. Mao also appealed to Lo's personal feelings: knowing that Lo was in love with a young woman, Mao arranged to have her transferred so that she could be with him.

In mid-April 1935, the Reds, still being pursued, entered Yunnan province, in the southwest corner of China. Mao ordered them to stay put and even to "expand southwards"—i.e., even farther away from the direction of Sichuan. But southward lay Vietnam, which was occupied by the French, who were extremely hostile to the Reds. Besides, this corner of China was mainly inhabited by an ethnic group called the Miao, who had given the Reds some very hard times at the beginning of the March, and were extremely warlike. Everyone could see that this was a dead end.

The field commanders were enraged by Mao's order. The night they received it, 25 April, Lin Biao cabled to demand that they "go immediately . . . into Sichuan . . . and be ready to join up" with Chang Kuo-tao. Peng concurred.

Mao could not drag his feet any longer. On 28 April he finally consented to head for Sichuan. Once the Red Army started northward, their path was trouble-free. Even facilitated. That day they found a truck carrying twenty very detailed maps (scale 1:100,000), as well as a load of local goodies—tea, ham and the famed baiyao—parked by the roadside waiting to be captured. Chiang or the Yunnan authorities had clearly organized this bounty to hasten the Reds out of Yunnan into Sichuan. When the Reds got near the provincial border, the Golden Sand River (the name of the Yangtze in these upper reaches), three crossing towns opened their gates, offering zero resistance, even handing over money and food.

It took the Reds seven days and nights to cross the Golden Sand River at the beginning of May. Chiang's troops stood close, but did not interfere. None of the ferry points was defended. Spotter planes wheeled overhead, but this time dropped no bombs. Long Marchers remembered "a frightening number" of flies being more of a nuisance.

But once across the river, Mao tried to avoid going farther north. He ordered a siege to be laid to a town just inside Sichuan called Huili, so it could be the center of a new base. Surrounded by a moat, and with thick walls and battlements dating from the fifteenth century, Huili was held by a local warlord, whose home it was, and who was prepared to go to any lengths to keep it. He burned down all the houses outside the city walls so as to leave no shelter for the besiegers, and killed scores of his own soldiers suspected of harboring Red sympathies. Chiang's planes now began bombing again, to drive the Reds on. Casualties were very high, and the Red Army, with no medicine, was unable to take care of them. Mao was indifferent, and never once visited the wounded.

For Peng De-huai, the level of casualties and failure to treat the wounded were the last straw. He decided to challenge Mao for the military leadership. Peng had wide support from other field commanders, not least Lin Biao, who pointed out that Mao had dragged the Red Army on a huge detour, and that they could have gone straight into Sichuan well over three months before. Lo Fu convened a meeting on 12 May, in a makeshift thatched shed.

With his back to the wall, Mao fought with fearsome willpower and enormous rage, condemning Peng with political labels like "right-wing," and accusing him of stirring up Lin Biao. When Lin tried to reason, Mao just bellowed: "You are a baby! You don't know a thing!" Lin could not compete with Mao in a shouting match, and was bludgeoned into silence. Peng was doomed by his own decency and decorum. Unlike Mao, he was shy about fighting for power for himself, even though his cause was good. Nor could he match Mao in mud-slinging and "political" smearing.

Mao got support from the deeply compromised Party No. 1, Lo Fu, who stigmatized Peng and Peng's supporters as "right-wing opportunists." In doing so, he acted against his own feelings, under the shadow of blackmail by Mao. Others were silent. Taking on Mao was no small thing. Apart from the terrifying atmosphere he created on the spot, and the sense of urgency and demoralization created by being on the run for some eight months, a sustained fight could well have led to the Party and the army being split. So Mao kept his job. His hatred for Peng because of Huili lasted for the rest of Peng's life, and he started to take revenge immediately. After the meeting, a close friend of Peng's, who had also brought up the tremendous casualties in the battles initiated by Mao, and had opposed marking time in Guizhou, found himself denounced. He understood that Peng was the implicit target: "it was inconvenient to denounce Peng De-huai by name, so I was denounced instead."

Mao was astute enough to agree to a trade-off. He withdrew the order to take Huili, and agreed, finally and explicitly, to "go north at once to join up with" Chang Kuo-tao. He had been putting this off for four months, and in doing so had lost some 30,000 men, more than half of the force with him. Because of him, the soldiers under him had walked at least an extra 2,000 km, often on lacerated feet.

But Mao had made tremendous headway towards achieving his goal. Not only did he now have a formal top military job, but his puppet Lo Fu had established himself as the de facto Party No. 1. These four months of ruthless sacrificial procrastination had made a critical difference. Mao had not entirely averted a power struggle with Chang Kuo-tao, but he had vastly improved his chances.

Mao at once began making preparations, and his most important step was to dispatch a reliable envoy to Moscow to establish his status. (Someone had to go in person as there was no radio communication.) The man he chose had no political ambitions of his own, was obliging, and senior enough to deal with any problems that might come up in Moscow. This was Chen Yun, a member of the Secretariat. Mao chose his spokesman well. In Moscow, Chen delivered a carefully crafted message which gave the impression that the majority of the high command had elected Mao as their leader at a proper meeting: "an enlarged Politburo meeting . . . removed the [old] leadership and put comrade Mao Tse-tung in the leadership."

MAO'S GROUP HAD now reached west-central Sichuan, near Tibet, marching straight north towards Chang Kuo-tao. This next stretch provided the backdrop for the primal myth about the Long March—the crossing of the bridge over the Dadu River. This river constituted a formidable natural barrier. In late May, swollen with the Himalayan snows, it was a raging torrent, trapped between towering cliffs. Its rock-strewn bed concealed treacherous whirlpools that made wading or swimming across impossible.

There was no way around, and only one bridge, which had been built in the early eighteenth century as part of the imperial road connecting Chengdu, the capital of Sichuan, to Lhasa, the capital of Tibet. It was a magnificent suspension bridge, 101 meters long and over 3 meters wide, carried by 13 thick iron chains, 9 on the bottom, with gaps a foot wide between each chain. Wooden planks paved the surface, and covered the gaps.

This bridge is the center of the Long March myth,* fed to the journalist Edgar Snow in 1936. Crossing the bridge, Snow wrote, "was the most critical single incident of the Long March." As he describes it:

> half this wooden flooring had been removed [by the Nationalists], and
> before them [the marchers] only the bare iron chains swung to a point

---

* A picture of it features on the cover of the 1985 book *The Long March*, by Harrison Salisbury, which purveys the official post-Mao version.

midway in the stream. At the northern bridgehead an enemy machine-gun nest faced them, and behind it were positions held by a regiment of White troops . . . [W]ho would have thought the Reds would insanely try to cross on the chains alone? But that was what they did.

He described men being shot and falling into the river.

Paraffin was thrown on the [remaining] planking, and it began to burn. By then about twenty Reds were moving forward on their hands and knees, tossing grenade after grenade into the enemy machine-gun nest.

This is complete invention. There was no battle at the Dadu Bridge. Most probably the legend was constructed because of the site itself: the chain bridge over the roiling river looked a good place for heroic deeds. There were no Nationalist troops at the bridge when the Reds arrived on 29 May. The Communists claim that the bridge was defended by a Nationalist regiment under one Li Quan-shan, but cables to and from this regiment locate it a long way away, at a place called Hualinping. There *had* been a different Nationalist unit headquartered in Luding, the town at one end of the bridge, but this unit had been moved out of town just before the Reds arrived.* The numerous Nationalist communications make no mention of any fighting on the bridge or in the town, while they do mention skirmishes en route to the bridge, and after the Communists crossed over it. Chiang had left the passage open for the Reds.

When the Red advance unit reached the area, it set up HQ in a Catholic church near the bridge, and shelled and fired across the river at Luding on the opposite side. A local woman, who was a sprightly 93-year-old when we met her in 1997, described to us what happened. In 1935 her family—all Catholics, like most locals in those days—was running a bean-curd shop right by the bridge on the side held by the Reds, and Red soldiers were billeted in her house. She remembered the Communists firing as "Only Yin a shell, and Yang a shot"—a Chinese expression for sporadic. She did not remember her side of the river being fired on at all.

Some planks of the bridge may have been removed or damaged. The 93-year-old remembered that the Reds borrowed her doors and those of her neighbors to put on the bridge, and after the troops had crossed over, the locals went to collect their doors. But the bridge was not reduced to its bare chains: the only time this happened was when Mao's regime made a propaganda film. Nor was the bridge set on fire. This claim was explicitly denied by the curator of the museum at the bridge in 1983.

* Nationalist plans on the 28th described the task of the unit, under Yu Song-lin, as "to defend Kangding," a city about 50 km away as the crow flies. The fact that Yu's troops were not at or near the bridge is demonstrated in a report of 3 June by the governor of the region.

The strongest evidence that there was no battle is that the Red Army crossed the bridge without incurring a single casualty. The vanguard consisted of twenty-two men, who, according to the myth, stormed the bridge in a suicide attack. But at a celebration immediately afterward, on June 2, all twenty-two were not only alive and well, they each received a Lenin suit, a fountain pen, a bowl and a pair of chopsticks. Not one was even wounded.

No one else died under fire. Chou En-lai's bodyguard described how Chou, having been upset when he heard that *a horse* had fallen into the river, went to check on human losses. "No men lost?" Chou asked the commander of the unit that had taken the bridge, Yang Cheng-wu, to which Yang replied: "None."*

In 1982, no less an authority than China's paramount leader, Deng Xiao-ping, himself a Dadu Bridge participant, confirmed that there was no battle. When a U.S. interlocutor described the crossing as "a great feat of arms," Deng smiled and said, "Well, that's the way it's presented in our propaganda. . . . In fact, it was a very easy military operation. There wasn't really much to it. The other side were just some troops of the warlord who were armed with old muskets and it really wasn't that much of a feat, but we felt we had to dramatize it."†

MAO WALKED ACROSS the Dadu bridge on 31 May 1935. He was now only about 300 km away from the dreaded meeting with Chang Kuo-tao. Between him and Kuo-tao's advance unit coming to meet him was a mountain called the Big Snowy, in a largely Tibetan area. In spite of its name—and myth—there was no snow where they climbed, locals told us. But it was cold, with sleet and biting winds, made worse by the fact that many men had abandoned their warm clothes in the semi-tropical lowlands, in an effort to shed some weight. All they had to provide some warmth was boiling chili water which they drank before they set off. Although it took only one day to cross, the mountain claimed many lives,

* When Peng De-huai, the most honest of all the Communist leaders, was asked about the Dadu crossing by a British writer in 1946, he gently, but very clearly, refused to endorse the myth. "It's a long time ago, and I cannot remember all of it. There were so many rivers—the Gold Sand river, the Hsiang river, the Wu and the Yangtse . . . I cannot remember very much, but I remember the people falling into the water . . ." He did not say one word about fighting, or a burning bridge. It seems that two or three people did die at the bridge, but only when they fell off while repairing it, when one old plank suddenly snapped, as Mrs. Zhu De and the 93-year-old local we interviewed remembered. For good measure, the Reds constructed an ancillary myth about more heroism around the other crossing of the Dadu River, at Anshunchang, some 75 km to the south. Although this ferry crossing was extremely exposed and it took the troops a whole week to cross, with spotter planes circling overhead, there was not a single battle casualty here, either.
† Zbigniew Brzezinski, former U.S. National Security adviser, speech at Stanford 2005, p. 3

partly because of the altitude (the pass was 10,000 feet high) but mainly because the marchers had been weakened by their privations.

They had been walking virtually non-stop for nearly eight months, half the time totally pointlessly from a military or survival point of view— though not from the point of view of Mao's ascent to power. In addition to being attacked by their enemies, they had been assailed by innumerable ailments. "All of us were unbelievably lice-ridden," Braun remembered. "Bleeding dysentery was rampant; the first cases of typhus appeared . . . More and more, our route was lined with the bodies of the slain, frozen or simply exhausted." It was hardest for those who had to carry the leaders in their litters and heavy loads. Some porters never got up again after they sat down to rest.

Mao climbed the mountain on foot, using a walking-stick. He fared far better than his young bodyguards, as he was much better nourished and rested.

Kuo-tao's men were waiting for them on the far side, in a Tibetan town of about 100 households, with a cornucopia of supplies—not only food, but clothes, shoes, woolen socks, blankets, gloves and delicacies like preserved yellow peas, tea and salt. This army was well fed and well kitted-out, and even had supplies to spare. Mao and the other leaders got extra food, horses or donkeys, and woolen suits. A docile horse was chosen for Mao, who was also given a male doctor to serve as his nurse.

A week later, on 25 June, Kuo-tao, having ridden over three days through virgin forests and rocky gorges, arrived to meet Mao and his companions at a village called Fubian. The two biggest Red armies were now formally linked up.

DAYS LATER, on 4 July, Chiang Kai-shek's brother-in-law, H. H. Kung (vice-premier and finance minister), called on Soviet ambassador Dmitri Bogomolov, ostensibly to discuss Japan's moves in northern China. At the very end, Kung remarked that the Generalissimo very much wanted to see his son. This was Chiang saying to Stalin: I have allowed two major Red armies to survive and join forces, would you please let me have my son? "We are not putting any obstacles in the way of him leaving," Bogomolov replied, lying smoothly, "but as far as I know, he does not want to go anywhere."

Although he did not get his son back now, Chiang had achieved his goal of bringing the three southwestern provinces under the central government. The Guizhou warlord had been forced to resign, and left the province after being lavishly bought off. The Yunnan governor stayed on and maintained a good relationship with Chiang (for the time being). With his own army now in Sichuan, following at Mao's heels, Chiang returned there in May to assume control of this strategically important—

and most populous—province. Here he spent months of intensive activity to build up Sichuan as his base for war against Japan.

Mao too had succeeded in his goal. The 2,000-kilometer detour he had forced upon the Red Army had bought the time to establish his puppet Lo Fu as de facto Party chief, and Mao had secured his grip on the Party leadership as the man behind the throne. Chang Kuo-tao's chances had been critically reduced. Mao's machinations had reduced the ranks under him by tens of thousands, to around 10,000 hungry and exhausted men in rags. But no matter to him. The army could be rebuilt.

As always, Mao regarded the Kremlin as his only hope if he was to conquer China. Now that he was nearer than ever to Russian-controlled territory, he began to talk about requesting "matériel and technical assistance" from Soviet Central Asia. His paramount aim now was to ensure that Chang Kuo-tao, who outgunned him by about 8 to 1, did not gain access to Soviet arms—or the Kremlin's ear—before he did.

LONG MARCH III: MONOPOLIZING THE MOSCOW CONNECTION

(1935 ★ AGE 41)

WHEN THE TWO Red armies joined up in June 1935, Mao's force—known as the Central Red Army, as it came directly under the Party leadership—was in a state of ruin. It had started the Long March with 80,000 men. Now it was down to some 10,000—one-eighth its original strength. The surviving remnant was on the verge of collapse. It had lost nearly all its heavy weapons, and its rifles had an average of only five bullets each. As Zhu De lamented to Chang Kuo-tao, who was an old friend, this army "had been a giant before, but now it's only a skeleton. It can no longer fight."

In contrast, Kuo-tao's army, 20,000 at the outset of their own march, had quadrupled to an impressive 80,000. They were well fed, well equipped with machine-guns and mortars and ample ammunition, and superbly trained.

It was thus from a position of considerable strength that Kuo-tao met his colleagues. He was "a tall, stately man about forty," Otto Braun recalled, who "received us as a host would his guests. He behaved with great self-confidence, fully aware of his military superiority and administrative power . . . His cadres . . . controlled most of the area's meager resources, which were essential for the care of tens of thousands of Red Army soldiers . . . He was every bit as ambitious as Mao . . ."

The moment had arrived when Kuo-tao had to be given a job, and he had an extremely strong case for being made head of either the Party or the army. Mao did not want him to have either. It was showdown time. Mao seemed to be at an overwhelming disadvantage, and yet he emerged from the link-up with Kuo-tao as the victor, thanks to the three political figures who had been with him and formed the core Party leadership, the Secretariat—Lo Fu, Chou En-lai and Po Ku.

As far as Lo Fu was concerned, he had no hope of holding on to his position as Party No. 1 without Mao. Moreover, when Mao had decided to drag the army off on a detour, Lo had given his consent rather than risk losing his newly won position. Chou En-lai had colluded with Mao all the way. The one who on the face of it might seem to have had the least to lose by switching sides was Po Ku, who had been elbowed out of his No. 1 position by Mao and Lo Fu. But he too was heavily compromised in the destruction of the army; he had put up no effective struggle on its behalf, and was now very much a broken man.

So, although there was now a chance to gang up with Kuo-tao and ditch Mao, the top men chose not to do so, out of personal interest. If they now blamed Mao for everything that had gone wrong, this was bound to raise the question: Where were you? This would imply that there had been a better alternative which they had failed to grasp. It would make them seem unfit to be leaders. Out of self-protection, they stuck with a simple story-line: that the Central Army had been wrecked by more powerful Nationalist forces. To bolster the image of their own resilience, they tried to denigrate Kuo-tao's army, which had been highly successful, in spite of the heavy fighting it had faced. As they could hardly fault its military performance, they resorted to political smear tactics, saying it suffered from "warlordism" and "political backwardness," and had "a bandit style."

These accusations enraged Kuo-tao's army. The two camps descended into a mud-slinging contest, in which Kuo-tao's men had a virtual walkover. The wretched state of the Central Red Army was plain for all to see, and the scorn poured on it clung to the whole of the leadership.

"How can such a Centre and Mao Tse-tung lead us?" was the widely voiced sentiment. This resentment was directed against the entire Center, not just Mao, and this was a key factor in throwing the three core leaders— Lo Fu, Chou En-lai and Po Ku—together with Mao, which gave him a majority in the Secretariat of 4 to 1 against Kuo-tao.

The trio felt it was "sink or swim" with Mao as their own officers and soldiers started to vent their outrage as well. There was a flood of complaints about military "incompetence" and indifference to the welfare of the rank-and-file. "They didn't know where they were running . . . so aimlessly," officers told Kuo-tao, and "should have let the army rest and recover." The rank-and-file, in turn, voiced bitter feelings about the way their leaders had abandoned the wounded, and turned ordinary soldiers into "sedan-chair bearers" for the VIPs and their wives.

This charge—that Mao and the other leaders had "sat in sedan chairs" all through the March—was the sorest issue of them all. A Long Marcher told us how angry the ordinary soldiers had felt: the leaders "talked about equality, but they lounged about in litters, like landlords. We talked in whispers . . ." The soldiers were told that "the leaders have a very hard life. Although they don't walk, nor carry loads, their brains and everything have it much rougher than we do. We only walk and eat, we don't have cares." Not surprisingly, this low-level sophistry failed to assuage the rank-and-file.

Not having to walk made the difference between life and death. Not a single one of the wounded or the weak with a high enough rank to qualify for the Cadres' Convalescent Company died on the March. Nor did any of the leaders who were carried, even those who were badly wounded. While the elite all survived, sheer exhaustion killed many of their much younger litter-carriers, nurses and bodyguards, who were often in their teens—and some as young as twelve or thirteen. One statistic reveals the stony-hearted hierarchy and privilege under Mao's dominion: the Central Red Army now had almost more officers than soldiers.

WITH THE CONNIVANCE of his three Party allies, Mao offered Kuo-tao only the token position of deputy chairman of the Military Council, which was now a hollow shell, not even a rubber stamp. Kuo-tao and his subordinates demanded that he must lead the army. Mao responded with a stony silence. During the stand-off, the troops began to run out of food. The two armies, totaling about 90,000 men, were crowded into a Tibetan highland region that was just able to sustain its own population, but whose economy was completely thrown out of kilter by the advent of this huge force. "We were reduced to fighting for food with the local population," one Red Army officer recalled. Marchers cut down fields of barley, depriving the locals of their livelihood for the coming year. Mao, characteristically, treated this plundering—which probably made the difference between life and death for many thousands—as a joke: "This is our only foreign debt," he said to his American spokesman Edgar Snow, in a manner that Snow described as "humorous."

The Tibetans, not surprisingly, hated the Reds. Excellent marksmen, they launched guerrilla attacks from the forests. Long March diaries recorded: "There were a lot of corpses along the way, mostly stragglers killed by the barbarians." "Came across three stragglers (cut down by barbarian cavalry)."

In the end, Mao had to let Kuo-tao have the top army job. On 18 July, Kuo-tao was appointed Chief Commissar of the Red Army, "directly commanding all the armies." But Mao kept control of the Party leadership.

AT THE BEGINNING of August 1935, a detailed plan was agreed for going north—in order, as Mao put it, to be "close to the Soviet Union, where we can receive help ... planes and artillery." The plan envisaged going first to Gansu, and then sending a unit on to Xinjiang, which was a Soviet satellite, "and building airports and arsenals." It was during this operation to move north that Mao machinated to scupper Kuo-tao's chances of making contact with the Russians before he himself did.

The agreed plan involved dividing the army: the main force under Kuo-tao and Zhu De would seize the town of Aba and then go on north, while a smaller force, known as the Right Column, was to take a different route farther east, via Banyou. By Mao's choice, he and the Center went with the Right Column, which contained the bulk of his old troops, under Lin Biao and Peng De-huai, though these now answered to two of Kuo-tao's commanders. Nine days after Kuo-tao and his force had departed, on 15 August, Mao cabled Kuo-tao in the name of the Politburo, dictating a total change of course: "the main force must go via Banyou," i.e., follow the same route as the Right Column. Mao was thus tearing up the agreed plan and demanding that Kuo-tao and the many tens of thousands of troops in the other column reverse course and come to him.

Kuo-tao replied on 19 August that he was very near Aba, where there was plenty of food, and that he planned to take the town in a couple of days. He argued hard for sticking to the Aba route, pointing out that there were "three or four parallel roads to the north, with plenty of people and food," whereas "the road to Banyou is totally unknown."

Mao used his control of the political leadership to put pressure on Kuo-tao. Next day he sent Kuo-tao a resolution in the name of the Politburo, saying that his forces were too far to the west. The route Kuo-tao had taken by a unanimous decision was suddenly described as "extremely disadvantageous," and Kuo-tao himself was accused of being "opportunist"—for "choosing the road with fewest obstacles." Using a label like "opportunist" was a way of threatening to condemn him with a political charge.

Mao's aim in all this was to keep himself always ahead of Kuo-tao. This would also mean that Kuo-tao and his army would be dragged through calamitous conditions. By now Mao had discovered that, whilst Kuo-tao's route was plain sailing, his own route, via Banyou (which he had chosen himself), was actually a dire one. It went through the most murderous terrain, a huge swampland that would take at least a week to cross and whose hazards included: no inhabitants—and therefore no food and shelter; an atrocious climate—dark fogs, lashing storms and hail; few trees, so really hard to make a fire; and treacherous, quicksand-like, and often poisonous mud that could swallow a person up with one false step. All this at an altitude of over 3,000 meters, and a night-time temperature below zero even in August.

Instead of trying to conserve the strength of the Red Army, Mao insisted that Kuo-tao must face the same evil conditions—after him. Having fired off his menacing ultimatum, Mao floated into the swamps on his litter, sacrificing a huge pile of books, including the complete set of his favorite *Twenty-four Histories*, before departing. By the end of the first day, Long March records show that the troops had trudged "with not a single person in sight, crossed 5 rivers, 3 of which had no bridges," and were "soaked to the skin ... sitting huddled in the rain for the night." Braun has left a vivid description of what most endured:

> A deceptive green cover hid a black vicious swamp, which sucked in anyone who broke through the thin crust or strayed from the narrow path ... We drove native cattle or horses before us which instinctively found the least dangerous way. Grey clouds almost always hung just over the ground. Cold rain fell several times a day, at night it turned to wet snow or sleet. There was not a dwelling, tree, or shrub as far as the eye could see. We slept in squatted positions on the small hills which rose over the moor. Thin blankets, large straw hats, oil-paper umbrellas or, in some cases, stolen capes, were our only protection. Some did not awaken in the morning, victims of cold and exhaustion. And this was the middle of August! ... Outbreaks of bloody dysentery and typhus ... again won the upper hand.

Another Long Marcher remembered: "I once saw several men under a blanket and thought they were stragglers. So I tried to rouse them." The men were dead. There was little to eat: "When a horse died, we ate it: the troops at the front ate the meat, the ones at the back gnawed the bones. When everything ran out, we ate the roots of grass, and chewed leather belts."

> Mrs. Lo Fu saw the corpses of friends all the time ... On the sixth day, I got dysentery. I couldn't worry about embarrassment and just squatted down and shat all the time. Then I would tie my trousers and rush to catch up. I spent two days like this, and gritted my teeth to get through. For seven days and nights, it was a world of no human beings. On the eighth day, when I walked out of the swamp and saw villages, people, cattle, and smoke coming out of chimneys, when I saw turnips in the fields, my happiness was beyond words ... Those seven days and nights were the hardest time in the Long March. When I arrived in Banyou, I felt as if I had just returned to the human world from the world of death.

A night at Banyou, in a hut made of dried yak droppings plastered over wicker, able to dry one's clothes by a bonfire of the all-purpose dung, was the lap of luxury for those who survived. In Lin Biao's corps alone, 400 had died—some 15 percent of its complement.

This was the ordeal that Mao was demanding that Kuo-tao's tens of thousands of troops should go through, instead of marching along proper roads on the route first assigned. Invoking the name of the Politburo, Mao kept piling on the pressure, urging Kuo-tao to "move fast to Banyou."

In one cable written after he had emerged from the swampland and knew full well what it was like, Mao lied through his teeth: "From Maoergai [where he had started] to Banyou, it is short in distance and plentiful in shelter." He then advised Kuo-tao: "Suggest you . . . bring all the wounded and sick who can manage to walk, plus the matériel and equipment . . ." On the surface, this seemed to be telling Kuo-tao: Don't abandon your wounded, but its real intention was to cause maximum suffering.

If Kuo-tao refused to obey, Mao could get him formally condemned and removed from command. Reluctantly, Kuo-tao agreed to come to Mao, and directed his huge army into the swampland. A couple of days' taste of what lay ahead made him even less keen than before. On 2 September his force reached a river in spate. He cabled Mao: "We have reconnoitred 30 *li* [15 km] up and down the river, and cannot find anywhere we can ford. Difficult to find bridge-making material. Have food for only 4 days . . ."

A day later, he decided to go no further. "Have reconnoitred 70 *li* [35 km] upstream, and still cannot ford or build a bridge," he told Mao. "There is food for only 3 days for all the units . . . The swampland looks boundless. Impossible to go forward, and seem to be waiting for our death. Cannot find guide. Sheer misery. Have decided to start back to Aba from tomorrow morning." He barely hid his fury against Mao: "The whole strategy is affected. Last time . . . the troops ran out of food and suffered great damage. This time, you force us to move to Banyou, and get us into this . . ." Kuo-tao turned back.

By now, Kuo-tao and the main body of the army had been shunted around for a month, thanks to Mao. Moreover, in these highlands, murderous weather was setting in. Kuo-tao now made a decision that was just the one Mao had been angling for: to suspend the journey north and stay put until spring the next year. "The window of opportunity to go north has been lost," he told Mao. Two-thirds of his troops had contracted foot infections and could hardly walk. If they were to embark on the long march north, nearly all the wounded and sick would have to be abandoned.

Mao, of course, knew all this; indeed, the whole point of hustling Kuo-tao's army from pillar to post was to reduce it to this state. Mao had now achieved his key objective: he had made sure he would get to the Russians first, knocking Kuo-tao out of the running by penning him up in the south till the following year.

ONCE KUO-TAO GAVE the order not to go on north, Mao faced a major problem. Kuo-tao had issued this order as military supremo. Mao could issue orders in the name of the Party, but he was not at all sure that he could take any of the army, even his own troops, with him, if they were allowed a choice. Crisis time came on 8 September when Kuo-tao ordered his two commanders with Mao to bring the Right Column down south to him.

Aware that he lacked prestige among the troops, Mao ducked a straight confrontation. He did not dare challenge Kuo-tao's order openly, even in the name of the Party. Instead, he kidnapped his own troops, using false pretenses. On the night of 9–10 September, he and Lo Fu told a select few an egregious lie—that Kuo-tao had ordered his men to harm the Party leaders; so, Mao said, they must secretly muster their subordinates and decamp that night.* Mrs. Lo Fu remembered being woken up in the middle of the night and told: " 'Get up! Get up! Set off at once!' We asked: 'What happened?' 'Where are we going?' [and were told]: 'No questions, just get a move on and go! . . . No noise, no torches . . . follow me!' We rushed for about 10 *li* [5 km] and did not pause to catch our breath until after we crossed a mountain pass."

At the same time as he was abducting his own troops, Mao got one of his top men to extract the 2nd Bureau, which handled radio communications, from HQ, and steal the detailed maps.

On this occasion, Mao had help from a crucial new ally—Peng De-huai. Just over three months before, Peng had challenged Mao for the military leadership, and had been friendly towards Kuo-tao, who had tried to cultivate him. But now Peng sided with Mao. The reason was not only that Mao controlled the Party leadership, but that he had also grabbed pole position for the Russian connection.

At dawn on 10 September, Kuo-tao's commanders with the Right Column woke up to find Mao and Co. gone, as well as the maps. Moreover, they were told that the rear guard of Mao's escape party had their guns cocked and would open fire on any pursuers. Officers stationed along the route the escapers were taking rang to ask whether they should use force to stop Mao and his band, as it was obvious that they were leaving surreptitiously. Kuo-tao's commanders decided that "Red Army must not shoot Red Army," so Mao was allowed to get away.

As Mao and his men went on their way, a propaganda team from Kuo-

---

* At the time, the lie was told in very vague words to only a few people. Mao later embellished it into a vivid story about how Kuo-tao had sent a cable to his men ordering them to "liquidate" him and the Center. And this became the official version. But Mao did not produce this claim until eighteen months later, on 30 March 1937, when he was trying to purge Kuo-tao. Until then, although there had been a Party resolution denouncing Kuo-tao for "splitting the Red Army," it did not include this charge. Nor was the accusation mentioned in any of the many subsequent telegrams to Kuo-tao from Mao and his armies. Even Mao's cable to Moscow denouncing Kuo-tao as soon as radio links were restored in June 1936 did not have a word about it. All this proves that there was no order from Kuo-tao to harm Mao.

tao's army appeared and began to wave and shout: "Don't follow Big Nose! Please turn back!" "Big Nose" meant foreigner, in this case Otto Braun. Braun had also been told the lie that Kuo-tao had given an order "to break the resistance of the Central Committee, by force if necessary." The shouting disclosed for the first time to the rank-and-file that there was a split in the army, and caused great confusion and anxiety. Mao's political department immediately sent staff to urge the soldiers on, in case some took the opportunity to go with Kuo-tao.

At this point, Mao had fewer than 8,000 troops, and they were desperately bewildered men, who had not chosen to take his side. Most unusually for him, he now appeared in front of the troops. He did not address them, but just stood in silence by the roadside, watching them go by, counting their strength, trying to gauge their mood. He made sure to have Peng stand beside him, to lend authority. For most, even quite senior officers, this was the only time they got this close to Mao, who preferred to wield power in the shadows.

Mao's next move was to make sure that Chiang Kai-shek gave his contingent no trouble. By now there could be no doubt that Chiang had been letting him through, but would allow only a weakened army to reach its destination. During the Long March, while Mao's force had been given little trouble, Kuo-tao's had had to fight every inch of the way—and the reason was that it was too large and too powerful.

It was thus to Mao's advantage for Chiang to know that only a small branch was now going north, and that the CCP leadership was with it. Sure enough, within hours of Mao's splitting, the Nationalists knew both these facts, and exactly which troops had gone with Mao, and how debilitated they were. On 11 September, the day after Mao bolted, Chiang told his governor in the area that he had "received information that Mao, Peng, Lin and their bandits are fleeing north, and they are all totally starved and worn out ..."

Kuo-tao seems to have had no doubt that the information was deliberately leaked by Mao, as a cable he sent to Mao and Co. next day read: "The morning after you left, [the enemy] knew straight away that Peng De-huai's unit had fled northward. Please beware of reactionaries ... leaking secrets. No matter what differences we have, we must not reveal military movements to our enemy."

This leak ensured Mao a smooth run for himself all the way to his destination—the Yellow Earth Plateau. There in North Shaanxi the only secure base in the whole of China awaited him, courtesy of Chiang Kai-shek. Mao and the core leaders had known about this base before the Long March, and Moscow had told them to expand it as far back as 3 May 1934, well before the March set off.

★

MAO ENJOYED A helping hand from Chiang, and the next thousand kilometers were virtually obstacle-free, militarily. "Except for native snipers," Braun recorded, "this stretch was void of enemies."* Chiang's forces shadowed them, but only to prevent Mao straying back into the heartland of China.

This final stretch was a cakewalk compared with before. Instead of snow and hail, and Tibetans sniping from the woods, here in south Gansu the Reds saw golden ears of grain in glorious sunshine, sheep at pasture and farmers tending fields. The locals were friendly, and Mao made an effort to keep them that way. He did not want another reception like the one from the Tibetans, and enjoined "strict discipline." Muslims made up 60 percent of the population, and the Red Army was forbidden to slaughter or eat pigs, and ordered not to rob any Muslims, even the rich.

The locals allowed the Red Army into their homes, where the men had a hot bath for the first time in months, enjoyed a shave and a haircut, and ate hearty Muslim meals, with pancakes and noodles, mutton and chicken, garlic and pepper. The hospitality, Braun remembered, "astonished me greatly."

But this friendly atmosphere became the cause of a major headache for Mao, as desertions soared. A Nationalist report showed that while Mao's troops were in one county alone, Minxian, over 1,000 Red Army men gave themselves up. On 2 October Mao ordered the security forces to "collect" stragglers. "Collect" often meant execution. One senior officer (later army chief of staff in Communist China) recalled: "During the march to north Shaanxi, there were continual stragglers. The army political security organization . . . adopted cruel means of punishment again." He was scared: "I followed the troops carefully, worried all the time that I might fall behind and be dealt with as a straggler." "Deal with" was akin to the Mafia's "take care of," a euphemism for killing. One day, "on the verge of collapse," he thought he might not make it: "my heart only settled back to its place when I got to quarters at 11 o'clock at night."

When Mao finally arrived at the Red area in north Shaanxi that was to be his base, his army was down to well below 4,000. In the last—and easiest—month of the journey, he actually lost more than half his remaining men, between deserters, stragglers, and deaths both from illness and

---

* There was one small skirmish at a pass called Lazikou, on 17 September. Although this involved only a handful of men, it was later blown up into a major battle—and a major victory. The reason for this fabrication was that, for Mao to validate his split from Kuo-tao, he had to show at least one feat of arms in the period after he broke away from him. In fact, Mao was simply let through at Lazikou.

at the hands of his own security men. His force was just about the same size as when he had left the outlaw land back in January 1929, seven years earlier. And the troops were in the worst possible shape. One officer recalled:

> We were famished and exhausted. Our clothes, in particular, were in shreds. We had no shoes or socks, and many people wrapped their feet with strips of blanket . . . Wuqi [where they arrived] was already a very poor place, but even the . . . local comrades kept questioning me: how come you got into such a sorry state? You really looked like nothing but a bunch of beggars.

But Mao was not feeling at all defeated when he set foot in the Red territory on 18 October 1935. "The darkest moment" in his life—as he described the threat from Kuo-tao—was over, and he was the winner. The Red Army might be on its last legs after a trek of some 10,000 km, lasting an entire year, of which four months were extra, thanks to him, but the Party was now, to all intents and purposes, his.

HIS ENVOY, Chen Yun, had reached Moscow, and delivered his message to the Comintern on 15 October. With Mao the clear winner on the ground, Moscow accepted, for the first time, that he was now the boss of the CCP. In November the Russians published a carefully edited version of Chen Yun's report, proclaiming Mao by name as "the tried and tested political" leader of the Chinese Party. Two weeks later, Pravda published a feature article entitled "The leader of the Chinese people, Mao Tse-tung," which portrayed Mao in florid, tear-jerking language as an almost Chekhovian invalid struggling heroically against illness and privation.

In mid-November a messenger arrived in North Shaanxi from Moscow, the first direct liaison for well over a year. He had traveled through the Gobi Desert disguised as a trader wearing a sheepskin coat. In his head he carried codes for resuming radio contact with Moscow, and he brought a radio operator with him. Within a matter of months, the radio link with Moscow was restored, and the person who controlled it at the Chinese end was Mao.

The messenger brought Stalin's word that the Chinese Reds should "get close to the Soviet Union" by making for the border with Russia's satellite, Outer Mongolia. The move "to link up with the Soviet Union" could now start.

CHIANG KAI-SHEK WAS less successful in achieving his private agenda. On 18 October, the day the Long March ended for Mao, Chiang saw Soviet ambassador Bogomolov for the first time since just before the

March had started. Chiang proposed a "secret military treaty" with Russia. This could only be aimed against Japan, which had stepped up its efforts to detach five provinces from northern China by offering them bogus "independence." The Russian response was that Chiang must first "regulate relations with the CCP." The Generalissimo's close associate and founder of the Chinese FBI, Chen Li-fu, began secret talks straightaway with Bogomolov and Soviet military attaché Lepin on the nuts and bolts of a deal with the CCP—even referring to "cooperation" with the Reds.

During these talks Chen Li-fu asked Bogomolov for the release of Chiang's son Ching-kuo. Chen told us: "I said to him: We two countries are signing a treaty now, and we are on very good terms. Why do you still detain our leader's son? Why can't you release him?" (Loyally, Chen added that he was acting without telling Chiang—"He would not have wanted me to make this request." This remark reflects the understanding among the few people in on Chiang's Reds-for-son exchange that the deal must never be attributed to him, or allowed to leak out.)

But Stalin still refused to free his hostage. Ching-kuo had by now been separated from his parents for exactly ten years. In March that year, in his heavy machinery plant in the Urals, love had softened the young man's bleak life when he married a Russian technician called Faina Vakhreva. In December they were to have their first child, born into the same captivity that Ching-kuo himself would endure for many more moons, as Mao's fortunes rose, and rose again.

PART THREE

BUILDING HIS POWER BASE

THE TIMELY DEATH
OF MAO'S HOST

(1935–36 ★ AGE 41–42)

MAO'S HOME for the next decade was the Yellow Earth Plateau in northwest China, near the Yellow River, the second biggest in China after the Yangtze, and the cradle of Chinese civilization. The base had a population of nearly one million, occupying well over 30,000 sq km, mainly in northern Shaanxi, and straddling the border with Gansu province to the west. Far from the country's heartland, in those days it was the only secure Red territory in the whole of China.

The landscape was dominated by vast stretches of loess, yellow earth, that looked bleak and barren, broken only by long jagged gorges, often hundreds of meters deep, slicing dramatically through the soft substrate formed with the passage of time by minuscule particles of dust blown in from the nearby Gobi Desert. Most of the dwellings were carved into the yellow hillsides. One could gaze far into the distance and often not see a single soul. Wuqi, the first "town" Mao saw on arrival, had only some thirty residents. This area was unique in being relatively underpopulated, and enjoyed something unheard-of elsewhere in China—arable land to spare. Chiang Kai-shek had picked the locality to keep the Red Army alive, but small.

The founder of the base was a local Communist called Liu Chih-tan, who had an army of 5,000 men—more than Mao. For the local Red sympathizers, Chih-tan was a hero. For the Spanish Catholic bishop of the area, whose brand-new cathedral and other properties were seized by Chih-tan's men in July 1935, he was "daring, and a conspirator in everything that was subversive."

As Mao approached Chih-tan's base, he pointedly remarked that Chih-tan's leadership "does not seem to be correct," meaning Chih-tan was politically unsound. And it seems that Mao gave secret orders to the Party bureau whose jurisdiction covered Chih-tan's area (the Northern Bureau) to carry out a purge there. In mid-September Party envoys descended on the base, where they were joined on the 15th by a Red Army unit 3,400 strong which had been driven there from a different part of China. Together, these new arrivals struck out in a savage purge. Although Chih-tan's forces were superior in strength, he offered no resistance either to the takeover or to the purge. When he was recalled from the front, and discovered on the way that he was going to be arrested, he turned himself in.

The Party envoys condemned Chih-tan for being "consistently right-wing" (newspeak for moderate), and charged him with being an agent of Chiang's who had "created a Red Army base in order to wipe out the Red Army." His willingness to submit to Party authority, far from being appreciated as an act of loyalty, was twisted against him, and he was accused of being "cunning, in order to deceive the Party into trusting him." Hideous torture was applied. A colleague of Chih-tan's had his right thigh pierced to the bone by a red-hot wire. Many were buried alive. One survivor wrote in 1992: "We were imprisoned in heavy leg-irons . . . We heard that the pit to bury us alive had already been dug . . ." Between 200 and 300 people are estimated to have been killed.

It was at this moment that Mao arrived—in time to play the benign arbiter. He ordered arrests and executions to be suspended, and released Chih-tan and his comrades at the end of November. The purge against them was ruled to have been "a serious error." Two scapegoats were reprimanded.

Mao thus managed both to sabotage the local Red leadership *and* to present himself as the man who saved them. This put him in a position to take over their base. Thanks to the purge, Chih-tan and his comrades were already sufficiently intimidated by the time Mao turned up (Chih-tan could barely walk after being heavily shackled), and Mao was able to exclude them from decision-making positions and from key military jobs without prompting major resistance. Chih-tan, the founder of the base, was given a lowly post as commander of a detachment titled "the 28th Army," which was really just a bunch of new recruits, onto whom Mao foisted a trusted man of his own as commissar, and therefore Chih-tan's boss. Chih-tan did not demur; he endorsed Mao's authority publicly, and asked his comrades who had been victimized to put the interests of the revolution before their personal sufferings.

Mao did not want to be seen to be purging Chih-tan, as he meant to exploit his name to lend legitimacy and prestige to his own rule. But nor did he intend to retain him—because he was a local. Mao was going to be involved in extorting food, money, soldiers and laborers out of the population, as the CCP had done in other bases before; and, as in the case of virtually all other Red bases, he knew that these policies were sure to meet resistance from local leaders, who might well lead a popular upris-ing against the Party. Mao had a different method for dealing with Chih-tan from those he used against other potential threats.

★

AS SOON AS he settled down, Mao went ahead with his project of trying to open a passage to a Russian-controlled border where he could pick up supplies, and especially arms. His plan involved crossing the Yellow River into the much richer province of Shanxi to the east, to acquire new manpower and provisions, even possibly to build a base, before turning north towards Russian-controlled Outer Mongolia.

The expedition began in February 1936.* It garnered some spoils and recruits, but was rapidly driven back west of the Yellow River by Chiang's troops, without getting anywhere near the Mongolian border. During this brief operation Chih-tan met his death, at the age of thirty-three. According to history books, he died in combat, but the overwhelming evidence points to murder.

Chih-tan was shot on 14 April 1936, at a place called Sanjiao, a ferry town on the Yellow River. The official account claimed that an enemy machine-gun that had engaged an advancing Red Army unit put a round in his heart. Chih-tan was not with the assaulting unit, nor caught in cross-fire. He was about 200 meters away, up a small hill from which he was observing through a telescope. The machine-gun that reportedly killed him was firing in a totally different direction, and if the official story is to be believed, it suddenly swiveled round and loosed a single burst that miraculously hit Chih-tan in the heart—at 200 meters. This machine-gun seems to have had a sniper's accuracy.

Only two people were with Chih-tan when he was hit. One was the Political Security man in his unit, whose name was Pei, a star of the Chinese KGB. On the Long March, he had been given the crucial job of watching over the porters carrying the assets of the regime's bank. The other man present was a bodyguard. After Chih-tan was shot, Pei sent the bodyguard to "fetch a doctor," according to his own account, leaving himself the only man around when Chih-tan "completely stopped breathing." There seems little doubt that Chih-tan was killed by Pei.

The sequence of events surrounding Chih-tan's death strongly suggests that it was choreographed by Mao. A week before, Mao cabled Chih-tan that the 28th Army unit, "from now on comes directly under this HQ." There was no discernible reason for this order—except, of course, that this way whatever happened to Chih-tan from then on would not be reported through the normal chain of command, but directly to Mao. Two days after that, Mao appointed Chih-tan to the Military Council, from which he had previously been excluded. This amounted to Chih-

---

* As with the Long March, the Reds pretended that the goal was to fight the Japanese, and called it the "Anti-Japanese Vanguard," with slogans like "Going east to fight Japan." But this was pure propaganda. Mao's force did not even try to get near the Japanese.

tan's elevation to a major military position. If he died now, he would have the status of a hero and his men would be kept happy. Finally, on the 13th, it was Mao himself who ordered Chih-tan to go to Sanjiao, where he was killed the very next day.

When Chih-tan was buried, his widow was kept away from the interment. "You are not well," Chou En-lai told her, "and seeing him will make you sadder." This was an order. Seven years were to pass before she was allowed to have him exhumed, by which time the corpse had decomposed. The coffin was opened, at her request, when Chih-tan was given a public burial in a special shrine. Mao wrote an inscription, calling Chih-tan's death "a surprise." This was at a time when Mao particularly needed to ensure that there would not be any trouble in the base, and he was using the dead Chih-tan to lend himself authority.

Chih-tan was the only top leader of a Red base ever to die at the front. In addition, his former left- and right-hand commanders both fell dead in quick succession within weeks of him being killed—Yang Qi in March, and Yang Sen at the beginning of May. Within a few months of Mao arriving, all three top Shaanxi commanders were killed—a fate that befell none of the commanders from any other Red Army unit.

With the deaths of Chih-tan and these two top colleagues, any serious potential danger of rebellion against Mao's rule over the base was removed. Thereafter, although there were small-scale revolts among the locals, there was no uprising big enough to threaten Mao's regime.

CHIANG KAI-SHEK KIDNAPPED

(1935–36 ★ AGE 41–42)

WHEN MAO arrived in the northwest at the end of the Long March in October 1935, his aim, other than sheer survival, was to open up a passage to the border of a Russian-controlled territory so as to receive the arms and other supplies that would enable him to expand. Chiang Kai-shek wanted the Reds kept penned in their corral. The man he assigned to the task was the former warlord of Manchuria, Chang Hsueh-liang, "the Young Marshal," who had his HQ in the city of Xian, the capital of Shaanxi province. Mao was in the same province, some 300 km to the north.

There were two Russian-controlled territories through which arms could be delivered: Xinjiang, over 1,000 km to the west-northwest, and Outer Mongolia, more than 500 km due north. The Young Marshal's vast army of some 300,000 was stationed in the provinces giving access to both of these.

The Young Marshal's American pilot, Royal Leonard, has left a description of a worldly man: "My first impression . . . was that here was the president of a Rotary Club: rotund, prosperous, with an easy, affable manner . . . We were friends in five minutes . . ." After inheriting Manchuria when his warlord father ("the Old Marshal") was assassinated in June 1928,* the Young Marshal placed his domain under Chiang's central government, while remaining its chief until Japan invaded it in 1931. He then retreated into China proper with 200,000 troops, and was subsequently given various important posts by Chiang. He had an apparently intimate relationship with Chiang and his wife. Thirteen years the Generalissimo's junior, he was fond of saying that Chiang was "like a daddy to me."

---

* This assassination is generally attributed to the Japanese, but Russian intelligence sources have recently claimed that it was in fact organized, on Stalin's orders, by the man later responsible for the death of Trotsky, Naum Eitingon, and dressed up as the work of the Japanese.

But behind the Generalissimo's back, the Young Marshal plotted to supplant him. Having governed a land larger than France and England together, it irked him to be Chiang's subordinate. He aspired to rule all of China. To this end, he had earlier made approaches to the Russians and had tried to visit the Soviet Union when he was in Europe in 1933, but the Russians were very wary and turned him down. Only four years earlier, in 1929, Stalin had invaded Manchuria and fought a brief war against him after he had seized the Russian-controlled railway in Manchuria. Moreover, the Young Marshal had expressed admiration for fascism, and was friendly with Mussolini and his family. In August 1935 a statement put out from Moscow under the name of the CCP called him "scum" and a "traitor."

But once he was appointed Mao's warden later that year, Moscow performed a U-turn. The Young Marshal had become worth courting. He could make the CCP's life easier and, more importantly, help them link up with Russian supplies. Within weeks of Mao arriving in the northwest, Russian diplomats were deep in talks with the Young Marshal.

He traveled to Shanghai and Nanjing, the capital, to meet the Russians in secret. To cover his tracks, he wove a camouflage of frivolity. He had a reputation as a playboy, and happily played up this image. One day, his American pilot recalled, the Young Marshal got him to "fly the plane in a vertical bank, one wing in the street, past the windows of the Park Hotel where his friends lived. We passed within ten feet of the façade, the noise of the motor rattling the panes like castanets." This flamboyant show was staged outside the hotel room where one of the Young Marshal's girl-friends was staying. "Perhaps this will make you smile," the Young Marshal, aged ninety-one in 1993, chuckled to us. "At that time, Tai Li [Chiang's intelligence chief] tried everything he could to find out my whereabouts, and he thought I went to have a good time with my girlfriends. But in fact, I was doing deals . . ."

The Young Marshal made clear to the Russians that he was ready to form an alliance with the Chinese Reds *and* engage in "decisive struggle against the Japanese"—i.e., declare war on Japan, which Chiang had not done. In return, he wanted Moscow to back him to replace Chiang as the head of the country.

This package contained extremely attractive features for Stalin, including the one thing the Kremlin boss most wanted—for China to wage all-out war against Japan. Japan had been encroaching on China since 1931, and had been nibbling away ever since. After annexing Manchuria, Tokyo set up another puppet regime in part of northern China in November 1935, but Chiang had been avoiding all-out war. Stalin was anxious that Tokyo might turn north and attack the Soviet Union.

Stalin's goal was to use China to steer Tokyo away from the Soviet

Union by dragging the Japanese into the vast interior of China and bogging them down there. Moscow worked hard to fan sentiment in China for such an all-out war with Japan, while keeping its own agenda under wraps. It took a hand in major student demonstrations; and its many agents, particularly Mme Sun Yat-sen, Chiang Kai-shek's sister-in-law, formed pressure groups to lobby Nanjing for action.

Chiang did not want to surrender to Japan, but nor did he want to declare war. He thought that China had no realistic chance of winning, and that taking on Tokyo would lead to his country's destruction. He opted for a very unusual limbo—neither surrendering nor fighting a full-scale war. He was able to hang on in this state thanks to China's size, and the fact that the Japanese were only encroaching gradually. Chiang may even have harbored the hope that Japan would soon turn on Russia and leave the rest of China alone.

The Young Marshal's proposal suited Stalin, but Stalin did not trust him. Nor did he believe that the former Manchurian warlord was capable of holding China together to fight such a war. If China lapsed into internecine strife, it would facilitate the Japanese conquest—and, a fortiori, redouble the Japanese threat to the Soviet Union.

Moscow was too canny to reject the Young Marshal's offer outright. The Russians led him on, deluding him that they were considering it—so that he would help the Chinese Reds. Russian diplomats told him to establish direct contact with the CCP in secret. The first talks between a CCP negotiator and the Young Marshal took place on 20 January 1936.

WHILE THE RUSSIANS were merely stringing the Young Marshal along, Mao was happy to support him to replace Chiang, and wanted a real alliance with him. This was an ideal scenario for Mao. As the Young Marshal would be dependent on the Soviet Union, the CCP would have a pivotal role, and Mao might even become the power behind the throne for the whole of China. He instructed his negotiator, Li Ke-nong, to propose an anti-Chiang alliance with the Young Marshal, and to promise to back him as head of a new national government in place of Chiang. The negotiator was told to "hint" that the offer had Moscow's authorization, by suggesting that funds and arms would be no problem.

The Young Marshal naturally wanted to have Mao's promises nailed down by the Russians themselves. And it seemed this was very much on the cards when a scheme was soon put to him to get a senior envoy of his to Moscow. In January, a certain "Pastor Dong" arrived at the Young Marshal's HQ from Shanghai. Dong, who had once been a pastor at St. Peter's in Shanghai in the 1920s, was a Communist intelligence operative. The lapsed Pastor told the Young Marshal that Mao's sons were secretly in his care in Shanghai, and that there was a plan to send them to Russia, to the special school for the children of foreign Communist leaders run by the Comintern. He proposed that the Young Marshal assign an envoy to accompany them there.

Mao had three sons by his second wife, Kai-hui, who had been executed by the Nationalists in 1930. After their mother's death, the boys had been taken to Shanghai and looked after by the Communist underground.

The children had been having a tough time. The youngest, An-long, died at the age of four soon after he came to Shanghai. The other two, An-ying and An-ching, had to live a secret life, unable to go to school or to make friends outside the Dong family, where there was constant tension. Dong had deposited them with his ex-wife, whose life was thrown into danger and upheaval by their arrival, and who had no particular affection for these boys anyway. Sometimes they would run away and live as street urchins. Years later, watching a film about an orphan in Shanghai, An-ying became very emotional and told his wife that his brother and he had led a similar life, sleeping on the pavements and scavenging through rubbish dumps for food and cigarette stubs. During all these years, Mao had never sent a word to them.

Moscow now decided to bring Mao's sons to Russia, where they could be looked after and put through school. As in the case of Chiang Kai-shek's son when Chiang was rising to the top, the aim was also to keep the boys as hostages. Stalin was personally involved with this decision. Mao had no objection.

Moscow's offer to the Young Marshal to have an envoy of his escort the boys to Soviet Russia thus killed two birds with one stone. This way, the Young Marshal would guarantee the boys' safety during the journey and look after all the logistics, as well as footing the considerable bill for an entourage, which included a nanny. And, most important, the Young Marshal would see the invitation to send an envoy as a sign that Moscow was seriously interested in doing a deal, which could not be done under Chiang Kai-shek's surveillance in China.

The Young Marshal was delighted, and quickly made all the arrangements. His representative and the boys sailed from China for Marseille on 26 June. Moscow had told the Young Marshal they could collect their Russian visas in Paris.

THAT JUNE, two provinces in southern China, Guangdong and Guangxi, formed an alliance and rebelled against Chiang's government. Mao tried to persuade the Young Marshal to seize this opportunity to do likewise and turn the northwest into a breakaway state in alliance with the Reds. His aim, he told his Politburo, was to create an entity "like Outer Mongolia"—i.e., a Russian satellite.

But the Young Marshal was not keen. He wanted to run the whole of

China, not just part of it. And Moscow was downright hostile to the plan. At this time, in late June, the CCP's radio links with Moscow were re-established after a gap of twenty months. In the first telegram to the Comintern after the break, Mao requested endorsement for a breakaway northwest state. The plan was sent to Stalin, who was not pleased. He wanted a united China that would drag the Japanese into an all-out war, not a dismembered China.

Within days of Mao sending his telegram, the rebellion by Guangdong and Guangxi collapsed, ignominiously, not least because popular opinion was vehemently against any separatist movement. Stalin was confirmed in his belief that Chiang was the only person who could hold China together. On 15 August Moscow sent the CCP a milestone order, telling them to stop treating Chiang as an enemy, and count him as an ally. "It is incorrect to treat Chiang Kai-shek the same as the Japanese . . . You must work for the cessation of hostilities between the Red Army and Chiang Kai-shek's army, and for an agreement . . . to struggle jointly against the Japanese . . ."; "everything must be subordinated to the anti-Japanese cause." Stalin now wanted the CCP to support Chiang as the head of an undivided China, at least for the time being.

Moscow brusquely ordered the CCP to enter serious negotiations with Chiang for an alliance. Mao had to accede, and talks about a "United Front" began in September between the CCP and Chiang's representa-tives. Chiang had initiated the rapprochement. At the time the Long March ended, he had made overtures to Moscow, but the Russians told him he had to talk "directly with the Chinese [CP]," as a way of promot-ing the CCP.

Both Moscow and Mao kept the Young Marshal in the dark about this policy shift, and continued to mislead him on the issue that most concerned him—replacing Chiang. When the Young Marshal told Soviet ambassador Bogomolov in late July that he "hoped" that his "bloc with the [CCP], directed against Chiang Kai-shek and the Japanese, would be supported by the USSR," the ambassador said absolutely nothing to suggest that Moscow was dead set against this notion. For his part, Mao encouraged the Young Marshal to go on thinking that Moscow might back him.

ALTHOUGH HE HAD decided to back Chiang as the head of China, Stalin was in no way cutting back on his clandestine efforts to build up the Chinese Red Army. In early September 1936 he endorsed a plan to ship a large cargo of arms to the CCP through Outer Mongolia. Mao's wish list had included "monthly aid of 3 million dollars," as well as "planes, heavy artillery, shells, infantry rifles, anti-aircraft machine-guns, pontoons," together with Soviet personnel to fly the planes and operate the artillery. On 18 October he heard from the Comintern that "The goods are not as many as you requested in your cable of the 2nd [October] . . . and there are no planes or heavy artillery . . ." Still, the "foreign company" handling the shipment, a GRU dummy, would "supply 150 vehicles and provide drivers and gasoline; they can make two return trips . . . with about 550 tons to 600 tons" each trip. The number of rifles was almost exactly the same as the Russians sent to Spain, where the civil war had just broken out.

In October the Chinese Red Army began its operation to smash through to a delivery point in the desert near the Outer Mongolian border. At this stage, Mao had 20,000 troops in the base, and the other Red Army branches were about to converge there in response to his summons to join him. They included the troops led by his now disabled rival Chang Kuo-tao, who had spent the winter on the Tibetan border, at the mercy of Nationalist bombing. Thousands froze to death, and many others developed snow blindness. During the previous year, Kuo-tao had lost half the 80,000 troops he had commanded when he met up with Mao in June 1935.

Although he still had twice as many men, Kuo-tao now came as a junior partner. Sensing that he was done for, he became "very emotional," as his colleagues witnessed. "He even shed tears. He said: 'I'm finished. When we get to North Shaanxi, I'm going to prison . . .'" Though Kuo-tao was not exactly imprisoned, Mao was eventually to wreck his army further—and then purge him. But for now, Mao needed Kuo-tao's large and efficient force to fight to the Outer Mongolia border.

The other branch of the Red Army that came to Mao now was headed by Ho Lung, a tough former outlaw. He had been herded to North Shaanxi by Chiang Kai-shek from his base on the Hunan–Hubei border.* The three branches of the Red Army joined hands on 9 October 1936, making Mao the chief of an army of almost 80,000 men, twenty times the number he had fielded just a year before.

This was a formidable force, but in order to get to the Russian arms the Reds had to break through a powerful Nationalist army, and Chiang was determined to stop them. On 22 October he flew to Xian to take

---

* This base also went through bloody purges conducted by the Reds between 1932 and 1934. Ho Lung himself said later: "in this one purge alone, over 10,000 were killed. Now [1961] there are only a few women comrades alive, and this is because men were killed first . . . and then the enemy came before [the purgers] got around to the women . . ." "Even today in the area . . . they dig out bones from one big pit after another." Survivors recalled that many had been "put in jute sacks and thrown into Lake Hong with big stones tied to them. Fishermen did not dare to go fishing in the lake, because so many corpses came up, and the color of the lake changed."

personal command, and this put the Young Marshal in a jam. The Young Marshal duly alerted the Reds about Chiang's plans, as well as giving them cash and winter clothes, but that was his limit: he could not defy Chiang's orders openly. So his men ended up fighting the Reds. Within a week, Mao's push for the Russian supplies had been thwarted. A contingent 21,800 strong that had crossed the Yellow River was stranded on the other side. The main body of the Red Army pulled back to its corral in North Shaanxi, and was hemmed in again.

Mao asked Moscow for money urgently: "Be quick," he cabled. The Comintern immediately sent US$550,000,* but it could not solve the long-term problems. For food, there was just coarse black beans. Housing in this region was mainly *yao-dong*, quarters dug into hills, like grander caves, and many of the troops lacked even these. It had started to snow, and the soldiers had threadbare clothes and straw sandals. At the front, Peng De-huai, the chief commander, was living in a shepherd's shelter, a hole in the ground one meter deep and two meters wide, on the edge of the desert, battered by furious sandstorms. Even Mao was enduring discomfort, as the Party Center had been forced into the small town of Baoan, where he and his heavily pregnant wife were living in a dank cave, with water dripping from the roof. Once, when a bodyguard tried to push the door open, he was stung by an outsize scorpion. Plague-bearing rats abounded, half the size of house cats, and so bold that they would sit on people's chests while they slept and flick their tails across their faces, waking them up with a start.

BY THE END OF October 1936, the Reds were desperate. The Young Marshal saw an opportunity to rescue them, and gain favor with Moscow. His plan was simple, and extreme: to kidnap Chiang, who was about to step onto his turf. Even though the Young Marshal had not received the explicit commitment from Moscow that he had been seeking (his envoy had been given the runaround about his Russian visa), he calculated that saving the Chinese Red Army and having Chiang in his custody would change the whole equation for Stalin. This was a gamble, but the Young Marshal was a gambler. "My philosophy is gamble," he had once said to his inner circle. "I might lose once or twice, but as long as the game goes on, the time will come when I get all my stakes back." Having Chiang on his own turf was a once-in-a-lifetime opportunity.

The Young Marshal discussed his plan with Mao's secret liaison, Yeh Jian-ying, telling Yeh he intended to stage a "coup d'état," using this term

---

* These funds, as well as some further transfers, were sent through Mme Sun Yat-sen, from America.

(which in Chinese is transliterated as *ku-die-da*). On 29 October, Yeh cabled Mao, using veiled language, that "there is a proposal to stay Chiang." On 5 November, Yeh left for Mao's place, carrying the coup plan.

The idea of kidnapping Chiang was the Young Marshal's—but it was undoubtedly spurred on by Mao through his envoy, Yeh. The Soviet intelligence insider Aleksandr Titov records that "the question of arresting Chiang Kai-shek was discussed by ... Yeh Jian-ying and Chang Hsueh-liang in November 1936." And Mao very deliberately concealed the plan from Moscow, knowing that Stalin would be dead set against it. Mao was now acting directly contrary to Stalin's interests. Chiang was more crucial to Stalin than ever. On 25 November Germany and Japan had signed a treaty known as the Anti-Comintern Pact, confronting the USSR with its worst nightmare—belligerent enemies on both flanks in an alliance, with Japanese-backed forces on the move westward along the southern flank of Mongolia, towards Soviet Central Asia. The very day the pact was announced, Stalin urgently ordered the Comintern chief Georgi Dimitrov to impress yet more strongly on the CCP that it had to abandon its anti-Chiang position and support a united government: "We need ... a government of national defence" in China, Stalin told Dimitrov. "Work out a plan ..."

Mao was running a considerable risk of infuriating Stalin by endangering Chiang. He tried to play safe by keeping his distance from the kidnap. Before taking the plunge, the Young Marshal cabled Yeh to return: "Vital thing to discuss. Please come instantly." Mao held Yeh back, while pretending to the Young Marshal that Yeh was on his way. Then he spurred the Young Marshal on by wiring him that there was no prospect of the Communists reaching any compromise with Chiang, and saying the Reds were determined to continue their war against the Generalissimo. Mao gave the Young Marshal the impression that he, the Young Marshal, was their only possible partner, implying that Moscow would accept this.

WHEN HE GOT to Xian on 4 December, Chiang made no exceptional arrangements for his personal security. His immediate quarters were guarded by several dozen of his own staff, but the gate and outer perimeter of the residence were patrolled by the Young Marshal's men. The Young Marshal was even able to bring the kidnappers to reconnoiter Chiang's residence, at a hot spring on the outskirts of town, and to check out the Generalissimo's bedroom.

At dawn on 12 December, Chiang was kidnapped. He had just finished his morning exercises, part of his strict routine, and was getting dressed when he heard gunfire. His quarters were attacked by some 400 of the

Young Marshal's men. Chiang's guards resisted, and many were shot dead, including his chief of security. Chiang managed to escape into the hills behind, where he was found hours later hiding in a crevasse, clad only in his nightshirt, barefoot and covered with dust, and with an injured back.

Just beforehand, the Young Marshal had informed Mao that he was about to act. When Mao received the cable from his secretary, he beamed: "Go back to bed. There will be good news in the morning!"

A NATIONAL PLAYER

(1936 ⋆ AGE 42−43)

WHEN THE NEWS reached Party HQ that Chiang Kai-shek had been kidnapped, jubilant leaders crowded into Mao's cave. Mao was "laughing like mad," a colleague recalled. Now that Chiang was caught, Mao had one paramount goal: to see him dead. If Chiang was killed, there would be a power vacuum—and therefore a good opportunity for Russia to intervene and help to bring the CCP, and himself, to power.

In his first cables to Moscow after the event, Mao implored the Russians to get seriously involved. Choosing his words with care, he solicited their consent to killing Chiang, saying that the CCP wanted to "demand that Nanjing sack Chiang Kai-shek and deliver him to the people for trial." This was a euphemistic expression, unmistakably implying a death sentence. Knowing that his own goals were different from Stalin's, Mao pretended not to have heard about the kidnapping until after it had happened, and promised that the CCP "would not issue public statements for a few days."

Meanwhile, he was maneuvering busily behind Moscow's back to get Chiang killed. In his first cable to the Young Marshal after the kidnapping, on 12 December, Mao urged: "The best option is to kill [Chiang]." Mao tried to dispatch his ace diplomat, Chou En-lai, to Xian at once. Chou had negotiated with the Young Marshal earlier in the year, and they seemed to have hit it off. Mao wanted Chou to persuade the Young Marshal "to carry out the final measure" (in Chou's words), i.e., to kill Chiang.

Without spelling out the real purpose of Chou's mission, Mao solicited an invitation for Chou from the Young Marshal. At the time, the Reds' HQ was several days' ride on horseback from Xian, at Baoan, nearly 300 km to the north; so Mao asked the Young Marshal to send a plane to collect Chou at the nearby city of Yenan (then held by the Young Marshal), where there was an airstrip which Standard Oil had built when it was prospecting in the area earlier in the century. To encourage the

Young Marshal to act quickly, Mao made him a spurious promise on the 13th: "We have made arrangements with the Comintern, the details of which we will tell you later." The clear implication was that Chou would be bringing news of a plan coordinated with Moscow.

What the Young Marshal needed was not off-the-record promises relayed by the CCP, but Russia's public endorsement. Yet on the 14th, front-page articles in the two main Soviet papers, *Pravda* and *Izvestia*, strongly condemned his action as helping the Japanese, and unambiguously endorsed Chiang. Two days into the kidnapping, the Young Marshal could see that the game was up.

He turned a deaf ear to Mao's suggestion to send Chou. But Mao dispatched Chou anyway, telling the Young Marshal on the 15th that Chou was coming, and asking for a plane to pick him up in Yenan. When Chou reached Yenan, there was no plane, and the city gate was closed to him; he had to wait all night outside the walls, in sub-zero temperatures. "The guards refused to open the gate and refused to listen to reason," Mao wired the Young Marshal, exhorting him to do something. The Young Marshal was literally freezing Chou out, an indication of how bitter he felt about the Reds misleading him over Moscow's attitude.

On the 17th he relented. He was looking for a way to end the fiasco, so he sent his Boeing to fetch Chou. His American pilot, Royal Leonard, was shocked to find he was carrying Reds (who had only recently been peppering his plane). En route back that snowy afternoon, he played a trick on his passengers. "I deliberately picked rough air," he wrote in his memoirs. "Occasionally, I peeked back into the cabin and enjoyed watching the Communists . . . holding their black beards aside with one hand and vomiting into a can held in the other."

The Young Marshal accepted Chou through gritted teeth, though he presented an amicable façade and played along with his guest.* When Chou urged him to kill the Generalissimo, he pretended he would do so "when civil war is unavoidable and Xian is besieged" by government forces.

Mao had in fact been trying to provoke a war between Nanjing and Xian. He hoped to trigger this off by moving Red troops towards Nanjing. On the 15th he secretly ordered his top commanders to "strike at the enemy's head: the Nanjing government . . ." But he had to scrap the plan, as it would have been suicidal for the Red Army, and there was no guarantee it would set off a Nanjing–Xian war. To his delight, on the 16th Nanjing declared war on the Young Marshal, moving armies towards Xian

---

* The Young Marshal's bitterness against Moscow and the CCP flared briefly during our otherwise very friendly meeting with him fifty-six years later. When we asked him whether the Chinese Communists had told him about the real Soviet attitude towards him before the coup, he snapped back with sudden hostility: "Of course not. You ask a very strange question."

and bombing the Young Marshal's troops outside the city. Mao urged the Young Marshal not just to fight back, but to broaden the fighting into a major war by striking out towards Nanjing. The following day, Mao cabled him, saying: "The enemy's jugulars are Nanjing and [two key railway lines]. If 20 to 30 thousand . . . troops can be dispatched to strike these railway lines . . . the overall situation will change at once. Please do consider this." Mao's hope was that by taking such action, the Young Marshal would burn his bridges with Nanjing and thus be more likely to kill Chiang.

WHILE MAO WAS maneuvering to have Chiang killed, Stalin put his foot down to save the Generalissimo. On 13 December, the day after Chiang was seized, the Soviet chargé d'affaires in Nanjing was summoned by acting prime minister H. H. Kung (Chiang's brother-in-law) to be told that "word was around" that the CCP was involved in the coup, and that "if Mr. Chiang's safety was endangered, the anger of the nation would extend from the CCP to the Soviet Union and could put pressure on [the Chinese government] to join with Japan against the Soviet Union." Stalin understood that the kidnapping might pose an urgent threat to his strategic interests.

At midnight on the 14th, the phone rang in the office of Comintern chief Dimitrov. Stalin was on the line. "Was it with your permission that the events in China took place?" he asked. Dimitrov hastily answered: "No! That would be the greatest service anyone could possibly render Japan. Our position on these events is the same." Using ominous language, Stalin went on to question the role of the CCP's delegate at the Comintern, who had submitted to Stalin the draft of a cable to be sent to the CCP in favor of executing Chiang: "Who is this Wang Ming of yours? Is he a provocateur? I hear he wanted to send a telegram to have Chiang killed." At the time, Dimitrov's Chinese assistant recalled, "you could not find anyone" at Comintern HQ who did not think that "Chiang must be finished off." Even Stalin's top man at the Comintern, the normally cool Manuilsky, "rubbed his hands, embraced me, and exclaimed: 'Our dear friend has been caught, aha!' "

Wang Ming pleaded that the draft cable had been suggested by the deputy head of the GRU, Artur Artuzov. Artuzov was soon arrested and accused of being a spy. Before he was shot, he protested his innocence in a letter written in his own blood, which, his jailer noted icily, had come "from his nose." Stalin spared Wang Ming. And Dimitrov scrambled to clear himself and lay the blame on Mao. He wrote to Stalin: "in spite of our warnings, the . . . Chinese Party in fact entered into very close, friendly relations with [the Young Marshal]." More damningly, Dimitrov told Stalin: "it is hard to imagine [the Young Marshal] would have undertaken his adventurist action without coordination with them [Mao and his colleagues] or even without their participation." This was clearly suggesting that Mao was lying about having no prior knowledge of the event, and that Mao had flouted Moscow's orders.

Stalin was suspicious that Mao might be in cahoots with the Japanese. Stalin had already begun to have almost all the Soviet "old China hands" denounced and interrogated under torture. Four days after Chiang was kidnapped, a leading detainee "confessed" to being involved in a Trotskyist plot to provoke an attack by Japan (and Germany) on Russia. Mao's own name soon surfaced in confessions, and a hefty dossier on him was compiled, with accusations that he was an agent of the Japanese, as well as a Trotskyist.

Dimitrov sent a stern message to Mao on the 16th. It condemned the kidnapping, saying that it "can objectively only damage the anti-Japanese united front and help Japan's aggression against China." Its key point was that "the CCP must take a decisive stand in favour of a peaceful resolution." This was an order to secure the release and reinstatement of the Generalissimo.

WHEN THE CABLE arrived, Mao reportedly "flew into a rage . . . swore and stamped his feet." His next move was to pretend that the message had never reached him. He kept it secret from his Politburo, from the Young Marshal, and also from Chou En-lai, who was en route to Xian to try to persuade the Young Marshal to kill Chiang.* Mao went on maneuvering for Chiang to be killed.

This was a high-risk tactic vis-à-vis Moscow. Mao was not simply withholding from the Kremlin the fact that he had encouraged the kidnap plot, he was also suppressing—and defying—a direct order from Stalin. But for Mao, the vistas opened up by the elimination of Chiang outweighed the risks.

But the Generalissimo was not about to disappear off the map. Once the Young Marshal knew he had no Moscow backing, which was immediately after the kidnap, he decided to keep Chiang safe. Mao had proved worthless. In spite of all its posturing in private communications, the CCP kept a public silence for three long days after the kidnapping, voicing no support for the Young Marshal. Its first official statement did not

---

* Mao later tried to claim that the Comintern's cable of 16 December "was garbled, and could not be decoded," and that the CCP asked Moscow, on the 18th, to retransmit it. This has to be a fabrication. Radio operators at the core of CCP operations told us that the standard procedure was that if a cable was illegible, they would instantly ask Moscow to retransmit and would definitely not wait for two days—least of all at a time of crisis. Mao told his Politburo on the 19th: "Comintern instructions have not arrived."

emerge till the 15th. It made no mention of backing the Young Marshal to be head of China, as Mao had specifically offered earlier. Instead, it recognized the authority of Nanjing.

The Young Marshal's only option was to stick with Chiang. That meant he had to set Chiang free. Moreover, he realized that the only way he himself could survive was to leave Xian with Chiang and place himself in Chiang's hands. There were many in Nanjing who wanted him dead and who were sure to send assassins after him. Chiang's custody was the only place where he could be safe. And by escorting Chiang out of captivity he could also hope to win the Generalissimo's goodwill. His gamble that Chiang would not kill him turned out to be a good bet. After house arrest under Chiang and his successors for over half a century, when he was both detained and protected, he was released, and died in his bed in Hawaii, aged 100, in 2001, having outlived Chiang and Mao by over a quarter of a century.

On 14 December, the day Moscow publicly condemned the coup, the Young Marshal went to see Chiang, and stood in front of him in silence, weeping. Chiang registered that his captor showed "considerable remorse." Later that day the Young Marshal told Chiang he realized that the kidnap was "a foolish and ill-considered action" and wanted to release him, secretly. Chiang gave him active cooperation by making sure Nanjing did not rock the boat. When Nanjing declared war on the Young Marshal on the 16th, Chiang got a message out at once telling Nanjing to hold its fire. Nanjing suspended military operations, and sent Chiang's brother-in-law T. V. Soong (known as T.V.) "as a private citizen" to negotiate a deal, as Chiang himself could not be seen to be negotiating with his captors. T.V. arrived in Xian on the 20th, followed two days later by Mme Chiang.

On the 20th, Moscow repeated its cable to the CCP, which Mao had been suppressing, ordering a "peaceful resolution." Now, Mao had to forward the cable to Chou En-lai, with instructions to help "restore Chiang Kai-shek's freedom."

MAO THUS BROUGHT his goals back into alignment with Stalin's. The CCP demanded that Chiang promise to "stop the policy of 'exterminating Communists.'" It also insisted that Chiang meet Chou, who was right there in Xian. For Chou to talk to Chiang would accord the CCP the status of a major player in national politics, an act whose modern-day equivalent would be for the top man in some notorious terrorist group suddenly to be received by the US president.

At a talk on the 23rd between T. V. Soong, the Young Marshal and Chou, T.V. said he personally agreed to what Chou asked, and would convey the CCP's demands to the Generalissimo. But Chiang refused to talk to Chou directly, even though he was told he would not be released unless he saw Chou. The talks deadlocked.

Moscow knew what would get the Generalissimo to see Chou. Chiang's most recent signal to Moscow had been just before the kidnap, in November, when the Chinese Red Army had its back to the wall after failing to reach the Russian arms supplies. On that occasion, Chiang's ambassador in Moscow had asked for the return of Chiang's son, Ching-kuo, and Moscow had said "No." Now it was ready to respond. Late on 24 December the former Party leader, Po Ku, arrived in Xian, bearing special news. This piece of news got Chou into Chiang's bedroom on Christmas Day. Chou told Chiang that his son Ching-kuo "would return." It was only after receiving this promise from Stalin that Chiang agreed to the Reds' demands, and invited Chou "to come to Nanjing for direct negotiations." From this moment on, the CCP stopped being officially regarded as bandits, and was treated as a proper political party.

The Chiang–Chou meeting in Xian was brief, but it wrapped up the Reds-for-son deal that Chiang had been working on for years. This marked the end of the civil war between the CCP and the Nationalists.

THAT AFTERNOON the Chiangs left Xian. So did the Young Marshal, flying voluntarily into house arrest.* Chiang was at the peak of his popularity. When his car drove into Nanjing, spontaneous crowds lined the streets to hail him. Fireworks crackled all night long. People who experienced those days say that Chiang's prestige shone like the midday sun. Yet his triumph was short-lived, and the deal that regained his son rebounded against him. His calculation that he could contain Mao and outsmart Stalin was wishful thinking. Mao was uncontainable—and the small CCP had just been promoted to a major "opposition party."

---

* Since then, he has become one of the biggest legends in Chinese history, the subject of endless books and articles, and both admired and denounced. But even his adversaries hardly mention his machinations with the Russians, or that these were the result of personal ambition. To the end of his long life he claimed that the kidnapping was inspired by "pure motives." To us in 1993, he said: "Mme Chiang understood me well . . . she said I didn't want money, I didn't want territory, I only wanted sacrifice [*sic*]."

NEW IMAGE, NEW LIFE
AND NEW WIFE

(1937–38 ★ AGE 43–44)

A S S O O N A S the dust from the kidnapping settled, in January 1937 Moscow told Mao exactly how it viewed the next stage. The CCP was to abandon its policy of trying to overthrow the government by violence, and stop confiscating land and robbing the rich; instead, it would in effect recognize Nanjing as the legitimate government, and put the Red territory and Red Army under Chiang. Mao accepted the shift as a purely tactical expedient, and the CCP made a public pledge to Nanjing that embodied the policy changes willed by Moscow. This opened a new phase for the Party.

As a quid pro quo, Chiang was to assign some territory to the Red Army, and fund the Communist administration and army. Mao naturally went all out to get the largest possible swath of territory and the highest level of funding. In the end, the Reds were allocated 129,600 square kilometers of ground, with a population of about 2 million, and Yenan as their capital. This settlement brought substantial government funding. Chiang also armed and paid for over 46,000 regular Red troops (the number he officially recognized).

In order to help Mao achieve these gains, Stalin held on to Chiang's son. Not until he was satisfied about Chiang's concessions did he deliver. On 3 March the Soviet Politburo decreed, in its peculiar crabbed idiom, "Not to oppose the return to China of Chiang Kai-shek's son." Ching-kuo returned to China on 19 April, and was reunited with his father after more than eleven years as a hostage.[*]

During the week-long train journey across Siberia, Ching-kuo was in the custody of the future CCP intelligence chief, Kang Sheng. Only a few weeks before, Kang Sheng had brought Mao's sons from Paris to Moscow.

---

[*] Before Ching-kuo left Russia, he was worked on by Stalin in person, as well as being subjected to a blitz of blandishments and threats by Dimitrov. Ching-kuo played along, cabling Dimitrov en route that: "All your instructions will be fulfillled." When he reached Vladivostok he was taken to the KGB office, where he performed his last formal act of obeisance to Moscow, promising: "I will strictly follow Party discipline."

An-ying and An-ching, aged fourteen and twelve, had been waiting for Russian visas in Paris for months. The Russians had not wanted to admit the Young Marshal's envoy, who was escorting them, but had not wanted to give a straightforward refusal, so they withheld visas for the whole group. After the Xian kidnap was over, the envoy was told he would not get a visa. The Mao boys arrived in Moscow at the beginning of 1937, and became boarders in the special school for children of foreign Communist leaders. They wrote to their father, sending photos. He rarely replied.

WHILE MAO'S ATTITUDE to his sons was one of indifference, Chiang Kai-shek's amounted to obsession. In February 1937, when Stalin was still holding Ching-kuo, and Chiang was impatiently waiting for him to be returned, the Generalissimo did another favor to the CCP, which had far-reaching repercussions. He appointed the mole Shao Li-tzu (who had taken Chiang's son to Russia in 1925) as head of the Nationalists' Propaganda Department, in charge of the media. Shao's job was to bring about a change of attitude in the press and in public opinion, which were both fiercely anti-Communist. It was an enormous gesture of good will to Moscow.

Soviet Russia henceforth received wide and enthusiastic coverage. A benign and positive image of the Chinese Communists began to emerge. By summer, Shao and Mao had concocted the idea of publishing a Mao autobiography portraying Mao as a good and kindly man, complete with an appendix of his pronouncements on war with Japan that depicted him as committed to fighting the Japanese. Mao wrote an inscription in the tone of an ardent patriot: "Fight the Japanese imperialists unwaveringly through to the end . . ." The book came out on 1 November and was a hit. It was this period that gave birth to the myth, which was vital to Mao's success, that the CCP was the most dedicated anti-Japanese force. It was thanks to this myth that many tens of thousands joined the Communists, including many of those who were later to staff Mao's regime.

The *Mao Tse-tung Autobiography* consisted largely of interviews Mao had done with the American journalist Edgar Snow in summer 1936—the only extensive account of his life Mao ever gave. Snow also produced his own book, *Red Star Over China*, which relied overwhelmingly on interviews with Mao and other Communists, and laid the foundation for the rehabilitation of the Reds, not least by brushing out their blood-soaked past.

The encounter with Snow was no accident. That spring, Mao had asked the Shanghai underground to find a foreign journalist who could publicize his story, plus a doctor. After careful vetting, Mao invited Snow, who combined all the necessary qualities: he was American, wrote for the influential *Saturday Evening Post* and *New York Herald-Tribune*, and was sympathetic. Snow arrived in the Red area in July, with a Lebanese-American doctor, George Hatem, who brought top-secret documents from the Comintern in his medicine case. Snow stayed for three months, while Hatem remained with the Reds for the rest of his life, becoming one of Mao's doctors, and working in the CCP's foreign intelligence apparatus.

Mao left nothing to chance, and dictated detailed instructions on handling Snow's visit: "Security, secrecy, warmth and red carpet." The Politburo carefully coordinated answers to a questionnaire Snow had to submit beforehand. Mao offered Snow a mixture of valuable information and colossal falsification, which Snow swallowed in toto, calling Mao and the CCP leadership "direct, frank, simple, undevious." Mao covered up years of torture and murder, such as the AB purges, and invented battles and heroism like the crossing of the Dadu bridge in the trek across China, astutely now titled "the Long March." He led Snow to believe that, except when he was ill, he had "walked most of the 6,000 miles of the Long March, like the rank and file." Mao also completely suppressed his links with Moscow, and claimed he wanted friendship with America—a claim that fooled many.

Mao took the added precaution of checking everything Snow wrote afterwards, and amending and rewriting parts. On 26 July 1937 (before *Red Star* came out) Snow wrote to his wife Helen, who was then in Yenan: "Don't send me any more notes about people reneging on their stories to me ... As it is, with so many things cut out it begins to read like Childe Harold." Snow omitted to mention this background in *Red Star*, and instead alleged that Mao "never imposed any censorship on me." The Chinese edition even gilded Snow, and had him say that he found Mao's words "honest and true."

Red Star was published in English in winter 1937–38, and played a big role in swaying Western opinion in favor of Mao. The CCP organized its publication in Chinese, under the title *Stories of a Journey to the West*, to make it appear impartial. In addition to this book and the *Mao Tse-tung Autobiography*, a third book was produced out of the Snow material, under another neutral-sounding title, *Impressions of Mao Tse-tung*.

Red Star—and the two books of edited excerpts—profoundly influenced radical youth in China. Many, like one of the first Tibetan Communists, joined the Communists as a result of reading Snow. It was the beginning of the CCP's renaissance. Mao was to say that its publication "had a merit no less than the Great Yu controlling floods." The Great Yu was the mythical emperor who had brought floods under control, thus starting Chinese civilization.

As Chiang Kai-shek's media chief, Shao played an indispensable role in assisting Snow and promoting Mao and the Reds. By the time Chiang removed Shao from the post after nearly a year, Mao and the Reds had sanitized their image.

★

FOR THE NEXT DECADE, Mao lived in Yenan, the capital of the territories Chiang assigned to the Reds. He moved into the city on New Year's Day 1937, through a huge gate, which majestically and silently opened up to columns of Red Army soldiers, marching along the broad dirt road that stretched into the infinity of yellow earth. This ancient city (whose name means "extending peace") was enclosed by high thick walls that mounted the chain of loess hills far above the city, with battlements exuding warrior stateliness. In dry, crisp air beneath a high blue sky, it was dominated by a nine-story pagoda, built 1,000 years before. Beneath the pagoda was a complex of temples, many appearing to be clinging to the cliffs. Further down, the heavily silted River Yan was joined by the Tu Fu River, named after the great eighth-century poet, who reputedly came here to admire the peonies, a local claim to fame.

Yenan was not only a cultural center, but also a hub of commercial activities. Oil had been discovered in the region. Living quarters built by Standard Oil were now taken over by the Reds, who also appropriated substantial buildings owned by the Spanish Franciscans, including a just-completed cathedral, in which many key Party meetings were to take place. The problem of housing was further eased by the fact that many locals had fled, particularly the relatively wealthy, leaving empty hundreds of houses, some large and beautiful. Mao occupied one such mansion in a place called Phoenix Village. The big courtyard was by local standards grand, with a decorated wall immediately inside, facing the gate, to ward off evil spirits—and for privacy. For the first time in over two years, he settled into some comfort.

One considerable luxury for its place and time was wall heating, which Mao had installed. The usual way of heating a house in northern China was to heat the brick bed, the *kang*, from underneath, but Mao preferred his proper wooden bed, and for heating, he selected this most deluxe form. Another indulgence was to have several residences. When he later moved to an area called Yang Hill, he kept the house in Phoenix Village, and he kept both when he settled in the compound of the Chinese KGB, the picturesque area known as the Date Garden. In addition to these publicly known residences, Mao had secret dwellings built in secluded valleys, one behind Yang Hill and another behind the Date Garden. Few knew of their existence, then or now.

The most public residence was Yang Hill, which was also the least grand, and closest to the local peasants. Ten households lived in the face of a ravine, against a hill thickly wooded in those days with elms, cypresses and redwood poplar. The houses were *yao-dong*, unique to this part of the country, which looked like caves hollowed out of the loess slopes. Mao had a row of *yao-dong* in a courtyard with a small gate surmounted by a tiled roof. One of his neighbors, a peasant family, did the laundry for him. Mao's cook he had brought with him, for security—as well as culinary—reasons. He also declined to share the peasants' stone roller for grinding his grain: "Chairman Mao considered things from a safety point of view," the locals told us. He was surrounded by very tight security, some visible, some not.

For Mao, Yenan provided the first relatively stable and non-violent period for nearly a decade. With peace and a rather good life—and the sudden availability of glamorous, educated young women, who were beginning to trickle into Yenan to the lure of the Reds' benign new image—Mao started to womanize more or less openly. He confided to a fellow-philanderer that he could only go without sex "for forty days at the most."

ONE OF THE FIRST young women on the scene was a beautiful (and married) 26-year-old actress, Lily Wu, who arrived in early 1937 and became the star actress of Yenan. Her elegant clothes and manners turned heads in this back-country region, and her flowing, shoulder-length hair, in particular, was the symbol of desirability. Communist women mostly wore bulky uniforms and had shaved off their hair to get rid of lice. Mao started a relationship with her.

Lily struck up a friendship with a visiting American writer, Agnes Smedley, who was an outspoken radical feminist. Smedley had worked for the Comintern, but was something of a loose cannon, and Moscow had sent instructions "to isolate her." Even so, and although she found that Mao had a "sinister quality," both "feminine" and "physically repulsive," Mao cultivated her, and gave her a long interview, because she was American. Mao sent a copy of the interview to Snow, asking him to give it "wide publicity."

While Lily Wu's good looks stirred Mao's lust, the much less good-looking Smedley caused a tornado by organizing square-dancing, accompanied by phonograph records. The dances were swamped. At first, Smedley observed, "Pride prevented him [Mao] from trying to dance. He had no rhythm in his being." He basically just "walked the floor," the women who danced with him noted. But he soon came to see the advantage of the dances as a form of exercise—and as a way to pick up women. Weekly dances were organized, some in the open air, others in a former church. Yenan went wild about dancing.

Together with other Long March women, Mao's wife, Gui-yuan, at first refused to attend. According to Snow, "The close embrace of bodies involved seemed positively indecent to the old guard." Jealousy seems to have played a big—if unavowed—role. Also repressed was their secret fondness for this pleasure: Gui-yuan later came to love dancing and was good at it.

She found Mao's womanizing intolerable. One night in June, Smedley heard Gui-yuan screaming from the adjacent cave, where Lily lived. "Son of a pig, turtle's egg, whoremongering no-good! How dare you sneak in here to sleep with the little bourgeois bitch!" Smedley went next door and found Gui-yuan lashing out at Mao with a flashlight, while his bodyguard looked on. Mao's protestations that he had only been talking to Lily cut no ice. Gui-yuan turned on Lily, scratching her face and pulling her hair, while Mao stood by.

Gui-yuan then rounded on Smedley. "Imperialist bitch!" she cried. "You who are the cause of it all, get out of here!" She hit Smedley, who hit her back. Gui-yuan was felled to her knees, and appealed to Mao: "What kind of man are you, what kind of husband and Communist? You let an imperialist whore beat me before your very eyes!" When Mao told his bodyguard to lift her up, Gui-yuan tripped the bodyguard and knocked him down, and in the end it took three bodyguards to carry her off, trailed by a silent Mao.

Smedley was soon sent packing. Lily was not simply banished from Yenan, but written out of Chinese Communist sources, and disappeared off the map forever.

Mao conducted other flirtations, including one with the writer Ding Ling. Though boyish and stout and not exactly a beauty, she had talent and character. Mao sent her a very complimentary poem which included the lines: "To what do I compare your slender pen? Three thousand Mausers and best men." She recalled in later years how she often visited Mao. One day he half-jokingly compared Yenan to a small imperial court, and started writing down his colleagues' names under the various imperial titles, which she shouted out to him. "After we finished this, he suddenly said to me: 'Ding Ling, we have got the Hundred Civil and Military Courtiers sorted out. Now that we are a royal court, no matter how small, we've got to have the imperial concubines in Three Palaces and Six Courtyards! Come on, give me some names, and I will bestow titles on them.' "

For Gui-yuan, Mao's flagrant womanizing was the last straw. Over their marriage of nearly ten years, she had had to live with her husband's heartlessness. She was particularly hurt by his callousness towards her painful pregnancies and childbirth—including one on the Long March—and by his crack that she gave birth to babies "as easily as a hen dropping eggs." And she was bitter that although he was indifferent to children, and had not cared when four of theirs had died or been abandoned, he repeatedly made her pregnant. Their fifth child, a daughter called Chiao-

chiao, was born in 1936 in Baoan, where conditions were appalling, with scorpions and rats running all over the place. A year later, Gui-yuan was pregnant again, which plunged her into depression. Repeated child-bearing in harsh circumstances had severely damaged her health, without the compensation of family life. Now, on top of this, her husband was openly sleeping with other women.

After the Communists settled in Yenan, some senior Reds who had been wounded were able to go to Russia for treatment. Ostensibly to get rid of the painful shrapnel still lodged in her body, Gui-yuan left for Russia in early October 1937. Their one-year-old daughter remained in Yenan.

Gui-yuan reached Moscow in the depths of winter. She and the other new arrivals were immediately warned by fellow Chinese there not to get in touch with anyone they had known previously. A great purge was sweeping Soviet Russia, and many Chinese were being arrested. It was in this freezing world of isolation and fear that she gave birth to a boy, to whom she gave the Russian name Lyova. He died of pneumonia after only six months, and Gui-yuan sank into inconsolable grief. For days she sat on a bench facing the tiny mound where he was buried in the back garden, murmuring his name, weeping.

There was no warmth from her husband. When the baby was born, she had written to Mao to say that the boy looked just like him. Mao did not reply. No word either for his son's death. Then, in summer 1939, nearly two years after they had parted, Gui-yuan learned by chance that Mao had remarried. She and a group of non-Russian-speaking Chinese met regularly to have items from the Soviet press read out to them in Chinese. On this occasion, the translator was reading an article by a famous Russian film-maker, Roman Karmen, about meeting Mao. Karmen mentioned that Mao and "his wife" had seen him off outside their cave in moonlight. The phrase "Mao's wife," so casually mentioned, set Gui-yuan's stomach churning. In the following days, people who shared a room with her said she was tossing and turning all night. She was already suffering from severe insomnia. Now she came to the brink of a nervous breakdown. Her condition worsened further when she received a brief letter from Mao. It was dry stuff: hope you will study hard and make progress politically. In one lapidary sentence Mao announced the dissolution of their marriage: From now on, we are only comrades.

Because he had remarried, Mao did not want Gui-yuan back in China. When the friends with whom she had traveled to Russia were returning to China in 1939, a cable from Yenan specifically ordered her to stay behind. As a result, the infant daughter she had left in Yenan spent her first few years as a virtual orphan. Chiao-chiao had had to live as a boarder in the elite's nursery. When the other children were taken home by their parents at the end of the day, nobody came for her. Later in life she recalled that there was also a boy who always stayed behind. He would cry and shout: "I want Papa! I want Mama! I want Home!" Chiao-chiao had no idea what these words meant. As a grown-up, she told a friend, quietly but not without an edge: "In those days, I was an 'orphan' who was not exactly an orphan!"

When she was four, Chiao-chiao was taken to Russia to join her mother. Gui-yuan hugged her daughter long and hard when they were reunited, in streams of tears, which made Chiao-chiao extremely happy. She was also fascinated by her mother's permed hair, skirts, and leather shoes with heels, all very different from the women in Yenan, who wore baggy pants and un-smart cotton shoes, attire that even those who came to Yenan from Nationalist cities had to adopt. But Gui-yuan was already crushed by poor health, the result of frequent pregnancies, injuries suffered during the Long March, and painful memories of her dead and abandoned children, as well as years of grinding loneliness. The horrors she had experienced in the revolution may also have haunted her mind. Soon she had a breakdown, and the brunt of her rage was borne by her daughter; other children often heard Chiao-chiao screaming as her mother beat her. Gui-yuan was put in a mental institution, howling as she was torn away from her room and bundled into a car. Her terrified seven-year-old daughter ran away and hid in the woods, and grew into an introverted and silent girl.

IN SUMMER 1937, before Gui-yuan left for Russia, Mao had spotted a young actress called Jiang Qing, who was to become his fourth wife. Jiang Qing cut a stylish figure even in Communist garb, her belt tightly cinching her svelte waist, and her rakishly tilted army cap exposing waves of shining black hair. She exuded femininity and sexiness. She had a soft and pliant posture and a very sweet—to some an affected—voice.

Born in 1914, Jiang Qing was the daughter of a concubine to an alcoholic inn-owner. Her mother let her grow up willful, even allowing her to unbind her feet, after the bones had been broken when she was six. Jiang Qing was tough, and in the frequent fights between her parents she would help her mother by clinging to her father's legs and biting his arms. In one of these fights she lost part of a front tooth. Her fellow pupils recalled her as a bully, and she was expelled from school at the age of twelve after she spat at a teacher. She ran away from home at fourteen to join a traveling opera troupe, fetching up in Shanghai, where she made her name as an actress. But acting was a precarious career, and in summer 1937, out of work and unable to stand her lover's seven-year-old son, she came to Yenan, which also appealed to her radical chic side.

She knew how to get herself noticed, sitting in the front row at Mao's lectures, and asking wide-eyed questions. One day, Mao came to a Peking opera—a genre he loved—in which she was starring. Afterwards, he went backstage and put his coat around her shoulders. Next day she went to Mao's place to return the coat, and stayed the night.

The couple began to appear in public together. This caused a scandal, as she was a woman with a past. She had already been married to, or lived with, four men, and had left a trail in the Shanghai gossip columns. Her stormy relationship with one of her husbands had provided fodder for the tabloids, especially after he tried to commit suicide by gulping down a bottle of surgical spirit with crushed match heads in it.

If cosmopolitan Shanghai found her difficult to stomach, puritanical Yenan positively gagged. On top of that, there was also tremendous sympathy for the woman she supplanted. One of Gui-yuan's former Long March companions recalled: "The students in my college were all upset. Some wrote to Mao openly, some wrote secretly . . . I wrote three letters. They went roughly like this: Chairman Mao, we hope you won't marry Jiang Qing. [Gui-yuan] is in very poor health, and you have had five or six children together . . . Jiang Qing's reputation is pretty bad."

For the Party, there was a more serious concern. Jiang Qing had once been imprisoned by the Nationalists as a Communist suspect, and had got out by signing a recantation—an act that the Party considered as "betrayal." Moreover, there were allegations that she had entertained her jailers by being their dinner—and even their bed—companion. Underground organizations in Shanghai and other areas wired Yenan with formal complaints that she was "unsuitable to marry Chairman Mao." Nominal Party chief Lo Fu wrote to Mao with his own objections and those of many others. When Mao received the letter, he tore it up on the spot and announced to the messenger: "I will get married tomorrow. Everyone else can mind their own business!" Next day he gave a "wedding" banquet to two dozen of Yenan's elite, to which Lo Fu was not invited.

Mao got security chief Kang Sheng to vouch for Jiang Qing. While working in Russia, Kang had been the escort for Mao's sons to Moscow, and for Chiang Kai-shek's son on his way out of Russia. He had come to Yenan in November 1937, and quickly attached himself to Mao, who made him the head of his KGB. In this world of yellow earth, Kang stood out as he was often dressed completely in black, from head (black cap) to toe (unusual leather riding boots). His horse was black, and he was frequently seen cuddling a black dog, which was about the only pet around. Although Kang had proof that Jiang Qing's conduct while in prison had been dubious, he provided Mao with an official verdict which cleared her by saying that "her past is no problem politically." In fact, Mao knew that the charges were true, as he acknowledged near his death. But he did not care. He wanted her.

Mrs. Mao number 4 was to become the notorious Mme Mao.

RED MOLE TRIGGERS
CHINA–JAPAN WAR
(1937–38 ★ AGE 43–44)

ON 7 JULY 1937, fighting broke out between Chinese and Japanese troops at a place just outside Peking called the Marco Polo Bridge. By the end of the month the Japanese had occupied the two main cities in northern China, Peking and Tianjin. Chiang did not declare war. He did not want a full-scale war—not yet, anyway. And neither did the Japanese.

At this point Japan did not aim to extend the fighting beyond northern China. Yet, within a matter of weeks, all-out war had broken out 1,000 km to the south, in Shanghai, a place where neither Chiang nor Japan wished, or planned, to have a war. Japan had only some 3,000 marines stationed near Shanghai, under the 1932 truce agreement. Tokyo's plan until mid-August remained: "Army to North China only." It added specifically: "There is no need to send the Army to Shanghai."

The well-informed *New York Times* correspondent H. Abend wrote afterwards:

> It was a commonplace ... to declare that the Japanese attacked Shanghai. Nothing was further from their intentions or from the truth. The Japanese did not want and did not expect hostilities in the Yangtse Valley. They ... had so small a force there even as late as August 13th ... that they were nearly pushed into the river on the 18th and 19th.

ABEND REALIZED that there were "clever plans to upset the Japanese scheme for confining the hostilities entirely to North China." He was right about there being "clever plans"—he was only wrong about one thing: the plans were not Chiang's (as Abend thought), but almost certainly Stalin's.

Japan's swift occupation of northern China in July posed a very direct danger to Stalin. Tokyo's huge armies were now in a position to turn north and attack Russia anywhere along a border many thousands of kilometers long. The year before, Stalin had publicly identified Japan as the principal menace. Now, we believe, he activated a long-term Communist agent in the heart of the Nationalist army, and detonated a full-scale war in Shanghai, which drew the Japanese inextricably into the vast heartland of China—and away from Russia.

The "sleeper" now wakened was a general called Zhang Zhi-zhong (whom we shall refer to as ZZZ), commander of the Shanghai–Nanjing garrison. In 1925 he had been a teacher at Whampoa, the Russian-funded and Russian-staffed military academy near Canton. From the day of its founding, Moscow made a determined effort to plant high-level agents in the Nationalist military. In his memoirs, ZZZ acknowledged that: "In summer 1925 I was completely in sympathy with the Communist Party, and ... was called 'red teacher,' 'red regiment commander' ... I wanted to join the CCP, and told Mr. Chou En-lai." Chou told him to stay in the Nationalists and collaborate "covertly" with the CCP. During the mid-1930s, ZZZ kept in close contact with the Soviet embassy.

At the time of the Marco Polo Bridge clash, ZZZ held the pivotal job of chief of the Shanghai–Nanjing garrison. He tried to talk Chiang into launching a "first strike" against Japan—not in northern China, where the fighting was, but 1,000 kilometers to the south, in Shanghai, where the small Japanese garrison was not involved in any military action at this stage. Chiang did not reply to this proposal, even though ZZZ repeated it many times. Shanghai was the industrial and financial heart of China, an international metropolis, and Chiang did not want to see it turned into a battleground. Moreover, it was very close to his capital, Nanjing. He had even transferred troops and artillery away from the Shanghai area, to give Japan no excuse for war there.

At the end of July, right after the Japanese occupied Peking and Tianjin, ZZZ cabled Chiang again, arguing strongly for "taking the initiative" to start a war. After ZZZ said he would only do so if the Japanese showed unmistakable signs of attacking Shanghai, Chiang gave his conditional consent, stressing: "You must wait for orders about when this should happen."

But on 9 August, at Shanghai airport, an army unit hand-picked by ZZZ killed a Japanese marine lieutenant and a private. A Chinese prisoner under sentence of death was then dressed in Chinese uniform and shot dead at the airport gate, to make it seem that the Japanese had fired first. The Japanese gave every sign of wishing to defuse the incident, but ZZZ still bombarded Chiang with requests to launch an offensive, which Chiang vetoed. On the morning of the 13th, the Generalissimo told ZZZ not to launch a war "on impulse," but to "study and discuss" all the angles again, and then submit his plan. ZZZ pressed the next day: "This army is determined to start the offensive against the enemy at 5:00 PM today. Here is the plan ..." On the 14th, Chinese planes bombed the Japanese flagship *Izumo*, as well as troops and navy planes on the ground, and ZZZ ordered a general offensive. But Chiang stopped him: "You must not attack this evening. Wait for order."

When no order arrived, ZZZ outflanked Chiang by issuing a press release next day, claiming, falsely, that Japanese warships had shelled Shanghai and that Japanese troops had started attacking the Chinese. With anti-Japanese feeling running high, Chiang was put on the spot. The following day, 16 August, he finally gave the order: "General assault for dawn tomorrow."

But after one day's fighting, Chiang ordered a halt, on the 18th. ZZZ simply ignored the order and expanded his offensives. All-out war became unstoppable as large Japanese reinforcements began to arrive on 22 August.

The Japanese inflicted tremendous casualties. In Shanghai, 73 of China's 180 divisions—and the best one-third—over 400,000 men, were thrown in, and all but wiped out. The conflict here consumed virtually all of China's nascent air force (which Chiang so treasured that he had not sent a single plane to the northern front), and the main warships. It significantly weakened the military force Chiang had been painstakingly building up since the early 1930s. The Japanese suffered much fewer, though still heavy, casualties: about 40,000.

Once Chiang was forced into all-out war, Stalin moved with alacrity to bolster Chiang's capability to sustain a war. He signed a non-aggression treaty with Nanjing on 21 August, and started to supply Chiang with weapons. China could not manufacture any weapons except rifles. Stalin advanced Chiang US$250 million for arms purchases from Russia, which included some 1,000 planes, plus tanks and artillery, and committed a sizable Soviet air force contingent.* Moscow sent hundreds of military advisers, headed for a time by the Chinese-speaking General Vasili Chuikov, later of Stalingrad fame. For the next four years, Russia was not only China's main supplier of arms, but virtually its only source of heavy weapons, artillery and planes.

Moscow was exhilarated by the turn of events, as the Soviet foreign minister, Maksim Litvinov, admitted to French vice-premier Léon Blum. According to Blum, Litvinov told him that "he [Litvinov] and the Soviet Union were perfectly delighted that Japan had attacked China [adding] that the Soviet Union hoped that war between China and Japan would continue just as long as possible . . ." Both of the Russians who dealt with ZZZ, the military attaché Lepin and Ambassador Bogomolov, were immediately recalled and executed.

---

* From December 1937 to the end of 1939 more than 2,000 Russian pilots flew combat missions, destroying about 1,000 Japanese planes, and even bombing Japanese-occupied Taiwan.

ZZZ was quickly forced to resign, in September, by an angry, frustrated and undoubtedly suspicious Chiang. But the Generalissimo continued to employ him. When the Nationalists fled to Taiwan in 1949, ZZZ stayed with the Communists, as did super-mole Shao Li-tzu.

The outbreak of full-scale war between Japan and China brought Mao immediate benefits. Chiang Kai-shek finally acceded to the Communists' key demand, which he had till now refused to consider—that the Red Army could keep its autonomy. Mao thus kept control of his own army, even though it was supposed to be part of the armed forces of the central government. Though Chiang was supreme commander of the Chinese army, he could not give orders to the Red Army, and had to couch his commands in the form of "requests." In addition, the CCP was now, in effect, legitimized. Communist prisoners were released and the CCP was allowed to open offices in key cities, and to publish its own papers in Nationalist areas.

And yet this was just the beginning of Mao's gains from the Sino-Japanese War, which lasted eight years and took some 20 million Chinese lives. It ended up weakening Chiang's state enormously, and enabling Mao to emerge in possession of a giant army of 1.3 million. At the beginning of the war, the ratio of Chiang's army to Mao's was 60:1; at the end, it was 3:1.

HAVING MASTERMINDED the detonation of all-out war between China and Japan, Stalin ordered the Chinese Red Army to get actively involved, telling the CCP in no uncertain terms that it must cooperate properly with the Nationalists, and not do anything to give Chiang the slightest excuse not to fight Japan.

At this time, the Chinese Red Army had some 60,000 regular troops. Of these, 46,000 were in the northwest Red region, with Yenan as its capital. These were now renamed "the 8th Route Army" (8RA), led by Zhu De, with Peng De-huai as his deputy. Ten thousand were in the Eastern Yangtze valley in the heartland of China. These were guerrillas who had been left behind by the Long March, and they now became the "New 4th Army" (N4A). Xiang Ying, the head of the stay-behinds (and Mao's old nemesis, who had argued vigorously against Mao being taken along on the Long March), became the head of the N4A.

From late August, the three divisions that made up the 8RA began to cross the Yellow River towards the front, which lay several hundred kilometers to the east, in Shanxi province. Red Army commanders as well as soldiers were very keen to fight the Japanese. So were most of the CCP leaders.

But not Mao. Mao did not regard the Sino-Japanese War as a conflict in which all Chinese would fight together against Japan. He did not see himself as on the same side as Chiang at all. Years later, he was to say to his inner circle that he had regarded the war as a three-sided affair. "Chiang, Japan and us—Three Kingdoms," he said, evoking the period in Chinese history known as the Three Warring Kingdoms. The war was to him an opportunity to have Chiang destroyed by the Japanese. In later years he more than once thanked the Japanese for "lending a big hand." When after the war some Japanese visitors apologized to him for Japan having invaded China, he told them: "I would rather thank the Japanese warlords." Without them occupying much of China, "we would still be in the mountains today." He meant every word.

Mao had no strategy to drive the Japanese out of China without Chiang. Nor could he dream that the CCP could cope with the Japanese occupying army once Chiang was defeated. All his hopes hinged on Stalin. Mao had made his calculation clear in an interview with Edgar Snow in 1936, saying that Soviet Russia

> cannot ignore events in the Far East. It cannot remain passive. Will it complacently watch Japan conquer all China and make of it a strategic base from which to attack the USSR? Or will it help the Chinese people . . . ? We think Russia will choose the latter course.

Mao's basic plan for the Sino-Japanese War, therefore, was to preserve his forces and expand the sphere of the Chinese Reds, while waiting for Stalin to act. So when the Japanese pushed deeper into the interior from northern China as well as from the Shanghai area, Mao got Chiang to agree that the Red Army would not be put into any battles, and would operate only as auxiliaries to government troops. Mao did not want the Red Army to fight the invaders at all. He ordered Red commanders to wait for Japanese troops to defeat the Nationalists, and then, as the Japanese swept on, to seize territories behind the Japanese lines. The Japanese could not garrison the vast areas of China they conquered— which were eventually much larger than Japan itself. They could only control the railways and the big cities, leaving the smaller towns and the countryside up for grabs. Mao also ordered his men to round up defeated Nationalist troops in order to expand the Red ranks. His plan was to ride on the coat-tails of the Japanese to expand Red territory.

He bombarded his military commanders with telegrams such as: "Focus on creating base areas . . . Not on fighting battles . . ." And when the Japanese were sweeping across the province of Shanxi, he ordered: "Set up our territory in the whole of Shanxi province." He said years later that his attitude had been: "The more land Japan took, the better."

Mao's approach met with resistance from his own commanders, who were keen to fight the Japanese. On 25 September the Red Army had its first engagement with the Japanese, when a unit under Lin Biao ambushed the tail end of a Japanese transport convoy at the pass of Pingxingguan, in northeast Shanxi, near the Great Wall. Although this was a minor clash—and against a non-combat unit, which, according to Lin, was mainly asleep—it was the first time Communists had killed any Japanese (outside Manchuria). If Mao had had his way, this fight would not have happened at all. According to a report Lin Biao wrote in 1941 in Russia (where he was receiving treatment for bullet wounds), Mao had repeatedly refused to authorize the action: "When battles started between the Japanese army and the Nationalist army, I more than once asked the CC [Central Committee: i.e., Mao] for a decision to organise a powerful strike against the Japanese. I never received an answer, and I ended up giving battle near Pingxingguan on my own initiative."

Mao was furious about Pingxingguan. This fighting, he said, was "helping Chiang Kai-shek," and had done nothing to advance his goal—which was to establish Red territory. But for propaganda purposes, Mao had Pingxingguan inflated out of all proportion in an effort to demonstrate that the CCP was more committed to fighting the Japanese than the Nationalists were. One reason the Communists kept citing it was because it was, literally, the *only* "battle" they had with the Japanese for years,* one that killed a couple of hundred Japanese at the very most.

The Red Army had a few other small successes, as minor players in collaboration with Nationalist troops. But all the time, Mao was urging them to stop fighting the Japanese and concentrate on taking over territory. By mid-November, the first new Communist base in the Japanese rear was formed, near Peking, called Jinchaji, with a population of some 12 million, making it many times larger than the Yenan base. This and other huge Red territories "created the condition for our victory" in conquering China, Mao told a Japanese visitor years later.

STALIN, HOWEVER, wanted the Chinese Reds to fight Japan, and to get his policy enforced he flew his most loyal Chinese acolyte to Yenan in a special plane in November 1937. This was Wang Ming, who had been working for years in the Comintern as the CCP representative. Just before he left, Stalin called him in and laid down the line: "The main thing *now* is the war [i.e., to fight Japan] . . . when that is over we will face the question of how to fight each other [i.e., Reds fighting Chiang]."

Most CCP leaders agreed with Stalin's line. When the Politburo met in December for the first time after Wang Ming's return, Wang Ming became the champion of the "fight Japan first" policy. The Politburo decided that the Red Army must take orders from the national military

---

* Confirmed by Lin Biao himself in his report for the Russians of February 1941. The CCP "to this day exploits this battle for agitational [propaganda] purposes. In all our documents this is the only important battle cited . . ."

HQ, of which Chiang was the head and the CCP a part. Mao argued against this. But faced with a clear order from Stalin, he had to accept.

Mao's colleagues showed their disapproval of his agenda by making a decision that would oust Mao from his No. 1 position. Moscow had told the CCP to convene a congress, which was long overdue (the last had been in 1928). The person the Politburo chose to deliver the political report at the congress, which by strict Communist protocol devolved on the Party No. 1, was not Mao but Wang Ming. This was the Party leadership saying they wanted Wang Ming to be the future chief.

Although Mao was de facto leader of the Party, and was recognized by Moscow as such, his position was not formalized, most unusually for the ritual-obsessed Communist world. The Party chief was still nominally Lo Fu. Nor did Mao command the kind of unchallengeable awe that Stalin did.

Mao had also lost control of the core decision-making group, the Secretariat. For the first time since the break with the Nationalists in 1927, all of its nine members had come together in one place, and five of them did not support Mao. The leader of the majority opposition was Wang Ming. Xiang Ying, head of the N4A, had long been an outspoken opponent of Mao. Chang Kuo-tao, the man Mao had so massively sabotaged on the Long March, hated Mao. And Chou En-lai and Po Ku both backed Wang Ming. Chou was in favor of fighting Japan actively, and gladly went along with the majority. Mao was in the minority.*

Wang Ming had Moscow's authority, and the credentials of having been the Party's representative there, of having met Stalin, and of having hobnobbed with international Communist leaders. Fluent in Russian, and wise to the Kremlin's ways, he was also ambitious and ruthless. During the great purge in Russia, he had sent many Chinese Communists to prison or death. Though baby-faced, short and fleshy, this super-confident 33-year-old posed an acute threat to Mao.

Mao would often hark back with great bitterness to that December 1937 when Wang Ming prevailed. This stands in stark contrast to the fact that not once in his long life did he mention another event that took place at exactly the same time—a huge massacre in Nanjing, in which an estimated up to 300,000 Chinese civilians and prisoners of war were slaughtered by the Japanese. Mao never made any comment, then or later, about this, the single biggest human tragedy of the Sino-Japanese War for his fellow countrymen.

After Nanjing fell on 13 December, Chiang Kai-shek established his temporary capital farther inland, at Wuhan on the Yangtze. Wang Ming went there as CCP liaison on 18 December, with Chou and Po Ku as his

---

* The other three members of the Secretariat were Lo Fu, Chen Yun and Kang Sheng.

deputies. They formed a good working relationship with Chiang. Red Army commanders were going there too, to liaise with the Nationalists. Mao was marginalized in Yenan. He referred resentfully to his peripheral position as "house-sitting," although this complaint masked a critical reality: he used this time and the fact that the others were deeply involved in the war, to build up Yenan as his fiefdom.

From Yenan Mao waged an unrelenting struggle to prevent the Red Army from acting on the plans made in the national HQ headed by Chiang. When Zhu De wired on 19 February 1938 to say that the 8RA HQ was moving east in line with the general plan, Mao tried to turn the army back, by claiming that the Japanese were about to attack Yenan. In fact, Japan never attempted to attack Yenan, apart from occasional bombing.

Zhu declined to turn back, saying that Mao was probably falling for a ruse whose purpose was precisely to entice the 8RA away from the front. Mao persisted, showering Zhu with telegrams ordering him and Peng back to Yenan: "In particular, you two must return." Zhu and Peng replied with a definitive "No" on 7 March and continued east with their troops.

To stop Mao from constantly issuing orders that countermanded agreed strategy, the Politburo met again at the end of February. Wang Ming had demanded the meeting for this purpose—and to sort out another urgent matter. In January, under Mao's aegis and without Chiang Kai-shek's consent, the new Red territory of Jinchaji had been publicly proclaimed as a Red base. This had triggered off a wave of anti-communism in the country, with many asking: "What are we fighting the Japanese for? After Japan is defeated all we will get is a Communist takeover!" Wang Ming and his group in Wuhan were extremely unhappy about this in-your-face act by Mao.

Once again the majority of the Politburo sided with Wang Ming (and confirmed that he would deliver the political report at the forthcoming Party congress). The summary of the meeting, written by Wang Ming, said that the Red Army must be subject to "the supreme commander," i.e., Chiang Kai-shek, with "completely unified command . . . unified discipline, unified war plans and unified operations." Any new Red bases "must obtain the consent and authorisation of . . . the Nationalist government beforehand." Wang Ming also said, most ominously for Mao, that: "Today, only the Japanese Fascists . . . and their running-dogs . . . and the Trotskyists are attempting to overthrow the Nationalists . . ."

These were Moscow's words, and the charge was potentially deadly. So Mao pretended that he accepted the "fight Japan first" policy. He told Red commanders that they could take orders from the national HQ, and promised not to "interfere" in the future.

Mao was so nervous that he had been taking steps to prevent Moscow learning his real position. At the end of the December 1937 Politburo meeting, he had had all the participants' notes confiscated under the pretense of "safe-keeping," so that no one could cite him if they decided to report him. When a new envoy was sent to Moscow, Mao engineered for an ally of his, Ren Bi-shi, to get the job. Ren told the Russians that Mao's policy was no different from Moscow's.

In late January 1938 an emissary from the Soviet General Staff, V. V. Andrianov, had secretly visited Yenan—the highest-ranking Russian ever to do so. He had brought the huge sum of US$3 million (equivalent to roughly US$40 million today) for the specific purpose of building up the Red Army to fight the Japanese. Stalin had said he wanted the Chinese Red Army to have "not three but thirty divisions." Moscow was ready to bankroll this huge expansion—for fighting Japan.[*]

Andrianov asked Mao what his plans were for the war. Mao gave him a detailed, but false, account, saying that he intended to concentrate large contingents to strike the Japanese through "mobile warfare," and claiming that the Nationalists were spurning his efforts to cooperate with them. He even tried to demonstrate his enthusiasm by suggesting that the Japanese—whom he portrayed as ineffective and suffering from low morale—were an easier foe to fight than the Nationalists.

This was a most precarious time for Mao. He could not have failed to register that Moscow had noticeably scaled down public praise of him in the previous year, and had criticized the CCP in a key text on the anniversary of the Bolshevik Revolution. His complicity in the kidnapping of Chiang was bound to make Stalin suspect him. Indeed, Stalin had been nursing suspicions that Mao might be "a Japanese agent." Comintern officials who had had dealings with Mao were arrested and interrogated under torture. Comintern intelligence chief Osip Piatnitsky was one of them,[†] and in April 1938, he named Mao as a conspirator in an alleged "Bukharin group." Bukharin, the former head of the Comintern, was alleged to have spied for Japan.

The dossier on Mao included a denunciation of him as "the leader of Trotskyism in the inmost depths of the CCP"—a doubly menacing accusation, as Chinese Trotskyists were deemed to be Japanese spies. Moscow's

---

[*] When Wang Ming was still in Moscow, he told the Comintern that Mao "wired me repeatedly that they need money terribly [and] asked that you continue to send money every month."

[†] Piatnitsky was arrested on 7 July 1937, the day the Marco Polo Bridge incident occurred, leading to Japan's attack on northern China and threat to Russia. The first recorded interrogation of him is dated 11 November 1937; that same day Stalin saw Wang Ming before the latter left for Yenan to press the CCP and Mao to fight Japan. These were unmistakable indications that the arrest of Piatnitsky had to do with the war with Japan, the CCP—and Mao.

former top agent in China, Boris Melnikov, was accused of having recruited Mao and then gone over to the Japanese, along with other top CCP leaders. Stalin had Melnikov brought to the Kremlin for a face-to-face debriefing, and Melnikov's execution was delayed for eight months while he was grilled about the CCP. It was during this period that a huge number of former Soviet agents in China were executed on the charge of being Japanese spies. Mao's fate was in the balance.

FIGHT RIVALS AND
CHIANG—NOT JAPAN

(1937–40 ★ AGE 43–46)

ONE MAN who sought to exploit Mao's vulnerability was Chang Kuo-tao. He had met up with Mao in June 1935 during the Long March, with an army 80,000-strong in contrast to Mao's battered 10,000. He also had solid credentials to be the leader of the CCP. Over the next few months, however, Mao had methodically sabotaged his army, and monopolized the route north to link up with the Russians, leaving Kuo-tao to languish on the Tibetan border. By the time Kuo-tao reached Party HQ in northern Shaanxi in October 1936, his army had been halved in strength and he had become very much the junior partner. Even so, Mao was bent on further weakening Kuo-tao, because his army was still twice the size of Mao's, and he was still a potential rival.

That month, October 1936, when Mao dispatched the Red Army to try to open the way to the Russian arms supplies near the Outer Mongolia border, he designated Kuo-tao's combat-hardened units to break through the Nationalist force blocking the route. When this operation failed, 21,800 of Kuo-tao's troops—half of his remaining men—were cut off on the far side of the Yellow River. Moscow then floated the idea that the CCP might collect arms in another Soviet-controlled region, Xinjiang. The mission was hopeless, given that it involved crossing more than 1,500 kilometers, through uninhabited desert and territory held by a fierce anti-Communist Muslim army. But Mao jumped at this idea and assigned Kuo-tao's stranded force to this doomed mission. The force was named the Western Contingent.

Mao managed to make the journey even more futile by issuing a stream of contradictory orders that drove the Contingent from one hellish locale to another, continually plunging it into pitched battles. Its commander recorded bitterly that the tasks assigned him by Yenan were "elusive and changeable." When the Contingent cabled early in February 1937 from the middle of the desert that it could not hold out much longer, nor go on, and asked for permission to come to Yenan, Mao ordered it to hold on where it was, telling it to "fight to the last person and the last drop of blood."

By mid-March the Contingent, once the backbone of Kuo-tao's army, had been all but killed off. Those captured met horrible deaths. After one climactic battle in western Gansu, more than 1,000 were buried alive. Heart-rending photos were taken of a large group of unsuspecting prisoners before they were slaughtered. The 2,000 women were raped, some tortured and killed, others sold in the local slave markets. Of the original 21,800 men and women, only around 400 eventually made it to Xinjiang at the end of April, more dead than alive.

The extermination of this force allowed Mao to slam the lid on the coffin of Kuo-tao. Mao turned Kuo-tao, who was in Yenan, into the scapegoat, asserting that the Contingent had been following "the Chang Kuo-tao line." But Moscow refused to support Mao's attempt to get Kuo-tao kicked out of the Politburo. Still, Kuo-tao was denounced in front of his own officers.

Mao not only ended Kuo-tao's political prospects, he ended the lives of the few of the Western Contingent who eventually made it to Yenan. A local official described what happened:

When they were chased into our [area], we first of all gave them a welcome party and took over their arms. Then we said to them: "Comrades, you have been through a lot. You are transferred to the rear to have a good rest." We took them in batches into the valleys, and buried all these grandsons of turtles [i.e., bastards] alive.

It was such fun burying them. At first, we said to them with smiles: "Comrades, dig the pits well, we want to bury Nationalist troops alive." They really worked hard, one spade after another, wiping sweat from their faces . . . After they finished, we shoved them and kicked them all in. At first, they thought we were joking. But when we began to shovel earth in, they started shouting: "Comrades, we are not Nationalist troops!" We cursed: "Sons of bitches. We don't care whether you are Nationalist troops or not. We want you to die, and you die . . ."

At this point, the bragger was challenged: "I absolutely refuse to believe this was the order of the Party."

But the man went on: "What! It was our regimental commander who ordered us to do this. And he said it was the order of Comrade Gao Gang [local Communist leader], who of course was carrying out the order of Chairman Mao. We only recognise Chairman Mao's authority. Whatever Chairman Mao asks us to do, we do."

Kuo-tao himself was subjected to multiple "torments . . . masterminded by Mao," he later wrote. He was thrown out of his house by Mao's secretary so that Mao could take it over, and his orderly was arrested. Mao even tormented Kuo-tao's young son, who was cast as the leading

Trotskyist Chang Mu-tao in a school play. Kuo-tao described arriving at the school to find "a group of people were ridiculing my son. Mao Tse-tung was also there, having fun. He cackled maliciously: 'It fits perfectly to have Chang Kuo-tao's son play the role of Chang Mu-tao.' . . . I tore away the mask my son was wearing and led him away from the scene. I shouted in anger as I left: 'Barbarians! . . . Worse than beasts!' "*

BY SPRING 1938, Kuo-tao was at the end of his tether. This was right at the moment when Mao's own position was unusually weak, as he was out of line with Moscow's orders to fight Japan. Kuo-tao spotted a chance to join hands with Wang Ming, who represented Moscow's viewpoint. At the time, Wang Ming was in Wuhan, Chiang's temporary capital, with Chou En-lai and Po Ku. On 4 April, in his capacity as chairman of the Red region, Kuo-tao left Yenan for a joint Nationalist–CCP ceremony at the tomb of the mythical Yellow Emperor, outside the base area. After the ceremony he drove off to Xian, and from there he went on to Wuhan to see Wang Ming and his colleagues.

This was the rarest of rare opportunities, with the majority of the core Party leadership, all in disagreement with Mao, out of Yenan at the same time, and thus out of Mao's clutches. (Xiang Ying, Mao's fiercest critic and the head of the N4A, was near Wuhan.) The content of Kuo-tao's confabulations in Wuhan is one of the CCP's most closely guarded secrets. Almost certainly, Kuo-tao argued for ousting Mao. Yenan later told Moscow that Kuo-tao had "tried to break the unity of the Party" when he was in Wuhan. But he left empty-handed, probably because the Wuhan trio did not believe that Moscow would stand for dumping Mao. Whereas Kuo-tao was desperate, Wang Ming was at the peak of his confidence, and it may have been hard for him to appreciate that Mao's apparent acceptance of majority decisions masked a ferocious determination to claw his way back into control.

The talks went on for about a week. When Kuo-tao realized that he was getting nowhere, he decided to leave the Party for the Nationalists, which he did on 17 April. The Wuhan trio let him go. He then wrote to his wife, whom he had left behind in Yenan, pregnant, asking her to join him, with their twelve-year-old son. Mao stalled for two months, to make sure that Kuo-tao did no drastic damage, and then allowed them to leave.

* According to a Russian archive source declassified in 2005, Mao told Stalin's envoy Mikoyan on February 3, 1949 that the situation around the Zunyi Conference was "most unfavorable." The reason Mao gave (which was false) was that Chang Kuo-tao, with an army of 60,000 men, "was on the offensive against us." "But," Mao said, "we annihilated over 30,000 of his troops." (Tikhvinsky 2005, p. 65)

These words of Mao's reveal why he maneuvered so relentlessly to avoid entering Sichuan after the Zunyi Conference. They also show that he was prepared to kill huge numbers of fellow-Communist troops for his own ends.

When Kuo-tao's wife came to Wuhan, Chou advised her to tell her husband "not to burn his bridges with the Party." Kuo-tao took notice. He had once been the head of the CCP's Military Department, in charge of planting high-level agents in the Nationalist military, but he never revealed a single name to the Nationalists. In fact, he did little for them, and they were disappointed with him. His thousand-page-plus autobiography conspicuously failed to spill many beans. A sign that he kept his mouth shut was that after he fled the Mainland on the eve of Mao's conquest of China, one of his sons was allowed back to go to university in Canton in the mid-1950s. He outlived Mao and died in an old people's home in Toronto, Canada, in 1979, aged eighty-two, having converted to Christianity the year before.

Kuo-tao's defection to the Nationalists allowed Mao to discredit him in the eyes of his army; he was promptly expelled from the Party. Some of his old followers in Yenan were "extremely dissatisfied," Nationalist intelligence chief Tai Li reported to Chiang Kai-shek. They met in secret, whereupon Mao's forces "liquidated them all there and then. About 200 were buried alive."

Moscow waited two months before endorsing the expulsion. During this time, something most crucial for Mao happened: Stalin brought the Comintern purge to an end. Piatnitsky and Melnikov, who had implicated Mao as a Japanese spy, were executed (on the same day), along with a host of others connected to China. Mao's dossier remained on file, ready to be resuscitated when Stalin needed it again a decade later. But for now Mao was off the hook.

As soon as Mao learned that the Kremlin had approved the expulsion of Kuo-tao, and that he himself was in the clear, he turned to tackle Wang Ming.

AT THIS POINT Mao had a major ally in Moscow, his old fellow plotter on the Long March, Wang Jia-xiang, the Red Prof. Mao had pushed hard and bombarded Moscow with requests for the Red Prof to go to Russia, ostensibly for medical treatment, ever since radio contact with Moscow had been established in June 1936. The Red Prof arrived there in July 1937, and became the CCP's representative once Wang Ming returned to China. Now, in June 1938, Mao cabled the Red Prof to return. He was in the position to perform a signal service for Mao. Before he left, he saw Comintern leader Dimitrov, and in a conversation about Party unity, Dimitrov said that the CCP needed to solve its problems "under the leadership headed by Mao Tse-tung." Mao was to use this single expression to reverse his personal fortunes—and Party policy.

The Red Prof returned to Yenan in late August. Mao immediately had him summon Wang Ming and the others to a Central Committee plenum "to hear the Comintern's instructions." This was the first time the Central Committee had been convened since before the Long March, well over four years before. Wuhan, the temporary capital, was under fierce attack by the Japanese. Yet Mao recalled the field commanders and top men to Yenan, which was a backwater. Wang Ming objected, saying this was no time for the entire Party leadership to be absent from the nation's capital, and suggested holding the meeting in Wuhan. "I'm not going anywhere!" Mao declared. The Red Prof cabled Wang Ming threateningly: "Obey the Centre, or else."

Wang Ming came reluctantly, on 15 September. The Red Prof first addressed the Politburo, quoting the remark Dimitrov had made, upon which Mao said that *he* would deliver the political report at the plenum—thus re-establishing his position as No. 1. Wang Ming offered no resistance. When the plenum opened on the 29th in Yenan's Franciscan cathedral, the Red Prof, seated beneath Lenin's picture on the altar, repeated Dimitrov's words to the larger audience. Thus was planted in the minds of the CCP high command the idea that Moscow had explicitly endorsed Mao as their leader.

As a reward to the Red Prof, Mao gave him a slew of key posts, including vice-chairman of the Military Council. Mao also found the 32-year-old bachelor a pretty and coquettish bride, a 23-year-old medical graduate whose father had been an old friend of Mao's. So, having made nominal Party chief Lo Fu a happy man with a petite and vivacious spouse, Mao had spun the "red thread" around another useful heart, locking two vital allies to his belt. Mao enjoyed matchmaking, and was shrewd about the ways of the heart, particularly in sexually inhibited men.

Mao now set about discrediting Wang Ming. However, shattering Party unity was something Moscow had specifically vetoed—and Wang Ming could be expected to fight back if attacked to his face. So Mao resorted to his old trick of dragging the meeting out until Wang Ming and other key opponents had left before he set upon them.

Mao strung the plenum out for almost two months, making it the longest ever, even though it took place in the midst of a national crisis during which not only Wuhan but also the Nationalists' last major port, Canton, fell to the Japanese. Communist bases behind Japanese lines were threatened as well. Urgent pleas came flying in—"Emergency situation here. Please could Peng De-huai return soonest..."—but Mao refused to release the military commanders until he had achieved his goals.

Chiang Kai-shek moved his capital to Chongqing, further inland, where he was convening a new National Assembly for 28 October which Wang Ming was due to attend. Mao made sure that his plenum was still in session when Wang Ming had to depart for Chongqing—the same ploy he had used in 1929 to lay his hands on Red Fujian.

In order to prolong things, Mao insisted that every Politburo member make two virtually identical speeches—one to the Politburo and one to the plenum. He himself stalled his Political Report for two weeks, during which time participants were kept hanging around. When he finally spoke he was massively long-winded, and what with his habit of sleeping in the morning, he took up no less than three days.

By the end of October, all Mao's most powerful opponents—Chou, Xiang Ying, Po Ku and Wang Ming—had left town. Once they had gone, Mao launched an onslaught on them, and especially on Wang Ming, for "following Chiang Kai-shek's orders," and even for the bloody purges in the Red areas before the Long March, when Wang Ming was not even there.

With his opponents absent, Mao imposed his policy on the plenum: to expand Red bases aggressively, and wage war on Nationalist troops if necessary. This was the first time that Mao spelled out his real intentions. There were many Nationalist troops behind Japanese lines, and they were competing with the Communists for territory. Hitherto, the policy had been to avoid fighting them and make unity with Chiang the priority. Mao had expressed complete agreement while Wang Ming was present, called Chiang Kai-shek a "great leader," committed himself to placing new Red bases under the central government, and promised to "aim every gun at the Japanese." He even proclaimed: "The Chinese nation has stood up! The state of being bullied, insulted, invaded and oppressed for 100 years ... is over." These words are almost identical to those he used at the time of the founding of Communist China in 1949, when he said: "the Chinese have stood up." The 1949 remark is much quoted as— and widely assumed to be—a first. In fact, it was not. Moreover, when Mao originally used the phrase, China, in his words, was "under Mr. Chiang's leadership"!

With Wang Ming gone, Mao told the top men that the Generalissimo was their ultimate enemy, and that they must start *now* preparing to seize power from him. The Red Army must strike Nationalist troops who stood in the way of its expansion. This was a milestone order to the top echelon: Chiang remains your enemy No. 1. You can open fire on Chiang's army.

A KEY SUPPORTER of this approach was the future president, Liu Shao-chi, who had been running the underground network in northern China. Liu had spent two long periods in Russia, had met Lenin in 1921, and had had an affair with one of Lenin's closest friends, Larisa Reysner. A man of considerable far-sightedness, Liu shared Mao's hard-nosed strategy for seizing power. Immediately after the plenum, Mao made him Party chief of a large area in east central China where the N4A was operating—and thus the boss over Xiang Ying and the N4A.

Mao also had the support of Peng De-huai, the deputy chief of the 8RA, who could see that civil war was inevitable if the Reds were to expand—or even to stay on at all in some places. Zhu De, the 8RA chief, went along. Mao had secured the support of the chiefs of all the Red forces for his policy.

As his strategy directly contravened Stalin's instructions, Mao was afraid that the news might be leaked to Wang Ming, and through him to Moscow. So he ordered his speeches to be kept absolutely secret. To seal the mouths of his audience, Mao produced two cautionary "Resolutions on discipline," which banned anyone from "revealing secrets" to "anyone else inside or outside the Party." This meant that participants could not tell their colleagues, even those who had attended the early part of the plenum, that Mao had just ordered civil war against the Nationalists. And no one dared tell Wang Ming the full story about Mao's attacks on him.

To weave a blanket of fear, Mao relied on the later infamous security chief Kang Sheng. In Russia, Kang had supervised the purges of hundreds of Chinese, many of whom were tortured, executed, or worked to death in the gulag. He had been Wang Ming's deputy on the CCP delegation to the Comintern, and had followed him closely. When the two first arrived in Yenan, Kang had led the shouting of "Long live our Party's genius leader comrade Wang Ming!" at the security apparatus's training sessions. But Kang had quickly realized Mao was the winner, and switched allegiance. It was now that Kang vouched for Jiang Qing, enabling Mao to marry her, forming a further bond between him and Mao. Mao made him the head of the CCP's KGB, even trusting him to select his personal guards.

It was to this closely controlled Yenan that Wang Ming was ordered to return after the National Assembly session in Chongqing. He was made head of the United Front Department, nominally an important post, but was soon reduced to a figurehead. An eyewitness recalled seeing him in the street, "his head bent, his steps heavy . . . buried in his own thoughts." But Wang Ming was not openly denounced, as his link with Moscow was strong. So, for the average Party member, he was still one of the leaders—and popular. Many recalled him being "a good orator whose speeches were very lively and rousing. Young people liked him." Mao was no orator. Wang Ming remained his unfinished business.

FROM 1939, after Mao ordered the Party to adopt an aggressive stance towards the Nationalists, large-scale engagements were fought behind Japanese lines between Communist and Nationalist forces over territory, in which the Communists usually came off best. By January 1940 the 8RA, under Zhu De and Peng, had grown to at least 240,000 (from 46,000 at the beginning of the war). And the N4A, operating under Liu

Shao-chi near Shanghai and Nanjing, had tripled, to 30,000. A score of sizable bases sprang up in the Japanese rear. The base of Jinchaji alone, only some 80 km from Peking, expanded to control a population of 25 million. At this point, with the war more than two years old, when realism had replaced initial patriotic ardor, many Red leaders came to admire the brilliance of Mao's cold vision. Peng De-huai described Mao in a speech in February 1940 as "a wise leader with political foresight, who can foresee developments and is good at dealing with them." And it was in this period that Chou En-lai made a total conversion to Mao.

Mao had done well for the CCP. But he had to keep Stalin on board. For many months, he concealed the clashes with the Nationalists from Moscow. He only owned up when the fighting had grown conspicuous and serious in June 1939, and then he claimed that it was purely self-defensive, portraying the Nationalists as intent on wiping the Communists off the face of the earth.

Mao knew how to play to his audience in Moscow. In spring 1939, Stalin had sent his top documentary film-maker, Roman Karmen, to Yenan to film Mao. Mao left a book of Stalin's open in his study when Karmen arrived and then posed for a long take holding a text by Stalin, with a picture of the author prominent on the front cover. He toasted Stalin, saying that the only place abroad he wanted to go was Moscow, to see Stalin. When he bade farewell to Karmen at the entrance to his cave, in the dark, he made a point of asking which way Moscow lay, sighing deeply and then falling into a long silence. "With what warmth Mao talks of comrade Stalin!" Karmen wrote.*

Most crucially, Mao had his men in Moscow to bolster his position— and to denigrate his foes. He had made sure that the CCP's envoys in Moscow were his allies—first, the Red Prof, then Ren Bi-shi. As he embarked on a course of action towards Chiang that was in defiance of Stalin's orders, he sent a string of additional emissaries, starting with Lin Biao, who went to Russia at the end of 1938 for treatment for bullet wounds. Lin had been shot by Nationalist troops while he was wearing a captured Japanese coat, and was mistaken for a Japanese.

Lin took with him only documents that Mao wanted Moscow to see, so Stalin was kept in the dark about Mao's machinations and real policies. Lin built Mao up as "the solid, decisive and principled leader of the CCP," badmouthing Chou as a "swindler" and Zhu De ("the former gendarme") as "not one of us."

Lin was followed in June 1939 by Mao's brother, Tse-min, ostensibly

---

* Mao's first celluloid image shown in Moscow seems to have been in 1935, when a news-reel of CCP leaders was screened before the 7th Comintern Congress. Comintern No. 3 Piatnitsky, later executed by Stalin, said he thought Mao looked like a "hooligan."

also for "health" reasons—although, as the Russians observed, he did not spend a single day in the hospital. Tse-min's main task was to undermine Wang Ming, whom he called "a scoundrel," denouncing him for, amongst other things, exaggerating the strength of the Chinese Red Army in the presence of Stalin—a potentially deadly accusation. Another aim of Mao's was to have Wang Ming's role downgraded at the forthcoming Party congress. Wang Ming was scheduled to deliver the second report, on organization. But Tse-min told Moscow that Wang Ming was not the right person, making the false allegation that he "had never run practical org[anisation]work." Tse-min also threw mud at other foes of Mao, like Po Ku and Li Wei-han, an old Hunan Communist leader, both of whom he accused of "major crimes," saying they should be kept out of all leading bodies. He likened Po Ku to "opportunists, Trotskyists and bandits."

Mao's third "extra" emissary, Chou En-lai, arrived just as the war in Europe started, checking into the Kremlin hospital on 14 September for an operation on his right arm, which had been badly set after he broke it in a fall from a horse. Chou had just converted to Mao—an unconditional conversion that made him Mao's very faithful servant from then on. He worked assiduously to build up Mao, and told the Russians that the CCP leadership "considered that he [Mao] must be elected GenSec [General Secretary]." He assured Moscow that the CCP's policy remained that "the anti-Japanese war comes above everything else," and that the Party was committed to "the united front" with Chiang. He detailed the expansion of Red forces and territory, larding his account with a number of exaggerated claims, such as that the 8RA had fought no fewer than 2,689 battles against the Japanese. CCP membership, he stated, had "increased sevenfold [to] 498,000" since the war had started.

While using Chou, Mao also made sure he was cut down to size. After visiting Chou in the hospital, Tse-min told the Russians that Chou held "unhealthy" views on relations with the Nationalists, and claimed Chou had opposed shooting the prominent Trotskyist Chang Mu-tao.

Mao was also worried about Otto Braun, Moscow's adviser in China since before the Long March, who had come to Russia with Chou, and might tell the Russians things Mao did not want them to hear. Tse-min made a point of calling Braun's tactics "counter-revolutionary"—an accusation that could well have got Braun shot. Braun, who survived, claims that this was the intention. Chou also weighed in, calling his former friend and close colleague "an enemy of the Chinese revolution." (Braun described Chou as his "chief prosecutor.")

Mao later accused his rivals of "running others down to foreign daddies." But none of them engaged in anything remotely like the character assassination that Mao practiced.

MOST DESIRED SCENARIO: STALIN CARVES UP CHINA WITH JAPAN

(1939–40; AGE 45–46)

ON 23 AUGUST 1939 the Soviet Union signed a non-aggression pact with Nazi Germany, and the following month the two countries invaded Poland and divided it up between them. Many in China were outraged by Stalin's deal with Hitler. These feelings were perhaps best articulated by the founding father of the CCP, Chen Tu-hsiu, the man who had set Mao on the path of communism, but had been expelled from the Party for being too independent. After years imprisoned by the Nationalists, he had been released with other political prisoners when the Nationalist–Communist "United Front" was formed in 1937. Now he penned a poem expressing his "grief and anger," comparing Stalin to "a ferocious devil," who

> strides imperiously into his neighbouring country
> . . . And boils alive heroes and old friends in one fell swoop . . .
> Right and Wrong change like day and night,
> Black and White shift only at his bidding . . .

The Stalin–Hitler Pact opened up the prospect that Stalin might do a similar deal with Japan, with China a second Poland. Indeed, at this very moment, the Kremlin signed a ceasefire with Japan, bringing to a halt fighting that had been going on between the Soviet Red Army and the Japanese on the border of Outer Mongolia and Manchukuo. The Poland scenario caused Chiang Kai-shek acute concern, which he raised with Moscow. Mao's reaction, however, was one of delight. His whole strategy for the war with Japan was aimed at prevailing on Russia to step in. Now a real chance appeared that Stalin might occupy part of China, and put Mao in charge.

In late September that year, when Edgar Snow asked Mao how he felt about a Soviet–Japanese pact, Mao's reply was enthusiastic. He said that Russia might sign such a pact "as long as this does not hinder its support for . . . the interest of the world liberation movement [i.e., Mao himself and the CCP]." Asked whether "Soviet help to China's liberation movement may take a somewhat similar form" to Russian occupation of Poland, Mao gave a very positive reply: "It is quite within the possibilities of Leninism." The Poland scenario was now Mao's model for China.*

Similarly, Mao hailed Russia's seizure of eastern Finland in early 1940, though not for public consumption. In a secret directive on 25 June, he claimed that the Soviet–Finnish peace agreement, under which Moscow annexed large swaths of Finnish territory, "guarantees the victory of the world *and the Chinese revolution*" (italics added). After France was divided between a German-occupied half and a puppet regime based at Vichy, Mao again drew a comparison. He wrote in coded language in a circular issued to top commanders on 1 November 1940: "There is still the possibility of the Soviet Union stepping in to adjust China–Japan relations." Referring to a partition of the kind imposed on France, he went on to talk about the Reds "getting a better deal [relying on] the Soviet Union stepping in to do the adjustment, and us keeping trying." Again, Mao was hoping that Russia would partition China with Japan.

Mao even had an ideal demarcation line, the Yangtze, which flows across the middle of China. To his inner circle, Mao dreamed of "drawing a border... at the Yangtze, with us ruling one half..."

Replicating the Poland scenario was indeed at the front of Stalin's mind, and Russia began talks with Japan in September 1939, right after the signing of the Nazi–Soviet Pact, with the future of China very much at the center of the negotiations. Stalin thus had a very direct interest in the expansion both of the Chinese Red Army and of Red territory, as that would strengthen his bargaining position vis-à-vis Japan, and further his long-term goals for the postwar period.

Over the winter of 1939–40 there was a marked shift in what Mao told Moscow about the armed clashes between the Chinese Reds and Chiang's forces. He became much more candid about the level of fighting. Before Stalin's pact with Hitler, Mao had been presenting the clashes as the result of Nationalist attempts to wipe out Communist forces, claiming that the Reds were acting in self-defence. After the Nazi–Soviet Pact, he began to seek Stalin's approval for expanding aggressively at Chiang's expense. On 22 February 1940 he sent a highly belligerent report to Moscow, saying that in fighting Chiang's forces, "victory is generally ours." "We wiped out 6,000 [Nationalists] in Hebei, 10,000 ... in Shanxi," he reported.

---

* Mao's remarks about the Polish model and a Soviet–Japanese pact did not go down well in Moscow. They were too unvarnished, and a harsh reproof ensued. "The provocative essence of this statement must be unmasked," Comintern chief Dimitrov cabled Mao. "We urgently request that Mao Tse-tung and other Chinese comrades refrain from giving interviews to foreign correspondents like the interview with Edgar Snow, as this is being used for provocative purposes." Mao kept his mouth shut in public, and Snow was barred from Red-held China until the Sino-Soviet split, in 1960.

Stalin did not say "Stop!" On the contrary, three days later he authorized the huge sum of US$300,000 per month for the CCP. When Chou
En-lai left Moscow shortly afterwards, he brought with him a new radio
system for communicating with Moscow, which he delivered to Mao.*
Mao's Russian-language aide noted: "Chairman Mao alone had the right
to use it. He kept all communications personally, and decided to whom
he would show the information."

AFTER THE Nazi–Soviet Pact and the prospect that Stalin might do a
similar deal with Japan, in September 1939 Mao initiated a long, close
and little-known collaboration with Japanese intelligence, in the hope of
further sabotaging Chiang—and preserving his own forces. The CCP
operation was headed by a man called Pan Han-nian, who worked with
the Japanese vice-consul in Shanghai, Eiichi Iwai, a senior intelligence
officer. Pan was given a special Japanese ID, addressed: "To all Japanese
military, gendarme and police personnel: any enquiry regarding the bearer,
please contact the Japanese Consul-General." A radio operator from
Yenan was installed in Iwai's house, for direct contact with Yenan, though
in the end this channel was not used, as it was considered "too risky."

Pan supplied Iwai with information about Chiang's ability to resist
the Japanese, his conflicts with the CCP and his relations with foreign
powers, as well as about US and British agents in Hong Kong and
Chongqing. This intelligence rated high with the Japanese: one item
reportedly sent the Japanese ambassador to China "wild with joy." Before
Japan invaded Hong Kong in December 1941, Iwai helped arrange the
evacuation of CCP agents. As Pan assured Iwai, some of the agents would
continue to collect intelligence for the Japanese, while others would come
to Shanghai to "help with our 'peace movement.'" The "peace movement" was Japan's chief non-military drive to force China to surrender.
One prominent organization in this scheme was the "Revive Asia and
Build the Country Movement," which Pan helped to start, funded by
Tokyo and largely manned by secret Communists.

The Reds used the Japanese to stab the Nationalists in the back. "At
the time," one CCP intelligence man recalled,

> our Party's tactic with the Japanese and collaborators was: "Use the
> hand of the enemy to strike the other enemy . . ." Comrade Kang Sheng
> told us this many times . . . Collaborators' organisations were filled
> with our comrades, who used the knives of the Japanese to slaughter
> Nationalists . . . Of the things I knew personally, the Japanese annihi-
> lation of the [Nationalist underground army] south of the Yangtze

* The new system was highly effective. The Japanese could not even locate the radios,
much less break the codes.

[was one of the] masterpieces of cooperation between the Japanese and our Party.*

Apart from sabotaging Chiang, Pan's other task was to get the Japanese to allow the Reds to operate unmolested, and this went as far as floating the idea of a secret ceasefire in northern China to Japan's highest intelligence officer in China, Major-General Sadaaki Kagesa.

In east central China, a deal was struck under which the Communist New 4th Army left the railways alone in return for the Japanese leaving the N4A alone in the countryside. For years, Japanese trains ran smoothly, and the N4A expanded quietly. The underlying reasoning behind leaving the Reds in peace was spelled out to us by Emperor Hirohito's brother, Prince Mikasa, who was an officer in China at the time. He told us that the Japanese view was that while the Communists could be a nuisance, they had no strategic importance. The Japanese considered Chiang Kai-shek to be their main enemy.

BY SPRING 1940, huge tracts of countryside in northern China were in Communist hands. In one series of battles in March, immediately after Stalin's tacit go-ahead, the Communists concentrated 30,000–40,000 troops, and destroyed over 6,000 Nationalists. Having established a strong position in northern China, 8RA commanders Zhu De and Peng De-huai felt it incumbent on them to do something against the Japanese, and on 1 April they ordered preparations for large-scale sabotage operations against Japanese transportation lines. Mao refused to permit the attack. Instead, he ordered all available troops to be moved to east central China to seize more territory there. Zhu and Peng were forced to abandon their plan.

At this point, Chiang invited Zhu, who minded about the continuing internal strife, to Chongqing to discuss a solution. En route, Zhu stopped in Yenan, as Mao had told him that a Party congress was about to convene. Zhu found no congress—and no sign of one. Nonetheless, he was prevented from proceeding to Chongqing, and was in effect detained in Yenan for the rest of the war. Even though he was the C-in-C of the 8RA, he played no role in the war, and Mao basically used him as a rubber stamp.

Mao sent someone else to Chongqing—Chou En-lai, who was now the exclusive channel with Chiang. Mao had completed his stranglehold on communications with the two places that counted—Moscow and Chongqing.

---

* Mao's deal does not seem to have extended to actual military cooperation in the field, though the Russian GRU chief in Yenan reported one occasion when Communist troops attacked Nationalist forces in Shandong in summer 1943 "in coordination with Japanese troops."

At this time, in May 1940, the Sino-Japanese war entered a critical phase. The Japanese began to intensify their bombing of Chongqing, which soon became the most heavily bombed city in the world to date; over the next six months, the tonnage dropped on it equaled one-third of what the Allies dropped on all Japan throughout the Pacific War; up to 10,000 civilians died in one raid. The Japanese army meanwhile advanced up the Yangtze towards Chongqing. Tokyo demanded that France close the railway from Vietnam, and that Britain shut down the Burma Road—the only routes into now landlocked China other than from Russia. Both Western states acquiesced, on 20 June and 18 July, respectively (although Britain's closure was only for three months). In Chongqing, sentiment strengthened for a deal with Japan. Chiang—and China—were facing a momentous crisis.

To Mao the crisis was a godsend—the worse the better. He said later that he "had hoped they [the Japanese] would go as far as . . . Chongqing." That way, he reckoned, Russia would have to intervene.

But Peng De-huai, now de facto chief of the 8RA after Zhu's quasi-detention in Yenan, wanted to take some of the heat off Chongqing, and resuscitated his plans for a large operation to sabotage Japanese transportation lines in northern China, calling it by the resounding name of "Operation 100 Regiments." On 22 July he ordered the 8RA to get ready to launch on 10 August, and radioed the plan to Mao, twice. There was no reply. When Peng got no answer to a third cable, he gave the go-ahead for the 20th.

Peng knew that Mao would dislike his operation. Not only would it help Chiang, it would also hurt the Reds, as Tokyo was bound to retaliate against Red territories. Peng was putting country before Party.

The operation, which lasted about a month, mainly involved attacks on installations, not on Japanese troops. It took the Japanese "totally by surprise," in their own words. Damage to railways and highways in some sections was reported as "extremely serious" and "on an indescribably large scale" (the sabotage work was carried out partly by corvée labor). The Jingxing coal mines, which supplied the key Anshan iron and steel works in Manchuria, were badly hit, and the main mine put out of action "for at least half a year." The Japanese had to pull back one division from the front against Chiang, and briefly delay plans to capture two railways into southern China.

The main effect was on Chinese morale, especially in heavily bombed Nationalist areas. The Nationalist press there praised the 8RA for taking the offensive, and for "dealing a deadly blow to enemy rumours that we are split and sunk in internal strife." From Chongqing, Chou cabled Mao that the operation had had "an extremely big impact." "We are publicising it and propagating it everywhere . . . now is the time to spread our Party's influence . . ." Mao milked the fall-out to the hilt.

But in private he was seething, partly because the operation led to heavy Red casualties—90,000, according to Zhu De. The Japanese took extremely harsh reprisals against Red-controlled territory, which was soon reduced by about half; the population under Red rule fell from about 44 to some 25 million. But Peng soon got the 8RA and the bases back on their feet. In slightly over two years, the 8RA more than recovered its pre-1940 strength, to 400,000 men, and Peng had rebuilt its base areas.

But what most infuriated Mao was that the initiative lessened the chances of Chiang's defeat—and hence of Russia intervening. In future years, Mao was to make Peng pay dearly for this, the only large-scale operation carried out by any Communist forces during the whole eight years of the Japanese occupation.

MEANWHILE, IN SPITE of Japanese bombing, Chongqing still stood, and Chiang did not collapse. Mao had to find another way to try to draw the Russians in. Chiang now came up with a plan to end the Nationalist–Communist fighting by separating the two forces physically. By this time, the 8RA had control over most of the territories they could expect to lay their hands on in northern China, so fighting there had died down. The main theater of civil war had moved to the Yangtze Valley in east central China near Shanghai and Nanjing. Chiang's plan called for the Red N4A to move out of the Yangtze region and join the 8RA in the north, in return for letting the Reds keep virtually all of the territory seized in northern China. On 16 July 1940, Chiang offered this trade-off, couched in the form of an "order," and gave the N4A a deadline of a month.

Mao had no intention of giving up the rich and strategic heartland. He turned Chiang's order-offer down flat. Actually, he positively hoped that Chiang would use force to remove the N4A, and that there would be all-out civil war. "Mao's calculation," Russian ambassador Panyushkin wrote, was that "if there is a civil war, the Russians would back the CCP," and Mao wanted to "nudge such a development."

In his many cables to Moscow that summer, Mao kept urging the Russians to help him deal "serious blows" to the Nationalists. Instead of moving north, the N4A launched its biggest-ever attack on the Nationalists at the beginning of October, at a place called Yellow Bridge, wiping out 11,000 Nationalist troops and killing two generals. Chiang did not order any retaliation, and kept quiet about the defeat, as he had after many other defeats at the hands of the Reds. Unlike Mao, Chiang was afraid of igniting an all-out civil war, which would doom China's chances against Japan. He only reiterated on 19 October that the N4A must move to the "appointed areas" within one month.

Mao met this second deadline with silence. He wanted to goad the Generalissimo into resorting to force, so that an all-out civil war could start and, as Mao told Chou, "the Soviet Union would step in." Again Chiang took no action. Mao knew the Generalissimo's weak spots. He wrote to Chou on 3 November: "What Chiang fears most is civil war, and the Soviet Union. So we can bully him on this."

On 7 November 1940, the anniversary of the Bolshevik Revolution, Mao appealed to Moscow with his most overtly bellicose proposition yet. Signed by himself, the cable was addressed to Dimitrov *and Manuilsky*, Mao's main backer in the Comintern. Copies were sent to Stalin and defense minister Semyon Timoshenko. Mao's plan was to dispatch 150,000 soldiers "to deliver a blow" at Chiang's rear. He called this a "preventive counter-offensive," i.e., he would fire the first shot.

Mao was asking Moscow to endorse his starting a full-scale civil war, in the thick of the Sino-Japanese War. The reason he felt able to venture this far now was his perception that the latest developments might cause Stalin to favor a strike at Chiang. The Kremlin was considering joining the Tripartite Pact of which Japan was a member, together with Nazi Germany and Fascist Italy. If Mao struck now, in effect forming a pincer attack with Japan on Chiang, Chiang might well collapse. If Mao contributed to the defeat of Chiang, this would greatly strengthen Stalin's hand at the negotiating table with Tokyo.

Mao's entreaty to Moscow to allow him to enter this unholy de facto alliance with Japan arrived as Soviet foreign minister Molotov was about to set off for Berlin, where one of his goals was to get Hitler to help Moscow muscle in as a major interested party in the Sino-Japanese War. Molotov's agenda stated: "Discuss the necessity of reaching an honorable [*sic*] peace for China (Chiang Kai-shek), in which the USSR may with the participation of G[ermany] and I[taly] be ready to take on mediation . . . (Manchukuo stays for J[apan])." Molotov then told the Führer: "[We] must find a compromise exit from the situation prevailing between China and Japan . . . in this regard the USSR and Germany could play an important role." But the Führer was not interested.

The terms Japan offered on China did not begin to match Stalin's expectations. Tokyo would agree only to "a Russian sphere of influence in Outer Mongolia and Xinjiang," which was hardly alluring to Stalin, as these two places were already in his pocket. Japan also considered "recognising and accepting the three northwestern provinces (Shaanxi, Gansu, and Ningxia) remaining a Chinese Communist base"—on condition that Russia agreed to "restrain the anti-Japanese activities of the Chinese Communists." But this idea was again not nearly enough for Stalin, as the CCP was already occupying a much larger territory than these three provinces.

Moscow's failure to strike a deal with Tokyo meant that Stalin's priority remained staving off the possibility of a Japanese attack on Russia—and that meant Mao could not have his all-out war on Chiang yet. Stalin wanted a united China which could continue to bog down the Japanese. When Stalin dispatched General Chuikov as his new military adviser to Chongqing at this time, Chuikov asked why he was being sent "to Chiang Kai-shek, not the Chinese Red Army." Stalin answered: "Your job is firmly to tie the hands of the Japanese aggressor in China."*

So the Kremlin line to Mao was: hold your fire. An order went off to him on 25 November: "for the time being, play for time, manoeuvre, and bargain with Chiang Kai-shek in every possible way over removing your forces from Central China . . . It is essential you do not initiate military action [i.e., against Chiang] . . ." But Moscow did authorize Mao to fight back if attacked: "However, if Chiang Kai-shek . . . attacks [you], you must strike with all your might . . . In this case, the responsibility for the split and civil war will fall entirely on Chiang . . ."

This left Mao with one hope: that Chiang would fire the first shot. But as deadlines for the N4A to move north came and went, Mao reached the conclusion that "Chiang launching a big assault is not a possibility . . ."

Having failed to provoke Chiang into firing the first shot, Mao now set up a situation in which Chiang's finger would be forced to pull the trigger.

---

* Chuikov's other role, which he did not mention in his memoirs, was to give Moscow an expert assessment of whether the Chinese Reds could take power after Japan was defeated.

DEATH TRAP FOR HIS OWN MEN

(1940–41 ★ AGE 46–47)

THE POLITICAL commissar of the New 4th Army, the Red Army based in east central China, was an old nemesis of Mao's, Xiang Ying. A decade before, Mao had tried to have him eliminated when he opposed Mao's torturing and killing in the AB purge. And Xiang Ying had warned against taking Mao along on the Long March, predicting that he would scheme to seize power. He had remained outspoken about Mao, sometimes even mocking him.

Xiang Ying's HQ of about 1,000 staff and 8,000 escort troops was situated in a picturesque place called Cloud Peak, near perhaps the most strangely beautiful mountain in China, Huangshan, the Yellow Mountain, where, before one's astonished eyes, the clouds run, dance, storm and melt at dazzling speed around Gothic-looking rocks. By December 1940, Xiang Ying's group was the only part of the N4A south of the Yangtze, as Mao had sent 90 percent of the N4A north of the river, and put them under a separate headquarters run by his ally Liu Shao-chi.

That month, Mao set Xiang Ying's group up to be killed by the Nationalist army, in the hope that the massacre would persuade Stalin to let him off the leash against Chiang. Months before, in July, the Generalissimo had ordered the N4A to move to northern China, an order Mao had defied. In December, however, Mao told Xiang to decamp, and cross to the north of the Yangtze.

There were two routes Xiang could take. The shortest ran due north (the North Route). The second would take him southeast, and then over the Yangtze much farther downstream (the East Route). On 10 December the Generalissimo designated the North Route, and Mao confirmed it to Xiang on the 29th.

The next day, Mao suddenly told Xiang to take the East Route, the one the Generalissimo had vetoed, but did not tell Chiang this, so Chiang thought the Reds would take the route agreed. On 3 January 1941 a cable arrived at Xiang's HQ from the Generalissimo himself, specifying the itinerary and adding: "I have ordered all the armies along the way to ensure your safety."

Xiang replied at once, saying he would not be taking the route Chiang had designated, and asking to have the East Route cleared instead. But this crucial message never got to Chiang—thanks to Mao. Mao had banned all Communist commanders from communicating with the Generalissimo direct, and had ordered all contacts channeled through himself. Xiang sent the message via Mao, and Mao did not send it on. So Xiang set off in wintry chill and rain on the night of 4 January 1941 along Mao's chosen East Route not knowing that Chiang had never seen his cable.*

Xiang and his troops walked right into a much larger Nationalist force, who had not been told that Xiang's unit was coming, much less that it was only passing through, and thought this was an attack. Fighting broke out on the 6th. That day the local Nationalist commander, General Ku, gave orders to "exterminate" the Reds.

Xiang sent frantic telegrams to Yenan pleading for Mao to tell the Nationalists to hold their fire. But Mao did nothing. When Liu Shao-chi, who was with the main N4A force north of the Yangtze, wired Yenan on the 9th about the situation, Mao pretended ignorance, claiming that the last he had heard from Xiang was on the 5th, and "after that we do not know anything."

During the most critical period of bloody fighting, the four days from 6 to 9 January, Mao claimed he received no communication. During those days, Xiang's radio operators were sending out repeated, desperate SOS messages, and Liu Shao-chi had no problem receiving them. It is hard to believe that Mao's communications had conveniently "broken down" just for the four days when the N4A HQ was being massacred. And even if there was some glitch, this cannot explain how Mao did nothing—for days—to resume contact. Mao had a history of using "radio trouble" as an excuse to suppress information (after the kidnapping of Chiang Kai-shek in 1936, Mao had claimed he was unable to receive a vital message from Moscow). For Mao, the greater the bloodshed, the greater his excuse to turn on Chiang; *and* he was sacrificing someone he was glad to get rid of anyway, Xiang Ying.

After Liu brought up the subject of the N4A's plight on the 9th, Mao's radio miraculously started functioning again. From that day, urgent pleas from N4A HQ began to be recorded. On the 10th the HQ entreated

* We know that Mao suppressed this cable because he told Chou En-lai, his liaison with Chiang, on 13 January, nine days and many deaths later: "I have sent you the cable of the 4th from . . . Xiang to Chiang. Its wording is inappropriate, so if you haven't passed it on, please don't." The fact that Mao felt he still had time to withdraw the cable indicates he had only just recently sent it to Chou.

Mao: "on the brink of doom . . ." "Please could you quickly make representations to Chiang and Ku to call off the encirclement. Otherwise the entire force will be wiped out." Mao sat still.

That same day, Xiang Ying again tried to cable Chiang, again via Mao. That plea too was withheld from the Generalissimo, as Mao revealed to his liaison Chou (on the 13th): "I did not send it on to you . . . This cable must absolutely not be passed on."

On the evening of the 11th Chou was attending a reception in Chongqing to celebrate the third anniversary of the CCP's *New China Daily* when a message arrived from Mao. Chou announced to the assembled throng that N4A HQ had been surrounded and attacked. But even now the telegram Mao sent was not an order to act; it was merely "for your information."

It was only the next day that Mao finally instructed Chou to "make serious representations to have the encirclement called off." But the level of crisis was carefully toned down ("they say they can still hold out for seven days" was a distortion of much more desperate reports days before). Chou did not make any serious protest until the 13th. By that time Chiang had stopped the killing on his own initiative, on the 12th.

On 13 January, after the massacre had ended, Mao suddenly came to life, telling Chou to crank up a PR campaign for a righteous all-out war against Chiang. "Once the decision is made," Mao said, "we will strike all the way to Sichuan [Chiang's base]." "Now it is a matter of a total split . . . of how to overthrow Chiang."

AS HIS ARMY was no match for Chiang's, Mao could not possibly achieve these goals without Stalin's intervention. Chou saw the Russian ambassador on 15 January to impress on him that the Reds needed bailing out. He was given the cold shoulder. In his classified memoirs, Panyushkin recorded his suspicion that Mao had set Xiang Ying up—and that Chou had been lying.*

Mao, meanwhile, appealed directly to Moscow for all-out war against Chiang, with what a Russian intelligence source calls "one hysterical telegram after another," claiming that Chiang's plan was to wipe out first the N4A, then the 8RA, and then "crush the CCP." "There is a danger our army will be completely annihilated," Mao told Moscow.

"Danger of civil war," noted Comintern chief Dimitrov in his diary the day this cable arrived, 16 January, calling the N4A "our troops." Moscow did not believe Mao's claim that Chiang was about to try to

---

* Chou told the Russians that radio links between N4A HQ and Yenan had been broken from the afternoon of *the 13th*—different from the dates Mao gave: 6th–9th. Clearly, Mao's dates would have been bound to arouse suspicion in the Russians.

"annihilate" the CCP, and told Mao so. Mao responded with another alarmist cable, specifically asking that it go "to cde. [comrade] Stalin so that he could weigh the situation in China, and see whether he could not give us concrete military help soon." "Help" meant direct intervention, not just arms and aid. This importuning seems to have annoyed Stalin. At a ceremony for the anniversary of Lenin's death on 21 January, he talked disparagingly about the N4A's nominal commander, Ye Ting, whom the Russians had once considered sending to the gulag, calling him "an undisciplined partisan." "Need to check whether he did not provoke this incident. We, too, had a number of good partisans whom we were obliged to shoot because of their lack of discipline." Dimitrov told Mao again more firmly than before: "Don't take the initiative to break..."

Writing to Stalin, Dimitrov pinned the responsibility on Mao personally: "the Chinese comrades... are thoughtlessly pursuing the split; we have decided... to draw C[omrade] Mao Tse-tung's attention to his incorrect position..." On 13 February, Stalin endorsed Dimitrov's order to the CCP, marked for Mao personally. It was peremptory: "We consider that a split is not unavoidable. You should not strive for a split. On the contrary, you should... do everything possible... to prevent civil war erupting. Please reconsider your current position on this issue..." A cable from Mao that same day toed Moscow's line, but vibrated with determination to get Chiang: "the split," Mao insisted, "is inevitable in the future."

Mao had seen Moscow's decision coming days before. It had greatly depressed him, and led him to write a most unusual letter to his sons in Russia (to whom he very seldom wrote) on 31 January:

> My sons An-ying and An-ching:
>   ... Seeing what progress you have made, I am very happy. An-ying writes well, the Chinese characters are not bad at all, and you have aspiration for achievements: all this is very good. I have only one thing to suggest to you both: while you are young, study natural science more, and talk less politics. Politics needs to be talked about, but at the moment you should set your mind on studying natural science... Only science is real learning, and will have boundless use in the future...

Compared with his previous few rather dry and note-like letters to his sons, this one was long and intimate, even wistful. It reeked of fatigue. What was most extraordinary and absolutely unique was that Mao told his children to avoid politics!

MAO MIGHT HAVE failed to provoke full-scale war against Chiang, but he had won a number of far from negligible victories. Not the least gratifying was the death of his most outspoken critic. Xiang Ying had escaped after Chiang ordered the Nationalist army to stop fighting, but in the small hours of 14 March, while asleep in a mountain cave, he was shot dead by his aide-de-camp, who had turned against the Communists some time before. The aide took the gold and valuables Xiang Ying had in his pockets and gave himself up to the Nationalists.

Two months before Xiang Ying died, when he had just broken out of the death trap, Mao wrote a fierce condemnation of him to senior Party officials, insinuating that Xiang was "an enemy agent." (Even today, Xiang Ying is still often blamed, along with Chiang Kai-shek, for the deaths of the N4A men and women.)

Getting rid of Xiang Ying was only one of Mao's gains. Another was that the N4A was allowed to stay where it was. Chiang was desperate to avoid a total civil war in the middle of the war against Japan. The Russians now put tremendous heat on the Generalissimo not to impede—much less roll back—Red expansion. General Chuikov made an explicit link between Chiang agreeing to fall into line and the continuation of Russian aid to the Nationalists. The Russian ambassador noted how Chiang was beside himself with anger. He "received my statement very nervously," wrote Panyushkin. "He paced up and down the study and . . . I had to repeat my question three times."

Chiang was also highly vulnerable to pressure from America, which was his only hope of freeing himself from dependence on the Russians for arms. US president Franklin Roosevelt, whose overriding concern was (like Stalin's) to get China to do as much fighting against Japan as possible and bog Japan down, had no leverage with the Communists, so he put all the pressure on Chiang, linking the issue of aiding his government with an end to civil conflict—in effect, regardless of who was causing it. In the wake of the N4A incident, US media announced that Washington was discussing withholding a US$50 million loan because of the civil strife. This news came just when American aid could have played a big role, as the air route over the Himalayas, known as "the Hump," opened on 25 January.

Roosevelt leaned heavily for information about China on a private network that included Edgar Snow, largely bypassing the State Department, which he distrusted. His chief private informant on China was a Marine officer called Evans Carlson, who filed starry-eyed reports to the White House lauding the Reds, which Roosevelt recycled uncritically to members of his inner circle, one of whom told him that Carlson's version of events was corroborated by Snow's Red Star. Carlson was in Chongqing at the time of the N4A Incident, and immediately after it he returned to Washington to convey the Reds' version to Roosevelt in person.

Britain did not count as far as aid was concerned, but Chiang aspired to be close to the Anglo-US bloc, and so was susceptible to British pressure. Britain's prime minister Winston Churchill disliked Chiang, regarding him as militarily useless, and a potential menace to British interests in China. The British ambassador, Clark Kerr, told Chiang that in the event of civil war Britain would not support him, regardless of who started the fighting. In the period covering the N4A Incident, his advice to London heavily favored the Communists. He openly said that Chou En-lai was worth all the Nationalists rolled into one.

In the aftermath of the N4A Incident, Moscow organized an immense publicity campaign against Chiang in the West. Communist propaganda claimed that up to 10,000 were massacred. In fact, the total casualty figure was around 2,000. Three thousand had managed to escape back to their own side by turning around and taking the North Route across the Yangtze, the one designated by Chiang. They were unmolested along the way.

Chiang had not set a trap, but he presented his case poorly. His government unwisely announced the disbanding of the N4A, leaving the impression that the Nationalists had intentionally wiped it out. Chiang was also hampered by the fact that he had not protested publicly about the many earlier and much larger clashes in which his troops had been the victims, and had even suppressed news of them, on the grounds that civil strife was bad for domestic morale—and for international aid (which all the foreign powers had made conditional on there being no civil conflict). This silence on the Generalissimo's part had suited the Communists very well. As Red C-in-C Zhu De put it: "They [Nationalists] keep quiet, and we keep quiet, too. They are defeated and keep quiet; we win, so why should we publicise it?" As a result of all these factors, many in the West only knew about the N4A Incident, and saw it as a treacherous large-scale attack by the Nationalists on innocent Reds.

The Communist propaganda machine was effective. In Chongqing, Mao's disinformation symphony was conducted by Chou En-lai, who alone knew Mao's murderous role in the killing of their own men and women in the N4A. This accomplice of Mao's was extremely successful in spreading the lie, thanks to his charm. The American journalist Martha Gellhorn, who met him at this time, told us she would have followed Chou to the ends of the world had he beckoned. But the summing up by her husband, Ernest Hemingway, catches Chou's main attribute: "he does a fine job of selling the Communist standpoint on anything that comes up."

In America, on 22 January the *New York Herald-Tribune* carried a report highly favorable to the Reds' version of events by Edgar Snow, which opened with the words: "The first reliable account of the recent clashes . . ." Yet Snow's account was based entirely on a CCP intelligence man in Hong Kong.

While the Communists' version traveled all over the world, other observations were sidetracked by friends that Moscow and the CCP had in America. Hemingway, who was in China just after the N4A Incident, made some sharp observations about the Reds: "... as good Communists they will attempt to expand their sphere of influence ... no matter what territorial limits they may accept on paper." Thanks to the Reds' "excellent publicity," he wrote, "America has an exaggerated idea of the part they have played in the war against Japan. Their part has been very considerable but that of the Central Government troops has been a hundred times greater." "Communists," Hemingway noted, "in my experience in Spain, always try to give the impression that they are the only ones who really fight."

Given Hemingway's name, his assessment might have made a considerable impact on public opinion, but it did not see the light of day until 1965. He was dissuaded from publishing his views in 1941 by a Roosevelt aide called Lauchlin Currie, who told him "our policy was to discourage civil war."

Currie, chief White House economic adviser, visited China right after the N4A Incident. US intercepts of Soviet intelligence traffic (Venona) name Currie as helping the Russians, and some consider that he was a Soviet agent. A judicious recent study of Roosevelt and intelligence describes Currie as "a manipulable sympathizer," concluding that he was not a spy, but a "friend" of the Russians in the White House. On this trip to China, he certainly did the Reds sterling service. In Chongqing, he told Chiang that he had brought a verbal message from Roosevelt (as well as a written one). Currie opened the verbal message with this sentence: "It appears at ten thousand miles away that the Chinese Communists are what in our country we would call socialists. We like their attitude towards the peasants, towards women and towards Japan."

In his report to Roosevelt, Currie mainly spoke ill of Chiang, and painted an extremely rosy picture of the Reds. He claimed that "the Communists have been the only party which has been able to attract mass support," suggesting that this was the reason they had expanded. Currie gave Roosevelt the Communists' version of the N4A crisis.*

International pressure on Chiang was so strong that on 29 January he

---

* Another thing Currie did which was to Mao's great advantage was to thwart Chiang's attempt to establish a sympathetic channel to Roosevelt. Chiang requested Currie to ask Roosevelt to send him a political adviser who had access to the president. Chiang named his own choice, William Bullitt, the first US ambassador to the Soviet Union, whom Chiang knew personally, and knew to be anti-Communist. Currie rejected Chiang's request outright, off his own bat, and there is no sign he even told Roosevelt that Chiang wanted Bullitt. When Currie got back to America, he recommended an academic, Owen Lattimore, who had not even met Roosevelt, much less had the sort of access to the President that Chiang had specified. The upshot was that Currie had a tight grip on communications between Chiang and Roosevelt.

told his ambassador in Moscow to ask the Kremlin to intervene to help resolve the crisis with the Reds, effectively asking the Russians to dictate terms. Three days later, a jubilant Mao told his army chiefs: "No matter how hard Chiang Kai-shek tries to rebel, he can try this and that, but in the end will only get himself toppled." Mao was using the word "rebel" as if Chiang were the outlaw and he himself already on the throne. Chiang acceded to Russian demands to let Mao's men hang on to their territorial gains and stay in the heartland of China near Nanjing and Shanghai.

Mao had been quick to see how helpful Western journalists like Snow could be to his cause, but slow to appreciate how useful the British and American governments could be in tying Chiang's hands. His hostility to both states had been extreme. On 25 October 1940 he had told his top brass how he hoped Britain could be occupied by the Nazis, and the Japanese would continue to occupy China: "the most difficult, most dangerous and darkest scenario," he said, was Chiang "joining the Anglo-US bloc":

We must envisage this: that the Japanese are unable to take Singapore . . . which will be taken by the US navy; London does not fall . . . Japan surrenders to America; Japanese army leaves China; America finances and arms the pro-Anglo-American Chinese . . . It can't be darker than this.

This scenario was to Mao worse than Japanese occupation. But all of a sudden there was a spectacular change in his attitude. On 6 November he wrote to Chou En-lai: "I have this morning just read the important intelligence in your cable of the 3rd. So Chiang joining the Anglo-US bloc is only to our advantage . . . Let us oppose this no more . . . We must forge more links with Britain and America . . ."

Chou En-lai had clearly enlightened Mao about how useful the West could be to him. From now on, Chou devoted more energy to cultivating Westerners, particularly Americans. And his charm offensive intensified after the Japanese attacked Pearl Harbor in December 1941 and America's presence in China greatly increased.

ON 13 APRIL 1941 Russia signed a Neutrality Pact with Japan, which freed large numbers of Japanese troops to attack Southeast Asia and Pearl Harbor. But it did not include a carve-up of China between Russia and Japan. Mao did not get his Poland scenario.

BUILDING A POWER
BASE THROUGH TERROR
(1941–45 ★ AGE 47–51)

ON 22 JUNE 1941 Germany invaded the Soviet Union. This event radically altered Mao's calculus. Soviet Russia was his sponsor and his hope; a seriously weakened—or diverted—Russia was unlikely to offer much help. Mao could not sleep for days.*

To start with, there was absolutely no chance now that Russia would step in and bail him out if fighting with Chiang's troops turned perilous. Mao immediately halted attacks. "Stop any assaults on all Nationalist units," he ordered his armies.

Self-preservation dominated his relationship with newly weakened Russia. As a result of the German invasion, Moscow wanted the CCP to commit to engage militarily with Japanese troops if Japan should attack the Soviet Union. Stalin's nightmare was a giant pincer assault by Japan from the east coordinated with Hitler's attack from the west. How many Japanese troops could the CCP "divert" if that happened? Moscow asked Mao. To encourage Mao to act, Dimitrov cabled on 7 July that he was sending US$1 million in installments. Two days later, the Comintern told the CCP to draw up "concrete steps."

Most of Mao's colleagues thought they should take some action if Tokyo invaded the Soviet Union. The normally circumspect Liu Shao-chi wrote to Mao that if Japan attacked Russia, the CCP must launch offensives to tie up Japanese forces. Mao, however, was determined not to risk troops under any circumstances. On 18 July he told Liu that if Japan attacked Russia (which Mao had said on 2 July was "extremely likely"): "It is not

---

* Mao knew the German invasion was coming, and when, to within a matter of hours, and had alerted the Kremlin. Comintern chief Dimitrov records in his diary the tip-off from the CCP saying: "Germany will attack the USSR...the date—21 June 1941!" (bold in Dimitrov original). This is the only such warning singled out. This information had been acquired by CCP moles. When the Germans did invade on the 22nd, the Kremlin belatedly acknowledged the CCP's help, although it seems it discounted the warning.

a good idea ... to undertake large-scale action ... our armies are weak. Action will inevitably do irreparable damage." His approach was to let the Russians do the fighting: "Everything depends on victory by the Soviet Union."

Mao spelled this out to Peng De-huai, the acting commander of the 8th Route Army. Any coordination with the Russians was to be purely "strategic [i.e., in name only] and long-term—not in battles." To his troops Mao repeatedly cautioned: "Do not excessively upset the [Japanese] enemy."

To Moscow, Mao protested that his forces were too weak to be counted on: "our human and material resources [are diminishing], regions of oper-ation [are contracting], ammunition is running out—and the situation is becoming more difficult by the day." If his army acted, Mao argued, "there is a possibility that we will be defeated and will not be able to defend our partisan bases for long ... Such an action will not be good for either of us ..." He told Moscow not to expect much: "if Japan attacks the Soviet Union, our abilities in terms of coordinating military operations will not be great."

Mao virtually admitted that his army had not been fighting the Japanese and would not start now. Only recently he had been telling Moscow he had a huge army, with 329,899 men in the 8RA alone; now he was saying his troops could hardly fire a shot.

Stalin personally cabled Mao several times asking him to keep the Japanese occupied, when the Germans were at the gates of Moscow in late 1941 and just before the battle of Stalingrad, in July 1942—in vain. Mao's refusal to help infuriated Moscow, and he further riled his patrons by advising them to retreat to the Urals and fight a guerrilla war. Some Russians claim that Mao's behavior was also motivated by lack of confi-dence in the Soviet Union, and even (according to General Chuikov) by the desire to exploit Hitler's attack to supplant Russia. Word got around that Mao said: "Stalin cannot beat Hitler" and "24-year-old socialism cannot compete with eight-year-old fascism."

Years later, Molotov was asked: "We knew [what Mao was doing to us] and we still helped Mao?" To which Molotov mumbled: "Right. Yes, yes. I know that is hard for you to understand. But you must not look at things in such a stark way." "We looked like fools, but, in my opinion, we were not fools."

Indeed, even though they were at odds, Stalin and Mao understood each other perfectly. Their relationship was based on brutal self-interest and mutual use, and they shared the same long-term goals. However much Mao's actions displeased the Kremlin, Stalin never for one moment ceased doing business with him.

★

WITH NO FIGHTING against either the Japanese or the Nationalists, and with Russia in trouble and in no position to intervene, Mao seized the opportunity to go to work on his Party and mold it into an unquestioning machine in preparation for the forthcoming all-out civil war against Chiang Kai-shek.

By late 1941, Party membership had grown to some 700,000. Over 90 percent of these were people who had joined up since the start of the war against Japan, and many were young enthusiasts who had come to the Communist bases from Nationalist areas. These young volunteers were vital to Mao because they were relatively well educated, and he needed competent administrators to staff his future regime. Most of the Long Marchers and rural recruits from within the Communist bases were illiterate peasants. It was the young volunteers who were Mao's target.

These volunteers had almost all joined up in the late 1930s as the mood among the younger middle class swung significantly to the left. This was a time when Red Russia was China's main—and virtually only—ally and supplier of arms against Japan. Goodwill towards Russia rubbed off on the CCP. Many thought the Chinese Communists were truly dedicated to fighting Japan.

There was also widespread disenchantment with the Nationalists, who were seen as incapable of eradicating China's widespread poverty and injustice. The CCP's atrocities before the Long March were either unknown or forgotten, or dismissed as Nationalist propaganda. Some also believed the Party when it proclaimed that it had changed, and abandoned its old policies. And for a while the Communists' behavior seemed to confirm that this change was real. Many foreigners, and even some missionaries, accepted Red claims. The mole Shao Li-tzu, the Nationalists' media overlord during the crucial period 1937–38, did much to erase the Party's bloody past and project a benign image of the Reds. So too did Edgar Snow's *Red Star Over China*. Mao assiduously peddled the line that the Communists had been slandered. The CCP "has always been pretty," he told a group of new arrivals in Yenan; "it is just that it was painted badly..."

A large number of the young volunteers congregated in Yenan, Mao's capital. By the time Mao started his drive to condition them, some 40,000 had come there. Most were people in their late teens and early twenties who had joined the Party in the Nationalist areas, and then been sent on to Yenan.

They were tremendously excited when they first reached what had been portrayed as a revolutionary Mecca. One young volunteer described his feelings when he arrived: "At last we saw the heights of Yenan city.

We were so excited we wept. We cheered from our truck . . . We started to sing the 'Internationale,' and Russia's Motherland March."

The new arrivals, he wrote, "really envied the stinking and dirty worn-out padded uniforms [of the veterans]. They found everything fresh, exciting and mysterious."

The newcomers were mostly enrolled in various "schools" and "institutes" to be trained—and indoctrinated. But most very soon became disillusioned. The biggest letdown was that equality, the core of their idealism, was not only completely absent, but manifestly rejected by the regime. Inequality and privilege were ubiquitous. Every organization had three different levels of kitchen. The lowliest got roughly half the amount of meat and cooking oil allotted to middle-rankers, while the elite got much more. The very top leaders received special nutritious foods.

Likewise with clothes. The locally produced cotton was rough and uncomfortable, so softer cotton was imported for senior cadres. Mao, outwardly, dressed the same as the rest, but his underwear was made of fine material, as a servant who washed and mended for the Maos told us. The maid did not qualify for any underwear or socks at all, and kept getting colds as a result. Items like tobacco, candles and writing paper were similarly allocated by rank.

Children of the topmost leaders were sent to Russia, or had nannies of their own. Wives of senior cadres could expect to give birth in a hospital, and then have a personal nurse for a while. Officials on the next rungs down could send their children to an elite nursery. The relatively small number of ordinary Communists who were married either tended not to have children, or had to struggle if they did.

Spartan conditions and poor food led to many illnesses, but only high officials had access to scarce medicines, which were imported specially from Nationalist areas. Mao had a personal doctor from America, George Hatem, as well as Russian doctors. When he needed something—or somebody (like a physiotherapist)—he asked Moscow, or Chou En-lai in Chongqing. Senior cadres were given special hospital treatment, and no one could get into a hospital without authorization from their work unit. Food was graded in hospitals, too.

At the beginning of the Sino-Japanese War there was a Red Cross team in Yenan, which had been sent by the Nationalists. It treated local residents as well as average Communists. But the regime set about driving it away. Rumors were put about that its medicines were poisonous, and that it had been "sent by the Nationalists to murder our comrades! And to poison our drinking water, to spread germs!" Most of the team soon left. The rest were forcibly kept behind, mainly to minister to the Red elite.

The ultimate symbol of privilege in Yenan was highly visible—the only car, in fact an ambulance, which was a present from Chinese laundry workers in New York for carrying war wounded. But it never transported one injured soldier. Mao "privatised" it. It transported his guests as well, including Edgar Snow in 1939. Snow was blasé about it: "So this was Mao's extravagance that had shocked my missionary friend," he wrote, asserting that it was one of "a number of these laundrymen's gifts [which] had accumulated in Yenan, where sometimes they were used to carry civilian air-raid victims to near-by hospitals." In fact, it was the only car, and never carried any civilian wounded—and was known, appropriately, as "Chairman Mao's car." Even people near the top thought Mme Sun Yat-sen had given the car to Mao "for his personal use."

Many were extremely put out. One young volunteer saw Mao in the car in spring 1939, driving with his wife, who sported "a dark red spring outfit. She and Mao Tse-tung raced by, drawing a lot of attention, and the passersby looked askance at the couple."

Mao was well aware that his privileges were a sore point. One day an old devotee came to dine. Afterwards, Mao invited her to come back often, whereupon she blurted out: "So I"ll come to you every Sunday to treat myself to a good meal!" She noticed that "the Chairman's smile froze, and he looked a bit awkward. I knew I had said the wrong thing..."

The Party tried to make a case for privilege: "it is not the leading comrades who ask for privilege themselves," one leading ideologue opined. "It is the order of the Party. Take Chairman Mao, for example: the Party can order him to eat a chicken a day."

This sophistry failed to dissipate the widespread discontent. One crack doing the rounds went: "In Yenan, only three things are equal to all— the sun, the air and the toilets." The privilege system even extended to the group of Japanese Communists and POWs. The only one of them officially allowed to have sex was their leader, Sanzo Nosaka. "Mao wanted to keep him in a good mood," a former Japanese POW in Yenan told us, "so he gave him a woman comrade to keep him company...we didn't complain—not openly—people did have complaints, but they kept them to their own hearts."

NO MATTER HOW disillusioned they might feel, the young volunteers realized that they could not leave Yenan: trying to leave was treated as desertion, with execution a distinct likelihood. The Yenan region was run like a prison. The rest of China, including other Red bases, was called "the Outside." One volunteer described a scene he witnessed in a hospital. "We are not ill, why send us here?" two men were shouting. Their accents showed they were Long Marchers from Jiangxi. They were struggling and being pinned down by armed men.

"We've been asking for leave to go home to see our families, but we just don't get the permission. They insisted we were crazy, and sent us here."

The men wore the Long March veterans' medal. One cadre said: "Comrades, please remember your glorious revolutionary history!"

"Fart of use this thing. We were dead and wounded plenty of times. All we get is others become officials, and have good things to eat and wear. What's in it for us? It's better to go home and work on the land."

"Ha, it seems you are not crazy. You are just wavering in your revolutionary stand."

The eyewitness noticed that "among cadres in Yenan, old and new, homesickness was common." Cadres of peasant origin "often asked straight out to go home, and were stopped by their superiors. Some tried to run away, and once caught were immediately executed. The educated were much cleverer. They wouldn't say they wanted to go home, they would make up some story and ask the Party to transfer them Out . . ."

Escape was easier for army men on the border of the region—and the rate of desertion was colossal. The target of one brigade alone, as of 29 September 1943, was to catch *one thousand* of its own deserters. But in the heart of the Red area, escape was virtually impossible, and most young volunteers just willed themselves to settle down.

THESE WERE THE people Mao had to depend on for his future power base. And to that end they were clearly poor material. They had come to Yenan for a dream. To make them fight for the real CCP, Mao would have to change them fundamentally, to remold them. This enormous human engineering project Mao began from early 1942.* His first step was to strike at the champion of the young volunteers, a 35-year-old writer called Wang Shi-wei, a dedicated Communist who had translated Engels and Trotsky. An essay by him called "Wild Lilies," which was published in the main newspaper in Yenan, *Liberation Daily*, caught Mao's attention. In the first installment on 13 March, Shi-wei wrote:

> Young people in Yenan seem to have lost steam in their life lately, and seem to have discontent in their stomachs. Why? What do we lack in our life? Some might answer: we lack nutrition, we lack vitamins . . . Others say: the male–female ratio in Yenan is 18 to 1, and many young men cannot find a wife . . . Still others will say: life in Yenan is too monotonous, too drab . . .
>
> These answers are not unreasonable. But . . . young people . . . have come here to be in the revolution, and they are committed to self-sacrifice. They have not come to seek the satisfactions of food and sex or the pleasures of life.

* This project is known as *zheng-feng*, usually translated as "Rectification Campaign."

What had shattered their dreams, he said, was institutionalized privilege, accompanied by high-handedness and arrogance. He quoted a
conversation he had overheard between two young women about their
bosses:

> He's always accusing you of petty bourgeois egalitarianism. Yet he
> himself . . . only looks out for his own privileges . . . and is completely
> indifferent to comrades under his charge . . . !
>   All fine words—class friendship and warmth. And it all boils down
> to—fart! They don't have even elementary human sympathy! . . . There
> are just too damn few cadres who really care about us.

In the second installment ten days later, Shi-wei sharpened his key
points:

> Some say there is no system of hierarchy and privilege in Yenan. This
> is not true. It exists. Others say, yes, there is, but it is justified. This
> requires us to think with our heads.

SHI-WEI WAS calling on people to think for themselves. Moreover,
his arguments were reasonable and eloquent:

> I am no egalitarian. But I do not think it is necessary or justified to
> have multiple grades in food or clothing . . . If, while the sick can't even
> have a sip of noodle soup . . . some quite healthy big shots are indulging
> in extremely unnecessary and unjustified perks, the lower ranks will
> be alienated . . .

When Mao read this, he slammed the newspaper on his desk and
demanded angrily: "Who is in charge here? Wang Shi-wei, or Marxism?"
He picked up the phone and ordered a shake-up at *Liberation Daily*.

Shi-wei put some even sharper thoughts in a wall poster. Mao had
tolerated these as a safety-valve for the young intellectuals. Wall posters
had the advantage (for him) of having a restricted audience—and were
easily torn down or erased. Shi-wei's poster proclaimed: "Justice must be
established in the Party. Injustice must be done away with . . . Ask yourselves, comrades . . . Are you scared of telling the 'big shots' what's on your
mind . . . ? Or are you the kind that is good at persecuting the 'little men'
with trumped-up crimes?" Shi-wei went far beyond the issue of privilege, to the heart of darkness in the Party.

The poster with Shi-wei's words was hoisted outside the South Gate,
the busiest place in the city. People flocked to read these few sentences,
which articulated what many wanted to say but did not dare. Shi-wei
became a hero.

One night, Mao crossed the river to read the poster by the light of a
barn lantern. There he saw the eager crowds and registered Shi-wei's

enormous popularity. He said at once: "I now have a target." He later complained: "Many people rushed from far away to . . . read his article. But no one wants to read mine!" "Wang Shi-wei was the king and lord master . . . he was in command in Yenan . . . and we were defeated . . ."

Mao decided to condemn Shi-wei as a way of scaring his sympathizers, the young volunteers. As he could not confront Shi-wei's points head-on, he denounced him as a Trotskyist. Some remarks that Shi-wei had made in private about Trotsky and Stalin were made public. Trotsky, Shi-wei had said, was "a genius," while Stalin was "an unloveable person" who had "created untold countless evils" in the purges. The Moscow Trials he described as "dubious." Shi-wei was sent to prison. He spent the last years of his short life in solitary, where he was subjected to crushing pressure. In 1944, when some journalists from the Nationalist areas were allowed into Yenan, he was wheeled out to meet them and produced a robotic confession. "He said over and over again: 'I'm a Trotskyite. I attacked Mao. I deserve to be executed . . . But Mao is so magnanimous . . . I am extremely grateful for his mercy.' " One reporter observed: "When he mentioned his past 'mistakes,' his expression was severe to the point of frightening . . . In my observation, his mind had been badly disturbed . . ."

His interrogator later revealed the background: "He said what he was told to say. Of course, he had no option. Afterwards, he lay in bed in great anguish. He clenched his fists and showed extreme bitterness." When the Communists evacuated Yenan in 1947, he was taken along— and executed en route. One night he was hacked to death, and thrown into a dry well. He was forty-one.

AFTER MAO DESIGNATED Shi-wei as his prime target, meetings were held throughout the rest of 1942, at which the young volunteers were told to denounce him. Mao noticed that they expressed a lot of resistance. They were not sufficiently scared. He had to find another way to terrorize them.

So Mao and his KGB chief Kang Sheng devised a blanket accusation—that the vast majority of Communist organizations in the Nationalist areas were spy rings working for Chiang Kai-shek. This assertion turned virtually all the young volunteers into spy suspects, because they had either belonged to one of these organizations, or had come to Yenan under their auspices. To back this accusation there was one single piece of "evidence"—the confession of a nineteen-year-old volunteer who had been deprived of sleep and worked over by the security forces for seven days and nights, at the end of which he produced what he was told to say.

By deploying this charge, Mao found a way to place all the young volunteers in Yenan in one form of confinement or another for "screening," starting in April 1943. Thousands were arrested and thrown into prison-caves newly carved out of the loess hillsides. In one prison alone, in the ravine behind the Date Garden—the site of the Chinese KGB, where Mao also lived—cells were dug for over 3,000 prisoners. Most of the rest were detained in their own institutions, which now became virtual prisons, sealed off and patrolled by guards. Mao gave orders that every organization must "place sentries and impose a curfew. Ban visitors and freedom of movement in or out." The roles of jailers and interrogators were filled by those in each institution who were not suspects. These were mainly people who had not come from Nationalist areas, who were often a minority of the personnel, sometimes as few as 10–20 percent in any given institution.

Turning ordinary organizations into virtual prisons was a significant innovation of Mao's, which he was to apply throughout his rule. Here he went far beyond anything either Hitler or Stalin achieved: he converted people's colleagues into their jailers, with former colleagues, prisoners and jailers living in the same premises. (In Communist China, people's workplaces and living quarters were often the same.) In this way, Mao not only drove a massive wedge between people working and living side by side, he greatly enlarged the number of people directly involved in repression, including torture, making the orbit significantly wider than either Stalin or Hitler, who mostly used secret elites (KGB, Gestapo) that held their victims in separate and unseen locales.

In incarceration, the young volunteers came under tremendous pressure to confess to being spies, and to denounce others—not really in order to find spies, but for the sake of inducing terror. Genuine spy-hunting was conducted secretly all the time by the security forces, using conventional methods. Any real suspects were "taken care of without fuss," Mao's security assistant Shi Zhe told us, which often meant a speedy, secret and noiseless execution.*

The fake spy-hunting created the excuse for torture. Sleep deprivation was the standard technique, sometimes lasting as long as two weeks on end. There were also old-fashioned tortures like whipping, hanging by the wrists, and wrenching people's knees to breaking point (the "tiger-bench"); as well as psychological torment—from the threat of having poisonous snakes put in one's cave to mock execution. At night, amid the quiet of the hills, from inside the rows of caves screams of lacerating pain traveled far and wide, within earshot of most who lived in Yenan.

---

* Executions sometimes served other functions. Shi Zhe recounted visiting a hospital where he was shown a big basin: "inside was a male corpse, aged about thirty, soaked in formaldehyde." Hospital staff told him they had needed corpses for dissection, and "Kang Sheng authorised us" to kill three "counter-revolutionaries" for medical purposes.

Mao personally gave instructions about torture (which the regime euphemistically called *bi-gong-xin*, meaning use "force" to produce a "confession," which then provides "reliable evidence"): "it is not good to correct it too early or too late," he decreed on 15 August 1943. "Too early . . . the campaign cannot unfold properly; and too late . . . the damage [to torture victims] will be too profound. So the principle should be to watch meticulously and correct at the appropriate time." Mao wanted his victims to be in good enough shape to serve his purposes.

For month after month, life in Yenan centered on interrogations—and terrifying mass rallies, at which some young volunteers were forced to confess to being spies and to name others in front of large crowds who had been whipped into a frenzy. People who were named were then hoisted onto the platform and pressed to admit their guilt. Those who stuck to their innocence were trussed up on the spot and dragged away to prison, and some to mock execution, amidst hysterical slogan-screaming. The fear generated by these rallies was unbearable. A close colleague of Mao's remarked at the time that the rallies were "an extremely grave war on nerves. To some people, they are more devastating than any kind of torture."

Outside the interrogations and rallies, people were pounded flat at indoctrination meetings.* All forms of relaxation, like singing and dancing, were stopped. The only moments alone afforded no peace either, consumed as they were in writing "thought examinations"—a practice hitherto known only in fascist Japan. "Get everybody to write their thought examination," Mao ordered, "and write three times, five times, again and again . . . Tell everyone to spill out every single thing they have ever harboured that is not so good for the Party." In addition, everybody was told to write down information passed unofficially by other people— termed "small broadcasts" by the regime. "You had to write down what X or Y had said," one Yenan veteran told us, "as well as what you yourself had said which was supposed to be not so good. You had to dig into your memory endlessly and write endlessly. It was most loathsome." The criteria for "not so good" were kept deliberately vague, so that out of fear, people would err on the side of including more.

Many tried to resist. But any sign of doing so was considered "proof" that the person resisting was a spy, on the specious grounds that: "If you are innocent, there should be nothing that cannot be reported to the Party." The concept of privacy could not be evoked, because a Communist was required to reject the private. One man at the Administration College, which was the place where aversion was most outspoken, took a small but brave step to protest by quipping: "Do we have to write down our

---

* Using exhausting meetings to bend—and break—people was to solidify into an integral part of Mao's rule.

pillow talk with our wives at night?," which aroused chuckles all round. Naturally, the man and most others there were "found" to be spies. "Apart from one [*sic*] person, all teachers and administration staff are spies" in this college, Mao announced on 8 August 1943, and "many of the students are spies, too, probably more than half." Under this kind of pressure, one man wrote down no fewer than 800 items of conversation in a frantic attempt to get off the hook.

Through forcing people to report "small broadcasts," Mao succeeded to a very large extent in getting people to inform on each other. He thus broke trust between people, and scared them off exchanging views not just at the time in Yenan, but in the future too. By suppressing "small broadcasts," he also plugged what was virtually the only unofficial source of information, in a context where he completely controlled all other channels. No outside press was available, and no one had access to a radio. Nor could letters be exchanged with the outside world, including one's family: any communication from a Nationalist area was evidence of espionage. Information starvation gradually induced brain death—assisted vastly by the absence of any outlet for thinking, since one could not communicate with anyone, or put one's thoughts on paper, even privately. During the campaign, people were put under pressure to hand in their diaries. In many a mind, there also lurked the fear of thinking, which appeared not only futile but also dangerous. Independent thinking withered away.

Two years of this type of indoctrination and terror turned the lively young volunteers from passionate exponents of justice and equality into robots. When outside journalists were allowed into Yenan for the first time after many years in June 1944, a Chongqing correspondent observed an eerie uniformity: "if you ask the same question of twenty or thirty people, from intellectuals to workers [on any topic] their replies are always more or less the same . . . Even questions about love, there seems to be a point of view that has been decided by meetings." And, not surprisingly, "they unanimously and firmly deny the Party had any direct control over their thoughts."

The journalist felt "stifled" by "the air of nervous intensity." "Most people," he noticed, "had very earnest faces and serious expressions. Among the big chiefs, apart from Mr. Mao Tse-tung who often has a sense of humour, and Mr. Chou En-lai who is very good at chatting, the others rarely crack a joke." Helen Snow, wife of Edgar Snow, told us that in 1937, when she was in Yenan, people could still say things like "There goes God" behind Mao's back. But seven years on, no one dared to say anything remotely so flippant. Mao had not only banned irony and satire (officially, since spring 1942), but criminalized humor itself. The regime invented a new catch-all offense—"Speaking Weird Words"—under which anything from skepticism to complaining to simply wise-cracking could lead to being labeled a spy.

Mao had decided that he did not want active, willing cooperation (willingness, after all, could be withdrawn). He did not want volunteers. He needed a machine, so that when he pressed the button, all its cogs would operate in unison. And he got it.

BY EARLY 1944 Russia was on the offensive against Germany, and Mao could look to it entering the war against Japan. After Japan was defeated, Mao would need cadres to fight Chiang Kai-shek, so he now began to tone down the terror.

The victims remained locked up, still living in uncertainty and torment, while the security forces began to examine their cases, to see whether there were any genuine spy suspects at all from among the mountains of coerced confessions—a process that was predictably long and slow. But one thing the apparatus was sure of from the start: that true spy suspects were far less than 1 percent of the young volunteers.

At this time, Mao ordered other Red bases to start their spy-hunting, replicating the Yenan model. He specifically warned them not to get into examining individual cases just because Yenan was doing so. All must go through the full cycle of terrorization. To spur them to whip up the same kind of frenzy as in Yenan, Mao inflated his KGB's estimate of the proportion of spy suspects from 1 percent to 10 percent, claiming, falsely, that Yenan had uncovered a plethora of spies through his method.

It was not until another year elapsed, in spring 1945, that Mao ordered a wholesale rehabilitation of the victims. By then, he knew that Russia would be entering the war against Japan; soon he would be fighting for control of all of China, and he needed cadres fast.

The young volunteers, who numbered many tens of thousands in Yenan alone, had been through a hell of mental confusion and anguish. There had been many breakdowns—some lifelong. People who lived through Yenan remembered seeing caves in valleys crammed with people "many of whom had gone mad. Some were laughing wildly, some crying," producing "screams and howls like wolves every night."

The number who perished could be in the thousands. For many, suicide was the only way to end their ordeal. Some jumped off cliffs, others into wells. Those with children and spouses often killed them first. Repeat attempts were common: one physics teacher failed when he swallowed match heads (which were poisonous), then hanged himself, successfully. Survivors of suicide attempts were hounded mercilessly. One who had swallowed broken glass was brought back to life and immediately told to "write self-criticisms."

Suicide was sometimes also used as a way to stage a protest—in one case becoming a double protest. When one detainee killed himself by jumping off a cliff, his classmates buried him opposite the residence of his interrogators, one of whom registered the import of the gesture: the ghost will come back to haunt you!

As one official put it in a letter to the leadership in March 1945, the young volunteers had been dealt "a heavy blow to their revolutionary enthusiasm . . . the wounds carved in their minds and hearts are very deep indeed." All the same, Mao was confident he could rely on these people to serve him. However unhappy they might be, they were trapped in the Communist organization, and it was extraordinarily hard for them to leave, psychologically as well as physically. In the absence of options, many fell back on their faith, which made it easier for them to rationalize sacrifice. Mao adroitly exploited their idealism, convincing them to accept their maltreatment as part of "Serving the People" (a snappy expression he coined now, and which later acquired fame), and as a noble experience, soul-cleansing for the mission of saving China.

To defuse the bitterness that clung on in many hearts, Mao performed a few public "apologies" in spring 1945 before he sent his victims to the front to battle Chiang Kai-shek. What he typically did was to take off his cap and bow or salute his audience. But he would carefully present his apology as generously taking responsibility for others ("On behalf of the Centre, I apologise . . ."), and spread the blame—even to the victims themselves. "The whole of Yenan committed mistakes," he averred. "The intention was to give you a nice bath, but too much potassium permanganate [used to kill lice] was put in, and your delicate skin was hurt." This last remark implied that the victims had been too pampered and were easily hurt. Sophistry flowed liberally from Mao's lips: "We were fighting the enemy in the dark, and so wounded our own people." Or even: "It was like a father beating his sons. So please don't bear grudges." "Please just get up, dust the mud off your clothes and fight on."

At such moments, the audiences were usually in tears, tears which were a mixture of resignation and of relief. Most went on fighting for a system that had cruelly wronged them. After they had helped Mao come to power, they would function as part of the machine that ground down the entire population of China. Mao built this machine not through inspiration or magnetism, but fundamentally through terror.

During what can be called the Yenan Terror, the whole Party was worked over, even those members who did not become outright victims themselves. These were invariably coerced into denouncing others— colleagues, friends, even spouses—which caused lasting trauma to themselves as well as to the victims. Everyone who attended a rally witnessed haunting sights, involving people they knew, and lived with the fear that the next victim might be oneself. The relentless invasion of privacy, being forced to write endless "thought examinations," brought further stress. Mao was to say over a decade later that he did not just stamp on 80 percent of the Party—"it was in fact 100 percent, and by force, too."

MAO NOW HAD in his hands a formidable tool for use against Chiang Kai-shek. One supreme accomplishment of the terror campaign was to squeeze out every drop of information about any link whatever with the Nationalists. Mao introduced a special "Social Relationship" form: "Tell everyone to write down *every single social relationship* of any kind [our italics]." At the end of the campaign, the regime compiled a dossier on every Party member. The result was that Mao knew every channel the Nationalists might use to infiltrate in the forthcoming showdown. Indeed, during the civil war, while the Nationalists were penetrated like sieves, they had virtually zero success infiltrating the Communists. Mao had forged a machine that was virtually watertight.

Mao also prepared a "no-questions-asked" anti-Chiang force by fomenting hatred of Chiang. When most of the young volunteers joined up, the CCP was not at war with the Nationalists, and many did not hate Chiang the way Mao wanted them to. As Mao said, "Some people think the Nationalist Party is very good, very pretty." One senior official noted at the time that "new cadres cherish extremely big illusions about Chiang, while old cadres have weakened their class hatred" for the Generalissimo. Chiang was the undisputed leader of China's war against Japan. It was Chiang who got America and Britain to retrocede their territorial concessions (except Hong Kong) in 1943—an historic event for which even Mao felt obliged to order grand celebrations. And it was under Chiang that China was accepted as one of "the Big Four," along with America, Russia and Britain. China's permanent seat and veto on the UN Security Council, which Mao eventually inherited, were acquired thanks to Chiang.

At the time, Chiang was generally regarded as the nation-builder of modern China, who had done away with the warlords and unified the country—and led the war against Japan. Mao had to smash this image. In the terror campaign, he ordered the Party to be "re-educated" on the question: "Who is the nation-builder of China: the Nationalists or the CCP?" The corollary of the drive to break Chiang's image was to create the myth that Mao was the founder of modern China.

Mao manufactured the fault-lines and hate-lines against Chiang through his "spy hunt" campaign, in which it was spying for the Nationalists, not for the Japanese, that was made the key issue, sometimes identifying the Nationalists with the Japanese by vague assimilation. It was via the terror campaign that Mao turned Chiang into *the* enemy of the average Communist.

*

TO STIR UP anti-Chiang fervor in the CCP, Mao cogitated another "massacre" by the Nationalists like the one involving the New 4th Army HQ two years before. This time the sacrificial victims included his only surviving brother, Tse-min.

Tse-min had been working in Xinjiang, in the far northwest, which had been a Russian satellite for years. In 1942 the warlord there turned against the Reds. Sensing that their lives were in danger, Tse-min and the other regional CCP leaders cabled Mao repeatedly asking to be evacuated. But they were told to stay put. In early 1943, Tse-min and more than 140 other Communists and their families, including his wife and son, and a girl Mao had called his "daughter," Si-qi (Mao's future daughter-in-law), were imprisoned.

As the warlord had gone over to Chongqing, the obvious thing to do was for the CCP's liaison, Chou En-lai, to ask for their release from the Nationalist government, which is what the Russians urged Chou to do. The CCP leadership collectively (in the name of the Secretariat) also asked Chou to do this on 10 February. Two days later, on the 12th, Mao sent Chou a separate cable, signed only by him, with the agenda for talks with the Nationalists; the release of the Xinjiang group was not on it. Chou, by now taking orders from Mao alone, did not raise the matter of the Xinjiang group in his many meetings with the Nationalists.

Lin Biao was in Chongqing at the time, and on 16 June he got to a meeting with Russian ambassador Panyushkin ahead of Chou, and told Panyushkin that Chou had not done anything, and that "orders" had come from "Yenan." When Chou turned up, he started claiming he had written to Chiang some three months before, but had had no reply. At this point, Panyushkin reported to Moscow, Lin Biao "sat hanging his head." Chou was obviously lying. In fact, Chou and Lin had seen Chiang only days before, on the 7th, when Chiang had been friendly and Chou had said nothing about his imprisoned comrades in Xinjiang.

The upshot was that Mao's brother Tse-min and two other senior CCP figures were executed on 27 September on charges of plotting a coup. But with so few deaths—only three—Mao was unable to cry "Massacre." He did not make any announcement condemning the executions, either, as this might raise questions about whether the Communists were indeed guilty as charged.* For years, Tse-min's death remained a public non-event.

---

* The other detainees, including Tse-min's wife and their son Yuan-xin, were released later, with the Generalissimo's authorization.

UNCOWED OPPONENT POISONED

(1941–45 ★ AGE 47–51)

WHILE USING terror to turn ordinary Party members into cogs for his machine, Mao also went to work on his top colleagues. His aim was to break them and make them kowtow, with the ultimate goal of establishing himself as their undisputed leader, so that he would never have to rely on Moscow's blessing again. He picked the time when Stalin was preoccupied with the war against Germany.

In autumn 1941, Mao convened a series of Politburo meetings at which all those who had opposed him in the past in any way had to make groveling self-condemnations and pledge loyalty to him. Most did so meekly, including nominal Party chief Lo Fu, and former Party No. 1 Po Ku, the man who had reduced Mao to a figurehead before the Long March.* (Chou En-lai was away in Chongqing.) But one top figure in Yenan refused to crawl: this was Wang Ming, the man who had been the main threat to Mao since his return from Moscow late in 1937.

After the German invasion of Russia, Wang Ming figured that Stalin was bound to be displeased with Mao's refusal to take action against Japan to help the Soviet Union. In October 1941 he caught sight of a cable from Comintern chief Dimitrov to Mao posing fifteen extremely stern questions, including: What measures is the CCP adopting to strike at the Japanese army so that Japan cannot open up a second front against the Soviet Union? Armed with this hard evidence of Moscow's vexation with Mao, Wang Ming pounced on the chance to reverse his personal and political fortunes. He declined to perform self-flagellation, and criticized Mao's policy vis-à-vis both Chiang and the Japanese. He also demanded that Mao debate with him in a large Party forum, declaring that he was prepared to take the issue all the way up to the Comintern.

Mao's original plan had been to nail down absolute and unconditional submission from his colleagues and then call the long-delayed Party congress and mount the Party throne. He had been de facto Party No. 1

* Po Ku died in a plane crash in 1946.

for nearly seven years, but with no commensurate post or title. However, Wang Ming's challenge wrecked Mao's plan. If the stubborn challenger managed to open up a debate about Mao's war policies at the congress, the conclave could well take his side. Mao had to shelve the congress.

Mao was infuriated at this unexpected turn of events, and his wrath gushed forth from his pen. In this period, he wrote and rewrote nine ranting articles, cursing Wang Ming and his past allies, including Chou En-lai, even though Chou had since switched allegiance. These articles are still a closely guarded secret today. According to Mao's secretary they were a "huge release of emotions, with much shrill excessive language." One passage referred to his colleagues as "most pitiful little worms"; "inside these people, there is not even half a real Marx, living Marx, fragrant Marx . . . there is nothing but fake Marx, dead Marx, stinking Marx . . ."

Mao reworked these articles repeatedly, and then put them away. He remained obsessively attached to them right up to the end of his life three and a half decades later. In June 1974, after Wang Ming had died in exile in Moscow, and while Chou En-lai had terminal cancer of the bladder, Mao had the articles taken out of the archives and had them read out to him (Mao then was almost blind). And only one month before he died in 1976, he had them read to him yet again.

MEANWHILE, JUST AFTER he had challenged Mao in October 1941, Wang Ming collapsed from a sudden illness, and was hospitalized. He claimed he had been poisoned by Mao—which may or may not have been true on this occasion. What is certain is that Mao attempted to have him poisoned the following March, when Wang Ming was just about to be discharged from the hospital. Wang Ming remained defiant: "I will not bow my head even if all others are fawning," he vowed. In private, he had written poems calling Mao "anti-the Soviet Union, and anti-the Chinese Communist Party." Furthermore, he said, Mao was "setting up his personal dictatorship"; "Everything he does is for himself, and he does not care about anything else." Mao could expect the highly articulate Wang Ming to speak out against him.

The agent for Mao's poisoning operation was a doctor called Jin Mao-yue, who had originally come to Yenan as part of a Nationalist medical team, at the height of the cooperation between the Nationalists and the CCP. He was a qualified gynecologist and obstetrician, and so the Communists kept him in Yenan. When Wang Ming was admitted to the hospital, Jin was assigned as his chief doctor. That he poisoned Wang Ming was established by an official inquiry involving Yenan's leading doctors in mid-1943. Its findings, which we obtained, remain a well-kept secret.

As of the beginning of March 1942, Wang Ming was described as "ready to be discharged." Dr. Jin had been trying to keep him in the hospital by advocating a whole string of operations—"having his teeth taken out, piles excised and tonsils removed." These operations were dropped after another doctor objected. The inquiry found that the operations for both the tonsils and the piles (which were "large") "would have been dangerous."

But just as Wang Ming was about to leave the hospital on the 13th, Dr. Jin gave him some pills, after which Wang Ming collapsed. The inquiry recorded that: "On 13 March, after taking one pill, [Wang Ming] felt a headache. On 14 March, he took two, and started vomiting, his liver was in severe pain, his spleen was swollen, there was pain in the area of his heart." After more pills from Dr. Jin, Wang Ming "was diagnosed as having acute cholecystitis [of the gallbladder] and . . . hepatomegaly [enlarged liver]."

The inquiry never found out what the pills were, as there was no prescription. Under questioning, Dr. Jin gave "very vague answers" about the type of drug, and the amount. But the inquiry established that after taking the pills, Wang Ming showed "symptoms of poisoning."

Dr. Jin then prescribed further pills: large doses of calomel and soda—two medicines which, when taken in combination, produce poison in the form of corrosive mercury chloride. The inquiry found that these prescriptions were "enough to kill several people." The report detailed many "symptoms of mercury poisoning," and concluded: "It is a fact that he was poisoned."

Wang Ming would have died if he had taken all Dr. Jin's poisonous prescriptions. But he grew suspicious and stopped. In June, Dr. Jin halted his murderous treatment. The reason was that a new and very senior Russian liaison man, Pyotr Vladimirov, had just arrived in Yenan. Vladimirov, who held the rank of general, had worked in northwest China, spoke fluent Chinese and knew some of the CCP leaders personally. His reports went to Stalin. He also brought with him a GRU surgeon, Andrei Orlov, who also held the rank of general, plus an extra radio operator.

On 16 July, shortly after Vladimirov and Orlov arrived, Moscow was informed, for the first time, that Wang Ming "after nine months of treatment is at death's door." At this stage it seems Wang Ming did not tell the Russians that he suspected he was being poisoned. Not only was he in Mao's hands, but he had no proof. He first tried to drive a wedge between Stalin and Mao by telling Vladimirov that Mao had no intention of helping Russia out militarily. Wang Ming, Vladimirov recorded on 18 July, "says that if Japan attacks [Russia] . . . the Soviet Union ought not to count on the [CCP]."

Vladimirov quickly became very critical of Mao. "Spies watch our every step," he noted. "These last few days [Kang Sheng] has been foisting upon me a teacher of Russian whom I am supposed to accept as a pupil. I have never seen a Chinese girl of such striking beauty. The girl doesn't give us a day's peace . . ." Within weeks, Vladimirov had fired the cook who he was convinced was "a Kang Sheng informer."

At the beginning of 1943, Wang Ming's condition took a sharp turn for the worse. Doctors, who now had the Russian surgeon Orlov in their ranks, recommended treatment in the Nationalist area or Russia. Mao refused to let Wang Ming go.

To save his life and get himself to Moscow, Wang Ming knew he had to make Stalin feel that he was politically useful. On 8 January, he dictated a long cable to Vladimirov, addressed to Stalin by name. According to his own account, it detailed Mao's "many crimes," which he called "anti-Soviet and anti-Party." At the end, he "inquired if it was possible to send a plane for me and have me treated in Moscow, where I would also give the Comintern leadership particulars about Mao's crimes."

Wang Ming's message, much watered down by Vladimirov, reached Comintern chief Dimitrov on 1 February. Mao obviously found out that Wang Ming had got a dangerous message out to Russia, as he immediately cabled Dimitrov with counter-accusations against Wang Ming. Still, Dimitrov promised Wang Ming: "We'll have you flown to Moscow."

At this point Dr. Jin made another attempt on Wang Ming's life. On 12 February, right after Dimitrov's message, Jin prescribed the deadly combination of calomel and soda again. A week later, he prescribed tannic acid as an enema at a strength that would have been fatal. This time, Wang Ming not only did not follow the prescriptions, he kept them carefully.

Mao clearly felt a sense of acute urgency, as he now made a startling move. On 20 March, in total secrecy, he convened the Politburo—minus Wang Ming—and got himself made supreme leader of the Party, becoming chairman of both the Politburo and the Secretariat. The resolution gave Mao absolute power, and actually spelled out: "On all issues . . . the Chairman has the power to make final decisions." Wang Ming was dropped from the core group, the Secretariat.

This was the first time Mao became Party No. 1 on paper, as well as in fact. And yet this was a deeply surreptitious affair, which was kept entirely secret from his own Party, and from Moscow—and was to stay secret throughout Mao's life, probably known to no more than a handful of people.

Wang Ming may have got wind of Mao's maneuver, as he now, for the first time, exposed the poisoning attempt to the Russians. On 22 March he showed Orlov one of Dr. Jin's prescriptions, which Vladimirov cabled to Moscow. Moscow wired back immediately, saying that the prescription "causes slow poisoning" and "in grave cases—death." Wang Ming then showed the prescription to Yenan medical chief Dr. Nelson Fu, and this led to an inquiry, which found beyond doubt that Wang Ming had been poisoned.

But Mao, the ace schemer, turned the inquiry to his advantage. Whilst the inquiry did establish that attempts had been made on Wang Ming's life, Mao used the fact that it was still sitting as an excuse to stall Wang Ming's trip.

And for Mao, scapegoats were always to hand—in this case Dr. Jin. On 28 March, Mme Mao "came to see me quite unexpectedly," Vladimirov noted. "She talked at length about 'the unreliability of Doctor Jin who [she said] is probably a [Nationalist] agent . . .' "

FIFTY-SIX YEARS LATER, in a drab concrete building in dusty Peking, the only surviving member of the medical panel of fifteen that drew up the official findings in Yenan, Dr. Y, a physically energetic and mentally alert 87-year-old, gave us a tape-recorded interview.

Once the decision was taken to carry out a medical inquiry, Dr. Y was assigned to establish whether Wang Ming had indeed been poisoned. He "stayed with Wang Ming for a month, sleeping in his study," heating up his urine each day and then dipping a sliver of gold into it and examining it under a microscope. It proved to contain mercury: "He was being poisoned slowly," Dr. Y reported to his medical superior. But nothing was done for weeks. The medical inquiry finally opened on 30 June, more than three months after the poisoning was exposed. The findings, drawn up on 20 July, stated that Wang Ming had definitely been poisoned by Dr. Jin, and were signed by Jin himself. After his signature, he wrote in brackets: "Will make separate statement about several of the points." But he never did. In the middle of one meeting, in front of his colleagues, he threw himself at the feet of Wang Ming's wife, weeping. Dr. Y was present. He told us that Dr. Jin "went down on his knees, begged for forgiveness, saying he was wrong." "He admitted mistakes. Of course, he wouldn't admit it was deliberate." In fact, Dr. Jin had been carrying a pocket medical manual, which stated specifically that it was taboo to use calomel in combination with soda, and he had underlined these words. Dr. Y had actually confronted him on this: "Look, it's written here: taboo prescription, great harm. You have even underlined it!" Jin was silent.

Far from getting into trouble, however, Jin was protected by being taken to the haunt of the security apparatus, Date Garden, where he lived with the security elite. He continued to be one of the doctors for

Mao and other leaders, which would have been inconceivable if Mao had had the slightest doubt about either his competence or his trustworthiness.*

The inquiry did not mention Mao, of course, but the Russians had no doubt: "Wang Ming was being poisoned and ... Mao Tse-tung and Kang Sheng were involved."

MAO'S KEY ACCOMPLICE in preventing Wang Ming from making it to Moscow was, once again, Chou En-lai, his liaison in Chongqing. Chiang Kai-shek's permission was needed for Russian planes to come to Yenan so Mao hypocritically asked Chou to obtain permission from Chiang for a Russian plane to come and collect Wang Ming, while making it clear to Chou that he did not want Wang Ming to leave. Chou duly told the Russians that "the Nationalists would not allow cde. Wang Ming to leave Yenan." In fact, Lin Biao, who was in Chongqing at the time, told Soviet ambassador Panyushkin that Chou never raised the issue with the Nationalists, because of "instructions" from "Yenan."

At this very time, Chou got Chiang's clearance for a Russian plane to bring Mao's son An-ying back from Russia. An-ying, who had been in Russia since 1937, was now a 21-year-old gung-ho enthusiast at a military academy where he had joined the Soviet Communist Party. He had written three letters to Stalin asking to be assigned to the German front.

As he was not sent to the front, An-ying asked permission to return to China after graduation on 1 May 1943. He was not only Mao's eldest son, but also the only probable male heir, as Mao's other son, An-ching, was mentally handicapped. An-ying cabled his father (via Dimitrov), and Mao replied saying that Chiang had cleared the plane trip. An-ying got ready to go home, and asked the head of the International Communist School to look after his brother: "Don't let him out of your sight ... He is an honest person, only he has hearing ailments and his nerves are wrecked."

On 19 August, a Russian plane left for Yenan to collect Wang Ming, and An-ying was supposed to be on it. But that day he was called in to see Dimitrov. When the plane arrived in Yenan, there was no An-ying on board. This was Moscow saying to Mao that it wanted Wang Ming first before releasing his son.

But Mao held on to Wang Ming. Vladimirov recorded: "doctors were ... told to say Wang Ming ... couldn't stand the strain of the flight ...

---

* Dr. Jin remained particularly close to Mme Mao, on whom he had performed an induced abortion and oviduct ligation in summer 1942. When the Communists took power, he became head of the Peking Hospital, which catered for Party leaders and their families. On the night of 30 September 1950, Mao's daughter-in-law was taken to this hospital with appendicitis. The signature of the next-of-kin was needed to okay the operation. As her husband, An-ying, was not present, it was Dr. Jin who authorized the operation.

[The] crew kept delaying the flight as long as they could, but [Mao] got his way."

Another Soviet plane came on 20 October and stayed four days, before leaving with some Russian intelligence men—but again not Wang Ming. "On seeing [Dr Orlov]," Vladimirov recorded, "Wang Ming burst into tears . . . he is . . . still unable to walk . . . [his] friends have abandoned him . . . He is all alone in the full sense of the word . . ." It was two years now since his health crisis had begun, and a good nineteen months since the start of the poisoning. In those long and agonizing days, his wife looked after him devotedly, presenting a strong calm face to him. But occasionally she would lock the door and try to release her anguish. Her son told us that as a young boy he once caught her rolling and kicking on the earthen floor, muffling her sobbing and screaming with a towel. The son was too young to comprehend, but the traumatic scene was etched into his memory.

In Yenan, Dr. Y said, "many people knew that Wang Ming had been poisoned by mercury, and that someone was trying to murder him . . . Word got around." And not only among senior officials, but also among ordinary Party members who had connections to medical staff. So many people suspected the truth that Mao felt he had to flush out the undercurrent of suspicion and kill it off. That meant getting the Wang Mings to make a public denial.

On 1 November, a week after the second Russian plane had left, Mao convened a large meeting for senior officials. He himself sat on the platform. Wang Ming was kept away. The star witness was a veteran commander who was trotted out, from detention, to say that over a year before, Mrs. Wang Ming had told him her husband was being poisoned— and had strongly hinted that Mao was responsible. Mrs. Wang Ming then made a vehement denial onstage. On 15 November she wrote to Mao and the Politburo, vowing that she and her husband had not even harbored such a thought, and felt nothing but gratitude to Mao. The poisoning case was formally closed.

MAO HAD DEFIED Stalin's will to an astonishing degree, as Moscow would not send a plane all the way to Yenan for nothing. Furthermore, strange things happened to the Russians in Yenan around now. Their radio station was wrecked, apparently sabotaged. Their dogs, which they had brought to provide security and an alarm system—as well as protection against wolves—were shot. Mao dared to do all this because he knew he was the victor, and that Stalin needed him and was committed to him. It was during this same period that Stalin told the Americans, on 30 October 1943, he would eventually enter the war against Japan. Russian arms supplies to Mao were greatly stepped up.

When Dimitrov cabled Mao again on 17 November about getting Wang Ming to Russia, Mao did not respond. And when Dimitrov wrote to Wang Ming on 13 December it was in an unmistakably sad tone. After saying that Wang Ming's daughter, whom the Dimitrovs had adopted, was well, Dimitrov went on resignedly: "As regards your Party matters, try to settle them yourselves. It is not expedient to intervene from here for now."

But Stalin clearly decided that Mao should be served a warning. Shortly afterwards, on 22 December, he authorized Dimitrov to send a most unusual telegram, in which he told Mao:

> Needless to say, after the disbanding of the Comintern,∗ its leaders . . . can no longer intervene in the internal affairs of the CCP. But . . . I cannot help offering a few words about my worries caused by the situation in the CCP . . . I think the policy of curtailing the struggle against the foreign occupiers is politically wrong, and the current action to depart from the national united front is also wrong . . .

Saying that he had "suspicions" about Mao's intelligence chief, Kang Sheng, whom he described as "helping the enemy," Dimitrov told Mao that "the campaign conducted to incriminate" Wang Ming (and Chou En-lai) was "wrong."

Dimitrov opened the telegram with a very pointed passage about An-ying:

> Regarding your son. I have arranged for him to be enrolled in the Military-Political Academy . . . He is a talented young man, so I have no doubt that you will find in him a reliable and good assistant. He sends his regards.

Dimitrov did not say a word about An-ying's long-overdue return to China. And mentioning him in one breath with Wang Ming was the clearest possible way of saying to Mao that his own son was a hostage, just as Chiang Kai-shek's had been.

WHEN VLADIMIROV translated Dimitrov's cable to him on 2 January 1944, Mao's immediate reaction was one of defiance. He wrote an answer there and then. It was a blunt, point-by-point retort:

> To Comrade Dimitrov,
> 1. We have not curtailed the anti-Japanese struggle. On the contrary . . .
> 2. Our line as regards collaboration with the [Nationalists] remains unchanged . . .

∗ On 20 May 1943. This was largely a formality, to mollify Stalin's Western allies, and it brought little change in the relationship between Moscow and Mao.

3. Our relations with Chou En-lai are good. We are not going to cut him off from the Party at all. Chou En-lai has made great progress.
4. Wang Ming has been engaged in various anti-Party activities . . .
5. I assure you and can guarantee that the Chinese Communist Party loves and highly respects Comrade Stalin and the Soviet Union . . .
6. . . . Wang Ming is not trustworthy. He was once arrested in Shanghai. Several people have said that when he was in prison he admitted to being a member of the Communist Party. He was released after this.* There has also been talk about his suspicious connections with Mif [purged in Russia] . . .

> Kang Sheng is a trustworthy man . . .
> *Mao Tse-tung*

Mao was an impulsive man, but he usually held his impulses at bay. He once told staff who commented on his "unruffled calm" and "impeccable self-control": "It's not that I am not angry. Sometimes I am so angry I feel my lungs are bursting. But I know I must control myself, and not show anything."

Mao's hair-trigger reaction on this occasion was uncharacteristic. The reason he exploded was not that he cared so much for his son, but because this was the first time Moscow tried to blackmail him. But he instantly regretted his eruption. He could not afford to offend Moscow, especially now that the tide had turned against Germany, and Russia was likely to move against Japan soon—and sweep him to power.

Next day, Mao told Vladimirov he "had given much thought" to Dimitrov's telegram, and asked if his answer had been sent. If not, "he certainly would change its content."

But the cable had gone off, and over the following days a visibly anxious Mao set out to woo Vladimirov. On 4 January, he invited Vladimirov to an operatic show, and "immediately began speaking of his respect for the Soviet Union . . . and I. V. Stalin . . . Mao said he sincerely respected the Chinese comrades who had received education or worked in the USSR . . ." Next day, Mao called on Vladimirov again: "apparently he understands," Vladimirov noted, "that the telegram he sent to Dimitrov on January 2 was rude and ill-considered." On the 6th, Mao threw a dinner for the Russians: "Everything was ceremonious, friendly and . . . servile." The following day, Mao came alone to Vladimirov's place at 9:00 AM—for him, the middle of the night. "Suddenly," Mao "began to speak of Wang Ming—in an entirely different, almost friendly tone!" At the end, Mao sat down and wrote another telegram to Dimitrov, and asked Vladimirov

---

* This meant that Wang Ming's explanation of the way he got out of prison was unsatisfactory, and therefore suspicious.

to "tick it out" at once. "Mao looked perturbed, his gestures betraying tension and nervousness... He looked extremely tired, as if he hadn't had a minute's sleep."

The tone of the second telegram was groveling:

> I sincerely thank you for the instructions you gave me. I shall study them thoroughly... and take measures according to them... Regarding inner-Party questions, our policy is aimed at unity. The same policy will be conducted towards Wang Ming... I ask you to rest assured. All your thoughts, all your feelings are close to my heart...

Mao then paid Wang Ming two long visits.

Dimitrov wrote on 25 February saying that he was particularly pleased by Mao's second (groveling) telegram. This and subsequent missives had a we-can-work-together tone.

On 28 March, Mao asked Vladimirov to send a telegram to his son An-ying. It told him not to think about returning to China. Mao, it said, was "very happy about his successes in his studies." Mao asked his son "not to worry about his [Mao's] health. He feels well." He asked An-ying to convey "warm greetings" to Manuilsky and Dimitrov, who, Mao said, "have assisted... the Chinese revolution. It is to them that Chinese comrades and their children owe their education in [Russia], their upbringing and maintenance."

This was Mao saying to Moscow: I accept you keeping An-ying as a hostage. With this understanding, An-ying remained in Russia.

Dimitrov meanwhile told Wang Ming to compromise. While protesting that the rift was not his fault, a helpless Wang Ming promised to work with Mao, but asked Moscow to try to restrain him.

The result was a stand-off, but very much in Mao's favor. Mao was allowed to keep Wang Ming in Yenan, and do what he wanted with him, including vilifying him, so long as he did not kill him. In fact, vilification of Wang Ming was a major activity in the Yenan terror campaign from 1942. Endless indoctrination sessions were held to blacken his name among Party members. At one rally denouncing him in absentia (Mao made sure that Wang Ming was kept well away from the Party cadres), Wang Ming's wife managed to get onto the stage and say the accusations were untrue. She asked for Wang Ming to be fetched to clarify the facts. As no one stirred, she threw herself at Mao, sobbing loudly, clinging to his legs and asking him to be just. Mao sat there, unmoved as a stone.

By the end of the campaign, it was established in people's minds that Wang Ming was Party Enemy No. 1, and he was in no position thereafter to challenge Mao's supremacy—even though Mao still saw him as a threat, because he remained unbroken. Five years later another attempt was made on his life.*

WHILE EMPLOYING poisoning to tackle Wang Ming, in 1943 Mao also turned on Chou En-lai. This was in spite of the fact that Chou had collaborated in quite a bit of Mao's dirty work, not least in letting Tse-min be killed, and in preventing his old friend Wang Ming from getting out to Moscow for treatment.

Mao, however, wanted more than just slavish deference. He wanted Chou thoroughly scared and broken. The terror campaign in 1942–43 threatened to condemn Chou as the big spy chief. In fact, it was partly to frame Chou that Mao invented the charge that most Communist organizations in Nationalist areas were spies for Chiang, because Chou was in charge of these organizations. In order to have Chou on the spot in Yenan and put him through the terror mill, Mao sent menacing cables ordering him back from Chongqing. One, on 15 June 1943, read: "Don't linger . . . to avoid people talking." And when Chou came back in July the first thing Mao said to his face was a warning: "Don't leave your heart in the enemy camp!" Chou panicked, and responded with fulsome fawning, singing Mao's praises at length at his "welcome" party. Then, in November, he bashed himself for five days in front of the Politburo, saying he had "committed extremely big crimes," been "an accomplice" to Wang Ming, and had "the character of a slave"—for the wrong master, of course. He told larger Party audiences that he and other leaders had been disasters, and that it was Mao who had saved the Party from them. Thoroughly tamed, Chou became a self-abasing slave to Mao for more than three decades, until almost his last breath.

---

* In 1948, when Mao planned to go to Russia, he was concerned about what Wang Ming might get up to in his absence. So Wang Ming was given Lysol, ostensibly for his chronic constipation. Lysol was a powerful disinfectant used for cleaning urinals, and would wreck the intestines. Wang Ming survived because his wife immediately stopped administering it to him after he cried out in agony. No other top CCP leader had so many "medical accidents"—or indeed any serious accidents at all. The possibility of it being an accident can be ruled out by the fact that the doctor who prescribed the Lysol remained chief physician for Mao.

A restricted official circular dated 7 July 1948 and other medical documents acknowledged this "medical accident," but made the pharmacist the scapegoat. In September 1998, a friend of the pharmacist telephoned her for us. After greetings, the colleague said: "I have a writer here, and she would like to talk to you about the enema." To this question out of the blue, we heard the pharmacist answer without a second of hesitation or bafflement: "I don't know. I don't know."

"What medicine did you give?"

"I don't know what medicine I gave. I've forgotten."

It seems that for the past fifty years, the matter had remained at the forefront of the pharmacist's mind.

★

THE LAST MAN Mao set out to de-fang was Peng De-huai, the acting commander of the 8th Route Army. Peng had opposed Mao in the 1930s. In 1940 he had defied Mao's wishes and launched the only large-scale operation by the Reds against the Japanese during the entire Sino-Japanese War. And he had done something else equally infuriating to Mao—tried to implement some of the ideals which in Mao's lexicon were to be brandished solely as propaganda. "Democracy, freedom, equality and fraternity," Mao said, were concepts to be deployed only "for our political needs." He berated Peng for "talking about them as genuine ideals."

Mao had tolerated Peng because Peng had played an extremely useful role in expanding the army and running the base areas. (The bases under Peng enjoyed a much better relationship with the local people, and a much less oppressive atmosphere than Yenan.) In autumn 1943, Mao brought him back to Yenan, although he did not put Peng on the hit list immediately because he did not want to have to deal with too many enemies all at the same time. Peng did not mince his words over the many things that galled him in Yenan, including Mao's effort to build a cult of himself, which Peng called plain "wrong." One day, talking to a young Party member who had just been released from Mao's prison, he said pensively: "It is hard to stand alone honorably."

From early 1945 Mao set out to tarnish Peng's credibility and reputation—and to unnerve him. In a series of long harassment meetings, Mao's henchmen bombarded him with insults and accusations—an experience he described as "being fucked for forty days." The sessions attacking Peng went on intermittently right up to the eve of the Japanese surrender, when they stopped because Mao needed commanders of Peng's caliber to fight Chiang Kai-shek. By this point, Mao had systematically subdued all his opponents.

SUPREME PARTY LEADER AT LAST

(1942–45 ★ AGE 48–51)

MAO'S TERROR campaign made him so many enemies, from raw recruits to veteran Party leaders, that he came to feel more unsafe than ever, and redoubled his personal security. In autumn 1942 a special Praetorian Guard was inaugurated. Mao gave up his public residence at Yang Hill altogether and lived full-time in Date Garden, the isolated haunt of his KGB, several kilometers outside Yenan. Surrounded by high walls and heavily guarded, the estate was a place to stay away from. Anyone venturing near could easily draw suspicion as a spy. There Mao had a special residence built, designed to withstand the heaviest aerial bombing.

But even Date Garden was not safe enough. Beyond it, shielded by willows, birch-leaf pears and red-trunk poplars, a path led through wild chrysanthemums into the depths of the hills—and an even more secret lair. There, in a place called the Back Ravine, a group of dwellings was prepared for Mao in a fastness in the hillside. The path was broadened so that Mao's car could be driven virtually to his door. Only a handful of people knew he lived here.

Mao's main room here, as in most of his residences, had a second door, leading to a bolthole dug through to the other side of the hill. The secret passage also ran all the way up to the stage of a large auditorium, so that Mao could step onto it without having to go outside. The auditorium and Mao's caves were so well camouflaged by the hills and woods that one would not suspect their existence until one virtually reached the doorstep. But from Mao's place, it was easy to monitor the path leading up. The auditorium was designed, like most public buildings in Yenan, by a man who had studied architecture in Italy, and it looked like a Catholic church. But it was never used, except for a few gatherings of the security force. Mao wanted it kept ultra-secret, exclusively his own. Today Mao's caves nestle in total seclusion, and the grand hall stands in ruins like a dilapidated cathedral, spectral, in a landscape of loess gullies extending as far as the eye can see.

Mao's security assistant Shi Zhe told us: "I controlled that entrance to the path. No one was allowed in just because they wanted to come." Few leaders ever came. Any who did could take only one bodyguard in, but "not near where Mao Tse-tung lived." Mao's own men escorted the leader, alone, to Mao's place.

MAO'S CAMPAIGN terrorized even the terrorizers like his deputy and main hatchet man, Kang Sheng. Shi Zhe observed that Kang was living in a state of deep fear of Mao in this period. Though Kang had helped concoct the charge of a vast spy ring in the CCP, it could rebound, as Kang himself had a murky background. Where and when he had joined the CCP was a mystery: he had no witness to the event, and the sponsors he named denied his claim. Many letters had reached Mao casting doubts on Kang, some saying he had buckled when arrested by the Nationalists. Most damning of all, Dimitrov (i.e., Stalin) condemned Kang to Mao in December 1943 as "dubious," saying that Kang was "helping the enemy." In fact, back in 1940, the Russians had urged that Kang be kept out of the leadership.

Far from being put off by Kang's murky past, Mao positively relished it. Like Stalin, who employed ex-Mensheviks like Vyshinsky, Mao used people's vulnerability as a way of giving himself a hold over subordinates. He kept Kang on as the chief of his KGB, in charge of vetting and condemning others. Kang remained in fear of Mao right up to his death in 1975; one of his last acts was to plead with Mao that he was "clean."

Mao made full use of Kang's penchant for persecution and twisted personality. Kang had been in Moscow during the show trials and had participated in Stalin-type purging. He enjoyed watching people being stricken with terror at mass rallies, and liked to play with his victims' anguish. Like Stalin, who sometimes invited victims to his study for a last talk, Kang savored the pleasure of watching the condemned fall into the abyss at the very moment they thought they were safe. He was a sadist. One story he particularly liked telling was about a landlord in his home district who thrashed his farmhands with a whip made from asses' penises. Kang was also a voyeur. After one fifteen-year-old girl invented a story of how she had used her body for spying, he had her repeat it all over the region, while he listened again and again. One of Kang's closest bonds with Mao came from supplying him with erotica, and swapping lewd tales.

Kang later became a scapegoat for the Yenan Terror, but everything he did was on Mao's orders. Actually, during the campaign, Mao limited his power by making Party bosses in each unit—rather than Kang's KGB— responsible for designating and taking charge of most victims in their institution. In the future Communist China, there was to be no exact equivalent of the Soviet KGB.

ANOTHER ASSOCIATE who was dealt a tremendous scare in the campaign was Liu Shao-chi. Not only did some of the organizations named as spy outfits come under his domain, but he had also been arrested by the Nationalists—in fact, several times, which qualified him to be a prime suspect as a possible turncoat. If he gave any cause for dissatisfaction, Mao could easily have him condemned as a spymaster. Liu had actually been against the terror campaign when he first came back to Yenan at the end of 1942; but after this brief flutter of distaste, Russian liaison Vladimirov described him as "changing his views rapidly," and cozying up to Kang Sheng. Thereafter, Liu toed Mao's line, and played an ignominious role in the campaign.* As he was extremely able, Mao picked him to be his second-in-command, a position Liu held until his downfall in the Cultural Revolution in 1966.

TWO WOMEN WHO were to become extremely powerful in the future entered the realm of persecution now: Mao's wife and the wife of the man who was to be his deputy in the Cultural Revolution, Lin Biao. Both women had come to Yenan through Party organizations that were being condemned as spy centers. One day in 1943, while Lin Biao was in Chongqing, his wife, Ye Qun, was tied onto a horse and dragged off into detention. Luckily for her, Lin Biao was someone who enjoyed a most uncommon crony relationship with Mao. When Lin returned to Yenan in July, he marched into the Party office dealing with his wife's case. "Fuck you!" he shouted, throwing his whip on the desk. "We fight wars at the front, and you screw my wife in the rear!" His wife was released, and given the all-clear. This brief experience of intense fear was the beginning of the sclerosis of the heart for Ye Qun. When she rose with her husband in the Cultural Revolution, she became a victimizer.

The later notorious Mme Mao, Jiang Qing, also learned terror during the Yenan campaign. She had been arrested by the Nationalists years before, and had got out of prison by recanting, and entertaining her jailers—and, according to Kang Sheng (later), sleeping with them. Her past had been a big issue in 1938, when Mao wanted to marry her. Now, although no one dared to denounce her, because she was Mao's wife, she

---

* Later, Liu encouraged some cadres to speak up against the terror, but not until it was over in 1945. In 1950 he told Soviet ambassador Nikolai Roshchin that its methods were "perversions which cost a great number of victims."

lived in dread that somebody might, particularly as she too had to perform "self-examinations" and endure criticisms from others. She tried to hide by asking for sick leave, but unlike Lin Biao, who simply told his wife to stay at home, Mao ordered his wife to go back to her unit and experience the scare cycle. Although what she went through was nothing compared with the ordeal suffered by the vast majority, it was enough to make her live in fear about her past for the rest of her life. More than two decades later, when she acquired enormous power, this obsessive fear contributed to the imprisonment and death of many people who knew about her. Above all, Jiang Qing was afraid of her husband. Unlike her predecessor Gui-yuan, she never dared to make a scene about Mao's womanizing, much less to contemplate leaving him. Whatever squalid jobs he assigned her, she would do.

The terror campaign in Yenan also marked her debut at persecuting others, for which she developed a taste. Her first victim was her daughter's nineteen-year-old nanny, whom she got thrown into prison, as the nanny revealed fifty-five years later.

Mao and Jiang Qing had one child together, a daughter, Li Na, born on 3 August 1940. By the time Li Na was one and a half, she was on her third nanny, who came from a poor peasant family in Shanxi. The nanny's father had died humping goods across the freezing Yellow River for the Reds. She herself started making shoes for the Red Army from a young age, and was promoted to her district Communist bureaucracy. She and some other "reliable" women were then selected to be nannies for the leaders.

After a health check and some training, she was taken on as the Maos' nanny and servant. One of her chores was to wash Mme Mao's hair. She described how Mme Mao would lose her temper if her hair was not washed exactly the way she wanted. One day in 1943, the nanny was suddenly summoned to appear in front of Mme Mao and two staff members. "You have come here with poison! Confess!" screamed Mme Mao. That night the nanny was taken to the prison in the Back Ravine behind Date Garden.

She was accused of poisoning the Maos' milk, which came from their own specially guarded cow at the security apparatus' compound. What had happened was that Mme Mao developed diarrhea. After grilling the chef and the orderly, she told Kang Sheng she wanted the nanny imprisoned and interrogated.

In prison, the nanny shared a cave with a large number of other women. During the day, the main activity was spinning, with a very high quota, which she had to work flat out to fill. The regime had spotted that this was an ideal occupation for prisoners, as they were forced to be stationary, thus easy to guard, while being economically productive. The evenings were a time for interrogations, during which the nanny was copiously abused with remarks like: "Why don't you simply confess and get it over with, you shit-making machine!" During the night, guards poked their heads into the cave to watch against suicide and escape. After nine months she was released, but the gut-wrenching fear she experienced stayed with her forever.

IT WAS THROUGH the Yenan Terror that Mao accomplished another most important goal: building up his own personality cult. People who lived through this period all remembered it as a turning point when they "firmly established in our minds that Chairman Mao is our only wise leader." Till then it had been possible to admire Mao while having reservations about him, and to gossip about his marriage to Jiang Qing while still supporting him as the leader. When they were first told to "study" a Mao speech, many had responded with an audible groan: "the same old thing," "can't be bothered to go over it again," "too simplistic." Quite a few had been reluctant to chant "Long live Chairman Mao." One recalled thinking: "This was a slogan for emperors. Why are we doing this? I felt creepy and refused to shout it." This kind of independent talk—and thinking—was killed off by the campaign, and the deification of Mao established. This worship had nothing to do with spontaneous popularity; it stemmed from terror.

Every step in the construction of his cult was choreographed by Mao himself. He minutely controlled its main vehicle, *Liberation Daily*, using giant headlines like "Comrade Mao Tse-tung is the Saviour of the Chinese People!" And it was Mao who initiated the phenomenon of badges of his head, which he first issued to the elite during the campaign. In 1943 he got a huge head of himself carved in gold relief on the façade of a major auditorium. It was in that year that Mao's portraits were first printed en masse and sold to private homes, and that the Mao anthem, "The East Is Red," became a household song.

It was also in 1943 that a later widely used expression, "Mao Tse-tung Thought," first saw the light of day, in an article by the Red Prof, Wang Jia-xiang. Mao stage-managed this eulogy himself. The Red Prof's wife described how Mao dropped in one sunny day when the dates were green on the trees. After some banter about mah-jong, Mao asked her husband to write an article to commemorate the twenty-second anniversary of the Party that July, dropping heavy hints as to what it should say. Mao checked the final text and made it obligatory reading for all.

Every day, at the interminable meetings, Mao's simplistic formula was hammered in: for everything wrong in the Party, blame others; for every success—himself. To achieve this end, history was rewritten, and indeed often stood on its head. The battle of Tucheng, the biggest disaster on the Long March, fought under Mao's command, was now cited as an example of what happened when the army "violated Mao Tse-tung's principles." The first action against Japan, Pingxingguan, was credited to Mao, although it had been fought against his wishes. "Just make it clear to Party members and cadres that the leadership headed by Comrade Mao Tse-tung is completely correct," Mao instructed.*

IN EARLY 1945 Mao was ready to convene the long-delayed Party congress and have himself inaugurated as the supreme leader of the CCP. The 7th Party Congress opened in Yenan on 23 April, seventeen years after the 6th, in 1928. Mao had been postponing it for years, to make sure he had absolute control.

Mao had not only weeded the list of delegates with a fine-tooth comb, he had held most of them in virtual imprisonment for five years, *and* put them through the grinder of his long-drawn-out terror campaign. Of the original 500 or so delegates, half were victimized as spy suspects and suffered appallingly, with some committing suicide and others having mental breakdowns. Many were then dropped. Hundreds of new delegates were appointed, guaranteed loyal to Mao.

The congress hall was dominated by a huge slogan hung over the platform: "March Forward under the Banner of Mao Tse-tung!" Mao was voted chairman of all three top bodies: the Central Committee, the Politburo and the Secretariat. For the first time since the founding of the Party, Mao formally, and publicly, became its head. It had taken him twenty-four years. It was an emotional moment for Mao, and, as always when his emotions were in play, self-pity was never far off. As he raked over his tale of woes, he was on the verge of tears.

Mao Tse-tung had become the Stalin of the CCP.

---

* In 1943, a booklet was published in Yenan, entitled *A Brief History of China's Labour Movement*, written by Deng Zhong-xia, a labor leader executed by the Nationalists. The original text had been published in 1930 in Russia, and contained no mention of Mao's role. Now a passage was inserted: "In 1922, thanks to the leadership of comrade Mao Tse-tung, the workers' movement in Hunan developed stormily . . ."

PART FOUR

TO CONQUER
CHINA

"REVOLUTIONARY OPIUM WAR"

(1937–45 ★ AGE 43–51)

Y ENAN, MAO'S HQ during the Sino-Japanese War, was run somewhat differently from former Red bases like Ruijin. With the policy
changes the CCP introduced for the "United Front," the practice
of designating "class enemies" for slave labor and dispossession was drastically scaled down. But the maximum extraction went on, through taxation.

This was despite the fact that Yenan enjoyed two enormous external
subsidies: substantial funding from the Nationalists (for the first few
years), and massive clandestine sponsorship from Moscow, which Stalin
personally set at US$300,000 per month in February 1940 (worth
perhaps some US$45–50 million a year today).

The chief domestic source of revenue was grain tax, which rose steeply
during the years of Communist occupation. Official figures for grain tax
for the first five years of Red rule, for which records are available, were
(in *shi*, equivalent to roughly 150 kg at the time):

1937:	13,859
1938:	15,972
1939:	52,250
1940:	97,354
1941:	200,000

The sharp increases from 1939 on were to fund Mao's aggressive
expansion of both territory and army. Coercion and violence were clearly
rife, as the region's Communist chief secretary, Xie Jue-zai, noted in his
diary for 21 June 1939 that peasants were being "driven to death" by tax
collectors. (Xie was one of the few to keep a diary, thanks to his high
position and his long relationship with Mao, which went back to Mao's
youth.) In 1940, grain tax doubled in spite of severe bad weather and
famine. And it doubled again in 1941, even though the harvest was 20–30
percent down on the previous year.

Mao was disliked by the locals—a fact he knew, but had no impact on his policy. He later told senior cadres a story about a peasant complaining about heavy taxation. After a county chief was struck dead by lightning, the peasant said: "Heaven has no eyes! Why didn't it strike Mao dead?" Mao told the story as a way of saying he was responsive to discontent, and claimed he had had grain tax reduced as a result. As a matter of fact, the lightning and the peasant's curse occurred on 3 June 1941, well before that year's unprecedentedly high tax was announced, on 15 October. Mao doubled the tax *after* he heard about the peasant's anger. And that November he added a new tax, on horse feed.

On another occasion, Mao revealed that someone who, according to him, "was feigning madness" lunged at him and tried to assault him— because of the heavy taxes. Mao did not quote other stories that went the rounds, including one about a peasant who cut the eyes out of a portrait of Mao. When interrogated, he said: "Chairman Mao has no eyes," meaning: "There is no justice under his rule." Mao's response was simply to cook the figures. In 1942 and 1943, government announcements understated taxes by at least 20 percent.

The Communists claimed that taxation in Yenan was much lower than in Nationalist-ruled areas. But Chief Secretary Xie himself noted in his diary that grain tax per capita in 1943 was "high by the standards of the Big Rear [Nationalist area]." Sometimes, he recorded, grain tax "almost equals the entire year's harvest"; the state took the astronomical figure of 92 percent in the case of one family he cited. For many, "there was no food left after paying the tax." Large numbers tried to flee. According to the Communists' own records, in 1943 over 1,000 families fled from Yenan County alone, which was no small feat, as the whole place was guarded around the clock, and the county was not on the border of the Red area, which was roughly the size of France.

THE REDS FOSTERED the myth that Yenan was under tight economic blockade by Chiang Kai-shek. In fact, there was plenty of trade with Nationalist areas, and the person Chiang selected to place on Yenan's northern frontier, General Teng Pao-shan, was a man who had long-standing ties with the Communists. His daughter was a Party member, and actually lived in Yenan, which he sometimes visited; he also had a Communist secretary. He let the Reds take over two crucial border crossing points on the Yellow River, which gave them uninterrupted communications with their other bases. In addition, his men bought arms and ammunition for the Reds. Chiang tolerated this state of affairs because he did not want an all-out civil war, which Mao promised to start if he did not get his way.

The Yenan region had considerable assets. The most important marketable one was salt. There were seven salt lakes, where all that had to be done, as one 1941 report noted, was "just to collect it." In the first four years of their occupation, the Reds produced no new salt, and simply used up the reserve built up before they arrived. "The salt stock of decades has been sold out," the 1941 report said, and the territory "is in a salt famine." The regime was not only extremely slow to maximize this asset, it had no plan. This reflected the fact that Mao treated Yenan, like the other areas he occupied, as a stopover, inflicting an economic approach akin to slash and burn, with no attention to long-term output.

By mid-1941, the regime had belatedly come to recognize salt as "the second-biggest source of [domestic] revenue" after the grain tax, and a key money-spinner, which soon came to account for over 90 percent of export earnings. The salt was in the northeast of the region, but the export market was over the southern border. As there was no railway or navigable river, let alone motor vehicles, it had to be carried some 700 km on steep, twisting paths. "Transporting salt is the harshest form of taxation," one Yenan governor wrote to the emperor under the Manchu Dynasty; "those who are poor and cannot afford animals have to carry it on their backs and shoulders, and their hardship is untold . . ." "Today," Chief Secretary Xie noted, "it is not much different from the old days."

The regime imposed corvée labor (unpaid porterage) on innumerable peasant families. Xie and other moderates wrote to Mao many times arguing against this harsh method, but Mao told them flatly that the policy "is not only nothing to criticise, but is also completely correct." Peasants, he said, must be "forced" to do it, and, he specifically enjoined, "in the *slack season*." The underline was Mao's, to stress that they must not neglect farm work.

THE LOCAL PEASANTS were having to support an administration that was both huge and inefficient. A British radio expert who was in Yenan in 1944–45, Michael Lindsay, was so frustrated by the inefficiency that he produced a document called "What's Wrong with Yenan." The system stifled initiative, Lindsay wrote, and made people frightened of proposing improvements, as any suggestion could be twisted into a lethal political accusation. "Technical people all [*sic*] run away at the first opportune moment." A copy was given to Chou En-lai. Lindsay heard nothing more.

Others had raised their voices against the bloated bureaucracy earlier. In November 1941 a non-CCP member of the region's dummy parliament had proposed cutting down on the army and administration, quoting a traditional adage that a good government should have "fewer but better troops, smaller and simpler administration." For propaganda purposes, Mao made a public show of adopting the adage. But he was not interested in reducing the number of cadres, or soldiers. He wanted more of them, not fewer, in order to conquer China.

It is part of the founding myth of Communist China that in Yenan both the army and the administration were reduced, and that this relieved the burden on the population. In fact, what the regime did was to weed out the politically unreliable (termed "backward"), and the old and the sick, and reassign them to manual labor. The rules for relocating them said they "must be placed round the centre of the region to avoid the Nationalists enticing them away." In other words, to prevent them flee-ing. But even with these reductions, as a secret document of March 1943 noted, there was actually "an overall increase" in employees in the region's administration, mainly at lower levels, in order to intensify control at the grassroots. Meanwhile, Mao used the drive to merge departments and carry out a reshuffle at the top to tighten his grip.

THE GERMAN INVASION of Russia in June 1941 made Mao look around for an alternative source of funding in case Moscow was unable to continue its subsidy. The answer was opium. Within a matter of weeks, Yenan brought in large quantities of opium seeds. In 1942, extensive opium-growing and trading began.

To a small circle, Mao dubbed his operation "the Revolutionary Opium War." In Yenan, opium was known by the euphemism "*te-huo*," "Special Product." When we asked Mao's old assistant, Shi Zhe, about growing opium, he answered: "It did happen," and added: "If this thing gets known, it's going to be very bad for us Communists." He also told us that conven-tional crops, mainly sorghum, were planted around the opium to hide it. When a Russian liaison man asked Mao outright over a game of mah-jong in August 1942 how Communists could "openly engage in opium production," Mao was silent. One of his hatchet men, Teng Fa, supplied the answer: opium, he said, "bring[s] back a caravan loaded with money . . . and with it we'll whip the [Nationalists]!" That year a care-fully researched study put the opium-growing area at 30,000 acres of the region's best land.

The major opium-producing counties lay on the borders with the friendly Nationalist general to the north, Teng Pao-shan, who was actu-ally known as "the Opium King." Mao received invaluable collaboration from him, which he reciprocated by facilitating Teng's own opium-trafficking. When Chiang Kai-shek was thinking of transferring Teng, Mao sprang into action to prevent this: "Ask Chiang to stop at once," he told Chou in Chongqing, saying that he (Mao) was "determined to wipe out" the unit scheduled to replace Teng. Chiang canceled the transfer. Mao showed how much he appreciated Teng by mentioning him twice when he addressed the 7th Congress in 1945, once even in the same breath as Marx, leading the Russian liaison Vladimirov to ask: "What sort of man is this Teng Pao-shan whom Mao Tse-tung cited . . . alongside Marx?" Yet

Mao never trusted his benefactor. After the Communist takeover in 1949, Teng remained on the Mainland and was rewarded with high nominal posts. But when he asked to travel abroad, the request was denied.

In one year, opium solved Mao's problems. On 9 February 1943 he told Chou that Yenan had "overcome its financial difficulties, and had accumulated savings . . . worth 250 million *fabi*." *Fabi* was the currency used in the Nationalist areas, which Mao had been stockpiling, along with gold and silver, "for when we enter Nationalist areas," i.e., once all-out war began against Chiang. This sum was six times the official Yenan region budget for 1942, and it represented pure saving. In 1943 the Russians estimated Mao's opium sales at 44,760 kg, worth an astronomical 2.4 billion *fabi* (roughly US$60 million at then current exchange rates, or some US$640 million today).

By early 1944 the Communists were "very rich," according to Chief Secretary Xie. The huge *fabi* reserve "is without doubt thanks to the Special Product," Xie wrote in his diary. The lives of Party members in Yenan improved dramatically too, especially for senior officials. Cadres arriving from other base areas marveled at how well they ate. One described a meal with "several dozen dishes," and "every table left many dishes unfinished."

Mao put on weight. When Opium King Teng met him in June 1943 after some time, his first words of greeting were: "Chairman Mao has grown fatter!" He meant it as a compliment.

FOR THE PEASANTS, the main benefit opium brought was that it lessened the impositions visited on them. Up till now, they had been liable to have their meager household possessions and vital farm tools commandeered. After he became opium-rich, Mao ordered steps to improve relations with the locals. The army began to return goods it had taken, and even to help peasants work the land. Mao himself later admitted that the locals' attitude towards the Party until spring 1944 had been to "keep an awe-struck and fearful distance as if it were deity and devil," i.e., to try to steer well clear of the Reds. And this was seven years after the Communists had occupied Yenan. Throughout, the Communists had little contact with the locals, except when their work required it, or on token New Year visits to villages to exchange ritual greetings. Intermarriage, and social relations, were rare.

Opium wealth, however, did not improve the locals' standard of living, which remained far below that of the occupying Communists. The lowest-grade Communist's annual meat ration was almost five times (12 kg) the average local's (2.5 kg). While conserving its vast hoard of cash, the regime still lost no opportunity to milk the population. In June 1943, on the grounds that Chiang was about to attack Yenan (which he did not), civilians were made to "voluntarily donate" firewood, vegetables, pigs and sheep, and what little gold they had, which was often their life savings.

A mention of the CCP's huge reserves in Xie's diary on 12 October 1944 is sandwiched between dire descriptions of peasants' lives: the mortality rate was not only rising, it was vastly outstripping the birth rate, in one district by nearly 5 to 1. The reasons, Xie noted, were "inadequate clothing, food and accommodation," foul drinking water, and "no doctors." The regime had introduced a major cause of mortality by banning firearms. Wolves sauntered into people's front yards, and leopards roamed freely in the hills.* So people had to bring their precious livestock into their dwellings, or risk losing them. The resulting abysmal hygiene led to many diseases. Access to game as food was also strangled by the firearms ban.

Mortality was highest among immigrants, who formed a sizable part of the population. They had been moving to the Yenan area because it had spare arable land. Mao encouraged them to keep coming, but then did little for them when they got there. Herded into mountain country and left to fend for themselves, they died like flies—31 percent within two years in one area. Mao knew that the mortality rate for children was 60 percent (and nearly all who survived grew up illiterate). And yet, as a top administrator recalled, "the massive death tolls in people and livestock were never given proper attention." When pressed to do something, in April 1944, Mao said: Let's discuss this in the winter. Public health did become the focus of discussion in November that year, *for the first time* since the Communists had arrived in the area nearly a decade before; but there was no mention of spending money on it.

FOR THE LOCALS, opium also brought astronomical inflation, much worse than in Nationalist areas. "We have caused great inflation," Xie wrote in his diary on 6 March 1944, "not because we are poor, but because we are rich."

Mao played a key role in this. In June 1941 he had personally ordered unrestrained printing of the local Communist currency, *bianbi*. The orig-

---

* Control of guns was watertight. An Austrian doctor kidnapped by the Communists in the later 1940s observed that if you heard wolves, you knew you were in a Red area. No one we interviewed recalled hearing a shot in Yenan throughout the war. One night, when a Russian radio operator on the outskirts of Yenan shot a wolf that had killed one of their two guard dogs, Mao's guards immediately appeared to complain that the sound of the shots had "very much unsettled" Mao. Another time, Russian liaison Vladimirov shot a rabid dog (rabies was common) that was attacking his guard dog. A group of Mao's guards instantly descended, saying that Mao "was very agitated" and that the shooting "had interrupted his work."

inal plan had had a ceiling. After he saw the budget, Mao wrote: "don't get fixated on the idea that *bianbi* should be kept within 10 million yuan . . . don't tie our hands." He urged spending "generously" on administration and the army, showing a total disregard for the local economy: "If in the future [the system] collapses, so be it." In 1944 the price of salt was 2,131 times that in 1937, cooking oil 2,250 times, cotton 6,750 times, cloth 11,250 times, and matches 25,000 times, according to Chief Secretary Xie.

This hyper-inflation did not hurt those feeding at the state trough. Russian ambassador Panyushkin, who probably had a better picture than most, said it hurt the "toilers," i.e., the peasants, who needed cash to buy basics like cloth, salt, matches, utensils and farm tools—and medical care, which was never free for non-state employees, if they could get it at all. A hospital official in one Red area revealed: "Only when we want wheat do we admit the *lao-pai-shing* [man-in-the-street]."

One practice where cash was needed, and the impact of inflation can be measured, was buying a bride. In 1939 a bride cost 64 yuan. By 1942 the prices were: seven-year-old girl: 700; adolescent: 1,300; widow: 3,000. By 1944 the price for a widow was 1.5 million.

Loan-sharking flourished, with average interest rates running at 30–50 percent *monthly*, according to Chief Secretary Xie, who also recorded the astronomical rate of 15–20 percent from one market day to the next—which was five days. These rates were as bad as the worst before the Communists. To raise cash, many peasants presold crops, which sometimes meant accepting as little as 5 percent of the harvest-time price.

"Reducing loan interest" was one of the Communists' two main economic pledges at the time; the other was to lower land rent. But, whilst there were specific regulations about the latter (which actually meant little, as the peasants just had to hand over their harvest to the state instead of to landlords), the regime set no ceiling on loan interest. All it said was: "it should be left to the people themselves to fix . . . and the government should not fix too low an interest rate, in case lending dries up." As the regime advanced virtually no loans, it had to find some other way to get credit floated. Some Red areas enforced low ceilings on interest rates, but in the Yenan region the regime let loose the most rapacious forces of the private sector on the most helpless of its subjects.

In March 1944 the regime stopped the runaway printing of money and started to call in *bianbi*. This was partly prompted by the imminent arrival of the first non-Russian outsiders for five years—an American mission, and some journalists. Hyper-inflation did not look good. But deflation was no boon to those in debt either, as Xie noted on 22 April: "No matter whether the currency goes down or up, those who suffer are always the poor . . . the debt they owed when prices were high now has to be paid back by selling more of their possessions. I heard that many are selling their draft animals."

Opium-growing stopped at this point. Apart from not wanting the Americans to see, there was overproduction. In fact, the surplus had become a headache. Some hard-liners advocated dumping it on the population within Yenan, which Mao vetoed. A drug-addicted peasantry was no use to him. But some peasants had inevitably become hooked by growing the stuff. The regime ordered locals to kick the habit, with tough deadlines, promising to "assist addicts with medicine" and saying that "the poor" did not have to pay for treatment, clearly showing that one had to pay if one could remotely afford it.

To officials in the know, Mao met the widespread disquiet about opium-growing by calling it one of the Party's "two mistakes," but he went on to justify both in the same breath. One mistake, he said on 15 January 1945, "was that during the Long March we took people's things" — "but," he immediately added, "we couldn't have survived if we hadn't"; "the other," he said, "was to grow a certain thing [*mou-wu*, i.e., opium] — but without growing this we couldn't have got through our crisis."

YENAN STAYED extremely poor even years after Mao had taken control of China. A visitor from Communist Hungary, itself by no means rich, commented on "indescribably squalid and poverty-stricken villages" near Yenan in 1954. In fact, all the Red bases remained among the poorest areas in China, and the reason was precisely that they had been Red bases. An exchange between Mao and a Swedish enthusiast in 1962 ran:

> J. MYRDAL: I have just come back from a trip to the Yenan area.
> MAO: That is a very poor, backward, underdeveloped . . . part of the country.
> MYRDAL: I lived in a village . . . I wanted to study the change in the countryside . . .
> MAO: Then I think it was a very bad idea that you went to Yenan . . . Yenan is only poor and backward. It was not a good idea that you went to a village there.
> MYRDAL: But it has a great tradition—the revolution and the war—I mean, after all, Yenan is the beginning—
> MAO [interrupting]: Traditions—[laughing]. Traditions—[laughing].

THE RUSSIANS ARE COMING!

(1945-46 ★ AGE 51-52)

IN FEBRUARY 1945, at Yalta in the Crimea, Stalin confirmed to Roosevelt and Churchill that Russia would enter the Pacific War two or three months after Germany's defeat. This meant the Soviet army would enter China, and thus give Mao his long-awaited chance to take the country. Mao had made a shrewd assessment as far back as 1923: communism, he had said then, "had to be brought into China from the north by the Russian army." Now, twenty-two years later, this was about to become reality.

Stalin did not have to persuade Roosevelt and Churchill to let him tail-end on the war against Japan. They wanted him involved. At the time, the US atomic bomb had not been tested, and the feeling was that Soviet entry would hasten the defeat of Japan and save Allied lives. The two Western leaders accepted Stalin's demands for "compensation," neither seeming to realize that Stalin needed no inducement at all to come in. They agreed not only to accept "the status quo" in Outer Mongolia (in effect, allowing Stalin to keep it), but to turn the clock back decades and restore the Tsarist privileges in China, including extraterritorial control over the Chinese Eastern Railway and two major ports in Manchuria.*

Stalin used the excuse of fighting Japan, at the very last minute, to invade China and create the conditions for Mao to seize power. A hint

---

* In the Yalta Declaration, these are presented as reparations due Russia by Japan, but the reality was that they were gouged out of *China*. Churchill welcomed this, on the grounds that "any claim by Russia for indemnity at the expense of China would be favorable to our resolve about Hong Kong." Though the deals involved Chinese territory, the Chinese government was not even informed, much less consulted. Moreover, the US put itself at Stalin's mercy by committing to wait for his permission before it told Chiang Kai-shek—and placed itself in the uniquely constrained position of then being responsible for obtaining Chiang's compliance. As a result, the Generalissimo was not given a full account by the US until 15 June, over four months later. This was shabby treatment of an ally, and it stored up trouble.

came right after Yalta, on 18 February, when Russia's governmental mouthpiece, *Izvestia*, wrote of Moscow's "desire to solve the Far Eastern problem taking due account of the interests of the Chinese Communists."

Mao was ecstatic, and his goodwill towards the Russians extended to their sex lives. Within days, he was trying to fix them up. "Haven't you liked a single pretty woman here?" Mao asked Russian liaison Vladimirov on 26 February. "Don't be shy . . ." He returned to the theme a week later: "Well, there are attractive girls, aren't there? And extremely healthy. Don't you think so? Maybe Orlov would like to look around for one? And maybe you, too, have an eye for someone?"

Vladimirov wrote:

> towards evening a girl appeared . . . She shyly greeted me, saying she had come to tidy up the house . . .
> I took out a stool, and placed it under our only tree, near the wall. She sat down, tense, but smiling. Then she amiably answered my questions, and was all the while waiting cautiously, her legs crossed, small slender legs in woven slippers . . .
> She was a smashing girl, indeed!
> . . . she told me she was a university student, just enrolled. How young she was . . .

On 5 April, Moscow told Tokyo it was breaking their Neutrality Pact. One month later Germany surrendered. This came right in the middle of the CCP congress that ratified Mao's supremacy. Mao fired up the delegates with the sense that victory was imminent for the CCP as well. The Soviet army would definitely come to help them, he said, and then, with a big smile, he put the side of his hand to his neck like an ax head, and announced: "If not, you can chop my head off!" Mao delivered the most effusive comments he ever made about Stalin in his entire life. "Is Stalin the leader of the world revolution? Of course he is." "Who is our leader? It is Stalin. Is there a second person? No." "Every member of our Chinese Communist Party is Stalin's pupil," Mao intoned. "Stalin is the teacher to us all."

AT TEN PAST MIDNIGHT on 9 August 1945, three days after America dropped the first atomic bomb on Hiroshima, over 1.5 million Soviet and Mongolian troops swept into China along a huge front stretching more than 4,600 km, from the shores of the Pacific to the province of Chahar—far wider than the European front from the Baltic to the Adriatic. In April, Mao had ordered those of his troops who were near the Russian points of entry to be ready to "fight in coordination with the Soviet Union." As soon as the Russo-Mongolian army entered China, Mao went to work around the clock dispatching troops to link up with them and seize the territory they rolled over. He moved his office to an auditorium at Date Garden, where he received a stream of military commanders, drafting telegrams on a Ping-Pong table he used as a desk, pausing only to wolf down food.

Under the Yalta agreements, before entering China, Russia was supposed to sign a treaty with Chiang Kai-shek, but it stormed in anyway without one. A week after the Russians invaded, with their army driving hundreds of kilometers into China, Chiang's foreign minister reluctantly put his signature on a Sino-Soviet Treaty of Friendship and Alliance, which formally severed Outer Mongolia from China. Chiang compromised in return for the Russians recognizing him as the sole legitimate government of China and promising to hand back all the territory they occupied to him and only to him.

In spite of his promise, Stalin found myriad ways to assist Mao. His first ploy was to refuse to commit to a timetable for withdrawal. He made a verbal promise to withdraw his troops within three months, but refused to incorporate this in the agreement; and it was attached only as a nonbinding "minute." In fact, Stalin was to stay much longer than three months, and was to use the period of occupation to thwart Chiang and secretly transfer territory and assets to Mao.*

Japan surrendered on 15 August. The occasion was greeted in China with firecrackers and street parties, tears and toasts, drums and gongs. Most of China had been at war for eight years, and some regions for fourteen years. During that time at least one-third of the population had been occupied by the Japanese. Tens of millions of Chinese had died, untold millions had been crippled, and more than 95 million people— the largest number in history—had been made refugees. People yearned for peace.

What they got instead was an all-engulfing nationwide civil war, which broke out in earnest at once. In this, Stalin was right behind Mao; in fact, the Russians did not stop their drive south when Japan surrendered, but pressed on for several weeks afterwards. The area Russian troops moved into in northern China was larger than the entire territory they occupied in Eastern Europe. Russian paratroopers landed as far west as Baotou, the railhead due north of Mao's base, some 750 km west of the Manchurian border. By the end of August, with Russian help, the CCP had occupied much of Chahar and Jehol provinces, including their capitals, Zhangjiakou and Chengde, both only some 150 km from Peking, to

---

* Stalin also had his own aggressive agenda: a tentative scheme to detach part of the Mongolian region of China adjacent to Outer Mongolia and merge it with the Soviet satellite. Russo–Mongolian occupation forces actually formed an Inner Mongolia provisional government, ready for the merger, but the scheme was then dropped.

the northwest and northeast respectively. For a while Mao planned to move his capital to Kalgan, and camel trains carrying documents and luggage set off thither from Yenan.

The key prize was Manchuria, which contained China's best deposits of coal, iron and gold, giant forests—and 70 percent of its heavy industry. Manchuria was bordered on three sides by Soviet-controlled territory—Siberia, Mongolia and North Korea. The border with Siberia alone was over two thousand kilometers long. "If we have Manchuria," Mao had told his Party, "our victory will be guaranteed."

Neither the Communists nor the Nationalists had armies in the region, which had been occupied by the Japanese, efficiently and ruthlessly, for fourteen years. But Red guerrillas were far closer than Chiang's troops. The Russians immediately opened up Japanese arms depots to these Reds, including the biggest arsenal, in Shenyang, which alone contained about "100,000 guns, thousands of artillery pieces, and large quantities of ammunition, textiles and food," according to a secret CCP circular. Only a few months earlier, the Communist 8th Route Army had had only 154 pieces of heavy artillery.

The bonanza was not just in weapons, but also in soldiers. The troops of the Japanese puppet Manchukuo regime, almost 200,000 strong, had surrendered en masse to the Soviet army, and were now made available by the Russians to be "re-enlisted" by the CCP. So were hundreds of thousands of men newly unemployed as a result of Russian depredations and outright destruction. The Soviet occupation forces carted off whole factories and machinery as "war booty," and even demolished industrial installations. The equipment removed by the Russians was estimated to be worth US$858 million (US$2 billion at current replacement cost). Many local people were deprived of their livelihood. The CCP, which had originally dispatched 60,000 troops into Manchuria, saw its force snowball to well over 300,000.

THIS EMPOWERMENT of the CCP was carried out by the Russians in maximum secrecy, as it was in stark violation of the treaty Moscow had just signed with Chiang. The Generalissimo's best, combat-hardened troops, who were American-trained and equipped, were stuck in South China and Burma, far away from the areas Russia held. To get them to Manchuria fast, he desperately needed American ships. America wanted him to talk with Mao about peace; so under American pressure, the Generalissimo invited Mao to come to Chongqing for talks. America's China policy had been defined by the late President Roosevelt (who had died on 12 April 1945 and was succeeded by his vice-president, Harry Truman) as to "knock heads together," and the US ambassador in China had earlier suggested the idea of bringing the Generalissimo and Mao to the White House together if the two Chinese leaders reached a deal.

Mao did not want to go to Chongqing, and twice turned down Chiang's invitation, mainly because he did not trust Chiang not to harm him. This would be Mao's first venture out of his lair since he had started running his own military force in 1927. He told Chiang he was sending Chou En-lai instead. But Chiang insisted the summit must take place with Mao, and in the end Mao had to accept. Stalin had cabled him no fewer than three times to go. While secretly helping Mao to seize territory, Stalin wanted him to play the negotiations game. If Mao refused to show up, he would look as though he were rejecting peace, and America would be more likely to give its full commitment to Chiang.

Mao resented this pressure from Stalin. It was to be his biggest grievance against Stalin, and one he would keep bringing up for the rest of his life.

Stalin told Mao that his safety would be assured by both Russia and the US. The Founder of Chiang's FBI, Chen Li-fu, told us that the Nationalists had no designs on Mao's life "because the Americans guaranteed his safety." Mao knew he would also have secret protection from his strategically placed moles, especially the Chongqing garrison chief, Chang Chen. Even so, he insisted on US ambassador Patrick Hurley coming to Yenan and escorting him to Chongqing as insurance against being bumped off in mid-air.

With all these precautions in place, Mao at last flew off to Chongqing in an American plane on 28 August, leaving Liu Shao-chi in charge in Yenan. When the plane landed, Mao stuck close to Hurley, and got into Hurley's car, shunning the one Chiang had sent for him.

Mao also took out insurance of the kind he knew best, by ordering an offensive against Nationalist forces while he was in Chongqing, which demonstrated that the Reds would escalate the civil war if anything happened to him. He told his top generals, who were about to be flown (by the Americans) to 8th Route Army HQ: Fight without any restraint. The better you fight, the safer I am. When his troops won the battle at a place called Shangdang, Mao beamed: "Very good! The bigger the battle, the bigger the victory, the more hope I will be able to return."

Mao flew into one moment of panic in Chongqing, when Hurley left on 22 September, followed by Chiang on the 26th, and he feared he was being set up for a hit. Chou was dispatched to the Soviet embassy to ask if the Russians would let Mao stay there, but Ambassador Apollon Petrov was non-committal, and got no reply when he wired Moscow for instructions. Mao was furious.

Mao gained a lot by going to Chongqing. He talked to Chiang as an equal, "as though the convicts were negotiating with the warders," one observer remarked. Foreign embassies invited him not as a rebel, but as a statesman, and he played the part, behaving diplomatically, and laughing off a pointed challenge from Churchill's no-nonsense envoy General Carton de Wiart, who told Mao that he did "not consider that [the Reds] contributed much towards defeating the Japs," and that Mao's troops only "had a nuisance value, but no more." Even when put on the spot in a tough face-to-face encounter with the US commander in China, General Albert Wedemeyer, about the murder and mutilation by the Reds of an American officer called John Birch, Mao showed aplomb. And he kept his cool when Wedemeyer told him, with more than a hint of a threat, that the US was planning to bring atomic bombs into China, as well as up to half a million troops. By appearing conciliatory, Mao scored a propaganda victory.

The peace talks lasted forty-five days, but the whole episode was theater. Mao went around exclaiming "Long live Generalissimo Chiang!" and saying he supported Chiang as the leader of China. But this meant nothing. Mao wanted China for himself, and he knew he could only get it through civil war.

Chiang also knew that war was inevitable, but he needed a peace agreement to satisfy the Americans. Although he had no intention of observing it, he endorsed an agreement that was signed on 10 October. And this behavior brought benefits, at least in the short term. While Mao was in Chongqing, US forces occupied the two main cities in northern China, Tianjin and Peking, and held them for Chiang, and started to ferry his troops to Manchuria.

After the treaty was signed, Chiang invited Mao to stay with him for the night; and the next day they had breakfast together before Mao departed for Yenan. The moment Mao's back was turned, the Generalissimo gave vent to his true feelings in his diary: "The Communist Party is perfidious, base, and worse than beasts."

WHEN MAO RETURNED to Yenan on 11 October he immediately started military operations to keep Chiang's army out of Manchuria. Lin Biao was appointed commander of the Red forces there. Tens of thousands of cadres had already been dispatched, coming under a new Manchuria Bureau whose leaders the Russians flew secretly from Yenan to Shenyang in mid-September.

Mao ordered troops deployed around Shanhaiguan, at the eastern end of the Great Wall. His forces had occupied this strategic pass from China proper into Manchuria in cooperation with the Soviet army on 29 August. He asked the Russians to take care of the seaports and the airports. With

Russian encouragement, CCP units posing as bandits fired on US ships trying to land Chiang's troops, in one case shooting up the launch of the US commander, Admiral Daniel Barbey, and forcing him back out to sea.

The US 7th Fleet finally had to dock at Qinhuangdao, a port just south of Manchuria, and one of Chiang's best armies disembarked. On the night of 15–16 November it stormed the Shanhaiguan pass. Mao had called for a "decisive battle" and told his troops to hold out at the pass, but Chiang's divisions simply swept through them. Mao's forces disintegrated so overwhelmingly that one Nationalist commander lamented proudly that "we don't even have enough people to accept all the arms being surrendered."

The Communist forces had no experience of trench warfare, or of any kind of modern warfare. As guerrillas, their first principle, as laid down by Mao himself, was "retreat when the enemy advances." And that is what they did now. Chiang's armies, on the other hand, had fought large-scale engagements with the Japanese: in Burma, they had put more Japanese out of action in one campaign than the entire Communist army had in eight years in the whole of China. The Nationalist supremo in Manchuria, General Tu Yu-ming, had been in command of major battles against the Japanese, whereas Mao's commander, Lin Biao, had taken part in one single ambush in September 1937, eight years before, since when he had hardly smelled gunpowder. By studiously avoiding combat with the Japanese, Mao had ended up with an army that could not fight a modern war.

The Reds had been in some frontal engagements during the Japan war, but mostly against weak Nationalist units. They had not faced the cream of Chiang's forces, who, as one top Red commander wrote to Mao, were fresh, well-trained, "US-style troops," and battle-ready.

The CCP troops were not only badly trained, but also poorly motivated. After the Japanese war, many just wanted peace. The Reds had been using a propaganda song called "Defeat Japan so we can go home." After Japan's surrender, the song was quietly banned, but the sentiment— let's go home—could not be quenched as easily as the song.

When Red troops were marched to Manchuria, mainly from Shandong, pep talks focused not on high ideals but on material enticements. Commissar Chen Yi told officers: "When I left Yenan, Chairman Mao asked me to tell you that you are going to a good place, a place of great fun. There are electric lights and high-rises, and gold and silver in plenty . . ." Others told their subordinates: "In Manchuria we'll be eating rice and white flour [desirable foods] all the time," and "everyone will be given a promotion." Even so some officers found it impossible to motivate the soldiers, and kept the destination secret until the troops were safely on board ship en route to Manchuria.

Communist officers who trekked to Manchuria remembered abysmal morale. One officer recalled:

The thing that gave us the worst headache was desertions . . . Generally speaking, all of us Party members, squad commanders, combat team leaders had our own "wobblies" to watch. We would do everything— sentry duty, chores, and errands—together . . . When the wobblies wanted to take a leak, we would say "I want to have a piss, too" . . . Signs of depression, homesickness, complaints—all had to be dealt with instantly . . . After fighting, particularly defeats, we kept our eyes peeled.

Most of those who ran away did so after camp was pitched, so . . . as well as normal sentries, we placed secret sentries . . . Some of us tied ourselves surreptitiously to our wobblies at night . . . Some of us were so desperate we adopted the method the Japanese used with their labourers—collected the men's trousers and stowed them in the company HQ at night.

Yet even some of these trusted cadres deserted.

The commander of one division that had transferred from Shandong to Manchuria reported to Mao on 15 November that between "deserters, stragglers and the sick" he had lost 3,000 men out of the 32,500 he had set off with. Earlier, the commander of another unit reported: "Last night alone . . . over 80 escaped." One unit suffered a desertion rate of over 50 percent, ending up with fewer than 2,000 out of its original 4,000-plus men. Local Manchurian recruits also defected in droves when they realized they would be fighting the national government. During a ten-day period in late December 1945 to early January 1946, over 40,000 went over to the Nationalists, according to the Reds' own statistics. Although CCP troops in Manchuria far outnumbered the Nationalists, and were well armed with Japanese weapons, they were still unable to hold their own.

MAO'S NO. 2, Liu Shao-chi, had foreseen that the Reds would not be able to shut Chiang out of Manchuria. He had a different strategy from Mao. While Mao was in Chongqing, Liu had instructed the CCP in Manchuria to focus on building a solid base on the borders with Russia and its satellites, where the troops could receive proper training in modern warfare. On 2 October 1945, he had sent an order: "Do not deploy the main forces at the gate to Manchuria to try to keep Chiang out, but at the borders with the USSR, Mongolia and Korea, and dig our heels in." In addition, Liu had told the Reds to be ready to abandon big cities and go and build bases in the countryside surrounding the cities.

But when Mao returned to Yenan from Chongqing, he overruled Liu. Concentrate the main forces at the pass into Manchuria and at big railway junctions, he ordered on 19 October. Mao could not wait to "possess the whole of Manchuria," as another order put it. But his army was not up to the job.

Mao's relationship with his army was in many ways a remote one. He never tried to inspire his troops in person, never visited the front, nor went to meet the troops in the rear. He did not care about them. Many of the soldiers sent to Manchuria had malaria. In order to drag these feverish men the many hundreds of kilometers, each sick man was sandwiched between two able-bodied soldiers and pulled along by a rope around the waist. Mao's preferred method for dealing with wounded soldiers was to leave them with local peasants, who were usually living on a knife-edge between subsistence and starvation, and had no access to medicine.*

His army's performance showed that Mao had no prospect of victory anytime soon, and Stalin adjusted rapidly. On 17 November 1945, after Chiang's army stormed into southern Manchuria, Chiang noted a "sudden change of attitude" in the Russians. They told the CCP it would have to vacate the cities, putting an end to Mao's hopes of becoming immediate master of all Manchuria, and of a quick victory nationwide.

Stalin knew this decision would be devastating for Mao, so he made a gesture to reassure him. On the 18th, a cable was dispatched from Russia: "MAO AN YIN[G] asks for your permission to go to '41' [code name for Yenan]." Stalin was finally returning Mao's son. This was good news for Mao, but no help in seizing Manchuria. Desperate entreaties to the Russians followed, and futile orders for his troops to hold out. When both failed, Mao collapsed with a nervous breakdown. On the 22nd he moved out of Date Garden into a special elite clinic (after all the patients had first been turfed out). For days on end, he was unable to rise from his bed, or to sleep a wink. He lay trembling all over, his hands and feet convulsing, pouring cold sweat.

At his wits' end, Mao's assistant Shi Zhe suggested asking Stalin for help. Mao agreed, and Shi cabled Stalin, who replied at once, offering to send doctors. Mao accepted the offer, but two hours later he seems to have had second thoughts about laying himself so bare to Stalin's eyes and asked Shi to hold the telegram. But it had already gone off.

Only days before, Stalin had recalled Mao's GRU doctor Orlov, together with the whole GRU mission in Yenan. Orlov had been in Yenan for three and a half years without a break, but the minute he arrived in Moscow, Stalin ordered him back to Mao. The hapless Orlov arrived back

---

* When two years later he urged sending large forces deep into Nationalist areas, the commanders asked what would happen to the wounded without a base area to fall back on. Mao's airy response was: "It's easy . . . leave the wounded and the sick to the masses."

on 7 January 1946, accompanied by a second doctor called Melnikov from the KGB. They found nothing seriously wrong with Mao, except for mental exhaustion and nervous stress. Mao was advised to delegate work more, relax, take walks and get plenty of fresh air. Orlov, however, was soon pleading nervous tension himself and begging Moscow to recall him. In vain.

On the plane with the doctors came Mao's son, An-ying, to whom Stalin had personally presented an inscribed pistol before he left. It was over eighteen years since Mao had seen his son, then four years old, in 1927, when Mao had left his wife Kai-hui and three sons and begun his outlaw career. Now An-ying was a good-looking young man of twenty-three. At the airfield Mao hugged him, exclaiming: "How tall you have grown!" That evening, Mao wrote a thank-you letter to Stalin.

Mao had moved out of the clinic by now and settled in the HQ of the military, a beautiful place known as Peony Pavilion. It was surrounded by a large garden of peonies, including some of China's most gorgeous varieties. To this rich splendor the plant-loving nominal C-in-C, Zhu De, and his staff had added a delicate peach orchard, a fish pond and a basketball court. Mao spent a lot of time with An-ying, often sitting at a square stone table chatting outside his adobe house, which stood right next to his deep—and private—air-raid shelter. A frequent mah-jong and card partner of the Maos at the time noticed that Mao acted very affectionately towards his son. Mao's health gradually improved. By spring, he had made a good recovery.

The most comforting thing for Mao was that most of Manchuria was still in Communist hands. Stalin maintained overall control of the area, having hung on way beyond the three months he had promised, and had refused to allow anything but a skeleton Nationalist staff into the cities. Though the CCP had to move its organizations out of most cities, they entrenched in the vast countryside.

THE RUSSIAN ARMY did not finally leave Manchuria until 3 May 1946, nearly ten months after it had entered. To maximize the CCP's chances, they kept the Nationalists in the dark until the very last minute about the pull-out schedule, while coordinating their departure with the CCP so that it could take over the area's assets, including major cities, which the Reds now re-entered. Mao ordered his army again to hold out in key cities on the railway line, which he insisted were to be defended "regardless of the sacrifice," "like Madrid," evoking the heroic image of defending the capital to the death in the Spanish civil war.

Mao's second in command, Liu Shao-chi, again cautioned that the Reds were not up to stopping Chiang's army, and that most cities would have to be abandoned. The Manchuria commander, Lin Biao, also warned

Mao that "there is no great likelihood of holding on to [the cities]," and suggested their strategy should be "to eliminate enemy forces, not defend cities." He agreed with Liu Shao-chi that the priority was to build up rural bases. Mao insisted that the cities must be defended "to the death."*

But the next round of battles showed that his army was still no match for Chiang's. Within weeks of the Russian withdrawal the Nationalists had seized every major city in Manchuria except Harbin, the nearest to Russia, and the Communist forces had been reduced to a state of collapse. They retreated north in chaos, under aerial bombardment, harried by Nationalist tanks and motorized troops. Lin Biao's political commissar later admitted that "the whole army had disintegrated" and fallen into what he called "utter anarchy." One officer recalled being chased northward non-stop for forty-two days: "It really looked as though we'd had it . . ."

Not only were the Reds collapsing militarily, but they were at a huge disadvantage with the civilian population, which longed for national unity after fourteen years of brutal Japanese rule, and saw the Nationalists as representing the government. Lin Biao reported to Mao: "People are saying that the 8th Route Army shouldn't be fighting the government army . . . They regard the Nationalists as the Central Government."

The CCP had a further disadvantage, that of being linked in people's minds with the much-hated Russians. Russian troops plundered not only industrial equipment, but people's homes; and rape by Russian soldiers was frequent. When the belated publication of the Yalta Agreement in February 1946 revealed the huge extraterritorial privileges Stalin had grabbed in Manchuria, anti-Soviet demonstrations erupted in many cities there, as well as in other parts of China. There was a widespread feeling that the CCP had got into Manchuria on the back of the Russians and was not working for the interests of China. When demonstrators shouted slogans like "The CCP should love our country," onlookers applauded. Rumors circulated that the Party was offering the Russians women in exchange for weapons.

The locals treated the Chinese Reds quite differently from the Nationalists. One Red officer recalled: "We were hungry and thirsty when we got to Jilin . . . There was not a soul in the street . . . But when the enemy entered the city, somehow the folks all appeared, waving little flags and cheering . . . Imagine our anger!"

---

* Since then, a cultivated myth has credited Mao with the strategies of "surrounding the cities from the countryside" and of "aiming mainly to eliminate enemy forces, not to defend or capture cities." In fact, the former idea came from Liu Shao-chi, and was vigorously opposed by Mao before practicality forced him to adopt it; and the latter was Lin Biao's.

The Red troops were disheartened, and vented their fury even on their top brass. Lin Biao was once caught in his jeep in a crowd of retreating troops. When his guard asked the men to make way for "the chief," he was greeted with yells like: "Ask that chief, are we retreating to the land of the Big Hairy Ones?" The sobriquet was the locals' derogatory term for the Russians.

At this point it looked as though the Chinese Reds might be driven across the border into Russia, or be scattered into small guerrilla units in the mountains, which Lin Biao anticipated. On 1 June, he asked Mao for permission to abandon Harbin, the last big city the Reds held, about 500 km from the Russian border. The CCP's Manchuria Bureau gave Mao the same fatalistic message the next day: "We have told Brother Chen [code name for the Russians] that we are ready to leave [Harbin] . . ." Mao twice implored Stalin to intervene directly, in the form of either a "military umbrella" or "joint operations." Stalin declined, as intervention would have international implications, although he allowed CCP units to cross into Russia. On 3 June, Mao had to endorse plans to abandon Harbin and go over to guerrilla warfare "on a long-term basis."

Mao was on the ropes. Then he was rescued—by the Americans.

SAVED BY WASHINGTON

(1944–47 ⋆ AGE 50–53)

IT WAS NO secret that many US officials were decidedly unenthusiastic about Chiang, and so Mao acted to exploit this ambivalence in the hope that America would withhold support from the Generalissimo and perhaps take a friendlier line towards the Reds. Mao carefully fostered the delusion that the CCP was not a real Communist party, but one of moderate agrarian reformers, who wanted to cooperate with the US.

In mid-1944 Roosevelt sent a mission to Yenan. Just after the first Americans arrived, Mao floated the idea of changing the Party's name: "We've been thinking of renaming our Party," he told the Russian liaison in Yenan, Vladimirov, on 12 August: "of calling it not 'Communist' but something else. Then the situation . . . will be more favorable, especially with the Americans . . ." The Russians immediately chimed in. Later that month, Molotov fed the same line to Roosevelt's then special envoy to China, General Patrick Hurley, telling him that in China "some . . . people called themselves 'Communists' but they had no relation whatever to communism. They were merely expressing their dissatisfaction at their economic condition by calling themselves Communists. However, once their economic conditions had improved, they would forget this political inclination. The Soviet Government . . . [was not] associated with the 'Communist elements.' "*

Red deception became especially important when Roosevelt's successor, Harry Truman, sent America's top general, George Marshall, to China in December 1945 to try to stop the civil war. Marshall, who had served in China in the 1920s, was already ill-disposed towards Chiang, mainly because of the corruption of Chiang's relatives, and was susceptible to

---

* The Moscow–Mao double act deceived many into suggesting for decades that Mao could have been won over by the US, and that the US had lost the chance to detach Mao from the Soviet camp. In fact, in secret, Mao always told his Party that the friendliness towards America "is only a tactic of expedience in our struggle against Chiang."

CCP claims that it and the US had a lot in common. At their first meeting, Chou En-lai soft-soaped Marshall by telling him how much the CCP "desired a democracy based . . . on the American style." A month later, Chou egregiously suggested that Mao preferred America to Russia, telling Marshall "a small anecdote which might be of interest to you. It has been rumored recently, that Chairman Mao is going to pay a visit to Moscow. On learning this, Chairman Mao laughed and remarked half-jokingly that if ever he would take a furlough abroad . . . he would rather go to the United States . . ." Marshall relayed these remarks uncritically to Truman. Even years later, he was maintaining to Truman that the Reds had been more cooperative than the Nationalists.

Marshall did not understand Mao, or Mao's relationship with Stalin. On 26 December 1945 he told Chiang that "it was very important to determine whether or not the Russian Government was in contact with and was advising the Chinese Communist party"—as though this still needed verification. Later (in February 1948), he told the US Congress that "in China we have no concrete evidence that [the Communist army] is supported by Communists from the outside." This ignorance is particularly striking because the Americans, like the British, had been intercepting cables from Russia, some of them addressed to Yenan, clearly showing the relationship. Marshall was also given strong warnings by other American officials, including the head of the US mission in Yenan, who opened his final report with a three-word alarm: "Communism is International!"*

Marshall visited Yenan on 4–5 March 1946. For the occasion, Mao made doubly sure that everything was shipshape and watertight. One step was to pack his son An-ying off to a village. He told An-ying this was to help him to learn farm labor and Chinese ways, but the real reason was that Mao was vexed by the attention the Americans were paying his English-speaking son. Soon after An-ying had arrived from Russia, Mao had introduced him to the Associated Press correspondent John Roderick, who then interviewed An-ying on the edge of the dance floor at a Saturday night party. Afterwards Mao exploded. He "did not even read the interview through," An-ying recalled, "before he crushed it into a ball, and then told me sternly: . . . How dare you give an interview to a foreign reporter just like that, off the top of your head, without instructions?" An-ying had been schooled in the hard world of Stalin's Russia, but even that had not prepared him for the super-steely discipline of his father's laager. While An-ying was banished to the sticks, the non-

---

* Washington's savvy ambassador in Moscow, Averell Harriman, had been concerned about Marshall's appointment precisely because he felt Marshall was not sufficiently aware of the "Russian danger."

English-speaking Mme Mao was very much on hand for her debut as First Lady.

Marshall's report to Truman about Yenan oozed illusions: "I had a long talk with Mao Tze-tung, and I was frank to an extreme. He showed no resentment and gave me every assurance of cooperation." Marshall informed Truman that Communist forces in Manchuria were "little more than loosely organized bands"; and, even more astonishingly, that: "It has been all but impossible for the Yenan headquarters to reach the leaders' in Manchuria. This was after the Russians had flown CCP leaders to Manchuria from Yenan (in a DC-3) and when Yenan was in daily contact with CCP forces in the field that numbered hundreds of thousands.

While Marshall was still in Yenan, Mao summoned the GRU liaison, Dr. Orlov, and briefed him on the talks.

MARSHALL WAS to perform a monumental service to Mao. When Mao had his back to the wall in what could be called his Dunkirk in late spring 1946, Marshall put heavy—and decisive—pressure on Chiang to stop pursuing the Communists into northern Manchuria, saying that the US would not help him if he pushed further, and threatening to stop ferrying Nationalist troops to Manchuria. On 31 May, Marshall wrote to Chiang, invoking his personal honor:

> Under the circumstances of the continued advance of the Government troops in Manchuria, I must . . . repeat that . . . a point is being reached where the integrity of my position is open to serious question. Therefore I request you again to immediately issue an order terminating advances, attacks or pursuits by Government troops . . .

Chiang gave in and agreed to a fifteen-day ceasefire. This came at the very moment when Mao had become resigned to abandoning the last big Red-held city in Manchuria, Harbin, and dispersing his army into guerrilla units. In fact, he had issued the order on 3 June but on the 5th, when he learned about the ceasefire, he dashed off a new order: "Hang on . . . especially keep Harbin." The tide had turned.

Marshall's diktat was probably the single most important decision affecting the outcome of the civil war. The Reds who experienced that period, from Lin Biao to army veterans, concurred in private that this truce was a fatal mistake on Chiang's part. Had he pressed on, then at the very least he might have prevented the Reds establishing a large and secure base on the Soviet border, with rail links with Russia, over which huge amounts of heavy artillery were brought in. Furthermore, having agreed to a truce of two weeks, Chiang then found Marshall proposing that it be extended to nearly four months and cover the whole of Manchuria—and that the Communists be allowed to keep northern

Manchuria. For Chiang to press on would have meant a head-on collision with Marshall, who, Chiang noted, "was in an exceptionally violent
fury" in this period.

The Generalissimo found pressure bearing down on him not only from
Marshall, but from President Truman himself. In mid-July, two prominent anti-Nationalist intellectuals were gunned down in the Nationalist
area. That month, a public opinion poll in the US showed that only 13
percent favored aiding Chiang, while 50 percent wanted to "Stay Out."
On 10 August, Truman wrote to Chiang using very tough language, citing
the two assassinations and saying that the American people "view with
violent repugnance" events in China. Truman threatened that he might
have to "redefine" America's position if there was no progress "toward a
peaceful settlement."

Under these circumstances, Chiang held his fire in Manchuria
(although he pursued Mao's forces elsewhere, with some success). One
of Chiang's closest colleagues, Chen Li-fu, disagreed with his restraint.
"Be like Franco of Spain," he told Chiang; "if you want to fight communism, fight it to the end." A "stop-go" approach would not work, he told
Chiang: "No good to fire and cease fire, cease fire and fire . . ." But Chiang
needed American aid, which came to some US$3 billion for the whole
civil war (almost $1.6 billion in outright grants, and about $850 million
in de facto gifts of arms), and bowed to American pressure.

Mao thus gained a secure base in northern Manchuria some 1,000 km
by 500 km, an area far bigger than Germany, with long land borders and
railway links with Russia and its satellites. To his top brass, Mao compared
this base to a comfortable armchair, with Russia as a solid back to lean
on, and North Korea and Outer Mongolia on each side on which to rest
his arms.

WITH FOUR MONTHS' RESPITE, the Reds had the time to inte-
grate the nearly 200,000-strong Manchukuo puppet army and the other
new recruits, and to retrain and recondition the old troops. Any soldier
the Communists could not control was "cleansed" (qing-xi), which often
meant killed. Classified figures reveal that for the Red Army in this
theater, the total for those "cleansed," together with those who "escaped,"
came to a staggering 150,000 in three years, almost as many as the total
killed in action, assumed captured and invalided out (172,400).

Motivating the troops to fight Chiang was a key part of the recondi-
tioning. This was mainly done through rallies at which soldiers were
pushed to "speak bitterness." Most had been poor peasants, and had histories of hunger and injustice. Bitter memories were stirred up, bringing
out personal traumas. The crowds became febrile. A report to Mao said
that one soldier had burst out at a rally with such a storm of grief and

anger that "he passed out. And when he came to, he never recovered sanity and is now an idiot." When the rallies reached their emotional climax, the Party would tell the inflamed crowds that they were now fighting to "take revenge on Chiang Kai-shek," whose regime was the source of all their woes. The soldiers thus found personal motivation to fight. People who went through the process testify to its effectiveness, even though they find this hard to believe when they reflect in a calmer state of mind.

Many, however, declined to be psyched up, and some made skeptical remarks. They quickly found themselves condemned as members of "the exploiting classes," and joined the ranks of those destined for "cleansing."

The military training was as intensive as the political reorientation. Here, the Russians were indispensable. When the first Chinese Red units arrived in Manchuria, the Russians had taken some of them for bandits. They did not look like regular troops, and could not handle modern weapons. During the truce, the Russians opened at least sixteen major military institutions, including air force, artillery and engineering schools. Many Chinese officers went to Russia for training, and others to the Russian enclaves of Port Arthur and Dalian. These two ports that Stalin had acquired at Yalta now also served as sanctuaries for Mao's shattered units and cadres in southern Manchuria; here they were given refuge, trained and rearmed.

Moscow's arming of Mao accelerated. The Russians transferred some 900 Japanese aircraft, 700 tanks, more than 3,700 artillery pieces, mortars and grenade-launchers, nearly 12,000 machine-guns, plus the sizeable Sungari River flotilla, as well as numerous armored cars and anti-aircraft guns, and hundreds of thousands of rifles. More than 2,000 wagonloads of arms and war matériel came by rail from North Korea, which had housed major Japanese arsenals, and more captured Japanese weapons arrived from Outer Mongolia. Russian-made arms were also shipped in, plus captured German weapons with the markings chiseled out, which the Reds then pretended were captured American arms.

In addition, the Russians secretly transferred tens of thousands of Japanese POWs to the CCP. These troops played a major role in turning the ragtag Communist army into a formidable battle machine, and were crucial in training Red forces to use the Japanese arms on which they chiefly depended, as well as for servicing and repairing these weapons. It was Japanese, too, who founded the CCP air force, with Japanese pilots serving as flight instructors. Thousands of well-trained Japanese medical staff brought the Red wounded a new level of professional and much-welcomed treatment. Some Japanese troops even took part in combat operations.

Another vital factor was Soviet-occupied North Korea. From there the Russians supplied not only arms but also a Japanese- and Russian-trained contingent of 200,000 hardened Korean regulars. In addition, with its 800-km border with Manchuria, North Korea became what the CCP called "our clandestine rear" and bolthole. In June 1946, when they were on the run, the Chinese Reds moved troops, wounded and matériel there. As the Nationalists took much of central Manchuria, splitting the Red forces in two, the Communists were able to use North Korea as a link between their forces in north and south Manchuria, and between Manchuria and the east coast of China, particularly the vital province of Shandong. To supervise this vast transportation complex, the CCP set up offices in Pyongyang and four Korean ports.

By no means the least of the Russians' contributions was to get the railway system running. Once the northern Manchuria base was consolidated, in late 1946, a team of Russian experts restored the extensive railway network in Mao's territory and had it linked with Russia by spring 1947. In June 1948, when Mao's army was preparing for its final push to take all Manchuria, Stalin sent his former railways minister, Ivan Kovalev, to oversee the work. Altogether, the Russians supervised the repair of more than 10,000 km of track and 120 major bridges. This railway system was critical in allowing the Communists to move vast numbers of troops, and heavy artillery, at speed, to attack the main cities that autumn.

The gigantic assistance from Russia, North Korea and Mongolia was carried out in the greatest secrecy—and is still little known today. The Reds went to great lengths to conceal it. Mao told Lin Biao to delete mention of the fact that their base "was supported by Korea, the Soviet Union, Outer Mongolia" even from a secret inner-Party document.* Moscow played its customary part by calling reports of Soviet assistance "fabrications from start to finish." The real fabrication was Mao's claim that the CCP was fighting with "only millet plus rifles."

This Russian help, however, came at a grievous price for those living under Mao's rule. Mao did not want to be beholden to Stalin for this aid, and he wanted to feel free to ask for more. Twice, in August and October 1946, he offered to pay for it with food, an offer Russia's trade representative in Harbin at first declined. So in November Mao sent one of his most dependable acolytes, Liu Ya-lou, to Moscow to insist. A secret agreement was reached for the CCP to send Russia one million tons of food every year.

The result was famine and deaths from starvation in some areas of China occupied by the Communists. In the Yenan region, according to

---

* Lin was also told: "say we struggle for political, economic and military democracy . . . Do not put forward the slogan of class struggle."

Mao's logistics manager, over 10,000 peasants died of starvation in 1947. Mao knew the situation very well, as he was traveling in the region that year, and saw village children hunting for stray peas in the stables of his entourage, and women scrabbling for the water in which his rice had been washed, for the sake of its driblets of nutrient. In the neighboring Red base in Shanxi, his guard chief told him after a visit home that people were starving, and that his own family was lucky to be alive—and this was soon after harvest time. In Manchuria itself, civilian deaths from starvation were in the hundreds of thousands in 1948, and even Communist troops were often half-starved.

Few knew that the famine in Red areas in those years was largely due to the fact that Mao was exporting food; the shortage was put down to "war." Here was a foretaste of the future Great Famine, which was likewise Mao's creation: again the result of his decision to export food to Russia.

AT THE TIME of the Marshall-dictated ceasefire, in June 1946, Chiang was militarily still far superior to Mao. The Nationalist army stood at 4.3 million, easily outnumbering Mao's 1.27 million. For a while, the Generalissimo seemed to prevail. While he left the Reds in peace in Manchuria, he drove them out of most of their strongholds in China proper, including the only important city they still held, Zhangjiakou, in October. Farther south, the Reds were swept virtually completely out of the Yangtze area. In all theaters, Mao repeated his failed Manchuria approach, and urged his generals to seize big cities at any cost. His plan for eastern China on 22 June, for instance, called for closing in on Nanjing, where Chiang had just reinstalled his capital. Though Mao called this a "no-risk" undertaking, it had to be abandoned, like his other plans.

In spite of these substantial losses, Mao remained totally confident—because he had the north Manchuria base. When Chiang did begin to attack it, in October 1946, after the ceasefire had given the Reds more than four months to consolidate, he was unable to break their defenses. In that winter of 1946–47, the coldest in many people's memory, the Nationalists found themselves fighting hard see-saw battles with the transformed Communist forces under Lin Biao, whose military talent came into its own in these harsh months. Mao summed up Lin's style appreciatively as "merciless and devious." One method of Lin's was to make use of the cold weather. In temperatures as low as −40°C, when passing water could cause frostbite on the penis, his troops lay in ambush in ice and snow for days on end. Red veterans estimated their own dead and crippled from frostbite at up to 100,000. The Nationalists suffered much less because they had better clothes—and less ruthless commanders.

By spring 1947, the Reds' north Manchuria base had become unshakable. Marshall had left China in January, marking the end of US mediation efforts. The US later gave considerable aid to Chiang, but it made no difference. The goal the Communists had been secretly seeking for more than two decades, "linking up with the Soviet Union," had been accomplished—with help from Washington, however unwitting. Mao's victory nationwide was only a matter of time.

MOLES, BETRAYALS AND POOR
LEADERSHIP DOOM CHIANG

(1945–49 ★ AGE 51–55)

BY EARLY 1947, when the Nationalists had failed to crack Mao's vast base on the borders with Russia, Chiang knew he was in trouble. Many in the country knew, too. He badly needed a victory to boost morale. He came up with the idea of taking Yenan, Mao's capital. Its capture would have "the greatest significance," he wrote in his diary on 1 March. On that day, he gave this vital task to a man who enjoyed his unconditional trust. General Hu Tsung-nan was the guardian of his younger (and adopted) son, Weigo, and had stood proxy for Chiang at Weigo's wedding.

Our investigations have convinced us that General Hu was a Red "sleeper." He started his career at the Nationalists' Whampoa Military Academy in 1924, which Moscow founded, bankrolled and staffed, at a time when Sun Yat-sen was trying to use Russian sponsorship to conquer China. Chiang Kai-shek was the head of the Academy, and Chou En-lai the director of its pivotal Political Department. Many secret Communist agents were planted there, and went on to become officers in the Nationalist military.

At Whampoa, Hu Tsung-nan was strongly suspected of being a secret Communist,* but he had well-placed friends who vouched for him. He then struck up a friendship with Chiang's intelligence chief, Tai Li, who match-made his marriage. The two became so close that Tai ordered his subordinates in Hu's units to send copies of all their intelligence reports to Hu as well as to himself, the result of which was that none of them dared report any suspicions about Hu.

In 1947, Chiang assigned him to take Yenan. On the day he received the assignment, the message appeared on Mao's desk. Mao ordered the

---

* This was partly on account of his close friendship with a man called Hu Kung-mien, who at the time was commonly assumed to be a secret Communist, and who has now been acknowledged by Peking as an agent. During the war against Japan, when Hu Tsung-nan was stationed south of Yenan, he made this man his representative to Mao.

city to be evacuated, and the local population was herded out into the hills by armed militia. The bulk of the Red administration went to the Red base east of the Yellow River.

On 18–19 March, Hu took Yenan, which the Nationalists trumpeted as a great victory. But all they acquired was a ghost town. On Mao's orders, the evacuees and the locals had buried not only their food, but all their household goods, down to cooking utensils.

Mao himself had left only hours before, in an ostentatiously leisurely, even nonchalant manner, pausing awhile to gaze at the pagoda which was the symbol of Yenan, while his driver revved the engine of his American jeep (donated by the departing US mission) as a reminder that the Nationalists were nearby. Mao staged this performance to build confidence in people around him. A short time before, Mao's top brass had been awe-struck when he sent most of the troops in Yenan away, keeping only 20,000 men with him for the whole of the region—less than one-tenth of the force Hu had at his disposal, which totaled some 250,000.

Mao set off north, riding with Chou En-lai, now his chief of staff, and Mme Mao. On the way, he and Chou chatted and laughed, as if, in the words of a bodyguard, "this was an outing."

About 30 km northeast of Yenan, at a place called Qinghuabian, Mao asked the driver to slow down in a deep valley where the loess slopes had been scoured by rain and floods into deep canyons. His bodyguards were puzzled to see him pointing and nodding thoughtfully with Chou. It was only a week later that the explanation dawned on them, when Hu's 31st Brigade HQ and 2,900 troops walked into an ambush at this exact spot on 25 March.

The brigade had been given the order to follow this road by Hu only the day before. But Mao's men had started taking up positions days earlier—and Mao had committed his entire force of 20,000 to this one operation. Before the first shots were fired, the brigade spotted the ambushers, and radioed the information to Hu. General Hu told his force to press on, threatening court martial if they did not, and the 2,900 men were wiped out. Meanwhile, Hu had dispatched the bulk of his army in another direction, due west, making it impossible for it to come to the rescue of the trapped brigade.

Three weeks later, on 14 April, Mao scored another victory in exactly the same fashion at a place called Yangmahe, when one of Hu's units marched straight into an ambush. Five thousand men were killed, wounded or captured. Just as before, Hu had moved his main force away, so the doomed brigade was cut off from it by impassable ravines.

On 4 May came a third pushover, when the Communists took Hu's main forward depot, Panlong. Once again, Hu had sent his main force away on a wild goose chase, leaving the depot lightly defended. Both the defenders and the main force had reported Red units "lying in hiding" near the depot, but Hu said they were crying wolf. When the main force reached its target, it found an empty city.

The depot at Panlong handed the Reds vast stores of food, clothing, ammunition and medical supplies, while the Nationalists were left starving. Some were reduced to taking shoes from rotting Communist corpses. "No matter how we washed them," one recalled, "we still couldn't get rid of the horrible stench." Many fell ill, but they had been cleaned out of medicine.

After these three victories within two months of the Nationalists taking Yenan, the Communists broadcast the news that Mao had remained in the Yenan region. The import was that even though he was not actually in the capital, the CCP supremo was able to survive and operate in the area, and was very much in control of events.

Mao remained within some 150 km of Hu's HQ in Yenan city for a whole year, traveling with an entourage of 800 people, which eventually grew to 1,400, including a cavalry company. A sizable radio corps operated twenty-four hours a day, keeping contact with Red armies and bases all over China and with Russia.

Mao moved about from place to place for the first time since he had come to rule this region a decade before. A litter was kept at the ready, but Mao preferred walking and riding, unlike his custom on the Long March, and became very fit. His chef carried his favorite foods like chili and sausages. Mao almost never ate with the locals or in restaurants, for fear of poor hygiene, or poison. He slept so well that he even dispensed with sleeping pills, and was in marked high spirits. He did quite a bit of sightseeing, and posed for a newsreel crew who came from Manchuria to film him. Mme Mao acquired a stills camera, and took a lot of photographs, embarking on a hobby at which she later became quite accomplished. The Russian doctors came over frequently from the Red base east of the Yellow River to give Mao check-ups and report on his condition to Stalin.

During this year, most of the Yenan region remained under Communist control, and Hu's vast army was sent into one large ambush after another, always following the same pattern: isolated units surrounded and overwhelmed by concentrated Communist forces while Hu's main forces chased their own tails elsewhere. Hu's superbly trained artillery battalion fell wholesale to the Reds, and came to form a significant part of Mao's artillery. Yet another spectacular ambush buried one of Hu's crack units when he ordered it back to Yenan, claiming that the city was under threat. It was trapped in a narrow mountain valley and shelled to smithereens. While Hu's army was thus destroyed on a massive scale, Mao came across as a military genius who could pull spectacular victories out of a hat.

MAO HAD ONE CLOSE SHAVE. It came in June 1947, when he had lingered nearly two months in a village called Wangjiawan, staying with a peasant's family, the first time he lived in intimate proximity to the locals. Here he took walks and went riding for pleasure. When the weather got hotter, he decided he wanted a shady place to read outdoors, so his bodyguards felled some trees to make pillars, weaving the twigs and leaves into a bower, where Mao read every day, studying English for relaxation.

On 8 June, one of Hu's commanders, Liou Kan, suddenly appeared nearby with a large force. He had been tipped off about Mao's presence by a local who had managed to escape from the Red area. Mao erupted with unprecedented rage, bellowing at Chou En-lai, and a heated discussion ensued about which way to run. The nearest safe haven was a Red base east of the Yellow River, where boats and cars were on constant standby at the crossing. But it was too far away, so Mao decided to go west, towards the Gobi Desert—after taking the precaution of rounding up a large group of villagers, who were forcibly evacuated in the opposite direction as decoys.

Mao made off through thunderstorms, carried on the backs of bodyguards along mountain paths too slippery for horses. Radio silence was imposed to minimize the chances of detection—except for one radio, which worked non-stop, almost certainly to contact Hu to call his troops off.*

Which is exactly what happened. On 11 June, Liou Kan was so close on Mao's heels that the Reds could hear his troops and see their torches. Mao's guards said they felt their hair seemed to "stand on end." As they were getting ready to defend him to the death, Mao emerged from a cave all smiles, predicting that the enemy would pass them by. At that instant, right in front of the guards' astonished eyes, the Nationalist troops rushed by, and left them totally unmolested. Hu had ordered Liou Kan to drop everything and race on to his original destination, Baoan, Mao's old capital.

This incident may well have triggered an urgent request to Stalin to get Mao out to Russia. A cable from Stalin on 15 June was clearly in reply to such a request. Stalin offered to send a plane to pick up Mao.

By then, Mao was safe. The day before Stalin's telegram, Mao had

---

* Mao's radios had been maintaining regular communication with Communist agents in Hu's army, "so their action was entirely under our control," one of Mao's radio men told us, adding that "some of the identities of the underground are not disclosed even today" (1999).

wired a cheerful message to his colleagues in the Red base east of the Yellow River: "On 9–11 this month, Liou Kan's 4 brigades held a parade where we were . . . Apart from a little loss to the population, no losses. Now the Liou [Kan] army is running to and fro between Yenan and Baoan." Mao did not take up Stalin's offer to evacuate him this time. All the same, he ordered an airstrip built at once just east of the Yellow River, in case.

Liou Kan soon met his death. In February 1948 he was ordered to reinforce the town of Yichuan, between Yenan and the Yellow River. There were three possible routes, and the one picked for him, by General Hu, ran through a narrow wooded valley. Scouts found a heavy concentration of Communist troops, clearly indicating an ambush. Liou Kan radioed Hu for permission to attack the ambushers and then change course. Hu flatly refused.

One of Liou Kan's division commanders, Wang Ying-tsun, later wrote: "After this order, which completely ignored the real situation and our interests, officers and soldiers lost heart . . . everyone marched in silence, with their heads bowed . . ." They walked straight into the encirclement and were virtually annihilated. Half a dozen generals were killed, and Liou Kan committed suicide. The division commander managed to escape, and later saw General Hu. According to him, the general "hypocritically expressed his regret, and said why did you press on when you did not have enough troops? I thought: it was your order, and my men were pounded and killed . . ." The division commander testified: "After Liou Kan's 29th Army was wiped out, it went without saying that Hu Tsung-nan's troops had no morale to speak of. Moreover, the state of mind of the whole Chiang area was tremendously shaken . . ." This defeat sealed the Nationalists' fate in the Yenan theater, and negated Chiang's whole aim in capturing Yenan, which had been to boost morale and confidence in the country at large.

Chiang knew that Hu wrecked everything he touched. In his diary of 2 March 1948, the Generalissimo wrote: "This catastrophe cost over one third of the main force [under Hu]," and that Hu was "following the same fatal road again and again." And yet, when Hu disingenuously offered his resignation, Chiang turned it down, with only a lamentation: "The loss of our troops at Yichuan is not only the biggest setback in the Nationalist Army's campaign against the bandits, but also an entirely senseless sacrifice. Good generals killed, a whole army wiped out. Grief and anguish are consuming me . . ." A half-hearted investigation blamed the debacle on the dead Liou Kan. The Nationalist system followed its tradition of closing ranks, especially once others saw that Hu was so secure in Chiang's favor.

The fact that the Generalissimo allowed Hu to get away with a whole year of incredible defeats, all clearly following the same pattern, says a lot about his leadership and judgment. He trusted people he liked, and would back them come what may, often sentimentally. He was also stubborn, and would stick by his own mistakes. Chiang even allowed Hu to siphon off troops from other vital theaters. The chief US military adviser, Major General David Barr, observed that Hu "prevailed on" Chiang "to reinforce his Xian garrison to an extent which was later to prove disastrous to the Nationalists in east central China"; key losses there were "a direct result of this shift of troops to the west," where, Barr noted, they were either useless or destroyed.

When Mao finally left the Yenan region and headed east over the Yellow River to the Red base on 23 March 1948, he did so publicly, with organized crowds of peasants seeing him off at the river crossing. And he shook hands with local cadres before he boarded the boat. This unusual openness was to demonstrate that he was not running away furtively. And the general point that the Reds were riding high was reinforced a month later when Hu abandoned Yenan altogether. Over the past year he had lost 100,000 troops. Recovering Yenan was potentially a propaganda windfall for the Reds, but Mao adopted an extremely low-key position. His assistant, Shi Zhe, expected him to make the most of the occasion: "so I waited by his side . . . But nothing happened." Mao did not want to attract more attention to Hu in case he was sacked.

Hu went on to cause even more spectacular catastrophes for Chiang, ultimately losing many hundreds of thousands of troops. When Chiang got to Taiwan, Hu went too. There he was immediately impeached, on the charge that he had "brought about the greatest damage to our army and country" of all the Nationalists. But the impeachment failed, thanks to Chiang's protection. Chiang even put Hu in charge of operations to infiltrate the Mainland: they all came to grief. Hu died in Taiwan in 1962. Chiang may have come to doubt his judgment in his later years. His chief of guards (and subsequently prime minister of Taiwan), Hau Po-tsun, told us that Chiang showed an aversion to the mention of the Whampoa Academy, which is generally assumed to have been his base. Many moles had hailed from there.

MOLES CONTINUED to play a key role in the defeats Chiang suffered in the three military campaigns in 1948–49 that clinched the civil war. The first was in Manchuria, where Chiang picked as his supreme commander a general called Wei Li-huang. In this case, Chiang had not only been told that Wei was a Communist agent, but actually suspected this to be true. Even so, he put Wei in charge of all the 550,000 best troops in this critical theater in January 1948.

Wei had asked to join the CCP in 1938. Mao passed the news to

Moscow in 1940, telling the Russians that the CCP had instructed Wei to stay undercover with the Nationalists. It seems that Wei decided on his betrayal out of a mighty grudge against Chiang for not promoting him as high as he felt he deserved. Wei had told cronies then: "I am going for the Communists . . . Yenan is nice to me . . . Let's work with the Communists to bring him [Chiang] down."

Chiang had been told about Wei's secret liaisons by a Communist defector at the time, and so he passed Wei over again for a top army post after 1945, even though Wei had fought well in Burma against the Japanese, and earned the title "Hundred Victories Wei." Wei became even more disgruntled, and went into self-imposed exile abroad.

The reason Wei was brought back in 1948 and given such a crucial job was that Chiang was frantically trying to woo the Americans, who thought highly of Wei's performance in Burma and regarded him as an important "liberal." The then US vice-consul in Shenyang, William Stokes, told us that Chiang appointed Wei "in a futile attempt to gain more American equipment and funding, because Wei was recognised by the Americans as a proven military leader."

The moment Wei received the call from Chiang, he let the Russian embassy in Paris know, and thenceforth coordinated his every move with the CCP. First of all, he pulled his troops back into a few big cities, thus allowing the Communists to take control of 90 percent of Manchuria without a fight and then to surround these cities.

Mao wanted Wei to make sure that all the Nationalist troops under him stayed in Manchuria so that they could be wiped out there. Wei therefore ignored repeated orders from Chiang to move his troops to Jinzhou, the southernmost railway junction in Manchuria, preparatory to withdrawing from Manchuria completely (a move the chief US adviser, Major General Barr, had also recommended). Instead of sacking Wei, Chiang went on arguing with him for months—until the Communists took Jinzhou, on 15 October, trapping most of the hundreds of thousands of Nationalist troops in Manchuria. Mao's troops then swiftly isolated Wei's forces in the remaining Nationalist-held cities, and attacked them one by one. With the fall of Shenyang on 2 November, the whole of Manchuria was in Mao's hands.

For his performance in Manchuria, Chiang put Wei under house arrest, and there were calls for him to be court-martialed. But the Generalissimo, who rarely executed, or even imprisoned, any of his top commanders or opponents, let Wei go, and he sailed off unmolested to Hong Kong. A year later, two days after the proclamation of Communist China, Wei cabled Mao, wagging his tail: "wise guidance . . . magnificent triumph . . . great leader . . . rejoice and cheer and whole-hearted support . . . Am leaping up ten thousand feet like a bird . . ." But he cynically declined to go and live under Mao, and tried to contact the CIA in 1951 to back him to lead a third force. He finally moved to the Mainland in 1955.

Mao spoke to his nephew about Wei in withering terms: "Wei Li-huang didn't return until he went bankrupt doing business in Hong Kong. A man like Wei Li-huang is contemptible . . ." And Mao made sure his contempt was demonstrated. Wei's old Communist contacts were told to turn down his invitations to dinner, and the snubbing lasted until Wei's death in Peking in 1960. His critical help for Mao is still hushed up, as Mao's military genius would look a lot less brilliant if it were known that the enemy's top commander had offered up much of his force—and many of Chiang's best troops—on a platter.

DURING THE WHOLE of the Manchuria campaign, Mao never went there. He was at his new HQ at Xibaipo, 240 km southwest of Peking. After Manchuria fell in early November 1948, he ordered the army there under Lin Biao to come south. This army now stood at upwards of 1.3 million strong, and its new mission was to tackle the 600,000-man Nationalist army in northern China led by Fu Tso-yi, a celebrated general who had fought China's first winning battle against Japanese puppets in 1936. The encounter between Lin and Fu, known as the Peking–Tianjin Campaign, was the second of the three key campaigns that decided the civil war.

Unlike Wei, General Fu was not a secret Communist. But he was surrounded by people who were, not least his own daughter, who was assigned by the Party to stay with her father in this period and report his every move. Chiang had some idea about this situation, but took no action to remedy it.

By November, even before Lin was on his way south from Manchuria, Fu had made up his mind to surrender, without telling Chiang. He had lost faith in Chiang's regime, and decided to try to save the area under him from pointless devastation—not least Peking itself, the nation's cultural capital, where his HQ was located. He did not do this out of any illusions about Communist rule, which, he said publicly at the time, would bring "cruelty . . . terror and tyranny," and the decision to surrender caused him great anguish. He began to fall to pieces, and was seen slapping his own face, and contemplating suicide.

Chiang knew what was happening to Fu. On 12 December he wrote in his diary that Fu was "deeply depressed . . . and seems to be going insane." But he still refused to sack him, and when Fu offered to resign, Chiang turned him down with a maudlin "10,000 Nos."

Mao kept close tabs on Fu's mental condition through Fu's daughter, and he decided he could extract more from the situation than just a surrender. He could establish himself in the public eye as a military genius who had beaten Fu, the renowned war hero. So, when Fu sued for surrender, Mao strung Fu's envoys along for two months, not accepting the surrender but not saying "No" either, while all the time keeping up attacks on Fu's army. By now Fu was quite unfit to command. One officer recalled how during one key battle, when asked for instructions, "Fu dithered and faltered and then said listlessly: 'Play it by ear.' At that moment, I thought, we are finished . . ." Predictably, Mao's army took city after city, including Tianjin, the third largest in China, which fell on 15 January 1949. Only when he had created an image of himself as a military giant-killer did Mao accept Fu's standing offer to surrender Peking. Mao was thus able to say that Fu had opted for peace only after being thoroughly defeated on the battlefield—by Mao himself. The truth is that the whole campaign, which cost tens of thousands of lives, did not have to be fought at all. A broken Fu collaborated with Mao until his death on the Mainland in 1974.

AT ABOUT THE SAME TIME as the sham Peking–Tianjin Campaign, a third huge, and more genuine, campaign was being fought in the heartland of China to the north of Chiang's capital, Nanjing. Known as the Huai–Hai Campaign, this involved well over one million men, and lasted from November 1948 to January 1949. The chief commander on the Nationalist side here was not a Communist agent, or a mental wreck. But just below him there were strategically placed Red sleepers, including two generals who had been secret Party members for ten and twenty years respectively, who opened up the gateway to this battleground within forty-eight hours of the campaign starting.

The major saboteurs were two other men in Chiang's own HQ called Liu Fei and Kuo Ju-kui, who were intimately involved in drawing up the battle plans for the campaign. They placed the Nationalists on the defensive in every move by deliberately making wrong deployments and recommendations, while passing the plans to the Communists.

Chiang was particularly dependent on Kuo, to whom he spoke on the phone almost every day, and whose ruinous advice he heeded. Kuo actually fell under suspicion at this time from field commanders, and was even denounced as a spy by no less a person than Chiang's adopted son, Weigo. But the Generalissimo did nothing until it was too late, and even then he merely transferred Kuo to Sichuan—on the recommendation of the other key mole, Liu Fei. In Sichuan, Kuo would later surrender an entire army.

By mid-January 1949, Mao had wrapped up all three major campaigns triumphantly. The country north of the Yangtze, where 80 percent of Chiang's troops had been stationed, was Mao's. He now wanted moles to be posted to unconquered areas south of the river, to wait for his army to arrive and then surrender at the opportune moment. Nationalist bigwigs jumped ship in droves. On 7 January Mao informed Stalin that "many prominent" Chiang men, including former defense minister Pai, were seeking deals: "Pai Chung-hsi asked our people—whatever orders come from the CCP, I would fulfill them immediately . . ." (Pai in fact did not go with Mao.) Mao told supplicants to stay with Chiang, and in some cases even to put up resistance and wait for the right moment. Though the Yangtze was a formidable barrier, and Chiang had a sizable navy, these old and new betrayals made sure that the road was open to the capital, Nanjing, and the financial center, Shanghai—and to the rest of China. On 9–10 January, Mao confidently informed Stalin that his government "can be created in summer," or "earlier."

Mao's victory in the civil war was enormously helped by Chiang's very poor judgment about people—although it was also not easy to detect and root out the Communist moles. Mao's own policy was not to take the slightest chance. The terror campaigns in Yenan and the other Red areas had exposed and severed virtually every connection individual Communists had with the Nationalists, and the Communists' total destruction of privacy meant there was no way those under their rule could contact the Nationalists even if they wanted to.

And Mao never let up. Each time he acquired more territory and personnel, he took relentless steps to enforce control, requiring each new Party enlistee to write down all his or her family and social relations— and this was just for starters. He never stopped seeking, never stopped plugging, every conceivable loophole. Very few agents, Nationalist or foreign, survived his attention, certainly none who reached any position of importance.

CHIANG'S STRONG FEELINGS for his wife contributed heavily to him losing China. His first prime minister after the Sino-Japanese War was T.V. Soong, who was Mme Chiang's brother. The Soongs and the family Mme Chiang's elder sister had married into, the Kungs, grew fat on T.V.'s policies. After the Japanese surrender, T.V. set the exchange rate for the currency of the puppet government outside Manchuria at the absurd level of 1 to 200. This saw the family wealth swell, but impoverished the entire population in the former Japanese-occupied areas in China proper, which included the main cities like Shanghai and Nanjing, with the bulk of the nation's middle class. Under T.V., takeover officials engaged in widespread extortion, shaking down the rich by designating them "collaborators." Chiang himself acknowledged that his officials were "indulging in extreme extravagance, whoring wildly and gambling with no restraint . . . They brag, swagger and extort and stop at nothing . . ."

The room where Mao was born, on 26 December 1893, in Shaoshan village, Hunan province.

Mao Tse-tung (right), in the only photograph of him with his mother, taken in Changsha in 1919, shortly before she died. Mao, aged twenty-five, is dressed in scholar's garb, while his two younger brothers, Tse-tan (far left) and Tse-min, are still wearing peasant clothes.

Mao Tse-tung (right), wearing a black armband just after the death of his mother, with his father (second from left), uncle (second from right), and brother Tse-tan (far left), Changsha, 13 November 1919.

Yang Kai-hui, Mao's second wife, with their two eldest sons, An-ying (right), aged two, and An-ching, aged one, Shanghai, 1924. Kai-hui was soon to be deserted by Mao, and executed by the Nationalists because of Mao. She left poignant manuscripts describing her disillusionment with communism and with Mao, whom she loved.

Moscow's key agents in China. Grigori Voitinsky (above left) founded the Chinese Communist Party in 1920. Maring (above right), the Dutch agitator, co-presided over the first congress of the Chinese Communist Party in Shanghai in 1921. He later broke with communism and was executed by the Nazis. (Below) Mikhail Borodin (far right) steered both the Nationalists and the Communists in 1923–27. He was in Canton, 1925, with Chiang Kai-shek (next to him), soon to become the Nationalists' leader, and Wang Ching-wei (front), Mao's patron in the Nationalist Party, and later head of the Japanese puppet government.

Ruijin, 7 November 1931, the day the first Chinese Red state was founded, when Mao (second from right) became the "Chairman." To his left Wang Jia-xiang; to his right: Xiang Ying, Deng Fa, military chief Zhu De, Ren Bi-shi and Gu Zuo-lin.

The leadership of the Red state held its first formal meeting on 1 December 1931. Mao standing, back to camera. Zhu De to Mao's right. The Red state collapsed in October 1934, when the Long March began.

The bridge over the Dadu River at Luding, the site of the core myth about the Long March. Communist claims of fierce fighting here in 1935 were invented.

Mao (standing, third from left, looking Oscar Wilde-ish), in his post–Long March HQ, Yenan, September 1937, with some of the participants in the "Autumn Harvest Uprising" of 1927, the founding moment of the myth of Mao as a peasant leader. His third wife, Gui-yuan, is standing far right.

Mao (seated, second from left), with Red Army officers, including Zhu De (seated, third from left) and Mao's closest crony, Lin Biao (seated, fourth from left), Yenan, 1937.

The four moles who helped doom the Nationalists. Shao Li-tzu (right) delivered Chiang Kai-shek's son to Moscow in 1925 to be Stalin's hostage for over a decade. To get his son back, Chiang let the Reds survive during the Long March.

Gen. Zhang Zhi-zhong (above) triggered off all-out war with Japan in 1937, diverting the Japanese into the heartland of China and away from Russia.

Gen. Hu Tsung-nan (below) offered up Nationalist forces en masse to Mao to be wiped out in 1947–48. "Hundred Victories" Gen. Wei Li-huang (below right, center), photographed for *Life* magazine, delivered over half a million of Chiang's best troops and Manchuria to Mao in 1948.

Generalissimo Chiang Kai-shek (front right) with Chang Hsueh-liang ("the Young Marshal"), the former warlord of Manchuria, who kidnapped Chiang at Xian in December 1936. The kidnap, which was co-ordinated with Mao, dealt the marginalized Reds back into the game.

Mao's main Party rivals. Chang Kuo-tao (above left) with Mao in Yenan, 1937. Mao sabotaged Chang's much larger army on the Long March; he then sent half the remainder to its doom in the Northwest desert, finally burying the survivors alive. Chang fled the Reds in 1938. Wang Ming (above right) with Mao shortly after arriving in Yenan from Moscow in late 1937, bringing Stalin's orders for the CCP to fight Japan. Mao, who welcomed the Japanese invasion as a way to destroy Chiang Kai-shek, felt threatened by Wang Ming, and had him poisoned. Mao was in the minority in the Politburo over his "don't fight Japan" policy, but reversed his political fortunes by scheming in autumn 1938, when the Politburo gathered in Yenan, here seen (below) in front of the Spanish Franciscan cathedral. From left: Mao, Peng De-huai, Wang Jia-xiang, Lo Fu, Zhu De, Po Ku (who tried to leave Mao behind on the Long March), Wang Ming, Kang Sheng, Xiang Ying, Liu Shao-chi, Chen Yun, Chou En-lai.

January 1937: Red Army troops entering Yenan, which became Mao's home for a decade.

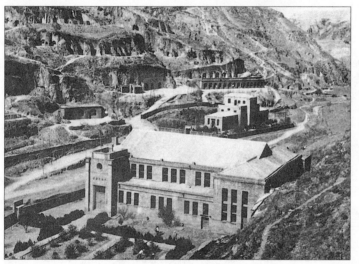

Yenan: the building constructed specially for the Party congress that enthroned Mao in 1945. Cave dwellings visible in the background, dug into the soft loess hills.

The Spanish Franciscan cathedral of Our Lady of Begoña in Yenan. Completed in 1935, it was seized by the local Red leader, Liu Chih-tan, whom Mao soon eliminated. The site of many key Party meetings, including the one which reversed Mao's fortunes.

Jung Chang, outside Mao's official Yenan residence, interviewing a local farmer whose mother used to do Mao's laundry.

Jon Halliday at the ruins of a churchlike edifice specially built in a remote valley outside Yenan for Party meetings; it was never used, as Mao had a secret residence next door and wanted to keep the place to himself. This secret compound (below) is unknown to this day. Mao lived in the "cave" to the right, with tunnels through the hills. The entrance was covered, and even had a sun awning. The only neighbors were several thousand well-guarded prisoners.

Mao with his third wife, Gui-yuan, in Yenan, 1937. She soon left him and went to Russia. She lived the rest of her life in and out of mental breakdowns.

Mao's two surviving sons at the special school for children of foreign Communist leaders at Ivanovo, outside Moscow. An-ying, the eldest son, is the tall boy in the middle row, center. The banner above the portrait of Mao reads: "Long live the Communist International— the Organiser of the Struggle for the Victory of the Workers!"

Mao posing outside one of his residences in 1939 reading Stalin for a documentary by Stalin's favorite film-maker, Roman Karmen, who duly reported back on Mao's "devotion."

A receipt signed by Mao for US$300,000 (worth about US$4 million in 2005) received from a Russian called Mikhailov, dated 28 April 1938.

In August 1945, when Japan surrendered, Stalin told Mao to go to Chongqing to play the negotiating game with Chiang Kai-shek. (Above) Mao in topee on arrival at Chongqing, with U.S. Ambassador Patrick Hurley (center). Chou En-lai to right of Hurley. When the civil war heated up, and Mao was on the verge of defeat, he was saved, unwittingly, by America's mediator, General George C. Marshall. (Left) Marshall was seen off from Yenan on 5 March 1946 by Mao's fourth wife, Jiang Qing, the later notorious "Mme Mao," on her first outing as would-be "First Lady."

(Right) A downcast Chiang Kai-shek visiting his ancestral temple for the last time before leaving Mainland China in 1949, with his son and heir, Ching-kuo (to left in hat).

(Below) Red troops entering Nanjing to a conspicuously cool welcome. The Communists later filmed reconstructions of the takeover of cities and showed them as if they were real events.

(Above) Mao proclaiming the founding of Communist China from the top of Tiananmen Gate, 1 October 1949. His first political campaign centered on mass executions, in front of organized crowds (below). "Only when this thing is properly done can our power be secure," Mao pronounced. The people being exhibited carry plaques announcing that they are "landlords" and "spies."

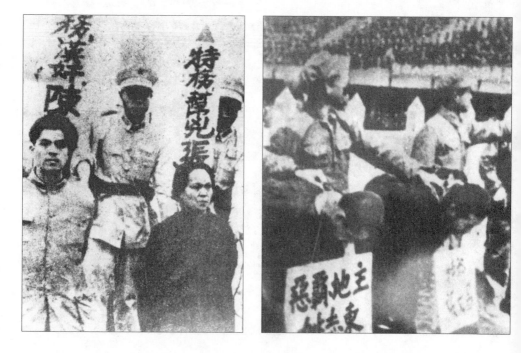

"The Calamity of Victory" was how the influential *Ta Kung Pao* newspaper described the takeover.

At the time of the Japanese surrender, Chiang seemed to be a glorious victor, yet within a very short time he was plunging into decline. Hyper-inflation, food crises, hoarding and panic buying became endemic in the cities. Under T.V., the government managed to squander not only its own reserves, but also the sizable holdings of gold and foreign currency that it inherited from the puppet government.

The Soongs and the Kungs had access to China's foreign currency reserves at preferential rates, which enabled them to sell US goods in China at a huge profit, causing the largest trade deficit in China's history in 1946. This dumping bankrupted swaths of industry and commerce, and T.V. was forced to resign as prime minister on 1 March 1947, after being fiercely attacked in the National Assembly and the press. Chiang ordered an investigation, which concluded that Soong and Kung companies had illegally converted more than US$380 million.

But all the Generalissimo did was demote T.V., which outraged and alienated many devoted, and uncorrupt, followers. Demoralization accelerated throughout the population, while many denounced the regime as "a bunch of robbers" and "bloodsuckers." Chiang's failure to clean up, and especially to come to grips with the malfeasance of his wife's family, also lost him support in America.

The report of the investigation into Chiang's relatives was kept secret. Then the Nationalists' own newspaper, the *Central Daily*, got hold of a copy and published it on 29 July, causing a sensation. Two days later, after irate phone calls from Mme Chiang to her husband, the paper had to carry a notice claiming it had got the decimal point wrong, and lowered the sum taken by the families from over US$300 million to US$3 million.

Chiang consistently let personal feelings dictate his political and military actions. He lost China to a man who had none of his weak spots.

CHINA CONQUERED

(1946–49 ★ AGE 52–55)

MAO'S MOST FORMIDABLE weapon was pitilessness. In 1948, when he moved on Changchun, in Manchuria, and a direct assault failed to take it, an order was given to starve it into surrender. The actual words used on 30 May by Mao's commander on the spot, Lin Biao, were: "Turn Changchun into a city of death."

The defending commander, General Cheng Tung-kuo, was a hero of the war against Japan, and refused to capitulate. As there was only enough food to see the 500,000 civilians through until the end of July, he tried to evacuate civilians.

Lin Biao's response, endorsed by Mao, was: "Strictly ban civilians from leaving the city." The Communists let people go who had arms or ammunition, so as to encourage Nationalist soldiers to defect, but specifically blocked civilians. Mao's calculation was that General Cheng was "a nice sort of guy," as he described him to Lin Biao, and could be pressured into surrendering by massive civilian deaths. Though completely without pity himself, Mao knew how to manipulate it in others. As it happened, Cheng stuck it out to the end, although he was very torn.

Three months after the city was sealed off, Lin Biao reported to Mao:

> The blockade . . . has produced remarkable results, and has caused grave famine in the city . . . The civilian inhabitants are mainly living on tree leaves and grass, and many have died of starvation . . .

"Our main policy has been to forbid exit," Lin wrote.

> On the front line, we have placed one sentry every 50 metres, plus wire and ditches, and blocked all the gaps . . . Those who got out, we persuaded [*sic*] to return . . . When starvation got worse and worse, hungry people . . . flocked out; after we drove them back, they were pressed into No Man's Land . . . Many died of starvation there. In [one place] alone, there were about 2,000 deaths . . .

This policy was so brutal that the troops balked at enforcing it. Lin told Mao:

The starving people knelt in front of our soldiers en masse, begging to be allowed to go. Some put their babies down in front of the troops and turned back themselves, some hanged themselves in the sentry posts. The sentries could not bear the sight of the misery. Some knelt with the starving people and wept with them . . . others secretly released refugees. After we corrected this, we discovered another tendency. Soldiers beat up, abused and tied up refugees [to push them back] and went as far as opening fire on refugees, causing deaths.

Even the hard-hearted Lin recommended letting the refugees go. There was no reply from Mao. Lin, familiar with Mao's tactic of veto by silence, then took it upon himself to issue an order on 11 September: "Release Changchun refugees . . . at once." But the order was not carried out, which can only mean that Mao rescinded it. The only people allowed to leave were those with something useful to the Reds, which usually meant they were relatively rich. One survivor remembered that Communist soldiers "walked up and down announcing: 'Anyone who has a gun, ammunition, a camera—hand it over and we'll fill out a pass for you to leave.' " Nationalist deserters and their families were given preferential treatment. This survivor's family got out on 16 September, thanks to the fact that her husband was a doctor, and useful to the Reds.

After mid-September, Changchun's mayor recorded a massive rise in deaths, when tree leaves, the last food, were falling. By the end of the five-month siege the civilian population had dropped from half a million to 170,000. The death toll was higher than the highest estimate for the Japanese massacre at Nanjing in 1937.*

A Red veteran in the besieging army described how he and his comrades felt:

When we heard outside the city that so many people had died of hunger, we weren't too shocked. We had been in and out of piles of corpses, and our hearts had been hardened. We were blasé. But when we entered the city and saw what it was like, we were devastated. Many of us wept. A lot of us said: We're supposed to be fighting for the poor, but of all these dead here, how many are the rich? Which of them are Nationalists? Aren't they all poor people?

News of this mammoth atrocity was suppressed. The few inhabitants who were let out had four "refugee rules" stamped on their passes, one

---

* Even the watered-down official CCP figure for civilian deaths from starvation in Changchun was 120,000.

of which was "no spreading rumors"—i.e., don't talk. The Changchun model, based on starving civilians to death in order to force the defending troops to surrender was used in "quite a few cities," according to the Communist general Su Yu, who was understandably unspecific.

CIVILIANS IN THE communist-held territories were also ruthlessly exploited. Most men of working age were either drafted into the Reds' expanding army, or into hard, often dangerous labor at the front. The latter involved particularly large numbers. In Manchuria the Reds conscripted 1.6 million laborers, roughly two to each fighter. In the Peking–Tianjin campaign the figure was 1.5 million, and in the Huai–Hai Campaign, 5.43 million. This gigantic corvée performed numerous front-line tasks for which the Nationalists used regular troops, such as dismantling fortifications and transporting ammunition and wounded.

Women were left to do most of the farm work, along with children and men unfit for the front. They also had to care for the wounded, mend uniforms, make countless shoes for the army, and cook for the giant army of troops and laborers. Every household had to hand over a designated amount of food—which came to a staggering 225 million kg of grain alone in the Huai–Hai Campaign. In addition to feeding Red soldiers, food was also used in psychological warfare to entice Nationalist troops to defect.

The Nationalists were constantly short of food, as they relied heavily on supplies brought in by railway, and sporadic airlifts. One Nationalist veteran recalled how hundreds of thousands of men sat for a month in one pocket, starving and freezing in a temperature of −10°C. Soldiers fought—and sometimes killed—each other to get to air-dropped food. Later on, tree bark "was a good meal," and soldiers turned to eating their leather belts and shoe soles. The veteran remembered digging up a dead rat: "Delicious! It was meat." At the end, he said, there was no need for the Reds even to shell them: "In an area no bigger than your bum, all you'd have to do was just throw stones at the 300,000 starving ghosts and they would have had it." Some went over to the Communists as a result of being bombarded by loudspeakers shouting: "Hey, Chiang Kai-shek, we've got pancakes here, come on over and eat." "No amount of politics was as good as food," the vet remarked. "Everyone knew that stewed pork was better than shoe soles."

Apart from enduring Red requisitioning and being drafted, many peasants also lost their houses, pulled down to provide fuel for cooking and materials for building bridges. The whole of Communist-held territory was turned into a giant war machine encompassing every aspect of every person's life. The entire population was made to live and work flat out, night and day, for the war, and very often in the thick of it. Mao called this "People's War."

But "the People" did not volunteer this all-consuming type of support, much less with the zeal that Communist mythology proclaims. Only intense terrorization coerced them into providing services for the war "for a long time without getting tired," as Mao put it. The process went under the misnomer "land reform."

DURING THE WAR against Japan the Communists had suspended their policy of confiscating and redistributing land and replaced it with one of reducing land rent. When the war against Chiang started in earnest, they reverted to their earlier radical approach. But land redistribution was not the main aspect of Mao's land reform. The part that really mattered was a practice called *dou di-zhu*, "struggle against the landlords," which in reality meant violence against the relatively better-off. (In China, unlike pre-Communist Russia, there were very few large landowners.) When people recall the land reform, it is this practice that dominates their memories.

The violence typically took place at rallies, which all villagers had to attend. Those designated as targets were made to stand facing large crowds, and people were psyched up and organized to come forward and pour out their grievances against them. The crowds would be led to shout slogans while brandishing fists and farm tools. Village militants and thugs would then inflict physical abuse, which could range from making the victims kneel on broken tiles on their bare knees, to hanging them up by their wrists or feet, or to beating them, sometimes to death, often with farm implements. And there was often torture of even more ghastly kinds.

The Party's orders to its cadres were not to try to stop the violence, the line being that these were legitimate acts of revenge by the downtrodden. Cadres were told they must "let the people do what they want" to those who had oppressed and exploited them. In fact, the Party wanted to encourage violence, and where there was no violence, local cadres were accused of obstructing the land reform movement, and promptly replaced.

A model was created between March and June 1947 by Mao's terror expert, Kang Sheng. Cadres in all other Red areas were instructed to copy his methods. The fact that land reform was entrusted to a man who was an expert not in agrarian reform, but in terror (and who knew nothing about land issues), makes clear the nature of the program. Kang went to a village in northwest Shanxi called Haojiapo. After the first rally, he berated the local cadres and activists for being "far too polite." "There must be abuse," he said. "Educate the peasants to . . . have no mercy . . . There will be deaths. But let's not be afraid of deaths."

Kang told the cadres and activists to treat whole families as targets, even children. He stood by smiling when village children beat up "little landlords," as children from the wrong families were called. These could be almost anybody, as Kang extended the criteria for condemning people far beyond the original "landlords" and "kulaks," in order to create victims where there were no landed rich. (This was especially the case in areas that had been occupied by the Reds for years, where the relatively wealthy had been impoverished.) Kang invented a new—and very vague—yard-stick: "how they are liked by the masses." This meant that anyone could be turned into a target, so those who had incurred feelings of indignation or jealousy on the part of their fellow villagers, for behavior like having "illicit affairs," became prime victims.

Appalling physical abuse swept the Red areas. One woman official described to us a rally where "four people were hanging in a row by their wrists from four ropes," watched by "every man, woman, the old, young, even children" of the village. There was a "female landlord" at the end of one of the ropes. "It is very painful thinking about it," the eyewitness told us.

> As a matter of fact, she hadn't got much land; she had only been short of labour and had hired a farmhand . . . They asked her where she had hidden the grain . . . I knew she did not have the grain. But they insisted she did and beat her . . . Her blouse was stripped off. She had just had a baby and her milk was dripping. The baby was crying and crawling on the ground, trying to lick up the milk. People lowered their heads and couldn't bear to look . . . Many loathed all this, but they were forced to watch. If they objected, they would come to disaster, too. Some village cadres were really thugs. True honest peasants did not dare to offend them.

Public displays like these brought shivers for decades to people who witnessed them. In many places people were obliged to watch even more gruesome sights. In one place, one elderly member of the gentry whose surname was Niu, which means Ox, had a wire run through his nose and his son was forced to pull him through the village by the wire, like an ox, with blood streaming down his face. Elsewhere, "entire families from the youngest to the oldest were killed. Babies still on milk, grabbed and torn apart at the limbs or just thrown into a well." Some grisly scenes took place right under Mao's nose in Jiaxian county in the Yenan region, where he was staying from 16 August to 21 November 1947, doing quite a bit of sightseeing. Reports to Mao about this county included descriptions of how one person was drowned in a vat of salt water, and another was killed by having boiling oil poured over his head. One place actually had *a rule* that "anyone not active in denouncing landlords will be stoned to death."

Mao saw violent scenes with his own eyes. His bodyguards described him going, in disguise, to watch a rally in the village where he was staying in late 1947, Yangjiagou, where dreadful things happened. Afterwards, he talked to the guards about the various forms of torture, and the fact that children had been severely beaten up.

The upshot was, as reports to Mao made clear: "Everyone is terrified."* Mao had achieved his goal.

BY THE BEGINNING of 1948 the Reds controlled some 160 million people. Peasants constituted the overwhelming majority, and they were all terrorized in traumatic ways. The Party dictated that 10 percent of the population qualified as families of "landlords" and "kulaks." This means that in these categories alone (and more were created by Kang Sheng's new criteria) at least some 16 million people were on the receiving end of some degree of physical abuse and humiliation. Hundreds of thousands, possibly as many as a million, were killed or driven to suicide.

In Yenan in 1942–43, Mao had built an efficient instrument by terrorizing his power base, the members of the Communist Party. Now he was terrorizing his economic and cannon-fodder base, the peasantry, in order to bring about total, unquestioning conformity. The result was that the peasants put up little resistance to Mao's requisitioning of soldiers, laborers, food, and anything else he wanted for his goals.

Mao regarded this process of terrorization as indispensable for winning the war. So when he was preparing for the last decisive campaign, Huai–Hai, he sent Kang Sheng to Shandong province, which was going to bear most of the logistics burden, to carry out a *second* land reform at the end of 1947, having decided that the first had not been fearsome enough. Kang decreed hideous public torture and executions on a scale so large that the Shandong Party organization revolted. It was purged en masse. A sense of the scale of the violence can be derived from the fact that in one small town, where relations had been good up till then, 120 people were beaten to death, some simply designated as landlord "sympathisers." Among them were two boys aged seven, who were killed by children in the Children's Corps. It was this generalized terror in Shandong that built the foundation for the Huai–Hai victory.

IN THE LAND REFORM, the people who implemented Mao's policy were Party cadres, who were also being terrorized and brutalized in the process. This was part of Mao's design. Most new Party members were

* The terror and the extraordinarily high level of killing were recorded on the spot in Hebei province by Jack Belden, an American reporter extremely sympathetic to the Reds, who told US diplomat John Melby about "the increasing use of terror against any form of opposition, and the extermination of large sections [*sic*] of the population." The Reds, Belden said, have "create[d] in the peasants a terror and furtiveness he has never before seen in Communist areas . . ."

sent to villages to be "educated" in the ways of land reform. One person Mao made a point of hardening was his 25-year-old son An-ying, whom he placed under Kang Sheng's tutelage in 1947–48, disguised as Mrs. Kang's nephew. Less than ten days after arriving at Kang's HQ, An-ying was already in torment. He was bombarded with criticisms and made to feel that his thoughts "smelled right-wing." He lay awake at night, and was in a constant state of self-criticism for his "petty bourgeois feelings." "I have not become proletarianised," he wrote in his diary, which remains a secret to this day. "My character is so rotten." He felt "extremely full of pain, so full of pain that I wept."

An-ying was shocked by the public, mass brutality, which was something he had not experienced in Stalin's Russia. This was exactly what his father wanted him to get used to, and to learn to incite, by being with Kang. After two months in Kang's company, he wrote to his father (using Red jargon) that "my own proletarian stand is firmer now." But he retained a sense of aversion, which emerges strongly from notes he wrote about mass rallies other people had described to him. In one case, 10,000 peasants had been herded to rallies that lasted for almost a week. "It was very cold that day," An-ying wrote. "Everyone was saying: 'How cold! There must be quite a few frozen to death today. What have we done to deserve this!' " He evinced palpable distaste about the rallies themselves: "After careful rehearsals, on the fifth day, denunciations began . . . all the masses were told to raise their weapons when the word was given and shout several times: 'Kill, Kill, Kill' . . . the rally site was in a chaotic storm, and ended in eight people being beaten to death." An-ying also registered that the Party was often relying on the worst people in the land reform: "Some of the activists promoted were thugs and dregs, [former] Japanese puppet soldiers and lackeys." Such people made up a sizable proportion of the Party's new recruits in rural areas.

LIKE AN-YING, many Party members who had joined up during the Sino-Japanese War, and who tended to have been idealists, were repelled by the atrocities, and some petitioned the Party about it. A few top leaders also feared that this level of violence might cost the Party its chance to capture power. Mao was not worried. He knew his power did not depend on popularity. As he had done in Yenan, he let terror sink deep into everyone's heart before he called a halt. This came in early 1948, when he circulated reports criticizing atrocities, which he pretended he was hearing about for the first time.

After the Yenan Terror, Mao had made some unapologetic apologies to pacify Party cadres. Now he designated a scapegoat for the violence and atrocities. On 6 March, he wrote to his No. 2, Liu Shao-chi, inform-

ing him that he was to be the fall guy: "I feel the many mistakes committed in all areas are mainly . . . the result of the leading body . . . not clearly
demarcating what was permissible and what was not . . . Can you please
do a critical review of yourselves." Liu resisted at first, but then caved in:
"most [mistakes] are my fault," he told top cadres. "It was not until
Chairman Mao made a systematic criticism . . . that these were
corrected." Thenceforth it was Liu, not Mao, whom Party officials tended
to blame for the violence in the land reform. To rise high under Mao you
had to carry the can for him.

This acknowledgement of "mistakes" was kept strictly within the Party.
The public knew nothing about it, as the Party remained a secret organization. There was no apology to the public. Mao's calculation was that
he did not need to placate the common people, because they did not
count. This went for both the Red-held areas and the Nationalist-held
areas.

Although people in the White areas knew quite a lot about the brutality in the land reform, not least through the hundreds of thousands who
escaped, they often attributed it to passing excesses by the oppressed. In
any case, they had no way of doing anything to stop Mao's advance, and
having no great affection for the existing regime, often willed themselves
to give Mao the benefit of the doubt.

Nationalist captain Hsu Chen had seen some terrors, which had made
him strongly anti-Communist. In early 1948, when he came home to
Ningbo, near Shanghai, he found that people did not want to listen to
what he had to say, and saw him as a pain:

> [M]any relatives and friends came to see me . . . I talked to every visi-
> tor, till my tongue dried up and my lips cracked . . . I told them about
> the heartless and bestial deeds of the Communist bandits . . . But I
> was unable to wake them up from their dreams, but rather aroused
> their aversion . . . I realized that most of them thought as follows:
> "These words are Nationalist propaganda. How can you believe
> them all?"
> "In a violent war like this, these are only transitional means . . ."
> "We've been through Japanese occupation, and survived. You can't
> say the Communists are worse than the Japanese."
> These views could be said to represent the way of thinking in the
> middle and lower echelons of society . . . People always have to learn
> from their own experience . . .

People were in denial—and helpless against Mao's juggernaut. This
fatalism was buttressed by disillusion with the Nationalists, who also
committed atrocities, often against groups more visible to urban dwellers,

and in a milieu far more open than under Mao—with public opinion, a much freer press, and where people could talk, gossip and complain. The Nationalists openly arrested large numbers of students and intellectuals, many of whom were tortured, and some killed. A Nationalist student wrote in April 1948 to the famous pro-Chiang intellectual leader, Hu Shih: "The government mustn't be so stupid, and treat all students as Communists." Four months later, he wrote again saying: "Now they are being slaughtered in great numbers." Although Nationalist killings were a drop in the ocean compared with Mao's, they raised strong feelings, and some even thought that the Reds were the lesser of two evils.

But however averse people were to the Nationalists, only a small number of radicals embraced communism. As late as January 1949, when the Reds were clearly on the verge of total victory, Mao told Stalin's envoy Anastas Mikoyan that even among workers in Shanghai, who should have been the Communists' core constituency, the Nationalists were much stronger than the Reds. Even right at the end, in Canton, a hotbed of radicals in the 1920s, the Russian consul noted that there was "practically no Communist underground . . . Therefore people did not go out to welcome the arrival" of the Communist army. In central China, Lin Biao told the Russians in January 1950: "the population is not evincing great joy at the change of power." There was not a single uprising, urban or rural, in the CCP's favor in the whole of China— unlike in Russia, Vietnam or Cuba during their revolutions. There were defections by Nationalist troops (as opposed to surrender on the battle-field), but these were not mutinies by the rank-and-file, but by top commanders, mostly prearranged "moles," who brought their troops with them.

ON 20 APRIL 1949 a Communist army of 1.2 million men began pour-ing across the Yangtze. On the 23rd it took Chiang's capital, Nanjing, in practice ending twenty-two years of Nationalist rule over the Mainland. On that day, Chiang flew to his ancestral home, Xikou. Knowing that this would probably be his last visit, he spent much of the time kneeling by his mother's tomb, praying in tears. (Soon afterwards the victorious Mao issued an order to protect the tomb, Chiang's family house and clan temple.) Then a ship carried Chiang away to Shanghai, and eventually he crossed the strait to the island of Taiwan.

A few months later, Mao asked Stalin for Soviet-crewed planes and submarines to help take Taiwan in 1950 or "even earlier," telling Stalin that the CCP had a large number of well-placed moles who had "fled" there with Chiang. Stalin, however, was not prepared to risk a direct confrontation with America in such a high-visibility, high-tension area, and Mao had to shelve his plan, allowing Chiang to turn Taiwan into an island stronghold.*

However much Chiang hated the Communists, he did not carry out a scorched-earth policy when he fled. He took most of China's civil aviation—and many art treasures—but only tried to move a small number of factories, mainly electronics plants, to Taiwan. This attempt was blocked by a senior Nationalist official, and virtually all significant industrial facilities were preserved and taken over by the Communists, including sixty-eight ordnance factories. Chiang did far less damage in industrial terms in the entire Mainland than the Russians did just in Manchuria. Mao did not inherit a wasteland in 1949; in fact, he was bequeathed a relatively intact, albeit small, industrial structure, no fewer than 1,000 factories and mines—as well as a functioning state. Chiang was not nearly as ruthless as Mao. As a critic of both regimes observed, "Old Mr. Chiang was not like old Mr. Mao. Perhaps this was why Chiang was beaten by Mao."

THAT SPRING, Mao floated into the outskirts of Peking amidst pear blossoms from Xibaipo, where he had been staying for the past year. Peking had been the capital of China for many dynasties from the twelfth century, and he had decided to make it his capital. In the heart of the city, a huge imperial compound called Zhongnanhai, Central-South Lake, with waterfalls, villas and pavilions, became the main official residence and workplace for him and the rest of the leaders, the equivalent of the Kremlin, which the Russians sometimes called it.

While Zhongnanhai was being prepared, Mao stayed for several months in a beauty spot on the western outskirts called the Fragrant Hills. The inhabitants were moved out, and the whole mountain cordoned off for the leaders, the Praetorian Guard, and some 6,000 staff. To preserve secrecy, a plaque was hung at the entrance bearing the words "Labour University," but this drew so many young people wanting to enroll that another sign had to be put up saying: The Labor University is not ready; consult the newspapers for enrollment dates.

Mao moved into Zhongnanhai in September. There, and anywhere else he might set foot, the grounds were swept by Russian mine-

---

* But Stalin responded eagerly to Mao's request to help subdue the vast and remote north-western deserts and annihilate a fierce anti-Communist Muslim army there. No problem, Stalin said. The Muslim horsemen "could be destroyed by artillery very easily. If you wish, we can give you 40 fighter planes which can rout . . . this cavalry very fast." A senior Russian diplomat told us, with accompanying "rat-a-tat" of machine-guns and mowing-down hand gestures, that this is what Stalin's air force had done, far from prying eyes, in the wastes of the Gobi.

detectors—and Chinese soldiers walking shoulder-to-shoulder as human minesweepers. An extraordinary but unobtrusive security system was installed, for which the watchword was *wai-song nei-jin*—"Outwardly relaxed, inwardly tight."* The system was so slick that even Stalin's former interpreter, with extensive security experience, was unable to spot it.

And yet, with all his watertight security, on the eve of his inauguration as supreme leader of China, deep fear was lurking in the recesses of Mao's mind. A friend from the past, Mrs. Lo Fu, described visiting him and Mme Mao at this time. Mao was "in high spirits . . . When I asked about his health, Jiang Qing said he was all right, except he would tremble when he saw strangers. At first I didn't understand . . . and I said: But he looks all right today! Chairman Mao interjected with a smile: You are an old friend, not a stranger." It seems Mao knew that his terrorization had produced not only mass conformity, but quite a few would-be assassins.

On 1 October 1949, Mao appeared standing on top of Tiananmen Gate, a stone's throw from Zhongnanhai, in front of the Forbidden City, and inaugurated the People's Republic of China (PRC). This was his first-ever public appearance before a large crowd of hundreds of thousands. The crowd was well organized, and very distant from the Gate high above. From now on Mao would ascend the Gate on special occasions, a practice he modeled on Soviet leaders mounting Lenin's tomb in Red Square, which was far lower and less grand. On this occasion Mao made the only speech he ever delivered from the Gate in his entire reign of twenty-seven years. (On other occasions when he appeared there, he would at most mouth a slogan or two.) He cleared his throat every other sentence, in the manner of a nervous speaker rather than a rousing orator. Moreover, the content was extraordinarily flat, mainly a list of appointments. Its most salient feature was what he did *not* say. Mao did not outline any program to benefit "the people" in whose name the regime had been installed.

The crowd of over 100,000 cried "Long live Chairman Mao!" Mao appeared excited, waving as he walked from one end of the magnificent Gate to the other, and occasionally shouting into the microphone: "Long live the people!" He had that day established himself as the absolute ruler of some 550 million people.

---

* This system fooled foreigners into thinking that security was light, from which many concluded, wrongly, that the regime was popular, and so did not need much protection. A not untypical reaction was that of a French journalist who watched Chou En-lai drive across Tiananmen Square with India's Premier Nehru in October 1954: "Assassinating Chou En-lai . . . would have been child's play," he wrote.

TOTALITARIAN STATE, EXTRAVAGANT LIFESTYLE

(1949 – 53 ★ AGE 55 – 59)

THE TRANSITION FROM Nationalist to Communist rule was managed without great disruption. The advancing Communist army took over all civilian institutions, and recruited educated young urban men and women to staff them, in addition to seasoned Party cadres. This machine immediately assumed control of the country.

Many old administrators stayed on, under their new Party bosses, and for a time the economy ran much as before. Private businessmen were told that their property would not be touched for a long while and that they must keep their factories functioning and shops open. Industry and commerce were not nationalized for some years, and the collectivization of agriculture was not carried out until the mid-1950s.

In these few years, with much of the economy still in private hands, the country quickly recovered from well over a decade of war. Agriculture saw considerable growth, as the new government issued loans and invested in water works. In the cities, subsidies were doled out to alleviate starvation. Death rates dropped.

Some sectors were subjected to instant drastic change. One was the law, where courts were replaced by Party committees. Another was the media, on which tight censorship was imposed at once; public opinion was stamped out. Mao would digest the rest of society gradually.

Mao had an able team, headed by his No. 2 Liu Shao-chi, with Chou En-lai, the No. 3, as prime minister. In June 1949 Mao sent Liu to Russia to learn about the Soviet model in detail. Liu stayed there for nearly two months, and saw Stalin an unprecedented six times. He held meetings with a stream of top Soviet ministers and managers and visited a wide range of institutions. Hundreds of Soviet advisers were assigned to China, some returning with Liu on his train. A Stalinist state was being constructed even before Mao had formally assumed power.

The new regime ran into armed resistance in the countryside and dealt with it without mercy. Once the state was secure, Mao began systematic terrorization of the population, to induce long-term conformity and obedience. His methods were uniquely Maoist.

Mao was viscerally hostile to law, and his subjects were utterly shorn of legal protection. He described himself to Edgar Snow in 1970 as "a man without law or limit" (which was mistranslated as him saying he was "a lone monk"). Instead of laws, the regime issued edicts, resolutions and press editorials. It accompanied these with "campaigns" conducted by the Party system. There was a paper facade of law, which formally allowed the "right of appeal," but exercising it was treated as an offense, a "demand for further punishment," as one ex-prisoner put it, which could result in one's sentence being doubled, for daring to doubt the wisdom of "the people."

In October 1950 Mao launched a nationwide "campaign to suppress counter-revolutionaries," and devoted much energy to this, his first major onslaught since taking power, ordering his police chief to "send reports directly to me." The targets were what remained of the old Nationalist regime. They came under the general heading of "class enemies," broken down into categories like "Bandits," which referred to anyone involved in armed resistance: these alone ran into many millions. Another group was "Spies," which meant not people actually spying, but anyone who had worked in Nationalist intelligence. Grassroots Nationalist chiefs also fell victim en bloc—although senior Nationalists were protected, as bait to entice others back from abroad. "We don't kill a single one of those big Chiang Kai-sheks," Mao said. "What we kill are small Chiang Kai-sheks."

Mao issued order after order berating provincial cadres for being too soft, and urged more "massive arrests, massive killings." On 23 January 1951, for instance, he criticized one province for "being much too lenient, and not killing [enough]"; when it raised its execution rate, he said this "improvement" made him feel "very delighted."

This nationwide campaign went hand in hand with the land reform in the newly occupied areas, where some two-thirds of China's population lived. Some 3 million perished either by execution, mob violence, or suicide.* Mao wanted the killings performed with maximum impact, and that meant having them carried out in public. On 30 March 1951 he instructed: "Many places . . . don't dare to kill counter-revolutionaries on a grand scale with big publicity. This situation must be changed." In Peking alone, some 30,000 sentencing and execution rallies were held, attended by nearly 3.4 million people. A young half-Chinese woman from Britain

---

* Mao claimed that the total number executed was 700,000, but this did not include those beaten or tortured to death in the post-1949 land reform, which would at the very least be as many again. Then there were suicides, which, based on several local inquiries, were very probably about equal to the number of those killed.

witnessed one rally in the center of Peking, when some 200 people were paraded and then shot in the head so that their brains splattered out onto bystanders. Even those who managed to evade the rallies could not always avoid seeing horrific things, like trucks carrying corpses through the streets, dripping blood.

Mao intended most of the population—children and adults alike—to witness violence and killing. His aim was to scare and brutalize the entire population, in a way that went much further than either Stalin or Hitler, who largely kept their foulest crimes out of sight.

More might well have been killed if it had not been for their value as slave labor. Mao said as much in one order: some people had "committed crimes that deserve to be punished by death," but they must not be killed, partly because "we would lose a large labour force." So millions were spared to be shipped to labor camps. With advice from Russian gulag experts on deportation and camp management, Mao sowed a vast archipelago of camps, the official term for which was *lao-gai*: "reform through labour." To be sent to *lao-gai* meant being condemned to back-breaking labor in the most hostile wastelands and down the most contaminating mines, while being hectored and harassed incessantly. Hidden away in these camps, the physically weaker, and the spiritually stronger, were worked to death. Many inmates were executed, while others committed suicide by any means, like diving into a wheat-chopper. In all, during Mao's rule, the numbers who were executed, and met other premature deaths in prisons and labor camps, could well amount to 27 million.[*]

In addition to execution and incarceration in prisons and camps, there was a third, and typically Maoist, form of punishment that was imposed on many tens of millions of people during Mao's reign. It was called being placed "under surveillance" while the victim remained in society. What it meant was "doing time on the outside," kept on a kind of permanent knife-edge parole, one of the usual suspects to be rounded up and tormented afresh with any new bout of suppression. It meant one's whole family living like outcasts. The high-visibility stigma served as a warning to the general public never to cross the regime.[†]

The terror worked. A report to Mao on 9 February 1951, only a few

---

[*] The number of people in detention in any one year under Mao has been calculated at roughly 10 million. It is reasonable to estimate that on average 10 percent of these were executed or died of other causes.

[†] A Soviet diplomat who served ten years in both Nationalist and Red China, and witnessed Mao's campaigns close up, later observed in a classified source that however cruel the Nationalists could be, it was never anything like as bad as under the Communists. He estimated that Mao killed more Chinese in these early campaigns alone than died in the civil war.

months into the campaign, said that after this first bout of killings, "rumor-mongering died down and social order stabilised." What the state called "rumors" were often the only way people had to express their real sentiments. In one case, a seemingly bizarre alert spread not just from village to village, but from province to province: "Chairman Mao sends people to the villages to cut off [men's] balls to give to the Soviet Union to make atom bombs." (In Chinese, "balls" and "bombs" share the same pronunciation: *dan*.) In some places, when what looked like a tax collector appeared, the shout went up: "The ball-cutters are here!," and the whole village would run for cover. This story reflects the fact that Mao was already imposing extortionate food levies on the peasants, some of whom had clearly surmised that the food was being sent to Russia.

This campaign clamped the lid down hard on any such expression of dissent, but there were still a few cracks in the system in those early years. Victims could sometimes still hide. A small landowner from Anhui province managed to stay on the run with her son for 636 days, without ever being informed on, even by people sent to catch them. When the fugitives eventually returned to their village, "the overwhelming majority of people, particularly women . . . shed tears of pity," the son recalled. As the campaign was over by then, they survived.

But control became increasingly pervasive, and with it the loss of freedom on every front: of speech, movement, work, information. A nationwide system of concierges called Order-Keeping Committees was established in every factory, village and street, composed of members of the public, often the nosiest and most hyper-active busybodies, now made complicit with the regime's repression. These committees kept an eye on everyone, not just political suspects and petty criminals. Above all, the regime nailed every person in China to a fixed, and usually immutable, job and place of residence through a registration system (*hu-kou*) begun in July 1951, which soon became iron-clad.

The government also used the "suppression of counter-revolutionaries" campaign to move against all sorts of non-political offenses, such as ordinary banditry, gangsterism, murder, robbery, gambling, drug-dealing and prostitution ("liberated" prostitutes were organized to do manual labor). Thanks to phenomenal organization and ruthlessness, these actions were extremely successful. By the end of 1952, drug-dealing was virtually wiped out, as were brothels.

Mao repeatedly said that his killings "were extremely necessary." "Only when this thing is properly done can our power be secure," he pronounced.

WHILE NUMEROUS CHINESE were executed, only two foreigners are known to have suffered this fate—one Italian, Antonio Riva, and a

Japanese called Ryuichi Yamaguchi. The charge was no minor one: planning to kill Mao with a mortar bomb as he stood on Tiananmen on 1 October 1950, National Day. The two men were arrested days before, together with several other foreigners. Ten months later, on 17 August 1951, these two were driven through central Peking standing up in jeeps, and then shot in public near the Bridge of Heaven. The news was splashed across next day's *People's Daily* under the headline "The Case of US Spies Plotting Armed Rebellion," alleging that the assassination had been ordered by the former US assistant military attaché, Colonel David Barrett.

For anyone, let alone a foreigner, to contemplate assassinating Mao on a maximum-security occasion like National Day, amid a throng of hundreds of thousands of organized and hyper-vigilant Chinese, not to mention some 10,000 police and another 10,000 troops, was a very tall order. Actually, Barrett, the alleged ringleader, had left China many months before. Two decades later, Chou En-lai apologized, in a vague way, about implicating him, and invited him back to China. This was an indirect acknowledgment that the accusation was faked.

Linking the plot to Barrett helped whip up anti-American feeling, which was not as fervid as the regime wished. The trumped-up charge was also used to tarnish another major target of Mao's—the Roman Catholic Church, whose leading foreign representative, an Italian Monsignor, was one of those arrested. China had about 3.3 million Catholics at the time. Mao was very interested in the Vatican, especially its ability to command allegiance beyond national boundaries, and his Italian visitors often found themselves being peppered with questions about the Pope's authority. The tenacity and effectiveness of the Catholics perturbed the regime, which used the phony assassination case to accelerate the takeover of Catholic institutions, including schools, hospitals and orphanages. A high-decibel smear campaign accused Catholic priests and nuns of heinous actions ranging from plain murder to cannibalism and medical experiments on babies. Hundreds of Chinese Catholics were executed, and many foreign priests suffered physical abuse.

In general, religious and quasi-religious organizations were either branded reactionary and suppressed, or brought under tight control. Almost all foreign clergy were expelled, along with most foreign businessmen, virtually clearing China of non-Communist foreigners by about 1953. Non-Communist foreign press and radio were, it goes without saying, banned.

THE "CAMPAIGN to suppress counter-revolutionaries" lasted over a year though routine suppression continued unabated after that. Mao then focused his attention on securing watertight control of the state coffers, to make sure that the funds the state extracted from the people did not revert to private hands. In late 1951 he started a campaign known as "the Three-Antis," targeting embezzlement, waste and "bureaucratism" (which meant slacking, not bureaucracy per se). The primary aim was to scare anyone with access to government money from pocketing it. Alleged embezzlers were called "tigers." "Big Tigers," involving cases over 10,000 yuan, qualified for death.

As corruption had been epidemic under the Nationalists, the campaign had genuine appeal. Many thought that the Communists were trying to root out corruption. What people did not realize was that while it was true that after this campaign few who had access to state money dared dip their hand in the till, the funds thus amassed in the state coffers were not going to be used for the interests of the people.

Mao was hands-on about what had now, in effect, become his money. He bombarded government ministers, and provincial and army leaders, with cables urging them to catch "Big Tigers," and setting quotas: "We must probably execute 10,000 to several tens of thousands of embezzlers nationwide before we can solve our problem." He whipped up a competition among the provinces, goading them on to higher targets, threatening: "Whoever disobeys is either a bureaucratist or an embezzler himself."

The method for uncovering those deemed to be offenders was, as Mao enjoined, "confession and informing." Using these techniques, some 3.83 million civilian officials were grilled and screened (and more in the army). Though torture was not encouraged as a public spectacle this time, it was nevertheless used in some places, and Mao was kept informed. Russians working on the railway in Manchuria reported hearing screams ("like from Japanese dungeons") from nearby offices. These turned out to be coming from Chinese colleagues who were being "checked" by having their testicles crushed in bamboo pliers.

In the end, relatively few officials were found to have embezzled sums large enough to qualify them as "Big Tigers." But Mao had achieved his goal, to instill fear. From now on, few dared to pilfer state funds.

As for its second target, waste, the campaign caused more loss than it prevented. By tying up skilled managers and technicians in sterile meetings for months on end, it deprived the economy of badly needed human assets. On 14 February 1952, Tianjin reported that wholesale trade was down by half, banks had stopped loans, and private businesses dared not buy goods. Industrial production was declining, tax income collapsing, and the economy was heading into recession. In Manchuria, production plummeted by half. In fact, the system of repression itself was a prime source of waste. One Belgian priest worked out that he was interrogated—to no effect—for more than 3,000 hours over three years, which involved at least three or four people full time (at least 10,000 man-hours), as well as vast amounts of scarce paper.

In January 1952, shortly after the Three-Antis began, Mao ordered another campaign to run in tandem with it, this one called "the Five-Antis." The offenses were: bribery, tax evasion, pilfering state property, cheating, and stealing economic information. It was aimed at private businessmen, whose property had not been confiscated, to force them to disgorge money, as well as to frighten them out of acts like bribery and tax evasion. One person involved at a high level put the number of suicides in these two campaigns as at least 200,000–300,000. In Shanghai so many people jumped from skyscrapers that they acquired the nickname "parachutes." One eyewitness wondered why people jumped into the street rather than into the river. The reason, he discovered, was that they wanted to safeguard their families: "If you jumped into the Huangpu River and were swept away so the Communists didn't have a corpse, they would accuse you of having escaped to Hong Kong, and your family would suffer. So the best way was to leap down to the street."

BY MAY 1953, when Mao brought the campaigns to an end, he had accomplished what he had set out to do, namely to scare people away from touching state money. Communist officialdom did become relatively uncorrupt in the conventional sense, such as not taking bribes, but it was granted a privileged standard of living, which was minutely graded hierarchically.

Mao himself did not embezzle in the conventional way, like lesser dictators who kept Swiss bank accounts. But this was simply because he did not need to hedge against losing power. He just made absolutely sure such a day would never come. Rather than embezzling, he treated the funds of the state as his own, and used them however he wanted, disregarding the needs of the population and persecuting any who advocated different spending priorities from the ones he laid down. When it came to personal lifestyle, Mao's was one of royal self-indulgence, practiced at tremendous cost to the country. This corrupt behavior emerged as soon as he conquered China.

Mao lived behind an impenetrable wall of secrecy, so that very few knew anything about his life and his world, including where he lived, or where he was (he made few public appearances). Even up close, he did not give an obvious impression of high living. He had no taste for opulence, and positively shunned the sort of objects usually associated with luxury, such as gold taps, antiques, paintings, vast wardrobes, elegant furniture. But these absences involved no restraint of his desires. In fact, Mao indulged every whim in his daily life.

Mao liked villas. During his twenty-seven-year rule, well over fifty estates were created for him, no fewer than five in Peking. Many he never set foot in. These estates were set in enormous grounds, mostly in gorgeous locations. So, in many places of great beauty, the whole mountain (like Jade Spring Hills outside Peking), or long stretches of lakes (such as along the famed Western Lake in Hangzhou), were cordoned off for his exclusive use. There were often old villas on these spots, many of architectural splendor. These were torn down to make room for new buildings designed and constructed under the supervision of his security forces, with safety and comfort à la Mao as the priorities. These purpose-built edifices were bullet- and bomb-proof; some had deep nuclear shelters. Most were in the same style: a warehouse clone with identical wings, one for Mao and the other for his wife, with a huge sitting room in the middle. All were one-story, as Mao feared being trapped upstairs.

The one floor was very high, sometimes as high as a normal two- or three-story building, to cater for Mao's sense of the grandiose. One villa built in the mid-1960s outside Nanchang was about 50 feet high, a single floor, like a monstrous gray hangar. When many of them were turned into guest houses after Mao died, their corridors were so enormous that, even after creating a row of sizable rooms inside them, there was space enough for a normal-width corridor.

Construction on his first new villas had started in 1949, the moment he entered Peking. These were followed by others, during the Three-Antis campaign. One, completed in 1954, was at Beidaihe on the east coast. This had been a seaside resort from the turn of the century, and had over 600 villas, many of them large and elegant, but none met Mao's security specifications, so an enormous Mao-style identikit building was plonked down in an enclave with a spectacular view overlooking the beach, protected by lushly forested hills with bunkers and tunnels hollowed out inside them. The whole expanse of sea was placed out of bounds to all but an authorized few.

In 1952 Mao's security chief sent word to Hunan indicating that a villa should be built in the provincial capital, Changsha, for Mao's possible homecoming. The Hunan leaders were unsure whether this was really Mao's wish. As this was at the height of the Three-Antis, it seemed too blatant to be true. So they vacated their own houses, and had them refurbished for Mao. But Mao did not come. Then it dawned on them that a new estate was indeed what he desired, and construction work began. It was not until it was completed that Mao deigned to come back for a visit. Later, a second villa was built only a stone's throw away. More villas were built in his home village of Shaoshan. Other provinces, which naturally all wanted visits from Mao, would be told "But you have no place for the Chairman to stay," and would then build the necessary mansions.

The houses were constantly upgraded for security and comfort. In his old age, an enclosed outer corridor was added so that Mao could take walks without risking catching cold. To minimize the risk of assassination, the outside windows in these corridors were staggered with those in Mao's rooms, so that from either direction only a wall was visible. Another security refinement in the later villas was steel gates at both ends of the portico, which became incorporated into the house, so Mao's car effectively drove right into the sitting room.

Sometimes, even Mao's train drove into his villa—or strictly speaking, into the front garden, along a spur laid specially for him. In many places, an exclusive underground tunnel ran all the way from the villa to the local military airport. Mao frequently slept in his train parked at military airports, ready to make a quick getaway by train or plane, in case of emergency. Throughout his reign, he lived in his own country as if in a war zone.

Mao mostly traveled with three sets of transport—train, plane, and ship (when applicable). Even if he was using only one kind of transport, the other two would follow wherever possible, just in case. When he flew, every other plane in China was grounded. And when his special train moved, always setting off at a moment's notice, the country's railway system was thrown into chaos, as other trains were not allowed to be anywhere near his. These disruptions were not infrequent, as Mao was constantly on the move by train. The crew were on permanent standby, not allowed home sometimes for weeks, even months on end.

One particular extravagance was swimming pools, as Mao loved swimming. Pools were rare in those years, in what was a very poor country. (In Chengdu, the capital of Sichuan province, when a pool was built for Mao, the attendants did not know how much chlorine to put in the water. As a result, the few who had the privilege of swimming in the pool had red eyes. Mao suspected poison.) The first pool built for him was in Jade Spring Hills, right in the middle of the Three-Antis campaign. By Mao's own account, the pool cost 50,000 yuan, which was five times the amount that would condemn an embezzler to the execution ground as a "Big Tiger." In Zhongnanhai, his official residence in Peking, well hidden behind a large sign saying "Serve the People," an indoor pool was built for him shortly after the campaign, even though there was already an exclusive outdoor pool, which until Mao came to power had been open to the public.

Keeping these pools warm for months on end, in case Mao should fancy a dip, cost a fortune. The water was heated by hot steam running through a pipe, and burned up large amounts of scarce fuel.

MAO DID NOT stint on any side of life that he enjoyed. He was a gourmet, and had his favorite foods shipped in from all over the country. (Mao and the top leaders rarely went out to restaurants, whose numbers dwindled under the Communists.) A special fish from Wuhan that he liked had to be couriered alive 1,000 km in a plastic bag filled with water and kept oxygenated. With his rice, Mao demanded that the membrane between the husk and the kernel be kept for its taste, which meant the husking had to be done manually and with great care. Once, he complained he could not taste the membrane, and told his house-keeper he had developed beriberi as a result. The housekeeper raced to the special farm at Jade Spring Hills and had some rice carefully husked the way Mao wanted.

This farm was specially set up to grow rice for Mao, as the water there was supposed to be the very best. In the olden days the spring had supplied drinking water for the imperial courts. Now it fed Mao's rice paddies. The vegetables Mao liked, as well as poultry and milk, were produced in another special farm called Jushan. The tea Mao chose was the one renowned as the best in China, Dragon Well, and the very best leaves were picked for him, at the ideal time. All Mao's food was put through a meticulous medical check, and the cooking was supervised by his house-keeper, who doubled as taster. Stir-fried dishes had to be served immediately, but as the kitchen was located at a distance, so that no smells would waft Mao's way, servants would race all the way to his table with each dish.

Mao did not like getting into baths, or showers, and did not have a bath for a quarter of a century. Instead, his servants rubbed him every day with a hot towel. He enjoyed daily massages. He never went to a hospital. The hospital facilities, along with the top specialists, came to him. If he was not in the mood to see them, they would be kept hanging around, sometimes for weeks.

Mao never fancied smart clothes. What he loved was comfort. He wore the same shoes for years, because, as he said, old shoes were more comfortable; and he got bodyguards to wear in new shoes for him. His bathrobe, face towel and quilts were heavily patched—but no ordinary patching: they were taken specially to Shanghai and mended by the best craftsmen, costing immeasurably more than new ones. Far from being indications of asceticism, these were the quirks of the hedonistic super-powerful.

It was perhaps not unreasonable for a leader to enjoy villas and other luxuries, but Mao was gratifying himself while he was executing others for taking a fraction of what he was burning up. And doing so while preaching and imposing abstinence and having himself portrayed as "Serving the People." Mao's double standards had a comprehensive cynicism that put him in a league of his own.

In no area of life did these double standards cause more misery than in the sphere of sexuality. Mao required his people to endure ultra-puritanical constraints. Married couples posted to different parts of China were given only twelve days a year to be together, so tens of millions were condemned to almost year-round sexual abstinence. Efforts to relieve sexual frustration privately could lead to public humiliation. One patriotic Chinese who had returned to "the Motherland" was made to put a sign up over his dormitory bed criticizing himself for masturbating.

And all the while, Mao was indulging in every sexual caprice in well-guarded secrecy. On 9 July 1953 the army was ordered to select young women from their entertainment groups to form a special troupe in the Praetorian Guard. Everyone involved knew that its major function was to provide bed mates for Mao. Army chief Peng De-huai termed this "selecting imperial concubines"—a complaint that would cost him dear in time to come. But his objection had no effect on Mao, and more army entertainment groups were turned into procurement agencies. Apart from singers and dancers, nurses and maids were handpicked for Mao's villas to provide a pool of women from which he could choose whoever he wanted to have sex with.

A few of these women received subsidies from Mao, as did some of his staff and relatives. The sums involved were petty cash, but he made a point of authorizing each transaction personally. Mao was very aware of the value of money, and for years checked his household accounts with a peasant's beady eye.

Mao's handouts came from a secret personal account, the Special Account. This was where he stashed the royalties from his writings, for on top of all his other privileges he cornered the book market by forcing the entire population to buy his own works, while preventing the vast majority of writers from being published. At its peak, this account held well over 2 million yuan, an astronomical sum. As a yardstick of what this was worth, Mao's staff earned on average about 400 yuan a year. A peasant's cash income, in a better year, could be a few yuan. Even privileged Chinese rarely had savings of more than a few hundred yuan.

Mao was the only millionaire created in Mao's China.

PART FIVE

CHASING A SUPERPOWER DREAM

RIVALRY WITH STALIN

(1947–49 ★ AGE 53–55)

EVEN BEFORE he conquered China, Mao had set his sights on the wider world. He started to get active as soon as victory hove in sight in the civil war.

Mao hoped to repeat the huge PR success he had had with Edgar Snow and *Red Star Over China*, a success which was unique for the Communist world. But Snow had meanwhile been banned by Moscow, and so Mao had to fall back on a second-rate American journalist called Anna Louise Strong, who had nothing like Snow's influence globally, and was generally perceived as a lackey.

In 1947, Mao sent Strong on a world tour to promote him. She was given documents that Mao told her to pass "to the world Communist parties." He particularly wanted her to "show them to Party leaders in the United States and Eastern Europe," adding pointedly that he "did not think it was necessary for her to take them to Moscow."*

Strong duly churned out an article called "The Thought of Mao Tse-tung," and a book called *Dawn Out of China*. They contained encomia like the claim that Mao's "great work has been to change Marxism from a European to an Asiatic form . . . On every kind of problem . . . in ways of which neither Marx nor Lenin could dream"; that "all Asia will learn from [China] more than they will learn from the USSR"; and that Mao's works "highly likely influenced the later forms of government in parts of post-war Europe." These claims trod hard on Stalin's toes. Not surprisingly, publication of her book was stonewalled in Russia, and the US CP demanded that half the book be deleted. The full version came out in India and, more significantly, in several countries in Eastern Europe, including Yugoslavia.

---

* In America, the CCP had its own people operating inside the US Communist Party, and a powerful intelligence network with access to information unavailable to the Russians. When Moscow denounced US CP head Earl Browder, an old China hand, whose secret "China Bureau" had close links to Mao, Mao had very publicly continued to call him "comrade."

To promote Mao internationally without Stalin's endorsement, to suggest that Mao had improved on Stalin, and could offer more than Stalin, were red rags to the Kremlin. But Mao clearly understood that acquiring a sphere of influence needed elbow. And he now had real clout.

There were also signs that Stalin was prepared to cede some turf. In September 1947 he set up a new organization called the Communist Information Bureau (Cominform), which included only European parties. This left open the possibility of a separate Asian grouping. In November, within weeks of the Cominform being established, and while he was still wandering near Yenan, Mao had the name of his entourage changed to "Unit Asia."

STALIN REMAINED totally committed to backing Mao, but he now took steps to contain him, and to remind him who was master.

On 30 November 1947, when Mao became confident that he would win the civil war soon, he proposed to Stalin that he should visit Russia. Stalin decided that the visit was the ideal vehicle to make Mao sweat. Stalin's office cabled back a welcome on 16 December. Dr. Orlov, the recipient of the cable, was clearly under orders from Stalin to report in detail on Mao's reactions. Next day he informed Stalin that Mao was "extremely pleased," "rather animated" in fact, and "said immediately: 'Very good, I can go there [in] 3 months...'"

Three months passed, with no sign of an invitation from Stalin. Mao brought it up again on 22 April 1948, the day after the CCP retook Yenan; he told Orlov he planned to depart on 4–5 May. This time Stalin said "Yes." Mao asked to take both Russian doctors with him, on health grounds—but really to prevent any of his colleagues communicating with the Russians during his absence. Stalin agreed. Mao also wanted to visit Eastern Europe, a proposal Stalin pointedly did not endorse.

On 10 May, days after Mao's self-appointed departure date, Stalin suddenly postponed the visit. And as spring slid into summer, there was no sign of him reviving his invitation. Mao was anxious to get going. He was with his colleagues at Party HQ at Xibaipo at the time, and they all knew he was going to Moscow to see Stalin. The impression was that he was leaving any minute. One sign was that nothing was done to the frogs that were disturbing Mao's sleep. Ordinarily, any noisy animals like chickens and dogs were brought "under control" wherever Mao stayed. His bodyguards proposed using dynamite to silence the frogs, which were croaking away happily in a reedy pond. The plan was not carried out, because it was assumed that Mao's stay at Xibaipo was going to be short. Mao felt the need to head off any negative impact of the delay, and arranged for his bête noire, Wang Ming, to suffer another medical "accident." On 25 June Wang Ming was given the urinal cleaner Lysol as an enema, which wrecked his intestines.

On 4 July, Mao cabled Stalin: "I have decided to visit you in the near future." He set his departure date for ten days ahead: "we shall leave anyway about the 15th of this month," and told Stalin "it is necessary to send two transport (passenger) airplanes."

On the 14th, the eve of the date he had told Stalin he would be leaving, instead of a plane, what came from Stalin was a cable to Dr. Orlov, putting off the visit until the winter:

> Tell Mao Tse-tung the following: In view of the start of the grain harvest, top Party officials are leaving for the provinces in August, and will remain there until November. Therefore, the Central Committee requests Comrade Mao Tse-tung to delay his visit to Moscow until the end of November in order to have the opportunity to meet with all the top Party comrades.

This pretext was openly derisive. Orlov reported back that Mao "listened with a slight smile," saying "fine, fine." But he asked Orlov: " 'Can it be . . . that in the USSR they attach such great importance to the grain harvest that leading members of the Party . . . go off for it?' " "I have known Mao Tse-tung for more than six years," Orlov reported, "and if I understand him right, his smile and the words *hao, hao* (fine, fine) . . . in no way indicate he was pleased . . ." "Melnikov [the other Russian doctor] told me that on July 15 Mao Tse-tung asked him a similar question about the harvest." "He [Mao] was confident he would be leaving just now." "Evidently, the visit has become necessary to him . . ." "[His] suitcases had already been packed, plus leather shoes had been bought . . . and a woolen coat made . . ."

It was clear to Mao that Stalin was annoyed with him, and was yo-yoing him over his trip. He scrambled to make amends, starting with his own personality cult. On 15 August, Mao vetoed the new North China University's program "mainly to study Mao Tse-tung-ism," saying: "There is no benefit, only harm." He also changed the term "Mao Tse-tung Thought" to "Marxism-Leninism" in documents. Promoting his own formulations to a "Thought" had not gone down well with Stalin: Soviet media never mentioned Mao's "Thought," and red-penciled the expression when they published CCP documents containing it.

Finally, with autumn setting in, Mao sent an unusually ingratiating telegram on 28 September, in which he addressed Stalin by the sobriquet "the Master," and begged: "it is essential to report personally to . . . the Master . . . I hope sincerely that they [the Soviet Party and Stalin] would give instructions to us."

Stalin had shown who was boss. Mao had groveled. Having made his point, Stalin replied on 17 October, aloof yet reassuring, confirming Mao's trip for "the end of November." Mao was now confident enough to respond by requesting a brief postponement. The first round of Stalin's punishment of Mao for harboring ambitions beyond China was over.

MAO HAD BLINKED first. But he also stood firm vis-à-vis Stalin when his fundamental interests were involved. In the last stage of the civil war, before Chiang Kai-shek fled to Taiwan, Nanjing sued for a ceasefire and peace on 9 January 1949. Stalin told Mao to respond and say the CCP "supports negotiations." Mao was furious ("spoke more sharply," Orlov reported to Stalin). Stalin most uncharacteristically sent another telegram the next day, attempting to reposition himself, and claiming that his proposal had been purely tactical, to make it seem that it was the Nationalists who were responsible for continuing the war: "our draft of your response . . . is designed to undermine the peace negotiations."

Mao's attitude was that the Nationalists should not be allowed a day's peace, even for appearances' sake. He told Stalin he wanted "the unconditional surrender of the Nanjing government . . . we no longer need to undertake any more political detours." For the first time ever, Mao told Stalin what to say, telling the Master: "We think you should give the following answer . . ." to the Nationalists, who had requested Russian mediation. Mao had gained a definite edge over Stalin, which was noticed in the Kremlin: one of Stalin's top China advisers confirmed to us that Stalin's staff felt the Master had been "told off" by Mao in no uncertain terms.

Stalin fired back next day, 14 January, with a lengthy lecture, telling Mao that turning down talks was bad PR, and raising the specter of foreign intervention. Mao did not believe that this was likely, but he found a way to stick to his guns while also satisfying Stalin, by publishing a list of conditions for peace talks that were tantamount to demanding unconditional surrender. He then artfully quoted back to Stalin the latter's own expressed position: "With regard to the basic line (to undermine the peace talks with the Nationalists, to continue the revolutionary war up to the end), we are absolutely unanimous with you." Stalin folded the following day: "we have reached complete agreement . . . Hence, the issue is now closed."

Stalin seems to have been impressed. It was just after this that he commented to Yugoslav and Bulgarian leaders that Mao was insubordinate, but successful. Mao had fought his corner fiercely—and effectively. So when on 14 January Stalin "insisted" that Mao postpone his trip to Moscow yet again, it seems that he genuinely meant it when he said "because your presence in China is essential." Instead, Stalin offered to send an "authoritative" member of the Politburo to see Mao "immediately."

Mao's first reaction to this further postponement was irritation. His secretary remembered him throwing the telegram on the table, saying: "So be it!" But on second thoughts, he saw that Stalin was actually conveying an accolade. Stalin had never sent a member of his Politburo into a war zone to visit a Communist party involved in a civil war—and, moreover, a civil war against a government with which Moscow had diplomatic relations. On 17 January Mao responded "very much welcoming" a visit by Stalin's envoy.

The envoy was Stalin's old confidant, Anastas Mikoyan. He arrived at Mao's HQ at Xibaipo on 30 January, bringing two specialists in neutralizing delayed-action bombs and bugging equipment. Mao "was extremely pleased," Mikoyan reported, "and thanked comrade Stalin for his good care." With Mikoyan came former railways minister Ivan Kovalev, who had been fixing the railroads in Manchuria, and who was now to be Stalin's personal liaison with Mao.

Mao showed his self-confidence straightaway. The day after Mikoyan arrived, the Nationalist government moved from Nanjing to Canton. The only ambassador to accompany the Nationalists was the Soviet ambassador, Roshchin. On 1 and 2 February, Mao absented himself from meeting Mikoyan in a show of pique, and Chou En-lai was deputized to ask for an explanation. Describing it as "quite natural," Mikoyan said it "would not at all cause detriment to our common cause, but on the contrary, would facilitate it."* Mao was not assuaged and Stalin knew it. Soon afterwards Stalin tried to explain to Mao's No. 2, Liu Shao-chi, that the move had been made in order to gather intelligence. But Mao remained displeased, and took his displeasure out on Roshchin when Stalin sent him back to China as Russia's first ambassador to Mao's government. When Roshchin threw his first dinner for the Chinese Politburo, Mao sat through it without saying a word all evening, displaying what one Russian diplomat described as "a mocking-indifferent attitude."

During Mikoyan's visit Mao curbed his annoyance. To Mikoyan's astonishment, Mao did not complain about Russia's 1945 treaty with Chiang Kai-shek, under which Russia had regained extraterritorial concessions; he even went so far as to call it "patriotic." Mao wanted a lot from Stalin. His shopping list started with a request for a US$300 million loan—exclusively for military purposes—and moved on to a vast range of arms, including heavy tanks and anti-aircraft guns, plus advisers on reorganizing the army. Even more important was long-term help for factories to produce his own aircraft, tanks and other heavy weapons. Mao wanted Stalin's help to become a major military power.

---

* Mao learned from Stalin's duplicity about conducting an open, even apparently friendly relationship with a government while secretly trying to overthrow that same government. When he came to power, he was to copy Stalin in his dealings with other countries.

Stalin had recently expelled Tito, the Yugoslav leader, from the Communist camp. Tito had shown too much independence and an inclination to carve out his own sphere of influence. In an earlier message to Stalin, Mao had referred to Tito's experience, seemingly placing it alongside Russia's as a possible model, and had been slapped down hard in return. Mao now made the right noises about Tito, commending Stalin's criticism of Yugoslav nationalism. This was Mao's effort to reassure Stalin that he would not be another Tito.

Mao also made a point of stressing to Mikoyan how much he regarded himself as Stalin's subordinate. Toasting Stalin's health, Mao "emphasised that . . . Stalin was . . . the teacher of the Chinese people and the peoples of the whole world," Mikoyan reported to Stalin. Mao "emphasised several times that he was a disciple of comrade Stalin," and "was awaiting instructions . . . and deliberately downgraded his own role . . . as a leader and as a theoretician . . . [saying] that he . . . had made no new contribution to Marxism, etc." But the astute Mikoyan was not taken in. "This," he told Stalin, "does not correspond to what Mao Tse-tung is in reality, nor to what he thinks about himself."

Indeed, when Mikoyan brought up the subject of "coordination" among Asian Communist parties, Mao was ready with his plan, which was to create an Asian Cominform, which he proposed starting to organize as soon as he had completed his conquest of China. He wanted the group to consist of "several" other Asian parties, listing the Koreans, the Indo-Chinese and the Filipinos, to begin with.

Mikoyan then produced Stalin's offer, which restricted Mao to China's immediate backyard, saying that Mao should "head" a bureau of *East* Asian parties, consisting initially of only three members: China, Japan and Korea. "Later on," he said, others "could also be involved gradually."

Stalin was conceding some ground. At the same time, he sent a signal for Mao not to push too hard. The day after the conversation about turf, Stalin sent Mikoyan a very strong cable telling him to order Mao to arrest an American working with the CCP called Sidney Rittenberg—"as a spy." Stalin linked Rittenberg with Anna Louise Strong, the American whom Mao had sent abroad to promote himself; according to Stalin, Strong too was an American spy. (Mikoyan said Stalin had given him special orders to check for US and British "spies" in the entourage of the CCP leadership.) Rittenberg was duly arrested.

Strong herself was at that moment stranded in Moscow, denied an exit visa for China. On 13 February, the day after Mikoyan returned to Moscow and saw Stalin, she was thrown into the Lubyanka prison. Most unusually, her arrest, on a charge of "espionage," was reported in *Pravda* the next day, which made the warning more emphatic for Mao, and for Communist satellite regimes. After Strong was deported shortly afterwards, she wrote to a CCP intermediary: "Please tell Chairman Mao . . . that, so far as I could learn, it was my too persistent search into the road to China [*sic*] that the Russians finally attacked as 'spying.' "

One of Strong's contacts in Moscow was Mikhail Borodin, Stalin's main operative in China in the 1920s, who had been trying to help get her book promoting Mao published in Russia. Two weeks after Strong's arrest, Borodin too was arrested and tortured for information about Mao.

Though these arrests were shots across Mao's bows, he was unruffled. Stalin was saying: Don't mess with America, or Europe. But Mikoyan had already promised him East Asia. Mao was now demarcating turf with Stalin. So it was in a cheerful mood that he thought out loud on this subject to a pre-victory Central Committee plenum on 13 March 1949.

At this meeting, his old challenger Wang Ming, who by now had conceded defeat, curried favor instead, declaiming that Mao's Thought was "the . . . development of Marxism-Leninism in colonial and semi-colonial countries." Not East Asia, or just Asia, but all "colonial and semi-colonial countries."

Wang Ming had spelled out what Mao had in mind, and Mao was so delighted that he got rather carried away: "Comrade Wang Ming's phrase gives off a smell of dividing a 'market.' Colonial and semi-colonial countries take up a very large part of the world. Once they come under us, doesn't that mean Stalin only takes charge of the developed industrial regions, and [the rest of the world] is under our charge . . . ?" Persisting with the royal "we," Mao continued: ". . . we say colonial and semi-colonial countries belong to us. But what if one of them doesn't buy our goods and goes straight to Moscow . . . ? . . . Of course, let's not be in a hurry to think too big; let's fix China first."

Mao had begun to dream about dividing the world with Stalin.

STALIN CLEARLY decided that if he allowed Mao stewardship over even a limited slice of turf his own power would be eroded. So when Liu Shao-chi visited Russia that summer and delicately broached the subject by asking Stalin whether China could join the Cominform, he got a taste of the Master at his slyest. "I think it is not really necessary," Stalin replied. China should, instead, be "organising a union of Communist parties of East Asia." But this seeming confirmation of his earlier offer was followed at once by: "Since the USSR is a country situated both in Europe and Asia, it will participate in [this] union." The Master was not backing off at all.

As before, Stalin served up sharp warnings to Mao by arresting a whole string of operatives who had been in China. While Liu was in Moscow, many of the key Russian agents who had been with Mao followed Borodin into the torture cells: Mao's GRU doctor, Orlov, was recalled and savagely tortured by KGB chief Viktor Abakumov in person. Orlov was accused of links with "the American and Japanese spy" Mao. Orlov's arrest was signaled to Mao, as the Russians approached Shi Zhe, Liu's interpreter and Mao's assistant, and asked him to inform on Orlov. These were signals that Stalin was preparing the ground to denounce Mao as a spy or a Titoist if it became opportune to do so.*

Stalin was baring his fangs. But Mao was not scared, and flexed his muscles on an issue of great importance to him: the first international Communist gathering scheduled to be held in his new capital, Peking. This was a huge trade union conference, which would be the springboard for putting Mao on the world map, as it covered not only the whole of Asia, but also Australasia, an advanced capitalist continent. It was also highly political, more like an international conference of Communist parties than a trade union gathering. Stalin tinkered with the idea of blocking it, or moving the venue, but Mao had Liu insist that it "should be held in China at the scheduled time." Liu promised that it "would not carry out any work of organization," meaning that Mao would not try to exploit it to set up his own international network.

When the conference opened, on 16 November 1949, Mao had just founded his regime, on 1 October. In his keynote speech, Liu proclaimed "the Mao Tse-tung road," and did not mention Stalin, or the Russian model, once. The theme of the conference was seizing power via the "Mao Tse-tung road" throughout Asia—and beyond: "The road that the Chinese people have followed is the road that the peoples of many colonial and semi-colonial areas should traverse . . ." Liu was categorical: "It is impossible for the revolutionary . . . people in such areas to avoid taking [this] road . . . [and] it will be wrong if they do so." "Armed struggles," he said, "should be the principal form of struggle."

This was strong stuff, and what followed showed how much headway Mao had made. When the Russian delegate complained that Liu's speech was "ultra-left," Stalin denounced his own man as "a turncoat." The hapless delegate, Leonid Solovyov, was obliged to admit error at a meeting chaired by Mao. This was a first for Mao—a senior Russian apologizing to him in front of his colleagues. Mao then grandly asked Stalin to "pardon" Solovyov.

Even bolder, Mao reneged on his commitment that there would be no organizational follow-up to the conference. On 23 November, Liu

---

* Many of Stalin's agents with Mao were soon to die abnormal deaths. Orlov died shortly afterwards in a plane crash. Mao's KGB doctor, Melnikov, vanished without trace after accompanying Mao on his trip in Russia in winter 1949–50. Borodin perished from torture in 1951. Vladimirov died at the age of forty-seven, in 1953—murdered by security overlord Lavrenti Beria with slow-acting poison, according to Vladimirov's son, the post-Communist presidential candidate (and Olympic weight-lifting champion) Yuri Vlasov.

Shao-chi announced that a Liaison Bureau would be set up, in Peking, through which the participating countries "can form their ties." Mao was gearing up to give orders to foreign Reds. Stalin let it pass.

Mao knew the Master was not going to swallow all this lying down. Some punishment was sure to result. But he now owned China, and with it a quarter of the world's population. He had significantly increased the scope and weight of the Communist camp as a whole. Stalin could not afford to disown him. Mao fully intended to force Stalin to help him advance his own global ambitions.

TWO TYRANTS WRESTLE

(1949–50 ★ AGE 55–56)

MAO'S PARAMOUNT requirement from Stalin was help to build a world-class war machine and turn China into a global power. The key to this was not how many weapons Stalin would provide, but the technology and infrastructure to manufacture armaments in China. At the time, China's ordnance factories could only produce small arms. If Mao was to move at the tempo he desired—faster than Japan had done when building up an advanced arms industry from scratch in the nineteenth century—he needed foreign assistance. And Stalin was not just Mao's best bet; he was his only bet. The Cold War had recently begun. There was no way the West could possibly help him achieve his goals without him changing the nature of his regime, which was out of the question.

But Mao had a problem: he needed to persuade Stalin that his ambitions were manageable from Stalin's own perspective. So he made ostentatious demonstrations of loyalty, lavishing praise on Stalin to the Master's top envoy Mikoyan, and putting on an act for his liaison man Kovalev. The latter reported to Stalin that Mao once "sprang up, raised his arms and cried out three times: 'May Stalin live ten thousand years.' " Along with the froth, Mao offered something very substantial—to cut China's ties with the West. "We would be glad if all the embassies of capitalist countries got out of China for good," Mao told Kovalev.

This attitude was also motivated by domestic concerns. "Recognition would facilitate subversive activities [by] the USA and Britain," Mao told Mikoyan on 31 January 1949. He feared that any Western presence at all would embolden liberals and give his opponents an opening, however slight. So he battened down the hatches, imposing a policy he called "cleaning house before inviting guests." "Cleaning house" was a euphemism for drastic, bloody purges and the installation of an airtight control system nationwide, which included sealing off the whole country, banning Chinese from leaving, and expelling virtually all Westerners. Shutting out foreigners was also a way to ensure there were no outside observers to the purges. Only after he had "cleaned"—or rather cleansed—house, would Mao open the door a crack to admit a few closely controlled foreigners, who were always known as "guests," not visitors.

Given the kind of regime he had in mind, Mao had cause to feel worried. Western influence was strong in China. "Many representatives of the Chinese intelligentsia received their education in America, Britain, Germany and Japan," Mao told Mikoyan. Virtually all modern educational institutions were either founded by Westerners (often missionaries) or heavily influenced by the West. "In addition to newspapers, magazines and news agencies," Liu wrote to Stalin in summer 1949, America and Britain alone had 31 universities and specialized schools, 32 religious educational institutions and 29 libraries in China, as well as 2,688 schools, 3,822 religious missions and organizations, and 147 hospitals.

China was short of educated people, especially skilled personnel, and Mao needed these people to get the country working, particularly the cities. Contrary to common assumption, it was the cities he cared about most. If we can't run the cities, he told top officials in March 1949, "we won't last." His aim was to scare the educated class out of their liberal Western attitudes. This would be much easier to achieve if potential dissidents knew there were no Western representatives in the country to whom they could appeal, or any foreign media to tell their story.

Mao was also concerned about the appeal the West had inside his own Party. His army loved American weapons: his own bodyguards compared Soviet sub-machine-guns contemptuously with US-made carbines. "The [US] carbines are so light and accurate. Why can't we have more carbines?" they pleaded with Mao. American cars positively inspired awe. One CCP official in the Russian-occupied port of Dalian had a shiny black 1946 Ford: "It was great to show off with," he recalled, "and roused the interest of the highest command of the Soviet army," who asked to borrow it for a day, which put him one up on the Russians. Mao's aim was to nip in the bud any chance of the West exerting any influence on his Party, in any field, from ideas to consumer goods. In this Mao was more thorough even than Stalin.

Control was one key reason Mao decided to shun Western recognition. But his primary purpose was to show Stalin that the new China was committed 100 percent to the Communist bloc. This was the main reason Peking did not establish diplomatic relations with America and most Western countries when the regime was founded. It is widely thought that it was the US that refused to recognize Mao's China. In fact, Mao went out of his way to make recognition impossible by engaging in overtly hostile acts. When the Communists captured Shenyang in November 1948, there were three Western consulates there (US, British and French), and the local CCP was friendly towards them at first. But orders soon came from Mao to "force [them] out." Chou was explicit to Mikoyan: "We created intolerable conditions for them in order to get them to leave."* On 18 November, US consul general Ward and his staff were put under house arrest. Ward was later accused of spying and expelled. In the same aggressive spirit, Red troops broke into the residence of US ambassador J. Leighton Stuart in Nanjing in April 1949 when they took the Nationalist capital.

Mao was equally hostile to the British. When the Communists were crossing the Yangtze in late April, moving south, there were two British ships on that stretch of the river, HMS *Amethyst* and HMS *Consort*. Mao ordered that "all warships which get in the way of our crossing may be bombarded. Treat them as Nationalist ships." Forty-two British sailors were killed, more than all other Western military deaths in the entire civil war. *Consort* got away, but *Amethyst* became grounded. Back in Britain, enraged sailors beat up CP chief Harry Pollitt, who landed up in the hospital. Winston Churchill, then leader of the Opposition, asked in Parliament why Britain did not have "in Chinese waters one aircraft carrier, if not two, capable of . . . effective power of retaliation."

The incident greatly alarmed Stalin, who placed Soviet forces throughout the Far East on full alert—the only time this occurred in connection with the Chinese civil war. Stalin was worried that the West might intervene militarily and involve Russia, and he cabled Mao urgently to play down their relationship: "We do not think now is the right moment to publicise the friendship between the USSR and Democratic China." Mao had to tone down his aggressiveness and issued new orders to "avoid clashes with foreign ships. No firing at [them] without the order of the Center. Extremely, extremely important." He told his commanders to "protect . . . especially diplomats from America and Britain," "or else big disaster could happen." On 27 April he suspended the advance on Shanghai, which was the most important economic and financial center in the country, and the focus of Western interests—and therefore the most likely place where the West, which had sizable military forces there, might make a stand.

To lessen the risk of Western intervention, on 10 May Mao took diversionary steps by authorizing talks with US ambassador Stuart, who had stayed on in Nanjing after the Nationalist government had left. Stuart was an "old China hand" who wishfully thought he could bring Washington and Mao together. Decades later, Mao's then negotiator and future foreign minister, Huang Hua, spelled out Mao's intent: "Mao and

---

* Chou used the expression "iron curtain" to describe what the CCP wanted: "to drive at having Manchuria covered by the iron curtain against foreign powers," "except the USSR and people's democracies."

Chou ... were not looking for friendly relations. They had but one concern: to forestall a major American intervention which might rescue the Nationalists at the eleventh hour ..."

As further insurance against a backlash from foreign powers, Mao spun a web of disinformation. On 30 May, Chou En-lai gave a verbal message to an intermediary to be passed to Truman. The message was carefully tailored to American hopes at the time. It said there was a split in the CCP between the pro-Western "liberals" headed by Chou himself, and pro-Soviet "radicals" headed by Liu Shao-chi, and that if America would back Chou he might be able to influence CCP foreign policy. This was a hoax, but it contributed to the delusion that the CCP might throw itself into the West's embrace.*

This flurry of pseudo-diplomacy, like the temporary lull on the battlefield, in no way implied any diminution in Mao's resolve to shun the West. By mid-May, he had given the go-ahead for a general offensive against Shanghai, which fell by the end of the month. When foreign warships withdrew from Shanghai as the Reds approached, and US forces quickly left their last base on the Mainland, at Qingdao, Mao was more convinced than ever that Western powers would not invade China, where they would only get bogged down, as the Japanese experience had shown.

Mao now demonstrated all-out hostility towards the West. In a signed article in *People's Daily* on 30 June, he stated that his foreign policy would be to "side exclusively with one camp": *yi-bian-dao*. This did not just mean staying firmly in the Communist camp. It meant freezing relations with the West. A few days later the US vice-consul in Shanghai, William Olive, was arrested in the street, thrown in jail, and so badly beaten up that he soon died. The US recalled ambassador Stuart at once. At the end of July, when *Amethyst* tried to leave, Mao gave orders to "strike it hard." *Amethyst* got away, but a Chinese passenger ship it had been hiding behind was sunk.

That same month, July, Mao spelled out to Stalin that his preferred policy was to "wait and not hurry to gain recognition from these [Western] states." Stalin was delighted. "Yes! Better not to hurry," he wrote in the margin, underlining Mao's words.

SEVERING TIES with the West was Mao's gift to Stalin before they met up. Mao was keen to visit him as soon as his regime was proclaimed in October 1949. Stalin was the boss of the Communist camp, and Mao had to have an audience with him. Mao also knew that the kind of deals he wanted to do had to be transacted face-to-face.

A visit had been pending for two years, but Stalin had been stringing

---

* It was also a source of the lasting misconception that Liu Shao-chi was more hard-line than Chou.

Mao along, manipulating his patent desire for a meeting to punish him for ambitions beyond his borders. Even after Mao was inaugurated as supreme leader of China, there was still no invitation. By the end of October, Chou had to go to the Russian ambassador and tell him that Mao wanted to go to Moscow to pay his respects to Stalin on his seventieth birthday, on 21 December 1949. Stalin agreed, but he did not offer Mao the sort of state visit in his own right that someone who had just brought a quarter of the world's population into the Communist camp might feel entitled to expect. Mao was coming merely as one of a flock of Party leaders from around the globe converging to pay court on Stalin's birthday.

Mao set off by train on 6 December, on what was his first trip out of China. He did not bring a single senior colleague. The highest-ranking person in the delegation was a secretary. Stalin's liaison, Kovalev, rightly surmised that this was so that when Stalin humiliated Mao, which was inevitable, it would be "without Chinese witnesses." When Mao met Stalin the first time, he even excluded his ambassador from the session. Face was power. A snub from the Master could weaken his hold over his colleagues.

Mao got to see Stalin the day he arrived, and he reiterated that China was bound exclusively to Russia. "Several countries," he told Stalin, "especially Britain, are actively campaigning to recognise the People's Republic of China. However, we believe that we should not rush to be recognised." He laid out his core requests: help in building a comprehensive military–industrial system, with emphasis on an aircraft industry, and a modern military, especially a navy.

In exchange, Mao was ready to make significant concessions. He had come to Moscow wanting to secure a new Sino-Soviet treaty to replace the Soviet Union's old treaty with Chiang Kai-shek, but after learning that Stalin had "decided not to modify any of the points of this treaty for now," on the grounds that discarding the old treaty would have complications involving the Yalta Agreement, Mao conceded at once. "We must act in a way that is best for the common cause . . . the treaty should not be modified at the present time." The treaty with Chiang had given Russia territorial concessions. Mao enthusiastically offered to leave them in Russian hands. The status quo, he said, "corresponds well with Chinese interests . . ."

Mao's readiness to make major concessions in the interests of achieving his goal—help towards furthering his global aspirations—was transparent. What Stalin had to gauge was how far those aspirations would affect his own position. A militarily powerful China would be very much a two-edged sword: a tremendous asset for the Communist camp—and for him; but also a potential threat. Stalin needed time to mull things over. Should he offer Mao anything at all, and if so, what, and how much?

Mao was packed off to his bugged residence, Stalin's No. 2 dacha, 27 km outside Moscow. For days there was no follow-up meeting. Mao was left gazing out of the picture window at the snow-covered garden, and took out his anger on his staff. Stalin sent various underlings to see Mao, but they were not empowered to talk business. Rather, their job was, as Stalin put it to Molotov, "to find out what sort of type" Mao was, and to monitor him. When liaison man Kovalev reported to Stalin that Mao was "upset and anxious," Stalin answered: "We have many foreign visitors here now. Comrade Mao should not be singled out" for exceptional treatment.

But, in fact, Mao *was* singled out for special treatment—*ill*-treatment—precisely in relation to these "visitors." Mao was eager to meet Communist leaders from other countries, and they were equally keen to meet him—the man who had just brought off a triumph that could be called the second October Revolution. But Stalin blocked Mao from getting together with any of them, except for meaningless exchanges with the lackluster Hungarian, Mátyás Rákosi. Mao asked to meet the Italian Communist chief Palmiro Togliatti, "but," Mao told an Italian Communist delegation (after Stalin died), "Stalin managed, with a thousand stratagems, to deny me that."*

For the actual birthday celebration itself, on 21 December, Mao donned the obligatory mask, and newsreels record him applauding Stalin expansively. Stalin, for his part, appeared solicitous to Mao, whom he seated on his right on the platform, and *Pravda* reported that Mao was the only foreign speaker for whom the audience stood at the end of his speech. At the show that followed, Mao was greeted with an ovation "the like of which the Bolshoi had undoubtedly never seen," Rákosi observed, with the audience chanting "Stalin, Mao Tse-tung!" Mao shouted back: "Long live Stalin! Glory belongs to Stalin!"

As soon as that was over, the next day, Mao demanded a meeting with Stalin. "I'm not here just for the birthday," he exploded to Kovalev. "I'm here to do business!" Colorful language was used: "Am I here just to eat, shit and sleep?"

Of this trio of bodily functions, none was problem-free. On the food front, Mao vented his discontent on the fact that his hosts were delivering frozen fish, which he hated. "I will only eat live fish," he told his staff. "Throw these back at them!" Shitting was a major problem, as Mao not only suffered from constipation, but could not adapt to the pedestal toilet, preferring to squat. And he did not like the soft Russian mattress, or the pillows: "How can you sleep on this?" he said, poking at the down-filled pillows. "Your head will disappear!" He had them swapped for his own,

* British Communist leader John Gollan's notes of what Mao said to him in 1957 (about 1949) read: "Not even freedom of meeting leaders. 70th birthday—Didn't dare although there."

filled with buckwheat husks, and had the mattress replaced by wooden planks.

Mao saw Stalin two days later, on the 24th, but the Master declined to discuss his requests about building up China's military power, and would only talk about the issue they had not touched on at their first meeting: Mao's role vis-à-vis other Communist parties such as those in Vietnam, Japan and India. After probing Mao's appetite for turf, Stalin went silent again for days, during which time Mao's own birthday, his fifty-sixth, came along on 26 December, but went unmarked. Mao spent all his time cooped up in the dacha, dealing with domestic matters by cable. He said later that he made "an attempt to phone him [Stalin] in his apartment, but they told me Stalin is not at home, and recommended that I meet with Mikoyan. All this offended me . . ." Stalin rang Mao a few times, but the calls were brief and neither here nor there. Mao declined invitations to go sightseeing, saying he was not interested, and that he was in Moscow to work. If there was no work to do, then he would rather stay in the dacha and sleep. Mao was frustrated and furious; at times, to his close assistants, he appeared "desolate."

It seems that Mao now decided to play "the West card" to prod Stalin into action. He let it be known, not least by speaking out loud in his bugged residence, that he was "prepared to do business with . . . Britain, Japan and America." And contrary to what he had told Stalin upon his arrival in Moscow (that he was not going to "rush to be recognised" by Britain), talks went ahead with Britain which led to London recognizing Mao's regime on 6 January 1950. The British press, meanwhile, reported that Mao had been put under house arrest by Stalin, and this "leak" could well have been planted by Mao's men. It was "possible," Mao later said, that this shift in policy towards the West helped "in Stalin's change of position," noting that real negotiations "began right after this."

BY NEW YEAR'S DAY 1950, Stalin had made up his mind. On 2 January, *Pravda* ran an "interview" with Mao, which, Mao said sarcastically years later, Stalin had "drafted for me, acting as my secretary." The text prepared by Stalin made it clear that Stalin was willing to sign a new treaty; to Mao this meant that Stalin was ready to deal with the key issue of turning China into a major military power. Mao now summoned Chou En-lai from Peking, along with his main industry and trade managers, to do the detailed negotiations, specifying that Chou must travel by train, not by plane, for safety reasons. Chou would have had to come in a Russian plane, and Mao was hinting that he was taking precautions.

Mao, however, was not about to swallow his treatment without taking a kick at Stalin. An opportunity quickly presented itself when US Secretary of State Dean Acheson made a speech at the National Press

Club in Washington on 12 January, timed to coincide with Mao's protracted stay in Moscow, accusing Russia of "detaching the northern provinces of China . . . and . . . attaching them to the Soviet Union," with the process "complete" in Outer Mongolia, "nearly complete" in Manchuria, and under way in Inner Mongolia and Xinjiang. Stalin sent his right-hand man, Molotov, to tell Mao he must rebut the speech in the name of the Chinese Foreign Ministry, and that Mongolia and Russia would do the same. Mao agreed to do so, but instead of a rebuttal by the Foreign Ministry, he wrote a text in the name of his press chief, a relatively low-level figure. The piece referred to the Soviet satellite of Outer Mongolia, which was formally independent, in the same breath as Chinese regions, which seemed to be saying that China did not accept Russia's de facto annexation of the territory.

The evening this article appeared in Mao's main newspaper, *People's Daily*, on 21 January, Stalin hauled Mao into the Kremlin for a mighty dressing-down, which included the accusation that China's "own Tito" was emerging. This was delivered mainly by his faithful lackey Molotov, in the presence of Beria. Stalin made a point of staging the tongue-lashing in front of Chou En-lai, who had just arrived the day before. Even though Chou for Mao was a kind of eunuch, and the one among all Mao's senior colleagues that he least minded seeing him take a caning, Mao was livid.

Having chastised Mao, Stalin invited him and Chou to his dacha for dinner. Stalin knew that Mao was in no position to stake a claim to Outer Mongolia, as Peking had recognized it diplomatically in October 1949. Mao's insubordinate behavior about rebutting Acheson was an expression of resentment rather than a statement of policy (though Stalin still demanded an official exchange of notes regarding the status of Mongolia). For the drive to dinner, Stalin and Shi Zhe, Mao's interpreter, sat on the jump seats, while Mao and Chou were given the main seats. In the car, Shi Zhe recalled, everyone was silent, and the air was like lead:

> To lighten the tension, I chatted a little with Stalin, and then asked him: "Didn't you promise to visit our delegation?"
> He answered at once: "I did, and I have not abandoned this wish."
> Before he finished, Chairman Mao asked me: "What are you talking to him about? Don't invite him to visit us."
> I immediately admitted I had indeed just been talking about this with him.
> Chairman Mao said: "Take it back. No more invitation."
> . . . Silence again. The air was heavy, as if new lead had been poured into it. We sat like this for thirty minutes.
> . . . The atmosphere at the dinner was also cold and bored . . . The Chairman remained silent, not speaking a word . . .

>   To break the ice, Stalin got up to turn on the gramophone...
> Although three or four men took turns trying to pull Chairman Mao
> onto the floor to dance, they never succeeded...The whole thing
> ended in bad odour..."

The two sides finally signed a new treaty on 14 February 1950. The published text was a formality. The essence of the treaty was in secret annexes. The US$300 million loan China had requested was confirmed, although it was spread over five years, and of the first year's tranche China actually got only one-third (US$20 million), on the grounds that the rest was owed for past "purchases." The entire loan was allocated to military purchases from Russia (in Mao's inner circle it was referred to as "a military loan"). Half of the total loan, US$150 million, was earmarked for the navy. Stalin gave the go-ahead for fifty large-scale industrial projects—far fewer than Mao had wanted.

In return, Mao agreed that Manchuria and Xinjiang were to be designated Soviet spheres of influence, with Russia given exclusive access to their "industrial, financial, and commercial...activities." As these two huge regions were the main areas with known rich and exploitable mineral resources, Mao was effectively signing away most of China's tradable assets. To his inner circle he himself referred to the two provinces as "colonies." To the Americans, decades later, he said that the Russians "grabbed half of Xinjiang. It was called a sphere of influence. And Manchukuo [*sic*] was also called their sphere of influence." He gave Russia a monopoly on all China's "surplus" tungsten, tin and antimony for fourteen years, thus depriving China of the chance to sell about 90 percent of its marketable raw materials on the world market into the mid-1960s.

In 1989, the post-Mao leader Deng Xiao-ping told Russian leader Mikhail Gorbachev: "Of all the foreign powers that invaded, bullied and enslaved China since the Opium War (in 1842), Japan inflicted the greatest damage; but in the end, the country that got most benefit out of China was Tsarist Russia, including [*sic*] the Soviet Union during a certain period..." Deng was certainly referring to this treaty.

Mao went to great lengths to conceal how much the treaty gave away. When he went over the draft of the announcement he carefully erased any phrases like "supplementary agreements," and "appendix," which might make people suspect the existence of these secret documents, marking his deletions: "Extremely crucial, extremely crucial!"*

---

* When a news item in March 1950 mentioned joint companies, Liu Shao-chi noted that the news "has aroused tremendous waves among Peking students, who suspect these... might be damaging China's sovereignty. Many Youth League members demanded an... explanation; some even charged out loud...that the people's government had sold out the country." And this was without knowing the half of it.

At Stalin's insistence, China not only paid huge salaries to Soviet technicians in China, plus extensive benefits for them and their families, but had to pay compensation to Russian enterprises for the loss of the services of the technicians who came to China. But the concession Mao was most anxious to hide was that he had exempted Russians from Chinese jurisdiction. This had been *the* issue the CCP had always harped on as the embodiment of "imperialist humiliation." Now Mao himself had secretly introduced it.

Mao wanted to end his trip on a high note, so he pleaded with Stalin, who did not go to parties outside the Kremlin, to attend a celebration he was throwing at the Metropol Hotel on the evening of the signing: "we do hope you can come for a minute. You can leave early any time . . ." Stalin decided to grant Mao this moment of glory. When Stalin showed up at 9:00 PM, bringing his own bottle, the flabbergasted guests went into a frenzy.

But Stalin did not come just to show good will. He had a message to send. In his toast he brought up Yugoslavia's leader, Tito, whom he had recently cast out of the Communist camp. Any Communist country that went its own way, Stalin observed pointedly, would end up badly, and would only return to the fold under a different leader. The warning was clear—and would have been even more threatening if Stalin's plans to assassinate Tito had been known.

None of this dampened Mao's ambitions. Earlier that day, at the treaty-signing ceremony, when photographs were being taken, the diminutive Stalin had taken one step forward. To his staff afterwards, Mao remarked, with a smile: "So he will look as tall as I am!" (Mao was 1.8 meters tall.)

Mao was bent on pursuing his dream of making China, his base, a superpower. Stalin was equally determined to thwart this ambition—as Mao could tell from the fact that, in return for the huge concessions he had made, he got relatively little from Stalin. What Stalin let him have fell far short of even the skeleton basis for a world-class military machine. Mao was going to have to find other ways to squeeze more out of Stalin.

WHY MAO AND STALIN
STARTED THE KOREAN WAR

(1949−50 ⋆ AGE 55−56)

STALIN RECOGNIZED that Mao had the drive and the resources, especially the human resources, to expand the frontiers of communism in Asia significantly. In order not to erode his own power, Stalin decided not to form an Asian Cominform, which would give the Chinese leader a formal pan-Asia set-up, but instead to dole out individual countries to Mao, in such a way that he, Stalin, remained the ultimate boss. At their second meeting, during Mao's stay in Moscow, Stalin assigned him to supervise Vietnam.

Stalin had hitherto shown little interest in Vietnam. In 1945, when the Vietnamese Communist leader Ho Chi Minh led an uprising against French colonial rule and declared a provisional independent government, Moscow had not even bothered to answer his cables. But, even though he did not entirely trust Ho, Stalin changed his attitude radically once Mao took power and Chinese troops reached the border with Vietnam in late 1949. On 30 January 1950, while Mao was in Moscow, Stalin recognized Ho's regime, some days after Mao did. The lack of a common frontier with Vietnam made it difficult for Stalin to command from afar, whereas China could supply arms, goods and training across its border with Vietnam (and Laos). By giving Mao custody of Vietnam, Stalin gave himself a way of reaching into Vietnam, *and* gratified Mao, while passing on to China the enormous expense of sustaining the Indochina insurgencies.

Mao had already been trying to bring the Vietnamese under his tutelage. Ho had lived in China for more than a decade, including a stretch in Yenan, and spoke fluent Chinese. Mao had been training, funding and arming the Vietnamese, but when he developed a plan to send in Chinese troops once he controlled the border with Vietnam, in late 1949, Stalin called him to heel. Stalin wanted to gather all the strings together in his own hands first.

Ho Chi Minh was brought to Moscow, via Peking, arriving in time to make a dramatic appearance at Stalin's farewell dinner for Mao in the Kremlin on 16 February 1950. Stalin told Ho that aid to Vietnam was

China's responsibility—and cost. Ho was the only foreign Communist leader with whom Mao was allowed to have proper talks on this trip, and the two returned to China on the same train, in a convoy between one train carrying Soviet airmen going to protect Shanghai and China's coastal cities, and one loaded with MiG-15s.

Mao now began to take personal charge of action in Vietnam, vetting both grand strategy and the minutiae of military operations. The first objective was to link up the Vietnamese Communists' base with China, as the CCP had done with Russia in 1945–46. Inside China, a road-building blitz to the border was completed in August 1950. Within two months this enabled the Vietnamese to win a crucial series of battles known as the Border Campaign, as a result of which the French army lost control of the frontier with China. Thereafter, China poured in aid. On 19 August, Mao told Stalin's emissary Pavel Yudin that he planned to train 60,000–70,000 Vietnamese soldiers. It was having China as a secure rear and supply depot that made it possible for the Vietnamese to fight for twenty-five years and beat first the French and then the Americans.

In most of these years, the huge logistics burden of the fighting in Indochina fell almost entirely on China. To Mao, the cost was irrelevant. When the French Party's first emissary to Ho mentioned ways the French Communists could help the Vietnamese, he was told by Liu Shao-chi: "Don't waste your time on this. Don't get into things like medical aid. We can do that. After all there are 600 million Chinese . . ."

It was not long before Mao started trying to "Maoise" his client, imposing a much-hated land reform on Vietnam in the 1950s, in which Chinese advisers even presided over kangaroo tribunals that sentenced Vietnamese to death in their own country. Vietnam's "poet laureate," To Huu, hymned Mao's role in surprisingly frank doggerel:

> *Kill, kill more . . .*
> *For the farm, good rice, quick collection of taxes . . .*
> *Worship Chairman Mao, Worship Stalin . . .*

Even though some Vietnamese leaders raised strenuous objections to the Mao-style land reform, Ho Chi Minh put up only feeble and belated resistance to Mao's attempt to turn the Vietnamese revolution into a clone of China's.

IN SEPTEMBER to October 1950, Mao downgraded operations in Vietnam, in order to focus on a much larger war on another patch of turf that Stalin had decided to assign him. This was Korea.

At the end of World War II, Korea, which had been annexed by Japan early in the century, was divided across the middle, along the 38th Parallel, with Russia occupying the northern half and the US the South. After

formal independence in 1948, the North came under a Communist dictator, Kim Il Sung. In March 1949, as Mao's armies were rolling towards
victory, Kim went to Moscow to try to persuade Stalin to help him seize
the South. Stalin said "No," as this might involve confronting America.
Kim then turned to Mao, and one month later sent his deputy defense
minister to China. Mao gave Kim a firm commitment, saying he would
be glad to help Pyongyang attack the South, but could they wait until he
had taken the whole of China: "It would be much better if the North
Korean government launched an all-out attack against the South in the
first half of 1950 . . ." Mao said, adding emphatically: "If necessary, we can
stealthily put in Chinese soldiers for you." Koreans and Chinese, he said,
had black hair, and the Americans would not be able to tell the difference: "They will not notice."

Mao encouraged Pyongyang to invade the South and take on the
USA—and volunteered Chinese manpower—as early as May 1949. At
this stage he was talking about sending in Chinese troops clandestinely,
posing as Koreans, and not about China having an open collision with
America. During his visit to Russia, however, Mao changed. He became
determined to fight America openly—because only such a war would
enable him to gouge out of Stalin what he needed to build his own world-
class war machine. What Mao had in mind boiled down to a deal: Chinese
soldiers would fight the Americans for Stalin in exchange for Soviet technology and equipment.

Stalin received reports from both his ambassador in Korea and his
liaison with Mao about Mao's eagerness to have a war in Korea. As a
result of this new factor, Stalin began to reconsider his previous refusal
to let Kim invade the South.

Stalin was given a push by Kim. On 19 January 1950, the Soviet ambassador to Pyongyang, Terentii Shtykov, reported that Kim had told him,
"excitedly" that "now that China is completing its liberation," South
Korea's was "next in line." Kim "thinks that he needs to visit comrade
Stalin again, in order to receive instructions and authorization to launch
an offensive." Kim added that "if it was not possible to meet comrade
Stalin now, he will try to meet with Mao." He stressed that Mao had
"promised to render him assistance after the conclusion of the war in
China." Playing "the Mao card," Kim told Shtykov that "he also has other
questions for Mao Tse-tung, in particular the question of the possibility
of setting up an Eastern bureau of the Cominform" (no mention of talking to *Stalin* about this). Mao, he said, "would have instructions on all
issues." Kim was telling Stalin that Mao was keen to give him military
support, and that if Stalin would still not endorse an invasion, he (Kim)
would go to Mao direct and place himself under Mao.

Eleven days later, on 30 January, Stalin wired Shtykov to tell Kim that he was "prepared to help him on this." This is the first documented evidence of Stalin agreeing to start a war in Korea, and he shifted his position because of Mao, who possessed the critical asset—an inexhaustible supply of men. When Kim came to Moscow two months later, Stalin said that the international environment had "changed sufficiently to permit a more active stance on the unification of Korea." He went on to make it explicit that this was because "the Chinese were now in a position to devote more attention to the Korean issue." There was "one vital condition—Peking's support" for the war. Kim "must rely on Mao, who understands Asian affairs beautifully."*

A war in Korea fought by Chinese and Koreans would give the Soviet Union incalculable advantages: it could field-test both its own new equipment, especially its MiG jets, and America's technology, as well as acquiring some of this technology, along with valuable intelligence on America. Both China and Korea would be completely dependent on Russian arms, so Stalin could fine-tune the degree of Russia's involvement. Moreover, he could test how far America would go in a war with the Communist camp.

But for Stalin, the greatest attraction of a war in Korea was that the Chinese, with their massive numbers, which Mao was eager to use, might be able to eliminate, and in any case tie down, so many American troops that the balance of power might tilt in Stalin's favor and enable him to turn his schemes into reality. These schemes included seizing various European countries, among them Germany, Spain and Italy. One scenario Stalin discussed during the Korean War was an air attack on the US fleet on the high seas between Japan and Korea (en route to Inchon, in September 1950). In fact, Stalin told Mao on 5 October 1950 that the period provided a unique—and short-lived—window of opportunity because two of the major capitalist states, Germany and Japan, were out of action militarily. Discussing the possibility of what amounted to a *Third World War*, Stalin said: "Should we fear this? In my opinion, we should not . . . If a war is inevitable, then let it be waged now, and not in a few years' time . . ."†

Mao repeatedly spelled out this potential to Stalin, as a way of stressing his usefulness. On 1 July 1950, within a week of the North invading the South, and long before Chinese troops had gone in, he had Chou tell

---

* Kim Il Sung later told the head of the Spanish Communist Party, Santiago Carrillo (who told us), that he had started the war—and that Mao had been far more strongly for launching it than Stalin.

† In late 1950 a top French government adviser in Indochina (Jean Sainteny) summed up the thinking of the French commanding general there, Jean de Lattre de Tassigny, in these words: "that the Russians are looking for one billion human beings, human beings from Asia, a sort of human livestock, to get them to fight the West." The same thought had occurred earlier to US Senator Henry Cabot Lodge. Questioning the head of the US Military Advisory Group to the Chinese Nationalists, Major General Barr,

the Russian ambassador: "Now we must energetically build up our aviation and fleet," adding pointedly for Stalin's ears: "so as to deal a knockout blow . . . to the armed forces of the USA." On 19 August Mao himself told Stalin's emissary, Yudin, that America could send in thirty to forty divisions but that Chinese troops could "grind" these up. He reiterated this message to Yudin a week later. Then, on 1 March 1951, he summed up his overall plan for the Korean War to Stalin in chilling language: "to spend several years consuming several hundred thousand American lives."

With Mao's expendables on offer, Stalin positively desired a war with the West in Korea. When Kim invaded the South on 25 June 1950, the UN Security Council quickly passed a resolution committing troops to support South Korea. Stalin's ambassador to the UN, Yakov Malik, had been boycotting proceedings since January, ostensibly over Taiwan continuing to occupy China's seat. Everyone expected Malik, who remained in New York, to return to the chamber and veto the resolution, but he stayed away. Malik had in fact requested permission to return to the Security Council, but Stalin rang him up and told him to stay out. The Soviet failure to exercise its veto has perplexed observers ever since, as it seemed to throw away a golden opportunity to block the West's involvement in Korea. But if Stalin decided not to use his veto, it can only have been for one reason: that he did not want to keep Western forces out. He wanted them *in*, where Mao's sheer weight of numbers could grind them up.

IT WAS NOW very much in Stalin's interest to make Mao the sub-chief over Kim, but this was a different case from Vietnam. Because of the enormous ramifications of taking on the USA, Stalin decided to keep an extra degree of control. He had to make absolutely sure that Kim understood that he, Stalin, was the ultimate boss before he put Kim in Mao's hands. So even though Mao was in Moscow on 30 January, when Stalin gave Kim his consent to go to war, he did not breathe a word to Mao, and ordered Kim not to inform the Chinese. Stalin brought Kim to Moscow only at the end of March, after Mao had left. Stalin went over battle plans in detail with Kim, and at their last talk, in April 1950, he laid it on the line to Kim: "If you should get kicked in the teeth, I shall not lift a finger. You have to ask Mao for all the help." With this comradely envoi, Kim was waved away to Mao's care.

---

in March 1949, Lodge asked: "Do you think the Russians can regiment those Chinese . . . and make them a military asset outside the borders of China, and use them in Europe or . . . somewhere else?" After an interjection by Senator Alexander Wiley ("Genghis Khan was a Chinese, was he not?"), Barr replied: ". . . could the Russians organize a Chinese division and take it over to Germany or in that area . . . I am afraid that idea would appeal to some of the Chinese Communists."

On 13 May a Russian plane flew Kim to Peking. He went straight to Mao to announce that Stalin had given the go-ahead. At 11:30 that night, Chou was dispatched to ask the Soviet ambassador, Roshchin, to get Moscow's confirmation. Stalin's stilted message came the next morning: "North Korea can move toward actions; however, this question should be discussed . . . personally with comrade Mao." Next day (15 May), Mao gave Kim his full commitment, and on the most vital issue: "if the Americans were to take part . . . [China] would assist North Korea with its own troops." He went out of his way to exclude the participation of Russian troops, saying that: "Since the Soviet Union is bound by a demarcation agreement on the 38th Parallel [dividing Korea] with America, it would be 'inconvenient' [for it] to take part in military actions [but as] China is not bound by any such obligations, it can therefore fully render assistance to the northerners." Mao offered to deploy troops at once on the Korean border.

Mao endorsed the Kim–Stalin plan, and Stalin wired consent on the 16th. On 25 June the North Korean army smashed across the 38th Parallel. Mao, it seems, was not told the exact launch day. Kim wanted Chinese troops kept out until they were absolutely needed. Stalin, too, wanted them in only when America committed large numbers of troops for the Chinese to "consume."

TRUMAN REACTED fast to the invasion. Within two days, on the 27th, he announced that he was sending troops into Korea, as well as upping aid to the French in Indochina. Furthermore, he now reversed the policy of "non-intervention" towards Taiwan. It was thanks to this new US commitment that neither Mao nor his successors were ever able to take Taiwan.

By early August, the North Koreans had occupied 90 percent of the South, but the US poured in well-armed reinforcements, and on 15 September landed troops at Inchon, just below the 38th Parallel, cutting off much of the North Korean army in the South, and positioning itself for a move into the North. On the 29th Kim sent an SOS to Stalin, in which he asked for "volunteer units" from China.

On 1 October, Stalin signaled to Mao that the moment had come for him to act, dissociating himself shamelessly from any responsibility for defeat: "I am far away from Moscow on vacation and somewhat detached from events in Korea . . ." After this barefaced lie came his real point: "I think that if . . . you consider it possible to send troops to assist the Koreans, then you should move at least five–six divisions towards the 38th Parallel . . . [These] could be called volunteers . . ."

Mao leapt into action. At 2:00 AM on 2 October he issued an order to the troops he had already moved up to the Korean border: "Stand by for order to go into [Korea] at any moment . . ."

Poverty-stricken, exhausted China was about to be thrown into war with the USA. It seems it was only now, at the beginning of October, that Mao convened the regime's top body, the Politburo, to discuss this momentous issue. The Politburo was not a team to make important decisions, but to serve as a sounding-board for Mao. On this occasion, he specifically invited differing views, because of the colossal implications of war with America. Nearly all his colleagues were strongly against going into Korea, including his No. 2 Liu Shao-chi and nominal military chief Zhu De. Lin Biao was the most vocal opponent. Chou En-lai took a cautious and equivocal position. Mao said later that going into Korea was "decided by one man and a half": himself the "one" and Chou the "half." Among the huge problems voiced were: that the US had complete air supremacy, and artillery superiority of about 40:1; that if China got involved, America might bomb China's big cities and destroy its industrial base; and that America might drop atomic bombs on China.

Mao himself had been losing sleep over these questions. He needed a functioning China as the base for his wider ambitions. But Mao gambled that America would not expand the war to China. Chinese cities and industrial bases could be protected from US bombing by the Russian air force. And as for atomic bombs, his gut feeling was that America would be deterred by international public opinion, particularly as Truman had already dropped two—both on an Asian country. Mao took precautions for himself, though. During the Korean War, he mostly holed up in a top-secret military estate outside Peking in the Jade Spring Hills, well equipped with air-raid shelters.

Mao was convinced that America could not defeat him, because of his one fundamental asset—millions of expendable Chinese, including quite a few that he was pretty keen to get rid of. In fact, the war provided a perfect chance to consign former Nationalist troops to their deaths. These were men who had surrendered wholesale in the last stages of the civil war, and it was a deliberate decision on Mao's part to send them into Korea, where they formed the bulk of the Chinese forces. In case UN troops should fail to do the job, there were special execution squads in the rear to take care of anyone hanging back.

Mao knew that America just would not be able to compete in sacrificing men. He was ready to wager all because having Chinese troops fighting the USA was the only chance he had to claw out of Stalin what he needed to make China a world-class military power.

Mao hand-drafted a cable to Stalin on 2 October, committing to "sending Chinese army to Korea." Then it seems he had second thoughts. In his eagerness to go in, he had not informed Stalin of any of his problems. Playing them up could raise his price. So he held back the cable committing Chinese forces, and sent a quite different one, saying that Chinese entry "may entail extremely serious consequences . . . Many comrades . . . judge that it is necessary to show caution . . . Therefore it is better to . . . refrain from advancing troops . . ." However, he left open the option of going in: "A final decision has not been taken," he ended; "we wish to consult with you."

AT THE SAME TIME, Mao prepared the ground for going into Korea by pretending to give America "fair warning." For this purpose, Chou En-lai staged an elaborate charade, waking the Indian ambassador in the small hours of 3 October to tell him "we will intervene" if American troops crossed the 38th Parallel. Choosing this roundabout channel, using an ambassador whose credit in the West was minimal, when it would have been perfectly simple to make an official statement, suggests compellingly that Mao wanted his "warning" to be ignored: thus he could go into Korea claiming he was acting out of self-defense.

By the 5th of October, with UN forces already pushing into the North, Stalin was showing impatience. That day he replied to Mao's cable of the 2nd which had suggested that Mao might hold back. He reminded Mao that he, Mao, had made a commitment:

> I considered it possible to turn to You with the question of five–six Chinese volunteer divisions because I was well aware of a number of statements made by the leading Chinese comrades [i.e., *you*] regarding their readiness to move several armies in support of the Korean comrades . . .

Stalin referred ominously to what he called "a passive wait-and-see policy," which, he said, would cost Mao Taiwan. Mao had been using Taiwan as an argument to persuade Stalin to help him build an air force and a navy. Stalin was now telling Mao he would get neither if he stalled about his mission in Korea.

But Mao was not really trying to opt out. He was raising his price. By the time he received Stalin's reply, he had already appointed a commander-in-chief for the Chinese forces slated for Korea: Peng De-huai. Mao moved at his own pace. On 8 October, having ordered his troops to be redesignated as "Chinese People's Volunteers," he wired Kim that "we have decided to dispatch the Volunteers into Korea to help you." He also sent Chou En-lai and Lin Biao to see Stalin about arms supplies. En route, Lin sent Mao a long cable urging him to abandon the idea of going in. The reason Mao sent Lin Biao to see Stalin when Lin was such a strong opponent of intervention, was to impress on Stalin the military difficulties facing the Chinese and thus extract the maximum out of the Master.

Chou and Lin got to Stalin's villa on the Black Sea on the 10th, and talked through the night until 5 in the morning. Stalin promised them "planes, artillery, tanks and other equipment." Chou did not even negotiate a price. But out of the blue Stalin reneged about the key requirement: air cover for Chinese troops. Stalin had promised this ("a division of jet fighter planes—124 pieces for covering [Chinese] troops") on 13 July. Now he claimed that the planes would not be ready for another two months. Without air cover, Chinese troops would be sitting ducks. Chou and Lin Biao argued that Russian air cover was essential. An impasse was reached. Stalin then wired Mao to tell him that China did not have to join the war.

Stalin was calling Mao's bluff by saying, as Mao put it later, "Forget it!" Mao climbed down at once. "With or without air cover from the Soviet Union," he told Stalin, "we go in." Mao needed the war. He wired Chou on 13 October: "We should enter the war. We must enter the war . . ." When Chou received the cable he buried his head in his hands. That same day Mao told the Russian ambassador that China was going in, only expressing the "hope" that Russian air cover would arrive "as soon as possible, but not later than in two months," which was, in fact, Stalin's own timetable.

So it was that out of the global ambitions of the two Communist tyrants, Stalin and Mao, as well as the more local ambition of Kim, China was hurled into the inferno of the Korean War on 19 October 1950.

MAO MILKS THE KOREAN WAR

(1950–53 ★ AGE 56–59)

WHEN CHINESE troops went into Korea in October 1950, the North Koreans were on the run. Two months later, Mao's army had pushed the UN out of North Korea and restored Kim Il Sung's dictatorship. But Kim was now militarily powerless, with his depleted 75,000-man army outnumbered 6:1 by the 450,000 troops Mao had in Korea. On 7 December, the day after the Chinese recovered Kim's capital, Pyongyang, Kim ceded command to the Chinese. The Chinese commander Peng De-huai cabled Mao that Kim had "agreed . . . not to intervene in the future in matters of military command." Peng was made the head of a joint Chinese–Korean HQ. Mao had taken over Kim's war.

Peng wanted to stop north of the 38th Parallel, the original boundary between North and South Korea, but Mao refused. Peng pleaded that his supply lines were over-extended, leaving them seriously exposed to US bombing: "our troops are unable to receive supplies of food, ammunition, shoes, oil or salt . . . The main problem is no air cover, and no guaranteed railway transport; the moment we repair them, they are bombed again . . ." Mao insisted. He was determined not to stop fighting until he had squeezed the utmost out of Stalin. "Must cross the 38th Parallel," he ordered Peng on 13 December. Early in January 1951 the Chinese took Seoul, the Southern capital, eventually pushing about 100 km south of the Parallel.

Chinese military successes greatly boosted Mao's standing with Stalin, who sent extraordinarily enthusiastic congratulations, which he had not done for Mao's triumph in taking China. Stalin particularly remarked that the victories had been won "against American troops."

Mao had dealt an enormous psychological blow to the USA. On 15 December 1950, Truman went on radio to declare a State of National Emergency, something that did not happen in either World War II or the Vietnam War. Using almost apocalyptic language, he told the American people: "Our homes, our Nation . . . are in great danger." The Chinese by then had already driven the Americans back some 200 km in a matter of weeks, in appalling conditions, with sub-zero temperatures compounded by icy winds. Secretary of State Dean Acheson described the reverse as the "worst defeat" for US forces in a century.

The Chinese won their victories at horrendous cost to their own men. Peng told Mao on 19 December:

> The temperature has dropped to minus 30 degrees centigrade. The troops are very run down, their feet are incapacitated by frostbite, and they have to sleep in the open . . . Most troops have not received coats and padded shoes. Their padded jackets and blankets have been burned out by napalm. Many soldiers are still wearing thin cotton shoes, and some are even bare-foot . . .

"Unimaginable losses may happen," Peng warned. Mao's logistics manager told the Russians on 2 January 1951 that whole units had died from cold. Many "Volunteers" developed night blindness from lack of nutrition. HQ's answer was: Gather pine needles to make soup. Eat live tadpoles to provide some vitamins and protein.

The Chinese fought with "human wave tactics" (*ren-hai zhan-shu*), using the only advantage they had—superiority in numbers. The British actor Michael Caine, who was drafted into the war, told us he had gone into it feeling sympathetic to communism, coming as he did from a poor family. But the experience left him permanently repelled. Chinese soldiers charged in one wave after another, to exhaust Western bullets. He could not help thinking: If they don't care about the lives of their own people, how can I expect them to care about me?

The Chinese advance was soon halted. On 25 January 1951 the UN launched a counter-offensive, and the tide began to turn. Chinese casualties were extremely heavy. Peng went back to Peking on 21 February to tell Mao to his face about the "grave difficulties" and the "massive unnecessary casualties." From the airport he raced to Zhongnanhai, only to find that Mao was staying out at Jade Spring Hill in his bunker. When Peng got there he was told Mao was having a siesta, but he pushed his way past the bodyguards and burst into Mao's bedroom (practically *lèse-majesté*). Mao let him say his piece, but brushed his concerns aside, and told him to expect the war to be a long one: "Don't try to win a quick victory."

Mao outlined his "overall strategy" to Stalin in a cable on 1 March, which opened with the sentence: "The enemy will not leave Korea without being eliminated in great masses . . ." He then told Stalin that his plan was to use his bottomless reserves of manpower to exhaust the Americans. The Chinese army, he reported (which was true), had already taken "more than 100,000 casualties . . . and is expecting another 300,000 this year and next." But, he told Stalin, he was replenishing the losses with 120,000 more troops, and would send a further 300,000 to replenish future losses.

"To sum up," Mao said, he was "ready to persist in a long-term war, to spend several years consuming several hundred thousand American lives, so they will back down . . ." Mao was reminding Stalin that he could seriously weaken America,* but Stalin must help him build a first-class army and arms industry.

MAO GOT MOVING on this fundamental objective from the moment China entered the war in October 1950. That very month, China's navy chief was sent to Russia to ask for assistance to build up the navy. He was followed in December by a top-level air force mission, which had considerable success. On 19 February 1951, Moscow endorsed a draft agreement to start building factories in China to repair and service planes, as a large number were being damaged, and required advanced repair facilities in the theater. The Chinese plan was to convert these repair facilities to actually making aircraft. By the end of the war, China, a very poor country, had the third largest air force in the world, with more than 3,000 planes, including advanced MiGs. And factories were being built to churn out 3,600 fighter planes annually which, it was projected (over-optimistically, as it turned out), would come on stream in three to five years' time. Discussions had even begun about manufacturing bombers.

Immediately after the aircraft deal in early 1951—and after Stalin endorsed Mao's plan "to spend several years consuming several hundred thousand American lives"—Mao upped the ante by asking for the blue-prints for all the weapons the Chinese were using in Korea, and for Russian help to build factories to produce them, as well as the arms to equip no fewer than sixty divisions. He sent his chief of staff to Russia in May to negotiate these requests.

Although Stalin wanted China to do his fighting for him, and was happy to sell Mao the weapons for the sixty divisions, he had no intention of endowing Mao with a full-blown arms industry, so the Chinese delegation was stonewalled in Russia for months. Mao told his chief of staff to keep on pushing, and in October the Russians reluctantly agreed to transfer the technology for producing seven kinds of small arms including machine-guns, but declined to divulge more.

By now the war had lasted for a year, during which North Korea had been pulverized by US bombing. Kim saw that he might end up ruling over a wasteland, and possibly a shrunken one at that. He wanted an end to the war. On 3 June 1951 he went to China in secret to discuss opening negotiations with the US. As Mao was nowhere near his goal, the last thing he was interested in was stopping the war. In fact, he had just

---

* Altogether, China put at least 3 million troops into Korea. The US committed roughly 1 million military personnel.

ordered Chinese troops to draw UN forces deeper into North Korea: "the farther north the better," he said, provided it was not too near the Chinese border. Mao had hijacked the war, and was using Korea regardless of Kim's interests.

But, as his troops had been suffering heavy defeats, a breathing space was tactically useful for Mao, so he sent his Manchuria chief with Kim to consult with Stalin—and to press for more arms factories. Afterwards, Stalin cabled Mao, treating Kim as Mao's satrap, to propitiate Mao, as he was turning him down on the arms factories. After talking "with your representatives from Manchuria and Korea" (*sic*), Stalin told Mao, "a truce is now advantageous." This did not mean Stalin wanted to stop the war. He wanted Mao's soldiers to inflict more damage on the US, but he saw that engaging in talks could be expedient, and seeming to show an interest in peace would help the Communists' image. Interim ceasefire talks opened in Korea between UN and Chinese–Korean military teams on 10 July.

Most items were settled fairly swiftly, but Mao and Stalin turned one issue into a sticking point: the repatriation of POWs. America wanted voluntary, "non-forcible," repatriation; Mao insisted it had to be wholesale. The UN held over 20,000 Chinese, mainly former Nationalist troops, most of whom did not want to go back to Communist China. With the memory of handing back prisoners to Stalin at the end of World War II, many to their deaths, America rejected non-voluntary repatriation, for both humanitarian and political reasons. But Mao's line to his negotiators was: "Not a single one is to get away!" Mao's chilling mantra prolonged the war for a year and a half, during which hundreds of thousands of Chinese, and many more Koreans, died. Kim had been only too keen to concede, and argued that "there was no point in putting up a fight" to recover "politically unstable" ex-Nationalists. But this cut no ice with Mao, as that was not his point. Mao did not care about the POWs. He needed an issue to string out the war so that he could extract more from Stalin.

BY EARLY 1952, Kim was absolutely desperate to end the war. On 14 July 1952 he cabled Mao begging him to accept a compromise. American bombing was reducing his country to rubble. "There was nothing left to bomb," US Assistant Secretary of State Dean Rusk observed. The population was declining to almost critical survival levels, with perhaps one-third of adult males killed.

Mao turned Kim down by return telegram, with the cold-blooded argument that "Rejecting the proposal of the enemy will bring only one harmful consequence—further losses for the Korean people and Chinese people's volunteers. However . . ." Mao then proceeded to list the "advantages" in these human losses, such as the sufferers being "tempered and acquiring experience in the struggle against American imperialism." He signed off menacingly by saying he would report to Stalin and then get back to Kim "upon receiving an answer."

Without waiting for Mao to tell him what Stalin thought, Kim replied at once to say that Mao was, of course, "correct," and that he, Kim, was determined to fight on. Kim simultaneously cabled Stalin, pathetically trying to explain his wavering.

Stalin wired Mao on the 17th with his verdict: "We consider your position in the negotiations on an armistice to be completely correct. Today we received a report from Pyongyang that comrade Kim Il Sung also agrees with your position."

Kim was frantic, but he was powerless to stop the war in his own country. Moreover, his own fate was in peril. An ominous conversation between Stalin and Chou En-lai a month later shows that he had reason to feel insecure. After Chou said that China was preparing for "the possibility of another two to three years of war," Stalin asked about the attitude of the Korean leaders. The meeting record runs as follows (our comments in brackets):

> STALIN says that the American[s] have not frightened China. Could it be said that they have also failed to frighten Korea?
> CHOU EN-LAI affirms that one could essentially say that.
> STALIN: [obviously skeptically] If that is true, then it's not too bad.
> CHOU EN-LAI [picking up on Stalin's skepticism] adds that Korea is wavering somewhat . . . Among certain elements of the Korean leadership one can detect a state of panic, even.
> STALIN reminds that he has been already informed of these feelings through Kim Il Sung's telegram to Mao Tse-tung.
> CHOU EN-LAI confirms this.

Kim's panic about America paled beside his fear of Mao and Stalin. American bombing could kill a large part of his population, but Stalin and Mao could depose him (something Mao in fact later plotted doing) — or worse.

So the war went on.

BY AUGUST 1952, Mao decided to push Stalin harder and nail down his twin key demands: turf and arms industries. He sent Chou to Moscow with these requests. Chou first established that Mao had done Stalin an invaluable service. At their first meeting, on 20 August, he told Stalin that Mao "believes that the continuation of the war is advantageous to us." "Mao Tse-tung is right," Stalin answered. "This war is getting on

America's nerves." Echoing Mao's dismissive comments about casualties on their own side, Stalin produced the bone-chilling remark: "The North Koreans have lost nothing, except for casualties." "The war in Korea has shown America's weakness," he commented to Chou, and then said "jokingly": "America's primary weapons are stockings, cigarettes, and other merchandise. They want to subjugate the world, and yet they cannot subdue little Korea. No, Americans don't know how to fight." "Americans are not capable of waging a large-scale war at all, especially after the Korean War."

It was Mao who had made it possible for Stalin to draw this conclusion. America was losing more aircraft than it could afford militarily, and more men than the public would accept. Altogether, the US lost well over 3,000 aircraft in Korea, and could not replenish these losses fast enough to feel safe about being able to fight a two-front war simultaneously in Asia and Europe. Equally important, the US lost some 37,000 dead.

Although the American death toll was only a small percentage of the Chinese, democratic America could not compete with totalitarian China when it came to body bags. As America headed into a presidential campaign in 1952, support in the US for continuing the war stood at only about 33 percent, and the Republican candidate, ex-General Dwight D. Eisenhower, campaigned on the slogan "I Will Go to Korea," which was widely taken to mean ending the war.

China's role in taking on the US gave Chou the cards to shoot for the moon, and he asked the Master for no fewer than 147 large military-related enterprises, including plants to produce warplanes and ships, 1,000 light tanks per year, with one factory for medium tanks to be ready within five years.

Stalin prevaricated, responding with platitudes ("China must be well armed, especially with air and naval forces"; "China must become the flagship of Asia"). But he never signed Chou's list.

Then there was the question of turf. Stalin had been doling out parts of Asia to Mao since he had begun to think about the war in Korea. Mao had extruded tentacles into half a dozen Asian countries stretching from Japan (the Japanese Communists had come to Peking in spring 1950 to prepare for armed action in coordination with the Korean War) to the Philippines (where the US had strategic bases) and Malaya, where a sizable, and largely ethnic Chinese, insurgency was fighting British rule. In Southeast Asia, Burmese Communist insurgent forces had been moving towards the Chinese border to link up with China to receive supplies and training, just as Ho Chi Minh's army had done in Vietnam. One evil harbinger who was soon to come to China for training was the future leader of the Cambodian Khmer Rouge, Pol Pot.

In September 1952, Chou talked to Stalin about Southeast Asia as if its fate were to be entirely decided by Peking, and the Chinese army could just walk in if Peking so wished. The minutes of their meeting on 3 September record that Chou: "says that in their relations with Southeast Asian countries they are maintaining a strategy of exerting peaceful influence without sending armed forces. He offers the example of Burma . . . The same in Tibet. Asks whether this is a good strategy." Chou was treating Burma in the same vein as Tibet. Stalin replied wryly: "Tibet is part of China. There must be Chinese troops deployed in Tibet. As for Burma, you should proceed carefully." But Stalin immediately added, confirming that Burma was Mao's: "It would be good if there was a pro-China government in Burma." (Stalin monitored Burma closely through his ambassador, the long-time liaison in Yenan, Vladimirov.)

Mao was now planning to form his regional conglomerate, using a "Peace Congress" of the Asia–Pacific region scheduled to convene in Peking. This was on Chou's agenda for his talks with Stalin. Stalin was obliged to acknowledge that China should play "the principal role." That he was not at all pleased can be seen from what followed. Chou asked "what specific actions" the Russian delegation would take, which was a subtle invitation for Stalin to confirm that the Russians would not grab leadership. Stalin replied sarcastically with one word: "Peace."

Undeterred, Chou forged on to say that during the imminent Soviet Party Congress Liu Shao-chi would like to meet Asian Communist leaders. This was a way of trying to secure Stalin's blessing for Mao to take charge of Asian parties, but dragging endorsements out of the Master was like getting water out of a stone. First mentioned were the Indonesians. The minutes record:

> CHOU EN-LAI . . . asks whether it would be timely to discuss party
> issues in Moscow with them.
> STALIN says that it is difficult to tell yet . . .
> CHOU EN-LAI reports that the Japanese should arrive, and it is
> likely they will also want to discuss party issues.
> STALIN answers that older brothers cannot refuse their younger
> brothers in such a matter. He says that this should be discussed
> with Liu Shao-chi . . .
> CHOU EN-LAI points out that Liu Shao-chi intends to bring with
> him appropriate material, in order to discuss a number of questions.
> STALIN notes that if the Chinese comrades want to discuss these
> issues, then of course we will have no objection, but if they do not
> want it, then we will not have to discuss anything.
> CHOU EN-LAI answers that the Chinese comrades will definitely
> want to talk.

How forceful Chou En-lai was! Relentlessly pursuing the Master as he tried to evade. Two and a half years and a devastating war before, when Mao was in wintry Moscow, Stalin had blocked him from any such meetings. Now, Stalin was forced to concede: "in this case, we shall find the time." Then, another little sarcasm when the smooth Chou, "ending the conversation, says they would like to receive instructions concerning all these issues."

> STALIN asks—instructions or suggestions?
> CHOU EN-LAI answers that from comrade Stalin's perspective this would be advice, but in their perception these would be instructions.

Chou's tact masked a startling new degree of assertiveness on Mao's part. In fact, Mao had even begun conspiratorial operations in the USSR itself.

CHOU'S MISSION in August–September 1952, transparently aimed at enabling Mao to become a major power and a rival to Stalin, drastically sharpened Stalin's sense of the threat from Mao, and so he set about undermining Mao by exhibiting special intimacy towards Mao's top colleagues. Stalin first cultivated army chief Peng De-huai, who came to Moscow in early September, with Kim, for the only tripartite Russo-Sino-Korean summit of the war. At the end of one meeting, most unusually, Stalin took Peng aside for a tête-à-tête, without Chou, which Chou reported to a furious Mao. Peng explained to Mao that Stalin had only talked about the way the North Koreans had been maltreating POWs (which had been causing problems for the Communists diplomatically). Mao remained suspicious, but seems to have concluded that this was just a ploy of Stalin's to unsettle him.

Then came another attempt by Stalin to drive a wedge—this time between Mao and Liu Shao-chi, who came to Moscow for the Soviet Party Congress in October. Stalin was extraordinarily, and noticeably, attentive to Liu, demonstrating a degree of intimacy that amazed Liu's entourage. "Stalin even mentioned his personal matters and moods," Liu's interpreter, Shi Zhe, observed. Shi had also interpreted for Mao, and saw the sharp contrast with the way that Stalin had treated Mao. Chou En-lai was to comment to a small circle that Stalin had given a far warmer welcome to Liu than to Mao.

Stalin then fired a salvo across Mao's bows with an unprecedented gesture, unique in the annals of world communism. On 9 October, *Pravda* published Peking's congratulations to the Congress, which Liu had delivered the previous day. In large type, Liu was billed as "General Secretary" of the CCP (the highest post in other parties). But, as Moscow well knew, the CCP did not have a general secretary. It was inconceivable that this was an accident. "*Pravda* in those days didn't make mistakes," one Russian ambassador to Britain commented to us. Stalin was saying to Mao: I *could* make your No. 2 the No. 1!

Liu had to clear himself, so he immediately wrote a note to Stalin's No. 2, Georgi Malenkov, saying that he was not general secretary, and that the CCP was "all under the leadership of Comrade Mao Tse-tung [who] is the Chairman." Clearly deciding that the wise thing to do was not to panic, he sent no frantic excuses home to Mao. After the congress, he stayed on as planned to talk to other Asian Communist leaders, including Ho Chi Minh, and together the two discussed not only Vietnam, but also Japan and Indonesia with Stalin. Stalin then kept Liu in Russia for months, until January 1953, to meet the people who were at the top of Mao's list—the Indonesians. On the night of 6–7 January 1953 Liu finally joined Stalin and Russia's top agent in Indonesia for an unusually long meeting with the Indonesian Communist leaders Aidit and Njoto, to discuss Peking "taking over" the Indonesian Party. Afterwards, Aidit celebrated by going out into the freezing night to throw snowballs, unaware that little more than a decade later, in 1965, Mao's tutelage would condemn him and Njoto and hundreds of thousands of their followers to premature and ghastly deaths.

As soon as the meeting with the Indonesians was over, Liu left Moscow for home that same day. Altogether, he had stayed in Russia for three months. Mao could do nothing about Stalin's machinations to needle him and stir up suspicion, nor was he able to take it out on Liu, which would play into Stalin's hands. But he flashed a warning signal to Liu the moment Liu returned to Peking, which amounted to: Don't get ideas!*

Meanwhile, Mao kept on bombarding Stalin with requests relating to arms industries. A blockbuster eight-page cable on 17 December 1952 bluntly demanded of Stalin: "Please could the Soviet government satisfy our arms order for war in Korea in 1953, and our orders for arms industries." Prefaced to this was Mao's vision for the war: "in the next phase (suppose one year), it will become more intense." As an added inducement to Stalin to cough up, Mao offered to carry Kim's bankrupt state, informing Stalin that Peking would subsidize Pyongyang for three years— to the tune of US$60 million p.a., which happened to be exactly the amount Stalin had "lent" to Mao in February 1950; but, per capita, fifty times the amount Stalin had been willing to advance—and from a much poorer country. And, unlike Stalin's loan, Mao's to Kim carried no inter-

---

* Mao did this by denouncing the head of the trade unions, Li Li-san, for advocating greater independence for unions. Those in the know were well aware that this was a line that Liu had strongly espoused.

est. A few weeks later, in January 1953, Mao put in another large request for his navy. Stalin said he would send the armaments requested, and approved Mao's fleet taking part in naval operations on the high seas for the first time, but he firmly declined to meet Mao's demands about arms industries.

AT THIS POINT, the armistice talks had long been in recess, while heavy fighting had continued. On 2 February 1953 the new US president, Eisenhower, suggested in his State of the Union address that he might use the atomic bomb on China. This threat was actually music to Mao's ears, as he now had an excuse to ask Stalin for what he wanted most: nuclear weapons.

Ever since the first Bomb had been dropped on Hiroshima in 1945, Mao had longed to possess one. One of his economic managers, Bo Yi-bo, recalled that all through the early 1950s, "at all meetings and on all occasions, Chairman Mao would talk about the fact that we had no atom bombs. He talked and talked. Chairman Mao was really anxious!" Mao successfully concealed this hankering from the public, affecting instead an image of nonchalant contempt for atomic weapons, and pretending that he preferred to rely on "the people," a position made famous by his remark in 1946 that the atom bomb was "a paper tiger."

As soon as Eisenhower made his remarks about possibly using the Bomb, Mao dispatched his top nuclear scientist, Qian San-qiang, to Moscow. Mao's message boiled down to this: Give me the Bomb, so that you will not be drawn into a nuclear war with America. This confronted Stalin with a serious dilemma, as Russia had a mutual defense pact with China.

Stalin did not want to give Mao the Bomb, but he was worried about Eisenhower. It was under this unremitting pressure—from Mao as much as from the West—that Stalin, it seems, decided to end the Korean War. According to Dmitri Volkogonov, the Russian general who had access to the highest-level secret archives, Stalin made the decision to end the war on 28 February, and told his colleagues he was planning to act the next day. That night Stalin was felled by a stroke, which killed him on 5 March. Mao may well have been a factor in the stroke. At the last dinner Stalin had talked about the Korean War, connecting the failure to keep Yugoslavia's Tito in the camp with the Communists losing the chance to win in Korea. He also brought up the Comintern in the Far East, and how it had failed in Japan. After dinner, he read some documents, and the last was a report that his attempt to assassinate Tito had failed. Stalin had suspected Mao of being a Japanese spy in the past, and was viewing Mao as a potential Tito. His obsessive mind may have been revolving around Mao, reflecting that getting rid of Mao would be just as daunting a task as trying to finish off Tito.* Mao may have helped cause Stalin's stroke.

Mao went to the Soviet embassy to mark Stalin's death. An embassy staffer claims that Mao had tears in his eyes and had trouble standing up straight, and that Chou wept. Actually, Stalin's death was Mao's moment of liberation.

On 9 March a giant memorial service was held in Tiananmen Square, with an organized crowd of hundreds of thousands. Strict orders were issued to the populace, including the injunction "Don't laugh!" A huge portrait of Stalin was draped above the central archway, and the ceremony opened with Mao bowing before the portrait and laying a wreath. Many speeches were made, but none by Mao. Nor did he go to the funeral in Moscow, though Mme Mao, who was then in Russia, visited Stalin's bier. Chou attended the funeral in Red Square, and was the only foreigner to march with the top Russian mourners, walking next to security chief Beria, in bitter cold (among Chou's gifts was immunity to temperature).

Stalin's death brought instant changes. During an all-night meeting on 21 March, the new Russian leaders, headed by premier Georgi Malenkov, told Chou they had decided to end the war in Korea. Stalin's successors were keen to lessen tension with the West, and made it clear that if Mao cooperated over stopping the war he would be rewarded with a large number of arms enterprises—ninety-one—which Stalin had been delaying. Unlike Stalin, who saw Mao as his personal rival, the new Soviet leaders took the attitude that a militarily powerful China was good for the Communist camp.

But Mao insisted on keeping the Korean War going. He wanted one more thing: the Bomb. In fact, this was the main goal of Chou's trip, along with arms industries. Chou tried hard to get the nuclear physicist Qian San-qiang's group into Russian nuclear research institutes, but their repeated requests for the transfer of nuclear technology were turned down. Qian kept pushing for two months, a period that coincided exactly with Mao's foot-dragging over ending the war. Then, in May, Moscow put its foot down.

The Communist camp had for some time been waging a huge campaign accusing the US of using germ warfare in Korea and China, and had vaguely claimed large numbers of deaths from germ attacks. Captured US airmen were made to confess to dropping germ bombs, sometimes on camera.

---

* The Korean War also boomeranged in spectacular fashion on its third instigator, Kim Il Sung. In 1994, forty-four years after he started it, Kim was found dead, sitting holding copies of the dossier the post-Communist Russian government was about to release revealing the inside story of the war and his role in starting it.

Mao used the issue to whip up hatred for the US inside China. But the accusations were concocted.* When Stalin died, the Kremlin immediately decided to drop the charges, which, Beria wrote to Malenkov on 21 April 1953, had caused Russia to "suffer[ed] real political damage in the international arena."

The accusation of fabricating the charges was now used to put pressure on Mao to end the war. Soviet foreign minister Molotov wrote to his colleagues that the Chinese had given the North Koreans "an intentionally false statement . . . about the use of bacteriological weapons by the Americans." The Koreans, he said, were "presented with a fait accompli." The Russians were laying the groundwork for throwing all the blame onto Mao.

On 2 May the Kremlin told its new ambassador in Peking, V. V. Kuznetsov, to deliver an unprecedentedly harsh message to Mao, which read:

> The Soviet government and the Central Committee of the CPSU [Soviet Party] were misled. The dissemination in the press of information about the use by the Americans of bacteriological weapons in Korea was based on false information. The accusations against the Americans were fictitious.

The message "recommended" that Peking drop the accusations, and informed Mao menacingly that the Russians "responsible for participation in the fabrication . . . will receive severe punishment." Indeed, the Soviet ambassador to Pyongyang, V. N. Razuvayev, had already been recalled, as Mao certainly knew, and tortured by Beria's men.

Kuznetsov saw Mao and Chou at midnight on 11–12 May. Afterwards he reported to Moscow that Mao back-pedaled. According to Kuznetsov, Mao said "that the campaign was begun on the basis of reports from the [Chinese] command . . . It is difficult now to establish the authenticity of these reports . . . If falsification is discovered, then these reports from below should not be credited." Kuznetsov was clearly under orders to give a detailed account of Mao's reactions. He reported that: "some nervousness was noticed on the part of Mao Tse-tung; he . . . crushed cigarettes . . . Towards the end of the conversation he laughed and joked, and

---

* Peking is still sticking to the allegation, although its official claim now is a grand total of 81 deaths from 804 US germ attacks—45 Koreans from cholera and plague, and 36 Chinese of plague, meningitis, and "other diseases." Two Russian generals who were in Korea, Valentin Sozinov, chief adviser to North Korean chief of staff Nam Il, and the chief medical adviser to the North Korean army, Igor Selivanov, both told us they had never seen any evidence of germ warfare, and Selivanov stressed that in his position he would have known about it if it had happened. Other leading Russian officers and diplomats involved concurred.

calmed down. Chou En-lai behaved with studied seriousness and some uneasiness."

Mao had every reason to feel uneasy. Moscow's language was uncommonly severe. It showed how determined the Kremlin was to end the war, and signaled a readiness to apply extreme pressure, and to disavow something that Stalin must have approved. Coming fast on the heels of the Kremlin disowning Stalin's last fake conspiracy, the "Doctors' Plot" (the first time any action of Stalin's was publicly repudiated, which came as a bombshell to the Communist world), the new Kremlin was telling Mao it was determined to have its way. Mao was clearly taken aback, as he gave orders to end the war that very night.*

Mao could see that getting the Bomb from Russia was out of the question for now, as the new Kremlin was bent on lowering tension with America. So he recalled his nuclear delegation from Moscow, and settled for the arms projects that the new Kremlin leaders had offered. He ordered his negotiators in Korea to accept voluntary repatriation of POWs, which had been on the table for over eighteen months.

Two-thirds of the 21,374 Chinese POWs refused to return to Communist China, and most went to Taiwan.† The one-third who returned to the Mainland found themselves labeled as "traitors" for having surrendered, and suffered appallingly for the rest of Mao's reign. One other dire, and little-known, contribution Mao made to the misery of the Korean nation was to help consign over 60,000 South Korean prisoners, who were illegally retained by the North at the time of the armistice, to a terrible fate. Mao told Kim to hold on to them. These unfortunate men were dispersed to the remotest corners of North Korea to conceal them from prying eyes and minimize their chances of escape, and this is where any survivors are probably held to this day.

AN ARMISTICE WAS finally signed on 27 July 1953. The Korean War, which had lasted three years and brought millions of deaths and numerous wounded, was over.

---

* Kim's regime was eager to put the boot into Mao. The Soviet chargé in Pyongyang, S. P. Suzdalev, reported to Moscow on 1 June that on hearing the Kremlin's new "recommendations," the Korean official to whom he conveyed the message, Pak Chang-ok, jumped at the chance to disown the Chinese, even suggesting "the possibility that the bombs and containers were thrown from Chinese planes."

† Twenty-one Americans and one Scot opted to go to China, where most soon became disillusioned and left, often after great difficulties. Their defection stoked fears in the West about "brainwashing," as did captured airmen's "confessions" about dropping germ bombs. While the top brass worried that some of those who "confessed" might spill hi-tech knowledge of great use to an enemy, FBI chief J. Edgar Hoover mounted a vast surveillance campaign on returned POWs, fearing "Manchurian Candidates," the then US Attorney General Herbert Brownell told us.

More than 3 million Chinese men were put into Korea, among whom at least 400,000 died.* An official Russian document puts Chinese dead at 1 million.

Among those who died in Korea was Mao's eldest son, An-ying, killed in an American air raid on Peng De-huai's HQ, where he was working as Peng's Russian translator. It was 25 November 1950, just over a month after he had entered Korea. He was twenty-eight.

He had married only a year before, on 15 October 1949. His wife, Si-qi, was a kind of adopted daughter to Mao, and she and An-ying had known each other for some years. When An-ying told his father in late 1948 that he wanted to marry her, Mao had flown into a ferocious rage and bellowed at him so terrifyingly that An-ying fainted, his hands going so cold they did not react even to a boiling hot water bottle, which left two big blisters. Mao's furious reaction suggests sexual jealousy (the beautiful and elegant Si-qi had been around Mao for much of her teens). Mao withheld consent for many months, and then told the couple to delay getting married until his regime was formally proclaimed, on 1 October 1949. By the time of his first wedding anniversary, An-ying was gone. As was the rule, he did not tell his wife where, and she did not ask.

When Mao was given the news of his son's death, he was silent for some time, and then murmured: "In a war, how can there be no deaths?" Mao's secretary observed: "He really didn't show any expression of great pain." Even Mme Mao shed some tears, although she had not quite got on with her stepson.

Nobody informed An-ying's young widow for over two and a half years. While the war was still going on, she accepted An-ying's silence, as she was used to Party secrecy. But in summer 1953, after the signing of the armistice, she found his continued silence puzzling, and asked Mao, who told her that An-ying was dead. During those years she had been seeing Mao constantly, spending weekends and vacations with him, and he had not shown any sadness, not even a flicker to suggest that anything was wrong. He had even cracked jokes about An-ying as though he were alive.

---

* The official claim is 152,000 deaths, but in private Deng Xiao-ping told Japanese Communist leaders that the number of Chinese killed was 400,000. The same figure was given by Kang Sheng to Albania's Enver Hoxha. These sacrifices did not earn China much gratitude from North Korea. When we tried to gain access to the Chinese war memorial in Pyongyang, Korean officials refused permission. To the question, "How many Chinese died in the Korean War?," the reply came, most grudgingly, after two refusals to answer: "Perhaps 10,000."

LAUNCHING THE SECRET SUPERPOWER PROGRAM

(1953–54 ★ AGE 59–60)

AFTER MAO had accepted an end to the Korean War, in May 1953, Stalin's successors in the Kremlin agreed to sell China ninety-one large industrial enterprises. With these assured, on top of the fifty projects agreed to by Stalin, Mao was able to launch his blueprint for industrialization on 15 June. This focused exclusively on building up arms industries, to make China a superpower. It was in effect Mao's Superpower Program. Its utterly military nature was concealed, and is little known in China today.

Mao wanted to channel every resource the nation had into this program. The whole "industrialisation" process had to be completed "in ten to fifteen years," or at most a bit longer. Speed, he said over and over again, was everything—"the essence." What he did not spell out was his real goal: to become a military power in his own lifetime, and have the world listen when he spoke.

Mao was approaching sixty, and he often referred to his own age and mortality when discussing this industrialization. Talking to a group of his guards on one occasion, he stressed: "We will make it in fifteen years," then out of nowhere came the words: "Confucius died at seventy-three." The subtext was: Surely I can live longer than Confucius, and thus be able to see results within fifteen years.

On another occasion he said that "we can overtake Britain ... in fifteen years or slightly more," and then added: "I myself also have a Five-Year Plan: to live ... another fifteen years, then I will be satisfied; of course, it will be even better to over-fulfill"—i.e., live even longer.

Mao was not interested in posterity. Back in 1918 he had written: "Some say one has a responsibility for history. I don't believe it ... *People like me are not building achievements to leave for future generations ...*" (our italics). These remained his views throughout his life. In 1950, after visiting Lenin's mausoleum, Mao said to his entourage that the superb preservation of the corpse was only for the sake of others; it was irrelevant to

Lenin. Once Lenin died, he felt nothing, and it did not matter to him how his corpse was kept.

When Mao died, he left neither a will nor an heir—and, in fact, unlike most Chinese parents, especially Chinese emperors, he was indifferent about having an heir, which was extremely unusual (in stark contrast to Chiang Kai-shek, who went to inordinate lengths to protect his heir). Mao's eldest son, who died in the Korean War, had no offspring, as his wife did not want to have children while she was still studying. Mao put no pressure on him to produce an heir, even though he was the only one of Mao's sons who was of sound mind, as the younger son was mentally handicapped.

For decades to come, Mao's determination to preside over a military superpower in his own lifetime was the single most important factor affecting the fate of the Chinese population.

MAO WAS IN a rush for his arsenal. In September 1952, when Chou En-lai gave Stalin Peking's shopping list for its First Five-Year Plan (1953–57), Stalin's reaction was: "This is a very unbalanced ratio. Even during wartime we didn't have such high military expenses." "The question here is . . . whether we will be able to produce this much equipment." According to official statistics, spending during this period on the military, plus arms-related industries, took up 61 percent of the budget—although in reality the percentage was higher, and would rise as the years progressed.

In contrast, spending on education, culture and health combined was a miserable 8.2 percent, and there was no private sector to fall back on when the state failed to provide. Education and health care were never free, except in the case of epidemics, and often not available, for either the peasants or the urban underclass. In order to save money on health, the regime resorted to schemes like hygiene drives, which called for killing not only flies and rats, but in some areas also cats and dogs, although, curiously, it never extended to cleaning up China's stinking, and pestiferous, toilets, which survived uncleansed throughout Mao's reign.

The Chinese people were told, vaguely but deliberately, that equipment from the USSR used in China's industrialization was "Soviet aid," implying that the "aid" was a gift. But it was not. Everything had to be paid for—and that meant mainly with food, a fact that was strictly concealed from the Chinese people, and still largely is. China in those days had little else to sell. Trade with Russia, Chou told a small circle, "boils down to us selling agricultural products to buy machines."*

---

* Chou told Stalin in September 1952 that China could also "collect" up to £1.6 billion sterling plus US$200m over five years, "mostly" through what he called "contraband."

Throughout the 1950s, "the main exports were rice, soybeans, vegetable oil, pigs' bristles, sausage skins, raw silk, pork, cashmere, tea and eggs," according to today's official statistics. In this period Mao told the Indonesian President Sukarno, almost flippantly: "Frankly speaking, we haven't got a lot of things [for export] apart from some apples, peanuts, pig bristles, soybeans."

What China was exporting to Russia, and its satellites, consisted overwhelmingly of items that were basic essentials for its own people, and included all the main products on which China's own population depended for protein: soybeans, vegetable oil, eggs and pork, which were always in extremely short supply. With only 7 percent of the world's arable land, and 22 percent of its population, land was too precious to raise livestock in most places, so most Chinese had no dairy products and very little meat. Even grain, the staple, was on Mao's export list, while China's grain production was woefully inadequate, and the country had traditionally been a large importer of grain.

Mao was ready to deprive his people of food so that he could export it. One instruction to the Foreign Trade Ministry in October 1953 read:

> Regarding commodities that are crucial to the survival of the nation (e.g., grain, soybeans and vegetable oil), it is true we need to supply the Chinese population, but we cannot only stress this . . . *We must think of every way to squeeze them out for export* [our italics] . . . As for commodities (such as meats, peanuts) that are less essential to the survival of the population, we have all the more reason to cut down on consumption inside China, to satisfy the need for export.

Another order in July 1954 read:

> For commodities like meats, the internal market should be reduced and shrunk to guarantee exports. Other commodities like fruits, teas . . . should be exported as much as possible, and *should only supply the internal market if there is anything left* . . . [our italics]

The main impact fell on the peasants. Policy was to guarantee basic food to the urban population, with strict rationing, and leave the peasants to starve when the inevitable food shortages struck. Anyone registered as a peasant at the time Mao took power was forbidden to move into urban areas or to change their status. Peasants were not even allowed to move to another village except with special permission (e.g., if they got married). Otherwise, they were nailed to their village for life. And so were their children and grandchildren. This total immobility was something new in China. Traditionally, peasants had always been able to move geographically as well as socially. They had been able to aspire to fame and fortune— as Mao had done. If there was a famine, they had been able to flee into towns or other regions and at least try their luck. Now, even at the best of times, they could never hope to improve their lot, except when the government enrolled them into the army, or into a factory. And when disaster struck, they would starve or die in their villages.*

Once, as he was promising to send East Germany more soybeans, Chou En-lai told his German interlocutors: "If people starve here it will be in the countryside not in the cities, the way it is with you." In other words: our starving won't be seen.

The peasants had to produce the food for export with virtually no help from the state, a fact confirmed to the rubber-stamp Supreme Council on 27 February 1957 by Premier Chou when he said bluntly: "Nothing to agriculture." For raising output, Mao's agriculture chief spelled out to his staff, "we depend on the peasants" two shoulders and one bottom"—i.e., manual labor and excrement used as manure.

As well as having to produce food to pay for military imports from Russia and Eastern Europe, the peasants were having to part with precious produce to make up the massive donations Mao was dispensing to boost his turf aspirations. China not only provided food for poor countries like North Korea and North Vietnam, it gave liberally to very much richer European Communist regimes, especially after Stalin's death, when Peking floated the idea of Mao becoming the head of the world Communist camp. When Romania staged a youth jamboree, Mao donated 3,000 tons of vegetable oil—while the peasants in China who produced the oil were getting about one kilogram per year, which had to do for both cooking and lighting, as electricity was non-existent in most of the countryside. After the 1956 uprising in immeasurably wealthier Hungary, Peking sent the regime 30 million rubles' worth of goods and a £3.5 million "loan" in sterling; and loans, as Mao kept saying, did not have to be repaid.

When the first big revolt in Eastern Europe erupted in East Germany in June 1953, just after Stalin died, Mao jumped in to bolster the dictatorship there, immediately offering 50 million rubles' worth of food. But the Germans wanted more, offering in exchange machines that China had no use for. Peking's foreign trade managers had actually decided to turn the exchange down, but Mao intervened and ordered them to accept, with the ludicrous argument that *"They are much harder-up than we are. We must make it our business to take care of them"* (Mao's emphasis). It was thanks to Chinese food that East Germany was able to lift food rationing in May 1958.

---

* The threat of rustication functioned as a powerful deterrent to urban-dwellers not to step out of line. Everyone knew that being cast into the peasantry would bring on themselves and their families not only back-breaking labor, but the loss of any certainty of earning a livelihood, and that this misfortune would extend to future generations as well.

Ordinary Chinese not only had no say in Mao's largesse, they had no idea they had made such generous donations. The pleasure was all Mao's. When East Germany's brutish leader, Walter Ulbricht, came to China in 1956 and paid Mao a ritual compliment, Mao responded grandly: "You must not copy us to the dot." Mao was talking like a mentor. He also wanted to ascertain that Ulbricht was oppressive enough. "After the 17th of June [1953 uprising in East Berlin]," Mao asked, "did you take a large number of them prisoner?" He suggested one Chinese "model" the East Germans might consider copying: the Great Wall. A wall, he said, was a great help with keeping out people like "fascists." A few years later the Berlin Wall went up.

The highest proportion of GNP the richest countries gave as foreign aid barely ever exceeded 0.5 percent, and the US figure at the turn of the millennium was far below 0.01 percent. Under Mao, China's reached an unbelievable 6.92 percent (in 1973)—by far the highest the world has ever known.

CHINESE PEASANTS were amongst the poorest in the world, as Mao knew very well. He knew equally well that peasants were starving under him. On 21 April 1953, on the eve of launching the Superpower Program, he noted on a report: "About 10 percent of agricultural households are going to suffer food scarcity in spring and summer . . . even out of food altogether." This was happening "every year," he wrote. How could the country's limited stock of food pay for Mao's vast ambitions? Elementary arithmetic alone would suggest there were going to be massive deaths from starvation if he went ahead sending food abroad at these levels.

Mao did not care. He would make dismissive remarks like: "Having only tree leaves to eat? So be it." All economic statistics and information were top-secret, and ordinary people were kept completely in the dark. They were also powerless to influence policies. But the men at the top were in the picture, and one of them, Mao's No. 2, Liu Shao-chi, balked at the colossal consequences of Mao's program. He was in favor of industrialization and superpower status, but he wanted to reach these goals at a more gradual tempo, by building a stronger economic foundation and raising living standards first.

"We cannot develop heavy industry first," he told a small audience on 5 July 1951, because it "consumes a tremendous amount of money with no returns . . . and the only way available to us to raise the money is by depriving our people . . . Now people's life is very miserable. We must raise people's living standards first," a process he suggested would take ten years. This, he said, should be the Party's priority. "People are very poor," he wrote. "They desperately need to lead a better life, a well-to-do and cultured life." "The [Party's] most basic task must be to fulfill this wish..." "Peasants," he said on another occasion, "want to have new clothes, to buy socks, to wear shoes, to use...mirrors, soap and hand-kerchiefs...their children want to go to school." This was the kind of language Mao never used.

Five years Mao's junior, Liu also came from a village in Hunan, only a few kilometers away from Mao's. He had gone to Moscow in 1921 and joined the Party there as a 23-year-old student. Enormously attractive to women, he was a very serious young man, with no hobbies except read-ing, and disliked idle chatter. He first met Mao when he returned to Hunan in 1922, but the two did not strike up any special relationship until the late 1930s, when Liu became Mao's ally through sharing his cold vision of using the war with Japan to destroy Chiang Kai-shek. Mao promoted him to be his No. 2 in 1943. In 1945, when Mao had to go to Chongqing, and again in 1949–50, when he was in Moscow, he appointed Liu as his stand-in. Mao relied on him as his chief executive.

Liu was the most able all-round lieutenant Mao had found. He also combined total discretion with a willingness to be at Mao's beck and call day and night. Mao slept during the day and worked at night, and Liu changed his routine to try to synchronize with Mao. But Mao was erratic, and would often summon Liu when the latter was heavily drugged from the very strong pills he, like almost all of Mao's lieutenants, needed to sleep. One of Liu's secretaries recalled: "Whenever Chairman Mao's secre-tary rang, the message was always: 'Come this minute.'...As the sleep-ing pills were working, [Liu] would look very tired, in agony. He often didn't even have time to take a sip of the strong tea his man-servant made him, and set off to Mao's place at once." Most importantly for Mao, Liu harbored no ambitions to supplant him.

But around the time the Communists took power, serious disagree-ments emerged between the two about whether to give priority to becom-ing a military superpower via a forced march, or to improving living standards. Mao constantly mocked Liu's espousal of the latter, retorting: " 'Oh, peasants' lives are so hard'—the end of the world! I have never thought so."

While Stalin was still alive, Mao held his fire so as not to give the Master any pretext to muscle in and sabotage him. Stalin had been trying to undermine Mao by showering attention on Liu during Liu's visits to Russia; and, not least, by taking the unprecedented step of having *Pravda* call Liu "the General Secretary" of the CCP.

As soon as Mao learned that Stalin was dying, at the beginning of March 1953, he leaped into action. First he sent out signals that Liu might be removed. At the time, Liu was in the hospital, having had an appen-dectomy in late February. Mao made sure he stayed there, even going as far as blocking the news of Stalin's death from him. Mao went to the Soviet embassy twice in connection with Stalin's illness and death, both times accompanied by other top leaders, but not Liu, although Liu was well enough to move around. When *People's Daily* published a cable of good wishes for Stalin from the Sino-Soviet Friendship Association, the message was not signed by Liu, who was president of the Association, but by a subordinate, which was extraordinary in terms of protocol. And Liu was excluded from the memorial ceremony on Tiananmen Square.

In May Mao sent Liu a sharp, indeed menacing, letter saying: "all documents and telegrams issued in the name of the Center can only be issued after I have seen them. *Otherwise, they are invalid* [Mao's emphasis]. Be careful." Another told Liu (and Chou and army chief Peng) to "check all telegrams and documents issued in the name of the Center or the Military Council . . . to see whether there are any . . . that have not been seen by me . . . In the past, several decisions . . . have been issued unauthorized, without me having seen them. This is intolerably wrong, and is a sabotage of rules . . ." These were very strong words indeed, and they were designed to make Liu sweat all the more.

Next came a direct and open attack on Liu to a small but crucial audience. On 15 June, when the Politburo gathered to hear Mao announce his industrialization program, Mao sharply condemned Liu, calling him "right-wing." Even though he did not name Liu, every listener knew whom he was driving at. Mao had taken precautions for the most unlikely eventuality of Liu using the Praetorian Guard, which also guarded Liu, to fight back. He had had a hush-hush investigation conducted beforehand to gauge individual members' relationships with Liu. On the day of the meeting, some of the guards were rounded up and transferred out of Peking.

Over the following months, Mao denounced Liu by proxy to ever larger audiences, criticizing key Liu protégés like finance minister Bo Yi-bo, who had devised a tax system that would not produce anything like the revenue that Mao's program demanded. Then in September Mao handpicked a lower-rank official to insinuate to a Party conference that Liu and his protégés had suspect pasts, and could be enemy agents. This was a frightening accusation. Liu was in danger of losing far more than just his job.

Mao let Liu stew for months, and then on 24 December 1953 he suddenly announced to the Politburo that he was going away on holiday, and was appointing Liu to stand in for him, which meant that Liu was still No. 2. The psychological effect of being thus pulled back from the precipice was considerable, and Liu caved in to Mao's demands that he recant his old views to his top colleagues, which he did, groveling for three days and nights non-stop. Mao had what he wanted: a hyper-intimidated Liu.

★

MAO HAD BEEN threatening to replace Liu with another man called Gao Gang, the head of Manchuria. Gao was a hard-liner and supported Mao's Superpower Program 100 percent. He had been the most vocal critic of Liu's views in the top circle. Mao showed that he liked Gao and disliked Liu, and hinted to Gao that he was considering giving him Liu's job. Gao talked to other top people about what Mao had said, and played the key role in attacking Liu. Many in the inner circle assumed that Gao was about to take Liu's place.

Then, out of the blue, Mao reinstated Liu—and purged Gao, who was charged with "plotting to split the Party in order to usurp the power of the Party and the state." This was the first top-level purge since the regime had come to power, and it spread an atmosphere of disquiet and dread. When the Dalai Lama arrived in Peking just after Gao was condemned, his entourage immediately alerted him to the purge as an ill omen. It was the first topic the Dalai Lama himself wanted to discuss with us when we interviewed him forty-five years later.

The real reason for the purge involved Soviet Russia. As boss of Manchuria, Gao had had a lot to do with the Russians, and he had shot his mouth off to them, even telling Stalin's liaison Kovalev about disagreements in the Politburo, where he claimed that Liu headed a "pro-American faction." Mao got to know about this when he was in Moscow in 1949, when Stalin gave him a report by Kovalev, partly based on talks with Gao. Gao told other Russians that Liu was too soft on the bourgeoisie. He complained about Chou, too, telling the Russians that he had had a "serious clash" with Chou over the Korean War in the Politburo.*

That Gao was a talker had been noticed by a British couple in Yenan a decade before. Gao, they wrote, was "perhaps the most indiscreet of all the Communists whom we interviewed." They must have been quite struck, as Gao was then a complete unknown.

For Mao, to have underlings talking about the inner workings of his regime to any outsider was an absolute taboo. By purging Gao he wanted to send a message: you can never be too tight-lipped, even—and especially—with the Russians. As the Superpower Program depended overwhelmingly on the Soviet Union, there was going to be a lot of contact with Russians. Mao feared that fraternization might lead to a loosening of his grip, and conceivably threaten his power. On this score, Mao never took the slightest chance. His vigilance in anticipating potential threats

---

* That Gao said too much was indirectly confirmed by the top Soviet adviser in China, Arkhipov. When we pushed him on the subject, he threw us a steely stare and said in a different tone of voice: "Why do you want to know so much about Gao Gang?"

was the main reason he died in his bed. Mao could not ban all contacts with Russians, so he moved to put an invisible barrier between his men and "the brothers." Gao provided a perfect vehicle for warning his underlings: Don't get too fraternal with the Russians!

Soon, Mao used the Gao case explicitly to order his top echelon to disclose any relationships with any Russians, what he termed "illicit contacts with foreign countries":

> Do we have such people in China, who give information to foreigners behind the back of the Centre [i.e., *me*]? I think there are—Gao Gang for one ... I hope those comrades will disgorge totally ... Everything should go through the Centre [*me* again]. As for information, don't pass it ... Those who have passed information, own up and you won't be pursued. If you don't, we'll check, and we will find out. You will be in trouble.

Mao did not define what counted as information, so the rule of thumb was simply not to talk to foreigners about *anything*.

Mao designated Chou En-lai chief "prosecutor" against Gao, while he absented himself. At the meeting in February 1954 when Chou delivered his onslaught on Gao (who was present), tea mugs were, unusually, filled beforehand, to prevent servants eavesdropping. But as the leaders were unable to proceed without more hot water, a tea boy was allowed in. He was stunned to see the usually suave Chou transformed, contorted into a picture of ferocity, a side that the outside world never got to see. Chou, the old assassin, had taken the precaution of getting two trusted subordinates to bring along pistols, something normally absolutely unthinkable at top-level meetings.

Gao was beside himself with shock about how Mao had set him up, and he tried to electrocute himself, unsuccessfully, on 17 February. For this he was forced to apologize, but his apology was rejected with the Party's customary pitilessness; this act of despair was branded "an out-and-out traitor's action against the Party." He was kept under house arrest, and finally succeeded in ending his life six months later, after accumulating enough sleeping pills to do the trick.

In the Communist world a conspiracy was always preferred to a lone schemer. To make up a "conspiracy," Mao picked on the head of the Organization Department, Rao Shu-shi, who was accused of forming an "anti-Party alliance" with Gao, although the two were not particularly close. Rao had been the head of the CCP intelligence network in America, inter alia, and this was very possibly why Mao wanted him behind bars, as Mao was gearing up for a purge in his intelligence system. Rao was arrested, and died in prison twenty years later, in March 1975.

*

ON 26 DECEMBER 1953, having lit the fuse for Gao's demise, Mao merrily celebrated his sixtieth birthday with his staff, drinking more wine than usual, even eating peaches, a symbol of longevity, though normally he did not like fruit. During the meal he hummed along to records of Peking opera and beat time on his thigh. Stalin had died, and Mao had successfully completed two maneuvers that were key for his Superpower Program: hammering his chief executive, Liu, into shape; and inoculating his top subordinates against any possible Russian contagion that might endanger his power.

Next day, when he arrived in picturesque lakeside Hangzhou, near Shanghai, he was in such good spirits that he could hardly wait to settle in before he ordered a game of mah-jong. Mao had been in Hangzhou thirty-two years before, in summer 1921, after the 1st Congress of the Communist Party. Then he had been a hard-up provincial teacher travelling on a Russian allowance. Now he was the master of China. His coming had been suitably prepared. A famous turn-of-the-century estate called Water and Bamboo had been picked for him. It was adorned with ponds and bamboo groves, and vines and palm trees, and enjoyed a panoramic view over the Western Lake. Villas next to it, and the hills behind it, were all incorporated into a single enormous estate, covering 36 hectares. The hill behind was hollowed out to provide a nuclear shelter. Mao stayed in an exquisite building, combining classical Chinese and exotic foreign styles, with pillars, doors and decorations which had been lovingly shipped in piece by piece by the original owner. But shortly afterwards, Mao had it torn down and replaced with his usual nondescript identikit structure. The creaking of the old timber had rattled his nerves with thoughts about assassins. He only felt safe in a reinforced concrete bunker.

Mao fell in love with the view. Every day, even in drizzle, he climbed the nearby peaks, which were specially cordoned off for him. He lingered over plum blossoms, sniffing at the petals. He chatted and joked with his staff. His mood was captured by his photographer, in a picture of a beaming plump-cheeked Mao, bathed in sunshine.

Soon the biggest snowfall in decades descended. Mao got up at the, for him, outlandish hour of 7:00 AM, and stood transfixed by the snow-clad southern garden. He then walked along a path blanketed with snow, which he ordered left unswept, to marvel at the lake in white. He tinkered with a poem.

Spring came, alternating between misty drizzle and dazzling sunshine, each day unfolding its masses of blossoms. During one pleasure trip, his female photographer, Hou Bo, gathered a bunch of wildflowers and presented them to Mao. Nobody seemed to know what the flower was called, so Mao said: Let's name it the Hou Bo Flower.

Mao fancied a visit to the home of his favorite tea, Dragon Well village, which was nearby. The peasants were duly removed "for a mass meeting"—in fact for his security. But occasional surprise drop-ins were deemed safe enough, and so, on another occasion, Mao called in on one peasant house. The couple could not understand a word of his Hunan dialect, nor he theirs. Curious villagers started to converge, so Mao's guards whisked him away.

On one excursion to the top of a hill, Mao saw a thatched hut on fire in the distance. The inhabitants were standing outside, helpless as the flames swallowed their home. According to Mao's photographer, Mao "turned to me with a glance, and said coolly: 'Good fire. It's good to burn down, good to burn down!' "

The photographer was astonished. Sensing this, Mao said: " 'Without the fire, they will have to go on living in a thatched hut.' "

" 'But now it's burnt down, where are they going to live? . . .'

"He did not answer my question, as if he hadn't heard . . ."

Mao had no answer to this question. Throughout his reign, peasants had to fend for themselves when it came to housing. The state provided no funds. Even in urban areas, other than apartments for the elite and residential blocks in industrial complexes, virtually no new dwellings were built.

Watching the thatched cottage turned to ashes, Mao eventually said to himself: "Um, Really clean if the earth has fallen to complete void and nothingness!"

This was a line of poetry from the classic *Dream of the Red Chamber*. But Mao was doing more than just reciting poetry. This was an echo of the attraction to destruction that he had alarmingly expressed as a young man. He continued: "This is called: 'No destruction, no construction.' "

Construction for Mao was exclusively related to becoming a superpower. Here in Hangzhou, he began revising the draft of the first "Constitution," something he had only just got around to after more than four years in power. Among the things he wanted revised was the promise that his regime "protects all citizens' safety and legal rights . . ." Mao underlined the words "all citizens" and wrote in the margin: "What exactly is a citizen?"

Flatterers had suggested that the document should be named the "Mao Tse-tung Code," clearly with the Napoleonic Code in mind. Mao rejected the idea. He was averse to law, and wanted there to be nothing that could bind him. Indeed, hopelessly feeble as it was, the Constitution was soon to be discarded altogether.

One day Mao toured a temple, which had, as usual, been emptied for security reasons, except for one blind monk. On the altar was a wooden holder with bamboo slips for divination, and Mao asked his photographer to pick a slip for him. She shook the holder, took out a slip, and went to a bookcase containing old poetry books to find the line referred to on the slip. It read: "No peace, either inside or outside home." There could be no question of presenting this inauspicious line, so she quickly picked another. It had a cheery message, and brought laughter.

The divination was eerily accurate. Mme Mao had come with their daughter, Li Na, to spend Chinese New Year, the traditional time of family reunion. But the visit had ended with Mme Mao in tears, asking for a plane to take her away. Hangzhou, famed not only for its scenery but also for its women, had caught Mao's sexual fancy. He was to return forty-one times, partly for this reason. He liked young and apparently innocent women, whom underlings procured as partners for the weekly dances and for subsequent fornication.

Mao no longer felt sexual interest in his wife. Even before 1949, his Russian doctor Orlov had been treating him "for sexual problems" with her (Orlov acidly referred to Mme Mao as "the Queen" in a cable to Stalin). Then Mme Mao had suffered serious gynecological problems, for which she was treated in Russia, under the pseudonym "Yusupova," as she stayed in a palace in Yalta that had belonged to Prince Yusupov, the man who killed Rasputin. (Stalin himself had stayed in it during the Yalta conference.) Her illness almost certainly put Mao further off her. He became more and more brazen in his philandering. Mme Mao was once found weeping by the lake in Zhongnanhai. "Don't tell anyone," she said to the man who saw her, Mao's doctor. "The Chairman is someone no one can beat in political fighting, not even Stalin; nor can anyone beat him in having women, either." Mme Mao grew increasingly difficult and hysterical, and vented her fury and frustration on the staff, routinely accusing her nurses of "deliberately tormenting" her, striking them, and demanding they be punished.

Meanwhile, as the divination on the bamboo slip uncannily described, quite a few of Mao's colleagues were going through turmoil and dread. For the nation as a whole, economic policy was about to become drastically harsher as the Superpower Program got under way.

WAR ON PEASANTS

(1953–56 ★ AGE 59–62)

FROM AUTUMN 1953, nationwide requisitioning was imposed, in order to extract more food to pay for the Superpower Program. The system followed that of a labor camp: leave the population just enough to keep them alive, and take all the rest. The regime decided that what constituted subsistence was an amount of food equivalent to 200 kg of processed grain per year, and this was called "basic food."

But this figure was rarely achieved under Mao. In 1976, the year he died, after twenty-seven years in power, the average figure nationwide was only 190 kg. As city-dwellers got more, the average peasant's consumption was considerably lower than 190 kg.

Mao wanted the peasants to have far less than this. They "only need 140 kg of grain, and some only need 110," he declared. This latter figure was barely half the amount needed for mere subsistence. Even though Mao's chosen minimum was not enforced at this stage, the results of his "squeeze-all" approach were painfully spelled out by some peasants to a sympathetic official within a year of the introduction of requisitioning. "Not a family has enough to eat." "I worked for a year, and in the end I have to starve for a few months . . . My neighbors are the same." "The harvest isn't bad, but what's the use? No matter how much we get in we don't have enough to eat anyway . . ." As for the "basic food," "no one has had that much." In theory, anyone starving was supposed to be able to buy some food back, but the amounts were never adequate, and Mao was constantly berating officials that "Too much grain is sold back!" and urging them to slash the amount "enormously."

Mao's answer to the peasants' plight was pitiless. They should eat sweet potato leaves, which were traditionally used only to feed pigs. "Educate peasants to eat less, and have more thin gruel," he instructed. "The State should try its hardest . . . to prevent peasants eating too much."

One of Mao's economic managers, Bo Yi-bo, later acknowledged that under the requisitioning policy, "Most of the food the peasants produced was taken away." And "force," he said, was commonplace; people were "driven to death." This violence was specifically endorsed by Mao, who discussed the consequences of the requisitioning with its architect, Chen Yun, on 1 October 1953. Next day, Mao told the Politburo that they were "at war" with the whole population: "This is a war on food producers—as well as on food consumers," meaning the urban population who were now subjected to unprecedentedly low rationing. To justify treating peasants as enemies, Mao's fatuous rationale was that "Marx and Engels never said peasants were all good." When, days later, Chen Yun conveyed Mao's instructions to provincial leaders in charge of extracting food, he told them they must be prepared for deaths and riots in 100,000 villages—one-tenth of all the villages in China. But this would not jeopardize Communist rule, he assured them, making a comparison with Manchukuo, where the occupying Japanese had requisitioned large amounts of grain. "Manchukuo," he said, "would not have fallen if the Soviet Red Army had not come." In other words, brute force *à la japonaise* would guarantee that peasants could not endanger the regime, no matter how hard it was squeezing them.

BY EARLY 1955, requisitioning had brought utter misery. Numerous reports reached Mao about peasants having to eat tree bark, and abandoning their babies because they had no food. Mao had installed many channels for gathering feedback at the grassroots, as he needed to keep his ear to the ground to maintain control. One channel was his guards. When they went home for visits that year, he asked them to report back about their villages. The picture they painted was bleak. One wrote that 50 percent of households in his village were short of food, and had had to eat tree leaves that spring. Another reported that people were having to depend on wild herbs for food, and were dying of starvation.

From other channels Mao learned that people were saying things like "What's so good about socialism? Even now when we've just begun we are not allowed cooking oil"; and "The Communist Party is driving people to death!" A then unknown official in Guangdong province called Zhao Zi-yang (who became Party chief in the post-Mao era) reported that cadres were searching houses, tying peasants up and beating them to force them to surrender food, and sealing the houses of those who said they had nothing left. He cited the case of an old woman who hanged herself after being imprisoned inside her house. In one not atypical county, Gaoyao, 110 people were driven to suicide. If this figure is extrapolated to China's 2,000-plus counties, the number of suicides in rural areas in this short period would be approaching a quarter of a million.

Some courageous individuals petitioned Mao. One prominent fellow traveler wrote to Mao that he had received many letters saying that peasants did not have enough energy to work because they were left too little food. Mao summed up: "10,000 reports ['10,000' expresses hugeness] about deaths of humans, deaths of animals, about people raiding granaries: 10,000 reports of darkness . . ." But Mao was completely unmoved. He would punish the fellow traveler with what he disdainfully called "a good bit of persecution." He was given to say airily that people were "not without food all the year round—only six . . . or four months" (*sic*). Senior officials who invoked the traditional concept of conscience (*liang-xin*) to beg him to go easy found themselves being slapped down with remarks like: "You'd better have less conscience. Some of our comrades have too much mercy, not enough brutality, which means they are not so Marxist." "On this matter," Mao said, "we indeed have no conscience! Marxism is that brutal."

Mao turned the screw even tighter from mid-1955 by forcing the entire countryside into collective farms. This was to make it easier to enforce requisitioning. Previously, peasants could harvest their own crops and bring them home before handing over the state's "share." To Mao, this left a loophole: peasants could underreport the harvest and hide some of it, and checking nearly a hundred million households was not easy. With collectivization, however, the whole harvest went straight from the fields into the state's hands, giving the regime complete control over how it was allocated. As one peasant said: "Once you join the collective, you only get food the government doles out to you."

The other huge advantage of collectivization for Mao was that it made it much easier to keep the peasants under surveillance when they were working. With collectivization came slave-driving. Henceforth, the state dictated what hours peasants worked, and how hard. A *People's Daily* editorial on New Year's Day 1956 made it clear that the aim was to get peasants to double their working hours. Mao especially targeted women; those who used not to work in the fields would do so now.

To stifle resistance to both requisitioning and collectivization, Mao wielded his old panacea: terror. In May 1955 he talked about another "Five-Year Plan," this time for suppression: "We must arrest 1.5 million counter-revolutionaries in five years . . . I am all for more arrests . . . Our emphasis is: arrest in a big way, a giant way . . ." Using the scatological language of which he was enamored, Mao added: "My farts [i.e., orders] are socialist farts, they have to be fragrant," i.e., obeyed. Anyone resisting food confiscation or collectivization, and any official sympathetic to them, was termed a criminal, and notices announcing their sentences were plastered up across the country.

Collectivization of agriculture marked a big stride towards making China even more totalitarian. At the same time, Mao ordered the nationalization of industry and commerce in urban areas, to channel every single resource into the Superpower Program. However, businessmen were not persecuted like rural landlords, for pragmatic reasons. "The bourgeoisie," Mao said, "are much more useful than . . . landlords. They have technical know-how and management skills." Though he then proceeded to squander these managerial and technical talents spectacularly. In addition, China's glorious handicrafts withered over the coming years. Repair and maintenance shops would dwindle in number, greatly increasing the misery of everyday life. "We started socialism, and everything disappears," Liu Shao-chi remarked pithily.

To scare state employees into conforming, Mao launched a purge campaign in which no fewer than 14.3 million men and women on the state payroll were put through terrifying vetting that involved "confessions and informing," frequent public denunciation meetings, and physical abuse. Offices and residential buildings were turned into detention centers, as were sports halls and university dormitories. Mao decreed that "Counter-revolutionaries . . . make up . . . around 5 percent" of those vetted, which would mean that 715,000 people were condemned and received various punishments, including execution. In fact, Mao indicated that more people than this could be done in, as one of his instructions reads: "Whenever this figure [5 percent] is exceeded, authorization should be obtained."

This campaign was accompanied by a clampdown on literature and the arts. With his characteristic thoroughness, Mao had begun to strangle culture from the moment he took power. The cinema industry was almost shut down. In 1950, 39 feature films were produced; in 1952 the figure was 5. In 1954 he had started a drive to eradicate the influence of the great non-Communist writers, historians and scholars, some of whom had fled abroad, or to Taiwan. Now he turned to those who had stayed and who showed some independence. Mao picked on a well-known writer called Hu Feng, who had called for a more liberal artistic environment, and had a following. In May 1955, Hu was publicly denounced and thrown into prison, from which he only emerged, his mind destroyed, after Mao died more than two decades later.

The Hu Feng case was headlined in the press. And it served another purpose—to scare people out of writing to each other about their views. Letters that Hu and his followers had exchanged were published, revealing thoughts critical of the regime, and these were presented as evidence against them. As a result, people became wary of putting any thoughts on paper. Not being able to write one's thoughts down, on top of not being able to voice them, or having to censor them all the time, undermined people's ability to form their own independent judgment.

Terror worked. At the beginning of 1956, Mao told the top echelon:

The first half of 1955 was simply foul . . . with black clouds all over the sky . . . There were curses against us everywhere. People said we were no good. All because [we took] a few bits of grain. In the latter half of the year, the curses disappeared. Some happy events emerged. A good harvest and collectivisation were two big happy events, and then there was the purge of counter-revolutionaries, another happy event.

Another "happy" event, which Mao kept quiet about, was in many ways the most significant of all. He had acquired the single thing dearest to his heart: the start-up technology to make the atomic bomb.

In 1953, Mao had failed to get the Bomb out of Moscow through the device of trying to prolong the Korean War. But he soon found another way—by starting *another* war, this one concerning Taiwan. In July 1954, Peking gave the appearance of seriously preparing to go to war over Taiwan. Chou En-lai went to Moscow and gave Mao's message to the Kremlin: he must have a war to "liberate Taiwan."

In fact, China's military chiefs had told Mao there was little chance of a sea crossing succeeding, and he had actually decided not to make a move on Taiwan until he was ready. The point of this hullabaloo about attacking Taiwan was really to push the situation to the brink of nuclear confrontation with America, which would face Russia with the possibility of having to retaliate on China's behalf unless it let Mao have the Bomb.

On 3 September, Mainland artillery opened fire on the Nationalist-held island of Quemoy, which lies only a few kilometers off the coast, and was considered the jumping-off point for any move on Taiwan. This detonated what became known as the "first Taiwan Strait crisis." Washington perceived the crisis to be between itself and Peking, but in fact it was a ploy by Mao to exert pressure on Moscow.

Soon afterwards, Nikita Khrushchev, who had just established himself as No. 1 in the Kremlin, arrived in Peking for the fifth anniversary of the Communist regime on 1 October 1954, accompanied by an array of senior colleagues, something unimaginable under Stalin. Khrushchev came determined to establish the best possible relations. He wiped much of Stalin's slate clean, offering to scrap the secret annexes in the 1950 treaty which infringed on China's interests. He also agreed to supply more equipment for the 141 arms factories already under way, and to sell Mao another 15 enterprises, and extend a new loan of 520m rubles.

Mao immediately seized the initiative and requested help to build his own Bomb to deter the Americans. Asked by Khrushchev what might prompt a US attack, he cited the Taiwan crisis. Khrushchev attempted to talk him out of making his own Bomb by promising shelter under Russia's nuclear umbrella, and guaranteeing to retaliate if China was attacked. Khrushchev also adduced the economic argument that making the Bomb was too expensive for China. Mao acted as though his national pride was offended. Though this irritated Khrushchev, the Soviet leader reluctantly promised to consider helping China build a nuclear reactor.

Soon after Khrushchev left, Mao escalated the crisis by bombing and strafing more Nationalist-held islands. US President Eisenhower responded by agreeing to sign a mutual defense treaty with Taiwan. Mao pressed on, apparently intent on taking the offshore islands of Quemoy and Matsu—and more. His calculation was to nudge America into threatening to use nuclear weapons. In March 1955 the US said it would use nuclear weapons under certain circumstances. Eisenhower very deliberately told a press conference on the 16th that he could see no reason why they should not be used "just exactly as you would use a bullet or anything else." Mao had what he had aimed for—a situation in which China seemed to be in real danger of a US nuclear strike.

Not wishing to be drawn into a nuclear confrontation with America, Khrushchev took the momentous decision to provide China with the technical assistance to make the Bomb.

At this time, substantial uranium deposits had just been confirmed in Guangxi province. Mao was extremely excited, and immediately ordered a demonstration on 14 January. Geology chief Liu Jie recalled:

> I put the uranium ore on the table, and . . . waved a Geiger counter across it. The Geiger counter went "ga-ga-ga . . ." Chairman Mao looked so intrigued. He laughed like a child, and picked up the Geiger counter himself, waving it across the ore, listening to the "ga-ga" sounds again . . . When I said goodbye . . . Mao held my hand and said: "Liu Jie—ah! I want you to know that what you are doing is the thing that decides our destiny!"

Afterwards, there was a banquet. Mao's toast was straight to the point: "Bottoms up . . . to having our own atom bombs as quickly as possible!"

In April, the Russians agreed to build China the two key items needed to make a Bomb: a cyclotron and a nuclear reactor. Mao was en route to becoming a nuclear power. Large groups of Chinese scientists set off to be trained in Russia. In December, news came that the Russians had committed to help build a comprehensive nuclear industry in China. Mao was ecstatic. On the advice of Russian scientists, a twelve-year nuclear plan was drawn up. As 1956 dawned, Mao told his aides he was in better spirits than when he had taken China six years before. He felt on top of the world, and announced grandly to his inner circle: "We must control the Earth!"

TO CORRESPOND WITH the twelve-year nuclear plan, in January 1956 Mao and a group of his cronies drafted a twelve-year plan for agriculture. This was really Mao's scheme to extract much more food to fund his upgraded and expanded Superpower Program. It ordered peasants to produce the equivalent of 500 billion kg of grain per annum by the end of the twelve years, more than triple the highest-ever previous annual output (in 1936). And this tall order had to be achieved with virtually no investment, not even of fertilizer.

At this point, Mao met with new resistance—this time from virtually the whole Politburo, spearheaded by the usually doglike Chou En-lai, who was in charge of planning, and Chou was backed by Liu. They all knew that Mao's astronomical output target was unattainable. Mao had set the figure by a process of "back-calculation," starting not from reality, but from the amount of food that he would need to fund his purchases, and working back from there. The obvious conclusion was that Mao's plan would involve extracting a much larger percentage of the harvest from the peasantry than before. As the peasants were already living on a knife-edge, millions, at a minimum, would be tipped over the edge into starvation and death.

Realizing the implications, in February 1956, Chou cut spending on industrial projects by over a quarter. He was just as keen as Mao for China to be a superpower, but he was willing to face up to the fact that the country did not have nearly enough resources to pay for everything Mao wanted, much less simultaneously. So he opted for focusing on the nuclear program and key projects, and cutting back on other projects, which was necessitated anyway by shortages of basic materials like steel, cement and timber.

Mao, however, wanted all the projects, and all at once. Quite apart from his devil-may-care attitude to his subjects' welfare, Mao had no grasp of economics. According to Bo Yi-bo, Mao asked to read and listen to reports from the ministries at this time, but "he found it extremely taxing," and complained that the reports contained "only dull lists and figures, and no stories." Once, as he listened to a minister, he knitted his eyebrows, and said it was "worse than being in prison" (where he had never been). Chou En-lai found himself being admonished for "flooding Chairman Mao with boring materials and figures." Mao had trouble even with basic numbers. Once, while he was talking about trade with Japan, his prepared notes contained a figure of US$280 million, but one line later he wrote this as US$380 million, throwing the whole calculation out by US$100 million. "Statistics and numbers were not in any way sacred to him," Yugoslavia's No. 2, Edvard Kardelj, observed after he met Mao in 1957. "He said, for example, 'In two hundred years' time, or perhaps in forty.' " The chief Soviet economic adviser in China, Ivan Arkhipov, told us, with a sigh of exasperation, that Mao "had no understanding, absolutely no understanding at all" of economics.

In April 1956, Mao told his colleagues that the cuts must be restored, but for once they dug their heels in. Mao dismissed the meeting in a fury. Afterwards, Chou went to see him and begged him to accept the cuts, saying, most extraordinarily, that his "*conscience* would not allow" him to obey Mao's orders. This sent Mao into a mad rage, but he could not stop the cuts going through.

Mao's colleagues stood up to him because, hard men though they were, the consequences—millions dying of starvation—were too appalling. They were also emboldened by an event that had just occurred in Moscow. There, on 24 February 1956, at the 20th Congress of the the Soviet Party, Khrushchev had denounced Stalin for his killings and tyrannical behavior—and for the costs of his forced-march industrialization, a process which in fact was a lot less extreme than Mao's was to be. Mao's colleagues now started criticizing Stalin on these same issues (always within the confines of the inner circle). Liu called Stalin's peasant policy one of his "major mistakes." Former Party No. 1 Lo Fu observed that Stalin "put too much emphasis on . . . heavy industry." "When I was ambassador to Russia," he noted, "I went to the shops and found almost nothing to buy. They are also always short of food . . . We should draw a big lesson." "We will be making big mistakes if we ignore agriculture," Chou told the State Council on 20 April. "The lessons in the Soviet Union and Eastern European countries all proved this." The parallels with Mao's practices hardly needed laboring.

Mao did not mind seeing Stalin denounced, but not over these issues, which were at the core of his own rule. He tried to hold the line with the crude formulation that Stalin was 70 percent correct and only 30 percent mistaken. The 30 percent was not to do with murder, torture and economic misrule, but mostly with how Stalin had treated Mao Tse-tung.

But Mao could not come out openly against Khrushchev, who carried the authority of the Soviet Union, the head of the Communist camp—and was giving Mao so many arms factories, plus the Bomb. What was more, Khrushchev's sudden and drastic denunciation of Stalin had taken Mao by surprise and made him sit up and take notice of Khrushchev. As Mao observed, Khrushchev's move had destabilized the whole Communist camp and "shaken the entire world." It struck awe into Mao, and made him feel he was dealing with somebody unusually bold, unpredictable and not to be trifled with. He commented several times in a pensive mood: "Khrushchev really has guts, he dares to touch Stalin." "This indeed needs courage."

Mao felt he had to be careful. In this situation, he could not rebut his colleagues when they cited Khrushchev to oppose his policies. Frustrated and angry, he left Peking to ponder a solution in the provinces. The provincial bosses (known as first secretaries) were a special group selected for their blind devotion. They had to be 100 percent yes-men, as they were the on-the-spot enforcers who made sure that every corner of the vast country did what Mao said.

Sudden unscheduled departures were routine for Mao, but this time he left Peking in an unprecedented manner. He got on the phone himself to his trusted follower, air force chief Liu Ya-lou, out of the blue, in the deep of one night at the end of April, and told him to have planes standing by. Mao had never taken a plane, except in 1945, to Chongqing, under pressure from Stalin. Now he could not wait to be among his cronies.

Because this was Mao's first flight with his own air fleet, inordinate measures were taken in the way of both comfort and security. A large wooden bed was installed in his plane, and the crew were only told who their passenger was at the last minute. To them, Mao appeared somewhat distracted; sitting in silence, he let his cigarette burn into a long column of ash before he suddenly seemed to wake up, and ordered the plane to take off. Mao landed first at Wuhan, where he was met by the local chief, an arch-devotee, who had installed a big statue of Mao in the airport waiting room—perhaps one of the first in China. Mao showed annoyance, as this was just after Khrushchev's denunciation of the cult of personality, and told the devotee to get rid of it; but the man could not tell whether Mao really meant it or not, and the statue stayed.

Mao then flew on to the southern provincial capital of Canton, to be met by another major acolyte, as well as by Mme Mao. His vast estate here, "the Islet," sat on the Pearl River, so river traffic was stopped and that stretch of the waterway was sealed off. Mao's entourage was banned from receiving visitors or letters, or making telephone calls, much less going out. The weather was steamy, and even five giant barrels of ice in Mao's room made little difference. The grounds, blooming with tropical shrubs, swarmed with mosquitoes and midges. DDT was bought from Hong Kong to kill them, without total success. Mao lost his temper with the servants, whom he blamed for doing too little swatting.

What was really getting to Mao was events in Peking, where his colleagues, particularly his Nos. 2 and 3, Liu and Chou, continued to defy his wishes, and even pressed harder to cut back on military–industrial projects. In thwarted fury, Mao decided to flash them a unique warning signal. At the end of May, he left Canton for Wuhan to swim in the Yangtze, the biggest river in China. He wanted to demonstrate his resolve to take on his opponents, and his stamina to see the battle through.

At Wuhan, the Yangtze spreads wide, and many of his entourage tried to dissuade him from plunging in. But Mao felt safe. As one of his chief guards remarked, he "would not do anything... that was risky." Later, Mao wanted to swim in the Yangtze Gorges, but he dropped the idea the minute he learned that the water was seriously treacherous. In Wuhan, scores of officials, from the province chief downward, joined security men to test the eddies and undertows. When Mao actually got into the water, dozens of specially trained guards formed a cordon around him, followed by three boats.

Mao swam across the river on three occasions. There were high winds and big waves, but he was unperturbed, flaunting his strength. Before his first swim, he stood and posed for photographs at the prow of the boat, looking to his entourage "like an unshakeable mountain." On the last day that he swam, in drizzle, several tens of thousands of people were organized to watch him from a distance, shouting "Long Live Chairman Mao!" This rare public appearance was Mao's way to get his message out to his colleagues. He further showed his determination in a poem about the swims. Part of it read:

> I don't care—whether the winds thrash me or the waves pound me,
> I meet them all, more leisurely than strolling in the garden-court.

Back in Peking, Mao's colleagues stuck to their guns. On 4 June the Politburo endorsed further spending cuts, and canceled more industrial projects. Mao returned to Peking that afternoon, but his presence made no difference.

On the 12th, Liu sent Mao a draft of an editorial he (Liu) had commissioned for *People's Daily*. Its target, as its title stated, was "the mindset of impatience." It criticized people who "plan actions beyond their means, and try to force things that cannot be achieved" and "want to achieve everything in one morning," and "so create waste." "This mindset of impatience," it said, "exists first and foremost among the leading cadres," who were "forcing" the country into it. As Mao was later to say, these strictures were plainly aimed at him. In a fury, he jotted three characters on it: "I won't read." But the editorial came out nonetheless.

Mao's problem was that this was a time of great uncertainty for him—in some ways even more uncertain than under Stalin, who had fundamentally been committed to Mao because Mao was a Stalinist. But Khrushchev had rejected Stalinism, and there was no telling if this bulldozer might not turn on Stalinist leaders—maybe even on Mao himself. Indeed, Khrushchev had just brought down the Stalinist Hungarian Party chief, Rákosi, the only European Communist leader Stalin had trusted to talk to the Chinese leader during Mao's visit to Russia. Furthermore, in August, emboldened by Khrushchev's denunciation of Stalin, a move had been made to try to vote North Korea's seemingly well-entrenched dictator Kim Il Sung out of power at a Party plenum.

Mao, too, was facing a Party conclave: the first congress of his own Party since taking power, which was set for September. He could not delay it, as it had been widely publicized, and the new climate since Khrushchev's exposure of Stalin was very much one of abiding by the rules. Mao's concern was that if his colleagues felt cornered they might try something at the congress, like kicking him upstairs, or even voting him out, by exposing the full implications of the Superpower Program. Only a few weeks before, Khrushchev's delegate to Mao's congress, Anastas Mikoyan, had supervised the dethronement of Rákosi in Hungary.

Mao took a series of steps to make sure that the congress posed no threat. First he fired warning shots across his colleagues' bows. A few days before the congress, on 10 September, he reminisced to them about how much opposition he had faced in the past, and how he had always prevailed. Most unusually, he volunteered that he had made "mistakes" in the past, mentioning the purge in the early 1930s, and the two biggest disasters on the Long March, Tucheng and Maotai, which he called "the real mistakes." This was not, as it might seem, an apology, but a way of driving home the message: Nothing can topple me; none of these mistakes, however disastrous, made the slightest difference. So don't even try.

But Mao's main tactic was to appear conciliatory and willing to compromise. He allowed his own cult to be played down by letting the phrase "Mao Tse-tung Thought" be dropped from the Party Charter— although he made up for this with other forms of self-promotion, like having himself portrayed as the wise leader who had always rejected the cult. In the end he managed to turn the anti-personality cult tide to his advantage by having portraits of his colleagues taken down, and by getting rid of slogans like "Long live Commander-in-Chief Zhu De!," making himself the sole focus of worship.

Mao gave the impression that he was making other important concessions, not least by letting colleagues speak about the rule of law. Liu Shao-chi promised to stop massive killings and violence, and to set up a legal system: "We must ... convince everyone ... that as long as he does not violate the law, his citizen's rights are guaranteed and he will not be violated ..." Another report criticized "campaigns," which were the essence of Mao's rule. Mao had the last laugh, though. He let a criminal code be drafted, but then made sure it was never approved in his lifetime.

Mao's most important concession was to relax the timetable for the Superpower Program. In the main report to the congress, he deleted his own pet slogan "More and Faster ... ," and allowed the deadline of fifteen years to be replaced with "in a rather long time." The report reprised Liu's criticisms of over-hasty industrialization that "places too much burden on the people ... and causes waste." Mao endorsed lower levels of food requisitioning. The result was that in 1956 the average food allowance was 205 kg of grain (equivalent)—the highest amount there was ever to be under Mao. He accepted a further cut of 21 percent in investment in arms industries for 1957. As a result, 1957 was, like 1956, a relatively better year for ordinary people.

For Mao, however, these concessions were intolerable; they slowed down his Program. Within a year he found ways to roll them back and reassert his old master plan.

UNDERMINING KHRUSHCHEV
(1956–59 ★ AGE 62–65)

WITHIN MONTHS of denouncing Stalin, Khrushchev had run into trouble. In June 1956, protests erupted in Poland at a factory suitably named "the Stalin Works" in the city of Poznan, and more than fifty workers were killed. Wladyslaw Gomulka, a former Party leader who had been imprisoned under Stalin, returned to power, espousing a more independent relationship with Moscow. On 19 October the Russians told Mao that anti-Soviet feelings were running high in Poland, and that they were thinking of using force to keep control.

Mao saw this as an ideal opening to undermine Khrushchev by presenting himself as the champion of the Poles and the opponent of "Soviet military intervention." As this might involve a clash with Khrushchev, Mao weighed the pros and cons long and carefully, lying in bed. He convened the Politburo on the afternoon of the 20th. None counseled caution. Then, clad in a toweling robe, he summoned Russian ambassador Yudin and told him: If the Soviet army uses force in Poland, we will condemn you publicly. He asked Yudin to phone Khrushchev straight away. By now, Mao had concluded that Khrushchev was something of a "blunderer," who was "disaster-prone." The awe he had felt for Khrushchev at the time when the Soviet leader denounced Stalin was rapidly fading, replaced by a confidence that he could turn Khrushchev's vulnerability to his own advantage.

Before Yudin's message reached the Kremlin, Khrushchev had already made the decision not to use troops. On the 21st he invited the CCP and four other ruling parties to Moscow to discuss the crisis. Mao sent Liu Shao-chi, with instructions to criticize Russia for its "great-power chauvinism" and for envisaging "military intervention." In Moscow, Liu proposed that the Soviet leadership make "self-criticisms." Mao was aiming to cut Khrushchev down to size as leader of the Communist bloc, and make his own bid for the leadership, which had been his dream since Stalin's death. Now an opportunity had come.

At this juncture, another satellite, Hungary, exploded. The Hungarian

Uprising was to be the biggest crisis to date for the Communist world—an attempt not just to gain more independence from Moscow (which was the aim in Poland), but to overthrow the Communist regime and break away completely from the bloc. On 29 October the Russians decided to withdraw their troops from Hungary, and informed Peking. Up till this point, Mao had been urging a pull-back of Soviet forces from Eastern Europe, but he now realized that the regime in Hungary would collapse if the Russians left. So the next day he strongly recommended that the Soviet army stay on in Hungary and crush the uprising. Keeping Eastern Europe under communism took priority over weakening Khrushchev. Mao's bid to become the head of the Communist camp would be worthless if the camp ceased to exist.

On 1 November, Moscow reversed itself. Its army remained in Hungary, and put down the Uprising with much bloodshed. The realisation that Russian troops were essential to keep the European satellites under Communist rule was a blow to Mao's designs to ease these countries out of Moscow's clutches. But he did not give up. On 4 November, as Russian tanks were rolling into Budapest, he told his Politburo: The Hungarians have to find a new way to control their country—and we must help. What he meant was that Eastern European regimes should adopt his method of rule and do their own brutal repression: that way, they would not have to rely on Russian tanks. Back in 1954, Mao had dispensed his ideas on statecraft to the man who was to be Hungary's prime minister when the Uprising started, András Hegedüs. Hegedüs told us that Mao had urged him to keep a total grip on the army, and all but told him that the Hungarian regime should make its power unchallengeable through killing. When Mao heard about the Yugoslav dictator Tito arresting his liberal opponent Milovan Djilas, he showed "such delight," army chief Peng noticed, "that his face lit up." Mao was to continue advocating his Stalinist ways to Eastern European countries, hoping they would emulate his model of repression and embrace his leadership.

IN JANUARY 1957, Mao sent Chou En-lai to Poland to try to pull Gomulka into his fold. "The key to all questions," Chou told Gomulka, was "to attack right-wing forces and hidden counter-revolutionaries ... targeting one particular group at a time." This advice held no appeal for Gomulka, who had spent years in Stalin's prisons. Chou's résumé to Mao afterwards revealed both Peking's patronizing designs and its failure: "Polish leadership is correct ... but still has not grasped the key question." Later that year, in Moscow, Mao tried again by repeatedly offering Gomulka advice on how to hang on to power, referring to Gomulka's government as "your *court*" (our italics). Mao did not get very far. Gomulka did not aspire to be a tyrant.

Mao hoped to prod the Poles into proposing him as head of the Communist camp. His convoluted way of doing this was to keep telling Gomulka that the Communist camp had to be "headed by the Soviet Union." By saying that the camp must have a head, Mao was trying to broach the issue of who that head should be, hoping the Poles would look his way. Gomulka simply frowned each time Chou used the formula.

What the Poles wanted was more freedom, not more Stalinism, or more poverty. A vivid illustration of the yawning gap between Mao's vision and Polish reality came when a group of Polish visitors told Mao that their fellow countrymen were unhappy with their low living standards, and that their Party felt it had to do something to meet its people's wishes. Mao replied: "I do not believe the standard of living in Poland is too low. On the contrary, I feel that it is relatively very high: the Poles are eating more than two or three thousand calories every day, while [about 1,500] could be sufficient. If the people feel that there are too few consumer goods available, the [regime] should increase their propaganda efforts." After Mao's "monologue," a Polish diplomat wrote, the Poles "realized that Chinese assistance could not be substantial or long-lasting because their program was even more 'anti-people' than the Soviet one."*

When Chou En-lai saw that it was unlikely he could line up the Poles to propose Mao as the head of the Communist camp, Mao turned at once to the other most anti-Moscow Communist country, Yugoslavia. An envoy already there in January 1957 was instantly instructed to request an ultra-private meeting with Tito, at which he asked the Yugoslav president to co-sponsor a world Communist summit with Peking, using the argument that the Soviet Party was in such disrepute that no one would listen to it. At that very moment, Mao was trashing Tito to his inner circle as an enemy—just as he trashed Gomulka. Mao's cultivation of these two Communist countries was completely opportunistic, based solely on the fact that they were the most anti-Soviet. After listening to Mao's pitch, Tito not only declined to co-sponsor such a conference, but would not even commit to attend it.

At the same time, Mao was trying again to weaken the Kremlin by getting the Russians to humiliate themselves. In Moscow in January 1957 Chou demanded that the Soviet leaders make groveling "open self-criticisms" and re-evaluate Stalin along Mao's lines. The Russians bristled, and rebuffed him on both scores. Mao's reaction was a rant to Chou, as he told his provincial chiefs: "I told Comrade En-lai on the phone that these people have been turned into cretins by their material gains, and

---

* A joke went the rounds in Budapest about a man buying tea. When asked: Which tea do you want—Russian or Chinese? he replied: I'll have coffee instead!

the best way to deal with them is to give them a good round of stinking curses. What do they actually have? No more than 50 million tons of steel, 400 million tons of coal, and 80 million tons of oil ... Big deal!" Mao was blaming his failure to supplant Khrushchev on China's lack of economic muscle.

MAO HAD OTHER sources of frustration. One was the Middle East, where a major crisis erupted at the same time as Hungary, over the Suez Canal, which Egypt had nationalized in July 1956. On 29 October Israel attacked Egypt, as the spearhead of a secretly coordinated Israeli-Anglo-French invasion.

Mao was itching to act as Egypt's protector and teacher. He staged mammoth demonstrations against the British and the French, involving nearly 100 million people. To a visitor from Franco's Spain attending one in Peking, it was: "Worse than fascist meeting. There are leaders in all stands who start to cheer and everybody shout when they shout. These are not true demonstrators ... very boring." Mao dispensed advice to Egypt's ambassador, General Hassan Ragab, on everything from how to handle the exiled King Farouk to how Egypt's President Gamal Abdel Nasser could avoid assassination, urging the ambassador to "study the experience of China," which was "very much worth studying." Voicing barely veiled rivalry with Russia, Mao pressed aid on Ragab: "The Soviet Union will be doing all it can to help Egypt. China also would like to do our best to help Egypt, and our help does not have any strings attached. Whatever you need, just name it ... Our aid to you does not have to be paid back ... if you insist on paying back ... then pay back in a hundred years." China gave Nasser 20 million Swiss francs in cash, and rigged the bilateral trade balance heavily in Egypt's favor.

Mao was so keen to play a role that on 3 November he sent Nasser a war plan. True to form, he offered cannon-fodder: 250,000 Chinese volunteers. An offer Nasser did not take up—fortunately for the "volunteers," but also for Mao, as China had no way of transporting this number of people to the Middle East.

Nasser paid scant attention. Nasser's top adviser Mohamed Heikal told us that the president left Mao's war plan at the bottom of his pile of correspondence. What Nasser really wanted was arms. He had decided to recognize Peking that spring so that China, which was outside the UN, could serve as a conduit for Russian arms in case there was a UN arms embargo.

When Cairo asked for arms in December, China at once offered to donate whatever it produced, cost-free. But it could only make small arms such as rifles, and the offer was not taken up. Mao found himself left on the sidelines. All this made him more impatient to speed up his

Superpower Program, and to possess the Bomb; otherwise, as he put it, "people just won't listen to you."

FOR THIS HE NEEDED Khrushchev. Luckily for Mao, Khrushchev needed him too. Hardly had the tumult in Poland and Hungary subsided than Khrushchev was faced with a domestic crisis. In June 1957, Molotov, Malenkov and a group of old Stalinists tried to overthrow him. Khrushchev thwarted the attempt, but felt he needed to get explicit support from foreign Communist parties. Other Communist leaders sent their endorsements promptly, but not Mao. So Khrushchev dispatched Mikoyan to see Mao, who was in the southern lake city of Hangzhou. "I think they wanted someone senior to come to them," Mikoyan's interpreter told us. Mao let Mikoyan talk for much of the night before gesturing languidly over his shoulder to his former ambassador to Moscow: "Old Wang [Jia-xiang], where's our cable?" The telegram of support had been ready all the time. Mao would, of course, back Khrushchev, who was, after all, the power in the Kremlin. He just wanted to make Khrushchev plead, and to up his price. China immediately asked to renegotiate the technology transfer agreement.

Moscow responded extremely positively, saying that it was happy to help China build atom bombs, and missiles, as well as more advanced fighter planes. It turned out that Moscow needed even more support from Mao. The Communist world's biggest-ever summit was set for 7 November, the fortieth anniversary of the Bolshevik Revolution. For this event to go smoothly, Moscow had to have Mao on board.

Mao exploited this situation to the hilt. He said he would attend the summit only on condition that the Russians signed a prior agreement guaranteeing to hand over "the materials and the models for the production of an atomic weapon and the means to deliver it." On 15 October, three weeks before the summit was to convene, Moscow signed a fateful deal agreeing to provide Mao with a sample A-bomb. Russian ministries were told "to supply the Chinese with everything they required to build their own Bomb." So many missile experts were suddenly transferred to China that it caused "havoc" in Russia's own program, according to one Russian expert.* Russian experts also helped China choose missile and nuclear test sites deep in the interior.

Although the "father of the Russian Bomb," Igor Kurchatov, strongly objected, Khrushchev sent a top nuclear scientist, Yevgenii Vorobyov, to supervise the construction of Mao's Bomb, and during Vorobyov's stay

---

* Khrushchev handed over two R-2 short-range, ground-to-ground missiles, which China copied, though he declined to transfer rockets with a range of more than 2,900 km. The Russians also stationed a missile regiment outside Peking, with sixty-three R-1 and R-2 missiles, on which they trained the Chinese.

in China the number of Chinese nuclear specialists increased from 60 to 6,000. Russia "is willing to let us have all the blueprints," Chou told a small circle. "Whatever it has made, including atom bombs and missiles, it is willing to give us. This is maximum trust, maximum help." When Khrushchev later said: "they received a lot from us . . . ," Mikoyan chipped in: "We built [nuclear weapons] plants for the Chinese."

Soviet know-how enabled the Chinese to copy every shortcut the Russians had made, secure in the knowledge that these shortcuts worked, thus greatly speeding up Mao's Bomb. China was the only country in the world that had anything like this level of help to manufacture nuclear weapons. Mao was told by his delegation just before the signing of the new agreement that with this degree of Russian assistance, he could possess all the attributes of a military superpower by the end of 1962. The undertaking cost a fortune. An authoritative Western source estimated the cost to China of making the Bomb alone at US$4.1 billion (in 1957 prices). A large part of this was paid for by agricultural products.

And Mao wanted more than the Bomb and missiles. On 4 October 1957, Russia launched a satellite called Sputnik, the first man-made object in space—and the first time the Communist world had "overtaken" the West in any technical sphere. Mao wanted to get into the space race right away. "Whatever happens, we must have Sputniks," he announced to his top echelon in May 1958. "Not the one-kilo, two-kilo kind . . . it has to be several tens of thousands of kilos . . . We won't do ones the size of chicken eggs like America's." The first US satellite, launched in January 1958, had weighed 8.22 kg, compared with Sputnik's 83.6 kg. Mao wanted his to be bigger than either America's or Russia's, and he wanted it launched in 1960.

MAO FLEW OFF to Moscow on 2 November 1957 for the Communist summit, having decided to be cooperative so as to get what he wanted out of Khrushchev, while at the same time to try to place himself on the map of the Communist camp as Khrushchev's equal, even superior. The summit, the biggest of its kind ever, was attended by leaders of 64 Communist and friendly parties, among which 12 of the Communist parties were in power. Just before leaving Peking, Mao floated to the Russians the idea of the final declaration being signed only by himself and them.

Mao did not quite bring this off, but China was the sole co-drafter, with the Russians, of the final declaration, and Mao himself was accorded special treatment in Moscow, being the only foreign leader put up in the Kremlin, where everything was arranged to his taste, with a large wooden bed, and the toilet turned into a squat one, by making a platform on the seat. At the ceremony on the eve of the anniversary of the Bolshevik Revolution, Mao and Khrushchev appeared hand in hand. At parades on

Gorky Street and Red Square people waved Chinese flags, and shouted "Long live Mao and China!"

Mao's great asset in his drive for equal status with Russia was China's manpower. A Muscovite said to a top Finnish Communist at the time: "We don't need to be afraid of America any more. The Chinese army and our friendship with China have altered the whole world situation, and America can't do a thing about it." And it was the asset Mao himself promoted while he was in Moscow. There, he totted up to Khrushchev how many army divisions each country could raise, based on its population. China outnumbered Russia and all its other allies combined by two to one. Immediately after returning from Moscow, Mao definitively rejected birth control for China, a policy on which the regime had earlier kept a fairly open mind.

As a way of showing that he was equal to his Russian host and above the rest of the participants, Mao brushed away the conference standing order that every speaker must provide an advance text, saying: "I have no text. I want to be able to speak freely." He did indeed eschew a written text, but he had prepared his seemingly off-the-cuff speeches with intense care. Before entering the conference hall, Mao was in a state of super-concentration, so intensely focused that when his Chinese interpreter moved to button up his collar as they were waiting for the lift, Mao seemed totally oblivious of what his aide was doing.

Mao was also the only person to speak sitting down, from his seat. He said he had been "sick in the head." This, as the Yugoslav ambassador wryly put it, "came as a surprise to the majority of those present."

Mao talked about war and death with a gross, even flippant, indifference to human suffering:

> Let's contemplate this, how many people would die if war breaks out. There are 2.7 billion people in the world. One-third could be lost; or, a little more, it could be half . . . I say that, taking the extreme situation, half dies, half lives, but imperialism would be razed to the ground and the whole world would become socialist.

An Italian participant, Pietro Ingrao, told us the audience was "shocked" and "upset." Mao gave the impression that not only did he not mind a nuclear war, he might actually welcome it. Yugoslavia's chief delegate Kardelj came away with no doubt: "It was perfectly clear that Mao Tsetung wanted a war . . ." Even the Stalinist French were appalled.

Mao dismissed concerns about improving living standards:

> People say that poverty is bad, but in fact poverty is good. The poorer people are, the more revolutionary they are. It is dreadful to imagine a time when everyone will be rich . . . From a surplus of calories people will have two heads and four legs.

Mao's views ran dead against the mood of the post-Stalin Communist regimes, which wanted to avoid war and raise living standards. He was not a success. Although he met plenty of Communist leaders this time, unlike on his previous visit, when Stalin had banned any such meetings, and although he missed no opportunity to dispense advice, few took his words seriously. Notes by Britain's John Gollan of Mao's advice to the tiny and irrelevant British Party read: ". . . wait for opportune moment— one day England will be yours.—when win victory don't kill them, give them a house." To the third-rate Bulgarian Todor Zhivkov, one of the youngest present, Mao remarked: "you are young and clever . . . When socialism is victorious in the whole world, we will propose you for president of the world community." No one but Zhivkov himself thought Mao meant it. Mao fascinated some, but he did not command the kind of respect that translated into allegiance, or confidence.

Mao attributed this failure to China's lack of economic and military muscle. "We are a short tree and the Soviet Union is a tall tree," he told Poland's Gomulka, citing steel output as the yardstick. He was determined to remedy this. In his final speech he announced: "Comrade Khrushchev told me that in fifteen years the Soviet Union can overtake America. I can also say that in fifteen years we may catch up or overtake Britain." The subtext was that he was in the race, as much a player as Khrushchev.

To put Khrushchev down, Mao adopted a grand style, talking to the Soviet leader like a teacher: "You have a quick temper, which tends to make enemies . . . let people voice their different views, and talk to them slowly . . ." In the presence of a large audience, Mao sounded even more superior:

> Everyone needs support. An able fellow needs the help of three other people, a fence needs three stakes to support it. These are Chinese proverbs. Still another Chinese proverb says that with all its beauty the lotus needs the green of its leaves to set it off. You, comrade Khrushchev, even though you are a beautiful lotus, you too need the leaves to set you off . . .

At this point, according to one participant, Khrushchev "hung his head and went very red."*

---

* Mao decided to play the superior philosopher, and used a language full of Chinese metaphors, oblique for a non-Chinese audience, and almost impossible to translate. One of the Italian interpreters recalled: "From the Russian translation I heard, no one could understand what Mao said. I remember our translators put their heads in their hands." In fact, even Chinese audiences had to guess what Mao was driving at when he employed this style.

Worse, in front of delegates from all 64 countries, Mao brought up the attempt to oust Khrushchev a few months earlier, and described Molotov, the chief plotter, as "an old comrade with a long history of struggle," saying that Khrushchev's line was only "relatively correct"; at this point a deathly silence fell over the hall. Mao repeatedly said things to top Russians in private like "We loved Molotov very much." (In 1955 the highly unlovable Molotov had called China the "co-leader" of the Communist camp.)

In his memoirs, Khrushchev wrote about Mao's "megalomania": "Mao thought of himself as a man sent by God to do God's bidding. In fact, Mao probably thought God did Mao's *own* bidding." But Mao was not just being megalomaniac, he was also deliberately aiming to diminish Khrushchev's stature, and elevate his own. Khrushchev put up with all this in the interests of preserving the unity of the Communist camp. This concern tied Khrushchev's hands vis-à-vis Mao, and Mao exploited this weak spot to the full.

AFTER RETURNING from Moscow, Mao added to his shopping list another item dear to his heart: nuclear submarines, which Peking regarded as "the ace in the modern arsenal." In June 1958 Chou wrote to ask Khrushchev for the technology and equipment to manufacture these, as well as aircraft-carriers and other large warships.

But this time Khrushchev did not just hand over what Mao asked for. Instead, he tried to secure a quid pro quo: use of China's long coastline, which had easy access to the high seas, unlike Russia's. Khrushchev suggested that China (and Vietnam) could co-crew ships with the Russians in return for these ships using Chinese (and Vietnamese) ports. Ambassador Yudin put this to Mao on 21 July.

Mao wanted a fleet of his own, and to build his own ships. In order to give himself an excuse to turn down the Russian proposal for cooperation, he staged a tantrum. Next day, on 22 July, he summoned Yudin back and told him: "You upset me so much that I didn't sleep all night." He then distorted Moscow's proposal into an issue of sovereignty, accusing the Russians of "wanting to control us" through a "joint fleet." "It boils down to you don't trust the Chinese . . ." In among the bluster, Mao inserted his real demand: "You must help us to build a navy! . . . We want to have *two or three hundred* [nuclear] submarines" (our italics).

Khrushchev was alarmed by Mao's outburst, as Mao had hoped he would be, and rushed to Peking in secret on 31 July. Mao gave him an ostentatiously frosty welcome. As the leaders drove into their first talk, Khrushchev declared straightaway that: "There was no thought of a joint fleet." After much bombast, Mao backed down and conceded that his interpretation of Khrushchev's proposal was unfounded, that he had "lost sleep" for nothing, though he continued to act as if his national pride had been mortally wounded. But Mao's theatrics had got Khrushchev to come more than halfway, and the Soviet leader offered to build China "a big plant . . . to manufacture a large number of nuclear submarines." To keep the pressure on, Mao strongly hinted that otherwise the Russians might be drawn into a war: "Now that we don't have a nuclear submarine fleet, we might as well hand our entire coast over to you, for you to fight for us." Then, to hammer this point home, as soon as Khrushchev departed, Mao manufactured a war situation, once again using Taiwan.

The second Taiwan Strait crisis was very like the first in 1954–55, which Mao had staged to twist his ally's arm for A-bomb technology. This time his target was nuclear submarines and other high-tech military know-how. On 23 August Mao opened up a huge artillery barrage against the island of Quemoy, the springboard to Taiwan, blanketing the tiny island with over 30,000 (mainly Russian-made) shells. Washington thought Mao might really be going for Taiwan. No one in the West suspected his true goal: to force the USA to threaten a nuclear war in order to scare his own ally—a ruse unique in the annals of statecraft.

The US moved a large fleet into the area, and on 4 September Secretary of State John Foster Dulles announced that the US was committed to defending not only Taiwan, but also Quemoy, and threatened to bomb the Mainland. The Kremlin got very nervous about an armed confrontation with the US, and sent foreign minister Andrei Gromyko secretly to Peking the next day. Gromyko brought the draft of a letter from Khrushchev to Eisenhower, which said that an attack on China "is an attack on the Soviet Union." Khrushchev was inviting Mao's comment, which he hoped would be a reassurance that things would not go that far. Mao obliged, telling Gromyko that "this time we are not going to strike Taiwan, nor are we going to fight the Americans, so there will not be a world war." But he made it clear that a war over Taiwan was definitely on the cards "for the future," and that it would most likely be a nuclear war.

Khrushchev thought Mao could well trigger off such a war, but he wrote in his memoirs: "We made no move to restrain our Chinese comrades because we thought they were absolutely right in trying to unify all the territories of China." This was the beauty of Taiwan as an issue for Mao: even if it threatened to cause a third world war, Moscow could not fault him.

Having established this scenario of a future nuclear war with America over Taiwan, Mao scraped hard at the Russians' nerves. He told Gromyko he would like to discuss with Khrushchev at some stage how to coordinate in such a war, and then raised the specter of Russia being wiped out. When the war was over, he asked, "Where shall we build the capital of the socialist world?," implying that Moscow would be gone. He proceeded to propose that the new capital be located on a man-made island in the Pacific. This remark so startled Gromyko that he wanted to exclude it from his telegram home; there the Kremlin "paid particular attention" to Mao's sally, according to the aide who drafted the cable.

Having thus shaken up Gromyko, Mao then proceeded to mollify him by saying that China would take all the heat of the coming nuclear war. "Our policy is that we will take the full consequences of this war ourselves. We will deal with America, and . . . we will not drag the Soviet Union into this war." Except, Mao said, "we have to make preparations to fight the war with America," and that included "material preparations." Chou En-lai spelled it out to the Russian chargé: "We have made plans to produce modern weapons with the help of the Soviet Union." Mao had made his position clear: You can opt out, if you enable me to fight the war myself.

Khrushchev got the point. On 27 September he wrote to Mao: "Thank you for your willingness to take on yourselves a strike, without involving the Soviet Union," and followed this up on 5 October by announcing that the Taiwan crisis was an "internal" matter and that Russia would not get involved in what he called this "civil war." For Khrushchev to say that he would let Mao deal with a nuclear war with America on his own signaled his agreement to arm the Chinese to do so. The very next day, Mao wrote a statement in the name of his defense minister, suspending the shelling of Quemoy. This ended the second Taiwan Strait crisis.

Mao then wrote to Khrushchev confirming that he would be only too happy for China to fight a nuclear war with America alone. "For our ultimate victory," he offered, "for the total eradication of the imperialists, we [i.e., the Chinese people, who had not been consulted] are willing to endure the first [US nuclear] strike. *All it is is a big pile of people dying* [our italics]."*

To keep the Taiwan issue alight, Mao ordered the shelling of Quemoy to resume, eventually cutting it back to alternate days. This characteristically Maoist extravagance put tremendous strain on the economy. The army chief of staff, who was not let in on Mao's intentions, protested: "There is little point in the shelling. It costs a lot of money . . . Why do it?" Mao could find nothing to say except to accuse the general of being "right-wing," and he was soon purged. Firing expensive shells onto the rocky island went on for twenty years, and stopped only after Mao's death,

---

* Mao had said similar things before, in less overtly callous language. In 1955 he told the Finnish ambassador that "America's atom bombs are too few to wipe out the Chinese. Even if the US atom bombs . . . were dropped on China, blasted a hole in the Earth or blew it to pieces, this might be a big thing for the solar system, but it would still be an insignificant matter as far as the universe as a whole is concerned."

on New Year's Day 1979, the day Peking and Washington established diplomatic relations.

Meanwhile, Khrushchev endorsed a number of high-end technology transfers, which led to an astonishing deal on 4 February 1959 under which Russia committed to helping China to make a whole range of advanced ships and weapons, including conventional-powered ballistic missile submarines and submarine-to-surface missiles. The first Taiwan Strait crisis had panicked the secrets of the Bomb out of Moscow; now, four years later, with the second Taiwan Strait crisis, Mao had prised out of Khrushchev an agreement to transfer no less than the whole range of equipment needed to deliver the Bomb.

Over the years from 1953 when Mao had first outlined his Superpower Program, its scale had grown prodigiously, but each expansion had only aggravated his fundamental problem: how to squeeze out enough food to pay for his purchases. In 1956, when the scope of the Program was much smaller, deaths from starvation had become so shocking that his usually docile Politburo had balked at the plan and forced him to slow down. Now a far worse death toll was in the offing. But this time Mao did not have to make concessions to his colleagues at home. In the course of 1957 he had altered one fundamental thing. Khrushchev no longer had any authority in Peking, and Mao no longer felt constrained by him.

KILLING THE "HUNDRED FLOWERS"

(1957–58 ★ AGE 63–64)

TERRORIZATION HAD always been Mao's panacea whenever he wanted to achieve anything. But in 1956, after Khrushchev condemned Stalin's use of terror, Mao had to lower the rate of arrests and killings. On 29 February, as soon as he learned about Khrushchev's secret speech, Mao had ordered his police chief to revise established plans: "This year the number of arrests must be greatly reduced from last year . . . The number of executions especially must be fewer . . ."

But when Khrushchev's tanks rolled into Hungary later that year, Mao saw his chance to revive persecution. His colleagues were still saying that the troubles in Eastern Europe were the result of over-concentration on heavy industry and neglecting living standards. Liu Shao-chi argued that China should go "slower" with industrialization, so that "people won't be going onto the streets to demonstrate . . . and moreover will be fairly happy." Chou, too, wanted to scrap some arms factories. Although wholly in agreement with Mao over giving priority to nuclear weapons, he remarked pointedly: "We can't eat cannons, or guns."

Mao's view of the "lessons from Eastern Europe" was completely different. "In Hungary," he told his top echelon on 15 November, "it's true the standard of living did not improve much, but it wasn't too bad. And yet . . . there were great troubles there." "The basic problem with some Eastern European countries," he said, "is that they didn't eliminate all those counter-revolutionaries . . . Now they are eating their own bitter fruit." "Eastern Europe just didn't kill on a grand scale." "We must kill," Mao declared. "And we say it's good to kill."

But with the trend in the Communist world blowing towards de-Stalinization, Mao decided it was not wise to be too blatant about launching a purge. To create a justification, he cooked up a devious plan. He did so mainly while lying in bed, where he spent most of his time that winter of 1956–57. He ate in bed, sitting on the edge, and only got up to go to the toilet.

⋆

ON 27 FEBRUARY 1957, Mao delivered a four-hour speech to the rubber-stamp Supreme Council announcing that he was inviting criticisms of the Communist Party. The Party, he said, needed to be accountable and "under supervision." He sounded reasonable, criticizing Stalin for his "excessive" purges, and giving the impression there were going to be no more of these in China. In this context, he cited an adage, "Let a hundred flowers bloom."

Few guessed that Mao was setting a trap, and that he was inviting people to speak out so that he could then use what they said as an excuse to victimize them. Mao's targets were intellectuals and the educated, the people most likely to speak up. After taking power, Mao's policy had been to give them a generally better standard of living than the average. Those who were well-known or "useful" were given special privileges. But Mao had them put through the grinder several times, not least with "thought reform," which he himself described as brainwashing: "Some foreigners say our thought reform is brainwashing. I think that's right, it is exactly brainwashing." In fact, even the fearsome term "brainwashing" does not conjure up the mental anguish of the process, which bent and twisted people's minds. Now Mao was planning to persecute the educated en masse.

Mao confided his scheme only to a very few special cronies like the boss of Shanghai, Ke Qing-shi, keeping even most of the Politburo in the dark. In early April, he told these few cronies that as a result of him soliciting criticisms, "intellectuals are beginning to . . . change their mood from cautious to more open . . . One day punishment will come down on their heads . . . We want to let them speak out. You must stiffen your scalps and let them attack! . . . Let all those ox devils and snake demons . . . curse us for a few months." To these same few cronies, Mao spelled out that he was "casting a long line to bait big fish." He later described his ensnaring like this: "How can we catch the snakes if we don't let them out of their lairs? We wanted those sons-of-turtles [bastards] to wriggle out and sing and fart . . . that way we can catch them."

Mao's trap was extremely successful. Once the lid was loosened just a fraction, a deluge of dissent burst out, mostly in wall posters and small-scale meetings called "seminars," which were the only forums allowed.

One of the very first things to be challenged was the Communists' monopoly of power, which one critic described as "the source of all ills." One poster was entitled "Totalitarian power is peril!" The Communists' exercise of power was compared to Hitler's. One man said in a seminar that "in not protecting citizens' rights, today's government is worse than the feudal dynasties or Chiang Kai-shek." One professor called the Constitution "toilet paper." Another, an economist, went right to the core of Mao's methods, and called for banning public denunciations, "which are much worse than being in prison"—"just the thought of them makes one tremble from heart to flesh." Democracy was the popular demand.

So was the rule of law. One vice-minister called for the independence of the judiciary. Another administrator said he wanted to be able "just to follow the law, not the orders of the Party." Referring to the CCP's smothering methods of controlling everything, one well-known playwright asked: "Why is it necessary to have 'leadership' in the arts? Who led Shakespeare, Tolstoy, Beethoven, Molière?"

Foreign policy, too, came in for questioning by some of the elite who had access to partial information. The former Nationalist governor of Yunnan province, who had crossed over to the Communists, protested that "it is unfair that China should pay all the costs in the Korean War"—and called for reducing the level of aid being lavished on foreign countries.

The regime's secretiveness also came under attack. "All absolute economic statistics are state secrets," protested one critic, "even the output of alkali . . . What is this but an attempt to keep people in a state of stupidity?" He demanded information about the industrialization program. Another wrote: "I have indeed heard about peasants . . . dying from having just grass roots to eat, in areas so rich in produce that they are known as the land of fish and rice. But the newspapers say nothing about any of this . . ."

Many contrasted the harsh life of the peasants with that of the leaders (which they could only glimpse). *People's Daily* had reported a banquet for the Russian president Kliment Voroshilov, attended by 1,000 people. "Why such grandeur?," one poster enquired, when " 'local Party emperors' are using methods like abuse, torture and detention to gouge food out of the peasants . . . ?" "We must know that dissatisfied peasants could throw Chairman Mao's portrait into the toilet," this daring author warned.

Most of this criticism never reached the general public, as Mao only allowed carefully selected snippets to appear in the press. The rest was confined to the two channels—seminars and wall posters—which were impermanent and easy to erase. And Mao made sure that these outlets were restricted to isolated campuses and individual institutions, to which the general public was not allowed access. Nor were these institutions permitted to contact each other, and people inside them were banned from going outside to spread their views. When some students tried to distribute handwritten journals, their *samizdats* were instantly confiscated, and they were punished as "counter-revolutionaries." Dissent was thus kept rigidly fragmented, so a popular uprising was impossible.

ON 6 JUNE 1957, Mao read a mimeographed pamphlet which speculated that the leadership was split, with himself cast as the champion of dissent, ranged against "conservatives." In the information void he had created, some had mistakenly come to think that he was a liberal, and appeals had been heard like: "Let us unite around Mao Tse-tung– Khrushchev!" Some even expressed concern for Mao: "It seems our dear comrade Mao Tse-tung is in a very difficult position." This suggestion that Mao was a liberal was dangerous for him, because it could well embolden dissent.

The next day, Mao ordered an editorial for *People's Daily* to be broadcast that evening, saying that challenging the Party was forbidden. Once he pressed this button, the persecution machine started rolling for what was called the "Anti-Rightist Campaign," which lasted a year. The brief exciting moment of "a hundred flowers" was over.

On 12 June, Mao issued a circular to the Party, to be read to all members "except unreliable ones," in which he made it explicit that he had set a trap. He did not want his Party to think he was a liberal—in case they themselves should turn liberal.

In this circular, Mao set a quota for victims: between 1 and 10 percent of "intellectuals" (which meant the better-educated), who numbered some 5 million at the time. As a result, at least 550,000-plus people were labeled as "Rightists." While many had spoken out, some had not said anything against the regime, and were pulled in just to fill Mao's quota.

To Mao, writers, artists and historians were superfluous. Scientists and technicians, however, were largely exempted from persecution—"especially those who have major achievements," a September 1957 order decreed; these "must be absolutely protected." Scientists who had returned from Europe and America, in particular, were to be "neither labelled nor denounced." Nuclear physicists and rocket scientists were treated extra well. (Throughout Mao's reign, top scientists were given privileges superior even to those enjoyed by very senior officials.)

As the ultimate aim of this crackdown was to create the atmosphere for harsher extraction to finance the Superpower Program, Mao made a particular point of hammering any challenge directed against his policies towards the peasantry. One *People's Daily* headline screamed: "Rebuke the rubbish that 'peasants' lives are hard!' " To drive home his message, Mao personally arranged a piece of sadistic theater. One well-known figure had been saying that peasants were "on the verge of dying from starvation," so a "fact-finding" tour was arranged for him. *People's Daily* reported that wherever he went he was pursued by crowds up to 50,000 strong, "refuting his rubbish," and was finally forced to flee, hidden under jute sacks in the boot of a car.

Parallel with theater came executions. Mao revealed later to his top echelon that one province, Hunan, "denounced 100,000, arrested 10,000 and killed 1,000. The other provinces did the same. So our problems were solved."

A particular example was made of three teachers in one county town in Hubei province who were executed for allegedly stirring up a demonstration by schoolchildren over education cuts. The effect of the cuts was that only one in twenty children would now be able to go on to high school. The demonstration was branded "a Little Hungary," and a special point was made of publicizing the executions nationwide. It is almost certain that Mao personally ordered the death sentences, as he had just arrived in the province the day before they were passed, and up till that moment the authorities had been undecided about imposing the death penalty. The huge publicity was intended to instill fear in rural schools, which bore the brunt of the education cuts Mao had introduced to squeeze out more funds for the Superpower Program.

Funding for education was already minuscule. Now it was to be cut back even further. Mao's approach was not to raise the general standard of education in society as a whole, but to focus on a small elite, predominantly in science and other "useful" subjects, and leave the rest of the population to be illiterate or semi-illiterate slave-laborers. What funds were allotted to education went mainly to the cities; village schools received no funding, and schools in small towns very little. As a result, only tiny numbers of rural youth were able to go on to higher education.

Even in the cities, young people's chances of education were drastically slashed in 1957, when 80 percent of the 5 million urban elementary school leavers (i.e., 4 million people) and 800,000 of 1 million middle-school leavers were told that they could not continue their education. There had been widespread discontent in the cities, and the executions of the teachers in the "Little Hungary" case were a warning to urbanites too.

Execution was not the only cause of death in this campaign: suicides were rife among those condemned as "Rightists." In the Summer Palace in Peking, early morning exercise-takers frequently encountered corpses hanging from trees, and feet sticking out of the lake.

Most of those branded as "Rightists" were put through hellish, though largely non-violent, denunciation meetings. Their families became outcasts, their spouses were shunted to undesirable jobs, and their children lost all hope of a decent education. To protect their children—and themselves—many people divorced their spouses when they were labeled as Rightists. Numerous families were broken up, causing lifelong tragedy to children and parents alike.

After they were denounced, most Rightists were deported to do hard labor in remote areas. Mao needed labor, particularly to open up virgin lands. A journalist called Dai Huang described how deportees were just dumped in places like the far north of Manchuria, known as "the Great Northern Wilderness," and had to rig up a shelter "in a hurry, using wheat stems to make a roof" in a temperature of −38°C. Even with a fire, "it was still a dozen or so degrees below zero . . ."

> The grass and beaten earth huts we lived in had wind coming in from all sides . . . there were hardly any vegetables or meat . . . We got up . . . just after 4 at dawn, and did not stop until 7 or 8 in the evening . . . In these 15–16 hours . . . we basically worked non-stop . . . in summer . . . We had to get up at 2 am . . . We had at most three hours' sleep.

While being subjected to ceaseless, relentless harangues—"You're here to redeem your crime! Don't dare to make trouble, or look for ways to be lazy!"—the deportees had to work on less than subsistence-level rations. Many died from malnutrition, illness, cold, overwork and in accidents doing unfamiliar jobs like felling trees.

This journalist, Dai, had actually spoken up after he knew that Mao had set a trap. He wrote a petition to Mao, objecting to "the new ruling class" holding sumptuous "receptions and banquets," while "tens of thousands of people . . . are chewing grass roots or tree bark." He even took a swipe at Mao's personality cult. "A chef cooking a good meal is said to be 'thanks to Chairman Mao's leadership.' " "Don't think you are a wise god," he warned Mao.

Dai Huang's wife divorced him, and his relatives suffered discrimination. A schoolteacher nephew was denied funds for a life-saving operation because of the family connection. Dai himself barely survived the Northern Wilderness, from which many were never to return.

HAVING SUPPRESSED dissent among the educated in general, starting in 1958, immediately after returning from the Moscow summit, Mao moved to strike fear into his top echelon by threatening to label as "Rightists" any of them who opposed the relaunch of the Superpower Program. His main concern was with his Nos. 2 and 3, Liu Shao-chi and Chou En-lai, who had championed the cuts in the Program in 1956.

The tactic Mao chose this time was new—to abase his most senior colleagues in front of dozens of provincial chiefs. This was the first time that Mao involved these second-rank officials in directly attacking his top colleagues and their own superiors. It was a means both of humiliating Chou and Liu, and of putting pressure on them; especially as Mao personally delivered stinging assaults on his two colleagues in front of their subordinates. Bringing in these provincial chiefs to witness the working of power at the very top—and the humiliation of the regime's Nos. 2 and 3—was also a way for Mao to empower the men responsible for supervising the actual collection of the food.

He focused on Chou, who was in charge of planning and administering the Program. Mao described Chou as being "only 50 metres away from being a Rightist"; Chou's attempts to curb investment in arms industries in 1956, Mao said, were on a par with the Hungarian Uprising, and had "considerably influenced the Rightists." These were ominous charges, carrying the direst potential consequences. To make things even more menacing, Mao removed Chou as foreign minister in February 1958, and senior diplomats close to Chou were encouraged to attack him.

The heat around Mao was unbearable, even by the usual nerve-racking standards of his regime. One minister who had been in the firing line had a fatal breakdown. When Mao's doctor went to give the minister a check-up, he found him lying in bed, "muttering again and again: 'Spare me! Please spare me!'" The minister was flown off to a hospital in Canton. In the plane, he suddenly sank to his knees and banged his head on the floor, begging: "Please spare me . . ." He died in Canton within weeks, aged forty-six.*

As the climax of this process of intimidation and abasement, Mao ordered Chou to make a self-criticism that would imply that he was a quasi-Rightist in front of the 1,360 delegates to a special Party Congress in May 1958. Chou apologized for his previous efforts to hamper Mao's desired rate of "industrialisation," whose military nature was not revealed even to this high-level gathering, nor its catastrophic implications. This self-denunciation caused Chou a great deal of pain. It took him ten days to write his speech. The normally dapper premier spent days on end shut up in his room, unshaven and unkempt, not even getting dressed. The secretary taking his dictation recalled that Chou spoke extremely slowly,

> sometimes unable to say a word for five or six minutes . . . So I suggested I leave his office and let him compose quietly . . . It was midnight, and I returned to my room and lay in bed with my clothes on, waiting to be called.
>
> At about 2 am [Mrs. Chou] summoned me. She said: "En-lai is sitting in the office staring blankly. How come you went to bed? . . ." So I followed [her] to [his] office, where she and comrade Chou En-lai argued for a long time . . .

---

* This minister, Huang Jing, had been the second husband of Mme Mao. They married when he was a handsome twenty-year-old radical student and she an eighteen-year-old librarian in 1932, and she joined the Party under his influence. After she married Mao, she occasionally invited her ex-husband over "for a chat," but he declined every time. The pressure on him now was nothing personal on Mao's part, as Mao was never jealous. In fact, in Chongqing in 1945 Mao had made a point of inviting another of his wife's former husbands, Tang Na, to a reception, and greeted him with a twinkle in his eye and a crack, as Tang Na had once attempted suicide over the future Mme Mao. Tang Na settled in Paris after Mao took power, and subsequently died there.

Chou then dictated, on the verge of tears. Chou had chosen his wife not out of love, but out of mutual devotion to the Communist cause, and she lived right up to that specification.

Chou duly delivered his speech, to Mao's satisfaction. The atmosphere at the congress was more frightening than usual, as reflected in the language of the press announcement, which said the meeting had "denounced Rightists who have wormed their way into the Party"—in Communist jargon, barely one step away from damning such people as enemy agents. Orchestrated by Mao, a host of provinces announced how they had uncovered Rightists among their own provincial leaders. The provincial chief of Henan was condemned and dismissed for saying the peasants could not afford to hand over too much to the state as they were "starving." Henan, he said, had endured "endless floods, droughts and other natural disasters," and its inhabitants were "having to pull ploughs, since many draft animals have died because of the shortage of food."

Liu Shao-chi also came under bitter attack from Mao's henchmen at the congress for his role in the 1956 cuts. Like Chou, he too capitulated fulsomely, as did everyone who had a managerial role in Mao's Superpower Program. Mao's notes show that he had been ready to charge anyone who refused to toe his line with what amounted to treason ("using illegal methods . . . to carry out opposition activities"). In the end he did not need to go this far, as all surrendered.

Liu stayed on as No. 2. Chou was so battered that he asked Mao "whether it is appropriate for me to go on being prime minister." He was told to carry on, and he remained foreign affairs supremo, even though he was not reinstated as foreign minister. Mao was well aware that no one else could put so seductive a face on his regime. The man who took Chou's place as foreign minister, Chen Yi, remarked ruefully that he found himself being "no more than a glorified entertainer."

MAO MADE ONE most important personnel shift at the congress. He promoted his old crony Lin Biao to be one of the Party's vice-chairmen (alongside Liu, Chou, Zhu De and Chen Yun). This gave Mao an ally-in-need in the core, one who also held a top army rank: a marshal. Formal military ranks had been introduced in 1955, when Lin and nine other generals were made marshals.

Along with these steps, Mao intensified his personality cult, which he had started to promote from the time of the Yenan Terror in 1942–43. In March 1958 he told his top echelon (colleagues, provincial chiefs and ministers): "There has to be a personality cult . . . It is absolutely necessary." His henchmen vied to declare their "blind faith" in Mao, with Shanghai boss Ke actually advocating the herd instinct: "We must follow the Chairman like a blind herd."

To stoke his cult, Mao took the most unwonted step of visiting places like factories and agricultural cooperatives, and these visits were reported with huge fanfare. Mao was filmed for newsreels that were shown nation-wide, and featured in a painting aptly titled *Chairman Mao Walks All Over China*, which became a household image. After Mao visited a village outside Chengdu in Sichuan, huge publicity was given to the story that the excited villagers changed its name to "Happiness Co-operative." When Mao lifted a few bits of earth on a shovel at the Ming Tomb Reservoir on the outskirts of Peking, *People's Daily* wrote: "As soon as Chairman Mao put down the spade, a soldier named Yu Bing-sen wrapped the spade up in his clothes. He said with brimming emotions: 'Whenever we see this spade we will think of Chairman Mao, and we will have greater energy.' An agricultural co-op member wept and told the reporter..."* These exaltations of Mao in the press were then force-fed to the entire population, the illiterate as well as the literate, at newspaper-study sessions that were a permanent fixture of life under Mao.

On 13 August, for the only time throughout his 27-year reign, Mao ate in a restaurant, in Tianjin. There he was sighted, undoubtedly as intended, as he not only got out of the car in front of the restaurant, but appeared at the window upstairs. "Chairman Mao! Chairman Mao!" people began to chant. Word spread fast, and soon a hysterical crowd of tens of thou-sands surrounded the restaurant for several blocks, jumping up and down and screaming "Long Live Chairman Mao!" One of Mao's secretaries got worried about security, and suggested that Mao should leave while a body-guard with a build similar to Mao's drew the crowd off. But Mao vetoed it. He had come to the place to be seen, and he was not in any danger, as this was a surprise visit, and he was distant enough from the crowd, none of whom could possibly have a gun anyway. (One of his regime's first acts had been to confiscate weapons.) And the people around the restaurant had almost certainly been preselected, as happened in other places where Mao appeared. Mao waved at the crowd, who replied with more frenzy and weeping. All of which was reported in great detail in the papers.

When Mao eventually left, after several hours, he described his depar-ture to his inner circle in almost godlike language: "I gave one wave, and the crowd receded." He reveled in the way his cult was thriving and told his coterie that he "was deeply impressed." Years of force-feeding his personality cult had endowed him with awesome power.

---

* Shoveling earth at the Ming Tomb Reservoir for those few minutes was the only phys-ical labor Mao put in during his entire rule, although he made heavy labor compulsory and routine for nearly everyone in China, children included, on the grounds that it helped maintain their ideological purity.

THE GREAT LEAP: "HALF OF CHINA MAY WELL HAVE TO DIE"

(1958–61 ★ AGE 64–67)

WITH HIS cult fed and watered among the population, his colleagues cowed into submission, and potential voices of dissent silenced through the "Anti-Rightist" campaign, Mao proceeded vastly to accelerate his Superpower Program, though he still concealed its military nature. The original 1953 schedule of completing "industri-alisation" in "ten to fifteen years" was now shortened to eight, seven, or even five—*or possibly three*—years. Mao had been informed that acquisi-tions from Russia could enable him to break into the superpower league in five years. He fancied he could fulfill his ambition in one "big bang," declaring that "Our nation is like an atom." He called the process the "Great Leap Forward," and launched it in May 1958.

While the nation was told, vaguely, that the goal of the Leap was for China to "overtake all capitalist countries in a fairly short time, and become one of the richest, most advanced and powerful countries in the world," Mao spelled out to small audiences, and strictly confidentially, just what he meant to do once the Leap was completed. On 28 June, he told an elite army group: "Now the Pacific Ocean is not peaceful. It can only be peaceful when we take it over." At this point Lin Biao interjected: "We must build big ships, and be prepared to land [sc. militarily] in Japan, the Philippines and San Francisco." Mao continued: "How many years before we can build such ships? In 1962, when we have xx–xx tons of steel [figures concealed in original] . . ." On 19 August, Mao told select provincial chiefs: "In the future we will set up the Earth Control Committee, and make a uniform plan for the Earth." Mao dominated China. He intended to dominate the world.

For the Chinese population, the Great Leap was indeed an enormous jump—but in the amount of food extracted. This was calculated on the basis, not of what the peasants could afford, but of what was needed for Mao's Program. Mao proceeded by simply asserting that there was going to be an enormous increase in the harvest, and got the provincial chiefs to proclaim that their area would produce an astronomical output. When harvest time came, the chiefs got selected lackeys down at the grassroots to declare that their areas had indeed produced fantastic crops. Mao's propaganda machine then publicized these claims with great fanfare. The stratospheric harvests and other sky-high claims were called "sputniks," reflecting Mao's obsession with the Russian satellite. On 12 June *People's Daily* reported that in Henan, Mao's No. 1 model province, a "Sputnik Co-operative" had produced 1.8 tons of wheat on one *mu* (1/6th acre)—more than ten times the norm. Claims in this vein were not, as official Chinese history would have us believe, the result of spontaneous boasting by local cadres and peasants. The press was Mao's voice, not the public's.

"Sputnik fields" mushroomed. They were usually created by trans-planting ripe crops from a number of fields into a single artificial plot. These were the Maoist equivalent of Potemkin fields—with the key difference that Mao's plots were not intended to fool the ruler, but instead produced *by* the ruler for the eyes of his distant underlings, grassroots cadres from other collective farms. These cadres were most important to Mao, as they were the people immediately in charge of physically hand-ing over the harvests to the state. Mao wanted them to see these Sputnik fields and then go back and make similar claims, so that the state could say: since you've produced more, we can take more. Cadres who declined to go along were condemned and replaced with others who would. Charades of sky-high yields filled the press, though Peking eventually quietly stopped the transplanting theater, as it caused big losses.

By late July, *People's Daily* was declaring that "we can produce as much food as we want," setting the stage for Mao to assert publicly on 4 August: "We must consider what to do with all this surplus food." This claim about there being surplus food was one that Mao himself could not possi-bly have believed. Barely six months before, on 28 January, he had acknowledged to the Supreme Council that there was a shortage of food: "What are we going to do as there isn't enough food to eat?" he had asked. His solution was as follows: "No worse than eat less . . . Oriental style . . . It's good for health. Westerners have a lot of fat in their food; the further west one goes the more fat they eat. I say that Western meat-eaters are contemptible." "I think it is good to eat less. What's the point of eating a lot and growing a big stomach, like the foreign capitalists in cartoons?" These airy remarks might well apply to Mao, who had a paunch, but they were irrelevant to famished peasants. In January, Mao had been saying: There isn't enough food, but people can eat less. Six months later, he was saying: There is too much food. Both of these contradictory remarks had the same purpose: to gouge more food out of the peasants.

In September, *People's Daily* reported that "the biggest rice sputnik" yet had produced over 70 tons from less than 1/5th of an acre, which was hundreds of times the norm. This sputnik field was faked by an ambitious new county boss in Guangxi. At the end of the year, his county reported a grain output that was over three times the true figure. The state then demanded an impossible 4.8 times what it had taken the year before.

Grassroots cadres often resorted to brute force. And if they were judged ineffective, armed police were sent in. On 19 August 1958, Mao instructed his provincial chiefs: "When you order things handed over and they are not handed over, back up your orders with force." Under such pressure, state violence raged across the countryside.

To produce a "justification," Mao repeatedly accused peasants and village cadres of hiding grain. On one occasion, on 27 February 1959, he told his top echelon: "All production teams hide their food to divide among themselves. They even hide it in deep secret cellars, and place guards and sentries..." Next day, he asserted again that peasants were "eating carrot leaves during the day, and rice at night..." By this he meant that peasants were pretending they had run out of proper food but in fact had good food, which they consumed in secret. Mao revealed his contempt for the peasantry to his inner circle: "Peasants are hiding food ... and are very bad. There is no Communist spirit in them! Peasants are after all peasants. That's the only way they can behave..."

Mao knew perfectly well that the peasants had no food to hide. He had an efficient reporting system, and was on top of what was happening daily around the country. On one batch of reports in April 1959 he noted that there was severe starvation in half the country: "a big problem: 15 provinces—25.17 million people no food to eat"; his response was to ask the provinces to "deal with it," but he did not say how. A report that reached his desk from Yunnan province, dated 18 November 1958, described a wave of deaths from edema—swelling caused by severe malnutrition. Again, Mao's response was to pass the buck: "This mistake is mainly the fault of county-level cadres." Mao knew that in many places people were reduced to eating compounds of earth. In some cases, whole villages died as a result, when people's intestines became blocked.

This nationwide squeeze made it possible for Mao to export 4.74 million tons of grain, worth US$935 million, in 1959. Exports of other foods also soared, particularly of pork.

The claim about China "having too much food" was trundled out to Khrushchev. When he came to Peking in summer 1958, Mao pressed him for help to make nuclear submarines, which were going to be extremely expensive. Khrushchev asked how China was going to pay. Mao's response was that China had unlimited supplies of food.

Food was also used as a raw material in the nuclear program, which required high-quality fuel. Grain was turned into the purest alcohol. On 8 September, having claimed that there was food to spare, Mao told the Supreme Council that "we have to find outlets for grain in industries, for example to produce ethyl alcohol for fuel." Grain was therefore used for missile tests, each of which consumed 10 million kg of grain, enough to radically deplete the food intake of 1–2 million people for a whole year.

THE PEASANTS WERE now having to work much harder, and much longer hours, than before. As Mao wanted to raise output without spending any money, he latched on to methods that depended on labor, not investment. It was for this reason that he ordered huge drives to build irrigation systems—dams, reservoirs, canals. Over the four years from 1958, about 100 million peasants were coerced into such projects, moving a quantity of earth and masonry equivalent to excavating 950 Suez Canals, mostly using only hammers, picks and shovels, and sometimes even doors and bed planks from their homes to improvise makeshift carts. Peasants corvéed for these projects often had to bring not only their own food but their own tools, and in many cases their own materials to put up shelters.

In the absence of safety measures and medical care, accidents were frequent, as were deaths, which Mao well knew. His talks with provincial chiefs about these waterworks are littered with mentions of death tolls. In April 1958 he observed that as Henan (his model) had promised to move 30 billion cubic meters that coming winter, "I think 30,000 people will die." Anhui, another of Mao's favorite provinces, "said 20 billion cubic metres, and I think 20,000 people will die . . ." When senior officials in Gansu province appealed against "destroying human lives" in these projects, Mao had them condemned and punished as a "Rightist anti-Party clique."

Mao wanted instant results, so he promoted a typical slogan: "Survey, Design and Execute Simultaneously," known as the "Three Simultaneouslys." Geological surveying was therefore scanty, or non-existent, so a fourth "simultaneous" usually soon had to be added: Revision.

One well-known project was a canal 1,400 km long across the drought-plagued Yellow Earth Plateau in the northwest. It had to cross 800 mountains and valleys and the 170,000 laborers had to dig caves to sleep in, and forage for herbs to eke out their meager food. Months into the project, tunnels which they had already started digging, by hand, were abandoned in favor of culverts. After more months, this approach in turn was abandoned, and some of the tunnels reinstated. The project went on in this way for three years, during which at least 2,000 laborers died, and was then abandoned. The official account admitted that not one plot of land had benefited.

Most of the projects turned out to be a stupendous waste. Many had to be abandoned halfway: out of the over 500 large reservoirs (100 million cubic meters capacity or more), 200 had already been abandoned by late

1959. Many others collapsed during Mao's lifetime. The worst dam disaster in human history happened in 1975 in Mao's model province of Henan, when scores of reservoirs built during the Leap crumbled in a storm, drowning an estimated 230,000–240,000 people (official death toll: 85,600). Other Mao-era follies went on killing people long after his death, and as of 1999, no fewer than 33,000 were considered a risk to human life. The dams also uprooted untold millions from their homes, and more than two decades later there were still 10.2 million "reservoir displaced persons."

MAO INFLICTED MANY other half-baked schemes on the peasants, like forcing them to dig up soil by hand to a depth of half a meter. "Use the human wave tactic, and turn every field over," he ordered. Grossly excessive close planting was another. Close planting needed fertilizer, but Mao refused the requisite investments, and in late 1958 he actually ordered: "Reduce chemical fertiliser imports." On another occasion he said: "Turn China into a country of pigs . . . so there will be lots of manure . . . and more than enough meat, which can be exported in exchange for iron and steel." But he did not say where the feed was to come from for these pigs. In fact, under Mao's stewardship the number of pigs fell by no less than 48 percent between 1957 and 1961.

Over the centuries, Chinese peasants had applied their ingenuity to find every possible substance that could be used as fertilizer. In urban areas, every spot where human waste was dumped was allocated to a particular village, and peasants coming in before dawn to collect this waste with their special oblong barrels on carts were a feature of life. Human waste was so precious that frequent fights broke out between people from different villages over poaching, using their long-handled ladles. Desperate to find new sources for fertilizer, people started to mix human and animal manure with the thatched roofs and earth walls of old houses, into which smoke and grease had seeped. Millions of peasant houses were torn down to feed into manure pits, known as "shit lakes and piss seas."

One day it hit Mao that a good way to keep food safe would be to get rid of sparrows, as they ate grain. He designated sparrows as one of "Four Pests" to be eliminated, along with rats, mosquitoes and flies, and mobilized the entire population to wave sticks and brooms and make a giant din to scare sparrows off landing so that they would fall from fatigue and be caught and killed by the crowds. There was much to be said for eradicating the other three, which were genuine pests, though one side-effect was that whatever slight privacy people had once had in performing their bodily functions disappeared, as eager fly-collectors loitered in droves at public lavatories. But the case for eliminating sparrows was not so clearcut, as sparrows got rid of many pests, as well as eating grain—and, needless to say, many other birds died in the killing spree. Pests once kept down by sparrows and other birds now flourished, with catastrophic results. Pleas from scientists that the ecological balance would be upset were ignored.

It was not long before a request from the Chinese government marked "Top Secret" reached the Soviet embassy in Peking. In the name of socialist internationalism, it read, please send us 200,000 sparrows from the Soviet Far East as soon as possible. Mao had to accept that his anti-sparrow drive was counter-productive, and it gradually petered out.*

The "Four Pests" campaign was a sort of Maoist DIY substitute for a health service, as it was labor-intensive and investment-free. Mao had wanted to get rid of dogs, which consumed food, but relented, when he was advised that peasants needed them to guard their houses when they were out at work.

ANOTHER FIASCO that drained the peasants' energy, and brought disaster, was an order from Mao that the entire nation had to "make steel." The Superpower Program needed a lot of steel—and steel was also Mao's yardstick for superpower status. When he boasted to Communist leaders in Moscow in 1957 that China would "overtake Britain in fifteen years" (which he later shortened to three) and when he told the Chinese he was fully confident that China could "overtake America" in ten years, steel output was what he had in mind. Mao set the 1958 target at 10.7 million tons. How this came about illustrates his broad-brush approach to economics. Sitting by his swimming pool in Zhongnanhai on 19 June he said to the metallurgy minister: "Last year, steel output was 5.3 million tons. Can you double it this year?" The yes-man said: "All right." And that was that.

Steel mills and related industries like coal mines were ordered to go flat out to speed up production. Rules, and common sense, were cast aside. Equipment was overworked to the point of breakdown, and over 30,000 workers were killed in serious accidents alone within a few months. Experts who tried to talk sense were persecuted. Mao set the tone for discrediting rationality by saying that "bourgeois professors' knowledge should be treated as dogs' fart, worth nothing, deserving only disdain, scorn, contempt . . ."

Even going flat out, the existing steel mills could not fulfill Mao's target. His response was to order the general population to build "back-yard furnaces." At least 90 million people were "forced," as Mao said matter-of-factly, to construct such furnaces, which Khrushchev not

---

* North Korea's Kim Il Sung turned out to be less stupid than Mao on this issue. Mao had pressed him to emulate China's anti-sparrow campaign. To humor Mao, Kim drafted a "3-Year Plan for Punishing Sparrows," but then did nothing while he watched to see how Mao's campaign turned out.

unfairly dubbed "samovar" furnaces, and which produced not steel at all, but pig iron, if that.

To feed these furnaces, the population was coerced into donating virtually every piece of metal they had, regardless of whether this was being used in productive, even essential, objects. Farm tools, even water wagons, were carted off and melted down, as were cooking utensils, iron door handles and women's hair-clips. The regime slogan was: "To hand in one pickaxe is to wipe out one imperialist, and to hide one nail is to hide one counter-revolutionary."

Across China yet more peasant houses were torn down, and their occupants made homeless, so that the timber and thatch could be burned as fuel. Most accessible mountains and hillsides were stripped bare of trees. The resulting deforestation was still causing floods decades later.

The furnaces required constant attention, consuming vast amounts of labor time. Tens of millions of peasants, plus a large proportion of draft animals, were pulled out of agriculture, leaving only women and children to bring in the crops in many places. By the end of the year, some 10 billion work-days had been lost to agriculture, about one-third of the time that would normally have gone to producing grain. Though the total 1958 crop output was slightly up on 1957, there was no increase in the amount harvested.

As the year-end deadline approached for his steel output goal, every time Mao saw his managers he would use his fingers to count the days left, and urge them: "We must make it!" By 31 December, the 10.7 million tons figure was reached, but as Mao acknowledged to his top echelon, "only 40 percent is good steel"; and more than 3 million tons were completely useless. The "good" steel had been produced by proper steel mills; the useless stuff from the backyard furnaces, almost all of which were soon abandoned. The whole venture, a gigantic waste of resources and manpower, triggered further losses: in one place, local bosses hijacked shipments of high-quality Russian alloys and had them melted down so that they could claim a bumper output, called an "Iron and Steel Sputnik." "No good at constructing, but super-good at destruction": never was Mao's own assessment of himself more accurate.

MAO WASTED MUCH of the technology and equipment bought from Russia, along with the skills of the accompanying specialists. Machinery often lay idle, as the gigantic industrial infrastructure they required was lacking. The equipment that was working was overworked, often twenty-four hours a day, while maintenance was neglected or dismissed as irrelevant. Mao encouraged ignoring regulations, and told those Chinese who were working with Russian advisers that they must not be "slaves" to Russian expertise. Russian pleas for common sense got nowhere. Even the very pro-Chinese chief adviser Arkhipov was rebuffed. In 1958, he told us, "I asked Chou and Chen Yun to try to persuade Mao to keep his ideas to himself, but Mao wouldn't listen ... They said to me: Very sorry; Mao didn't agree with the Soviet side." In June 1959, Soviet deputy premier Aleksandr Zasyadko, a metallurgy and missile silo expert, visited China and afterwards reported to Khrushchev that "They've let the whole thing go to pot."

By the end of 1958, the number of *large* arms-centered industrial projects that were under construction had reached a staggering 1,639—yet only 28 had been completed and were producing anything at all. Many were never finished, because of a lack of basic materials like steel, cement, coal and electricity. The regime itself called these "greybeard projects." Mao was the only ruler in history to produce a rust-bowl at the start of industrialization rather than at its end.

All this was destructive to Mao's own dreams. The breakneck speed he imposed sabotaged quality and created a long-term problem that was to plague arms production throughout his reign. China ended up with planes that could not fly, tanks that would not go in a straight line (on one occasion a tank swerved round and charged at watching VIPs), and ships that were almost a greater hazard to those who sailed in them than to China's enemies. When Mao decided to give Ho Chi Minh a helicopter, the manufacturers were so scared it might crash that they detained it at the border.

The four-year Leap was a monumental waste of both natural resources and human effort, unique in scale in the history of the world. One big difference between other wasteful and inefficient regimes and Mao's is that most predatory regimes have robbed their populations after relatively low-intensity labor, and less systematically, but Mao first worked everyone to the bone unrelentingly, then took everything—and then squandered it.

Mao demanded a fever pitch of work, using non-stop "emulation" drives to make people vie with each other. Undernourished and exhausted men, women and children were made to move soil at the double, often having to run while carrying extremely heavy loads, and in all weathers, from blazing sun to freezing cold. They had to trot for kilometers along mountain paths carrying water for the fields, from dawn till dusk. They had to stay up all night to keep the useless "backyard furnaces" going. Mao called this way of working "Communist spirit." In one of his many bits of theater, on 6 November 1958 he first asserted that peasants refused to take breaks ("even if you want them to rest, they won't"), and then played magnanimous and codified his optimal day: "Change from 1 January next year: guarantee 8 hours sleep, 4 hours eating and breaks, 2 hours studies [i.e., indoctrination] ... 8–4–2–10," with the "10" referring to the hours of work. In the same generous tone, he bestowed a few days off: two a month, and five for women (up from the three he had originally contemplated).

In fact, these tiny concessions resulted in part from reports of epidemics, which Mao took seriously, not least because they affected the workforce. One account that startled Mao involved a typhoid epidemic near Peking. He called for "greatly reducing diseases" so that people "can go labouring every day."

IN SUMMER 1958 Mao pitchforked the entire rural population into new and larger units called "People's Communes." The aim was to make slave-driving more efficient. He himself said that by concentrating the peasants into fewer units—26,000-plus in the whole of China—"it's easier to control." The first commune, "Chayashan Sputnik," was set up in his model province, Henan. Its charter, which Mao edited, and touted as "a great treasure," laid down that every aspect of its members' lives was to be controlled by the commune. All the 9,369 households had to "hand over entirely their private plots . . . their houses, animals and trees." They had to live in dormitories, "in accordance with the principles of benefiting production and control"; and the charter actually stipulated that their homes were to be "dismantled" "if the commune needs the bricks, tiles or timber." Every peasant's life must revolve around "labour." All members were to be treated as though in the army, with a three-tier regimentation system: commune, brigade, production team (usually a village). Peasants were allowed negligible amounts of cash. The communes were de facto camps for slave-laborers.

Mao even toyed with getting rid of people's names and replacing them with numbers. In Henan and other model areas, people worked in the fields with a number sewn on their backs. Mao's aim was to dehuman-ize China's 550 million peasants and turn them into the human equiva-lent of draft animals.

As befitted the labor-camp culture, inmates had to eat in canteens. Peasants were not only banned from eating at home, their woks and stoves were smashed. Total control over food gave the state a terrifying weapon, and withholding food became a commonplace form of "light" punish-ment, which grassroots officials could deploy against anyone they felt like.

As the canteens were sometimes hours' walk away from where people lived or worked, many tended to move to the site of the canteen. There, men, women, children and old people lived like animals, crammed into whatever space was available, with no privacy or family life. This also hugely increased the incidence of disease. Meanwhile, many of their own homes, which were often made of mud and bamboo, collapsed from neglect, in addition to all those torn down to make fertilizer, or to feed the backyard furnaces as fuel. When Liu Shao-chi inspected one area near his home village in spring 1961, of the previous 1,415 abodes, only 621 decrepit huts remained.

Mao's claim about there being "too much food" contributed in another way to increasing the peasants' misery. When the canteens were first set up, many cadres allowed the hungry peasants to fill their stomachs. This spree only lasted a couple of months, but it hastened the onset of famine— and wholesale deaths—in many areas before the end of 1958. Three years later, Mao reluctantly agreed to abandon canteens. Yet closing down the canteens, though hugely popular in itself, was almost as painful as their opening had been, as the many peasants who had gone to live where the canteens were located now had no home to return to. Even when their dwellings had survived, their stoves and their woks had not.

UNDERNOURISHMENT and overwork quickly reduced tens of millions of peasants to a state where they were simply too enfeebled to work. When he found out that one county was doling out food to those too ill to work, Mao's response was: "This won't do. Give them this amount and they don't work. Best halve the basic ration, so if they're hungry they have to try harder."

The people who drove the peasants on were the commune cadres, who were Party men. These were the resident slave-drivers. Knowing that if they failed to do their job, they and their families would swiftly join the ranks of the starving, many adopted the attitude articulated by one man: people were "slaves who have to be beaten, abused, or have their food suspended to get them to work."

These cadres doubled as jailers, keeping the peasants penned inside their villages. On 19 August 1958, Mao clamped down even further on anyone moving without authorization, what he called "people roaming around uncontrolled." The traditional possibility of escaping a famine by fleeing to a place where there was food, which had long been made illegal, was now blocked off. One peasant described the situation as worse than under the Japanese occupation: "Even when the Japanese came," he said, "we could run away. This year [1960] ... we are simply shut in to die at home. My family had six members and four have died ..."

The cadres' other job was to stop peasants "stealing" their own harvest. Horrific punishments were widespread: some people were buried alive, others strangled with ropes, others had their noses cut off. In one village, four terrorized young children were saved from being buried alive for taking some food only when the earth was at their waists, after desperate pleas from their parents. In another village, a child had four fingers chopped off for trying to steal a scrap of unripe food; in another, two children who tried to steal food had wires run through their ears, and were then hung up by the wire from a wall. Brutality of this kind crops up in virtually every account of this period, nationwide.

AS PART OF his Leap, in 1958 Mao also tried to turn the cities into slave-labor camps by organizing urban communes. His plan was to abolish wages and put the whole society on a non-cash barracks system. This did not work out, as the slave system could not be made to fit onto modern cities, where life had more complex dimensions.

But this failure did not mean that Mao left the cities unravaged. His guideline for them was "Production first, Life takes second place." His ideal city was a purely industrial center. Standing on Tiananmen Gate and looking out over the gorgeous palaces and temples and pagodas which in those days decorated Peking's skyline, he told the mayor: "In the future, I want to look around and see chimneys everywhere!"

Worse, Mao wanted to destroy existing cities on a massive scale and build industrial centers on the ruins. In 1958 the regime did a survey of historic monuments in Peking. It listed 8,000—and decided to keep *seventy-eight*. Everyone who heard of the scheme, from the mayor down, pleaded against this level of destruction. Eventually, the order was not carried out so drastically—for a while. But at Mao's insistence, the centuries-old city walls and gates were mostly razed to the ground, and the earth used to fill in a beautiful lake in the city. "I am delighted that city walls in Nanjing, Jinan, and so on, are [also] torn down," Mao said. He was fond of mocking cultural figures who shed tears of anguish at such senseless destruction, and intellectuals were deliberately made to work on the wrecking crews. Many of the visible signs of Chinese civilization disappeared forever from the face of the earth.

Time and again, Mao expressed his loathing for Chinese architecture, while praising European and Japanese buildings, which he saw as representing the achievements of militaristic states. "I can't stand the houses in Peking and Kaifeng [old capitals]. I much prefer the ones in Qingdao and Changchun," he remarked to his inner circle in January 1958. Qingdao was a former German colony, while Changchun had been built by the Japanese as the capital for the puppet state of Manchukuo. Mao repeatedly called these two cities "the best."

Mao permitted few things with a Chinese character to be built. In the early years of his rule, some buildings in old Chinese style had been put up, but these were soon denounced for their traditional design. When new edifices were put up to mark the tenth anniversary of the regime in 1959, they were built in the Soviet style. They were actually the only Mao-era buildings with even a nod to aesthetics. The rest were factories and utilitarian, gray concrete matchbox blocks.

The best-known of the new buildings was the Great Hall of the People, in central Peking. This was where Mao intended to hold large prestigious meetings, and he specifically ordered the auditorium to be designed to hold as many as 10,000 people. The Great Hall itself, 171,800 square meters in area, was erected on one side of Tiananmen Square in front of the old imperial palace, the Forbidden City. Determined to outdo other totalitarian rulers in gigantism, Mao gave orders to make the Square into "the biggest square in the world, capable of holding a rally of one million people." What had been a square of 11 hectares, with great character, was quadrupled in size, destroying large swaths of the old city. The result was a vast concrete space devoid of human warmth, the dehumanized heart of Mao's regime.

PEOPLE STARVED in the cities too, although death tolls were much lower than in the countryside. Nonetheless, most urban dwellers could barely survive on the rations they got. "Life seemed to proceed in slow motion," a Polish witness observed in Peking. "Rickshaw drivers barely able to pedal . . . tens of thousands of comatose cyclists . . . dejection stared out of the eyes of passersby." The urban meat ration declined annually from 5.1 kg per person in 1957 to an all-time low of just over 1.5 kg in 1960. People were told to eat "food substitutes." One was a green roe-like substance called chlorella, which grew in urine and contained some protein. After Chou En-lai tasted and approved this disgusting stuff, it soon provided a high proportion of the urban population's protein.

This famine, which was nationwide, started in 1958 and lasted through 1961, peaking in 1960. That year, the regime's own statistics recorded, average daily calorie intake fell to 1,534.8. According to a major apologist for the regime, Han Suyin, urban housewives were getting a maximum 1,200 calories a day in 1960. At Auschwitz, slave-laborers got between 1,300 and 1,700 calories per day. They were worked about eleven hours a day, and most who did not find extra food died within several months.

During the famine, some resorted to cannibalism. One post-Mao study (promptly suppressed), of Fengyang county in Anhui province, recorded sixty-three cases of cannibalism in the spring of 1960 alone, including that of a couple who strangled and ate their eight-year-old son. And Fengyang was probably not the worst. In one county in Gansu where one-third of the population died, cannibalism was rife. One village cadre, whose wife, sister and children all died then, later told journalists: "So many people in the village have eaten human flesh . . . See those people squatting outside the commune office sunning themselves? Some of them ate human flesh . . . People were just driven crazy by hunger."

While all this was happening, there was plenty of food in state granaries, which were guarded by the army. Some food was simply allowed to rot. A Polish student saw fruit "rotting by the ton" in southeast China in summer–autumn 1959. But the order from above was: "Absolutely no opening the granary door even if people are dying of starvation" (*e-si bu-kai-cang*).

CLOSE TO 38 million people died of starvation and overwork in the Great Leap Forward and the famine, which lasted four years.* The figure is confirmed by Mao's No. 2, Liu Shao-chi himself. Even before the famine had ended, he told Soviet ambassador Stepan Chervonenko that 30 million had already died.

This was the greatest famine of the twentieth century—and of all recorded human history. Mao knowingly starved and worked these tens of millions of people to death. During the two critical years 1958–59, grain exports alone, almost exactly 7 million tons, would have provided the equivalent of over 840 calories per day for 38 million people—the difference between life and death. And this was only grain; it does not include the meat, cooking oil, eggs and other foodstuffs that were exported in very large quantities. Had this food not been exported (and instead distributed according to humane criteria), very probably not a single person in China would have had to die of hunger.

Mao had actually allowed for many more deaths. Although slaughter was not his purpose with the Leap, he was more than ready for myriad deaths to result, and had hinted to his top echelon that they should not be too shocked if they happened. At the May 1958 congress that kicked off the Leap, he told his audience they should not only not fear, but should actively welcome, people dying as a result of their Party's policy. "Wouldn't it be disastrous if Confucius were still alive today?" he said. The Taoist philosopher Chuang Tzu, he said, "was right to lounge and sing when his wife died. There should be celebration rallies when people die." Death, said Mao, "is indeed to be rejoiced over . . . We believe in dialectics, and so we can't not be in favor of death."

This airy yet ghoulish "philosophy" was relayed down to grassroots officials. In Fengyang county in Anhui, when one cadre was shown the corpses of people who had died from starvation and overwork, he repeated almost word for word what Mao had said: "If people don't die, the earth

---

* This figure is based on the following calculation. Chinese demographers have concluded that death rates in the four years 1958–61 were 1.20 percent, 1.45 percent, 4.34 percent and 2.83 percent, respectively. The average death rate in the three years immediately before and after the famine was 1.03 percent (1957: 1.08 percent; 1962: 1 percent; and 1963:1 percent). The death rates over and above this average could only have been caused by starvation and overwork during the famine. The "extra" death figure comes to 37.67 million, based on population figures of 646.53, 659.94, 666.71, and 651.71 million for 1957, 1958, 1959 and 1960. The official statistics published in 1983 are recognized as partly defective, because local policemen understated the number of deaths in the years 1959–61 after some were purged for "over-reporting deaths."

won't be able to hold them! People live and people die. Who doesn't die?" Even wearing mourning was forbidden; even shedding tears—since Mao said that death should be celebrated.

Mao saw practical advantage in massive deaths. "Deaths have benefits," he told the top echelon on 9 December 1958. "They can fertilise the ground." Peasants were therefore ordered to plant crops over burial plots, which caused intense anguish.

We can now say with assurance how many people Mao was ready to dispense with. When he was in Moscow in 1957, he had said: "We are prepared to sacrifice 300 million Chinese for the victory of the world revolution." That was about half the population of China then. Indeed, Mao told the Party congress on 17 May 1958: "Don't make a fuss about a world war. At most, people die . . . Half the population wiped out—this happened quite a few times in Chinese history . . . It's best if half the population is left, next best one-third . . ."

Nor was Mao just thinking about a war situation. On 21 November 1958, talking to his inner circle about the labor-intensive projects like waterworks and making "steel," and tacitly, almost casually, assuming a context where peasants had too little to eat and were being worked to exhaustion, Mao said: "Working like this, with all these projects, half of China may well have to die. If not half, one-third, or one-tenth—50 million—die." Aware that these remarks might sound too shocking, he tried to shirk his own responsibility. "Fifty million deaths," he went on, "I could be fired, and I might even lose my head . . . but if you insist, I'll just have to let you do it, and you can't blame me when people die."

DEFENSE MINISTER
PENG'S LONELY BATTLE

(1958–59 ★ AGE 64–65)

I N THE FIRST two years of the Great Leap Forward, most of Mao's colleagues went along with him. Only one man in the Politburo, Marshal Peng De-huai, the defense minister, had the courage to dissent.

Peng had stayed close to his poverty-stricken peasant roots. In an account of his life written later while imprisoned by Mao he recorded that he often reminded himself of his famished childhood to avoid "becoming corrupt, or callous about the lives of the poor." In the 1950s he spoke up among the top echelon about Mao's corrupt lifestyle: the villas all over China, and the procurement of pretty girls, which Peng described as "selecting imperial concubines."

Peng had crossed swords with Mao over the years. In the 1930s he had criticized Mao's vicious treatment of other military commanders. On the Long March he had challenged Mao for the military leadership when Mao was dragging the Red Army to near-ruin for his personal goals. In the 1940s, when Mao began his personality cult during the Yenan Terror, Peng had raised objections to rituals like shouting "Long Live Chairman Mao!," and singing the Mao anthem, "The East Is Red." Once Khrushchev denounced Stalin in 1956, Peng spoke out more forcefully against the personality cult, and even advocated changing the oath that servicemen took, from one that pledged allegiance to Mao personally, to one that pledged allegiance to the nation, arguing that "Our army belongs to the nation."

This was guaranteed to rile Mao. Besides, Mao loathed the fact that Peng had not only expressed esteem for Khrushchev over de-Stalinization, but had also urged that spending on defense industries in peacetime "must be compatible with people's standard of living."

Peng had often voiced independent, unorthodox views. He openly admired the concepts of "Liberty, Equality and Fraternity," which Mao denounced as "anti-Marxist." Peng also advocated observing traditional Chinese ethical codes like "A prince and the man in the street are equal before the law" and "Do not do to others what you don't want done to yourself." My "principle," Mao said, "is exactly the opposite: Do to others precisely what I don't want done to myself."

Peng had been a thorn in Mao's side for three decades, although he had also cooperated with Mao at certain key moments, like going into Korea in 1950. It was as a result of this that Mao made him defense minister in 1954—reluctantly, as Mao himself revealed later. Throughout Peng's tenure, Mao undermined him by creating competing chains of command. Still, Peng retained a fearlessness vis-à-vis Mao that was unique among top leaders.

WHEN HE LAUNCHED the Leap in May 1958, Mao plunged Peng and some 1,500 senior army officers into daily "criticism and self-criticism" meetings, at which they were made to attack each other for weeks on end. Such sessions, which had become a Maoist staple since the Yenan Terror, were full of bitter character-assassination, and were emotionally utterly draining.* Peng felt so demoralized that he offered to resign, an offer Mao rejected because he wanted to purge Peng. Meanwhile, he elevated his crony Marshal Lin Biao to be a vice-chairman of the Party, which put Lin above Peng, in the army as well as the Party.

These upheavals consumed Peng's time and energy until late July, when the criticism meetings were brought to a close. Only then was he able to start taking stock of the fearsome panorama around him. He could see that Mao was fixated on acquiring an absolutely gigantic strike force— no fewer than 200–300 nuclear submarines, as Mao had insisted to the Russians, and every other state-of-the art weapon Russia possessed—and that Mao would go to any lengths to achieve this goal. One step towards this end was to shell the Nationalist-held island of Quemoy in August, with the aim of triggering nuclear threats from America in order to put pressure on Khrushchev. (Peng was deliberately excluded from this exercise, even though he was the army chief.) Then there was the flood of bogus harvest figures, which could only mean one thing: that Mao was aiming to squeeze out far greater quantities of food to pay for the enormous amount of hardware he was acquiring from Russia.

On the evening of 3 September, shortly after the shelling of Quemoy had started, Peng disappeared while at the seaside resort of Beidaihe for a round of meetings. Eventually, after a long search, the Praetorian Guard found him pacing a remote stretch of beach in the moonlight, alone. With a darkened face, he returned to his villa, where he lay awake all night.

---

* At the end of these sessions, Mao victimized a host of prominent generals, to make the point that the top brass must keep their distance from the Russians. Mao's message was: The only thing you are to learn from the Russians is how to use modern weapons.

Afterwards, he set off on an inspection tour of northern China, during which he learned that the crop figures were indeed inflated, and that peasants were dying of starvation. He saw for the first time the disastrous impact of Mao's pet obsession, the backyard furnaces. Passing through Henan, Mao's model province, he saw the furnaces getting denser, with crowds and carts and shovels and ladders and baskets, and flames stretching out like a blazing sea to the horizon. Gazing out of the train window, he turned to his aide-de-camp and shook his head: "These fires are going to burn up everything we have."

At the beginning of December, at a conference in Wuhan, Peng heard Mao announce that the harvest figure for 1958 was more than double 1957's, which had been a very good year. Peng said that this was impossible, but Mao's agriculture chiefs shut him up with what amounted to "We know better than you."

Peng decided to go back to his home area in Hunan, which was in the same county as Mao's home village, to find out what was really happening. There, he got confirmation that the harvest figures were false. Peasants had had their homes torn down to feed the backyard furnaces; they were being worked to the point of collapse; and grassroots cadres were using violence to force them to work. "In some areas, it has become common practice to beat people up," Peng wrote. "People are beaten up when they can't fulfill their work quota, beaten up when they are late going out to work, beaten up even for saying things some don't like." Peng also registered the special misery that Mao's slave-driving was inflicting on women: overwork, he noted, had caused "many women to suffer prolapses of the womb, or premature stoppage of menstruation."

Peng's childhood friends had famished, waxen faces. They showed him their canteen wok, which contained only vegetable leaves and a few grains of rice, with no oil. Their beds were just cold bamboo mats with flimsy quilts, in freezing December. As his coevals were sixty-ish, they were living in the commune's quarters for the old, called the "Happiness Court." "What sort of Happiness is this?" Peng exploded. The beds in the kindergarten had only thin rags. Many children were ill. Peng gave the kindergarten 200 yuan out of his own pocket, and left another 200 yuan to buy bedding for the old. A Red Army veteran who had been disabled in the 1930s tucked a piece of paper into his palm. It was an entreaty for Peng to "cry out for us."

On 18 December, Peng met one of the top economic managers, Bo Yi-bo, and told him Mao's figure for the grain harvest was unreal, and that they must not collect food on the basis of this exaggeration. Bo agreed with him. In fact, all Mao's economic managers, as well as Politburo members, knew the truth. But when Peng suggested that he and Bo send a joint telegram to Mao, Bo declined. So Peng cabled Mao on his own, urging that food collection be reduced. There was no response.

Peng knew his report was not news to Mao, who had reprised his offhand views about death at Wuhan earlier that month: "A few children die in the kindergarten, a few old men die in the Happiness Court . . . If there's no death, human beings can't exist. From Confucius to now, it would be disastrous if people didn't die."

How could Mao be stopped? Even though he was defense minister, Peng had little power—nothing like the power which defense ministers had in other countries. The army was completely controlled by Mao, and Peng could not move troops without Mao's explicit permission. Peng began to contemplate seeking help from the only possible source—abroad.

With no access to the West, Peng's only hope was Eastern Europe, and Khrushchev. This was an extremely long shot. He decided, it seems, to try and make a sounding, on the off-chance.

PENG HAD long-standing invitations to visit Eastern Europe. Getting there meant passing through Moscow, and Mao had indicated that he was not keen on Peng taking up the invitations. But he agreed on 28 February 1959, after Peng had taken the uncharacteristic step of pressing him for his consent.

The beady Mao guessed Peng was up to something. On 5 April, shortly before Peng's scheduled departure, Mao exploded to a top Party gathering: "Is comrade Peng De-huai here? . . . you really hate me to death . . ." Mao then flew into a temper the like of which those close to him said they had never seen. "We have always been battling each other . . ." Mao exclaimed. "My principle is: You don't mess with me and I won't mess with you; but mess with me, and I sure as hell will mess with you!"

That night, Peng was seen pacing up and down his office. When a secretary came to consult him about plans for the following day, Peng, who never mentioned private matters, astonished him by suddenly speaking with melancholy about how much he missed his former wife. His current wife was a scared and "correct" Party person, from whom he could not expect understanding or support for the course of action on which he was about to embark.

On 20 April, just before leaving for Europe, Peng attended a reception given by ambassadors of the countries he was to visit. There he did something unprecedented. He took Soviet ambassador Yudin into a separate room and, with only a Russian embassy interpreter present, which was a major breach of the rules, initiated a conversation about the Great Leap Forward. According to the interpreter, Peng's sounding was cautious: "Only by the character of his questions and the tone in which they were

put was it possible to understand his negative attitude towards 'the leap.' "
The interpreter told us: "It seemed Peng wanted to see what the ambassador would say about the Great Leap—to get the ambassador's opinion." Yudin waffled about the "positive" aspects of the Leap. "What stuck in my mind," the interpreter recalled, "were the Marshal's mournful eyes, reflecting a gamut of feelings: from alarm for the fate of his country to firm determination to fight for its future."

Peng found no more sympathy when he got to Europe. East Germany's leader, Ulbricht, said he knew that China was enjoying fantastic growth in agriculture, and could it send more meat so that they could match West Germany's annual consumption of 80 kg per capita? In China, even in the cities, the meat ration for the whole year was only a few kilos.

After Ulbricht spoke, Peng fell silent for a long time before telling his host that there was actually a tremendous food shortage. Ulbricht, an old Stalinist who had concocted a few claims himself, was unmoved. Whether Mao's claims were true or not was immaterial to him. In fact, food imports from China had just allowed East Germany, with a standard of living incomparably higher than China's, to end rationing, in May 1958. (Later, when tens of millions of Chinese had already died of starvation, Ulbricht asked Mao for more food, on 11 January 1961. When Chou told East European ambassadors that China could not deliver all the food it had contracted to send, and asked to postpone or cancel some contracts, Poland showed understanding, but East Germany flatly refused even to consider a postponement, and pressed for delivery on the dot. "Great Germany above all," Chou remarked, but still sent 23,000 tons of soybeans.)

After his conversation with Ulbricht, Peng burst out to his staff: "How would our people feel if they heard they were being asked to help others have 80 kg of meat a year?" His next stop was Czechoslovakia. When he told the Czechs about what was really happening in China, and said that anyone but the Chinese would be taking to the streets, he got little reaction. Peng realized that the East European regimes were a lost cause. They "all pay great attention to arms," he noted. "They all have a privileged class trained by the Soviet Union." The bottom line was that these regimes did not care what it cost the Chinese people to supply food to them, even if it meant Chinese dying; Eastern Europe's imports of food from China reached their highest levels yet in 1958.* Throughout the trip, Peng was downcast.

Peng's last stop in Europe was Albania. When he arrived there, on 28 May, he found that Khrushchev had just turned up, unexpectedly, for his

---

* Eastern Europe also allowed Peng to anticipate Mao's gruesome mausoleum. "We have seen the corpses of the leaders: Lenin, Stalin, Gottwald, Dimitrov. Every country has one. The Asian countries probably will also have these in the future."

first-ever visit. Any hopes Peng might have entertained about Khrushchev perhaps having come specially to meet him were dashed at once. Khrushchev had no Chinese-language interpreter with him.

Khrushchev was in Albania for a very different reason. Albania provided Russia with a unique submarine base in the heart of the Mediterranean, on Sazan Island. Peng's own mission, dictated by Mao, was also geared to this base. On his first full day in Albania, 29 May, Peng got up at 5:30 AM and headed straight there. The purpose of Khrushchev's visit was to try to prevent the Albanians doing a deal with China over the base.* Peng saw that he could not count on Khrushchev, or any of the Communist countries, for help.

It seems that Peng then, in desperation, contemplated something akin to a military coup. When he returned to Peking on 13 June, the first thing he did was to try to move some military forces "to transport grain to famine-stricken areas," he told the army chief of staff, Huang Ke-cheng, who was a close friend and a kindred spirit. Huang clearly understood what Peng wanted the troops for, as he expressed a degree of reluctance that he would not have shown if he had thought the proposal was really about transporting food. Mao seems to have got wind of this conversation, and had Peng grilled intensely about it later. As all troop movements had to have Mao's authorization, Peng was unable to move any forces. All he could do was try to exert pressure on Mao by sending him annotated reports about the famine, and lobby others to do likewise. Seeing famished peasants from the train, he would say to his companions: "If China's workers and peasants weren't so nice, we would have had to invite in the Soviet Red Army [to prop up the Communist regime]!"

Mao had followed Peng's every step in Europe through spies in the delegation, and knew Peng had got nowhere. Mao was soon to remark complacently that Peng had gone abroad "to sniff around," but had been unable to do any more than that. As soon as he was convinced that Peng had secured no foreign backing, Mao decided to pounce. Part of his calculation was to use the purge of Peng to kick off a wider terror campaign. Mao badly needed to keep up the great squeeze, as China was falling behind on payments to Russia. The trouble for Mao was that grassroots officials, out of pity, were often holding off taking food that the peasants needed to survive. Mao knew that much of his own machine, as well as the entire nation, was resisting his policies. In February and March 1959

---

* When Albania broke with Russia, control of the submarines there was at the core of the bust-up. In January 1961, Peking gave the Albanian leader, Enver Hoxha, the gigantic sum of 500m rubles, and when the Russians tried to pull their submarines out in early June that year, Hoxha used force to hold four of them back, and almost certainly gave Mao access to them.

he had said quite a few times: "Several hundred million peasants and production team leaders are united against the Party." Even his provincial bosses now mostly kept an awkward silence when he pressed them to cough up more food. Mao needed his stand-by, terror, to steel his machine.

ON 20 JUNE 1959, a week after Peng returned from Europe, Mao left Peking by train. It was ferociously hot, and the electric fan was switched off in case Mao caught cold. A big bowl of ice was placed in his carriage, to little avail. All the men, Mao included, stripped down to their underpants. (Immediately after this, an air-conditioned train was ordered for Mao from East Germany.) To cool himself off, Mao went swimming in the Yangtze and the Xiang River—which doubled up for him as baths. He had not taken a bath or a shower, or washed his hair, since 1949, almost a decade before, when he discovered the pleasure of being rubbed by a servant with a hot towel and having his hair and skull combed by his barber.

Meanwhile, he began to make ready for his showdown. On the 24th, he told his secretary to telephone Peking to call a conference at Lushan, the mountain resort above the Yangtze. Mao dictated a list of the participants, but did not spell out that this was to be a forum to condemn Peng.

Having decided on the highest-level purge since he took power, it seems that Mao felt he needed personal confirmation that he still held godlike status, and was invincible. He was staying at the time near his home village, Shaoshan. On the spur of the moment, he decided to go there to sniff the air.

This was Mao's first visit home in thirty-two years, even though he had passed by the area frequently. The local authorities had built a villa for him, at his express wish. Pine Hill No. 1, situated in pine woods, had been on standby for years. They had also evicted any "undesirable" families years before, to prevent them from getting near Mao—or bumping into visiting foreigners.

Mao stayed two nights in Shaoshan. Having invited complaints, he got them aplenty. The harvests, the villagers told him, had been inflated. Those who had made objections had been put through denunciation meetings and beaten up. An old man inquired whether it was Mao's idea that men and women should live segregated lives in barracks conditions (which had come with the communes in many parts of China). Above all, they were hungry, as they were getting only *between one-third and one-quarter* of what was traditionally considered enough in this area. When Mao gave a meal to several dozen villagers, they wolfed it all down unceremoniously.

There was not a word of support for Mao's policies, even here in his home village, which was extremely privileged and was receiving large state subsidies. But Mao could also see that although the discontent was massive, no one dared to do more than grumble, and some complaints had to be dressed up as flattery. "Chairman," one said, "if you hadn't come to Shaoshan, soon we would all die of hunger." When one young man complained more bitterly than others, Mao pulled a long face and snapped: "After all, it's better than the old days." Though this was a pathetic untruth (he himself had said in "the old days" that in Shaoshan "it is easy to get rich"), nobody called Mao's bluff. Neither did anyone challenge his subsequent instruction, which was transparently irrelevant: "Eat more in busy seasons and eat less in slack seasons. And be thrifty with food . . ." When he turned to the provincial leaders and said unashamedly that the complaints were "appeals against you; it is your responsibility, write them down," the scapegoats took it in silence.

Mao's personality cult had ensured that he was untouchable. A young servant at the guest house had spent three sleepless nights and days cleaning the place up. Decades later, she recounted how the manager had called her in. " 'Can I give you the best and most glorious task?' I said: 'Certainly . . .' " It turned out to be washing Mao's dirty underwear.

> Wow, it was Chairman Mao's clothes. This is really, really fantastic . . .
> They had been drenched in sweat. This color, yellow. One shirt, one pair of long underpants . . . I thought of Chairman Mao: he was the leader of the people of the world and yet he lived such a hard life. [!] The underwear felt so flimsy I didn't dare to rub, so I stroked them gently. What was I to do if I messed them up? . . . I was afraid someone might see them [hanging out to dry], and might do something . . . so every few minutes I went out and felt them to see whether they were dry . . . There was no electricity and no electric iron.* But I had to make the clothes look pretty. So before they were dry, I folded them and put them under the glass top of the desk to press them . . . When I delivered them to the director, he said: "Very good, very good." But I was thinking: it won't do if Chairman Mao doesn't like my work . . .

Mao left Shaoshan with no doubt that he would come out on top against Peng.

RISING ALMOST 1,500 meters sheer out of the steamy Yangtze plain, Lushan had the air of a magic mountain divorced from life below. It was permanently veiled by swiftly massing and evaporating clouds. A great poet, Su Shi, has left an immortal poem about its mystery:

> *Unable to see the true face of Lushan*
> *No surprise, as you are inside it.*

---

* Electricity was installed for Mao the next time he was nearby, on 18 May 1960. This took 470 workers, who had to battle a force-8 gale. Even so, Mao did not drop in again.

Clouds of the most fabulous shapes gushed from the gorges up the cliffs, swaying in front of pedestrians on the paved streets. Sometimes, as one sat chatting, clouds would imperceptibly envelop one's interlocutors—only to unwrap them an instant later. One could even catch the surreal moment of a cloud curling and floating in through an open window, then turning and sailing out of another.

Europeans turned Lushan into a summer resort in the late nineteenth century. Here, bamboo and pines, waterfalls and mossy rocks, offered blissful relief from the stifling heat of the lowlands. At its center, Kuling, there were over 800 villas in different European styles. It became Chiang Kai-shek's summer capital for thirteen years. A villa originally built for an Englishman had been Chiang's residence, and it now became Mao's. During the Chiangs' last stay, in August 1948, Chiang had named it "Villa of Beauty"—"Mei-lu" (the character "beauty" being part of Mme Chiang's given name, Mei-ling). Knowing that his days on the Mainland were numbered, Chiang inscribed the name and had it carved into the rock at the villa entrance. When Mao saw masons trying to chisel it out, he stopped them.

Chiang and earlier residents had ascended Lushan in sedan chairs if they did not fancy a steep walk up of 7–8 km. The Communists had built a road. When Mao's motorcade was on it, no other cars were allowed from top to bottom. The whole mountain was sealed off during his stay; even residents outside the villa area were sent away. Mao's security was immeasurably tighter than Chiang's. In fact, after this one visit, Mao became dissatisfied with Chiang's villa, as he was with all the old villas selected for him all over China. Here too he ordered one of his enormous bullet- and bomb-proof warehouse-style bunkers of cement, steel and stone. This new estate, Reeds Wood No. 1, which was completed two years later, was built beside a reservoir, so that Mao could go swimming at his leisure. This, like many other villas of Mao's, was built during the worst years of the famine.

In the face of raging mass starvation, Mao made a point of generating a holiday atmosphere at Lushan. Participants had been specially instructed to bring their wives and children. (For many of the children, this was their first experience inside European villas, whose flush toilets and stone walls mesmerized them.) The food was excellent; even the staff canteen served more than half a dozen dishes at each meal. In the evenings, there were local operas chosen by Mao, and dances in a former Catholic church, with dancing girls bussed in. At least one of the dancers and one of the resort nurses were summoned to Mao's villa "for a chat."

Mao's womanizing was now more brazen than ever. In Zhongnanhai, a new lounge was added to the dance hall, and a bed installed there. Mao would take one or several girls into it to engage in sexual play or orgies.

The lounge was well insulated so the noise did not carry, and the thick floor-to-ceiling velvet curtain would be drawn behind them. It was obvious what Mao disappeared in there for, but he did not care.

WHEN PENG arrived at Lushan for the conference, he was stopped as he entered the villa area by guards with little flags: "Group One"—code-name for Mao—was resting. Peng had to get out and walk. His villa, No. 176, was about 100 meters from Mao's—so Mao's security men could monitor him easily.

The conference of over 100 top officials began on 2 July 1959. Mao's first tactic was to split the participants into six groups, each chaired and controlled by a trusted provincial chief, who reported directly to Mao. Discussions were confined to these groups, so any unwanted views would have only a restricted audience. The rest of the participants could find out only what Mao wanted them to read in the conference bulletin, which was printed by his office.

When Peng spoke to his group, the Northwest Group, he voiced his views about the Leap, raising the issue of the phantom harvest claims, and basically called Mao a liar: "The growth figure claimed by . . . Chairman Mao's home place for last year was far higher than the real figure. I was there and asked around and learned that the increase was only 16 percent . . . and even that was because the state gave large subsidies and loans."/"The Chairman has also been to this commune. I asked the Chairman: What was your information through your investigation? He said he didn't talk about it. I think he did."

Peng spelled out Mao's responsibility again the next day: "The 10.7 million [tons of steel, the 1958 target] was decided by Chairman Mao. You cannot say he didn't have responsibility." Over the following days, Peng called into question Mao's role in the villa-building spree, and warned that Mao "must not abuse his prestige." Peng also hit out at Mao's policy of squeezing out food for export "at the cost of domestic consumption."

But, as Mao had made sure would be the case, Peng's words did not percolate beyond his group. In frustration, on 14 July, Peng wrote a letter to Mao, criticizing the Great Leap Forward, using carefully phrased language. His hope was that this would set off a real debate about the Leap. Mao circulated the letter to the other participants, only to turn it into an excuse to purge Peng.

Mao had been watching Peng like a cobra to see whether Peng was involved in any conspiracy, which was the only way Mao could really be threatened. He wanted to know who was coming to see Peng so he could round them all up.

In fact, Peng had put out some feelers. He knew that Lo Fu, the former Party No. 1, was opposed to Mao's policies, and Peng had asked Lo to read the letter he was sending to Mao. But Lo declined; and when Peng tried to read it out to him, Lo jumped up and fled. Mao had instilled such fear about "plotting" that people were simply paralyzed when there was any whiff of it. Under Mao, as under Stalin, only one person was allowed to plot—and that, as Stalin's sidekick Molotov observed, was the boss.

Mao brought all the participants together for the first time on 23 July. He opened in a characteristically thuggish, and plaintive, manner: "You have talked so much. Now allow me to talk for an hour or so, will you? I have taken sleeping pills three times and still couldn't sleep." He made it sound as if someone had been preventing him speaking, and even sleeping. To create an atmosphere where rational debate would be smothered and he could evade the real issues, Mao worked himself into a rage, and belittled the catastrophe his policy had caused with remarks like: "All it means is a little less pork, fewer hairpins, and no soap for a while." Then he unsheathed the ultimate deterrent. If I am opposed, he declared, "I will leave . . . to lead the peasants [!] to overthrow the government . . . If the army follows you, I will go up the mountains and start guerrilla warfare . . . But I think the army will follow me." One general recalled: "We felt the atmosphere in the hall freeze." Mao had polarized the issue into one of: Peng or me; and if you back Peng, I will fight you to the death.

Everyone knew that Mao was unbeatable. He drove home the point about the army obeying him by arranging for his crony Marshal Lin Biao, whose prestige in the military was as high as Peng's, to appear at the conference the next day. Up to this moment, Lin had not been in Lushan itself; he had been on hand, lurking at the foot of the mountain.

When Lin got up to Lushan, he attacked Peng venomously, and gave Mao his total and demonstrative support. There was nothing Peng or anyone else could do to defy Mao or to reason with him. Mao had also made it easier for people to go along with him by pretending to make some concessions—on food extraction levels, steel output targets, and expenditure on arms factories—and by expressing a willingness to put some money into agriculture. Mao had no intention of honoring any of these promises, and was soon to renege on them all.

Mao labeled Peng and other critics, including Chief of Staff Huang Ke-cheng and former Party No. 1 Lo Fu, as an "anti-Party clique." He now enlarged the conference to a plenum of the Central Committee, so that his critics could be condemned more formally. Mao read out the resolution himself, and simply announced that it was passed, without even going through the motions of asking the participants to raise their hands. After the obligatory degrading denunciation meetings, Peng was put under house arrest, and the others suffered various punishments. Their families became outcasts with them. Huang's wife went out of her mind. The youngest and most junior of the group, Mao's occasional secretary

Li Rui, went through nearly 100 denunciation meetings, and was then sent to do forced labor in the Great Northern Wilderness. His wife divorced him, and under her influence his children disowned him with a frosty letter, turning down his request to have a photograph of them. He spent virtually all of the next two decades in and out of forced labor camps and solitary confinement in prison, narrowly escaping a death sentence. This bravest of men emerged with his sanity, intellect, and moral courage undiminished, and continued to speak out against injustice in the post-Mao years.

AFTER LUSHAN, Peng was replaced as defense minister by Lin Biao, who immediately started to purge Peng's sympathizers in the army. He also set about promoting Mao's cult on an even grander scale. From January 1960 he ordered the armed forces to memorize quotations from Mao—a move that was to develop into the compendium known as "the Little Red Book." Mao was overjoyed. He later told the Australian Maoist Edward Hill that Lin "has invented a new method, that is, to compile quotations . . . Confucius's *Analects* is a collection of quotations. Buddhism also has collections of quotations." Mao then mentioned the Bible. This was the company in which he thought his aphorisms belonged.

Across the nation anyone resisting hyper-requisition and slave-driving was hounded down. Over the next couple of years, according to post-Mao leader Deng Xiao-ping later on, an "estimated 10 million" people were made victims in this drive, which in addition jeopardized the life of "several tens of millions" of their relations. Many of the 10 million victims were grassroots cadres. Their replacements were people willing to slave-drive as harshly as ordered.

One other group particularly persecuted in this purge cycle was doctors, for the reason that they had so often identified starvation as the true cause of the tidal wave of illness and death. Mao wanted to ensure that the gigantic tragedy he had created remained a non-event. Even the names of diseases that suggested starvation were tabooed, like edema, which was just called "No. 2 Illness." Years later, Mao was still flagellating doctors for doing their job professionally: "Why were there so many . . . hepatitis cases in [those days]? Weren't they all you doctors' doing? You went looking for them, didn't you?"

In the following year, 1960, 22 million people died of hunger. This was the largest number in one year in any country in the history of the world.

LUSHAN ALSO SEALED the fate of Mao's ex-wife, Gui-yuan. Twenty-two years before, unable to bear his blatant womanizing and general callousness towards her, she had left Mao and gone to Moscow. In Russia she had a mental breakdown, and spent two years in a provincial psychiatric hospital where she went through a nightmare regime. She got out in autumn 1946, stable, if a little slow, and was allowed to return to China. She was banned from Peking, and in 1959, at the time of Lushan, was living nearby, in Nanchang. She had made a good recovery, but her life was lonely, as she lived on her own. She had not set eyes on Mao for twenty-two years.

On 7 July 1959, while Mao was watching Peng before pouncing, he was seized by a whim to see Gui-yuan. He sent the savvy wife of a local boss to fetch her, but specifically asked the woman not to tell Gui-yuan who it was that she was going to see, and just to say that she was invited to Lushan for a holiday—because, Mao told the intermediary, Gui-yuan "could well collapse mentally if she got too excited." Mao was well aware that Gui-yuan was in a fragile emotional state, and the shock might be more than she could take. Their daughter had told him her mother had had a relapse at the unexpected sound of Mao's voice on the radio in 1954 (one of the very rare occasions his voice was broadcast—for which the radio was reprimanded). He was prepared to risk her having a breakdown merely to gratify his whim.

Mao's selfishness cost Gui-yuan dearly. When she suddenly saw him standing in front of her, her nerves gave way. The damage was worsened by the fact that when Mao was saying goodbye he promised to see her again "tomorrow." But the next morning she was forcibly taken back to Nanchang, on his orders. This time her breakdown was worse than ever. She did not even recognize her own daughter, and would not wash, or change her clothes. Every now and then she would escape to the gate of the provincial Party HQ, hair disheveled, drooling at the mouth, demanding to know who had schemed to prevent her from seeing Mao again. She never fully recovered.

THE TIBETANS REBEL

(1950–61 ★ AGE 56–67)

FROM THE TIME he conquered China, Mao was determined to take Tibet by force. When he saw Stalin on 22 January 1950, he asked if the Soviet air force could transport supplies to Chinese troops "currently preparing for an attack on Tibet." Stalin's reply was: "It's good that you are preparing to attack. The Tibetans need to be subdued . . ." Stalin also advised flooding Tibet and other border regions with Han Chinese: "Since ethnic Chinese make up no more than 5 percent of Xinjiang's population, the percentage of ethnic Chinese should be brought to 30 . . . In fact, all the border territories should be populated by Chinese . . ." This is exactly what the Chinese Communist regime then proceeded to do.

During 1950–51, 20,000 Chinese Communist troops forced their way into Tibet. But Mao realized he was unable to send in larger numbers to occupy the whole place. There were no proper roads to supply a large army, and Mao's soldiers were not used to the altitude, while the Tibetan army was not a negligible force. So Mao played the negotiation game, pretending that he would allow the area virtual autonomy. Acting the benign moderate, he recognized the Dalai Lama, Tibet's spiritual and governmental leader, as the head of Tibet, sent him gifts like a 16mm film projector, and said reassuring things to Tibetan delegations. Meanwhile he pressed ahead with building two roads into Tibet.

In September 1954, the nineteen-year-old Dalai Lama went to Peking to attend the rubber-stamp National Assembly, of which he had been appointed a member. Mao met him at least a dozen times during his stay, which lasted half a year, and set out to charm—and disarm—him. Mao knew about his interest in science: "I know you are a reform-minded man, like myself," Mao said. "We have a lot of things in common," citing education reform. "That was the danger with Mao," the Dalai Lama told us, "everything he said—*half* true! *Half* true!" But along with the lulling, Mao was also patronizing and bullying, berating the Dalai Lama for not accepting that "religion is poison."

In an effort to do the best he could for his people, the Dalai Lama applied to join the CCP. His application was turned down. He tried to keep Mao in a good mood, and after returning to Lhasa, wrote to him in summer 1955 enclosing a Tibetan flower. Mao responded in almost sentimental language:

> Dear Dalai Lama, I was very happy to receive your letter ... I often miss you, missing the happy times when you were in Peking. When can I see you again? ... I was very happy to see the Tibetan flower which you enclosed ... I'm here enclosing one flower to you ...

Early in 1956, once the two major roads had been completed into Tibet, Mao set about requisitioning food, attacking religion and confiscating arms in a region called Kham, adjacent to Tibet and inhabited by some half a million Tibetans. The people rebelled, and by the end of March had mustered an armed force of over 60,000 men with more than 50,000 guns. Rebellions spread like wildfire in other regions where Tibetans formed a majority. Mao found himself with major wars on his hands covering huge areas of the interior; he resorted to using heavy artillery and aerial bombardment.

The mass participation and the combativeness of the rebels brought home to Mao what kind of resistance he would face in Tibet itself. In September he suspended his plans to "Maoise" Tibet.

However, two years later, with the Great Leap in 1958, food requisitioning was drastically stepped up nationwide. This encountered tenacious resistance in Tibet and the four large provinces in Western China with sizable Tibetan populations—Gansu, Qinghai, Yunnan and Sichuan. Many Tibetans had managed to retain their firearms, which for herdsmen were essential for their livelihood. They also had horses, which gave them mobility. But above all they had their own separate identity, language and religion, which enabled them to organize in secret.

In Qinghai, which is larger than France, the rebellion spread through the province. Mao gave instant orders to quell it, on 24 June. At the same time, he told his army chiefs to "be ready to deal with an all-out rebellion in Tibet" itself. He made it explicit that he positively wanted a violent, crushing solution. "In Tibet," he wrote on 22 January the following year, "there has to be a general decisive war before we can solve the problem thoroughly. The Tibetan rulers ... now have a 10,000-strong rebelling armed force with high morale, and they are our serious enemies. But this is ... a good thing. Because this makes it possible to solve our problems through war." Mao was saying: They have given me an excuse to start a war. A month later, he wrote: "The bigger the upheaval the better."

On 10 March 1959, an uprising broke out in Lhasa, after word spread that the Chinese planned to kidnap the Dalai Lama. Thousands paraded in front of his palace and through Lhasa, shouting "Chinese get out!" Next day, Mao cabled an order to let the Dalai Lama escape. His calculation was that if the Dalai Lama was killed it would inflame world opinion, particularly in the Buddhist countries and India, which Mao was courting. On the night of the 17th the Dalai Lama made his way out of Lhasa and set off for India. Once his escape was confirmed, Mao told his men: "Do all you can to hold the enemies in Lhasa . . . so when our main force arrives we can surround them and wipe them out."

THE PHYSICAL WAR had its propaganda chorus. On 7 April, Mao made inquiries about Tibetan practices. One thing he was particularly keen to know was whether the Tibetan ruling class used torture, and whether disobedient lamas were skinned alive and had their tendons severed. On the 29th, following Mao's orders, a vigorous media campaign began, painting Tibet as a terrifying place, where gruesome tortures of the kinds Mao had mentioned, plus gouging out eyes, were everyday occurrences. Aided by age-old prejudices, this propaganda drive was effective, and Mao succeeded in planting the idea in people's minds that Tibet was a land of barbarism.

There had been a very dark side to the rule of the old Tibetan theocracy, but in terms of overall brutality and suffering, Mao's rule was far worse. This is shown in a 70,000-word letter written to Chou En-lai by the second-ranking spiritual leader in Tibet, the Panchen Lama, in 1962, describing what happened in the years 1959–61. What gives the letter particular weight is that the Panchen Lama had initially welcomed Mao's troops into Tibet, and even accepted the suppression of the Lhasa rebellion in 1959. Moreover, Chou himself acknowledged that the letter was accurate.

Mao had imposed a level of requisitioning on the Tibetan economy far higher than it could possibly sustain. In the old days, the Panchen Lama wrote, "food was not that short . . . there was no death from starvation." But in 1959 and 1960 "too much grain was collected, even the food and tsampa [barley flour, Tibetans' staple food] in people's offering bags were confiscated." Requisitioning was brutal: "nearly all the reserve food, meat and butter were confiscated . . . There was no oil to light lamps, not even firewood . . ." "To survive, herdsmen had to eat many of their animals . . ." The population was herded into canteens, where they were fed "weeds, even inedible tree bark, leaves, grass roots and seeds." Food traditionally fed to animals had "now become rare nutritious delicious foods." People's health declined dramatically: "A tiny infectious illness like a cold led to . . . masses of deaths. Quite a lot . . . also died directly of starvation . . . Death rate was really terrible . . . Such awful pain of hunger had never existed in Tibetan history."

While he was writing the letter, the Panchen Lama toured Tibetan regions. He found that in Qinghai, people did not even have food bowls. "In the old society, even beggars had bowls," the Panchen Lama observed. Under Chiang Kai-shek and the Muslim warlord Ma Pu-fang, the Tibetans in Qinghai "were never so poor as not to be able to afford bowls!" Later, people even took to trying to break into labor camps and prisons to search for food.

Large numbers of Tibetans were put through violent denunciation meetings, including the father and family of the Panchen Lama, who wrote: "People were beaten till they bled from eyes, ears, mouths, noses, they passed out, their arms or legs broken . . . others died on the spot." For the first time in Tibet, suicide became a common practice.

With so many Tibetans joining rebellions against Mao's regime, Chinese troops treated most Tibetans as enemies, rounding up the majority of adult males in many places, leaving only "women, the old, the children and extremely few young and middle-aged men." After Mao's death, the Panchen Lama revealed what he had not dared put in his original letter: that a staggering 15 to 20 percent of all Tibetans—perhaps half of all adult males—were thrown into prison, where they were basically worked to death. They were treated like subhumans. Lama Palden Gyatso, a brave long-term prisoner, told us he and other prisoners were flogged with wire whips as they pulled heavy plows.

The crushing of the rebellions produced atrocious behavior on the part of Chinese troops. In one place, the Panchen Lama described (speaking after Mao died) how "corpses were dragged down from the mountains" and buried in a big pit, and the relatives were then summoned and told: " 'We have wiped out the rebel bandits, and today is a day of festivity. You will all dance on the pit of the corpses.' "

Atrocities went in parallel with cultural annihilation. This period witnessed a campaign officially called "Big Destruction," in which the entire Tibetan way of life came under violent physical assault for being "backward, dirty and useless." Mao was bent on destroying religion, the essence of most Tibetans' lives. When he met the Dalai Lama in 1954–55 he told him there were too many monks in Tibet, which, he said, was bad for reproducing the labor force. Now lamas and nuns were forced to break their vows of celibacy and get married. "Holy Scriptures were used for manure, and pictures of the Buddha and sutras were deliberately used to make shoes," the Panchen Lama wrote. The destruction was of a kind that "even lunatics would hardly carry out." Most monasteries were destroyed, "the sites looking as if they had just been through a war and bombardments." According to the Panchen Lama, the number of monasteries in Tibet fell from over 2,500 before 1959 to "only just over 70" in

1961, and the number of monks and nuns from over 110,000 to 7,000 (some 10,000 fled abroad).

One particularly painful order for Tibetans was that Buddhist ceremonies for the dead were banned. "When a person dies," the Panchen Lama wrote:

> if there is no ceremony to expiate his sins for his soul to be released from purgatory, this is to treat the dead with the utmost ... cruelty ... People were saying: "We die too late ... Now when we die, we are going to be like a dog being tossed outside the door!"

On his tours in the early 1960s, Tibetans came at great risk to see the Panchen Lama, crying out and weeping: "Don't let us starve! Don't let Buddhism be exterminated! Don't let the people of the Land of Snows become extinct!" Mao was "greatly displeased" with the Panchen Lama's letter, and visited much suffering on him, including ten years in prison.

To Tibet, as to the whole of China, Mao's rule brought unprecedented misery.

MAOISM GOES GLOBAL

(1959–64 ★ AGE 65–70)

I N FEBRUARY 1959, Russia signed an agreement to provide China with the means to make nuclear submarines. This marked the high point of the Kremlin's cooperation on technology transfers. But even while the deal was being signed, Khrushchev was having second thoughts about endowing Mao with such enormous military power.

One incident in particular had prompted Khrushchev to rethink. In September 1958 a US air-to-air Sidewinder missile had come down over China unexploded from a Taiwanese plane. Urgent requests from Khrushchev to let the Russians examine this state-of-the-art windfall went unanswered. The Chinese then claimed they could not find it. Khrushchev's son Sergei, a leading rocket scientist, recalled:

> For the first time, Father sensed the deep fissures that had appeared in our "fraternal friendship." For the first time he wondered whether it made sense to transfer the newest military technology and teach the Chinese how to build missiles and nuclear warheads.
> ... in February [1959], he decided to exert pressure for the first time ... he held up transfer of instructions for the R-12 [missile]. It did the trick. The [Sidewinder] missile was immediately found.

The Chinese had dismantled the missile and the critical guidance system was missing. "This was offensive and insulting to us," Khrushchev senior wrote in his memoirs. "Anybody in our place would have felt pain. We held no secrets back from China. We gave them everything ... Yet when they got a trophy they refused to share it." Khrushchev reached the conclusion that Mao was just using Russia for his own goals, and did not care about the interests of the Communist camp as a whole. Mao, he felt, "was bursting with an impatient desire to rule the world." Khrushchev gave orders to go slow on transferring nuclear know-how, and on 20 June 1959 he suspended assistance on the Bomb.

This was not a fatal blow, as by now China had the basic know-how, and the key equipment, for a Bomb. But Mao could see that from here on it was going to be hard to tap Khrushchev for more.

In September, Khrushchev went to America on the first-ever visit by a Soviet leader. He believed there was a real possibility of peaceful coexistence with the West. Afterwards he went on to Peking for the tenth anniversary of Mao's regime. Khrushchev urged Mao to be conciliatory towards the West, "to avoid anything that could be exploited . . . to drive the world back into the cold war 'rut,' " as Russia's chief ideologist put it.

Mao saw Khrushchev's rapprochement with the West as a historic opportunity to put himself forward as the champion of all those around the world who saw peaceful coexistence as favoring—and possibly freezing—the status quo. The timing seemed particularly good, with decolonization in full swing. There were numerous anti-colonial movements in Africa that were keen on guerrilla war, of which Mao was perceived to be the advocate and expert in a way that Khrushchev was not. Communist parties, too, seemed soft targets, as they had little hope of getting into power except through violence. Mao envisaged a situation where "Communist parties all over the world will not believe in [Russia] but believe in us." He saw a chance to establish his own "centre for world revolution."

To have his own camp, and not have to play second fiddle to Khrushchev, had long been Mao's dream. As Khrushchev had begun to dry up as a source of military hardware, Mao felt less concerned about annoying him. But nor did he want a split from him either, as Russia was still handing over a wealth of military technology, with no fewer than 1,010 blueprints transferred in 1960 alone—more even than in 1958. So Mao formulated a policy of "not to denounce" the Russians "for the time being," and sought to milk them of everything he could as fast as he could. "China will become powerful in eight years," he told his top echelon, and Khrushchev "will be completely bankrupt."

The goal for now, he told his inner circle at the beginning of 1960, was "to propagate Mao Tse-tung Thought" around the world. At first, the drive should not be too aggressive, in order, as he put it, not to be seen to be trying to "export our fragrant intestines" (to which Mao compared his "Thought"). The resulting propaganda campaign brought the world "Maoism."

THE IDEA OF promoting China's experience as a model when the Chinese were dying of starvation in their millions might seem a tall order, but Mao was not perturbed: he had watertight filters on what foreigners could see and hear. As of February 1959, the CIA's "preliminary judgement" about Chinese food output was that there were "remarkable increases in production." Mao could easily pull the wool over most visitors' eyes. When the French writer Simone de Beauvoir visited in 1955, even the French-speaking Chinese woman assigned to accompany her had to get special permission to speak to her directly without going through the interpreter. After her short visit, de Beauvoir pontificated that "the power he [Mao] exercises is no more dictatorial than, for example, Roosevelt's was. New China's Constitution renders impossible the concentration of authority in one man's hands." She wrote a lengthy book about the trip, titled *The Long March*. Its index has one entry for the word "violence," which reads: "[Mao] on violence, avoidance of."

Mao made sure that no Chinese except a very carefully vetted elite could get out of the country. Among the few who could were diplomats, who became notorious for their leaden performances. They worked under straitjacket rules about exactly what they could say, the strictest orders to report every conversation, and permanent surveillance by each other. Communist China's first ambassadors were mostly army generals. Before sending them off, Mao told them, only half-jokingly: "You don't know any foreign language, and you are not [professional] diplomats; but I want you to be my diplomats—because in my view you won't be able to flee." And over half of these men were going to other Communist countries.

The only people who got out and would talk were a small number of daring ordinary citizens who risked their lives and swam to Hong Kong. They broke the wall of silence around Mao's famine and the dark realities of Red China in general. But their voices won little credence in the West.

Instead, when Mao told barefaced lies to France's Socialist leader (and future president) François Mitterrand during the famine in 1961 ("I repeat it, in order to be heard: there is no famine in China"), he was widely believed. The future Canadian prime minister Pierre Trudeau came in 1960 and co-wrote a starry-eyed book, *Two Innocents in Red China*, which rejected reports of famine. Even the former chief of the UN's Food and Agricultural Organization, Lord Boyd-Orr, was duped. In May 1959, after a trip to China, he opined that food production had risen 50–100 percent over 1955–58 and that China "seems capable of feeding [its population] well." Britain's Field Marshal Montgomery, a much more gullible figure, asserted after visits in 1960 and 1961 that there had been "no large-scale famine, only shortages in certain areas," and he certainly did not regard the "shortages" as Mao's fault, as he urged Mao to hang on to power: "China . . . needs the chairman. You mustn't abandon this ship."

Mao had no problem covering up the famine, and was confident he could promote himself as a credible international leader. For this job he brought in three dependable writer-journalists: Edgar Snow, the half-

Chinese Han Suyin, and Felix Greene, who did an interview with Chou on BBC TV during which Chou simply read out his answers from sheets of paper.

MAO'S SELF-PROMOTION abroad was fueled by vastly increased handouts of his usual trio: arms, money and food. On 21 January 1960 a new body called the Foreign Economic Liaison Bureau was formed, ranking on a par with the Foreign Trade Ministry and the Foreign Ministry, to handle the rise in foreign aid. Aid figures soared immediately. This spree of gifts by Mao coincided with the worst years of the greatest famine in world history. Over 22 million people died of starvation in 1960 alone.

China was not only the poorest country in the world to provide aid, but its aid was the highest ever given as a percentage of the donor country's per capita income—and, moreover, often went to countries with a standard of living much higher than itself, like Hungary. And the cost of these handouts was not just the standard of living, but Chinese *lives*. Moreover, they were literally handouts, as Peking constantly said that loans should be treated as gifts, or that repayment should be deferred indefinitely. As for arms, the regime liked to say "We are not arms merchants"; but this did not mean it did not export arms, only that the arms did not have to be paid for.

Mao saw that his best chance was where there was a war, so the main donee on his list was Indochina, on which he lavished more than US$20 billion during his reign. In Africa he tried to latch on to the decolonization movement: there he showered cash, goods and arms on the Algerians, who were fighting the biggest anti-colonial war on the continent, against the French.*

In Latin America, Peking made a beeline for Cuba after Fidel Castro took power in January 1959. When Castro's colleague Che Guevara came to China in November 1960, Mao doled out US$60m as a "loan," which Chou told Guevara "does not have to be repaid."

In the Communist bloc itself, Mao worked on trying to acquire influence in every country, but only managed to detach one client from Russia's sphere of influence: tiny poverty-stricken Albania. As early as 1958, its dictator, Enver Hoxha, had scrounged 50m rubles out of a willing Mao— a considerable sum for a country of fewer than 3 million people. Then, in January 1961, as the Peking–Moscow rift sharpened and Hoxha showed he could be relied on to spout venom against Khrushchev, Peking decupled this amount, lending Tirana 500 million rubles, and sent 2.2 million

---

* Algeria showed how dependent Mao was on there being an armed conflict. Once Algeria gained its independence, in 1962, his influence evaporated.

bushels of wheat, which China had bought from Canada for hard currency. Thanks to food donated by China, the Albanians did not even know what rationing was, while the Chinese were dying in their tens of millions. Albania's chief negotiator with Peking, Pupo Shyti, told us that in China "you could see the famine." But "the Chinese gave us everything." "When we needed anything, we just asked the Chinese ... I felt ashamed ..." When Mao's colleagues flinched he told them off.

Mao spent money trying to split Communist parties and to set up Maoist parties all over the world—a task he entrusted to his old intelligence chief, Kang Sheng. Spotting Peking's crude criteria for allegiance, freeloaders jumped aboard the gravy train. Albanian archives reveal a tetchy Kang in Tirana griping about Venezuelan leftists walking off with US$300,000 of China's money funneled through Albania. Dutch intelligence set up a bogus Maoist party, which was funded and feted by the Chinese. The CIA's top China hand, James Lilley, told us they were delighted to discover how easy it was to infiltrate China: simply get a few people to chant hosannas to Mao and set up a Maoist party, which Peking would then rush to fund—and invite to China. (These spies, however, were useless, as all foreigners were rigidly segregated from the Chinese.)*

TO LAUNCH "Maoism" on the world, Mao chose the ninetieth anniversary of Lenin's birth, in April 1960, in the form of a manifesto entitled Long Live Leninism!, which said that advocating a peaceful road to socialism was unacceptable—"revisionism," Peking called it—and that if Communists were to take power they would have to resort to violence. It did not attack Khrushchev by name, using Yugoslavia's Tito as its whipping-boy instead. Mao's calculation was that this way Khrushchev would have less excuse to punish him by withholding military know-how.

Simultaneously, Mao tried to move himself center-stage by inviting more than 700 sympathizers from the Third World for May Day. This was intended to be the founding moment of the Maoist camp. He received several groups of them himself, and the foreigners were reported "expressing adulation" for him and singing the Maoist anthem, "The East Is Red."

---

* At least one Chinese noticed how easily huge sums of money flooded into projects to do with promotion abroad and tried to take advantage. In March 1960 a clerk at the Foreign Trade Ministry walked off with the astronomical sum of 200,000 yuan, in the biggest known cash swindle to date, which he accomplished by forging just one letter, and faking one signature: Chou En-lai's. The one-page letter claimed a telephone call had come from Mao's staff to Chou's office asking for cash to be allotted to repair a temple in Tibet so that some foreign journalists could take photographs of it. The clerk had four hungry children, and wanted to buy them some extra food, which special state shops sold outside the rationing network at exorbitant prices for those with the money, mainly people with relatives abroad. Needless to say, this enterprising bureaucrat was easily discovered.

He ordered maximum publicity for these audiences, tinkering over the press reports himself phrase by phrase.

These encounters were timed to take place just before a major world event from which Mao was excluded—a summit of the Big Four (US, UK, France, Russia), which was due to open in Paris on 16 May, at which Khrushchev hoped to enshrine peaceful coexistence. Mao intended his to be a rival show, and for the world to see him as the champion of the disadvantaged. But his venture went virtually unnoticed, partly because his foreign followers were marginal figures. Mao did not inspire passionate faith, either, and acquired few fervent disciples. He was perceived as patronizing. A group of Africans heard him say that, to Westerners, "our race seems no better than you Africans."

Mao's hopes that Khrushchev would be seen as an appeaser, and himself as the antithesis, also received a blow from an unexpected quarter. Two weeks before the Paris summit, an American U-2 spy plane was shot down over Russia. When President Eisenhower refused to apologise, Khrushchev walked out and the summit collapsed. Peking had to praise Khrushchev for taking a tough stance.

Khrushchev's bellicosity towards America risked taking the wind out of Mao's sails, but he blasted ahead nonetheless, and a convenient occasion was to hand: a meeting of the World Federation of Trade Unions which opened in Peking on 5 June 1960. This was the most important international meeting to be held in China since Mao had taken power, with participants from some sixty countries combining delegates from ruling Communist parties and militant trade unionists from all five continents, some not subservient to Moscow. Mao mobilized all his top colleagues to lobby hard against Moscow, arguing that peaceful coexistence was a deception, and that "as long as capitalism exists, war cannot be avoided." The French and the Italians, who were close to Khrushchev's position, were singled out and called servants of imperialism. An Italian delegate, Vittorio Foa, told us that the hostility from the Chinese was so nerve-racking that the Italians feared for their physical safety and tried not to leave each other unaccompanied. The aggressiveness of the Chinese shocked even Albania's delegate Gogo Nushi, who described them, in private, as "bandits."*

The Chinese were "spitting in our face," remarked Khrushchev. Moscow perceived this event as the beginning of the Sino-Soviet split. So did the CIA. Its Acting Director, Charles Cabell, told the National Security Council two weeks later that Chinese behavior at the meeting

---

* An Albanian Politburo member, Liri Belishova, was in China at this time, and let the Russians know what was happening, for which she suffered thirty years in Hoxha's gulag—not "strangled" or "eliminated," as Khrushchev wrote in his memoirs. She emerged with remarkable bounce, as we saw in 1996.

had been "a challenge to USSR leadership of such a magnitude that Khrushchev has been compelled to meet it head-on." Up to now, differences between Moscow and Peking had been tightly concealed by Communist secrecy, and many had doubted that there really was a Sino-Soviet rift.

On 21 June Khrushchev addressed Communist leaders from fifty-one countries gathered in Bucharest. He refuted Mao's contention that war was needed to bring about socialism: "No world war is needed for the triumph of socialist ideas throughout the world," he declared. "Only madmen and maniacs can now call for another world war," in which, he said, using apocalyptic language, "millions of people might burn in the conflagration." In contrast, "people of sound mind" were "in the majority even among the most deadly enemies of communism." This was tantamount to saying that Mao was crazy, and suggesting that coexistence with the West was a better bet than continuing an alliance with Mao. "You want to dominate everyone, you want to dominate the world," Khrushchev told Mao's delegate, Peng Zhen, in private. Khrushchev also said to the Chinese: "Since you love Stalin so much, why don't you take his corpse to Peking?" He told his colleagues: "When I look at Mao I see Stalin, a perfect copy."

When Peng Zhen persisted with Mao's line, he found himself alone. "We were isolated in Bucharest," Mao noted. "There was not a single party that supported China. Not even . . . Albania." This isolation, and the sharpness of Khrushchev's attack, took Mao by surprise. A split under these circumstances was counterproductive, as he still needed Russian military technology. When Khrushchev refused to accept one word of Mao's views for the communiqué, Mao backed down and told Peng Zhen to sign.

By now the scales had completely fallen from Khrushchev's eyes. On his return from Bucharest, he immediately ordered the withdrawal of all the 1,000-plus Soviet advisers in China and halted assistance on the 155 industrial projects that were furthest from completion.

Mao had miscalculated. Russian retaliation came at a highly disadvantageous time. Although his scientists had secured the technology to make a Bomb, the Russians had not finished imparting their expertise in building the delivery system: the missiles. The Chinese scrambled, telling their scientists to seize every minute to dig things out of the Russians before they left, by hook or by crook. Song-and-dance girls were brought in to get Soviet minders drunk and detain them on the dance floor, while Russian scientists' notebooks were photographed. Even so, the missile program, and indeed the entire Superpower Program, was thrown into disarray. Mao's impatience to promote himself as a world leader, and rival to Khrushchev, had led him to shoot himself in the foot.

Mao had to backtrack. When eighty-one Communist parties met in

Moscow in November, the Chinese appeared conciliatory. Mao himself showed up at the Soviet embassy in Peking for the anniversary of the Bolshevik Revolution, and sent Khrushchev fulsome personal greetings for New Year's 1961. There was a reconciliation of sorts. In the end, the Russians continued to provide assistance to keep construction work going on 66 of the 155 unfinished industrial projects. But Mao did not get what he coveted most—renewed collaboration on high-end military technology transfers.

Scores of large-scale projects were canceled. Mao later blamed the famine that he himself had created on their cancellation, which he alleged had damaged China's economy, and his claim is believed in China to this day. In fact, the cancellations should have eased the famine: China could now export less food.

But instead of allowing the Chinese population to benefit from a respite, Mao found a new way to spend the food. He insisted on continuing to export it to repay Russian loans *ahead of* schedule—in the space of five years, instead of the sixteen that the agreements allowed. He did this because he knew Russia needed food, and Chinese food made up two-thirds of Russia's food imports. By continuing to supply the same large amounts as before, he was encouraging Russia's dependence on Chinese food, in the hope that Khrushchev would sell him more of what he wanted. Mao later fabricated the myth that Khrushchev had pressured China to pay back its debts during the famine, and that this was one major reason why the Chinese starved. In fact, as a briefing for China's post-Mao leaders stated categorically, Russia "did not ask for the debt to be repaid" then, let alone try to "force" China to do so. It was Mao who insisted on repaying far ahead of schedule.

Russia's ambassador to Peking at the time, Chervonenko, told us that Moscow instructed him to try to refuse Chinese food exports, and that Russia had sometimes declined to accept shipments of grain. The Russians knew only too well about the famine. "You didn't have to do any investigation," Chervonenko said. "It was enough just to drive in from the airport. You could see there were no leaves on the trees." On one occasion, when the Chinese said they were going to increase meat shipments, the Russians asked how. The answer was: "None of your business!"

Far from demanding accelerated repayment, Khrushchev was extraordinarily obliging, even revaluing the yuan:ruble exchange rate in China's favor. According to a Russian source, this reduced China's indebtedness to Russia by 77.5 percent. In February 1961, Khrushchev offered Mao one million tons of grain and half a million tons of Cuban sugar. Mao bought the sugar but rejected the grain. This was not out of pride. He had just grabbed at an offer from Khrushchev of technology and experts to manufacture MiG-21 fighters.

For the next two years Mao's tactic was to keep one foot in the Kremlin door, in the hope of maintaining access to military technology, while taking a swipe at Khrushchev on every possible occasion—even over the Berlin Wall, the ultimate symbol of the Cold War. An East German diplomat then in Peking told us that when the Wall went up in summer 1961, Chou En-lai made it clear to the East Germans that Mao saw this as a sign of Khrushchev "capitulating to the US imperialists."

WITH MAO SHOWING himself to be such a tricky customer, Khrushchev had to cover his back when he made any important move. In October 1962, Khrushchev was secretly deploying nuclear missiles in Cuba, the most adventurous act he undertook in his decade in power, and the peak of his "anti-imperialism." Given the danger of a confrontation with the USA, he wanted to ensure that Mao would not stab him in the back. He decided to throw him a bone, a big one: the Kremlin's blessing for China to attack India, even though this meant Russia betraying the interests of India, a major friendly state that Khrushchev had long been wooing.

Mao had been planning war with India on the border issue for some time. China had refused to recognize the boundary that had been delineated by the British in colonial times, and insisted it be renegotiated, or at least formalized by the two now sovereign states. India regarded the border as settled, and not negotiable, and the two sides were deadlocked. As border clashes worsened, Peking quietly prepared for war during May–June 1962. Chou later told the Americans that "Nehru was getting very cocky... and we tried to keep down his cockiness." But Mao was chary of starting a war, as he was worried about the security of the nuclear test site at Lop Nor in northwest China, which was beyond the range of American U-2 spy planes flying from Taiwan, but lay within range from India. Part of the fallout from the war was that India allowed U-2s to fly from a base at Charbatia, from where they were able to photograph China's first A-bomb test in 1964.

Mao was also concerned that he might have to fight on two fronts. Chiang Kai-shek was making his most active preparations since 1949 to invade the Mainland, fired by the hope that the population would rise up and welcome him because of the famine. Mao took the prospect of a Nationalist invasion seriously, moving large forces to the southeast coast opposite Taiwan, while he himself hunkered down in his secret shelter in the Western Hills outside Peking.

The Chinese had been holding regular ambassador-level talks with America in Warsaw since 1955. Mao now used this channel to sound out whether Washington would support an invasion by Chiang. And he got a very reassuring and direct answer. The Americans said they would not back Chiang to go to war against the Mainland, and that Chiang had promised not to attack without Washington's consent.

But Mao still hesitated. The paramount factor was Russia, on which China was heavily dependent for oil. In China's previous border clashes with India, Khrushchev had ostentatiously declined to back Peking. He had then agreed to sell India planes that could fly at high altitudes, and in summer 1962 signed an agreement not only to sell India MiGs, but for India to manufacture MiG-21s.

By early October, the Himalayan winter was approaching, and the window of opportunity narrowing. Mao sent out a feeler to the Russian ambassador about how Moscow would react if China attacked India. Khrushchev seized this chance to make a startling démarche. On the 14th he laid on a four-hour farewell banquet for the outgoing Chinese ambassador, at which the Soviet leader pledged that Moscow would stand by Peking if China got into a border war with India, and would delay the sale of MiG-21s to India. He revealed that he had been secretly installing nuclear missiles in Cuba and said he hoped the Chinese would give him their support.

This was a hefty horse-trade, one well concealed from the world.* On the morning of 20 October, just as the Cuba crisis was about to break, Mao gave the go-ahead for crack troops to storm Indian positions along two widely separated sectors of the border. Five days later, with the Cuba crisis at fever pitch, Khrushchev came through with his support for Mao in the form of a statement in *Pravda* that mortified Nehru.

Chinese forces rapidly advanced more than 150 km into northeast India. Then, having demonstrated military superiority, Mao withdrew his forces, leaving each country holding some disputed territory, a situation that prevails to this day. Mao had achieved his objective: long-term stability on this border, leaving him free to focus on his broader ambitions. The war also dealt a lethal blow to Nehru, Mao's rival for leadership in the developing world, who died eighteen months later from a stroke.

MEANWHILE, THE Cuban missile crisis was basically settled on 28 October, after Khrushchev agreed to withdraw the missiles in return for a promise by US president John F. Kennedy not to invade Cuba (and an unpublished promise to pull US missiles out of Turkey). Mao immediately jettisoned his deal not to make trouble for Khrushchev during the crisis, and tried to horn in on Havana's resentment towards

* When one participant (Thomas Kuchel) in Oval Office discussions on 22 October asked whether there was any indication that Russia's move in Cuba was "associated with the Chinese operation against India," CIA chief John McCone answered: "No, we have no information whatsoever with respect to that at all."

Khrushchev for failing to consult it about his settlement with the US. Gigantic "pro-Cuba" demonstrations were staged in China, accompanied by bellicose statements containing barely veiled accusations against Moscow for "selling out." Mao bombarded the Cubans with messages, telling them that Moscow was an "untrustworthy ally," and urging them to hold out against Khrushchev's agreement to remove Russian missiles and planes. Mao tried to capitalize on the differences between Castro and Guevara, who was against the settlement. "Only one man got it right," Mao said: "Che Guevara."

Mao meddled and needled, but failed to get Havana to sign up to his anti-Soviet stance. However, he did benefit from Cuba's bitter feelings towards the Russians. When an advanced US rocket, a Thor-Able-Star, landed accidentally in Cuba, instead of letting the Russians have it, as he would normally have done, Castro played them off against the Chinese by auctioning it. The result was that Peking got some crucial components, which played a big part in enabling it to upgrade its missiles.

Khrushchev, for his part, backtracked from his previous support for China even while fighting was still going on inside India. A *Pravda* editorial on 5 November conspicuously contained not one word endorsing Peking's position. For him, as for Mao, the collaboration had been completely opportunistic, though he still wanted to keep the Communist camp together.

So did Mao, hoping that he could still finagle a few more nuclear secrets out of Khrushchev. These hopes were dashed definitively in July 1963, when Khrushchev signed a Nuclear Test Ban Treaty with America and Britain, which embargoed the signatories helping others acquire a Bomb.* This meant that Khrushchev was now virtually useless to Mao.

It was at this point, more than three years after he had started pushing Maoism onto the world stage, that Mao gave the order to denounce Khrushchev by name as a "revisionist." A public slanging match quickly escalated. For Mao, the polemic acted as a sort of international advertising campaign for Maoism, whose essence was summed up in one of the main accusations against Khrushchev: "In the eyes of the modern revisionists, to survive is everything. The philosophy of survival has replaced Marxism-Leninism." It is hard now to cast oneself back to a time when anyone could think this approach might appeal. But to deny people's desire—and right—to live was central to Maoism.

---

* Kennedy had in fact been trying to use the treaty to widen the rift between Moscow and Peking.

AMBUSHED BY THE PRESIDENT

(1961–62 ★ AGE 67–68)

WHEN MAO LAUNCHED the Great Leap Forward in 1958, his No. 2, Liu Shao-chi, went along with him, even though he disagreed with Mao's position. And when defense minister Peng De-huai spoke up against Mao's policies at Lushan in 1959, when the famine was well under way, Liu, who was now state president as well as Party No. 2, failed to take Peng's side.

But Liu was deeply troubled by the famine, which he knew had consumed some 30 million lives by early 1961. He was particularly affected after he went back to his home area in Hunan in April–May that year, and saw at first hand the horrific suffering he had helped create. He made up his mind to find a way to stop Mao.

During the trip Liu visited his sister. She had married into the family of a "landlord," who was categorized as a "class enemy." When she had written to Liu at the beginning of Mao's regime about their hardships during the land reform, he had written back giving her all the "correct" and comfortless advice. Now he came with food: 2.5 kg of rice, 1 kg of biscuits, 1 kg of sweets, 9 salted eggs and a jar of lard. His sister was lying in bed famished and extremely ill. She wept as she talked about her husband, who had died not long before in great agony after eating a bun made of unhusked grain, which their daughter had specially saved for him. His weakened stomach could not cope with the coarse food. There were no doctors to call, no hospitals to turn to.

This brother-in-law had written a letter to Liu in 1959, after Liu became president, to tell him about the starvation in the village. The letter was intercepted, and he was punished by being tied to a tree and left out to freeze in bitter winds until he was on the verge of passing out.

Everywhere he went Liu encountered heart-rending sights and tragic stories. He could sense how much people hated the Communists—and him. In his home village a twelve-year-old boy had written "Down with Liu Shao-chi" outside Liu's old family house. This boy had seen six members of his family succumb to starvation-induced illness within one year, the last being his youngest brother, who had died in his arms; he had been carrying the baby around looking for someone to breast-feed him, as their mother had just died. Liu told the police not to punish the boy as a "counter-revolutionary," which would normally have been the charge for such an act.

He also stopped the local authorities punishing peasants for "stealing" food, making a striking admission to the villagers that it was the regime that was robbing them. "Commune members think this way," Liu said. "Since you take from us, why can't I take from you? Since you take a lot, why can't I take a little?"

Liu did something else unprecedented. He apologized to the peasants for the misrule the Communists had brought. After nearly forty years away, he said, "I am shocked to see my fellow-villagers are leading such a harsh life . . . I feel responsible for causing so much suffering to you, and I must apologise . . ." He started to sob, and bowed to the villagers.

The trip marked Liu profoundly. After he returned to Peking, he told the top managers: "We cannot go on like this."

IN AUGUST 1961, as autumn harvest time approached, Mao once again gathered his managers under the clouds of Mount Lushan to fix the food extraction figures. Liu pressed him to set them lower. The two men had many arguments, and the tension in their relationship seeped through to their outward behavior, as the teenage son of a provincial boss observed. He was swimming in the reservoir with other children of high officials when Mao arrived. The children clambered excitedly onto the wooden platform where Mao was sitting with bodyguards and dancing girls. The boy told Mao he had swallowed some water while swimming. Mao said: "It's nothing to be choked by thousands of mouthfuls of water when swimming, you have to be choked by ten thousand mouthfuls before you master it." Choking when learning to swim was a metaphor for "learning comes at a price," one that Mao often enlisted to explain away his repeated economic disasters. Soon Liu Shao-chi swam over with his bodyguards, and climbed onto the platform. He and Mao did not exchange so much as a nod. They just sat apart, in a space of about 30 square meters, smoking, not speaking a word. The boy remembered wondering: "How come they don't greet each other?"

Mao's other colleagues had also been trying to reason with him. After touring an old Red base area in Hebei, Chou En-lai told Mao that people "have only tree leaves, salted vegetables and wild herbs, and absolutely nothing else. There is genuinely no grain left." Mao was mightily irritated, and once, while Chou was describing what he had seen, snapped: "What's all the fuss about?"

Nevertheless, under intense pressure at Lushan, Mao accepted a cut in food requisitions of over 34 percent from the figure he had set at the beginning of the year. As a result, deaths from starvation in 1961 fell by nearly half from the year before—though they still approached 12 million.

Mao made this concession partly because a large number of big industrial projects were having to be closed down anyway as a result of the lack of essentials like steel, coal and electricity. Closing them down was a good idea, as they had caused stupendous waste, but the result was huge upheaval, in which over 26 million people lost their jobs. Most of these had been sucked into the cities in the past three years; now they were kicked back to their villages—the largest such yo-yo movement of population in human history. "How wonderful our Chinese people and our cadres are!" Mao exclaimed. "Twenty million people: we call and they come; we dismiss and they go." He continued: "Which party can manage this except the Communist Party?" Once back in their villages, these people lost whatever borderline livelihood and welfare guaranteed them as factory workers. In addition, families were broken up if one spouse was accorded an urban job and did not wish to go and live as a peasant and face starvation. Such couples faced the prospect of living permanently apart, allowed only twelve days a year together.

But having conceded lower food levies in 1961, Mao warned his audience at Lushan: "We have retreated to the bottom of the valley," meaning the only way requisitioning could go from there on was up. Next year, his managers were told, the levies would have to rise again.

To anyone in his court who might be contemplating drastic measures against him, Mao sent a warning signal through a somewhat unusual channel, the visiting retired British Field Marshal Montgomery. Quite unprompted, Mao told Montgomery: "I am prepared for destruction any time," before launching into five possible ways he might be assassinated: "shooting to death by enemies, a plane crash, a train crash, drowning, and killing with germs. I have made preparations for all these five ways." As it was standard procedure for Mao's talks with foreigners to be circulated among top leaders, Mao was serving notice on his colleagues: Don't try anything. I have taken precautions.

Mao had reason to worry. Even his Praetorian Guard, the people he relied on for his life, voiced bitter sentiments against him. "Where is all this grain that has been harvested?" one soldier said. "Is it Chairman Mao's order that people should only eat grass?" asked another. "He can't just take no notice of whether people live or die . . ." Yet another: "Now the folks in the villages don't even have the food that dogs used to eat. In the old days, dogs had chaff and grain . . . And the commune members are saying: Does Chairman Mao want to starve us all to death?" The Guards were promptly purged.

★

A MORE URGENT CONCERN for Mao in September 1961 was the chance of losing power at a Party congress. Mao's "biggest worry," Lin Biao wrote in his diary, "is whether he can get the majority in a vote." And a congress was due that very month. The previous one had been held in September 1956, and the Party charter stipulated one every five years. Mao had to fend off the threat of being deposed.

As far back as 1959, Mao had sensed profound discontent towards him among the top echelon. "If you don't vote for me," he had told a Party plenum then, "so be it." Since then, officials had been shattered by the impact of the famine. At Party gatherings in the provinces, cadres would burst into tears when reporting what they had seen in the villages. Moreover, Mao's policies had brought starvation to themselves and their families. Their monthly rations were about 10 kg of rice, a few ounces of cooking oil and a small lump of meat. In Zhongnanhai, officials like Liu's staff grew wheat and vegetables outside their offices to supplement their inadequate rations. Hunger had made Mao's officials almost universally yearn for a change of policy.

Mao tried to deflect dissatisfaction by his usual method of designating scapegoats. The people he picked on were first of all village cadres, whom he blamed for "beating people up and beating them to death," and for "causing grain harvests to drop and people not to have enough food to eat." Next he blamed the Russians, and his third scapegoat was "extraordinarily big natural calamities." As a matter of fact, meteorological records show that not only were there no natural calamities in the famine years, but the weather was better than average. But even if cadres had no general picture, and half believed Mao, hungry officials still felt that something must be terribly wrong with the way their Party was running the country if the entire population, including themselves, was brought to such a state of wretchedness.

Mao also tried to win his cadres' sympathy vote by announcing to Party members that he would "share weal and woe with the nation," and give up eating meat. In fact, all he did, for a while, was to eat fish instead, which he loved anyway. Nor did his meatless regime last long. Indeed, it was right in the middle of the famine that he developed a fancy for meat-rich European cuisine. On 26 April 1961, a comprehensive set of European menus was presented to him, under seven headings: seafood, chicken, duck, pork, lamb, beef and soup—each with scores of dishes.

Mao went to the greatest lengths to keep his daily life completely secret. His daughter Li Na was boarding at the university, so she lived during the week on normal rations and was starving. After one weekend at home, she smuggled a few of her father's usual luxuries out of the house. Mao ordered her never to do it again. Nothing must puncture the illusion that he was tightening his belt along with the rest of the nation.

As a result, Li Na contracted edema in 1960 and she stopped menstruating. The following year she abandoned the university altogether and stayed at home.

To his staff, who could see what Mao was eating, and who themselves were half-starved, like their families, Mao claimed that his food was a reward to him "from the People," and that others had "no right" to it. When Mao's housekeeper took some scraps home, he found himself exiled to the freezing Great Northern Wilderness and was never heard of again.

Mao's attempt to win the sympathy vote did not work; the deprivation was just too great. One of the things that had completely disappeared was soap, because Mao was exporting the fat required to make it. Mao wanted people to accept doing without soap, so he told the Party that he himself was forgoing the use of soap to wash his hands. "Of course he doesn't use soap," one official snapped, in private. "He doesn't do any proper work!" Senior officials were saying other unthinkable things to one another such as: "Why doesn't he just kick off!" Mao knew what bitter comments they were making. One remark that reached his ears was: "If what's happening had happened in the past, the ruler would have had to resign long ago."

When Mao's daughter Chiao-chiao went to sweep the tomb of his late wife Kai-hui, she heard people cursing Mao, and reported it back to him. When the purged former defense minister Peng De-huai, who had been under house arrest since 1959, was allowed to visit his home area in October 1961, he got a very warm welcome from officials as well as ordinary villagers, as they had heard he had been purged for opposing Mao's policies. Two thousand "pilgrims," some of whom had walked up to 100 km on half-empty stomachs, poured into Peng's old family home to thank him for speaking up. Peng talked till he lost his voice.

If the scheduled congress met and held a vote, there was a strong possibility that Mao would be voted out. His fears were spelled out later by one of his closest henchmen (Zhang Chun-qiao, one of the notorious "Gang of Four"): "If the old Party charter had been followed, and the 9th Congress had been held then . . . Liu Shao-chi would have become the Chairman . . ."

Many officials called for a congress to be convened to address the catastrophic situation. Mao vetoed the idea, and came up with the device of convening a conference that would not have voting powers, thus averting the threat of being removed. The conference would be attended by the top few people in each ministry, province, city, region, county and major industrial enterprise.

In January 1962, these officials—7,000 in all—came to Peking from all over China for the largest gathering in the Party's history, known as the Conference of the Seven Thousand. It proved to be a landmark, because it was after this conference that famine was brought to a halt. But what is little known is that this victory was only secured by Liu Shao-chi ambushing Mao.

When he called the conference, Mao had had no intention of stopping his deadly policies. On the contrary, his aim had been to use the occasion to spur on his officials, so that they would go back home and turn the screws tighter. He had said then to his inner circle: "It's not the case that we don't have things [food]. True, there are not enough pigs, but there are plenty of other foods. We just don't seem to be able to lay our hands on them. We need a spur."

The method Mao used to lay down his line was to give the delegates the text of the keynote speech before it was delivered. The text glossed over past disasters, which were only vaguely and briefly referred to as "mistakes," before announcing that "the most difficult time is over." Most ominously, it not only claimed that "our domestic situation is on the whole good," but also declared that there would be another Great Leap in the coming years.

The delegates were told to voice their views, and that their amendments would be taken into account before the speech was delivered. But Mao made sure it was extremely hard for anyone to speak up, by organizing the discussions in groups, each chaired by an intimidating henchman. Anyone who ventured sharper questions was instantly gagged with heavy-handed threats. As one brave delegate wrote in an anonymous letter to the leadership, the sessions were simply "for everyone to sit there and kill time."

This went on for two weeks. Mao kept tabs on the delegates, and smugly read discussion bulletins while lounging in bed in his girlfriends' arms. His plan was that Liu Shao-chi would deliver the finalized speech to the one and only plenary session on 27 January, and the conference would then close. His program would thus be set in stone, and Liu and all the participants would be co-responsible.

BUT MAO'S COZY PLAN fell apart. On the 27th, Liu did something that took Mao utterly by surprise. With Mao in the chair, Liu gave a different speech from the circulated keynote text he was supposed to deliver.

With this huge audience of all the 7,000 top officials in the country listening, Liu laid into Mao's policies. "People do not have enough food, clothes or other essentials," he said; "agricultural output, far from rising in 1959, 1960 and 1961, dropped, not a little, but tremendously . . . there is not only no Great Leap Forward, but a great deal of falling backward." Liu dismissed the official explanation for the calamities, saying there was "no serious bad weather" in the areas he had visited, nor, he strongly hinted, anywhere. He called on delegates to question the new Leap that

Mao had advocated, and raised the possibility of scrapping the communes and even the Mao-style industrialization program.

Liu established beyond a glimmer of a doubt that past policies had been disastrous, and had to be discarded. He openly rejected a standard Mao formula that "Mistakes are only one finger whereas achievements are nine fingers." This, he said flatly, was untrue. When Mao cut in and insisted it was true in many places, Liu contradicted him.

Liu's speech brought a torrential response from his audience, who could hardly wait to raise their voices. The discussions that day took on a totally different tone and mood. Now they knew that the president was behind them, delegates spoke their minds, condemning the old policies passionately, and insisting they absolutely must not be repeated.

Mao had not expected the normally ultra-prudent Liu to pull a fast one. Inwardly, he was black with rage, but he decided it was wise to hold his fire, as Liu clearly had the support of the 7,000 participants, and Mao could not afford to have a head-on collision with this vast body of officials, which included just about everybody who ran the country. So he had to pretend there were no differences between himself and them. His first move was to extend the conference, presenting this as a sympathetic response on his part to the delegates' sentiments, telling them it was so they could "get their anger off their chest" (*chu-qi*). Privately he was fuming, and called it "letting their farts off" (*fang-pi*).

Mao plunged into damage control, to kill any idea that he was responsible for the famine. He designated some provincial bosses and agricultural chiefs and planners to make speeches taking responsibility for the disasters, thus implicitly exonerating him. But his most important maneuver was to wheel out his crony, Defense Minister Lin Biao, who was the first person to speak after the conference was extended, on 29 January. The marshal had started his collusion with Mao as far back as 1929, and he was someone Mao could rely on for support, however awful the cause.

To the 7,000, Lin Biao trotted out the kind of heartless clichés Mao loved to hear: disasters were inevitable "tuition fees"; Chairman Mao's ideas were "always correct"; "in times of difficulty . . . we must all the more follow Chairman Mao." When he finished, Mao was the first to clap, and praised Lin fulsomely to the audience. Only now did Mao feel safe enough to hint at his loathing for what Liu Shao-chi had done, using an ominous expression that amounted to "I'll get you later." Lin Biao had saved Mao's bacon.

Once he saw Lin Biao appear, Liu Shao-chi's heart sank. His widow told us that Liu murmured: "Lin Biao comes, and talks like this. Trouble." This total solidarity with Mao from the army chief, expressed in the kind of peremptory language which signaled that there could be no rational debate, immediately cast a frightening shadow over the participants. In the following days, they toned down their language and the ways they expressed their anger, though continuing to criticize the disastrous economic policies. The result was that Mao's policies did not get the scrutiny and forceful condemnation Liu had hoped for. And no one dared to criticize Mao directly, least of all by name.

Nonetheless, Mao could feel the force of the sentiment of the 7,000, and felt compelled to produce a "self-criticism" in front of them, on 30 January—his first ever since coming to power in 1949. Although he characteristically made it sound as if the disasters had been other people's fault and that he was rather altruistically accepting the blame, using carefully slanted formulae like "I am responsible . . . because I am the Chairman," he had to admit that there was much to be blamed for. Having made this admission, Mao had to swallow a policy change. He was forced to abandon the lethal scale of food levies planned for 1962 and onwards. As a result, tens of millions of people were spared death by starvation.

AS SOON AS the conference was over, on 7 February, Mao stormed off to Shanghai to be among his cronies, under local boss Ke Qing-shi. He had to take a back seat while Liu and his other colleagues, mainly Chou En-lai, Chen Yun and a rising star, Deng Xiao-ping, made major changes to his policies. Requisitioning was greatly lowered. Costly and unrealistic projects like nuclear submarines were suspended, although the basic nuclear program was unaffected. Spending on arms factories was enormously scaled down, while consumer goods industries received unprecedented funding. In a blow to the promotion of Maoism, overseas aid was slashed drastically—to virtually zero for the year. Mao's extravagance had been extremely unpopular with officials who knew about it. The man who ran military aid later wrote: "Every time I saw foreigners' smiling faces after signing yet another aid agreement, my heart would be filled with guilt towards my own people."

Investment in agriculture rose sharply. In many places, peasants were allowed to lease land from the commune, and effectively were able to return to being individual farmers. This alleviated starvation and motivated productivity. It was in defense of this practice that Deng Xiao-ping quoted an old saying, which became his most famous remark: "It doesn't matter whether it's a yellow cat or a black cat, as long as it catches mice." In the cities, working hours were reduced so that the malnourished population could recover some energy, and this also allowed more private time and family life. In less than a year people's lives improved perceptibly. By and large, deaths from hunger stopped.

The regime even allowed a number of people to leave the country. Normally, people trying to escape abroad were sent to labor camps, but now the authorities opened the fence to Hong Kong for a few days to let some 50,000 people flee. Border guards even lent a hand to lift children over the barbed wire.

The year 1962 was to be one of the most liberal periods since Mao's reign had begun. That spring, Liu and his colleagues rehabilitated wholesale those condemned following the purge of Peng De-huai in 1959, who totaled a staggering 10 million. Some "Rightists" (victimized in 1957–58) were also rehabilitated. In the arts and literature a host of creations burst forth. It had taken tens of millions of deaths to bring this degree of relief to the survivors. It was also in this year that the Panchen Lama felt able to write to Chou En-lai, chronicling the brutality the Tibetans had suffered. There was some relaxation in Tibet; some monasteries were restored and religious practices tolerated.

BEING FORCED TO change policy by his own Party—without the backing of Moscow—was the biggest setback Mao had suffered since taking power. First he had been outsmarted by the seemingly ultra-cautious Liu. Then he had effectively been given the thumbs-down by virtually all of the stratum that ran the country. From this moment on, Mao nurtured a volcanic hatred for Liu and the officials who had attended the conference—as well as for his Party, which these people obviously represented. He was out for revenge. The president of China and the backbone of his Party were his target. That is why, a few years later, he launched his Great Purge, the Cultural Revolution, in which Liu and most of the officials in that hall, and numerous others, were to be put through hell. As Mme Mao spelled out, Mao had "choked back this grievance at the Conference of the Seven Thousand, and was only able to avenge it in the Cultural Revolution." Of course Mao was not just in quest of revenge, savage and devastating though that was. It was obvious to him that this set of officials was not prepared to run the country the way he wanted. He would purge them and install new enforcers.

Quite a few left the conference with a sense of foreboding for Liu. Liu himself knew that this was the biggest turning-point in his life, but he had decided that his priority was to fend off more tens of millions of deaths. During this period the normally reserved Liu was unusually passionate and vocal about the plight of the Chinese people, who had suffered so terribly at the hands of the regime of which he was a leading member.

Over the next few years, Liu and his like-minded colleagues worked at getting the economy back into shape—while Mao planned revenge.

THE BOMB
(1962–64 ★ AGE 68–70)

B Y LATE 1962, famine had eased. In the following years, while toler-
ating food levies on a scale that allowed his subjects to subsist, Mao
began to resuscitate the pet projects that had been shelved as the
result of the famine, such as satellites and nuclear submarines. And new
projects joined them. When Mao was told about lasers, at the time seen
only as a deadly weapon, and translated into Chinese as "the Light of
Death," *si-guang*, he instantly decided on huge investments in laser research,
giving a characteristic order: "The Light of Death: get some people to
devote entirely to this. Feed them and don't let them do anything else."

For now, the focus of Mao's attention was the atomic bomb. In
November 1962, a special committee was formed, chaired by Chou En-
lai, to coordinate the several hundred thousand people involved and pool
the whole country's resources to produce a Bomb within two years. The
concentration of resources was on a scale that astonished even a top echelon accustomed to totalitarian organization. Each of the numerous
preparatory tests would take up nearly half of all China's telecommuni-
cation lines, and much of the country, including factories, would recur-
rently find itself without electricity or transport, because power had been
diverted for these tests.

How to protect the Bomb, and indeed his entire nuclear complex, was
Mao's constant preoccupation; and not without reason. At the tripartite
(US–UK–USSR) Nuclear Test Ban talks in Moscow in July 1963,
President Kennedy told his negotiator, Averell Harriman, to sound out
Khrushchev about destroying Mao's nuclear facilities: "try to elicit
K[hrushchev]'s view of means of limiting or preventing Chinese nuclear
development and his willingness either to take Soviet action or to accept
U.S. action aimed in this direction." Khrushchev rebuffed the approach.
But Kennedy told a press conference on 1 August that a nuclear China—
which, he emphasized, was "Stalinist," "with a government determined
on war as a means of bringing about its ultimate success"—posed "potentially a more dangerous situation than any we faced since the end of the

Second [World] War . . . and we would like to take some steps now which would lessen that prospect . . ."

Kennedy seriously considered air strikes on China's nuclear facilities. He was advised that the Lanzhou gaseous diffusion plant could be destroyed in such a way as to make it look like an accident, but that nuclear strikes might be needed to destroy the plutonium plant at Baotou.

After Kennedy was assassinated in November 1963 (by an "oil king," Mao told Albania's defense minister) his successor, Lyndon Johnson, was soon toying with the idea of dropping Taiwan saboteurs to blow up the facilities at Lop Nor, China's atomic test site.

Lop Nor and other nuclear sites deep in the Gobi Desert were sealed off by land, and everyone there, from top scientists to laborers, was completely isolated from their families and society for years, even decades. But the sites were exposed to America's spy planes—and attack from the air, which Mao feared most.

In April 1964, Mao was told that the Bomb could be exploded that autumn. He moved at once on every front to minimize the danger of a strike on the nuclear facilities. He dealt with the Russian end by going public to remind Khrushchev that China was still a member of the Communist camp. On 12 April, the day after the test details were decided, he stepped in to rewrite a telegram to Khrushchev for the latter's seventieth birthday. The original draft had reflected the acrimonious public relationship between the two states. Mao changed the text to make it ultra-friendly, adding a most unusual "Dear Comrade," and stressing that their discord was "only temporary." "In the event of a major world crisis," he said, they would "undoubtedly stand together against our common enemy." To conclude, he added a phrase evoking their past relationship: "Let the imperialists and reactionaries tremble before our unity . . ." The cable was given wide publicity in the Chinese media, and amazed everyone, as this was after months of fire-breathing public polemics targeting Khrushchev. On the eve of National Day that year, on 1 October, Mao stunned the Russians by greeting their delegate warmly, holding his hand, and repeating: "Everything will be fine; our peoples will be together."

Mao's main worry was America. To deter it he tried hard to deal himself some cards. His options for stirring up trouble in the US itself or in its immediate vicinity were limited. Shortly after the Test Ban Treaty, he had fired off a statement on 8 August 1963, to support the blacks in America. However, it only amounted to what he himself later called an "empty cannon." The black American radical whom Mao credited with urging him to issue the statement, Robert Williams, told us that Mao "didn't understand a lot of things about blacks in America." Williams compared Mao unfavorably on this score with Ho Chi Minh. Mao issued more statements supporting anti-American movements in countries near the US, like those in Panama and the Dominican Republic. These were just words.

There was one spot, though, near China, where there were Americans, and that was Vietnam. By the end of 1963 there were some 15,000 American military advisers in South Vietnam. Mao's plan was to create a situation whereby America would send more troops to South Vietnam, and even invade North Vietnam, which bordered with China. This way, if Washington were to strike his nuclear facilities, the Chinese army would pour into Vietnam and engulf the American troops as they had done in the Korean War. To try to make this happen, in 1964 Mao started pressing the Vietnamese hard to step up the war in Indochina. Their fighting, he told them, had "made no great impact and was just scratching the surface . . . Best turn it into a bigger war." "I'm afraid you really ought to send more troops to the South." "Don't be afraid of US intervention," he urged; "at most, it's no worse than having another Korean War. The Chinese army is prepared, and if America takes the risk of attacking North Vietnam, the Chinese army will march in at once. Our troops want a war now."

Mao asked the North Vietnamese to escalate fighting in other countries which were neighbors of China: "Better also send several thousand troops to Laos," he said. Laos "has been fighting for several years; but nothing has come of it. You should think of a way: get 3,000 or 4,000 men and . . . train them so they stop believing in Buddhism and become tough combat troops . . ." He particularly urged the Vietnamese to help build up a guerrilla army in Thailand, where America had military bases.

Hanoi's policy, in fact, was to get the USA to de-escalate, and the Vietnamese told Mao they did not want to "provoke" America. Mao nonetheless ordered 300,000–500,000 Chinese troops deployed along the border with Vietnam, ready to pour in. Chou En-lai paid a visit to China's South Sea fleet and told its commander to get ready to attack *South* Vietnam. Funds were allocated to move the fleet much closer to Vietnam, to the port of Zhanjiang.

Mao's agenda, as Chou En-lai later spelled out to Egypt's President Nasser, was to draw the maximum number of American troops into Vietnam as "an insurance policy" for China against a possible US nuclear attack,

> because we will have a lot of their flesh close to our nails.
>   So the more troops they send to Vietnam, the happier we will be, for we feel that we will have them in our power, we can have their blood . . .
>   . . . They will be close to China . . . in our grasp. They . . . will be our hostages.

Chou also told Tanzania's President Julius Nyerere that to protect its nuclear facilities, Peking would act in Vietnam regardless of what the Vietnamese themselves wanted. "Tell the US," Chou said, that if America attacks China's nuclear facilities, Peking will "respect no borders" and will go into North Vietnam "with or without the consent of the Vietnamese."

MAO DID NOT worry only about air strikes on his nuclear facilities, he feared that all his arms-centered industries could be targets. As a lot of these were situated in coastal plains, he decided to move them to China's mountainous hinterland.

In June 1964 he ordered this massive relocation, which he described to his inner circle as a nationwide "house-moving" of industries to cope with "the Era of the Bomb." The undertaking went by the general name of the "Third Front" (coastal and border areas were "the First Front"; "the Second Front" was the rest of China). No fewer than some 1,100 large enterprises were dismantled and moved to remote areas, where major installations like steel and electricity plants had to be constructed. Some nuclear facilities were even duplicated. Mountains were hollowed out to make giant caves to accommodate them. The upheaval and cost were colossal. Over the decade the Third Front was being built, it cost an astronomical 200 billion-plus yuan, and at its peak it sucked in at least two-thirds of the entire nation's investment. The waste it created was more than the total material losses caused by the Great Leap Forward.

From a strategic point of view, the whole project was nonsensical. The vast majority of plants in the Third Front were utterly dependent on road transport—sometimes even for water supplies—while the oil refineries were left exposed. China's main oil field, which had just come on stream, lay on the Manchurian plain. The relocation did not give China any greater security from attack.

Characteristically, Mao insisted that everything be built at breakneck speed, usually without any proper surveying. Irrational siting alone at least doubled normal construction costs, and left the new factories, which were frequently jerry-built, at the mercy of floods, avalanches and rock- and mud-falls. Many expensive plants, including tank factories and shipyards, were never finished, or overran by years. "Perhaps the most colossal failure," one study concluded, was the Jiuquan steel mill in Gansu, which took twenty-seven years to produce any steel at all.

The human costs were immeasurable. Over 4 million people were thrown into the mountains to build factories, lay railways and open mines, working and living in appalling conditions, in airless caves; water, often polluted, was in constant short supply. Many died. Countless families were torn apart for up to two decades. Only in 1984, long after Mao's death, were separated couples allowed to be reunited—and then only if the one in the Third Front was over forty, and had worked for twenty years.

Liu Shao-chi and Mao's other colleagues put up no resistance to this lunacy. Mao told them his mind was made up. To make it easier for them to swallow the idea, he gave the nearest thing in his lexicon to a commitment that people would not have to die from starvation, by telling his planners: "Be careful: Don't do a 1958, 1959 and 1960." In addition, although the Third Front was economic folly, it did not involve persecutions. For Mao to forgo deaths and political victimization seems to have been the best his colleagues thought they could expect—and enough to make them feel they might as well go along with him. It was, it seems, a good day if the boss waived a few million deaths.

CHINA'S FIRST BOMB was detonated on 16 October 1964 at Lop Nor in the Gobi Desert. The Silk Road had passed through here, linking central China with the shores of the Mediterranean Sea across the vast continents of Europe and Asia. Via this most barren and uninhabitable desert had flowed silk, spices, precious stones, art and culture with all their richness and splendor, exchanges that had excited ancient civilizations, and infused them with new life. Lop Nor had thus witnessed numerous life-enhancing impacts. Now, nearly two millennia later, it was the cradle of another "big bang," that of destruction and death.

The nuclear test site had originally been chosen by the Russians. There, army engineers, scientists and workers had been living for years in mud huts and tents, and in total isolation, working through sandstorms, searing heat and freezing winds.

On the day itself, Mao was waiting for the big moment in his suite in the Great Hall—baptized "of the People," although off limits to anyone uninvited. Situated on Tiananmen Square, a stone's throw from Zhongnanhai, it was designed to withstand any kind of military assault, and had its own nuclear bunker. The suite tailor-made for Mao was code-named Suite 118, in line with his usual clandestine style. Mao could drive straight into it in his car. Inside, there was a lift down into an escape tunnel wide enough for two trucks abreast, which led to the underground military centers on the edge of Peking. The suite was adjacent to the stage of a giant auditorium, so that Mao could emerge, and leave, without any close contact with the audience.

On that day, waiting next to Mao's suite were 3,000 performers involved in a musical extravaganza promoting his cult, *The East Is Red*, which Chou En-lai had staged. The title had been taken from the Mao "anthem":

> *The East is red,*
> *The sun rises,*

China has produced a Mao Tse-tung.
He seeks happiness for the people,
He is the people's great saviour.

Once the success of the test was confirmed, the music of the anthem started, bright lights came on, and a beaming Mao stepped out, flanked by his whole top Party team. Waving to the 3,000 performers, he signaled for Chou En-lai to speak. Chou stepped in front of the microphones: "Chairman Mao has asked me to give you some good news . . ." Then he announced that a Bomb had been detonated. The crowd was silent at first, not knowing how to react, having been given no prior instructions. Chou then provided a cue: "You can rejoice to your hearts' content, just don't jump through the floor!" Whereupon they started yelling and leaping up and down in an apparent frenzy. Mao was the only leader of any country to greet the birth of this monster of mass destruction with festivity. In private, he composed two lines of doggerel:

Atom bomb goes off when it is told.
Ah, what boundless joy!

Celebrations were organized throughout the country. Among the population, who learned for the first time that evening that China had been making a Bomb, there was genuine exultation. To possess nuclear weapons was regarded as a sign of the nation's achievement, and many felt tremendous pride—especially since they were told that China had produced the Bomb single-handed, with no foreign assistance. The decisive role that Russia played was strictly suppressed, and is little known today.

With hunger only a couple of years behind, and painful memories raw, some among the elite wondered how much the Bomb had cost. The regime registered the import of the questions, and Chou made a point of telling a small audience that China had made the Bomb very cheaply, and had spent only a few billion yuan on it. In fact, the cost of China's Bomb has been estimated at US$4.1 billion (in 1957 prices). This amount in hard currency could have bought enough wheat to provide an extra 300 calories per day for two years for the entire population—enough to save the lives of every single one of the nearly 38 million people who died in the famine. Mao's Bomb caused 100 times as many deaths as both of the Bombs the Americans dropped on Japan.

A TIME OF
UNCERTAINTY AND SETBACKS
(1962–65 ★ AGE 68–71)

IN THE YEARS after 1962, while China was recovering economically, Mao nursed his revenge. Liu Shao-chi, his normally circumspect and seemingly obliging No. 2, had ambushed and outsmarted him at the Conference of the Seven Thousand in January 1962. Under the collective pressure of virtually the whole Chinese establishment, Mao had been forced to abandon his lethal policies. Mao was not going to let Liu or anyone who sympathized with Liu get away with thwarting him.

Mao started clearing the ground for a big purge from the moment the famine abated. He put the brakes on liberal measures such as letting peasants lease some land, and rehabilitating political victims, and he steadily fueled his personality cult. Eulogies of Mao increasingly dominated school texts, publications, the media and every sphere that affected people's minds, so that wherever anyone's eye fell there were slogans hailing him, and whenever a song was heard it was in the vein of the one called "Father is close, Mother is close, but neither is as close as Chairman Mao." Mao was making everything more thoroughly politicized than ever, in a context where only adulation of him was permitted to exist.

He opened with novels, saying sarcastically to a Party audience in September 1962: "Aren't there a lot of novels and publications at the moment? Using novels to carry out anti-Party activities is a big invention." Mao later laid into all books: "The more books you read, the more stupid you become." "You can read a little," he would say, "but reading too much ruins you, really ruins you." This was unashamedly cynical, as he himself was well-read, and loved reading. His beds were tailor-made to be extra large, with enough space for loads of books to be piled on one side (and sloping, so that the books would not topple over onto him), and his favorite hobby was reading in bed. But he wanted the Chinese people to be ignorant. He told his inner circle that "We need the policy of 'keep people stupid.' "

In spring 1963, Mao turned his attention to traditional Chinese opera.

Unlike opera in the West, Chinese opera was popular entertainment. For hundreds of years, different regions had developed their own distinctive styles, performed in village markets as well as city theaters, danced in the northern mountains amidst winds and dust, and sung under moonlight and kerosene lamps on southern islets, listened to by fishermen on house-boats. Mao himself was a fan, indeed a connoisseur of regional operas. He had a collection of over 2,000 cassettes and records, and would discuss interpretations of arias knowledgeably with opera singers. The only time he let people see him wearing glasses was at operas. He was a very involved viewer as well, and once he became so engrossed that he not only sobbed and blew his nose loudly, but shot straight up from his seat, whereupon his trousers fell down, as his servant had loosened his belt to make him more comfortable. He had a particular taste for those operas his own regime deemed "pornographic."

Mao's passion for the opera did not prevent him suppressing a large number of them soon after his reign began. But when he embarked on this new purge he set out to get the old repertoires banned *in toto*, start-ing with a genre known as "Ghost Dramas," in which dead victims' spir-its took revenge on those who had driven them to their death. Mao had the genre banned in March 1963; having just been the agent of tens of millions of deaths, he regarded these on-stage avengers as uncomfortably close to reality.

At the end of 1963, he accused "all art forms—operas, theater, folk arts (including ballad-singing, traditional story-telling and stage comics), music, the fine arts, dance, cinema, poetry and literature" of being "feudal or capitalist," and "very murky." Even works produced under his own regime to sing the praises of the Communists were condemned as "poisonous weeds." Mao ordered artists to be sent down to villages to be "seriously reformed." "Throw singers, poets, playwrights, and writers out of the cities," he said in his quintessentially blunt style in February 1964. "Drive the whole lot of them down to the villages. No food for those who don't go."

Ancient monuments, the visible signs of China's long civilization, fell victim too. Mao had started having city walls and commemorative arches knocked down indiscriminately soon after he came to power; by the end of the 1950s the vast majority were destroyed. He now added temples and old tombs to his hit list, and complained to one of his secretaries in December 1964 about the slow obedience to his order: "Only a few piles of rotten bones [i.e., tombs] have been dug out . . . You take the enemies [i.e., those resisting] too lightly. As for the temples, not one of them has been touched."

Mao even pushed for the elimination of horticulture: "growing flowers is a hangover from the old society," he said, "a pastime for the feudal scholar class, bourgeois class and other layabouts." "We must change it now," he ordered in July 1964. "Get rid of most gardeners."

What Mao had in mind was a completely arid society, devoid of civilization, deprived of representation of human feelings, inhabited by a herd with no sensibility, which would automatically obey his orders. He wanted the nation to be brain-dead in order to carry out his big purge—and to live in this state permanently. In this he was more extreme than Hitler or Stalin, as Hitler allowed apolitical entertainment, and Stalin preserved the classics. In fact, Mao criticized Stalin on this score; in February 1966, Mao said: "Stalin took over the so-called classics of Russia and Europe uncritically, and this caused grave consequences."

IN THE YEARS 1962–65 Mao made some headway in turning every facet of life into something "political" and killing culture, but the result was far from satisfactory for him. He had to rely on the Party machine to execute his orders, and virtually everyone had reservations about his policies, all the way from the Politburo downward. Few welcomed a life without entertainment or color. Mao found that almost everyone was dragging their feet, and that recreations patently harmless to the regime, like the classics and flowers, continued to exist. He was angry and frustrated, but was unable to have his way.

He was more successful in one area, indoctrinating the population, for whom he created a role model: a safely dead soldier called Lei Feng. Lei Feng had most conveniently kept a diary in which he allegedly recorded how he was inspired by Mao to do good deeds, and swore that for Mao he was ready to "go up mountains of knives and down into seas of flames." Total obedience to Mao, to be what the regime lauded as perfect "little cogs" in Mao's machine, was elevated to the ultimate virtue. This cult of impersonality, the necessary obverse of the cult of Mao's personality, was cloaked in a deceptive appeal to be selfless—for "our country" or "the people."

Apart from symbolizing total loyalty to Mao, soldier Lei Feng exemplified another vital point: the idea that hate was good, which was drilled into the population, especially the young. Lei Feng had reportedly written: "Like spring, I treat my comrades warmly ... And to class enemies, I am cruel and ruthless like harsh winter." Hatred was dressed up as something necessary if one loved the people.

As a particular hate figure, Mao built up Khrushchev, on the grounds that he practiced "revisionism." The Chinese press was flooded with polemics demonizing the Soviet leader, which the population was force-fed at weekly indoctrination sessions. It was thus drilled into people's minds that Khrushchev and other "revisionists" were villains (like murderers in a normal society). Eventually, the other shoe would drop: Mao would condemn Liu Shao-chi as "China's Khrushchev," and disobedient Party officials as "revisionists."

The first time Mao raised the specter of a Chinese Khrushchev was to his top echelon on 8 June 1964. Liu knew that Mao was driving at him, and that the tornado was about to strike. His options were limited. All he could do was try to entrench his own position to make it harder for Mao to get him. Then, in October, something happened in Moscow that gave Liu an opening.

ON 14 OCTOBER 1964, Khrushchev was ousted in a palace coup. Mao saw an opportunity to resuscitate Soviet assistance for his missile program, which had fallen far behind schedule. He found himself in the position of finally possessing the atomic bomb, but lacking the means to deliver it. For this, he needed foreign know-how, and he set his sights on improving relations with the new leadership in the Kremlin, now headed by Leonid Brezhnev. Within days, Chou was telling Soviet ambassador Chervonenko that it was Mao's "utmost wish" to have a better relationship. Chou requested an invitation to the anniversary of the Bolshevik Revolution in Moscow on 7 November.

The new Soviet leadership was also interested in finding out whether a rapprochement was possible, and made sure that Mao was the first to hear about Khrushchev's downfall, before it was made public. But the Kremlin quickly realized that the prospect was extremely dim as long as Mao remained in charge. Ambassador Chervonenko recalled what happened when he went to tell Mao. "It was about 11 pm when I entered Mao's residence." After hearing the news, Mao

> thought for a moment or two, and then said: "Nice move you have made, but this is not enough" ... After the meeting, Mao ... saw me off. The car wouldn't start, so the driver took a bucket and went to the kitchen with Mao's bodyguard. The moon was shining on the lake. Mao was standing beside my stalled car: "There are still a few things that need fixing," he said, "and your Plenum hasn't done them all."

Mao insisted that Moscow must repeal its Party program and, in effect, disown de-Stalinization. This was out of the question for the new Soviet leaders, and so it seems that they used Chou's visit to test the water to see whether there was a possibility of the CCP dumping Mao.

At the reception in the Kremlin on 7 November, the big day, Chou and his delegation were walking round toasting old acquaintances when Soviet defense minister Rodion Malinovsky approached Chou, bringing along Russia's top Chinese-language interpreter. Out of the blue, Malinovsky said to Chou: "We don't want any Mao, or any Khrushchev, to stand in the way of our relationship." "I don't understand what you are talking about," Chou replied, and walked away at once. Malinovsky then turned to Marshal Ho Lung, China's acting army chief: "We've got rid of our fool Khrushchev, now you get rid of yours, Mao. And then we can have friendly relations again." Malinovsky used barrack-room language: "The marshal's uniform I am wearing was Stalin's dog-shit, and the marshal's uniform you are wearing is Mao Tse-tung's dog-shit . . ." Ho Lung argued with him, and then the Chinese delegation left the reception.

Chou sat up all night composing a cable to Mao. The next morning, Brezhnev came with four senior colleagues (but not Malinovsky) to the Chinese delegation's residence, where Chou made a formal protest. The Russians apologized, saying that Malinovsky's words did not reflect their views, and that he was drunk. But, quite apart from the fact that Malinovsky was a man who could hold his liquor, such words could never be spoken lightly by the army chief of one country to the premier and an army chief of another country, particularly when the countries involved were totalitarian Russia and China. Moreover, the Soviet leadership did not censure Malinovsky, which they surely would have done had this been a genuine gaffe. All the evidence suggests that Malinovsky acted deliberately, in a way that could be disowned. A top Russian intelligence expert on China used a telling formulation to us: "We learned that we could not divide Chou and Mao."

This episode enormously stoked Mao's suspicions that there might be a vast plot against him involving senior colleagues in cahoots with the Russians. Nothing could be more dangerous for him than the Kremlin expressing a serious wish to oust him. Neither the challenge by Peng De-huai in 1959, nor that by Liu in 1962, had shaken his position. But if the Kremlin really wanted to get rid of him, that would be a different story. Interest on the part of Russia might well embolden some of his colleagues to take drastic steps. The distance from the border of Russia's satellite Outer Mongolia to Peking was only some 500 km, over mainly flat and open land, which Russian tanks could easily overrun, and China lacked effective anti-tank defenses. The very next month, December 1964, on Mao's instructions, the army drew up a plan to construct artificial mountains, each like a giant military fortress, on the North China plain, as obstacles to Russian tanks—a huge project that was abandoned as useless after several years and immense cost.

Chou managed to retain Mao's favor, as Mao figured Chou was too shrewd to try anything rash. But Chou knew that a cloud of suspicion was hanging over his head. Before leaving Moscow, members of his entourage heard him say that he had visited Moscow ten times since the founding of Communist China, but that it was most unlikely that he would ever be returning. Indeed, this was his last visit—and none of Mao's colleagues ever visited Moscow as long as Mao lived.*

Mao was chary about anyone in his top circle going to Russia in case they schemed with the Russians to overthrow him. Even being present at the same occasion as high-level Russians in a third country—i.e., outside Mao's control—was to be avoided. In September 1969, Chou faced the possibility of bumping into some Soviet leader at the funeral of Ho Chi Minh in Hanoi, so he rushed to Hanoi ahead of the funeral, ignoring Vietnamese protests that they were not ready for visitors. And Chou left well before the ceremony itself, to which China sent a second-level delegation.

In the forthcoming purge, any connection with Russia became a key issue, especially among the top echelon. Marshal Ho Lung and a huge number of his old subordinates were arrested and interrogated. Ho Lung himself died in detention in appalling conditions in 1969.

So did Deputy Defense Minister General Xu Guang-da, who was brutally tortured over a period of eighteen months, being interrogated no fewer than 416 times. He had the misfortune to be the only senior military figure to visit Russia after Malinovsky's remarks, and so was suspected of being a link between Mao's domestic foes and Moscow. Xu had gone to Russia in May 1965 because at the time there was still some nuclear cooperation with Russia. Immediately after his trip, Mao withdrew all the Chinese at the Russian nuclear center at Dubna, shutting off nuclear collaboration completely.

Thanks to the Malinovsky episode, Mao had absolutely no relationship with Brezhnev. China's relations with the Soviet Union deteriorated to their worst ever under Brezhnev, who remained in power for the rest of Mao's lifetime.

But at the time of the Kremlin's heavy-handed feeler in November 1964, Mao did not order Chou to leave. Chou stayed on in Moscow, and held meetings with a host of foreign delegates, whom Mao was keen for him to see. He returned to Peking on 14 November, according to schedule. Mao turned up to greet him at the airport with his whole team. The message was for the Russians: that the Chinese leadership was united. But the Russians drew mixed inferences. Soviet diplomats at the airport observed that Mao did not look at all well—"close to prostration," they thought.

THIS WAS AN exceptionally unsure time for Mao, and Liu Shao-chi exploited it. He made a bid to strengthen his position by having himself

---

* Except for a stop-over by Deng Xiao-ping en route to a Party congress in Romania in July 1965, which shows Mao's trust in Deng.

reconfirmed as state president. This would provide an opportunity for a huge burst of profile-building, as a sort of personality cult for himself. Reconfirmation of his tenure was long overdue. Mao had not allowed the body that "elected" the president, the National Assembly, to convene as it should have in 1963, because he only wanted it to meet when he was ready to purge Liu. But within weeks of Malinovsky's remarks about getting rid of Mao, Liu convened the Assembly on extraordinarily short notice, calculating that Mao would feel too insecure either to veto this move or to purge him. Mao saw what Liu was up to, and erupted. "Let's do the handover now," he said sarcastically to Liu on 26 November: "You take over and be the chairman. You be Qinshihuang [the First Emperor] . . ."

Mao could not prevent the Assembly meeting. All he could do was to withhold his blessing by not calling a Party plenum beforehand to set the agenda—the only time such an omission ever happened during his reign. In the Politburo the day before the Assembly opened, Mao snapped at Liu repeatedly: "I just won't endorse [you]." At one point, he told Liu: "You're no good."

Outside the meeting room, Mao exploded to a couple of his devotees: "Someone is shitting on my head!" Then, on his seventy-first birthday, on 26 December, he took the most unusual step of inviting Liu for dinner. Mao almost never socialized with Liu or his other colleagues, except for being on the dance floor at the same time. Beforehand, Mao said to his daughter Li Na: "You are not coming today, because your father is going to curse the mother-fucker." Mao sat at one table with a few favorites, while Liu was put at a separate table. There was not an iota of birthday atmosphere. While everyone else sat in frigid silence, Mao ranted on with accusations about "revisionism," and "running an independent kingdom," transparently directed at Liu.

No one said anything in support of Mao, not even the equivalent of "You're right, Boss"—except his secretary, Chen Bo-da. Mao so appreci-ated this that afterwards he summoned Chen, drowsy with sleeping pills, in the small hours of the night, and confided to him that he intended to get Liu, making Chen one of the first people to be told this explicitly. (Mao was soon to catapult Chen to No. 4 in the Party.)

On 3 January 1965, Liu was reappointed president, to a blaze of public-ity, quite unlike the occasion of his original appointment in 1959, when there had been little fanfare. This time there were rallies and parades, with his portrait carried alongside Mao's, and firecrackers, drums and gongs. Newspapers ran headlines like "Chairman Mao and Chairman Liu are both our most beloved leaders." (The president is also called "chair-man" in Chinese.) Liu plainly had many supporters rooting for him. He had earned a lot of credit with senior Party officials for extricating China from the famine. Even devoted Mao followers in the inner circle showed signs of switching allegiance. Most incredibly, the idea was mooted of hanging Liu's portrait on Tiananmen Gate—alone, *without Mao's!*—which Liu had to veto at once.

On the day Liu was being re-elected, his wife was summoned, for the first time ever, to a meeting in Mao's Suite 118 in the Great Hall. The Lius were very much in love, and Mao knew it. He chose this day to signal his intention to make them both suffer. When Liu walked in after the vote, he was taken aback when he saw his wife was present. Mao pounced, bellowing a long tirade. Mme Liu felt immense hatred radiating from Mao. She and Liu looked at each other in silence. Mao wanted Mme Liu to witness her husband being abused, and for Liu to register: I will make your wife pay too.

Yet, even after such an overt display of hostility, no colleague took Mao's side and denounced Liu. Most just expressed concern about the discord between "the two chairmen," and urged Liu to adopt a more obsequious posture towards Mao. Liu eventually apologized to Mao for not being respectful enough. Mao's response was as menacing as it was arbitrary: "This is not a matter of respect or disrespect. This is a question of Marxism versus Revisionism."

Echoing Stalin's remark about Tito ("I will wag my little finger and there will be no more Tito"), Mao told Liu: "Who do you think you are? I can wag my little finger and there will be no more you!" But in fact, for now, there was a stand-off. Mao could not get Liu condemned just on his own say-so.

AT THIS POINT Mao resorted to a potent symbolic gesture—a trip to the Jinggang Mountains, where he had set up his first base in 1927. Unlike his other trips, which were spur-of-the-moment, this one was publicized well in advance among his top circle, so all his colleagues knew he was going. Six years before, facing a rebellious Peng De-huai, Mao had threatened that if he were challenged he would "go up into the mountains and start guerrilla warfare." Now he was actually going to the mountains, which made the message altogether louder, more actual and more powerful.

A portable squat toilet was constructed. An advance team scouted the destination. "Class enemies" were detained and stashed well away from Mao's route. Duplicate cars were prepared, and heavy machine-guns positioned on commanding points. The Praetorian Guard lurked in plain clothes, their weapons concealed, like Hollywood gangsters', in musical instrument cases.

Mao left Peking in late February 1965, moving slowly, feeling his way. En route, on 9 April, he learned of the death of a favorite retainer, the 63-year-old boss of Shanghai, Ke Qing-shi, of misdiagnosed pancreatitis. For such an invaluable acolyte to die by human error at this juncture was alarming, so Mao stayed put in Wuhan. There, he summoned his long-term accomplice, defense minister Marshal Lin Biao, for a tête-à-tête meeting on 22 April. The marshal, who had rescued Mao at the Conference of the Seven Thousand in January 1962, was in on Mao's plans to purge President Liu. Mao told him to keep a particularly tight grip on the army and a sharp lookout in case the president, who was overseeing things in the capital, should try to gain support among the military.

On 19 May, Lin Biao made a spectacular démarche in line with Mao's request. On that day, in his capacity as president, Liu was receiving the participants at a high-level army meeting when the marshal turned up unexpectedly, having earlier declined the invitation on health grounds. At the end of the meeting, when the president announced that it had reached a satisfactory conclusion the marshal suddenly stood up and launched into a harangue that basically contradicted what Liu had said. He thus made it unmistakably clear to the top brass that he, not the president, was their boss, massively undermining Liu's authority.

While the marshal kept an eye on President Liu in Peking, Mao proceeded to his old outlaw stamping-ground on 21 May. He stayed there seven nights, going nowhere apart from short walks in the immediate vicinity of the guest house. A stop had been scheduled at his old residence, the Octagonal Pavilion, but as he got out of the car, Mao heard faint noises. These were actually hammers and chisels clanging from some masons at work on a distant slope, but here in the mountains noise traveled far. Just as his foot was touching the ground, Mao shrank back into the car, and ordered it to drive off at once.

Mao did not see any local people until minutes before his departure, when organized crowds were brought to stand outside the guest house, and he waved at them and had photographs taken. His presence had been kept secret until the last minute. During his stay, and for some time after he left, all communications with the outside world for the locals were cut off.

The guest house where Mao stayed, which had been built during the famine, was not up to his standards, so work on another soon began, to the usual specifications: one-story and totally bomb-proof. But Mao never returned. He had come for one purpose only: to make a threat.

WHILE MAO WAS in the mountains, Liu was busy building up his own profile. On 27 May an article appeared in *People's Daily*, replete with vintage cult language: "The hills were extraordinarily green, and the water was exceptionally blue . . . the scenery of the Ming Tombs Reservoir displayed unprecedented splendour." But instead of being just about Mao, it was about both Mao and Liu, and both of them were engaged in the quintessential Mao cult activity of swimming:

After 3 in the afternoon, two cars stopped ... Two towering, kindly-looking men stepped out of the cars, and with firm steps walked towards the water.

... these were our most revered and beloved leaders, Chairman Mao and Chairman Liu. The crowd immediately burst into loud cheers:

"Chairman Mao has come swimming!"

"Chairman Liu has come swimming!"

The youth saw that Chairman Mao and Chairman Liu were glowing with tremendous health and spirits, and felt a surge of happiness through their bodies ...

Chairman Mao and Chairman Liu ... swam forward shoulder to shoulder ...

But this was not a "news" report at all. The swim had actually taken place the previous year, on 16 June 1964. That it was resurrected suggests that the story was inserted to promote Liu's image, at a time when Mao's absence from Peking meant *People's Daily* did not have to clear it with Mao. For this and other acts of disobedience, Mao later visited ghastly punishment on his media chiefs.

AFTER HIS TRIP to the Jinggang Mountains to make his threat, Mao did not act at once. It seems that the reason he held his fire was that he was waiting for a particular international event to take place. This was the second Afro-Asian summit, scheduled for June 1965 in Algiers. As president, Liu had had dealings with many heads of state who would be there, and to purge him just before the gathering would create a bad impression. The summit was crucial to Mao, who wanted to use it to establish a dominant role in the Third World. As he was not prepared to leave his home turf, for security reasons, he had to pull the strings from afar. His man for the job was Chou En-lai.

The first Afro-Asian summit had taken place ten years before at Bandung in Indonesia, where Chou had had considerable success in wooing newly independent Third World countries. Since then, Peking's influence had grown substantially, thanks, not least, to its extravagant aid. Nehru, the star at Bandung, was dead, and meanwhile China had acquired the Bomb. Mao entertained the idea that at this second summit he could be seen as the patron—if Russia did not take part. In the preparations for the Algiers summit Mao's goal had been to keep the Russians out.

To this end, Peking courted Indonesia's President Sukarno, as he was the man vetting the invitations, in his capacity as host of the first summit. China offered him lavish gifts, quite possibly including soldiers for a war he was waging against Malaysia. Top of the list of offers was to train Indonesian nuclear scientists, enabling Sukarno to announce that Indonesia would soon explode an atom bomb. China dangled the same lure of nuclear secrets in front of Egypt, another key Third World country, when in fact Mao had no intention of sharing his nuclear knowledge; when Nasser later asked Chou to deliver on his promise, Chou told him to be "self-reliant."

To buy votes for the Algiers summit, Mao committed China to its biggest-ever overseas project—a railway nearly 2,000 km long from land-locked Zambia across Tanzania to the Indian Ocean. Informed that Tanzania's President Julius Nyerere was interested in such a railway and could not get the West to put up the money, Chou said: "Chairman Mao said whatever the imperialists oppose, we support; the imperialists oppose this, so we sponsor it..." Mao was not concerned whether the railway was viable. When Nyerere expressed hesitation about accepting the offer, Chou pressed harder, claiming that Chinese railway-building materials and personnel would be going to waste if they were not used in Tanzania. The project cost about US$1 billion, which Mao dismissed as "No big deal."

Ten days before the summit was due to open, Algeria's President Ahmed Ben Bella was overthrown in a military coup. A short while before, Mao had called him "my dear brother." Now he dropped Ben Bella like a hot potato, and ordered Chou to back the new military government and ensure the summit went ahead on schedule.

Peking's diplomats started lobbying frantically, even though it was clear that the vast majority of governments due to attend favored a postponement. Even the very pro-Chinese Nyerere gave Peking's lobbyist a piece of his mind: "Chou En-lai is my most respected statesman. But I don't understand why he insists on the conference being held on schedule," Ben Bella, Nyerere said, was an "anti-colonialist hero recognised all over Africa," adding: "I must tell you [that China's lobbying] has damaged the reputation of China and Premier Chou himself."

The summit was postponed. Peking's hustling boomeranged. Within weeks, Nasser, in many ways the decisive voice, was backing Russian participation. If the Russians attended, Mao would be unable to play the leading role. So the Chinese announced that they would not take part. The summit never convened.

AS HIS DREAM of playing the leader to Asian and African countries collapsed, in fury, Mao lashed out. Longing to score a victory somewhere, he went to the brink of war with India.

Three years before he had trounced India satisfactorily. But now, in autumn 1965, he could not guarantee success, as India was much better prepared. So he resorted to parasitizing on someone else's conflict, always a risky undertaking. On 6 September, Pakistan got into a war with India. Over the previous years, Pakistan had grown much closer to China, and become one of the two biggest non-Communist recipients of Chinese aid.*

Pakistan's war with India seemed to Mao to offer a chance to score another victory over India, which would be forced to fight on two fronts if China intervened. He moved troops up to the border, and issued two ultimatums, demanding that India dismantle alleged outposts on some territory Peking claimed, within three days, by 22 September. When Delhi replied in a conciliatory vein, denying it had outposts there, but calling for a "joint investigation" and promising that if outposts were found, it "would not oppose dismantling them," Peking answered thuggishly that "there is no need for investigation," and that there just were outposts. Mao was bent on war.

But the scheme collapsed when Pakistan suddenly accepted a UN call for a ceasefire before China's deadline had expired. The Pakistanis told Mao that the cost of continuing fighting was too high, both diplomatically and economically, but Mao pressed them to fight on, reportedly giving Pakistan's President Ayub Khan the message: "If there is a nuclear war, it is Peking and not Rawalpindi that will be a target." When the Pakistanis declined to oblige, Mao was left out on a limb, and Peking had to climb down in public, lamely alleging that India had secretly dismantled its outposts—when in fact India had not stirred. Mao ended up deeply frustrated.

IMPATIENT FOR A SUCCESS, Mao tried to ignite violent insurrections wherever he could. In Thailand, the Communist Party fostered by Mao (and composed overwhelmingly of ethnic Chinese) now launched into armed insurgency, clashing for the first time with government forces on 7 August 1965, thenceforth known as "Gun-Firing Day." It got nowhere.

The biggest—and most tragic—fiasco came in Indonesia. The Communist Party there, the PKI, was the largest in the non-Communist world, with some 3.5 million members, and had the kind of secret intimate relationship with Peking which the Chinese Communists had had with Stalin before they conquered China.† The head of the Japanese

---

* In 1965 China began talking about transferring nuclear know-how to Pakistan—or, more accurately, dangling the prospect. Pakistan had grown more and more useful to Mao as a staging post to the Middle East, and Peking aggressively backed Pakistan's ambitions over Kashmir, training Kashmiri guerrillas for what China presented as a "national liberation" war.
† In September 1963, Chou En-lai brought PKI chief Aidit to a secret summit at Conghua in South China with Vietnam's Ho Chi Minh and the head of the Laotian Communists, to coordinate military strategy in Indonesia with the war in Indochina. This summit placed Indonesia on a strategic par with Indochina, and linked developments in Indonesia with the much more advanced military conflict in Indochina.

Communist Party at the time, Kenji Miyamoto, told us that Peking continually told the PKI, and the Japanese Party: "Whenever there is a chance to seize power, you must rise up in armed struggle." In 1964, Miyamoto discussed this with Aidit. Whilst the Japanese Communists were cautious, Aidit, who had great faith in Mao, was very eager to swing into action. After the Algiers summit folded, in lashing-out mood, Mao set the PKI in motion to seize power.

In early August Aidit came to China, where he met Mao. Aidit then proceeded to Indonesia with a team of Chinese doctors, who within days reported that President Sukarno (who was pro-Peking) had terminal kidney problems, and did not have long to live; so if the PKI were going to act, now was the time.

The plan was to decapitate the anti-Communist top brass of the army, over which President Sukarno held very limited sway. Peking had been pressing Sukarno to overhaul the army radically, and with Sukarno's support the PKI had been infiltrating the army with some success. The PKI believed, wildly over-optimistically, that it could secretly control over half the army, two-thirds of the airforce and one-third of the navy. According to the plan, once the generals were disposed of, Sukarno would step in and take over the army, while the Communists in the army kept the rank-and-file in line.

On 30 September a group of officers arrested and killed Indonesia's army chief and five other generals. Speaking shortly afterwards to Japanese Communist Party chief Miyamoto, Mao referred to this coup as "the Communist Party of Indonesia's ... uprising." But the PKI failed to cope with an unforeseen occurrence which derailed its whole plot. An informer had tipped off a then little-known general called Suharto, who was not on the arrest list. Thus prepared, Suharto waited for the arrests and killings of the other generals to be completed and then took immediate control of the army, unleashing a massacre of hundreds of thousands of Communists and sympathizers—and innocent people. Almost the entire PKI leadership was captured and executed. Only one member of the Politburo survived, Jusuf Adjitorop, who was in China at the time, and whom we met there, a disillusioned man, three decades later.

President Sukarno was forced out, and General Suharto established a military dictatorship that was fiercely anti-Peking and hostile to the large ethnic Chinese community at home.

Mao blamed the PKI for the failure. "The Indonesian party committed two errors," he told the Japanese Communists. First, "they blindly believed in Sukarno, and overestimated the power of the Party in the army." The second error, Mao said, was that the PKI "wavered without

fighting it out."* In fact, the slaughter unleashed by Suharto was so ferocious, and so instantaneous, that it had been impossible for the PKI to
fight back. Mao, in any case, was to blame, as he had started the action
for his own self-centered reasons. He just could not wait to have a victory
after his pipedream of Afro-Asian leadership collapsed.

By the end of 1965, Mao's global schemes had suffered one setback
after another. In a dark and vehement state of mind, he turned to deal
with his foes inside China.

---

* These parts of Mao's talks were withheld from the published version, and were made
available to us by the Japanese Communist Party Central Committee.

UNSWEET
REVENGE

8

A HORSE-TRADE SECURES
THE CULTURAL REVOLUTION
(1965–66 ★ AGE 71–72)

IN NOVEMBER 1965, Mao was finally ready to launch the Great Purge he had long been planning, to "punish this Party of ours," as he put it.

Mao proceeded in stages. He decided to fire his first shot at culture, and this is why the Great Purge was called the Cultural Revolution. Mme Mao spearheaded the assault. She was an ex-actress who actually loved culture, but cared nothing about denying it to other Chinese. And she enjoyed the chance to vent her venom, which she possessed in abundance. "Jiang Qing is as deadly poisonous as a scorpion," Mao once observed to a family member, wiggling his little finger, like a scorpion's tail. Mao knew exactly how to exploit her potential as a persecution zealot. In 1963 he had assigned her to the Ministry of Culture as his private supervisor to try to get operas and films condemned. Officials there had largely ignored her. She was already paranoid, and had been accusing her nurses of trying to poison her with sleeping pills and scald her when she took a bath. Now, she claimed that the officials she dealt with "suppressed and bullied" her—and she began revenging herself on them mercilessly. Mao made her his police chief for stamping out culture nationwide.

One of her tasks was to draw up a manifesto denouncing every form of culture, on the grounds that they had all been run by officials who were following a "black line opposed to Mao Tse-tung Thought." Mao told her to do this in collaboration with Lin Biao, the army chief. On the night of 26 November, Mme Mao telephoned Mrs. Lin Biao, who usually took her husband's calls, and acted as his chief assistant. Lin Biao pledged his help for the undertaking.

Mao and Lin Biao actually rarely met socially, but their collaboration went back nearly four decades—to 1929, when the two struck up an alliance to sabotage Zhu De, whom Lin Biao loathed and Mao was bent on dominating. From then on, a special crony relationship evolved between Mao and Lin. Mao tolerated an extraordinary degree of independence on Lin's part. For example, when Lin was in Russia during the Sino-Japanese War, he had spoken his mind to the Russians about Mao's unwillingness to fight the Japanese and how eager Mao was to turn on Chiang Kai-shek— an act Mao would never have swallowed from anyone else. During the Yenan Terror, Lin again did what no one else was allowed to: he simply removed his wife from detention and refused to let her be interrogated. Under Mao, everyone had to do humiliating "self-criticisms" in public, but not Lin. In return for giving Lin this degree of license, Mao expected him to come through for him in times of need, which Lin always did.

When Mao was launching the Great Leap Forward in 1958, he promoted Lin to be one of the Party's vice-chairmen, as a counter-weight to his other colleagues. When former defense minister Peng De-huai challenged Mao over the famine in 1959, Lin's staunch backing for Mao ensured that few dared to take Peng's side. Mao then moved Lin in to replace Peng as defense minister. Throughout the famine, Lin propped up Mao's image by promoting the cult of Mao's personality, especially in the army. He invented the Little Red Book, a collection of very short quotations by Mao, as a mechanism of indoctrination. At the Conference of the Seven Thousand in 1962, Lin saved Mao's skin by championing the equivalent of papal infallibility for him. Afterwards, when Mao was laying the ground for his Great Purge, Lin continued to build the army into the bastion of the cult of Mao.

Lin lauded Mao to the skies in public, although he felt no true devotion to Mao, and at home would often make disparaging and even disdainful remarks about him, some of which he entered in his diary. It was out of pure ambition that Lin stood by Mao and boosted him—the ambition to be Mao's No. 2 and successor. He told his wife that he wanted to be "Engels to Marx, Stalin to Lenin, and Chiang Kai-shek to Sun Yat-sen." With the Great Purge, which had Liu, the president, as its primary target, Lin Biao could expect his advancement.

The man who was about to rise to the top suffered from many phobias and looked like a drug addict. His most extreme phobias were about water and air. His hydrophobia was so acute that he had not taken a bath for years, and would only be wiped with a dry towel. He could not stand the sight of the sea, which kept his contact with the navy to zero. He had a villa by the seaside, but it was located among hills, so that he would not actually see the sea. His residences had numerous wind-sensitive devices hanging from the ceilings. One visitor was told by Mrs. Lin to walk slowly in Lin's presence in case the stir of air when he moved triggered her husband's breeze phobia.

Lin was a man, as his own wife observed in her diary, "who specialises in hate, in contempt (friendship, children, father and brother—all mean nothing to him), in thinking the worst and basest of people, in selfish calculation . . . and in scheming and doing other people down."

The man Lin particularly hated as of 1965 was the army chief of staff, Luo Rui-qing, one of Mao's long-time favorites, whom Mao fondly called Luo the Tall. Mao often routed his orders to the army via Luo the Tall, even orders to Lin himself, which was partly the result of Lin often being out of action nursing his phobias. Luo the Tall was super-energetic as well as able—and had incomparable access to Mao. He had been Mao's top security man for years, and Mao had enormous confidence in him. "As soon as Luo the Tall steps closer, I feel very safe," Mao said. These were words not spoken lightly. Lin felt overshadowed, and had been plotting to get rid of the chief of staff for some time. When he received Mme Mao's call in November 1965, which signaled that Mao needed him for a major task, Lin Biao seized his chance. Four days later, he dispatched his wife to see Mao in Hangzhou (the Lins were staying nearby in the garden city of Suzhou), with a letter in his own hand, enclosing some extremely flimsy charges against Luo the Tall. Lin was asking Mao to sacrifice a highly valued retainer.

Mao had Lin Biao himself brought to Hangzhou, and on the night of 1 December the two men had an ultra-secret talk. Mao told Lin about his plans for the Great Purge, and promised to make Lin his No. 2 and successor. He told Lin he must make sure the army was fully under control—and be ready to assume a completely new role: to step in and take over the jobs of the huge number of Party officials Mao intended to purge.

Lin insisted that Luo the Tall must be purged as well. The fact that Lin drove such a hard bargain shows that both he and Mao understood his unique value. Without Lin, Mao could not bring off his Purge.

MAO HAD BEEN trying hard, without success, to have one particular period opera condemned. This was called *Hai Rui Dismissed from Office*, and was based on a traditional story of a mandarin who was punished by the emperor for having spoken up for the peasants. Mao accused it of being a veiled attack on what he (the "emperor") had done to the purged defense minister Peng De-huai, and ordered it to be denounced, along with Marshal Peng himself. An article to this effect was written with Mao's sponsorship, and published in Shanghai on 10 November 1965.

To Mao's fury, the article was not carried anywhere else in China. Province after province, even the capital, Peking, ignored it. They were able to do this because the culture overlord at the time, Peng Zhen (no relative of Peng De-huai), blocked it from being reprinted. Peng Zhen was a loyal long-time follower, trusted enough to hold the vital strategic job of mayor of the capital, and few men were closer to Mao. But while his allegiance does not seem to have been in question, Mayor Peng, who had been made national overseer of culture in 1964, was strongly averse to Mao's demands to annihilate culture. And being at the heart of things, he realized that this time Mao intended to use the field of culture to start a purge that would engulf the whole Party.

Mayor Peng cared about the Party. He was also gutsy. He even complained to foreigners about Mao, something quite amazing among the tight-lipped CCP leadership. When a Japanese Communist asked him about the *Hai Rui* opera, Mayor Peng replied that: "It is not a political issue, but a historical play. Chairman Mao says it is a political issue. How troublesome!" This was unbelievably outspoken language for someone in the inner circle to use to an outsider.

With Mayor Peng taking the responsibility for blocking the Mao-sponsored article, even the *People's Daily* refused to reprint it. The editor, one Wu Leng-xi, knew that he was crossing Mao, as an eyewitness at a small meeting with him and Mao saw. Mao asked smokers to hold up cigarettes, and then said: "It seems on this point too I am in the minority." "At that remark," the witness recalled, "I saw Wu Leng-xi . . . turn chalky white, stop taking notes and go rigid. Something about what Mao had just said had frightened [him]."

And yet the editor held out for a week more, until Chou En-lai stepped in and ordered him to run the article, citing instructions from Mao. But the editor still managed to half-bury the article way back on page 5, in a section called "Academic Discussions," which meant that it was not a Party order to start a persecution campaign. The editor ended up in prison. To his successor Mao said menacingly: "Wu Leng-xi disobeyed me. And I wonder how you would behave." The successor was so panic-stricken that he could not stammer out what he wanted to say: "I will definitely obey Chairman Mao."

The fact that an article so overtly sponsored by Mao was treated in this way showed the degree of resistance he was facing from very powerful forces in the Party. Mao needed a system to carry out his will, and that made Lin Biao's instant help essential. Lin knew it, and he knew what he wanted in return: Chief of Staff Luo must suffer. So Mao conceded, even though Luo the Tall had been ultra-loyal, and Mao needed such men more than ever at this of all times. But Lin was the man he could not do without: there was no one with comparable clout who would do Mao's bidding. Luo the Tall was able and loyal, but he was not a marshal, and did not have long-established prestige in the army, and so he was sacrificed.

On 8 December, Mrs. Lin Biao addressed a Politburo meeting chaired by Mao, and spoke for a full ten hours about the alleged crimes of Luo the Tall, accusing him of having "bottomless" ambitions, starting with coveting Lin's job as defense minister. For Lin's wife to play such a role at a Politburo meeting was unheard-of, as she was neither a Politburo member nor even a high official, and wives of the top leaders had till now been kept very much in the background.

Luo the Tall was not present at the meeting. When he learned about his downfall, his legs turned to jelly. This powerfully built man was unable to walk upstairs. He was put under house arrest.

For his family, a nightmare began. One day very soon after this, his daughter, who attended a boarding school and had not heard the news about her father, was cycling home across Beihai Bridge opposite Zhongnanhai. The arch was flanked by elegant carved white marble balustrades. Through the dense dust borne by the cold wind from Siberia, she noticed three boys riding after her, close friends whose parents were also friends with hers. As they passed by her, they turned round and fixed her with a look of such coldness and disdain that it nearly knocked her off her bicycle. They knew something which she did not—that her father was now an enemy. That look, chilling, cruel, intended to hurt and break, from people whom only yesterday one had assumed to be friends, was to become a hallmark of the forthcoming years.

But Lin Biao was still not satisfied with the level of pain inflicted on Luo the Tall. He asked Mao to have Luo condemned for the equivalent of high treason: "wanting to usurp the Party and state." Mao was reluctant to allow this, as to do so would mean casting his old stalwart away irrevocably. So, for a few months, Luo the Tall was not charged with treason.

Lin therefore held back about helping Mao. When Mme Mao came to see him on 21 January 1966 about writing the planned "manifesto" against the arts in the name of the army, he made a show of willingness, and assigned a few writers from the army, but behind her back he told them: "Jiang Qing is sick . . . and paranoid . . . Just listen to what she says and say as little as you can . . . Don't make any criticisms about how the arts are run . . ." As a result, when their draft was submitted to Mme Mao in February, she called it "totally useless."

MEANWHILE, MAO WAS getting desperate. That same February, with the backing of Liu Shao-chi, Mayor Peng issued a national "guideline" forbidding the use of political accusations to trample on culture and the custodians of culture. Moreover, he went further, and actually suppressed Mao's instructions aimed at starting a persecution campaign. The obstruction from the Party was being highly effective.

Nor was this all. As soon as he issued the guideline, Mayor Peng flew to Sichuan, ostensibly to inspect arms industries relocated in this mountainous province. There he did something truly astonishing. He had a secret tête-à-tête with Marshal Peng who had been banished there the previous November when Mao began clearing the decks for the Great

Purge. What the two Pengs talked about has never been revealed, but judging from the timing, and the colossal risk Mayor Peng took in visiting a major foe of Mao's, without permission, *in secret*, it is highly likely that they discussed the feasibility of using the army to stop Mao.

Although Marshal Peng was under virtual house arrest and was powerless, he still commanded great respect and loyalty in the army, especially among his old subordinates. While he was under house arrest in Peking, a few of them, including one man high up in Mao's security apparatus, had risked a lot to see him.

News of the clandestine visit by Mayor Peng to the marshal may not have reached Mao's ears, but he certainly suspected Mayor Peng was up to something in Sichuan, and his suspicions deepened when Marshal Ho Lung, the man to whom Soviet defense minister Malinovsky had said "Get rid of Mao," soon also went to Sichuan, also in the name of inspecting the arms industries. Mao suspected a conspiracy was being cooked up down there, and soon accused his opponents of hatching a plot, dubbed "the February military coup."* Mao's state of mind was shown by the dosage of sleeping pills he was now taking, which rose to ten times his normal, to a level that could kill an average man.

And there was more that was gnawing at Mao's mind. It seems that Mayor Peng was contemplating getting in touch with the Russians, and may have thought of seeking Russian help to avert Mao's Purge. The Kremlin had invited the CCP to attend the next Soviet Party congress (the 23rd) in April 1966. Mao's colleagues knew that ever since Malinovsky's remarks in November 1964, Mao did not want any of them to go to Russia, in case they colluded with the Kremlin against him, and so they had recommended declining the invitation.

But in early March 1966, after his secret meeting with Marshal Peng in Sichuan, Mayor Peng revised this position, with the agreement of President Liu Shao-chi, and suggested to Mao that the Party should consider accepting the invitation. This was an extraordinary shift, and undoubtedly deepened Mao's suspicions. Mayor Peng was soon accused of trying to "liaise with a foreign country" and "attempt a coup." Mao's anxiety can hardly have been assuaged when the new Soviet ambassador, Sergei Lapin, with whom President Liu had earlier had an unusually frank talk, contrived an unscripted encounter with Liu on the tarmac at Peking airport on 24 February 1966 as they were awaiting the arrival of Ghana's President Kwame Nkrumah (who had been overthrown in a coup that same day). Lapin said he had an invitation for the Chinese to the Soviet

---

* This suspicion sealed the fate of Sichuan chief Li Jing-quan, who was supposed to be Peng De-huai's minder. Li, who had been one of Mao's favorites, suffered greatly in the years ahead, and his wife committed suicide.

congress. "Give me the document," Liu replied. Lapin said it was at the embassy; but all subsequent efforts to get it to Liu failed.

Mao was already suspicious that there might be a vast conspiracy between his colleagues and Moscow against him. The previous November, in the opening stage of the Purge, one of his first moves had been to fire the man who handled the leadership's communications with Moscow, the Russian-speaking director of the Central Secretaries' Office, Yang Shang-kun, and exile him to Canton, in the far south. Later, Yang was grilled intensely in prison about contacts with Moscow, as were the leadership's Russian-language interpreters.

There was one thing in Yang's past that especially roused Mao's suspicion. Yang's office had tape-recorded Mao. Mao did not want any record kept of what he said and did, unless it was carefully sanitized. In the old days, he would light a match to telegrams once they were sent. After he came to power, he would constantly ask his listeners not to take notes. But this caused insoluble problems, as Mao's words were commands, and the absence of written records made it hard for subordinates to know what he had really said and thus, at times, to carry out his orders. So he had to allow some of what he said to be noted down or taped. With Mao's approval, Yang's office began installing recording systems in the late 1950s. But a couple of years later, the tape operator unwisely teased a girlfriend of Mao's about overhearing her with Mao on his train. "I heard everything," he claimed, though in fact he had not. The girlfriend told Mao, who instantly ordered the systems dismantled and the tapes destroyed.* All Mao's houses and cars were combed for bugs. Although none was found, Mao was not convinced. He suspected the taping was part of a plot linked with President Liu and the Russians. All those involved would in time be interrogated, quite a few meeting gruesome deaths.

In March 1966, all the strands of Mao's suspicions meshed together. In January Brezhnev had visited Mongolia—the first Soviet leader ever to do so—and had been joined there by none other than defense minister Malinovsky, the man who had put out the feeler about ditching Mao. Brezhnev had never had dealings with Mao, but knew Liu Shao-chi, having been Liu's host when he visited Russia for a summit of the world Communist parties in 1960. Brezhnev, then No. 2 to Khrushchev, had spent more than a week with Liu traveling in Russia and to the Soviet Far East on the Trans-Siberian train, and the two had got on well. Now

---

* Although most were kept, and the man in charge told us that he privately saw to it that the ones destroyed were first transcribed. This was accomplished with the approval of his superior, who, it so happened, was Mayor Peng Zhen, who said: "I'll just tell the Chairman they are all destroyed."

Brezhnev signed a military treaty with Mongolian chief Yumjaagiyn Tsedenbal. Russian units were moved into Mongolia and stationed only about 500 km from Peking, across open country, accompanied by ground-to-ground missiles, apparently armed with nuclear warheads. Tsedenbal, who had been on the receiving end of Mao's plots to overthrow him earlier in the 1960s, volunteered to carry the fight against "the Mao clique" into China itself.

This was a real crisis for Mao, and he needed forceful support from Lin Biao—at once. He consented to Lin's demand to have Chief of Staff Luo condemned for "treason." On 18 March, Luo threw himself off the roof of his house, in a failed attempt to kill himself. This was regarded, as always, as "betraying" the Party, and qualified him for the nastiest punishment. Later, he was subjected to mass denunciation meetings, and as he had broken both ankles when he jumped off the roof, he would be dragged up onto the stage in a big basket, his crippled feet dangling over the rim, oozing blood.

The day after Luo's suicide attempt, Mme Mao wrote to Lin Biao asking him to endorse her "kill culture" manifesto, which Mao himself had meantime revised, writing Lin's name into the heading ("Comrade Lin Biao Has Authorized Comrade Jiang Qing to . . .") so as to highlight Lin's backing. Lin endorsed it at once in writing, and before the end of the month he had presented a formal demand to the Party, in the name of the army, for a comprehensive purge.

THIS MOVE BY Lin propelled another crucial man into affirming his stand. This was Chou En-lai, who had so far managed to maintain an ambivalent position. Chou now told Mayor Peng that he, Chou, was with Mao. It was with Chou on board that the unbeatable trio of Mao, Marshal Lin and Chou was complete, thus dooming any hope of resistance.

On 14 April 1966, Mme Mao's "kill culture" manifesto was made public. A month later, the Politburo met to rubber-stamp the first list of victims of the Great Purge, four big names described as an "anti-Party clique": Mayor Peng, Chief of Staff Luo, Yang Shang-kun, the liaison with Russia and the tape-recording suspect, and old media chief Lu Ding-yi. Mao did not bother to come to the occasion, and just ordered it to pass a document he had had prepared condemning the four. A fatalistic atmosphere dominated the gathering, which included two of the four-man "clique" and was actually chaired by Liu Shao-chi, who knew he was chairing an event that was ultimately going to bring him to ruin, even though for now he was not named. For once, his steely Communist training failed him. With unwontedly visible anger, he made a protest aimed at Mao: "we are ordered to discuss this document, but no revision is allowed . . . Is this not dictatorial?" He then asked Mayor Peng, who was condemned by name in the document, whether he had "any complaints." The mayor, who had acted so bravely up to now, answered: "No complaints." Liu gave him another chance to say something by asking: "Are you for it or against it?" The mayor hung his head and was silent. Liu then asked all in favor to raise their hands. All did, including Mayor Peng and Liu himself.

The members of the "clique" were soon hauled off and incarcerated. Mao's cynicism about his case is revealed in a conversation he had the following month with Vietnam's Ho Chi Minh. Mao claimed the four men "are with the Nationalists." When Ho queried this absurd assertion, Mao replied, without batting an eyelid: "We still do not have firm evidence, but just a suspicion of sorts."

At this May Politburo gathering it was Lin Biao who acted as Mao's intimidator. Raising his clenched fist, he surveyed the audience threateningly, and announced that anyone opposing Mao must be "put to death . . . the whole country must call for their blood." His speech was larded with coarse personal abuse, with foes referred to simply as "sons of bitches."

Most unusually, in the speech Lin spoke explicitly about the possibility of a coup d'état, a subject which was normally taboo. Mao had him talk in this way in order to knock any lingering dreams of a palace coup on the head. Mao had been making preparations against a coup for years, Lin disclosed, and particularly "in recent months," when Mao had "paid special attention to the adoption of many measures toward preventing a . . . coup." Mao had "deployed troops and key personnel . . . and made arrangements in critical departments like radio stations, the army and the police. This is what Chairman Mao has been doing in the past few months . . ." He also divulged that Mao had taken the possibility of a coup so seriously that he (Mao) had "lost sleep for many days."

Mao had indeed been making arrangements to forestall a coup. Army units officered by Lin men had been moved into the capital. "We transferred two more garrison divisions [into Peking]," Mao told Albania's defense minister. "Now in Peking we have three infantry divisions and one mechanised division, altogether four divisions. It is only because of these that you can go anywhere, and we can go anywhere." The Praetorian Guard was drastically purged, including three deputy chiefs, one dying a terrible death, two barely surviving. The only person left unscathed was its chief, Mao's trusted chamberlain Wang Dong-xing. Likewise, in the only other organization with access to weapons, the police, chiefs of both the ministry and its Peking bureau were arrested, because they had had ties to President Liu in the past. Another victim of Mao's precautions was the ethnic Mongolian chief of Inner Mongolia, Ulanhu. This province occupied a vital position bordering on Russia's satellite Mongolia. Ulanhu was detained that fateful May.

★

WHILE SHORING UP Mao, Lin Biao also attended to some personal business. Apart from Chief of Staff Luo, there was another member of the four-man "clique" he hated: media chief Lu Ding-yi, and for a rather unusual reason. Lu Ding-yi's wife was a schizophrenic who was fixated on Mrs. Lin, and had written the Lins over fifty scabrous anonymous letters claiming that Mrs. Lin had had a string of affairs, including one with Wang Shi-wei, the dissident leader of the young volunteers in Yenan, and that Lin might not be the father of their children. Some of the letters were addressed to the Lins' children, with lewd descriptions of their mother's alleged sex life, some signed with the name of Dumas' avenger, "Monte Cristo." Instead of receiving mental treatment, which was what she clearly needed, Mrs. Lu was arrested on 28 April 1966, and went through hell for the next twelve years.

At one session of the May Politburo gathering, Lin had a document placed in front of the participants. It read:

> I solemnly declare:
> 1. Ye Qun [Mrs. Lin] was a pure virgin when she married me. Since then, she has always been proper;
> 2. Ye Qun had no love relationship whatsoever with Wang Shi-wei;
> 3. Tiger and Dodo are blood son and daughter of mine with Ye Qun;
> 4. Everything written in the counter-revolutionary letters by [Mrs. Lu] is rubbish.
>
> *Lin Biao*
> 14 May 1966.

It was the first time such a colorful text had ever come before the Politburo.

Although this behavior seems ludicrous, it had a practical aim. Lin was clearing his wife's name, as she was now to be a fixture on the political scene, acting as his representative. He himself disliked attending meetings, or seeing people.

Mrs. Lin was a rather batty woman, a bundle of energy who received little love from the marshal and lived in a state of unremitting sexual frustration. She grew to be erratic, and managed to drive her own daughter, Dodo, to attempt suicide more than once, the first time in 1964. Like Mme Mao, who was also hysterical from frustration, Mrs. Lin now sought compensation and fulfillment in political scheming and persecution, although she was less awful than Mme Mao. She acted as her husband's assistant, and issued orders on his behalf.

Mao's Great Purge was rolling thanks to a horse-trade with his crony Lin Biao.

THE GREAT PURGE

(1966–67 ★ AGE 72–73)

A T T H E E N D of May 1966, Mao set up a new office, the Cultural Revolution Small Group, to help run the Purge. Mme Mao headed it for him, with Mao's former secretary, Chen Bo-da, its nominal director, and purge expert Kang Sheng its "adviser." This office, in addition to Lin Biao and Chou En-lai, formed Mao's latest inner circle.

Under the new cabal, the cult of Mao was escalated to fever pitch. Mao's face dominated the front page of *People's Daily*, which also ran a column of his quotations every day. Soon, badges started appearing with Mao's head on them, of which, altogether, some 4.8 billion were manufactured. More copies of Mao's *Selected Works* were printed—and more portraits of him (1.2 billion)—than China had inhabitants. It was this summer that the Little Red Book was handed out to everyone. It had to be carried and brandished on all public occasions, and its prescriptions recited daily.

In June, Mao intensified the terrorization of society. He picked as his first instrument of terror young people in schools and universities, the natural hotbeds for activists. These students were told to condemn their teachers and those in charge of education for poisoning their heads with "bourgeois ideas"—and for persecuting them with exams, which henceforth were abolished. The message was splashed in outsize characters on the front page of *People's Daily*, and declaimed in strident voices on the radio, carried by loudspeakers that had been rigged up everywhere, creating an atmosphere that was both blood-boiling and blood-curdling. Teachers and administrators in education were selected as the first victims because they were the people instilling culture, and because they were the group most conveniently placed to offer up to the youthful mobs, being right there to hand.

The young were told that their role was to "safeguard" Mao, although how their teachers could possibly harm "the great Helmsman," or what perils might beset him, was not disclosed. Nevertheless, many responded enthusiastically. Taking part in politics was something no one had been allowed to do under Mao, and the country was seething with frustrated activists who had been denied the normal outlets available in most societies, even to sit around and argue issues. Now, suddenly, there seemed to be a chance to get involved. To those interested in politics, the prospect was tremendously exciting. Young people began to form groups.

To make sure that students were fully available to carry out his wishes, Mao ordered schooling suspended from 13 June. "Now lessons are stopped," he said, and young people "are given food. With food they have energy and they want to riot. What are they expected to do if not to riot?" Violence broke out within days. On 18 June, scores of teachers and cadres at Peking University were dragged in front of crowds and manhandled, their faces blackened, and dunces' hats put on their heads. They were forced to kneel, some were beaten up, and women were sexually molested. Similar episodes happened all over China, producing a cascade of suicides.

On 24 June, a group from a middle school in Peking put up a wall poster, which they signed with the snappy name of "Red Guards," to show that they wanted to safeguard Mao. Their writing was full of remarks like: "Stuff 'human feelings!'" "We will be brutal!" "We will strike you [Mao's enemies] to the ground and trample you!" The seeds of hate that Mao had sown were being reaped. Now he was able to unleash the thuggery of these infected youth, the most malleable and violent element of society.

MAO ORCHESTRATED THESE events from the provinces. He had left the capital the previous November as soon as he had set the Purge in motion. Peking was no longer safe: it was full of foes he wanted to purge, and uncomfortably close to Russian troops on the Outer Mongolia border. For more than eight months, Mao stayed way down south, travelling incessantly.

He was also relaxing and storing up energy for the coming tempest. He took walks in the misty hills along the lake at Hangzhou, and flirted at his twice-weekly dancing parties. That June, while mayhem was rising, he spent some time in a particularly serene villa that he had never been to, outside his home village of Shaoshan. He had ordered this villa built during his previous visit seven years before. While swimming in a reservoir there, he had been much taken by the secluded beauty of the surroundings, and said to the provincial boss: "Mm, this place is pretty quiet. Would you build a straw hut here for my retirement?" As the man was soon purged, nothing was done until Mao brought it up again a year later, in the depth of the famine. So began "Project 203," the building of a giant steel and cement edifice called Dripping Grotto. The whole mountain range was sealed off, and the local peasants evicted. A helicopter pad and a special railway line were planned, and an earthquake- and atom bomb—proof building, with shock-absorbers, was later incorporated. Altogether, Mao stayed here for all of eleven days in that violent June, and never again.

This grey monstrosity was surrounded, incongruously, by soft green hills alive with blazing wildflowers, and the back abutted onto the Mao family's ancestral burial ground. Its front door faced a peak called Dragon's Head, auspicious in the view of geomancy. This delighted Mao, who chatted jovially with his entourage about the *feng shui* assets of the place.

Though he was just on the edge of his native village, Mao did not meet a single villager. On his way, a little girl had caught a glimpse of him in his car, and told her family. Police descended at once, and warned the family: "You didn't see Chairman Mao! Don't you dare to say that again!" Meetings were called to warn the villagers not to think that Mao was there. Mao spent most of his time reading and thinking. He did not even go swimming, although the reservoir was right on his doorstep.

By the end of June, he was ready to head back to Peking and start the next stage of his Purge. En route, he stopped at Wuhan, where on 16 July he swam for more than an hour in the Yangtze, watched by tens of thousands of people. Like his swim a decade before, this was to send the message to his foes that, at the age of seventy-two, he had the health, the strength and the will for a gigantic fight. And this time the symbolic gesture was also intended for the population at large, especially the young. The message was distilled into one slogan: "Follow Chairman Mao forward through high winds and waves!" Chanted repeatedly from the now ubiquitous loudspeakers, it fanned the flames in many restless heads. Having cranked up his media to ballyhoo this swim to the maximum, even making it famous abroad, Mao returned to Peking on 18 July. He immediately adopted a hands-on approach, frequently chairing meetings with the Small Group that ran the Purge, and meeting every day with Chou En-lai, who was in charge of day-to-day business.

Mao did not go back to his old house, claiming he did not like the way it had been redecorated. Instead, he moved into unexpected quarters in another part of Zhongnanhai—the changing-rooms of the swimming pools, which he made his main residence for the next ten years. He did not move there to swim. He was taking precautions against the possibility that bugging devices—or worse—had been installed during his absence.

IT WAS IN these nondescript changing-rooms that Mao created the terror of "Red August," with the aim of frightening the whole nation into an even greater degree of conformity. On 1 August he wrote to the first group of Red Guards, who had vowed in their posters to "be brutal" and to "trample" Mao's enemies, to announce his "fiery support." He circulated this letter, together with the bellicose Red Guard posters, to the Central Committee, telling these high officials that they must promote the Red Guards. Many of these officials were actually on Mao's hit list, but for now he used them to spread terror—one that would soon engulf themselves. Following Mao's instructions, these officials encouraged their children to form Red Guard groups, and these children passed the word to their friends. Red Guard groups mushroomed as a result, invariably headed by the children of high officials.

Learning from their fathers and friends that Mao was encouraging violence, the Red Guards immediately embarked on atrocities. On 5 August, in a Peking girls' school packed with high officials' children (which Mao's two daughters had attended), the first known death by torture took place. The headmistress, a fifty-year-old mother of four, was kicked and trampled by the girls, and boiling water was poured over her. She was ordered to carry heavy bricks back and forth; as she stumbled past, she was thrashed with leather army belts with brass buckles, and with wooden sticks studded with nails. She soon collapsed and died. Afterwards, leading activists reported to the new authority. They were not told to stop—which meant carry on.

A more explicit incitement to violence soon came from Mao himself. On 18 August, dressed in army uniform for the first time since 1949, he stood on Tiananmen Gate to review hundreds of thousands of Red Guards. This was when the Red Guards were written about in the national press and introduced to the nation, and the world. A leading perpetrator of atrocities in the girls' school where the headmistress had just been killed was given the signal honor of putting a Red Guard armband on Mao. The dialogue that followed was made public: "Chairman Mao asked her: 'What's your name?' She said 'Song Bin-bin.' Chairman Mao asked: 'Is it the "Bin" as in "Educated and Gentle?"' She said: 'Yes.' Chairman Mao said: 'Be violent!'"

Song Bin-bin changed her name to "Be Violent," and her school changed its name to "The Red Violent School." Atrocities now multiplied in schools and universities. They started in Peking, then spread across the country, as Peking Red Guards were sent all over China to demonstrate how to do things like thrash victims and make them lick their own blood off the ground. Provincial youngsters were encouraged to visit Peking to learn that Mao had given them enormous destructive license. To facilitate this process, Mao ordered that travel be made free, together with food and accommodation while traveling. Over the next four months, 11 million young people came to Peking and Mao made seven more appearances at Tiananmen Square, where they gathered in massive, frenzied, yet well-drilled crowds.

There was not one school in the whole of China where atrocities did not occur. And teachers were not the only victims. In his letter to the Red Guards on 1 August 1966, Mao singled out for praise some militant teenagers who had been dividing pupils by family background and abusing those from undesirable families, whom they labeled "Blacks." Mao announced specifically that these militants had his "fiery support," which was unequivocal endorsement for what they were doing. In the girls' school where the headmistress was tortured to death, "Blacks" had ropes tied around their necks, were beaten up, and forced to say: "I'm the bastard of a bitch. I deserve to die."

With models set up by Mao, this practice then spread to all schools, accompanied by a "theory of the bloodline," summed up in a couplet as ridiculous as it was brutal: "The son of a hero father is always a great man; a reactionary father produces nothing but a bastard!" This was chanted by many children of officials' families, who dominated the early Red Guards, little knowing that their "hero fathers" were Mao's real targets. At this initial stage, Mao simply used these children as his tools, setting them upon other children. When the Sichuan boss returned from Peking, he told his son, who was organizing a Red Guard group: "The Cultural Revolution is the continuation of the Communists against the Nationalists... Now our sons and daughters must fight their [Nationalists'] sons and daughters." This man could not possibly have given such an order unless it had come from Mao.

AFTER TERROR IN SCHOOLS, Mao directed his Red Guards to fan out into society at large. The targets at this stage were the custodians of culture, and culture itself. On 18 August, Mao stood next to Lin Biao on Tiananmen while Lin called on Red Guards throughout the country to "smash... old culture." The youngsters first went for objects like traditional shop signs and street names, which they attacked with hammers, and renamed. As in many revolutions, puritans turned on the softer and more flamboyant. Long hair, skirts and shoes with any hint of high heels were pounced on in the streets, and sheared by scissors-wielding teenagers. From now on, only flat shoes, and uniform-like, ill-fitting jackets and trousers, in only a few colors, were available.

But Mao wanted something much more vicious. On 23 August he told the new authorities: "Peking is not chaotic enough... Peking is too civilised." As Peking was the trail-blazer and the provinces all copied the capital, this was a way to pump up terror nationwide. That afternoon, groups of teenage Red Guards, many of them girls, descended on the countryard of the Peking Writers' Association. By then, a "uniform" was firmly in fashion for the Red Guards: green army-style clothes, often ordinary clothes dyed army green, or sometimes real army uniforms handed down by parents, red armband on the left arm, Little Red Book in hand—and a leather belt with brass buckles. Thus attired, the Red Guards rained blows with their heavy belts on some two dozen of the country's best-known writers. Large insulting wooden plaques were hung on thin wire from the writers' necks, as they were thrashed in the scorching sun.

The victims were then trucked to an old Confucian temple, which housed Peking's major library. There, opera costumes and props had been brought to make a bonfire. About thirty of the country's leading writers, opera singers and other artists were made to kneel in front of the bonfire and were set upon again with kicks and punches, sticks and brass-buckled belts. One of the victims was the 69-year-old writer Lao She, who had been lauded by the regime as "the people's artist." The following day, he drowned himself in a lake.

The site, props and victims had all been chosen to symbolize "old culture." The selection of the victims, all household names, was unquestionably done at the very top, since till now they had all been official stars. There can be no doubt that the whole event was staged by the authorities; the loosely-banded teenage Red Guards could not possibly have organized all this on their own.

Mao had also cleared the way for the atrocities to escalate by issuing explicit orders to the army and police on the 21st and 22nd, saying that they must "absolutely not intervene" against the youngsters, using uncommonly specific language such as "even firing blanks . . . is absolutely forbidden."

To spread terror deeper and closer to home, Mao got the young thugs to make violent raids on victims selected by the state, which gave their names and addresses to the Red Guards. The boss of Sichuan, for instance, ordered the department in his province that looked after prominent cultural figures to hand out a list to his son's Red Guard organization—something he could only have done if Mao had told him to.

On 24 August, national police chief Xie Fu-zhi told his subordinates to pass out such information. Clearly responding to questions like "What if the Red Guards kill these people?," Xie said: "If people are beaten to death . . . it's none of our business." "Don't be bound by rules set in the past." "If you detain those who beat people to death . . . you will be making a big mistake." Xie assured his reluctant subordinates: "Premier Chou supports it."

It was with the authorities' blessing that Red Guards broke into homes where they burned books, cut up paintings, trampled phonograph records and musical instruments—generally wrecking anything to do with "culture." They "confiscated" valuables, and beat up the owners. Bloody house raids swept across China, which People's Daily hailed as "simply splendid." Many of those raided were tortured to death in their own homes. Some were carted off to makeshift torture chambers in what had been cinemas, theaters and sports stadiums. Red Guards tramping down the street, the bonfires of destruction, and the screams of victims being set upon—these were the sights and sounds of the summer nights of 1966.

There was a short list of notables to be exempted, drawn up by Chou En-lai. This later brought Chou totally unmerited plaudits for allegedly "saving" people. In fact, it was Mao who got Chou to draw the list up, on 30 August, and the purpose was purely utilitarian. The only reason Chou had charge of it was because he was running the whole show, not because he stepped in to save people. The list comprised a few dozen names. By contrast, later official statistics show that in August–September, in Peking alone, 33,695 homes were raided (which invariably involved physical violence), and 1,772 people were tortured, or beaten, to death.

To cover himself, Mao had Chou En-lai announce to a Red Guard rally on Tiananmen on 31 August: "Denounce by words, and not by violence." This announcement allowed most Red Guards to opt out of violence by saying that Mao was against it. Some victims were also able to protect themselves by quoting this back to their persecutors. But as perpetrators of atrocities went unpunished, violence raged on.

One of Mao's aims with the house raids was to use the Red Guards as proxy bandits. They confiscated tons of gold, silver, platinum, jewelry, and millions of dollars in hard currency, which all went into the state coffers, as well as many priceless antiques, paintings and ancient books. The looting, along with mindless on-site destruction, cleaned virtually all valuable possessions out of private hands. Some of the plunder was exported to earn foreign currency.

The top few leaders were allowed to take their pick of the booty. Mme Mao selected an 18-carat gold French pendant watch, studded with pearls and diamonds, for which she paid the princely sum of 7 yuan. This was in line with the Maoist leadership's "un-corrupt" practice of insisting on paying for paltry items like tea leaves at meetings, but paying nothing at all for their scores of villas and servants, and having the de facto private use of planes and trains and other expensive perks. Kang Sheng, an antiques lover, privatized some house raids by sending in his own personal looters disguised as Red Guards. Mao himself pilfered thousands of old books. Sterilized by ultraviolet rays, they lined the shelves of his enormous sitting room, forming the backdrop to photographs of him receiving world leaders and impressing foreign visitors. The room, Kissinger mused, looked like "the retreat of a scholar." In fact, unknown to the American visitors, it had more in common with one of Goering's mansions adorned with art seized from victims of Nazism.

The regime squeezed something else out of these raids: housing space. The housing shortage was acute, as virtually no new dwellings had been built for ordinary urban residents under the Communists. Now the battered families who had been raided were squeezed into one or two rooms, and neighbors were moved into the rest of the raided houses, often resulting, not surprisingly, in excruciatingly bitter relations.

Some families who had been raided were exiled to villages, escalating a process which Mao had already initiated in order to turn cities into "pure" industrial centers. In Peking, nearly 100,000 were expelled in less than a month from late August. One eyewitness saw the vast waiting room at Peking railway station crammed with children waiting to be exiled with their parents. Red Guards ordered the children to kneel down, and then walked around aiming blows at their heads with brass-buckled belts. Some even poured scalding hot water over them as a farewell souvenir, while other passengers tried to find a place to hide.

IN SUMMER 1966 Red Guards ravaged every city and town, and some areas in the countryside. "Home," with books and anything associated with culture, became a dangerous place. Fearing that the Red Guards might burst in and torture them if "culture" was found in their possession, frightened citizens burned their own books or sold them as scrap paper, and destroyed their own art objects. Mao thus succeeded in largely wiping out culture from Chinese homes. Outside, he was also fulfilling his long-held goal of erasing China's past from the minds of his subjects. A large number of historical monuments, the most visible manifestation of the nation's civilization, which had so far survived Mao's loathing, was demolished. In Peking, of 6,843 monuments still standing in 1958, 4,922 were now obliterated.

Like the list of people to be spared, the list of monuments to be preserved was a short one. Mao did want to keep some monuments, like Tiananmen Gate, where he could stand to be hailed by "the masses." The Forbidden City and a number of other historical sites were put under protection and many were closed down, thus depriving the population of access even to the fraction of their cultural inheritance that survived. Not spared was China's leading architect, Liang Si-cheng, who had described Mao's wish to see "chimneys everywhere" in Peking as "too horrifying a picture to bear thinking about." Now he was subjected to public humiliation and abuse, and brutal house raids. His collection of books was destroyed, and his family expelled to one small room, with broken windows and ice-covered floor and walls. Chronically ill, Liang died in 1972.

Contrary to what is widely believed, the vast majority of the destruction was not spontaneous, but state-sponsored. Before Mao chided the

Red Guards for being "too civilized" on 23 August, there had been no vandalism against historical monuments. It was on that day, only after Mao spoke, that the first statue was broken—a Buddha in the Summer Palace in Peking. From then on, when important sites were being wrecked, official specialists were present to pick out the most valuable objects for the state, while the rest were carted off and melted down, or pulped.

It was Mao's office, the Small Group, which ordered the desecration of the home of the man whose name was synonymous with Chinese culture, Confucius. The home, in Shandong, was a rich museum, as emperors and artists had come there to pay homage, commissioning monuments and donating their art. The locals had been ordered to wreck it, but had responded by going slow. So Red Guards were dispatched from Peking. In their pledge before setting off, they said that the sage was "the enemy rival to death of Mao Tse-tung Thought." Mao did, indeed, hate Confucius, because Confucianism enjoined that a ruler must care for his subjects, and as Mao himself put it, "Confucius is humanism ... that is to say, People-centred-ism."

In the annihilation of culture, Mme Mao played a key role as her husband's police chief for this field. And she made sure there was no resurrection of culture for the rest of Mao's life. Partly thanks to her, for a decade, until Mao's death in 1976, old books remained banned, and among the handful of new books of general interest that were published, all of them sported Mao's quotations, in bold, on every other page. There were a few paintings and some songs around, but they all served propaganda purposes, and eulogized Mao. Virtually the only performing arts allowed were eight "revolutionary model shows" and a few films that Mme Mao had had a hand in producing. China became a cultural desert.

BY MID-SEPTEMBER 1966, the country was thoroughly terrorized and Mao felt confident enough to start stalking his real target: Party officials. On 15 September, Lin Biao instructed a Red Guards' rally on Tiananmen Square that they were to shift their target and "focus on denouncing those power-holders inside the Party pursuing a capitalist road," known as "capitalist-roaders." What Lin—and Mao—really meant was the old enforcers who had shown distaste for Mao's extremist policies. Mao aimed to get rid of them en masse, and the call went out to attack them right across China.

For this job, new groups were formed, who sometimes called themselves Red Guards but were generally known as "Rebels," because they were taking on their bosses. And these Rebels were mostly adults. The original Red Guard groups, most of them made up of teenagers, now fell apart, as they had been organized around the children of those same high officials who now became targets. Mao had used the young Red Guards to terrorize society at large. Now he was moving against his real enemies, Party officials; and for this he used a broader, mainly older force.

With Mao's explicit support, Rebels denounced their bosses in wall posters and at violent rallies. But anyone who thought the Party dictatorship might be weakened had their hopes dashed fast. People who tried to get access to their own files (which the regime held on everyone), or to rehabilitate those the Party had persecuted, were instantly blocked. Orders poured out from Peking making it clear that, although Party officials were under attack, the Party's rule was not to be loosened one bit. Victims of past persecutions were banned from joining Rebel organizations.

After some months to generate momentum, in January 1967 Mao called on Rebels to "seize power" from their Party bosses. Mao did not differentiate between disaffected officials and those who were actually totally loyal to him and had not wavered even during the famine. In fact, there was no way he could tell who was which. So he resolved to overthrow them all first, and then have them investigated by his new enforcers. The population was told that the Party had been in the hands of villains ("the black line") ever since the founding of the Communist regime. It was an index of how deeply fear had been embedded that no one dared to ask the obvious questions, like: "In that case, why should the Party go on ruling?," or "Where was Mao all these seventeen years?"

The Rebels' basic assignment was to punish Party cadres, which is what Mao had been longing to do for years. Some Rebels hated their Party bosses, and jumped at the chance to take revenge. Others were hungry for power, and knew that the only way to rise was to be merciless towards "capitalist-roaders." There were also plenty of thugs and sadists.

Stalin had carried out his purges using an elite, the KGB, who swiftly hustled their victims out of sight to prison, the gulag or death. Mao made sure that much violence and humiliation was carried out in public, and he vastly increased the number of persecutors by getting his victims tormented and tortured by their own direct subordinates.

A British engineer who was working in Lanzhou in 1967 caught a glimpse of life in one remote corner of the northwest. Two nights after being entertained at an official dinner, he saw a corpse strung up from a lamp-post. It was his host of two nights before. Later, he saw two men being deliberately deafened into unconsciousness by loudhailers—"so that no more reactionary remarks enter their ears," his minder told him.

The first senior official tortured to death was the minister of coal, on 21 January 1967. Mao hated him because he had complained about the Great Leap Forward—and about Mao himself. He was exhibited in front of organized crowds, and had his arms twisted ferociously backwards in the form of torment known as being "jet-planed." One day he was shoved onto a bench, bleeding, shirtless in a temperature well below freezing, while thugs rushed forward to cut him with small knives. Finally, a huge iron stove was hung around his neck, dragging his head down to the cement floor, where his skull was bashed in with heavy brass belt buckles. During all this, photographs were taken, which were later shown to Chou—and doubtless to Mao.

Photographing torture had hitherto been rare under Mao, but it was done extensively in the Cultural Revolution, especially where Mao's personal enemies were concerned. As Mao's usual practice was not to keep records for posterity, let alone proof of torture, the most likely explanation for this departure from his norm is that he took pleasure in viewing pictures of his foes in agony. Film cameras also recorded gruesome denunciation rallies, and Mao watched these displays in his villas. Selected films of this sort were shown on TV, accompanied by the soundtrack of Mme Mao's "model shows," and people were organized to watch. (Very few individuals had TV in those days.)

Mao was intimately acquainted with the types of ordeal visited on his former colleagues and subordinates. Vice-Premier Ji Deng-kui later recalled Mao doing an imitation for his entourage of the agonizing "jet-plane" posture which was routine at denunciation meetings, and Mao laughing heartily as Ji described what he had been through.

Eventually, after two or three years of suffering in this manner, millions of officials were exiled to de facto labor camps which went under the anodyne name of "May 7 Cadre Schools." These camps also housed the custodians of culture—artists, writers, scholars, actors and journalists—who had become superfluous in Mao's new order.

THE REPLACEMENTS FOR the ousted cadres came mainly from the army, which Mao ordered into every institution in January 1967. Altogether, over the next few years, 2.8 million army men became the new controllers, and of these, 50,000 took over the jobs of former medium- to high-ranking Party officials. These army men were assisted in their new roles by the Rebels and some veteran cadres who were kept on for continuity and expertise. But the army provided the core of the new enforcers—at the expense of doing its job of defending the country. When one army unit was moved away from the coast opposite Taiwan to take control of a province in the interior, its commander asked Chou En-lai what would happen if there was a war. Chou's answer was: "There will be no war in the next ten years." Mao did not believe Chiang would invade.

In March, with the new enforcers in place, pupils and students were ordered back to their schools—although, once there, they could only kick their heels, as the old textbooks, teaching methods and teachers had all been condemned, and nobody knew what to do. Normal schooling did not exist for most young people until after Mao's death, a decade later.

In society at large, the economy ran much as usual, except for relatively minor disruptions caused by the personnel changes. People went to work as before. Shops were open, as were banks. Hospitals, factories, mines, the post, and, with some interruptions, transport, all operated fairly normally. The Superpower Program, far from being paralyzed, as is often thought, was given unprecedented priority in the Cultural Revolution, and investment in it increased. Agriculture did no worse than before.

What changed, apart from the bosses, was life outside work. Leisure disappeared. Instead, there were endless mind-numbing—but nerve-racking—meetings to read and reread Mao's works and *People's Daily* articles. People were herded into numerous violent denunciation rallies against "capitalist-roaders" and other appointed enemies. Public brutality became an inescapable part of daily life. Each institution ran its de facto prison, in which victims were tortured, some to death. Moreover, there were no ways to relax, as there were now virtually no books to read, or magazines, or films, plays, opera; no light music on the radio. For entertainment there were only Mao Thought Propaganda Teams, who sang Mao's quotations set to raucous music, and danced militantly waving the Little Red Book. Not even Mme Mao's eight "model shows" were performed for the public yet, as their staging had to be under draconian central control.

ONE TASK OF the new enforcers was to screen the old cadres to explore whether they had ever resisted Mao's orders, even passively. Each of the millions of ousted officials had a "case team" combing through his or her past. At the very top was a Central Special Case Team, a highly secret group chaired by Chou En-lai, with Kang Sheng as his deputy, and staffed by middle-ranking army officers. This was the body that investigated people personally designated by Mao. Since he especially wanted to find out whether any of his top echelon had been plotting against him with the Russians, the key case in the military was that of Marshal Ho Lung, the unlucky recipient of Russian defense minister Malinovsky's remarks about getting rid of Mao. All Ho's old subordinates were implicated in this case, and Ho himself died as a result.

The Central Special Case Team had the power to arrest, interrogate—and torture. They also recommended what punishments should be meted out. Chou's signature appeared on many arrest warrants and recommendations for punishment, including death sentences.

While suspects were being interrogated under torture, and while his old power base endured unprecedented suffering, Mao cavorted. The dancing still went on at Zhongnanhai with girls called in, some to share his large bed. To the tune of "The Pleasure-Seeking Dragon Flirts with the Phoenix," which was deemed "pornographic" by his own regime, and long banned, Mao danced on. One by one, as the days went by, his colleagues disappeared from the dance floor, either purged, or simply having lost any appetite for fun. Eventually, Mao alone of the leaders still trod the floor.

Out of his remaining top echelon, there came only one burst of defiance. In February 1967, some of the Politburo members who had not fallen spoke up, voicing rage at what was happening to their fellow Party cadres. Mao's old follower Tan Zhen-lin, who had been in charge of agriculture during the famine (showing how far he was prepared to go along with Mao), exploded to the Small Group: "Your purpose is to get rid of all the old cadres . . . They made revolution for decades, and end up with their families broken and themselves dying. It is the cruellest struggle in Party history, worse than any time before." Next day, he wrote to Lin Biao: "I have come to the absolute end of my tether . . . I am ready to die . . . to stop them." Foreign Minister Chen Yi called the Cultural Revolution "one big torture chamber."

But these elite survivors were either devoted veteran followers of Mao's, or men already broken by him. Faced with his wrath, they folded. With the critical duo of Lin Biao and Chou behind him, Mao had the dissenters harassed; then, when they had been suitably cowed, he extended them an olive branch. The mini-revolt was easily quelled.

Not cowed as easily as the Politburo members was a brigadier called Cai Tie-gen, who even contemplated organizing a guerrilla force, making him the only senior cadre known to have thought of trying to "do a Mao" to Mao. He was shot, the highest-ranking officer executed in the Purge. Saying farewell to a friend who was nearly shot with him, he encouraged him to continue the fight, and then went calmly to the execution ground.

There was other truly heroic resistance from ordinary people. One was a remarkable woman of nineteen, a student of German called Wang Rong-fen, who had attended the Tiananmen rally on 18 August 1966, and whose reaction to it showed astonishing freshness and independence of spirit, as well as courage. She thought that it was "just like Hitler's," and wrote to Mao posing a number of sharp questions: "What are you doing? Where are you leading China?" "The Cultural Revolution," she told Mao, "is not a mass movement. It is one man with the gun manipulating the masses. I declare I resign from the Communist Youth League . . ."

One letter she wrote in German, and with that in her pocket she got hold of four bottles of insecticide and drank them outside the Soviet embassy, hoping the Russians would discover her corpse and publicize her protest to the world. Instead, she woke up in a police hospital. She was sentenced to life imprisonment. For months on end, her hands were tightly handcuffed behind her back and she had to roll herself along the floor to get her mouth to the food that was just tossed onto the floor of her cell. When the handcuffs were finally removed, they had to be sawn off, as the lock was jammed with rust. This extraordinary young woman survived prison—and Mao—with her spirit undimmed.

UNSWEET REVENGE

(1966–74 ★ AGE 72–80)

IN AUGUST 1966, Mao toppled Liu Shao-chi. On the 5th, after Liu met a delegation from Zambia in his capacity as president, Mao had Chou En-lai telephone Liu and tell him to stop meeting foreigners, or appearing in public, unless told to do so. That day, Mao wrote a tirade against Liu which he himself read out to the Central Committee two days later, in Liu's presence, breaking the news of Liu's downfall (the general population was not told). Just before this, on the 6th, Mao had had Lin Biao specially fetched to Peking to lend him weight, in case there was unmanageable opposition. Lin Biao formally replaced Liu as Mao's No. 2.

Mao's persecution of the man he hated most could now begin. He started with Liu's wife, Wang Guang-mei. Mao knew that the two were devoted to each other, and that making Guang-mei suffer would hurt Liu greatly.

Guang-mei came from a distinguished cosmopolitan family: her father had been a government minister and diplomat, and her mother a well-known figure in education. Guang-mei had graduated in physics from an American missionary university, and had been about to take up an offer from Michigan University to study in America in 1946 when she decided to join the Communists, under the influence of her radical mother. People remembered how at dancing parties in the Communist base in those civil war days, Liu would cross the threshing-ground that served as a dance floor with his characteristic sure steps and, bowing, ask for a dance, in a manner unusual for a Party leader. Guang-mei had elegance and style, and Liu was smitten. They were married in 1948, and the marriage was an exceptionally happy one, particularly for Liu, who had had a string of unsuccessful relationships (and one wife executed by the Nationalists).

From the moment it was clear that Mao was coming after Liu, from the Conference of the Seven Thousand in January 1962, Guang-mei encouraged her husband to stand up to Mao. This was in vivid contrast to the behavior of many leaders' wives, who urged their spouses to kowtow. In the ensuing years, she helped Liu to entrench his position. In June 1966, when Mao was fomenting violence in schools and universities, Liu made a last-ditch attempt to curb the mayhem by sending in "work teams," and Guang-mei became a member of the one sent to Qinghua University in Peking. There she came into collision with a twenty-year-old militant called Kuai Da-fu. Kuai's original interest in politics had been sparked by a sense of justice: as a boy of thirteen in a village during the famine, he had petitioned Peking about grassroots officials ill-treating peasants. But when, in summer 1966, the Cultural Revolution was presented by the media as a "struggle for power," Kuai developed an appetite for power and led riotous actions to "seize power from the work team." He was put under dormitory arrest by the work team for eighteen days, which Liu authorized.

In the small hours of 1 August, Kuai was woken up by cars screeching to a halt to find before him none other than Chou En-lai. Kuai was completely overwhelmed. He could not make himself sit properly on the sofa, but perched on the edge. Suavely putting him at his ease, Chou told him he had come on behalf of Mao, and quizzed him about the work team—and the role of Mme Liu. Even though he had a stenographer with him, Chou took notes himself. The session lasted three hours, until after 5:00 AM, when Chou invited Kuai to come to the Great Hall of the People that evening. There they talked for another three hours. Mao used Kuai's complaints as ammunition, and from now on Kuai was Mao's point man against the Lius.

On 25 December, the eve of Mao's seventy-third birthday, on the orders of the Small Group, Kuai led 5,000 students in a parade through Peking with trucks fitted with loudspeakers blaring "Down with Liu Shao-chi!" This unusual demonstration was a step towards preparing people for the fact that the president of China was about to become an enemy, and even though it was not announced in the media, it made Liu's fall known to the nation. Kuai and his "demonstration" also enabled Mao to make it seem that Liu's downfall was by some sort of popular demand.

From here on, the Lius were tormented in countless ways. At dawn on New Year's Day 1967, Mao sent New Year greetings to his old colleague by getting staff in Zhongnanhai to daub giant insults inside the Lius' house. Similar menaces followed, all choreographed—except one.

This was on 6 January, when Kuai's group seized the Lius' teenage daughter, Ping-ping, and then telephoned Guang-mei to tell her that the girl had been hit by a car and was in a hospital, which needed consent to perform an amputation. Both parents raced to the hospital, which discomfited the Rebels. Kuai recounted:

The students never thought Liu Shao-chi would come, and they were all frightened. They knew they couldn't touch Liu Shao-chi ... the Centre had given no instructions [about handling Liu in person]. We dared not be rash ... We knew this kind of "Down with" in politics could well turn to "Up with" ... Without clear and specific instructions from the Centre, when it came to blame, we would have had it. So my pals asked Liu to go back, and kept Wang Guang-mei.

This is a good self-confession of how the Rebels really worked; they were tools, and cowards, and they knew it.

As this stunt had not been centrally orchestrated, soldiers descended on the hospital within minutes. The students scurried nervously through the motions of denouncing Guang-mei in just half an hour. While this was going on, Kuai was called to the phone, which, he remembered,

gave me a big fright when the voice on the line said. "This is Chou En-lai." Chou told me to release Wang Guang-mei: "No beating, no humiliation. Do you understand?" I said: "I understand" ... He hung up. Less than a minute later, another call came. It was from Jiang Qing—my only call ever from her. As I took the phone, I heard her giggling. She said: "You got Wang Guang-mei. What's all this? Are you fooling around? Don't beat her, don't humiliate her." She repeated Chou En-lai's words and said: "The premier is anxious, and asked me to telephone you. As soon as you finish denouncing Wang Guang-mei, send her back."

So ended the only spontaneous move by the Rebels against the Lius. Chou's order to spare Guang-mei was not made out of the kindness of his heart. Kuai's action was unauthorized, and did not fit in with Mao's timetable.

Mao's next step was to have Liu brought to Suite 118 in the Great Hall for a tête-à-tête in the middle of the night on 13 January. Mao showed he was well aware of the hoax played on the Lius by inquiring: "How are Ping-ping's legs?" He then advised Liu to "read some books," mentioning two titles both having the word "mechanical" in them, which Mao claimed were by Haeckel and Diderot. This was a way of advising Liu to be less stiff-necked, meaning he should do some kowtowing. Liu did not grovel, but repeated the offer he had made many times: to resign and go and work as a peasant. He asked Mao to stop the Cultural Revolution and punish only him, and not to harm anybody else. Mao waxed non-committal, and merely asked Liu to look after his health. With this he saw Liu, his closest colleague for nearly three decades, to the door for the last time—and to a slow and agonizing death.

WITHIN DAYS THE Lius' telephones were cut off. House arrest was now total, with the walls covered with enormous insulting posters and slogans. On 1 April, Mao made Liu's purge official to the general public by having him condemned as "the biggest capitalist-roader" in *People's Daily*. Right after this, Kuai organized a rally 300,000 strong to humiliate and abuse Guang-mei. Chou discussed the details with Kuai beforehand, and on the day itself Chou's office kept in constant contact by phone with Kuai's group. Mme Mao added her personal touch by telling Kuai: "When Wang Guang-mei was in Indonesia, she lost all face for the Chinese. She even wore a necklace!" Mme Mao also accused Guang-mei of wearing traditional Chinese dresses "to make herself a whore with Sukarno in Indonesia," and told Kuai: "You must find those things and make her wear them." Mme Mao had been bitterly jealous of Guang-mei being able to wear glamorous clothes when she went abroad as the president's wife, while she herself was cooped up in China, where these things were not allowed.

Kuai recalled that Mme Mao "was telling me explicitly, in effect, to humiliate Wang Guang-mei . . . We could insult her any way we wanted." So a traditional Chinese tight dress was forced on to Guang-mei, over her padded clothing, making her body appear bulging and ugly. A string of ping-pong balls was hung around her neck to signify a pearl necklace. The whole rally was filmed by cameramen, undoubtedly for Mao, as it could not have been done without his authorization.

But the Maos failed to break Guang-mei. During the pre-rally interrogation, she showed extraordinary fearlessness—and a quick wit—and defended her husband eloquently. When she was hauled onto the stage to face the crowd's blood-curdling screams and upthrust fists, her interrogators asked her: "Aren't you scared?" Her calm answer impressed them: "No, I am not."

Decades later, Kuai spoke with admiration about Guang-mei: "She was very strong . . . She stood straight, and refused to bow her head when ordered to. The students went at her with force, great force. She was pushed down to her knees . . . but instantly she stood up straight. Wang Guang-mei would not be cowed. She was full of bitterness against Mao Tse-tung, only she could not say it straight out." Afterwards, she wrote to Mao to protest.

Liu did likewise, again and again. Mao's response was to ratchet up the punishment, leaving detailed instructions with the Small Group before he left Peking on 13 July. The moment he was gone, several hundred thousand Rebels were summoned to camp outside Zhongnanhai, blasting insults like "pile of dog shit" at the Lius through scores of loudspeakers. Liu's subordinates were dragged outside the walls of Zhongnanhai to be denounced in a sort of grotesque road show.

At the height of this, Liu was presented with a demand to "bow your head obediently and admit your crimes to Chairman Mao." This was purportedly in the name of some Rebels, to pretend that it had come from "the masses." But it was presented to Liu by Mao's chamberlain and chief of the Praetorian Guard, Wang Dong-xing, which left no doubt who was the puppeteer. Liu turned the demand down flat. Anticipating the worst after this defiance, Guang-mei held up a bottle of sleeping pills in front of her husband, offering to commit suicide with him. Neither spoke a word for fear of bugging, which would almost certainly have led to the pills being confiscated. Liu shook his head.

Knowing how much Liu's strength had come from his wife, Mao ordered the couple separated. On 18 July, they were told they would be denounced at separate meetings that evening. More than three decades later Guang-mei wrote about the moment:

> I said: "It looks as if it really is goodbye this time!" I just couldn't stop my tears falling . . .
> . . . For the only time in our lives, Shao-chi did my packing for me, and he folded my clothes neatly. In the last few minutes, we sat gazing at each other . . . Then he who rarely cracked a joke said: "This is like waiting for a sedan-chair to come and carry you off [to be married]!" . . . We burst out laughing.

After brutal denunciation meetings, the Lius were put in separate virtual solitary confinement. They met again only once, when they were dragged in front of a kangaroo court as a couple, on 5 August, the first anniversary of Mao's written tirade against Liu. Mao's point man Kuai had prepared a big event at Tiananmen Square, where a stage had been specially constructed for the Lius to be paraded in front of an organized crowd of hundreds of thousands. In the end, Mao vetoed the idea. He could not risk this being seen by foreigners. If they were to witness the savagery towards his former closest colleague, here in the heart of Peking, i.e., clearly backed by him, the whole charade could easily backfire. Not least, this could affect foreign Maoists, many of whom had already been alienated by Mao's Purge.[*] Nor could Mao risk the Lius speaking. Mao could count on the Lius to produce sharp rebuttals, as they had done in letters to himself and in their retorts to Rebels. Mao did not dare risk a Stalin-type show trial. So the Lius ended up receiving their salvo of abuse only inside Zhongnanhai, from Praetorian Guards dressed in mufti and from Zhongnanhai staff.

On that day, 5 August, the "capitalist-roaders" Nos. 2 and 3, Deng Xiao-ping and Tao Zhu (Liu was the "No. 1"), were denounced outside their own houses too. They had both fallen into disgrace, like many other

---

[*] The Belgian Communist Jacques Grippa, the most senior Maoist in Western Europe and a man who had himself been tortured in a Nazi camp, now wrote to Liu, as president, in Zhongnanhai. The letter was returned marked "Does not live at this address."

old Mao favorites, because they had declined to cooperate with Mao's Great Purge. But as Mao did not hate them as much as he did Liu, they were treated less fiercely. Tao Zhu's wife, Zeng Zhi, was an old friend of Mao's, and was spared. She recounted a telling episode which reveals how precise Mao's control was. While her husband was being beaten up, she was allowed to sit down. A militant woman was about to set upon her when Zeng Zhi noticed a man in the audience shaking his head at the woman, who promptly backed off.

Zeng Zhi knew that Mao's "friendship" and protection could vanish as soon as she did anything that displeased the Great Helmsman. Later, when her terminally ill husband was sent into internal exile, she was given the option of accompanying him. Both she and her husband knew that if she did so she would lose Mao's goodwill, which would ruin her and their only daughter. So the couple decided she should not go with him, and he died in exile alone.

At the kangaroo court inside Zhongnanhai on 5 August 1967, Liu stood his ground and gave succinct answers; but as soon as he tried to say more, Little Red Books rained down on his head, and he was shouted down by the crowd yelling mindless slogans. The Lius were punched, kicked, "jet-planed," and had their hair pulled ferociously back to expose their faces for photographers and a film crew. At one moment, the meeting was adjourned and an order was given by a Mao point man to make it more ferocious for the cameras. The film shows Liu then being trampled on the ground. In a supreme act of sadism, the Lius' six-year-old daughter and their other children were brought to watch their parents being assaulted. The whole vile episode was also attended by Mao's special observer—his own daughter Li Na.

Mao may have derived satisfaction from the Lius' ordeal, but he can hardly have failed to register that they were not crushed. At one point, Guang-mei tore free and clung to a corner of her husband's clothes. For a few minutes, under a rain of kicks and punches, the couple held each other's hands tight, struggling to stand up straight.

Guang-mei was to pay a hefty price for her courage. A little over a month later, she was charged with spying for America—plus, for good measure, Japan and Chiang Kai-shek. For twelve years, until after Mao's death, she was locked up in the top-security prison, Qincheng, where for long periods she was not allowed even to walk, so that years later she still could not stand up straight. She remained undaunted. Her case team called for her execution. Mao said "No." He did not want her put out of her misery so soon.

Guang-mei's siblings were incarcerated, as was her septuagenarian mother, who died in prison a few years later. The Lius' children became homeless, and were subjected to beatings and imprisonment. One son of

Liu's from a previous marriage committed suicide. Meanwhile, Liu's house, a short walk from Mao's, was turned into a uniquely Maoist slow-death cell.

LIU WAS NEARLY seventy, and his health deteriorated fast. One leg became paralyzed, and he was in a state of permanent sleep deprivation, as the sleeping pills on which he had been dependent were now withheld. He was kept alive, barely. On 20 December 1967, his jailers recorded that they were "only keeping him alive, just short of starvation." "Tea has been stopped . . ." His life-threatening ailments, pneumonia and diabetes, were treated, although, in a further Maoist turn of the screw, the doctors would curse him while patching him up. But his mental health was deliberately allowed to collapse. On 19 May 1968, his jailers reported that he "brushed his teeth with a comb and soap, put his socks on over his shoes and his underpants outside his trousers . . ." And in the cruel style that was the order of the day, they wrote that Liu "plays the idiot, and makes one disgusting fool of himself after another."

, That summer, Mao twice gave orders through Wang Dong-xing to the doctors and the guards that they must "keep him [Liu] alive until after the 9th Congress," when Mao planned to have Liu expelled from the Party. If Liu was dead, this rigmarole would not provide Mao with the same satisfaction. Once the congress was over, the clear implication was that Liu should be left to die.

By October 1968, Liu had to be drip-fed through the nose, and it seemed he might die any minute. Mao was not ready for the congress, so the Central Committee—in fact, a rump minority which contained only 47 percent of the original members, the rest having been purged—was hastily convened to expel Liu from the Party. It also removed him from the presidency, an act that did not even pretend to follow constitutional procedure.

Liu's case team had signally failed to come up with a case. Mao had told it he wanted a spy charge, which was a way of avoiding any policy issues, and of steering the investigators away from Liu's links with himself. In fact, Mao was so nervous about Liu speaking to anyone that the team investigating Liu was forbidden even to set eyes on him, let alone ask him any questions. Instead, a large number of other people were imprisoned and interrogated, to try to turn up evidence against him. It was partly to accommodate key detainees in the Liu case that Qincheng, the prison for the "elite," which had been built with the help of Russian advisers in the 1950s, was expanded by 50 percent. Its first inmate in the Cultural Revolution was Shi Zhe, who had interpreted for Liu with Stalin and who was pressed to say that Liu was a Russian spy. Also imprisoned here was the American Sidney Rittenberg, who had known Mme Liu in the 1940s. Pressure was put on him to say that he had recruited her, and Liu, for American intelligence. (Rittenberg observed that the interrogators, while going through the required frenzied motions, did not seem to believe their own case.) Attempts were also made to get former Nationalist intelligence chiefs to say that Guang-mei had spied for them.

Most of those detained and called upon to tell blatant lies tried their hardest not to comply. Among those who paid dearly for sticking to their guns were two former Party chiefs, Li Li-san and Lo Fu. Their families were thrown into prison, and the two men themselves were both to meet their deaths. Li-san's Russian wife, who had stood by him through the purges in Russia in the 1930s when he had been imprisoned there for two years, now spent eight years in Mao's prison.

Even some of the members of the Lius' case team declined to fabricate evidence. As a result, the team itself had to be purged three times, and two of its three chiefs ended up in prison. It found itself in a Catch-22 situation, as concocting evidence could be as dangerous as failing to unearth it. On one occasion, the team claimed that Liu had wanted American troops to invade China in 1946, and that Liu had wanted to see President Truman about this. "Making such a claim," Mao said, "is . . . to treat us like fools. America sending in troops en masse: even the Nationalists did not want that." In the end, the team just piled up a list of assertions, one being that Liu "married the American spy Wang Guang-mei who had been sent to Yenan by the American Strategic Intelligence." Its report, which was delivered to the Central Committee by Mao's faithful slave, Chou En-lai, called Liu a "traitor, enemy agent and scab," and recommended the death sentence. But Mao rejected it, as he did for Mme Liu.

Mao was kept fully informed about Liu's last sufferings. Photographs were taken showing Liu in such agony that he had squeezed two hard plastic bottles right out of shape. In April 1969, when the 9th Congress convened at last, Mao announced in a voice devoid of even a show of pity, that Liu was at death's door.

In his lucid hours, Liu had maintained his dignity. On 11 February 1968 he had written a last self-defense, in which he even had a go at Mao about his dictatorial style from back in the early 1920s. After that, Liu went totally silent. Mao's whole modus operandi depended on breaking people, but he had failed to make Liu crawl.

On a cold October night, half-naked under a quilt, Liu was put on a plane to the city of Kaifeng. There, local doctors' requests for an X-ray or hospitalization were denied. Death came within weeks, on 12 November 1969. Altogether, Liu had endured three years of physical suffering and mental anguish. He was cremated under a pseudonym, his face wrapped in white cloth. The crematorium staff had been told to vacate the premises, on the grounds that the corpse had a deadly infectious disease.

The extraordinary coda to Liu's story is that his death was never made public during Mao's lifetime. This seemingly anomalous behavior (most dictators like to dance on their enemies' graves) was an indication of how insecure Mao felt. He was afraid that if the news got out, it would arouse sympathy for the dead man. In fact, the vilification of Liu continued for the rest of Mao's life, with never a hint to the public that Liu was dead. Mao had got his revenge by making Liu die a painful and lingering death. But it cannot have tasted very sweet.

NOR DID MAO emerge a victor vis-à-vis his second-biggest hate, Marshal Peng De-huai. The first Rebel leader sent to Sichuan in December 1966 to haul Peng back to detention in Peking was so moved by Peng after he talked to him that he started to appeal on Peng's behalf. The Rebel ended up in prison, but said he had no regrets for having stuck his neck out. Another Rebel leader who manhandled Peng expressed deep remorse later for what he had done. There is no question where people's feelings lay when they knew what Peng stood for, or met him.

In Peking, Peng was dragged to scores of denunciation meetings, on Mao's orders, at each one of which he was kicked by Rebels wearing heavy leather boots and beaten ferociously with staves. His ribs were broken, and he passed out repeatedly.

Unlike Liu, Peng was interrogated, some 260 times, as Mao genuinely feared he might have had some connection with Khrushchev. In solitary, Peng's mind began to crack, but his redoubtable core never did. He wrote a lucid account of his life, refuting Mao's accusations. The ending, written in September 1970, proclaimed: "I will still lift my head and shout a hundred times: my conscience is clear!"

Peng was a man of rugged constitution, and his ordeal lasted even longer than Liu's—eight years, until 29 November 1974, when he was finally felled by cancer of the rectum. Like Liu, he was cremated under a pseudonym, and his death, too, was never announced while Mao remained alive.

THE CHAIRMAN'S NEW OUTFIT

(1967–70 ★ AGE 73–76)

B
Y EARLY 1967, Mao had axed millions of Party officials and replaced them mainly with army men. But he immediately found himself facing problems with the replacements. Most lacked sufficient brutality, and often protected and even re-employed purged officials, a feat they achieved by enlisting Mao's hypocritical remark that "most of the old cadres are all right." This was bad enough, but there was an additional cause for concern on Mao's part. He had to rely on army officers to choose Rebels to staff the new set-up. The trouble was that in every region and institution there were different, rival groups, all calling themselves Rebels, and the military tended to incorporate the more moderate ones, even though Mao told them to promote "the Left," i.e., those harshest in persecuting "capitalist-roaders."

If the army men were allowed to have their way, Mao's revenge would be incomplete. More important, if these new army enforcers turned out to be like the old officials, he would be back where he started. He had intended the Great Purge to install much more merciless enforcers.

One place that was giving Mao a headache was the city of Wuhan, his favorite spot for symbolic swims in the Yangtze. The commander there, Chen Zai-dao, had joined the Red Army in 1927 as a poverty-stricken peasant of eighteen, and risen through the ranks. General Chen was deeply averse to the Cultural Revolution, and had even shown sympathy for Mao's primary target, Liu Shao-chi. In the province under his control, he reinstated large numbers of old officials, disbanded the most militant Rebel groups and arrested their leaders. In May 1967, when the moderates united into a province-wide organization called "the Million Peerless Troops," which boasted a membership of 1.2 million, he supported them.

In mid-July, Mao came to Wuhan in person to order General Chen to change his position. Assuming that General Chen would just cave in, Mao planned then to use Wuhan as an example to get army units all over the country to follow suit.

But Mao was in for a huge shock. When he told General Chen that the Peerless was a "Conservative" organization, and that the military had committed grave errors in backing it, Chen told Mao to his face: "We don't admit that."

Next came something equally unheard-of: rank-and-file members of the Peerless, together with sympathizers in the army, reacted to Mao's verdict with defiance. On the night of 19–20 July, when the message was relayed to them by military and civilian grandees whom Mao had brought with him from Peking, outraged crowds took to the streets, with hundreds of trucks carrying nearly 1,000 soldiers with machine-guns, as well as tens of thousands of workers armed with iron bars. The demonstrators blasted protests through loudspeakers at Mao's villa compound. Many knew that this ultra-mysterious, top-security lakeside estate was Mao's, and, seeing the lights on, guessed that he was in residence. Though no one dared to attack Mao openly, giant posters in the streets carried slogans attacking the Small Group and its leader, Mme Mao, indirectly aiming at Mao himself: "Jiang Qing keep away from power!" "Chairman Mao is being hoodwinked!" General Chen received extraordinary letters; one even urged him to "use your power . . . to wipe off the face of the Earth those worst dictators in the world who want no history and no culture . . ."

Most scary for Mao, hundreds of demonstrators and armed soldiers broke into the grounds of his villa, and got within a stone's throw of him, carrying off a key member of his entourage, Small Group member Wang Li, who took a fearsome beating.

Never in eighteen years of compulsive, all-inclusive, self-protection had Mao faced so concrete a threat, both to his personal safety and to his sense of total power.

Chou En-lai, who had come to Wuhan ahead of Mao to arrange his security, had just returned to Peking, but had to fly straight back with 200 fully armed Praetorian Guards. He reverted smoothly to his old underground style, though this time operating in the state whose prime minister he was: waiting until dark before proceeding to Mao's place, changing clothes and donning dark glasses. At 2:00 AM on 21 July, Mao was whisked away through the back door of his villa. All his three forms of transportation were on standby—his special train, his plane, and warships. Mao gave the order to leave by train, but once he was on board he switched to a plane—though not his own. The pilot was not told the destination, Shanghai, until he was airborne.

This was Mao's last flight ever—and it was a *flight*. Soldiers rampaging right inside his estate was something utterly unthinkable. So was a demonstration openly hostile to his orders—and moreover, one involving fully armed troops.

The regime acted swiftly to show that it would not tolerate Wuhan. Chou got Small Group member Wang Li released, and embraced him

demonstratively, putting his unshaven cheek to his. Wang Li returned to
Peking to a staged welcome the like of which the country had never seen.
A crowd of tens of thousands greeted him at Peking airport, headed by
a teary Chou. This was followed by a million-strong rally on Tiananmen
Square, presided over by Lin Biao.

General Chen was purged, and replaced by a man of unquestioning
loyalty to Lin Biao. Army units involved in the defiance were disbanded,
and sent to do forced labor. The Peerless disintegrated, and those who
tried to hold out were physically beaten into collapse. Over the next few
months, as many as 184,000 ordinary citizens and cadres were injured,
crippled or killed in the province. General Chen and his deputies were
ordered to Peking. There something else extraordinary happened, probably a world "first." The Wuhan generals were beaten up—and not in
some squalid dungeon, but at a Politburo meeting chaired by Chou En-
lai. The perpetrators were senior officers headed by air force commander-
in-chief Wu Fa-xian. The scene in the Politburo chamber was just like a
street denunciation meeting, with the victims made to stand bent double,
their arms twisted back in the jet-plane position, while they were punched
and kicked. General Chen was knocked down and trampled on. Even in
Mao's gangster world, for the Politburo to become the scene of physical
violence was unprecedented.

THE UPRISING IN Wuhan led Mao to conclude that over 75 percent
of army officers were unreliable. He had a stab at initiating a huge purge
among the military, and started denouncing "capitalist-roaders within the
army," but he had to pull back almost immediately. Having sacked most
civilian officials, he simply could not afford to create more enemies in
what was now his only power base.

Mao had to placate the army, so he threw it a few sops, pretending
that he was not responsible for having tried to purge it. One sop was Small
Group member Wang Li, of the Wuhan episode. Mao now made him a
scapegoat. On 30 August, Wang Li was arrested. Hardly a month before,
he had stood on Tiananmen Gate being hailed by a million people as the
hero of Wuhan, the only occasion when leaders ever lined up there without Mao. Actually, this prominence was his undoing. The sight of him on
Tiananmen, Mao's preserve, annoyed the Great Helmsman, who said
Wang Li had "got too big for his boots, and must be cut down to size."

Purging Wang Li, however, did not solve Mao's problem. He still had
to find a way to make sure the new army enforcers would be men who
would do what they were told unconditionally. To select such men, he
depended on Lin Biao, who had to dig into the second tier of the army
to find them. Mao thus found that he had no alternative but to allow Lin
to turn the army leadership into a personal fiefdom, run by Lin's cronies

and working on the basis of what amounted to gang loyalty. On 17 August 1967, Mao authorized Lin to form a new body called "the Administration Office" to run the army. This consisted of Lin's wife and a few generals who owed their careers, and sometimes even their lives, to Lin.

Typical of these was General Qiu Hui-zuo, the head of Army Logistics. At the beginning of the Cultural Revolution he had been denounced and beaten up. One of his ribs was broken, and his shoulder joints and muscles severely torn. He passed out on stage and was brought around by cold water for more beatings. Just when he thought he was going to die, an order came from Lin Biao to release him. He wrote afterwards to the Lins: "Hour 0:40 on 25 Jan 1967 was the moment of my second life, the moment I, my wife and children will never forget..."

Qiu promoted a personal coterie and indulged in a vendetta against those who had made him suffer. In his old department alone, 462 subordinates were arrested and tortured; among their lesser torments were being forced to eat bread soaked in excrement, and being kicked in the genitals. Eight died.

Qiu was an example of a person who had become totally cynical, for reasons that went back much further than the Cultural Revolution, and related to the unscrupulous nature of the Party itself from the earliest days. On the eve of the Long March, he and several other Red Army youngsters, including one aged eleven, had been ordered to hide some Party documents, which they sealed and sank in a river tied to stones. As they were climbing back up the river bank, they found themselves staring into the gun-barrels of their own comrades who had been sent to eliminate them so that no trail would be left. Qiu only survived because of a chance intervention.

Lin let Qiu and his other cronies wage their vendettas and build their own gangs as long as they obeyed him. Mao did the same with Lin. For a while, Mao tried to keep his own men in the army, and appointed one of his acolytes, General Yang Cheng-wu, as acting chief of staff. But Lin did not want General Yang on his back, and eventually got Mao to clap him in prison in March 1968. Mao even suspended the Military Council, the old supreme authority which he himself chaired. Mao retained just one vital veto: moving any force from battalion-strength up required his direct authorization.

Lin installed a sidekick called Huang Yong-sheng to be army chief of staff. Huang was so junior that Mao could not even put a face to his name. A well-known womanizer, he soon became Mrs. Lin's lover. Ye Qun was a woman of voracious sexual appetite, for which she had little outlet with the clearly impotent marshal, whom she described as "a frozen corpse." The relationship between her and her lover is revealed in a three-hour telephone conversation that was bugged.

YE QUN [YQ]: I am so worried you might get into trouble for pursuing physical satisfaction. I can tell you, this life of mine is linked with you, political life and personal life ... Don't you know what 101 [Lin Biao's code name] is like at home? I live with his abuse ... I can sense you value feelings ... The country is big. Our children can each take up one key position! Am I not right?

HUANG: Yes, you are absolutely right.

YQ: ... Our children put together, there must be five of them. They will be like five generals and will get on. Each will take one key position, and they can all be your assistants.

HUANG: Oh? I am so grateful to you!

YQ: ... I took that measure [implying contraceptive]. Just in case I have it and have to get rid of it [implying baby], I hope you will come and visit me once. [Sound of sobbing]

HUANG: I will come! I will come! Don't be like this. This makes me very sad.

YQ: Another thing: you mustn't be restricted by me. You can fool around ... I'm not narrow-minded. You can have other women, and be hot with them. Don't worry about me ...

HUANG: ... I'm faithful to you alone.

YQ: If you fancy other women, that's all right. But just one thing. She must be absolutely tight-lipped. If she talks, and if I am implicated, there will be tragedy ...

HUANG [speechless] ...

YQ: I feel that if we handle it well, it will be good for you, good for me ... Do you believe this?

HUANG: I do! I do! I do!

With this mixture of genuine personal feeling and bare-faced political calculation, the fate of the new chief of staff was bound up with that of the Lins.

Lin turned the air force into his main base. His lackey there made the Lins' 24-year-old son "Tiger" deputy chief of its war department and told the air force it "must report everything to [Tiger], and take orders from [Tiger]." Lin's daughter Dodo was made deputy editor of the air force paper.

IN SUMMER 1967, dissatisfied with the army, Mao contemplated forming a kind of "storm trooper" force, composed of those Rebels whom he called "the Left." After the Wuhan scare in July, in a vengeful mood, Mao incited "the Left" to stage assaults on other groups that he termed "the Conservatives." When Mao fled to Shanghai, he got "the Left" there to attack the rival group. The result was the biggest single factional battle in Shanghai during the Cultural Revolution, which took place two weeks after Mao arrived. That day, 4 August, over 100,000 "Left" militants,

armed with spears and iron bars, surrounded some 25,000 of their rivals
in a factory by the sea, with the exit sealed off by the navy—a deploy-
ment inconceivable without Mao's orders. By the end of the day, over
900 people had been wounded, many of them crippled and some dying.
Two helicopters filmed the scene—again impossible unless Mao gave the
word—and a camera crew had set up in an ideal vantage point two days
ahead. A 2½-hour documentary of the event was shown to organized
crowds. Mao watched it in his villa. The man who led the attack, Wang
Hong-wen, was subsequently promoted by Mao to be his national No. 3.
"I've seen your film," Mao told him, congratulating him on "winning a
victory."

On the day of the battle, Mao gave orders to form his "storm troopers." "Arm the Left," he wrote to his wife, the leader of the Small Group.
"Why can't we arm the Left? They [the Conservatives] beat us up, we
can beat them up, too."

But this order to distribute arms to civilians opened up a can of worms.
While in some places, like Wuhan, the distinction between moderates
and "the Left" was fairly clear, in many others even the most devoted
Mao followers could not tell which group was more militant, as all the
groups were vying to appear the most aggressive. Typical was Anhui
province, where the two opposing blocs rejoiced in the ultra-political
names of "Wonderful" and "Fart." Because the former had got into the
old government offices first, it declared that it had seized power from
the capitalist-roaders, and proclaimed: "Our seizing power is wonderful."
The latter snorted: " 'Wonderful'? What a load of fart!"

Neither in fact was more militant than the other; both were just
competing to be incorporated into the new power structure. Lacking any
criterion more precise than the ill-defined "militancy" towards capitalist-
roaders, army units handed out weapons to whichever faction they
decided was "the Left." Other factions then raided arsenals to seize
weapons for themselves, often with the collusion of their own sympathizers in the army. As a result, guns became widely available. Factional
fighting escalated into mini–civil wars across China, involving practically
all urban areas. The regime began sliding into something close to anarchy for the first time since taking power nearly two decades before.

Mao quickly realized that his "storm troopers" notion would not work
everywhere. So, while he continued to build up a force of them 1 million
strong in Shanghai, where he had particularly strict control, elsewhere he
had to rescind his decree to "arm the Left," and on 5 September ordered
that all guns must be returned. However, those who had acquired them
were often reluctant to give them up. More than a year later, Mao told
Albania's defense minister that 360,000 weapons had been collected in
Sichuan alone (a province of 70 million people), and a lot more were

still out there. With guns now in unofficial hands, "bandits" appeared in remote areas.

Mao had unleashed a dynamic that was undermining his own power. He had to abandon his attempt to identify factions as Left and Conservative, and called for all groups to unite. But his orders were ignored. Claiming that they were crushing "Conservatives," young men, mostly, carried on fighting, finding it more fun than doing boring jobs.

People stopped going to work. The economy was now seriously interrupted. Arms industries, even the nuclear program, were upset for the first time since the Cultural Revolution had started. An element of anarchy even crept into the Praetorian Guard. One of its members gave Mao's travel schedule to a student who fancied himself as a detective, who was able to tail Mao covertly. Although both were soon arrested, such a lapse in security had never happened before.

A YEAR LATER, in 1968, factional clashes with firearms had shown little sign of abating, despite a flood of commands from Peking. One man who was being conspicuously unruly was Kuai Da-fu, the Qinghua University student whom Mao had used to torment Liu Shao-chi and his wife. Kuai had by now become the most famous "leftist" in the country, and he was determined to bring his opponents in the university to their knees. He ignored repeated orders to stop, as he claimed that his rivals were "Conservatives," and therefore fair game to beat up, in accordance with Mao's earlier directive. Mao had to step in personally to get him to toe the line, and simultaneously made an example of him to send a warning to the whole country that factional wars had to stop.

On 27 July, 40,000 unarmed workers were dispatched to Kuai's university to disarm his group. Not knowing that the order came from Mao, Kuai resisted, and his group killed five workers and wounded more than 700. Next day Kuai was summoned to the Great Hall of the People. There he was astonished to see Mao, flanked by all the top leaders. Kuai threw himself into Mao's arms—probably the only time an outsider ever did this—and sobbed his heart out. Mao, too, apparently cried, quite possibly out of frustration at his own inability to reconcile his impulses with his practical needs. The impulse side of Mao wanted the many "Conservatives" he knew were out there to be beaten to a pulp. But the practical side recognized that in his own interest he had to restore order. He told Kuai and the other top Rebel leaders present that he himself had been behind the disarming of Kuai's faction, and that if they, or anyone else, went on fighting, the army would "eliminate" them. Kuai and his colleagues signed a record of this message, which was made public.

Kuai was packed off to a plant in far Ningxia. All university student organizations were now disbanded, and the students put to work in ordinary jobs, with many dispersed to the hinterland. This diaspora was followed by that of well over 10 million middle-school pupils, who were scattered to villages and state farms across China. In the following years, over 16 million urban youth were rusticated—which was also a way of dealing with unemployment. This ended the era of the student Red Guards.

But among non-student Rebel groups, sporadic mini–civil wars dragged on in many places. To stop them, a phantom conspiracy called "the May 16 Corps" was invented as a catch-all to condemn anyone who disobeyed orders. Kuai, who was nationally famous, was turned into its "chief" and detained. Altogether, under this rubric, a staggering 10 million Rebels were condemned, of whom 3.5 million were arrested.

STATE TERROR NOT ONLY hugely raised the level of violence, but was much more horrific than the factional fighting itself. The clearest illustration of this came in the southern province of Guangxi in summer 1968. There, one faction refused to recognize the authority of Mao's point man, General Wei Guo-qing (who had helped direct the climactic battle against the French at Dien Bien Phu in Vietnam in 1954). Wei was determined to use any degree of force to crush his opponents.

This involved not only using machine-guns, mortars and artillery, but also inciting gruesome murders of large numbers of people designated by the regime as "class enemies." As the boss of Binyang County, an army officer, told his subordinates: "I'm now going to reveal the bottom line to you: in this campaign, we must put to death about one-third or a quarter of the class enemies by bludgeoning or stoning." Killing by straightforward execution was rated not frightening enough: "It's OK to execute a few to start with, but we must guide people to use fists, stones and clubs. Only this way can we educate the masses." Over a period of eleven days after the order was given, between 26 July and 6 August 1968, 3,681 people in this county were beaten to death, many in ghastly ways; by comparison, the death toll in the previous two years of the Cultural Revolution had been "only" 68. This bout of killing claimed some 100,000 lives in the province.

The authorities staged "model demonstrations of killing" to show people how to apply maximum cruelty, and in some cases police supervised the killings. In the general atmosphere of fostered cruelty, cannibalism broke out in many parts of the province, the best-known being the county of Wuxuan, where a post-Mao official investigation (in 1983, promptly halted and its findings suppressed) produced a list of 76 names of victims. The practice of cannibalism usually started with the Maoist staple, "denunciation rallies." Victims were slaughtered immediately afterwards, and choice parts of their bodies—hearts, livers and sometimes penises—were excised, often before the victims were dead, and cooked on the spot to be eaten in what were called at the time "human flesh banquets."

Guangxi is the region with perhaps the most picturesque landscape in China: exquisite hills rising and falling over crystal-clear waters in which the peaks look as real as they do above. It was against these heavenly double silhouettes, by the purest rivers, that these "human flesh banquets" were laid out.

An 86-year-old peasant who, in broad daylight, had slit open the chest of a boy whose only crime was to be the son of a former landlord, showed how people had no trouble finding justifications for their actions in Mao's words. "Yes, I killed him," he told an investigative writer later. "The person I killed is an enemy . . . Ha, ha! I make revolution, and my heart is red! Didn't Chairman Mao say: It's either we kill them, or they kill us? You die and I live, this is class struggle!"

STATE-SPONSORED KILLINGS reached their extreme in every province in 1968. That year was dominated by a mammoth campaign called "Sort Out Class Ranks." The aim of this drive was to make an inventory of every single "class enemy" in the entire population, and to impose various punishments on them, including execution. So all the victims from both before and during the Cultural Revolution were dragged out and persecuted again. In addition, the regime set out to uncover new enemies by scrutinizing the history and conduct of every adult in the nation, and looking into every unsolved suspicion. The number of labels for official outcasts ran to as many as twenty-three, and the number of people persecuted amounted to many tens of millions—more than ever before.

An eyewitness described how the new boss of Anhui province, an army general, made decisions about executions. Flipping languidly through a list of "counter-revolutionaries" presented to him by the police, he paused every now and then, and raised his voice in a quintessentially official inflection (drawing on the end of a sentence in a pinched nasal tone, sounding rather bored): "Are you still keeping this one? Might as well kill him." "What about this one? Mm—finish her off." Then he asked how many people the provinces next to his planned to execute: "How many is Jiangsu killing this month? And how many is Zhejiang?" When told, he said: "Let's take the average between the two." People were executed accordingly.

One of the worst-ravaged provinces was Inner Mongolia, where Mao harbored suspicions about a plot to detach the province and link it up with Outer Mongolia and the Russians. The new boss there, General Teng Hai-qing, vigorously investigated this suspicion of Mao's, using torture on a large scale. According to post-Mao revelations, cases included a Muslim woman having her teeth pulled out by pliers, then her nose and ears twisted off, before being hacked to death. Another woman was raped with a pole (she then committed suicide). One man had nails driven into his skull. Another had his tongue cut out and then his eyes gouged out. Another was beaten with clubs on the genitals before having gunpowder forced up his nostrils and set alight. Post-Mao official figures revealed that over 346,000 people were condemned and 16,222 died as a result in this one case. The number of people in the province who "suffered" in some way was later officially put at over 1 million—of whom 75 percent were ethnic Mongols.

Another province that went through great trauma was Yunnan, in the southwest, where (according to official figures) in one trumped-up case alone nearly 1,400,000 people were persecuted under the new provincial boss, General Tan Fu-ren. Seventeen thousand of them were either executed or beaten to death, or driven to suicide. In a rare dramatic example of how those who rule by the sword can be felled by the sword, General Tan himself was assassinated in December 1970, making him the highest official ever to have died this way in Mao's China, where assassinations were extremely rare. The shooter was an HQ staff officer called Wang Zi-zheng, who actually held no personal grudge against General Tan. It was Mao's regime he hated. Back in 1947, he had been involved with an anti-Communist force that had shot dead a Communist militia chief. He had then escaped. Now, over two decades later, his home village had started a manhunt for him. Even though he was more than a thousand miles away and had changed his name, he was found and detained in April 1970. Knowing what his fate was likely to be, he decided he would try to kill General Tan, who was not only the biggest VIP around, but was doing terrible things to Yunnan. One night, the staff officer escaped from detention, went home to say goodbye to his wife and son, stole two pistols and twenty bullets from the HQ, where they were locked in a safe (as always), climbed into General Tan's house and shot him dead. When his pursuers came for him, this unique avenger shot and wounded two of them before turning the gun on himself.

BY EARLY 1969 Mao's new power apparatus was secured. In April he convened a Party Congress, the 9th, to formalize his reconstructed regime. The previous congress had been in 1956. Although the Party charter stipulated one every five years, Mao had held off letting this one convene for thirteen years, until he felt that all opposition had been thoroughly purged.

The new delegates were selected exclusively for their loyalty to Mao, and the yardstick of loyalty was how cruel and harsh they had been to Mao's enemies. Inside the congress hall, where no such enemies were present, they tried to demonstrate their fealty by jumping up incessantly, shouting slogans such as "Long live Chairman Mao!" while Mao was speaking. It took Mao twenty minutes to get through two pages of his opening address. This farce was not something he wanted from his top echelon, which was meant to be a practical machine. He looked irritated, and cut short his speech. After the session, he had the congress secretariat issue rules banning unscheduled slogan chanting.

The core leadership under Mao now consisted of Lin Biao, Chou En-lai and two chiefs of the Small Group: Chen Bo-da and Kang Sheng. The Small Group, Mao's office dealing with the Cultural Revolution, was wound up. Mme Mao was brought into the Politburo. So were Lin Biao's wife and his main cronies, such as army chief of staff (and Lin's wife's lover) Huang Yong-sheng. In the Central Committee, 81 percent of the members were new, and nearly half the new intake were army men, including the generals who had presided over the atrocities in Guangxi, Yunnan and Inner Mongolia. Lin himself collected the ultimate prize of being written into the Party charter as Mao's No. 2 and successor, an unprecedented badge of power and glory.

Mao had completed his Great Purge, though this did not mean that killings ceased. In the ten years from when Mao started the Purge until his death in 1976, at least 3 million people died violent deaths, and post-Mao leaders acknowledged that 100 million people, one-ninth of the entire population, suffered in one way or another. The killings were sponsored by the state. Only a small percentage was at the hands of Red Guards. Most were the direct work of Mao's reconstructed regime.

A WAR SCARE

(1969–71 ∗ AGE 75–77)

MAO HAD PRESENTED the Cultural Revolution as a move to rid China of Soviet-style "revisionists." So, when he was gearing up to declare victory and inaugurate his post-Purge regime at the 9th Congress in April 1969, he looked for a symbol of triumph over the Soviet Union. He set his mind on a small, controlled, armed engagement with Russia, a border clash.

There had been many clashes along the 7,000-kilometer Sino-Soviet border. For the site of his battle, Mao chose a small uninhabited island called Zhenbao (Damansky in Russian), in the Ussuri River on the northeast border. This was a clever choice, as Russia's claim to the island was far from established.

On 2 March, using a specially trained and equipped elite unit, the Chinese laid an ambush that left 32 Russians dead and between 50 and 100 Chinese wounded or killed. The Russians brought up heavy artillery and tanks, and on the night of 14–15 March a much bigger encounter ensued, in which the Russians fired missiles 20 kilometers into China. About 60 Russians and at least 800 Chinese were killed. One CIA photo expert said that the Chinese side of the Ussuri was "so pockmarked by Soviet artillery that it looked like a 'moonscape.'" The Russians were obviously serious.

The fierceness of the retaliation took Mao aback, and he became worried that the Russians might invade, which he described to his inner circle as a possibility. He urgently ordered his army to stop fighting, and to do nothing even when the Russians continued shelling.

A week later, the old hot line from Moscow unexpectedly came alive. It was the Soviet premier Aleksei Kosygin asking to speak to either Mao or Chou En-lai. By this time, China and Russia had had virtually no diplomatic contacts for some three years. The operator refused to put the call through, saying on the fourth attempt that they could not take a call for Chairman Mao from "that scoundrel revisionist Kosygin." Next day, the Chinese detected Russian troop movements near the disputed island.

Mao at once told the Foreign Ministry to inform Moscow that it was "ready to hold diplomatic negotiations"—meaning he did not want a war. Mao was especially scared that the Russians might target a surprise air strike on the 9th Congress, which was due to open in Peking in ten days' time, and at which he himself had no choice but to make an appearance.

So the congress met in conditions of secrecy extraordinary even by the regime's ultra-secretive standards. The event was not announced until it was already over, and the 2,000 delegates and staff were imprisoned in their hotels with the curtains closed, and banned from opening windows facing the streets. Instead of being driven direct from their hotel to the venue, the Great Hall of the People, delegates were bused by circuitous routes round Peking before being delivered to the Hall surreptitiously, at intervals. On the day of the opening, 1 April, when Mao was scheduled to attend, the Hall was made to look as if nothing was happening there at all. Thick curtains concealed the fact that the lights were on (the session did not open until 5:00 PM) and that the building was full of people.

Mao had grounds for alarm. A few months later, on 13 August 1969, the Russians attacked thousands of miles to the west, on the Kazakhstan–Xinjiang border, where they had overwhelming logistical advantages. Scores of Russian tanks and armored vehicles drove deep inside China, surrounding and destroying Chinese troops.

Mao had no effective defense against Soviet tanks, if they chose to target Peking. He had always banked on the size of China and its population as insurance against anyone wanting to invade. But ever since Malinovsky had sounded his close colleagues out about getting rid of him in late 1964, the idea of a quick Soviet thrust at his capital in coordination with his opponents had preyed on Mao's mind. He had issued an order: "Pile up some mountains if there aren't any," and spent a fortune in money and labor building "mountains" to block Russian tanks. Each of these was designed to be 20–40 meters high, 250–400 meters wide, and 120–220 meters deep. Earth and rocks were moved from far away, and elaborate defense works were constructed inside, before the project was abandoned some years later. All who saw these "mountains" (among them former US defense secretary and ex-CIA chief James Schlesinger) concluded that they were completely useless.

Mao was also worried about a nuclear strike against his atomic installations. In fact, Moscow did envisage such an operation, and went as far as sounding out Washington. Mao got so nervous that he broke his rule about shunning all contact with the Kremlin, and agreed to Kosygin stopping over in Peking in September 1969 on his way back from the funeral of Ho Chi Minh in Hanoi. The Soviet premier was confined to the airport, where Chou En-lai met him in the lounge. The first point Chou raised was a Russian strike, but he failed to extract a commitment from Kosygin that Russia would not attack China. A week later, when Chou wrote asking Kosygin to confirm that both sides had agreed that neither would launch a nuclear attack on the other, Moscow declined to confirm Chou's "understanding."

In the meantime, an article was published in a London newspaper by a KGB-linked Russian journalist called Victor Louis (who had recently acted as Moscow's first known emissary to Taiwan). Louis said the Kremlin was discussing bombing Mao's nuclear test site, *and* planning to set up an "alternative leadership" for the CCP.

Mao was seriously unnerved. He had agreed to a Russian delegation coming to Peking for negotiations on the border dispute. This itself now became a source of anxiety. The delegation was due to fly in on 18 October. Mao and his cabal feared that the aircraft might be carrying atomic bombs rather than negotiators, so he and Lin Biao both left Peking for the south: Mao to Wuhan on the 15th, and Lin for Suzhou on the 17th. On the 18th the marshal forwent his regular siesta to follow the Russian plane's flight path, and only went to lie down after the Russians had alighted from the plane.

Just before the Russians arrived, Chou En-lai decamped from his residence in Zhongnanhai and moved into the nuclear bunkers in the Western Hills, where he stayed until February 1970. Mme Mao holed up there too, most likely to keep an eye on Chou.

This war scare lasted nearly four months. The entire army was put on red alert, which involved moving 4,100 planes, 600 ships and 940,000 troops. The army now resumed serious military training, which had largely fallen into abeyance since the beginning of the Cultural Revolution.

Zhongnanhai was dug up in order to build a giant underground shelter, linked by tunnels wide enough for four cars abreast, running to Tiananmen, the Great Hall of the People, a major hospital (Hospital 305, specially built for Mao and the top leaders, with all his security requirements, although he never set foot in it), Lin Biao's residence, and the secret underground military HQ in the Western Hills. Tens of millions of civilians were corvéed to build underground shelters and tunnels in every city, at punishing expense. This whole scare, started by Mao's miscalculation, cost China dearly.

In the end, the scare remained only a scare, which restored Mao's confidence in his old belief that no country, Russia included, would really want to invade China. To make doubly sure, he set out to mollify the Russians. On May Day 1970 he made a point of greeting the deputy chief Soviet delegate to the border talks, who was present on Tiananmen Gate, and told him he wanted to be a "friendly neighbor" with Russia, and did not want war. Relations were restored to ambassadorial level, with a new

Russian ambassador arriving in Peking in October, making a Soviet strike still more unlikely.

THOUGH CONFIDENT THAT there would not be a war, Mao continued scare propaganda inside China, judging that a war atmosphere was advantageous to the Superpower Program.

Becoming a superpower had remained Mao's dearest dream. This was partly why he had carried out the Purge—to install new enforcers who were more in tune with his demands. After this process was complete, he started to accelerate the Program. To this end, in August 1970 he opened a plenum in Lushan, the mountain of volatile clouds, where the Central Committee had met twice before, in 1959 and 1961, both times for the same goal of pushing the Program ahead, resulting in nearly 38 million deaths from starvation and overwork.

On both those occasions Mao had met with considerable resistance. This time his new enforcers showed few qualms about obliging him, even though his latest plans involved investing as much in the nuclear program for the five years 1971–75 as had been expended in all the previous fifteen years. This was at a time when per capita income in China was lower than in dirt-poor Somalia, and calorie intake less than it had been under the Nationalists in 1930. But Mao met no opposition. Lin Biao and his coterie actually advocated that the question of whether or not the country could afford this level of spending should not matter. The new boss of Jiangxi, General Cheng Shi-qing, offered to cough up more than seven times as much food annually to the central government as the province was currently contributing—when the people of Jiangxi were already on the margin of survival. The new slave-drivers were willing to dragoon the population more harshly then ever before.

Mao was in a satisfied mood. As he drove up the mountain from the steaming plain, he itched for a swim. As soon as he arrived, he tore off his clothes and dived into the reservoir, ignoring the bodyguards who cautioned that the water was too cold, and that he had sweated too much. Laughing and joking, he swam for nearly an hour in water that made the young men around him shiver. At seventy-six, he was in excellent shape. His appetite impressed his chef and his housekeeper. He still had boundless energy.

But at this point, events took an unexpected turn. Mao and Lin Biao fell out. The post-Purge set-up began to unravel.

FALLING OUT WITH LIN BIAO

(1970–71 ★ AGE 76–77)

UP TO NOW, August 1970, the Mao–Lin partnership had worked extremely well. For the past four years Lin Biao had delivered the support from the army that Mao needed to purge the Party and reconstruct his regime. And Mao had done the maximum to satisfy Lin Biao's thirst for power, basically handing the army to him, and writing him into the Party charter as No. 2 and successor. Lin's wife had been brought into the Politburo (making her one of only two women members, along with Mme Mao), breaking a long-standing taboo against wife-promotion. Mao even tolerated a Lin mini-cult. Each day, when the chant went up: "May the Great Helmsman [etc.] Chairman Mao live for ever and ever!," accompanied by the brandishing of the Little Red Book, the homage was followed by: "May Vice-Chairman Lin be very healthy, and for ever healthy!"

But at Lushan, it was brought home to Mao that he had let Lin grow too powerful, and that this now posed a threat to himself. It started with a seemingly innocuous dispute about the presidency, a post last occupied by Liu Shao-chi. Mao wanted the post abolished. Lin insisted that it should stay, and that Mao should be the president. The reason Lin stuck to his contrary position was because he wanted to be vice-president, which would make him the formal No. 2 in the state hierarchy. Among the top five (Mao, Lin, Chou, Kang Sheng and Chen Bo-da), the line-up was four in favor of Lin's view, against Mao's solitary one. This was an amazing sign of Lin's power, as it showed that for Mao's top colleagues, Lin's interests overrode Mao's wishes.

Mao was further enraged when Lin went ahead and announced his proposal to the conclave on 23 August without first clearing it with Mao. Immediately after Lin spoke, the head of the Praetorian Guard, Wang Dong-xing, backed him up, demanding in fevered language that Mao become president, *and Lin vice-president*—even though he, too, knew that this was diametrically opposed to what Mao wanted. The man on whom Mao relied for his life was also putting Lin's wishes before Mao's.

The reason the head of the Praetorian Guard acted this way was because he felt Lin's patronage was essential. He had seen the fate that befell his de facto predecessor, Luo the Tall, who had been as close to Mao as it was possible to be, and yet whom Mao had sacrificed when Lin had demanded it. And now he saw Mao apparently making another similar sacrifice: Mao had just endorsed Lin's request to victimize yet another man who had Mao's deep trust, the Party No. 7, Zhang Chun-qiao.

The 53-year-old Zhang had been a middle-ranking functionary in Shanghai who had caught Mao's eye with his ability to churn out articles that dressed up Mao's self-serving deeds in Marxist garb. At the start of the Cultural Revolution, Mao had jumped him to the top to perform the crucial job of packaging the Purge in ideological phraseology. Zhang was the person largely responsible for the texts that caused many people in China and abroad to entertain illusions about the true nature of the Cultural Revolution.

Zhang was reticent and reserved, and wore a face that colleagues found hard to read. He had been dubbed "the Cobra" by Lin and his coterie, partly because he wore glasses, and partly because of his snakelike qualities. Lin Biao hated him because he was not one of his own cronies, and because Mao, ever one to sow discord among his underlings, had told Lin that the Cobra might one day succeed Lin when Lin got old. For some time, Lin had been trying to undermine the Cobra by sending Mao dirt on him. Just before delivering his speech at Lushan, Lin told Mao that he intended to condemn the Cobra in it, and Mao gave Lin the nod to proceed. After Lin's speech, which was fierce, other participants piled in, demanding, in the brutal language of the day, that the Cobra be "put to the death of the thousand cuts."

The lesson was clear: however close or important anyone was to Mao, that person had to have Lin's blessing to survive. Mao's favor on its own was not enough. This was a huge power shift. The thought that Lin's patronage was now more critical than his own rocked Mao.

He set out at once to demonstrate that Lin was not omnipotent. He vetoed any possibility of having a presidency, and called a halt to attacks on the Cobra, and to any further discussion of Lin's speech. Mao proceeded to show enormous displeasure towards Lin, and then condemned his old secretary Chen Bo-da, the Party No. 5, who had become too pally with Lin. As usual in such cases, Chen was put under house arrest, and then thrown into prison—an experience he described as like being "hit on the head by an atom bomb."

Mao asked Lin to make a self-criticism in front of the top echelon and say that he had been "deceived" by Chen. Lin declined. Until now, thanks to his special relationship with Mao, he had always avoided having to subject himself to this humiliating ritual. Even though Mao insisted,

Lin refused to budge. There was an impasse. After four decades, the Mao–Lin relationship began to fall apart.

AFTER LUSHAN, which ended inconclusively on 6 September, Mao moved to reduce Lin's power—and also to ensure his personal safety. He summoned trusted generals who were not in Lin's coterie to take over the military command of Peking, and inserted them into the army leadership. He also cleaned up his own household, by dismissing some of his favorite girlfriends who had come from the air force's song and dance troupe, a procuring service for Mao, which had links to Lin.

Mao had to tread very gingerly so as not to make Lin feel personally threatened. He could ill afford to break with Lin completely. Virtually the entire regime was staffed with people selected by Lin and his personal network. Mao wanted to neutralize him as much as possible without purging him. The interminable machinations needed to achieve this sapped Mao's energy, and that winter he fell ill with pneumonia. It was now, at seventy-seven, that old age suddenly set in, and he who had enjoyed extraordinary good health began to be besieged by illness.

Meanwhile, Lin Biao continued to refuse to perform the self-abasement that Mao demanded. Always a loner, he became even more withdrawn, and spent most of his time pacing his room, occasionally watching war films. He dictated a letter to Mao, making it clear that in the event of his being purged, Mao would have to restaff the entire machine that Lin had installed; the only possible replacements would have to be the old Party cadres, and that would mean repudiating the Cultural Revolution. But at his wife's urging, Lin did not send the letter. Mao would not tolerate being threatened in such a way.

A more realistic option for Lin was to cut and run, as past foes of Mao's had done: Chang Kuo-tao to the Nationalists in the 1930s, and Wang Ming to Moscow in the 1950s. With his control of the air force, Lin could escape overseas. The obvious choice was Russia. He had spent over four years there altogether, and his wife spoke workable Russian, having had a Russian officer lover. It was a sign of Lin Biao's mistrust of Communist regimes that Russia was only his fall-back choice, and his preferred destination was the British colony of Hong Kong.

Lin's plan was to fly first to Canton, which is very close to Hong Kong, and where the military were exceptionally devoted to him. To secure this escape route, he relied on his only son, Li-guo, whom he called "Tiger," who was in his mid-twenties. In November 1970, soon after Lin's breach with Mao at Lushan, Tiger started to see people from the Canton military. His intimates made frequent secret visits to Canton, got hold of small arms, radios and cars, and learned to fly helicopters. During all these extensive activities, no one informed on Tiger, who inspired loyalty.

Tiger had been a physics student at Peking University when the Cultural Revolution started. Unusually for a young man of his background, he only joined the Red Guards reluctantly, and quickly left, showing no inclination for violence, or for persecuting people. He seems to have been a decent person. He was something of a playboy, and had many girlfriends. His parents worshipped him, and his mother had sent agents all over China to look for the most beautiful young woman to be his wife. Tiger chose a sexy fiancée who was intelligent, and a character. With her he listened to Western rock music, which he adored, and told her: "There will be a day when I will let the Chinese know there is such wonderful music in the world!"

Being able to enjoy Western music was only one of Tiger's many rare privileges as the son of Lin Biao. Another was access to Western science magazines, which he devoured, often expressing admiration for the advances being made in the West. (He was an avid inventor of military equipment, with some effective ideas of his own.) But above all, he was able to read some top-secret documents, with the result that he was exceptionally well informed.

Tiger came to be sharply critical of Mao's tyranny. In March 1971, he and three friends put their thoughts on paper:

- Senior officials feel anger but dare not speak up;
- Peasants lack food and clothing;
- Educated youth rusticated: prison labour in disguise;
- The Red Guards were deceived and used at the beginning . . . as cannon fodder [and then] scapegoats . . .
- Workers' . . . wages have been frozen: disguised exploitation.

These words were part of a document called "Outline of Project 571." Tiger chose the name because "571"—*wu-qi-yi*—has the same pronunciation in Chinese as "armed uprising," and a coup was what the friends had in mind. The Outline was a razor-sharp indictment of Mao, describing China under his rule as "state rich, people impoverished," which they wanted to change to "people rich and state powerful." Their aim was "to give the people enough food and clothing and a peaceful life"—the antithesis of Mao's goals.

They described Mao as "the biggest promoter of violence," who "sets . . . people against people," "a paranoid and a sadist," and "the biggest feudal tyrant in Chinese history." They accused him of "turning the Chinese state machine into a meat grinder, slaughtering and crushing people." These observations were truly remarkable for the times. Tiger dubbed Mao "B-52" after the US heavy bomber, referring to the fact that Mao, as he put it, had a big stomach full of evil thoughts, each one like a heavy bomb that would kill masses of people. Tiger's attitude to Mao was completely different from that of Mao's opponents among the old guard. He saw right through Mao, whom he regarded as evil, and unfit to run the country. He also realized that with him no dialogue or compromise was possible. In this sense, he was the nearest thing China produced to a Claus von Stauffenberg, the German officer who tried to assassinate Hitler in 1944.

Tiger and his friends began to talk about assassinating Mao when Tiger saw that Mao was coming after his parents. The friends mooted many ideas, but all in very general terms, like "using poison gas, germ weapons, bombing...," and there is no sign that they ever got as far as actually preparing any of these. Mao had the most stringent rules on arms and troop movements, and phenomenal security. Moreover, as Tiger's group themselves observed, "the blind faith of the masses in B-52 is very deep" (thanks partly, ironically, to Tiger's father), and so they did not dare to reveal their project to most of their friends, or to Lin's major cronies at the top of the military. Tiger left a copy with his parents, but Lin was non-committal.

IN MARCH 1971, some seven months after the rift with Lin erupted at Lushan, Mao decided to convene a conference for about a hundred of the elite to hear Lin's wife and major army cronies perform their self-abasements. Mao sent Chou En-lai in person to ask Lin, in unusually strong terms, to appear and "say a few words." Lin refused. This was a huge snub to Mao's authority, and he went berserk. He ordered Chou to deliver a blistering denunciation of Lin on 29 April (though not naming him), saying that the army leadership had been "following a wrong political line."

A furious Lin retaliated. Two days later was May Day, when the leadership traditionally gathered on Tiananmen Gate. Protocol was very important in the Communist world, and any absence could be interpreted as signifying discord at the top. On the night, however, there was no sign of Lin. Chou stared anxiously at the empty seat facing Mao and Prince Norodom Sihanouk of Cambodia, next to the prince's wife, while frantic phone calls were made to Lin's home. A dejected-looking Lin eventually appeared, long after the fireworks display had begun.

The official photographer, Du, described the scene to us:

> When I saw Lin Biao sitting down, I snapped a shot. I didn't intend it to be published at all. I wanted to wait for [Mao and Lin] to start talking... But they didn't even look at each other... Then Lin Biao got up and left. I thought he had gone to the toilet, but half an hour later and he was still not back. I wondered how come Vice-Chairman Lin took so long in the toilet. In fact, he had left. We were all dumbfounded. As soon as the show was over, Premier Chou asked me: "Did

you take a photo of Vice-Chairman Lin?" ... I said: "One." He said: "What about film and television?" I said I didn't know. The premier had the crews fetched, and gave them a dressing-down those old guys remember today as if it had been yesterday.

Lin had stayed less than a minute, and had greeted no one, not the Sihanouks, not Mao.

Lin knew that Mao would not forgive him for what happened. After this, Tiger went to Canton to check out the Hong Kong escape route. He went right up to Lowu, the main crossing-point into Hong Kong, getting so close to the actual border that his entourage was worried the Hong Kong police might open fire.

Lin would soon defy Mao again, in June, when Romania's tyrant duo, the Ceauşescus, came to town. Lin declined to come to a meeting with them, claiming that he was "sweating," and Mrs. Lin had to go down on her knees to get him to go. Lin did finally show up, but left the room after Mao made a few digs at him, and went and sat outside the door in a slouching posture, his head lolling. Shortly afterwards, Tiger made another recce of the border with Hong Kong, by helicopter.

By mid-August, a year after Lushan, Mao was ready to purge Lin. On the 14th he left Peking to prepare provincial leaders. He had to make sure that these men, most of them Lin appointees, would not side with Lin in a showdown. During his tour, Mao made repeated damning remarks about Lin, like: "He wants to split the Party and can't wait to seize power." Although Mao told his audiences not to report to Lin on what he said, a few of Lin's followers disobeyed. Mao's words reached the Lins at the seaside resort of Beidaihe, east of Peking, on 6 September. The Lin villa occupied a whole hill, well shielded from the sea by luxuriant vegetation, as Lin could not stand the sight of water, though he liked the sea air. For kilometers there was not a soul around, except guards and staff.

Lin and his wife and Tiger decided to flee abroad at once. They planned to depart from the nearby airport at Shanhaiguan, where the Great Wall meets the sea. Tiger flew to Peking on the 8th to secure planes for the escape. He brought with him a handwritten note from his father: "Please follow the orders relayed by comrades Li-guo [Tiger] and Yu-chi [Tiger's closest friend]. (Signed) Lin Biao 8 September." The man in charge of dispatching planes at Peking military airport agreed to bypass regular channels to get Tiger the planes.

But Tiger did not want to flee without first making an attempt to assassinate Mao. At that moment Mao was in the Shanghai area, where officers loyal to Lin held key positions, and even had partial charge of Mao's security in the outer ring. It seems that at the eleventh hour, Lin Biao agreed that Tiger could try. Mrs. Lin was all for having a go. When

Tiger kissed his fiancée goodbye at Beidaihe, he said: "In case something happens to me, you don't know anything; I won't incriminate you."

In Peking, Tiger asked the deputy chief of staff of the air force, Wang Fei, to mount an assault on the compound where Mme Mao and her coterie were living, the Imperial Fishing Villa. Tiger told him that simultaneous action would be taken "in the south," where Mao was. Wang Fei was a good friend, but his reply was disappointing. He did not think he could persuade any troops to do what Tiger was asking. In any case, his troops were not allowed to carry weapons into Peking.

Next, Tiger met a senior air force officer called Jiang Teng-jiao, who was the youngest general in China, and who, for various reasons, hated Mao. Tiger asked him to try to kill Mao while Mao was still near Shanghai. Jiang agreed, and the two aired various ideas. One was to shoot up Mao's train with flame-throwers and bazookas; another was to shell it; a third was for the Shanghai military chief, a man trusted by the Lins, to shoot Mao on his train. The fourth was to bomb Mao's train from the air. But the man they approached to drop the bombs, a Korean War ace, replied that there were no bomber aircraft available. He took fright, and asked his wife, who was a doctor, to rub salt water and old aureomycin into his eyes so that they would swell up, and he thus got himself hospitalized. The other ideas also proved non-viable, as it was impossible to get lethal firepower anywhere near Mao's closely guarded and heavily armor-plated train.

Over the next couple of days, tense discussions continued. "I just can't stomach him any longer!" Tiger would shout, waving his fists. "OK," he would say, "the fish dies, but it breaks the net!," indicating that he was ready to make a suicidal attack if that was what it took to bring down the Mao regime.

Fast running out of ideas, Tiger sent a friend back to Beidaihe on the 10th to get his father to write to Army Chief of Staff Huang Yong-sheng, asking him to cooperate with Tiger. Lin wrote the letter, but it was not delivered. The plotters could not trust Huang not to betray them.

It was also too late. Next day, news came that Mao had left Shanghai by train. Several of Tiger's friends offered to fly helicopters on a suicide attack against Mao on Tiananmen Gate on National Day, 1 October. Tiger vetoed the idea, in tears. He had not anticipated any action of this magnitude.

All assassination plans were aborted, and Tiger decided to revert to the plan to flee to Canton, and then Hong Kong. On the evening of 12 September he flew back to Beidaihe in Lin's plane, a Trident, intending to leave with his family next morning.

Mao had returned to Peking late that afternoon, completely unaware that an assassination plot had been afoot. His train stopped outside the capital at a station called Fengtai, where he was given a routine briefing by his newly appointed Peking commanders on what had been happening in the capital. The meeting opened with a report about an army delegation's visit to Albania. Back in Zhongnanhai, it was like the end of any other trip. Mao's security chiefs and the head of his guards, who lived outside the compound, went home. Some of them took sleeping pills. Mao, too, went to sleep.

AT THE TIME Mao and his entourage went to bed, the Lins were getting ready to decamp. Tiger had reached Beidaihe about 9:00 PM, and went over plans with his parents. The staff were told that the Lins were leaving at 6:00 AM for Dalian, a nearby port city, which was an old haunt of Lin's, so this did not arouse suspicion. Then, fatally, Tiger asked his sister Dodo to be ready to leave in the morning.

Two years older than Tiger, Dodo was a very brainwashed young woman. Her parents had not wanted to let her in on their escape plans, in case she might turn them in. But Tiger was worried about what might happen to his sister after they fled, and had disclosed part of the plans to her a few days before. As their parents had foreseen, she got scared. Unlike her brother, Dodo was a product of the fear and twisted logic of Mao's China. For her, attempting to flee abroad was defection, and therefore treason, even though she knew that her sick father, whom she loved, was not likely to survive long in prison under Mao. When Tiger told her they were leaving the following morning, she reported the news to the Praetorian Guards who were stationed in a separate building at the bottom of the drive. This action doomed her family.

The Guards phoned Chou En-lai, and he began to check on the movements of planes, particularly the Trident, which was Lin's plane. Tiger's friends immediately let him know that Chou was asking questions, and Lin Biao decided to leave at once rather than wait till morning. He also decided to fly not to Canton, but to their fallback destination, Russia, via Outer Mongolia, as this route would mean much less time in Chinese airspace, just over an hour.

Tiger rang his friends about the change of route, and phoned the captain of the Trident to get the plane ready. Unaware that Chou's enquiry had been triggered by his sister's betrayal, Tiger told Dodo they were taking off right away. She went straight back to the Praetorian Guards and stayed at their post.

Around 11:50 PM, Lin Biao, Mme Lin and Tiger, plus a friend of Tiger's, sped off for the airport, accompanied by Lin's butler. As the car raced out of the estate, the Praetorian Guards tried to stop it. At this point Lin's butler surmised that they were going to flee the country. Thinking of the fate that awaited his family if he became a defector, he shouted "Stop the car!" and jumped out. Gunshots followed, one hitting his arm. The shot came from Tiger, the butler said; some suggest that it was self-inflicted, to protect himself.

The Praetorian Guards set off in hot pursuit, in several vehicles. About half an hour later the Lins' car screeched to a halt beside the Trident at Shanhaiguan airport, with one pursuing jeep only 200 meters behind. Mrs. Lin hit the tarmac screaming that Lin was in danger, shouting: "We are leaving!" Tiger had a pistol in his hand. The group clambered frantically up the small ladder to the pilot's cabin.

The Trident took off in a rush at 12:32 AM, carrying the three Lins, plus Tiger's friend and Lin's driver. Out of the full nine-man crew, only four, the captain and three mechanics, had time to get on board. The mechanics had just readied the plane for departure, and were only beginning to refuel it when the Lins arrived and Mrs. Lin yelled for the fuel tanker to be moved away. As a result, the plane had only 12.5 tons of fuel on board, enough for between two and three hours in the air, depending on altitude and speed.

They had to fly low for most of the time to dodge radar, and this used up more fuel. Two hours later, over the Mongolian grassland, they would have had only about 2.5 tons of fuel left—at which point the fuel gauge would have been flashing for some time. At 2:30 AM on 13 September 1971, the plane crash-landed in a flat basin and exploded on impact, killing all nine people on board.

A HEAVILY SEDATED Mao had been woken up by Chou soon after Lin's plane took off. Mao stayed in his bedroom, which was one of the former changing-rooms of the swimming pool in Zhongnanhai. The nearest telephone was in a room at the other end of the 50-meter pool. When the people monitoring Lin's plane rang, the head of the Guard, Wang Dong-xing (whom Mao had forgiven for supporting Lin at Lushan a year before), would rush to the phone, then back to Mao, then to the phone again. The plane did not cross the border into Mongolia until 1:50 AM, so Mao had about an hour to act.

It seems Mao was only presented with one option if he wanted to strike: interception by fighter planes. China apparently had no usable ground-to-air missiles. Mao vetoed interception.* The unspoken reason was that he could not trust the air force, which was honeycombed with Lin men. Instead, Mao had every plane in China grounded, while the

---

* A letter from Chou to Mao on the night of 13 September shows unequivocally that the plane was not shot down by the Chinese.

land army took over all the airports, blocking the runways to prevent any planes taking off. The only planes allowed into the air were eight closely monitored fighters sent up later to force down a helicopter carrying three friends of Tiger's. When the three men were brought back to the outskirts of Peking, they agreed to shoot themselves together. Two did. The third, who had said that his last bullet was "reserved for B-52," meaning Mao, weakened at the last moment, and fired into the air.

Mao was moved to his Suite 118 in the Great Hall, where there was a lift to a nuclear-proof bunker and a tunnel to the Western Hills. His servants were told to be ready for war, and his guards went onto top alert, and started digging trenches around Mao's residences. The head of Mao's guards for twenty-seven years said he had never seen Mao look so strained, so exhausted and so furious.

Mao remained sleepless and wiped out until the afternoon of 14 September, when news came that the Lins had crashed in Mongolia. This was an ideal outcome from his point of view, and he swigged some *mao-tai*, the powerful liquor he did not normally touch, in celebration.*

But Mao's relief that Lin was dead was quickly overshadowed by the news that there had been a plot to assassinate him, which came to light right after he heard that Lin had crashed. This was the first assassination plot against Mao by his top echelon, and it came as a profound shock. Equally alarming was the fact that quite a few people had known about these plans, and not one had informed. For days Mao hardly slept, in spite of downing fistfuls of sleeping pills. He ran a temperature and coughed incessantly. Breathing problems made it impossible for him to lie down, so he sat on a sofa day and night for three weeks, developing bedsores on his bottom. Then a heart condition was discovered. On 8 October, when he met Ethiopia's Emperor Haile Selassie, he barely spoke a word. One official present, who had last seen Mao the day before Lin fled, less than a month before, could not believe how washed-out Mao looked. Chou brought the meeting to an early close.

Mao had to struggle to deal with endless details in order to tighten his already incredibly tight security. Everybody near him had to report in detail on their every dealing with the Lins. A deputy chief of the Praetorian Guard, Zhang Yao-ci, owned up to having received some bamboo shoots "and two dead pheasants" from Mrs. Lin one New Year, and to having

---

* The Russians sent their top investigator, KGB general Aleksandr Zagvozdin, to Mongolia to make sure it really was Lin on the plane. Zagvozdin dug up the corpses. But, he told us, his report failed to satisfy his bosses, and he was sent back to exhume the bodies again from the now frozen ground. The corpses of Lin and his wife were boiled in a huge pot and the skeletons taken to Moscow, where Lin's was checked against old Russian medical records and X-rays from his earlier visits, and a squeamish Yuri Andropov and Brezhnev were finally satisfied that it really was Lin.

given her some tangerines. Mao's warning to him tells a lot about the bleak world surrounding the Boss:

1. Don't cultivate connections;
2. Don't visit people;
3. Don't give dinners or gifts;
4. Don't invite people to operas [i.e. Mme Mao's model shows] or films;
5. Don't have photographs taken with people.

An altogether more monumental task was sorting out the armed forces, which were crammed with Lin men, especially at the top. Mao had no way of knowing who was involved in the assassination plot, or where anyone's allegiance lay. One small but alarming incident came days later when senior air force officers were gathered to be briefed about the Lins. One of the men raced to the top of the building, shouted anti-Mao slogans and jumped to his death.

The only marshal Mao could trust to take over running the army was Yeh Jian-ying. He had been a faithful follower in the past, but had spoken his mind against the Cultural Revolution, and as a result had been cast into semi-disgrace, for a while living under virtual house arrest. At the time Mao brought him back to high office, several of his children and other close relatives were still languishing in prison.

But Mao had nobody else. He was also forced to reinstate purged Party officials, because they were the only alternative to the people installed by Lin's network. These officials were mostly in camps. Now many were rehabilitated and re-employed. Mao loathed having to let this happen, and tried to limit the scale of the rehabilitations. He knew that these officials felt extremely bitter towards him after the appalling ordeals they had been put through. One former deputy chief of the Praetorian Guard spoke for many people when he told us how he felt then: "What Chairman Mao, what Party? I stopped caring about any of them . . ."

At this juncture, Marshal Chen Yi, one of the more outspoken opponents of the Great Purge, who had suffered much in it, died of cancer, on 6 January 1972. The memorial service was scheduled for the 10th, as a low-key affair, with limitations put on the size of his portrait, the number of wreaths, how many people could attend—and the number of stoves permitted to heat a big hall: just two. Mao had no wish to attend the funeral.

But in the days after Chen Yi's death, although the news was not announced, word got out, and large numbers of old cadres gathered outside the hospital, demanding to be allowed to bid farewell to his corpse. The mood of the crowds was angry as well as mournful. And there was no doubt that the anger was directed against the Cultural Revolution—and against Mao himself. Mao felt tremendous pressure to make a gesture to placate the old power base which he had treated so abominably, and on which he now had to rely again.

On the day of the service, shortly before it was due to begin, Mao suddenly declared that he would attend. His staff observed that "his face was hung with dark clouds" and he looked "irritated and frustrated," remaining totally silent. But he could see it was wise to go and use the occasion to put across the message to old cadres that he "cares for us." He also did some scapegoating, telling Chen Yi's family that it was Lin Biao who had "plotted . . . to get rid of all us old stagers." Word went out that the persecutions in the Cultural Revolution were Lin Biao's fault, and that Mao was coming to his senses. Afterwards, a photo was published of Mao at the service, looking suitably sad (though with his unshaven stubble airbrushed out), with Chen Yi's grief-stricken widow clinging to his arm, and this did much to abate the bitterness among "capitalist-roaders."

The day of Chen Yi's funeral was bitterly cold, but Mao was in such a foul mood at having to go that he refused to put on a warm coat. His staff tried to get him to dress sensibly, but he pushed the clothes away. He ended up wearing only a thin coat over his pajamas, and that was all he had on for the whole service in the poorly heated hall. As a result he fell ill. He was seventy-eight, and he got sicker and sicker. On 12 February he passed out, and lay at the brink of death.

Physical and political vulnerability forced Mao to allow the rehabilitation of cadres to be speeded up, and the regime became markedly more moderate for the first time since the start of the Cultural Revolution nearly six years before. Abusive practices in prisons decreased greatly. Violent denunciation meetings were scrapped, even for Lin Biao's men, who, although detained,* suffered little physically compared with Mao's previous routine. Incredibly, given that an attempted assassination—of Mao, no less—was involved, not a single person was executed.

After years of living surrounded by daily brutality, and with almost nothing constructive to see or do in the way of entertainment, tension in society had built up to an almost unbearable pitch. An Italian psychoanalyst who was in China just before this time observed to us that he had never seen anything like the number of facial tics and extreme tension in people's faces. Now there was a let-up. A few old books and tunes, and some leisure activities, were allowed again. Some historical sites were reopened. Although relaxation stayed within very strict limits, still there was a lightness in the air when spring came in 1972.

---

* Among those detained was Lin Biao's daughter Dodo.

MAOISM FALLS FLAT
ON THE WORLD STAGE

(1966–70 ★ AGE 72–76)

MAO'S ULTIMATE AMBITION was to dominate the world. In November 1968 he told the Australian Maoist leader Hill:

> In my opinion, the world needs to be unified ... In the past, many, including the Mongols, the Romans ... Alexander the Great, Napoleon, and the British Empire, wanted to unify the world. Today, both the United States and the Soviet Union want to unify the world. Hitler wanted to unify the world ... But they all failed. It seems to me that the possibility of unifying the world has not disappeared ... In my view, the world can be unified.

Mao clearly felt that he was the man for the job, as he dismissed America and Russia as possible unifiers, using arguments that rested solely on China's huge population. "But these two countries [America and Russia]," he went on, "have too small populations, and they will not have enough manpower if it is dispersed. Further, they are also afraid of fighting a nuclear war. They are not afraid of eliminating populations in other countries, but they are afraid of their own populations being eliminated." It was hardly necessary to read between the lines to see that the ruler with the largest population—and the least fear of it being wiped out— was Mao himself. He saw China's role as follows: "In another five years, our country ... will be in a better position ... In another five years ..."

It was for the sake of this world ambition that Mao had embarked on his Superpower Program in 1953, insisting on breakneck speed, and taking hair-raising risks in the nuclear field. The most scary of these came on 27 October 1966, when a missile armed with an atomic warhead was fired 800 km across northwest China, over sizable towns—the only such test ever undertaken by any nation on earth, and with a missile known to be far from accurate, putting the lives of those in its flight path at risk. Three days beforehand, Mao told the man in charge to proceed, saying that he was prepared for the test to fail.

Almost all those involved in the test felt that a catastrophe was likely. The people in the launch control room expected to die. The commander of the target zone was so nervous that he moved his HQ to the top of a mountain, comforting himself and his colleagues with the argument that if the missile went off course, they might be able to shield themselves from the atomic blast by scrambling down the opposite side of the mountain.

As it happened, the test succeeded, an outcome that was attributed to Mao's "Thought," summed up in the slogan "The spiritual atomic bomb detonating the material atomic bomb." In fact the success was a fluke. Subsequent tests of the same missile failed, as it began gyrating wildly shortly after lift-off.*

The whole missile program suffered from insuperable problems. The regime blamed sabotage, and scientists were put through hideous persecutions, including mock executions, to extract "confessions." Many died violent deaths. In this climate, not surprisingly, Mao never possessed an intercontinental missile in his lifetime. The first successful launch of a Chinese ICBM took place only in 1980, years after his death.

But in October 1966, thanks to the one nuclear-armed missile landing on target, Mao assumed that he would soon be able to deliver the Bomb wherever he liked. On 11 December, a decision was made that China must possess the entire missile arsenal, including intercontinental missiles, within four years.

Mao's optimism was given a big boost when China's first hydrogen bomb was detonated on 17 June 1967. Mao told its makers on 7 July: "Our new weaponry, missiles and atom bombs have gone really fast. We made our hydrogen bomb in just two years and eight months [since the first A-bomb]. Our speed has overtaken America, Britain, France and the Soviet Union. We are the No. 4 in the world." Actually, much of this was due to assistance Russia had provided earlier (and which had only ended completely in 1965); without Soviet help, it would have been impossible to develop either the A- or the H-bomb nearly so soon. But Mao was not about to dwell on this aspect. His emphasis was rather on what he could do with the technology. Using the royal "we," he declared to the Bomb-makers: "We are not only the political centre of the world revolution, we must become the centre of the world revolution militarily, and technologically. We must give them arms, Chinese arms engraved

---

* The October 1966 success coincided with the presence in China of one of Hitler's top rocket experts, Wolfgang Pilz, who was spotted in Peking by an Indian diplomat that month, along with three German colleagues. Pilz had previously been supervising Egypt's missile program and had been lured away to China with offers of large sums of money and more exciting technical conditions. When China tried to attract other German scientists, the US offered them more money to entice them to America.

with our labels ... We must openly support them. We must become the arsenal of the world revolution."

It was now, between October 1966 and summer 1967, with the nuclear program seemingly riding high, that Mao vastly expanded the worldwide promotion of his cult. In the year before, 1965, he had suffered some major setbacks. Now "to propagate Mao Tse-tung Thought" was made the "central task" of foreign policy. Peking proclaimed that "the world has entered the new era of Mao," and sweated blood to make sure that the Little Red Book got into over 100 countries. Supposedly this was "an event of immense joy for the people of the world," who "love Chairman Mao's books more than any other books," and to whom the Little Red Book "is like the sweet rain to crops withering in a long drought, and the shining beacon to ships sailing in thick fog." China's entire diplomatic and clandestine machine was thrown into attempts to induce adulation of Mao in foreign countries.

Burma was not atypical of the countries where Peking had a foothold. A hard-sell campaign pressured the sizeable ethnic Chinese minority to wave the Little Red Book, wear Mao badges, sing songs of Mao quotes and salute Mao's portrait. Regarding these practices as challenging its own authority, the Burmese government banned them in mid-1967. Peking then goaded ethnic Chinese to defy the ban and confront the government. The result was much bloodshed and many deaths, and severe retribution against ethnic Chinese.

Mao then unleashed the Burmese Communist Party, which was completely dependent on China for its survival, in a new wave of insurgency. On 7 July 1967, in the afterglow of the H-bomb test, he instructed in secret: "It is better that the Burmese government is against us. I hope they break off diplomatic relations with us, so we can more openly support the Burmese Communist Party." Chou summoned the Burmese Communist officers being trained in China to the Great Hall of the People to inform them that they were to be sent home to start a war. They were accompanied to Burma by their Chinese wives, who had been selected in a distinctly unceremonious manner. Each Burmese man would go out into the street, with a Chinese officer, and pick a woman who caught his eye. If the woman and her family passed a security check, the authorities would work on her to marry the Burmese. Some women entered into marriage willingly, others were coerced.

The insurgency was geared around promoting Mao. When a victory was won, it was celebrated with a Mao Thought propaganda team dancing, waving the Little Red Book, and chanting "Long live the great leader of the peoples of the world Chairman Mao!"

To spread Maoism all over the world, secret training camps were set up in China. One was in the Western Hills just outside Peking, where many young people from the Third World and quite a few Westerners were instructed in the use of arms and explosives. Mao Thought was the unvarying and ineluctable staple of camp life.

HOWEVER, ON HIS doorstep the Great Leader of World Revolution was faced with an uncomfortable reality. Two portions of Chinese territory remained under colonial rule: Macau under the Portuguese and Hong Kong under the British. And taking them back would have been easy, as both depended on China for water and food. Khrushchev had taunted Mao that he was living next door to "the colonialists' latrine." After Mao accused him of climbing down in the Cuba missile crisis in 1962, Khrushchev had compared Mao's inaction over the two colonies unfavorably with Nehru's recent seizure of Portugal's colonies in India: "The odour coming from [Hong Kong and Macau] is by no means sweeter than that which was released by colonialism in Goa." Mao had clearly felt that he had to explain himself to those he was claiming to champion, so he made rather a point of telling the Somali prime minister, somewhat defensively, that Hong Kong "is a special case and we are not planning to touch it. You may not understand this."

Mao chose not to recover Hong Kong and Macau for purely pragmatic reasons. Hong Kong was China's biggest source of hard currency, and a vital channel for acquiring technology and equipment from the West, which fell under a strict US embargo. Mao knew that Hong Kong would no longer be of use for his Superpower Program if it reverted to Peking's rule.

In order to do good business in Hong Kong, Peking had to disrupt Taiwan's intelligence network, which was helping the US identify Western companies breaking the embargo. Peking's methods had at times been drastic. In April 1955, Chou En-lai was due to go to Indonesia for the first Afro-Asian conference in Bandung, and Peking chartered an Indian airliner, the *Kashmir Princess*, to fly to Indonesia from Hong Kong. Taiwan agents apparently thought that the plane was going to carry Chou, and concocted a plan to place a bomb on board at the Hong Kong airport. Peking had all the details well in advance, but let the operation go ahead, without telling either Air India, or the British mission in Peking, or the Hong Kong government—or the passengers, eleven relatively low-level officials and journalists (in a plane that seated over 100). The plane blew up in mid-air, killing all the passengers and five of the eight Indian crew.

Peking immediately declared that Taiwan agents had planted a bomb, and Chou En-lai gave the British names of people Peking wanted expelled from Hong Kong. The British went along, and over the following year deported over forty key Nationalist agents on Chou's list, even though there was not enough evidence to charge any of them with an offense in court. This put a sizable part of Chiang's network in Hong Kong out of action, and it was after this that Peking secured a series of clandestine deals for its nuclear program via the colony; one purchase alone from Western Europe cost 150 tons of gold.

When the Cultural Revolution started and Mao revved up his campaign to be the leader of the world revolution, he wanted to show the world that he was the true master of the colony, by making the British "go down on their knees" and publicly offer "unconditional surrender," in the words of Chinese diplomats at internal meetings. The only way this could be achieved was to put the British in the wrong—and that needed a massacre of Chinese.

So Peking seized on a labor dispute in May 1967, and urged Hong Kong radicals to escalate violence, especially to break the law in a confrontational manner. To spur them on, Peking hinted strongly and publicly that it might take the colony back before the lease expired in 1997, and activists there were given to understand that this was Peking's intention.

Mao's real line was the one he imparted to Chou En-lai, in secret: "Hong Kong remains the same"—i.e., it stays under British rule. Chou's assignment was to stir up enough violence to provoke reprisals, and then a kowtow, from the British, but not so much violence that it "might lead to us having to take Hong Kong back ahead of time," which Chou privately made clear would be disastrous.

In the riots that ensued, Hong Kong police killed some demonstrators; but the number of deaths fell short of a massacre and the colonial authorities refused to apologize. Peking then incited Hong Kong radicals to kill policemen. "Do to them [the police] as they have done to us," urged *People's Daily*. "Those who kill must pay with their lives." As the Hong Kong rioters were unable to kill policemen, Chou had to infiltrate soldiers into the colony. These men slipped across the border on 8 July, dressed in mufti, and shot dead five police. Chou expressed his satisfaction with the results, but vetoed any more such operations in case the situation evolved to a point where Peking's bluff might be openly called. Instead, Peking fostered an indiscriminate bombing campaign, and over the next two months there were about 160 bomb incidents, some fatal.

But the British refused to resort to a massacre, and focused on methodically rounding up activists, quietly, at night. Mao's hope of getting Britain to kowtow collapsed. In frustration, he fell back on hooliganism on his own turf. On 22 August a crowd of over 10,000 torched the British Mission in Peking, trapping the staff inside and almost burning them alive, and subjecting women to gross sexual harassment.

THE MISSIONS OF a score of other countries also found themselves on the receiving end of Mao's fury. In 1967, violent assaults were made on the Soviet embassy, followed by the embassies of Indonesia, India, Burma and Mongolia. These attacks had official sanction, with the Foreign Ministry telling the mobs which missions to assail, and how intensely. The "punishments" ranged from million-strong demonstrations besieging the missions, unfurling giant portraits of Mao, and blasting insults through loudhailers, to breaking in, setting fire to cars, manhandling diplomats and their spouses and terrorizing their children, while yelling slogans like "Beat to death, beat to death."

This treatment was even meted out to North Korea, as Kim Il Sung had declined to submit to Mao's tutelage. Mao had over the years tried to subvert Kim, for which he had once been obliged to apologize. At the Moscow Communist summit in November 1957 he waylaid Kim to mend fences, to forestall Kim spilling the beans to other Communist leaders. According to an official Korean report that was relayed to a large meeting in Pyongyang, Mao "repeatedly expressed his apologies [to Kim] for the Chinese Communist Party's unjustified interference in the affairs of the Korean [Party]." Kim seized the chance to reduce Mao's clout in Korea by demanding the withdrawal of all the Chinese troops still there, to which Mao had to accede.

Mao did not give up. In January 1967, his man in charge of clandestine missions abroad, Kang Sheng, told the Albanians: "Kim Il Sung should be overthrown, so that the situation in Korea can be changed." Unable to fulfill this wish, Mao directed crowds to swamp the Korean embassy, denouncing "fat Kim." Kim retaliated by renaming Mao Tsetung Square in Pyongyang, closing the rooms commemorating China's role in the Korean War Museum, "re-sizing" the Russian and Chinese war memorials in Pyongyang, and drawing much closer to Russia.

By the end of September 1967, China had become embroiled in rows with most of the forty-eight countries with which it had diplomatic or semi-diplomatic relations. Many of these countries lowered their level of representation, and some closed their embassies. National Day that year saw only a sprinkling of foreign government delegates on Tiananmen.* Mao later blamed his debacles on "extreme leftists." The truth is that China's foreign policy was never out of his hands.

BY THE END of the 1960s, Mao's self-promotion had been going on for a decade, and had raised his profile sky-high in the outside world. In the West, many were mesmerized by him. The Little Red Book was taken up by intellectuals and students. Mao was termed a philosopher. The

---

* Not surprisingly, when even committed friends could find themselves at risk. When the Albanian premier Mehmet Shehu and his colleague Ramiz Alia returned to Peking after traveling around the country, Mao greeted them by asking: "Did anyone hit you?"

influential French writer Jean-Paul Sartre praised the "revolutionary violence" of Mao as "profoundly moral."

However, it was apparent that this general fascination had not translated into substance. No Maoist party in the West—even the largest one, in Portugal—ever gained more than a minuscule following. Most Western "Maoists" were fantasists, or freeloaders, and had no appetite for sustained action, least of all if it was physically uncomfortable or dangerous. When large-scale student unrest erupted in Western Europe in 1968, Mao hailed this as "a new phenomenon in European history," and sent European Maoists who had been trained in sabotage back home to exploit the situation. But they generated no action of significance.

Nor were Maoist groups making much headway in the Third World. Africa, once full of promise, had proved a thorough disappointment, as a jingle by a Chinese diplomat summed up:

> *Big, big tribalism,*
> *Small, small nationalism,*
> *Much, much imperialism,*
> *Little, little Mao Tse-tung Thought.*

African radicals rather astutely took Mao's money, as one Chinese diplomat put it, with a big smile, but his instructions with a deaf ear. Some years later, meeting one of the heads of state he had tried hardest to topple, Zaïre's President Mobutu, Mao admitted failure, in the guise of a rueful quip. His opening sally was: "Is that really you, Mobutu? I've spent a lot of money trying to have you overthrown—even killed. But here you are." "We gave them money and arms, but they just couldn't fight. They just couldn't win. What can I do then?"

Mao had even less success in the Middle East. When the Six-Day War broke out between Israel and the Arab states in June 1967, Mao offered Nasser US$10 million and 150,000 tons of wheat, as well as military "volunteers," if Nasser would take his advice "to fight to the end." He sent Nasser a battle plan for a Mao-style "people's war," telling him to "lure the enemy in deep," by withdrawing into the Sinai Peninsula, even to Khartoum, the capital of *Sudan*. Nasser declined to follow the Maoist road, explaining to his distant adviser that Sinai "is a desert and we cannot conduct a people's liberation war in Sinai because there are no people there." Peking withdrew its offers of aid, and tried to promote opposition against Nasser. But Mao built up no groups of disciples in the Middle East. When he and Chou died in 1976, among the 104 parties from 51 countries—many of them tiny groupings—listed as sending condolences, there was not one in the Arab world.

One key factor behind this failure was Mao's insistence that foreign radicals had to take sides with him against Russia. This lost him many potential sympathizers—not least in Latin America. There, Mao had disbursed money and food to try to swing Cuba against Moscow. This largesse produced few returns. In 1964 a delegation of nine Latin American Communist parties, headed by Cuban Party chief Carlos Rafael Rodríguez, came to China to ask Mao to halt public polemics with Russia, and "factional activities," i.e., trying to split Communist parties. An infuriated Mao told them that his fight with Russia "will go on for 10,000 years," and abused Castro. When the delegate from Uruguay (pop. 3 million) tried to get a word in, Mao rounded on him, saying that he, Mao, was "speaking in the name of 650 million people" and how many people did *he* represent?

Castro, who never visited China during Mao's lifetime, described Mao as "a shit," and then went public in front of a large international audience, on 2 January 1966, accusing Peking of applying economic pressure to try to lever him away from Moscow. One month later, he charged Peking with resorting to "brutal reprisals," in particular trying to subvert the Cuban army. Mao called Castro "a jackal and a wolf."

Mao had placed high hopes on Castro's colleague Che Guevara. On Guevara's first visit to China in 1960, Mao demonstrated uncommon intimacy with him, holding his hand while talking eagerly to him, and fulsomely praising a pamphlet of his. Guevara had reciprocated, recommending copying Mao's methods in Cuba. And he had proved the closest in the Havana leadership to Mao's position during the 1962 Cuban missile crisis. But in the end, Mao could not get Guevara to take his side against the Russians. When Guevara returned to China in 1965, just before going off to try to launch guerrilla ventures in Africa, and then Bolivia, Mao did not see him, and a request from Guevara in Bolivia for China's help to build a radio station that could broadcast worldwide was refused. When Guevara was killed in 1967, Peking privately expressed delight. Kang Sheng told Albania's defense minister in October 1968: "The revolution in Latin America is going very well, *especially after the defeat of Guevara*; revisionism is being unmasked . . ." (italics added).

During Mao's lifetime, there were no influential Maoist parties in Latin America. The only notable one, the "Shining Path" in Peru, was founded in 1980, four years after Mao's death.*

ON HIS OWN doorstep in Asia, Mao's influence failed to spread, even against deadbeat regimes like that of Ne Win in Burma. But Mao's biggest

---

* Its failed leader, Abimael Guzmán, called himself "Chairman of the World Revolution." The year "Shining Path" was founded, it celebrated Mao's birthday by hanging dogs from lamp-posts in Lima wrapped in slogans excoriating the post-Mao leader Deng Xiaoping, whom it regarded as having betrayed Mao's legacy, as "a son of a bitch."

Looking grim, next to his patron and rival, Stalin, at the ceremony for Stalin's seventieth birth-day, Moscow, December 1949. To Stalin's left is East Germany's leader Walter Ulbricht, to whom Mao suggested building a wall; Mongolia's Tsedenbal far right; Soviet Marshal Bulganin in the center (rear). Behind Mao's right shoulder is his interpreter Shi Zhe, who provided us with much valuable information about Mao's relationship with Stalin.

A long-faced Mao being shown the glories of Soviet animal husbandry in a freezing cowshed at Krasnogorsk, January 1950. Interpreter Shi Zhe on the left.

Tiananmen Gate bedecked with a portrait of the dead Stalin, 9 March 1953 (leaders just visible below Stalin's portrait). Orders to the hundreds of thousands of people brought to the giant ceremony included "Don't laugh."

Mao holding up a wreath to Stalin's portrait. Stalin's death was Mao's moment of liberation.

Post–Stalin Soviet supremo Nikita Khrushchev was willing to help turn China into a military superpower, which was Mao's long-cherished dream. The two leaders embrace at Peking airport in August 1958. Interpreter Li Yueran on the left.

Riveted at the sight of a jet fighter (personal security overlord Luo Rui-qing on right).

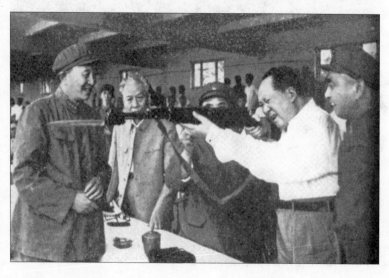

"Power comes out of the barrel of the gun": Mao at a military exercise, with (from left) Luo Rui-qing and President Liu Shao-chi.

A blonde dummy catches Mao's eye at a Japanese exhibition in Peking in 1956. Mao was not here to check out fashion for Chinese women, who were restricted mostly to "Mao suits," but to court the Japanese for strategic goods for his Superpower Program.

Mao liked to rule from bed, often summoning his colleagues from their own beds in the middle of the night. Chairs for his Politburo were set out at the foot of his huge book-strewn bed, on which he also romped with his numerous girlfriends.

In the Great Leap Forward (1958–61) Mao toyed with the idea of getting rid of names and identifying people by numbers. Peasants in his model province, Henan, working with numbers on their shirts.

China Surpasses U.S.A. in Wheat Production

False bumper harvests were invented in order to extract the maximum amount of food for export.

People were worked much harder in the Leap: a girl pulling a cart.

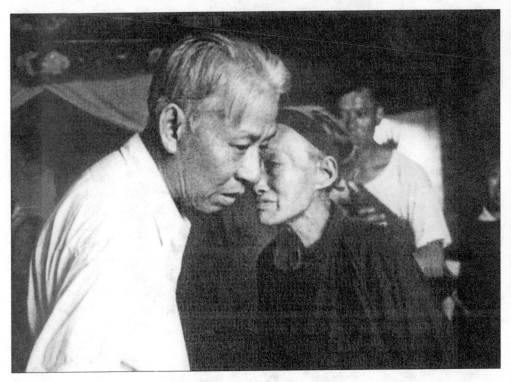

President Liu Shao-chi visiting his home village in Hunan in spring 1961. (Above) He listens aghast to an elderly peasant and (below) stares at an empty food utensil, with his wife, Wang Guang-mei. This trip propelled him to ambush Mao and halt the Leap—and the famine.

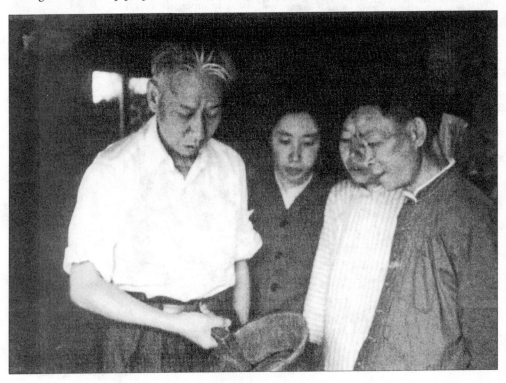

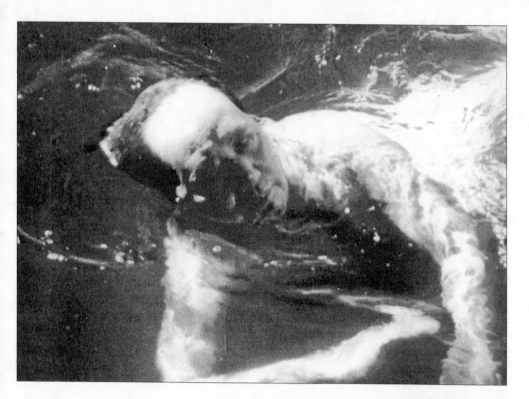

Determined to fight back, Mao used his favorite hobby, swimming, as a political gesture to demonstrate strength and willpower.

Contemplating a map of the world during the famine in 1961. He told his inner circle: "We must control the earth!"

反革命修正主义分子
彭德怀

Anyone who spoke up
was persecuted. (Top)
Tibet's Panchen Lama
being denounced in
front of a portrait of
Mao; and ex-defense
minister Peng De-huai
(inset) paraded (left)
in the Cultural
Revolution; he was
made to suffer a
lingering death.

During the Cultural Revolution, Mao took revenge against Liu Shao-chi, seen here being struck by Little Red Book–wielding staff inside the leaders' compound, Zhongnanhai, and then (below) trampled to the ground. He died an agonizing death in captivity. (Inset) Liu's brave wife, Wang Guang-mei, being manhandled wearing a necklace of Ping-Pong balls and a label calling her a "political thief."

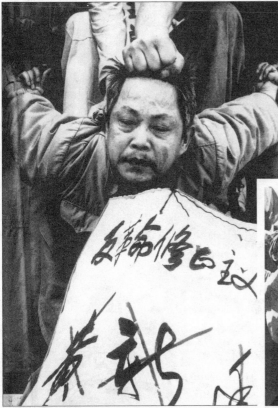

Everyday scenes in the Cultural Revolution. The "jet-plane" position (left), and brutal hair-cutting, always under a picture of Mao.

A rare picture catches how the population really looked during these years.

Defiant dissidents
being shot before
a crowd outside
Harbin during the
Cultural Revolution.

The Cultural Revolution was made possible by a horse-trade between Mao and Marshal Lin Biao. (Left) Lin alongside Mao (wearing Red Guard armband) on Tiananmen Gate, 1966. (Note Mao's black teeth, which he rarely brushed. He did not have a bath or a shower throughout his twenty-seven-year reign.) Eventually, Mao and Lin fell out; (below) on May Day 1971 a sulking Lin (in cap, right) defied protocol and turned up on Tiananmen for only one minute, refusing to talk to Mao, or Cambodia's Prince Sihanouk (next to Mao) or Princess Monique (next to Lin).

Lin Biao's son, "Tiger" (right), is the only person known to have planned to assassinate Mao. In September 1971, Lin, his wife (center) and Tiger fled China by plane and crashed to their deaths in Mongolia, after Lin's brainwashed daughter, Dodo (left), informed on them.

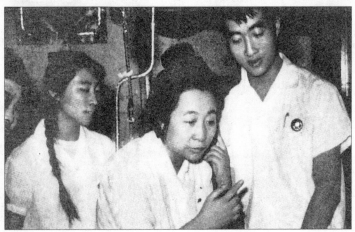

Wooing Cuba's
Che Guevara in 1960;
Guevara was cut off when
he came to be seen as too
much of a competitor.

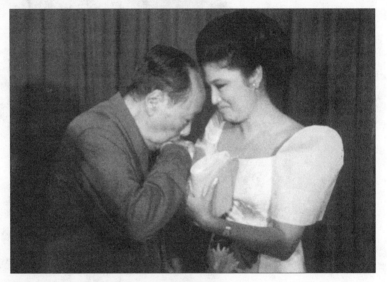

Flirting with the
Philippines'
first lady Imelda
Marcos, 1974.

Congratulating the
Khmer Rouge in 1975,
for bringing about a slave
society in one fell swoop:
Pol Pot (center); Foreign
Minister Ieng Sary (right).

Premier Chou En-lai was the charming face of Mao's tyranny. Mao used his services while blackmailing him for nearly half a century. In February 1972 Chou had a comfortable armchair (top) when U.S. president Nixon came calling. From left: Chou, Nancy Tang, Mao, Nixon, Kissinger, Winston Lord. By December 1973, Mao had banished Chou to a humiliating hard chair when meeting the Nepalese king (middle). At this time, Mao was withholding permission for Chou to have treatment for cancer, thus ensuring that Chou died before he did.

(Far left) In 1974, the newly rehabilitated Deng Xiao-ping (shortest, in front) formed an alliance with Marshal Ye Jian-ying (second from left) and Chou En-Lai (far right) against the Gang of Four, three of whose members are here: Mme Mao (in scarf), Wang Hong-wen (behind Deng) and Yao Wen-yuan (far left).

(Left) Mme Mao being restrained at her trial after Mao's death. To her prosecutors, she said: "I was Chairman Mao's dog. Whoever Chairman Mao asked me to bite, I bit." She committed suicide in 1991.

In his last years, Mao increasingly identified with fallen leaders, especially disgraced U.S. ex-president Nixon, whom he flew to China for a private farewell in February 1976.

The last photograph of Mao was with Pakistan's premier Zulfikar Ali Bhutto, 27 May 1976. Mao died on 9 September 1976. His twenty-seven-year rule brought death to well over seventy million Chinese.

setback was "losing" Vietnam. In the 1950s and early 1960s, China had been Hanoi's almost sole backer in its wars against first the French and then the Americans, ever since Stalin had allocated it to Mao in 1950. But the Vietnamese had developed suspicions about Mao from as early as 1954. That year, after he launched his Superpower Program, while doing everything to attract Russian assistance, Mao began trying to gain access to embargoed Western technology and equipment. One prime candidate for cracking the embargo was France.

At the time, France was bogged down in Indochina. Mao's plan was to make the Vietnamese intensify the war "to increase the internal problems of France" (as Chou put it), and then, when France was on the ropes, to step in and broker a settlement. The idea was that France would then reciprocate by acceding to Mao's embargo-breaking approaches.

Mao had been co-directing the war in Indochina. During the Korean War, he had halted large-scale offensives in Indochina to focus China's resources on Korea. In May 1953, when he decided to end the Korean War, he sent Chinese officers straight from Korea to Indochina. In October that year, the Chinese got hold of a copy of the French strategic plan, the Navarre Plan, named after the French commander, General Henri Navarre. China's chief military adviser to Vietnam, General Wei Guo-qing, carried this from Peking and delivered it to Ho Chi Minh in person. It was this vital intelligence coup that led to the decision by the Communist side to give battle at Dien Bien Phu, a French base in northwest Vietnam, where the Vietnamese, with massive Chinese military aid and advice, won a decisive victory in May 1954.

Dien Bien Phu was fought in the lead-up to, and during, the Geneva conference about Indochina (and Korea), which had opened on 26 April with Chou En-lai leading the Chinese delegation. Mao had decided well over a month before it opened that he "definitely must have a settlement," but he did not inform the Vietnamese. The role he had in mind for them was to do the fighting, and escalate the war, at whatever cost, to create as big a crisis for Paris as possible. Mao wrote to chief military adviser Wei on 4 April, about an ostensible next stage: "Try to complete the Dien Bien Phu campaign by . . . early May . . . Begin attacking Luang Prabang and Vientiane in August or September and liberate them." These were the twin capitals of Laos. Then, Mao went on: "actively make ready to attack Hanoi and Haiphong this coming winter and at the latest early spring next year, aiming to liberate the [Red River] Delta in 1955." Mao specifically ordered Wei to discuss this plan with Vietnam's defense minister General Vo Nguyen Giap, to give the Vietnamese the impression that he would sponsor them to expand the war well into the following year—when in fact he had secretly decided on a ceasefire in the coming months.

The Vietnamese took Dien Bien Phu on 7 May, and the French government fell on 17 June. This was China's moment to step in. On the 23rd, Chou met the new French prime minister, Pierre Mendès-France, in Switzerland, without the Vietnamese, and worked out a deal.

Chou now put immense pressure on the Vietnamese Communists to settle for the terms he had negotiated with the French, which were far inferior to what the Vietnamese had hoped for. Vietnam's later leader Le Duan said that Chou threatened "that if the Vietnamese continued to fight they would have to fend for themselves. He would not help any longer and pressured us to stop fighting." (These remarks incidentally reveal how dependent the Vietnamese were on the Chinese.) Ho Chi Minh told his negotiator, Pham Van Dong, to concede, which Dong did, in tears. Le Duan was sent to break the news to Communist forces in the south. "I travelled by wagon to the south," he recalled. "Along the way, compatriots came out to greet me, for they thought we had won a victory. It was so painful." Seeds of anger and suspicion towards Peking took root among the Vietnamese.

Early in 1965 the new Brezhnev–Kosygin team in Moscow began stepping up military assistance to Hanoi, supplying the key heavy equipment it needed: anti-aircraft guns and ground-to-air missiles, some manned by Russians. Mao could not compete. So he tried to talk the Russians out of helping the Vietnamese. "The people of North Vietnam," he told Russian premier Kosygin that February, "are fighting well without the help of the USSR ... and they themselves will drive the Americans out." "The Vietnamese can take care of themselves," Mao said, adding (untruly) that "only a small number of people have been killed in the air raids, and it is not so terrible that some amount of people were killed ..." Peking suggested that the Russians should take on the Americans elsewhere. Soviet ambassador Chervonenko was told that the best thing Russia could do was "exercise pressure on imperialist forces in a western direction"— i.e., in Europe.

At the same time, Mao tried to compel Hanoi to break with Moscow. He wooed Ho Chi Minh, who had intimate ties with China, where he spent much time. The CCP found him a Chinese wife, but the marriage was vetoed by the Vietnamese leadership, ostensibly on the grounds that it would be better for their cause if their leader remained self-sacrificingly celibate.

Ho and his colleagues were urged to reject Soviet assistance. "It will be better without Soviet aid," Chou told Premier Pham Van Dong. "I do not support the idea of Soviet volunteers going to Vietnam, nor Soviet aid to Vietnam." Chou even claimed to Ho that "The purpose of Soviet aid to Vietnam [is] ... to improve Soviet–US relations." Such arguments strained even Chou's silver tongue. Mao's only way to try to exert influence was to pour in more money, goods, and soldiers,* but he could not prevent Hanoi moving close to the Russians.

Mao was equally powerless to dissuade it from opening talks with the US, which Hanoi announced on 3 April 1968. Arguing against this initiative, Chou even blamed Hanoi for the murder of US black civil rights leader Martin Luther King, Jr. on 4 April. The assassination, he said, came "one day after your statement had been issued. Had your statement been issued one or two days later, the murder might have been stopped." Claiming to represent "the world's people," Chou went on to say: "So many people don't understand why [you] were so hurried in making this statement . . . It is the judgement of the world's people. In the eyes of the world's people, you have compromised twice."

Hanoi just ignored Peking, and started negotiating with the US in May. Mao then tried to muscle in, with Chou telling the Vietnamese that the Chinese had more experience at negotiating than Hanoi did. This cut no ice. Mao was hopping mad. In early October, Chou told the Vietnamese that a delegation due to visit China for more aid need not come, saying Chinese leaders would be too busy to receive them. But Mao soon had to backtrack and continue splashing out aid. The Great Teacher of the World's Revolutionary People could not afford not to play a part in the foremost revolutionary war on the planet.

More galling to Mao was that he had to stand by helplessly while the Vietnamese expanded their own sphere of influence at his expense. In spite of massive sponsorship from China, the Red guerrillas in Laos chose Vietnam as their patron, and by September 1968 had asked the Chinese advisers there to "take home leave" permanently, a request the Chinese had to comply with. The Laotians and the Vietnamese both aligned themselves with Moscow.

AFTER A DECADE of unremitting machinations and expenditure to promote Maoism as a serious international alternative to Moscow, Mao had failed. It was still Moscow, not Peking, that the world saw as the chief anti-American force. Mao's tirades against Moscow for "helping the imperialists" were widely perceived as untrue, and listeners were frequently irritated, bored, even embarrassed. On at least one occasion, some Third World Communists simply asked the Chinese to shut up.

* China had over 320,000 soldiers in Vietnam during the years 1965–68, including more than 150,000 anti-aircraft troops, some of whom stayed into late 1973. The presence of these troops in North Vietnam allowed Hanoi to send many more of its own forces into the South, where some Chinese accompanied them. In 1965 a Chinese general was present to watch US forces landing at Danang, on the coast of South Vietnam.

By the end of the 1960s, US officials considered that the Maoist model was no longer a threat in the Third World, a fact that Mao himself could see. He told his coterie in 1969: "Now we are isolated, nobody wants to have anything to do with us." The foreign Maoists were useless, he said, and ordered their funding cut back.

Mao needed a solution. A chance cropped up when Cambodia's neutralist leader, Prince Sihanouk, was deposed on 18 March 1970 in a coup that was widely perceived to be CIA-inspired. Mao decided to back Sihanouk if the prince was willing to fight America. His calculation was that the Vietnam War could now be turned into a pan-Indochina war, and by being Sihanouk's sponsor, he could play a leading role in the whole of Indochina.

Not long before, in summer 1967, Mao had been plotting *against* Sihanouk. Peking, according to the prince, was "implicitly advocating my overthrow"—something that Chou En-lai later admitted was true, though he disowned responsibility, not very convincingly. In March 1968, Sihanouk had gone public about Peking's patronage of a then little-known rebel group in Cambodia, the Khmer Rouge. "Below the surface," he announced, the Communist nations were "playing a dirty game because the Khmer Reds are their offspring . . . The other day we seized a large quantity of arms of all sorts coming from China, in particular."

But now, in March 1970, Mao latched on to Sihanouk. As it happened, the prince had been scheduled to visit China the day after the coup. The moment he stepped off the plane, Chou ascertained that he was determined to fight the US, and then declared total support for him. Chou contacted the Vietnamese at once, and proposed a pan-Indochina summit in Sihanouk's name. The summit, which was held in China the following month, boiled down to forming a joint Indochina command.

Since Sihanouk was so vital to Mao, the Chinese catered to his princely tastes, providing him with seven cooks and seven pastry-chefs, and flew foie gras in for him from Paris. They gave him special trains, and two planes for his foreign trips, one of which was just to carry his gifts and his luggage. Mao told Sihanouk: "Tell us what you need. Just ask. We can do more for you. It's nothing." Mao waved away any question of repayment: "We're not arms merchants." When Sihanouk protested about the burden on China, Mao replied: "I ask you to burden us still more." Mao's Cambodian creature, Pol Pot, the leader of the Khmer Rouge, who was in China secretly at the time, was persuaded to give formal support to Sihanouk.

But the Vietnamese did not let Mao take over, and the world continued to perceive Vietnam as the leading player in Indochina. Sihanouk's "return to power," the London *Times* said, "depends on the goodwill of

Hanoi." US National Security Adviser Henry Kissinger talked about "Hanoi's designs on Cambodia."

Mao had tried to impress the Vietnamese by launching China's first satellite on the day the Indochina summit opened, which Chou presented as a "gift" to the summit and "a victory for us all." But it made no difference to the Vietnamese, or to the world.

The satellite was an ego-trip for Mao, as it orbited the globe warbling the Maoist anthem, "The East Is Red." Mao was thrilled to bits about being hailed from space. On May Day on Tiananmen Gate he shook hands with each of the people who had worked on the satellite, with a big grin on his face, exclaiming "Amazing! Amazing!"; while they shouted slogans saying it had all been the product of Mao's Thought.

Boosted by the satellite, Mao made yet another effort to advertise himself to the world as the leader of the Indochina war. On 20 May he issued a statement titled "People of the world, unite, and defeat American aggressors and all their running dogs!" Next day, he ascended Tiananmen Gate and had the text declaimed to a crowd of half a million, with Sihanouk by his side. As the title made clear, Mao was issuing a command. But the presentation was as farcical as the document's pretensions. It was read out by Mao's then No. 2, Lin Biao, who had to be specially injected with a stimulant beforehand. Sihanouk noticed that before the rally Lin "seemed . . . to be somewhat intoxicated. He would periodically interrupt Mao, gesticulating and loudly launching himself into anti-U.S. tirades." When Lin started reading the statement, the words that came out were: "I am going to issue a speech!—I am going to talk about Vietnam—Two Vietnams—Half a Vietnam—" When he got to the written text, he misread it at several places, saying "Pakistan" instead of "Palestine."

The statement condemned US president Richard Nixon by name. Nixon was incensed and, in a drunken rage, wanted ships moved into attack positions. Kissinger calmed him down by pointing out that Mao had "offered little to Hanoi except verbal encouragement." Mao was ignored. In pique, he lashed out at Kissinger for failing to recognize him as a player, calling him "a stinking scholar," "a university professor who does not know anything about diplomacy." An exasperated and vexed Mao had this exchange with Vietnam's premier Dong:

> MAO: Why have the Americans not made a fuss about the fact that more than 100,000 Chinese troops help you building railways, roads and airports although they knew about it?*
>
> DONG: Of course, they are afraid.

* Chinese troops wore Chinese uniforms so the Americans would know they were there.

MAO: They should have made a fuss about it. Also, their estimate of the number of Chinese troops in Vietnam is less than their real number.

The promotion of Maoism had reached the end of the road, in Indochina as in the world at large. Ever resourceful, Mao came up with a new scheme that would hoist him into the limelight: to get the president of the United States to come to China.

NIXON: THE RED-BAITER BAITED

(1970–73 ★ AGE 76–79)

WHEN HE FOUNDED his regime in 1949, Mao had deliberately made it impossible for the USA to recognize it, mainly so as to reassure Stalin, hoping that this would encourage Stalin to build up China's military machine. After Stalin died in 1953, Mao began seeking relations with America, in order to gain access to Western technology for his Superpower Program. But memories of fighting the Chinese in the Korean War were too recent, and Washington snubbed Peking. Though the two countries established a diplomatic channel for discussing specific issues, overall, relations remained frozen. Mao hewed to an aggressively anti-US posture, and in 1960, when he was promoting Maoism, he made this bellicosity his hallmark, setting himself apart from the Kremlin, which he accused of going soft on America.

In 1969, the new US president, Nixon, publicly voiced interest in improving relations with China. Mao did not respond. Establishing a relationship with Washington would jeopardize his identity and image as a revolutionary leader. It was only in June 1970, after his anti-American manifesto of 20 May had flopped, and when it was inescapably clear that Maoism was getting nowhere in the world, that Mao decided to invite Nixon to China. The motive was not to have a reconciliation with America, but to relaunch himself on the international stage.

Mao did not want to be seen as courting the US president, and he went to considerable lengths to make the invitation deniable. In November, Chou sent a message through the Romanians, who had good relations with both China and America, saying that Nixon would be welcome in Peking. The invitation reached the White House on 11 January 1971. As Mao had feared might happen, Nixon "noted on it that we should not appear too eager to respond," according to Kissinger. When Kissinger replied to Peking, on 29 January, he made "no reference to a Presidential visit," regarding the idea as "premature and potentially embarrassing."

Mao was not deterred. He soon found another way to tempt Nixon to China.

On 21 March, a Chinese table tennis team arrived in Japan for the world championships—one of the first sports teams to travel abroad since the start of the Cultural Revolution five years before. China was good at table tennis, and Mao personally authorized the trip. So as not to appear too outlandish, the players were exempted from having to wave the Little Red Book.

They were given precise instructions on how to behave with the Americans: no shaking hands; no initiating conversation. But on 4 April, an American player, Glenn Cowan, got on the Chinese bus, and the Chinese men's champion Zhuang Ze-dong decided to talk to him. Photographs of the two shaking hands were front-page news in the Japanese papers. When Mao was informed, his eyes lit up and he called Zhuang "a good diplomat." Nonetheless, when the American team expressed a desire to visit China, after other foreign teams had been invited, Mao endorsed a Foreign Ministry recommendation to turn down the request.

But he was clearly uneasy with this decision, and staff noticed that he seemed preoccupied for the rest of the day. That night at eleven o'clock he took a large dose of sleeping pills, and then had dinner with his female nurse-cum-assistant, Wu Xu-jun. Mao sometimes invited one or two members of his staff to dine with him. He seldom dined with his wife at this stage, and almost never with colleagues. His routine was to take sleeping pills before dinner, so he would fall asleep right after the meal, which he ate sitting on the edge of his bed. The pills were so powerful they would sometimes hit him while he was chewing, and his staff would have to pick food out of his mouth, so he never had fish for dinner, because of the bones. This time, Wu recalled,

> after he finished eating, he slumped on the table ... But suddenly he spoke, mumbling, and it took me a long time to work out that he wanted me to telephone the Foreign Ministry ... "Invite the American team to China." ...
>
> I was dumbstruck. I thought: this is just the opposite of what he had authorised during the day!

Mao's standing orders were that:

> his "words after taking sleeping pills don't count." Did they count now? I was really in a dilemma ... I must make him say it again.
>
> ... I pretended nothing was happening and went on eating ... After a little while, Mao lifted his head and tried very hard to open his eyes and said to me:
>
> "Little Wu ... Why don't you go and do what I asked you to do?"
> Mao ... only called me "Little Wu" when he was very serious.

I asked deliberately in a loud voice: "Chairman, what did you say to me? I was eating and didn't hear you clearly. Please say it again."

So Mao repeated, word for word, haltingly, what he had said.

Wu then checked with Mao about the pills rule:

"You've taken sleeping pills. Do your words count?"

Mao waved at me: "Yes they do! Do it quickly. Otherwise there won't be time."

Mao kept himself awake until Wu returned with the news that she had done what he asked.

Mao's change of mind changed his fortunes. The invitation, the first ever from Red China to an American group, caused a sensation. The fact that it was a sports team helped capture the world's imagination. Chou En-lai switched on his charm, and his totalitarian regime's meticulously orchestrated theater, to produce what Kissinger called "a dazzling welcome" for the Ping-Pong team. Glowing and fascinated reports littered the American and major Western press day after day. Mao the old newspaperman had hit exactly the right button. "Nixon," wrote one commentator, "was truly amazed at how the story jumped off the sports pages and onto the front page." With one move, Mao had created the climate in which a visit to China would be a political asset for Nixon in the run-up to the 1972 presidential election.

"Nixon was excited to the point of euphoria," Kissinger wrote, and "now wanted to skip the emissary stage lest it take the glow off his own journey." By the end of May it was settled, in secret, that Nixon was going.

MAO HAD NOT only got Nixon, he had managed to conceal that this had been his objective. Nixon was coming thinking that he was the keener of the two. So when Kissinger made his first, secret, visit in July 1971 to pave the way for the president, he bore many and weighty gifts, and asked for nothing in return. The most startling offer concerned Taiwan, to which the US was bound by a mutual defense treaty. Nixon offered to drop Washington's old ally, promising to accord full diplomatic recognition to Peking by January 1975, provided he was re-elected in 1972.

By the end of the trip Chou was talking as if Peking pocketing Taiwan was a matter of course. It was only at this point that Kissinger made a feeble gesture: "We hope very much that the Taiwan issue will be solved peacefully." But he did not press Chou for a promise not to use force.*

As part of the recognition package, Nixon offered to get Peking into

---

* The records of Kissinger's 1971 visits were held back until 2002. In his memoirs Kissinger claimed Taiwan was "mentioned only briefly." When confronted with the record in 2002, he said: "The way I expressed it was very unfortunate and I regret it."

the UN straight away: "you would get the China seat now," Kissinger told Chou when proposing this behind-the-scenes fix, adding that "the President wanted me to discuss this matter with you before we adopted a position."

And there was more, including an offer to tell the Chinese everything about America's dealings with Russia. Kissinger: "Specially, I am prepared to give you any information you may wish to know regarding any bilateral negotiations we are having with the Soviet Union on such issues as SALT [Strategic Arms Limitation Talks]." A few months later Kissinger told the Chinese: "we tell you about our conversations with the Soviets; we do not tell the Soviets about our conversations with you."

Along with this came top-level intelligence. Future Vice-President Nelson Rockefeller was reported as being "almost mesmerised at hearing . . . the amount of sensitive information that we had made available to the Chinese." The intelligence included information about Soviet troop deployments on China's border.

Kissinger also made two commitments on Indochina: to pull out all US forces, mentioning a twelve-month deadline; and to abandon the South Vietnamese regime, promising to withdraw "unilaterally" even if there were no negotiations—and that US troops would not return. "After a peace is made," Kissinger said, "we will be 10,000 miles away, and [Hanoi] will still be there." Kissinger even made a promise that "most, if not all, American troops" would be out of *Korea* before the end of Nixon's next term, without even trying to extract any guarantee that Mao would not support another Communist invasion of South Korea.

Mao was being given a lot, and on a platter. Kissinger specifically said that he was not asking China to stop giving aid to Vietnam, and Mao was not even requested to soften his bellicose anti-American tone, either in the world at large or during the meetings. The minutes show that Chou was hectoring ("you should answer that question . . . you must answer that question"), and constantly referring to "your oppression, your subversion, and your intervention." He in effect suggested that Nixon must make more and more concessions for the privilege of coming to China, and being allowed to recognize Peking. Kissinger did not ask for reciprocal concessions. Chou's outlandish claim that China was not "aggressive"—"because of our new [Communist] system," no less—went unchallenged. And Chou's reference to American "cruelties" in Vietnam earned no reproof about Mao's cruelties in China. On a different occasion, when North Vietnam's negotiator had obliquely criticized the Nixon administration, Kissinger had shot back: "You are the representative of one of the most tyrannical governments on this planet . . ." Now, Kissinger described Chou's presentation as "very moving."

When Mao heard the report of the first day's talks, his ego soared, and he remarked to his top diplomats that America was "changing from monkey to man, not quite man yet, the tail is still there ... but it is no longer a monkey, it's a chimpanzee, and its tail is not very long." "America should start its life anew," he proclaimed, expanding on his Darwinian approach, viewing America as a slowly evolving lower primate. "This is evolution!" Chou, for his part, compared Nixon to a loose woman "tarting herself up and offering herself at the door." It was now, during this first Kissinger visit, that Mao drew the conclusion that Nixon could be manipulated, and that Peking could get a lot out of America without having to modify its tyranny, or its anti-American ranting.

IMMEDIATELY AFTER KISSINGER'S secret visit, it was announced that Nixon had been invited to China and had accepted. Kissinger returned to Peking in October 1971 to prepare for the president's visit. His second trip coincided with the annual UN vote on China's seat, which Taiwan held, and the public presence in Peking of the president's top adviser turned the tide. On 25 October, Peking displaced Taipei in the UN, giving Mao a seat, and a veto, on the Security Council.

This was just over a month after the flight and death of Lin Biao. The news that there had been a plot to kill him had left Mao in a state of deep depression. Taiwan's defeat and Nixon's coming visit lifted his spirits immeasurably. Laughing broadly and joking, he talked for nearly three hours in full flow to his top diplomats. Looking at the UN vote, he declared that: "Britain, France, Holland, Belgium, Canada, Italy—they have all become Red Guards ..."

Before China's delegates left for the UN, Mao made a point of reminding them that they must continue to treat the USA as Public Enemy No. 1, and fiercely denounce it "by name, an absolute must." He wanted to make his debut on the world stage as the anti-American champion, using the UN as a new platform.

Nine days before Nixon was scheduled to arrive in China on 21 February 1972, Mao passed out, and came very close to death. The prospect of Nixon's imminent arrival helped to restore him. New shoes and clothes were made for him, as his body had become swollen. The sitting-room where he was to receive Nixon had been converted into a makeshift ward, with a large bed and medical facilities. Staff moved some of these out of the room, and screened off the bed and the other medical equipment. The vast room was lined with old books, which impressed the Americans, who did not know that many were loot from brutal house raids in the not-so-distant past.

On the morning when Nixon arrived, Mao was tremendously excited, and kept checking on the president's progress. As soon as he heard that Nixon had reached the guest house, the Imperial Fishing Villa, Mao said he wanted to see him, straightaway. Nixon was getting ready to take a shower, when Chou, behaving "slightly impatiently," Kissinger noted, hustled them to be on their way.

During the relatively brief 65-minute meeting (the only one between Nixon and Mao on this trip), Mao parried every attempt to engage him in serious issues. This was not because he had been ill, but because he did not want to leave a record of his positions in the hands of the Americans. Nothing must damage his claim to be the global anti-American leader.* He had invited Nixon to Peking to promote that claim, not to waive it. So when Nixon proposed discussing "current issues like Taiwan, Vietnam and Korea," Mao acted as if he were above such lesser chores. "Those questions are not questions to be discussed in my place," he said, conveying an impression of lofty detachment. "They should be discussed with the Premier," adding that: "All those troublesome problems I don't want to get into very much." Then he cut the Americans short by saying: "As a suggestion, may I suggest you do a little less briefing?" When Nixon persisted in talking about finding "common ground" and building a "world structure," Mao ignored him, turned to Chou to ask what time it was, and said: "Haven't we talked enough now?"

Mao was especially careful not to pay Nixon any compliments, while Nixon and Kissinger both flattered Mao fulsomely. Nixon told Mao: "The Chairman's writings moved a nation and have changed the world." Mao returned no thanks and made only one, condescending, comment on Nixon: "Your book, *Six Crises*, is not a bad book."

Instead, Mao used banter to put Nixon and Kissinger down, exploring how much they would swallow. When Nixon said: "I have read the Chairman's poems and speeches, and I knew he was a professional philosopher," Mao turned away to look at Kissinger, and started this exchange.

MAO: He is a doctor of philosophy?
NIXON: He is a doctor of brains.
MAO: What about asking him to be the main speaker today?

Mao kept disrupting his exchanges with Nixon to make remarks like: "We two must not monopolise the whole show. It won't do if we don't let Dr. Kissinger have a say." This transgressed both protocol and common politeness, and was definitely slighting Nixon. Mao would never have dared to talk this way to Stalin. But, having upgraded Kissinger at Nixon's expense, Mao did not really invite Kissinger's views. He merely engaged in repartee about Kissinger using "pretty girls as a cover."

Mao clearly felt he could push Nixon quite far. At the end of the visit

---

* Mao made doubly sure of controlling the record by not allowing an American interpreter to be present. Nixon caved in to this diktat without demur.

there was to be a joint communiqué. Mao dictated one in which he could denounce America. "Aren't they talking peace, security . . . and what not?" he said to Chou. "We will do the opposite and talk revolution, talk liberating the oppressed nations and people all over the world . . ." So the communiqué took the form of each side stating its own position. The Chinese used their space for a tirade against America (though not by name). The American side did not say one word critical of Mao's regime, going no further than a vague and much qualified platitude about supporting "individual freedom."*

IN SPITE OF all his efforts to come across as the champion of anti-Americanism, Mao caught a lot of flak from his old allies. The fiercest came from Albania, which mattered to Mao because it was the only Eastern European regime he had detached from Russia's orbit. Albania's dictator, Hoxha, penned Mao a nineteen-page letter expressing his fury over what he called "this shitty business." Actually, Hoxha cunningly used rhetoric to extract colossal amounts of extra aid, basically saying: You are consorting with the enemy, but you can buy our silence for more money. Mao paid up.

The biggest problem was Vietnam, which counted far more than Albania internationally. The Vietnamese were worried that Mao was trying to use them as a bargaining chip with the US. When Chou went to Hanoi immediately after Kissinger's first visit, to explain Peking's move, he got an earful from North Vietnam's leader. "Vietnam is our country," Le Duan protested; "you have no right to discuss the question of Vietnam with the United States." After Nixon's visit, Chou returned to Hanoi, and got an even worse reception. Prince Sihanouk was there at the time, having decamped from Peking in indignation during Nixon's stay in China. He has left a rare picture of a flustered Chou, who, he records, "looked worn and still appeared heated by the discussion he just had with his North Vietnamese 'comrades.' He seemed irritated," and "not himself." Mao tried to salvage some influence by pouring in even more aid, which rose to unprecedented levels from 1971, peaking in 1974.

All these bribes to keep old allies quiet meant a tighter squeeze on the Chinese population. Nor did its extra burdens stop there. As more and more countries recognized Peking in the wake of Nixon's visit, the number of states to which China sent aid jumped from 31 prior to 1970

---

* This was not because the stifling repression was not visible. The political commentator William Buckley noticed how people had been cleared away everywhere they went. "Where are the people?" he asked a Chinese official. "What people?" the official replied. To which Buckley retorted: "The People, as in the People's Republic of China!"

to 66. On tiny and immeasurably more prosperous Malta (pop. *c.* 300,000), Mao lavished no less than US$25 million in April 1972. Its prime minister, Dom Mintoff, returned from China sporting a Mao badge.

Mao often had to pay over the odds to buy himself back into favor with states he had earlier tried to subvert. One former target, President Mobutu of Zaïre, told us how generously he was funded by Mao, who— unlike the IMF and the World Bank—let him defer loans indefinitely, or repay them in worthless Zaïrean currency. In the years 1971–75, foreign aid took up a staggering average of 5.88 percent of China's entire expenditure, peaking at 6.92 percent in 1973—by far the highest percentage in the world, and at least seventy times the US level.

While Mao dished out money and food, and built expensive underground railway systems, shipyards and infrastructure for countries far richer than China, most of the 900 million Chinese hovered just above survival levels. In many areas, peasants recall that the hungriest years after the Great Famine of 1958–61 were those from 1973 to Mao's death in 1976—the years immediately after Nixon's visit.

Nixon has often been credited with opening the door to China. Inasmuch as a number of Western statesmen and businessmen, plus some press and tourists, were able to enter China, he did increase the Western presence in China. But he did not open the door *of*—much less *from*— China, and the increased Western presence did not have any appreciable impact on Chinese society while Mao was alive. Mao made sure that for the vast majority of its population, China remained a tightly sealed prison. The only people who benefited at all from the rapprochement were a small elite. Some of these were allowed to see relatives from abroad—under heavy supervision. And a tiny number could lay hands on the half-dozen or so contemporary Western books translated in classified editions, one of which was Nixon's own *Six Crises*. From 1973 some foreign-language students were sent abroad, but the very few who were lucky enough to be allowed out had to be politically ultra-reliable, and lived and worked under the closest surveillance, forbidden even to step out of their residence unescorted.

The population as a whole remained rigidly quarantined from the few foreigners allowed into China, who were subject to rigorous control. Any unauthorized conversation with them could bring catastrophe to the locals involved. The lengths to which the regime would go were extraordinary. For Nixon's one-day visit to Shanghai, which coincided with Chinese New Year, the traditional occasion for family reunions (like Christmas), thousands of rusticated youths who were visiting their families were expelled back to their villages of exile, as a precaution against the extremely remote possibility of any of them trying to complain to the president.

The real beneficiaries of Nixon's visit were Mao himself, and his regime. For his own electoral ends, Nixon de-demonized Mao for mainstream opinion in the West. Briefing White House staff on his return, Nixon spoke of the "dedication" of Mao's cynical coterie, whom Kissinger called "a group of monks ... who have ... kept their revolutionary purity." Nixon's men asserted, falsely, that "under Mao the lives of the Chinese masses have been greatly improved." Nixon's favorite evangelist, Billy Graham, lauded Mao's virtues to British businessmen. Kissinger suggested that Mao's callous crew would "challenge us in a moral way." The result was an image of Mao a whole lot further from the truth than the one that Nixon himself had helped purvey as a fierce anti-Communist in the 1950s.

Mao became not merely a credible international figure, but one with incomparable allure. World statesmen beat a path to his door. A meeting with Mao was, and sometimes still is, regarded as the highlight of many a career, and life. When the call came for Mexico's president Luis Echeverria, his entourage literally fought to join the audience group. The Australian ambassador told us that he did not dare go to the toilet, even though his bladder was bursting, in case the privileged few should suddenly leave without him. Japan's prime minister Kakuei Tanaka, on the other hand, relieved himself at Mao's place. Mao escorted him to the lavatory, and waited for him outside the door.

Statesmen put up with slights that they would never have condoned from other leaders. Not only were they not told in advance if they would see Mao, they were summoned peremptorily at the moment most convenient to the chairman, whatever they were doing, even in the middle of a meal. Canada's prime minister Pierre Trudeau, who had not even asked to see Mao, suddenly found himself being bossed about by Chou—"Well, we have to adjourn now. I have other business and so do you"—without even telling him what for.

When Mao met foreigners, he flaunted his cynical and dictatorial views. "Napoleon's methods were the best," he told France's president Georges Pompidou: "He dissolved all the assemblies and simply appointed those who were to govern with him." When former British prime minister Edward Heath expressed surprise that Stalin's portrait was still hanging in Tiananmen Square and brought up the fact that Stalin had slaughtered millions of people, Mao gave a dismissive flip of the hand to signal how little he cared, and answered: "But he is there because he was a Marxist." Mao even managed to infect Western leaders with his own jargon. After Australian premier Gough Whitlam showed some uncertainty about the right answer to a question about Darwin, he wrote Mao what he calls in his memoirs "a self-criticism." As recently as 1997, when much more was known about Mao, Kissinger described him as a "philosopher," and claimed that Mao's goal was a "quest for egalitarian virtue."

Mao liked giving audiences to star-struck visitors, and continued to do so until his dying days, when oxygen tubing lay on his side table, concealed by a book or a newspaper. For him these audiences represented global glory.

NIXON'S VISIT ALSO opened up for Mao the possibility of laying his hands on advanced Western military technology and equipment. "The only objective of these relations," he told the North Korean dictator Kim, "is to obtain developed technology." Mao knew that he could only achieve his goal if America considered him an ally. To offer a plausible explanation for this shift from his long-standing anti-American posture, Mao claimed that he lived in fear of a Russian attack and desperately needed protection. Having laid the groundwork from the time of Kissinger's first visit, Mao spoke explicitly about a military alliance in February 1973. "The Soviet Union dominated our conversations," Kissinger reported to Nixon; as he put it in his memoirs, he was given to understand that "China's conflict with the Soviet Union was both ineradicable and beyond its capacity to manage by itself." Mao then told Kissinger: "we should draw a horizontal line [sc., alliance]—the US, Japan, China, Pakistan, Iran, Turkey and Europe."* All the places Mao cited except China were American allies.

To make the idea more attractive, Mao and Chou said that China would like the alliance to be *led by America*. Kissinger recorded that Chou "called on us to take the lead in organising an anti-Soviet coalition."

Mao was not *that* frightened of a Soviet strike. Although he genuinely feared it, as he had shown in the 1969 scare, it had become obvious to him since then that the chances of such an event were extremely remote. The way he angled for American military secrets followed a pattern similar to his past approach with Moscow. Twice, in 1954 and 1958, he had exploited the fear of America using atom bombs in his staged confrontations with Taiwan to get Khrushchev to help him; in the first instance, to build his own Bomb, and in the second, to extract a deal that almost gave him an across-the-board modern arsenal. Now he was using the specter of war again to conjure a similar prize out of America.

At one point in February 1973, Mao revealed a glimpse of what he really thought about the "Soviet threat." When Kissinger promised that the US would come to China's rescue "if the Soviet Union overruns China," Mao, who had earlier evoked this scenario himself, replied, laughing: "How will that happen? How could that be? . . . do you think they would feel good if they were bogged down in China?" Seeing that

* In the published minutes in English, which had been supplied by the Chinese, there is no mention of "China," but the word is in the Chinese record.

Kissinger was a little nonplussed, Mao quickly checked this line of reasoning, and reverted to crying wolf.

To persuade the US to think that he really wanted them as an ally, Mao hinted that he and Washington shared a mutual enemy: Hanoi. Kissinger came away feeling that "in Indochina, American and Chinese interests were nearly parallel. A united Communist Vietnam dominant in Indochina was a strategic nightmare for China . . ." Mao's position not only double-crossed the Vietnamese, it was also a huge betrayal of the Chinese people, who had been starved of essentials for decades so as to aid the Vietnamese—against "US imperialism."

Mao added a personal touch to soften up Kissinger, by alluding to Kissinger's success with women. "There were some rumours that said that you were about to collapse. (laughter)," the meeting record runs. "And women folk seated here were all dissatisfied with that. (laughter, especially pronounced among the women) They said if the Doctor [Kissinger] is going to collapse, we would be out of work." "Do you want our Chinese women? We can give you ten million. (laughter, particularly among the women)."

A few weeks later, on 16 March, Nixon wrote Mao a secret letter, stating that the territorial integrity of China was a "fundamental element" of US foreign policy, in language which suggested a commitment to come to China's defense militarily if it was attacked. The Chinese wanted to know exactly what this meant.

Kissinger told the Chinese on 6 July that he had set up "a very secret group of four or five of the best officers I can find" to study what the US could do. Among scenarios considered was airlifting American nuclear artillery shells and battlefield nuclear missiles to Chinese forces in the event of war. The only practical option, the group recommended, was to ferry American tactical bombers into China loaded with nuclear weapons, and launch nuclear attacks on Soviet forces from Chinese airfields. This opened up the prospect of US nuclear weapons being stationed on Chinese soil.

To his close circle on 19 July, Kissinger spelled out how the White House was thinking: "All this talk about 25 years of mutual estrangement was crap. What the Chinese wanted was support in a military contingency."* The memo reveals that Kissinger was well aware that he and Nixon were contemplating doing something almost unimaginable: "We might not be able to pull it off, but at least [Kissinger] and the President understood this. Alex Eckstein and other chowder-headed liberals loved

---

* Kissinger had made a sounding about how much the Chinese really wanted an alliance by suggesting "Chinese military help" against India during the Bangladesh crisis in December 1971.

China but if you asked them about military actions in a contingency they'd have 600 heart attacks."

Nixon and Kissinger knew that Mao had his eye on military know-how, and they agreed to fix substantial acquisitions for him. On 6 July, Kissinger told Mao's envoy:

> I have talked to the French Foreign Minister about our interest in strengthening the PRC [Communist China]. We will do what we can to encourage our allies to speed up requests they receive from you on items for Chinese defense.
>
> In particular, you have asked for some Rolls-Royce [engine] technology. Under existing regulations we have to oppose this, but we have worked out a procedure with the British where they will go ahead anyway. We will take a formal position in opposition, but only that. Don't be confused by what we do publicly . . .

This decision was vital for China's aircraft industry, which was entirely military-oriented—and decrepit. In April 1972 Chou had warned the Albanians not to try to fly their Chinese-made MiG-19s. Six months later, a plane supplied to another country exploded in mid-air, after which all shipments of arms overseas were halted. Chou told Third World heads of state that he could not satisfy their pressing requests for Chinese helicopters, as they were unsafe.

Access to Western technology revolutionized China's aircraft industry, and may also have boosted its flagging missile program, as rocket chiefs were deeply involved in the Rolls-Royce negotiations. In addition, Kissinger secretly encouraged Britain and France to sell strictly prohibited nuclear reactor technology to China. Mao had made a lot of headway towards getting what had always been his core objective.

The Russians were alarmed by Mao's overtures towards the Americans. In June 1973 Brezhnev warned Nixon and Kissinger that (as Kissinger paraphrased it to China's liaison): "if military arrangements were made between the US and the PRC, this would have the most serious consequences and would lead the Soviets to take drastic measures." This conversation with Brezhnev, which concerned US national security, was promptly related to Mao's envoy, who was present at the Western White House during Nixon's talks with Brezhnev, but not to America's allies— or to the US government itself. "We have told no one in our government of this conversation," Kissinger confided to Mao's envoy. "It must be kept totally secret."

One ostensible purpose of Nixon's journey to Peking had been to lessen the danger of war with Russia. Thanks to Mao, this danger had if anything increased.

THE BOSS DENIES
CHOU CANCER TREATMENT
(1972–74 ⋆ AGE 78–80)

IN MID-MAY 1972, shortly after Nixon's visit, it was discovered that Chou En-lai had cancer of the bladder. Under Mao, even a life-threatening illness was not just a medical matter. Mao controlled when and how his Politburo members could receive treatment. The doctors had to report first to Mao. They requested immediate surgery for Chou, stressing that the cancer was at an early stage, and that prompt action could cure it.

On 31 May, Mao decreed: "First: keep it secret, and don't tell the premier or [his wife]. Second: no examination. Third: no surgery..."

Mao's pretexts for vetoing treatment were that Chou was "old" (he was seventy-four), had "heart trouble," and that surgery was "useless." But Mao himself was seventy-eight, and had worse heart problems, yet surgeons and anesthetists were on stand-by for him.

One reason Mao did not want Chou to go to a hospital and be treated was in order for Chou to be available to work around the clock to deal with foreign statesmen, who were queuing at the gate after Nixon's visit. Ever since the early 1940s, Chou had been Mao's essential diplomat. During the war against Japan he was stationed for years in Chiang Kai-shek's capital Chongqing, and, with his combination of charm, skill and attention to detail, had won the Communists many sympathizers among foreigners. When civil war started after the Japanese surrender, he ran rings around President Truman's envoy George Marshall, whose decisions contributed significantly to Mao's conquest of China. After the founding of Red China, Chou was the executor of Mao's foreign policy, and his greatest diplomatic asset. After his first three days of talks in 1971, Kissinger gushed about Chou's "heroic stature" in his report to Nixon:

> my extensive discussions with Chou in particular, had all the flavor, texture, variety and delicacy of a Chinese banquet. Prepared from the long sweep of tradition and culture, meticulously cooked by hands of experience, and served in splendidly simple surroundings, our feast

consisted of many courses, some sweet and some sour [etc., etc.] . . . and one went away, as after all good Chinese meals, very satisfied but not at all satiated.

Yet, though a star, Chou deferred slavishly to Mao in front of foreigners. In Mao's presence, Kissinger commented, Chou "seemed a secondary figure." Japan's premier Tanaka went even further. "Chou is a nobody before Mao," he said on returning from China in September 1972, when diplomatic relations were established (and Mao grandly waived all claims to war compensation). Chou's motto in dealing with Mao was: "Always act as if treading on thin ice."

But entertaining visiting statesmen was not the sole, or even the principal reason why Mao vetoed surgery for Chou. Mao wanted Chou around in the short term, but he did not want him cured, as he did not want Chou, four years his junior, to outlive him. This was miserable reward for decades of service, which had involved a care for his master's health that reached far beyond the call of any duty. Chou had even tested some of Mao's medicines on himself, and tried out Mao's eye-drops—"to see whether this stings," as he put it.

ALTHOUGH DOCTORS WERE under orders not to tell Chou that he had cancer, he sensed it from the frequent urine tests they asked him to take, and the evasive way they behaved. He resorted to reading medical books himself. Mao knew that Chou was extremely anxious to have treatment, and seized the chance to exercise a bit of blackmail. Ever since Lin Biao had fled to his death the previous September, Mao had been wary about the amount of power Chou held in his hands, as Chou was running everything—Party, government and army. Mao decided to exploit Chou's anxiety to get him to do something that would weaken him to the maximum. He demanded that Chou make a detailed self-denunciation about his past "errors" in front of 300 top officials.

In addition, Mao ordered Chou to circulate to these 300 officials a highly self-incriminating document. Back in 1932, just after Chou had superseded Mao as Party boss of the Red state, Ruijin, a "recantation notice" had mysteriously appeared in the Shanghai press, bearing Chou's then pseudonym, and averring that its author condemned the Communist Party and was renouncing it. Chou had taken fright at this smear, in particular fearing that it might have been planted by Mao, and had cozied up to Mao. From then on Mao knew that he had an effective blackmail weapon. When the Cultural Revolution started, more than three decades later, Mao dangled it over Chou's head. Now, Mao dragged it out again.

Chou spent many days and nights composing the humiliating speech, which was so long that it took him three evenings to deliver. He was so harsh on himself, and so pathetic, that some of his listeners cringed with pain and embarrassment. At the end, he announced: "I have always thought, and will always think that I cannot be at the helm, and can only be an assistant." This was a desperate attempt to pledge that he had no ambition to supplant Mao, and was no threat.

In this period, Chou lived an extraordinary double life, unique in the annals of modern politics. Hidden from outside eyes both in China and abroad, he was a blackmailed slave, living in dread of untreated cancer and of being purged; for the world at large, he was a virtuoso who dazzled visiting statesmen, many of whom regarded him as the most impressive political figure they had dealt with and the most attractive man they had ever met.

Yet even after Chou did what was required of him, Mao still refused him treatment. At the beginning of 1973, Chou's urine contained a lot of blood, a sign that the tumor had worsened critically. It was only now that he was officially informed he had cancer. But when doctors pleaded to be allowed to conduct a full examination and give him treatment, Mao told them off through his chamberlain on 7 February, using words to the effect that Chou was quite old enough to die; adding: "What the hell do you want an examination for?"

Then, a week later, Chou performed a sterling service for Mao, which put the boss in a good mood. When Kissinger was in Peking that February and Mao pretended he wanted an alliance, Chou did an excellent job of making Mao's pretense plausible. Mao finally agreed to let him have treatment, after Chou had humbly requested it. But Mao set conditions: he ordered it done "in two stages," authorizing only an examination, and specifying that the surgeons must leave the removal of any tumor to a "second stage." When it came to keeping Chou from being cured, Mao's ingenuity and resourcefulness were infinite.

The chief surgeon realized that "there won't be a second stage," and decided to risk Mao's displeasure and remove the cancer during the examination, which took place on 10 March.

Just beforehand, Mrs. Chou reminded the surgeons: "You do know that you must do it in two stages, don't you?" The chief surgeon asked: "But if I see a little lump during the examination . . . should I leave it there . . . ?" and she agreed he could remove it. When Chou regained consciousness and learned that the tumor had been removed, he adroitly performed a bit of Maoist theater and berated the doctors: "Weren't you told to do it in two stages?" But he was visibly delighted, and invited the medical team to a Peking duck dinner.

The doctors had been nervous about how Mao would react to what they had done, and were relieved to receive a telephone message saying:

"It's good that the doctors combined two stages into one." Though the praise was hypocritical, it signaled that Mao had accepted their fait accompli. But it was not a full-scale operation.

MAO'S BENIGN MOOD did not last long. On 22 June 1973, Brezhnev and Nixon signed an Agreement on the Prevention of Nuclear War. When Mao read a Foreign Ministry analysis which concluded that this showed that "the world is more than ever dominated by the two powers, the US and the USSR," he flew into a monumental rage. Nixon's visit to Peking had raised Mao's hopes that (in Kissinger's words) "The bipolarity of the postwar period was over." But Mao saw that it was not, and that he had not tipped the scales of world power after all. And in the meantime his dalliance with America had cost him his international image. "My reputation has gone bad in the last couple of years," Mao told acolytes. "The only Marx in the world, the only beacon, is now in Europe. Over there [he meant Albania, which had come down hard on him over Nixon's visit], even their farts are considered fragrant and are treated as imperial edicts ... And I have come to be regarded as a right-wing opportunist."

Mao took it out on Chou. He had bottled up much resentment against Chou over the whole business with America. Though Mao had masterminded the US president's visit and the end to Peking's diplomatic isolation, it was mostly Chou who seemed to get the credit. (There are some parallels with Nixon's jealousy towards Kissinger.) On 4 July, Mao sent word to the Politburo that Chou was a "revisionist," and Chou was condemned to one more round of self-abasement.

Barely was this crisis over when another, far worse one came crashing down on Chou's head. Kissinger returned to China in November (now as secretary of state), bringing a terminal blow to Mao's ambitions. Nine months before, Kissinger had promised that Washington would move towards full diplomatic relations "after the 1974 [mid-term] elections." Now he said that the US "domestic situation" precluded severing relations with Taiwan "immediately"—which Peking had insisted on as a prerequisite for diplomatic relations. Mao was never to rule in Taiwan, or to have diplomatic recognition from America.

Worse still for Mao, his dreams of enjoying military might by courtesy of the USA came to nothing. All Kissinger could offer was an "early warning" system to detect Soviet missile launches. "I will have to study it," Chou replied, but Kissinger heard no more. The proposal held no interest for Mao, as he did not really believe in a Russian attack. The Chinese stopped talking about a military alliance with America.*

---

* Kissinger later said (to the Russian ambassador in Washington) that he "had been wrong in basing his concepts on the inevitability of a Soviet attack against China."

Mao blamed these setbacks on the Watergate scandal, which was then threatening Nixon's presidency, and made it impossible for Nixon to take any big risks. Mao spent some time talking to Kissinger about Watergate, saying that he was "not happy about it," and could not understand what all the "farting" was about. And he railed tirelessly against Watergate to other foreign statesmen. To France's president Pompidou he said he could not understand what all "the fuss" was about. "What's wrong with having a tape recorder?" he asked Thailand's prime minister. "Do rulers not have the right to rule?" he would demand. In May 1974, when Nixon was on the ropes, Mao asked former British prime minister Heath: "Can you lend him a hand to help him through?"

Because of Watergate, Nixon was forced to resign on 9 August 1974. Less known is that Watergate also helped finish off Mao's dreams of becoming a superpower.

By now, Mao's Superpower Program was in seriously bad shape, despite two decades spent consuming a huge proportion of the nation's investment. The entire higher-tech end of the arsenal was producing defective and unusable equipment, and it desperately needed foreign input. With Russia now a lost cause, Mao had hoped that America would bestow the kiss of life. But Kissinger's November 1973 trip, conducted under the shadow of Watergate, closed this door. Mao was unable to come up with any new strategy. Ace schemer though he was, even he had reached the bottom of the barrel.

MAO WAS NOW EIGHTY, and very ill. He finally resigned himself to the reality that he could not become a superpower in his lifetime. He could not dominate the world, or any part of it other than China.*

Mao's disenchantment immediately became apparent to the Americans. Meetings were canceled by the Chinese side, and cooperation sagged. Sino-US relations became "substantially frozen," Kissinger noted, and his next trips to China "either were downright chilly or were holding actions." He did not see Mao for two years, and, unbeknownst to Kissinger, Mao was constantly bad-mouthing him to his close circle, and even to ex-British prime minister Heath in 1974: "I think Henry Kissinger is just a funny little man. He is shuddering all over with nerves every time he comes to see me." On 21 October 1975, when Kissinger saw Mao again, to negotiate a visit by Nixon's successor, Gerald Ford, he

---

* Mao could see that the whole process of technology transfer from the West was far too slow for him. The Rolls-Royce engine deal encouraged by Kissinger was not signed for another two years, and the first engines were not produced in China until well after Mao's death. The first significant high-technology agreement with the US, for fast computers, was only signed in October 1976, after Mao was dead. Mao could not impose his own timetable on democratic countries, or on modern industry.

offered American military assistance, clearly expecting that Mao was still interested. But Mao brushed the offer away: "As for military aspects, we should not discuss that now." When Ford visited China later that year, Mao was amicable, but uninvolved.

MAO'S FURY AND disappointment were mainly vented on Chou. During Kissinger's watershed visit, in November 1973, the secretary of state noticed that Chou "seemed uncharacteristically tentative"; "the old bite and sparkle were missing." As soon as Kissinger left, Chou's subordinates in the Foreign Ministry, including close associates who had worked with him for decades, were forced to attack him to his face for weeks on end, for alleged failings in dealing with the Americans. Chou's cancer had just returned, and he was passing large quantities of blood in the midst of these sessions. Mao kept himself informed about Chou's miserable state through two young female upstarts in the Foreign Ministry who enjoyed an intimate relationship with him: one was his niece, the other his English-language interpreter, Nancy Tang.

Mao also unleashed his wife, who accused Chou of "capitulating" to the Americans. When Chou tried to defend himself, she interrupted him: "You really are a blatherer!"

During these weeks of torment, Chou kept working. On 9 December he was present when Mao met Nepal's king and queen. After the royal couple left, Mao said to Chou with a smirk: "Premier, haven't you been having a tough time being done in?" "The premier is really pitiful. Done in so sorrily by these few hussies." When Chou left, the "hussies"—Mao's niece and Nancy Tang—berated Mao: "How can you possibly say this about us?" Mao acted coquettish: "But it's true, it's all your doing!" He was having fun tormenting Chou.

An official photograph was published of the meeting with the Nepalese, which shows Chou sitting on a hard chair normally reserved for a junior interpreter, on the edge of an arc of armchairs for the distinguished. This was more than petty humiliation. In the Communist world, placement was the most potent signal of a top leader's rise or fall. People began to avoid Chou's staff.

Eventually, Mao passed the word that Chou was not to be hounded further. Having played with Chou's dignity and energy, Mao still wanted to have his services on call. Chou's last major contribution to Mao's foreign policy was to supervise the seizure from South Vietnam in January 1974, of the strategic Paracel (aka Xisha) Islands in the South China Sea, before they fell into the hands of Peking's Vietnamese "comrades."

At this time, Chou was losing so much blood that he needed twice-weekly transfusions. The blood often clogged his urethra so that he could not pass urine, and his doctors saw him jumping up and down and rolling from side to side in agony, trying to loosen the coagulated blood. Even in this state, he was still pursued. During one transfusion, a message came summoning him to a Politburo meeting at once. His physician asked for twenty minutes' grace to finish the transfusion. Minutes later, another note appeared under the door, this time from Chou's wife, saying: Please tell the premier to go. Chou showed only a flicker of anger as he said: Pull the needle out! As the doctors learned later, there was nothing urgent.

The doctors' entreaty to Mao for proper surgery met with a brutal reply on 9 May 1974: "Operations are ruled out for now. Absolutely no room for argument." Mao intended to let the tumor eat Chou to death unimpeded. Chou himself then practically begged, via the four top leaders designated by Mao to supervise his medical "care." At this point, Mao reluctantly gave his consent: "Let him see Tun Razak and then we'll talk about it." Razak, the Malaysian prime minister, was due at the end of the month, and Chou went into the hospital on 1 June—after he had signed the communiqué establishing diplomatic relations with Malaysia. It was only now that he was allowed his first proper operation, two years after his cancer had been diagnosed. This delay made sure that he died nineteen months later, and before Mao.

Mao only finally granted Chou surgery because he was feeling highly vulnerable himself, as a result of a deterioration in his own physical condition. He was nearly blind, and, of more concern to him, was beginning to lose control over parts of his body. In this state, he did not want to drive Chou into a corner and make him feel he had nothing to lose and might as well take extreme measures.

Just over a month after his operation, Chou received a startling piece of news: Mao was suffering from a rare and incurable disease, and had only two years to live. Chou decided not to pass on the information to Mao.

This knowledge transformed the Chou–Mao relationship. Chou now became a much bolder man.

MME MAO IN
THE CULTURAL REVOLUTION
(1966–75 ★ AGE 72–81)

MAO'S LAST WIFE, Jiang Qing, is often thought of as the evil woman who manipulated Mao. Evil she was, but she never originated policy, and she was always Mao's obedient servant, from the time of their marriage in 1938. Their relationship was aptly described by herself after Mao died: "I was Chairman Mao's dog. Whoever Chairman Mao asked me to bite, I bit." In the first few years of the Great Purge, she headed the Small Group, Mao's office that dealt with the Purge, and afterwards she was a member of the Politburo. In these posts, she played a big part in ruining the lives of tens of millions of people. She also helped Mao to destroy Chinese culture and keep China a cultural desert.

The only individual initiative that she took in the Purge was to use her position to engage in personal vendettas. One was against an actress called Wang Ying, who decades before had won a theatrical role Mme Mao herself had coveted, and who then spent glamorous years in America, even performing in the White House for the Roosevelts. Wang Ying died in prison.

Mme Mao had one vulnerable spot, her Shanghai past. She lived in constant dread that her scandals, and her behavior in prison under the Nationalists, would be exposed. So former colleagues, friends, a lover, lovers' friends, and even a maid who had been devoted to her, were thrown into prison, many of them never to emerge alive.

Another obsession was to retrieve a letter she had once written after a row with Mao, back in 1958. In a fit of frenzy she had dashed off a letter to an old friend, a film director, asking for the address of a former husband, Tang Na, who was living in Paris. The potentially fatal consequences of this rash act had been nagging at her ever since. Eight years later, as soon as she had the power, she had the hapless film director and several other former mutual friends arrested and their houses ransacked. The director died from torture, pleading in vain that he had destroyed her letter.

With so much blood on her hands, Mme Mao was haunted by the specter of assassins. At the peak of her power, she developed an intense fear of strangers coming near her, as well as of unexpected sounds, just as Mao had on the eve of conquering China. When a new secretary joined her staff in 1967, his predecessor greeted him by saying: "Comrade Jiang Qing is not very well... She is particularly afraid of sounds, and of strangers. As soon as she hears a noise or sees a stranger, she ... starts to sweat and flies into a temper. Whatever we do in this building—talking, walking, opening and closing windows and doors—we must take special care to be noiseless. Please do be very, very careful. Don't see her for a while, and try your best to stay out of her way. If the worst comes to the worst and you can't hide, don't try to run ..."

Her nurse also advised the new secretary that "she is particularly frightened of seeing strangers. If she sets eyes on you now, there will be big trouble." For more than three months, the secretary lurked in his office. Then his predecessor left—in fact for prison. Next day, the new man was summoned: "I went into her office trembling with fear. I saw her reclining on a sofa, with her feet on a soft footstool, reading some documents in a languid manner." After a few exchanges, "She raised her head, opened her eyes, and fixed me with a peevish, dissatisfied stare. She said: 'You can't talk to me standing. When you talk to me, your head can't be higher than mine. I am sitting, so you should crouch down and talk to me. Didn't they even tell you this rule?' ... So I crouched down ..."

After the secretary answered one or two of her questions, Mme Mao snapped: "'... You speak so loud, so fast, it's like firing a machine-gun. It gives me a headache, and makes me sweat. If I fall ill because of your carelessness about the volume and rate of your speech, your responsibility will be too gigantic.' She pointed at her forehead and said in a loud voice: 'Look, you look, I'm sweating!'

"I lowered my voice and said: 'Please forgive me. I will take care with my voice and speed.'

"Jiang Qing knitted her eyebrows... and shrieked loudly and impatiently: 'What are you saying? I can't hear you. Now your voice is too low. If I can't hear you clearly, I will also become tense, and will also sweat...'" The secretary was waved away.

Life at close quarters with Mme Mao was a nightmare, as everyone around her whom we interviewed testified. She would send servants to jail at the drop of a hat for phantom crimes. When Chou En-lai went to her place, his entourage preferred to sit in their cars and freeze rather than go into her villa, in case they bumped into her, which could land them in disaster. Chou's chief bodyguard, Cheng Yuan-gong, was in charge of security at a meeting she was coming to in 1968. Her staff asked him to have some food ready, so he invited her to eat first. He described what happened next: "She burst in on the premier and said: 'Cheng Yuan-gong wanted to stop me from coming in. What's going on here? What sort of meeting are you having?' She yelled and screamed at the premier." Chou had to spend hours straightening things out. Two days later she told Chou: "Cheng Yuan-gong is a scoundrel. He had a shady past. And he has always been trying to prevent me from seeing the premier . . ." The bodyguard had been with Chou for twenty-three years, but Chou had to get rid of him, and the man was packed off to detention, and then to a camp.

Mao knew what a monumental, time-consuming pain his wife was, as some people occasionally grumbled to him; and he knew that her behavior interfered with the smooth functioning of his regime. But for him it was worth it to keep everybody off balance and maintain a climate of insecurity and capriciousness, and to keep things on the paranoid track. With Mao himself, of course, she was as meek and quiet as a mouse. She feared him. Only he could do her harm.

IN 1969, WHEN Mao's reconstructed regime was set up, Mao wound up the Small Group, keeping Mme Mao on as his attack dog. She had no administrative role. While on standby for Mao, she spent a lot of time playing cards, amusing herself with her pets, including a monkey (when pets were banned for everyone else), and riding in Beihai Park in the center of Peking, formerly a public park, now closed to the public. She watched foreign films practically every night—all, naturally, prohibited for ordinary Chinese.

Her lifestyle was the acme of extravagance. One of her hobbies was photography. For this she would get warships to cruise up and down, and anti-aircraft guns to fire salvos. Her swimming pools had to be kept permanently heated, and for one of them built exclusively for her, in Canton, mineral water was channeled from dozens of kilometers away. Roads were built specially for her to scenic mountain spots, often requiring extraordinary means. In one case, because her villa was nearby, the army engineers building the road were forbidden to use dynamite in case the explosions alarmed her, and they had to break the rocks manually. Planes were kept on tap for her every whim, even to fly a particular jacket that she suddenly felt like wearing from Peking to Canton, or a favorite chaise longue. Her special train, like Mao's, would stop at will, snarling up the transport system. Far from feeling ashamed, she would say: "In order for me to have a good rest, and a good time, it is worth sacrificing some other people's interests."

One such sacrifice was blood. Always on the lookout for methods to improve her health and looks, she learned about an unusual technique: blood transfusions from healthy young men. So scores of Praetorian Guards were put through a rigorous health check, and from a short list of four, blood was taken from two of them for her. Afterwards, she gave the two a dinner, telling them what a "glorious" deed they had done to "donate" their blood to her. "When you know your blood is circulating inside me . . . you must feel very proud," she added—before warning them to keep their mouths shut. The transfusions did not become a routine, as she got so excited that she told Mao about them, and he advised against them on health grounds.

In spite of her constant complaining, Mme Mao was in fact in very good health. But she was a nervous wreck. She had to down three lots of sleeping pills before she could drop off, which was usually about 4:00 AM, and she also took tranquillizers twice a day. When she was indoors in daytime, she had natural light shut out, just as Mao did, by three layers of curtains, and read by a lamp, with a black cloth draped over the shade, producing an atmosphere her secretary described as spooky.

Noise bothered her to an absurd degree. In her main residence in Peking, the Imperial Fishing Villa, staff were ordered to drive away birds and cicadas—and even, at times, not to wear shoes, and to walk with their arms aloft and legs apart, to prevent their clothes from rustling. Even though her villa sat in a garden of 420,000 square meters, she ordered the park next door, Yuyuantan, one of the few public parks left in the capital, closed down. A similar thing happened in Canton, where her villa lay beside the Pearl River, so traffic on this commercially important thoroughfare was suspended during her stays, and even a distant shipyard had to stop work.

Heat and drafts also obsessed her. Her rooms had to be kept at exactly 21.5 degrees centigrade in winter, and 26 degrees in summer. But even when the thermostat showed that the temperature was exactly what she demanded, she would accuse her attendants: "You falsify temperature! You conspire to harm me!" Once she threw a big pair of scissors at a nurse, missing her by inches, because the nurse could not locate the source of a draft.

"To serve me is to serve the people" was her constant refrain to her staff.

AFTER LIN BIAO crashed to his death, and the assassination plot against Mao—and herself—surfaced in late 1971, Mme Mao became plagued by nightmares about the Lins' ghosts pursuing her. She confided to her secretary: "I have been feeling as if I am about to die any minute . . . as if some catastrophe is about to happen tomorrow. I feel full of terror all the time."

Her paranoia had been flipped into overdrive by an incident that occurred just before the Lins fled. She had gone to Qingdao to photograph warships (she had ordered six of them to roam about at sea to pick the best angle), and found the lavatory in the local villa wanting. So she used a spittoon instead, which, she complained, was too hard for her bottom. So her staff rigged up a seat for it, using a rubber ring from the swimming pool. She had to be supported by her nurses while she relieved herself, but she was accustomed to this. One night, however, she used the spittoon-toilet without assistance after taking three lots of sleeping pills, and fell and broke her collarbone. After the Lins fled, she insisted that this accident had been part of the assassination plot, and that her sleeping pills had been poisoned. This caused a huge commotion, with all her medicines sealed up and carted away to be tested, and her entire medical staff detained and interrogated in front of Chou En-lai and the Politburo. Chou had to talk to her for a whole night, from 9:00 PM to 7:00 AM, trying to calm her down.

The Nixons' visit in February 1972 came as an enormous tonic. With them and with the subsequent stream of international visitors, she could indulge her craving to play the First Lady. There was also the chance to publicize herself to the world by having her biography written. In August that year, an American woman academic, Roxane Witke, was invited to write about her and hopefully turn her into a global celebrity, as Edgar Snow had done for Mao.

Mme Mao talked to Witke for sixty hours. But her performance annoyed Mao, who had originally endorsed the project. True to form, she shot her mouth off. To the horror of her entourage, she confessed to a deep "love" and nostalgia for Shanghai in pre-Communist days, and even hummed to Witke a flirtatious song popular there in the 1930s. "My life was extremely romantic then . . . I had so many boyfriends, suitors who chased after me . . ." This was bad enough, but she nearly caused heart failure in the Chinese present by describing how an American marine had once tried to pick her up. "Perhaps he was drunk. He was staggering towards me along the Bund in Shanghai, and stood in front of me. He barred my way, clicked his heels and gave me a military salute . . . He put out his arms . . . I raised my hand and slapped him. He went on smiling, and gave me another salute, clicking his heels. He even said 'Sorry.' You Americans are so polite . . ."

Mme Mao gushed that she "worshipped" Greta Garbo, and adored *Gone with the Wind*, which she said she had watched some ten times: "Each time I was very moved." "Can China produce a film like this?" she asked, as though she and her husband had nothing to do with the suppression of Chinese cinema. Her adulation of *Gone with the Wind* seems to have made Mao's press controller Yao Wen-yuan uneasy, as he started spouting Party clichés: ". . . the film has shortcomings. She [the writer] sympathized with slave-owners." Mme Mao shut him up with a baffling observation: "But I didn't see any praise in the film for the Ku Klux Klan."

In the end, on Mao's orders, only some transcripts were shipped to Witke, who published a full-length biography. Jiang Qing continued to play the First Lady with foreigners, though her chances to do so were far fewer than she would have liked. As a result, she constantly tried to shoe-horn her way in. When Danish prime minister Poul Hartling came in 1974, she accompanied him and his wife to a show, but was not included in the state banquet, so she barged in just beforehand and detained the Danes for half an hour, keeping 400 people waiting. She talked in what seemed to the Hartlings a "haughty" and "show-off" manner, and was embarrassing. When an American swimming team came, she lurked around the corner of a glass wall to eye them practising. "Oh, they were so beautiful! . . . such beautiful movements," she enthused afterwards. (She herself had earlier declined to take to the water with Witke on the grounds that "the masses would become too excited" if they saw their "First Lady" swimming.)

MME MAO'S THIRST for contact with foreigners was matched only by her yearning for feminine clothes. In her husband's China, women were only allowed shapeless jackets and trousers. Only on extremely rare occasions could she wear a dress or a skirt. In 1972, she longed to wear a dress to accompany the US president (who described her as "unpleasantly abrasive and aggressive") and Mrs. Nixon to the ballet *The Red Detachment of Women*, one of her eight "model shows." But after much agonizing, she abandoned the idea, since it would look too incongruous in front of large numbers of Chinese in the audience who, though specially invited, would all be wearing drab Mao-issue clothes. When Imelda Marcos of the Philippines visited China in September 1974 in her glorious national costume, Mme Mao had to appear in *her* shapeless uniform and cap, which showed her up most unfavorably next to the former beauty queen. Both the Chinese photographer and Mrs. Marcos noticed that she kept staring at Mrs. Marcos enviously out of the corner of her eye.

Mme Mao set her heart on designing a "national costume" for Chinese women. Her design was a collarless top with a three-quarter-length pleated skirt. The ensemble was so unflattering that when pictures of China's female athletes wearing it abroad were published in the newspapers, Chinese women, even though fashion starved, greeted it with universal derision. Still, although her design was a failure as fashion, Mme Mao's love of clothes helped to lift the taboo on women wearing skirts and dresses, which cautiously returned after nearly a decade in 1975.

Mme Mao tried to have her design made official "national costume." This required a decision from the Politburo, which decided against, on budgetary grounds. A long pleated skirt would use a lot of material, and if it went into production as "national" garb, huge quantities would be needed. She tried to persuade Mao to reverse the decision by getting his favorite girlfriends to wear the dress for him. But when he heard it had come from her, he rejected it with annoyance, even disgust.

MME MAO WAS now reduced to currying favor with Mao's girlfriends to gain access to her husband. Since the beginning of the Cultural Revolution, the couple had been living in separate residences even when they were both in Peking: she in the Imperial Fishing Villa, he in Zhongnanhai. In the early years of the Cultural Revolution, when she was actively involved in running things, she could visit him freely. But as her political role grew less, he restricted her access, and often barred her from his house. The plain fact was that Mao could not stand his wife. But the more she was shunned, the more desperately she tried to get close. She could not afford to be discarded. She would beg Mao's girlfriends to put in a word for her, giving them presents like pretty material for making clothes, even a Swiss watch. On one occasion she talked her way into Mao's house, telling the guards she was there to check "hygiene." Mao yelled at her to get out, and afterwards told the guards angrily: "Arrest her if she tries to barge in again!"

On Mao's eighty-second (and last) birthday on 26 December 1975, his wife was admitted, bringing two of his favorite dishes. Mao acted as though she did not exist, giving her no more than a vacant glance, and not addressing one word to her. She soon left, in a forlorn state, while five young women, mostly former girlfriends, joined Mao for his birthday dinner.

These girlfriends were not treated like royal mistresses and showered with gifts and favors. Mao used them, as he did his wife. They provided him with sex, and served him as maids and nurses. In his final year, because he was afraid of assassination, only two people were allowed into his bedroom without his express permission; both were girlfriends-turned-nurses: Zhang Yu-feng, a former stewardess on his train, and Meng Jin-yun, a former actress from the air force song-and-dance troupe. They took turns to do all the work around Mao, on their feet for up to twenty hours a day, on standby around the clock, and usually having to sleep in their clothes. They had little family life, no holidays, no weekends. Mao refused to increase the nursing staff, as they were the only two people he trusted to be constantly near him.

Meng, the former actress, longed to leave, and asked her fellow nurse Yu-feng to put in a plea for her, saying that she was nearly thirty years old and wanted to spend some time with her husband so that she could have a child. "Wait till after I die and then she can have a child," was Mao's reply. Yu-feng herself had a baby daughter who needed her milk (there was no baby food in China in those days). As she was unable to go home every day, she tried to feed the baby by squeezing her milk into a bottle and putting it in a fridge at Mao's, and taking it home when she had a moment to spare. But the baby became ill from the milk. She felt anxious all the time about her child. Sometimes, when she was reading to Mao in a state of utter exhaustion, she would start to mumble her daughter's name. None of this moved Mao enough to lessen her workload.

Few of the many women Mao had eyes for turned him down, but one does seem to have done so: his elegant English teacher and interpreter, Zhang Han-zhi. One day in late 1972, after she had been interpreting for Mao, he took her to a staff room down the corridor, and burst out in tremendous agitation: "You don't have me in your heart! You just don't have me in your heart!" Taken aback, she blurted out: "Chairman, how can I possibly not have you in my heart? Everyone in China has you in their heart." He let her go. She continued to be his interpreter, and Mao even promoted the man she loved (and went on to marry) to be foreign minister. But Mao visited punishment on him by subjecting him to bouts of denunciation at the hands of Foreign Ministry staff.

ONE PERSON WHO did love Mao was his youngest daughter, Li Na, his only child with Jiang Qing. Born in 1940, Li Na had grown up by his side, and as a child her patter had helped to relax him. She had worshipped her father, as is clear from a letter she wrote him when she was fourteen, on 8 February 1955:

> Dear Daddy,
>   Are you asleep? You must be having a sweet, sweet sleep.
>   You must be surprised why I'm writing to you all of a sudden. What happened was: when you were having your birthday, I wanted to give you a present, but before I finished embroidering a handkerchief, your birthday was gone. Also my embroidery was so bad, so I didn't give it to you. Because I know you wouldn't be angry with me, and you are my good Daddy, right? This time, Mummy's birthday is coming, so I wanted to take this chance to make it up. You might not like the thing I'm giving you, but I made it myself. It's small, but shows my feelings: I wish my dearest Little Daddy always young, kind and optimistic . . .

It was signed "Kisses, Your daughter who passionately loves you."

Mao wanted his daughter to grow up to be useful politically, and steered her in that direction. Back in 1947, when the Communists were vacating Yenan, he insisted that she stay within earshot of the shelling and the shooting, even though she was only six years old. A tearful Mme Mao pleaded for her to be evacuated, but Mao shouted at his wife: "Get the hell out of here! The child is not going. I want her here to listen to gunfire!"

Mao started to groom her as his assistant when the Cultural Revolution started in 1966. Aged twenty-six, she had just graduated from Peking University in modern Chinese history, a subject she said she did not particularly like, but accepted, because the Party wanted more children from elite families to become Party historians. Her father assigned her to the army's main newspaper, where she started work as one of the special reporters, gathering information for him. Mao's goal was for her to take control of the paper, which she accomplished in August 1967, while the editorial and management boards were carted off to prison. A cult was then fostered around her. The paper's offices—and even staffers' homes— were covered with posters "saluting" her, and slogans shouted at rallies proclaimed that whoever opposed her was a counter-revolutionary. An exhibition room was opened at the paper to display her "great merit," showing things like her tea mug and her bicycle, implying that it was saintly of her not to be using fine china or a limousine.

Her behavior changed at this time. Having at first seemed unpretentious, now she would scream at senior staff to stand to attention in front of her, shrieking: "I really wish I could have you shot!" She declared that she was going to impose "thug rule," using an arcane expression that she had clearly learned from her father. Over 60 percent of the old staff at the newspaper suffered appalling persecution for allegedly opposing her. Among the many who were tortured was a former personal friend who had expressed disagreement with her over some minor matter.

Early in 1968, because Mao was shutting down his personal channels in the army in order to please Lin Biao, Li Na was taken off the paper. Her next job was no less critical: director of the Small Group's private office. The position was vacated for her by a simple expedient, typical of Mme Mao's modus operandi. Mme Mao accused the existing director of being a spy and had him clapped in jail. Li Na then took over his job until the Small Group was dissolved in 1969.

Mao had intended her for even higher office—controller of Peking. But in 1972 she had a nervous breakdown, and floated in and out of insanity for years, until after his death. It seems that, unlike her parents, Li Na did not thrive on persecution, and that after her early zealousness to enforce her father's orders, she was driven out of her mind by the constant victimizations she was expected to carry out. On one occasion, she picked up a pile of documents about the purge and suicide of a man she knew, and threw them out of the window, shouting: "Don't give me any more of this rubbish! I've been sick and tired of it for ages!"

She longed for affection. Her mother, who had loved her when she was a child, now, like her father, narrowed their relationship down to one based exclusively on politics, and gave her no warmth or comfort. When she was heading for a nervous breakdown, reliant for short-term relief on more and more massive amounts of sleeping pills, Li Na had no one to turn to. As a young woman, she yearned for a love relationship, but with Mao for a father, and especially with Jiang Qing for a mother, no man dared to court her, and no match-making enthusiast fancied inviting trouble. It was only when she was thirty-one, in 1971, that she herself approached a young servant. When she wrote to her father for permission to marry, he only asked the messenger a few basic questions, and then wrote on the letter simply: "Agree." Mao's wedding present was a set of leaden tomes which he himself never read: the works of Marx and Engels.

Neither of her parents came to her simple wedding, which Mme Mao had only grudgingly accepted, regarding the bridegroom as beneath her daughter, since he had been a servant. For a while after the marriage, Li Na seemed to be prone to colds and high temperatures, which Mme Mao blamed on her daughter having sex with the son-in-law, and insultingly ordered him to have a physical check-up. It did not take her long to have her son-in-law banished to another city, claiming that he "looks like a spy." The marriage collapsed, and Li Na sank into a deep depression.

In May 1972, Li Na gave birth to a son, which briefly brightened up her life. But Jiang Qing disliked the baby because she despised its father, and never once held it in her arms. Mao showed zero interest in this grandson, as in his other three grandchildren.

With no love or joy in her life, Li Na lapsed into insanity. As far as Mao was concerned, she had run out of use. He saw less and less of her, and evinced no concern about her mental or physical condition.*

MAO HAD SIMILARLY lost interest in his other daughter, Chiao-chiao, who had no political flair. Years before, when she returned from Russia as a pretty twelve-year-old, exotic in her Russian wool skirt and leather shoes, with Russian manners, and speaking Russian, Mao had showered her with affection, and shown her off, calling her "my little foreigner." And she had been deliriously happy. But when she lost the entertainment value she had had as a child, and turned out politically worthless as an adult, she found she had diminishing access to Mao. In the last few years of his life, she only very rarely got to see him. She went to the gate of Zhongnanhai several times, but he refused to let her in. She had a nervous breakdown, and was in and out of depression for years.

Mao's oldest son An-ying had been killed in the Korean War in 1950. The only surviving son, An-ching, was mentally ill. Mao provided him with a comfortable life, but hardly ever saw him, and did not regard him as a member of the family. Mao was wont to say that his family consisted

---

* Today, Li Na has recovered, and leads a normal life. She appears to have "forgotten" her role in the Cultural Revolution.

of five members: himself and Mme Mao, the two daughters, and his only nephew, Yuan-xin.

The nephew had spent much of his youth in Mao's family. During the Cultural Revolution, when he was still in his early thirties, he was catapulted into the post of political commissar of the Shenyang Military Region, in which capacity he helped Mao control Manchuria, the critical area in the northeast bordering with Russia. One of his later best-known acts there was to order the execution of a brave female Party member called Zhang Zhi-xin, who had openly challenged Mme Mao and the Great Purge. Just before she was shot, she was pinned to the floor of her cell and her windpipe was slit, to prevent her from speaking out at the execution ground, even though it was a secret execution. This cruelty was gratuitous, as execution victims routinely had a cord put around their neck that could be yanked to choke them if they tried to speak.

As well as being ruthless, Yuan-xin belonged to the family. Mao made him his liaison with the Politburo in the final year of his life, 1975–76. Actually, Yuan-xin's own father, Mao's brother Tse-min, had been killed partly as the result of Mao giving instructions not to try to save him when he was in prison in Xinjiang in the early 1940s—a fact carefully concealed from Yuan-xin, as from everyone else.

Mao had been the cause of the death of his second wife too. After being abandoned by Mao, Kai-hui had been executed in 1930 as a direct result of his attacking Changsha, where she was living, for reasons that were entirely to do with his drive for personal power. And he was also largely responsible for the repeated and eventually irreversible mental breakdowns of his third wife, Gui-yuan (who died, aged seventy-five, in 1984).

Over the decades, Mao had brought ill fortune to virtually every member of his family. His final betrayal was towards his fourth and last wife, Jiang Qing. After getting her to do much of his dirty work, and knowing how much she was loathed, he made no provision for safeguarding her after he died. On the contrary, he offered her up as a trade-off to the "opposition" that emerged near the end of his life. In return for guaranteeing his own safety while he was alive, they were told that after he died, they could do as they pleased with Mme Mao and her group of cronies, which included Mao's nephew Yuan-xin. Less than a month after Mao's death, the whole group ended up in prison. In 1991 Mme Mao committed suicide.

ENFEEBLED MAO HEDGES HIS BETS

(1973–76 ★ AGE 79–82)

IN THE LAST two years of Mao's life a formidable "opposition" to his policies emerged, in the shape of an alliance that centered on Deng Xiao-ping, the man who later dismantled much of Mao's legacy after Mao died. Mao had purged Deng in 1966, at the beginning of the Cultural Revolution, but brought him back to the top in 1973.

Born in Sichuan in 1904, and thus eleven years Mao's junior, Deng went to France in 1920 on a work-and-study program at the age of sixteen, and there became a Communist, working under Chou En-lai. Five years in France left him with a lifelong fondness for many things French: wine, cheese, croissants, coffee and cafés—all, it would seem, to do with food. Late in life, he would often compare French cafés nostalgically with the teahouses in his home province of Sichuan, reminiscing about a little café he had frequented in the Place d'Italie in Paris.

His fellow Chinese in France remembered Deng, who was just over 5 feet tall, as a plump ball of energy, full of jokes. Since then, decades of life in the Party had caused him to metamorphose into a man of deep reserve and few words. One advantage of this reticence was that he kept meetings brief. The first session of the committee in charge of southwest China after the Communist takeover lasted a mere nine minutes, in contrast with those under the long-winded Chou En-lai, who once talked for nine hours. Deng was decisive, with the ability to cut straight through complicated matters, which he sometimes did while playing bridge, for which he developed a passion.

Deng had joined the Communists in France, but his grounding was in Russia, where he spent a year after being kicked out of France, and where he received Party training. When the Long March started in 1934, he was already chief secretary of the Party leadership, and he was a top army commander during the Sino-Japanese War of 1937–45. In the civil war after 1945 he became chief of the half of the Communist army which won the decisive Huai–Hai Campaign that clinched the Red victory and then took much of China south of the Yangtze. Afterwards, he was in charge of several provinces, including his native Sichuan, before Mao promoted him to the core leadership in Peking in the early 1950s.

He was deeply loyal to Mao, and during the suppression of intellectuals in the anti-Rightist campaign in 1957–58 he was Mao's chief lieutenant. But he had a breaking-point, and supported Liu Shao-chi's efforts to stop the famine in the early 1960s. He tried to keep at arm's length from Mao—a fact that Mao took note of, remarking that Deng was "keeping a respectful distance from me as though I were a devil or a deity."

When Mao launched the Cultural Revolution in 1966, he tried all kinds of inducements to keep Deng on board, but failed. Deng was branded "the second-biggest capitalist-roader," after Liu, and put under house arrest in 1967, and his children and stepmother were evicted from their home. He was subjected to denunciation meetings, though with much less physical abuse than Liu. Mao calibrated the punishment of his foes meticulously. He did not hate Deng the way he hated Liu, so he ordered that Deng "must be denounced . . . but differentiate him from Liu." Unlike Liu, Deng was not separated from his wife, which gave him the companionship that often made the difference between life and death.

But even Mao's "better" treatment was hell. In May 1968, Deng's eldest son and a daughter were taken, blindfolded, to Peking University, and told to "expose" their father. Over sixty other people who had been imprisoned there had committed suicide or been tortured to death. Deng's 24-year-old son, Pu-fang, soon threw himself out of an upstairs window, and was permanently paralyzed from the chest down. Deng and his wife were not told about this until a year later, when they were briefly allowed to see their other children shortly before being exiled from Peking in October 1969. In exile, Deng worked on the factory floor in a tractor plant in Jiangxi province, living under house arrest, with armed guards.

Mrs. Deng wept for days when she heard about Pu-fang. She later told Deng's stepmother that she almost lost the will to live. Deng was forbidden to see his paralyzed son, and was deeply affected by what happened to his children. Once, after his youngest son, who had turned up starving and in rags, had to leave for his own place of exile, Deng collapsed on the factory floor. In June 1971, when the paralyzed Pu-fang arrived, Deng was visibly shaken. His son had been a buoyant young man. Deng nursed Pu-fang devotedly, helping him to turn every two hours to prevent bedsores, which was no light work (Pu-fang was big), and wiping his body several times a day, as the climate in Jiangxi was hot and humid.

The Cultural Revolution years, Deng was to say later, were the most painful time of his life. The pressure crept into his sleep. One night he woke up the whole building, screaming during a nightmare. But those years also helped him rethink the system the CCP had imposed on China. As a result, he turned his back on the essence of Maoism and Stalinism, and after Mao died he changed the course of China. In exile, Deng kept his mouth shut, tried to stay healthy, and waited for a chance to return to the political center.

AFTER TWO YEARS, in September 1971, came a ray of hope. Deng's son Pu-fang was an electronic whiz, and had fixed up a radio that could receive short-wave broadcasts. This he did with his parents' acquiescence, even though listening to foreign radio stations was a prison offense (and, moreover, one his father had helped enforce). It was from these foreign broadcasts that the Dengs first surmised that Lin Biao was dead.

The regime carefully controlled the way it dribbled out information about Lin's death. Deng heard the news officially two months later, when a document was read out to workers in his tractor factory. The document mentioned Lin's "crimes of persecuting veteran comrades." The official who was chairing the meeting said: "Chairman Mao would never have driven old cadres to death" (i.e., as Lin had done), and turned to Deng: "Old Deng is sitting here, he can vouch for this. Old Deng, wouldn't you say so?" Deng stolidly declined the invitation to advertise Mao's innocence, remaining totally silent, his expression not changing one flicker.

When he came home that day, Deng allowed himself to show excitement and condemned Lin explicitly, which for him was really letting rip, as he never talked politics with his family. Two days later, he wrote to Mao for the first time since his downfall five years before, asking for a job. With Mao's major prop gone, he sensed that Mao might have to repeal the Cultural Revolution.

No reply came from Mao. To reinstate the man he had publicly condemned as "the second-biggest capitalist-roader" would be an admission of failure. Even when Chou En-lai was diagnosed with cancer in May 1972, and Mao had no one else but Deng with the caliber to run his vast kingdom, still he would not send for Deng.

Instead, Mao promoted Wang Hong-wen, the former Rebel leader in Shanghai, one of the products of the Cultural Revolution. Wang was a faceless good-looking 37-year-old, who had been a security man in a textile factory before the Purge. He was clever, and, like a lot of Rebel leaders, had a certain flair for inspiring gang allegiance. Mao brought him to Peking and began to train him up, and a year later, in August 1973, made him his No. 3, after Chou.

But the Protégé was not up to filling Chou's shoes, especially when it came to dealing with foreigners. The Australian ambassador, Stephen FitzGerald, who met him with Mao in November 1973, noted that he was extremely jumpy, and did not speak a word during the entire meeting, except at the end. The Australian prime minister, Whitlam, had mentioned the Communist "Nanchang Uprising" of 1927, and had observed that the youngish man could not have been born at the time. When the meeting was over, the Protégé piped up nervously: "Prime Minister, you said that at the time of the Nanchang Uprising I was not born. But I have been making revolution for a long time." This was his only contribution.

Mao felt he had to have a standby. So, when Chou's cancer worsened, Mao had Deng brought to Peking in February 1973, and made him a vice-premier, mainly to entertain visiting foreign statesmen. Although Deng lacked Chou's polish, and spat constantly during meetings, which unsettled quite a few of his interlocutors, he had stature.

Late that year, Chou's health deteriorated drastically. Mao made the momentous decision to put Deng in charge of the army (for which Deng was restored to the Politburo). Deng was the only person who could guarantee stability in the military, where Mao's Protégé had zero influence. Marshal Yeh, the man Mao had appointed army chief after Lin Biao's death, lacked the necessary gravitas.

Giving Deng this much power was a gamble, but it proved well judged. Deng never made a move against Mao's person while Mao was alive, and even after Mao's death, insisted that Mao must not be denounced personally, although he repealed much of Mao's core legacy.

As soon as Deng assumed power, he started to push through his own program. Central to this was rolling back the Cultural Revolution. He tried to rehabilitate and re-employ more purged cadres en masse, to resurrect some culture, and to raise living standards, a concern that had been condemned as "revisionist." Mao regarded the Cultural Revolution as his greatest achievement since taking power in 1949 and kept four remaining Cultural Revolution Rottweilers in place to counter Deng: Mme Mao, Zhang "the Cobra," media chief Yao, and Protégé Wang—a group that Mao dubbed "the Gang of Four." (Kang Sheng was out of action by now with terminal cancer, and was to die in 1975.) This was Mao's own gang, who represented his true policy.

FOR HIS PART, Deng formed his own counter-alliance with army chief Marshal Yeh and premier Chou En-lai soon after he returned to Peking in spring 1973. Of this trio, Deng and Yeh had been on the receiving end of the Purge, while Chou had collaborated with Mao. Chou had even changed the name of his house to "Drawn to the Sun [i.e., Mao] Courtyard." When Mao gave the word, Chou would send anyone to their death. Chou's only adopted child, Sun Wei-shi, had been imprisoned because she had been a top-flight Russian interpreter, and met many Russian leaders, including Stalin; so Mao suspected her as he did most others who had such connections. Mme Mao also hated her because she was very beautiful, and because Mao had once taken a shine to her. Chou, who was widely thought to be in love with her, did not lift a finger to save her. She died in prison, and he kept an ignoble distance even in death.

Deng felt fairly cool towards Chou, and after Mao died said publicly that Chou had "done many things against his heart" during the Cultural Revolution, though Deng claimed that "the people forgave him." However, Deng decided to set personal feelings aside and form an alliance with Chou. On 9 April, shortly after getting back to Peking, he went to see him—their first meeting in nearly seven years. At first, they just sat facing each other in silence. Finally, Chou spoke. The first thing he said was: "Zhang Chun-qiao betrayed the Party, but the Chairman forbids us to investigate it." Zhang, "the Cobra," was a major star of the Cultural Revolution. By saying this, Chou was not just condemning the Cobra, he was complaining about Mao. This was no indiscretion from the super-prudent Chou; it was his way of conveying that he was on Deng's side, against the Cultural Revolution. This, plus the fact that Chou had become terminally ill thanks to Mao, melted the ice between him and Deng. From that moment on, the two were allies.

This was a milestone. The two most important colleagues of Mao had formed a league of a kind, which also incorporated army chief Marshal Yeh. Mao's decades-long ability to enforce a ban on his colleagues forming alliances was broken. And with it, his awesome hold over them.

MAO WAS REDUCED to these straits because his health was ebbing fast as he entered his eighties. It was now that he had to kick his lifelong addiction to smoking. By early 1974 he was nearly blind. This, like his other ailments, was kept top-secret. Losing his sight made Mao extremely anxious about security, so his staff were given special instructions to "walk noisily to let him know someone was coming so that he would not be frightened."

He was also depressed because he could not read. He had ordered some banned works of classical literature to be specially printed. Two print shops, one in Peking and one in Shanghai, were purpose-built to do the printing, and each print-run was five copies, all for Mao, plus a few extra copies, which were placed under lock and key, and even the people who had been involved in annotating the texts for him were forbidden to keep a copy. As his eyesight got worse, the characters grew larger, eventually reaching a height of 12 mm. When Mao finally found he could not read at all, even with a magnifying glass, he broke down and cried. Thenceforth, he had to rely on staff to read to him, and sometimes to sign documents for him.

Because of his condition, Mao did not want to appear at meetings and look vulnerable, so he left the capital on 17 July 1974 and went south.

Soon he was told that the trouble was cataracts, and that they could be removed by a simple operation once they matured. The news came as a huge relief, even though it meant nearly a year of hardly being able to see. Meanwhile he stayed away from Peking—for nine months altogether, on what turned out to be his last trip.

There was another discovery made at the same time: that he was suffering from a rare and incurable motor neurone illness called amyotrophic lateral sclerosis, sometimes known as Lou Gehrig's disease. This gradually paralyzes the muscles in the arms, legs, throat and tongue, strangling speech, preventing food going down the right way, and finally causing death by respiratory failure. The diagnosis was that he had about two years to live.

The doctors did not tell Mao. Their reporting channel was to his chamberlain and chief of the Praetorian Guard, Wang Dong-xing, who told only Chou En-lai. It was now that Chou became much more daring.

Chou's allies, Deng and Marshal Yeh, were put in the picture about Mao's state of health. They decided not to tell the Gang of Four, even Mao's wife, who was anyway a walking incentive for others to keep her out of the loop. Two years before, after Mao had passed out, she had accused medical staff of being "spies" and "counter-revolutionaries." When Chou had discussed Mao's illnesses with her, she had accused him of trying to force Mao to surrender power. But the decision to exclude her was determined by more than just the fact that she was trouble. It was politically motivated.

Mao himself was not informed. If Mao knew his days were numbered, there was no knowing what he might do. Instead, he was assured that he was in good health, and still had a long time to live. To make doubly sure he did not find out, none of his regular staff was told. One doctor who blurted out "I'm afraid the Chairman's illness is hard to treat..." was instantly removed. Mao's symptoms were passed off as harmless. This did not satisfy him, but there was nothing he could do.

With the knowledge of the time frame of Mao's life, and with Chou himself in inexorable decline, the Deng-Chou-Yeh Alliance moved to press Mao to institutionalize Deng's role as Chou's stand-in and successor, and to restore to high office a large number of old cadres who had been ousted in the Purge. In December 1974, Chou left his hospital bed and flew to Changsha to see Mao with a slate of new appointments. Mao knew about the Alliance's activities from the Gang of Four, who were keeping a look-out in Peking on his behalf. Mme Mao had written to say she was "shocked and aghast" at what was going on. But Mao was in no condition to veto the Chou–Deng list. He could not hand over the country to the Gang of Four, and neither could he try to get rid of the Alliance—if he wanted to die in his bed. The Gang of Four were powerless in the army and Mao had nobody in the military who could take on the Alliance on his behalf. And he himself was physically too feeble to create a new force that could trump the Alliance.

Lou Gehrig's disease had been nibbling away at his body. At the start of his trip to the south in summer 1974, Mao could still take walks in the garden; but within a few months, all he could do was drag one leg after the other for a short distance. On 5 December he found he had to say goodbye to swimming, his lifelong passion. He had taken a few dips in his indoor pool in Changsha, but that day he nearly choked in the water, and this was to be his last swim. His bodyguard of twenty-seven years heard Mao let out a long sigh of melancholy and resignation, something he had never heard, and could not imagine coming from Mao.

As his muscular coordination failed, Mao's speech became increasingly slurred, and food kept getting into his lungs, causing choking and infection. He had to lie on his side to be fed. Life became excruciatingly uncomfortable.

In this condition, Mao had to endorse Chou's slate, especially the promotion of Deng to first vice-premier and stand-in for Chou. But Mao promoted one of the Gang of Four, the Cobra, and made him second to Deng in the military and the government. He also insisted that the media remain in the hands of the Gang, so that only his message could reach the country at large.

The Alliance's strategy was to dislodge the Cobra and Mme Mao, exploiting their less than spotless pasts. On 26 December, Mao's eighty-first birthday, Chou told Mao that these two had had connections with Nationalist intelligence in the 1930s. Mao's reply was that he had known about their pasts all along, and he effectively said that he could not care less.

Telling Mao to his face that his wife and one of his top acolytes were suspected enemy agents was startling behavior on Chou's part. Mao could see that battle had been well and truly joined, with himself and the Gang of Four pitted against the Deng–Chou–Yeh Alliance and the old cadres who were now being re-employed en masse.

Mao tried to regain some ground by getting the Gang of Four to start a media campaign in March 1975 to smear the authority of the reinstated cadres. In April, after Mao returned to Peking, Deng gave Mao a piece of his mind and asked him to call a halt. Mao was forced to yield, and blamed the Gang of Four. On 3 May, in front of the Politburo, Mao ordered the campaign stopped and said he had "made a mistake." This was an unprecedented climb-down, brought about by the fact that he was patently vulnerable. As everyone at the meeting could see, he was extremely frail, completely blind, and his speech was barely intelligible. It was his last appearance at a Politburo meeting.

On this occasion, for the first time since he had come to power, Mao all but threw himself on the mercy of his colleagues by asking them not to contemplate a coup. Again and again, he implored them: "Don't practice revisionism; don't split; don't plot." The first point meant: Stick with the Cultural Revolution. The rest meant: Don't plot against me. Several times during this period, he recounted a historical tale to Deng and his allies, whose implicit, but unmistakable, message was: If you are thinking of a coup, do it to my wife and the Gang, *after I die*.

MAO HAD TO beg like this because he had virtually lost control of the army. The Alliance had rehabilitated many generals who had been victims of Mao's, and put them in high office. If it came to a showdown, Mao would have no top men in the army on his side. He had tried to insert his own men, two members of the Gang of Four, into leading army jobs, but they had been frozen out.

In June 1975 the army made a powerful gesture of defiance towards Mao. The occasion was the sixth anniversary of the death of Marshal Ho Lung, the man to whom Russian defense minister Malinovsky had said "get rid of Mao" a decade before. As a result of Mao's suspicions, Marshal Ho had died in incarceration in appalling circumstances in 1969. The army now decided to hold a memorial service for him, which was both a sign of the changing times and a huge snub to Mao. Mao could not prevent the service taking place, but he ordered that it be extremely low-key— without even wreaths or speeches. With the support of the top brass, Ho's family wrote to Mao, threatening to boycott the service if these restrictions were not lifted, and making a point of saying that Ho had many loyal comrades alive. Mao had to give in. The most he could salvage was to keep the news of the service out of the media.

The service was dominated by bitter emotions, and the atmosphere was heightened by the extraordinarily demonstrative sorrow exhibited by Chou En-lai, who got up from what was manifestly his deathbed to attend, and delivered the eulogy. He entered the hall crying out the name of the marshal's widow, sobbed loudly while hugging her shoulders, and told her he felt "very sorry" for "not having been able to protect" her husband.

Chou had been in charge of the investigation into Ho during the Cultural Revolution, which had resulted in Ho's death, and a host of Ho's subordinates being imprisoned and tortured, some to death. There were strong feelings against Chou, which he was aware of, and his apology to Ho's widow was partly an attempt to exonerate himself and put the blame on Mao. This, and the fact he turned up when he himself was dying— which he made a point of telling the congregation—dissipated much of the anger people felt towards him and redirected it towards Mao.

Mao, who was used to passing the buck, did not like having the blame laid on himself, and he hit back at Chou—as soon as he recovered his eyesight. On 23 July, Mao had the cataract removed from his left eye. To accompany the seven-minute operation, he chose a piece of soaring music to give himself a boost. He was delighted by the ease of the operation, and asked the surgeon to perform it on his right eye the following year. In the meantime, he consented to have special glasses made. They were made in two pairs, one with only a left arm, the other with only a right arm, which were swapped around by an attendant when Mao turned over in bed, so that the side of his face would never be resting on an arm.

Being able to see again gave Mao a renewed sense of confidence. Within two weeks he had initiated a new media campaign against Chou. Mao announced that one of the most famous classic Chinese novels, *The Water Margin*, was really all about "capitulationists," who deserved to be condemned. "Capitulationists" was an allusion to the fake 1932 "recantation notice" that bore Chou's name. Chou was so worried that Mao might blacken his name, particularly after his death, that at the very last moment before a big operation for his cancer, after he had been given the pre-op medication, just as he was about to be wheeled into the operating theater, he insisted on devoting an hour to go over his self-defense about the notice. He only got on the waiting trolley after he had signed the document, in a shaky hand, and passed it to his wife. Deng confronted Mao about the campaign the next time he saw him, and Mao had to back down, again. He tried to blame it on his wife, using his characteristic language: "Shit!" he said of her. "Barking up the wrong tree!" The campaign petered out.

ALL THE WHILE, Deng was trying to undo the practices of the Cultural Revolution and improve standards of living. In this, the twenty-fifth year of Mao's reign, most of the population were living in dire poverty and misery. In the urban areas, which were privileged, extremely severe rationing of food, clothing and virtually all daily essentials was still in force. Families of three generations were often crammed into one small room, as the urban population had increased by 100 million under Mao and yet very little housing had been built, and maintenance was non-existent. Mao's priorities—and the quality of life—may be gauged from the fact that total investment in urban upkeep (including water, electricity, transport, sewage, etc.) in the eleven years 1965–75 was less than 4 percent of that in arms-centered industries. Health and education were getting well under half of the already tiny percentage of investment that they had been receiving at the outset of Mao's rule. In the countryside, most people were still living on the verge of starvation. In places, there were adult women who had no clothes to cover themselves and had to go stark naked. In Mao's old capital, Yenan city, people were poorer than when the Communists had first arrived four decades before. The city was teeming with hungry beggars, who would be roped up and shoved into detention when foreigners came to admire Mao's old base, and then deported back to their villages.

Mao knew beyond a doubt how bad things were. He kept himself extremely well informed by reading (or having read to him) daily reports from a network of feedback channels he had installed. In September 1975 he told Le Duan, the Party chief of Vietnam, which had just been through thirty years of nonstop war, including devastating US bombing: "Now the poorest nation in the world is not you, but us." And yet he directed the media to attack Deng's efforts to raise living standards with absurd slogans like: "The weeds of socialism are better than the crops of capitalism."

Deng also tried to lift the virtual blanket ban on books, arts and entertainment that had lasted for nearly a decade. Most immediately, he tried to release a few feature films to give the population some entertainment. Though all of these kept well within the bounds of socialist realism, Mme Mao, acting on Mao's behalf, tried to get them withdrawn, accusing them of "crimes" such as using pretty actresses.

Mao himself had plenty of entertainment. One was to watch his favorite Peking operas in the comfort of his home. For this, opera stars were summoned back from their camps to be filmed in the now empty Peking TV Studio by crews who had also been recalled from exile. After years in the backwoods they were rusty, so they were first kept isolated for months and told to recover their lost art, and ask no questions. As no one would explain to them why they were to perform these still banned— and therefore extremely dangerous—"poisonous weeds," most spent these months in a state of great apprehension. The films were then broadcast for Mao from a TV van parked next to his house. He also watched films from pre-Communist days, from Hong Kong, and from the West.

But Mao refused to let the population savor so much as a drop of what he himself enjoyed. Deng often fought with Mao's wife, sometimes shouting at her and banging on the table—not treatment she was used to from anyone except her husband. Deng also denounced Jiang Qing's action to Mao's face, and encouraged people like film directors to write letters to Mao complaining about her. Mao wanted to stop Deng's initiatives by getting him to put on paper a pledge to stick to Cultural Revolution practices. In November 1975 he demanded that Deng draw up a Party resolution that would set the Cultural Revolution in stone.

Deng not only declined, he did so point-blank in front of some 130 senior cadres, thus defying Mao in no uncertain terms. Mao had to give up on the resolution. For him, this was the last straw. He made up his mind to discard Deng.

Chou and Yeh had been urging Deng not to be too confrontational with Mao: just to pay lip-service and wait for him to die. But Deng would not wait. He calculated that he could force Mao to swallow what he was doing, provided that he did not harm Mao personally.

Mao was fading fast. The muscular paralysis had invaded his vital organs, including his throat, severely affecting his ability to eat. But beneath this crumbling shell, he preserved his phenomenal determination not to be beaten.

MAO'S MOMENT CAME on 8 January 1976, when Deng's chief ally Chou En-lai died, at the age of seventy-eight. Mao moved at once. He fired Deng, put him under house arrest, and publicly denounced him by name. Simultaneously, he suspended Marshal Yeh, the third key member of the Alliance, claiming that Yeh was ill. To succeed Chou, Mao appointed a hitherto unknown middle-level disciple called Hua Guo-feng. An equally unknown low-ranking general called Chen Xi-lian was appointed to run the army. Mao chose these relatively neutral new faces, rather than members of the Gang of Four, to minimize adverse reactions from the Party and the army, most of whom loathed the Gang.

However, Chou's death detonated something that hitherto had not existed in Mao's China: public opinion. In the previous year, under Deng, information about who stood for what at the top had been made available for the first time through the networks of reinstated Communist officials and their children, and had circulated around the country. The public came to have some idea that Chou had been persecuted (while learning nothing about his squalid role in the Cultural Revolution). The news of Chou's death triggered off an unprecedented outpouring of public grief, especially as the media played it down. On the day when his body was taken from the hospital to the crematorium, over a million people lined the streets of Peking. This was the first time under Mao that anything remotely resembling this number of people had gathered without being organized. On the day of Chou's memorial service, even Mao's extremely prudent nurse-cum-secretary suggested that perhaps he should attend, an idea Mao rejected. People took Mao's absence as a snub to Chou, and when firecrackers were set off some days later at Mao's residence in Zhongnanhai for Chinese New Year, staff started whispering that he was celebrating Chou's death.

Popular protests broke out all over China, using the breach blown open by Chou's death to express loathing for Mao's policies. In early April the volcano erupted during the Tomb-Sweeping Festival, when the Chinese traditionally pay respects to their dead. Spontaneous crowds filled Tiananmen Square to mourn Chou with wreaths and poems and to denounce the Cultural Revolution. Even more amazing, in the heart of the capital crowds destroyed police vehicles broadcasting orders for them to clear the square, and set fire to the headquarters of the militia, who were organized by the Gang of Four and were trying to disperse the demonstrators violently. This defiance of Mao's rule took place a stone's throw from his house.

The regime suppressed the protests with much bloodshed. Mme Mao toasted this as a victory, and Mao wrote: "Great morale-booster. Good. Good. Good." A crackdown followed on across the country, but Mao was unable to crank up great terror like before.

Although Deng had nothing to do with organizing the demonstrations, a single device announced his popularity: the assortment of little bottles that hung from the pine trees around Tiananmen Square. Deng's given name, Xiao-ping, is pronounced the same as "little bottles." Mao felt extremely threatened by this sign. For the public to join hands with his Party opponents was an act without precedent. Mao had Deng hauled off from house arrest at home to detention in another part of Peking.

But instead of punishing Deng by the same cruel methods he had inflicted on other foes, Mao left him unharmed. This was not because he was fond of Deng. He simply could not take the risk of creating a situation where Deng's many supporters in the army might feel forced to take action. Although Mao had had Deng's ally Marshal Yeh suspended, Yeh continued to exercise virtual control over the military. At his home in the exclusive army compound in the Western Hills, he received a stream of generals and top officers, telling them defiantly that he was not ill at all, as Mao had been claiming. Among friends, Yeh now referred to Mao not as "the Chairman," which was the de rigueur respectful norm, but as na-mo-wen, the Chinese transliteration of the English "number one," which was irreverent. Army chiefs were discussing semi-openly what to do. One, nicknamed the "Bearded General," urged Yeh to act at once and "simply grab" the Gang of Four. Not speaking out loud, for fear of bugs, Yeh stuck his thumb upwards, shook it a couple of times and then turned it downwards, meaning: Wait for Mao to die. The "Bearded General" then had a word with the head of the Praetorian Guard, Wang Dong-xing, who was a former subordinate of his, to say that Deng must be well protected.

Mao knew what was going on in the Western Hills, but his new enforcers in the army were in no position to take on the veterans, and he himself was too ill to act. He had to lump it. It was in this frustrated state of mind that he had a massive heart attack at the beginning of June 1976, which left him at death's door.

THE POLITBURO AND Mao's leading doctors were told. Another person who was instantly informed, by a sympathetic doctor, was Deng's wife, who was in Hospital 301, a special hospital for top leaders, even those in disgrace. It was a sign of Mao's slackening grip that top-secret news like this about his condition could leak to his political foes. Once Deng himself heard, he wrote to Mao on 10 June, asking to be allowed to go home; in effect, demanding to be released.

Mao had to say "Yes," which he did after his condition stabilized at the end of the month; but Deng's release was delayed for some days because of another event that made Mao feel insecure. On 6 July, Marshal Zhu De, the most senior army leader, who enjoyed considerable respect, died, at the age of ninety. Mao feared that Zhu's death might touch off mass protests similar to those that followed Chou's death earlier in the year—and that Deng might get involved. Zhu had been Mao's earliest opponent, back in the late 1920s. Mao had made him suffer in the Cultural Revolution, but had refrained from purging him. Eventually, as unrest did not materialize after Zhu's death, Deng was allowed to go home on 19 July—driven through deserted streets in the dead of night.

Deng's detention had lasted only three months. Although he was still under house arrest, he was among his family. Mao had failed to destroy him, and Deng was very much around to fight another day.

LAST DAYS

(1974–76 ★ AGE 80–82)

HATRED, FRUSTRATION AND self-pity dominated Mao's last days. Mao expressed these feelings, long prominent in his character, in unique ways. He was very fond of a sixth-century poem called "The Sere Trees," which was a lamentation and elegy about a grove of sublime trees that ended up withered and lifeless. The poet, Yu Xin, attributed the trees' ill fortune to their having been uprooted and transplanted, which echoed his own life as an exile. But on 29 May 1975, Mao told the scholars annotating poems specially for him that the fate of the trees had "nothing to do with being transplanted." It was, he asserted, "the result of the trees being battered by harsh malevolent waves and hacked by human hands." Mao was thinking of himself as someone who was being (in his wife's words) "bullied" by Deng Xiao-ping and Deng's allies. Days before, they had forced Mao into an unprecedented climbdown by having him cancel his media campaign against them, and concede that he had "made a mistake."

After he had to release Deng from detention in July 1976, which made him furious, Mao had the "The Sere Trees" read aloud to him twice. He then began reciting it himself, very slowly, in his strangulated voice, brimming with bitterness. After this, he never asked to hear, or read, another poem.

Deng was only one of many old Party foes whom Mao took to scourging in his head in his last years. Another was Chou En-lai. In June 1974, Chou finally had the cancer operation that Mao had been blocking for two years. Mao had only finally consented because his own enfeebled physical condition had made him feel insecure himself. While Chou was in the hospital, Mao dug out some old diatribes he had written against Chou and other opponents back in 1941. They were full of insults, and Mao had never felt it was wise to publish them. Now, thirty-three years later, he spent a lot of time reading them, cursing Chou in his mind.

Going over them was also a way for Mao to vent his hatred for another foe, Liu Shao-chi, who had died five years before, at Mao's hands, but whose death Mao had still not dared to announce publicly. When Mao had originally written the articles, Liu had been his ally, and he had praised Liu in them. Now he made a point of crossing out each reference to Liu.

There was yet another man whom Mao was flaying in his head, and that was his chief rival at the time the articles were written: Wang Ming, who had died in exile in Russia on 27 March 1974, two months before Mao reread his old tirades. Mao had tried to murder Wang Ming by poisoning him in the 1940s, but then had had to allow him to take refuge in Russia, where Wang had remained something of a time-bomb. Khrushchev and Wang Ming's son both confirmed that Mao tried to poison Wang Ming in Russia. The attempt was unsuccessful, but only because the vigilant exile tested the food on his dog, Tek, which died. In Moscow, Wang Ming turned out anti-Mao material which was broadcast to China, and during the Cultural Revolution he started planning a return to China to set up a base in Xinjiang, near the Russian border, and then try a coup against Mao (a proposal that got short shrift from the Kremlin).

Wang Ming's death had been long drawn-out, and came after decades of ruined health, the legacy of Mao's attempts to kill him. He was bedridden in his final years, and it took him three hours to swallow enough tiny morsels of food to constitute a meal. But his painful death did not assuage Mao's grievance, just as the similarly agonizing deaths of both Liu and Chou brought Mao little relief. A month before he himself died, Mao had his old tirades read to him again, to bring himself the temporary pleasure of savaging all these foes one more time.

By the end of Mao's life, almost all his former close colleagues were dead, most of them thanks to him. Yet their deaths had somehow not quite satisfied him. Those of Liu and Peng De-huai, his two main victims in the Cultural Revolution, he had to keep secret for fear of public sympathy. Chou's death *had* been made public, but the outcome was to rock Mao's rule. Wang Ming had died in Russia, out of his reach. Zhu De he had been unable to purge. Lin Biao, Mao's chief collaborator in setting up the Great Purge, had managed to flee the country before the plane that carried him across the border crashed; moreover, Lin had bequeathed a legacy that haunted Mao—a plot to assassinate him. Deng was alive, and more than just alive: Mao had had to give in and let him live in the comfort of his own home, among his family. On his deathbed, Mao's thirst for revenge was unslaked.

DISSATISFACTION CONSUMED MAO. He had not risen to be a superpower, in spite of his decades of craving. Although he had the Bomb, he could not cash it, not least because the delivery system could barely loft it over China's border. The country's industrial bases were a shambles, turning out heaps of defective equipment—including fleets of planes that could not fly, even though an aircraft industry had topped his agenda from the very beginning of his rule, and the Korean War had been fought partly to acquire it. Nor was the navy much better. Mao's last words to his navy chief in 1975, a year before his death, were: "Our navy is only like this!," sticking out his little finger, looking immensely disconsolate. That October, Mao remarked ruefully to Kissinger that he did not belong to the major league. "There are only two superpowers in the world . . . We are backward . . ." Counting on his fingers, he said: "We come last. America, Soviet Union, Europe, Japan, China—look!" When US president Ford came to China a few weeks later, Mao told him: "We can only fire . . . empty cannons" and "curse."

Mao had made a last-ditch effort to promote himself as a world leader in 1974, by trying to capitalize on something that did not require military prowess, and was the one point where he could claim to lead the world: poverty. He proclaimed a new way of defining "Three Worlds," announcing that the "Third World" meant countries that were poor, excluding Russia, and dropped heavy hints that he should be seen as the leader of the Third World. But although he was regarded, in a very general way, as a leader of the Third World, it did not take orders from him, and he provided no tangible leadership. Besides, as one hard-nosed American diplomat put it, "would it really make all that difference?"

Even his own creatures refused to acknowledge his authority. Mao had played a vital part in installing the Khmer Rouge regime in Cambodia in 1975. Pol Pot, its leader, under whom up to one quarter of the Cambodian people perished in the space of a few years, was a soul-mate of Mao's. Immediately after Pol Pot took power, Mao congratulated him face to face on his slave-labor-camp state: "You have scored a splendid victory. Just a single blow and no more classes." What Mao meant was that everyone had become a slave. And Mao sent Prince Sihanouk, who had been living in luxurious exile in China, back to Cambodia, where the prince was put under house arrest and his name was exploited by Pol Pot. But though Mao was Pol Pot's sponsor and mentor, he got no gratitude. A colleague of Pol Pot's called Keo Meas, who had referred to Mao in eulogistic terms, was tortured to death. Written on the dead man's dossier were the words: "This contemptible Mao who got the horrible death he deserved was worthless. You shouldn't think, you antique bastard, that the Kampuchean Party has been influenced by Mao."

On the world stage, Mao had to cling to a vague halo. When Nixon's daughter Julie turned up wearing a Mao badge, "he reacted with a child-like delight and impulsively clasped my hand," she wrote. To sustain his profile, he continued to "receive" foreign statesmen until three months before his death. But he often rather spoiled the effect of these audiences. Thailand's leaders found him "snoring" as they entered the room.

Singapore's premier Lee Kuan Yew, Mao's penultimate foreign visitor, described an almost inarticulate Mao grunting, head lolling against the back of his armchair. Indeed, as the last photos of him confirm, Mao looked anything but a world leader. Dribbling saliva, waxen-faced and slack-jawed, he projected an image of senility and wretchedness. When he saw how bad he looked in photos with Pakistan's prime minister Bhutto at the end of May 1976, Mao stopped meeting foreigners altogether.

WHILE FEELING DEEPLY discontented at having failed to achieve his world ambition, Mao spared no thought for the mammoth human and material losses that his destructive quest had cost his people. Well over 70 million people had perished—in peacetime—as a result of his misrule, yet Mao felt sorry only for himself. He would cry as he talked about anything he could connect with his past glory and current failure, even watching his own regime's propaganda films. His staff often saw tears flooding down his face, "like a spring" as one of them put it. Self-pity, to which Mao had always been prone, was the paramount emotion of the utterly unpitying Mao in his last days.

Mao became very attached to some classical poems which convey a mood of great men brought down, kings fallen, and heroes' brilliant prospects in ruins. He empathized with the unfulfilled heroes and kings.

This state of mind led him to an extraordinary sense of fraternity with those he regarded as "fallen kings" around the world. Top of the list was former US president Richard Nixon, who had been forced from office by Watergate in August 1974. Time and again Mao went out of his way to proclaim his fond feelings for Nixon. Weeks after Nixon had been ejected from the White House, Mao asked Imelda Marcos of the Philippines to pass on his good wishes and an invitation to Nixon to revisit China. Nixon's daughter Julie and her husband, David Eisenhower, were given an astonishing welcome in December the following year. Mao told Julie: "Write to your father at once, tell him I miss him." When Julie got back to America, Peking's envoy told her that Mao "considers you part of his family"—a remark that was absolutely unique.

When the disgraced Nixon came, in February 1976, Mao sent a Boeing 707 to Los Angeles for him, complete with the protocol chief of the Foreign Ministry, another unheard-of gesture. The fact that the plane ran the risk of being seized as collateral against US assets expropriated in China was immaterial for Mao. When he saw Nixon again, Mao clinked teacups with him, and when Nixon took his leave, Mao struggled to the door, standing unaided, to see him off, looking melancholy. Mao had invited him to China for what was, in effect, a private farewell. He personally selected an evening's entertainment for the former US president which included the singing of Mao's favorite classical poems set to music, which conjured up the mood of the tragic ending of great men. The program meant nothing to Nixon, who showed he was tired—and bored. But Mao was expressing his own sentiments, for himself, even though he was not present at the performance.

Another even more unlikely recipient of Mao's sentimental affinity was Chiang Kai-shek, the man he had deposed—and had slaughtered millions of Chinese to keep deposed. Chiang died in Taiwan on 5 April 1975 at the age of eighty-nine, leaving a will decreeing that his coffin was not to be buried in Taiwan, but kept in a shrine to await a return to the Mainland when communism collapsed. Around the time of Chiang's funeral, Mao mourned the Generalissimo for an entire day, in private. On that day, Mao did not eat, or speak. He had an eight-minute tape of stirring music played over and over again all day long to create a funereal atmosphere, while he beat time on his bed, wearing a solemn expression. The music was set specially for Mao to a twelfth-century poem, in which the writer bade farewell to a friend who bore an uncanny resemblance to Chiang—a patriotic high mandarin whose career ended tragically and unfulfillled, and who was being exiled to a remote part of China. The writer told his friend:

> *You and I are men of history*
> *No little men chattering about minor affairs!*

This was exactly how Mao felt towards Chiang.

Days later, Mao rewrote the last two lines of the poem so that they read:

> *Go, let go, my honored friend,*
> *Do not look back.*

This change turned the poem into an unmistakable valediction. Mao was writing his own envoi to a fellow thwarted giant. It was re-recorded to music, and was one of the poems sung to Nixon when Mao brought the former US president over to say his personal goodbye.

MAO SHOWED UNCOMMON sympathy in private for other ousted rulers. When the emperor of Ethiopia, Haile Selassie, whom he had met only once and very briefly, died in prison in 1975 after being dethroned by a military coup, Mao sank into melancholy. "The emperor was doing fine," Mao kept saying. "Why did he have to come to this? Why did it have to end like this?!"

This new empathy with deposed rulers was an extension of Mao's old fear of being toppled himself. In this final phase of his life, he was more obsessed than ever with a coup. It was to avert such a possibility that he intimated to Deng Xiao-ping and his allies in 1975 that they were welcome to crush Mme Mao and her Gang after his death.

It was partly for this same reason—fear of a coup—that Mao did not appoint a successor. He never bestowed that title on the head of his last coterie, Hua Guo-feng, as he had earlier on Lin Biao. He feared that an official heir apparent might be in too much haste to succeed, and would try to jump the gun. So, although Hua showed manifest loyalty (when Mao was fed through the nose for the first time, Hua took on Chou's guinea-pig role and tested a tube on himself first), and although Mao obviously trusted Hua enough to put him in charge, he declined to confirm that Hua would take over after he died.

Mao did not care one iota what happened after his death. In fact, he had scant confidence in the staying power of his own "achievements." On the only occasion he said a few words to his inner circle about the future, when he knew he was dying, he told them that there would be "upheaval," indeed "blood rains and winds smelling of blood." And then Mao said: "What's going to happen to you, heaven only knows."

So Mao did not leave a will, even though he had been expecting death for at least a year, and had had ample time to prepare one.

THE LAST FEW weeks of Mao's life were spent in a nondescript building which had been specially built for him in Zhongnanhai, with all the usual security specifications, and was earthquake-proof. Characteristically, it only had a code-name, "202." He was carried there at the end of July 1976, after Peking was shaken by a huge earthquake that measured 7.8 on the Richter scale and which flattened Tangshan, an industrial city 160 km to the east, where somewhere between 240,000 (official figure) and 600,000 (unofficial estimate) people were killed. In Peking and many other cities, tens of millions of people had to sleep out in the open. In true Mao style, the regime turned down foreign help, which could have greatly lowered the death toll. A media campaign was launched exhorting rescuers to "denounce Deng on the ruins."

Mao was still giving orders. When Mme Mao wanted to go out of Peking on 2 September, she came to ask her husband for permission. He was peevish at being bothered, and refused the first time, but granted it when she persisted. Three days later, Mao suddenly lost consciousness, and she was summoned back by the new team headed by Hua. In the past weeks they had been taking turns to keep vigil by Mao's bed, and when Mme Mao got back, she joined them, but stood behind the bed, as he had shown annoyance before when he woke up and set eyes on her. None of Mao's children was present.

On 8 September an unintelligible croak came from Mao's throat. His barber and servant of seventeen years tucked a pencil into his trembling hand, and Mao laboriously drew three shaky lines, and then feebly touched the wooden edge of his bed three times. The barber figured out that Mao wanted to know what was happening to the Japanese prime minister, Takeo Miki (whose name in Chinese means "Three Woods"). Mao had never met Miki, and had shown no special interest in him until now, when Miki was fighting to prevent being toppled by a coup within his own party.

One of Mao's two girlfriends-turned-nurse, Meng, held up the news bulletin, and Mao read it for a few minutes. This report about yet another leader on the ropes was the very last thing he read.

Soon after this, Meng heard Mao say: "I feel very ill. Call the doctors." These were the last words he spoke. Shortly afterwards, he slipped into unconsciousness. At ten minutes past midnight on the morning of 9 September 1976, Mao Tse-tung died. His mind remained lucid to the end, and in it stirred just one thought: himself and his power.

EPILOGUE

TODAY, MAO'S PORTRAIT and his corpse still dominate Tiananmen Square in the heart of the Chinese capital. The current Communist regime declares itself to be Mao's heir and fiercely perpetuates the myth of Mao.

ACKNOWLEDGMENTS

Our gratitude goes first to the several hundred interviewees, who provided us with vital information, as well as much color to bring Mao alive. None is responsible for any of the views expressed in the book.

The following people kindly sent us material, answered queries, effected introductions, or gave us other valuable help. To all of them we are most grateful. We regret that we have not been able to differentiate their contributions more distinctively. Our apologies for any omissions (including some titles), which we will be glad to correct in future editions. We feel very sad that those in Mainland China cannot be named, and hope that this situation will change one day.

Eric Aarons, Aldo Agosti, Aziza Allard, Kirill Anderson, Eugenio Anguiano, Oscar Armstrong, Kazuko Aso, Prof. Ivo Banac, Luciano Barca, Mr. & Mrs. C. D. Barkman, Antony Beevor, Edward Behr, Csaba Békés, Prof. Gregor Benton, Prof. Barton Bernstein, Prof. Charles Bettelheim, Praful Bidwai, Prof. Herbert P. Bix, Dennis Bloodworth, Nenne Bodell, Countess Resy Bonacossa, Dominique & Christian Bourgois, Horst Brie, Marina Brodskaya, Aleksandr Bukh, Boriana Buzhashka, Lord (Peter) Carrington, Prof. Carolle Carter, Fr. John Carven, Fr. Santiago Cepeda, Prof. Chang Yu-fa, Prof. Chen Jian, Prof. Chen Peng-jen, Prof. Chiang Yung-ching, Chin Hsiao-i, Chou Wei-peng, Thomas B. Cochran, Dr. Alex Colas, William Colby, Les Coleman, Prof. Richard Crampton, Bernard R. Crystal, Cui Kuang-chung, David Cutler, Prof. Alexander Dallin, John Paton Davies, Fr. Thomas Davitt, Prof. Wolfgang Deckers, Prof. Lev Delyusin, Jonathan Demme, Veselin Dimitrov, Prof. John Dower, Harald & Elke Einsmann, Carlos Elbirt, Robert Elegant, Hans Magnus Enzensberger, Prof. Grant Evans, Edmund Fawcett, Prof. Roland Felber, Prof. Stephan Feuchtwang, Léo Figuères, Fou Ts'ong, Guido Franzinetti, Prof. Edward Friedman, Hiroaki Fujii, Tetsuzo Fuwa, Gao Anhua, Sam Gerovich, Patrick Gilkes, Siegmund Ginzberg, John Gittings, Antonio Giustozzi, Sir Alastair Goodlad, Aleksandr Grigoriev, Tom Grunfeld,

A. Guindi, Edward Gurvich, Dr. Jürgen Haacke, Lord Hailsham, David Halliday, Eric Hanson, Harry Harding, Dr. Hope M. Harrison, John Haynes, Dieter Heinzig, Sir Nicholas Henderson, Jim Hershberg, Fr. Jeroom Heyndrickx, Stefan Hermlin, Andrew Higgins, Lord (Geoffrey) Howe, Lord (David) Howell, Jason Hu, Peter Huber, Sir Christopher & Lady Hum, Jean Hung, Gen. & Mrs. I Fu-en, Lord (Peter) Inge, Ji Wei, Nelson Jobim, Monty Johnstone, Jong Fang-ling, Prof. Harold Kahn, Prof. Thomas Kampen, Hideaki & Toshikazu Kase, Maneesha Kaul, Prof. Pauline Keating, Dr. Edward Keene, Michael Keon, Vladimir Khanjenkov, Dr. Sergei Khrushchev, Prof. Ben Kiernan, Takuji Kimura, Gen. Yuri Kobaladze, Hanako Koyama, Ina Krymova, Rishat Kudashev, Dr. Peter M. Kuhfus, Boris T. Kulik, Kuo Kuan-ying, Kisho Kurokawa, Andrei Lankov, Eugene K. Lawson, Boyka Leader, Dr. Andrei Ledovsky, Dr. Milton Leitenberg, Rob Lemkin, David Lie, Helmut & Marianne Liebermann, Georges Liébert, Maria Sofia Lilli, Dr. Frederick Litten, Liu Shao-tang, Gary Lundell, Lorenz Luthi, Peter Lyon, Fr. Patrick McCloskey, Sir Colin McColl, Prof. Gavan McCormack, Prof. Ruth McVey, Ukeru Magosaki, John Maher, Sean Malloy, Prof. Giorgio Mantici, Anto Marden, Aglika Markova, Barry Martin, Fr. Michel Masson, Prof. James Mayall, Sonny Mehta, Werner Meissner, George Melly, Dr. Jonathan Mirsky, Eileen Moffett, Simon Sebag Montefiore, Kimitoshi Morihara, Aziz Naim, Kazuko Nakajima, Kujtim Nako, Premier Fatos Nano, Prof. Vitaly Naumkin, Richard Needham, Richard Neustadt, Ngo Manh Lan, Ngo Thi Minh-Hoang, Nguyen Co Thach, Masaki Orita, Prof. Alexander Pantsov, Gabriel Partos, Fr. James Perluzzi, Leonid S. Polevoy, Prof. David Pollard, Brian Pollitt, John W. (Bill) Powell, Lord (Charles) Powell, Wen & Michael Powles, Fr. P. Pycke, Sergey Radchenko, Prof. Kimmo Rentola, Lord (Gordon) & Lady Richardson, Florentino Rodao, Peter Rodman, Helge Ronning, Prof. Robert Ross, Lord (Jacob) Rothschild, Rosa Rust, Lord (John) Sainsbury, Akira Sakaguchi, Sang Ye, Bernd Schäfer, Fritz Schatten, Prof. Michael Schoenhals, Prof. Stuart Schram, Kathryn Seitz, Prof. Mark Selden, Aldo Serafini, Rostislav Sergeyev, John Service, Hugh Seymour, Prof. Shaw Yu-ming, Prof. Michael Sheng, Sokol Shtylla, Zamir Shtylla, Prof. Harry Shukman, Larry Shyu, Vasily Sidikhmenov, Boris Slavinsky, Daniel Southerland, Tilman Spengler, Sergei Stanishev, Sir Nicholas Stern, William & Jadwiga Stokes, Richard Stolz, Judy Stowe, Dr. Viktor Sumsky, Hideya Taida, Takashi Inoue, David Tang, Prof. William Taubman, Tsering Tashi, Dick Taverne, Fr. P. Taveirne, Jay Taylor, Prof. Frederick Teiwes, Anne Thurston, Victoria Tomkinson, Count Francesco Tonci, Tong Kraisak, Prof. Tong Te-kong, Thomas Torrance, Tania Tourlakova, Nasir Tyabji, Oleg Troyanovsky, Achin Vanaik, Nicholas Villiers, Lyuba Vinogradova, Stephen Vizinczey, Peter von Bagh, William

Waack, Bob Walther, Wang Dan-zhi, S. G. Wheatcroft, J. Williams, Paul Wingrove, Wu Wei-shi, Jim Yang, Prof. Yu Maochun, Gen. Yu Song Chol, Joe Zhang, Prof. Zhang Shuguang, Dr. Valentina Zhuravlyeva, James Zobel, Suzanna Zsohar.

We owe a special thank you to: Aleksandr Borodin, William Burr, Prof. Chen Yung-fa, Prof. Fred Halliday, Col. James Jordan, Lida Kita, Dr. Alexandre Mansourov, Connie Rudat, Roger Sandilands, Andrei Sidorov, Konstantin Shevelyov, Viktor Usov, Michael Wall, Robert Wampler, Lisa & Stanley Weiss, Prof. Arne Westad, Col. William J. Williams, Xue Yi-wei.

We are immensely indebted to our editor at Knopf, Dan Frank, who did so much to improve the text, and whose thought-provoking queries led to the solving of major historical puzzles. Deep gratitude also to our editor at Cape, Dan Franklin; to assistant editor Alex Milner; to Steve Cox, who did an excellent line edit on the penultimate draft; and to all who worked on the book; to our agent, Gillon Aitken, and his associates and staff; and to our indispensable assistant, Alexandra Adamson.

It is impossible to exaggerate the role of Pu Zhang, who over the years bounced our ideas and hypotheses back at us with vigor and insight.

LIST OF INTERVIEWEES
(T: by telephone)

MAINLAND CHINA
(fifteen were informal conversations)

I FAMILY AND RELATIVES OF MAO

Cao Quan-fu	son-in-law of Mao's brother, Tse-min; political secretary to Zhu De
Cao Yun-shan	grandson of Mao's brother, Tse-min
Han Jin-xing	relative
Li Na	daughter
Liu Si-qi	wife of Mao's eldest son, An-ying; adopted daughter
Mao Xin-yu	grandson
Mao Ze-lian	cousin
Zhang Wen-qiu	mother-in-law to Mao's two sons

II OLD FRIENDS AND COLLEAGUES

Li Shu-yi	friend of Mao and his wife, 1920s
Liu Ying	friend of Mao from early 1930s; wife of Lo Fu; Long Marcher
Luo Zhang-long	close friend and colleague, 1915–27
Wang Hui-wu	witness to CCP 1st Congress; she and her husband Li Da friends with Mao
Xiao Ke	subordinate to Mao from 1928; Long Marcher
Yi Li-rong	closest friend for a decade until 1927
Zeng Zhi	friend from 1928 for four decades; wife of Tao Zhu
Zheng Chao-lin	in Shanghai with Mao, 1924; together at 7 August 1927 meeting; last

surviving leader of Shanghai
Uprising, 1927

III CLOSE STAFF (SECRETARIES, INTERPRETERS,
BODYGUARDS, HOUSEHOLD STAFF, MEDICAL STAFF,
GIRLFRIENDS)
Chen Hui-min, Feng Yao-song, Gao Zhi, He Qing-hua, Hu Xiu-yun, Li Jin, Li
Yue-ran, Meng Jin-yun, Shang Lai-bao, Shi Zhe, Tian Yun-yu, Wang He-bin,
Wu Lian-deng, Xie Jing-yi, Yan Ming-fu, Zhang Han-zhi, Zhang Yu-feng, Zhou
Fu-ming

IV FAMILIES OF MAO'S COLLEAGUES

Chen Hao-su	son of Chen Yi
He Ping-sheng	daughter of He Chang-gong
Li Inna	daughter of Li Li-san
Li Lisa	wife of Li Li-san
Li Te-te	daughter of Li Fu-chun and Cai Chang
Lin Li-heng (Dodo)	daughter of Lin Biao
Liu Shi-kun	son-in-law of Yeh Jian-ying; famous pianist
Liu Xiang-ping	Minister of Health; wife of Xie Fu-zhi
Luo Dian-dian	daughter of Luo Rui-qing
Luo Ping-hai	son of Luo Zhang-long
Qin Ji-ma	daughter of Po Ku
Shen Zai-wang	son of Li Jing-quan
Tan Sheng-yuan	daughter of Tan Zhen-lin
Tao Si-liang	daughter of Tao Zhu and Zeng Zhi
Wang Dan-zhi	son of Wang Ming
Wang Guang-mei	wife of Liu Shao-chi
Wang Ning	wife of Zhou Xiao-zhou
Xia Bo-gen	stepmother of Deng Xiao-ping
Xie Fei	former wife of Liu Shao-chi; Long Marcher
Xue Ming	wife of Ho Lung
Zhang Ning	fiancée of Lin Biao's son, Tiger
Zhang Qing-lin	son-in-law of Lin Biao
Zhu Zhong-li	wife of Wang Jia-xiang; friend of Mao from 1930s

V STAFF FOR THE LEADERSHIP

Cheng Yuan-gong	long-time chief bodyguard to Chou En-lai
Du Xiu-xian	photographer
Guan Wei-xun	secretary to Mrs. Lin Biao

Guo Wen	secretary to Yao Wen-yuan
Hou Bo	photographer
Jin Shan-wang	senior Praetorian Guard officer
Kang Yi-min	chief radio operator; Long Marcher
Liu Ji-chun	member of Lin Biao's staff
Liu Yu-qin	temporary companion to Li Na
Lü Hou-min	photographer
Qian Si-jie	photographer
Wang Ru-qin	nurse to Lin Biao
Wang Sheng-rong	Praetorian Guard chief
Wu Ji-cheng	Praetorian Guard chief; in charge of arresting the guards of the Gang of Four, 1976
Xu Xiao-bing	photographer
Yang Jun	confidential secretary to Liu Shao-chi
Zhang Zuo-liang	doctor of Chou En-lai

VI TOP ECHELON, KEY WITNESSES TO HISTORICAL EVENTS

Chen Ying-qian	top doctor
Gao Liang	senior diplomat
Hou Zheng	Mao's wife Gui-yuan's company chief on Long March
Hu Min	wife of Qiu Hui-zuo
Hu Ping	air force officer involved in the Lin Biao affair
Hua Jun-wu	Yenan witness; foremost cartoonist
Huang Huo-qing	Long Marcher; survivor of Western Contingent
Jiang Wen	chief prosecutor at the trial of Jiang Qing
Jin Shu-wang	intelligence operative, 1920s and 1930s; Yenan Terror victim
Kuai Da-fu	leading Red Guard
Li Jian-tong	author of novel singled out for condemnation by Mao, 1962
Li Pu	high official, close to Tao Zhu
Li Qiong	wife of Yang Fan
Li Rui	one-time secretary to Mao; major liberal in CCP
Li Yun	CCP liaison with Mme Sun Yat-sen
Liao Gai-long	leading Party theoretician
Lin Xiao-xia	son of Zhang Hao; senior official
Lu Min	air force officer involved in Tiger's plot to assassinate Mao
Luo Fu	senior operative in Hong Kong

Mu Xin	Cultural Revolution Small Group member
Qian San-qiang	director, the Institute of Atomic Energy
Qin Chuan	*People's Daily* editor-in-chief
Shen Rong	senior official; one-time colleague of Wang Guang-mei
Shui Jing	wife of Jiangxi province chief, Yang Shang-kui
Su Fei	wife of Mao's American doctor, George Hatem
Tu Men	chief prosecutor in the trial of the Lin Biao group
Wang Fan-xi	in Shanghai with Chou En-lai, 1920s
Wang Li	Cultural Revolution Small Group member
Wang Shu	senior diplomat
Wang Zun-ji	Yenan Terror victim
Wen Ji-ze	Yenan Terror witness
Wu Zu-guang	leading playwright
Xia Yan	leading cultural figure
Xie He-geng	intelligence operative in the USA; husband of Wang Ying
Yang Chao	Yenan Terror witness; one-time secretary to Chou En-lai
Yang Fan	intelligence chief
Yang Yi	senior Xinhua News Agency official
Yu Zhan-bang	secretary to Zhang Zhi-zhong
Yuan Jing-shen	Party supervisor for architecture
Zhao Di-sheng	senior Xinhua News Agency official
Zheng Xing-he	air force officer involved in Tiger's plot to assassinate Mao
Zhu Tie-zheng	air force officer, deputy head of the Ho Lung Case Team

VII WITNESSES TO MAJOR EVENTS

Chen Kai-ge	Red Guard; later leading film director
Li Hsiao-li	Yenan witness
Li Xiu-zhen	93-year-old living by the Dadu Bridge
Li Da-zhong	son of Mao's doctor, Li Zhi-sui
Liu Dong-lin	son of Jiangxi province chief Liu Jun-xiu
Lu Hong	friend and victim of Li Na
Liu Xiao-ang	son of Li Shu-yi
Qiu Lu-guang	son of Qiu Hui-zuo
Qu Lei-lei	son of author of one of Mme Mao's model operas; working in

	television studio when special videos were made for Mao
Shi Da-zheng (T)	son of film director who was the first famous cultural figure to commit suicide after Communist takeover
Sima Lu	Yenan witness
Song Yong-yi (T)	Shanghai Cultural Revolution violence eyewitness; later scholar on Cultural Revolution
Wang Da-zhang	son of Wang Wei-guo; involved in the Tiger plot to assassinate Mao
Wei Jing-sheng	Red Guard; later leading democracy campaigner
Weiss, Ruth	long-time foreign resident in China
Wu Hong-da (Harry)	labor camp survivor and campaigner
Wu Peng-qing	Long Marcher
Wu Yi-man	daughter of Wu Xiu-quan
Zhang Xiao-ji	daughter of Zhang Ming-yuan (involved with Gao Gang)
Zhang Yan-sheng	daughter of Zhang Xiu-shan (involved with Gao Gang)
Zhang Yi-jiu	sorted out Mao's books after Mao died
Zhou Chun	German-language interpreter
Zhu Luo-jun	sister-in-law of the Young Marshal

VIII HISTORIANS AND WRITERS WITH SPECIAL ACCESS

Cao Chun-rong, Cao Zhong-bin (T), Chen Dong-lin, Chen Jian, Cheng Zhong-yuan, Dai Qing, Ding Shu (T), Dong Bao-cun, Dong Sheng, Gao Wen-qian, Gong Yu-zhi, Gu Bao-zi, He Di, He Ding, Huang Zheng, Jin Chong-ji, Jin Zhen-lin, Li Dan-hui, Li Hai-wen, Li Chun-lin, Liao Xin-wen, Lin Ying, Liu Bin-zhen, Liu Jia-ju, Liu Xiao-nong, Ma Zhen-du, Mao Bing-hua, Niu Jun, Quan Yan-chi, Shen Zhi-hua, Shi Dong-bing, Song Ke, Wang Nian-yi, Wang Xing-juan, Wang You-qin (T), Wang Yu-xiang, Wen Rui, Wu Qi-quan, Xu Chun-hua, Yan Jia-qi, Yang Kui-song, Yang Bu-sheng (T), Ye Yong-lie, Yin Qi, Yu Guo-lu, Zhang De-xiang, Zhang Guo-qi, Zhang Xi, Zhang Xue-xin, Zhang Zheng-long, Zheng Yi (T), Zhu Bing-feng, Zhu Yu, Zhu Zheng

TAIWAN

HISTORICAL FIGURES AND KEY WITNESSES

Chang Hsueh-liang	warlord of Manchuria; kidnapped Chiang Kai-shek, 1936
Chen Li-fu	close associate of Chiang Kai-shek; founded Nationalists' FBI
Chiang Weigo	Chiang Kai-shek's adopted son

Chien Fu	English-language secretary to Chiang; Foreign Minister
Chin Hsiao-i	secretary to Chiang
Hau Po-tsun	chief of Chiang's Guard; Prime Minister
Hu Chiu-yuan	leading political and cultural figure
I Fu-en	Chiang's pilot, close to Chiang and sons
Kao Kui-yuan	at Whampoa with Lin Biao; later military assistant to Chiang (interviewed via Kuo Tian-you)
Li Huan	Chiang Ching-kuo's confidant
Lu Keng (T)	leading investigative journalist
Mao Chia-hua	Nationalist member of parliament
Tsai Meng-chien (T)	Nationalist intelligence man who caught Gu Shun-zhang
Wang Sheng	Chiang Ching-kuo's confidant
Yang Hsi-kun	leading diplomat
Yu Ta-wei	Defense Minister

REST OF THE WORLD
(Italic: met Mao in a substantial way)

ALBANIA

Alia, Ramiz	Hoxha's heir; later President
Belishova, Liri	Politburo member; key witness in Sino-Soviet split, 1960
Çomo, Maqo	Minister of Agriculture; at Khrushchev–Peng De-huai dinner, Tirana, May 1959
Fagu, Agim	basketball star; extensive trips to China
Hoxha, Nexhmije	wife of Party chief Enver Hoxha
Paçrami, Adil	Minister of Culture; editor, Party daily
Pllumi, Zef	Catholic priest imprisoned 22 years over China issue
Shehu, Bashkim	son of Premier Mehmet Shehu
Shyti, Pupo	Vice-Chairman, Planning Commission; chief trade negotiator with China

AUSTRALIA

| Aarons, Eric (T) | head of Australian Communist Party study group, in China early 1950s |
| *FitzGerald, Stephen* | ambassador to China |

BELGIUM

Grippa, Madeleine	Maoist leader, 1960s
Pairoux, Serge	Maoist activist
Tindemans, Léo	Prime Minister

BRAZIL

Amazonas, Joao — Maoist leader

Prestes, Fernanda (T) — schoolmate of Mao's sons in Russia

Prestes, Yuri — schoolmate of Mao's sons in Russia

CAMBODIA

Hor Namhong — Foreign Minister; with Sihanouk in Peking 1970–75

DENMARK

Hartling, Poul — Prime Minister (and Mrs.)

EGYPT

Farid, Col. Abdul Magid — Secretary-General of the presidency under Nasser; later adviser to the Algerian presidency

Heikal, Mohammed Hasanein — senior adviser and confidant to Nasser; Minister of Foreign Affairs; editor, *Al Ahram*

FRANCE

Behr, Edward — journalist; in China, 1964

Bettencourt, André — Secretary of State for Foreign-Affairs; Minister

Bloch, Adm. René — head of De Gaulle's force de frappe (nuclear program)

Figuères, Léo — Communist Party envoy to Ho Chi Minh, 1950

Meadmore, Jean — embassy, Nanjing, 1940s

Pasqualini, Jean — prisoner in Chinese labor camps, 1950s–1960s

Vergès, Jacques — Maoist, lawyer

GERMANY

Brie, Horst — East German embassy, Peking

Felber, Prof. Roland — East German student, China, 1950s; China scholar

Siao, Eva — wife of old friend of Mao; Yenan resident

Werner, Ruth — GRU officer in Sorge group, China, 1930s

Wolf, Markus — at Mao's banquet for Stalin (East German-chargé d'affaires), Moscow, 1950; later East German Foreign Intelligence chief

HONG KONG
Grove, Dan   head, FBI office, Hong Kong

HUNGARY
Hegedüs, András   Prime Minister
Szall, Jozsef   embassy, Peking
Tálas, Barna   embassy, Peking

INDIA
Dalai Lama   exiled Tibetan leader
Kaul, T. K.   embassy, Peking, 1950s; foreign
                                                      policy adviser to Nehru
Mahta, Peter (T)   head of Air India office, Hong
                                                      Kong, 1955
Mehta, Jagad Singh   chief negotiator, border talks with
                                                      China, 1960
Palden Gyatso   Tibetan lama; long-term labor
                                                      camp prisoner
Paranjpe, Vasant V.   interpreter for Nehru–Mao talks
Ranganathan, C. V.   ambassador to China
Tyabji, Nasir   Nehru expert, Nehru Memorial,
                                                      Delhi

INDONESIA
Adjitorop, Jusuf   sole survivor of Communist Party
                                                      Politburo, 1965; exile in China

IRAN
Alikhani, Alinaghi (T)   emissary to China, 1960

IRAQ
Abdulrazak, Nouri   Secretary-General, Afro-Asian
                                                      People's Solidarity Organization

IRELAND
O'Reilly, Fr. Luke   Catholic priest in Jiangxi during
                                                      Communist takeover

ITALY
Barca, Luciano   Communist Party leader
Foa, Vittorio   Socialist trade union leader; present
                                                      at milestone meeting in Peking,
                                                      1960, at start of Sino-Soviet split
Graziosi, Prof. Franco   microbiologist; germ warfare
                                                      investigation team, 1952

Ingrao, Pietro   Communist Party leader; at
  Moscow summit, 1957
Jotti, Nilde   companion of Party chief Togliatti;
  at Moscow summit, 1957
Longo, Luigi Libero   interpreter at Moscow summit,
  1957; son of Party No. 2
Pesce, Osvaldo   Maoist activist

JAPAN

Arisue, Lt. Gen. Seizo   head of wartime military intelligence
  and atomic bomb program
Eto, Prof. Shinkichi   China expert, historian
Fuwa, Tetsuzo   head, Communist Party
Fujita, Kimio   diplomat; at secret Chou-Sukarno
  meeting, 1965
Fujiwara, Prof. Akira   China expert, historian
Hata, Prof. Ikuhiko   China expert, historian
Kanazawa, Yukio   prominent Maoist journalist
Koizumi, Seiichi   intelligence officer, China, 1940s,
  dealing with CCP
Maeda, Mitsushige   POW, Yenan
Mikasa, Prince   brother of Emperor Hirohito;
  army officer, China, 1940s
Miyamoto, Kenji   head, Communist Party
Nakajima, Prof. Mineo   China expert, historian
Nikaido, Susumu   Chief Cabinet Secretary
Nosaka, Sanzo   head, Communist Party
Shimizu, Masao   director, Matsuzawa Ballet
Tachiki, Hiroshi   Communist Party official;
  long-term resident in China
Takeuchi, Prof. Minoru   leading Mao expert; editor, Mao's works

KOREA (NORTH)

Kang Sang Ho   Deputy Minister of the Interior
  during Korean War

MALAYSIA

Chin Peng   Party chief; guerrilla leader,
  1948–61; exile in China

MEXICO

Anguiano, Eugenio   ambassador, Peking
Cárdenas, Cuauhtémoc   Mayor of Mexico City; presidential
  candidate
Echeverría, Luis   President

NEW ZEALAND
Corner, Frank   Foreign Minister

NIGERIA
Gowon, Gen. Yakubu   President

NORWAY
Steigan, Pal   Maoist leader

PHILIPPINES
Marcos, Imelda   First Lady

POLAND
Rowinski, Jan   student, then diplomat, Peking,
  (and Hala)   1950s–60s
Walesa, Lech   President
Werblan, Andrzej (T)   chief foreign policy adviser to
                                      Party chief Gomulka

RUSSIA
Arkhipov, Ivan V.   chief economic adviser to the
                                      Chinese government, 1950–51,
                                      1953–58; later 1st Deputy Premier
Berezhkov, Valentin   interpreter for Stalin
Blake, George   British intelligence officer, Korea;
                                      spy for Russia
Brezhnev,   embassy, Peking
  Aleksandr A. (T)
Chervonenko, Stepan V.   ambassador to China, 1959–1965,
                                      during famine and Sino-Soviet
                                      split
Delyusin, Prof. Lev   *Pravda* correspondent, China;
                                      China scholar
Galenovich, Yuri   embassy, Peking; interpreter at talks
                                      with Mao
Glunin, Prof. V. I.   historian; expert on CCP and the
                                      Comintern
Kapitsa, Mikhail S.   top China expert throughout
                                      Mao period; Deputy Foreign
                                      Minister
Karpov, Col. Vladimir   spokesman for Security Service
                                      (FSB)
Kartunova, Anastasia   escort for Mme Mao in Russia,
                                      1949, 1952–53

Kudashev, Rishat S.	senior interpreter for Khrushchev, Mikoyan and Kosygin in talks with Mao
Kukushkin, K. V.	Expert in CCP–Moscow relations
Kulik, Boris T.	head, China Department, International Department, Soviet CP
Ledovsky, Andrei M.	Consul General, Shenyang, 1950–52; embassy, 1940s; China scholar with special archive access
Lobov, Lt. Gen. Georgi	Commander, Soviet Air Force in Korean War
Mirovitskaya, Dr. Raisa A.	China scholar with special access to Defense Ministry archives
Plotnikov, Col. Georgi	senior North Korea expert, Institute of Military History
Rogachev, Igor	ambassador to China
Selivanov, Gen. Igor V.	adviser to the head of the Medical Department of the North Korean army, 1950–52
Shevelyov, Konstantin	top expert on Comintern archives and CCP
Sidikhmenov, Vasili	interpreter on secret Russian mission to Yenan, 1945; head, interpreters' bureau, Moscow summit, 1957
Sozinov, Gen. Valentin	Chief Soviet adviser to chief of staff, North Korean Army in Korean War, 1950–52
Tikhvinsky, Sergei L.	intelligence officer; special access to archives
Troyanovsky, Oleg	senior foreign policy adviser to Khrushchev and Kosygin; ambassador to China
Zagvozdin, Gen. (KGB) Aleksandr	supervised exhumation of Lin Biao in Mongolia, 1971

SINGAPORE

Lee Khoon Choy	senior China policy adviser to Lee Kuan Yew
Lee Kuan Yew	Prime Minister
Rajaratnam, S.	Foreign Minister

SPAIN

Carrillo, Santiago	head, Communist Party; at Comintern, 1930s–1940s

TANZANIA

Babu, Abdul Rahman　　　　　　Minister of Trade and Commerce,
　　　　　　　　　　　　　　　　　1965 (negotiated Tan-Zam Railway);
　　　　　　　　　　　　　　　　　earlier, Foreign Minister, Zanzibar

THAILAND

Chatichai Choonhavan　　　　　Foreign Minister; later Premier
Mme Pridi　　　　　　　　　　　wife of former Thai Premier;
　　　　　　　　　　　　　　　　　long-term exile in China

UK

Bosshardt, Alfred　　　　　　　Swiss missionary kidnapped on
　　　　　　　　　　　　　　　　　Long March

Condron, Andrew　　　　　　　Korean War POW who went to China
Croft, John　　　　　　　　　　code-breaker on intercepts of
　　　　　　　　　　　　　　　　　Russian broadcasts to foreign
　　　　　　　　　　　　　　　　　Communist Parties, 1940s

Gordievsky, Oleg　　　　　　　Former Soviet intelligence officer
Heath, Edward　　　　　　　　Prime Minister
Morgan, Sir John　　　　　　　British diplomat, Peking, 1970
Needham, Joseph　　　　　　　British embryologist; on germ
　　　　　　　　　　　　　　　　　warfare investigation team, 1952

USA

Bush, George H. W.　　　　　　head, US Liaison Office, Peking
　　　　　　　　　　　　　　　　　1974–75; CIA Director; President

Colby, William　　　　　　　　CIA Director under Nixon and Ford
Colling, John　　　　　　　　　US mission to Yenan ("Dixie" Mission)
Davies, John Paton　　　　　　US State Department; to Yenan
Ford, Gerald　　　　　　　　　President
Haig, Gen. Alexander　　　　　head, advance party for Nixon
　　　　　　　　　　　　　　　　　visit, 1972

Helms, Richard　　　　　　　　CIA Director
Hitch, Herbert　　　　　　　　US mission to Yenan ("Dixie"
　　　　　　　　　　　　　　　　　Mission); on Marshall Mission
Kissinger, Henry　　　　　　　National Security Adviser, 1969–73;
　　　　　　　　　　　　　　　　　Secretary of State, 1973–77
Lilley, James　　　　　　　　　Top CIA China expert; CIA
　　　　　　　　　　　　　　　　　station chief, Peking
Lord, Winston　　　　　　　　Assistant Secretary of State
Odeen, Philip (T)　　　　　　　National Security Council staff
Polevoy, Leonid S. (T)　　　　son of man who tried to teach
　　　　　　　　　　　　　　　　　young Mao Russian
Roderick, John　　　　　　　　AP correspondent, Yenan, 1945–47
Rusk, Dean (T)　　　　　　　　Secretary of State

Schlesinger, James — Secretary of Defense; CIA Director

Scowcroft, Gen. Brent — National Security Adviser

Service, John — State Department; mission to Yenan ("Dixie" Mission)

Solomon, Richard — Assistant Secretary of State

Snow, Helen Foster [Nym Wales] — Yenan, 1937; first wife of Edgar Snow

Snow, Lois Wheeler — second wife of Edgar Snow; to China with Snow, 1970

Stokes, William — Vice-Consul, Shenyang (and Jadwiga)

Williams, Robert (T) — black militant; resident in China, 1960s

Yang Chen Ning (T) — Nobel Prize–winning physicist

VIETNAM

Bui Diem — South Vietnamese ambassador to USA

Bui Tin, Col. — North Vietnamese army, at Dien Bien Phu

Ngo Manh Lan — adviser to Gen. Giap

Nguyen Dinh Uoc, Lt. Gen. — North Vietnamese army, at Dien Bien Phu; director, Institute of Military History, Hanoi

YUGOSLAVIA (FORMER)

Jojic, Prof. Dimitri — former army officer (exile in Albania); worked in Radio Peking, 1960s and 1970s

ZAIRE (NOW CONGO)

Mobutu Sese Seko — President

INFORMAL CONVERSATIONS WITH:

Michelangelo Antonioni, Sir Leonard Appleyard, Algerian President *Abdel Aziz Bouteflika* (via intermediary), Herbert Brownell, William Buckley, Romanian ambassador to China Romulus Budura, Barbara Bush, *Gen. Henry Byroade* (T), Lord (James) Callaghan, Sir Michael Caine, Lord (Peter) Carrington, Henri Cartier-Bresson, Brian Crozier, Helen De Vries, Milovan Djilas, Everett Drumright (T), *Nikolai T. Fedorenko* (T), Russian ambassador Yuri Fokine, *Betty Ford,* J. K. Galbraith, Martha Gellhorn, Sergei Goncharov, Anthony Grey, Marshall Green, Prof. Aleksandr Grigoriev, Penny Gummer, Han Suyin, Hon. Alan Hare, *Ed Hauck* (T), Lord (Michael) Heseltine, John Holdridge, Lord (Douglas) Hurd, Giovanni Jervis, *Ismail Kadare,* R. N. Kao, Lady Clare Keswick, Henry Keswick, *Nancy Kissinger,* Ina Krymova, *Owen Lattimore,* Helmut & Marianne Liebermann (T), North Vietnamese ambassador to France Ho Nam, Mieczyslaw Maneli (T), Prof. Arlen Meliksetov, Sergo Mikoyan (T), Prof. Vladimir

Myasnikov, Albanian Premier Fatos Nano, Gen. Paek Sun-yop, Prof. Moisei Persits, *Phoumi Vongvichit* (via Prof. Grant Evans), Chris Pocock, *János Radványi* (T), Krishna Rasgotra, Norman Reddaway, Claude Roy, Egyptian Premier Aziz Sidky (T), Prof. Nodari Simoniya, Boris Slavinsky, Sir Nicholas Stern, Viktor Suvorov (T), Viktor Usov, Arkady Vaksberg, Bianca Vidali (T), Lord (William) Waldegrave, George Walden, Sir John and Lady Weston.

ARCHIVES CONSULTED

We regret not being able to name archives consulted in Mainland China.

ALBANIA
Arkivi Qëndror i Shtetit i Republikës së Shqipërisë (Central State Archive of the Republic of Albania)

BULGARIA
Tsentralen Durzhaven Arkhiv (Central State Archive)

GERMANY
Stiftung Archiv der Parteien and Massenorganisationen der ehemaligen DDR im Bundesarchiv (Foundation for the Archives of the Parties and Mass Organizations of the Former GDR [East Germany] in the Federal Archives)

ITALY
Franciscan Order, Curia Generale; Istituto Gramsci; Vincentian Order

JAPAN
Japanese Communist Party, Central Committee; Japanese Foreign Ministry, Archives of the Gaiko Shiryokan

RUSSIA
Arkhiv Prezidenta Rossiiskoy Federatsii (Archive of the President of the Russian Federation); Arkhiv Vneshney Politiki Rossiiskoy Federatsii (Archive of Foreign Policy of the Russian Federation); Rossiiskii Gosudarstvennyi Arkhiv Sotsialno-politicheskoi Istorii (Russian State Archive of Socio-political History)

SWITZERLAND
League of Nations Archives, United Nations

TAIWAN
Academia Historica; Archive of the Investigation Bureau; Nationalist Party History Archive

UK

Archive of the Communist Party of Great Britain; National Archives; Oxford University, Bodleian Library

USA

Columbia University, Rare Book and Manuscript Library, New York; Cornell University, Carl A. Kroch Library, Ithaca, NY; Emory University, Robert W. Woodruff Library, Atlanta; Harvard-Yenching Library, Harvard University, Cambridge, Mass.; Hoover Institution Library, Stanford, California; Library of Congress, Manuscript Division, Washington, D.C.; National Archives and Records Administration, Washington, D.C.; Schlesinger Library, Cambridge, Mass.; Syracuse University, George Arents Research Library, Syracuse, NY; University of Washington, Special Collections, Manuscripts and University Archives, Seattle; Lauchlin Currie Papers in the possession of Roger Sandilands.

NOTES

Asterisks indicate written Chinese-language sources, using the *pinyin* spelling system (with a few exceptions). References to English translations are given in brackets, denoted by "E:." Abbreviations used in the Notes are given at the start of the Bibliographies.

CHAPTER 1 *On the Cusp from Ancient to Modern*

Page

3   Found out emperor's death: Snow 1973, p. 138.

4–5   Parents: Snow 1973, pp. 130–4; *Mao Clan Chronicle*; Mao's father-in-law Yang Chang-chi's diary, 5 Apr. 1915, in *Mao 1990, p. 636 (E: *MRTP* vol. 2, p. 60); *Li Xiangwen, pp. 25–51; *Zhao Zhichao, pp. 273–4; visit to Shaoshan and conversations with locals.

4   Name preordained in 18th century: *Mao Clan Chronicle*.

5   "Boy of Stone": *Li Xiangwen, p. 51. Mao about his mother: Snow 1973, p. 132; *Shi Zhe 1992, p. 180; *Yan Changlin, p. 321. Carefree childhood: Mao letter to a cousin, 27 Nov. 1937, in *Mao 1984, pp. 114–15; *Zhao Zhichao, pp. 271–81; *Yan Changlin, pp. 320–1.

5–6   Did well in Confucian classics: *Li Rui 1992, pp. 1–3. Clashes with tutors: Snow 1973, pp. 131ff; *Zhao Zhichao, pp. 103–12, 122–3.

6   "jet-plane" father: Mao to Red Guard leaders, 28 July 1968, in *IIR, p. 546 (E: *Mao Miscellany* vol. 2, p. 496).

6   Rows with father: Snow 1973, pp. 132–3; *Shi Zhe 1992, p. 182.

7   First marriage: *Mao Clan Chronicle*; *Li Xiangwen, p. 66; Snow 1973, p. 147; Cheng 1973, p. 68. "In families in the West": "The Question of Miss Zhao's Personality," 18 Nov. 1919, *Mao 1990, pp. 416–17 (E: *MRTP* vol. 1, p. 423).

8   In modern school: Snow 1973, pp. 136–7; *Zhao Zhichao, pp. 282–4. "exceedingly excited": Snow 1973, p. 139.

8   Claims early concern for peasants: ibid., pp. 135–6, 139.

8–9 No trace of Millstone Maker: interview with local Party historians, 21 Oct. 1994. Yang Chang-chi, 5 Apr. 1915: *Mao 1990, p. 636 (E: *MRTP* vol. 1, p. 60). "bowled over" by Tseng Kuo-fan: letter to Li Jinxi, 23 Aug. 1917, *Mao 1990, p. 85 (E: *MRTP* vol. 1, p. 131). "sea of bitterness": "The Great Union of the Popular Masses," 21 July 1919, *Mao 1990, pp. 373–5 (E: *MRTP* vol. 1, p. 382). 71 items: "Statutes of the Problem Study Society," 1 Sept. 1919, *Mao 1990, p. 397 (E: *MRTP* vol. 1, p. 409). "workers and peasants": "Clearing up the Doubt," 27 Sept. 1920, *Mao 1990, p. 519 (E: *MRTP* vol. 1, pp. 558–9). "proletariat": "Letter to Xiao Xudong [Siao-yu], Cai Linbin [Cai He-sen] and the Other Members in France," 1 Dec. 1920, *XXZ*, pp. 149–50 (E: *MRTP* vol. 2, p. 10). Friend's diary: *Xie Juezai, pp. 49–50.

CHAPTER 2 *Becoming a Communist*

10 Russell: Russell to *The Nation,* 28 Oct. 1920, in id. 1968, p. 139; cf. ibid.: pp. 126–7; our visit to Changsha. Newspaper addiction: Snow 1973, p. 139. First political essay: ibid., p. 140. "be prepared for war": *Mao 1990, p. 647.

11 Dazzling range of choices: Snow 1973, p. 143. like a buffalo: Siao 1953, p. 36. Teacher-training college: visit to the college, Changsha, and conversations with locals, Oct. 1994. Real "Hundred Flowers": *INT.

12 Swimming poem: *Mao 1920–27, p. 303 (E: *MRTP* vol. 1, p. 159). Summer 1917 round countryside: Siao 1953.

12 Mao extreme remarks: Zhang Kundi diary, 23 Sept. 1917, in *Mao 1990, p. 639 (E: *MRTP* vol. 1, p. 139).

13–14 Notes on Paulsen: "Marginal Notes to Friedrich Paulsen, *A System of Ethics,*" 1917–18, *Mao 1990, pp. 116–275 (E: *MRTP* vol. 1, pp. 175–313). "all there only for me": ibid. *pp. 147–8 (p. 205). "no duty to other people": ibid.*p. 235 (p. 277). "responsible to no one": ibid.*pp. 204–5 (pp. 252–3). "not my own reality": ibid. *p. 205 (p. 252). "not . . . for future generations": ibid. *p. 206 (p. 253). Conscience "for better completion of impulse": ibid. *pp. 210–11 (pp. 255–7). Don't kill "out of self-interest": ibid.*p. 120 (p. 179). "purely calculation for oneself": ibid. *p. 219 (p. 263). "Great Heroes": ibid. *pp. 218–19 (pp. 263–4). "Long-lasting peace . . . unendurable": ibid. *pp. 184–6 (pp. 237–8). Death "fantastic": ibid. *pp. 197–8 (p. 247). "How do we change" China: ibid. *pp. 201–2 (p. 250).

15 Yang Chang-chi wrote: "Journal," 5 Apr. 1915, in *Mao 1990, p. 636 (E: *MRTP* vol. 1, p. 60). Another teacher: Xu Teli, in Band & Band, p. 250. Not elected leader: New People's Study Society Report, no. 1, winter 1920, in *XXZ*, p. 4.

15–16 "my mind is filled": Letter to Tao Yi [Tao Siyong], *Mao 1990, p. 467 (E: *MRTP* vol. 1, p. 494). Cannot learn Russian: Leonid Polevoy (son of Sergei) telephone interview, 24 May 1998, and letter to authors; S. Polevoy role: *VKP* vol.1, pp. 28, 48, 744. Life in Peking: New People's Study Society Report, no. 1, winter 1920, in *XXZ*, p. 6; Snow 1973, pp. 151ff; *Luo Zhanglong, pp. 8–9. "did not treat me like a human": Snow 1973, p. 151.

16   Unkempt: *INT; Cadart & Cheng, p. 159.

17   "we must now doubt": "Manifesto on the Founding of the *Xiang River Review*," 14 July 1919, *Mao 1990, p. 292 (E: *MRTP* vol. 1, p. 318). Mao and mother: "Letter to Seventh and Eighth Maternal Uncles," Aug. 1918, *Mao 1990, p. 288 (E: *MRTP* vol. 1, p. 174). "When my mother was dying": Wu Xujun, in *Remembering Mao Zedong* vol. 2, p. 663.

18   Father longing to see Mao: visit to the Mao clan temple, Shaoshan. "On Women's Independence": 21 Nov. 1919, *Mao 1990, pp. 422–3 (E: "Concerning the Incident of Miss Zhao's Suicide," *MRTP* vol. 1, pp. 432–3). "participate in production": Kau & Leung, p. 175. Second trip to Peking: Snow 1973, pp. 153ff; relationship with Hu, *Mao 1990, p. 494; with Li, ibid., p. 467; *Zhou Zuoren, p. 115. Mao on Chen: "The Arrest and Rescue of Chen Duxiu [Chen Tu-hsiu]," 14 July 1919, *Mao 1990, pp. 302–6 (E: *MRTP* vol. 1, p. 329).

18–19   Idea of CCP from Moscow: Shevelyov 1981, p. 128; *YD, pp. 22–3; *Chen Duxiu, p. 119. Voitinsky in China: Shevelyov 1981, pp. 128, 130; Glunin in Astafiev et al. 1970, pp. 66–87; *VKP* vol. 1, pp. 28, 38, 48. Party founded Aug. 1920: Maring to Zinoviev et al., 20 June 1923, in Saich 1991, p. 611; Yu-Ang-Li, p. 422. *New Youth* subsidized by Comintern: Shevelyov 1981, p. 131.

19–20   Bookshop: Mao, "The Founding of the Cultural Book Society," 31 July 1920, *Mao 1990, pp. 498–500 (E: *MRTP* vol. 1, pp. 534–5); bookshop business report, Nov. 1920, in *XXZ, pp. 255–9 (E: *MRTP* vol. 1, pp. 584–5); *Mao 1993b, vol. 1, p. 61. "special liaison man": *XXZ, pp. 530–1. Counted as "one of us": Zhang Wenliang diary, 17 Nov. 1920, *Mao 1990, pp. 703–4 (E: Li Rui 1977, p. 164).

20   First expression of Communist belief: Letter to Xiao Xudong, Cai Linbin et al., 1 Dec. 1920, *Mao 1920–27, pp. 4–7 (E: *MRTP* vol. 2, pp. 7–8). "Russian-style wrong": ibid., p. 4 (E: *MRTP* vol. 2, p. 7). Mao argument against: ibid., pp. 4–6 (E: *MRTP* vol. 2, pp. 8–10).

CHAPTER 3   *Lukewarm Believer*

All quotes from Kai-hui: *Yang Kai-hui, no. 7 (unless otherwise stated).

22   Kai-hui home: visit to Bancang; interview with one of Mao's group, Luo Zhanglong, 6 Oct. 1993; Snow 1973, pp. 91, 152, 153. Recommendation for Mao: *Zhang Suhua et al., p. 290.

23   Mao "Resisting Marriage": Letter to Luo Xuezan, 26 Nov. 1920, *Mao 1990, p. 567 (E: *MRTP* vol. 1, p. 609).

23   Relationship with Kai-hui: interviews with their old friends, Yi Li-rong, 20 Sept. 1993, 1 & 8 Oct. 1995, and Luo Zhang-long, 6 Oct. 1993.

23   Mao poem: interviews with Yi, 20 Sept. 1993, 1 & 8 Oct. 1995; *Bai Yang, p. 60. Mao changes rule: *INT; visit to site, Changsha. Girlfriend Si-yung: *INT ;*Mao 1990, p. 566; *XXZ, pp. 26, 28, 35, 40.

25   Kai-hui feminist writing: *Yang Kai-hui, no. 4. Russian subversion operations: documents in *VKP* vol. 1, and Malyisheva & Poznansky; cf. Usov 2002; Persits 1996, pp. 122ff; Persits 1997, pp. 79ff; Isaacs, p. 102; biographies in Kolpakidi & Prokhorov 2000b, pp. 278–440 (cf. ids., 2000a, pp. 178–83); ids., 2001, pp. 94ff; Lurye & Kochik, pp. 98–534. Nikolsky and Maring: Maring, 11 July 1922 in Saich 1991, pp. 307, 310. Biographical data on Nikolsky: Piatnitsky, p. 457; Usov 2002, pp. 172–3, 348–9n; Kolpakidi & Prokhorov 2001, pp. 305–6; ids., 2000b, p. 385.

25–26   Mao to 1st Congress: *YD, pp. 25, 67, 247; *Xie Juezai, p. 49; visit to site, Shanghai. Length of speeches: *YD, pp. 149, 166, 175, 191, etc. "I confronted him": *YD, p. 351. Check out Bolshevism: Chang Kuo-tao, vol. 1, pp. 137–8. Mao little impact: *YD, pp. 26, 173, 227.

26–27   Meeting on the lake: interview with the woman who rented the boat and kept watch on it, Wang Hui-wu, 29 Mar. 1993; visit to Jiaxing; Chou Fo-hai (participant), in Hsüeh, pp. 428–31. Mao sightseeing: *YD, p. 242; *Mao 1993b, vol. 1, p. 85. Chen against taking Moscow money: *YD, pp. 28, 61, 150, 178, 229, 245–6, 250–1, 321; *Luo Zhanglong, p. 291.

27–28   Moscow funding essential: Chen report to the 3rd Congress, June 1923, Saich 1991, p. 573; Maring to Moscow, 11 July 1922, Saich 1991, p. 310; cf. *Yang Kuisong 1992, pp. 24–5. Russian funds to Mao: Yi Li-rong, in *YD, p. 112; interview with Yi, 17 Mar. 1996. "My life is really too hard": to Luo Xuezan, 26 Nov. 1920, *Mao 1990, pp. 562, 565 (E: *MRTP* vol. 1, pp. 605, 607). "baking bread": in "Report on the Affairs of the New People's Study Society," no. 2, summer 1921, *XXZ, p. 39 (E: *MRTP* vol. 2, pp. 84–5). "Wow, what fun": 28 Sept. 1921, in *Mao 1993b, vol. 1, p. 87.

28   Set up house with Kai-hui: visit to Clear Water Pond, Changsha; interviews with Yi Li-rong, 30 Sept. 1993, 1 & 8 Oct. 1995; *INT.

28   Off on holiday: Mao to Ouyang Ze, 25 Nov. 1920, *Mao 1990, p. 551; *Mao 1993b, vol. 1, pp. 70–1; interview with Yi, 5 Nov. 1995. "research education": *Mao 1990, p. 703. Recruiting friends and family: Yi Li-rong in *YD, pp. 111–12; interview with Yi, 8 Oct. 1995; *ZR vol. 14, p. 250; *Shu Long, pp. 284–5; *INT.

29–30   Ho Min-fan: Cadart & Sheng, pp. 151–62; *Jin & Huang, pp. 24–5; Liu letter, 11 Feb. 1968, in ibid., p. 41. Had been courteous: Siao-yu, pp. 38–9. Just Mao giving orders: interview with Yi Li-rong, 1 & 8 Oct. 1995; Yi in *YD, p. 112. "Only scholars suffer": Letter to Luo Xuezan, 26 Nov. 1920, *Mao 1990, p. 565 (E: *MRTP* vol. 1, p. 607).

30   Mao first trip to Anyuan: Liu Shaoqi & Zhu Shaolian article about the history of labor movement in Anyuan, 10 Aug. 1923, in *CCP Pingxiang Committee, p. 117. Mao at "his wits' end": Maring letter, 20 June 1923 to Zinoviev et al., in Saich 1991, pp. 608–9, 617; van de Ven 1991, p. 123 for explanation of original. Mao no threat: Schram interview with Governor Chao (Schram note to Li Rui 1977, p. 266); Schram e-mail to authors, 21 Dec. 2000. Mao not at 2nd Congress: Snow 1973, p. 158; Titov, vol. 1, p. 82; Nikiforov, p. 123. Spurred to act: *Mao 1993b, vol. 1, pp. 93–107.

31   Hunan Committee set up: ibid., p. 95. How Committee worked: Liu letter, 11 Feb. 1968, in *Huang Zheng, p. 86. Sun and Outer Mongolia: Elleman, pp. 58ff, 63–4; Roshchin, pp. 102–7.

31–32 "an army with arms": *VKP* vol. 1, pp. 126–9 (Sun to Gekker, 26 Sept. 1922). Xinjiang: Joffe cable to Chicherin, 7–8 Nov. 1922, in *VKP* vol. 1, p. 139. Suggests invasion of Sichuan: Report by Sokolov-Strakhov, 21 Apr. 1921, in *VKP* vol. 1, p. 60; Kriukov, p. 57. "Give full backing": 4 Jan. 1923, in *VKP* vol. 1, p. 170. Joffe told Lenin: 26 Jan. 1923, in *VKP* vol. 1, pp. 194, 198. Stalin spelled out: Stalin 2001a, p. 157; the authentic text of this speech was suppressed until 2001 (Stalin 2001b, p. 79, n. 23 re Stalin editing). CCP views on Sun: Chen Report to 3rd Congress in Saich 1991, p. 574; minutes of ECCI meeting, 6 Jan. 1923, in *VKP* vol. 1, pp. 172–5; Chen letter to Voitinsky in Saich 1991, p. 257; CCP CC letter to Borodin (not later than 10 Oct. 1924), *VKP* vol. 1, pp. 483–5.

32–33 Mao "[only] supporter": Titov, vol. 1, p. 93 (Cai to ECCI, 10 Feb. 1926). Mao relying on Russian invasion: Maring report June 1923, Saich 1991, p. 590; Maring letter to Zinoviev et al., 20 June 1923 in Saich 1991, p. 616; Titov, vol. 1, pp. 90, 92, 93. Vilde as bagman: Usov 2002, p. 176. Vilde singles out Mao: Vilde to Voitinsky, 26 July 1923 in *VKP* vol. 1, p. 238; Mao wrote to Moscow: 2 July 1923, *Mao 1993c, p. 27; signature in *ZZWX vol. 1, p. 284.

33–34 Mao seldom attending CCP meetings: *Mao 1993b, vol. 1, pp. 118, 121–6; interview with Zheng Chao-lin, a Communist in whose house most meetings took place, 16 Apr. 1996. "our organisation lost": Titov, vol. 1, p. 93 (Cai He-sen to ECCI, 10 Feb. 1926). "Mao at that time": Deng Zhong-xia, cited in Titov, vol. 1, p. 92.

34   Dalin to Voitinsky: Dalin 1975, p. 149; cf. Dalin 1982, p. 182. Mao criticized, off Central Committee: cf. 4th Congress documents, *ZZWX vol. 1, pp. 328, 335–6; cf. Sladkovsky, p. 459. Health downturn: interview with Luo Zhang-long, 6 Oct. 1993; *YD, p. 173. "convalescing": *Li Weihan, p. 62.

CHAPTER 4 *Rise and Demise in the Nationalist Party*

35   Mao in Shaoshan: *INT. Wang Ching-wei got on well with Mao: records of meetings of the Nationalist Shanghai Executive Committee, 25 Feb. 1925ff. (at which Mao often served as note-taker), Nationalist Party History Archive, Taipei; interview with Zheng Chao-lin, 16 Apr. 1996.

35–36 Brothers to Canton: *Li Xiangwen, pp. 162, 201. Active from June: *HNYZ, p. 388; *Shaoshan Chronicle Committee, p. 409; *INT; *Mao 1993b, vol. 1, pp. 133–5. Co-worker recorded in diary: He Erkang, in *HNYZ, pp. 389–94. To Borodin, 18 Jan. 1924: *VKP* vol. 1, pp. 425–6.

36–37 Wang Hsien-tsung: *HNYZ, pp. 388, 395–8. Mao suspected of stirring things up: ibid., p. 388. President of Yale-in-China: NARA, RG 84.800. Changsha, 1925, vol. 26, no. 1240. Mao decamp: *HNYZ, p. 388; *Mao 1993b, vol. 1, pp. 135–6.

37–38   Poem by Xiang River: *MRTP* vol. 2, pp. 225–6. Clutch of key jobs: *Mao 1993b, vol. 1, pp. 137–40; *Mao 1920–27, pp. 249–50; cf. Mao writings between 20 Oct. 1925 and 19 May 1926, in *Mao 1920–27 (E: *MRTP* vol. 2, pp. 227–385). Discovery of sleeping pills: MacFarquhar et al., 1989, p. 167 (27 Feb. 1957); cf. Mao, 22 Mar. 1958 in Schram 1974, pp. 118, 119 (compared to Marx). Nov. 1925 form: 21 Nov. 1925, *Mao 1993b, vol. 1, p. 141 (E: *MRTP* vol. 2, p. 238). Articles about peasantry: "Analysis of All the Classes in Chinese Society," *MRTP* vol. 2, pp. 249ff., in journal *Revolution*, 1 Dec. 1925, *Mao 1920–27, pp. 219–31; "An Analysis of Classes in Chinese Peasants and Their Attitudes towards the Revolution," *Chinese Peasants*, 1 Jan. 1926, in *Mao 1993b, vol. 1, pp. 149–50 (E: *MRTP* vol. 2, pp. 303–9).

38   Moscow order on peasantry, Oct. 1925: *VKP* vol. 1, pp. 633–6 (Vasiliev to Voitinsky, 2 Oct. 1925). CCP first issued "Letter to Peasants," 10 Oct. 1925, in *ZZWX vol. 1, pp. 509–17; CCP told Hunan to start peasant movement also in that October, ibid., p. 500; Nationalist Hunan Committee report of Aug. 1926 (delivered by Yi Li-rong) says Hunan peasant movement started in Nov. 1925, *HNYZ, p. 201, Nationalist Party Central Committee report of 1926 says the same, ibid., p. 28. Back in May 1923: Comintern instruction to CCP 3rd Congress, May 1923, in *ZZWX vol. 1, p. 586; Eudin & North, p. 344. Mao's view in 1924: Dalin 1985, p. 182; id., 1975, p. 149 (letter to Voitinsky, 30 Mar. 1924). Russian criticizes Mao: "V-n" (S. N. Belenkii), *Kanton*, nos. 8–9 (1926), pp. 149–61; reprinted, with introduction by L. P. Delyusin, pp. 128–9, in *Voprosi Filosofii*, no. 6, 1969, pp. 130–6; AVPRF, 0100/11/141/81, p. 146. Wang Ching-wei appointed Mao: *GNYJ, p. 25; *Mao 1993b, vol. 1, pp. 133–6.

39   Russians in Changsha: Mitarevsky, p. 79 (figure corrected); cf. Leonard 1999, pp. 63, 67, 81, n. 53; NA, FO 405/256, pp. 271ff. W(alsworth) Tyng to his mother, Dec. 1926 (Mary Tyng Higgins Papers, Carton 1, Folder 6, Schlesinger Library). Peasant movement develops under Nationalists: Mao, "Report on the Peasant Movement in Hunan," Mar. 1927, *Mao 1920–27, p. 419 (E: *MRTP* vol. 2, pp. 429–64); *HNYZ, pp. 793ff.

39–40   Mao speech 20 Dec. 1926: *HNYZ, pp. 445–7 (E: *MRTP* vol. 2, p. 422). Freyer says Mao moderate: RGASPI, 495/154/294, p. 3 (Freyer, report to Far Eastern Bureau, 18 Jan. 1927). "completely change my attitude": 7 Aug. 1927, *ZDJC vol. 14, p. 5 (E: *MRTP* vol. 3, p. 30).

40–41   Quotes from Mao's Hunan Report: "Report on the Peasant Movement in Hunan," *Mao 1920–27, pp. 418–55: "terrifying in their hands": ibid., *pp. 424–5 (E: *MRTP* vol. 2, p. 44). "terror in the countryside": ibid., *pp. 422–3 (E: pp. 433–5). "forever broken" and not "a moment's peace": ibid., *pp. 436–7 (E: p. 446). sharp, twin-edged knife: ibid., *p. 441 (E: p. 450). "kind of ecstasy," "wonderful": ibid., *p. 422 (E: p. 432).

41   "one or two beaten to death": *INT. Admonishes attempts to lower violence: CCP Hunan Committee report, Jan. 1927, in *HNYZ, p. 456; *Mao 1920–27, p. 424 (E: *MRTP* vol. 2, pp. 434–5). Proposals about land redistribution: e.g. Chen Tu-hsiu's, in *HNYZ, pp. 710–11. Mao's view: *Mao 1993b, vol. 1, p. 193; cf. Schram 1966, p. 99. Published in

Comintern journal: 15 June 1927; cf. Glunin 1975, p. 301, n. 2; *Mao 1993b, vol. 1, p. 185.

42 One text Mao selected: *HNYZ, pp. 333–5. Chen report: 15 June 1927, *ZDJC vol. 13, p. 583.

43 Peking raid documents: NA, FO 405/256, FO 371/12500; Mitarevsky; Wilbur & How, pp. 442–835; Oudendyk, pp. 348ff. Mao on wanted list: *Chang Yu-fa, p. 351; *Chiang, p. 167. Chiang regarded as left-wing: VKP vol. 1, p. 261 (memo re Nationalist delegation, not later than 10 Sept. 1923); on 13 Dec. 1925 Mao placed Chiang alongside Wang Ching-wei (MRTP vol. 2, p. 291). Borodin impression: VKP vol. 1, p. 347 (talk with Chu Chiu-pai, 16 Dec. 1923).

44 "liquidation of Chiang": VKP vol. 2, p. 153 (Solovyov to Karakhan, 24 Mar. 1926); cf. Glunin 1975, pp. 61–3; Trampedach, pp. 128ff. Secret order to arrest Chiang: Smith, p. 156; *Zhang Guotao, vol. 2, pp. 192–5 (E: id., vol.1, p. 582). Chiang notice: *Chiang, p. 153. Chiang broke Communists in Shanghai: description based on documents in *ZDJC vol. 13, pp. 463–522; *Shanghai Archive. More than 300 deaths: various contemporary figures, in *CCP Shanghai Committee, pp. 358–9; Smith, p. 204.

44–45 "I felt desolate": *Mao 1993b, vol. 1, p. 198. "with the mighty waves": ibid., p. 198 (E: MRTP vol. 2, p. 484). "Only after Comrade Mao": Appendix 10, in a written testimony by Li Weihan, in *DYZ, 1982, no. 4, pp. 377–8.

CHAPTER 5 *Hijacking a Red Force and Taking Over Bandit Land*

49 Stalin: military option for CCP: cable to Borodin, 30 May 1927 (signed "Instantsiya" (Stalin), VKP vol. 2, p. 764; this option envisaged since 1919–20: Vilensky report, 1 Sept. 1920, VKP vol. 1, p. 37; cf. Malyisheva & Poznansky. Records of the Soviet Consulate in Changsha show it checking separate Red military units in 1926, AVPRF, 0100/10/129/78, pp. 5–6, 28–30, 43, 47 (report covering period 13 Mar. to 28 Dec. 1926). Khmelyev ("Appen") report, 6 May 1927, VKP vol. 2, pp. 715–17; Piatnitsky, p. 219 (Berzin plan). Lominadze, Berzin: Grigoriev 1976, p. 15; Leonard 1999, pp. 170–1; Mirovitskaya 1993, p. 308. GRU operations: Vinarov (deputy GRU head, China, 1926–29), pp. 294, 323–9, 342–3, 369, 373–7; Mirovitskaya 1975, pp. 61–2.

49–50 Peasant uprisings ordered: minutes of 7 Aug. 1927 emergency meeting under Lominadze, *ZDJC vol. 14, p. 10; cf. Saich 1996, pp. 296ff; Mao, 20 Aug. 1927, in *Central Archive 1982a, p. 16; *Mao 1993b, vol. 1, pp. 211–12. "barrel of the gun": *ZDJC vol. 14, p. 5 (E: MRTP vol. 3, p. 31).

50–51 Kumanin ("Zigon"): his report in RGASPI, 514/1/254, pp. 70–100; GRU post mortem, 14 Sept. 1927, VKP vol. 3, pp. 84–110; Freyer report on Nanchang, 25 Aug. 1927, RGASPI, 495/154/247; Mirovitskaya 1975, pp. 37–41. Mao proposes uprising in S. Hunan: *Mao 1993b, vol. 1, p. 207. Shanghai approves: 8 Aug. 1927, *Central Archive 1982a, p. 10. Meetings at Russian consulate: location, *INT, and Luo Zhanglong's unpublished memoirs on the "Autumn Harvest Uprising"; meetings described in Hunan Party secretary Peng Gongda's report, 8 Oct. 1927, *Central Archive 1982a, p. III (E: Saich 1996, pp. 322–31). Mao on outskirts: *Mao 1993b, vol. I, pp. 209–10. Moved into consulate: *INT. Excuse: Mao report, 20 Aug. 1927, *Central Archive 1982a, p. 17; *Mao 1993b, vol. I, pp. 209–10.

50 Stalin to Comintern, 27 Sept. 1927, *VKP* vol. 3, p. 129 (falsified published text: ibid., p. 130); cf. ibid., p. 61. Mikoyan: *VKP* vol. 3, pp. 72, 74, 76–7 (Soviet Politburo minutes).

51–52 Mao demanded uprising in S. Hunan be canceled: Peng Gongda report, 8 Oct. 1927, *Central Archive 1982a, p. 117 (E: Saich 1996, pp. 90n, 327, 504). "three hundred times": *Central Archive 1982a, p. 16.

52 Mao not with troops, but stayed in Wenjiashi: He Changgong, who was very close to Mao at this time, was categorical about this point in an interview on 22 Mar. 1977 with Party historians for the record, in *CCP Ninggang Committee, pp. 26–7; cf. other memoirs, *JGG vol. 2, pp. 129, 140, 153, 171; *Chen Shiju, pp. 10–11; cf. Lo Jung-huan, p. 10.

52–53 Action aborted: *Central Archive 1982a, pp. 43–4, 53, 133. "most despicable": Maier report, 16 Sept. 1927 in Pak, p. 173. "joke of an uprising": resolution of emergency meeting on Hunan, late Oct. 1927 in *Central Archive 1982a, p. 139. Link with outlaw: *CCP Ninggang Committee, p. 81; interview with a local Party historian, 4 Apr. 1996. Wenjiashi meeting: He Changgong, one of the men Mao sought out, *CCP Ninggang Committee, pp. 20–2.

52n Lo Jung-huan, p. 10.

53 Mao and troops: *JGG vol. 2, pp. 176–7; *Chen Shiju, pp.13–23; *CCP Ninggang Committee, pp. 28–31; *Central Archive 1982a, pp. 133, 161. "single spark": Mao letter to Lin Biao, 5 Jan. 1930, *MRTP* vol. 3, p. 237.

53–54 Deal with outlaws: *JGG vol. 2, pp. 90–1. Finale of takeover, eyewitness description: ibid., pp. 93–4. Rally Chinese New Year 1928: *JGG vol. 2, pp. 278–9.

54–55 Contact with Party HQ established: *He Changgong, pp. 109–14. Mao expelled from posts: "Political and Disciplinary Resolution," 14 Nov. 1927, *ZZWX vol. 3, pp. 483–4; *Li Weihan, pp. 182, 196–9. Shanghai order, 31 Dec. 1927: *JGG vol. I, pp. 64–5. Hunan committee arrested: *CCP Hunan Committee, pp. 375–6.

55–56 Bandit country: visit to Jinggang Mountains, and conversations with locals. Mao told troops: *JGG vol. 2, p. 458. One Red soldier recalled: ibid., p. 156.

56 Another described: ibid., p. 489.

56 Mao almost lost army: ibid., pp. 56–8, 168–9, 293. Security measures: ibid., p. 462; interview with a local Party historian, 4 Apr. 1996, and visits to Mao's houses. Long March houses: interview with a Party historian who had visited all the dwellings, 31 Aug. 1997.

57 Mao houses: visits and interviews with local historians.

57 Sizeable staff: *JGG vol. 2, pp. 461–2, 550.

58–59 Gui-yuan: *Wang Xingjuan 1987, pp. 1–47; interviews with a local Party historian, and with Yuan's relatives, Apr. 1996.

58–59 Marriage to Mao: ibid. interviews; visit to the site of the wedding banquet. Mao "too old": interview with close friend Zeng Zhi, 24 Sept. 1994. Gui-yuan chose Mao because: interview with her confidante, 14 Sept. 1997. Avoided appearing together: interview with veteran Xiao Ke, 30 Sept. 1993; *Wang Xingjuan 1987, p. 104. Tried to leave Mao: interview with Zeng Zhi; cf. *Wang Xingjuan 1987, pp. 105–6.

59–60 Policy: "kill every single": "Report about the South Hunan Uprising," June 1928, *ZDJC vol. 14, p. 206; interview with Zeng Zhi; *Kuo Hua-lun, vol. 1, p. 290 (E: Kuo, W., vol. 1, p. 383). Razing towns to ground, rebellions against Reds: *ZDJC vol. 14, p. 206; *Huang Kecheng, pp. 36–7; *Zeng Zhi, pp. 52–8; Le Missioni Francescane vol. 6 (1928), p. 150 (letter of Fr. Prandi, eyewitness at Leiyang). "use Red terror": *ZDJC vol. 14, p. 206. "I had suppressed": *JGG vol. 2, p. 454.

60 Mamaev report, 15 Apr. 1930, VKP vol. 3, p. 846.

60 Chrysanthemum Sister: *Li Xiangwen, pp. 239–40; photograph of two pages of her will, in *Yang Liuqing. 10,60–61 butchered: Kuo, W., vol. 1, p. 384; *Kuo Hua-lun, vol. 1, p. 290.

60–61 *GS vol. 4, pp. 793, 772, 761 (in order of quotes); *Zhong Yimou, p. 92; Maestrini, p. 146.

61 Moscow stops "aimless and disorderly pogrom": Titov, vol. 1, p. 198; *ZZWX vol. 4, p. 174; *JGG vol. 1, p. 105. Mao letter, 2 May 1928: in *Jiangxi Archive, pp. 29–30.

61–62 "over 1,000": Shanghai inspector, 15 June 1928, in *JGG vol. 1, p. 130. Began land redistribution: ibid., pp. 130–1. Mao letter reaches Stalin: VKP vol. 3, n. 1, p. 413. "bandit character": 6th Congress, Stenograficheskii otchet, Book 5, pp. 12–13. Mao as key leader: ibid. (Chou's Military Report) and Book 3, p. 70 (Chu Chiu-pai); Titov, vol. 1, pp. 153, 145. Establish Red Army: Chou notes of meeting with Stalin, VKP vol. 3, pp. 426–31. Military training, plans: Mirovitskaya 1975, pp. 57ff; ibid. 1993, pp. 313–15; Krivitsky, pp. 127–36 (counterfeiting).

62 Stalin to Yugoslavs: Dimitrov, 10 Feb. 1948. Demands met in full: Shanghai letter to Mao and Zhu, *ZZWX vol. 4, pp. 256–7; *Mao 1993b, vol. 1, pp. 256–7.

CHAPTER 6 Subjugating the Red Army Supremo

63–64 "collapsing by the day": 25 Feb. 1929, in *JGG vol. 1, p. 249. Hundreds killed: *JGG vol. 2, p. 99–101, 564–5; visit to site. Stay-behind committee report: *JGG vol. 1, p. 309. "Alliance with bandits": *ZZWX vol. 4, p. 399; 14 Jan. 1929 report from Special Party Committee to Hunan Provincial Committee, describing plan to "annihilate" Yuan's followers (RGASPI, 495/25/668, p. 30). Red search unit report: *JGG vol. 2, p. 643.

64   Mao cheerful: Zeng Zhi, in *"Mao and I" Collection Committee 1993a, p. 81. Moscow aid for Mao: *VKP* vol. 3, p. 518 (Comintern meeting minutes, 29 Jan. 1929). Zhu De's wife: Smedley 1956, pp. 223–4; *JGG* vol. 2, pp. 520, 552; *HDT, 1984, no. 1, p. 22. Mao abolishes Zhu post: Mao later report, 1 June 1929, *ZDJC vol. 14, p. 222 (E: *MRTP* vol. 3, p. 171). Curry favor with Shanghai: Mao, 20 Mar. & 5 Apr. 1929, *JGG vol. 1, pp. 289, 292, 302 (E: *MRTP* vol. 3, pp. 148, 161).

65   "suddenly turned back": Mao, 20 Mar. 1929, *JGG vol. 1, p. 291 (E: *MRTP* vol. 3, p. 150). "supply is no problem": Mao, 5 Apr. 1929, *JGG vol. 1, p. 301 (E: *MRTP* vol. 3, p. 159). Fascist shirt: *Le Missioni Francescane* vol. 6 (1928), p. 151. Mao in Tingzhou: Mao, 20 Mar. 1929, *JGG vol. 1, p. 289 (E: *MRTP* vol. 3, p. 147); *CCP Changting Committee, pp. 43–4; interview with a local Party historian, 9 Apr. 1996. An-gong charged Mao: *DDWX, 1989, no. 5, pp. 37–8; 1994, no. 4, p. 87; *Jin Chongji et al. 1993, p. 178.

66   Mao 1 June 1929 report: *ZDJC vol. 14, pp. 221–4 (E: *MRTP* vol. 3, pp. 171–4). Mao unpopular: Chin I-sun (Chen Yi), "Report . . . on the Question of the Red Army [and] Zhu De and Mao Tse-tung," 9 Jan. 1930, RGASPI, 514/1/1009, p. 5; cf. *VKP* vol. 3, p. 1263. *DDWX, 1989, no. 5, pp. 38–9. Criticisms of Zhu: *Xin Ziling 1995, vol. 1, p. 385. Mao voted out: *Xiao Ke 1993, 101; *DDWX, 1994, no. 4, p. 88; Zeng Zhi, in *"Mao and I" Collection Committee 1993a, p. 85. "work with locals": Mao letter, 14 June 1929, *Mao 1993–9, vol. 1, p. 75 (E: *MRTP* vol. 3, p. 188).

66–67   "rather crestfallen": Jiang Hua, in *DDWX, 1989, no. 5, p. 41. Mao got crony to call congress: *Deng Zihui Biography Committee, p. 88. Mao not ill: Jiang Hua, *DDWX, 1989, no. 5, p. 41. Jiaoyang congress: description and quotes from the report, "About the First Congress of the CCP West Fujian," July 1929, in *Jiangxi Archive & CCP Jiangxi Committee, vol. 2, pp. 102–5.

67–68   Lin Biao: *Xiao Ke 1993, pp. 19, 28; *Xin Ziling 2002, p. 56. Mao befriended Lin: Titov, vol. 1, pp. 189–91; *Xin Ziling 2002, pp. 42–4. Lin disobeyed Zhu: *Jin Chongji et al. 1993, p. 180; interview with Xiao Ke, 30 Sept. 1993; cf. *Xiao Ke 1993, p. 26.

68   European agents: Grigoriev 2002a, pp. 156–7; Adibekov et al., p. 134, n. 89 (Stalin order to use non-Russians, 23 Apr. 1928); Russian archive details on scores of agents in China in Kolpakidi & Prokhorov 2000a, 2000b, 2001; Lurye & Kochik; *Yang Kuisong 1997, pp. 255–70; Cai He-sen, in *Central Archive 1982b, p. 135.

69–70   "What beautiful girls": *Han Suyin, pp. 66–7 (E: Han Suyin 1994, p. 59). Girlfriend: *Jin Chongji et al. 1990, p. 78. "I chose your aunt": ibid. Chou to create Chinese Red Army: *Zhou 1991, pp. 68, 114, 125; Mirovitskaya 1993; Grigoriev 2002b, p. 312. "Charge!": Nie, pp. 59–60. Genius at clandestine work: Wang Fan-xi interview, 20 June 1995.

70   Set up Chinese KGB: Krymov, pp. 344–64; Usov 2002, pp. 194–206; *Zhou 1991, p. 115. Chou self-criticism: 3 Jan. 1931, in *ZZWX vol. 6, p. 359. "smack him on the bottom": Conclusion by the Comintern representative at the 4th Plenum, 1931, *ZZWX vol. 7, p. 39. "Once he

started talking": *Wang Fanxi, pp. 136–7. Talk for 8 hours: once in Tingzhou, interview with a Tingzhou museum curator, 9 Apr. 1996. Chou letter, 21 Aug. 1929: *DDWX, 1991, no. 2, pp. 39–42.

71n   Cited in Lih et al., p. 118 n. 5.

71   Stalin prepared to invade Manchuria: VKP vol. 3, p. 583 (Politburo, 6 Aug. 1929); Lih et al., p. 182 (Stalin to Molotov, 7 Oct. 1929); Kolpakidi & Prokhorov 2000a, p. 183. "defend the Soviet Union with arms": CCP Politburo to CCP delegation to Comintern repeats this order, 21 Aug. 1929, *ZZWX vol. 5, pp. 412–13. Soviet Politburo named Mao: VKP vol. 3, p. 616 (15 Oct. 1929); cf. ibid., pp. 483–4.

71–72   "tune of roubles": Chen letter to CCP leadership, 28 July 1929, *ZZWX vol. 5, p. 395. Mao in *Pravda*: 28 July 1929, 2 & 6 Dec. 1929; 2 Feb. 1930; "*vozhd*" on 13 Dec. 1935. "I can eat a lot": Zeng Zhi, in *"Mao and I" Collection Committee 1993a, p. 86, and in *Reminiscences of Deng Zihui*, p. 76. Lingering in village: interview with Zeng Zhi, who was with Mao then, 24 Sept. 1994; *"Mao and I" Collection Committee 1993a, pp. 86–7.

72–73   "wrote again and again": *Chen Yi, p. 140. Show of submission: *Mao 1993b, vol. 1, p. 290. "very positive": Chou "letter of instruction," 1 Feb. 1930, *ZDJC vol. 14, p. 238. Deference to Moscow: Mao, 28 Nov. 1929, *Mao 1984, p. 28 (E: MRTP vol. 3, p. 193); Mao to Shanghai, 6 Jan. 1930, *ZDJC vol. 14, pp. 236, 245; *DDWX, 1995, no. 3, p. 89. "plaything": VKP vol. 3, p. 1274 (Bespalov minutes of meeting with Po Ku, 11 Feb. 1931); cf. ibid., p. 1263 (Gailis to Berzin, 12 Feb. 1931).

73   "Deserters would be executed": *ZDJC vol. 14, p. 253.

73–74   Mao announcement to abolish: ibid. Item later disappeared: Gutian Resolutions, *ZZWX vol. 5, pp. 800–34. Gutian Resolutions: ibid. (E: MRTP vol. 3, pp. 195–230, xlvii); cf. Titov vol. 1, pp. 228–32. "Where do I go now?": (MRTP vol. 3, p. 233).

CHAPTER 7   *Takeover Leads to Death of Second Wife*

75   Chou to Moscow: VKP vol. 3, pp. 1047–51 (CCP letter to Stalin et al. re Chou–Stalin meeting 21 July 1930 and funding for CCP); Chou's reports to Comintern, 30 Apr., 4 May, in RGASPI, 495/154/416. *Zhou 1991, p. 180. Li-san ambitious plan: May–June 1930, in *ZDJC vol. 14, pp. 452–9.

75   Mao reluctance at first: Li-san speech, 9 June 1930, *Mao 1993b, pp. 308–9; letter to Mao, 15 June 1930, *ZDJC vol. 14, p. 451. Changed to zeal: Mao order, 22 June 1930, *Mao 1993b, vol. 1, p. 311; Mao to Shanghai, 19 & 24 Aug. 1930, *ZDJC vol. 14, pp. 496–7; cf. Titov, vol. 1, pp. 233–61.

76   Peng childhood and youth: *Peng 1981, pp. 1–5, 15 (E: pp. 19–27); *Wang Yan et al., pp. 8–16.

77   Meeting Mao, defending Jinggang: Peng report to Shanghai, Oct. 1929, *JGG vol. 1, pp. 401–18. Treated as subordinate: Mao to Shanghai, 20 Mar. 1929, *JGG vol. 1, p. 289 (E: MRTP vol. 3, pp. 148–9); Peng

to Shanghai, 4 Apr. 1929, ibid., p. 295. Shanghai made Peng independent of Mao: *ZDJC vol. 14, p. 455; *Peng 1981, pp. 149–51, 157.

77   Party inspector report: 22 July 1930, *Jiangxi Archive & CCP Jiangxi Committee, vol. 1, p. 239. Mao assignment Nanchang: *ZDJC vol. 14, p. 455; *Peng 1981, p. 149. Move towards Peng: *Mao 1993b, vol. 1, pp. 311–13. Alarm bells in the West: Hoyt, pp. 240ff. Elkin, *Palos*: NARA, RG 80 (1926–1940), Box 200, File EF 16/P9-2 (300101–301030); *FRUS* 1930, vol. 2, p. 142; NARA, RG 84, Records of the Bureau of Naval Personnel, Log Book of the USS *Palos*, Jan. 1–Dec. 31, 1930, LL. Log no. 15; cf. Peng, pp. 291, 297. Mao to Shanghai, 19 Aug. 1930: in *ZDJC vol. 14, p. 496 (E: *MRTP* vol. 3, p. 482).

78   Mao took over Peng: *Mao 1993b, vol. 1, pp. 313–14; *He Changgong, p. 283; *Peng 1981, p. 157; Zhu De talk, in *JDZ, no. 7, p. 225. Mao insisted on attacking Changsha: Mao to Yudin, 22 July 1958, *CWB*, nos. 6–7 (1995–1996), p. 159. Peng and Zhu against: *Peng 1981, pp. 157–8 (E: pp. 300–1); *Jin Chongji et al. 1993, p. 212. Mao stoked Shanghai delusions: Mao to Shanghai, 19 & 24 Aug. 1930, *ZDJC vol. 14, pp. 496–7. GRU told Moscow: Gailis, 7 May 1931, *VKP* vol. 3, pp. 1431–2. Resistance from Peng's officers: *Peng 1981, pp. 160–1; *Dai & Luo, p. 91.

78   Proclaimed an All-China . . . defying Shanghai: *Mao 1993b, vol. 1, p. 314; *Fang Xiao, p. 351; *Liou Di, letter to Shanghai, 11 Jan. 1931, RGASPI, 514/1/1008.

79   Politburo membership restored: *Jin Chongji et al. 1990, p. 221. Li-san condemned: *VKP* vol. 3, pp. 1018–19 (Soviet Politburo minutes, 25 Aug. 1930), 1031–2 (Comintern letter to Chou and Chu Chiu-pai, 16 Sept. 1930); Titov, vol. 1, pp. 249–61, 371; *Tang Chunliang 1999, pp. 175ff; *ZDJC vol. 14, pp. 581–5.

79   Interview with the man's daughter, 1–2 Aug. 1995; Moscow "Report on the Activities of Li [Lisan]," sent 30 Apr. 1945, NA, HW 17/66 (ISCOT 1358).

80   Kai-hui no Communist activities: clear from her writings; visit to her home and interview with a local Party historian, 1 Apr. 1996; interview with Yi Li-rong, 30 Sept. 1993.

80   Kai-hui arrest and execution: records of interrogations of executioners in the 1960s, unpublished; contemporary newspaper reports; interview with a local Party historian, 1 Apr. 1996.

80–81 Mao on Kai-hui: *Li Xiangwen, pp. 86–8; all Mao's relatives and staff we interviewed testify that Mao talked fondly about her. Writings discovered: visit to her home village, Bancang, and interview with local Party historians, Apr. 1996. "First Cousin" to Mao: This is Yang Kai-ming, see his report to Shanghai, 25 Feb. 1929, *JGG vol. 1, p. 269; visit to Bancang.

81   "Thoughts": *Yang Kai-hui, no. 1, in *HDT, 1984, no. 1, p. 21.

82   To First Cousin: *Yang Kai-hui, no. 2, unpublished.

82   "Feeling of Sadness on Reading about the Enjoyment of a Human Head": *Yang Kai-hui, no. 3, in *HDT, 1984, no. 1, pp. 21–2.

83   Abolition of death penalty: *ZZWX* vol. 1, p. 142. Mao killings in papers: a selection in *JGG* vol. 1, pp. 446–67. Eight agonized lines: *Yang Kai-hui, no. 5, unpublished. Party ordered Mao to Shanghai: *JGG* vol. 1, p. 241.

83   "Father Young's Own Story" (typescript, 1929); id., 1929, pp. 890–8; "Mandate Against Rev. Edward Young," signed by Zhu De, "Soviet Delegate of Mao [Tse] Tung," Vincentian Archive, Rome.

83   "If the financial situation allows": *Yang Kai-hui, no. 6, unpublished. Story of her life: *Yang Kai-hui, no. 7, unpublished.

85   Her last piece: *Yang Kai-hui, no. 8, unpublished.

86   First Cousin death: visit to Bancang, and interview with local Party historians, Apr. 1996.

CHAPTER 8   *Bloody Purge Paves the Way for "Chairman Mao"*

87   Lee Wen-lin: *Jishui County Chronicle* Committee, p. 576; *Xiao Ke 1993, p. 133. Mao declared himself boss: Mao, 20 Mar. 1929, in *JGG* vol. 1, p. 289; 1 June 1929, *ZDJC* vol. 14, p. 222. Tse-tan: *ZR vol. 3, p. 307; inspector, 22 July 1930, in *Jiangxi Archive & CCP Jiangxi Committee, vol. 1, p. 254; *JDZ, no. 7, p. 105.

87   Lieu Shi-qi: *Yongxin County Chronicle* Committee, p. 804; Lieu, 28 Feb. & 7 Oct. 1930, in *ZDJC* vol. 14, pp. 271–3, 280–3; cf. Titov, vol. 1, pp. 232, 269; interview with a local Party historian, 5 Apr. 1996.

88   Mao juggled timetable: Lieu, 7 Oct. 1930, *ZDJC* vol. 14, p. 283; *Mao 1993b, vol. 1, pp. 297–8; other reports, *ZDJC* vol. 14, pp. 244, 350; *Jiangxi Archive & CCP Jiangxi Committee, vol. 1, p. 200. Pitou: conference announcement, 16 Feb. 1930, ibid., pp. 172–4; *Mao 1993b, vol. 1, pp. 297–8; Lieu, 7 Oct. 1930, *ZDJC* vol. 14, p. 284; cf. Titov, vol. 1, pp. 231–2, 267–78 on Pitou. Execution of four: Lieu, ibid.; other reports, 5 Apr. & 22 July 1930, *Jiangxi Archive & CCP Jiangxi Committee, vol. 1, pp. 192, 200, 256. "have you executed!": report, 22 July 1930, ibid., p. 256. "kulaks": 16 Feb. 1930, ibid., vol. 2, p. 173 (E: *MRTP* vol. 3, p. 269).

88   Cai Shen-xi: *ZDJC* vol. 14, p. 409; *Provincial Action Committee, Emergency Announcement no. 9, 15 Dec. 1930, RGASPI, 514/1/1008. Jiang Han-bo: Jiang had been opposing the takeovers by Mao and his brother-in-law, *ZDJC* vol. 14, pp. 272–4; and yet a report to Shanghai in Jiang's name dated 5 Apr. 1930 entirely took Mao's line and condemned his own positions, *Jiangxi Archive & CCP Jiangxi Committee, vol. 1, pp. 180–212. The day before the report, Mao had issued an announcement saying that Jiang was expelled from the Party (expulsion was usually a prelude to execution), and, rather gratuitously, saying that Jiang was away (which could well be a ploy to cover up for Jiang's disappearance), *ZDJC* vol. 14, pp. 273–4.

88   *JGG* vol. 1, p. 496; *Dai & Luo, pp. 161–3.

89   Mao obituary: *International Press Correspondence* (English edition) 20 Mar. 1930.

89   Shanghai discovered Mao takeover: *ZDJC vol. 14, pp. 424–5. 3 Apr.
            circular: ibid., p. 426. Revolts against regime: Lieu to Mao, 22 May
            1930, *JDZ, no. 7, pp. 103–4; Lieu report, 7 Oct. 1930, *ZDJC vol. 14,
            pp. 281–8; *JDZ, no. 10, pp. 12–15; *Mao 1983, p. 266; CCP Agitprop
            Department, "Material for Agitprop work . . .," 25 Mar. 1930, RGASPI,
            495/154/430, p. 155 ("quiet life"). "seized and punished": 25 June 1930,
            *ZDJC vol. 14, pp. 624–6. "AB elements": 18 May 1930, *Jiangxi Archive
            & CCP Jiangxi Committee, vol. 1, pp. 599–600. AB standing for:
            according to founder and chief Duan Xipeng, 15 Apr. 1931, in *Dai &
            Luo, p. 10. Thousands killed: Shanghai inspector, 22 July 1930, *Jiangxi
            Archive & CCP Jiangxi Committee, vol. 1, p. 248; 5 Oct. 1930, *ZDZ,
            no. 7, p. 169. Jiangxi Reds fired Lieu: Description of the meeting
            (Second Plenary of the Southwest Special Committee) is contained in
            Lieu's report to Shanghai on 7 Oct. 1930. This particular passage is
            withheld even in the classified ZDJC vol. 14. Resolution of the meet-
            ing, 27 Aug. 1930, in *ZDJC vol. 14, pp. 649–50; Shanghai inspector,
            5 Oct. 1930, *ZDZ, no. 7, pp. 170–1; cf. Titov, vol. 1, pp. 278ff.

90   Lieu killed: *Sheng Ping et al., pp. 677–8. Mao denounced Jiangxi Reds:
            *Mao 1993b, vol. 1, p. 319 (E: MRTP vol. 3, pp. 552–6). Mao learned
            of Moscow promotion: Comintern Far Eastern Bureau letter to CCP,
            10 Nov. 1930, ordering that Mao be made head of the Revolutionary
            Military Council and given senior job in government (VKP vol. 3, p.
            1109). Mao signs Dec. 1930 document as "Chairman of the
            Revolutionary Committee of China": RGASPI, 514/1/1008. "scales on
            a fish": *Dai & Luo, p. 91; *Chen, Xiao et al., p. 162.

91   "Never trusted Mao": *Liou Di, letter to Shanghai, 11 Jan. 1931,
            RGASPI, 514/1/1008 (extracts in Vladimirov, 10 Nov. 1943, with Lie
            Shau-joe written "Liu Shao-chi" and Yongyang written "Yenan" in
            English-language editions). "wicked schemer": *ZDJC vol. 14, pp. 634–5
            (E: MRTP vol. 3, p. 707). Lie Shau-joe: *Liou Di, letter, 11 Jan. 1931,
            RGASPI, cit.; Shanghai inspector, 22 July 1930, *Jiangxi Archive & CCP
            Jiangxi Committee, vol. 1, p. 238. According to an officer: Xiao Ke, in
            *Dai & Luo, pp. 92–3. "over 4,400": *ZDJC vol. 14, p. 634; cf. Chou's
            weasel explanations to Mordvinov (KGB), 4 Mar. 1940, RGASPI,
            514/1/1006, pp. 48–9; Mao Tse-min, "Struggle with Counter-revolu-
            tionaries," 22 Aug. 1939, RGASPI, 514/1/1044, pp. 1a–12. Mao order,
            3 Dec. 1930: in *Dai & Luo, pp. 94–6; see a follow-up letter on 5 Dec.,
            in Vladimirov, 10 Nov. 1943 (mis-dated 15th). "AB meeting": Mao to
            Shanghai, 20 Dec. 1930, *ZDJC vol. 14, p. 636 (E: MRTP vol. 3, pp.
            704–5); *Liou Di, letter to Shanghai, 11 Jan. 1931, RGASPI, cit.;
            *Provincial Action Committee, Emergency Announcement no. 9, 15
            Dec. 1930, RGASPI, 514/1/1008.

91   Lie torture: ibid. Mutiny in Futian: *Liou Di, letter to Shanghai, 11 Jan.
            1931, RGASPI, cit.; *Jiangxi Party Committee, report to Shanghai,
            12 Jan. 1931, RGASPI, 514/1/1008; *Chen, Xiao et al., pp. 20–2,
            218–22; Shanghai inspector, 20 Feb. 1931, in *Dai & Luo, pp. 114–15.

92–93   "Extremely devious": *Provincial Action Committee, Emergency
            Announcement no. 9, 15 Dec. 1930, RGASPI, cit., Entrust fate to
            Shanghai: ibid.; cf. VKP vol. 3, p. 1272 (Bespalov report, 11 Feb. 1931,

cit.); *Jiangxi Party Committee. Showed torture marks: *VKP* vol. 3, p. 1272 (Bespalov report, 11 Feb. 1931, *cit.*).

93—94   "ignored the letters": *Provincial Action Committee. Chou told Pole: *VKP* vol. 3, pp. 1279—80 (Rylsky report of talk with Chou and Hsiang Chung-fa, 19 Feb. 1931). Moscow backed Mao: Comintern resolution on Futian, 18 Mar. 1931 (RGASPI, 514/1/1006, p. 90); cf. *VKP* vol. 3, p. 1348); "Politburo Resolution on Futian Incident," 28 Mar. 1931, *ZZWX* vol. 7, pp. 203—9. Hand of Kang Sheng: RGASPI, 514/1/1008.

94   Liou Di execution: Titov, vol. 1, p. 312; cf. Smedley 1934, p. 279; *Chen, Xiao et al., pp. 22—3.

94   Cited in Titov, vol. 1, p. 340.

94   Secret report revealed: May 1932, *Jiangxi Archive & CCP Jiangxi Committee, vol. 1, pp. 478—80; interview with a local Party historian, 4—5 Apr. 1996. Tens of thousands died: ibid. written source, p. 436. Purge in Fujian: *Deng Zihui Biography* Committee, pp. 112—13; "West Fujian Special Committee Circular no. 10," in *Nationalist Party Organization Department, p. 137; *Gong Chu, pp. 247—8; *Wen Yu, pp. 68—75; Kuo Chien, *FBIS-CHI-91-016* (24 Jan. 1991), p. 31. Head of Red Fujian fled: *Gong Chu, pp. 246—50.

95   "black and lightless": 20 Dec. 1930; *Hsiao Tso-liang, vol. 2, pp. 262—3; *Jiangxi Party Committee, report to Shanghai, 12 Jan. 1931, RGASPI, *cit.* "So many old comrades": *Gong Chu, pp. 266—7. Purging Zhu's staff: *Chen, Xiao et al., p. 184. "Peng might be mixed up": Gailis to GRU chief Berzin, 10 Feb. 1931 (*VKP* vol. 3, p. 1260). Zhu on panel: *Fan Hao, p. 109. Never halted purge: report, May 1932, *Jiangxi Archive & CCP Jiangxi Committee, vol. 1, pp. 477—80.

96   Few agreed with Mao strategy: *Provincial Action Committee, Emergency Announcement no. 9, 15 Dec. 1930, RGASPI, *cit.*; *Jiangxi Party Committee, report to Shanghai, 12 Jan. 1931, RGASPI, *cit.*; *Fan Hao, pp. 40—1. "we saw no people": *WZX*, no. 45, pp. 85—6. Chiang reflected: 12 Aug. 1931, *Chiang, p. 376.

96   Russian assistance: Mirovitskaya 1975, pp. 47—52, 61—2; id. 1993, pp. 307—15; Vinarov, pp. 328, 373—6; Mader, pp. 94—6.

96   Sorge role in China: Vinarov, pp. 373—6; Mader, pp. 64—117, 233—4; Werner interview, 20 Nov. 1999; Werner, pp. 38ff. Zhang Wen-qiu: interview with her, 29 Oct. 1995; *Zhang Wenqiu, pp. 231—8. Smedley confirmed as Comintern agent: *VKP*, vol. 4, p.585 (Comintern Protocol, 3 April 1934 records decision: "To send c[omrade] Agnes Smedley to China for the publication of [the magazine] *China Forum*.").

97   Ambush, 30 Dec. 1930: *Mao 1993b, vol. 1, pp. 329—30; *Fan Hao, pp. 50—2. "Chop his head": *Chen, Xiao et al., pp. 94, 186—7; *Huang Kecheng, p. 83. Mao asked for poison gas: 14 Oct. 1930 (*MRTP* vol. 3, p. 555). Radios: *VKP* vol. 3, pp. 1282 (Chou, 19 Feb. 1931: "big" radio sent to Mao); ibid., p. 1371 (Far Eastern Bureau, 28 Mar. 1931); ibid., p. 1466 (Rylsky, 10 June 1931); cf. Snow, H. 1979, pp. 251, 255; *Chen, Xiao et al., pp. 189—92; *Fan Hao, pp. 57—8.

97–98   Verge of collapse: Reds' report about the war, *ZDJC vol. 15, pp. 44–5; *Chen, Xiao et al., pp. 125–6. Domestic Stability First: 23 July 1931, *Chiang, p. 372. "Non-resistance only feasible policy": interview with the Young Marshal, 17 Feb. 1993. "This misfortune": 20 Sept. 1931, *Chiang, pp. 386–7. "suspend plan": 21 Sept. 1931, ibid., p. 387.

98   CCP rejected United Front: CCP declaration, 30 Sept. 1930, *ZZWX vol. 7, pp. 426–30. "defending the Soviet Union": CCP declaration, 22 Sept. 1930, ibid., pp. 416–21. Red state size: *Ma Qibin et al., pp. 448–9; *Xia & Chen, pp. 235–6; *Ma Juxian et al., p. 55.

98   *CCP Organization Department, pp. 25, 89.

99   First person to use "Chairman Mao": *Fan Hao, pp. 98, 109.

CHAPTER 9   *Mao and the First Red State*

100   Sites of Red government: visit to Ruijin and conversations with locals, Apr. 1996.

101   Grand celebration: *Chen, Xiao et al., pp. 457–8; Smedley 1934, p. 307. Moscow had considered Mao for head of military: Far Eastern Bureau to CCP, 10 Nov. 1930, in *VKP vol. 3, pp. 1008–09; *Mao 1993b, vol. 1, p. 360.

102   Village committees: *Mao 1983, pp. 297–300. Web of control: *Mao 1983, pp. 300, 326.

102–103   *Hsu En-tseng, et al., pp. 171–4 (E: Hsu, U. T., pp. 70–1); *DSYJ, 1980, no. 4, pp. 76–8; *ZDY, 1989, no. 3, pp. 1–2; interview with an old underground worker, 3 Sept. 1998.

103–104   "relied entirely on": resolution under Chou, 7 Jan. 1932, *ZZWX vol. 8, p. 19. "burned on the spot": *Chen, Xiao et al., p. 225. "Relaxing about purges": report, May 1932, *Jiangxi Archive & CCP Jiangxi Committee, vol. 1. pp. 480–8. Tungsten, trade: *Shu Long, pp. 72–7; *Chen, Xiao et al., pp. 380–95.

104   Hand over silver hairpins: Mao, "Changgang Investigation," Nov. 1933, *Mao 1983, p. 324; *Ruijin County Chronicle Committee, p. 783; "Communists' bonds worse": Reds' own report, 18 May 1934, *GS vol. 5, p. 345; Hsu, K., pp. 285–93, 291; Mao orders re bonds, *Mao 1993c, pp. 59–65 (E: MRTP vol. 4, pp. 357–60); bonds, *HZ, passim, a summary in *Wen & Xie, pp. 189–91. "lend grain": Mao, 1 Mar. 1933, *Mao 1993c, p. 62; (E: MRTP vol. 4, pp. 402ff, 408ff). Most men of working age: *Gong Chu, p. 414. Women main labor force: *Mao 1983, pp. 280, 302, 311–12, 325, 343.

105   Meetings "rest time": ibid., p. 308 (E: MRTP vol. 4, p. 603). Hospital moved to Ruijin: *Mao 1993b, vol. 1, p. 394. His own mug: *Chen, Xiao et al., p. 450. Sand Islet: the well is turned into a Mao-cult shrine, presenting him as a source (associated to "well") of benevolence to the people. Visit to the well and conversations with locals, Apr. 1996; *Zeng & Yan, pp. 239–40. Education in Ruijin: *Mao 1983, pp. 317–18, 326; *Gong Chu, pp. 419–21; visit to Ruijin and interviews with local museum curators, Apr. 1996; Snow 1973, p. 186.

105–106   Uncover "hidden landlords": this drive was called "Land Investigation Campaign [*chatian yundong*]." Mao orders, from June 1933, *GS vol. 5, pp. 284–306. "limitless forced labour": 10 Oct. 1933, ibid., p. 333. "Confiscate every last single": ibid., p. 298. Buffalo sheds: interview with a local Party historian, 8 Apr. 1996. Authorities reported: Sept. 1933, *GS vol. 5, pp. 321–5.

106   Gong Chu story: *Gong Chu, pp. 421–5.

107   "find counter-revolutionaries": *Liu Ying, pp. 48–9. Cai Dun-song: *Chen, Xiao et al., pp. 487–91.Manager tried to flee: *HZ, 18 Feb. 1934. Old-timers recalled: *Chen, Xiao et al., pp. 495–6.

107   President acknowledged: interview with an official present, 1 Apr. 1996. Back to Mainland: *First Front Army History Committee, p. 631.

107–108   "Suicides are the most shameful": *Qingnian shihua (Honest Words for the Youth), Ruijin periodical, vol. 2, no. 13. Yang Yue-bin: visit to Ruijin and conversations with local museum curators, Apr. 1996; *First Front Army History Committee, pp. 248–9. Escapes, rebellions: report, Sept. 1933, *GS vol. 5, p. 323; *Wang Qisen et al., pp. 223–5, 238, 244–5; *ZDZ, no. 21, p. 142; *Chen, Xiao et al., pp. 504–6. "killed together with the visitor": *Chen, Xiao et al., p. 496. Death toll: *Ma Juxian et al., pp. 54–6; *Fu & Chen, p. 40.

108   *Ma Juxian et al., p. 54.

108   "not one member of the CCP": "Report on Mission . . . by S. Tikhvinsky," 26 Jan. 1950, AVPRF, 0100/43/302/4, p. 79 (interview with CCP chief of Jiangxi, Shao Shi-ping, 3 Jan. 1950); the Russian Foreign Ministry Archive declined to let this page be photocopied; cf. Kulik 1994, p. 117.

CHAPTER 10   *Troublemaker to Figurehead*

109   Mao accused of "kulak line": Political Resolution, First Party Congress of the Central Soviet Area, 1–5 Nov. 1931, *ZZWX vol. 7, pp. 448–63; *Fan Hao, pp. 97–100, 106. Mao unseated, "sick leave": *Mao 1993b, vol. 1, pp. 365–6. In Buddhist temple: *Wang Xingjuan 1987, pp. 167–8; *Fan Hao, pp. 116–17.

109–110   "recantation notice": *Shun Pao, Shanghai newspaper, 20 Feb. 1932; *Jin Chongji et al. 1990, pp. 248–9. Mao to crisis meeting: *Wang Xingjuan 1987, p. 169; *Mao 1993b, vol. 1, p. 367; Red Army Political Dept. order, 17 Mar. 1932, *ZDJC vol. 15, pp. 164–6; *Fan Hao, pp. 103–4; cable from Chou, Wang Jia-xiang, Ren Bi-shi and Zhu De to Shanghai (forwarded to Moscow, arrived 3 May 1932), RGASPI, 495/19/217a, p. 82.

110–111   Chou gave Mao two-thirds of army: *Mao 1993b, vol. 1, p. 368; *Zhou 1991, p. 218; Chou et al. cable (arrived 3 May 1932), RGASPI, 495/19/217a, p. 82. Mao changed route to coast: Military Council's order of routes, 18 Mar. 1932, in *Jin Chongji et al. 1993, p. 284; but Mao: *Mao 1993b, vol. 1, pp. 368–9; *Fan Hao, p. 104; *Mao 1993a, vol. 1, pp. 263–8; Ningdu meeting bulletin, 21 Oct. 1932, *ZZWX vol. 8, p. 528; cable from Chou et al. (arrived 3 May 1932), cit. cf. Titov, vol. 1, pp. 376–7 and later report by Mao Tse-min to Comintern defending Mao Tse-tung's actions, cited ibid.

III　　Sent colleagues press cuttings: *Mao 1993b, vol. 1, p. 374. Ewert stressed to Ruijin: Ewert to Moscow, Oct. 1932, cited in Titov, vol. 1, pp. 381–2; cf. Ewert to Piatnitsky, 8 Oct. 1932, VKP vol. 4, pp. 193–4. Private fortune in cave: Salisbury, pp. 49–50; interview with a local Party historian, 23 May 1997; *Shu Long, pp. 234–5.

112　　Party leadership "utterly wrong": Mao, 3 May 1932, *Mao 1993a, vol. 1, pp. 271–2 (E: MRTP vol. 4, p. 217). Had to return to Jiangxi: *Mao 1993b, vol. 1, pp. 375–8; *Gong Chu, pp. 324–5; *Chen, Xiao et al., pp. 332, 346.

112n　　*Zhang Xuexin et al., p. 227; *Xiao Jingguang, pp. 112–16; *Chen, Xiao et al., pp. 334–8.

113　　MRTP vol. 4, p. 207; intra-CCP communications, e.g. Mao to Chou, 22 Apr. 1932, *Mao 1993a, vol. 1, pp. 269–70. (E: MRTP vol. 4, pp. 215–16).

113　　"right opportunism": cable from Chou et al. (arrived Moscow 3 May 1932), original in English, RGASPI, 495/19/217a, p. 82. Keep Mao on board: CCP cable to Comintern, 27 May 1932 ("concerning relation to Mao . . . perfectly agree"), RGASPI, 495/19/217a, p. 97; and Ruijin to Shanghai, 9 June 1932 referring to "Comintern directive" of 15 May 1932, RGASPI, 495/19/217a, p. 109. 25 July: *DDWX, 1990, no. 2, pp. 31–3. Mao chief political commissar: *ZDJC vol. 15, p. 168.

114　　Mao sat for a month: Mao cables and orders, Sept. 1932, *Mao 1993a, vol. 1, pp. 284–307; *Mao 1993b, vol. 1, pp. 382–8. Moscow strategy: *DDWX, 1990, no. 2, p. 39. Mao wait and see: Mao, 26 Sept. 1932, *Mao 1993a, vol. 1, pp. 298–304. "extremely dangerous": *DDWX, 1990, no. 2, p. 38. "Sometimes arguments": in *Zhang Xuexin et al., p. 245. Ningdu meeting: Shanghai to Ruijin, 30 Sept. 1932, RGASPI, 495/19/217a, p. 248; Shanghai to Ruijin, 7 Oct. 1932, RGASPI, 495/19/217a, p. 253; Ewert to Piatnitsky, 8 Oct. 1932, VKP vol. 4, pp. 193–4; cf. Shanghai to Comintern, 16 Oct. (ibid., p. 197); Wang Ming to Soviet Party at Comintern, 2 Nov., ibid., p. 199; Shanghai to Comintern, 11 Nov., RGASPI, 495/19/217a, p. 276; Titov vol. 1, pp. 377–85; bulletin, 21 Oct. 1932, *ZZWX vol. 8, pp. 528–31; report, 12 Nov. 1932, *Zhang Xuexin et al., pp. 244–5. Po Ku infuriated: *Mao 1993b, vol. 1, p. 389.

114　　Suggestion to expel Mao: Mao mentioned this, 1 Aug. 1959, in *Li Rui 1989, p. 231; and 24 Oct. 1966, CLG vol. 1, no. 4 (1968–69), p. 97. "temporarily returning": 12 Oct. 1932, *DDWX, 1990, no. 2, p. 39. Moscow told: Shanghai to Moscow, 11 Nov. 1932, RGASPI, 495/19/217a, p. 276. Mao cabled twice: Po Ku told Ewert (Titov, vol. 1, p. 385). Ewert: Ewert letter cited in Titov, vol. 1, pp. 381–2, cf. Ewert to Piatnitsky, 8 Oct. 1932, VKP vol. 4, pp. 192–6. "Regarding your differences": Shanghai to Ruijin, 16 Oct. 1932, RGASPI, 495/19/217a, p. 233; similar language in Comintern directive to CCP, 19–22 Mar. 1933, VKP vol. 4, p. 295 (E: Web/Dimitrov); *DDWX, 1990, no. 2, pp. 40–1, 55. Stalin's view asked: Wang Ming to Soviet Party at Comintern,

2 Nov. 1932, *VKP* vol. 4, p. 200. Chou's gentle handling praised: *Zhou 1991, pp. 233–4.

115   Hospital of the Gospel: visit, Apr. 1996. Mao ran competing HQ: Lo Fu, 18 Feb. 1933, in *Hsiao Tso-liang, pp. 666–7 (E: précis in id., 1961, pp. 236–7); *Mao 1993b, vol. 1, p. 391; article, 6 May 1933, *ZZWX vol. 8, pp. 491–502. "quick and subtle": Snow 1968, p. 15.

116   "nasty character" etc.: Titov, vol. 1, pp. 385, 386. Had to work with Mao: Titov, vol. 1, p. 386. Mao's brother Tse-min later told the Comintern that Po was like "Trotskyists," which was tantamount to requesting a death sentence (Mao Tse-min Report, 6 Dec. 1939, RGASPI, 514/1/1044, p. 102); cf. Titov, vol. 1, p. 389. Mao followers retained posts: *ZR vol. 48, pp. 381–3; *Reminiscences about Tan Zhenlin, pp. 72–4; *Mao 1993, p. 320.

117   Lepin: Mirovitskaya 1975, pp. 94–9. "impetus . . . from me": Braun 1982, p. 35. "tolerance and conciliation": Titov, vol. 1, pp. 392–5 (Po Ku reporting Ewert); cf. Comintern directive to CCP, 19–22 Mar. 1933, *VKP* vol. 4, p. 295; Far Eastern Bureau to Ruijin, 28 Mar. 1933, ibid., p. 298.

117   "I really stank": *Wang Dongxing 1997a, p. 116; *Wang Xingjuan 1987, p. 172. Not on Moscow list: Herbert (Comintern Shanghai) to Piatnitsky, 27 Dec. 1932, *VKP* vol. 4, p. 243; cable exchanges, Po Ku and Moscow, *ZDC, 1987, no. 5, p. 15. "diplomatic disorder": Braun 1982, p. 49. "Old Mao is": *Li Weihan, p. 353.

CHAPTER 11   *How Mao Got onto the Long March*

119   "shrink gradually": *Peng 1981, p. 188.

119–120   Stern: Krymov, pp. 308–19, 339; Brun-Zechowoj, pp. 62–4, 156–7 (Stern letter to Stalin from the gulag, Oct. 1952). Braun: Litten 1997. "stay inside my house": Braun 1982, pp. 34–5. "She had to be big": *Kang Keqing, p. 104; *Zhu Zhongli 1989, p. 56. According to Mrs. Zhu De: *Kang Keqing, p. 104. Mao cracked a joke: *Zhu Zhongli 1989, p. 56. Braun and CCP leaders: Braun 1982, pp. 54–5; *Wu Xiuquan 1992, pp. 97–100.

120–121   On 25 Mar.: Comintern to Ewert and CCP CC, NA, HW 17/3, cable 063; this is one of a number of transmissions between Moscow and China intercepted by British intelligence in 1934; the transmissions were in French; some of the same documents since released from Russian archives are in *VKP* vol. 4 (in Russian); this one pp. 583–4; cf. Comintern to Voroshilov, Mar. 1934, Mirovitskaya 1975, p. 97. 27 Mar.: Shanghai to Piatnitsky, *VKP* vol. 4, p. 585. 9 Apr.: Comintern to Ewert, *VKP* vol. 4, p. 586; following on Comintern meeting, 3 Apr., ibid., pp. 585–6; cf. Moscow to China, 7 May 1934, NA, HW 17/3, cable 123, which was the first Moscow cable decoded by the British (on 6 June; and the only one re-decoded, on 2 Aug). "My health is good": *Chen, Xiao et al., p. 486. Leave Mao behind: *Wu Xiuquan 1992, p. 105. No one wanted to be left behind: Chen Yi, in *Chen, Xiao et al., pp. 543–4; *Li Weihan, pp. 346–7; *Zhang Wentian 1943, p. 78.

121–122   Mao to southern front: *He Changgong, pp. 313–23; *Mao 1993b, vol. 1, pp. 426–32; *Chen, Xiao et al., pp. 507, 510–16, 524–7. Exit point changed in July: Braun 1982, p. 74; *Xiao Ke 1997, pp. 189–92; *Mao 1993b, vol. 1, pp. 432–3.

122   Mao squatted in Yudu: visit to the site, Apr. 1996; *Chen, Xiao et al., pp. 530–1. Treasure hoard to Po Ku: *Shu Long, pp. 234–5; Salisbury, p. 50. Begging Moscow to send money: Mirovitskaya 1975, pp. 96–7; cf. Moscow to Shanghai, 26 May 1934, NA, HW 17/3, cable 156; *VKP* vol. 4, pp. 598–9. Xiang Ying: *Wang Fuyi, pp. 98–101; *Dai & Luo, pp. 138–41.

122   Comintern to Shanghai, 1 July 1934, *VKP* vol. 4, p. 619.

123   Frame Xiang: Panyushkin, p. 122 ("doing away with Xiang"); Titov, vol. 1, p. 370; Chou tries to shrug off accusations in talk in Moscow with the KGB's Mordvinov, 4 Mar. 1940, RGASPI, 514/1/1006, p. 48. Xiang against taking Mao along, Po Ku optimistic: Braun 1982, pp. 87–8. Troublemaking until July: *Chen, Xiao et al., pp. 490–4, 511–16, 524–5; Hu Chi-hsi 1982, pp. 102–5. "very disciplined": *Nie 1991, pp. 188–9 (E: pp. 180–1).

123   Little Mao, other children: *Wang Xingjuan 1987, pp. 135–7; 163–7; 186–7, 269; *Wang Xingjuan 1993, pp. 108–9, 237–40.

124–125   Interview with Zeng Zhi, 24 Sept. 1994.

125   Last weeks before departure: *Gong Chu, pp. 395–9.

126   Nelson Fu: *Fu Lianzhang, pp. 3–12; *Li Yong et al., pp. 158–60.

126   "link up with the Soviet Union": Moscow to China, 3 May 1934, NA, HW 17/3, cables 106–115; Vinarov, pp. 373–4; cf. Mirovitskaya 1975, pp. 44–5: Borodin plan from mid-1927. Decoy of 6,000: Mao and Co. declaration, 15 July 1934, *Jiangxi Archive & CCP Jiangxi Committee, vol. 2, pp. 726–9 (E: *MRTP* vol. 4, pp. 768–9); Mao talk, 31 July 1934, *Mao 1993a, vol. 1, pp. 351–5 (E: *MRTP* vol. 4, p. 776); *Su Yu, pp. 110–33; Xiang, L, pp. 24–5; Yang, B. 1990, pp. 82–5.

126   Braun 1982, p. 77; *Jin Chongji et al. 1990, p. 277.

127   Executions before evacuation: *Gong Chu, pp. 430–2. Expert marksman: *Kang Keqing, pp. 121–4. "active shop-assistants": interview with a local Party historian, 8 Apr. 1996. He made abundantly clear: conversation, 7 Apr. 1996. Mao departure: *Wu Jiqing, pp. 168–9; *Kang Keqing, p. 131.

CHAPTER 12   *Long March I: Chiang Lets the Reds Go*

128   Long March numbers: Braun 1982, pp. 81, 84; *Zhou 1972, p. 66; *Li Weihan, pp.343–8. Mao's treasure: *Li Weihan, p. 345; "The autumn rain": *Liu Ying, pp. 58–9; *Guo Chen, p. 27.

128–129   Cantonese troops: *Chen, Xiao et al., p. 526; *Mao 1993b, vol. 1, pp. 436–7; cf. Sladkovsky, p. 139. Chiang told prime minister: *Chiang, pp. 751–2. A close aide: *Yan Daogang, p. 9. Red Army walks through fortified lines: Nationalists' telegram exchanges in *Second Archive & Hunan Archive; *Li Weihan, p. 348; *Nie 1991, pp. 191–5 (E: Nie, pp. 180ff.); *Peng 1981, pp. 193–4 (E: Peng, pp. 359–60); *Jin Chongji et al., 1993, pp. 329–31; *Yan Daogang, pp. 9–10; *Xue Yue, section notes under the heading "Xiangsheng zhuijiao." Chiang appoints Ho Chien: *Second Archive & Hunan Archive, pp. 220–1.

129   Crossing Xiang River: *Yan Daogang, p. 13; Nationalist army orders, in *Second Archive, pp. 186–91; *CCP Guilin Committee, pp. 25–8; *Museum of the Chinese Revolution, pp. 20–1; Zhu De cable, 1 Dec. 1934, in *Central Archive 1996, p. 46; Tong & Li, pp. 295ff., *Li Zongren, pp. 638–41; *Pai Chung-hsi, p. 90; Braun 1982, pp. 91–2.

129–130   Chiang monitoring: *Yan Daogang, p. 12. Ho Chien cable: *Military History Bureau MND, p. 861. Chiang plan to conquer southwest: Sichuan as "the base": *Chiang, p. 825.

129n   *Military History Bureau MND, p. 861; Braun 1982, pp. 91–2.

130   To his secretary: *Yan Daogang, p. 15. Nation-building blueprint: *Chiang, pp. 776–80. Warlords blamed and praised: *Chiang, pp. 762–3; *Military History Bureau MND, pp. 971–2; *Jin Chongji et al. 1993, pp. 329–30.

131   Ching-kuo sole heir of Chiang: Taylor 2000, pp. 7–8; *Wang Shichun, p. 20. Ching-kuo to Russia: Chiang Ching-kuo 1937 in Cline, pp. 154–7, and *Chiang Ching-kuo, pp. 66ff.; Tikhvinsky 2000, pp. 341–8 (Dossier on Chiang Ching-kuo for Brezhnev, 1969); TsDA, 146/6/1607, p. 5 (Ching-kuo letter to Dimitrov, Dec. 1936); n.a. "Jiang Jingguo in Russia," p. 179; Yu Miin-ling, pp. 112, 121.

131–132   Shao Li-tzu was mole: Interview with Shao, July 1956, in *YD, pp. 81–3; *CPPCC 1985a, p. 241. Shao telegram to Moscow, 23 Apr. 1927, VKP vol. 2, p. 696. Ching-kuo kept in Russia: Chiang Ching-kuo, pp. 179ff. Peggy: Dennis, p. 86. As of 2003 Tim Dennis was still in Russia, where he was a well-known Sinologist, under the name "Timur Timofeyev." Mme Sun Soviet agent: VKP vol. 4, p. 1100 (Wang Ming cable to CCP, 13 Mar. 1937); cf. NA, HW 17/3 (1934 Moscow cables to CCP intercepted by British).

132   RGASPI, 495/74/281, pp. 34–5 (to "Comrade Wang Ming" for "advise" [sic], 26 Jan. 1937, in English); VKP vol. 4, pp. 1092–3.

132   Proposed hostage swap: Chiang diary, 16 Dec. 1931, in *Yang Tianshi, p. 370. Chiang diaries: ibid., pp. 370–4.

133   Death of Shao junior: *CPPCC 1985a, pp. 37, 240; "The tragic end of a Chinese who had wounded his lover," Corriere della Sera, 22 Dec. 1931, p. 8.

133   Shaanxi Red base built: *CPPCC 1985a, pp. 34, 114, 240–1; *Chiang, pp. 755, 759; *Wang Zicheng, p. 25.

134   *Wu Changyi, pp. 92–103.

134–135   Chiang to American emissary: Currie, "Notes on Interviews with Chiang Kai-shek" (typescript, 17 Mar. 1941), p. 30. Reds steered by radio: *Radio Corps History Committee, p. 95; Song Kaifu, in *Fourth Front Army Memoirs Collection team, pp. 274–5; *Yan Daogang, pp. 12–13. Shanghai radio station shut down: *Hsu En-tseng et al., pp. 189–90 (E: Hsu, U. T., pp. 97–9); *Radio Corps History Committee, p. 98; *Yue Xia, p. 137; NA, HW 17/3, Moscow cables to Shanghai, 5 July 1934 (no. 225), 7 July 1934 (nos. 226, 227); cf. Titov, vol. 2, p. 135. 2 Sept. diary: in *Yang Tianshi, p. 375.

135 Chiang absents himself: *Chiang, pp. 752–65. Ching-kuo held hostage: Chiang Ching-kuo, pp. 178ff. "family calamity": *Yang Tianshi, p. 375.

CHAPTER 13   *Long March II: The Power Behind the Throne*

136 Guizhou warlord recalled: *Wang Jialie, pp. 85–6, 88. Chiang funnels Reds to Sichuan: Braun 1982, p. 91; *Chiang, p. 783; *Wang Jialie, pp. 87–8. Mao started active steps: *Zhou 1972, p. 67; *Zhang Wentian 1943, pp. 78–80; Mao speech, 13 Nov. 1943, in *Hu Qiaomu, p. 294; cf. Kampen 2000, pp. 66–77; Braun 1974, pp. 94ff.

137 Lo resentment: *Zhang Wentian 1943, p. 78; cf. Titov, vol. 2, pp. 122ff. Designing litter: *Liu Ying, p. 56. "lying in a litter": Mao told staff, 25 Dec. 1960, in *Ye Zilong, p. 38. Litter-carriers: *Guo Chen, p. 72–3. Plotting on litter: *Zhu Zhongli 1995, pp. 54, 60; *Cheng Zhongyuan 1993, p. 197; cf. Kampen 1989, p. 708.

137–138 Pointing a pistol: *Nie 1991, p. 206 (E: Nie, p. 198). Zunyi meeting: *Chen Yun 1935, pp. 36–41 (E: Chen Yun 1935, pp. 643–8); Braun 1982, pp. 102–4; cf. Kampen 2000, pp. 69–76; Titov, vol. 2, pp. 101–29; Titov 1976; Sladkovsky, pp. 139–43. Mao gets no top Party or army job, but enters Secretariat: *Chen Yun 1935, p. 42 (E: Chen Yun 1935, p. 648); Braun 1982, p. 104; *Xu Zehao, p. 223.

138–139 Resolution: *Chen Yun 1935, p. 42. Draft: Titov 1976, pp. 100, 103 and 103, n. 15. Final version: *ZHW, pp. 3, 21–2; Yang, B. 1986, pp. 262–5. Braun remark: Braun 1982, p. 98. "Helper": *Chen Yun 1935, p. 42 (E: Chen Yun 1935, p. 648). Red Prof job: *Xu Zehao, p. 223.

139 Lo Fu becomes No. 1: *Chen Yun 1935, p. 43 (E: Chen Yun 1935, p. 648); *Zhou 1972, pp. 68–9. Pressure on Po: Titov, vol. 2, p. 123. Kept secret: *Mao 1993b, vol. 1, p. 450. Decision to move into Sichuan: *Mao 1993b, vol. 1, p. 444. Stern proposal: 16 Sept. 1934, in VKP vol. 4, p. 688.

139–140 Lepin role: Mirovitskaya 1975, pp. 94ff. Li Li-san: Li Li-san report, 3 Aug. 1935, VKP vol. 4, pp. 897–903. Ringwalt report: NARA, RG 59, LM 83, roll 9 (US Department of State, file 893.00/12966, 11 Jan. 1935). Kim Philby: Philby, pp. 518–19.

140 Chang Kuo-tao bases: *Xu Xiangqian, pp. 121–2, 137, 221.

140–141 Purge: ibid., p. 103; Chang Kuo-tao report, 25 Nov. 1931, in *ZDJC vol. 15, pp. 330–4, cf. 345–9; Chen Chang-hao, Nov. 1931, in *ZZ4, Eyuwan period, vol. 2, pp. 433–4. Mao insists on ambush: *Mao 1993b, vol. 1,

p. 445; Mao talk, 10 Sept. 1956, in *DDWX*, 1991, no. 3, p. 7; CWB, no. 6–7 (1995–1996), p. 159 (Mao to Soviet ambassador Yudin, 22 July 1958). Original plan: 20 Jan. 1935, in *ZZWX* vol. 10, p. 479.

141   Tucheng: *Jin Chongji et al. 1996, p. 346; *Guo Chen, pp. 198–202. Casualties: *Ye Xinyu, pp. 207–8; *Song Renqiong, pp. 63–5; Xiao Hua, cited in Salisbury 1985, p. 372, n. 11.

142   Lin Biao: Braun 1982, p. 110. Original plan scrapped: *ZZWX vol. 10, p. 483. Retake Zunyi: *Wang Jialie, pp. 90–2.

142   Interview with one of the historians, Aug. 1997.

143   Mao appointment: *Mao 1993b, vol. 1, p. 450. Pyrrhic victory: *Wang Yan et al., p. 132–3; *Huang Kecheng, p. 134. 5 & 10 Mar.: *ZDJC vol. 15, p. 434.

144   Mao lost post: *Cheng Zhongyuan, pp. 218–19. Triumvirate formed: ibid.; *Zhou 1972, p. 69. Maotai defeat: Mao talk, 10 Sept. 1956, in *DDWX*, 1991, no. 3, p. 7; *Peng 1998, p. 118; *Chen Jiren, p. 90; *Ministry History Bureau MND, pp. 883–4; Nationalists' telegrams (and Lin Biao report), in *Guizhou Archive, pp. 123–5; also in *Guizhou Social Science* & Guizhou Museum, pp. 612–13.

144–145   "crossing to the east": *ZDJC vol. 15, pp. 436–7. "circling": Braun 1982, p. 110. Kuo-tao's army: *Xu Xiangqian, pp. 263, 268. "tour de force": Nie, p. 218. Chiang baffled: *Yan Daogang, pp. 18–20. Transferred army away from Sichuan border: *Sun Du, p. 136.

145   "forced marches": Braun 1982, pp. 113–14; *Guo Chen, pp. 213–14. 9th Corps: *Zhao Rong, pp. 167–88.

146–147   Baby girl birth: Interviews with Gui-yuan's fellow marchers, 23 Sept. & 15 Oct. 1993, 14 Sept. 1994; *Wang Xingjuan 1987, pp. 199–200; *Zhang Xinshi, pp. 12–13. Mao indifference: ibid. interviews; *Wang Xingjuan 1987, p. 200. "hen dropping an egg": Interview with Zeng Zhi, 24 Sept. 1994; *Wang Xingjuan 1993, p. 8.

147   hit by a bomb, Mao reaction: Interviews with fellow marchers, ibid., and 12 Sept. 1997; *Wang Xingjuan 1987, pp. 204–8. "Where are we going": *Cai Xiaoqian, p. 296. Lin Biao clamored: *Cheng Zhongyuan, pp. 220–1.

148   Lo Fu: Braun 1982, pp. 114–15. Mao livid: Braun 1982, p. 115. Young woman: *Liu Ying, pp. 66–9. "expand southward": order *Chen Jiren, p. 90. 25 Apr. cable: in *Chen Jiren, p. 90. Head for Sichuan: *Mao 1993b, vol. 1, pp. 453–4; *PLA Military Science Academy, p. 68.

148–149   Crossing Golden Sand River: Braun 1982, p. 113; *Song Renqiong, pp. 71–2; *PLA Military Science Academy, pp. 69–70; Nationalists' telegrams, in *Yunnan Archive, pp. 226–9; *Li Yimang, pp. 199–200; Salisbury, pp. 309–10. Huili, Peng: *Sichuan Party History Committee, pp. 60–2; Peng, pp. 368–71; *Liu Ying, pp. 71–3; *Nie 1991, p. 231 (E: Nie, pp. 222–3); Braun 1982, pp. 115–16; *Li Rui 1989, p. 259.

149   "I was denounced instead": *Huang Kecheng, pp. 135–6. "go north": *Mao 1993b, vol. 1, p. 455.

150 Chen Yun message in Moscow: RGASPI, 495/18/1011, pp. 13–14 (Chen Report to Comintern, 15 Oct. 1935, as delivered) & RGASPI, 495/18/1013, p. 73 (with handwritten changes and deletions, apparently by Manuilsky); *VKP* vol. 4, pp. 915–17 (notes to ECCI Secretariat minutes, 15 Oct. 1935) and ibid., p. 877; *Zhang Wentian 2000, p. 249.

151 No Nationalist troops at Dadu: Nationalist telegrams, in *Sichuan Archive, pp. 142, 150–3, 160. 93–year-old: Interview by the Dadu Bridge, 1 Sept. 1997.

152 Dadu myth: Snow 1973, pp. 194–9, esp. p. 199.

152 Bridge did not burn: *China Daily,* 1 & 2 Aug. 1983, cited in Hanson 1986, p. 281. No battle casualties: *Zhanshi* (Soldier), Red Army Political Department pamphlet, no. 186, 3 June 1935; *PLA Military Science Academy, p. 95. Chou bodyguard described: Wei Kouo-lou, p. 50.

152 Peng on Dadu: Payne 1947, p. 323 (Peng interview, 12 June 1946). Fell off: *Kang Keqing, p. 153; interview with the 93–year-old, 1 Sept. 1997. Ferry crossing myth: visit to site and interviews with the locals, Sept. 1997.

153 Hardship: Braun 1982, p. 120; *Guo Chen, p. 231. Mao climbing: *Wu Jiqing, pp. 245–9.

153 Kung–Bogomolov: *DVP* vol. 18 (1935), p. 438. "matériel": Braun 1982, p. 121; Mao cable, 16 June 1935, *Mao 1993a, vol. 1, p. 358; (E: *MRTP* vol. 5, p. 16).

CHAPTER 14 *Long March III: Monopolizing the Moscow Connection*

155 Zhu De lamented: *Zhang Guotao, vol. 3, pp. 221–2 (E: Chang Kuo-tao, vol. 2, p. 379). "as ambitious as Mao": Braun 1982, p. 123.

156 "warlordism": *Xu Xiangqian, pp. 285–6. "How can such": *Kuo Hua-lun, vol. 3, p. 60 (E: Kuo, W., vol. 3, p. 82).

156–157 Complain to Kuo-tao: *Zhang Guotao, vol. 3, pp. 245–6 (E: Chang Kuo-tao, vol. 2, p. 402). "sedan-chairs": ibid., p. 223; interview with a Long Marcher, 3 Sept. 1997. Difference between life and death: *Guo Chen, pp. 71–3; *Liu Ying, p. 74; *Su Ping, pp. 94–5; *Xu Xiangqian, p. 288.

157–158 "fighting for food": *Li Yimang, p. 168; *Xu Xiangqian, pp. 262–3. "foreign debt": Snow 1973, pp. 203–4. "barbarian cavalry": *Museum of the Chinese Revolution, pp. 205–7. 18 July: *Mao 1993b, vol. 1, p. 463. "close to the Soviet Union": Mao, 6 Aug. 1935, in *Ding Zhi, p. 19; Sheng, p. 24. Operation to move north: called "Operation Xiao-Tao," in *ZZ4, Long March Period, pp. 95–101.

158 Mao cable, 15 Aug.: ibid., p. 123. Kuo-tao reply: ibid., pp. 124–5.

159 Resolution: *ZZ4, Long March Period, pp. 126–8. Mao had discovered: *Yang Chengwu, pp. 214–17.

159 Into swamps on litter: interviews with historians who had done extensive research, Aug. & Sept. 1997. "huddled in the rain": Lin Biao report,

21 Aug. 1935, *Central Archive 1996, p. 297. Vivid description: Braun 1982, pp. 136–7. Another Long Marcher: *Li Weihan, pp. 362–3.

159	Mrs. Lo Fu: *Liu Ying, pp. 82–3.

159–160   400 died: *Zhou 1991, p. 290. Mao urging Kuo-tao: cables on 24 Aug. & 1 Sept. 1935, *ZZ4, Long March Period, pp. 132–3, 138. On 2 Sept.: *Central Archive 1996, p. 309.

160–161   A day later: *Central Archive 1996, p. 310. Stay put: Chang cables, 3 & 9 Sept. 1935, in *ZZ4, Long March Period, pp. 139, 144. 8 Sept.: ibid., p. 141. "Get up": *Liu Ying, p. 83. Maps: *Peng 1981, p. 203 (E: Peng, p. 377); *Xu Xiangqian, p. 302. Peng sided with Mao: *Peng 1981, p. 202 (E: Peng, p. 376).

161   Decamp that night: *Li Weihan, p. 364.

161   Cable, 10 Sept. 1935, *Central Archive 1996, p. 320; Saich 1996, pp. 685–6 (Resolution, 12 Sept. 1935); *ZZ4, Long March Period, pp. 153–4; Dallin & Firsov, p. 97 (CCP cable to Wang Ming, 26 June 1936); RGASPI, 495/2/267, pp. 19–27 (CCP cable to Dimitrov, 27 May 1938, enclosing 19 Apr. 1938 report about expulsion of Chang Kuo-tao).

162   "Red Army must not": *Xu Xiangqian, p. 302.

162   "Big Nose": *Cai Xiaoqian, pp. 376–7; Braun 1982, pp. 137–8. Only time close to Mao: *Cai Xiaoqian, p. 377. Chiang told governor: cable, 13 Sept., in *Shaanxi Archive, pp. 251–2. "The morning after": *ZZ4, Long March Period, p. 148.

163   Moscow to CCP re North Shaanxi base: NA, HW 17/3 (Moscow cable, 3 May 1934, nos. 106–15). "void of enemies": Braun 1982, p. 141; Mao cable, 18 Sept. 1935, *Mao 1993a, vol. 1, p. 369; *Hsu Chen 1990, p. 117; *Song Renqiong, p. 92. Hospitality: Braun 1982, p. 141; *Cai Xiaoqian, p. 382. 1,000 gave up: *Military History Bureau MND vol. 5, p. 964.

163   Cheng, J. Chester, "The Mystery of the Battle of La-tsu-k"ou in [sic] the Long March," *JAS*, vol. 31, no. 3 (1972), pp. 593–8.

163–164   "Collect": *Mao 1993b, vol. 1, p. 478. "During the march": *Huang Kecheng, pp. 144–5. "We were famished": *Li Yimang, pp. 213–14. "the darkest moment": Snow 1973, p. 432. Chen Yun message, Moscow endorsement: RGASPI, 495/18/1011, pp. 13–14; RGASPI, 495/18/1013, p. 73 (Chen Yun Report to Comintern, 15 Oct. 1935); *VKP* vol. 4, pp. 915–17 (notes to ECCI Secretariat minutes, 15 Oct. 1935); cf. ibid., p. 877; *Pravda*, 13 Dec. 1935 (signed by A.M. Khamadan).

164–165   Messenger, radio link with Moscow restored: *Xiong & Li, p. 92; Dallin & Firsov, p. 99 (CCP to Wang Ming, 26 June 1936). Liao Hui, in *PLA Historical Documents Committee, pp. 282–3. Stalin's word: Zhang Hao cable, 14 Feb. 1936, in *ZDJC vol. 15, p. 478. Chiang saw Bogomolov: *DVP* vol. 18 (1935), pp. 537–9 (Bogomolov cable, 19 Oct. 1935); *Huang Xiurong, pp. 64–5. Chen Li-fu: Interview, 15 Feb. 1993; AVPRF, 0100/20/184/11, pp. 11, 14–15.

165   Hostage stays: Chiang Ching-kuo, pp. 178ff.

CHAPTER 15   *The Timely Death of Mao's Host*

169–170   "a conspirator": Ybañez, p. 4; cf. Aguado, p. 258. Mao pointedly remarked: 12 Sept. 1935, *ZZ4, Long March Period, p. 151. Party envoys: *ZZ25, pp. 436–7; Nie Hong-jun, in *GZ, no. 1, 1981. Purge: *ZR vol. 3, pp. 218–19; *Sima Lu 1985, pp. 227–33; Xi Zhongxun, in *RR, 16 Oct. 1979; Vladimirov 27 Apr. 1945. Benign arbiter: *Mao 1993b, vol. 1, p. 484.

170–171   Lowly post: *ZR vol. 3, p. 221; Ma Wenrui, in *Remembering Mao Zedong vol. 1, p. 109; *Mao 1993b, vol. 1, pp. 499, 501. Expedition: strategy, Party resolution, 23 Dec. 1935, *Mao 1993a, vol. 1, pp. 413–21; MRTP vol. 5, pp. 77–83; *Peng 1981, pp. 210, 213–14 (E: Peng, pp. 391ff). Chih-tan's death: *Pei Zhouyu, pp. 70–1; cf. Apter & Saich, pp. 53–4; more on Pei, in *Song Renqiong, p. 106; *Shu Long, p. 238.

171   Sequence of events: *Mao 1993b, vol. 1, pp. 532–5. Widow kept away: interview with widow Tong Guirong, in *"Mao and I" Collection Committee 1993, p. 109.

172   "a surprise": *ZR vol. 3, p. 226. Deaths of left- and right-hand men: *ZR vol. 39, pp. 152–3; *Song Renqiong, p. 101; cf. *Wang Jianying 1986, pp. 271, 275.

CHAPTER 16   *Chiang Kai-shek Kidnapped*

173   "My first impression": Leonard 1942, p. 21. "like a daddy": *Chiang, p. 1020.

173   Kolpakidi & Prokhorov 2000, vol. 1, pp. 182–3 (from GRU sources); there is a photograph of the Old Marshal's bombed train in Vinarov's book (opposite p. 337), captioned "photograph by the author"; key role also attributed to the GRU chief in China, Salnin.

174   Tries to visit Russia: *Zhang Xueliang, pp. 651–2; Bertram, p. 98. "scum": 1 Aug. declaration, *ZZWX vol. 10, p. 519 (E: Saich 1996, p. 693). Deep in talks: Mirovitskaya 1975, p. 171; Titov, vol. 3, p. 81; cf. AVPRF, 0100/20/184/11 (Bogomolov report, 28 Nov. 1935); Mirovitskaya 1975, pp. 170–2; cf. AVPRF, 09/25/98/22, pp. 60–59 [sic] (Uritsky (GRU) report); *Zhang Xueliang, pp. 924, 938. "fly the plane in a vertical": Leonard 1942, p. 21. Chuckled to us: interview with the Young Marshal, 17 Feb. 1993.

174–175   He wanted Moscow: Titov, vol. 3, p. 81; cf. AVPRF, 0100/20/184/11, p. 109 (Bogomolov report of his meetings with the Young Marshal, 24 & 25 July 1936). Russians led him on: AVPRF, 0100/20/184/11, p. 109.

175–176   Mao instructed his negotiator: Mao cable, 20 Jan. 1936, in *Yang Kuisong 1995, p. 38. Mao's sons: *Ren & Yu, pp. 4–8; *Liu Yitao, pp. 52–5; interview with a member of Mao's family, 23 Oct. 1995.

176–177   Stalin personally involved: according to Boris Ponomaryov, top Soviet official involved in handling Mao's sons (interview in Russia, June 1995); "Moskvin" (Trilisser) to Stalin, 29 May 1936, in *Yang Kuisong 1995, p. 162. "like Outer Mongolia": in *Yang Kuisong 1995, pp. 89. First telegram: Dallin & Firsov, p. 99; *Yang Kuisong 1995, pp. 101–3;

for date, cf. *Shi Jixin, pp. 48–9; Mirovitskaya 1975, p. 104. Sent to Stalin: Dallin & Firsov, p. 96 (Dimitrov to Stalin, early July 1936).

177   15 Aug. milestone order: Dallin & Firsov, pp. 102, 104–5. Talks about United Front: *Huang Xiurong, pp. 79–82, 130. Chiang initiated rapprochement: *DVP* vol. 18 (1935), pp. 599, 602. Young Marshal still misled: AVPRF, 0100/20/184/11, pp. 108–9 (Bogomolov report); *Fan & Ding, pp. 220–5. Stalin endorsed a plan: Davies et al., pp. 351–2.

177–178   Mao's wish list; Comintern reply: in *Yang Kuisong 1995, pp. 218–19; cf. Sheng, pp. 28–9; Dimitrov, 11 & 20 Sept., 6 Nov., 2 Dec. 1936; Mirovitskaya 1975, p. 104; *MRTP* vol. 5, pp. 360–1 (Mao cable, 19 Sept. 1936); Cherepanov 1982, p. 307. "going to prison": *Xu Xiangqian, p. 334.

178   Ho Lung talk, 2 Feb. 1961, *ZZ2, pp. 657–8; *Wen Yu, p. 102.

179      $550,000: *Yang Kuisong 1995, p. 236; cf. Dimitrov, 2 Dec. 1936; Mirovitskaya 1975, p. 104 ($300,000 per month sent).

179–180   Plan to kidnap Chiang: Li Youwen, in *Yang Kuisong 1995, pp. 336–7. Gamble: to Sun Mingjiu and co, in *Wu Zuzhang, p. 216. Telling Yeh, Yeh to Mao: Titov 1981, p. 143. *Zhang Kuitang, p. 191; *Yang Kuisong 1995, pp. 264–5. Titov: Titov 1981, p. 143.

180   "Work out a plan": Dimitrov, 26 Nov. 1936. "come instantly": *Yang Kuisong 1995, p. 283. Pretending to Young Marshal: Mao cable, 10 Dec. 1936, in *Central Archive 1997, p. 174. "good news in the morning": *Ye Zilong, p. 39.

CHAPTER 17   *A National Player*

182   "laughing like mad": *Zhang Guotao, vol. 3, p. 330 (E: Chang Kuo-tao, vol. 2, p. 480). First cables to Moscow: *Zhang Xueliang, pp. 1124–5, 1133, 1149. "The best option": in *Zhang Xueliang, p. 1124. "carry out the final measure": cable to Mao, 17 Dec. 1936, in *Central Archive 1997, p. 213.

182–183   Asked for plane for Chou: two cables from Mao on 13 Dec. 1936, in *Central Archive 1997, pp. 181, 182 (E: one in *MRTP* vol. 5, p. 540). "made arrangements with the Comintern": *MRTP* vol. 5, p. 540 (13 Dec. 1936 cable). *Pravda* and *Izvestia*: in *Zhang Xueliang, pp. 1138–9. No plane for Chou: Mao cables, 15, 16, 17 Dec. 1936, in *Central Archive 1997, pp. 204, 211, 212 (E: 17 Dec. cable in *MRTP* vol. 5, p. 551). Sent his Boeing, Leonard: Leonard 1942, p. 99.

183–184   Pretended he would: Chou cable to Mao, 17 Dec. 1936, in *Central Archive 1997, p. 213. "Strike at the enemy's head": in *Central Archive 1997, p. 202, cf. 189 (E: *MRTP* vol. 5, p. 550). "The enemy's jugulars": in *Central Archive 1997, p. 212 (E: *MRTP* vol. 5, p. 551). H.H. Kung: *Kung Hsiang-hsi, p. 83.

184–185   Stalin was on the line: Dimitrov, 14 Dec. 1936; cf. Avreyski, p. 244. Dimitrov's Chinese assistant: Krymov, p. 289. Artuzov: Damaskin, pp. 153–4 (photo of letter); Piatnitsky, p. 422; interview with Wang Danzhi, 21 June 1999. Dimitrov wrote Stalin: *VKP* vol. 4, pp. 1084–5 (letter,

14 Dec. 1936); cf. Dimitrov, 14 Dec. 1936; Dallin & Firsov, p. 106. Mao in cahoots with Japan?: Vaksberg, pp. 220ff; Piatnitsky, p. 134. Dimitrov stern message: *VKP* vol. 4, pp. 1085–6; Dimitrov, 16 Dec. 1936; Dallin & Firsov, pp. 107–8.

185 "flew into a rage" (Mme Sun Yat-sen): Snow 1968, p. 2. CCP first official statement: *Central Archive 1997, pp. 200–1 (E: *MRTP* vol. 5, pp. 547–9).

185 Mao claim in *Yang Kuisong 1995, pp. 327, 329; normal procedure: our interview with Kang Yi-min, 9 Sept. 1997; no "re-sent" cable has been found in Comintern archives (*VKP* vol. 4, p. 886).

186 "considerable remorse": *Chiang, pp. 1022–3; Chiang 1985, p. 17. Chiang got message out: in *Zhang Xueliang, p. 1166. Moscow repeated cable, Mao: "restore Chiang Kai-shek's freedom": *Central Archive 1997, pp. 240, 244–5; *Yang Kuisong 1995, pp. 329, 333–4; cable of 21st in Saich 1996, p. 770. CCP demands: Mao to Chou, 21 Dec. 1936, *Central Archive 1997, pp. 244–5.

186–187 Chiang refused to see Chou: Snow 1968, p. 12. Chiang's ambassador in Moscow: *Li Yizhen, p. 409; *Jiang Tingfu, p. 184. Promise to free Ching-kuo: Wang Bingnan was by the door and overheard this, unpublished memoirs, cited in Han 1994, p. 154.

CHAPTER 18   *New Image, New Life and New Wife*

188 The next stage: *VKP* vol. 4, pp. 1091–2, 1097 (Comintern cables to CCP, 20 Jan. & 5 Feb. 1937; E: Web/Dimitrov); *Huang Xiurong, pp. 190, 202; *ZDY*, no. 3, 1988, p. 80. CCP public pledge: 10 Feb. 1937, *MRTP* vol. 5, pp. 606–7. Quid pro quo: *Huang Xiurong, pp. 204ff; *Wang Zicheng, p. 27. Hostage released: Tikhvinsky 2000, p. 40 (Soviet Politburo minutes); cf. Mirovitskaya 1999, pp. 43, 245; *Chiang, p. 1079.

188–189 Kang Sheng role: Taylor 2000, p. 76; *Wang Guangyuan, pp. 202–3. Mole Shao appointment: *CPPCC 1985a, p. 242. Mao autobiography: *Mao 1937.

188n Tikhvinsky 2000, p. 44 (Bogomolov to Poskryobyshev, head of Stalin's Secretariat); Larin, pp. 35–8; Chiang Ching-kuo, pp. 182ff; Dimitrov, 28 March 1937; Taylor 2000, p. 77 (from Vladivostok).

189–190 Mao inscription: in *Xun Yuanhu et al., p. 1 (E: *MRTP* vol. 5, p. 697). Snow visit: *Fang & Dan, pp. 138–49. George Hatem: interview with his widow, 17 Mar. 1998; *Yuan & Liang, pp. 210–15; *Sima Lu 1952. Snow swallowed in toto: Snow 1973, p. 355; cf. p. 95; *Mao 1993, pp. 67–8; *Mao 1937, p. 91.

190 Mao checks everything: Snow 1968, p. viii; id., 1973, p. 106. "Don't send me": Snow, H. 1961, p. 166. No "censorship": Snow 1973, p. 96. "Honest and true": in *Mao 1937, p. 91. *"Journey to the West"*: *Hu Yuzhi, pp. 184–5. "the Great Yu": translator Wu Liangping, in *Zhang Suhua et al., p. 129.

191 Mao dwellings: visit to Yenan and interviews with locals, Oct. 1994; *Cheng Zhongyuan, p. 480; *Shi Zhe 1992, p. 206.

192   "forty days": Mao to Gao Gang, interview with an insider, 3 Oct. 1994.
             Lily Wu: Snow, H. 1972, pp. 250–54. Smedley and Mao: Smedley
             1944, pp. 23, 121, 122; Marcuse, p. 286; *MRTP* vol. 5, pp. 611–23 (Mao
             interview, 1 Mar. 1937); ibid., p. 629 (Mao letter to E. Snow, 10 Mar.
             1937).

192–193   "walked the floor": interviews with several women who danced regu-
             larly with Mao; *Quan Yanchi 1991, p. 217. "close embrace": Snow 1956,
             p. 6. "Son of a pig": Snow 1956, pp. 10ff. Mao and Ding Ling: *Mao
             1993b, vol. 1, p. 660; *Yang Guixin, p. 43; *MRTP* vol. 5, p. 573 (Mao
             poem, Dec. 1936).

194   Karmen article: "U Mao Tsze-duna" (At Mao Zedong's), *Izvestia*, 8 July
             1939; Karmen 1941, p. 108.

194   Gui-yuan ordered not to return: *Liu Ying, p. 113.

195   Gui-yuan and daughter in Moscow: *Wang Xingjuan 1993, esp. pp.
             2–13, 27–59; *Liu Ying, pp. 113–15, *Wang Guiyi, p. 54; interview with
             people in Moscow with her, 6 Oct. 1993 & 7 Sept. 1998; Lee & Wiles,
             pp. 111ff.

195   Jiang Qing: Witke 1977, pp. 143ff; Terrill 1986, pp. 20ff; *Ye Zilong,
             pp. 64–5; *Wang Suping; *Ye Yonglie 1996; *Zhu Zhongli 1989, pp.
             72–3, 176–7.

196   "reputation is pretty bad": interviews with Xie Fei, the then Mrs. Liu
             Shao-chi, 14 Sept. 1994; Li Qiong, Mrs. Yang Fan, mentioned her
             husband's letter against the marriage, 17 Apr. 1996; Kuo, W., vol. 3,
             pp. 520–1. Entertained her jailors: *Shi Zhe 1992, p. 219; *Zhong Kan,
             p. 76. "I will get married tomorrow": *Liu Ying, pp. 117–18. Kang in
             black: interviews with Yenan veterans, 15 & 17 Oct. 1993; *Sima Lu
             2004, p. 83.

196   "her past is no problem": *Zhu Zhongli 1989, p. 174; *Shi Zhe 1992,
             pp. 218–21.

CHAPTER 19   *Red Mole Triggers China–Japan War*

197   Chiang did not declare war: Chiang diary, 8 Aug. 1937, *Chiang, p. 1144.
             Japan did not want full-scale war: *Ma Zhendu 1986, pp. 214–16,
             220–1; *CPPCC (Tianjin) vol. 1, pp. 334–6, 360–1. "It was a common-
             place": Abend, p. 245.

197–198   Very direct danger to Stalin: cf. *CPPCC (Tianjin), vol. 1, pp. 334–6,
             360–1; Mirovitskaya 1999, pp. 41ff; Haslam, pp. 88ff. "In summer
             1925": *Zhang Zhizhong, pp. 664–5. contact with Soviet embassy—
             and as mole: interview with two people who had access to ZZZ files,
             13 Sept. 1997, 7 Sept. 1998. ZZZ advocates "first strike" in Shanghai:
             ZZZ cable to Nanjing, 30 July 1937, and Nanjing reply, in *Zhang
             Zhizhong, p. 117; *Shi Shuo, p. 90.

198–199   Airport incident, Japanese wishing to defuse: *Zhang Zhizhong, p. 117;
             *Liu Jinchi, pp. 41–2; *Shi Shuo, p. 91; *Dong Kunwu, pp. 131–2. ZZZ
             urged war, Chiang reluctance: telegrams, in *Zhang Zhizhong,
             pp. 121–5; in *Second Archive 1987a, pp. 264–5, 287–8; in *ZS vol. 2,

no. 2, pp. 169–70. ZZZ expanded offensives, all-out war unstoppable 22 Aug.: *Zhang Zhizhong, pp. 125–6; *Chiang, p. 1150.

199   Russian aid: Garver, pp. 40–1; *DVP* vol. 22 (1939), book 2, pp. 507–8, n. 27; Mirovitskaya 1999, pp. 41ff; Vartanov. Russia "perfectly delighted": *FRUS* 1937, vol. 3, p. 636 (Bullitt to Washington, 23 Oct. 1937); cf. Haslam, pp. 92, 94. Russians dealing with ZZZ executed: Slavinsky 1999, pp. 123–6; cf. Dimitrov, 7 Nov. 1937 (Stalin to Dimitrov); Tikhvinsky 2000, pp. 136, 154–5 (Stalin to Yang Jie).

200   Stalin ordered CCP: Avreyski, pp. 282–4; Grigoriev 1982, p. 42.

201   "Three Kingdoms": in *Li Rui 1989, p. 223. "thank Japanese warlords": Mao to visiting Japanese, 24 Jan. 1961, *Mao 1994, pp. 460–1 (E: Mao 1998, p. 353); also to Japanese Communists, 28 Mar. 1966, Kojima, p. 207. Russia "cannot ignore events in Far East": Mao to Snow, 16 July 1936, *MRTP* vol. 5, p. 262. Got Chiang to agree: *Huang Xiurong, p. 264; *Zhou 1991, p. 377. Ordered Red commanders: many Mao cables, especially the three on 25 Sept. 1937, in *Mao 1993a, vol. 2, pp. 57–61 (E: one in Saich 1996, pp. 793–4), also on 12th, 21st, & 29th, in *Mao 1993a, vol. 2, pp. 44, 53, 66 (cable of 21st in Saich 1996, pp. 792–3).

201–202   "The more land Japan took": in *Li Rui 1989, p. 223; cf. Snow 1974, p. 169 (Mao to Snow, 9 Jan. 1965). Japanese "mainly asleep": Hanson 1939, p. 104 (Lin to Hanson). Lin report in Russia: RGASPI 495/74/97, pp. 1304–5 (Lin to Dimitrov, 5 Feb. 1941, sent on to Stalin). "helping Chiang": in *Li Rui 1989, p. 223; *Zhang Xuexin et al., p. 410.

202   Lin Biao report, 5 Feb. 1941, *cit.*, p. 1304.

202–203   Mao urged stop fighting Japan: cables, e.g. on 13 Nov. 1937, in *Mao 1993a, vol. 2, pp. 116–17; cf. p. 66. "created the condition for our victory": Mao to visiting Japanese, 24 Jan. 1961, in *Mao 1994, pp. 460–1 (E: Mao 1998, p. 353). Stalin laid down line: Dimitrov, 11 Nov. 1937; Tikhvinsky 2000, p. 151 (Stalin said he had a further meeting with Wang Ming on 18 Nov. 1937). Congress to convene, Wang Ming No. 1 speech: Politburo resolution, 13 Dec. 1937, *ZZWX vol. 11, pp. 405–7; *Hu Qiaomu, p. 367.

204   "house-sitting": in *Li Rui 1989, p. 329; *Xiao Jingguang, pp. 200–8.

204   Tried to turn army back: Mao–Zhu telegram exchanges, in *Jin Chongji et al. 1993, pp. 437–42. Summary of Politburo meeting: 11 Mar. 1938, in *ZZWX vol. 11, pp. 430–65 (E: Saich 1996, pp. 802–12).

204–205   Promised not to "interfere": Mao cable, 8 Mar. 1938, in *Mao 1993a vol. 2, p. 190 (E: *MRTP* vol. 5, p. 254). Participants' notes confiscated: Wang letter to Mao, 17 Aug. 1950, in *Cao & Dai, p. 381. Ren told Russians: Titov, vol. 3, pp. 234ff, 249–50 (Ren report to Comintern, 14 Apr. 1938); cf. Avreyski 1987, pp. 322, 333–4; *ZDJC vol. 16, pp. 45–55. Andrianov to Yenan: Titov, vol. 3, pp. 124, 197–200, 229–33; cf. Lurye & Kochik, p. 334 (Andrianov's career). "thirty divisions": Dimitrov, 11 Nov. 1937 (Stalin to Wang Ming, 11 Nov. 1937). Moscow criticizes CCP: Mif, p. 100; Nikiforov, pp. 115, 116.

205   Mao wired for money: Pan Hannian to Wang Ming in Wang to "Moskvin" (Trilisser), Sept. 1937, in Ovchinnikov, p. 10.

205   Purge of Piatnitsky, Melnikov: Piatnitsky, esp. pp. 78–9, 92, 108, 117, 120–4; Vaksberg, pp. 218ff. Mao dossier: Vaksberg, pp. 220–1, 235, cf. 212ff; cf. Piatnitsky, pp. 133–4.

CHAPTER 20   *Fight Rivals and Chiang—Not Japan*

207   Xinjiang as pick-up point for Russian arms: Comintern cable, 3 Nov. 1936, in *Yang Kuisong 1995, p. 224.

207–208   Mao assigned Western Contingent: CCP to Comintern, 13 Nov. 1936, in *Yang Kuisong 1995, p. 227; Titov, vol. 2, pp. 326–7. Contradictory orders: *Xu Xiangqian, p. 373. "last drop of blood": 22 Feb. 1937, in *Zhu Yu, pp. 272–3; cf. *Xu Xiangqian, pp. 365–6. Heart-rending photo: in *Gansu Archive. Survivors: RGASPI, 495/74/294, p. 19 (CCP, 9 Apr. 1937, in Dimitrov to Stalin, 13 Apr. 1937); *VKP* vol. 4, pp. 1117–18 (Dimitrov to Stalin, 17 June 1937); cf. Dallin & Firsov, pp. 109–10, n. 14; Dimitrov, 26 Nov., 2 Dec. 1936, 13 Apr. 1937; Titov, vol. 2, pp. 325–30. Kuo-tao denounced: Politburo resolution, 31 Mar. 1937, *ZZWX* vol. 11, pp. 164–8 (E: Saich 1996, pp. 755–8). Moscow order to keep him in Politburo: 22 Mar. 1937, Titov, vol. 2, pp. 333–4; Avreyski, pp. 267–9.

208   Burying survivors alive: *Sima Lu 1952, pp. 78–9.

208   "torments . . . master-minded by Mao": *Zhang Guotao, vol. 3, pp. 414–17 (E: Chang Kuo-tao, vol. 2, pp. 501ff, 563); *Ye Zilong, p. 48.

209   Kuo-tao in Wuhan: CCP letter to Dimitrov, 19 Apr. 1938, RGASPI, 495/2/267, pp. 19–27; CCP expulsion order (18th) and announcement to Party members (19th), *ZZWX* vol. 11, pp. 492–5. Statement by Wang Ming et al., 28 Apr. 1938, in *Jiang Xinli, pp. 381–6.

210   Post-defection: *Yang Zilie, pp. 352–4; *Tong Xiaopeng, vol. 1, pp. 165–7; *Cai Mengjian, pp. 20–5; *Jiang Xinli, p. 421; Titov vol. 2, pp. 344ff. "200 were buried alive": Report to Chiang, 10 July 1938, in *ZS* vol. 5, no. 4, p. 475. Moscow endorses expulsion: 11 June 1938, in Titarenko, p. 283 (E: Kuo, W. vol. 3 p. 410); *ZDJC* vol. 16, pp. 56–8. Comintern purge ends, Mao off hook: Piatnitsky, p. 454; Vaksberg, pp. 252–8. "under the leadership headed by Mao": outline of Wang Jia-xiang speech for the Politburo meeting of 14 Sept. 1938, and for the subsequent 6th plenum, in *WHY*, 1986, pp. 68–71; cf. Kampen 1987, pp. 712–16; Kampen 2000, pp. 93–6; Avreyski 1987, pp. 334–5; Titov, vol. 3, pp. 245–6. *Xu Zehao, pp. 296–305. Wang Ming summoned from Wuhan: *Xiao Jingguang, p. 233; *Zhu Zhongli 1995, pp. 99–100; *Zhou Guoquan et al., p. 351; Huang, J., p. 116.

211   Mao re-establishes No. 1 position: *Hu Qiaomu, p. 367; *Mao 1993b, vol. 2, pp. 90–1; *Xu Zehao, pp. 305–8. Strung plenum out: *Mao 1993b, vol. 2, pp. 90–5; footnote to Wang Jia-xiang speech, *WHY*, 1986, p. 68; *Zhou 1991, pp. 419–20; *Wang Xiuxin, pp. 230–6; *Peng 1998, pp. 205–6; *Xu Zehao, p. 308.

212   Opponents left town: *Zhou 1991, p. 420; *Wang Fuyi, p. 332; *Zhou Guoquan et al., p. 361. Mao: "Chinese nation has stood up" under Chiang: Mao report, 12–14 Oct. 1938, in *ZZWX* vol. 11, p. 561, also

pp. 560, 596, 606, 612–13, 642 (E: *MRTP* vol. 6, pp. 487, 461); cf. Titov, vol. 2, pp. 267ff. Identical words in 1949: 21 Sept. 1949, in *Mao 1993–9, vol. 5, p. 342 (E: Kau & Leung, p. 5).

212–213　　Liu shared Mao strategy: *Liu 1996, vol. 1, pp. 241ff; *Xie Youtian, p. 222; cf. Wang Ming, pp. 72–6; Titov, vol. 3, pp. 260–1; Huang, J., pp. 128ff. Mao imposed new policy, kept it secret: Luo Rui-qing article, in *Luo Diandian 1987, p. 102; *Mao 1991, vol. 2, pp. 537–40 (E: *MRTP* vol. 6, pp. 545–7); *Wang Shoudao, pp. 200, 213; orders in *ZZWX vol. 11, pp. 760–9 (E: Saich 1996, pp. 841–4).

213　　　　Kang switches allegiance: *Shi Zhe 1992, pp. 209–13, 220; *Sima Lu 1952, p. 73; Huang, J., pp. 125ff; Byron & Pack, pp. 145–50.

213–214　　Wang Ming return to Yenan: *Zhou Guoquan et al., p. 357; *ZR vol. 16, pp. 325–8; *Sima Lu 1952, p. 123. Peng: Mao "wise leader": *Wang Yan et al., p. 202. Chou conversion to Mao: Chou dated to May 1939 in a speech in Nov. 1943, *Jin Chongji et al. 1990, p. 563. Mao only told Moscow in June 1939: Anderson & Chubaryan, pp. 21–2 (extract of CCP Report to Comintern, June); cf. Titov, vol. 3, pp. 297ff.

214–215　　Karmen films Mao: Karmen 1941, pp. 109–15. Lin Biao in Russia: Titov, vol. 3, pp. 358–63, 369. Mao's brother to Russia: Titov, vol. 3, pp. 363ff. Tse-min on Wang: RGASPI, 514/1/1044, pp. 95–101 (Zhou Den [Mao Tse-min] report, "After Becoming Acquainted with Some Important Party Documents," 6 Dec. 1939); Titov, vol. 3, p. 375 (Tse-min report, 22 Jan. 1940); cf. *Hu Qiaomu, p. 367.

214n　　　Wang Dan-zhi interview, June 1995.

215　　　　On Po and others: RGASPI, 514/1/1044, pp. 13–29; *VKP* vol. 4, pp. 1129–39 (Tse-min report, 26 Aug. 1939, "On the Errors of Cdes. Po-Ku, Li-De [Braun] and Others in the Leadership of the Party and the Red Army"); Titov, vol. 3, p. 375 (22 Jan. 1940).

215　　　　Chou to Russia: Titov, vol. 3, pp. 386ff; Tikhvinsky 1996, pp. 341ff., 523–5; Dallin & Firsov pp. 111–25 (Chou reports in Moscow, early 1940); RGASPI 514/1/1006, pp. 48–9 (Chou grilled by KGB's Mordvinov, 4 Mar. 1940). Tse-min on Chou: Titov, vol. 3, pp. 376–7; cf. 368ff. Braun accused: Tse-min report, 26 Aug. 1939, *cit.*; Braun 1982, p. 263; *VKP* vol. 4, pp. 1144–51 (Braun report, "On My Errors in Work in China," 22 Sept. 1939); Titov, vol. 3, pp. 386–7 (Chou report to Comintern, early Jan. 1940).

CHAPTER 21　*Most Desired Scenario: Stalin Carves up China with Japan*

216　　　　Chen Tu-hsiu poem: in *YHCQ, 1994, no. 6, p. 81.

216–217　　Chiang concern: *DVP* vol. 22, book 1 (1939), p. 649 (to Panyushkin, 25 Aug. 1939); cf. *DVP* vol. 22, book 2 (1939), pp. 57–8, 64; Mirovitskaya 1999, pp. 63–4. Mao enthusiastic: *China Weekly Review*, 20 Jan. 1940, pp. 277–8 (Mao to Snow, 26 Sept. 1939); Snow in (London) *Daily Herald*, 21 Oct. 1939; Snow 1973, pp. 446–8; *Mao 1993, pp. 146–51. Hails Russia's seizure of eastern Finland: Titov, vol. 3, p. 411 (Mao secret directive, 25 June 1940). Compares China to partitioned France: restricted circular in *ZZWX vol. 12, p. 542. Demarcation line: Yangtze: Mao instruction on the strategy of development for N4A, 19 Jan. 1940, in *ZZWX vol. 12, p. 238 (E: Benton 1999, p. 741); Mao to Politburo, 11 Sept. 1940, in *Mao 1993b, vol. 2, p. 205.

217   Dimitrov to Mao, Oct. 1939, in Titarenko 1986, pp. 284–5 (E: Web/Dimitrov); cf. RGASPI, 514/1/1042, p. 8; Nikiforov, pp. 124–5; Titov, vol. 3, pp. 346–8; RGASPI, 514/1/1042, p. 7 (Mordvinov to Dimitrov, 13 Nov. 1939).

217–218   Mao report, 22 Feb. 1940: Titov, vol. 3, pp. 412–14. Money to Mao: Dimitrov, 23 Feb. 1940; Dallin & Firsov, p. 122; Anderson & Chubaryan, pp. 258–9 (Dimitrov to Voroshilov, 1 Feb. 1940). Radio to Mao: *Shi Zhe 1991, pp. 201–3.

218   Takahashi, p. 213.

218   Collaboration with Japanese intelligence: *Yin Qi 1996a, pp. 91ff.; *Yin Qi 1996b, pp. 198ff.; Iwai, pp. 80ff.; interview with Seiichi Koizumi, 8 Apr. 1999; Yick.

218   "our Party's tactic": *Sima Lu 1952, pp. 210–11.

219   Ovchinnikov, p. 95 (Vladimirov in Ilyichev to Dimitrov, 6 May 1944).

219   Why Japan left Reds in peace: interview with Prince Mikasa, 2 Mar. 1998. Zhu and Peng plan to attack Japanese, Mao veto: *Wang Yan et al., pp. 208–9; *Peng 1998, pp. 227–8. Zhu detained: *Jin Chongji et al. 1993, pp. 484–92.

220   Mao hopes Japanese get to Chongqing: Snow 1974, p. 169 (to Snow, 9 Jan. 1965). Peng launches Operation without Mao permission: *ZDJC vol. 16, pp. 368–70 also p. 320; *Peng 1981, p. 236 (E: Peng, p. 438); *Peng 1998, p. 232; *Li Rui 1989, p. 223; Van Slyke. Japanese on Operation: *CPPCC (Tianjin) vol. 1, pp. 574–5; *Japan Self-Defence Agency, pp. 309–10.

220–221   Chou cables Mao: *Zhou 1991, p. 465; *Revolutionary Military Museum, pp. 488–91. Mao to punish Peng: *Peng 1981, pp. 239–40 (E: Peng, pp. 442–5); *Wang Yan et al., p. 287. Chiang trade-off: *Chiang, pp. 1605–8. (Many documents on New 4th Army Incident in Benton 1999, pp. 754–818.)

221–222   Mao turns down offer: *Huang Xiurong, p. 437. Panyushkin: Panyushkin, p. 101. Mao cables to Moscow: Titov, vol. 3, pp. 418–22. Second deadline: *South Anhui Incident Committee, pp. 81–2. "bully him": Mao to Chou, 3 Nov. 1940, in *Central Archive 1982, pp. 38–9; also p. 75. 7 Nov. cable: in Dallin & Firsov, pp. 128–30;. cf. ibid. pp. 126–8 (Dimitrov to Stalin, 23 Nov. 1940 re Mao); cf. Panyushkin, p. 115, Titov, vol. 3, pp. 441ff.

222–223   Molotov's agenda for Berlin: DVP vol. 23, book 2, part 1 (1940–1941), p. 32. Molotov told Hitler: DVP vol. 23, book 2, part 1 (1940-1941), p. 71; Sontag & Beddie, pp. 246–7. "Russian sphere of influence": Documents on German Foreign Policy, Series D, vol. 11, pp. 512–13 (Ott to Ribbentrop, 11 Nov. 1940); cf. Slavinsky 1995, pp. 67ff. "recognising and accepting": "Draft Outline for the Adjustment of Japanese-Soviet Diplomatic Relations," Japanese Foreign Ministry, Archives of the Gaiko Shiryokan, Tokyo, File B100–JR/1, 2.100–23 (E: quoted in Hosoya in Morley 1980, p. 52; cf. ibid., pp. 23–4). Stalin to Chuikov: Chuikov 1981, pp. 56, 58.

223   Chuikov's other role: Chuikov 1971, p. 278.

223   Order to Mao, 25 Nov.: Dallin & Firsov, pp. 127–8 (dating: ibid., p. 126); cf. Titov, vol. 3, pp. 443–5.

223   Mao reached conclusion: Mao circular, 25 Dec. 1940, in *Central Archive 1982, p. 117.

CHAPTER 22   *Death Trap for His Own Men*

224   Xiang Ying mocking Mao: *Kuo Hua-lun, vol. 3, p. 276 (E: Kuo, W., vol. 3, p. 520, cf. p. 526). Xiang group the only N4A south of Yangtze: *N4A History Committee, pp. 534ff.; *Li Liangzhi, pp. 54–9; cf. Benton 1999, pp. 511ff. Mao told Xiang to decamp on 24 Dec. 1940, in *Central Archive 1982, p. 116.

224–225   Chiang designated North Route: Chiang order, 10 Dec., in *South Anhui Incident Committee, p. 94, cf. p. 84. Mao confirmed it: Mao to Xiang, 29 Dec., in *Central Archive 1982, p. 124. Mao changes route: Mao to Xiang, 30 Dec., in *Central Archive 1982, p. 125. Chiang not told: cable, 3 Jan. 1941, in *South Anhui Incident Committee, p. 102. Xiang reply to Chiang which never arrived: *Li Liangzhi, p. 211. All contacts to Chiang via Mao: from mid-1940, *Huang Xiurong, p. 436; *Jin Chongji et al. 1993, p. 487. Nationalists began to "exterminate" Reds on 6 Jan.: *ZDZ vol. 37, p. 33. Mao pretended he had not heard from Xiang 6th–9th: Mao to Liu, 9 Jan. 1941, in *Central Archive 1982, p. 130.

225   Mao to Chou, 13 Jan. 1941, in *Li Liangzhi, p. 211.

225–226   N4A HQ appeals to Mao: cables, in *Central Archive 1982, pp. 131ff. Xiang's cable of 10th to Chiang again suppressed: in *Li Liangzhi, p. 211. Mao informed Chou only on 11th: Mao cable in *Central Archive 1982, p. 135; Chou first raised it with Nationalist General Ku, in a tone more of sorrow than of anger, at 9–11 pm on 11th, cable in *ZS vol. 5, no. 2, p. 541; also *Tong Xiaopeng, vol. 1, p. 224. Mao toned down level of crisis on 12th: compare Mao to Chou that day with N4A HQ to Mao on 10th, in *Central Archive 1982, pp. 137, 132.

226   13th: Chou serious protest; Chiang had already stopped killing: Chou two cables to Mao on 13th, ibid., pp. 140, 142–3.

226–227   Mao cranked up PR campaigns: orders, ibid., pp. 138ff. "overthrow Chiang": Mao to Peng, 23 Jan. 1941, in *Li Liangzhi, p. 295, plus many other cables, ibid., pp. 294–7. Chou saw Russian ambassador, who suspected Mao: Panyushkin, pp. 113ff; cf. Mirovitskaya 1999, pp. 64–6; Tikhvinsky 2000, p. 628 (Chou–Panyushkin, 15 Jan. 1941). Mao appeals to Moscow for all-out civil war: Titov, vol. 3, pp. 461–2;

Dimitrov, 16 Jan. 1941; Panyushkin, pp. 129–30; cf. RGASPI, 495/74/317, p. 75. Dimitrov reaction: Dimitrov, 18 Jan. 1941; cf. Avreyski, pp. 384–5. Stalin annoyed: Dimitrov, 21 Jan. 1941. Ye Ting: RGASPI, 495/1/942; cf. ibid., 495/154/353, p. 3.

226   Tikhvinsky 2000, p. 628 (Chou–Panyushkin, 15 Jan. 1941).

227   Dimitrov blamed Mao: Dallin & Firsov, p. 135 (Dimitrov to Mao, 4 Feb. 1941, and to Stalin, 6 Feb. 1941); cf. Dimitrov, 4, 5 & 6 Feb. 1941. Order, 13 Feb.: Dimitrov, 12 Feb. 1941. Mao cable that day: to Dimitrov, in Dallin & Firsov, pp. 137–41; contrast with Mao to Dimitrov, 1 Feb. 1941, ibid., p. 136. Mao unusual letter to sons: 31 Jan. 1941, *Mao 1984, pp. 166–7. This and some other Mao letters to his sons in Usov 1997, pp. 109ff; three An-ying letters to Mao intercepted in NA, HW17/55 (ISCOT 297, sent 29 July 1944), HW17/66 (ISCOT 1359, sent 2 May 1945), HW17/67 (ISCOT 1475, sent 28 Nov. 1945); An-ying letters (to others) in Romanov & Kharitonov, pp. 159ff.

227–228   Xiang death: killer Liu Houzong's own account, in *LD, 1981, no. 2, pp. 81, 96; *Xu & Tang, pp. 613–19. Mao condemns Xiang: Resolution, Jan. 1941, in *ZZWX vol. 13, pp. 31–4 (E: Saich 1996, pp. 956–8); cf. Panyushkin, pp. 123–4. Russian heat on Chiang: Chuikov 1981, pp. 76, 78–9; Panyushkin, p. 127; Titov, vol. 3, p. 466; DVP vol. 23, book 2, part 1 (1940–1941), pp. 350ff. *Chiang, p. 1667. Pressure from US: Currie, "Notes . . .," cit. Currie report to Roosevelt: FRUS 1941, vol. 4, pp. 81–5; cf. Snow 1972, pp. 236–7. Carlson: Ickes, vol. 2, pp. 327–8; Wang, A., p. 328.

229   British ambassador: Panyushkin, pp. 117, 129; Hayter 1974, p. 51. Casualties: Mao cable, 1 Feb. 1941, in *Mao 1993a, vol. 2, p. 622; Ye Ting letter, Feb. 1941, in *South Anhui Incident Committee, p. 211. Chiang had not set a trap: ibid., pp. 388–419; *Li Liangzhi, pp. 232–45. Chiang and Reds kept quiet about clashes before: Ta Kung Pao editorial, 10 Mar. 1941, in *GS vol. 3, pp. 257–60; *Wang Yan et al., p. 205.

229–230   Hemingway on Chou: Morgenthau Diary vol. 1, p. 458 (letter to Morgenthau, 30 July 1941). Snow article: "Reds Fought off Chiang's Troops 9 Days in China," NY-HT, 22 Jan. 1941; cf. Thomas, pp. 239, 373, n. 39; Farnsworth, pp. 375–8. Hemingway on Reds: Morgenthau Diary vol. 1, p. 460 (to Morgenthau, 30 July 1941). Dissuaded from publishing by Currie: ibid., p. 461 (Hemingway to Morgenthau, 30 July 1941). Currie: Sandilands, pp. 107ff; Persico, p. 378 ("friend," not spy); *ZS vol. 3, no. 1, pp. 533ff.

230–231   Verbal message: Currie, "Notes . . .," cit., p. 2. Report to Roosevelt: FRUS 1941, vol. 4, pp. 81ff, 83. Chiang asked Kremlin to intervene: Tikhvinsky 2000, pp. 629–32 (Ambassador Shao Li-tzu to Lozovsky, 29 Jan. 1941). Mao referred to Chiang as "rebel": 1 Feb. 1941, *Mao 1993a, vol. 2, p. 623.

230n   Minutes of 22 Feb. 1941 Currie–Chiang meeting, p. 12; *ZS vol. 3, no. 1, pp. 579–80, 586, 591–5, 622–3, 725–37.

231   Mao scenario, 25 Oct. 1940: in *Central Archive 1982, p. 34 (E: Benton 1999, pp. 763–4). Spectacular change, 6 Nov.: in *ZZWX vol. 12, p. 551.

CHAPTER 23   *Building a Power Base through Terror*

232   Mao no sleep: *Yin Qi 1996a, p. 136. "Stop any assaults on all Nationalist
               units": 9 Sept. 1941, *Mao 1993a, vol. 2, p. 665. Moscow wanted CCP
               to tie down Japanese: Titov, vol. 3, pp. 470ff; Dallin & Firsov, pp. 141–6
               (Mao–Dimitrov cables, July 1941); Sidikhmenov 1993, p. 30; Dimitrov,
               9 July 1941 and ff.

232   Dimitrov, 21 June 1941; Andrew & Mitrokhin, p. 124; *OIRVR*, vol. 4,
               p. 214; cf. Peshchersky; Yan Baohang unpublished letter, in *Wang
               Lianjie, p. 337; *Yin Qi 1996a, pp. 134–5.

232–233   Mao determined not to fight Japanese: cables in *Mao 1993a, vol. 2,
               pp. 650–5; in *ZDJC vol. 17, p. 119; cf. Titov, vol. 3, pp. 472–4. Mao
               tells Moscow don't expect much: Titov, vol. 3, pp. 470ff; Dimitrov, 18,
               20 & 21 July 1941; Dallin & Firsov, p. 142. Stalin personally cabled:
               Panyushkin, p. 170; Titov, vol. 3, p. 472; *Shi Zhe 1991, pp. 213–17. Mao
               infuriated Moscow: Panyushkin, pp. 169–70; Titov, vol. 3, pp. 470,
               477–8; Chuikov 1981, pp. 201–2; Vereshchagin, p. 42.

233   Molotov: Chuev 1999, pp. 141–2.

234–235   CCP "always been pretty": Mao speech, 1 Apr. 1938, in *DSYJ, 1981,
               no. 4; (E: *MRTP* vol. 6, pp. 278–9). Young volunteer described: *Sima
               Lu 1952, pp. 45, 80. Inequality: *Central Party School, vol. 2, pp. 26,
               216–18; *Wen Jize et al. 1984, p. 50; *Mo Wenhua, p. 404; *Wang
               Enmao, vol. 3, p. 373; *Sima Lu 1952, pp. 50–1, 63–4; interviews with
               Yenan veterans in China.

235–236   Red Cross: *Sima Lu 1952, pp. 88–9; *ZDC, 1986, no. 3, pp. 71, 79.
               Mao's car: *Zhu Zhongli 1995, p. 125; Snow 1941, p. 281; Karmen, p. 114;
               *Sima Lu 1952, p. 123.

236   "the Chairman's smile froze": Zeng Zhi, in *"Mao and I" Collection
               Committee 1993a, p. 93. "a chicken a day": *Sima Lu 1952, p. 64. "only
               three things are equal": *Central Party School, vol. 1, p. 67. Japanese
               POW: interview with Mitsushige Maeda, 8 Mar. 1998. Could not leave:
               the writer Xiao Jun repeatedly asked Mao for a pass to leave; Mao
               personally stonewalled him, in *Wang Defen, pp. 105–10.

236   Scene in hospital: *Sima Lu 1952, pp. 64–6.

237   Catch 1,000 deserters: *Wang Enmao, vol. 3, p. 385.

237–238   "Wild Lilies": *Wang Shi-wei, pp. 125–32; (E: in Dai Qing 1994,
               pp. 2–9, 17–20).

238–239   Mao demanded angrily: *Hu Qiaomu, p. 449. Shi-wei's poster: *Wang
               Shiwei, pp. 139–40; *Wen Jize et al. 1984, p. 17. Mao on Shi-wei: Yang
               Guoyu diary, in *YQD, p. 292; *Huang Changyong, p. 183; cf. Saich
               1996, p. 1240 (Mao 24 Apr. 1945). Shi-wei on Trotsky and Stalin: *Wen
               Jize et al. 1993, pp. 83–5, 188, 191–3 (E: cf. Wen in Saich 1996, pp.
               1115–16 and Dai Qing 1994, pp. 47–8).

239   Robotic confession: Wei Jingmeng in Dai Qing, p. 65. *Zhao Chaogou
               et al., p. 49. Interrogator revealed: *Wen Jize et al. 1993, p. 78. Hacked

to death: *Huang Changyong, p. 191. Young volunteers turned into spy suspects: *Shi Zhe 1992, pp. 195–7; Li Yimin, pp. 29–43; Ling Yun, in *Wen Jize et al. 1993, p. 74; interviews with many Yenan veterans in China, 1993ff.

240   Mao orders: 15 Nov. 1943, in *ZDJC vol. 17, p. 385; 15 Aug. 1943, in *WHY, 1984, no. 9, pp. 10–14. Real spy suspects "taken care of": interviews with Shi Zhe, 7 Sept. 1994, 11 Sept. 1997.

240   *Shi Zhe 1992, p. 215.

241   Mao instructions about torture: in *WHY, 1984, no. 9, p. 12. Mass rallies "grave war on nerves": Ren Bi-shi, 13 May 1944, in *ZDJC vol. 17, p. 390; cf. Mao, 15 Nov. 1943, in *ZDJC vol. 17, p. 385; *Li Weihan, pp. 512–13; *YQD, p. 262; *Unity Publishing, pp. 3ff; *Chen Yung-fa, p. 112 (E: cf. Chen Yung-fa 1996); all our Yenan interviewees testify to this. "Get everybody to write their thought examination": 6 June 1943, in *WHY, 1984, no. 8, pp. 6–7; also p. 10.

242   "pillow talk": *Unity Publishing, pp. 66–9, cf. *Chen Yung-fa, pp. 215, 219. Mao announcement, 8 Aug.: in *Yang Kuisong 1997, p. 510. 800 items: *Central Party School, vol. 2, p. 140.

242   Chongqing journalist's observation: *Zhao Chaogou, pp. 15–19. Helen Snow: interview, 24 Oct. 1992.

243   Less than 1 percent: *Kang Sheng 1944; cf. *Chen Yung-fa, pp. 130–1; *Li Yimin, p. 40. Mao inflated the figure: 24 Jan. 1944, in *ZDJC vol. 17, p. 387. Rehabilitation spring 1945: interviews with victims; *Shi Zhe 1991, pp. 258–9; *Li Weihan, p. 514; *Wang Suyuan, p. 228. "many . . . gone mad": *Bo Yibo 1996, p. 362. Death figure: interview with Yenan veterans; cf. Byron & Pack, p. 470. Suicides: *Li Yimin, p. 38; *Wang Enmao, vol. 3, p. 386; *Cheng Min, pp. 151–99.

244   "heavy blow": *Jiang Nanxiang, pp. 64–71. Mao "apologies": *Shi Zhe 1991, p. 259; *Li Weihan, p. 514; *Cheng Min, p. 26; *Hu Qiaomu, p. 281; *Wang Suyuan, p. 229; *Central Party School, vol. 1, p. 65; *Wen Jize et al. 1993, p. 109; interviews with veterans, 25 Oct. 1994 & 17 Mar. 1998.

245   Stamp on "100 percent": *Li Rui 1989, pp. 349–50. "write down every single social relationship": Mao order, 6 June 1943, in *WHY, 1984, no. 8, pp. 6–7. "Some people think": *Mao 1995, p. 115; cf. *Mao 1993b, vol. 2, pp. 462–3. "illusions about Chiang": *Wang Enmao, vol. 3, p. 388.

245–246   "Who is the nation-builder of China": *Wang Enmao, vol. 3, pp. 376–7. Spying for Chiang the key issue: *Kang Sheng, 15 July 1943, and various Communist documents produced in the campaign, in the archive of the Investigation Bureau, Taipei. Tse-min told to stay put, imprisoned: *Zhu & Yi, pp. 368–89; *Shu Long, pp. 275–7; cf. Whiting & Sheng, pp. 238–9. Russians urged Chou to ask for their release: AVPRF, 0100/31/220/13, p. 257 (Panyushkin–Chou, 10 Apr. 1943). CCP and Mao cables, 10 & 12 Feb.; Chou did not raise issue: *Huang Xiurong, pp. 557–8; *Zhou 1991, pp. 549–57.

246   Lin told Panyushkin: AVPRF, 0100/31/220/13, pp. 240, 257; cf. Ovchinnikov, p. 62 (Godunov to Dimitrov, 14 Aug. 1943).

CHAPTER 24   *Uncowed Opponent Poisoned*

247   Autumn 1941 Politburo meetings: *Hu Qiaomu, pp. 193–9. Dimitrov 15 questions: Avreyski, pp. 409–11; Wang Ming, p. 38; in *Yang Kuisong 1999, pp. 130–1.

247–248   Wang demanded debate: *Hu Qiaomu, pp. 199–200. Mao shelves congress: *Hu Qiaomu, pp. 194, 222–32. Nine ranting articles: *Hu Qiaomu, p. 214; *Yang Kuisong 1997, pp. 507–8. Obsessively attached to them to the end of life: *Hu Qiaomu, pp. 214–15.

248–249   Wang defiant writings: Feb. 1942, in *Zhou Guoquan et al., p. 404. Dr. Jin: *ZDC, 1986, no. 3, pp. 71, 79. Inquiry findings: This document was entitled "Duiyu Wang Ming tongzhi bing guoqu zhenduan yu zhiliao de zongjie" (Summary of the Past Diagnosis and Treatment of Comrade Wang Ming's Illnesses), and was signed on 20 July 1943 by eleven top Yenan doctors. Wang described the poisoning in his own book: Wang Ming, pp. 38–46.

249–250   Vladimirov arrived: *ORK*, 11 May 1942. Wang "at death's door": Dimitrov, 16 July 1942. Wang: don't count on CCP: *ORK*, 18 July 1942. "Spies watch," beautiful girl, sack cook: *ORK*, 20 & 22 July 1942. Mao refused to let Wang go: *ORK*, 8 & 14 Jan. 1943; Dimitrov, 15 Jan. 1943. Wang to Stalin: Dimitrov, 1 Feb. 1943; Wang Ming, p. 40; cf. Avreyski, pp. 430–5; Pantsov, p. 5, n. 5 ("biggest Trotskyist in China"); Waack, p. 360, n. 16.

250   Mao to Dimitrov: Dimitrov, 3 Feb. 1943; cf. Avreyski, p. 433. Dimitrov promises to get Wang out: Avreyski, p. 434; Wang Ming, pp. 40–41. 12 Feb.: prescription in Mrs. Wang Ming's explanatory note to the "Summary" of the medical inquiry. Tannic acid: "Summary" of the medical inquiry. 20 Mar. Politburo resolution: in *ZDJC vol. 17, pp. 344–6; cf. Kampen 2000, pp. 104–7; Saich 1996, p. 986. Surreptitious affair: even somebody as senior as General Xiao Ke did not know: interview with the general, 30 Sept. 1993; other Yenan veterans did not know, either: interview, 11 Mar. 1998. Dr. Jin's prescription: *ORK*, 23, 25 Mar. 1943.

251   Mme Mao: Jin agent: *ORK*, 28 Mar. 1943. Jin protected: interview with Mao's security assistant Shi Zhe, 11 Mar. 1998, and other residents of Date Garden.

251–252   "Wang . . . poisoned": *ORK*, 24 July 1943. Accomplice Chou: AVPRF, 0100/31/220/13, pp. 173–4 (Panyushkin–Chou, 10 Apr. 1943), ibid., p. 240 (Panyushkin–Lin Biao, 9 June 1943). *Zhou 1991, pp. 551–7. Chiang clears An-ying's return: to Chou and Lin, 7 June, AVPRF, 0100/31/220/13, p. 240 (Lin–Panyushkin, 9 June 1943).

252   Interviews with Jin's elite patients and colleagues, 23 Oct. 1995, 17 Mar. & 6 Sept. 1998.

252–253   An-ying in Russia: Usov 1997, pp. 111–12; Dimitrov, 19 Aug. 1943. Mao held Wang back: *ORK*, 30 Aug. 1943. Second Soviet plane: *ORK*, 19 & 24 Oct. 1943; Siao, Eva, p. 131. "Wang Ming burst into tears": *ORK*, 28 Oct. 1943. Many suspected the truth: interviews with veterans, 11 Mar. 1998 & 18 Apr. 1999.

253   1 Nov. meeting, case closed: Mrs. Wang's letter to Mao, 15 Nov. 1943, in *ZDC, 1986, no. 3, pp. 78–80; Wang letter to Mao and Politburo, 1 Dec. 1943, in *Zhou Guoquan et al., pp. 413–14; cf. *Hu Qiaomu, p. 298.

253–254   Strange things happened: ORK, 29 Sept. & 3 Oct. 1943. Russian arms to Mao: Tikhvinsky 2000, p. 802 (Panyushkin to Molotov, 11 Feb. 1944). Dimitrov, 17 Nov.: NA, HW 17/54 (Moscow cable, 17 Nov. 1943, ISCOT 168). 13 Dec.: TsDA, 146/6/1206; cf. Dimitrov, 23 Nov. & 13 Dec. 1943. 22 Dec.: Dimitrov, 22 Dec. 1943.

254   Mao, 2 Jan. 1944: Ovchinnikov, pp. 84–5 (Vladimirov to Dimitrov); Dimitrov, 10 Jan. 1944.

255   "unruffled calm": *Shi Zhe 1991, pp. 238–9. "given much thought": Ovchinnikov, p. 82. Mao woos Vladimirov: ORK, 8 Jan. 1944.

256   "I sincerely thank you": Dimitrov, 10 Jan. 1944; Ovchinnikov, p. 83; cf. ORK, 6 & 8 Jan. 1944. Paid Wang visits: ORK, 23 & 25 Jan. 1944. Dimitrov, 25 Feb.: Dimitrov, 25 Feb. 1944. 28 Mar., to An-ying: ORK, 28 Mar. 1944; NA, HW 17/55 (An-ying to Mao, cabled 29 July 1944). Dimitrov–Wang: Dimitrov, 19 & 23 Jan., 7 Mar. 1944; ORK, 23 Jan. 1944.

256   Rally denouncing Wang: Liu Ying, in *YQD, p. 21; *Central Party School, vol. 1, p. 68.

257   cf. Wang Ming, pp. 46–7.

257–258   Threatened to condemn Chou: Dimitrov, 22 Dec. 1943 (to Mao); Yang Shangkun, in *Cheng Min, p. 25; *Yang Kuisong 1999, p. 153; *Li Weihan, p. 513; cf. AVPRF, 0100/29/205/11, pp. 276–8 (Chou–Panyushkin, 21 Sept. 1942) and RGASPI, 514/1/957, pp. 16–26 (Kogan & Shibanov report to Dimitrov, 12 Mar. 1943), which both suggest that Chou took out insurance with the Russians. "Don't linger": *Mao 1993b, vol. 2, p. 446. "Don't leave your heart": *Gao Wenqian, p. 76. "welcome" party: Chou speech, 2 Aug. 1943, in *Zhou 1981, p. 138. Chou bashed himself: Chou manuscript for speech at Politburo on 15 Nov. 1943, in *Gao Wenqian, pp. 78–9; cf. *Li Rui 1989, p. 287. "Democracy, freedom": 6 June 1943, in *Mao 1993b, vol. 2, pp. 444–5; (E: JPRS, vol. 9, part 1, pp. 130–1).

258   Plain "wrong": *Li Rui 1989, pp. 253, 287. "hard to stand alone": ibid., p. 304. "fucked for forty days": ibid., pp. 248, 279–80, 287; cf. *Bo Yibo 1996, pp. 367–73; *Peng 1998, pp. 294–9; Schram 1974, p. 194: Mao, 24 Sept. 1962.

CHAPTER 25 *Supreme Party Leader at Last*

259   Praetorian Guard inaugurated: Guard Di Fucai's account, in *ZHEN, 1994, no. 6, p. 26. Date Garden: interview with Li Hsiao-li, 22 Oct. 1995; ORK, 14 July 1942; *Shi Zhe 1992, p. 220; our visit to Yenan, Oct. 1994. Back Ravine: our visit to Yenan, Oct. 1994; interviews with Shi Zhe, 10 Oct. 1995 & 11 Mar. 1998, and with a Date Garden resident, 13 Mar. 1998.

260   "I controlled that entrance": interview, 10 Oct. 1995. Kang Sheng
       terrorized: *Shi Zhe 1991, pp. 260–1; *Shi Zhe 1992, pp. 208–9;
       *Cheng Min, p. 305. Moscow condemned Kang: Dimitrov to Mao, 22
       Dec. 1943, *cit.*; Titov, vol. 3, pp. 401–2. Pleaded with Mao: *Zhong Kan,
       p. 437; *Cheng Min, p. 307.

260   A sadist: Kang speech, Aug. 1943, in *Wen Jize et al. 1993, pp. 104–8.
       Asses' penises: *unpublished manuscript of a person present. A voyeur:
       *Shi Zhe 1992, p. 198; interviews with Yenan veterans. Mao limited
       Kang's power: the so-called "Nine Guidelines," 15 Aug. 1943, in *WHY,
       1984, no. 9, pp. 10–11; ORK, 20 Aug. 1944. "changing his views rapidly":
       ORK, 4 Apr. 1943; interview with a historian with access to Liu files,
       16 Mar. 1998.

261n   *Jiang Nanxiang; AVPRF, 0100/43/302/10, pp. 158–63 (Liu to
       Roshchin, 26 Aug. 1950).

261–262 "Fuck you": *Quan Yanchi 1997, pp. 176–9. Mao ordered wife to go
       back to unit: interview with Xie Fei, 14 Sept. 1994; *Zhu Zhongli 1989,
       pp. 221–4.

262   Her first victim, the nanny: interview with the nanny, 13 Mar. 1998;
       cf. *Zhu Zhongli 1988, pp. 55–67.

263   "only wise leader": *Deng Liqun, pp. 18–20; *YQD, p. 213; *Central
       Party School, vol. 1, pp. 42, 45. "same old thing," etc.: in *Wen Jize et
       al. 1984, pp. 234, 252, 259–60. Reluctant to chant "Long live": ibid.,
       p. 208; interview with Yenan veterans, 5 Oct. 1993. Giant headlines:
       *JR, 17 July 1943. Badges of his head: first to Central Party School
       members, *Central Party School, vol. 2, pp. 74, 79; *YQD, p. 196; cf.
       *Wang Enmao, vol. 3, p. 267; *Hu Qiaomu, p. 277. Head of himself
       carved: *Central Party School, vol. 2, pp. 208–9. Portraits printed:
       interview with Yenan veterans, 11 Mar. 1998. "The East Is Red": *PRC
       Encyclopaedia vol. 3, pp. 2889–90. Red Prof's wife described: *Zhu
       Zhongli 1995, pp. 120–3; Bodyguard Zhang Zhiyou also recalled this
       episode, in *Xu Zehao, pp. 374–5.

263–264 History rewritten: *Central Party School, vol. 2, pp. 40–1. Mao
       instructed: 28 Dec. 1943, *ZZWX vol. 14, p. 143. 7th Congress dele-
       gates: *YQD, pp. 43, 134, 154, 172, 201; *Shi Zhe 1992, pp. 3–4; *Central
       Party School, vol. 1, p. 24.

264n   1930 original, *Deng Zhongxia, p. 88; 1943 insert, *ZR vol. 35, p. 47;
       *CCP Xiangqu Committee Museum & Changsha Museum, pp. 122–3.

264   Verge of tears: *YQD, p. 61; *Lu Zhengchao, p. 513.

CHAPTER 26   *"Revolutionary Opium War"*

267   Funding from Nationalists: Shaanganning Border Region government
       report, Apr. 1941, *CASS vol. 2, p. 76; cf. Schran, pp. 171–2. From
       Moscow: Dimitrov, 25 Feb. 1940; Dallin & Firsov, pp. 122ff. (Chou asks
       Moscow to make up monthly deficit of US$358,280). Grain tax figures:
       Shaanganning Border Region government report, Apr. 1941, in *CASS
       vol. 2, p. 74; *Gansu Social Science Academy, vol. 2, p. 280.

267–268   "driven to death": *Xie Juezai, p. 309. Harvest 20–30 percent down: *Xie Juezai, p. 319. "strike Mao dead": Mao speech at the 7th Congress, 31 May 1945, in *Mao 1995, p. 211; also *Mao 1993b, vol. 2, p. 303; *JR, 5 June 1941. Doubled and added taxes: *Gansu Social Science Academy, vol. 2, pp. 270–2, 280, 287–8. "feigning madness": Mao speech, 12 Apr. 1945, in Yang Guoyu diary, *YQD, p. 202. "Mao has no eyes": interviews with Yenan veterans, 12 Sept. 1994 & 11 Mar. 1998. Cook figures: Mao figure: 160,000 *shi*, in Yenan Museum, visit, Oct. 1994, and in *RR, 26 Dec. 1981; but real figure 200,000 *shi*, *JR, 21 Sept. 1943; *Chen Yung-fa, p. 290; *Xie Juezai, p. 579. Xie noted in diary: 24 Feb. 1944, *Xie Juezai, pp. 579–80. 1,000 families fled: *Chen Yung-fa, p. 299.

268–269   Plenty of trade: Shaanganning Border Region government report, Apr. 1941, *CASS vol. 2, pp. 72, 76. Teng Pao-shan: Jin Cheng, in *Biographical Literature Pub., vol. 2, pp. 217–45; *Xiao Jingguang, pp. 258–63. 1941 report on salt: *CASS vol. 2, pp. 71–2. "second-biggest source": 19 July 1941, *Xie Juezai, p. 329. "Transporting salt": *Xie Juezai, pp. 322–3.

269–270   "Today": 19 July 1941, *Xie Juezai, p. 328. Mao told them flatly: Mao to Xie, 6 and 22 Aug. 1941, in *Mao 1984, pp. 176–8, 186–8; cf. *Xie Juezai, p. 332. Lindsay: Lindsay Hsiao-li, unpublished memoirs, pp. 372–3; id., interview, 22 Oct. 1995; cf. NA, WO 208/318 (M. Lindsay to M. Hall). In Nov. 1941: *"Shaanganning Border Region," pp. 7–9. Mao public show: ibid., pp. 1–6. What the regime did: ibid., pp. 11–15, 119, 128–37.

270   The answer was opium: contemporary publications, newspaper reports, Nationalist generals' telegrams to Chiang, and photographs of identity cards the CCP issued to opium dealers, in *ZS vol. 5, no. 3, pp. 217–71. "Revolutionary Opium War": interviews with Yenan veterans, Oct. 1995. "Special Product": *Xie Juezai, pp. 587, 589, 600; cf. Chen Yung-fa 1995; *Wang Enmao, vol. 3, p. 422; interviews with Yenan veterans, 12 Sept. 1994; Oct. 1995. "It did happen": interview with Shi Zhe, 28 Oct. 1995. Russian asked Mao: ORK, 2 Aug. 1943. 30,000 acres: contemporary investigation report, in *ZS vol. 5, no. 3, p. 257. "Ask Chiang to stop": *Mao 1993b, vol. 2, pp. 335, 355. "cited . . . alongside Marx": ORK, 27 Apr. 1945.

271   9 Feb. 1943: *Mao 1993b, vol. 2, p. 426; cf. *Mao 1993c, p. 156. Russians estimated: Panyushkin, p. 278; Ovchinnikov, pp. 69–70 (Fitin to Dimitrov, 29 Sept. 1943). "very rich": *Xie Juezai, pp. 584–5 (6 Mar. 1944), p. 600 (9 Apr. 1944). "several dozen dishes": *Wang Enmao, vol. 3, p. 299; *YQD, p. 197, *Central Party School, vol. 1, pp. 120–1, 236. "Mao has grown fatter": Jin Cheng, in *Biographical Literature Pub., vol. 2, p. 232. Steps to improve: e.g., 16 June 1943 at Politburo, *Mao 1993b, vol. 2, p. 446; cf. *Mo Wenhua, pp. 392–8. Mao later admitted: 24 Apr. 1945, *YQD, p. 3.

271   Meat ration: *Xie Juezai, p. 581 (26 Feb. 1944). Xie's diary: 9–16 Oct. 1944, ibid., pp. 694–7.

272n   Lippa, p. 265; ORK, 29 Sept. 1943, 10 May 1944.

272–273   31 percent mortality: Esherick, p. 1056, n. 22. 60 percent: *Li Weihan, p. 589. "never given proper attention": *Li Weihan, pp. 568, 587. Discuss in the winter: ibid. Public health: ibid., pp. 583, 587. 6 Mar.: *Xie Juezai, p. 584. Mao wrote: Mao letters, 13 & 15 June 1941, in *Mao 1984, pp. 170–1. Russian ambassador: Panyushkin, p. 278. Hospital official: Lippa, p. 179. Bride cost: *JR, 2 June 1942; Hua 1981, pp. 56–7.

273–274   1944 price: *Xie Juezai, pp. 591–2 (19 Mar. 1944), cf. p. 452. Interest rates: *Xie Juezai, pp. 696–7. All it said was: "CCP Decision on Land Policy in the Anti-Japanese Base Areas," 28 Jan. 1942, Appendix 1, *GS vol. 6, p. 5. Virtually no loans: Mao talk to senior cadres, Dec. 1942, in *GS vol. 6, p. 94. Some Red areas: e.g. Shangdong, *GS vol. 6, pp. 107, 117. Mar. 1944: *Xie Juezai, p. 586. 22 Apr.: ibid., pp. 608–9. Mao vetoed dumping opium: ibid., p. 734; *Wang Enmao, vol. 3, p. 422. "assist addicts": *Xie Juezai, pp. 485–6.

274   "two mistakes": ibid., p. 734; cf. Chen Yung-fa 1995, p. 277. "indescribably squalid": Aczél, p. 93. Swedish enthusiast: Myrdal, p. 29.

CHAPTER 27   *The Russians Are Coming!*

275   Churchill: Kimball, p. 287.

276   *Izvestia*: "Some Facts Concerning the Situation in China"; cf. ORK, 13 & 15 Mar. 1945. "Haven't you liked": ORK, 26 Feb. and 5 March 1945.

276   "chop my head off": 31 May 1945, in *Yang Kuisong 1997, pp. 519–20. "Stalin the leader": unpublished sections of Mao speeches at the 7th Congress, 1945, in *Yang Kuisong 1999, pp. 206–7. In Apr.: order of 13th, *Jinchaji Base Committee & Central Archive, vol. 3, p. 276; order of 18th, in *Niu Jun, p. 164. Dispatching troops: Xiao Ke, in *YQD, p. 126; *Shi Zhe 1991, p. 305.

277–278   Russian help, CCP occupied: Borisov 1982, p. 166; Zakharov, map opposite p. 68; Tsedenbal, p. 169, n. 3; Westad 1993, pp. 77ff; *Jinchaji Base Committee & Central Archive, vol. 3, pp. 285–90; Xiao Ke, in *YQD, p. 126; *Duan Suquan, p. 278. "If we have Manchuria": 31 May 1945, *Mao 1995, pp. 218–19.

277   Atwood, in Kotkin & Elleman, pp. 141ff; Luzianin, pp. 41–2; *Hao Weimin, pp. 437–8.

278   Secret CCP circular: *Zeng Kelin, pp. 112–13. Bonanza in soldiers: Borisov 1977, pp. 76, 168; *Liu Tong, pp. 42–3. America's China policy: Roosevelt cited in Wallace, p. 333, & Snow 1968, pp. 126–9; FRUS 1945, vol. 7, p. 177 (Hurley to Roosevelt, 14 Jan. 1945).

279   Stalin cabled Mao to go to Chongqing: interview with Kapitsa, who saw the cables, 21 June 1995; id. 1995, pp. 13–14; id. 1996, pp. 21–4; Borisov 1982, p. 85; Liu 2000, p. 105; interview with Shi Zhe, 10 Oct. 1995; Chiang–Mao telegram exchanges, in *Chiang, pp. 2639, 2647, 2651, *Mao 1993b, vol. 3, pp. 7, 9, 12. Chen Li-fu: interview, 15 Feb. 1993. Chang Chen: Kapitsa interview. Hurley escorts: Mao cable to Wedemeyer, 25 Aug. 1945, *Mao 1993b, vol. 3, p. 13; Morwood, p. 7. Ordering a battle: *Mao 1993b, vol. 3, p. 13; *Hu Qiaomu, p. 421; *Liu Bocheng, p. 300; cf. Tikhvinsky 2000, book 2, pp. 220–4 (minutes of

Mao–Petrov talk, 10 Oct. 1945; Mao–Petrov 6 Sept. talk, ibid., pp. 230–3). Moment of panic: Kapitsa 1996, pp. 23–4; cf. *FRUS* 1945, vol. 7, p. 466 (Hurley to Mao, 19 Sept. 1945).

280   One observer: Morwood, p. 11. Carton de Wiart: Carton de Wiart to Ismay, 6 Sept. 1945, Attlee Papers, Box 23, folio 48–9, Bodleian Library; cf. Carton de Wiart 1950, pp. 269–70. Wedemeyer: Milton Miles Papers, NARA, RG 38, Naval Group China, Box 40, Folder: Chinese Communists, pp. 3, 6 (Minutes of Mao–Wedemeyer talk, 30 Aug. 1945).

280–281   "worse than beasts": *Chiang, p. 2688. Keep Chiang out of Manchuria: Mao order, 19 Oct. 1945, *ZZWX vol. 15, p. 364. Russians fly CCP secretly to Manchuria: Sidikhmenov MS, pp. 15–18; interview with Sidikhmenov (on the plane), 24 June 1996. Russians to handle ports, airports: cable, 28 Oct. 1945, in *Yang Kuisong 1997, p. 543. CCP fire on US ships: Wedemeyer, p. 345; Westad 1993, p. 106; *Liu Tong, p. 62. "decisive battle": Mao cables, 14 & 15 Nov. 1945, *Mao 1993a, vol. 3, pp. 141–4. Lamented proudly: *WZX, no. 42, p. 23.

281–282   "US-style": Huang Kecheng cable, in *Zhang Zhenglong, pp. 105–6. Material enticements: Chen Yi in *Zhang Zhenglong, p. 35; also *Liu Tong, p. 34. Abysmal morale, desertion: quotes from *Zhang Zhenglong, pp. 34–8.

282–283   Over 40,000: ibid., p. 103. Liu had instructed: *Liu 1996, vol. 1, p. 507; also on 24 Sept., *Liu Tong, p. 41. Mao overruled Liu: *ZZWX vol. 15, p. 364. Another order: 23 Oct., *Liu Tong, p. 46.

283   "sudden change": *Chiang, p. 2727. They told the CCP: on 19th, *Liu 1996, vol. 1, pp. 530–1. Stalin returning Mao's son: NA, HW 17/63 (18 Nov. 1945, ISCOT 1475). Entreaties to Russians: Mao cable to Peng Zhen, 20 Nov. 1945, quoted in Borisov 1975, p. 107. Futile orders to troops: 22 Nov., *Zhang Zhenglong, p. 111. Mao nervous breakdown: Liu cable, *Liu 1996, vol. 1, p. 531; *Shi Zhe 1991, pp. 313–14; interview with Shi Zhe, 29 Sept. 1993.

283   *Yan Changlin, p. 136; *Mao 1993b, vol. 3, p. 227.

283–284   Dr. Orlov: *CWH* vol. 1, no. 1 (2000), p. 132 (Stalin cable to Molotov et al., 10 Nov. 1945); *ORK*, p. 544; Vlasov, p. 202; Ledovsky 1999, p. 79, n.2; *Shi Zhe 1991, pp. 316–17. An-ying: Usov 1997, p. 114; Usov 1992, p. 56; *Shi Zhe 1991, pp. 315–16. Affectionate towards son, recovery: interview with Mrs. George Hatem, 17 Mar. 1998; *Shi Zhe 1991, pp. 316–17.

284–285   Russians coordinated departure with CCP: Westad 1993, pp. 148, 156ff; Sheng, p. 132ff; Russian–CCP exchanges can be seen from Mao cable of 24 Mar. 1946, *ZZWX vol. 16, p. 100; *Yang Kuisong 1997, pp. 560–4; *Chiang, p. 2822. Hold out in key cities: Mao cables from 24 Mar. 1946 onwards, in *Mao 1993a, vol. 3, pp. 153, 177–8, 190, 198, etc., esp. on 20 Apr., in *Liu Tong, p. 170; 27 Apr., in *Zhang Zhenglong, p. 154. Liu cautioned: e.g., 13 Mar. 1946, *Liu 1996, vol. 2, p. 26. Lin Biao warned: 11 Apr. 1946, in *Zhang Zhenglong, p. 154, also pp. 186–7. Army disintegrated: ibid., pp. 170–2; *Liu Tong, pp. 194–5.

285   Lin Biao reported: *Zhang Zhenglong, p. 104. "We were hungry": ibid.,
             pp. 166–9. "Big Hairy Ones": ibid., p. 179. 1 June, Lin: ibid., p. 184,
             *Liu Tong, p. 203. Next day: *Zhang Zhenglong, p. 184.

286   Mao–Stalin: Liu 2000, pp. 106–7; Kozlov & Mironenko, p. 173. 3 June:
             *Mao 1993a, vol. 3, p. 250.

CHAPTER 28   *Saved by Washington*

287   Change Party name: ORK, 12 Aug. 1944. Molotov to Hurley: FRUS
             1944, vol. 6, p. 255 (31 Aug. 1944); cf. FRUS 1945, vol. 7, p. 448 (Kennan,
             18 Aug. 1945, reporting Stalin).

287   "tactic of expedience": 28 Nov. 1945, *ZZWX vol. 15, p. 455.

288   Soft-soaped Marshall: FRUS 1945, vol. 7, p. 804 (23 Dec. 1945
             Marshall–Chou meeting). "rather go to the US": FRUS 1946, vol. 9,
             p. 152; *Hu Qiaomu, pp. 428–9. Marshall told Chiang: FRUS 1945,
             vol. 7, p. 814. Told US Congress: Tsou, p. 368. US had intercepts:
             "COMINT," pp. 4, 6; texts of 1945–47 intercepts: NA, HW 17/67.
             Three-word alarm: FRUS 1946, vol. 9, p. 777 (Yeaton, 15 Apr. 1946).

288–289   An-ying to village: *Shi Zhe 1991, p. 316; interviews with Shi Zhe, Oct.
             1995. An-ying interview: *RR, 20 Feb. 1990; Roderick, e-mail to
             authors, 12 Oct. 2000; cf. Roderick, p. 40. Marshall illusions: FRUS
             1946, vol. 9, pp. 510 (Marshall to Truman, 6 Mar.), 501–2 (Marshall
             minutes of talk with Mao, 4 Mar.), 541, 542 (Marshall Memo to Truman,
             13 Mar.). Mao briefs Orlov: *Shi Zhe 1991, pp. 318–19. 31 May, Marshall:
             FRUS 1946, vol. 9, p. 926.

289–290   "Hang on": 5 June 1946, *Mao 1993a, vol. 3, p. 251. Concurred in private:
             *Zhang Zhenglong, p. 189; cf. *Liu Tong, p. 516. Chiang noted: 29 June
             1946, *Chiang, p. 2950. Truman wrote to Chiang: US Department of
             State *White Paper*, p. 652.

290–291   "Be like Franco": interview with Chen Li-fu, 15 Feb. 1993. Comfortable
             armchair: *YQD, pp. 166, 270. Classified figures: *Zhang Zhenglong,
             pp. 420–1. "now an idiot": *Zhang Zhenglong, p. 318.

291   Russian help: Lyudnikov, p. 308; Vereshchagin, p. 18; Zimonin, p. 47
             (new figures for Japanese arms captured); Borisov 1977, pp. 229–30,
             233, 248, 256, 264; APRF, 39/1/39, pp. 64–73 (Mao to Mikoyan, 5 Feb.
             1949); cf. FEA no. 3, 1995, p. 78; Ledovsky interviews, June 1995ff;
             documents in *ZS vol. 7, no. 1, pp. 596–615; *Liu Tong, pp. 304–5;
             *Zhang Zhenglong, p. 216. Japanese POWs: Gillin with Etter, pp.
             511–15; Zimonin, p. 47; FRUS 1946, vol. 9, p. 813; Sang Ye, p. 91; *Zeng
             Kelin, pp. 126–33; *Zhang Zhenglong, pp. 221–2.

291–292   North Korea: summary of CCP offices in North Korea during the civil
             war, based on archive documents and memoirs, *ZDZ, no. 17, pp.
             197–210; details of the Korean troops in China, *ZS vol. 7, no. 1, p.
             616; Chen Jian 1994, pp. 107–9; NA, WO 208/281. Restoring rail-
             ways: Tikhomirov & Tsukanov in Akimov; Silin, ibid., pp. 215–18;
             Borisov 1977, pp. 242ff; Kovalev 2004, p. 132; id. 1992a, p. 102. Mao
             told Lin Biao: 11 July 1946, *Mao 1993a, vol. 3, p. 334. Moscow disin-

formation: TASS, "Refutation," *Pravda*, 19 Oct. 1946, p. 6. Mao claim: *SW* vol. 4, p. 101 (6 Aug. 1946).

292–293   Mao paid with food: Liu Shao-chi letter to Stalin, 6 July 1949 (*FEA*, no. 5, 1996, pp. 87–8); cf. Vereshchagin, p. 19; Borisov 1977, p. 232 (Russian imports from CCP areas exceed exports to these areas, 1948, 1949); Wang Shoudao and Liu Yalou talks, in *Liu Tong, pp. 517–19. The result was famine: *YQD, pp. 49, 59; *Zhao Guilai, pp. 207, 223; *Zhang Zhenglong, pp. 237, 433–6. Mao urged seizing big cities: *Xiao Ke 1997, pp. 340–50; *Mao 1993a, vol. 3, pp. 277, 283–4, 290.

293   "merciless and devious": interview with an insider, 6 Sept. 1998. Up to 100,000: *Zhang Zhenglong, pp. 234–8.

CHAPTER 29   *Moles, Betrayals and Poor Leadership Doom Chiang*

295   1 Mar.: *Chiang, p. 3149. Hu suspected of being Communist: *Hsu Chen 1990, pp. 39–40.

295   *Hsu Chen 1990, p. 39; *Mao 1993–9, vol. 5, p. 322; *Shi Zhe 1991, p. 249.

295–296   Hu friendship with Tai Li: Meng Bingnan, in *WZX vol. 18, p. 133; Zhang Yanfo, in *WZX vol. 64, pp. 105–7. On Mao's desk: *Zhou 1991, p. 723. Mao leisurely departure: *Yan Changlin, pp. 53–6. 20,000 men: *Peng 1981, pp. 44–5 (E: Peng 453ff. and re below); cf. Quan, pp. 13ff; *Party Documents, pp. 229–30.

296   Qinghuabian ambush: *Yan Changlin, pp. 58–64; *Wang Enmao, vol. 5, pp. 95–8; Nationalist generals' accounts, *CPPCC 1992, pp. 115–16, 154–5.

296–297   Yangmahe ambush: Nationalist generals' accounts, *CPPCC 1992, pp. 118–20, 156–8; Peng cable to Mao, 16 Apr. 1947, *Peng 1998, pp. 340–1; *Party Documents, p. 233. Panlong: Nationalist generals' accounts, in *CPPCC 1992, pp. 120–4, 159–61; *Hsu Chen 1990, p. 321; *Peng 1981, p. 248; *Party Documents, p. 233; *Wang Enmao, vol. 5, pp. 119–20. "horrible stench": *Hsu Chen 1987, p. 254.

297–298   Mao in Yenan area a year: *Yan Changlin, pp. 64ff; *Zhao Guilai, pp. 99ff; *Wang Dongxing 1993, pp. 8ff; *Ren Bishi, pp. 538ff; *Shi Zhe 1991, pp. 337–52; interviews with Mao's entourage, 4 Sept. 1998 & 19 Apr. 1999; cf. Quan, pp. 29–34, 37–8. Artillery battalion: interview with a former member of the battalion, 29 Oct. 2000. Yet another ambush: *Hsu Chen 1987, pp. 251–3. Close shave: *Yan Changlin, pp. 94–117; *Hu Qiaomu, pp. 490–3; *Zhao Guilai, pp. 124–6; member of entourage Liao Zhigao, in *"Mao and I" Collection Committee 1993a, p. 46; interviews with Mao's entourage, 13 Mar. & 4 Sept. 1998, 19 Apr. 1999, 12 May 2001.

298   Hu ordered troops away: *Zhao Guilai, pp. 134–5; *Yan Changlin, p. 117; *Hsu Chen 1990, p. 318. Stalin offers plane: APRF, 39/1/31, p. 23 (Kuznetsov to Orlov 15 June 1947); cf. Ledovsky 1995a, p. 74; *Shi Zhe 1991, pp. 345–6.

299   "On 9–11": 14 June 1947, *Mao 1993a, vol. 4, pp. 101–2. Ordered airstrip: 27 June 1947, *Shi Zhe 1991, p. 345. Liou death: *Wang Yan et al., pp. 348–54; Wang Ying-tsun account, in *CPPCC 1992, pp. 243–9. Chiang diary of 2 Mar.: *Chiang, p. 3400. Turned down Hu resignation: *Chiang, pp. 3407–9.

300   Barr: US Department of State, *White Paper*, p. 326; cf. US Senate, p. 67 (Barr: Nationalists "always permitted themselves to get surrounded"). "so I waited": *Shi Zhe 1991, p. 365. Hu impeachment, failed: *Central Daily, Taipei, 19–22 May 1950; *Hsu Chen 1990, pp. 385–93.

300   Hau Po-tsun: interview, 2 Oct. 1996. Wei Li-huang: Titov, vol. 3, p. 453 (Mao message to Comintern, Dec. 1940); Wei's Communist secretary Zhao Rongsheng, in *Biographical Literature Pub., vol. 2, pp. 68–85; Wei's son Daoran, in *CPPCC (Beijing), p. 442; Stokes fax to authors, 4 June 1998.

301–302   Wei coordinated with CCP: through his nephew, French-trained nuclear scientist Wang Dezhao, *Wu Jiangxiong, pp. 1, 4, 10–13. Mao's strategy: 7 Feb. 1948, *Mao 1993a, vol. 4, p. 391; Lin Biao concurred on 10th, *Liu Tong, pp. 559–60. Wei therefore: Nationalist commanders' accounts, *CPPCC 1985b, pp. 9–13, 52, 60–1; *Zheng Dongguo, pp. 472–80. "wise guidance": *CPPCC (Beijing), pp. 443–4. Contacted the CIA: Singlaub, pp. 151–5, 534, n. 1. Mao in withering terms: Mar. 1964, *IIR, p. 503.

302   Fu's daughter: Titov 1995, pp. 82ff; Tikhvinsky 2002, pp. 7–11; *OIRVR* vol. 5, pp. 398–401; her CCP handler, in *Biographical Literature Pub., vol. 1, pp. 415–24. Nov. 1948, Fu decided to surrender: Mao cable, 18 Nov. 1948, in *Beijing Archive, p. 43; *CPPCC 1993, pp. 280–2, 309. "terror and tyranny": *China Magazine*, Jan. 1949, pp. 17, 18 (Fu, "Message to the People of North China," 12 Nov. 1948). Fall to pieces: *Biographical Literature Pub., vol. 1, p. 423; interview with General I Fu-en, 1 June 1998. Chiang, 12 Dec.: *Chiang, p. 3549.

303   Strung Fu along: *CPPCC 1993, pp. 282ff, chronology pp. 460–2; Mao cables, 27 Dec. 1948–9 Jan. 1949, *Beijing Archive, pp. 52–9. " 'Play it by ear' ": *CPPCC 1989, p. 95.

303   Opened up gateway: *Chang Shun et al., p. 656. Liu Fei: interview with Chen Li-fu, 15 Feb. 1993; *Liu Chi, p. 171. Kuo Ju-kui: his own account, in *Biographical Literature Pub., vol. 1, pp. 249–57; *CPPCC 1996, pp. 15–35; interview with Chiang Weigo, 4 Oct. 1996.

304   "Pai Chung-hsi": APRF, 39/1/31, pp. 54–8 (Orlov to Kuznetsov, 10 Jan. 1949); cf. Malukhin 1977, p. 123. "created in summer": APRF, 39/1/31, p. 60 (Mao to Stalin 10 Jan. 1949). Require each new enlistee: *Hu Qiaomu, pp. 523–6; e.g., Mao order, 7 Jan. 1948, *Mao 1991, pp. 1264–6 (E: Mao, SW vol. 4, pp. 177–9).

304   Under T.V.: articles in contemporary newspapers; *Hsu Yung-chang, vol. 8; interview with I Fu-en, 6 Oct. 1996; and with Mao Chia-hua, 6 Oct. 1996. Chiang acknowledged: 25 Oct. 1945, *Chiang, p. 2698.

305   *Central Daily*: *Lu Keng, pp. 159–80.

CHAPTER 30 *China Conquered*

306   "Turn Changchun": *Zhang Zhenglong, p. 441. Evacuate civilians: *Zheng Dongguo, pp. 500–4; Mayor Shang Chuandao, in *CPPCC 1985b, pp. 396, 403. "Strictly ban": *Zhang Zhenglong, p. 441. "nice sort of guy": *Chang Shun et al., p. 134.

306   Lin Biao reported to Mao: 9 Sept. 1948, in *Liu Tong, pp. 635–6; *Zhang Zhenglong, p. 469.

307   Lin order, 11 Sept.: in *Liu Tong, p. 639. One survivor remembered: *Zhang Zhenglong, p. 479. Changchun mayor recorded: *CPPCC 1985b, p. 403.

307–308   Death toll: *Zhang Zhenglong, p. 467; *Zheng Dongguo, p. 500; *Liu Tong, p. 638. A Red veteran: *Zhang Zhenglong, p. 482. "refugee rules": ibid., p. 486. Su Yu: *Su Yu, p. 622.

307n   *CPPCC 1985b, p. 403.

308   225 million kg: *Su Yu, p. 642. Nationalist veteran recalled: Sang Ye, pp. 90–1.

309   "without getting tired": 8 May 1946, *Central Archive 1981, p. 7.

309   Kang Sheng in Haojiapo: *Cheng Min, pp. 221–31, *Zeng Yanxiu, pp. 115–18.

310   Woman official described: interview, 16 Oct. 1993.

310–311   Wire run through nose: *Zhong Kan, p. 101. "entire families": Sang Ye, pp. 13, 14–15. Reports to Mao: *Central Archive 1981, pp. 101, 129. Mao saw: *Zhao Guilai, pp. 237–9. "Everyone is terrified": *Central Archive 1981, p. 129. 10 percent: ibid., pp. 121, 124.

311n   Melby, p. 243 (17 Oct. 1947).

311–312   Shandong to bear logistics: Su Yu on Huai–Hai campaign, *DDWX, 1989, no. 6., p. 10. Second land reform: *Zhong Kan, pp. 103–5; Gao 2001, p. 242. An-ying under Kang Sheng: *Shi Zhe 1992, p. 224; *Jin Zhenlin, pp. 199, 225. An-ying diaries: 14 Apr., 5 & 6 Nov. 1947, *handwritten, unpublished.

312–313   Wrote to father: *Jin Zhenlin, p. 210. An-ying notes about rallies: 16 Dec. 1947, *handwritten, unpublished. Circulated reports: 9 & 20 Jan. 1948, *Central Archive 1981, pp. 98–102, 128–31. Mao wrote Liu: ibid., pp. 261–2.

313   Liu caved in: Liu speech, and Mao remarks at Politburo, 13 Sept. 1948, *DDWX, 1989, no. 5, pp. 8–9; Liu, 12 Mar. 1949, *Liu 1981, p. 419 (E: Liu, SW vol. 1, p. 417). Nationalist captain: *Hsu Chen 1987, pp. 341–3.

314   Nationalist student wrote: *Zhuanji wenxue (Biographical Literature), Taipei, no. 245, pp. 28–30. Mao told Mikoyan: APRF, 31/1/31, 31 Jan. 1949. Russian consul noted: Malukhin 1989, pp. 30–1; cf. AVPRF, 0100/43/302/4, p. 118 (Tikhvinsky report, 26 Jan. 1950). Lin Biao told Russians: AVPRF, 0100/43/302/4, p. 130 (Tikhvinsky report, 26 Jan. 1950); cf. Kulik 1994, p. 117.

314–315   Chiang to ancestral home: our visit to Xikou, Nov. 2000; *Chiang, pp. 3632–3; entourage memoirs, in *WZX, no. 66, pp. 84–90. Mao issued order: 6 May 1949, *Mao 1993–9, vol. 5, p. 290. Mao–Stalin exchange re Taiwan: Kovalev 1992a, p. 108; Ledovsky 1996a, p. 71 (Liu report to Stalin, 4 July 1949); cf. Goncharov et al., p. 70. No scorched-earth: *Song Honggang, pp. 302ff., *China Today 1993, p. 24. "Old Mr. Chiang": *Lu Keng, p. 180.

315n   Ledovsky 1996a, p. 69 (Stalin to Liu, 27 June 1949); id., 1996b, pp. 89–91 (Mao cable 25 July 1949); cf. Goncharov et al., pp. 69–70.

315   "Labour University": *Zhang Suizhi, p. 71; *CCP Beijing Haidian Committee, p. 248. System so slick: Berezhkov, pp. 365–6.

316n   de Segonzac, p. 115.

316   Mrs. Lo Fu described: *Liu Ying, p. 154.

316   The only speech: *Mao 1993–9, vol. 6, pp. 1–2; sound recording issued.

CHAPTER 31   *Totalitarian State, Extravagant Lifestyle*

318   "man without law": *New China* (USA), summer 1975, p. 27 (Chou, 1971 interview with W. Hinton); Snow 1974, p. 149 (Mao, 10 Dec. 1970). "demand for further": Bao & Chelminski, pp. 78–9, 100. "campaign to suppress": Mao orders, *CCP Archive Study Office & Central Archive, 1949–52, pp. 235–49. His police chief: *Huang & Zhang, p. 263. "small Chiang Kai-sheks": *Mao 1977, p. 317 (E: Kau & Leung, p. 163). "massive arrests": 24 Mar. 1951, *Mao 1987–98, vol. 2, p. 192. Criticized one province: *ibid., pp. 62–3.

318–319   30 Mar.: *ibid., p. 202. Peking alone: *Han Yanlong, p. 95. Woman from Britain: Cheo Ying, pp. 56–61. Trucks dripping blood: Loh, p. 66. "labour force": 8 May 1951, *Mao 1987–98, vol. 2, p. 281 (E: Kau & Leung, p. 189). *Lao-gai*: interviews with ex-inmates; Bao & Chelminski; Rummel, pp. 228–33 (estimates).

318n   700,000: Mao, 27 Feb. 1957, *Mao CCRM, vol. 1, p. 198 (E: MacFarquhar et al., p. 142).

319–320   Report to Mao: *Mao 1987–98, vol. 2, p. 115. Bizarre alert: *Huang & Zhang, p. 261.

319n   10 million: Rummel, p. 232; Margolin, p. 498. Soviet diplomat: Ledovsky 1990, p. 128; cf. ibid., pp. 96–7, 99; Kulik 1994, esp. pp. 120–2.

320–321   A small landowner: *Yuan Maogeng, pp. 13–80. Mao repeatedly said: Apr. 1956, *Mao CCRM, vol. 1, p. 138; 24 Mar. 1951, *Mao 1987–98, vol. 2, p. 192. Execution of two foreigners: Lum, pp. 83ff; Domenach 1992, pp. 74, 654, n. 37.

321   Chou "apology": Kahn, p. 239; Service letter to authors, 8 Aug. 1994 and interview, 23 Apr. 1995. Mao interest in Vatican: Nenni, pp. 697–9; Malaparte, pp. 136ff; Barca interview, 2 June 1994; Pesce interview, 28 May 1994.

322   "Three-Antis": many Mao orders in *Mao 1987–98, vol. 3. "We must probably execute": 8 Dec. 1951, *Mao 1987–98, vol. 2, p. 549. "Whoever

disobeys": 4 Jan. 1952, *Mao 1987–98, vol. 3, p. 12. Mao enjoined: 8 Dec. 1951, *Mao 1987–98, vol. 2, p. 549. Mao kept informed: *Mao 1987–98, vol. 3, pp. 134, 167, 177, 195–7. Bamboo pliers: Ledovsky 1990, p. 93, confirmed by Ledovsky, interview, 19 June 1996.

322–323   Tianjin report: *Mao 1987–98, vol. 3, p. 214. In Manchuria: Ledovsky interview, 19 June 1996. Belgian priest: van Coillie, p. 258. "Five-Antis": Mao orders in *Mao 1987–98, vol. 3. Number of suicides: *Zhou Jingwen, pp. 224–5; cf. Chow, p. 133. "parachutes": *Ding Shu 1993, p. 128; Yue Qian, in *Kaifang (Open Magazine), Hong Kong, 1999, no. 3, p. 29.

324   Mao villas: visits to over two dozen of them, and interviews with Mao's personal staff.

324–325   Started in 1949: *Zhang Suizhi, pp. 72–5; *Li & Yang, p. 264. Sent word to Hunan: Hunan Party secretary Jin Ming, in *Gong Guzhong et al., pp. 301–2; visits to Hunan villas, Oct. 1994. "But you have no place": interviews with people who had been told, Oct. 1994 & Sept. 2000.

325–326   Mao travel: interviews with Mao's personal staff and provincial officials; *Li & Peng, pp. 10, 87, 104. Swimming pools: interviews with Mao's personal staff, villa attendants and people close to him; *Lin Ke et al., p. 128. The pool cost: Mao's own figure, 25 Apr. 1954, *Mao 1987–98, vol. 4, p. 483. A gourmet: interviews with Mao's personal staff.

326   No bath, massage: ibid.; *Li & Yang, pp. 69–71. Hospital came to him: *Li Zhisui, pp. 168–71; *Lin Ke et al.. Clothes: *SMMM, pp. 131–3, 154, 188–90, 217–18.

327   One patriotic Chinese: Aarons, p. 92. Sexual caprice: *Peng 1998, pp. 561–2; *Mao 1987–98, vol. 4, p. 389; *Li Zhisui, pp. 137–9, 283; interviews with Mao's girlfriends. Money: interview with Mao's personal staff; *SMMM, pp. 511–12, 532–3. Well over 2 million: interview with a staff member who knew about Mao's account, 19 Apr. 1999; cf. *SMMM, p. 511.

CHAPTER 32   *Rivalry with Stalin*

331   Mao sent Strong: Strong & Keyssar, pp. 228ff; Nikiforov, pp. 124–5, 131, n. 56.

331n   CCP intelligence in USA: AVPRF, 0100/43/302/4; cf. Kulik 1995. Mao and Browder: Schram 1965, p. 292 (Mao cable to Foster, 29 July 1945); Browder, p. 251; RGASPI, 485/184/15 (Mao to Dimitrov, 19 Aug. 1940).

331   Strong writings: Strong 1947, pp. 168ff; cf. id., 1948, pp. v–vi.

332   "Unit Asia": *Hu Qiaomu, p. 510.

332–333   Mao–Stalin exchanges 1947–49: APRF, 39/1/31, pp. 23–75; extracts in Ledovsky 1995a, pp. 74ff; complete texts of Mao to Stalin, 30 Nov. 1947 in PDV, 2001, no. 5, pp. 119–22; and Stalin to Mao, 20 Apr. 1948, in PDV, 2000, no. 6, p. 121.

332   Another "accident" for Wang Ming: medical documents that established the poisoning, including an official "circular" on 7 July 1948; Wang Ming, pp. 46–7.

333   15 Aug., Mao vetoed: *Mao 1993b, vol. 3, pp. 335–6, 397; *Hu Qiaomu, p. 329.

334–335   Stalin "told off" by Mao: interview with Kapitsa, 21 June 1995. Stalin to Yugoslavs: CWB no. 10, p. 131; Dimitrov, 10 Feb. 1948; our conversation with Djilas, 30 Mar. 1986. Stalin–Mao cable exchange 10–15 Jan. 1949: CWB nos. 6–7, pp. 27–9; cf. Ledovsky 1995a, pp. 81–4; id., 1995b, pp. 74–6. "So be it": *Ye Zilong, p. 136.

335   17 Jan. Mao response: APRF, 39/1/31, p. 75. Mikoyan at Xibaipo: Ledovsky 1995a, pp. 78–92 (Mikoyan 1966 report), 1995b; Mikoyan, S. 2002, pp. 154–9; Shi 1992, pp. 35–46; Heinzig, pp. 135–56. "quite natural": 1 Feb. 1949 (APRF 39/1/39); Ledovsky 1995b, pp. 76–7. Gather intelligence: Malukhin 1977, p. 127; *Shi Zhe 1991, p. 418 (E: Shi 1993, p. 88). Mao "mocking-indifferent": Malukhin 1977, pp. 149–50.

335–336   Mikoyan reports from Xibaipo: APRF, 39/1/39, pp. 1–95.

336–337   Strong, Rittenberg: Strong & Keyssar, p. 250; Mikoyan, S., p. 158 (Stalin's cable 4 Feb. 1949 re Rittenberg; Mikoyan on Stalin's "spymania"); CWB, nos. 12–13 (2001), p. 257 (Khrushchev to Mao, 31 July 1958); Rittenberg & Bennett, pp. 134ff. Borodin: Vaksberg, pp. 251ff; Strong & Keyssar, pp. 243–4. 13 Mar. 1949: *Mao 1993–9, vol. 5, pp. 259–60.

337   Stalin–Liu re Cominform: Heinzig, pp. 206–7; Kovalev 1992b, pp. 95–7; Shi 1993, pp. 83–6. Orlov: Vlasov, pp. 202–3, 205; Vaksberg, pp. 251ff; Li Haiwen, p. 60.

338–339   Liu insisted: *Liu 1996, vol. 2, p. 223. Liu speech: URI, *Liu*, vol. 2, pp. 178–9. Russian delegate: Heinzig, pp. 258–60. "form their ties": URI, *Liu*, vol. 2, pp. 183–5 (23 Nov. 1949); cf. Aarons, p. 87; Kovalev 1992b, p. 98.

CHAPTER 33   *Two Tyrants Wrestle*

340   Mao "sprang up": Kovalev 1992b, p. 108. "Capitalist embassies": Tikhvinsky 1994, p. 52 (Kovalev to Stalin, 23 May 1949); cf. id., 1996, pp. 467–8.

340   Mao to Mikoyan: APRF 39/1/39 (31 Jan., 5 Feb. 1949); extracts of talks in Ledovsky 1995a, 1995b.

341   Liu wrote Stalin: Ledovsky 1996a, p. 80 (Liu report, 4 July 1949). Cities as key: *Mao 1993b, vol. 3, p. 464. "[US] carbines": *Yan Changlin, pp. 335–7. 1946 Ford: *Li Yimang, pp. 383–4.

342   "force [them] out": *Yang Kuisong 1997, pp. 177–81. "intolerable conditions": APRF 39/1/39 (1 Feb. 1949). "all warships": 21 Apr. 1949, *Mao 1993b, vol. 3, p. 485; *Foreign Ministry 1990ff, vol. 1, p. 35. Churchill: U.K. *Hansard (Commons)* vol. 464, col. 34, cited in Murfett, p. 120.

342   APRF 39/1/39 (to Mikoyan, 1 Feb. 1949).

342–343 Stalin alert, cables Mao: Kapitsa 1996, p. 44; Malukhin 1977, pp. 135–6; Kovalev 1992a, p. 106; Tikhvinsky 1994a, p. 52. "avoid clashes": 27–9 Apr. 1949, *Mao 1993b, vol. 3, pp. 489–91. Mao's intent: Cohen 1987, p. 288 (paraphrasing Huang Hua). Chou verbal message: *FRUS* 1949, vol. 8, pp. 357–60 (Clubb, 1 June 1949). Hoax: Tikhvinsky 1994, p. 53.

343–344 "strike it hard": *Foreign Ministry 1990ff, vol. 1, pp. 44–5. "wait," Stalin says: "Yes!": Ledovsky 1996a, pp. 81–2; cf. Heinzig, pp. 174–231 on Liu visit. Chou to Russian ambassador: Westad 2003, p. 311; cf. Wingrove 1995, pp. 314–15.

344 "without Chinese witnesses": Kovalev 1992b, p. 108. Mao–Stalin first talk: 16 Dec. 1949, *CWB* nos. 6–7, pp. 5–7.

344–345 Mao in Moscow: Heinzig, pp. 263–367, 403ff; Wingrove 1995; Kapitsa 1996, pp. 48–55; Kapitsa interview; Fedorenko 1989, 1994, 1995, 1996; Shi 1989. *Li & Yang, pp. 108–9, 151; *Ye Zilong, pp. 178–9; interview with Shi Zhe, 14 Oct. 1993.

345 Molotov "to find out": Chuev, p. 163. Kovalev: Kovalev 1992b, p. 109. Togliatti: interview with Nilde Jotti (Togliatti's partner), 3 June 1994; Lajolo, p. 29. Ovation: Rákosi, p. 128; *Shi Zhe 1991, p. 441.

345n Gollan, Notes of talk with Mao, 10 Nov. 1957, p. 4 (Gollan Papers, Manchester University); Kapitsa interview.

345–346 Exploded to Kovalev: Kovalev 1992b, p. 109; *Pei Jianzhang, p. 19; *Shi Zhe 1991, pp. 437–8. Mao–Stalin, 24 Dec: *Pei Jianzhang, p. 18; cf. Westad 2003, p. 317. "attempt to phone him [Stalin]": *CWB* nos. 6–7, p. 165 (Mao to Yudin, 31 Mar. 1956). "do business with . . . Britain": *Mao 1987–98, vol. 1, p. 197; *Wang Dongxing 1993, p. 163.

346–347 "right after this": *CWB* nos. 6–7, p. 165 (Mao to Yudin, 31 Mar. 1956). "drafted for me": *Yang Kuisong 1999, p. 297. Not by plane: cable, 2 Jan. 1950, *Mao 1987–98, vol. 1, p. 212. Acheson and rebuttal: MacFarquhar 1972, p. 74; Heinzig, pp. 301–5; Wingrove 1995, p. 121; *Mao 1987–98, vol. 1, pp. 245–8.

347 Stalin's tongue-lashing: Kulik 2000, p. 31. Car ride: *Shi Zhe 1991, pp. 457–8.

348 Loan: Zazerskaya 1997, p. 175, n. 40; *Yang Kuisong 1997, p. 621. Soviet spheres of influence: *DDWX, 1996, no. 2, pp. 54–5; *CWB* nos. 6–7, p. 165 (Mao to Yudin, 31 Mar. 1956); cf. Ganshin & Zazerskaya, pp. 63ff. "colonies": Schram 1974, p. 101 (Mao, 10 Mar. 1958); *Sino–Russian Relations Studies Society, p. 249. "grabbed half": Burr 1999a, p. 91 (Mao to Kissinger, 17–18 Feb. 1973). Gave Russia monopoly: Chou cable to Politburo, 8 Feb. 1950, in *Jin Chongji et al. 1998, pp. 37–8; Wingrove 1995, pp. 327ff; Kapitsa interview. "Of all the foreign": quoted by Foreign Minister Qian Qichen, *Foreign Ministry 1990ff, vol. 5, p. 11. Carefully erased: 14 Feb. 1950 cable, *Mao 1987–98, vol. 1, pp. 262–3.

348n *Liu 1996, vol. 2, p. 246.

349 At Stalin's insistence, secretly introduced: Arkhipov interview; cf. Wingrove 1995, p. 330; *Shi Zhe 1991, pp. 415, 446 (E: Shi 1993, p. 86).

"We do hope": *Shi Zhe 1991, p. 463; *Zhu Zhongli 1995, pp. 190–1. Flabbergasted guests: interview with Markus Wolf, who was present, 18 Nov. 1999; Wolf, pp. 42–3. Stalin's toast: Fedorenko 1989, p. 148; id. 1995, p. 89; Kapitsa interview; *Shi Zhe 1991, p. 465. Mao on Stalin at photo: *Ye Zilong, p. 183; *Shi Zhe 1991, p. 462.

CHAPTER 34   *Why Mao and Stalin Started the Korean War*

350   Supervise Vietnam: cf. *Pei Jianzhang, p. 18.

350–351   plan to send in Chinese troops: Zhai, pp. 13–25. Ho to Moscow: *Luo Guibo, pp. 233–6; *Liu 1996, vol. 2, p. 241; Zhang Guanghua, in *BNC, 2000, no. 4, p. 12; Westad 2003, pp. 316–18; Heinzig, pp. 302–6. Mao told Yudin: Russian Ministry of Foreign Affairs, "Chronology," p. 45. Liu to French: Figuères interview, 13 Oct. 1998; Figuères' letter to authors, 11 May 1999. Mao-style land reform: Tin, pp. 14ff, 28ff; Boudarel.

352   Doggerel: To Huu, "October Song," *Daily Telegraph*, 19 Dec. 2002. Kim in Moscow 1949: Torkunov, pp. 12–13; *CWB*, no. 5, pp. 4–6 (Stalin–Kim, 5 Mar.); Weathersby, p. 4 (Stalin–Kim, 7 Mar.); Mansourov 1997, pp. 97–102. Mao commitment: APRF, 3/65/9, pp. 51–5 (Shtykov to Vyshinsky, 15 May 1949), APRF, 45/1/331, pp. 59–61 (Kovalev to Stalin, 18 May 1949); extracts in Torkunov, pp. 61–5; *Shen Zhihua, p. 211.

352   Push by Kim: *CWB*, no. 5, p. 8; Torkunov, pp. 51–3. 30 Jan. Stalin: *CWB*, no. 5, p. 9.

353   "Asian affairs beautifully": *DPRK Report,* no. 23 (2000); Torkunov, pp. 58–9; Weathersby, pp. 8–15. Stalin's schemes: *CWB*, nos. 6–7, p. 116 (Stalin to Mao in Stalin to Kim, 7[8] Oct. 1950); cf. Beria 2001, pp. 230–2. 1 July 1950: Russian Ministry of Foreign Affairs, "Chronology," p. 35.

353   interview, 27 Dec. 1995. Raphaël-Leygues, p. 118 (Sainteny); US Senate, p. 70 (Barr).

354   19 Aug.: ibid., pp. 45, 47 (28 Aug.). 1 Mar. 1951: *Mao 1987–98, vol. 2, p. 153. Stalin–Malik: Rusk, p. 141; Schoenbaum, pp. 208ff; telephone interview with Rusk, 17 Feb. 1992.

354–355   Ordered Kim: Torkunov, p. 56 (Stalin to Shtykov, 2 Feb. 1950). "I shall not lift a finger": Goncharov et al., p. 145 (citing Kapitsa); cf. Kapitsa 1996, pp. 215ff; Weathersby, pp. 9–11 (summarizes Stalin's shift to Kim, spring 1950). 13 May: *Shen Zhihua, pp. 218–19. Next morning: *CWB*, no. 4, p. 61. 15 May: Russian Ministry of Foreign Affairs, "Chronology," pp. 30–1. 16th: Mansourov, pp. 322–3 (Stalin to Roshchin, 16 May 1950); cf. Torkunov, p. 70.

355–356   SOS: *CWB* nos. 6–7, p. 112. "I am far": *CWB* nos. 6–7, p. 114. "Stand by": *Mao 1987–98, vol. 1, p. 538 (E: Zhang & Chen, p. 161). Only now Politburo: *Shen Zhihua, p. 251. Politburo discussion: Mao to Stalin, 2 Oct. 1950, *Mao 1987–98, vol. 1, pp. 539–40; *Lei Yingfu, pp. 156–8; Zhang 1993, pp. 6–15.

356 Two different cables, 2 Oct.: *Mao 1987–98, vol. I, pp. 539–41; Mansourov 1995–6, pp. 100, 106–7, 114–15; Shen 1996–7, pp. 237–8.

357 Chou–Indian ambassador: Zhang & Chen, pp. 163–4 (Chinese minutes); Panikkar, p. 110.

357–358 "I considered": CWB nos. 6–7, p. 116. Mao, 8 Oct.: *Mao 1987–98, vol. I, pp. 543–5; (E: Mao 1998, pp. 109–10). Lin sent Mao long cable: interview with Kang Yi-min, 2 Sept. 1998. Chou–Lin–Stalin talks: *Zhou 1997, vol. I, 85; *Shi Zhe 1991, pp. 495–8, 502; Kapitsa 1996, pp. 221–2; Zhang, X., pp. 70–4; CWB nos. 6–7, p. 119 (Roshchin to Stalin, 13 Oct. 1950).

358 "Forget it": Mao–Chou–Kim talk, 10 Oct. 1970, *ZQZS vol. 6, p. 70. "We should enter": *Mao 1987–98, vol. I, p. 556 (E: Zhang & Chen, p. 169; cf. Chen 1994, p. 202); *Shi Zhe 1991, p. 500. Mao to Russian ambassador: CWB nos. 6–7, pp. 118–19 (Roshchin to Stalin, 13 Oct. 1950; Torkunov, pp. 117–18).

CHAPTER 35 *Mao Milks the Korean War*

359 Kim "agreed . . .": *Peng 1998, p. 453; cf. Chen 2001, p. 320; Shen 2003–4, pp. 13–14. Peng–Mao exchange: *Peng 1998, p. 454 (E: Zhang & Chen, p. 215); cf. Chen 2001, pp. 92–4.

359–360 "against American": CWB nos. 6–7, p. 51 (1 Dec. 1950). "Our homes": *Public Papers: Truman 1950,* p. 741 (radio address, 15 Dec. 1950; "Declaration," 16 Dec.). "The temperature": *Peng 1998, p. 456. Logistics manager: Ledovsky 1990, pp. 73–4 (Li Fuchun, 2 Jan. 1951). HQ's answer: *Hong Xuezhi, pp. 240–1.

360 Peng raced to Mao: *Peng 1998, p. 480. "overall strategy": *Mao 1987–98, vol. 2, pp. 151–3; Torkunov, pp. 144, 146. 19 Feb. 1951: *Zhou 1997, vol. I, p. 132.

361–362 Chinese plan to make aircraft: *CCP Archive Study Office 1991, pp. 204–7. *He Changgong Biography team, pp. 487–8. 3,000 planes: Zhang, X., p. 210. Asking for blueprints: Mao cable to Stalin, 28 Apr. 1951, *Zhou 1997, vol. I, p. 151; delegation: *Xu Xiangqian, pp. 542–6 (E: Xu, p. 140ff). 3 June 1951: *Cai & Zhao, p. 125; *BNC, 2000, no. 10, p. 13. "the farther north": 26 May 1951, *Mao 1987–98, vol. 2, p. 332.

362 Truce "now advantageous": CWB nos. 6–7, p. 60 (13 June 1951). "Not a single": from someone who heard this order, interview, 11 Apr. 1999. Kim on POWs: Volokohova, pp. 83–4 (undated cable from Razuvayev, Soviet ambassador, Pyongyang, Feb–Mar. 1952). 14 July 1952: CWB nos. 6–7, p. 78. Rusk: interview for Thames TV, 1986. "Rejecting the proposal": CWB nos. 6–7, p. 78.

363 Kim: ibid., pp. 77–9. "We consider": ibid., pp. 77–8. Chou–Stalin: ibid., p. 14.

363–364 Mao plotted to depose Kim: AQSh, f. 14, 1967, d. 1, p. 2 (Kang Sheng to Albania's Hysni Kapo, 22 Jan. 1967); cf. Schäfer 2003–4, p. 60; id.

2004, pp. 7–10. Chou–Stalin, 20 Aug. & 3 Sept. 1952: CWB nos. 6–7, pp. 11–13, 16. US air losses: Stewart, p. 286; Jackson, p. 105.

364   Stalin never signed: *Bo Yibo 1993, 297; *Zhou 1997, vol. 1, pp. 261, 274, 288–9. Turf: Wada, pp. 18–19; Fuwa, p. 477. Pol Pot: *Quan & Du, pp. 2–9.

365–366   Chou–Stalin: 3, 19 Sept., CWB nos. 6–7, pp. 16–19.

366   Conspiratorial operations in USSR: Drozdov, p. 60. Stalin and Peng: probably on 12 Sept. 1952, *Zhou 1997, vol. 1, pp. 238–9; interview with an insider, 11 & 16 Apr. 1999; cf. CWB nos. 14–15, pp. 378–81 (minutes of 4 Sept. 1952 meeting). "Stalin even mentioned": *Shi Zhe 1991, p. 529 (E: Shi 1993, p. 88). Chou comment: *DDWX, 1996, no. 2, p. 53.

367   Liu wrote Malenkov: RGASPI, 17/137/944, p. 181; *Liu 1996, vol. 2, p. 304; Indonesians: *Istoricheskii Arkhiv*, no. 1, 1997, p. 34, (Stalin's appointments diary); interview with Russian insider, 1997; interview with Adjitorop (PKI Politburo), 5 Oct. 1994. "Please could the Soviet": Torkunov, pp. 264–9.

367n   *ZDJC vol. 19, p. 416; *Tang Chunliang 1999, pp. 263–71.

367–368   Jan. 1953, Mao: to "Semyonov" (Stalin), 7 Jan. 1953, Shifrtelegramma 17203. Stalin reaction: 27 Jan. 1953, Shifrtelegramma 372 to Mao. Eisenhower: *Public Papers 1953*, pp. 16–17. "really anxious: *Chen Xiaodong, p. 32. Nuclear scientist to Stalin: *Zhou 1997, vol. 1, p. 290; Hinton, pp. 222ff; Friedman, p. 82. Volkogonov: id., 1991, p. 570; id., 1998, pp. 172–3.

369   Staffer claims: Rakhmanin, p. 80.

369n   Kim death: interview with a Russian insider, 21 June 1995.

369–370   Stalin's successors: *Zhou 1997, vol. 1, pp. 288–90; Torkunov, pp. 272ff; AVPRF, 06/12a/59/395, pp. 4ff; Zazerskaya 1997, p. 173. Goal of Chou's trip: *Zhou 1997, vol. 1, p. 290; Lewis & Xue 1988, p. 43; Hinton, p. 227; Gobarev, pp. 16–20. Beria to Malenkov: CWB no. 11, p. 182; interview with Colonel Karpov (FSB), confirming authenticity, Moscow, June 1999.

370   Peking claim: *Military Science Academy, p. 150. Russian generals: interviews with Sozinov (29 Apr. 1992) and Selivanov (24 Apr. 1992).

370   Molotov wrote: CWB no. 11, p. 182. Harsh message: ibid., p. 183. Ambassador Razuvayev: Sozinov interview. Kuznetsov report: CWB no. 11, p. 183; cf. AVPRF 06/12a/59/395, p. 11 (Kuznetsov to Moscow, 11 May 1953). End the war: 12 May 1953, *Zhou 1997, vol. 1, p. 299; follow-up activities: pp. 301–4.

371   60,000 South: Volokhova, pp. 86, 89.

371   CWB no. 11, p. 184.

372   1 million: Beria 1994, p. 402. An-ying fainted: interview with a household member, 23 Oct. 1995. Secretary observed: Ye Zilong, in *ZQZS vol. 2, pp. 233–4.

371   Brownell: conversation, 17 Nov. 1988. 400,000 deaths: Kojima,
         pp. 78–9 (Liu and Deng to Japanese, 3 Mar. 1966); AQSh, f. 14, 1966,
         d. 31, p. 14 (Kang Sheng to Hoxha, 28 Oct. 1966).

371   As though he were alive: interview with a family member, 14 & 15 Apr.
         1999.

CHAPTER 36   *Launching the Secret Superpower Program*

373   15 June: *Zhou 1997, vol. 1, p. 309. "the essence": *ZDJC vol. 22, pp.
         457–8. "We will make it": 14 May 1955, in *Wang Dongxing 1997, p. 21.
         "we can overtake": 17 Nov. 1957, *Mao CCRM, vol.11A, p. 212.

373–374 "future generations": *Mao 1990, pp. 204–6. To his entourage: *Li &
         Yang, pp. 123–4. Indifferent about heir: interview with a family
         member, 23 Oct. 1995. Stalin: "unbalanced": CWB, nos. 6–7, pp. 15–16.
         Official statistics: *Finance Ministry, vol. 2, p. 436.

374–375 "boils down": 17 Feb. 1955, *Zhou 1997, vol. 1, pp. 449–50. "the main
         exports": *China Today 1992, vol. 2, pp. 8–9. "Frankly speaking": 30 Sept.
         1956, *Mao 1994, p. 273. Oct. 1953 instruction: *China Today 1992, vol. 1,
         pp. 15–16.

374n   CWB nos. 6–7, pp. 15, 16.

375   July 1954 order: ibid., p. 16.

376   Chou told German: interview with a former East German official, Nov.
         1999. "Nothing to": *Mao CCRM, vol. 1, p. 229. "one bottom":
         *Reminiscences about Deng Zihui, p. 337. Mao as head of camp: Kapitsa 1996,
         p. 58; Kapitsa interview; Tálas, p. 45; Pravda, 15 Feb. 1955 (Molotov).
         Romania: *Pei Jianzhang, p. 51. Hungary: ibid., p. 54. East Germany:
         ibid., p. 70; Mao letter, 16 Oct. 1953, *Mao 1987–98, vol. 4, p. 362.

376–377 Lift food rationing: *Wang Taiping 1998, p. 292; interview with Horst
         Brie, 22 Nov. 1999. Responded grandly: *Pei Jianzhang, p. 69. Great
         Wall: Meissner, pp. 85, 87 (Mao–Ulbricht, 16 Oct. 1956). 6.92 percent:
         *China Today 1989, p. 68. "About 10 percent": *Mao 1987–98, vol. 4,
         pp. 197–8. "So be it": 12 Aug. 1953, *Mao 1977, p. 97.

377   Liu quotes: *Liu 1993, pp. 169, 181–2, 204–5.

378–379 Secretary recalled: *Liu Zhende, pp. 23–4. "never thought so": 4 Nov.
         1953, *Mao 1977, p. 122. Liu in the hospital: his widow Wang
         Guangmei's reply to written questions (via secretary by phone), 16 Apr.
         1999; AVPRF, 06/12–a/59/395, p. 2 (Mao–Panyushkin, 4 Mar. 1953).
         No public appearances: *RR, 5–10 Mar. 1953. Menacing letter: *Mao
         1987–98, vol. 4, pp. 229–30 (E: Kau & Leung, p. 346).

379–380 Sharply condemned Liu: *Mao 1977, p. 81. Praetorian Guard: *Zhang
         Suizhi, pp. 85–6. Bo Yi-bo: *Bo Yibo 1993, pp. 231ff. To insinuate: the
         official was Zhang Xiushan, see Deng Xiaoping speech, 21 Mar. 1955,
         *ZDJC vol. 20, p. 515; interviews with people close to Zhang, 18 Apr.
         1999 & 20 Oct. 2000. 24 Dec. 1953: *Liu 1996, vol. 2, p. 315. Three
         days and nights: interview with a secretary of Liu's, 19 Apr. 1999; *Liu
         1996, vol. 2, pp. 317–21. Mao–Gao: Chou speech, 25 Feb. 1954, *ZDJC

vol. 20, pp. 267–9; Mao revision to Chou speech, *Mao 1987–98, vol. 4, pp. 451–2; *Bo Yi-bo 1993, pp. 308ff; Lin Yunhui, in *Han Taihua, pp. 448ff; interviews with people close to the Gao case, 18 & 20 Apr. 1999, 20 Oct. 2000; Wingrove 2000.

380   Dalai Lama: interview, 11 Feb. 1999. Kovalev report: *NiNI* no. 1, 2004, pp. 132–9; Ledovsky, "preface," ibid., pp. 128–31; *Wang Dongxing 1993, p. 168. Gao told Russians: interview with Ledovsky, 21 June 1999; Tálas, p. 52 (Kapitsa); Russian Ministry of Foreign Affairs, "Chronology," p. 61; Loboda, pp. 214, 228; Kulik 2000, pp. 41–2; interview with interpreter Li Yue-ran, 11 Oct. 1995. British couple: Band & Band, p. 248.

380   Arkhipov interview, 27 June 1995.

381   "Do we have": 15 Nov. 1956, *Mao 1977, p. 321. Tea boy: Li Weixin, in *Li Jian, pp. 23–4. Bring pistols: *ZQZS vol. 6, p. 40.

381   Gao suicides: Mao letter to Moscow, 1 Sept. 1954, *Mao 1987–98, vol. 4, pp. 537–8; Chou speech, *ZDJC vol. 20, p. 269; *ZQZS vol. 6, p. 42; *BNC, 1999, no. 11, pp. 48–9. Rao Shu-shi: in his intelligence role in USA in the mid–1930s, known as "Liang Pu," cf. 8 May 1936 document from RGASPI in Klehr et al., p. 65; *BNC, 1999, no. 11, p. 50.

382–383   Villa in Hangzhou: our visit, and interviews with Mao's staff, Nov. 2000; *Luo Yimin. Mao in Hangzhou: recollections in *CCP Zhejiang Committee, and *Li Linda; *Li & Yang, pp. 295–6. Thatched hut on fire: *CCP Zhejiang Committee, pp. 132–3, 221–2.

383   "all citizens": *Mao 1987–98, vol. 4, p. 457. Mao Code: *Li Linda, p. 9. Toured a temple: *CCP Zhejiang Committee, pp. 133–4.

384   Mme Mao: *CCP Zhejiang Committee, p. 134; Kapitsa interview; cf. Vlasov, p. 202; APRF, 39/1/31, pp. 61–2 (Orlov to Stalin, 10 Jan. 1949); cf. Kartunova 1992, pp. 1–2; Kudashev, p. 193; *Li Zhisui, pp. 137–8 (E: Li, pp. 144, 227ff); interview with Zeng Zhi, 24 Sept. 1994.

CHAPTER 37   *War on Peasants*

385   200 kg: *PRC Encyclopaedia* vol, 4, p. 5095; cf. Fei & Chang, p. 158. Grain equivalent: Yu & Buckwell, p. 225. 190 kg: *PRC Encyclopaedia* vol. 4, p. 5095. "only need 140": *Wang Dongxing, 1997, p. 23. "Not a family": *Zhou Jingwen, pp. 341–3.

385   Berating officials: *Wang Dongxing 1997, pp. 22–3; *Mao 1987–98, vol. 5: p. 267; *Mao CCRM, vol.1, p. 365.

385–386   Eat potato leaves: *Wang Dongxing, 1997, pp. 22–3. "Educate peasants": *Mao 1987–98, vol. 5, p. 267. Bo Yi-bo acknowledged: *Bo Yi-bo 1993, pp. 271, 282. 1 Oct. 1953: *Chen Yun 2000, p. 178. "at war": *Bo Yi-bo 1993, pp. 263–4. Chen Yun conveyed: *Sun & Xiong, pp. 90–1. Guards' reports: *Mao 1987–98, vol. 5, pp. 210–11.

386–387   Saying things like: *Wang Gengjin et al., p. 108; *Xin Ziling 1995, vol. 3, p. 529. Zhao Zi-yang: *Xin Ziling 1995, vol. 3, p. 529. Fellow traveler: Huang Yanpei, in *Mao 1987–98, vol. 5, p. 52; *Mao CCRM, vol. 1, p. 176; vol. 13, p. 20. "10,000 reports": *Mao CCRM, vol. 13, p. 18. Say airily: *Wang Dongxing, 1997, p. 22. "less conscience": *Bo Yi-bo 1993, pp. 350–1.

387–388   "Once you join": *Wang Gengjin et al., p. 98. "We must arrest": *Mao CCRM, vol. 13, p. 13. "My farts": ibid., p. 17. "The bourgeoisie": *Mao 1993c, pp. 377, 379–80. "We started": *Liu 1996, vol. 2, p. 350.

388–389   "5 percent": *Mao 1987–98, vol. 5, p. 149. "Whenever this figure": ibid., p. 472. Hu Feng: *Hu Feng, pp. 257ff; *Mei Zhi; *Xiao Feng, pp. 98–109; *Li Hui. "The first half": *Mao CCRM, vol. 11A, p. 88.

389   "liberate Taiwan": *Zhou 1997, vol. 1, p. 405. Sea crossing: *Peng 1998, p. 565; *Xu Yan 1992, p. 174. Taiwan Strait crisis: Lewis & Xue 1988, pp. 22ff; Chang, G. 1990, pp. 116ff.

389–390   Khrushchev offers: Zazerskaya, 1997, pp. 173ff; id. 2000, pp. 33ff; *Pei Jianzhang, p. 39; *Zhou 1997, vol. 1, p. 416. Help to build Bomb: Gobarev, pp. 17ff; Negin & Smirnov 2002 (Web/ PHP); Shepilov 2001, pp. 373–86; Russian Ministry of Foreign Affairs, *SSSR–KNR*, part. 1, pp. 144–7 (27 Apr. 1955 agreement); Arkhipov, Kapitsa interviews; Lewis & Xue 1988, pp. 39ff., 61–2; *Chen Xiaodong, pp. 36–8; *Peng 1998, p. 578.

390   "our destiny": *Chen Xiaodong, pp. 33–5. "Bottoms up": ibid., p. 43. Russians agreed: *China Today* 1987, pp. 20–1; Gobarev, p. 21. Told his aides: *Dong Bian et al., p. 50. "control the Earth": Li Shenzhi, in *YHCQ, 1999, no. 1, p. 7.

391–392   Chou cut spending: *Jin Chongji et al. 1998, pp. 264–7. "he found it": *Bo Yi-bo 1993, p. 470. "flooding Chairman Mao": ibid., p. 651. US$: *Mao 1987–98, vol. 7, pp. 119, 125. Yugoslavia's No. 2: Kardelj, p. 141. Apr. 1956: Hu Qiaomu, in *Jin Chongji et al. 1998, p. 269.

392   Liu, Lo Fu: *Wu Lengxi 1999, pp. 16, 9. Chou told State Council: *Zhou 1997, vol. 1, p. 567. "shaken the entire world": *Wu Lengxi 1999, p. 6. "really has guts": *Li Yueran, p. 147.

393   First flight: *Li & Peng, pp. 88–94. Mao statue: *Wang Renzhong, p. 9. In Canton: *Li Zhisui, pp. 126–7, 148 (E: id., pp. 132ff); interview with Zeng Zhi, 24 Sept. 1994.

393–394   "would not do": *Gong Guzhong et al., p. 356. Mao swam: *Wang Renzhong, pp. 6–9; *Zhang Yaoci, pp. 75–84. 4 June Politburo: *Zhou 1997, vol. 1, pp. 270–1. Liu editorial: *Jin & Huang, pp. 791–2; *Bo Yi-bo 1993, pp. 637–8.

394–395   North Korea: Fursenko, pp. 960–1 (based on Soviet Presidium archives); Lankov 1995, pp. 149–50; id. 2002, pp. 106–7; Mukhitdinov 1995, pp. 341ff; id. 1994, pp. 200ff; Kapitsa 1996, pp. 236–7; *Il Ponte* vol. 37, 1981, nos. 11–12, p. 1170 (Liu to Gomulka, Nov. 1960); confirmed by Werblan (present), phone interview, 8 Sept. 2003; Szalontai 2003–4, pp. 91–2. 10 Sept. reminisced: *DDWX, 1991, no. 3, pp. 5–8.

395   Conciliatory: Mao remarks on 8th Congress reports, *Mao 1987–98, vol. 6, pp. 136–69. Cult: *JYZW vol. 9, pp. 143, 314ff, *Mao 1994, p. 255; *Dai Huang, pp. 11–12. Legal system: *JYZW vol. 9, pp. 92–4, 268–9. Most important concession: *Shi Zhongquan et al., p. 157;

*JYZW vol. 9, pp. 42–3, 65; *PRC Encyclopaedia vol. 4, p. 5095; *Bo Yi-bo 1993, p. 560. *Jin Chongji et al. 1998, p. 296.

CHAPTER 38   Undermining Khrushchev

397   19 Oct.: *Pei Jianzhang, p. 61; *Wu Lengxi 1999, p. 38; Chen 2001, pp. 146–55. 20th: *Wu Lengxi 1999, pp. 34–9. Mao threat to Yudin: *Wu Lengxi 1999, pp. 39–40. "blunderer": *Li Yueran, p. 147. Chinese role in Polish crisis: Fursenko, pp. 174–9, 187–91, 967ff. (Soviet Presidium minutes); Kuo, M., p. 95; Werblan interview, 8 Sept. 2003; Chen 2001, pp. 149–50.

397–398   Criticize Russia: *Wu Lengxi 1999, p. 45. China and Hungarian crisis: Fursenko, pp. 176ff, 970ff; Kramer 1995–6, pp. 173, 181, n. 28; Rákosi, p. 130; Kuo, M., pp. 95–101; Luthi, pp. 109ff. Mao for crushing uprising: *Wu Lengxi 1999, pp. 51–3. 4 Nov.: ibid., p. 59. Hegedüs: interview, 15 Dec. 1994.

398–399   Mao re Djilas: *Peng 1962. Chou to Gomulka: minutes of Chou–Gomulka talks, 11 & 12 Jan. 1957, CWB no. 5, pp. 43–5; *Jin Chongji et al. 1998, p. 323. "Polish leadership": in *Jin Chongji et al. 1998, p. 324. "your court": *Wu Lengxi 1999, pp. 102–6, 145. "headed by": *Wang Taiping 1998, p. 285. Polish visitors: Maneli, pp. 81–2.

399   Turned to Tito: *Wang Taiping 1998, p. 349; *Wu Xiuquan 1992, pp. 251–2 (E: Wu, p. 118); Micunovic, p. 197. Trashing Tito and Gomulka: 18 Jan. 1957, *Mao 1977, pp. 333–4. Jan. 1957: Chou report of 24th, in *Jin Chongji et al. 1998, pp. 326–8; CWB nos. 6–7, pp. 153–4; cf. Vereshchagin, pp. 79–81, 87. Mao rant: 27 Jan. 1957, *Mao 1977, p. 344 (E: Leung & Kau, p. 252).

399n   Conversation with Stephen Vizinczey.

400   Spaniard: Croft, p. 168. Mao to Egyptian ambassador: 17 Sept. 1956, *Mao 1994, pp. 247–9 (E: Mao 1998, pp. 191–3). Gift, trade with Egypt: *Pei Jianzhang, p. 283; Shichor, pp. 41–5, 49–50. War plan: *Pei Jianzhang, p. 283. "volunteers": Croft, p. 172; Harris, p. 91; Shichor, pp. 65 n., 225; *RR, 14 Nov. 1956. Heikal: interview, 18 Jan. 1997. Offers arms: *Mao 1987–98, vol. 6, pp. 280–1; Trevelyan 1970, p. 34; Heikal 1972, pp. 65–6; Shichor, pp. 45–6.

401   "people just won't listen": *Chen Xiaodong, pp. 109–10. Mikoyan visit July 1957: interview with Kudashev (Mikoyan's interpreter), 28 June 1995; Xinhua, 5 July 1957 (CCP cable); Luthi, p. 120. Istochnik, no. 4, 1996, pp. 109–14 (Mao to Yudin, 29 Oct. 1957). To renegotiate: *Nie 1999, pp. 612–14. Attend summit on condition: Usov 2003, p. 4. Khrushchev gives Bomb: Gobarev pp. 18–31; Negin & Smirnov; Lewis & Xue 1988, pp. 62ff; *Nie 1999, p. 623; *Wu Lengxi 1999, pp. 94–5. Missiles: Goncharenko, pp. 153ff; Baturov, Vladimir, "Kosmicheskii Skachok Pekina" (Peking's Cosmic Leap), NV, nos. 2–3, pp. 38–9. Khrushchev, S., pp. 266–72.

402   "maximum help": in *Yang Kuisong 1999, p. 425. "they received a lot": Gobarev, pp. 22–3, citing document from presidential archive. Superpower by end 1962: *Nie 1999, p. 620. Cost of Bomb: Lewis &

Xue 1988, p. 108. "must have Sputniks": *Mao CCRM, vol. 8, pp. 38–9; *Chen Xiaodong, pp. 96–7; *Dong Sheng, p. 341.

401n   Baturov, p. 39; Khrushchev, S., pp. 266–72; Gobarev, p. 30; Goncharenko, pp. 156–9; Dolinin.

402–403   Mao floated idea: *Istochnik*, no. 4, 1996, p. 113 (to Yudin, 29 Oct. 1957); cf. Micunovic, p. 198; Fursenko, pp. 279–81, 1022, n. 3. Mao in Moscow: Schoenhals 1986; interviews with eight participants (Alia, Carrillo, Heikal, Ingrao, Jotti, Li Yueran, Longo, Sidikhmenov); Gollan notes, *cit.*; Togliatti report, "Verbali della Direzione," 26 Nov. 1957, p. 4 (Istituto Gramsci Archives, Rome); Sidikhmenov MS, pp. 213–15. Special treatment: *Li Yueran, pp. 131–2; interview with Li Yueran, 24 Oct. 2000. Muscovite to Finn: Kuusinen, p. 221. Mao totted up: Khrushchev 1977, vol. 2, p. 309; id. 1990, p. 198. Rejected birth control: *China Today* 1988, pp. 416–18; cf. *Mao 1987–98, vol. 6, p. 635.

403   "no text": Sidikhmenov interview, 24 June 1996; *Li Yueran, p. 144. "sick in the head": *Mao 1987–98, vol. 6, p. 630; Micunovic, p. 322; Kapitsa 1996, p. 60. "Let's contemplate": 18 Nov. 1957, *Mao 1987–98, vol. 6, p. 636. Audience "shocked": Ingrao interview, 17 July 1994. "four legs": Borisov 1982, p. 72 (from records); Kapitsa 1996, p. 60.

404   Gollan: Gollan Notes, *cit.*, p. 3. Zhivkov: id., p. 518; CWB nos. 14–15, p. 435 (to Deng, 7 May 1987). "tall tree": *Yang Kuisong 1999, p. 411. "overtake Britain": *Mao 1987–98, vol. 6, p. 635 (E: Schoenhals 1986, p. 118). Like a teacher: *Li Yueran, p. 137. "Everyone needs": *Mao 1987–98, vol. 6, p. 640 (E: Schoenhals 1986, pp. 121–2). "very red": Kardelj, p. 140.

404n   Italian interpreter: interview with Longo, 29 May 1996.

405   Mao on Molotov: *Mao 1987–98, vol. 6, p. 643 (E: Schoenhals 1986, p. 123); Micunovic, p. 322; cf. Vereshchagin, p. 93; *Istochnik*, no. 4, 1996, p. 112 (to Yudin, 29 Oct. 1957). Mao's "megalomania": Khrushchev 1977, vol. 2, pp. 300, 321; cf. id. 1990, p. 154. Chou asked for nuclear submarines: *Zhou 1997, vol. 2, p. 149; *China Today* 1992a, vol. 1, p. 342; cf. Fursenko, pp. 316, 1038–9. Mao–Yudin, 21 July 1958: Vereshchagin (present), pp. 119–21.

405–406   Mao–Yudin, 22 July: minutes in CWB nos. 6–7, pp. 155–9; *DDWX, 1994, no. 1, pp. 16–20; *Wu Lengxi 1999, pp. 158–66; *Wang Taiping 1998, pp. 226–7. Khrushchev–Mao talks in China: CWB nos. 12–13, pp. 250–62; Fedorenko 1990; Troyanovsky interviews, 20 June & 18 Aug. 1995; Khrushchev 1977, vol. 2, pp. 306ff; interview with Kudashev, 28 June 1995. Second Taiwan Crisis: *Wang Taiping 1998, p. 218; *Ye Fei, pp. 649ff; cf. Eliades, p. 355; Tucker, pp. 128–32.

406–407   Mao–Gromyko: Kapitsa 1996, pp. 61–3 (present); Kapitsa interview; Gobarev, pp. 25–7; Ford; Lewis & Xue 1994, p. 17; Khrushchev 1977, vol. 2, pp. 310–12; *Wang Taiping 1998, pp. 218–19; *Wu Lengxi 1999, p. 180. Chou to Russian chargé: *Dai Chaowu, p. 66.

407   Khrushchev letter, 27 Sept. 1958: in Russian Ministry of Foreign Affairs, *SSSR–KNR* vol. 1, p. 232; cf. ibid., p. 233. "people dying": *Yang Kuisong 1999, p. 434. "Why do it": *Huang Kecheng, p. 255.

407   *Mao 1977, pp. 136–7 (E: Kau & Leung, p. 516).

408   4 Feb. 1959 deal: *China Today 1989a, vol. 2, p. 157; Zazerskaya 1997, pp.
           173–4; Lewis & Xue 1994, p. 17.

CHAPTER 39   Killing the "Hundred Flowers"

409   "number of arrests": *Mao 1987–98, vol. 6, pp. 45–6. Colleagues on
           Eastern Europe: *Liu 1991, p. 647; *Zhou 1993, pp. 336, 344. Mao's
           view: *Mao CCRM, vol. IIA, p. 114; *Mao 1977, pp. 317–23 (E: Leung
           & Kau, pp. 163, 167); *Yang Kuisong 1999, p. 388.

410   27 Feb. 1957: *Mao CCRM, vol. 1, pp. 190–232 (E: MacFarquhar et
           al., pp. 131–89). "brainwashing": 17 Nov. 1957, *Mao CCRM, vol. IIA,
           p. 211 (E: Leung & Kau, p. 775). Told few cronies: *Mao CCRM, vol.
           IIA, pp. 168–72.

410   "catch the snakes": 6 Apr. 1958, *Mao CCRM, vol. 13, p. 115. Dissent:
           *Niu & Deng, pp. 122–3, 200, 204, 208–10, 269; *Ding Shu 1993,
           pp. 124, 132; *Zhu Zheng, pp. 384, 447, 470–2; *XB, 1957, no. 14,
           pp. 61–6.

411–412   Uprising impossible: cf. instruction, 6 June 1957, *Mao 1987–98, vol.
           6, pp. 491–2; *Niu & Deng, pp. 215–19. Pamphlet, appeals: in *Mao
           1987–98, vol. 6, p. 493; *Niu & Deng, pp. 34, 143–7, 262. Ordered
           editorial: *Wu Lengxi 1995, 39–42 (E: Leung & Kau, pp. 564–7).

412   Circular, 12 June: *Mao 1987–98, vol. 6, pp. 469–76. Scientists: *Jin
           Chongji et al. 1998, p. 396; *Zhu Zheng, p. 405. Sadistic theater: *Mao
           CCRM, vol. 1, 362; *Zhu Zheng, pp. 435–40. "denounced 100,000":
           *Mao CCRM, vol. 13, p. 201.

413   "Little Hungary": *Cai Gong; *CCP Hubei Committee, p. 330.
           Education budget: *Finance Ministry, vol. 2, p. 436; cf. Pan, p. 367.

413–414   Dai Huang: *Dai Huang.

414–415   Chou attacked: *Bo Yibo 1993, pp. 636–9; *Jin Chongji et al. 1998, p.
           409; *Mao 1977, pp. 225–6; Ke Hua, in *BNC, 1999, no. 3, p. 45. Fatal
           breakdown: *ZR vol. 10, pp. 187–9; *Li Zhisui, p. 219 (E: p. 230); *Bo
           Yibo 1993, p. 639.

415   Secretary recalled: Fan Ruoyu, in *Jin Chongji et al. 1998, pp. 434–5;
           Chou speech in Teiwes with Sun 1999, pp. 253–7.

416   Chief of Henan: Pan Fusheng, denounced by Mao, in *Mao 1987–98,
           vol. 7, pp. 201, 205, 209–10; in *Henan Ribao (Henan Daily), 4 July 1958;
           his successor Wu Zhipu, in *XB, 1957, no. 15, pp. 19–20, *Zhongzhou
           pinglun (Zhongzhou Comments), periodical, Henan, 1958, no. 1. Liu
           under attack: *Bo Yi-bo 1993, p. 642. Mao's notes: *Mao 1987–98,
           vol. 7, p. 205; *Bo Yi-bo 1993, pp. 642–3. Chou battered: *Jin Chongji
           et al. 1998, p. 438. "entertainer": interview with Chen Yi's son, 2 Oct.
           1994. "has to be a . . . cult": Schram 1974, pp. 99–100 (10 Mar. 1958,
           Chengdu); *Cong Jin, p. 116; cf. Mao 1998, pp. 424–5; Snow 1974, p.
           174 (talk with Mao, 9 Jan. 1965). "blind herd": *Cong Jin, p. 117.

417   *People's Daily* wrote: 26 May 1958. Mao at restaurant: Quan, pp. 87–9. Mao vetoed double: interview with the man who made the suggestion, 14 Oct. 1994.

417   "godlike language": *Mao CCRM, vol. 13, p. 133 (E: MacFarquhar et al., p. 412).

CHAPTER 40   *The Great Leap: "Half of China May Well Have to Die"*

418   Shortened to: 28 Jan. 1958. *Mao 1987–98, vol. 7, p. 42; *Mao CCRM, vol. 13, p. 90. "like an atom": ibid. (E: Schram 1974, p. 92). "Great Leap" launched: Teiwes with Sun 1999, pp. 71ff; Schoenhals 1987; MacFarquhar 1983, pp. 51ff; Yang, D., pp. 33ff; Becker, pp. 58ff. "overtake all": *RR editorial, 29 May 1958. "Pacific Ocean": *Mao CCRM, vol. 11B, p. 80.

418–419   "Earth Control Committee": *Mao CCRM, vol. 13, p. 131. Mao asserts enormous increase: *Bo Yibo 1993, pp. 684–5. Provincial chiefs proclaim: ibid., p. 688. Henan Mao's model: *Mao 1987–98, vol. 7, p. 114; *Wu Lengxi 1995, pp. 63–4; Domenach 1995. Potemkin fields: *Chen Han, pp. 74–5; Wang Ding, in *Xiao Ke et al., pp. 205–19. Transplanting stopped: *Chen Liming, p. 337.

419–420   "surplus food": *Qiu Shi, vol. 3, p. 235; *RR, 11 Aug. 1958. 28 Jan.: *Mao 1987–98, vol. 7, p. 44; *Mao CCRM, vol. 13, p. 92. Guangxi "sputnik": Wang Ding, in *Xiao Ke et al., pp. 205–19. "When you order": *Mao CCRM, vol. 13, p. 129. Mao repeatedly accused: *Mao CCRM, vol. 13, pp. 240, 253, 254.

420   "a big problem": *Mao 1987–98, vol. 8, p. 209. Yunnan report: *Mao 1987–98, vol. 7, pp. 584–5. Earth compounds: Becker, pp. 206–7. Exports: Yang, D., p. 66; Lardy, pp. 373, 381; Hussain & Feuchtwang, p. 51; Price, pp. 593, 601. Mao–Khrushchev 1958: CWB nos. 12–13, pp. 250ff (minutes of talks, 31 July & 3 Aug. 1958); *Li Yueran, pp. 149–50. Food as fuel: *Mao CCRM, vol. 13, p. 168 (E: CWB nos. 6–7, p. 220); *Dong Sheng, p. 493.

421   950 Suez Canals: Chi 1965, p. 50; cf. Becker, p. 78. "I think 30,000": *Jiang Weiqing, p. 421. Gansu: *RR, 17 May 1958; *Mao 1987–98, vol. 7, pp. 201, 205, 210. "Three Simultaneouslys": Lo Fu speech, 21 July 1959, in *Zhang Wentian 1990–5, vol. 4, 324; *Qiu Shi, vol. 3, p. 224. One well-known project: *Qiu Shi, vol. 3, pp. 222–32. Stupendous waste: *Reminiscences about Tan Zhenlin, p. 418; *Qian & Geng, pp. 771–8; Shapiro, pp. 63–4.

422   "human wave tactic": *Bo Yi-bo 1993, p. 683. "Reduce fertiliser imports": *Mao CCRM, vol. 13, p. 230. "country of pigs": 31 Oct. 1959, *Mao 1993c, p. 498. Pigs fell: Lardy, p. 373. "shit lakes": *Liu & Yi, pp. 144–5.

422–423   Sparrows: *Liu Zhende, pp. 80–1; *Mao 1987–98, vol. 9, p. 81; cf. Shapiro, pp. 86–9. Sparrows from Russia: interview with a Russian insider June 1995. Dogs: *SMMM, p. 271.

423n   Interview with a Russian insider, June 1995.

423–424   "Last year": *Bo Yibo 1993, p. 700. "bourgeois professors": 22 Mar. 1958, *Mao 1987–98, vol. 7, p. 118. "forced": 23 Nov. 1958, *Mao CCRM, vol. 13, p. 217 (E. MacFarquhar et al., p. 515); *Li Rui 1989, p. 236. "samovar" furnaces: Khrushchev 1977, vol. 1, p. 504. "To hand in": *CCP Zhenyuan Committee, p. 53.

424–425   Work-days lost: MacFarquhar 1983, p. 119. "We must make it!": *Bo Yibo 1993, p. 706. "only 40 percent": 21 Nov. 1958, *Mao CCRM, vol. 13, p. 204 (E: MacFarquhar et al., p. 495); cf. MacFarquhar 1984, p. 128. Russian alloys: Doumkova, p. 133. "No good at": *Li Rui 1989, p. 88. Wasted much from Russia: Brezhnev, pp. 59ff. "slaves": 16 May 1958, *Mao 1987–98, vol. 7, p. 231. Zasyadko: Khrushchev 1977, vol. 2, pp. 324–5, 81; Vereshchagin, p. 114.

425   "grey-beard": *Bo Yibo 1993, p. 713. Quality problems: *Huang & Zhang, p. 401; *Contemporary Chinese Biographies team, pp. 546–65. "Communist spirit": 30 Aug. 1958, *Mao CCRM, vol. 13, p. 147 (E: MacFarquhar et al., p. 434). "Change from 1 Jan.": *Mao CCRM, vol. 13, pp. 176–7.

426   Days off: *Mao CCRM, vol. 13, pp. 138, 180 (E: MacFarquhar et al., pp. 418, 443ff, 449, 455); Chayashan Commune Charter, in *ZDJC vol. 22, p. 500. Typhoid: Li Rui, in *Han Taihua, p. 583. "labouring every day": 30 Aug. 1958, *Mao CCRM, vol. 13, p. 151. "easier to control": 21 Aug. 1958, *Mao CCRM, vol. 13, p. 133. First commune: 19 Aug. 1958, *Mao CCRM, vol. 13, p. 130; *Mao 1987–98, vol. 7, pp. 345–7; *Chen Han, pp. 158–61; Chayashan Commune Charter, *ZDJC vol. 22, pp. 497–501. Rid of names: interview with Wang Guangmei, 27 Sept. 1994. See photo.

427   1,415 abodes: *Liu & Yi, pp. 75–7. "This won't do": 26 Sept. 1961, *Mao 1993c, p. 552. "people were slaves": *Wang Gengjin et al., p. 199; Becker, p. 144.

427–428   "people roaming": 19 Aug. 1958, *Mao CCRM, vol. 13, p. 130 (E: MacFarquhar et al., p. 407). Orders banning peasants from leaving their villages include those on 2 Mar. & 18 Dec. 1957, 9 Jan. 1958, 25 Feb. 1959, in *PRC Encyclopaedia vol. 2; 31 Mar. 1959, in *ZDJC vol. 23, pp. 17–18. "four have died": *Wang Gengjin et al., p. 195. Brutality: *Wang Gengjin et al., pp. 202–3; Becker, pp. 144–6. "Production first": *Yun & Bai, p. 7. "chimneys": Mrs. Liang Sicheng, *Li Yong et al., p. 271.

428–429   Keep seventy-eight: Terzani, pp. 27–8; Kordon, p. 11 (Mao to Kordon, Dec. 1962). "I am delighted": 28 Jan. 1958, *Mao CCRM, vol. 13, p. 91; also pp. 80–1. "I can't stand": Jan. 1958, Li Rui, in *Han Taihua, pp. 560–1. Qingdao and Changchun "the best": Mar. 1958, *Mao CCRM, vol. 11B, p. 46. Hold 10,000 people: interview with a chief architecture manager, 16 Oct. 2002. "biggest square": Ma Ju, Peng Zhen's secretary, *ZDZ, no. 76, p. 64.

429   Life in "slow motion": Rowinski, p. 89. Meat ration: *Cong Jin, p. 272. Daily calorie intake: Ashton et al., pp. 622–3; Han 1982, p. 361; Banister, pp. 866–7. Auschwitz ration: museum at Auschwitz. Cannibalism: *Wang Gengjin et al., p. 195; *Fu Shanglun et al., p. 26; Becker, pp. 212–13.

429   Polish student: Rowinski, p. 89. Liu said 30m dead: Chervonenko interview, 28 Oct. 1998. Grain exports: Yang, D., p. 66.

430   *Yang Zihui et al., pp. 1522, 1610–12; *China Statistics Bureau, p. 103; *China Today 1988, p. 9; *Dong Fu; cf. Yang, D., p. 38.

430–431   "in favour of death": 20 May 1958, *Mao 1987–98, vol. 7, p. 201; *Mao CCRM, vol. 11B, p. 68. Fengyang county: *Wang Gengjin et al., pp. 194–5. "Deaths have benefits": *Mao CCRM, vol. 11B, p. 148; *Wang Gengjin et al., p. 194. "prepared to sacrifice": Sidikhmenov MS, p. 215; cf. Kapitsa 1996, p. 60; Bonsov 1982, p. 72. "Don't make a fuss": *Mao CCRM, vol. 11B, p. 64; *Mao CCRM, vol. 8, p. 44. "half of China": *Mao CCRM, vol. 13, pp. 203–4 (E: MacFarquhar et al., pp. 494–5).

CHAPTER 41   *Defense Minister Peng's Lonely Battle*

432   Peng against corruption: *Peng 1981, p. 5 (E: Peng, p. 27); *Li Rui 1989, p. 342; *Peng 1998, pp. 561–2, 739. Against personality cult: *Li Rui 1989, pp. 253, 342; *Zheng Wenhan, p. 135.

432–433   Esteem for Khrushchev: *Li Rui 1989, p. 253. "must be compatible": *Peng 1962. Admired "Liberty, Equality": *Mao CCRM, vol. 10, p. 347 (E: JPRS, vol. 9, part 1, p. 13); *Li Rui 1989, pp. 235–6. Reluctantly made Peng defense minister: *Wang Dongxing 1997a, pp. 93–4, 121. Offered to resign: *Jin Chongji et al. 1998, p. 438.

433–434   Nuclear submarines: minutes of Mao's talk with Yudin, 22 July 1958, in *DDWX, 1994, no. 1, p. 19 (E: CWB nos. 6–7, pp. 155–9). Peng disappeared: *Zheng Wenhan, p. 338. Inspection tour: ibid., p. 366; *Jing Xizhen, pp. 69–71. Wuhan Conference: *Peng 1981, p. 265 (E: Peng, p. 487).

434   Peng visits home: *Peng 1981, pp. 266, 274–5 (E: Peng, pp. 487, 501); *Zheng Wenhan, pp. 389–92; *Jing Xizhen, pp. 72–3; *Wang Yan et al., p. 580.

434–435   18 Dec., Peng–Bo: *Peng 1981, p. 266 (E: Peng, p. 488); *Zheng Wenhan, p. 390; *Bo Yi-bo 1993, p. 857. "A few children die": 9 Dec. 1958, *Mao CCRM, vol. 11B, pp. 147–8.

435   Invitation to Eastern Europe: *Peng 1998, pp. 691, 717–22; *Peng 1962. Mao exploded: *Zheng Wenhan, pp. 413–14; cf. MacFarquhar 1984, pp. 172ff. Wives: *Zheng Wenhan, p. 414; interviews with people close to Peng. Peng–Yudin: Brezhnev, pp. 63–5; Brezhnev letter to authors, 6 Apr. 2000 and phone interview, 22 Apr. 2000.

436   East Germany: *Zhu Kaiyin, p. 20; *Zheng Wenhan, pp. 427–8; Wolf, Brie interviews, 18 & 22 Nov. 1999. Ulbricht wants more food: Meissner, p. 272 (Ulbricht letter to Mao, 11 Jan. 1961); *Wang Taiping 1998, p. 309. Peng on E. Europe: *Peng 1998, p. 736; *Wang Taiping 1998, p. 292; *Zhu Kaiyin, pp. 19–20.

436   Visit to Albania: *Zheng Wenhan, pp. 441–3; interview with Maqo Çomo, 13 Mar. 1996. "transport grain": *Peng 1981, p. 267 (E: Peng, p. 489).

436n   Mausoleum: *Peng 1998, p. 736. Submarines: Hoxha 1980, pp. 435–61. Loans: AQSh, f. 14, 1958, d. 1 (Hoxha to Mao, 7 Oct.; Hoxha to Chinese ambassador, 9 Oct.; Mao to Hoxha, 18 Dec. 1961); AQSh, f. 14, 1961, d. 1 (Chou–Koleka talks, 17 & 30 Jan. 1961).

437–438   "invite in Soviet Red Army": *Li Rui 1989, p. 126; cf. Vereshchagin, p. 115. "sniff around": 1 Aug. 1959, in *Li Rui 1989, p. 239; *Zheng Wenhan, p. 444. Payments to Russia: Li Xiannian report to Mao, 20 May 1959, in *ZDJC vol. 23, pp. 96–9. "peasants united against . . . Party": *Mao CCRM, vol. 13, pp. 253, 264–75. Provincial bosses: *Tao Lujia, pp. 82–4.

438   Mao to Shaoshan: our visit to Shaoshan, and interviews with Mao's entourage, relatives, local officials, Oct. 1994; *Gong Guzhong et al.; *Zhao Zhichao, pp. 495–531 (Li, Z., pp. 301–4).

439–440   Mao at Lushan: our visit to Lushan, and interview with a local insider, Apr. 1996; *Luo Shixu; *Li Rui 1989; *Li Zhisui, pp. 296–8 (E: pp. 309ff).

440–441   Zhongnanhai lounge: interviews with former girlfriends of Mao's, 29 Sept. 1994, 30 July 1999; *Li Zhisui, pp. 268–9, 342–5 (E: pp. 356–64). Peng arrived: visit to Lushan, Apr. 1996; *Wang Chengxian, pp. 238–9. Lushan conference: Teiwes with Sun 1999, pp. 202–12; Yang, D., pp. 51–6; Li Rui 1996, pp. 78–96. Peng views: *Peng 1998, pp. 738–40; Peng Dehuai's speeches at Lushan, 3–10 July 1959, URI, *Peng*, pp. 393–45; *Peng 1962.

441–442   Some feelers: *Peng 1998, pp. 740–1. Mao 23 July: *Li Rui 1989, pp. 165–76; *Deng Xiaoping, Jiang Zemin, et al., p. 504; Schram 1974, pp. 131–46; URI, *Peng*, pp. 405–12.

442   "We felt": Wang Yi, in *Han Taihua, p. 667. False concessions: *Liu 1993, p. 573; *ZDJC vol. 23, pp. 117–18, 132; *Cong Jin, pp. 236–8. "anti-Party clique": interviews with Li Rui, 1993–8; with the widows of two of the four-man "anti-Party clique," Lo Fu (7 Sept. 1998) and Zhou Xiaozhou (16 Oct. 1993); *Song Xiaomeng; *Huang Kecheng; *Zhou Xiaozhou Biography* team.

443   Lin "has invented": CWB, no. 11, p. 159 (28 Nov. 1968). Deng "estimated 10 million": *Cong Jin, pp. 393–4. "No. 2 Illness": Becker, p. 200. Flagellating doctors: interview with a doctor for the leaders, 22 Sept. 1994.

444   Mao's ex-wife: interviews with her friends (Zeng Zhi, 24 Sept. 1994; Liu Ying, 7 Sept. 1998) and Mao's messenger, Apr. 1996; *Shui Jing, pp. 211–28; *Wang Xingjuan 1993, pp. 67–85; 155–6; 209–13, 221.

CHAPTER 42   *The Tibetans Rebel*

445   Mao–Stalin 1950: CWB, nos. 6–7, p. 9. Stalin: "ethnic Chinese": FEA, no. 4, 1996, p. 69 (to Liu, 28 June 1949). Policy in early 1950s: Mao cables, *Mao 1987–98, vol. 1, pp. 475–7 (23 Aug. 1950), 488–9 (two on 29 Aug. 1950); vol. 2, pp. 451–2 (13 Sept. 1951); vol. 3, pp. 493 (11 July & 18 Aug. 1952), 583–4 (8 Oct. 1952). Le Yuhong, in

*Han Taihua, pp. 246–82; *CCP Tibet Committee; Tsering Shakya, pp. 33ff.

445   Mao–Dalai Lama talks: interview with the Dalai Lama, 11 Feb. 1999; Dalai Lama, pp. 88–9, 91, 97–100.

446   Dalai Lama applies to join CCP: Dalai Lama, p. 90; Dalai Lama interview. Mao–Dalai Lama correspondence: Mao letter of 24 Nov. 1955, *Mao 1987–98, vol. 5, pp. 451–2. Kham: *Mao 1987–98, vol. 6, pp. 113–14, 265–6; *CCP Tibet Committee; *Su Yu Biography team, pp. 923–8; interview with eyewitnesses, Sept. 1997.

446–447   24 June 1958: *Mao 1987–98, vol. 7, pp. 286–7, cf. p. 176. 22 Jan. 1959: *Mao 1987–98, vol. 8, pp. 10–11. "The bigger the upheaval": *Mao 1987–98, vol. 8, pp. 46–7 (18 Feb. 1959: E: in Wolff 2000, p. 59). Let Dalai Lama escape: *CCP Tibet Committee, p. 87. "wipe them out": *CCP Tibet Committee, pp. 90–1. Mao inquiries: *Mao 1987–98, vol. 8, pp. 198–9. Media campaign: *Mao 1987–98, vol. 8, p. 234; *RR, 30 Apr. 1959.

447   Chou acknowledged: *Cong Jin, p. 452.

447–448   All quotes and descriptions: *Panchen Lama (page numbers in order of quotes), pp. 26, 96, 111, 20–1, 93, 86, 109, 33, 107, 56, 87, 44, 45, 50, 97 (E: 29, 30, 112, 24, 102, 85, 189–90, 90, 102, 51, 52, 105, 113).

448   Palden Gyatso: interview, 10 Feb. 1999; Palden Gyatso, p. 78.

449   Mao "greatly displeased": Panchen Lama press conference, *RR, 5 Apr. 1988; *CCP Tibet Committee, pp. 141, 153, 167.

CHAPTER 43   *Maoism Goes Global*

450   Sidewinder: Khrushchev, S. 2000, pp. 269, 271–2; Khrushchev, N. 1990, p. 151; id. 1977, vol. 2, pp. 319–20.

450–451   "rule the world": Khrushchev, N. 1977, vol. 1, p. 504. Aid for Bomb stops: Khrushchev, S., pp. 270–1; Kapitsa 1996, p. 63; interview with Kapitsa, who drafted 20 June letter; Gobarev, pp. 25ff; Negin & Smirnov, pp. 3–13; Goncharenko, pp. 157–9; Zazerskaya 1997, pp. 177–8. Not fatal blow: Arkhipov, Kapitsa interviews; Gobarev, pp. 30–1; *Song Renqiong, p. 355. "avoid . . . 'rut' ": Wolff, p. 69 (Suslov, 24 Dec. 1959); cf. Taubman 1996–7, pp. 244, 248. "but believe in us": Dec. 1959, *Mao 1987–98, vol. 8, p. 601 (E: in Wolff, p. 74); *Qiu Shi, vol. 2, p. 551. 1,010 blueprints: Filatov, pp. 114–15.

451–452   Formulated a policy: Dec. 1959, *Mao 1987–98, vol. 8, pp. 600–1 (E: Wolff, p. 73); *Wu Lengxi 1999, pp. 234–5, 254–5. CIA: *FRUS 1958–1960* vol. 19, p. 521 (Feb. 1959 National Intelligence Estimate). de Beauvoir: Chen Xuezhao, p. 43; de Beauvoir, pp. 427, 429, 518, 119.

452–453   "you won't be able to flee": *Zhu Lin, p. 10; *Foreign Ministry 1990ff, vol. 4, p. 5; *Geng Biao, vol. 2, p. 24; Li, X., p. 22. Mitterrand: Mitterrand 1961, p. 30; cf. id., "Entretien avec Mao," *L'Express*, 23 Feb. 1961, pp. 13–14. Trudeau: Hébert & Trudeau. Boyd-Orr: *Facts on File*, 14–20 May

1959, p. 162 (statement, 13 May 1959). Montgomery: Montgomery, p. 64. BBC TV: Greene, p. 365. Aid figures: Copper 1976, pp. 125, 3.

453   Loans are gifts: *CCP Archive Study Office 1991, p. 261; Babu interview, 11 July 1994. Indochina: Hoan, p. 286. Algeria: *Wang Taiping 1998, p. 115. Guevara: ibid., p. 492; *Zhou 1997, p. 373; Anderson, pp. 489–90; cf. Copper 1976, pp. 33–4. Albania: AQSh, f. 14, 1958, d. 1; f. 14, 1961, d. 1, p. 7; Shyti interview, 14 Mar. 1996.

454   Venezuelans: AQSh, f.14, 1966, d.3 (9 Nov.). Dutch intelligence: Andrew Higgins, "In From the Cold," *Wall Street Journal*, 3 Dec. 2004. Lilley: interview, 1 May 1995.

454n   *Liu Guangren et al., pp. 247–57.

454–455   Founding Maoist camp: *Xiong Xianghui, pp. 361–80; *PRC Encyclopaedia* vol. 3, p. 2570. "no better than you Africans": 7 May 1960, Mao 1998, p. 311. Trade Union meeting: interview with Foa, 8 Aug. 2000, the first participant to go public about the split ("Dichiarazioni di Foa . . .," *l'Avanti!*, 14 June 1960); Prozumenshchikov 1999, pp. 80–2, 85, 95, n. 7 (from Russian archives); Grishin, pp. 179–82; Vereshchagin, pp. 159–60; Zubok, pp. 156–7. AQSh, f. 14, 1960, d. 1, 3, 4.

455n   Belishova interview, 13 Mar. 1996; AQSh, f. 14, 1960, d. 1, 3, 4; Yan Mingfu, in *Remembering Peng Zhen*, p. 178.

455–456   Cabell: FRUS 1958–1960, vol. 19, pp. 690–1 (22 June 1960); cf. ibid., p. 719 (Allen Dulles). Bucharest: interviews with three participants, two Russians and one Icelander. "No world war": CQ3 (1960), p. 120; Floyd, pp. 278–80; Zagoria, pp. 325ff. "We were isolated": Kojima, p. 206 (Mao, 28 Mar. 1966);

456–457   Mao backs down: *Wu Xiuquan 1995, pp. 337–42; *Wu Lengxi 1999, pp. 294–5. Russia withdraws experts: Russian Ministry of Foreign Affairs, SSSR-KNR vol. 1, pp. 265ff. (letter 16 July 1960); Chervonenko interview, 28 Oct. 1998; Zazerskaya 2000, pp. 133–70; Prozumenshchikov 1999, p. 91; Vereshchagin, pp. 159–61; Brezhnev, pp. 59ff; Chen 1996–97, pp. 246, 249–50. Dig things out of Russians: *Dong Sheng, pp. 401, 406–11. Missiles: Baturov. 66 of 155: *Wang Taiping 1998, p. 242; Zazerskaya 1997, p. 174.

457–458   Ahead of schedule: *Wu Lengxi 1999, p. 337; *Wang Taiping 1998, p. 241. Russia "did not ask for the debt": interview with an insider, 8 Sept. 1998; Chervonenko interview. Russia's ambassador: Chervonenko interview. Revaluing: Vladimirov, Y., pp. 22ff. Grain, sugar offer: *Wang Taiping 1998, p. 242; *CCP Archive Study Office, pp. 211–12; Russian Foreign Ministry, SSSR-KNR vol. 1, pp. 297–8 (Khrushchev letter to Mao, 27 Feb. 1961). Berlin Wall: Brie interview, 22 Nov. 1999.

458   May–June 1962: *Sino-Indian Border Self-defence War History*, pp. 465–6; Lin Biao report to Politburo 6 June 1962 about war preparation, *Liu 1996, p. 557. Nehru "cocky": Chou to Kissinger, 13 Nov. 1973 (Burr 1999b), p. 11. U-2, Charbatia: Pocock, pp. 96–100; *Weng & Pocock, pp. 165–9; interview with I Fu-en, 6 Oct. 1996. Preparation for Chiang invasion: *Huang & Zhang, pp. 370–2. Mao hunkered in Western Hills: interview with his entourage, Sept. 1994.

458–459   Sound out Washington: *Wang Bingnan, pp. 86–90; FRUS 1961–1963,
           vol. 22, doc. 131 (Cabot–Wang, 23 June 1962); Cabot, p. 128; Hilsman,
           p. 319; Fetzer, pp. 189–90. Feeler to Russian ambassador: *Wu Lengxi
           1999, p. 497. Khrushchev told Chinese about Cuba: *Zhang Dequn,
           pp. 7–8; *Liu Xiao, pp. 146–9. Cuba/India crises: Fursenko, pp. 596,
           616, 1106–9; Childs Papers, Box 2, Folder 3 (Khrushchev speech,
           14 Oct. 1962), Hoover Institution; conversations with Galbraith,
           22 Feb. 1995 & 24 Feb. 1997.

459n   May & Zelikow, p. 254.

460   "untrustworthy ally": May & Zelikow, pp. 637–8 (CIA chief McCone,
           29 Oct. 1962); Radványi 1972, pp. 136, 173n: Mikoyan briefing to
           Communist embassies in Washington after Cuba visit; Anderson, p.
           545; cf. CWB no. 5, pp. 109, 159 (Mikoyan to Guevara, 5 Nov. 1962).
           "Only one man": to Mexican President Echeverria, 20 Apr. 1973
           (Anguiano interview, 23 Nov. 1992). Castro played them off: Lewis &
           Xue 1994, p. 172; Prozumenshchikov 1996–7, pp. 254–6.

460   denounce Khrushchev by name: *Wu Lengxi 1999, pp. 633, 638–9.
           "philosophy of survival": URI, Liu, vol. 3, p. 244 (Liu Shao-chi, speech
           in Pyongyang, 18 Sept. 1963).

460n   FRUS 1961–1963, vol. 22, Doc. 180 (Kennedy to Harriman, 15 July
           1963); Harriman Papers, Boxes 539, 540, 542, 518, NARA.

CHAPTER 44   Ambushed by the President

461–462   Liu to home area 1961: quotes and descriptions from *Liu & Yi; *Liu
           Zhende, p. 132; interview with Liu's widow, Wang Guangmei, 27 Sept.
           1994. Liu, SW vol. 2, pp. 306–12 (talk with peasants, 7 May 1961).

462   "We cannot go on": *Liu 1993, p. 444 (E: Liu, SW vol. 2, p. 316). Teenage
           son observed: interview with the man, 12 Apr. 1996.

462–463   Chou: "no grain left": *Jin Chongji et al. 1998, p. 633. "What's all the
           fuss?": *Cong Jin, pp. 482–3. 34 percent: ibid., p. 399. "How wonder-
           ful": 9 Aug. 1962, Mao Miscellany vol. 2, pp. 22–7.

463–464   "We have retreated": *Mao 1987–98, vol. 9, p. 555. Managers were told:
           by Chou, end of 1961, *Jin Chongji et al. 1998, p. 656. Mao told
           Montgomery: *Xiong Xianghui, p. 388. Bitter sentiments: Wang Dong-
           xing report, Jan. 1961, in *Ding Wang, vol. 3, pp. 457–9. "biggest worry":
           *PRC Encyclopaedia vol. 2, p. 2438. "so be it": Apr. 1959, *Mao 1987–98,
           vol. 8, pp. 196–7.

464   Designating scapegoats: 15 Nov. 1960, 23–24 Jan. 1961, *Mao 1987–98,
           vol. 9, pp. 349–50, 425. Meteorological records: Becker, p. 283. Eat fish
           instead: interviews with Mao's personal staff, Oct. 2000. European
           menus: *SMMM, pp. 95–7. Daughter Li Na: conversation with Li Na,
           25 Mar. 1993; *Li Xiangwen, pp. 556, 558–60; *Li Yinqiao, pp. 165–6.

465   To his staff: interviews with Mao's personal staff, Oct. 1994, Apr. 1999,
           Oct. & Nov. 2000. Forgoing soap: *Gong Guzhong et al., p. 152;
           *SMMM, p. 161. Official snapped: JC father to mother, and with
           colleagues. "resign long ago": *Li Rui 1989, p. 60. Cursing Mao: *Quan

Yanchi 1991, p. 144. Peng visit home: *Peng 1998, pp. 764–8; *Wang Yan et al., pp. 668–76. "If the old Party charter": *Ding Shu 1991, pp. 271–2. Mao vetoed congress: *Pang & Jin, pp. 1184–5.

466   "need a spur": ibid., p. 1185. 7,000 Conference: MacFarquhar 1997, pp. 137–81. Text of keynote speech: *Liu 1993, pp. 458–67 (E: Liu, SW vol. 2, pp. 328–96); "kill time": *Dong Fu.

466–467   Different speech: interviews with Liu's widow Wang Guangmei, 27 Sept. 1994, 8 Nov. 1995; interview with Wang Li, 16 Oct. 1995; *Liu 1993, pp. 482–96; (E: Liu, SW vol. 2, pp. 397–422). Response: *Qiu Shi, vol. 1, p. 492; *Li Jian et al., pp. 457–60.

467–468   "Get their anger off": *Bo Yibo 1993, pp. 1017–19. "farts off": *Li Zhisui, p. 373 (E: p. 386). Lin Biao speech: *JYZW vol. 15, pp. 105–8. Praised Lin: *Pang & Jin, p. 1197. Loathing for Liu: ibid.; *Liao Gailong 1993, pp. 402–3. Liu murmured: interview with Wang Guangmei, 24 Sept. 1994. Liu had hoped: *Jin & Huang, p. 898. Mao "self-criticism": *JYZW vol. 15, p. 121 (E: Schram 1974, pp. 158–87).

468–469   Aid virtually zero: Copper 1976, p. 125; Kovner, p. 612. "Every time": Zhu Kaiyin, p. 17. "catches mice": 7 July 1962, *Deng 1989, p. 305 (E: Deng, SW vol. 1, p. 293). To Hong Kong: interview with a then CCP official in Hong Kong, 8 Oct. 2002; letter from a refugee.

469   "choked back": *Liao Gailong 1983, p. 140. Foreboding for Liu: Chang, J., p. 235; *Li Jian et al., p. 459. Liu knew: interview with Wang Guangmei, 24 Sept. 1994. Liu unusually passionate: *Wang Guangmei et al., p. 31; *Jin & Huang, pp. 896–8.

CHAPTER 45 *The Bomb*

470   "Light of Death": 16 Dec. 1963, *Chen Xiaodong, pp. 202–3. Half of China's lines: Qian Xuesen, in *CCP Archive Study Office 1991, pp. 289–91.

470–471   Kennedy and Mao's Bomb: FRUS 1961–1963 vol. 22, Doc. 180 (Kennedy to Harriman, 15 July 1963); Harriman Papers, Boxes 539, 540, 542, 518; Troyanovsky interviews; Seaborg, p. 245; Burr, 1999b; Kennedy press conference, 1 Aug. 1963 *Public Papers* (Web/Kennedy Library, p. 4).

471   Lanzhou/Baotou: Alsop, S., p. 9. "oil king": AQSh, f. 14, 1964, d. 38 (to Balluku). Johnson: FRUS 1964–1968 vol. 30, Doc. 2 (15 Jan. 1964, to Sen. Russell); cf. Garson; Burr, 1999b. 70th birthday cable: *Wu Lengxi 1999, pp. 745–53; English text in SCMP, no. 3203 (1964), pp. 29–30.

471–472   Stuns Russians: Grishin, pp. 240–1; Brezhnev, pp. 89–90. Statement on US blacks: Mao 1998, pp. 377–9. "didn't understand . . . blacks": Williams interviews by phone, 19 Mar. & 9 Apr. 1995. Panama, Dominican Republic: Mao 1998, pp. 390–1, 432–3 (12 Jan. 1964, 12 May 1965). Mao–Vietnamese: Yang Kuisong, in *Li Danhui, pp. 42–3 (E: Yang K. 2002, pp. 13ff); Le Duan, CWB, nos 12–13, p. 280; Westad et al. 1998, pp. 75–6 (Mao to Pham Van Dong, 5 Oct. 1964).

472 Laos, Thailand: Yang Kuisong 2002, pp. 17–18. South Sea fleet: *Wu Ruilin. US troops "hostages": Heikal, p. 277 (23 June 1965); Heikal confirmed in interview, 18 Jan. 1997. Chou to Nyerere: Babu, who was present, read to us from meeting notes, 11 July 1994; *Jin Chongji et al. 1998, p. 839.

473 "Third Front": quotes and description in *State Council, numbered volume compiled for the inner circle; *Bo Yibo 1993, pp. 1200–3; Naughton 1988; Lewis & Xue 1994, pp. 85–99; Shapiro, pp. 145–59.

474 "Be careful": *Mao 1993c, p. 622.

475 Mao celebrates the Bomb: *Chen Xiaodong, pp. 178–9; *Yang Mingwei, pp. 330–1. Doggerel: *Cong Jin, p. 459. Very cheaply: *CCP Archive Study Office 1991, p. 351.

475 US$4.1 billion: Lewis & Xue 1988, pp. 107–8. Lives saved calculation: based on *FRUS 1961–1963* vol. 22, Doc. 132 (Rusk to British prime minister Macmillan, 24 June 1962).

CHAPTER 46 *A Time of Uncertainty and Setbacks*

476 "Using novels": *Pang & Jin, p. 1254.

476–477 "The more books": 26 June 1965, *Mao CCRM & ARL, vol. VII, p. 3674 (E: Schram 1974, p. 232) . "ruins you": 27 Jan. 1965, ibid., p. 3670. "keep people stupid": *BNC, 1999, no. 3, p. 18. Mao opera fan: *SMMM, pp. 467–86; interviews with Mao's personal staff; Quan, pp. 44–7; Payne 1950, pp. 209–10. "all art forms": *Mao 1987–98, vol. 10, pp. 436–7.

477–478 "Throw singers": *Mao CCRM, vol. 4, pp. 3–4. Destruction: Terzani, pp. 26ff. Temples and tombs: *Mao 1987–98, vol. 11, pp. 232–6. "Get rid of most gardeners": *Mao CCRM, vol. 4, p. 26. Criticizing Stalin on classics: *ZDZ editorial board, p. 152.

478 Lei Feng: Marcuse, pp. 237–46. Hate: Chou, SW vol. 2, p. 432 ("Learn from Lei Feng"). 8 June 1964: *Bo Yibo 1993, p. 1148.

479 "utmost wish": Chou to Chervonenko (SAPMO, DY 30/3605, pp. 227–9: Podgorny to Ulbricht by phone, 29 Oct. 1964; Brezhnev, p. 96). Test rapprochement: Aleksandrov–Agentov, pp. 113–18; Kapitsa 1996, pp. 75–6; Troyanovsky interviews. Chervonenko recalled: interview.

479–480 Malinovsky episode: Kudashev (interpreter), pp. 198–9; Aleksandrov–Agentov, pp. 168–9; Arbatov (citing Andropov), p. 114; interviews with Kudashev, Kapitsa, Troyanovsky (present); record of Chou–Brezhnev talks, 8 Nov. 1964, in *Jin Chongji et al. 1998, pp. 827–8; *Yang Mingwei, pp. 389–90; interpreter Yan Mingfu's recollection, in *Han Taihua, pp. 757–9. Marshal's uniform: interview with Yan Mingfu, 14 Mar. 1998. Chou sat up all night: ibid.

480 Lacked effective anti-tank: *Li & Hao, pp. 273–4, 324. Artificial mountains: ibid., pp. 256–7.

481 Chou: no return to Moscow: *Yang Mingwei, pp. 397–8. Ho Chi Minh funeral: *Foreign Ministry 1990ff, vol. 2, pp. 158–60. Ho Lung: *Qiu Shi, vol. 3, pp. 494–524. General Xu: *Qiu Shi, vol. 3, pp. 500–19; *Xin Ziling 2002, p. 568; Zhang Songshan, p. 29. Withdrew from Dubna: Pashkovskaya & Zhdanovich, pp. 321, 323; Clemens, p. 255, n. 5.

481–482 "close to prostration": Brezhnev, p. 98. Convened the Assembly: 29 Nov. 1964, *Yang Shangkun, vol. 2, p. 427. Mao erupted: *Cong Jin, p. 602; *Mao 1993c, p. 615. Snapped at Liu: *Mao CCRM, vol. 4, pp. 66–72. "Someone is shitting": *Zeng Zhi, p. 432. Birthday: *Qi Li, p. 120; *Zeng Zhi, pp. 432–3; *Bo Yibo 1993, p. 1131; *Mao Miscellany* vol. 2, p. 427.

482–483 Chen Bo-da: *Bo Yibo 1993, p. 1133; *Ye Yonglie 1990, pp. 211–13. Liu's portrait: interview with Wang Guangmei, 27 Sept. 1994. In Suite 118: ibid.; *Wang Guangmei et al., p. 118; *Mao Miscellany* vol. 2, pp. 437ff. Colleagues–Liu–Mao: *Wang Guangmei et al., p. 119; *Jin & Huang, p. 973.

483 "wag my little finger": *Wang Guangmei et al., p. 118. Jinggang visit preparations: *Wang Dongxing 1993, p. 214; *Gong Guzhong et al., p. 247; interview with Mao's personal staff, 19 Apr. 1999, with a local official, 13 Apr. 1996.

484 Lin Biao démarche: *Xin Ziling 2002, pp. 497–8. Mao in Jinggang: visit to Jinggang Mountains and interviews with locals, Apr. 1996; *Wang Dongxing 1993, pp. 214–36; *Gong Guzhong et al., pp. 246–7.

485–486 Courted Sukarno: interview with Fujita (present at secret 5-hour Chou–Sukarno meeting, 1965), 6 Mar. 1998; Childs papers, Box 2, Folder 3 (Korianov briefing, 28 Feb. 1965); Taylor 1974, pp. 104–8; Copper 1983, p. 97. Egypt: Heikal, pp. 276–7, 282–3. Tan-Zam railway: Babu (original negotiator) interview; Snow, P., pp. 151–5, 160–72, 175–6, 181–2; *Foreign Ministry 1990ff, vol. 3, pp. 31–40; *BNC, 2000, no. 6, pp. 4–11. Ben Bella: *Mao 1987–98, vol. 11, pp. 187–90; *Zhou 1997, p. 738; cf. Liu, X., pp. 83–8; Snow, P., pp. 119–20.

486 Nyerere on Chou: *Xiong Xianghui, pp. 431–2.

486 Mao–Pakistan–India: Garver, pp. 202–4; *RR, 17, 20 & 22 Sept. 1965; *Wang Taiping 1998, pp. 87–8; *Foreign Ministry 1990ff. 1993, p. 478; conversation with Indian Foreign Secretary Krishna Rasgotra.

487n Garver, pp. 327–8.

487–488 Thailand: Marks, p. 23; cf. Stokes; interview with Pridi family, 1 May 1996. Miyamoto: interview, 22 Apr. 1996. PKI plan: interview with Indonesian Communist leader, Oct. 1994; cf. *Wang Taiping 1998, pp. 57–61.

488 Mao on Indonesia coup: to Japanese Communist Party delegation, 28 Mar. 1966, meeting record, courtesy of JCP Central Committee; Miyamoto interview, 22 Apr. 1996. Informer: Colonel Latief testimony in *Shadowplay* (BBC 4 television, 15 Aug. 2002).

489n *Tong Xiaopeng, vol. 2, p. 219; Zhai, pp. 117–19; cf. Armstrong, pp. 127, 131–2.

CHAPTER 47   *A Horse-trade Secures the Cultural Revolution*

493 "punish this Party": 20 Dec. 1964, *Mao CCRM, vol. 4, p. 60. "as a scorpion": interview with a person close to Mao, 14 Apr. 1999. "suppressed and bullied": Lin Mohan, in *BNC, 1994, no. 4, p. 26.

493 Mme Mao telephoned.: *Xin Ziling 2002, pp. 506–7. Disdainful remarks: interviews with Lin family members, 6 May & 20 Oct. 1995, 11 Sept. 1997; *Xin Ziling 2002, pp. 444, 480.

494–495 "Engels to Marx": *Xin Ziling 2002, p. 480. Lin phobias: interviews with Lin family members, 6 May, 14, 20 Oct. & 7 Nov. 1995, 11 & 12 Sept. 1997; *Deng Li, pp. 155–8; *Guan Weixun, p. 213; Li, Z, pp. 453–4; Jin, pp. 145–7; visit to Lin villas. "specializes in hate": Nov. 1961, in *Ming & Chi, p. 201. Luo the Tall: *Huang & Zhang, pp. 352, 433–538.

495 Mao–Lin, 1 Dec.: *Xin Ziling 2002, pp. 509–10. Mayor Peng complains to JCP: Kojima, p. 51.

496 Wu Leng-xi: Rittenberg & Bennett, p. 288; *Wu Lengxi 1995, pp. 150–4. "Wu disobeyed me": *Qiu Shi, vol. 2, p. 729. "bottomless" ambitions: *Huang & Zhang, pp. 540–1.

497 Luo's daughter: *Luo Diandian 1999, pp. 200–1. Mao reluctant: *Huang & Zhang, p. 540. "Jiang Qing is sick": *Zhang Tianrong, p. 71.

497–498 Suppressed Mao instructions: *Shi Dongbing, pp. 131–4, 139, 157. Peng–Peng tête-à-tête: ibid., pp. 208–22. Peng visitors: *Peng Meikui, p. 231. Mao suspected conspiracy: *He Long, p. 771; *Mao Mao 2000, p. 27. Sleeping pills: *Li Zhisui, p. 425 (E: pp. 440, 443).

498 Russian invitation: *Wu Lengxi 1999, pp. 934–9; *Shi Dongbing, p. 237; *Wang Li 2001, p. 582; *Mao Miscellany* vol. 2, p. 375 (Mao said "no" on 20 Mar. 1966).

498–499 "coup" accusation: *Wang Nianyi, p. 18. Lapin–Liu at airport: Galenovich 2000, pp. 130–1, and interview with Galenovich, 24 June 1996. Russian-speaking director: *Yang Shangkun, vol. 2, pp. 682–6; *Wang Lianjie, p. 438; interviews with Russian-language interpreters, Yan Mingfu, 14 Mar. 1998, and Li Yueran, 24 Oct. 2000.

499 Tape-recorded Mao: interview with the girlfriend of Mao, 2 Nov. 1995; interviews with officials involved in the taping, 17 Sept. 1994, 7 Nov. 1995, 9 Sept. 1997; Ye Zilong, in *ZQZS vol. 2, pp. 242–3; *Li Zhisui, pp. 281–2, 352–5 (E: pp. 292–3, 433, 439, 451).

499n Interview with Kang Yi-min, 17 Sept. 1994.

500 Tsedenbal: Radványi 1978, pp. 183, 185. Luo condemned: *Huang & Zhang, pp. 567–8.

500 Mme Mao writes Lin: *Cong Jin, pp. 621–2. Chou tells Mayor: *Shi Dongbing, pp. 239–43.

501 Politburo meeting May 1966: *WDYZ vol. 1, pp. 1–25; *Jin & Huang, pp. 1009–10; Li Xuefeng, in *BNC, 1998, no. 4, pp. 17–19. Mao to Ho: Schoenhals 1996a, p. 94. Lin speech: 18 May 1966, *WDYZ vol. 1, pp. 16–23 (E: Kau 1975, pp. 334, 328); *Xin Ziling 2002, p. 542. Mao told

Albanians: to Kapo and Balluku, 3 Feb. 1967, AQSh, f. 14, 1967, d. 6. Purging Praetorian Guard: interviews with victims, 17 & 25 Sept. 1994.

501   Purging police: *Tao Siju 1997, pp. 204ff.; *Liu Guangren et al., pp. 327ff. Ulanhu: *Ulanhu, pp. 9–11; Bulag, pp. 226–9.

502   Lin against Lu, colorful text: interviews with Lin family members and friends, 9 Oct. 1993, 20 & 31 Oct., 7 Nov. 1995; *WDYZ vol. 1, pp. 24–5; *Chen & Song, pp. 485ff.; *Ma Zhigang, pp. 187–211.

502   Mrs. Lin: interviews ibid.; *Zhang Yunsheng, pp. 256ff.; *Guan Weixun; Jin Qiu, pp. 145, 147–52.

CHAPTER 48   *The Great Purge*

503   Mme Mao heads Small Group: *Wang Li 1993, p. 26. 4.8 billion: *Zhou Jihou, p. 71. 1.2 billion: *Zhou 1997, vol. 3, p. 340.

504   24 June: 24 June seems to be the day when the poster signed "Red Guard" appeared in the middle school attached to Qinghua University, *WDYZ vol. 1, pp. 63–7. 13 June: *WDYZ vol. 1, pp. 44–5. "lessons are stopped": *Mao CCRM & ARL, vol. VII, p. 3684. 18 June: Yan & Gao, pp. 46–7.

504   Dripping Grotto: visit to the villa and interviews with local officials, Oct. 1994; interviews with Mao's personal staff; *Gong Guzhong et al., pp. 8–9, 13–14, 157–64; 167–8; *Zhang Yaoci, pp. 34–42.

505–506   Mao hands-on: Mao to Small Group: "Come to my place to have a meeting every week," in *Qiu Shi, vol. 3, p. 418; multiple interviews with Mao's and inner circle's personal staff, and with Small Group member Wang Li. Chou in charge: Schoenhals 1996a, pp. 90ff; id. 1996b, p. 363; *Jin Chongji et al. 1998, p. 894; interviews ibid. Changing-rooms: interviews ibid.; *Chen & Zhao, pp. 7, 10; *Li Zhisui, p. 462 (E: pp. 478–9). Officials' children form Red Guards: interviews with many high officials' children.

506   First known death: *Wang Youqin 1995, 1996; interviews with two then pupils of the school, 24 Sept. 1993, 8 Nov. 1998. Mao singled out: "Red Flag" team from the middle school attached to Peking University, who had started abusing "Blacks" on 1 July 1966, as well as beating up teachers, before Mao's "fiery support" on 1 Aug., see *Wang Youqin 1995, p. 43.

507   Sichuan boss: interview with an insider, 23 Mar. 1994. "Peking is not chaotic enough": *Mao CCRM, vol. 4, p. 115.

508   Orders to army and police: *WDYZ vol. 1, pp. 90–1; Schoenhals 1996a, pp. 48–9 (21 Aug.). Gave names and addresses: interview with an insider, 23 Mar. 1994.

508–509   Police chief: *Wang Nianyi, pp. 69, 73; *Qiu Shi, vol. 2, pp. 763–4; *Zhao Wumian, p. 137. Chou list: *Mao 1987–98, vol. 12, pp. 116–17; Schoenhals 1996, pp. 110–11. Official statistics: *Qiu Shi, vol. 2, p. 764.

509–510   Pick of booty: *Guan Weixun, pp. 130–3; Yang Yinlu, in *BNC, 1999, vol. 2, p. 67; interview with a member of Mao's personal staff, 19 Apr.

1999; Byron & Pack, pp. 364–8. Kissinger: Kissinger 1979, p. 1058. Housing space: *Wang Nianyi, p. 71; Kirkby, pp. 164–73. Eyewitness saw: *Zheng Yi, p. 48 (E: Zheng Yi, p. 59); cf. Schoenhals 1994, p. 10; telephone interview with Zheng Yi, 28 Aug. 2000.

510   Monuments obliterated: *Wang Nianyi, p. 70; Terzani, pp. 26–7. Leading architect: Liang's widow, in *Li Yong et al., pp. 265–78. First statue broken: *Wang Nianyi, p. 70. Specialists present: *Ya & Liang, pp. 116, 238–44.

511   Confucius' home: ibid., pp. 44–60. "People-centred-ism": 4 July 1973, in *Qiu Shi, vol. 3, p. 644. Lin speech: Kau 1975, pp. 363–6 (15 Sept. 1966).

512   Victims of past banned: 13 Jan. 1967, *WDYZ vol. I, p. 247. Mao resolved to overthrow all: *Wang Li 1993, p. 33.

512–513   British engineer: Watt, pp. 81, 91–2. Minister of coal: *Li Yong et al., pp. 89–97. Photographing torture: ibid., pp. 89–90; *Our Premier Zhou, pp. 32–3; *Tu & Kong, p. 73; *Zeng Zhi, p. 463; *Huang & Zhang, p. 575; *Yang Mu, p. 249; Wang Li 1994, p. 76 ("unbearable"). Vice-Premier Ji: *Si Ren, pp. 77–8; Wang Lingshu, p. 24.

513–514   Replacements: *Li & Hao, p. 241. Chou: "no war": *Li Desheng, p. 349. Superpower Program up: tables in *PRC Encyclopaedia vol. 4, p. 5094; interview with an economic manager, Sept. 2000.

514–515   Central Special Case Team: *Qiu Shi, vol. 3, pp. 489–525; *Li & Hao, p. 248; multiple interviews with victims of the team, and with an interrogator, 17 Apr. 1999; interview with Small Group member Wang Li, 16 Oct. 1995; *Wang Li 1994, p. 68; Schoenhals 1996a, 1996b. Mao danced on: interview with a girlfriend of Mao's, 29 Sept. 1994; *Quan Yanchi 1991, pp. 224–6.

515   Feb. 1967: *Qiu Shi, vol. 3, pp. 418ff.; *Wang Li 1993, pp. 31–2 (E: id. 1994, pp. 40–2; cf. id. 1999, pp. 69–81); interviews with family members of four main Politburo protesters; Suo, pp. 76ff; Yan & Gao, pp. 125–33. Brigadier: *Han Shangyu, pp. 1–7; interview with the friend of the brigadier, 30 Sept. 1993. Student of German: *Yu Xiguang, pp. 52–74; Schoenhals 1996, pp. 149–50 (text); conversation with Dai Qing, who interviewed her, 20 Oct. 2002.

CHAPTER 49   *Unsweet Revenge*

517   On the 5th: *Huang Zheng, p. 26 (E: id. 1999, pp. 31ff); cf. Galenovich 2000, pp. 55ff. Liu at dancing parties: interview with eyewitnesses, 13 Sept. 1994.

518   Kuai Da-fu story: interview with Kuai, 3 Oct. 1995.

519   Mao–Liu meeting: *Wang Guangmei et al., pp. 187–8; *Liu Zhende, pp. 282–4; Galenovich 2000, pp. 74–6. 300,000 rally: interview with Kuai, 3 Oct. 1995; Wang Guangmei interrogation in *Wang Nianyi, pp. 240–56 (E: Elegant 1971, pp. 347–67; Schoenhals 1996b, pp. 101–16).

520   Lius' protests to Mao: *Huang Zheng, pp. 102, 121–5. Mao left detailed instructions: through Qi Benyu, whom he appointed acting director

of the Central Secretariat's Office, *Zhang Zishen, pp. 320–3; *Chen & Zhao, p. 48.

521   Sleeping pills: Wang Guangmei reply to written questions by phone via secretary, 11 Apr. 2000; *Huang Zheng, p. 122. "burst out laughing": *Wang Guangmei et al., p. 34.

521   Grippa interview, 25 Jan. 1994.

522   Zeng Zhi: interview, 24 Sept. 1994; *Zeng Zhi, pp. 464–70.

522   Kangaroo court: Liu answers in *CCP Studies, pp. 629–30 (E: CLG vol. 1, no. 1 (1968), p. 75); *Wang Guangmei et al., pp. 202–3; Liu's valet Jia Lanxun, in *BNC, 2000, no. 2, pp. 22–4; *Tu & Kong, p. 73; Bonavia, p. 186; cf. Wang Li 1994, p. 76.

522–523   Guang-mei was to pay: her answer (by phone via secretary) to our questions, 11 Apr. 2000. Slow-death cell: quotes and descriptions from *Huang Zheng, pp. 126–30; Jia Lanxun, in *BNC, 2000, no. 2, pp. 26–9; *Tu & Kong, pp. 179–82.

523–524   Mao wants spy charge: *Tu & Kong, pp. 79–80. Forbidden to ask Liu: *Huang Zheng, p. 65 (E: id. 1999, p. 65). First inmate: *Shi Zhe 1992, pp. 237–9. Rittenberg: id. & Bennett, pp. 406–7. Nationalist intelligence: *Shen Zui, p. 214. Li Li-san: interview with Li's widow, Lisa, and daughter, Inna, 28 Oct. 1995; cf. Lescot, pp. 431–61. *Tang Chunliang 1989, pp. 204–10. Lo Fu: *Liu Ying, pp. 167–8.

524   Team purged: *Huang Zheng, p. 64. Catch-22: ibid., pp. 88–9. (E: id. 1999, p. 89). Chou delivered report damning Liu: CQ no. 37 (1969), pp. 175–80 (text). Death sentence: interview with Wang Guangmei, 8 Nov. 1995. Mao to 9th Congress: interview with a family member of Lin Biao, 20 Oct. 1995. Last self-defense: *Huang Zheng, pp. 86, 124–5 (E: id. 1999, pp. 84ff.).

525   Rebel leaders: *Peng 1998, p. 797; interview with Kuai Da-fu, 3 Oct. 1995. Peng's last days: *Peng 1998, pp. 806ff.

CHAPTER 50   *The Chairman's New Outfit*

526   General Chen: *Chen Zai-dao, pp. 295–311.

526–527   Wuhan shock for Mao: Chen Zai-dao, in *WDYZ vol. 1, p. 513; *Wang Li 1993, p. 39; *Wang Li 1994, pp. 59–61 (E: id. 1994, pp. 66ff). Mao verdict defied: *Chen & Zhao, pp. 59–61; *Wang Li 2001, pp. 1006–8; cf. Wang Li 1994, pp. 72–3; interview with Wang Li, 16 Oct. 1995; *Wang Nianyi, p. 263; Zhu, pp. 155–6; Huang, J., pp. 309–11.

527–528   Mao whisked away: *Zhang Zuoliang, pp. 153–5; *Chen & Zhao, pp. 62–5; *Zhang Zishen, pp. 344–6; cf. Yan & Gao, pp. 231–9. Unshaven cheek: *Wang Li 1994, p. 62. 184,000: Chen Zai-dao, in *WDYZ vol. 1, p. 524; cf. Schoenhals 1996b, p. 366; Zhu, pp. 157–61. World "first": Chen Zai-dao, in *WDYZ vol. 1, pp. 521–2; *Zhang Zuoliang, p. 158; *Zhou 1997, vol. 3, p. 173; *Wang Li 1993, p. 41.

528–529   75 percent: *Wang Li 1993, p. 53. Scapegoat: interview with Wang Li, 16 Oct. 1995; *Wang Li 1994, p. 66 (E: id. 1994, pp. 79–86); *Chen

Yangyong, p. 364. Lin's "Administration Office": Huang, J., pp. 312–13. General Qiu: *Xiao Sike, pp. 93–4, 289–97; interviews with Qiu family members, 5 & 8 Sept. 1998; interview with a member of Lin family, 20 Oct. 1995.

529   General Yang: *Zhang Zishen, pp. 395–6, 413ff; cf. Huang, J., pp. 312–13. Mao suspends Military Council: Zhu, pp. 31–2; Huang, J., p. 314. Vital veto: multiple interviews with Lin circle members; *Ji Xichen, pp. 364–5. Sidekick Huang: *Zhang Zishen, p. 419; *Guan Weixun, p. 184; *Wang Nianyi, p. 376; Zhu, p. 163.

530   Bugged conversation: *Xiao Sike, pp. 87–91.

530–531   Shanghai battle: interview with eyewitness Song Yong-yi, 8 Apr. 2000; *Li Xun, pp. 381–3, 391; *Ye Yonglie 1993, pp. 256–61; Perry & Li, pp. 44ff. Mao: "I've seen film": *Li Xun, pp. 384, 391. "Arm the Left": interview with an insider, Oct. 1995, and with Wang Li, 16 Oct. 1995; *Wang Li 1993, p. 54; cf. id. 1994, p. 75. "Wonderful": *Li Desheng, p. 347.

531–532   Mao told Albanian: to Defense Minister Balluku, 5 Oct. 1968, AQSh, f. 14, 1968, d. 6, p. 5. Student tails Mao: interview with a friend of the student, Oct. 1995.

532   Kuai story: interview with Kuai, 3 Oct. 1995; *Yang Mu, pp. 71–3; record of Mao's meeting with him, *IIR, pp. 524–47 (E: *Mao Miscellany*, pp. 469–97).

533   16 million rusticated: Pan, p. 373; cf. Schoenhals 1996b, pp. 370–1;

533–534   10 million condemned: Liu, X. p. 115. 3.5 million arrested: Schoenhals 1996b, p. 367. Binyang County: *Zheng Yi, pp. 8–12 (E: id., pp. 9ff). 100,000 lives: *Song Yongyi, pp. 239, 254; cf. Sutton, p. 137. 76 names: *Zheng Yi, p. 96 (E: id., p. 101). "human flesh banquets": ibid., pp. 68–9 (E: id., p. 13).

534   86-year-old: ibid., pp. 38–40 (E: id., pp. 48–9). Anhui executions: interview with the eyewitness, 15 Oct. 2002.

534   Inner Mongolia: Woody, pp. 3, 30–1; Sneath, pp. 422–6; Jankowiak, pp. 274–6; Sun in Walder & Gong 1993, pp. 15–17; *Tu & Zhu. Yunnan: *Ding & Ting, pp. 6, 339; cf. Schoenhals 1996b, pp. 368, 370. Assassination: *Wang Kexue, pp. 4–13.

535   9th Congress delegates: *unpublished memoirs of a key member of the congress staff; Zhang, Y. 1993, pp. 66–9.

536   Death estimates: *Ding Shu 2001; cf. Walder & Su, pp. 86–99; Leitenberg, pp. 11–12; Margolin, p. 513. 100 million: Ye Jianying, 13 Dec. 1978, in *Wang Nianyi, p. 623.

CHAPTER 51   *A War Scare*

537   Mao chose Zhenbao: *Li & Hao, pp. 319–20; *Yang Kuisong 1999, pp. 492–3 (E: id. 2000, p. 27); cf. Wishnick, p. 26. Clashes: Burr 2001, pp. 80–6; Kulik 2000, pp. 450–4. Casualties: Drannikov, p. 5; Ryabushkin, p. 151. "moonscape": Gates, p. 36; cf. Kapitsa 1996, p. 80

and interview. Mao orders stop fighting: *Yang Kuisong 1999, p. 493 (E: id. 2000, p. 30).

537–538   Kosygin phones: interview with Kudashev, Kosygin's interpreter who made the calls, 19 June 1996; Kudashev, pp. 199–200; *Wang Taiping 1998, p. 273. Ready to negotiate: *Mao 1987–98, vol. 13, p. 21. 9th Congress secrecy: *unpublished memoirs by a key member of the congress staff; Antonkin, pp. 105–6; Galenovich 2001, p. 159.

538   "Pile up some mountains": *Li & Hao, pp. 256–7.

538–539   Mao's "mountains": Schlesinger interview, 2 May 1995; *Zhang Yunsheng, pp. 293–5 (E: id., pp. 55–7). Nuclear strike sounding: Burr 2001, pp. 86–95; Bundy, pp. 102–6; Helms interview, 7 Apr. 1995; conversation with Kissinger, 1 July 1998. Chou–Kosygin meeting: interviews with three Russian participants, including Kapitsa, Kosygin's no. 2 at the meeting; Kapitsa 1996, pp. 81–92; Elizavetin (note-taker); Antonkin, p. 112. Chou–Kosygin letters: CWB no. 11, pp. 171–2 (Chou letter, 18 Sept. 1969); Goncharov & Usov, p. 112 (Kosygin reply, 26 Sept.). Victor Louis: *New York Times,* 18 Sept. 1969. Fear of Russian plane: *Zhang Yunsheng, pp. 316–20 (E: id., pp. 57–9); *Pang & Jin, p. 1563.

539   Chou and Mme Mao in Western Hills: *Yang Kuisong 1999, pp. 502–3, 508 (E: id. 2000, pp. 41, 47); *Yang Yinlu, p. 163. Red alert: *Li & Hao, pp. 124–5; cf. Teiwes & Sun 1996, pp. 111–15.

539–540   Giant shelter: multiple interviews with Mao's personal staff; *Deng Li, pp. 188–9; *Zhang Zuoliang, p. 331. Greets Soviet delegate: Galenovich 2001, pp. 220–1 (Chinese minutes); *Wang Taiping 1999, pp. 208, 211; this was Mao's last meeting with a Russian.

540   Investment in nuclear program: *China Today 1987, p. 77. Per capita income: Marer et al. (World Bank), p. 46; Li Rui 1996, p. 36. Calories: Rummel, p. 215. Lin Biao and coterie: proposal in June 1969, *ZDZ vol. 41, p. 212; cf. Huang, J., pp. 317–18. Boss of Jiangxi: *Chen Yun 1995, pp. 252–3. Mood and energy: interview with a member of Mao's personal staff, 19 Apr. 1999; *Chen & Zhao, pp. 126–30.

CHAPTER 52   *Falling Out with Lin Biao*

541   Mao solitary among top five: *Jin Chongji et al. 1998, pp. 1016–17.

541–542   Lin announced proposal: ibid., pp. 1017–18. Head of Praetorian Guard: *Wang Dongxing 1997a, p. 44; *Xin Ziling 2002, p. 622. "the Cobra": interview with an insider in Lin's coterie, 31 Oct. 2000; *Xin Ziling 2002, p. 621; *Ye Yonglie 1996a, pp. 81, 91–7; *Wang Nianyi, pp. 385, 388. Mao gave Lin the nod: Chen Boda, in *Ye Yonglie 1990, p. 441; *Xin Ziling 2002, p. 620; Jin, p. 123.

542–543   "atom bomb": *Ye Yonglie 1990, pp. 454, 466. Lin refuses self-criticism: *Xin Ziling 2002, pp. 627–30; Jin p. 131. Old age set in: interview with a member of Mao's personal staff, 24 Oct. 1995.

543–544   Lin letter to Mao: *Xin Ziling 2002, p. 628; Li Wenpu, in *Chi & Ming, p. 12. Plan to flee to Hong Kong: *Ming & Chi, pp. 351–66. Tiger: ibid., pp. 20–7; interviews with his fiancée, sister, brother-in-law, and a friend, 6 May, 14 & 20 Oct. 1995, 7 Sept. 1997; *Zhang Ning, p. 157; cf. Jin, pp. 155–61.

544 "Project 571": text in *WDYZ vol. 2, pp. 650–7 (E: Kau 1975, pp. 81–90). Tiger dubbed Mao B-52: interview with Tiger's fiancée, 6 May 1995.

545 Left copy with Lin: Li Weixin confession, in *Xin Ziling 2000, pp. 637–8. Mao sent Chou to Lin: *Li Desheng, p. 409; *Jin Chongji et al. 1998, pp. 1033–4. May Day night: Du interview, 17 Oct. 1995; *Zhang Zuoliang, p. 242.

546 Tiger checks out Hong Kong route: *Ming & Chi, pp. 351–4. Ceauşescus: ibid., pp. 358–9; *Xiao Sike, p. 85; Du interview. Another recce of Hong Kong border: *Ming & Chi, pp. 361, 366. Mao remarks about Lin: Kau 1975, p. 59 ("Summary of Mao's Talks"); cf. Jin, pp. 190–3.

546–547 Get Tiger planes: interview with the dispatcher of planes, 8 Sept. 1997. Lin Biao role: *Ming & Chi, pp. 386, 407–9, 412–13, 422. "I won't incriminate you": interview with Tiger's fiancée, 6 May 1995.

547 "breaks the net": Lu Min, in *YHCQ, 1998, no. 1, p. 16. Lin wrote to Chief of Staff: *Ming & Chi, pp. 407–8. Suicide attack: one volunteer's confession, ibid., pp. 422–3. Mao unaware of plot: interviews with members of Mao's personal staff, 24 Oct. & 4 Nov. 1995, 22 Oct. 2000; *Chen & Zhao, pp. 164–7; Wu De, in *An Jianshe, pp. 136–8; *Li Desheng, pp. 414–15.

548 Dodo: interview with Dodo and a friend, 20 Oct. 1995; *Shao Yihai, p. 282; *Ming & Chi, pp. 386, 442, 448–52; cf. Jin, pp. 153–4.

549 Petrol on board, crash-landing: *Guang Xin, pp. 27–8. Heavily sedated Mao: interview with the servant who woke up Mao, 22 Oct. 2000; *Qi Li, pp. 129–30; *Wang Dongxing 1997a, p. 208. Mao given one option: *Li Desheng, p. 421; *Shao Yihai, p. 298; Liu Yan, in *Chi & Ming, p. 367.

549n Chou letter to Mao, night of 13 Sept.: text in *Gao Wenqian, pp. 352–3; Zagvozdin: interview, 16 June 1995.

550 In Suite 118: interviews with Mao's personal staff, 21 Sept. 1994, 24 Oct. 1995, 22 Oct. 2000, 12 & 14 May 2001; *Chen & Zhao, pp. 170–1. Learned plot: interview with a plotter, 7 Sept. 1997; *Xiao Sike, p. 528; *Li Desheng, p. 427.

550–551 Mao very ill: interview with a member of Mao's intimate staff, 22 Oct. 1993; *SMMM, pp. 37–8; Li, Z., pp. 542–61. Ethiopia's Emperor: Wu De, in *An Jianshe, p. 150. Warning to Guard chief: *Zhang Yaoci, pp. 122–6. Jumped to death: *Ming & Chi, p. 481. Languishing in prison: interview with Yeh's son-in-law who was in prison, 2 Nov. 1993.

551 "What Chairman Mao?": interview with the deputy chief, 17 Sept. 1994.

552 Chen Yi funeral: *Gao Wenqian, p. 366; *Chen & Zhao, pp. 175–83; *Zhang Yufeng 1989 (E: id., pp. 17–19); Xiang, L., pp. 202–3; *Jin Chongji et al. 1998, p. 1053.

552 Brink of death: *Lin Ke et al., pp. 168–9.

CHAPTER 53   *Maoism Falls Flat on the World Stage*

553   Mao to Hill: 28 Nov. 1968, CWB no. 11, pp. 159–61.

553–554   27 Oct. 1966: *China Today 1992a, vol. 1, 252. Catastrophe likely: *Dong
             Sheng, p. 593; Zhang Yunyu, in *ZH editorial board, pp. 234–41; Lewis
             & Xue 1988, pp. 202–3. Subsequent tests failed: Gu Xiqiang, in *ZH
             editorial board, pp. 229–32.

554n   Meissner, p. 162 (East German ambassador Bierbach to Berlin, 10 Jan.
             1967); Heikal interview, 18 Jan. 1997; interview with Dan Grove, then
             FBI agent in Hong Kong, 6 Oct. 2002.

554–555   Entire missile arsenal: *Zhou 1997, vol. 3, p. 101. Mao speech 7 July:
             *Mao CCRM, vol. 13, pp. 376–7. Russian aid essential: Lewis & Xue
             1988, p. 199. "central task": *Wang Taiping 1998, p. 11. "shining beacon":
             *RR, 2 July 1967.

555   "Openly support the Burmese CP": *Mao CCRM, vol. 13, pp. 376–7.
             Chou summoned Burmese: *Yang Meihong, p. 69. Selecting Chinese
             wives: ibid., pp. 74–7. Promoting Mao: ibid., pp. 31–2, 230–40. Secret
             camps: interview with Belgian former trainee, 12 Nov. 1994.

556   "colonialists' latrine": Khrushchev speech, 12 Dec. 1962, in Floyd, p.
             329. Mao to Somali: 9 Aug. 1963, *Mao 1994, p. 502 (E: Mao 1998,
             pp. 383–4). *Kashmir Princess*: Chou "Intelligence no. 1 to Hong Kong
             Authorities," 15 May 1955, says Peking knew assassination plot in
             Mar., *Xiong Xianghui, p. 130; and Peking knew it involved a bomb
             on the *Kashmir Princess*, as Mao said Chou should change route and
             not take the plane: *Tao Siju 1996, p. 153; as a result, Chou settled
             on Burma route by 28 Mar.: *Zhou 1997, vol. 1, p. 459. Chou received
             details on 7 Apr. of how the bomb was going to be placed on the
             Kashmir Princess, a full four days before the explosion: *Cheng
             Yuangong, pp. 158–9. Peking withheld information: telephone inter-
             view with Peter Mahta, Air India's Hong Kong office director at the
             time, 21 Apr. 2000; NA, FO 371/115133–4, 115137–41; Tsang. Hong
             Kong expels Taiwan agents: *Foreign Ministry 1990ff, vol. 2, pp.
             146–7; *Xiong Xianghui, pp. 151–2; NA, FO 371/115139; Trevelyan
             1971, p. 159.

557   150 tons of gold: *Dong Sheng, pp. 322, 326. "unconditional surren-
             der": *Ran & Ma, pp. 22, 26, 33–5, 42. Urged Hong Kong radicals:
             *Zhou Yi, pp. 225–7, 251–5, 260. Mao's real line: *Ran & Ma, pp. 35,
             46. "Those who kill": *RR, 5 July 1967. Chou infiltrated soldiers: *Ran
             & Ma, pp. 45–6; *Zhou Yi, pp. 264–5.

557–558   Torching British mission: interviews with 4 trapped staff; cf. Petri in
             Schoenhals 1996b, p. 172; Grey, pp. 60–75. Official sanction: *Ran &
             Ma, pp. 5, 10–13, 22; Petri, cit., pp. 169–72. Mao apology to Kim:
             Lankov 2002, pp. 106–7; *Il Ponte* vol. 37 (1981), nos. 11–12, p. 1170
             (Liu to Gomulka, Nov. 1960). "Kim Il Sung should be overthrown":
             AQSh, f. 14, 1967, d. 7, p. 15 (Kang to Kapo, 22 Jan. 1967).

559   Sartre: Sartre, p. 13. 1968 "new phenomenon": CWB no. 11, pp. 159 (to
             Hill, 28 Nov. 1968), 156 (to Balluku, 1 Oct. 1968). Sent European

Maoists back: interview with one of them, 12 Nov. 1994; cf. Horne, p. 233. "Big, big": *Yun Shui, p. 186.

558n AQSh, f. 14, 1967, d. 20, p. 15 (Mao, 12 Oct. 1967).

559–560 African radicals: ibid., p. 198. Sally to Mobutu: Mobutu interview, 28 Oct. 1994; *Yun Shui, pp. 204–5. Offer to Nasser: Heikal, p. 283; Heikal interview; Harris, pp. 121–2; CQ no. 31 (1967), p. 217. Retreat to Khartoum: Elizavetin 1993, p. 64 (according to Chou to Kosygin, 11 Sept. 1969). No Arab condolences: Harris, p. 114. Latin American CPs' visit: Anderson, pp. 616, 620; Johnson, pp. 162–3; Balanta, . 32; *Wang Taiping 1998, p. 497; *Wang Li 1993, p. 144. Castro–Mao abuse: Feltrinelli, p. 300; *Wang Taiping 1998, pp. 497–8; *Mao CCRM, vol. 7, p. 92.

560 Subverting Cuban army: Dominguez, p. 161. Mao–Guevara: *Pang Bingan, pp. 169, 185–8; cf. Anderson, p. 620; Johnson, pp. 155–6. China refuses radio: Burr 1999b (Chou to Kissinger, 13 Nov. 1973). Kang on Guevara: AQSh, f. 14, 1968, d. 7 (to Balluku, 5 Oct. 1968).

560n Gorriti, pp. 131, 76.

561 Chou re pressure on France: proposal to Mao, Feb.–Mar. 1954, in *Jin Chongji et al. 1998, pp. 155–6; *Pei Jianzhang, pp. 317–18. Mao halts Vietnam offensive for Korean War: cable, 16 Oct. 1950 in Zhang 1995, p. 70; cf. id. 1992, pp. 176–8; *Qian Jiang, pp. 375–6. Navarre Plan: *Qian Jiang, p. 395; Zhai, p. 45. Dien Bien Phu: interviews with two North Vietnamese officers present: Lieutenant General Uoc (then regimental political commissar, artillery unit), 17 Sept. 1996; Colonel Bui Tin, 28 Sept. 1996; cf. Zhai, pp. 45–9. "must have a settlement": *Jin Chongji et al. 1998, p. 155. Mao to military adviser: Yang 2002, p. 4; *Qian Jiang, p. 578.

562 Chou's deal with French: *Jin Chongji et al. 1998, pp. 171–2; Joyaux, pp. 239–44. Pressure on Vietnamese: Zhai, pp. 55–63; Viet Nam, pp. 18–23. Le Duan recalled: CWB nos. 12–13, pp. 279–80, 286. Moscow ups aid to Hanoi: Gaiduk, pp. 27, 35ff. Mao–Kosygin: interviews with three Russian participants; Childs Papers, Box 2, Folder 1, p. 4 (Russian briefing); Troyanovsky, pp. 351–3. In western direction: Deng, in Brezhnev, p. 103.

562 Chinese wife for Ho: interview with Zeng Zhi (she and her husband Tao Zhu had a lot of dealings with Ho), 24 Sept. 1994. Chou against Soviet aid: in Westad et al., pp. 89–90 (9 Oct. 1964). Blames Hanoi for M. L. King murder: in ids., pp. 124–5 (13 Apr. 1968). Against Hanoi–US talks: ids., pp. 140–54 (Mao–Dong, 17 Nov. 1968). Too busy to receive: *Zhou 1997, vol. 3, p. 262; *Li Danhui, pp. 144–5.

563 Chen Jian 2001, pp. 221–9; Zhai 2000, pp. 179–80; Tucker, p. 345.

563–564 Splashing out aid: *Li Danhui, pp. 146–7. Red Laotians: *China Today 1989a, p. 560; *BNC, 2000, no. 7, pp. 16–24. Third World Communists: interview with Nouri Abdulrazak, 1 Sept. 2000. Mao model no threat: Burr 2001, p. 77. "we are isolated": Yang 2000, p. 43 (22 Mar. 1969). Plotting against Sihanouk: Sihanouk 1974, pp. 68–9; CQ no. 32 (1967), p. 224; CQ no. 34 (1968), p. 191.

564–565   Indochina summit: *Tian & Wang, pp. 151–6; cf. Sihanouk 1974, pp.
           201–2. Princely tastes: Fallaci, p. 86 (Sihanouk interview); Sihanouk
           1990, pp. 52, 112. Mao–Sihanouk: *Chen Xiaodong, p. 194; *SMMM,
           p. 43; *Wang Taiping 1999, p. 74; Sihanouk 1974, pp. 207–10; id. 1990,
           p. 84. Pol Pot: *Tian & Wang, pp. 166–71. London *Times*: 28 Apr. 1970.
           "Hanoi's designs": Kissinger 1979, p. 505. Satellite: *Tian & Wang, p.
           156; *New York Times*, 26 Apr. 1970; *Li Mingsheng, pp. 50–1.

565–566   Lin misreads: *Zhang Yunsheng, pp. 332–3; Sihanouk 1990, p. 84; text:
           Mao 1998, pp. 444–5. Nixon–Kissinger reaction: Summers, pp. 371–2;
           Kissinger 1979, pp. 695–6, 509. "stinking scholar": in Westad et al., p.
           177 (23 Sept. 1970). Mao–Dong exchange: ibid.

565n   Tucker, p. 519, n. 25.

CHAPTER 54   *Nixon: The Red-baiter Baited*

567   Only in June 1970: Kissinger: "by the end of June, we had received
           unmistakable signals from the Chinese that they were willing to reopen
           contacts with us" (Kissinger 1979, p. 509). Urgent invitation to Snow
           also in June: telephone interview with Lois Snow, 25 Apr. 2000; *Yin
           Jiamin, pp. 205–6.

567   Invitation to Nixon: Kissinger 1979, pp. 701–4.

569   Invites American Ping-Pong team: Wu Xu-jun, in *Lin Ke et al., pp.
           306–10; Zhuang & Sasaki, pp. 274–83. "dazzling welcome": Kissinger
           1979, p. 710.

569–570   One commentator: Tyler, p. 91. "Nixon was excited": Kissinger 1979,
           p. 711. US offer re Taiwan: Burr 2002, Doc. 34 (9 July), pp. 12, 13;
           Doc. 35 (10 July, afternoon), p. 16; Doc. 38 (11 July, last talk), p. 10;
           *Foreign Ministry 1990ff, vol. 2, p. 40; cf. Holdridge conversation, 3
           June 1998; Mann, pp. 32–5. Get Peking into UN: Burr 2002, Doc. 35
           (10 July), p. 17. Dealings with Russia: Burr 2002, Doc. 35 (10 July),
           pp. 28–9; Burr 1999, p. 49.

569n   Kissinger 1979, p. 749; *International Herald Tribune*, 1 Mar. 2002, p. 4;
           Holdridge conversation.

570   "mesmerised at": Holdridge, p. 76; Mann, pp. 35–6. Indochina: Burr
           2002, Doc. 34 (9 July), pp. 17, 18, 15, 33, 25–6, 30, 34. "10,000 miles":
           Burr 2002, Doc. 34 (9 July), pp. 17, 27. Pull out of Korea: ibid., p. 38.
           Not asking China to stop aid to Vietnam: Burr 2002, Doc. 35 (10 July),
           p. 26. Chou hectoring: Burr 2002, Doc. 34 (9 July), pp. 26, 27; Doc.
           35 (10 July), p. 7; China not "aggressive," US "cruelties": Burr 2002,
           Doc. 34 (9 July), pp. 42, 26. Kissinger to Vietnamese: Walters 1978,
           pp. 518–19. "very moving": Burr 2002, Doc. 35 (10 July), p. 14.

571   America as "monkey": *Foreign Ministry 1990ff, vol. 2, p. 41. Chou:
           Nixon loose woman: Barnouin & Yu 1998, p. 108. "Britain, France . . . all
           become Red Guards": *Xiong Xianghui, p. 347. US still enemy no. 1:
           ibid., p. 348. Nixon's arrival helped restore Mao: interviews with
           members of Mao's personal staff, 22 Oct. 1993, 24 Oct. 1995, 19 Apr.
           1999; *Zhang Yufeng 1989 (E: id., pp. 30–1).

572   See Nixon straightaway: interviews ibid.; *Lin Ke et al., p. 216; Kissinger 1979, p. 1057; Nixon, p. 560.

572   Mao–Nixon conversation: Burr 1999a, pp. 59–65.

573   Joint communiqué, Mao dictated: on 23 Oct. 1971, *Foreign Ministry 1990ff, vol. 3, p. 67 (E: Web/NSA, pp. 7–8).

573   conversation, 2 Mar. 1999.

573–574   Hoxha letter: AQSh, f. 14, 1971–1972, d. 3, pp. 48–66 (6 Aug. 1971); Hoxha 1979, p. 578; *Wang Taiping 1999, pp. 259–61; conversation with Fagu. Le Duan: Viet Nam, p. 43. Sihanouk on Chou: id. 1990, p. 58. Aid to Vietnam peak: *Wang Taiping 1999, p. 51; *Li Danhui, p. 147. From 31 to 66: *China Today 1989, pp. 55–7. Mintoff: Carrington, p. 246. Mobutu: interview, 28 Oct. 1994.

574   Staggering aid level: *China Today 1989, p. 68.

574   Hungriest years: *Fu Shanglun et al., p. 9. Nixon in Shanghai: *Ji Wei, p. 26.

575   Nixon de-demonized Mao: Nixon to Cabinet, 29 Feb. 1972; Kissinger briefing to White House Staff, 19 July 1971 (Nixon Project, President's Office Files, Memoranda for the President, Box 88, File Beginning 27 Feb. 1972, p. 10; Box 85, File Beginning 18 July 1971, p. 4); Judis, p. 338; Graham, p. 79). Echeverria: Anguiano interview, 23 Nov. 1992. Australian ambassador: FitzGerald interview, 22 Jan. 1993. Tanaka: Nikaido interview, 23 Feb. 1993. Trudeau: Trudeau, p. 209. "Napoleon's methods": *Nouvel Observateur*, 13 Sept. 1976, p. 24 (Mao, 12 Sept. 1973). Heath: Heath, p. 632; Heath interview, 5 Jan. 1993.

575–576   Australian premier: Whitlam, p. 60. "philosopher": Kissinger 1997, pp. 28, 31. "The only objective": *CWB* nos. 14–15, p. 60 (Kim to Honecker, 31 May 1984). Mao on military alliance: Burr 1999a, pp. 112 (Kissinger memo to Nixon, 2 Mar. 1973), 94 (Mao, 18 Feb. 1973); Kissinger 1982, p. 47; *Wang Taiping 1999, p. 367.

576   To be led by America: Kissinger 1982, p. 55. Real thinking about "Soviet threat": Burr 1999a, p. 99 (Mao, 18 Feb. 1973). Mutual enemy: Hanoi: Kissinger 1982, p. 57. Mao re women: Burr 1999a, pp. 92–5.

577–578   Nixon secret letter to Mao: Tyler, p. 158. Kissinger's "very secret group": Burr 1999a, p. 144 (Kissinger to envoy Huang Zhen, 6 July 1973). US nuclear weapons to China: Tyler, p. 163 (Odeen memo for Kissinger, 8 June 1973); Odeen to authors by phone, 16 Feb. 2003. To his close circle: Burr 1999a, p. 149. "I have talked to the French": Burr 1999a, p. 144.

577n   Burr 1999a, pp. 48–57.

578   Decrepit aircraft: Hoxha 1979, p. 700; AQSh, f. 14, 1972–73, d. 11, p. 32 (Chou to Balluku, 1 Dec. 1972); *CCP Archive Study Office 1991, pp. 209–20. Rocket chiefs involved: *Zhou 1997, vol. 3, p. 543. Selling nuclear technology: Tyler, p. 164. Brezhnev warned Nixon: Burr 1999a, p. 143. Mao envoy in Western White House: Tyler, p. 162; *Yin Jiamin, pp. 295–8. "We have told no one": Burr 1999a, p. 143 (Kissinger to Huang Zhen, 6 July 1973).

CHAPTER 55   *The Boss Denies Chou Cancer Treatment*

579   "no surgery": *Gao Wenqian, pp. 378, 512. Mao pretexts: interview with
               a doctor of Chou's, 22 Sept. 1994; *Deng Li, p. 170. Surgeons on stand-
               by for Mao: *Lin Ke et al., p. 162.

579–580   Gushing about Chou: Burr 2002, Doc. 40 (Memo for the President,
               14 July 1971), p. 26. "secondary figure": Kissinger 1979, p. 1059. "a
               nobody": Nikaido interview, 23 Feb. 1993. Chou's motto: *Shi Zhe 1991,
               p. 526. Tested Mao's medicines: interview with a doctor of Chou's, 2
               Nov. 1995; Yang Yinlu, in *BNC, 1999, no. 8, p. 55.

580–581   Mao demanded Chou self-denunciation: *Zhou 1997, vol. 3, pp. 527–31;
               cf. Zhu 208ff. Chou humiliating speech: *Gao Wenqian, pp. 375–7.
               Cancer worsened, Mao forbids surgery: ibid., pp. 512–13.

581–582   "in two stages": *Deng Li, p. 173. Removing cancer: ibid., pp. 173–4;
               interview with a doctor of Chou, 22 Sept. 1994. Mao hypocritical
               message: *Deng Li, p. 174. Foreign Ministry analysis: *Zhou 1997, vol.
               3, pp. 603–5; *Mao 1987–98, vol. 13, pp. 356–7; interview with an
               interpreter of Mao's, 21 Oct. 2000.

582   "bipolarity . . . was over": Kissinger 1979, p. 1096. "My reputation has
               gone bad": *Fan Daren, p. 123. Kissinger changes position on Taiwan:
               Burr 1999a, pp. 114–15 (re Feb. 1973), 186 (to Mao, 12 Nov. 1973).
               "early warning" system: Burr 1999a, p. 204 (to Chou, 13 Nov. 1973).
               Kissinger heard no more: ibid., pp. 206, 212.

582n   "had been wrong": Dobrynin, p. 282.

583   Mao to Kissinger about Watergate: *Yin Jiamin, p. 299 (E: Burr 1999a,
               pp. 181–2). Railed tirelessly: *Chen & Zhao, p. 247; *Nouvel Observateur*,
               13 Sept. 1976, p. 23. To Thais: Chatichai (present) interview, 5 Mar.
               1993 (to Kukrit, 1 July 1975). To Heath: 25 May 1974, *Mao 1987–98,
               vol. 13, p. 388 (E: Mao 1998, p. 456).

583   Rolls-Royce deal: *CCP Archive Study Office 1991, p. 214; Mann, p.
               76; Burr 1999a, pp. 175 n. 17, 423 n. 53.

583–584   Disenchantment apparent: Burr 1999a, p. 206; Tyler, pp. 175–6;
               Kissinger 1982, p. 698; our interviews with Kissinger, 4 May 1995, and
               Lord, 27 Apr. 1995. Mao bad-mouths Kissinger: interview with Mao's
               secretary, 24 Oct. 1995. To Heath: Heath, p. 495 (toned down in Mao
               1998, p. 457); cf. to Pompidou, *Nouvel Observateur*, 13 Sept. 1976, p. 24
               ("his remarks are often not very intelligent"). 21 Oct.: Burr 1999a,
               p. 400. Chou "sparkle . . . missing": Kissinger 1982, pp. 687–8; inter-
               view with Kissinger. Subordinates attack Chou: interview with a person
               present, 26 Sept. 1994, 21 Oct. 2000; *Zhou 1997, vol. 3, p. 634; *Zhang
               Hanzhi, pp. 64–5; *Zhang Zuoliang, pp. 310–11. After meeting with
               Nepal's king: interviews with two people present, 24 Oct. 1995, 21 Oct.
               2000; *Gao Wenqian, pp. 475–6.

584–585   Avoid Chou's staff: *Zhang Zuoliang, pp. 312–13. Chou supervised
               seizure of Paracels: *Zhou 1997, vol. 3, p. 645; Zhai, pp. 209–10, 264
               n. 84. Pursued during blood transfusion: interview with a member of
               Chou's staff, 22 Sept. 1994; *Zhang Zuoliang, pp. 322–9. "Operations
               ruled out": *Gao Wenqian, p. 514. Chou begged: *Deng Li, p. 178; *Zhou

1997, vol. 3, p. 668. "Let him see Razak": interview with a member of Chou's staff, 22 Sept. 1994.

585   Mao had two years to live: Li, Z,. p. 580.

CHAPTER 56   *Mme Mao in the Cultural Revolution*

586   "Chairman Mao's dog": interview with the public prosecutor of Jiang Qing, 13 Oct. 1993.

586   Personal vendettas: multiple interviews with victims like Wang Ying's husband, Xie He-geng, and witnesses; *Ye Yonglie 1996, pp. 1–18, 355–67.

587   New secretary's experience: the secretary, Yang Yinlu, in *BNC, 1998, no. 5, pp. 56–9.

587–588   Chou's chief bodyguard: interview with the bodyguard, 8 Nov. 1995. With Mao she was meek: interview with Wang Li, 16 Oct. 1995; *Ye Yonglie 1990, p. 343.

588   Mme Mao lifestyle: Yang Yinlu, in *BNC, 1998, no. 5—1999, no. 9; *Fu Chongbi, p. 243; interview with the secretary of one of the Gang of Four, 7 Oct. 1993. Blood from young guards: Li, Z., p. 593; *Yang Yinlu, pp. 32–5.

589   Nightmares: ibid., pp. 190–3. Incident in Qingdao: Yang Yinlu, in *BNC, 2000, no. 7, pp. 72–3; *Deng Li, pp. 164–8.

590   Mme Mao–Witke: *Zhang Ying, pp. 28–9, 56–7, 154–63; Witke 1977, pp. 17–26, 116–18; id. 1991, p. 65.

591   Danish prime minister: interview with Mr. and Mrs. Hartling, 20 Nov. 1993. American swimmers: *Zhang Ying, pp. 133–4 (remarks not to Witke). "masses too excited": Witke 1977, p. 303n. Nixon on Mme Mao: Nixon, p. 570; cf. interviews with Ford, 15 Apr. 1995, and Haig, 1 May 1995.

591–592   Envious looks at Marcos: interview with Imelda Marcos, 17 Mar. 1994; *Du & Gu, pp. 504, 521. "national costume": interview with two members of Mao's personal staff, Oct. 2000; Yang Yinlu, in *BNC, 1998, no. 6, p. 66. Currying favor with girlfriends: *Guo Jinrong, pp. 119–20; *Chen & Zhao, pp. 196–201. 82nd birthday: *Guo Jinrong, pp. 110–15.

592–593   Girlfriends no royal mistresses: multiple interviews with girlfriends; *Guo Jinrong, pp. 44–6, 122–3, 132–3. Turning Mao down: interview with an insider, 21 Oct. 2000.

593–594   Li Na letter: *Li Xiangwen, pp. 555–6. "listen to gunfire": *Yan Changlin, p. 52. Li Na at University: conversation with Li Na, 25 Mar. 1993.

594   On army newspaper: interview with a colleague of hers, 23 Sept. 1994; *BNC, 1999, no. 2, pp. 42–54; *Mu Xin, pp. 348–50; *Zhe Yongping et al., pp. 1–5. Predecessor to jail: Mu Xin, in *ZDZ, no. 69, pp. 83–9. Controller of Peking: *Yang Yinlu, p. 128. Nervous breakdown: ibid., pp. 125–33; interview with a friend of hers who visited her, 4 Sept. 1994.

595   Marriage and son: *Yang Yinlu, pp. 128–40; former husband Xu
             Zhiming article, in *"Mao and I" Collection Committee 1993b, pp.
             251–62; interviews with a relative and a former servant, 25 Sept. 1993,
             19 Sept. 1994.

595–596   "my little foreigner": *Wang Xingjuan 1993, p. 120. Mao refused to see
             her: ibid., pp. 265–6; interviews with members of Mao's personal staff,
             19 Oct. 1993, 24 Oct. 1995, 19 Apr. 1999. Son not counted as family:
             ibid., interviews. Yuan-xin: *Li Xiangwen, pp. 600–2. Zhang Zhi-xin:
             Yan & Gao, p. 276; *PRC Encyclopaedia, vol. 4, pp. 4822–47.

596   trade-off: *Yang Zhaolin, p. 292. For detail see below. Mme Mao's end:
             interviews with people close to Mao family; *Li Xiangwen, pp. 153–6;
             Witke 1991, pp. 52, 54–5; Rittenberg & Bennett, pp. 428–30 (in
             Qincheng prison).

CHAPTER 57   *Enfeebled Mao Hedges His Bets*

597   Nine minutes meeting: *Mao Mao 1993, p. 643.

598   "keeping a respectful distance": *Mao CCRM & ARL, pp. 3691, 3696;
             *Yu Shicheng, p. 239. Mao tried to keep Deng on board: Wang Jiaxiang's
             widow told us that, in autumn 1965, Chou came to brief her husband
             about the forthcoming Cultural Revolution, and said that Mao's plan
             was to replace Liu Shao-chi with either Lin Biao or Deng: interview
             with Zhu Zhongli, 28 Sept. 1993. Cf. *Zhu Zhongli 1995, p. 224; *Mao
             CCRM & ARL, pp. 3691, 3696; *Mao Mao 2000, pp. 40, 49; Li
             Xuefeng, in *CCP Archive Study Office 1998, pp. 223–5; *Wang Li
             1993, pp. 5, 63 (E: id. 1994, pp. 16, 49). "differentiate him from Liu":
             *Mao Mao 2000, p. 69.

598   Mrs. Deng told step-mother: interview with Deng's step-mother, Xia
             Bogen, 11 Sept. 1985. Most painful time: *Deng 1993, p. 54. Screaming
             during nightmare: interview with Deng's step-mother.

599–600   Declined to advertize Mao's innocence: *Huang Wenhua et al., pp.
             92–3. Australians noted: FitzGerald interview, 22 Jan. 1993. Deng
             comeback: Huang, J., pp. 328ff; Zhu, pp. 208ff.

600   Mao dubbed "Gang of Four": Chinese Communist Party, p. 364. Deng
             alliance with army chief Yeh: interview with a Yeh family member, 2
             Nov. 1993. Sun Wei-shi: interviews with a member of Chou's staff,
             20 Sep. 1994, and with Shi Zhe, 29 Sept. 1993, 7 Sept. 1994; *Li Yong
             et al., pp. 162–8; *Zhou 1997, vol. 3, p. 264.

601   "people forgave" Chou: Deng 1984, pp. 329–30; cf. *Guardian Weekly*,
             21 Sept. 1980, p. 18 (Deng to Fallaci, 21 & 23 Aug. 1980). Deng–Chou
             meeting, 9 Apr.: *Mao Mao 2000, pp. 318–19. "walk noisily": *Zhang
             Yufeng 1993, p. 635; cf. id., pp. 33–5. Books printed for Mao: *Wang
             Shoujia et al., pp. 5, 10, 15, 18.

601–602   Mao cried when couldn't read: *SMMM, p. 415. Lou Gehrig's disease:
             *Li Zhisui, pp. 556–8 (E: id., pp. 581–6). Chou and allies told, not
             Gang of Four, or Mao: Li, Z., p. 582; *Li Zhisui, pp. 556–60; *Chen &

Zhao, p. 237; interviews with three of the closest members of Mao's staff, 18, 19 & 22 Oct. 2000; *Guo Jinrong, p. 113.

602–603   "shocked and aghast": 19 Nov. 1974, *Wang Nianyi, p. 510; *Geng Biao, vol. 2, pp. 270–1. Goodbye to swimming: *Chen & Zhao, pp. 228–31.

603–604   Chou to Mao against Cobra and Mme Mao: *Mao Mao 2000, p. 384; *Gao Wenqian, pp. 540–1. Mao: "made a mistake": *Mao Mao 2000, pp. 409, 413. "don't plot": *Zhou 1997, vol. 3, p. 704. Historical tale: This story was about how, in the 2nd century BC, China's military chief Zhou Bo teamed up with Prime Minister Chen Ping, and successfully suppressed Empress Lü's family and gang—after the death of Emperor Liu Bang. Mao was hinting that the military chiefs should follow Zhou Bo's example. *Yang Zhaolin, p. 292. Mme Mao compared herself with Empress Lü: *Fan Shuo, pp. 92, 230 (E: id., p. 18).

604–605   Ho family letter to Mao: *Jin Chongji et al. 1998, p. 1180. Chou implying blame on Mao: Ho's widow Xue Ming, in *CCP Archive Study Office 1991, pp. 617–18. She also mentioned how Chou had sent his wife to her before the service to say that the extremely low-key arrangement was Mao's decision. Eye operation: Zhang, Y., 1989, pp. 34–5; Li, Z., pp. 604–5.

605   Media campaign against Chou: *Mao 1987–98, vol. 13, pp. 457–8; *Zhang Zuoliang, pp. 352–4; *Jin Chongji et al. 1998, p. 1187; cf. Yan & Gao, pp. 473–5; Zhu, pp. 210ff. "Barking up the wrong tree": 24 Sept. 1975, *Mao 1987–98, vol. 13, p. 399 (E: *PR*, 3 June, 1977, p. 22). Investment in urban upkeep: *China Today* 1989b, vol. 1, pp. 193–4; Kirkby 1985, pp. 165ff; Walder, pp. 193–201.

605–606   Health and education: Perkins, p. 491. Stark naked: Wei 1997, pp. 234–5. Yenan: *Fu Shanglun et al., pp. 4–17. "poorest nation in the world": *Mao Mao 2000, p. 475 (E: Westad et al., p. 194). Operas filmed for Mao: *Yue Meiti, pp. 22–6; interview with a technician in the film studio, 3 May 2000; *Qi Li, pp. 69–70.

606   Deng encouraged people to write Mao: interview with a letter writer, 2 Nov. 1993; *Yang Zhaolin, p. 290. *Mao Mao 2000, pp. 436, 476. Deng refuses to draw up "resolution": Huang, J., pp. 347–8; Yan & Gao, pp. 480–1. Chou, Yeh urge Deng not to be confrontational: *Gao Wenqian, pp. 575–6, 580–1.

607   Secretary suggests Mao attend funeral: Zhang, Y. 1989, pp. 35–6. "Great morale-booster": *Wang Nianyi, p. 583.

608   Yeh, army chiefs and "Bearded General": *Fan Shuo, pp. 169–70 (E: id., pp. 16–17); *Geng Biao, vol. 2, p. 286.

609   Mao had to release Deng: *Mao Mao 2000, pp. 571–4.

CHAPTER 58   *Last Days*

610   29 May 1975, Mao told scholars: *Wang Shoujia et al., pp. 12–13. "bullied" by Deng: *Fan Shuo, p. 91. Reciting "Sere Trees": *Zhang Yufeng 1993, p. 639.

610–611   Diatribes against Chou: the so-called "9 Articles," *Hu Qiaomu, p. 214. Crossing out references to Liu: ibid. Tried to poison Wang Ming in Russia: Khrushchev 1977, vol. 2, p. 300; interviews with Wang Dan-zhi, 24–5 June 1999. Tirades read a month before death: *Hu Qiaomu, p. 215.

612   "Our navy is only": *Yang Zhaolin, p. 285. Remarked ruefully to Kissinger: Burr 1999a, p. 391 (21 Oct. 1975). Mao told Ford: "Memorandum" of Mao–Ford talk, 2 Dec. 1975 (Burr 1999b), pp. 1, 2, 6; interviews with all five US participants (Ford, Kissinger, Scowcroft, Bush, Lord). "Third World": Mao to Zambian President Kaunda, 22 Feb. 1974, *Mao 1994, pp. 600–1 (E: Mao 1998, p. 454); *PRC Encyclopaedia vol. 4, pp. 4712–3.

612–613   No tangible leadership: Kim, S., p. 255. US diplomat: Roberts, p. 363 (quote is by Graham Martin, US ambassador to Vietnam, 15 Nov. 1973). Mao congratulated Pol Pot: SPK News Agency, p. 15 (from Pol Pot archive). Keo Meas: Kiernan, p. 33. "reacted with childlike delight": Eisenhower, J., p. 160. "snoring": Chatichai interview, 5 Mar. 1993. Singapore premier: interviews with Lee Kuan Yew, 16 Jan. 1993, and Rajaratnam, 15 Jan. 1993; cf. Wood, pp. 182–3.

613   Staff often saw tears: interviews with three people closest to him, 22 Oct. 1993, 29 Sept. 1994, & 21 Oct. 2000; *Zhang Yufeng 1993, pp. 638–9; *Guo Jinrong, p. 103. Imelda Marcos messenger to Nixon: interview with Marcos, 17 Mar. 1994; *Chen & Zhao, p. 247. Nixon's daughter told: Eisenhower J., p. 165 (talk 31 Dec. 1975–1 Jan. 1976). Nixon visit: Anson, pp. 126–33; Ambrose, pp. 491–2; *Xiong Xianghui, pp. 276–95; *Chen & Zhao, pp. 247–8. Mao selected entertainment: *Xiong Xianghui, pp. 287–90; cf. Anson, p. 130.

614   Mourning for entire day: *SMMM, pp. 460–2. Farewell poem: *Wang Shoujia et al., pp. 17, 871–4; *Yue Meiti, pp. 25–6; *Xiong Xianghui, pp. 289–90.

614–615   Melancholy for Haile Selassie: interview with the recipient of Mao's remark, 21 Oct. 2000. Did not appoint Hua successor, left no will: conversation with Mao's daughter Li Na, 25 Mar. 1993; interviews with Mao's last secretary, Zhang Yufeng, 24 Oct. 1995, 14 May 2001; Hua himself explicitly told Geng Biao, in *Geng Biao, vol. 2, pp. 288–90; *Guo Jinrong, pp. 222–5; *Chen & Zhao, p. 261. Hua guinea-pig: Li, Z. p. 624. "blood rains and winds": *Wang Nianyi, pp. 600–1; *Fan Shuo, p. 231.

615–616   Giving orders to wife days before death: *Chen & Zhao, pp. 259–60; *Guo Jinrong, p. 224. Last thing Mao read: interviews with the barber, 22 Oct. 2000, and with Meng, 29 Sept. 1994; *Guo Jinrong, pp. 73–4, 215; *Qi Li, p. 143. Last words to Meng: interviews with Meng, 19 Oct. 1993 & 29 Sept. 1994; *Guo Jinrong, pp. 224–5. Lucid to the end: stated by all Mao's personal staff by his deathbed, and shown in the medical record of his last two days, photographed pages at the front of *Lin Ke et al., and pp. 190–2.

BIBLIOGRAPHY OF
CHINESE-LANGUAGE SOURCES

I ABBREVIATIONS USED IN NOTES

BNC *Bainian chao* (Hundred Year Tide), periodical, Beijing

CASS (Chinese Academy of Social Sciences), ed., *Geming genjudi jingji shiliao xuanbian* (Archive Documents on the Economy of Revolutionary Bases), 3 vols, Jiangxi renmin chubanshe, Nanchang, 1986

CPPCC (Chinese People's Political Consultative Conference, National Committee), ed.:

Heping laoren Shao Lizi (Shao Lizi, an Old Man of Peace), Wenshi ziliao chubanshe, Beijing, 1985a

Liaoshen zhanyi qinliji—yuan Guomindang jiangling de huiyi (Personal Experiences of the Liao–Shen Campaign—Memoirs of Former Nationalist Generals), Zhongguo wenshi chubanshe, Beijing, 1985b

Bayisan Songhu kangzhan (The 13 August War against Japan in Shanghai), Zhongguo wenshi chubanshe, Beijing, 1987

Pingjin zhanyi qinliji—yuan Guomindang jiangling de huiyi (Personal Experiences of the Peking–Tianjin Campaign—Memoirs of Former Nationalist Generals), Zhongguo wenshi chubanshe, Beijing, 1989

Jiefang zhanzheng zhong de xibei zhanchang—yuan Guomindang jiangling de huiyi (The Northwest Theater of the Liberation War—Memoirs of Former Nationalist Generals), Zhongguo wenshi chubanshe, Beijing, 1992

Fu Zuoyi jiangjun (General Fu Zuoyi), a collection of memoirs, Zhongguo wenshi chubanshe, Beijing, 1993

Huaihai zhanyi qinliji—yuan Guomindang jiangling de huiyi (Personal Experiences of the Huai-Hai Campaign—Memoirs of Former Nationalist Generals), Zhongguo wenshi chubanshe, Beijing, 1996

CPPCC (Beijing), ed., *Zhou Enlai yu Beijing* (Zhou Enlai and Beijing), Zhongyang wenxian chubanshe, 1998

CPPCC (Tianjin), tr. & ed., *Riben junguozhuyi qinhua ziliao changbian* (Documents on the Japanese Militarist Invasion of China), 3 vols of Japanese documents compiled by Japan's Self-Defense Agency, Sichuan renmin chubanshe, Chengdu, 1987

DDWX   *Dang de wenxian* (Party Documents), periodical, Beijing

DSYJ   *Dangshi yanjiu* (Party History Studies), periodical, Beijing

DYZ   *Dangshi yanjiu ziliao* (Documents for Party History Studies), periodical, Beijing

DZS   *Dangdai Zhongguo shi yanjiu* (Contemporary China History Studies), periodical, Beijing

GNYJ   *Guangdong nongmin yundong jiangxisuo ziliao xuanbian* (Documents on the Guangdong Peasant Movement Institute), Guangdong Peasant Movement Training Institute Museum, ed., Renmin chubanshe, Beijing, 1987

GS   *Gongfei huoguo shiliao huibian* (Documents on the Communist Bandits Bringing Calamity to the Country), 6 vols, Republic of China Documents Editing Committee & Institute of International Relations, comp., Taipei, 1976

GZ   *Gemingshi ziliao* (Documents on the History of the Revolution), periodical, Beijing

HDT   *Hunan dangshi tongxun* (Correspondence on Party History in Hunan), periodical, Changsha

HNYZ   *Hunan nongmin yundong ziliao xuanbian* (Documents on the Hunan Peasant Movement), Museum of the Chinese Revolution & Hunan Museum, eds, Renmin chubanshe, Beijing, 1988

HZ   *Hongse Zhonghua* (Red China), newspaper, Ruijin

IIR   (Institute of International Relations), comp., *Zhonggong jimi wenjian huibian* (Classified Chinese Communist Documents: a Selection), Taipei, 1978

INT   Interview records with Mao's relatives, friends, and acquaintances, done in the 1960s, about Mao in Hunan up to 1927, unpublished

JDZ   *Jiangxi dangshi ziliao* (Documents on Party History in Jiangxi), periodical, Nanchang

JGG   *Jinggangshan geming genjudi* (Jinggangshan Revolutionary Base), documents and memoirs, 2 vols, Jinggangshan Base Party History team & Jinggangshan Revolutionary Museum, eds, Zhonggong dangshi ziliao chubanshe, Beijing, 1987

JR   *Jiefang Ribao* (Liberation Daily), newspaper, Yanan

JSY   *Jindaishi yanjiu* (Studies of Modern History), periodical, Beijing

JYZW   *Jianguo yilai zhongyao wenxian xuanbian* (Important Documents of the People's Republic), 20 vols, CCP Archive Study Office, ed., Zhongyang wenxian chubanshe, Beijing, 1992–8

LD   *Lishi dangan* (Historical Archives), periodical, Beijing

RR   *Renmin Ribao* (People's Daily), newspaper, Beijing

SMMM (Shaoshan Mao Memorial Museum), ed., *Mao Zedong yiwu shidian* (A Collection of Objects Left Behind by Mao Zedong), Hongqi chubanshe, Beijing, 1996

WDYZ *Wenhua dageming yanjiu ziliao* (Documents for Researching the Cultural Revolution), 3 vols, People's Liberation Army Defense University, ed., Beijing, 1988, unpublished

WHY *Wenxian he yanjiu* (Documents and Studies), periodical, Beijing

WZX *Wenshi ziliao xuanji* (Selected Historical Accounts), periodical, Beijing

WZX–S *Wenshi ziliao xuanji—Shanghai* (Selected Historical Accounts: Shanghai), periodical, Shanghai

XB *Xinhua banyue kan* (Xinhua Fortnightly), periodical, Beijing

XWS *Xin wenxue shiliao* (New Literature Materials), periodical, Beijing

XXZ *Xinmin xuehui ziliao* (Documents on the New People's Study Society), Museum of the Chinese Revolution & Hunan Museum, eds, Renmin chubanshe, Beijing, 1980

YD *Gongchanzhuyi xiaozu he dangde yida ziliao huibian* (A Collection of Documents and Interviews on the Early Communist Groups and the Party's First Congress), People's University, ed., Beijing, 1979, unpublished

YHCQ *Yanhuang chunqiu* (Annals of the Chinese People), periodical, Beijing

YQD *Yi qida* (Reminiscences about the 7th Congress), collection of memoirs, CCP Central Party History Study Office, comp. Heilongjiang jiaoyu chubanshe, Harbin, 2000

ZDC *Zhongyang danganguan congkan* (Central Archive Periodical), Beijing

ZDJC *Zhonggong dangshi jiaoxue cankao ziliao* (Reference Documents for the Teaching of CCP History), 24 vols, People's Liberation Army Defense University, ed., Beijing, 1986, unpublished

ZDY *Zhonggong dangshi yanjiu* (CCP History Studies), periodical, Beijing

ZDZ *Zhonggong dangshi ziliao* (CCP History Documents), periodical, Beijing

ZH *Zongheng* (Panorama), periodical, Beijing

ZHEN *Zhonghua ernu* (Sons and Daughters of China), periodical, Beijing

ZHW *Zunyi huiyi wenxian* (Documents on the Zunyi Meeting), CCP History Documents Collection Committee and Central Archive, eds, Renmin chubanshe, Beijing, 1985

ZQZS *Zhiqingzhe shuo* (Insiders Talk), a series of interviews with eyewitnesses and write-ups, Zhongguo qingnian chubanshe, Beijing, 1995–98

ZR *Zhonggong dangshi renwu zhuan* (Short Biographies of Important CCP Historical Figures) 75 vols, Important CCP Historical Figures Studies Society, ed., Shaanxi renmin chubanshe, Xian, 1980–

ZS *Zhonghua Minguo zhongyao shiliao chubian—dui Ri kangzhan shiqi* (Important Documents of the Republic of China—during the War against Japan), Nationalist Central Committee, ed., Zhongguo Guomindang zhongyang weiyuanhui dangshi weiyuanhui, Taipei, 1981

ZZ2   *Zhongguo gongnong hongjun dier fangmianjun zhanshi ziliao xuanbian* (Documents on the History of the 2nd Front Army of the Chinese Red Army), committee comp., Jiefangjun chubanshe, Beijing, 1995

ZZ4   *Zhongguo gongnong hongjun disi fangmianjun zhanshi ziliao xuanbian* (Documents on the History of the 4th Front Army of the Red Army), committee comp., Jiefangjun chubanshe, Beijing, 1993

ZZ25   *Zhongguo gongnong hongjun diershiwu jun zhanshi ziliao xuanbian* (Documents on the History of the 25th Army of the Chinese Red Army), committee comp., Jiefangjun chubanshe, Beijing, 1991

ZZWX   *Zhonggong zhongyang wenjian xuanji* (A Selection of CCP Documents), Central Archive, ed., 18 vols, Zhonggong zhongyang dangxiao chubanshe, Beijing, 1989–92

II   SOURCES BY AUTHOR NAMES

An Jianshe, ed., *Zhou Enlai de zuihou suiyue* (Zhou Enlai's Last Years), 1966–76, Zhongyang wenxian chubanshe, Beijing, 1996

Bai Hua, ed., *Mao Zedong shici quanji* (A Complete Collection of Mao Zedong's Poems), Chengdu chubanshe, Chengdu, 1995

Beijing Archive, ed., *Beijing heping jiefang qianhou* (Before and After the Peaceful Liberation of Beijing), Beijing chubanshe, Beijing, 1988

Biographical Literature Pub., ed., *Zhonggong dixiadang xianxingji* (CCP Underground Revealed), 2 vols, Zhuanji wenxue chubanshe, Taipei, 1993

Bo Yi-bo, *Ruogan zhongda juece yu shijian de huigu* (Recollections of Important Decisions and Events), Zhonggong zhongyang dangxiao chubanshe, Beijing, 1993

Bo Yi-bo, *Qishi nian fendou yu sikao* (Struggle of Seventy Years and Reflections), Zhonggong dangshi chubanshe, Beijing, 1996

Cai Dequan & Wang Sheng, *Wang Jingwei shengping jishi* (Wang Jingwei: A Life), Zhongguo wenshi chubanshe, Beijing, 1993

Cai Gong, " 'Xiao Xiongyali shijian' zhenxiang" (The Real Story of the "Little Hungary Incident"), in *Nanfang zhoumo* (Southern Weekend), Guangzhou, 15 Jan. 1999

Cai Mengjian, "Daonian fangong qiangren Zhang Guotao" (Mourning the anti-Communist Strongman Zhang Guotao), in *Zhuanji wenxue* (Biographical Literature), Taipei, vol. 36, no. 1

Cai Xiaoqian, *Jiangxi suqu hongjun xicuan huiyi* (Memories of the Jiangxi Soviet Area and the Westward Flight of the Red Army), Zhonggong yanjiu zazhishe, Taipei, 1978

Cao Zhongbin & Dai Maolin, *Wang Ming zhuan* (A Biography of Wang Ming), Jilin wenshi chubanshe, Changchun, 1991

CCP Archive Study Office, ed., *Bujin de sinian* (Endlessly Missing), Zhongyang wenxian chubanshe, Beijing, 1991

CCP Archive Study Office, ed., *Huiyi Deng Xiaoping* (Reminiscences about Deng Xiaoping), Zhongyang wenxian chubanshe, Beijing, 1998

CCP Archive Study Office & Central Archive, eds, *Gongheguo zouguo de lu—jianguo yilai zhongyao wenxian zhuanti xuanji* (The Road of the Republic—A Thematic Selection of Important Documents of the People's Republic), 1949–1952 & 1953–1956, Zhongyang wenxian chubanshe, Beijing, 1992

CCP Beijing Haidian Committee, ed., *Zhonggong zhongyang zai Xiangshan* (The CCP Leadership in the Fragrant Hills), Zhonggong dangshi chubanshe, Beijing, 1993

CCP Central Party History Study Office, tr. & ed., *Gongchan guoji, liangong (bu) yu*

Zhongguo geming dangan ziliao congshu (A Series of Archive Documents on the Comintern, A-UCP (B) and the Chinese Revolution), 6 vols, Beijing tushuguan chubanshe, Beijing, 1997–8

CCP Changting Committee, ed., *Changting renmin geming shi* (A History of Changting People's Revolution), Xiamen daxue chubanshe, Xiamen, 1990

CCP Guilin Committee, ed., *Hongjun changzheng guo Guangxi* (Long March Red Army Passing through Guangxi), Guangxi renmin chubanshe, Nanning, 1986

CCP Hubei Committee, ed., *Mao Zedong zai Hubei* (Mao Zedong in Hubei), Zhonggong dangshi chubanshe, Beijing, 1993

CCP Hunan Committee, *Hunan renmin geming shi* (A History of Hunan People's Revolution), Hunan chubanshe, Changsha, 1991

CCP Ninggang Committee, comp., *Ninggang—Jinggangshan geming genjudi de zhongxin* (Ninggang—Centre of Jinggangshan Revolutionary Base), a collection of Party historians' interviews with survivors and arguments about the base

CCP Organization Department, ed., *Zhongguo Gongchandang zuzhi gongzuo dashiji* (A Chronicle of Major Events of CCP Organization Work), Liaoning renmin chubanshe, Shenyang, 1992

CCP Pingxiang Committee, ed., *Anyuan lukuang gongren yundong* (the Labor Movement in the Anyuan Railway and Mines), Zhonggong dangshi ziliao chubanshe, Beijing, 1991

CCP Shanghai Committee, ed., *Shanghai gongren sanci wuzhuang qiyi yanjiu* (Studies and Documents on the Three Armed Uprisings of the Shanghai Workers), Zhishi chubanshe, Shanghai, 1987

CCP *Studies*, comp., *Liu Shaoqi wenti ziliao zhuanji* (A Collection of Documents on Liu Shaoqi), Zhonggong yanjiu zazhishe, Taipei, 1970

CCP Tibet Committee, *Zhonggong Xizang dangshi dashiji* (A Chronicle of Major Events of the CCP in Tibet), Xizang renmin chubanshe, Xizang, 1990

CCP Xiangqu Committee Museum & Changsha Museum, eds, *Zhongguo Gongchandang Xiangqu zhixing weiyuanhui shiliao huibian* (A Collection of Documents on the CCP Hunan Executive Committee), Hunan chubanshe, Changsha, 1993

CCP Zhejiang Committee, ed., *Mao Zedong yu Zhejiang* (Mao Zedong and Zhejiang), Zhonggong dangshi chubanshe, Beijing, 1993

CCP Zhenyuan Committee, "Dayuejin qijian de Zhenyuan yuanan" (The Unjust Zhenyuan Case during the Great Leap Forward), in BNC, no. 4, 1999

Central Archive, ed., *Jiefang zhanzheng shiqi tudi gaige wenjian xuanbian* (Documents on the Land Reform during the Liberation War), Zhonggong zhongyang dangxiao chubanshe, Beijing, 1981

Central Archive, ed., *Wannan shibian* (South Anhui Incident), a collection of archive documents, Zhonggong zhongyang dangxiao chubanshe, Beijing, 1982

Central Archive, ed., *Qiushou qiyi* (Autumn Harvest Uprising), a collection of archive documents, Zhonggong zhongyang dangxiao chubanshe, Beijing, 1982a

Central Archive, ed., *Zhonggong dangshi baogao xuanbian* (A Selection of Reports on the CCP History), Zhonggong zhongyang dangxiao chubanshe, Beijing, 1982b

Central Archive, ed., *Hongjun changzheng dangan shiliao xuanbian* (A Selection of Archive Documents on the Red Army's Long March), Xuexi chubanshe, Beijing, 1996

Central Archive, ed., *Zhongguo Gongchandang guanyu Xian shibian dangan shiliao xuanbian* (A Selection of CCP Archive Documents on the Xian Incident), Zhongguo dangan chubanshe, Beijing, 1997

Central Party School, ed., *Yanan zhongyang dangxiao de zhengfeng xuexi* (Rectification Campaign in Yanan's Central Party School), 2 vols, Zhonggong zhongyang dangxiao chubanshe, Beijing, 1989

Chang Shun et al., *Baiwan Guomindang jun qiyi toucheng jishi* (A Record of the Surrender of the Million-strong Nationalist Army), Zhongguo wenshi chubanshe, Beijing, 1991

Chang Yu-fa, *Zhongguo jindai xiandai shi* (Recent and Modern History of China), Donghua shuju, Taipei, 2001

Chen Changjiang & Zhao Guilai, *Mao Zedong zuihou shinian—jingwei duizhang de huiyi* (Mao Zedong's Last Ten Years—Memoirs of a Guard Chief), Zhonggong zhongyang dangxiao chubanshe, Beijing, 1998

Chen Duxiu, *Chen Duxiu nianpu* (A Chronological Record of Chen Duxiu), Tang Baolin & Lin Maosheng, eds, Shanghai renmin chubanshe, Shanghai, 1988

Chen Han, *Bayue de zuji—Mao Zedong 1958 nian Henan nongcun shicha jishi* (Footsteps in August—Mao Zedong's Inpection Tour of Henan in 1958), Zhongyang wenxian chubanshe, Beijing, 2001

Chen Jiren, "Sidu Chishui zhanlue mubiao zaitan" (Reconsidering the Strategic Objectives of the Four Crossings of the Chishui River), in *DDWX*, no. 1, 1991

Chen Liming, *Tan Zhenlin chuanqi* (The legend of Tan Zhenlin), Zhongguo wenshi chubanshe, Beijing, 1994

Chen Qingquan & Song Guangwei, *Lu Dingyi zhuan* (A Biography of Lu Dingyi), Zhonggong dangshi chubanshe, Beijing, 1999

Chen Shiju, *Cong Jinggangshan zoujin Zhongnanhai—Chen Shiju laojiangjun huiyi Mao Zedong* (From Jinggangshan to Zhongnanhai—General Chen Shiju Remembers Mao Zedong), Zhonggong zhongyang dangxiao chubanshe, Beijing, 1993

Chen Xiaodong, *Shenhuo zhiguang* (The Light of Magic Fire), Zhonggong zhongyang dangxiao chubanshe, Beijing, 1995

Chen Yangyong, *Kucheng weiju—Zhou Enlai zai 1967* (Managing a Dangerous Situation—Zhou Enlai in 1967), Zhongyang wenxian chubanshe, Beijing, 2000

Chen Yi, *Chen Yi nianpu* (A Chronological Record of Chen Yi), Liu Shufa et al., eds, Renmin chubanshe, Beijing, 1995

Chen Yi, Xiao Hua et al., *Huiyi zhongyang suqu* (Reminiscences about the Central Soviet Area), Jiangxi renmin chubanshe, Nanchang, 1981

Chen Yun, "Zunyi zhengzhiju kuoda huiyi chuanda tigang" (Outline for Relaying the Enlarged Politburo Meeting at Zunyi), in *ZHW*, manuscript, Feb.–Mar. 1935

Chen Yun, *Chen Yun wenxuan* (Selected Works of Chen Yun), vol. 3, Renmin chubanshe, Beijing, 1995

Chen Yun, *Chen Yun nianpu* (A Chronological Record of Chen Yun), 3 vols, CCP Archive Study Office, ed., Zhongyang wenxian chubanshe, Beijing, 2000

Chen Yung-fa, *Yanan de yinying* (Yanan's Shadow), Institute of Modern History, Academia Sinica, Taipei, 1990

Chai Chengwen & Zhao Yongtian, *Banmendian tanpan* (Panmunjom Negotiations), Jiefangjun chubanshe, Beijing, 1990

Chen Zaidao, *Chen Zaidao huiyilu* (Chen Zaidao Memoirs), Jiefangjun chubanshe, Beijing, 1991

Cheng Hua, *Zhou Enlai he ta de mishumen* (Zhou Enlai and his Secretaries), Zhongguo guangbo dianshi chubanshe, Beijing, 1993

Cheng Min, ed., *Dangnei dajian* (The Big Evil in the Party), Tuanjie chubanshe, Beijing, 1993

Cheng Yuangong, ed., *Zhou Enlai lixian jishi* (True Records of Zhou Enlai's Close Shaves), Zhongyang wenxian chubanshe, Beijing, 1994

Cheng Zhongyuan, *Zhang Wentian zhuan* (A Biography of Zhang Wentian), Dangdai zhongguo chubanshe, Beijing, 1993

Chi Nan & Ming Xiao, eds, *Lin Biao yuanshuai pantao shijian zuixin baogao* (Latest Report on Marshal Lin Biao's Defection), Zhonghua ernu chubanshe, Hong Kong, 2000

Chiang (Chiang Kai-shek), *Zongtong Jianggong dashi changbian chugao* (Draft of a Long Chronological Record of President Chiang Kai-shek), Chin Hsiao-i, ed., Taipei, 1978, courtesy of the editor

Chiang Ching-kuo, *Jiang Jingguo xiansheng quanji* (The Complete Works of Chiang Ching-kuo), vol. 1, Xingzhengyuan xinwenju, Taipei, 1991

China Statistics Bureau, ed., *Zhongguo tongji nianjian* (China Statistics Yearbook, 1983), Jingji daobaoshe, Hong Kong, 1983

China Today, ed., *Dangdai Zhongguo de hegongye* (China Today: Nuclear Industry), Zhongguo shehui kexue chubanshe, Beijing, 1987

China Today, ed., *Dangdai Zhongguo de renkou* (China Today: Population), Zhongguo shehui kexue chubanshe, Beijing, 1988

China Today, ed., *Dangdai Zhongguo de duiwai jingji hezuo* (China Today: Economic Co-operation with Foreign Countries), Zhongguo shehui kexue chubanshe, Beijing, 1989

China Today, ed., *Dangdai Zhongguo jundui de junshi gongzuo* (China Today: the Military Affairs of the Chinese Army), 2 vols, Zhongguo shehui kexue chubanshe, Beijing, 1989a

China Today, ed., *Dangdai Zhongguo de jiben jianshe* (China Today: Capital Construction), 2 vols, Zhongguo shehui kexue chubanshe, Beijing, 1989b

China Today, ed., *Dangdai Zhongguo duiwai maoyi* (China Today: Foreign Trade), 2 vols, Dangdai Zhongguo chubanshe, Beijing, 1992

China Today, ed., *Dangdai Zhongguo de guofang keji shiye* (China Today: Scientific and Technological Undertakings of National Defense), 2 vols, Dangdai Zhongguo chubanshe, Beijing, 1992a

China Today, ed., *Dangdai Zhongguo de bingqi gongye* (China Today: Ordnance Industry), Dangdai Zhongguo chubanshe, Beijing, 1993

Cong Jin, *Quzhe fazhan de suiyue* (Years of Tortuous Development), Henan renmin chubanshe, Zhengzhou, 1991

Contemporary Chinese Biographies team, *He Long zhuan* (A Biography of He Long), Dangdai Zhongguo chubanshe, Beijing, 1993

Dai Chaowu, "Zhongguo hewuqi de fazhan yu Zhongsu guanxi de polie" (The Development of China's Nuclear Weapons and the Sino-Soviet Split), in *DZS*, no. 5, 2001

Dai Huang, *Jiusi yisheng* (Narrow Escape from Death), Zhongyang bianyi chubanshe, Beijing, 1998

Dai Xiangqing & Luo Huilan, *AB tuan yu Futian shibian shimo* (The AB League and the Futian Incident), Henan renmin chubanshe, Zhengzhou, 1994

Deng Li, *Wu Jieping zhuan* (A Biography of Wu Jieping), Zhejiang renmin chubanshe, Hangzhou, 1999

Deng Liqun, "Huiyi Yanan zhengfeng" (Memories of the Yanan Rectification Campaign), in *DDWX*, no. 2, 1992

Deng Xiaoping, *Deng Xiaoping wenxuan* (Selected Works of Deng Xiaoping), 1938–65, Renmin chubanshe, Beijing, 1989

Deng Xiaoping, *Deng Xiaoping wenxuan* (Selected Works of Deng Xiaoping), vol. 3, Renmin chubanshe, Beijing, 1993

Deng Xiaoping, Jiang Zemin et al., *Weiwei fengbei* (A Towering Monument), Jiefangjun chubanshe, Beijing, 1996

Deng Zhongxia, *Zhongguo zhigong yundong jianshi* (A Brief History of the Chinese Labor Movement), Zhongyang chubanju, Russia, 1930

Deng Zihui Biography Committee, *Deng Zihui zhuan* (A Biography of Deng Zihui), Renmin chubanshe, Beijing, 1996

Ding Longjia & Ting Yu, *Kang Sheng yu Zhao Jianmin yuanan* (Kang Sheng and the Unjust Case of Zhao Jianmin), Renmin chubanshe, Beijing, 1999

Ding Shu, *Renhuo* (Man-made Calamity), Jiushi niandai zazhishe, Hong Kong, 1991

Ding Shu, *Yangmou* (Open Scheming), Jiushi niandai zazhishe, Hong Kong, 1993

Ding Shu, "Mao Zedong zhizheng qijian Zhongguo dalu de fei zhengchang siwang," in *Zhongguo zhichun* (China Spring), periodical, USA, Oct. 2001

Ding Wang, ed., *Zhonggong wenhua dageming ziliao huibian* (A Collection of Documents of the CCP's Cultural Revolution), Mingbao yuekanshe, Hong Kong, 1969

Ding Zhi, "Zhongyang hungjun beishang fangzhen de yanbian guocheng" (The Development of the Northbound Strategy of the Central Red Army), in *WHY*, no. 5, 1985

Dong Bian et al., eds, *Mao Zedong he ta de mishu Tian Jiaying* (Mao Zedong and his Secretary Tian Jiaying), Zhongyang wenxian chubanshe, Beijing, 1996

Dong Fu, "A record of famine in Sichuan," unpublished manuscript

Dong Kunwu, "Hongqiao shijian de jingguo" (The Hongqiao Incident), in *WZX*, no. 2

Dong Sheng, *Tiandi song* (Ode to Heaven and Earth), Xinhua chubanshe, Beijing, 2000

Du Xiuxian & Gu Baozi, *Hong jingtou—Zhongnanhai sheyingshi yanzhong de guoshi fengyun* (Red Lens—National Affairs through the Eyes of a Zhongnanhai Photographer), Liaoning renmin chubanshe, Shenyang, 1998

Duan Suquan, *Guwen jicun* (A Collection of Old Writings), Zhongguo wenshi chubanshe, Beijing, 1998

Fan Daren, *Wenge yubi chenfulu* (The Rise and Fall of a Court Scribe in the Cultural Revolution), Mingbao chubanshe, Hong Kong, 1999

Fan Hao, *Mao Zedong he ta de junshi jiaoyu guwen* (Mao Zedong and his Military Education Adviser), Renmin chubanshe, Beijing, 1993

Fan Shuo, *Ye Jianying zai 1976* (Ye Jianying in 1976), Zhonggong zhongyang dangxiao chubanshe, Beijing, 1995

Fan Shuo & Ding Jiaqi, *Ye Jianying zhuan* (A Biography of Ye Jianying), Dangdai Zhongguo chubanshe, Beijing, 1995

Fang Ke & Dan Mu, *Zhonggong qingbao shounao Li Kenong* (CCP Intelligence Chief Li Kenong), Zhongguo shehui kexue chubanshe, Beijing, 1996

Fang Xiao, ed., *Zhonggong dangshi bianyilu* (Queries about CCP History), 2 vols, Shanxi jiaoyu chubanshe, Taiyuan, 1991

Fang Zhou, *Qincheng chunqiu* (A History of Qincheng), Guanhai chuban youxian-gongsi, Hong Kong, 1997

Finance Ministry, ed., *Zhonghua Renmin Gongheguo caizheng shiliao* (Archive Documents on the Finance of the People's Republic of China), 5 vols, Zhongguo caizheng jingji chubanshe, Beijing, 1982–5

First Front Army History Committee, *Zhongguo gongnong hongjun diyi fangmianjun renwuzhi* (Who's Who in the First Front Army of the Chinese Red Army), Jiefangjun chubanshe, Beijing, 1995

Foreign Ministry, ed., *Xin Zhongguo waijiao fengyun* (Winds and Clouds of New China's Diplomacy), multiple vols, Shijie zhishi chubanshe, Beijing, 1990ff.

Foreign Ministry, ed., *Zhou Enlai waijiao huodong dashiji* (A Chronicle of Major Events in Zhou Enlai's Diplomatic Activities), Shijie zhishi chubanshe, Beijing, 1993

Fourth Front Army Memoirs Collection team, ed., *Jianku de licheng* (The Hard Journey), Renmin chubanshe, Beijing, 1984

Fu Chongbi, *Fu Chongbi huiyilu* (Fu Chongbi Memoirs), Zhonggong dangshi chubanshe, Beijing, 1999

Fu Lianzhang, "Mao zhuxi zai Yudu" (Chairman Mao in Yudu), in *Hongqi piaopiao* (Red Flags Fly), vol. 10, Zhongguo qingnian chubanshe, Beijing, 1959

Fu Shanglun et al., *Gaobie ji'e* (Goodbye to Hunger), Renmin chubanshe, Beijing, 1999

Fu Zude & Chen Jiayuan, eds, *Zhongguo renkou: Fujian fence* (Chinese Population: Fujian), Zhongguo caizheng jingji chubanshe, Beijing, 1990

Gansu Archive, ed., *Guomindangjun zhuidu hongjun changzheng he xilujun xijin dangan shiliao huibian* (Archive Documents on the Nationalist Army Chasing and Blocking the Red Army on the Long March and the Western Contingent), Zhongguo dangan chubanshe, Beijing, 1995

Gansu Social Science Academy, ed., *Shanganning geming genjudi shiliao xuanji* (Selections of Documents on the Shaanganning Revolutionary Base) 4 vols, Gansu renmin chubanshe, Lanzhou, 1983

Gao Hua, *Hongtaiyang shi zenyang shengqilai de* (How the Red Sun Rose), Zhongwen daxue chubanshe, Hong Kong, 2000

Gao Wenqian, *Wannian Zhou Enlai* (Zhou Enlai's Later Years), Mirror Books, USA, 2003

Geng Biao, *Geng Biao huiyilu* (Geng Biao Memoirs), 2 vols, Jiangsu renmin chubanshe, Nanjing, 1998

Gong Chu, *Wo yu hongjun* (The Red Army and I), Nanfeng chubanshe, Hong Kong, 1954

Gong Guzhong et al., eds, *Mao Zedong hui Hunan jishi* (Records of Mao Zedong's Trips to Hunan), Hunan chubanshe, Changsha, 1993

Gu Hongzhang, ed., *Zhongguo zhishi qingnian shangshan xiaxiang dashiji* (A Chronicle of Major Events of China's Educated Youth Going to Live in the Countryside), Zhongguo jiancha chubanshe, Beijing, 1997

Guan Weixun, *Wo suo zhidao de Ye Qun* (The Ye Qun I Knew), Zhongguo wenxue chubanshe, Beijing, 1993

Guang Xin, "Lin Biao canghuang chutao mujiji" (An Eyewitness Account of Lin Biao's Panic Flight), in *Zhuanji wenxue* (Biographical Literature), no. 4, Beijing, 1997

Guizhou Archive, ed., *Hongjun zhuanzhan Guizhou—jiu zhengquan dangan shiliao xuanbian* (The Red Army Fighting in Guizhou—Archive Documents from the Old Regime), Guizhou renmin chubanshe, Guiyang, 1984

Guizhou Social Science & Guizhou Museum, eds, *Hongjun changzheng zai Guizhou shiliao xuanji* (Archive Documents on the Long March Red Army in Guizhou), Guiyang, 1983

Guo Chen, *Teshu liandui* (A Special Company), Nongcun duwu chubanshe, Beijing, 1985

Guo Jinrong, *Mao Zedong de wannian shenghuo* (Mao Zedong's Later Years), Jiaoyu kexue chubanshe, Beijing, 1993

Han Shangyu, ed., *Wenge xiyuanlu* (The Unjust Cases in the Cultural Revolution), Tuanjie chubanshe, Beijing, 1993

Han Suyin, *Zhou Enlai yu ta de shiji* (Zhou Enlai and his Century), Zhongyang wenxian chubanshe, Beijing, 1992

Han Taihua, ed., *Zhongguo Gongchandang ruogan lishi wenti xiezhen* (Records of Various Historical Issues of the CCP), Yanshi chubanshe, Beijing, 1998

Han Yanlong, ed., *Zhonghua Renmin Gongheguo fazhi tongshi* (A History of the Legal System in the People's Republic of China), 2 vols, Zhonggong zhongyang dangxiao chubanshe, Beijing, 1998

Hao Weimin, ed., *Neimenggu gemingshi* (A Revolutionary History of Inner Mongolia), Neimenggu daxue chubanshe, Hohhot, 1997

He Changgong, *He Changgong huiyilu* (He Changgong Memoirs), Jiefangjun chubanshe, Beijing, 1987

He Changgong Biography team, *He Changgong zhuan* (A Biography of He Changgong), Zhongyang wenxian chubanshe, Beijing, 2000

He Long, *He Long nianpu* (A Chronological Record of He Long), Li Lie, ed., Renmin chubanshe, Beijing, 1996

Hong Xuezhi, *Kangmei yuanchao zhanzheng huiyi* (Recollections of the War to Resist US Aggression and Aid Korea), Jiefangjun wenyi chubanshe, Beijing, 1991

Hsiao Tso-liang, *Power Relations within the Chinese Communist Movement*, 1930–1934, vol. 2, the Chinese Documents, University of Washington Press, Seattle & London, 1967

Hsu Chen, *Amao congjun ji* (Amao in the Army), Fuji wenhua tushu youxian gongsi, Taipei, 1987

Hsu Chen, *Hu Zongnan xiansheng yu Guomin geming* (Mr. Hu Tsung-nan and the Nationalist Revolution), Wangqu shiqiqi tongxuehui, Taipei, 1990

Hsu En-tseng et al., *Xishuo zhongtong juntong* (Detailed Accounts of the Central Investigation Bureau and the Military Investigation Bureau), Zhuanji wenxue chubanshe, Taipei, 1992

Hsu Yung-chang, *Xu Yongchang riji* (The Diaries of General Hsu Yung-chang), 12 vols of bound photocopies, Institute of Modern History, Academia Sinica, Taipei, 1991

Hu Feng, *Hu Feng zizhuan* (The Autobiography of Hu Feng), Jiangsu wenyi chubanshe, Nanjing, 1996

Hu Qiaomu, *Hu Qiaomu huiyi Mao Zedong* (Hu Qiaomu's Recollections of Mao Zedong), Renmin chubanshe, Beijing, 1994

Hu Yuzhi, *Wo de huiyi* (My Reminiscences), Jiangsu renmin chubanshe, Nanjing, 1990

Huang Changyong, "Shengming de guanghua yu anying—Wang Shiwei zhuan" (The Brilliance and Shadow of a Life—A Biography of Wang Shiwei), in *XWS*, no. 1, 1994

Huang Kecheng, *Huang Kecheng zishu* (Huang Kecheng Tells His Story), Renmin chubanshe, Beijing, 1994

Huang Wenhua et al., *Deng Xiaoping Jiangxi mengnanji* (Deng Xiaoping's Hard Times in Jiangxi), Mingxing chubanshe, Hong Kong, 1990

Huang Xiurong, ed., *Kangri zhanzheng shiqi guogong guanxi jishi* (A Chronological Record of the Nationalist–Communist Relationship during the War against Japan), Zhonggong dangshi chubanshe, Beijing, 1995

Huang Yao & Zhang Mingzhe, *Luo Ruiqing zhuan* (A Biography of Luo Ruiqing), Dangdai Zhongguo chubanshe, Beijing, 1996

Huang Zheng, *Liu Shaoqi yuanan shimo* (The Whole Story of the Unjust Case of Liu Shaoqi), Zhongyang wenxian chubanshe, Beijing, 1998

I Fu-en, *Wo de huiyi* (My Memoirs), Liqing wenjiao jijinhui, Taipei, 2000

Japan Self-Defense Agency, ed., *Huabei zhian zhan* (North China Policing War), CPPCC (Tianjin), tr., vol. 1, Tianjin renmin chubanshe, Tianjin, 1982

Ji Wei, "Wo de zhiqing meng" (My Dream as an Educated Youth), in *Tianxia huaren* (Worldwide Chinese), July/Aug. issue, 1996

Ji Xichen, *Shiwuqianli de niandai* (Unprecedented Times), Renmin ribao chubanshe, Beijing, 2001

Jiang Nanxiang, letter to leadership, March 1945, in *ZDY*, no. 4, 1988

Jiang Tingfu, *Jiang Tingfu huiyilu* (Jiang Tingfu Memoirs), Zhuanji wenxue chubanshe, Taipei, 1984

Jiang Weiqing, *Qishinian zhengcheng—Jiang Weiqing huiyilu* (Seventy Years' Journey—Jiang Weiqing Memoirs), Jiangsu renmin chubanshe, Nanjing, 1996

Jiang Xinli, *Zhang Guotao de panghuang yu juexing* (Zhang Guotao's Wandering and Awakening), Youshi wenhua shiye gongsi, Taipei, 1981

Jiangxi Archive, ed., *Jinggangshan geming genjudi shiliao xuanbian* (Archive Documents about the Jinggangshan Revolutionary Base), Jiangxi renmin chubanshe, Nanchang, 1986

Jiangxi Archive & CCP Jiangxi Committee, eds, *Zhongyang geming genjudi shiliao xuanbian* (Archive Documents about the Central Revolutionary Base), 3 vols, Jiangxi renmin chubanshe, Nanchang, 1983

Jiangxi Party Committee, "Jiangxi shengwei guanyu shieryue qiri shibian baogao" (Jiangxi Party Committee's report to the Central Leadership about the Incident on 7 December), 12 Jan. 1931, Yongyang, RGASPI, 514/1/1008, Moscow

Jin Chongji et al., *Zhou Enlai zhuan* (A Biography of Zhou Enlai), 1898–1949, Renmin chubanshe & Zhongyang wenxian chubanshe, Beijing, 1990

Jin Chongji et al., *Zhu De zhuan* (A Biography of Zhu De), Renmin chubanshe & Zhongyang wenxian chubanshe, Beijing, 1993

Jin Chongji et al., *Mao Zedong zhuan* (A Biography of Mao Zedong), 1893–1949, Zhongyang wenxian chubanshe, Beijing, 1996

Jin Chongji et al., *Zhou Enlai zhuan* (A Biography of Zhou Enlai), 1949–1976, Zhongyang wenxian chubanshe, Beijing, 1998

Jin Chongji & Huang Zheng, *Liu Shaoqi zhuan* (A Biography of Liu Shaoqi), Zhongyang wenxian chubanshe, Beijing, 1998

Jin Zhenlin, *Mao An-ying* (Mao An-ying), Renmin chubanshe, Beijing, 1993

Jinchaji Base Committee & Central Archive, eds, *Jinchaji kangri genjudi* (Jinchaji Resisting Japan Base), documents, memoirs and a chronological record, 3 vols, Zhonggong dangshi chubanshe & Zhonggong dangshi ziliao chubanshe, Beijing, 1991

Jing Xizhen, *Zai Pengzong shenbian—jingwei canmou de huiyi* (Beside Chief Peng—Memories of an Aide-de-camp), Sichuan renmin chubanshe, Chengdu, 1979

Jishui County Chronicle Committee, ed., *Jishui xianzhi* (Jishui County Chronicle), Xinhua chubanshe, Beijing, 1989

Kang Keqing, *Kang Keqing huiyilu* (Kang Keqing Memoirs), Jiefangjun chubanshe, Beijing, 1993

Kang Sheng, "Qiangjiu shizu zhe" (Rescue the Fallen), speech, 15 July 1943, from the Archive of the Investigation Bureau, Taipei

Kang Sheng, "Sanshisan nian fanjian zhengfeng hou zhi zongjie chengji ji quedian" (Summary of Achievements and Shortcomings after the Anti-Spy and Rectification Campaign, 1944), 1944, from the Archive of the Investigation Bureau, Taipei

Kung Hsiang-hsi, "Xian shibian huiyilu" (Memories of the Xian Incident), in Li Jinzhou, ed.

Kuo Hua-lun, *Zhonggong shilun* (An Analytical History of the CCP), 4 vols, Guoli zhengzhi daxue guoji guanxi yanjiu zhongxin, Taipei, 1989

Lei Yingfu, *Zai zuigao tongshuaibu dang canmou* (A Staff Member at the Supreme HQ), Baihuazhou wenyi chubanshe, Nanchang, 1997

Li Danhui, ed., *Zhongguo yu Yinduzhina zhanzheng* (China and the Indochina War), Tiandi tushu, Hong Kong, 2000

Li Desheng, *Li Desheng huiyilu* (Li Desheng Memoirs), Jiefangjun chubanshe, Beijing, 1997

Li Guangan et al., eds, *Jinian Li Fuchun* (In Memory of Li Fuchun), Zhongguo jihua chubanshe, Beijing, 1990

Li Hui, *Hu Feng jituan yuanan shimo* (The Unjust Case of the Hu Feng Clique), Renmin ribao chubanshe, Beijing, 1989

Li Jiaji & Yang Qingwang, *Gensui hongtaiyang—wo zuo Mao Zedong tieshen weishi shisan nian* (Following the Red Sun—I Was Mao Zedong's Valet for Thirteen Years), Heilongjiang renmin chubanshe, Harbin, 1994

Li Jian, ed., *Deng Xiaoping sanjin sanchu Zhongnanhai* (Deng Xiaoping In and Out of Zhongnanhai Three Times), Zhongguo dadi chubanshe, Beijing, 1993

Li Jian et al., eds, *Guanjian huiyi qinli shilu* (Memoirs of Eyewitnesses of Key Meetings), vol. 2, Zhonggong zhongyang dangxiao chubanshe, Beijing, n.d.

Li Jinzhou, ed., *Xian shibian qinliji* (Personal Experiences of the Xian Incident), Zhuanji wenxue chubanshe, Taipei, 1982

Li Junshan, *Weizheng luexun—lun kangzhan chuqi Jinghu diqu zuozhan* (On the battles in Nanjing and Shanghai at the Beginning of the War against Japan), Guoli Taiwan daxue chuban weiyuanhui, Taipei, 1992

Li Ke & Hao Shengzhang, *Wenhua dageming zhong de renmin jiefangjun* (The People's Liberation Army in the Cultural Revolution), Zhonggong dangshi ziliao chubanshe, Beijing, 1989

Li Kefei & Peng Donghai, *Mimi zhuanji shang de lingxiumen* (Leaders on the Secret Special Planes), Zhonggong zhongyang dangxiao chubanshe, Beijing, 1997

Li Liangzhi, *Fenghuo Jiangnan hua qiyuan—xinsijun yu Wannan shibian* (A Great Tragedy—the New 4th Army and the South Anhui Incident), Zhongguo dangan chubanshe, Beijing, 1995

Li Linda, *Qingman Xihu* (Feelings Fill the Western Lake), Zhongyang wenxian chubanshe, Beijing, 1993

Li Mingsheng, "Zouchu diqiu cun" (Out of the Earth), in *Zhonghua wenxue xuankan* (Selected Chinese Literature), no. 5, Beijing, 1995

Li Rui, *Lushan huiyi shilu* (A True Record of the Lushan Conference), Chunqiu chubanshe & Hunan jiaoyu chubanshe, Beijing, 1989

Li Rui, *Mao Zedong zaonian dushu shenghuo* (The School Life of the Young Mao Zedong), Liaoning renmin chubanshe, Shenyang, 1992

Li Rui, *Zaonian Mao Zedong* (The Childhood and Youth of Mao Zedong), Liaoning renmin chubanshe, Shenyang, 1992a

Li Weihan, *Huiyi yu yanjiu* (Memories and Studies), Zhonggong dangshi ziliao chubanshe, Beijing, 1986

Li Xiangwen, ed. *Mao Zedong jiashi* (Mao Zedong's Family and Relatives), Renmin chubanshe, Beijing, 1996

Li Xun, *Da bengkui—Shanghai gongren zaofanpai xingwangshi* (Big Collapse—the Rise and Fall of Shanghai Worker Rebels), Shibao wenhua, Taipei, 1996

Li Yimang, *Mohu de yingping* (Obscure Screen), Renmin chubanshe, Beijing, 1992

Li Yimin, "Canjia Yanan qiangjiu yundong de pianduan huiyi" (Fragments of Recollections of My Participation in the Rescue Campaign in Yanan), in GZ, no. 3, 1981

Li Yinqiao, *Zai Mao Zedong shenbian shiwunian* (Fifteen Years by the Side of Mao Zedong), Hebei renmin chubanshe, Shijiazhuang, 1992

Li Yong et al., eds, *Wenhua dageming zhong de mingren zhi si* (The Deaths of Well-known Figures in the Cultural Revolution), Zhongyang minzu xueyuan chubanshe, Beijing, 1993

Li Yueran, *Waijiao wutai shang de xinzhongguo lingxiu* (New China's Leaders on the Diplomatic Stage), Waiyu jiaoxue yu yanjiu chubanshe, Beijing, 1994

Li Yuzhen, *Jiang Jingguo lusu shenghuo miwen* (The Secret Story of Chiang Ching-kuo's Life in the Soviet Union), Zhongguo youyi chubangongsi, Beijing, 1994

Li Zhisui, *Mao Zedong siren yisheng huiyilu* (The Private Life of Chairman Mao), Shibao wenhua, Taipei, 1994

Li Zongren, with Tang Degang, *Li Zongren huiyilu* (Li Zongren Memoirs), Liao chubanshe, Taipei, 1995

Liao Gailong, *Dangshi tansuo* (An Exploration of Party History), Zhonggong zhongyang dangxiao chubanshe, Beijing, 1983

Liao Gailong, *Mao Zedong sixiangshi* (A History of Mao Zedong Thought), Zhonghua shuju, Hong Kong, 1993

Lin Ke et al., *Lishi de zhenshi* (The True Life of Mao Zedong), Liwen chubanshe, Hong Kong, 1995

Liou Di (Liu Di), "Liu Di gei zhongyang xin" (Liu Di's Letter to the Central Leadership), 11 Jan. 1931, RGASPI, 514/1/1008, Moscow

Liu (Liu Shaoqi, also spelled Liu Shao-chi, as in text), *Liu Shaoqi xuanji* (Selected Works of Liu Shaoqi), Renmin chubanshe, Beijing, vol. 1: 1981; vol. 2: 1985

Liu, *Liu Shaoqi lun dang de jianshe* (Liu Shaoqi on Building the Party), Zhongyang wenxian chubanshe, Beijing, 1991

Liu, *Liu Shaoqi lun xinzhongguo jingji jianshe* (Liu Shaoqi on New China's Economy), Zhongyang wenxian chubanshe, Beijing, 1993

Liu, *Liu Shaoqi nianpu* (A Chronological Record of Liu Shaoqi), 2 vols, CCP Archive Study Office, ed., Zhongyang wenxian chubanshe, Beijing, 1996

Liu Bocheng, *Liu Bocheng junshi wenxuan* (Military Writings of Liu Bocheng), Jiefangjun chubanshe, Beijing, 1992

Liu Guangren et al., *Feng Jiping zhuan* (A Biography of Feng Jiping), Qunzhong chubanshe, Beijing, 1997

Liu Hansheng & Yi Fengkui, *1961, kurizi—Liu Shaoqi mimi huixiangji* (1961, Hard Days—Liu Shaoqi's Secret Home Visit), Zhongguo gongren chubanshe, Beijing, 1993

Liu Jinchi, "Songhu jingbei silingbu jianwen" (What I Saw and Heard in the Shanghai Garrison), in CPPCC 1987

Liu Tong, *Dongbei jiefang zhanzheng jishi* (A Record of the Liberation War in the Northeast), Dongfang chubanshe, Beijing, 1997

Liu Xiao, *Chushi Sulian banian* (Eight Years as Ambassador to the Soviet Union), Zhonggong dangshi chubanshe, Beijing, 1998

Liu Ying, *Zai lishi de jiliu zhong* (In the Tidal Waves of History), Zhonggong dangshi chubanshe, Beijing, 1992

Liu Yitao, "Mao An-ying, Mao An-qing, Mao An-long de xinsuan tongnian" (The Sad Childhood of Mao An-ying, Mao An-qing and Mao An-long), in *YHCQ*, no. 6, 1994

Liu Zhende, *Wo wei Shaoqi dang mishu* (I Was Shaoqi's Secretary), Zhongyang wenxian chubanshe, Beijing 1994

Liu Zhi, *Wo de huiyi* (My Reminiscences), Guanglong wenju yinshua gongsi, Taipei, 1966

Liu Zhijian, " 'Budui wenyi gongzuo zuotanhui jiyao' chansheng qianhou" (How the "Summary of the Army Arts Seminar" Was Produced), in ZDZ editorial board, vol. 5

Lu Keng, *Lu Keng huiyi yu chanhuilu* (Remembrance and Repentance of Lu Keng), Shibao wenhua, Taipei, 1998

Lu Zhengchao, *Lu Zhengchao huiyilu* (Lu Zhengchao Memoirs), Jiefangjun chubanshe, Beijing, 1987

Luo Diandian, *Feifan de niandai* (Extraordinary Times), Shanghai wenyi chubanshe, Shanghai, 1987

Luo Diandian, *Hongse jiazu dangan* (Records of a Red Family), Nanhai chuban gongsi, Haikou, 1999

Luo Guibo, "Shaoqi tongzhi pai wo chushi Yuenan" (Comrade Shaoqi Sent Me to Vietnam), 1987, in *Remembering Liu Shaoqi*, ed.

Luo Shixu, *Lushan bieshu daguan* (Villas in Lushan), Jiangxi meishu chubanshe, Nanchang, 1995

Luo Yimin, *Liuzhuang bainian* (A Hundred Years of the Liu Mansion), Shanxi renmin chubanshe, Taiyuan, 1998

Luo Zhanglong, *Chunyuan zaiji* (A Memoir), Sanlian shudian, Beijing, 1984

Ma Juxian et al., eds, *Zhongguo renkou: Jiangxi fence* (Chinese Population: Jiangxi), Zhongguo caizheng jingji chubanshe, Beijing, 1989

Ma Qibin et al., *Zhongyang geming genjudi shi* (A History of the Central Revolutionary Base), Renmin chubanshe, Beijing, 1986

Ma Zhendu, "Bayisan Songhu zhanyi qiyin bianzheng" (On the Cause of the 13 August War in Shanghai), in *JSY*, no. 6, 1986

Ma Zhendu, *Can sheng—kangri zhanzheng zhengmian zhanchang daxieyi* (Tragic Victory—A Panoramic Picture of the Frontal Battleground in the War against Japan), Guangxi shifan daxue chubanshe, Guilin, 1993

Ma Zhigang, ed., *Dayuanan yu dapingfan* (Big Unjust Cases and Big Rehabilitation), Tuanjie chubanshe, Beijing, 1993

Mao, (Mao Zedong, also spelled Mao Tse-tung, as in text), *Jiandang he dageming shiqi Mao Zedong zhuzuoji* (Mao Zedong Writings during the Period of the Formation of the Party and the Great Revolution), Dec. 1920–July 1927, CCP Archive Study Office & CCP Hunan Committee, comp., unpublished; in Notes as Mao 1920–27

Mao, *Mao Zedong zizhuan* (Mao Zedong Autobiography), 1937 (new edn, Jiefangjun wenyi chubanshe, Beijing, 2002)

Mao, *Mao Zedong xuanji* (Selected Works of Mao Zedong), Renmin chubanshe, Beijing, vol. 5, 1977

Mao, *Mao Zedong nongcun diaocha wenji* (Writings of Mao Zedong on Country Investigation), Renmin chubanshe, Beijing, 1983

Mao, *Mao Zedong shuxin xuanji* (Selected Letters of Mao Zedong), Renmin chubanshe, Beijing, 1984

Mao, *Jianguo yilai Mao Zedong wengao* (Manuscripts of Mao Zedong since the Founding of the People's Republic), 13 vols, CCP Archive Study Office, ed., Zhongyang wenxian chubanshe, Beijing, 1987–98

Mao, *Mao Zedong zaoqi wengao* (Early Manuscripts of Mao Zedong), June 1912–Nov. 1920, CCP Archive Study Office & CCP Hunan Committee, eds, Hunan chubanshe, Changsha, 1990

Mao, *Mao Zedong xuanji* (Selected Works of Mao Zedong), Renmin chubanshe, Beijing, vols 1–4, 1991

Mao, *Mao Zedong zishu* (Mao Zedong Tells His Story), Renmin chubanshe, Beijing, 1993

Mao, *Mao Zedong junshi wenji* (Mao Zedong Military Writings), 6 vols, CCP Archive Study Office & Military Science Academy, eds, Junshi kexue chubanshe & Zhongyang wenxian chubanshe, Beijing, 1993a

Mao, *Mao Zedong nianpu* (A Chronological Record of Mao Zedong), 1893–1949, 3 vols, CCP Archive Study Office, ed., Renmin chubanshe & Zhongyang wenxian chubanshe, Beijing, 1993b

Mao, *Mao Zedong jingji nianpu* (A Chronological Record of Mao Zedong on Economics), Gu Longsheng, ed., Zhonggong zhongyang dangxiao chubanshe, Beijing, 1993c

Mao, *Mao Zedong wenji* (Collected Writings of Mao Zedong), 8 vols, Renmin chubanshe, Beijing, 1993–9

Mao, *Mao Zedong waijiao wenxuan* (Mao Zedong on Diplomacy), Zhongyang wenxian chubanshe & Shijie zhishi chubanshe, Beijing, 1994

Mao, *Mao Zedong zai qida de baogao he jianghua ji* (Mao Zedong's Reports and Speeches at the 7th Congress), Zhongyang wenxian chubanshe, 1995

Mao CCRM (Center for Chinese Research Materials), comp., *Maozhu weikangao, "Mao Zedong sixiang wansui" bieji ji qita* (Unofficially Published Works of Mao Zedong, Additional Volumes of "Long Live Mao Zedong's Thought" and Other Secret Speeches of Mao), 15 vols, Virginia, USA (n.d.)

Mao CCRM & ARL (Center for Chinese Research Materials & Association of Research Libraries), comp., *Hongweibing ziliao xubian*, 1 (Red Guard Publications, Supplement 1), Washington, DC (n.d.)

"Mao and I" Collection Committee, ed., *Mao Zedong renji jiaowang ceji* (Sidelights on Mao Zedong's Personal Relationships), Shanxi renmin chubanshe, Taiyuan, 1993

"Mao and I" Collection Committee, ed., *Wo yu Mao Zedong de jiaowang* (My Relationship with Mao Zedong), Shanxi renmin chubanshe, Taiyuan, 1993a

"Mao and I" Collection Committee, ed., *Zai Mao Zedong shenbian* (Alongside Mao Zedong), Shanxi renmin chubanshe, Taiyuan, 1993b

Mao Clan Chronicle, Shaoshan Mao shi zupu (The Mao Clan Chronical, Shaoshan), 4 edns, 1737, 1881, 1911 and 1941, parts published in Li Xiangwen, pp. 3–6, 621ff.

[Deng] Mao Mao, *Wode fuqin Deng Xiaoping* (My Father Deng Xiaoping), Zhongyang wenxian chubanshe, Beijing, 1993

[Deng] Mao Mao, *Fuqin Deng Xiaoping wenge shinian ji* (My Father Deng Xiaoping in the Ten Years of the Cultural Revolution), Xianggang zhonghua ernu chubanshe, Hong Kong, 2000

Mei Zhi, *Wangshi ru yan—Hu Feng chenyuan lu* (The Past is Like Smoke—A Record of How Hu Feng was Wronged), Sanlian shudian, Hong Kong, 1989

Meng Qingshu, *Wang Ming zhuanji yu huiyi* (A Biography and Memoirs of Wang Ming), unpublished manuscript, courtesy of author's son, Wang Dan-zhi

Military History Bureau, MND, ed., *Jiaofei zhanshi* (A History of Military Actions against the Communist Rebellions during 1930–1945), 6 vols, Guofangbu shizhengju & Zhonghua dadian bianyinhui, Taipei, 1967

Military Science Academy, ed., *Zhongguo renmin zhiyuanjun kangmei yuanchao zhanshi* (A History of the Chinese People's Volunteers in the War to Resist America and Aid Korea), Junshi kexue chubanshe, Beijing, 1992

Ming Xiao & Chi Nan, *Mousha Mao Zedong de heise taizi* (The Black Prince Who Tried to Assassinate Mao Zedong), Zhonghua ernu chubanshe, Hong Kong, 2000

Mo Wenhua, *Mo Wenhua huiyilu* (Mo Wenhua Memoirs), Jiefangjun chubanshe, Beijing, 1996

Mu Xin, *Ban* Guangming Ribao *shinian zishu* (I Ran the *Guangming Daily* for Ten Years), Zhonggong dangshi chubanshe, Beijing, 1994

Museum of the Chinese Revolution, ed., *Hongjun changzheng riji* (Red Army Long March Diaries), Dangan chubanshe, Beijing, 1986

Nationalist Party Organization Department, ed., *Zhongguo Gongchandang zhi toushi* (A Perspective on the CCP), 1935, from the Archive of the Investigation Bureau, Taipei

N4A *History* Committee, *Xinsijun zhanshi* (A History of the New 4th Army), Jiefangjun chubanshe, Beijing, 2000

Nie Rongzhen, *Nie Rongzhen huiyilu* (Nie Rongzhen Memoirs), Mingbao chubanshe, Hong Kong, 1991

Nie Rongzhen, *Nie Rongzhen nianpu* (A Chronological Record of Nie Rongzhen), Zhou Junlun et al., eds, Renmin chubanshe, Beijing, 1999

Niu Han & Deng Jiuping, eds, *Yuan shang cao: jiyi zhong de fanyoupai yundong* (Grass on the Prairie: Documents and recollections of the Anti-Rightist Campaign), Jingji ribao chubanshe, Beijing, 1998

Niu Jun, *Cong Yanan zouxiang shijie* (From Yanan to the World), Fujian renmin chubanshe, Fuzhou, 1992

Our Premier Zhou, ed., *Women de Zhou zongli* (Our Premier Zhou), Zhongyang wenxian chubanshe, Beijing, 1990

Pai Chung-hsi, *Bai Chongxi huiyilu* (Memoirs of Pai Chung-hsi), Jiefangjun chubanshe, Beijing, 1987

Panchen Lama, *Qiwanyan shu* (70,000-word Letter), Tibet government-in-exile, Dharamsala, 1998

Pang Bingan, ed., *Lamei xiongying—Zhongguoren yanli de Qie Gewala* (A Latin American Eagle—Che Guevara in the Eyes of the Chinese), Shijie zhishi chubanshe, Beijing, 2000

Pang Xianzhi & Jin Chongji, *Mao Zedong zhuan* (A Biography of Mao Zedong), 1949–1976, Zhogyang wenxian chubanshe, Beijing, 2003

Party Documents, ed., *Cong Yanan dao Beijing* (From Yanan to Beijing), a collection of documents and studies about the civil war, Zhongyang wenxian chubanshe, Beijing, 1993

Pei Jianzhang, ed., *Zhonghua Renmin Gongheguo waijiaoshi* (A History of the Diplomacy of the People's Republic of China, 1949–1956), Shijie zhishi chubanshe, Beijing, 1994

Pei Zhouyu, "Liu Zhidan tongzhi he women zai yiqi" (Comrade Liu Zhidan is Always with Us), in *Xinghuo liaoyuan* (A Single Spark Can Start a Prairie Fire), vol. 4, Jiefangjun chubanshe, Beijing, 1997

Peng (Peng Dehuai), Peng's 80,000-word letter to Mao and leadership, 1962, unpublished

Peng, *Peng Dehuai zishu* (Peng Dehuai Tells his Story), Renmin chubanshe, Beijing, 1981

Peng, *Peng Dehuai nianpu* (A Chronological Record of Peng Dehuai), Wang Yan, ed., Renmin chubanshe, Beijing, 1998

Peng Dehuai Biography team, *Yige zhenzheng de ren—Peng Dehuai* (A True Man—Peng Dehuai), Renmin chubanshe, Beijing, 1995

Peng Meikui, *Wo de bofu Peng Dehuai* (My Uncle Peng Dehuai), Liaoning renmin chubanshe, Shenyang, 1997

People's Liberation Army Historical Documents Committee., ed., *Tongxinbing huiyi shiliao* (Recollections of the Radio Corps), Jiefangjun chubanshe, Beijing, 1995

People's Liberation Army Military Science Academy, ed., *Zhongguo gongnong hongjun changzheng shi* (A History of the Long March), Shanxi renmin chubanshe, Taiyuan, 1996

PRC Encyclopaedia, ed., *Zhonghua Renmin Gongheguo guoshi quanjian* (The Encyclopedia of the People's Republic of China), 6 vols, Tuanjie chubanshe, Beijing, 1996

Provincial Action Committee, "Sheng xingwei jinji tonggao dijiu hao" (Provincial Action Committee Emergency Announcement No. 9), 15 Dec. 1930, RGASPI, 514/1/1008, Moscow

Qi Gaoru, *Jiang Jingguo de yisheng* (The Life of Chiang Ching-kuo), Zhuanji wenxue chubanshe, Taipei, 1991

Qi Li, *Mao Zedong wannian shenghuo suoji* (Fragments of Memories about Mao Zedong's Last Years), Zhongyang wenxian chubanshe, Beijing, 1998

Qian Gang & Geng Qingguo, eds, *Ershi shiji Zhongguo zhongzai bailu* (Mammoth Disasters of Twentieth Century China), Shanghai renmin chubanshe, Shanghai, 1999

Qian Jiang, *Mimi zhengzhan—Zhongguo junshi guwentuan yuanyue kangfa jishi* (A Secret War—the True Story of Chinese Military Advisers in Vietnam against the French), Sichuan renmin chubanshe, Chengdu, 1999

Qiu Shi, ed., *Gongheguo zhongda juece chutai qianhou* (How Important Decisions of the People's Republic Were Launched), 4 vols, Jingji Ribao chubanshe, Beijing, 1997–8

Quan Yanchi, *Hongqiang neiwai* (Inside and Outside the Red Walls), Tiandi tushu, Hong Kong, 1991

Quan Yanchi, *Long kun—He Long yu Xue Ming* (The Plight of the Dragon—He Long and Xue Ming), Guangdong luyou chubanshe, Guangzhou, 1997

Quan Yanchi & Du Weidong, *Gongheguo mishi* (Secret Envoys of the People's Republic), Guangming Ribao chubanshe, Beijing, 1990

Radio Corps History Committee, "Hongjun wuxiandian tongxin de chuangjian, fazhan jiqi lishi zuoyong" (The Foundation, Development and Historical Role of the Red Army Radio Corps), in ZDZ, no. 30

Ran Longbo & Ma Jisen, *Zhou Enlai yu Xianggang liuqi baodong* (Zhou Enlai and the 1967 Riot in Hong Kong), Mingbao chubanshe, Hong Kong, 2001

Remembering Liu Shaoqi, ed., *Mianhuai Liu Shaoqi* (Remembering Liu Shaoqi), Zhongyang wenxian chubanshe, Beijing, 1988

Remembering Mao Zedong, ed., *Mianhuai Mao Zedong* (Remembering Mao Zedong), 2 vols, Zhongyang wenxian chubanshe, Beijing, 1993

Remembering Peng Zhen, ed., *Mianhuai Peng Zhen* (Remembering Peng Zhen), Zhongyang wenxian chubanshe, Beijing, 1998

Reminiscences about Deng Zihui, ed., *Huiyi Deng Zihui* (Reminiscences about Deng Zihui), Renmin chubanshe, Beijing, 1996

Reminiscences about Tan Zhenlin, ed., *Huiyi Tan Zhenlin* (Reminiscences about Tan Zhenlin), Zhejiang renmin chubanshe, Hangzhou, 1992

Ren Bishi, *Ren Bishi nianpu* (A Chronological Record of Ren Bishi), CCP Archive Study Office, ed., Renmin chubanshe & Zhongyang wenxian chubanshe, Beijing, 1993

Ren Wuxiong & Yu Weiping, "*Mao An-ying, Mao An-qing tongzhi younian zai Shanghai de yixie qingkuang*" (Some information about the Childhood of Comrades Mao An-ying and Mao An-qing in Shanghai), in WZX–S, no. 2, 1980

Revolutionary Military Museum, ed., *Baituan dazhan lishi wenxian ziliao xuanbian* (Archive Documents on Operation 100 Regiments), Jiefangjun chubanshe, Beijing, 1990

Ruijin County Chronicle Committee, ed., *Ruijin xianzhi* (Ruijin County Chronicle), Zhongyang wenxian chubanshe, Beijing, 1993

Second Archive, ed., *Guomindangjun zhuidu hongjun changzheng dangan shiliao xuanbian: zhongyang bufen* (Archive Documents on the Nationalist Army Chasing and Blocking the Red Army on the Long March: Central Red Army Part), Dangan chubanshe, Beijing, 1987

Second Archive, ed., *Kangri zhanzheng zhengmian zhanchang* (The Frontal Battleground of the War against Japan), Jiangsu guji chubanshe, Jiangsu, 1987a

Second Archive & Hunan Archive, eds, *Guomindangjun zhuidu hongjun changzheng dangan shiliao xuanbian: Hunan bufen* (Archive Documents on the Nationalist Army Chasing and Blocking the Red Army on the Long March: Hunan Part), Dangan chubanshe, Beijing, 1988

"Shaanganning Border Region," ed., *Shanganning bianqu de jingbing jianzheng ziliao xuanji* (Documents on Cutting Down Troops and Administration in the Shaanganning Border Region), Qiushi chubanshe, Beijing, 1982

Shaanxi Archive, ed., *Guomindangjun zhuidu hongjun changzheng dangan shiliao xuanbian: Shanxi bufen* (Archive Documents on the Nationalist Army Chasing and Blocking the Red Army on the Long March: Shaanxi Part), Zhongguo dangan chubanshe, Beijing, 1994

Shanghai Archive, ed., *Shanghai dangan shiliao congbian: Shanghai gongren sanci wuzhuang qiyi* (Collected Archive documents from Shanghai: Three Armed Uprisings of the Shanghai Workers), Shanghai renmin chubanshe, Shanghai, 1983

Shao Yihai, "Lin Biao jituan fumie neiqing" (The Inside Story of the Demise of the Lin Biao Clique), in *Zhongnanhai renshi chenfu* (The Rise and Fall of Figures in Zhongnanhai), Wenhui chubanshe, Hong Kong, 1992

Shaoshan Chronicle Committee, ed., *Shaoshan zhi* (Shaoshan Chronicle), Zhongguo dabaike quanshu chubanshe, Beijing, 1993

Shen Zhihua, *Mao Zedong, Sidalin yu Hanzhan* (Mao Zedong, Stalin and the Korean War), Tiandi tushu, Hong Kong, 1998

Shen Zui, *Wo zhe sanshinian* (Thirty Years in My Life), Beijing shiyue wenyi chubanshe, Beijing, 1994

Sheng Ping et al., eds, *Zhongguo Gongchandang lishi dacidian* (A Dictionary of CCP History), Zhongguo guoji guangbo chubanshe, Beijing, 1991

Shi Dongbing, *Zuichu de kangzheng—Peng Zhen zai wenhua dageming qianxi* (Resistance at the Beginning—Peng Zhen on the Eve of the Cultural Revolution), Zhonggong zhongyang dangxiao chubanshe, Beijing, 1993

Shi Jixin, "Hongjun changzheng hou Zhonggong zhongyang tong Gongchanguoji huifu dianxun lianxi wenti de kaozheng" (On the CCP's Restoring Radio Links with the Comintern after the Long March), in ZDC, no. 1, 1987

Shi Shuo, "Bayisan songhu kangzhan jilue" (A Brief Account of the 13 August War against Japan in Shanghai), in CPPCC 1987

Shi Zhe, *Zai lishi juren shenbian* (Alongside Giants of History), Zhongyang wenxian chubanshe, Beijing, 1991

Shi Zhe, *Feng yu gu* (Peaks and Valleys), Hongqi chubanshe, Beijing, 1992

Shi Zhongquan et al., *Zhonggong bada shi* (History of the CCP 8th Congress), Renmin chubanshe, Beijing, 1998

Shu Long, ed., *Mao Zemin* (Mao Zemin), Junshi kexue chubanshe, Beijing, 1996

Shui Jing, *Teshu de jiaowang* (Special Relationships), Jiangsu wenyi chubanshe, Nanjing, 1992

Si Ren, ed., *Wenhua dageming fengyun renwu fangtanlu* (Interviews with Celebrities of the Cultural Revolution), Zhongyang minzu xueyuan chubanshe, Beijing, 1993

Sichuan Archive, ed., *Guomindangjun zhuidu hongjun changzheng dangan shiliao xuanbian: Sichuan bufen* (Archive Documents on the Nationalist Army Chasing and Blocking the Red Army on the Long March: Sichuan Part), Dangan chubanshe, Beijing, 1986

Sichuan Party History Committee, *Hongjun changzheng zai Sichuan* (Long March Red Army in Sichuan), Sichuan sheng shehuikexue chubanshe, Chengdu, 1986

Sima Lu, *Douzheng shibanian* (Eighteen Years of Struggle), Yazhou chubanshe, Hong Kong, 1952

Sima Lu, *Hongjun changzheng yu zhonggong neizheng* (Red Army Long March and Infighting), Zilian chubanshe, Hong Kong, 1985

Sima Lu, *Zhonggong lishi de jianzheng—Sima Lu huiyilu* (Witnessing the Secret History of the Communist Party of China: Memoirs of Ex-Communist Smarlo Ma), Mirror Books, USA, 2004

Sino-Indian Border Self-Defence War History, ed., *Zhongyin bianjing ziwei fanji zuozhanshi* (A History of the Sino-Indian Border War of Self-Defense), Junshi kexue chubanshe, Beijing, 1994

Sino-Russian Relations Studies Society, ed., *Zhanhou Zhongsu guanxi zouxiang* (The Trend of Sino-Soviet Relations after the War), Shehui kexue wenxian chubanshe, Beijing, 1997

Song Honggang, *Sun Yueqi* (Sun Yueqi), Huashan wenyi chubanshe, Shijiazhuang, 1997

Song Renqiong, *Song Renqiong huiyilu* (Song Renqiong Memoirs), Jiefangjun chubanshe, Beijing, 1994

Song Xiaomeng, *Li Rui qiren* (The Story of Li Rui), Henan renmin chubanshe, Zhengzhou, 1999

Song Yongyi, ed., *Wenge datusha* (Massacres during the Cultural Revolution), Kaifang zazhishe, Hong Kong, 2002

South Anhui Incident Committee, ed., *Wannan shibian* (South Anhui Incident), Zhonggong dangshi chubanshe, Beijing, 1990

State Council, ed., *Sanxian jianshe* (Third Front), Beijing, 1991, unpublished

Su Ping, *Cai Chang zhuan* (A Biography of Cai Chang), Zhongguo funu chubanshe, Beijing, 1990

Su Yu, *Su Yu zhanzheng huiyilu* (War Memoirs of Su Yu), Jiefangjun chubanshe, Beijing, 1988

Su Yu Biography team, *Su Yu zhuan* (Su Yu Biography), Dangdai Zhongguo chubanshe, Beijing, 2000

Sun Du, "Dianjun ru Qian fangdu hongjun changzheng qinliji" (Personal Experience of the Yunnan Army to Guizhou to Cope with the Long March Red Army), in *WZX*, no. 62

Sun Yeli & Xiong Lianghua, *Gongheguo jingji fengyun zhongde Chen Yun* (Chen Yun and the Economy of the People's Republic), Zhongyang wenxian chubanshe, Beijing, 1996

Tang Chunliang, *Li Lisan zhuan* (A Biography of Li Lisan), Heilongjiang renmin chubanshe, Harbin, 1989

Tang Chunliang, *Li Lisan quanzhuan* (A Full Biography of Li Lisan), Anhui renmin chubanshe, Hefei, 1999

Tao Lujia, *Yige shengwei shuji huiyi Mao zhuxi* (A Provincial Secretary Remembers Chairman Mao), Shanxi renmin chubanshe, Taiyuan, 1993

Tao Siju, *Xinzhongguo diyi ren gongan buzhang Luo Ruiqing* (New China's First Public Security Minister Luo Ruiqing), Qunzhong chubanshe, Beijing, 1996

Tao Siju, *Xu Zirong zhuan* (A Biography of Xu Zirong), Qunzhong chubanshe, Beijing, 1997

Tian Zengpei & Wang Taiping, eds, *Lao waijiaoguan huiyi Zhou Enlai* (Old Diplomats Remember Zhou Enlai), Shijie zhishi chubanshe, Beijing, 1998

Tong Xiaopeng, *Fengyu sishinian* (Forty Years of Winds and Rains), 2 vols, Zhongyang wenxian chubanshe, Beijing, 1995

Tu Men & Kong Di, *Gongheguo zuida yuanan* (The Biggest Unjust Case of the People's Republic), Falu chubanshe, Beijing, 1993

Tu Men & Zhu Dongli, *Kang Sheng yu "Neirendang" yuanan* (Kang Sheng and the Unjust Case of "the Inner Mongolia People's Party"), Zhonggong zhongyang dangxiao chubanshe, Beijing, 1995

Ulanhu, *Wu Lanfu nianpu* (A Chronological Record of Ulanhu), vol. 2, Inner Mongolia Ulanhu Society, ed., Zhonggong dangshi chubanshe, Beijing, 1996

Unity Publishing, ed., *Zhonggong zuijin dang de douzheng neimu* (Recent Inner Party Struggle in the CCP), Tongyi chubanshe, Chongqing, 1944, from the Archive of the Investigation Bureau, Taipei

Wang Bingnan, *Zhongmei huitan jiunian huigu* (Recollections on Nine Years of Sino-US Talks), Shijie zhishi chubanshe, Beijing, 1985

Wang Chengxian, " 'Yijianshu' shi zenyang xiechengde" (How Peng Dehuai's Letter Was Written), in *Peng Dehuai Biography* team, pp. 237–53.

Wang Defen, "Xiao Jun zai Yanan" (Xiao Jun in Yanan), *XWS*, no. 4, 1987

Wang Dongxing, *Wang Dongxing riji* (The Diaries of Wang Dongxing), Zhongguo shehui kexue chubanshe, Beijing, 1993

Wang Dongxing, "Zhongnanhai li de yitang ke" (A Lesson in Zhongnanhai), in *BNC*, no. 1, 1997

Wang Dongxing, *Wang Dongxing huiyi Mao Zedong yu Lin Biao fangeming jituan de douzheng* (Wang Dongxing Remembers Mao Zedong's Struggle with the Lin Biao Counter-revolutionary Clique), Dangdai Zhongguo chubanshe, Beijing, 1997a

Wang Enmao, *Wang Enmao riji* (The Diaries of Wang Enmao), 5 vols, Zhongyang wenxian chubanshe, Beijing, 1995

Wang Fanxi, *Shuangshan huiyilu* (A Memoir), CHOW's CO, Hong Kong, 1977

Wang Fuyi, *Xiang Ying zhuan* (A Biography of Xiang Ying), Zhonggong dangshi chubanshe, Beijing, 1995

Wang Gengjin et al., eds, *Xiangcun sanshinian* (Thirty Years in the Countryside), Nongcun duwu chubanshe, Beijing, publication suppressed

Wang Guangmei et al., *Ni suo buzhidao de Liu Shaoqi* (The Liu Shaoqi You Don't Know), Henan renmin chubanshe, Zhengzhou, 2000

Wang Guangyuan, *Hongse mushi Dong Jianwu* (Red Pastor Dong Jianwu), Zhongyang wenxian chubanshe, Beijing, 2000

Wang Guiyi, "Weiren zhi nu Li Min de jinqing wangshi" (The Today and Yesterday of a Great Man's Daughter Li Min), in *YHCQ*, no. 7, 1993

Wang Hebin, *Ziyunxuan zhuren—wo suo jiechu de Mao Zedong* (The Master of the Purple Cloud Pavilion—the Mao Zedong I Knew), Zhonggong zhongyang dangxiao chubanshe, Beijing, 1991

Wang Jialie, "Zujie zhongyang hongjun changzheng guo Qian de huiyi" (Recollections of the Central Red Army Passing through Guizhou), in *WZX*, no. 62

Wang Jianying, *Zhongguo Gongchandang zuzhishi ziliao huibian—lingdao jigou yange he chengyuan minglu* (A History of the Organization of the CCP—Development of Leading Organizations and their Members), Hongqi chubanshe, Beijing, 1983

Wang Jianying, *Zhongguo gongnong hongjun fazhanshi jianbian* (A Brief History of the Chinese Red Army), Jiefangjun chubanshe, Beijing, 1986

Wang Kexue, "Tan Furen fufu beisha an jishi" (The True Account of the Killing of Tan Furen and his Wife), in *ZH*, no. 8, 1996

Wang Li, *Xianchang lishi—wenhua dageming jishi* (Witnessing the Cultural Revolution), Oxford University Press, Hong Kong, 1993

Wang Li, "Wuhan qi erling shijian shimo" (The Ins and Outs of the Wuhan 20 July Incident), in *Zhuanji wenxue* (Biographical Literature), Beijing, no. 2, 1994

Wang Li, *Wang Li fansilu* (Reflections of Wang Li), Beixing chubanshe, Hong Kong, 2001

Wang Lianjie, *Yan Baohang* (Yan Baohang), Heilongjiang renmin chubanshe, Harbin, 2002

Wang Nianyi, *Dadongluan de niandai* (The Years of Great Mayhem), Henan renmin chubanshe, Zhengzhou, 1992

Wang Qisen et al., eds, *Fujiansheng Suweiai zhengfu lishi wenxian ziliao huibian* (Collected Archive Documents on the Fujian Soviet Government), Lujiang chubanshe, Xiamen, 1992

Wang Renzhong, selected diaries, in CCP Hubei Committee, 1993

Wang Shichun, *Jiang Weiguo de rensheng zhilu* (The Journey of Chiang Weigo's Life), Tianxia wenhua, Taipei, 1996

Wang Shi-wei, *Wang Shiwei wencun* (Writings of Wang Shi-wei), with articles about him, collected by Zhu Hongzhao, Shanghai sanlian shudian, Shanghai, 1998

Wang Shoudao, *Wang Shoudao huiyilu* (Wang Shoudao Memoirs), Jiefangjun chubanshe, Beijing, 1987

Wang Shoujia et al., eds, *Mao Zedong wannian guoyan shiwenlu* (The Poems and Prose Mao Zedong Read during his Later Years), Balong shuwu, Hong Kong, 1993

Wang Suping, *Ta hai mei jiao Jiang Qing de shihou* (Before She Was Called Jiang Qing), Beijing shiyue wenyi chubanshe, Beijing, 1993

Wang Suyuan, "Shanganning bianqu qiangjiu yundong shimo" (The Rescue Campaign in the Shaanganning Border Region), in ZDZ, no. 37

Wang Taiping, ed., *Zhonghua Renmin Gongheguo waijiao shi* (A History of the People's Republic of China's Diplomacy), 1957–1969, Shijie zhishi chubanshe, Beijing, 1998

Wang Taiping, ed., *Zhonghua Renmin Gongheguo waijiao shi* (A History of the People's Republic of China's Diplomacy), 1970–1978, Shijie zhishi chubanshe, Beijing, 1999

Wang Xingjuan, *He Zizhen de lu* (The Road of He Zizhen), Zuojia chubanshe, Beijing, 1987

Wang Xingjuan, *Li Min, He Zizhen yu Mao Zedong* (Li Min, He Zizhen and Mao Zedong), Zhongguo wenlian chubangongsi, Beijing, 1993

Wang Xiuxin, "Zhonggong liujie liuzhong quanhui" (CCP's 6th Plenum of the 6th Congress), in ZDZ, no. 46

Wang Yan et al., *Peng Dehuai zhuan* (A Biography of Peng Dehuai), Dangdai Zhongguo chubanshe, Beijing, 1993

Wang Youqin, "1966: xuesheng da laoshi de geming" (1966: a Revolution of Pupils Beating Up Teachers), in *Ershiyi shiji* (Twenty-first Century), Hong Kong, Aug. issue, 1995

Wang Youqin, "Da laoshi he da tongxue zhi jian" (Between Beating Up Teachers and Pupils), in *Ershiyi shiji* (Twenty-first Century), Hong Kong, Oct. issue, 1996

Wang Zicheng, "Shanganning bianqu de xingcheng ji yanbian" (The Formation and Development of the Shaanganning Border Region), in ZDC, no. 5, 1987

Wen Jize et al., *Yanan zhongyang yanjiuyuan huiyilu* (Reminiscences about the Yanan Central Research Institute), Zhongguo shehui kexue chubanshe & Hunan renmin chubanshe, Changsha, 1984

Wen Jize et al., *Wang Shiwei yuanan pingfan jishi* (A Record of the Rehabilitation of Wang Shiwei), Qunzhong chubanshe, Beijing, 1993

Wen Rui & Xie Jianshe, *Zhongyang suqu tudi geming yanjiu* (A Study of Land Revolution in the Central Soviet Area), Nankai daxue chubanshe, Tianjin, 1991

Wen Yu, *Zhongguo zuohuo* (Leftist Perils in China), Zhaohua chubanshe, Beijing, 1993

Weng Taisheng & Chris Pocock, *Heimao zhongdui—U2 gaokong zhenchaji de gushi* (Black Cat Squadron—the Story of the U-2), Lianjing chuban shiyegongsi, Taipei, 1990

Wu Changyi, *Qiangu gongchen Yang Hucheng* (Yang Hucheng, the Man who Performed an Eternal Service), Zhongguo wenshi chubanshe, Beijing, 1993

Wu Fuzhang, ed., *Xian shibian qinliji* (Personal Experiences of the Xian Incident), Zhongguo wenshi chubanshe, Beijing, 1996

Wu Jiangxiong, ed., *Guomindang yaoyuan shenbian de Zhonggong dixiadang* (CCP Underground by the Side of Nationalist VIPs), 2 vols, Haitian chubanshe, Shenzhen, 1995

Wu Jiqing, *Zai Mao zhuxi shenbian de rizi li* (Days by the Side of Chairman Mao), Jiangxi renmin chubanshe, Nanchang, 1989

Wu Lengxi, *Yi Mao zhuxi* (Memories of Chairman Mao), Xinhua chubanshe, Beijing, 1995

Wu Lengxi, *Shinian lunzhan* (Ten Years of Debating War), Zhongyang wenxian chubanshe, Beijing, 1999

Wu Ruilin, "Zhou zongli de yici juemi zhixing" (One Top Secret Trip by Premier Zhou), in *Zuojia wenzhai* (Writers' Digest), 15 Oct. 2002

Wu Xiuquan, *Wangshi cangsang* (My Past), Shanghai wenyi chubanshe, Shanghai, 1992

Wu Xiuquan, *Huiyi yu huainian* (Cherish the Memories), Zhonggong zhongyang dangxiao chubanshe, Beijing, 1995

Xia Daohan & Chen Liming, *Jiangxi Suqu shi* (A History of the Jiangxi Soviet Area), Jiangxi renmin chubanshe, Nanchang, 1987

Xiao Feng, ed., *Wo yu Hu Feng* (Hu Feng and I), Ningxia renmin chubanshe, Yinchuan, 1993

Xiao Jingguang, *Xiao Jingguang huiyilu* (Xiao Jingguang Memoirs), Jiefangjun chubanshe, Beijing, 1987

Xiao Ke, *Zhu–Mao hongjun ceji* (Sidelights on the Zhu–Mao Red Army), Zhonggong zhongyang dangxiao chubanshe, Beijing, 1993

Xiao Ke, *Xiao Ke huiyilu* (Xiao Ke Memoirs), Jiefangjun chubanshe, Beijing, 1997

Xiao Ke et al., *Wo qinli de zhengzhi yundong* (The Political Campaigns I Experienced), Zhongyang bianyi chubanshe, Beijing, 1998

Xiao San, *Mao Zedong tongzhi luezhuan* (A Brief Biography of Comrade Mao Zedong), Xinhua shudian, Beijing, 1949

Xiao Sike, *Chaoji shenpan* (Super Trial), Jinan chubanshe, Jinan, 1993

Xie Juezai, *Xie Juezai riji* (Diaries of Xie Juezai), Renmin chubanshe, Beijing, 1984

Xie Liuqing, *Mao Zedong he ta de qinyoumen* (Mao Zedong and his Relatives and Friends), Hebei renmin chubanshe, Shijiazhuang, 1993

Xie Youtian, *Zhonggong zhuangda zhimi* (The Secrets of the CCP's Growth), Mirror Books, 2002

Xin Ziling, *Mao Zedong quanzhuan* (A Full Biography of Mao Zedong), 4 vols, Liwen chubanshe, Hong Kong, 1995

Xin Ziling, *Lin Biao zhengzhuan* (A Biography of Lin Biao), Liwen chubanshe, Hong Kong, 2002

Xinhua News Agency, ed., *Xinhuashe huiyilu* (Memoirs about the Xinhua News Agency), Xinhua chubanshe, Beijing, 1986

Xiong Jingyu & Li Haiwen, *Zhang Hao zhuanji* (A Biography of Zhang Hao), Huazhong shifan daxue chubanshe, Wuhan, 1991

Xiong Xianghui, *Wo de qingbao yu waijiao shengya* (My Intelligence and Diplomatic Career), Zhonggong dangshi chubanshe, Beijing, 1999

Xu Xiangqian, *Lishi de huigu* (A Memoir), Jiefangjun chubanshe, Beijing, 1998

Xu Yan, *Jinmen zhizhan* (The War of Quemoy), Zhongguo guangbo dianshi chubanshe, Beijing, 1992

Xu Yan, *Zhongyin bianjie zhizhan lishi zhenxiang* (The True Story of the Sino-Indian Border War), Tiandi tushu, Hong Kong, 1993

Xu Zehao, *Wang Jiaxiang zhuan* (A Biography of Wang Jiaxiang), Dangdai zhongguo chubanshe, Beijing, 1996

Xu Zehao & Tang Xiqiang, "Xiang Ying, Zhou Zikun lieshi beihai jingguo jishi" (How Xiang Ying and Zhou Zikun Were Murdered), in *DYZ*, no. 2, 1981

Xue Yue, *Jiaofei jishi* (A Record in the Campaign against the Communist Bandits), 1936, from the Archive of the Investigation Bureau, Taipei

Xun Yuanhu et al., "Xian faxian 64 nian qian Mao Zedong zizhuan" (A Mao Zedong

Autobiography Discovered in Xian after 64 Years), in *Zuojia wenzhai* (Writers' Digest), 29 June 2001

Ya Zi & Liang Zi, *Kongfu dajienan* (The Calamity to Confucius' Home), Tiandi tushu, Hong Kong, 1992

Yan Changlin, *Jingwei Mao Zedong jishi* (My Experience as a Guard to Mao Zedong), Jilin renmin chubanshe, Changchun, 1992

Yan Daogang, "Jiang Jieshi zhuidu changzheng hongjun de bushu jiqi shibai" (Chiang Kai-shek's Plans Regarding the Long March Red Army and His Failure), in *WZX*, no. 62

Yang Chengwu, *Yang Chengwu huiyilu* (Yang Chengwu Memoirs), Jiefangjun chubanshe, Beijing, 1987

Yang Guixin, "Wo Ding Ling jiushi Ding Ling!" (I Am Indeed Ding Ling!), in *YHCQ*, no. 7, 1993

Yang Kai-hui, writings (nos. 1, 3 & 4 published, in *HDT*, no. 1 (1984), pp. 21–3; the rest unpublished):
no. 1, "Ou gan" (Thoughts), Oct. 1928
no. 2, "Gei yidi de xin" (Letter to First Cousin), Mar. 1929
no. 3, "Jian xinshang rentou erqi de beigan" (Feeling of Sadness on Reading about the Enjoyment of a Human Head), Apr. 1929
no. 4, "Nuquan gaoyu nanquan?" (Women's Rights above Men's?), 1929
no. 5, "Ji yidi" (To First Cousin), 8th day of 4th lunar month, 1929
no. 6, "Ji yidi" (To First Cousin), 1929
no. 7, "Cong liu sui dao ershiba sui" (From Aged Six to Twenty-Eight), 20 June 1929
no. 8, untitled, 28 Jan. 1930

Yang Kuisong, *Zhongjian didai de geming* (Revolution in the Middle Region), Zhonggong zhongyang dangxiao chubanshe, Beijing, 1992

Yang Kuisong, *Xian shibian xintan* (A New Study of the Xian Incident), Dongda tushu gongsi, Taipei, 1995

Yang Kuisong, *Zhonggong yu Mosike de guanxi 1920–1960* (The Relationship between the CCP and Moscow, 1920–1960), Haixiao chuban shiye youxian gongsi, Taipei, 1997

Yang Kuisong, *Mao Zedong yu Mosike de enen yuanyuan* (The Love and Hate Relationship between Mao Zedong and Moscow), Jiangxi renmin chubanshe, Nanchang, 1999

Yang Meihong, *Yingsuhua hong—wo zai Miangong shiwu nian* (Red Poppies—Fifteen Years in the Burmese Communist Party), Tiandi tushu, Hong Kong, 2001

Yang Mingwei, *Zouchu kunjing—Zhou Enlai zai 1960–1965* (Out of Hard Times—Zhou Enlai in 1960–1965), Zhongyang wenxian chubanshe, Beijing, 2000

Yang Mu, ed., *Wenge chuangjiang fengshenbang* (Cultural Revolution Militants), Tuanjie chubanshe, Beijing, 1993

Yang Shangkun, *Yang Shangkun riji* (Diaries of Yang Shangkun), 2 vols, Zhongyang wenxian chubanshe, Beijing, 2001

Yang Tianshi, *Jiangshi midang yu Jiang Jieshi zhenxiang* (The Secret Archives of Chiang Kai-shek and the Truth about Him), Shehui kexue wenxian chubanshe, Beijing, 2002

Yang Yinlu, *Wo gei Jiang Qing dang mishu* (I was Secretary to Jiang Qing), Gonghe chuban youxian gongsi, Hong Kong, 2002

Yang Zhaolin, *Baizhan jiangxing Su Zhenhua* (Star General Su Zhenhua), Jiefangjun wenyi chubanshe, Beijing, 2000

Yang Zihui et al., eds, *Zhongguo lidai renkou tongji ziliao yanjiu* (Studies of Population Statistics over the Ages in China), Gaige chubanshe, Beijing, 1995

Yang Zilie, *Zhang Guotao furen huiyilu* (Memoirs of Mrs. Zhang Guotao), Zilian chubanshe, Hong Kong, 1970

Ye Fei, *Ye Fei huiyilu* (Ye Fei Memoirs), Jiefangjun chubanshe, Beijing, 1988

Ye Xinyu, "Hongjun Tucheng zhandou yu sidu Chishui" (The Red Army's Battle at Tucheng and the Four Crossings of the Chishui River), in ZDZ, no. 34

Ye Yonglie, *Chen Boda qiren* (Chen Boda), Shidai wenyi chubanshe, Changchun, 1990

Ye Yonglie, *Wang Hongwen zhuan* (A Biography of Wang Hongwen), Shidai wenyi chubanshe, Changchun, 1993

Ye Yonglie, *Jiang Qing zhuan* (A Biography of Jiang Qing), Shidai wenyi chubanshe, Changchun, 1996

Ye Yonglie, *Zhang Chunqiao zhuan* (A Biography of Zhang Chunqiao), Shidai wenyi chubanshe, Changchun, 1996a

Ye Zilong, *Ye Zilong huiyilu* (Ye Zilong Memoirs), Zhongyang wenxian chubanshe, Beijing, 2000

Yin Jiamin, *Huang Zhen jiangjun de dashi shengya* (The Ambassadorial Career of General Huang Zhen), Jiangsu renmin chubanshe, Nanjing, 1998

Yin Qi, *Pan Hannian de qingbao shengya* (Pan Hannian's Life in Intelligence), Renmin chubanshe, Beijing, 1996

Yin Qi, *Pan Hannian zhuan* (A Biography of Pan Hannian), Zhongguo renmin gongan daxue chubanshe, Beijing, 1996a

Yongxin County Chronicle Committee, ed., *Yongxin xianzhi* (Yongxin County Chronicle), Xinhua chubanshe, Beijing, Beijing, 1992

Yu Jinan, *Zhang Guotao qiren* (Zhang Guotao), Sichuan renmin chubanshe, Chengdu, 1980

Yu Shicheng, *Deng Xiaoping yu Mao Zedong* (Deng Xiaoping and Mao Zedong), Zhonggong zhongyang dangxiao chubanshe, Beijing, 1995

Yu Xiguang, *Weibei weigan wang youguo—wenhua dageming shangshuji* (A Humble Man does not Forget his Country—A Collection of Petitions in the Cultural Revolution), Hunan renmin chubanshe, Changsha, 1989

Yuan Maogeng, *Wo jia haojie* (My Family's Calamity), Baxi Meizhou Huabao, Brazil, 1994

Yuan Wuzhen & Liang Yuelan, "Guoji youren zai Yanan" (Foreign Friends in Yanan), in ZDZ, no. 46

Yue Meiti, "1975: yanchang Tangshi Songci zhimi" (1975: the Mystery of Singing Tang and Song Poems), in *Shanghai Tan*, no. 10, 1991

Yue Xia, "Yige tongxun zhanshi dui changzheng de huiyi" (A Radio Corps Member Remembers the Long March), in WZX, no. 72

Yun Shui, *Guoji fengyun zhong de Zhongguo waijiaoguan* (Chinese Diplomats in International Winds and Clouds), Shijie zhishi chubanshe, Beijing, 1992

Yun Zhiping & Bai Yihong, *Zhongguo zhufang zhidu gaige* (The Reform of China's Housing System), Zhongguo jingji chubanshe, Beijing, 1990

Yunnan Archive, ed., *Guomindangjun zhuidu hongjun changzheng dangan shiliao xuanbian: Yunnan bufen* (Archive Documents on the Nationalist Army Chasing and Blocking the Red Army on the Long March: Yunnan Part), Dangan chubanshe, Beijing, 1987

ZDZ editorial board, ed., *Qinli zhongda lishi shijian shilu* (Personal Experiences of Important Historical Events), 5 vols, Dangjian duwu chubanshe & Zhongguo wenlian chubanshe, Beijing, 2000

Zeng Kelin, *Zeng Kelin jiangjun zishu* (General Zeng Kelin tells his Story), Liaoning renmin chubanshe, Shenyang, 1997

Zeng Weidong & Yan Fan, *Mao Zedong de zuji* (The Footsteps of Mao Zedong), Qunzhong chubanshe, Beijing, 1993

Zeng Yanxiu, "Kang Sheng diandi" (A Few Things about Kang Sheng), in *Renwu* (People), no. 2, 1994

Zeng Zhi, *Yige geming de xingcunzhe* (A Survivor of Revolution), Guangdong renmin chubanshe, Guangzhou, 2000

ZH editorial board, ed., *Gongheguo junshi miwenlu* (Secret Stories in the Military Affairs of the People's Republic), Zhongguo wenshi chubanshe, Beijing, 2001

Zhang Dequn, "60 niandai zhongsu guanxi ehua de jijianshi" (Several Events during the Sino-Soviet Split in the 1960s), in *ZDZ* editorial board, vol. 5

Zhang Guotao (also spelled Chang Kuo-tao, as in text), *Wo de huiyi* (My Reminiscences), 3 vols, Dongfang chubanshe, Beijing, 1998

Zhang Hanzhi, *Wo yu Qiao Guanhua* (Qiao Guanhua and I), Zhongguo qingnian chubanshe, Beijing, 1994

Zhang Kuitang, *Zhang Xueliang zhuan* (A Biography of Zhang Xueliang), Dongfang chubanshe, Beijing, 1991

Zhang Ning, *Chen jie* (An Autobiography), Mingbao chubanshe, Hong Kong, 1997

Zhang Suhua et al., *Shuo bujin de Mao Zedong* (Endlessly Talking about Mao), 2 vols, Liaoning renmin chubanshe, Shenyang, 1993

Zhang Suizhi, *Hongqiang nei de jingwei shengya* (A Guard's Life inside the Red Walls), Zhongyang wenxian chubanshe, Beijing, 1998

Zhang Tianrong, "Budui wenyi gongzuo zuotanhui zhaokai ji 'jiyao' chansheng de lishi kaocha" (A Study into the Convening of the Army Arts Seminar and the Birth of the "Summary"), in *DSYJ*, no. 6, 1987

Zhang Wenqiu, *Ta bian qingshan—Mao Zedong de qinjia Zhang Wenqiu huiyilu* (All Those Green Mountains—the Memoirs of Mao Zedong's in-law Zhang Wenqiu), Guangdong jiaoyu chubanshe, Guangzhou, 1993

Zhang Wentian (alias Lo Fu, as in text), "Cong Fujian shibian dao Zunyi huiyi" (From the Fujian Incident to the Zunyi Meeting), in *ZHW*, speech of 16 Dec. 1943

Zhang Wentian, *Zhang Wentian wenji* (Collected Writings of Zhang Wentian), 4 vols, Zhonggong dangshi ziliao chubanshe (vol. 1), Zhonggong dangshi chubanshe (vols 2–4), Beijing, 1990–5

Zhang Wentian, *Zhang Wentian nianpu* (A Chronological Record of Zhang Wentian), Zhang Peisen et al., eds, Zhonggong dangshi chubanshe, Beijing, 2000

Zhang Xinshi, "He Zizhen de disi ge haizi" (He Zizhen's Fourth Child), in *Hunan dangshi yuekan* (Hunan Party History Monthly), Changsha, no. 12, 1990

Zhang Xueliang, *Zhang Xueliang nianpu* (A Chronological Record of Zhang Xueliang), Zhang Youkun & Qian Jin, eds, Shehui kexue wenxian chubanshe, Beijing, 1996

Zhang Xuexin et al., *Ren Bishi zhuan* (A Biography of Ren Bishi), Zhongyang wenxian chubanshe & Renmin chubanshe, Beijing, 1995

Zhang Yaoci, *Zhang Yaoci huiyi Mao Zedong* (Zhang Yaoci Remembers Mao Zedong), Zhonggong zhongyang dangxiao chubanshe, Beijing, 1996

Zhang Ying, *Fengyu wangshi—Weiteke caifang Jiang Qing shilu* (The Past in Winds and Rains—A True Record of Witke's Interviews with Jiang Qing), Henan renmin chubanshe, Zhengzhou, 1997

Zhang Yufeng, "Mao Zedong Zhou Enlai wannian ersanshi" (Anecdotes of Mao Zedong and Zhou Enlai in Their Old Age), in *Yanhuang Zisun*, no. 1, 1989

Zhang Yufeng, "Wo gei Mao zhuxi dang mishu" (I Was Secretary to Chairman Mao), 1993, in Qiu Shi, vol. 3

Zhang Yunsheng, *Maojiawan jishi—Lin Biao mishu huiyilu* (The True Account of

Maojiawan—Memoirs of a Secretary of Lin Biao's), Chunqiu chubanshe, Beijing, 1988

Zhang Zhenglong, *Xuebai xuehong* (Snow White and Blood Red), Dadi chubanshe, Hong Kong, 1991

Zhang Zhizhong, *Zhang Zhizhong huiyilu* (Zhang Zhizhong Memoirs), Zhongguo wenshi chubanshe, Beijing, 1993

Zhang Zishen, *Zhanjiang yu tongshuai—Yang Chengwu zai Mao Zedong huixia de sishiba nian* (A General and his Commander—Yang Chengwu's Forty-Eight Years of Service under Mao Zedong), Liaoning renmin chubanshe, Shenyang, 2000

Zhang Zuoliang, *Zhou Enlai de zuihou shi nian—yiwei baojian yisheng de huiyi* (Zhou Enlai's Last Ten Years—Memoirs of a Doctor of His), Shanghai renmin chubanshe, Shanghai, 1997

Zhao Chaogou et al., *Mao Zedong fangwenji* (An Interview with Mao Zedong), Changjiang wenyi chubanshe, Wuhan, 1992

Zhao Guilai, *Cong Baotashan dao Zhongnanhai—Gao Fuyou jiyi zhong de yidai weiren* (From the Pagoda Mountain to Zhongnanhai—a Great Man in Gao Fuyou's Memory), Zhongyang wenxian chubanshe, Beijing, 1998

Zhao Rong, "Changzheng tuzhong jiujuntuan zai Qiandianchuan de zhandou licheng" (The 9th Corps' Journey during the Long March in Guizhou, Yunnan and Sichuan), in WZX, no. 56

Zhao Wumian, *Wenge danianbiao* (Cultural Revolution Chronicle), Mingjing chubanshe, USA, 1996

Zhao Zhichao, *Mao Zedong he ta de fulao xiangqin* (Mao Zedong and his Fellow Villagers), Hunan wenyi chubanshe, Changsha, 1992

Zhe Yongping et al., eds, *Nage niandai zhong de women* (We in That Era), Yuanfang chubanshe, Hohhot, 1998

Zheng Dongguo, *Wo de rongma shengya—Zheng Dongguo huiyilu* (My Military Life—Zheng Dongguo Memoirs), Tuanjie chubanshe, Beijing, 1992

Zheng Wenhan, *Mishu riji li de Peng laozong* (Old Chief Peng in a Secretary's Diary), annotated diary, Junshi kexue chubanshe, Beijing, 1998

Zheng Yi, *Hongse jinianbei* (Red Monument), Huashi wenhua gongsi, Taipei, 1993

Zhong Kan, *Kang Sheng pingzhuan* (A Critical Biography of Kang Sheng), Hongqi chubanshe, Beijing, 1982

Zhong Yimou, *Hailufeng nongmin yundong* (the Peasant Movement in Hailufeng), Guangdong renmin chubanshe, Guangzhou, 1957

Zhou (Zhou Enlai, also spelt Chou En-lai, as in text), "Dangde lishi jiaoxun" (Historical Lessons of the Party), in ZHW, speech of 10 June 1972

Zhou, *Zhou Enlai xuanji* (Selected Works of Zhou Enlai), 2 vols, Renmin chubanshe, Beijing: vol. 1, 1981; vol. 2, 1984

Zhou, *Zhou Enlai shuxin xuanji* (Selected Letters of Zhou Enlai), Zhongyang wenxian chubanshe, Beijing, 1988

Zhou, *Zhou Enlai nianpu* (A Chronological Record of Zhou Enlai), 1898–1949, CCP Archive Study Office, ed., Renmin chubanshe & Zhongyang wenxian chubanshe, Beijing, 1991

Zhou, *Zhou Enlai jingji wenxuan* (Selected Works of Zhou Enlai on Economics), Zhongyang wenxian chubanshe, Beijing, 1993

Zhou, *Zhou Enlai nianpu* (A Chronological Record of Zhou Enlai), 1949–1976, 3 vols, CCP Archive Study Office, ed., Zhongyang wenxian chubanshe, Beijing, 1997

Zhou Guoquan et al., *Wang Ming pingzhuan* (A Critical Biography of Wang Ming), Anhui renmin chubanshe, Hefei, 1990

Zhou Jihou, *Mao Zedong xiangzhang zhimi* (The Mystery of the Mao Zedong Badge), Beiyue wenyi chubanshe, Taiyuan, 1993

Zhou Jingwen, *Fengbao shi nian* (Ten Years of Storm), Shidai piping chubanshe, Hong Kong, 1959

Zhou Ming, ed., *Lishi zai zheli chensi* (History Ponders Here), 3 vols, Huaxia chubanshe, Beijing, 1987

Zhou Xiaozhou Biography team, *Zhou Xiaozhou zhuan* (Zhou Xiaozhou Biography), Hunan renmin chubanshe, Changsha, 1985

Zhou Yi, *Xianggang zuopai douzheng shi* (A History of Struggle by the Hong Kong Left), Liwen chubanshe, Hong Kong, 2002

Zhou Zuoren, *Zhou Zuoren riji* (Diaries of Zhou Zuoren), Dajia chubanshe, Zhengzhou, 1996

Zhu De, *Zhu De nianpu* (A Chronological Record of Zhu De), CCP Archive Study Office, ed., Renmin chubanshe, Beijing, 1986

Zhu Kaiyin, "Wode junshi waijiaoguan shengya" (My Career as a Military Diplomat), in *YHCQ*, no. 9, 1994

Zhu Lin, *Dashi furen huiyilu* (The Memoirs of an Ambassador's Wife), Shijie zhishi chubanshe, Beijing, 1993

Zhu Tianhong & Yi Wan, *Mao Zemin zhuan* (A Biography of Mao Zemin), Hualing chubanshe, Beijing, 1994

Zhu Yu, ed., *Li Xiannian zhuan* (A Biography of Li Xiannian), Zhongyang wenxian chubanshe, Beijing, 1999

Zhu Zheng, *1957 nian de xiaji* (Summer 1957), Henan renmin chubanshe, Zhengzhou, 1998

Zhu Zhongli, *Nuhuang meng* (Dreaming of Being an Empress), Dongfang chubanshe, Beijing, 1988

Zhu Zhongli, *Yanyang zhaowo* (Under Bright Sunshine), Beifang funu ertong chubanshe, Changchun, 1989

Zhu Zhongli, *Mao Zedong Wang Jiaxiang zai wode shenghuo zhong* (Mao Zedong and Wang Jiaxiang in My Life), Zhonggong zhongyang dangxiao chubanshe, Beijing, 1995

Zhuang Zedong & Sasaki Atsuko, *Zhuang Zedong yu Zuozuomu Dunzi* (Zhuang Zedong and Sasaki Atsuko), Zuojia chubanshe, Beijing, 1996

BIBLIOGRAPHY OF
NON-CHINESE-LANGUAGE SOURCES

I ABBREVIATIONS USED IN NOTES

APRF   Arkhiv Prezidenta Rossiiskoy Federatsii (Archive of the President of the Russian Federation), Moscow; file numbers cited refer to, respectively, the "fond," "opis" and "delo": e.g., "39/1/39" refers to fond 39, opis 1, delo 39.

AQSh   Arkivi Qëndror i Shtetit i Republikës së Shqipërisë (Central State Archive of the Republic of Albania), Tirana; numbers cited refer to fondi 14, the file "PPSh–PKK" (ALP [Albanian Party of Labor] –CCP); thus "f. 14, 1958, d. 1" refers to fondi 14, for year 1958, dosje 1.

A–UCP(b)   All-Union Communist Party (bolshevik)

AVP RF   Arkhiv Vneshney Politiki Rossiiskoy Federatsii (Archive of Foreign Policy of the Ministry of Foreign Affairs of the Russian Federation), Moscow; file numbers cited refer to, respectively, the "fond," "opis," "papka" and "delo": e.g., "0100/29/205/11" refers to fond 0100, opis 29, papka 205, delo 11.

BKP   Bulgarian Communist Party

BR   *Beijing Review* (previously *Peking Review*)

CHOC   *The Cambridge History of China* (Cambridge, UK, et al., Cambridge University Press)

CHUS   *Chinese Historians in the United States*

CLG   *Chinese Law and Government*

CPC   Communist Party of China

CPSU   Communist Party of the Soviet Union

CQ   *China Quarterly*

CWB   *Cold War International History Project Bulletin*

CWH	*Cold War History*
DVP	*Dokumentyi Vneshney Politiki* (Foreign Policy Documents, Russian Ministry of Foreign Affairs)
ECCI	Executive Committee of the Communist International
FBIS	Foreign Broadcast Information Service (CIA)
FEA	*Far Eastern Affairs* (English-language edition of *PDV*)
FRUS	*Foreign Relations of the United States* (US Department of State)
IB	*Informatsyonnyi Byulleten* (Information Bulletin), Institute of the Far East, Moscow
JAS	*Journal of Asian Studies*
JPRS	Joint Publications Research Service (US Department of Commerce, Springfield, VA)
Mao Miscellany	*Miscellany of Mao Tse-tung Thought (1949–1968)*, 2 vols (JPRS, nos 612691 & 612692); on Web/JPRS
MAS	*Modern Asian Studies*
MRTP	Schram, Stuart, ed., *Mao's Road to Power: Revolutionary Writings 1912–1949*
NA	National Archives, UK (formerly PRO)
NARA	National Archives and Records Administration, USA
NiNI	*Novaya i Noveyshaya Istoriya* (Modern and Contemporary History), Moscow
NSA	National Security Archive, Washington, DC
NT	*New Times* (English-language edition of *Novoye Vremya*)
NV	*Novoye Vremya*, Moscow
OIRVR	*Ocherki Istorii Rossiiskoy Vneshney Razvedki*
ORK	*Osobyi Rayon Kitaya*; see: Vladimirov, P. P.
PDV	*Problemyi Dalnego Vostoka* (Problems of the Far East), Moscow
PHP	Parallel History Project on NATO and the Warsaw Pact, Zurich
PR	*Peking Review* (later *Beijing Review*)
RGASPI	Rossiiskii Gosudarstvennyi Arkhiv Sotsialno-politicheskoy Istorii (Russian State Archives of Socio-political History, formerly RTsKhIDNI); file numbers cited refer to, respectively, the "fond," "opis" and "delo": e.g., "514/1/1008" refers to fond 514, opis 1, delo 1008
SAPMO	Stiftung Archiv der Parteien und Massenorganisationen der ehemaligen DDR im Bundesarchiv (Foundation for the Archives of the Parties and Mass Organizations of the Former GDR [East Germany] in the Federal Archives), Berlin
SCMP	*Survey of the China Mainland Press*
SW	*Selected Works*

Titov	Titov, A. S., *Materialyi k politicheskoy biografii Mao Tsze-duna*
TsDA	Tsentralen Durzhaven Arkhiv (Central State Archive), Sofia
TsK	Central Committee
URI	Union Research Institute, Hong Kong
VKP	*VKP(b), Komintern i Kitay*

II SOURCES BY AUTHOR NAMES

Some entries are abbreviated. Translations of titles given only for Russian and
  Bulgarian entries.

Aarons, Eric, *What's Left? Memoirs of an Australian Communist,* Penguin, Ringwood,
  Australia, 1933
Abend, Hallett, *My Years in China 1926–1941,* J. Lane/Bodley Head, London, 1944
Aczél, Tamás, "Hungary: Glad Tidings from Nanking," CQ, no. 3 (1960)
Adibekov, G. M., et al., eds, *Organizatsionnaya Struktura Kominterna 1919–1943* (The
  Organizational Structure of the Comintern), Rosspen, Moscow, 1997
Adyrkhaev, Nikolai, "Stalin's Meetings with Japanese Communists in the Summer of
  1951," *FEA,* no. 3, 1990
Aguado, Fr. Angelus, Report ("Epistola") from Yenan, 7 June 1935, *Acta Ordinis Fratrum
  Minorum,* vol. 54, fasc. 1, Florence, 1935
Akimov, V. I., ed., *Iz Istorii Internatsionalnoy Pomoshchi Sovietskogo Soyuza Kitayu i Koreye*
  (From the History of the International Aid of the Soviet Union to China and
  Korea), Institute of the Far East, Moscow, 1985
Aleksandrov-Agentov, A. M., *Ot Kollontai do Gorbacheva* (From Kollontai to Gorbachev),
  Mezhdunarodnyie Otnosheniya, Moscow, 1994
Alsop, Joseph, "On China's Descending Spiral," CQ, no. 11 (1962)
Alsop, Stewart, "A Conversation with President Kennedy," *Saturday Evening Post,*
  1 January 1966
Ambrose, Stephen E., *Nixon,* vol. 3, Simon & Schuster, New York, 1991
Anderson, Jon Lee, *Che Guevara,* Bantam, London, 1997
Anderson, K. M., & Chubaryan, A. O., eds, *Komintern i Vtoraya Mirovaya Voyna* (The
  Comintern and the Second World War), Part 1: to 22 June 1941, Pamyatnik
  Istoricheskoy Myisli, Moscow, 1994
Andrew, Christopher, & Mitrokhin, Vasili, *The Mitrokhin Archive: The KGB in Europe and
  the West,* Allen Lane, London, 1999
Anson, Robert Sam, *Exile: The Unquiet Oblivion of Richard M. Nixon,* Touchstone, New
  York, 1985
Antonkin, Alexei, *Chiens de Faience,* Équinoxe, Paris, 1983
Apter, David E., & Saich, Tony, *Revolutionary Discourse in Mao's Republic,* Harvard
  University Press, Cambridge et al., 1994
Arbatov, Georgi, *The System,* Times Books, New York, 1992
Armstrong, J. D., *Revolutionary Diplomacy,* University of California Press, Berkeley et
  al., 1977
Ashton, Basil, et al., "Famine in China, 1958–1961," *Population and Development Review,*
  vol. 10, no. 4 (1984)
Atwood, Christopher P., "Sino-Soviet Diplomacy and the Second Partition of
  Mongolia, 1945–1946," in Kotkin, Stephen, & Elleman, Bruce A., eds, *Mongolia in
  the Twentieth Century,* Sharpe, Armonk et al., c.1999

Avreyski, Nikola, *Georgi Dimitrov i Revolyutsionnoto Dvizheniye v Kitaye* (Georgi Dimitrov and the Revolutionary Movement in China), Institute for the History of the BKP at the BKP CC, Sofia, 1987

Balanta, Martín, "Rupture Between Castro and Peiping," *Segunda Republica* (La Paz), 30 Jan 1966, in JPRS, *Translations on International Communist Developments*, no. 810

Band, Claire & William, *Dragon Fangs: Two Years with Chinese Guerrillas*, Allen & Unwin, London, 1947

Banister, Judith, "Population Policy and Trends," CQ, no. 100 (1984)

Bao Ruo-Wang (Jean Pasqualini) & Chelminski, Rudolph, *Prisoner of Mao*, Deutsch, London, 1975

Barmin, Valery, "Xinjiang in the History of Soviet-Chinese Relations in 1918–1931," *FEA*, no. 4, 1999

Barnouin, Barbara, & Yu Changgen, *Chinese Foreign Policy during the Cultural Revolution*, Kegan Paul, London & New York, 1998

Baturov, Vladimir, "Kosmicheskii Skachok Pekina" (Peking's Cosmic Leap), *NV*, nos 2–3, 1999

Becker, Jasper, *Hungry Ghosts: China's Secret Famine*, J. Murray, London, 1996

Benton, Gregor, *New Fourth Army*, University of California Press, Berkeley et al., 1999

Berezhkov, Valentin M., *At Stalin's Side*, Birch Lane, New York, 1994

Beria, Sergo, *Moy Otets—Lavrentii Beria* (My Father—Lavrentii Beria), Sovremmenik, Moscow, 1994

Beria, Sergo, *Beria: My Father*, Duckworth, London, 2001

Bertram, James M., *First Act in China*, Viking, New York, 1938

Blum, John Morton, ed., *The Price of Vision: The Diary of Henry A. Wallace, 1942–1946*, Houghton Mifflin, Boston, 1973

Bonavia, David, *Verdict in Peking*, Burnett Books, London, 1984

Borisov, O., *The Soviet Union and the Manchurian Revolutionary Base (1945–1949)*, Progress, Moscow, 1977

Borisov, Oleg, *From the History of Soviet-Chinese Relations in the 1950s*, Progress, Moscow, 1982

Boudarel, Georges, "L'idéocratie importée au Vietnam avec le maoisme," in Boudarel, Georges, et al., eds, *La bureaucratie au Vietnam*, L'Harmattan, Paris, 1983

Braun, Otto, "Mao Tse-tung's Climb to Power," *FEA* no. 1, 1974

Braun, Otto, *A Comintern Agent in China 1932–1939*, Hurst, London, 1982

Brezhnev, A. A., *Kitay: Ternistyi Put k Dobrososedstvu* (China: The Thorny Road to Good Neighborliness), Mezhdunarodnyie Otnosheniya, Moscow, 1998

Browder, Earl, "The American Communist Party in the Thirties," in Simon, Rita James, ed., *As We Saw the Thirties*, University of Illinois Press, Urbana, 1967

Brun-Zechowoj, Walerij, *Manfred Stern—General Kleber*, Trafo-Verl. Weist, Berlin, 2000

Bulag, Uradyn E., *The Mongols at China's Edge*, Rowman & Littlefield, Lanham et al., 2002

Bundy, William, *A Tangled Web: The Making of Foreign Policy in the Nixon Presidency*, Hill & Wang, New York, 1998

Burr, William, ed., *The Kissinger Transcripts: The Top-secret Talks with Beijing and Moscow*, Free Press, New York, 1999 [Burr 1999a] [Web/NSA]

Burr, William, ed., *China and the United States . . . 1960–1998*, NSA Electronic Briefing Book No.1, 1999 [Burr 1999b]

Burr, William, "Sino-American Relations, 1969: The Sino-Soviet Border War," *CWH*, vol. 1, no. 3 (2001)

Burr, William, ed., *The Beijing–Washington Back Channel and Henry Kissinger's Secret Trip to*

China, September 1970–July 1971, NSA Electronic Briefing Book No. 66, 2002 [Web/NSA]

Byron, John, and Pack, Robert, *The Claws of the Dragon: Kang Sheng*, Simon & Schuster, New York, 1992

Cabot, John Moors, *First Line of Defense*, Georgetown University, Washington, DC, n.d.

Cadart, Claude, & Cheng Yingxiang, eds, *Mémoires de Peng Shuzhi: L'Envol du communisme en Chine*, Gallimard, Paris, 1983

Carrington, Lord, *Reflect on Things Past*, Collins, London, 1988

Carton de Wiart, Adrian, *Happy Odyssey*, Cape, London, 1950

Chang, Gordon H., *Friends and Enemies: The United States, China, and the Soviet Union, 1948–1972*, Stanford University Press, Stanford, 1990

Chang, Jung, *Wild Swans: Three Daughters of China*, Simon & Schuster, New York, 1991

Chang Kuo-t'ao, *The Rise of the Chinese Communist Party*, University of Kansas Press, Lawrence, 1971, 1972, 2 vols

Chang, Sidney H., & Myers, Ramon H., eds, *The Storm Clouds Clear Over China: The Memoirs of Ch'en Li-fu*, Hoover Institution Press, Stanford, 1994

Chen Jian, *China's Road to the Korean War*, Columbia University Press, New York, 1994

Chen Jian, "A Crucial Step toward the Sino-Soviet Schism: The Withdrawal of Soviet Experts from China, July 1960," *CWB*, no. 8–9 (1996–7)

Chen Jian, *Mao's China and the Cold War*, University of North Carolina Press, Chapel Hill & London, 2001

Chen Zuezhao, *Surviving the Storm*, Sharpe, Armonk et al., 1990

Chen Yun, "Outline for Communicating the Zunyi Enlarged Politburo Meeting" (1935), in Saich 1996

Chen Yung-fa, "The Blooming Poppy under the Red Sun: The Yan'an Way and the Opium Trade," in Saich, Tony, and van de Ven, Hans J., eds, *New Perspectives on the Chinese Communist Revolution*, Sharpe, Armonk et al., 1995

Chen Yung-fa, "Suspect History," in Hershatter, Gail, et al., eds, *Remapping China*, Stanford University Press, Stanford, 1996

Cheng Hsueh-chia, "Mao Tse-tung Before the Formation of the Chinese Communist Party," *Issues & Studies*, Nov. 1973

Cheng, J. Chester, "The Mystery of the Battle of La-tzu-k'ou in the Long March," *JAS*, vol. 31, no. 3 (1972)

Cheo Ying, Esther, *Black Country to Red China*, Cresset, London et al., 1987

Cherepanov, A. I., *As Military Adviser in China*, Progress, Moscow, 1982

Chi, Wen-shun, "Water Conservancy in Communist China," *CQ*, no. 23 (1965)

Chiang Ching-kuo, "My Days in Soviet Russia" (1937) in Cline, Ray S., *Chiang Ching-kuo Remembered*, US Global Strategy Council, Washington, DC, 1989

Chiang Kai-shek, *A Fortnight in Sian: Extracts from a Diary*, China Publishing Co., Taipei, 1985

Chiang Kai-shek, *Soviet Russia in China*, Harrap, London, 1957

Chin Peng, *My Side of History*, Media Masters, Singapore, 2003

Chinese Communist Party, Central Committee, Party History Research Center, comp., *History of the Chinese Communist Party—A Chronology of Events*, Foreign Languages Publishing House, Beijing, 1991

Chow Ching-wen, *Ten Years of Storm*, Holt, Rinehart & Winston, New York, 1960

Chuev, F., *Molotov*, Terra, Moscow, 1999

Chuikov, Vasili, "Velik Internatsionalist" (A Great Internationalist), in Institut po Istoriya na BKP pri TsK na BKP, *Spomeni za Georgi Dimitrov* (Memories of Georgi Dimitrov), Partizdat, Sofia, 1971, vol. 2

Chuikov, V. I., *Missiya v Kitaye* (Mission to China), Nauka, Moscow, 1981

Clemens, Walter C., *The Arms Race and Sino-Soviet Relations*, Hoover, Stanford, 1968

Cohen, Warren, "Conversations with Chinese Friends: Zhou Enlai's Associates Reflect on Chinese-American Relations in the 1940s and the Korean War," *Diplomatic History*, vol. 11, no. 3 (1987)

"COMINT and the PRC intervention in the Korean War" [author's name deleted], *Cryptologic Quarterly*, summer 1996

Copper, John F., *China's Foreign Aid*, Heath, Lexington, 1976

Copper, John F., "China's Military Assistance," in Copper, John F., & Papp, Daniel S., eds, *Communist Nations' Military Assistance*, Westview, Boulder, 1983

Cressy-Marcks, Violet, *Journey into China*, Dutton, New York, 1942

Croft, Michael, *Red Carpet to China*, The Travel Book Club, London, 1958

Dai Qing, *Wang Shiwei and "Wild Lilies": Rectification and Purges in the Chinese Communist Party 1942–1944*, Sharpe, Armonk et al., 1994

Dalai Lama, *Freedom in Exile*, HarperCollins, New York, 1990

Dalin, S., "Chinese Memoirs," *FEA*, no. 2, 1975

Dalin, S., *Kitayskiye memuaryi* (Chinese Memoirs), Nauka, Moscow, 1982

Dallin, Alexander, & Firsov, F. I., eds, *Dimitrov and Stalin 1934–1943: Letters from the Soviet Archives*, Yale University Press, New Haven et al., 2000

Damaskin, Igor, with Elliott, Geoffrey, *Kitty Harris: The Spy with Seventeen Names*, St. Ermin's, London, 2001

Davies, R. W., et al., eds, *The Stalin-Kaganovich Correspondence 1931–36*, Yale University Press, New Haven et al., 2003

de Beauvoir, Simone, *The Long March*, World Publishing Co., Cleveland, 1958

de Segonzac, A., *Visa for Peking*, Heinemann, London et al., 1956

Deng Xiaoping, *Selected Works*, Foreign Languages Press, Beijing, 1984

Dennis, Peggy, *The Autobiography of an American Communist*, L. Hill, Westport, 1997

Dimitrov, Georgi, *Dnevnik* (Diary), Sofia, Izd. "Sv. Kliment Okhridski," 1997 [abbreviated English version: Banac, Ivo, ed., *The Diary of Georgi Dimitrov*, Yale University Press, New Haven et al., 2003]

Dimitrov, Georgi, cables regarding China 1935–1943 in English in *http://www.revolutionarydemocracy.org/rdv2n2/dimitrov.htm* [Web/Dimitrov]

Dobrynin, Anatoly, *In Confidence*, Random House, New York, 1995

Documents on German Foreign Policy, Series D, 1937–1945, vol. 11, HMSO, London, 1961

Dolinin, Aleksandr, "Kak nashi raketchiki kitaytsev obuchali" (How our Rocket Men Trained the Chinese), *Krasnaya Zvezda*, nos 105–6, 1995

Domenach, Jean-Luc, *Chine: l'archipel oublié*, Fayard, Paris, 1992

Domenach, Jean-Luc, *The Origins of the Great Leap Forward: The Case of One Chinese Province*, Westview, Boulder, 1995

Dominguez, Jorge I., *Cuba: Order & Revolution*, Harvard University Press, Cambridge, Mass., 1978

Doumkova, Iskra, "China After the 'Great Leap Forward'," in Näth

DPRK Report, no. 23 (Mar.–Apr. 2000), Center for Nonproliferation Studies, Monterey, CA, 2000

Drannikov, Valerii, "Iz istorii velikoy druzhbyi" (From the History of the Great Friendship), *Vlast*, no. 8, 1999

Drozdov, Yurii, *Vyimyisel Isklyuchen* (Fabrication Excluded), Almanakh Vyimpel, Moscow, 1996

Duclos, Jacques, *Mémoires: Dans la mêlée 1952–1958*, Fayard, Paris, 1972

Eisenhower, Dwight D., *Public Papers of the Presidents of the United States, Dwight D. Eisenhower, 1953*, US Government Printing Office, Washington, DC, 1953

Eisenhower, Julie Nixon, *Special People*, Simon & Schuster, New York, 1977

Elegant, Robert, *Mao's Great Revolution*, Weidenfeld & Nicolson, London, 1971

Eliades, George C., "Once More Unto the Breach: Eisenhower, Dulles, and Public Opinion during the Offshore Islands Crisis of 1958," *Journal of American-East Asian Relations*, vol. 2, no. 4 (1993)

Elizavetin, A., "Kosygin-Zhou Talks at Beijing Airport," *FEA*, nos. 4–6, 1992, & nos. 1–3, 1993

Elleman, Bruce A., *Diplomacy and Deception: The Secret History of Sino-Soviet Diplomatic Relations, 1917–1927*, Sharpe, Armonk et al., 1997

Esherick, Joseph W., "Deconstructing the Construction of the Party-State: Gulin County in the Shaan-Gan-Ning Border Region," *CQ*, no. 140 (1994)

Eudin, Xenia Joukoff, & North, Robert C., *Soviet Russia and the East 1920–1927*, Stanford University Press, Stanford, 1957

Fallaci, Oriana, *Intervista con la storia*, Rizzoli, Milan, 1990

Fan Shuo, "Tempestuous October—A Chronicle of the Complete Collapse of the 'Gang of Four'," *FBIS-CHI-89-029* (14 Feb. 1989)

Farid, Abdel Magid, *Nasser: The Final Years*, Ithaca/Garnet Press, Reading, 1994

Farnsworth, Robert M., *From Vagabond to Journalist: Edgar Snow in Asia 1928–1941*, University of Missouri Press, Columbia, 1996

Fedorenko, N., "The Stalin-Mao Summit in Moscow," *FEA*, no. 2, 1989

Fedorenko, N., "Khrushchev's Visit to Beijing," *FEA*, no. 2, 1990

Fedorenko, Nikolai, "Mne slushali zhivyiye bogi" (Living Gods Listened to Me), *NV*, no. 6, 1999

Fedorenko, Nikolai T., "Stalin and Mao Zedong," *Russian Politics and Law*, vol. 32, no. 4 (1994) & vol. 33, no. 1 (1995)

Fei, Hsiao-Tung, and Chang Chih-I, *Earthbound China*, Chicago University Press, Chicago, 1945

Felber, Roland, "China and the Claim for Democracy," in Näth

Feltrinelli, Carlo, *Senior Service*, Feltrinelli, Milan, 1999

Fetzer, James, "Clinging to Containment: China Policy," in Paterson, Thomas G., ed., *Kennedy's Quest for Victory: American Foreign Policy 1961–63*, Oxford University Press, Oxford et al., 1989

Filatov, L. V., "Nauchno-Tekhnicheskoye Sotrudnichestvo mezhdu SSSR i KNR (1949–1966)" (Scientific-Technical Co-operation between the USSR and the PRC), *IB*, no. 65 (1975)

Floyd, David, *Mao against Khrushchev: A Short History of the Sino-Soviet Conflict*, Pall Mall, London, 1964

Ford, Harold P., "Modern Weapons and the Sino-Soviet Estrangement," *CQ*, no. 18 (1964)

Foreign Relations of the United States (various years, 1930–68)

Friedman, Edward, "Nuclear Blackmail and the End of the Korean War," *Modern China*, vol. 1, no. 1 (1975)

Fursenko, A. A., et al., eds, *Prezidium TsK KPSS 1954–1964* (The Presidium of the CC of the CPSU), vol. 1, Rosspen, Moscow, 2003

Fuwa, Tetsuzo, *Interference & Betrayal: Japanese Communist Party Fights Back Against Soviet Hegemonism*, Japan Press Service, Tokyo, 1994

Gaiduk, Ilya V., *The Soviet Union and the Vietnam War*, Dee, Chicago, 1996

Galenovich, Y. M., *Gibel Liu Shaotsi* (The Fall of Liu Shao-chi), Vostochnaya Literatura/Russian Academy of Sciences, Moscow, 2000

Galenovich, Y. M., *Rossiya i Kitay v XX veke: Granitsa* (Russia and China in the 20th Century: The Frontier), "Izograf," Moscow, 2001

Ganshin, G., & Zazerskaya, T., "Pitfalls Along the Path of 'Brotherly Friendship'," *FEA*, no. 6. 1994

Gao, James Z., "From Rural Revolution to Urban Revolutionization: a case study of Luzhongnan," *Journal of Contemporary China*, no. 10, 2001

Garson, R., "Lyndon B. Johnson and the China Enigma," *Journal of Contemporary History*, vol. 32, no. 1 (1997)

Garver, John W., *Protracted Contest: Sino-Indian Rivalry in the Twentieth Century*, University of Washington Press, Seattle et al., 2001

Gates, Robert M., *From the Shadows*, Simon & Schuster, New York, 1997

Gillin, Donald G., with Etter, Charles, "Staying On: Japanese Soldiers and Civilians in China, 1945–1949," *JAS*, vol. 42, no. 1 (1983)

Glunin, V. I., *Kommunisticheskaya Partiya Kitaya nakanune i vo vremya natsionalnoy revolyutsii*, (The CCP on the eve of and at the time of the national revolution), 1921–27, vol. 2: *KPK v period vyisshego podyema i porazheniya revolyutsii* (The CCP in the period of the rise and defeat of the revolution), USSR Academy of Sciences/Institute of the Far East, Moscow, 1975

Glunin, V. I., "Grigori Voitinsky (1893–1953)" in Astafiev, G. V., et al., eds, *Vidnyie Soviet-skiye Kommunistyi—Uchastniki Kitayskoy Revolyutsii* (Eminent Soviet Communists—Participants in the Chinese Revolution), Nauka, Moscow, 1970

Gobarev, Viktor M., "Soviet Policy Toward China: Developing Nuclear Weapons 1949–69," *Journal of Slavic Military Studies*, vol. 12, no. 4 (1999)

Goncharenko, Sergei, "Sino-Soviet Military Cooperation," in Westad et al. 1998

Goncharov, Sergei, & Usov, Victor, "Kosygin-Zhou Talks at Beijing Airport," *FEA*, nos 4–6, 1992

Goncharov, Sergei N., et al., *Uncertain Partners: Stalin, Mao, and the Korean War*, Stanford University Press, Stanford, 1993

Gorriti, Gustavo, *The Shining Path*, University of North Carolina Press, Chapel Hill, 1999

Graham, Billy, speech, 2 Nov. 1971, in Institute of Directors, *Annual Conference of the Institute of Directors*, IoD, London, 1971

Greene, Felix, *The Wall has Two Sides*, J. Cape, London, 1970

Grey, Anthony, *Hostage in Peking*, Weidenfeld & Nicolson, London, 1988

Grigoriev, A. M. *Kommunisticheskaya Partiya Kitaya v nachalnyi period sovietskogo dvizheniya* (The CCP in the initial period of the soviet movement, July 1927—September 1931), USSR Academy of Sciences/Institute of the Far East, Moscow, 1976

Grigoriev, A. M. "Politika Kominterna v otnoshenii KPK" (Comintern Policy toward the CCP), *NiNI*, no. 2, 1982

Grigoriev, Alexander M., "The Far Eastern Bureau of the ECCI in China, 1929–1931," in Leutner [Grigoriev 2002a]

Grigoriev, A. M., "Kitayskaya politika VKP(b) i Kominterna, 1920–1937" (The China Policy of the A-UCP (b) and the Comintern), in Chubarian, A. O., ed., *Istoriya Kommunisticheskogo Internatsionala 1919–1943* (History of the Communist International), Nauka, Moscow, 2002 [Grigoriev 2002b]

Grishin, V. V., *Ot Khrushcheva do Gorbacheva* (From Khrushchev to Gorbachev), ASPOL, Moscow, 1996

Han Suyin, *My House Has Two Doors*, Triad/Granada, London, 1982

Han Suyin, *Eldest Son: Zhou Enlai and the Making of Modern China, 1898–1976*, Cape, London, 1994

Hanson, Haldore, *"Humane Endeavor": The Story of the China War*, Farrar & Rinehart, New York, 1939

Hanson, Haldore, *Fifty Years Around the Third World*, Fraser, Burlington, 1986

Harris, Lillian Craig, *China Considers the Middle East*, I. B. Tauris, London et al., 1993

Haslam, Jonathan, *The Soviet Union and the Threat from the East, 1933–41: Moscow, Tokyo and the Prelude to the Pacific War*, Macmillan, Basingstoke, 1992

Hayter, William, *A Double Life*, Hamish Hamilton, London, 1974

Heath, Edward, *The Course of My Life*, Hodder & Stoughton, London, 1998

Hébert, Jacques, & Trudeau, Pierre Elliott, *Two Innocents in Red China*, Oxford University Press, Toronto, 1968

Heikal, Mohamed, *Nasser*, New English Library, London, 1972

Heinzig, Dieter, *The Soviet Union and Communist China, 1945–1950*, Sharpe, Armonk et al., 2003

Hermes, Walter G., *Truce Tent and Fighting Front*, Office of the Chief of Military History, US Army, Washington, DC, 1966

Hilsman, Roger, *To Move a Nation*, Doubleday, Garden City, 1967

Hinton, Harold C., *Communist China in World Politics*, Macmillan, London, 1966

Hoan, Hoang Van, *A Drop in the Ocean*, Foreign Languages Press, Beijing, 1988

Holdridge, John H., *Crossing the Divide: An Insider's Account of the Normalization of U.S.–China Relations*, Rowman & Littlefield, Lanham et al., 1997

Horne, Gerald, *Race Woman: The Lives of Shirley Graham Du Bois*, New York University Press, New York et al., 2000

Hosoya, Chihiro, "The Japanese-Soviet Neutrality Pact," in Morley, James W., ed., *The Fateful Choice: Japan's Advance into Southeast Asia, 1939–1941*, Columbia University Press, New York, 1980

Hoxha, Enver, *Reflections on China*, vol. 1, 8 Nëntori, Tirana, 1979

Hoxha, Enver, *The Khrushchevites*, 8 Nëntori, Tirana, 1980

Hoyt, Frederick B., "The Summer of "30: American Policy and Chinese Communism," *Pacific Historical Review*, vol. 46, no. 2 (1977)

Hsiao, Tso-liang, *Power Relations Within the Chinese Communist Movement, 1930–1934*, University of Washington Press, Seattle, 1961

Hsu, King-yi, *Political Mobilization and Economic Extraction: Chinese Communist Agrarian Policies during the Kiangsi Period*, Garland, New York, 1980

Hsu, U.T., *The Invisible Conflict*, China Viewpoints, Hong Kong, 1958

Hsüeh, Chün-tu, "Chang Kuo-t'ao and the Chinese Communist Movement," in Hsüeh, Chün-tu, ed., *Revolutionary Leaders of Modern China*, Oxford University Press, New York, 1971

Hua Chang-ming, *La condition féminine et les communistes chinois en action: Yan'an 1935–1946*, Éditions de l'École des Hautes Études en Sciences Sociales, Paris, 1981

Huang, Jing, *Factionalism in Chinese Communist Politics*, Cambridge University Press, Cambridge et al., 2000

Huang Zheng, "The Injustice Done to Liu Shaoqi" (Siao, Richard, ed.), *CLG*, vol. 32, no. 3 (1999)

Hussain, Athar, & Feuchtwang, Stephan, "The People's Livelihood and the Incidence of Poverty," in Feuchtwang, Stephan, et al., eds, *Transforming China's Economy in the Eighties*, Zed, London, 1988

I Fu-En, *My Memoirs*, Li Ching Cultural & Educational Foundation, Taipei, 2003

Ickes, Harold L., *The Secret Diary of Harold L. Ickes*, vol. 2, Simon & Schuster, New York, 1954

Il Ponte, "Mosca Novembre 1960, Polacchi e Cinesi a Confronto" (minutes of Liu-Gomulka talk, Nov. 1960), vol. 37, nos. 11–12 (1981)

Isaacs, Harold R., "Notes on a Conversation with H. Sneevliet," *CQ*, no. 45 (1971)

Iwai, Eiichi, *Memories of Shanghai* (Nagoya, Memories of Shanghai Publishing Committee, 1983) [in Japanese]

Jackson, Robert, *Air War over Korea*, Ian Allan, London, 1973

Jankowiak, William R., "The Last Hurrah? Political Protest in Inner Mongolia," *Australian Journal of Chinese Affairs*, no. 19–20 (1988)

Jin Qiu, *The Culture of Power: The Lin Biao Incident in the Cultural Revolution*, Stanford University Press, Stanford, 1999

Johnson, Cecil, *Communist China and Latin America, 1959–1967*, Columbia University Press, New York et al., 1970

Joyaux, François, *La Chine et le règlement du premier conflit d'Indochine (Genève 1954)*, Sorbonne, Paris, 1979

JPRS, *Collected Works of Mao Tse-tung (1917–1949)*, vol. 9 [Web/JPRS]

Judis, John B., *William F. Buckley*, Simon & Schuster, New York et al., 1988

Kahn, E. J., *China Hands*, Viking, New York, 1975

Kampen, Thomas, "Wang Jiaxiang, Mao Zedong and the Triumph of Mao Zedong Thought (1935–1945)," *MAS*, vol. 23, no. 4 (1989)

Kampen, Thomas, *Mao Zedong, Zhou Enlai and the Evolution of the Chinese Communist Leadership*, NIAS, Copenhagen, 2000

Kapitsa, M., "Na raznyikh parallelyakh" (On Different Parallels), *Azia i Afrika*, no. 5, 1995

Kapitsa, M. S., *Na raznyikh parallelyakh* (On Different Parallels), Kniga i Biznes, Moscow, 1996

Kaple, Deborah A., *Dream of a Red Factory: The Legacy of High Stalinism in China*, Oxford University Press, New York, 1994

Kardelj, Edvard, *Reminiscences*, Blond & Briggs, London, 1982

Karmen, R., *God v Kitaye* (A Year in China), Sovietskii Pisatel, Moscow, 1941

Kartunova, A. I., "Vstrechi v Moskve s Tszyan Tsin, Zhenoy Mao Tszeduna" (Meetings in Moscow with Jiang Qing, the Wife of Mao Tse-tung), *Kentavr*, no. 1–2, 1992

Kase, Toshikazu, "A Failure of Diplomacy," in Cook, Haruko Taya & Cook, Theodore F., eds, *Japan at War*, New Press, New York, 1992

Kau, Michael Y. M., & Leung, John K., *The Writings of Mao Zedong 1949–1976*, vol. 1: September 1949–December 1955, Sharpe, Armonk et al., 1986; vol 2: see Leung & Kau

Kau, Michael Y. M., ed., *The Lin Piao Affair*, IASP, White Plains, 1975

Khrushchev, Nikita, *Khrushchev Remembers*, Penguin, Harmondsworth, 1977, 2 vols [Khrushchev 1977]

Khrushchev, Nikita, *Khrushchev Remembers: The Glasnost Tapes*, Little, Brown, Boston, 1990

Khrushchev, Sergei N., *Nikita Khrushchev and the Creation of a Superpower*, Pennsylvania State University, University Park, 2000

Kiernan, Ben, "Maoism and Cambodia," unpublished paper, 1991

Kim, Samuel S., *China, the United Nations, and World Order*, Princeton University Press, Princeton, 1979

Kimball, Warren F., *Forged in War: Roosevelt, Churchill, and the Second World War*, Morrow, New York, 1997

Kirkby, R. J. R., *Urbanisation in China*, Croom Helm, London et al., 1985

Kissinger, Henry, *White House Years*, Little, Brown, Boston, 1979

Kissinger, Henry, *Years of Upheaval*, Little, Brown, Boston, 1982

Kissinger, Henry, "The Philosopher and the Pragmatist," *Time*, 3 March 1997

Klehr, Harvey, et al., eds, *The Secret World of American Communism*, Yale University Press, New Haven et al., 1995

Kojima, Masaru, ed., *The Record of the Talks Between the Japanese Communist Party and the*

Communist Party of China: How Mao Zedong Scrapped the Joint Communiqué, Japanese Communist Party, Tokyo, 1980

Kolpakidi, Aleksandr, & Prokhorov, Dmitrii, *Imperiya GRU* (The GRU Empire), Olma-Press, Moscow, 2000, 2 vols [2000a, 2000b]

Kolpakidi, Aleksandr, & Prokhorov, Dmitrii, *Vneshnyaya Razvedka Rossii* (Russia's Foreign Intelligence), Olma-Press, Moscow, 2001

Kordon, Bernardo, "Mi entrevista con Mao Tse-Tung," in Bignozzi, Juana, ed., *Testigos de China*, Carlos Pérez, Buenos Aires, 1962

Kovalev, Ivan, "The Stalin-Mao Dialogue," *FEA*, nos. 1 & 2, 1992 [Kovalev 1992a, 1992b]

Kovalev, I. V., "Zapiska I. V. Kovaleva ot 24 dekabrya 1949" ("Report" of 24 Dec. 1949), *NiNI*, no. 1, 2004

Kovner, Milton, "Communist China's Foreign Aid to Less Developed Countries," in US Congress, Joint Economic Committee

Kozlov, V. A., & Mironenko, S. V., eds, *Arkhiv Noveyshey Istorii Rossii*, vol. 1: *"Osobaya Papka" I. V. Stalina* (Stalin's "Special File"), Blagovest, Moscow, 1994

Kramer, Mark, "The Soviet Foreign Ministry Appraisal of Sino-Soviet Relations on the Eve of the Split," *CWB*, nos. 6–7 (1995–6)

Kriukov, Mikhail, "The Tortuous Road to Alliance: Soviet Russia and Sun Yatsen (1918–1923)," part 2, *FEA*, no. 3, 1999

Krivitsky, W. G., *I Was Stalin's Agent*, Faulkner, Cambridge, 1992

Krymov, A. G. [Kuo Shao-tang], *Istoriko-memuarnyiye zapiski kitayskogo revolyutsionera* (Historical-Memoir Notes of a Chinese Revolutionary), Nauka, Moscow, 1990

Kudashev, R., "My Meetings with Mao and Jiang," *International Affairs* (Moscow), vol. 44, no. 3 (1998)

Kulik, B. T., "Kitayskaya Narodnaya Respublika v period stanovleniya (1949–1952)" (The PRC in the Period of its Establishment), (Part 1) *PDV*, no. 5, 1994

Kulik, B. T., "SShA i Tayvan protiv KNR, 1949–1952" (The USA and Taiwan versus the PRC), *NiNI*, no. 5, 1995

Kulik, B. T., *Sovietsko-Kitayskii Raskol* (The Soviet-Chinese Split), Russian Academy of Sciences/Institute of the Far East, Moscow, 2000

Kuo Chien, "The Novel *Battle of Xiang Jiang* is Banned," part 1, *FBIS-CHI-91-016* (24 Jan. 1991)

Kuo, Mercy A., *Contending with Contradictions: China's Policy toward Soviet Eastern Europe and the Origins of the Sino-Soviet Split, 1953–1960*, Lexington Books, Lanham, 2001

Kuo, Warren, *Analytical History of the Chinese Communist Party*, 4 vols, Institute of International Relations, Taipei, 1968–71

Kuusinen, Aino, *Before and After Stalin*, M. Joseph, London, 1974

Lajolo, Davide, "Mao dalla parte di Krusciov," *l'Europeo*, 18 Aug. 1963

Lankov, A. N., *Severnaya Koreya* (North Korea), Vostochnaya Literatura, Russian Academy of Sciences, Moscow, 1995

Lankov, Andrei N., "Kim Takes Control: The 'Great Purge' in North Korea, 1956–1960," *Korean Studies*, vol. 26, no. 1 (2002)

Lardy, Nicholas R., "The Chinese Economy under Stress, 1958–1965," in *CHOC*, vol. 14, part 1, Cambridge University Press, Cambridge et al., 1987

Larin, Aleksandr, *Dva Prezidenta* (Two Presidents), Academia, Moscow, 2000

Law Yu Fai, *Chinese Foreign Aid*, Breitenbach, Saarbrücken et al., 1984

Lebedeva, N. S., and Narinsky, M. M., Introduction to Anderson & Chubaryan

Ledovsky, A. M., *Delo Gao Gana–Zhao Shushi* (The Gao Gang–Rao Shushi Affair), USSR Academy of Sciences/Institute of the Far East, Moscow, 1990

Ledovsky, Andrei, "Mikoyan's Secret Mission to China in January and February 1949," *FEA*, nos. 2 & 3, 1995 [Ledovsky 1995a, Ledovsky 1995b]

Ledovsky, Andrei, "The Moscow Visit of a Delegation of the Communist Party of China in June to August 1949," *FEA* nos. 4 & 5, 1996 [Ledovsky 1996a, Ledovsky 1996b]

Ledovsky, A. M., *SSSR i Stalin v sudbakh Kitaya* (The USSR and Stalin in the Destinies of China), Pamyatnik Istoricheskoy Myisli, Moscow, 1999

Ledovsky, Andrei, "12 sovetov I. V. Stalina rukovodstvu kompartii Kitaya" (12 Recommendations of Stalin to the Leadership of the CCP), *NiNI*, no. 1, 2004

Lee, Lily Xiao Hong, & Wiles, Sue, *Women of the Long March*, Allen & Unwin, St. Leonard's, 1999

Leitenberg, Milton, "Deaths in Wars and Conflicts Between 1945 and 2000," Cornell University, Peace Studies Program, Occasional Paper 29, Ithaca, 2003

Leonard, Raymond W., *Secret Soldiers of the Revolution: Soviet Military Intelligence, 1918–1933*, Greenwood, Westport et al., 1999

Leonard, Royal, *I Flew for China: Chiang Kai-shek's Personal Pilot*, Doubleday, Doran, Garden City, 1942

Lescot, Patrick, *L'Empire Rouge: Moscou-Pékin 1919–1989*, Belfond, Paris, 1999

Leung, John K., & Kau, Michael Y. M., *The Writings of Mao Zedong 1949–1976*, vol. 2: January 1956–December 1957, Sharpe, Armonk et al., 1992

Leutner, Mechthild, et al., eds, *The Chinese Revolution in the 1920s*, RoutledgeCurzon, London et al., 2002

Lewis, John Wilson, and Xue Litai, *China Builds the Bomb*, Stanford University Press, Stanford, 1988

Lewis, John Wilson, and Xue Litai, *China's Strategic Seapower*, Stanford University Press, Stanford, 1994

Li Haiwen, interview with Shi Zhe, *CHUS*, vol. 5, no. 2 (1992)

Li Jui [Li Rui], *The Early Revolutionary Activities of Comrade Mao Tse-tung*, Sharpe, White Plains, 1977

Li Rui, "Lessons from the Lushan Plenum," *CLG*, vol. 29, no. 5 (1996)

Li, Xiaobing, et al., eds, *Mao's Generals Remember Korea*, University Press of Kansas, Lawrence, Kansas, 2001

Li, Zhisui, *The Private Life of Chairman Mao*, Chatto & Windus, London, 1994

Lih, Lars T., et al., eds, *Stalin's Letters to Molotov*, Yale University Press, New Haven et al., 1995

Lindsay, Michael, *The Unknown War: North China 1937–1945*, Bergström & Boyle, London, 1975

Lippa, Ernest M., *Captive Surgeon*, Morrow, New York, 1953

Litten, Frederick S., "Otto Braun's Curriculum Vitae—Translation and Commentary," *Twentieth-Century China*, vol. 23, no. 1 (1997)

Liu Jianping, "Mao Zedong's Perception of America and the Formation of New China's International Strategy of Leaning to One Side," *Social Sciences in China*, vol. 21, no. 3 (2000)

Liu Shao-chi, *Selected Works*, Foreign Languages Press, Peking, 1991, 2 vols

Liu Xiaohong, *Chinese Ambassadors*, University of Washington Press, Seattle, 2001

Lo Jung-huan, "Early Days of the Chinese Red Army," *PR*, 3 August 1963

Loboda, I. G., *Moskva–Pekin* (Moscow–Peking), Infra-M, Moscow, 1995

Loh, Robert, *Escape from Red China*, Coward-McCann, New York, 1962

Lum, Peter, *Peking 1950–1953*, Hale, London, 1958

Lurye, V. M., and Kochik, V. Y., *GRU: Dela i Lyudi* (The GRU: Deeds and People), Olma-Press, Moscow, 2002

Luthi, Lorens, "Les relations sino-soviétiques et l'effondrement de 'l'unité socialiste'," *Communisme*, nos. 74–75 (2003)

Luzianin, Sergei, "The Yalta Conference and Mongolia in International Law," *FEA*, no. 6, 1995

Lyudnikov, I. I., "Internationalist Assistance," in Chudodeyev, Y. V., ed., *Soviet Volunteers in China 1925–1945*, Progress, Moscow, 1980

MacFarquhar, Roderick, ed., *Sino-American Relations 1949–1971*, David & Charles/RIIA, Newton Abbot, 1972

MacFarquhar, Roderick, *The Origins of the Cultural Revolution*, Oxford University Press, London, 3 vols, 1974, 1983, 1997

MacFarquhar, Roderick, et al., eds, *The Secret Speeches of Chairman Mao: From the Hundred Flowers to the Great Leap Forward*, Harvard University Press, Cambridge, Mass., et al., 1989

MacKinnon, Janice R., & MacKinnon, Stephen R., *Agnes Smedley*, Virago, London, 1988

Mader, Julius, *Dr-Sorge-Report*, Militärverlag der DDR, Berlin, 1985

Maestrini, Nicholas, *My Twenty Years with the Chinese*, Magnificat Press, Avon, NJ, 1990

Malaparte, Curzio, *Io, in Russia e in Cina*, Mondadori, Milan, 1991

Malukhin, A. M., "Kulminatsiya osvoboditelnoy borbyi v Kitaye nakanune obrazovaniya KNR" (The Culmination of the liberation struggle in China on the eve of the formation of the PRC), *IB*, no. 87 (1977)

Malukhin, A., "Reminiscences of Veterans: A View from Guangzhou," *FEA*, no. 1, 1989

Malyisheva, M. P., & Poznansky, V. S., eds, *Dalnevostochnaya Politika Sovietskoy Rossii (1920–1922)* (The Far East Policy of Soviet Russia), Sibirskii Khronograf, Novosibirsk, 1996

Maneli, Mieczyslaw, *War of the Vanquished*, Harper & Row, New York et al., 1971

Mann, James, *About Face: A History of America's Curious Relationship with China, From Nixon to Clinton*, Knopf, New York, 1999

Mansourov, Alexandre Y., "Stalin, Mao, Kim, and China's Decision to Enter the Korean War, Sept. 16–Oct. 15, 1950: New Archival Evidence from the Russian Archives," *CWB*, nos 6–7 (1995–96)

Mansourov, Alexandre Y., "Communist War Coalition Formation and the Origins of the Korean War," Columbia University, PhD thesis, 1997

Mao Miscellany: Miscellany of Mao Tse-tung Thought (1949–1968), 2 parts, JPRS, Arlington, 1974

Mao Tse-tung, *Selected Works*, 5 vols, Foreign Languages Press, Peking, 1965, 1977

Mao Zedong, *Mao Zedong on Diplomacy*, Foreign Languages Publishing House, Beijing, 1998

Marcuse, Jacques, *The Peking Papers*, Dutton, New York, 1967

Marer, Paul, et al., *Historically Planned Economies*, World Bank, Washington, DC, 1992

Margolin, Jean-Louis, "China: A Long March into Night," in Courtois, Stéphane, et al., eds, *The Black Book of Communism*, Harvard University Press, Cambridge et al., 1999

Marks, Thomas A., *Maoist Insurgency Since Vietnam*, Cass, London, 1996

May, Ernest R., & Zelikow, Philip D., *The Kennedy Tapes*, Harvard University Press, Cambridge, 1997

Meissner, Werner, ed., *Die DDR und China 1949 bis 1990*, Akademie Verlag, Berlin, 1995

Melanson, Richard A., & Mayers, David, *Reevaluating Eisenhower: American Foreign Policy in the 1950s*, University of Illinois Press, Urbana et al., 1989

Melby, John F., *The Mandate of Heaven: Record of a Civil War, China 1945–49*, Chatto & Windus, London, 1969

Micunovic, Veljko, *Moscow Diary*, Doubleday, New York, 1980

Mif, P. (under pseudonym "Mao-Pin"), "Velikaya Oktyabrskaya revolyutsiya i Kitay" ("The Great October Revolution and China"), *Bolshevik*, no. 21, 1937

Mikoyan, Anastas, *Tak Byilo* (That's the Way It Was), Vagrius, Moscow, 1999

Mikoyan, Stepan Anastasovich, *Vospominaniya Voyennogo Letchik-Ispitatelya* (Memoirs of a Military Test Pilot), Tekhnika—molodezhi, Moscow, 2002

Mirovitskaya, R. A., *Sovietskii Soyuz i Kitay v period razryiva i vosstanovleniya otnoshenii (1928–1936)* (The Soviet Union and China in the period of the rupture and restoration of relations), *IB*, no. 67 (1975)

Mirovitskaya, R. A., "Sovietsko-kitayskiye otnosheniya: Problemyi voyennoy pomoshchi kompartii Kitaya v 1927–1929" (Military Aid to the CCP in 1927–1929), in Tikhvinsky, S. L., ed., *I Nye Raspalas Svyaz Vremen . . .* (And the Bond of Time did not Disintegrate . . .), Vostochnaya Literatura, Moscow, 1993

Mirovitskaya, R. A., *Kitayskaya Gosudarstvennost i Sovietsakaya Politika v Kitaye . . . 1941–1945* (Chinese Statehood and Soviet Policy in China), Pamyatnik Istoricheskoy Myisli, Moscow, 2000

Mitarevsky, N., *World Wide Soviet Plots*, Tientsin Press, Tientsin, 1927

Mitterrand, François, *La Chine au Défi*, Julliard, Paris, 1961

Montgomery, Bernard, *Three Continents*, Collins, London, 1962

Morgan, Kevin, *Harry Pollitt*, Manchester University Press, Manchester, 1993

Morgenthau Diary (China), US Senate, Committee on the Judiciary, Washington, DC, 1965, 2 vols

Morwood, William, *Duel for the Middle Kingdom*, Everest House, New York, 1980

Mukhitdinov, Nuriddin, *Godyi Provedennyiye v Kremlye* (Years in the Kremlin), Izd. Kadyiri, Tashkent, 1994

Mukhitdinov, Nuriddin, *Reka Vremeni* (The River of Time), "Rusti–Rosti," Moscow, 1995

Murfett, Malcolm H., *Hostage on the Yangtze: Britain, China and the Amethyst Crisis of 1949*, Naval Institute Press, Annapolis, 1991

Myrdal, Jan, *Report from a Chinese Village*, Pelican, Harmondsworth, 1967

N.a., "Jiang Jingguo in Russia," *FEA*, no. 2, 1992

Näth, Marie-Luise, ed., *Communist China in Retrospect: East European Sinologists Remember the First Fifteen Years of the PRC*, Lang, Frankfurt, 1995

Naughton, Barry, "The Third Front," *CQ*, no. 115 (1988)

Negin, Evgeny A., & Smirnov, Yuri N., "Did the USSR Share Atomic Secrets with China?," Parallel History Project, China and the Warsaw Pact, Web/PHP, 2002

Nenni, Pietro, *Tempo di Guerra Fredda*, Sugar, Milan, 1981

Nie Rongzhen, *Inside the Red Star: The Memoirs of Nie Rongzhen*, New World Press, Beijing, 1988

Nikiforov, V. N., "Maoistskaya Legenda i Sovietskaya Istoriografiya (1935–1939)" (The Mao Legend and Soviet Historiography), *IB*, no. 60 (1974)

Nixon, Richard, *The Memoirs of Richard Nixon*, Arrow Books, London, 1979

Ocherki Istorii Rossiiskoy Vneshnyey Razvedki (Essays in the History of Russian Foreign Intelligence), vols 4 (1941–5) & 5 (1945–65), Mezhdunarodnyie Otnosheniya, Moscow, 1999 & 2003

O'Reilly, Luke, *The Laughter and the Weeping*, Columba Press, Blackrock, 1991

Oudendyk, William J., *Ways and By-ways in Diplomacy*, P. Davies, London, 1939

Ovchinnikov, Yuri, ed., "Comintern–CCP Relations" (Part 2), *CLG*, vol. 30, no. 2 (1997)

Pak, Hyobom, ed., *Documents of the Chinese Communist Party 1927–1930*, URI, Hong Kong, 1971

Palden Gyatso, *Fire under the Snow: Testimony of a Tibetan Prisoner*, Harvill, London, 1998

Pan, Yihong, "An Examination of the Goals of the Rustication Program in the People's Republic of China," *Journal of Contemporary China*, no. 11, 2002

Panchen Lama, *A Poisoned Arrow: The Secret Report of the 10th Panchen Lama*, Tibet Information Network, London, 1997

Panikkar, K. M., *In Two Chinas*, Hyperion, Westport, 1981

Pantsov, Alexander, "The Soviet Impact and the Origins of 'Chinese Style' Socialism in Communist China in the 1950s," *Tamkang Journal of International Affairs*, vol. 6, no. 3 (2002)

Panyushkin, A. S., *Zapiski Posla: Kitay 1939–1944* (Notes of an Ambassador: China 1939–1944), USSR Academy of Sciences/Institute of the Far East, Moscow, 1981

Pashkovskaya, E. A., & Zhdanovich, V. G., "Khronologiya sovietsko-kitayskikh otnoshenii (1949–1965)" (Chronology of Soviet–Chinese Relations), *IB*, no. 25 (1969)

Paulsen, Friedrich (Frank Thilly, ed.), *A System of Ethics*, Scribner's, New York, 1899

Payne, Robert, *China Awake*, Heinemann, London et al., 1947

Payne, Robert, *Mao Tse-tung*, H. Schuman, New York, 1950

Peng Dehuai, *Memoirs of a Chinese Marshal*, Foreign Languages Publishing House, Beijing, 1984

Perkins, Dwight H., "Economic Policy," in *CHOC*, vol. 15, part 2 (1991)

Perry, Elizabeth J., & Li Xun, *Proletarian Power: Shanghai in the Cultural Revolution*, Westview, Boulder, 1997

Persico, Joseph E., *Roosevelt's Secret War: FDR and World War II Espionage*, Random House, New York, 2001

Persits, M., " 'Vostochnyi Front' Mirovoy Revolyutsii" ("The Eastern Front" of the World Revolution), *Svobodnaya Mysl*, no. 5, 1996

Persits, Moisei, "A New Collection of Documents on Soviet Policy in the Far East in 1920–1922," *FEA*, no. 5, 1997

Petri, Lennart, "Chinese Molestation of Diplomats," in Schoenhals 1996b

Peshchersky, V. L., " 'Vrag Moyego Vraga . . .' " (The Enemy of My Enemy . . .), *Voyenno-istoricheskii Zhurnal*, no. 3, 1998

Phandara, Y., *Retour à Phnom Penh*, Éditions Métailié, Paris, 1982

Philby, H. A. R., "Tibet: Bollwerk oder Durchzugsweg?" (Part 2), *Zeitschrift für Geopolitik*, vol. 13, no. 8 (1936)

Piatnitsky, Vladimir, *Zagovor protiv Stalina* (The Plot against Stalin), Sovremennik, Moscow, 1998

Pocock, Chris, *Dragon Lady: The History of the U-2 Spyplane*, Airlife, Shrewsbury, 1989

Prandi, Rev. Padre Pietro, letter in "La Rivoluzione comunista nelle lettere dei nostri missionari," *Le Missioni Francescane*, vol. 6 (1928)

Price, Robert L., "International Trade of Communist China, 1950–65," in US Congress, Joint Economic Committee

Prozumenshchikov, M. Y., "The Sino-India Conflict, the Cuban Missile Crisis, and the Sino-Soviet Split, October 1962," *CWB*, nos 8–9 (1996–7)

Prozumenshchikov, Mikhail, "The Year 1960 as Seen by Soviet and Chinese Leaders," *FEA*, no. 3, 1999

Quan Yanchi, *Mao Zedong: Man, not God*, Foreign Languages Publishing House, Beijing, 1992

Radványi, János, *Hungary and the Superpowers*, Hoover Institution Press, Stanford, 1972

Radványi, János, *Delusion & Reality*, Gateway, South Bend, 1978

Rakhmanin, O. B., "Vzaimootnosheniya I.V. Stalina i Mao Tszeduna Glazami

Ochevidna" (The Relations Between Stalin and Mao as Seen by an Eye-Witness), *NiNI*, no. 1, 1998

Rákosi, Mátyás, " 'Vidyel, kak voznikayet kult lichnosti': Mátyás Rákosi o Staline i o sebye" ("I saw how the cult of personality arises": Mátyás Rákosi on Stalin and himself), *Istochnik,* no. 1, 1997

Raphaël-Leygues, Jacques, *Ponts de Lianes: Missions en Indochine 1945–1954*, Hachette, Paris, 1976

Rittenberg, Sidney, & Bennett, Amanda, *The Man Who Stayed Behind*, Simon & Schuster, New York, 1993

Roberts, Priscilla, ed., *Window on the Forbidden City: The Beijing Diaries of David Bruce, 1973–1974*, Centre of Asian Studies, University of Hong Kong, Hong Kong, 2001

Roderick, John, *Covering China*, Imprint, Chicago, 1993

Romanov A. I., & Kharitonov, G. V., *"Podari solntse" Povest-khronika ob internatsionalnom detskom dome v Ivanove* ("Give the Sun": A Narrative Chronicle of the International Children's Home in Ivanovo), Yaroslavl, 1989

Roshchin, Sergei, review of Baabar, B., *Mongolia in the 20th Century, FEA*, no. 1, 1999

Rowinski, Jan, "China in the Crisis of Marxism-Leninism," in Näth

Rummel, R. J., *China's Bloody Century: Genocide and Mass Murder since 1900*, Transaction, New Brunswick et al., 1991

Rusk, Dean, *As I Saw It*, I. B. Tauris, London, 1991

Russell, Bertrand, *The Autobiography of Bertrand Russell*, vol. 2, Allen & Unwin, London, 1968

Russian [USSR] Ministry of Foreign Affairs, *SSSR-KNR (1949–1983): Dokumentyi i materialyi* (USSR-PRC (1949–1983): Documents and materials, vol. 1: 1949–63; vol. 2: 1964–83, Moscow, 1985

Russian [USSR] Ministry of Foreign Affairs, "Khronologiya Osnovnyikh Sobyitiya Kanuna i Nachalnogo Perioda Koreyskoy Voynyi (January 1949–October 1950)" (Chronology of Basic Events on the Eve of and in the early Period of the Korean War), unpublished, Moscow

Ryabushkin, D. S., "Ostrov Damansky, 2 marta 1969 goda" (Damansky Island, 2 March 1969), *Voprosyi Istorii*, no. 5, 2004

Saich, Tony, *The Origins of the First United Front in China: The Role of Sneevliet (alias Maring)*, 2 vols, Brill, Leiden et al., 1991

Saich, Tony, ed., *The Rise to Power of the Chinese Communist Party: Documents and Analysis*, Sharpe, Armonk et al., 1996

Salisbury, Harrison E., *The Long March*, Macmillan, London, 1985

Sandilands, Roger J., *The Life and Political Economy of Lauchlin Currie*, Duke University Press, Durham, NC et al., 1990

Sang Ye, *The Finish Line*, University of Queensland Press, St. Lucia, 1994

Sartre, Jean-Paul, "Introduction" ("Avant-propos") to Manceaux, Michèle, *Les Maos en France*, Gallimard, Paris, 1972

Schäfer, Bernd, "Weathering the Sino-Soviet Conflict: The GDR and North Korea, 1949–1989," *CWB*, nos 14–15 (2003–4)

Schäfer, Bernd, *North Korean "Adventurism" and China's Long Shadow, 1966–1972*, Washington DC, *Cold War International History Project Bulletin, Working Paper* no. 44, 2004

Schoenbaum, Thomas J., *Waging Peace and War: Dean Rusk*, Simon & Schuster, New York, 1988

Schoenhals, Michael, "Mao Zedong: Speeches at the 1957 'Moscow Conference'," *Journal of Communist Studies*, vol. 2, no. 2 (1986)

Schoenhals, Michael, *Saltationist Socialism: Mao Zedong and the Great Leap Forward 1958*,

Skrifter utgivna av Föreningen för Orientaliska Studier, 19, Stockholm University, Stockholm, 1987

Schoenhals, Michael, " 'Non-People' in the People's Republic of China: A Chronicle of Terminological Ambiguity," Indiana East Asian Working Paper on Language and Politics in Modern China, no. 4, Indiana University, Bloomington, 1994

Schoenhals, Michael, "The Central Case Examination Group," CQ, no. 145 (1996) [Schoenhals 1996a]

Schoenhals, Michael, ed., *China's Cultural Revolution, 1966–1969*, Sharpe, Armonk et al., 1996 [Schoenhals 1996b]

Schram, Stuart, ed., *The Political Thought of Mao Tse-tung*, Praeger, New York, 1965

Schram, Stuart, *Mao Tse-tung*, Penguin, Harmondsworth, 1966

Schram, Stuart, ed., *Mao Tse-tung Unrehearsed: Talks and Letters: 1956–71*, Penguin, Harmondsworth, 1974

Schram, Stuart, ed., *Mao's Road to Power*, 6 vols, Sharpe, Armonk et al., 1992–2004 [MRTP]

Schran, Peter, *Guerrilla Economy*, State University of New York Press, Albany, 1976

Seaborg, Glenn T., *Kennedy, Khrushchev and the Test Ban*, University of California Press, Berkeley et al., 1981

Semyonov, G. G., *Tri Goda v Pekine* (Three Years in Peking), Nauka, Moscow, 1978

Shapiro, Judith, *Mao's War Against Nature*, Cambridge University Press, Cambridge, 2001

Shen Zhihua, "The Discrepancy between the Russian and Chinese Versions of Mao's 2 October 1950 Message to Stalin on Chinese Entry into the Korean War," CWB, nos 8–9 (1996–7)

Shen Zhihua, "Sino-North Korean Conflict and its Resolution during the Korean War," CWB, nos 14–15 (2003–4)

Sheng, Michael M., *Battling Imperialism: Mao, Stalin, and the United States*, Princeton University Press, Princeton, 1997

Shepilov, Dmitrii, *Neprimknuvshii* (The Man Who Did Not Join), Vagrius, Moscow, 2001

Shevelyov, K., "On the History of the Formation of the Communist Party of China," FEA, no. 1, 1981

Shewmaker, Kenneth E., *Americans and Chinese Communists, 1927–1945: A Persuading Encounter*, Cornell University Press, Ithaca, 1971

Shi Zhe, "I Accompanied Chairman Mao," FEA, no. 2, 1989

Shi Zhe, "With Mao and Stalin," CHUS, vol. 5, no. 1 (1992)

Shi Zhe, "With Mao and Stalin (Part 2): Liu Shaoqi in Moscow," CHUS, vol. 6, no. 1 (1993)

Shichor, Yitzhak, *The Middle East in China's Foreign Policy 1949–1977*, Cambridge University Press, Cambridge, 1979

Siao, Emi, *Mao Tse-tung: His Childhood and Youth*, People's Publishing House, Bombay, 1953

Siao, Eva, *China—mein Traum, mein Leben*, ECON, Düsseldorf, 1994

Siao-yu, *Mao Tse-tung and I Were Beggars*, Collier, New York, 1973

Sidikhmenov, Vasili, "Stalin and Mao hearkened to us," NT, no. 5, 1993

Sidikhmenov MS: Sidikhmenov, Vasili, unpublished autobiography

Sihanouk, Norodom, *Charisma and Leadership*, Yohan, Tokyo, 1990

Sihanouk, Norodom, *My War with the CIA*, Penguin, Harmondsworth, 1974

Silin, K. S., "s missiyey druzhbyi" (With a mission of friendship), in Akimov

Singlaub, John K., *Hazardous Duty*, Summit Books, New York, 1991

Sladkovsky, M. I., ed., *Ocherki Istorii Kommunisticheskoy Partii Kitaya 1921–1969* (Essays in the history of the CCP), USSR Academy of Sciences/Institute of the Far East, Moscow, 1971

Slavinsky, Boris N., *Pakt o neutralitete mezhdu SSSR i Yaponiye* (The Neutrality Pact between the USSR and Japan), TOO "Novina," Moscow, 1995

Slavinsky, Boris, *SSSR i Yaponiya—na puti k voyne* (The USSR and Japan—On the Road to War), ZAO Segodnya, Moscow, 1999

Smedley, Agnes, *China's Red Army Marches*, International Publishers, New York, 1934

Smedley, Agnes, *Battle Hymn of China*, Gollancz, London, 1944

Smedley, Agnes, *The Great Road: The Life and Times of Chu Teh*, Monthly Review, New York, 1956

Smith, S. A., *A Road is Made: Communism in Shanghai 1920–1927*, Curzon, London, 2000

Sneath, David, "The Impact of the Cultural Revolution in China on the Mongolians of Inner Mongolia," *MAS*, vol. 28, no. 2 (1994)

Snow, Edgar, *Battle for Asia*, Random House, New York, 1941

Snow, Edgar, "The Divorce of Mao Tse-tung" (MS, c.1956)

Snow, Edgar, *Random Notes on Red China, 1936–1945*, Harvard University Press, Cambridge, Mass., 1968

Snow, Edgar, *Journey to the Beginning*, Vintage, New York, 1972

Snow, Edgar, *Red Star Over China*, Gollancz, London, 1973, revised and enlarged edn

Snow, Edgar, *China's Long Revolution*, Penguin, Harmondsworth, 1974

Snow, Helen Foster [Nym Wales], *My Yenan Notebooks*, mimeo 1961

Snow, Helen Foster [Nym Wales], *The Chinese Communists*, Book 2, Greenwood, Westport, 1972

Snow, Helen Foster, *Inside Red China*, Da Capo, New York, 1979

Snow, Philip, *The Star Raft: China's Encounter with Africa*, Cornell University Press, Ithaca, 1988

Sontag, Raymond James, & Beddie, James Stuart, *Nazi–Soviet Relations 1939–1941: Documents from the Archives of The German Foreign Office*, US Department of State, Washington, DC, 1948

SPK News Agency, *The People's Republic of Kampuchea*, SPK, Phnom Penh, 1979

Stalin, Iosif, "Joseph Stalin's Unpublished Speech on China" (5 April 1927), *PDV*, no. 1, 2001 [Stalin 2001a]; *FEA*, no. 1, 2001 [Stalin 2001b]

Stanchi, Fr. Giacinto, Changsha, 1 March 1929, letter in *Le Missioni Francescane*, vol. 6, 1928

Stenograficheskii otchet VI-go Syezda Kommunisticheskoy Partii Kitaya (Stenographic Report of the 6th Congress of the CCP), Nauchno Issledovatelskii Institut po Kitayu (Scientific Research Institute on China) Moscow, 1930, 6 vols

Stewart, James T., ed., *Airpower: The Decisive Force in Korea*, Van Nostrand, Princeton, 1957

Stokes, William, "Maoist Insurgency in Thailand," in Green, Marshall, et al., eds, *War and Peace in China*, DACOR-Bacon House, Bethesda, 1994

Strong, Anna Louise, *Dawn out of China*, People's Publishing House, Bombay, 1948

Strong, Anna Louise, "The Thought of Mao Tse-tung," *Amerasia*, June 1947

Strong, Tracy B., & Keyssar, Helene, *Right in her Soul: The Life of Anna Louise Strong*, Random House, New York, 1983

Summers, Anthony, *The Arrogance of Power: The Secret World of Richard Nixon*, Gollancz, London, 2000

Sun Xiaolei, "Blood and Tears on the Balin Grasslands," in Walder, Andrew G., & Gong Xiaoxia, eds, "China's Great Terror," *Chinese Sociology and Anthropology*, vol. 26, no. 1 (1993)

Suo Guoxin, "78 Days in 1967: The True Story of the 'February Countercurrent' " (Forster, Keith, ed.), *CLG*, vol. 22, no. 1 (1989)

Sutton, Donald S., "Consuming Counterrevolution: The Ritual and Culture of Cannibalism in Wuxuan, Guangxi, China, May to July 1968," *Comparative Studies in Society and History*, vol. 37, no. 1 (1995)

Szalontai, Balázs, " 'You Have No Political Line of Your Own': Kim Il Sung and the Soviets, 1953–1964," *CWB*, nos. 14–15 (2003–4)

Takahashi, Hisashi, "Japanese Intelligence Estimates of China, 1931–1945," in Hitchcock, Walter T., ed., *The Intelligence Revolution*, US Air Force Academy et al., Washington, DC, 1991

Tálas, Barna, "China in the Early 1950s," in Näth

Taubman, William, "Khrushchev vs. Mao: A Preliminary Sketch of the Role of Personality in the Sino-Soviet Split," *CWB*, nos 8–9 (1996–7)

Taylor, Jay, *China and Southeast Asia: Peking's Relations with Revolutionary Movements*, Praeger, New York, 1974

Taylor, Jay, *The Generalissimo's Son: Chiang Ching-kuo and the Revolutions in China and Taiwan*, Harvard University Press, Cambridge, Mass., 2000

Teiwes, Frederick C., *Politics at Mao's Court: Gao Gang and Party Factionalism in the Early 1950s*, Sharpe, Armonk et al., 1990

Teiwes, Frederick C., *Politics and Purges in China*, Sharpe, Armonk et al., 2nd. edn, 1993

Teiwes, Frederick C., & Sun, Warren, *The Tragedy of Lin Biao*, University of Hawaii Press, Honolulu, 1996

Teiwes, Frederick C., with Sun, Warren, *China's Road to Disaster: Mao, Central Politicians, and Provincial Leaders in the Unfolding of the Great Leap Forward 1955–1959*, Sharpe, Armonk et al., 1999

Terrill, Ross, *Madame Mao*, Bantam, New York, 1986

Terzani, Tiziano, *The Forbidden Door*, Asia 2000, Hong Kong, 1985

Thomas, S. Bernard, *Season of High Adventure: Edgar Snow in China*, University of California Press, Berkeley et al., 1996

Tikhomirov, V. V., & Tsukanov, A. M., "Komandirovka v Manchzhuriyu" (Assignment to Manchuria), in Akimov

Tikhvinsky, S., "New Facts About Zhou Enlai's 'Secret Démarche' and the CPC's Informal Negotiations with the Americans in June 1949," *FEA*, no. 1, 1994

Tikhvinsky, S. L., *Put Kitaya k Obyedineniyu i Nezavisimosti 1898–1949: Po materialam biografii Zhou Enlaya* (China's Route to Unity and Independence: On Materials of a Biography of Chou En-lai, 1898–1949), Vostochnaya Literatura, Russian Academy of Sciences, Moscow, 1996

Tikhvinsky, S. L., et al., eds, *Russko-kitayskiye otnosheniya v XX veke: sovietsko-kitayskiye otnosheniya: Materialyi i dokumentyi* (Russo-Chinese Relations in the 20th Century: Materials & Documents), vol. 4 (1937–1945); book 1: 1937–1944; book 2: 1945, Pamyatnik Istoricheskoy Myisli, Moscow, 2000

Tikhvinsky, S. L., *Vozvrashcheniye k Vorotam Nebesnogo Spokoystviya* (Return to the Gate of Heavenly Peace), Pamyatnik Istoricheskoy Myisli, Moscow, 2002

Tin, Bui, *Following Ho Chi Minh: Memoirs of a North Vietnamese Colonel*, Hurst, London, 1995

Titarenko, M. L., ed., *Kommunisticheskii Internatsional i kitayskaya revolyutsiya: Dokumentyi i materialyi* (The Communist International and the Chinese Revolution: Documents & Materials), Nauka, Moscow, 2002 [many of the documents in this volume regarding China are in English on Web/Dimitrov]

Titov, A. S., *Materialyi k politicheskoy biografii Mao Tsze-duna* (Materials towards a Political Biography of Mao Tse-tung), 3 vols, USSR Academy of Sciences/Institute of the

Far East, Moscow; vol. 1: to 1935 (1969); vol. 2: 1935–7 (1970); vol. 3 (titled *Borba Mao Tsze-duna za Vlast, 1936–1945*) (Mao Tse-tung's Struggle for Power), (1974) [Titov, vol. 1, 2, 3]

Titov, A., "About the Tsunyi Conference," *FEA*, no. 1, 1976

Titov, Alexander, "Looking Back on My Work in China in 1948–1950," *FEA*, no. 5, 1995

Titov, A. S., *Borba za Yedinyi Natsionalnyi Front v Kitaye 1935–1937* (The Struggle for a United National Front in China), Nauka, Moscow, 1979

Tong, Te-kong, & Li Tsung-jen, *The Memoirs of Li Tsung-jen*, Westview, Boulder, 1979

Torkunov, A. V., *Zagadochnaya Voyna: Koreyskii Konflikt 1950–1953* (A Mysterious War: The Korean Conflict), Rosspen, Moscow, 2000

Trampedach, Tim, "Chiang Kaishek between revolution and militarism, 1926/27," in Leutner

Trevelyan, Humphrey, *The Middle East in Revolution*, Macmillan, London, 1970

Trevelyan, Humphrey, *Living with the Communists*, Gambit, Boston, 1971

Troyanovsky, Oleg, *Cherez godyi i rasstoyaniya ...* (Through the Years and Distances ...), Vagrius, Moscow, 1997

Trudeau, Pierre Elliott, *Memoirs*, McLelland & Stewart, Toronto, 1993

Tsang, Steve, "Target Zhou Enlai: The 'Kashmir Princess' Incident of 1955," *CQ*, no. 139 (1994)

Tsedenbal, Y., "Iz vospominanii Yumzhagiyna Tsedenbala" (From the Memoirs of Y. Tsedenbal), *Vostok*, no. 5, 1994

Tsering Shakya, *The Dragon in the Land of the Snows*, Pimlico, London, 1999

Tsou, Tang, *America's Failure in China, 1941–1950*, University of Chicago Press, Chicago et al., 1963

Tucker, Nancy Bernkopf, ed., *China Confidential: American Diplomats and Sino-American Relations, 1945–1996*, Columbia University Press, New York, 2001

Tyler, Patrick, *A Great Wall: Six Presidents and China*, Public Affairs, New York, 1999

Union Research Institute, *The Case of Peng Teh-huai 1959–1968*, URI, Hong Kong, 1968

Union Research Institute, *Collected Works of Liu Shao Ch'i*, 3 vols, URI, Hong Kong, 1969

US Congress, Joint Economic Committee, *An Economic Profile of Mainland China*, Praeger, New York, 1968

US Department of State, *United States Relations with China* ["White Paper"], US Department of State, Washington, DC, 1949

US Senate, Foreign Relations Committee, *Economic Assistance to China and Korea 1949–50*, Garland, New York et al., 1979

Usov, Viktor, "Ubit v chuzhoy strane: Na chuzhoy voyne: Starshii syin 'velikogo kormchego' " ("To Be Killed in a Foreign Land, in a Foreign War: The Eldest Son of the 'Great Helmsman' "), *NV*, no. 38, 1992

Usov, V., "Kitayskiye vospitanniki interdomov Rossii" (Chinese Pupils in International Homes in Russia), *PDV*, no. 4, 1997

Usov, Viktor, *Sovietskaya Razvedka v Kitaye: 20-e godyi XX veka* (Soviet Intelligence in China in the 1920s), Olma-Press, Moscow, 2002

Usov, Viktor, "Ryichaniye 'bumazhnogo tigra': Kak atomnyi vopros isportil druzhbu SSSR i Kitaya" ("The Growl of the 'Paper Tiger': How the atomic Issue spoiled the Friendship between the USSR and China"), *Stolichniye Novosti*, no. 31, 2003

Vaksberg, Arkadi, *Hôtel Lux: Les partis frères au service de l'Internationale communiste*, Fayard, Paris, 1993

van Coillie, Dries, *I Was Brainwashed in Peking*, 's-Hertogenbosch, 1969 van de Ven, Hans J., *From Friend to Comrade: The Founding of the Chinese Communist Party, 1920–1927*, University of California Press, Berkeley et al., 1991

van de Ven, Hans J., *War and Nationalism in China 1925–1945*, RoutledgeCurzon, London, 2003

Van Slyke, Lyman, "The Battle of the Hundred Regiments," *MAS*, vol. 30, no. 4 (1996)

Vartanov, V. N., *Operatsiya "Z": Sovietskiye dobrovoltsyi v antiyaponskoy voyne kitayskogo naroda v 30–40 gg.* (Operation "Z": Soviet volunteers in the anti-Japanese war of the Chinese people in the 1930s–1940s), Institute of Military History, Moscow, 1992

Vereshchagin, B. N., *V starom i novom Kitaye* (In Old and New China), Institute of the Far East, Moscow, 1999

Viet Nam, *The Truth about Vietnam–China Relations over the Last Thirty Years*, Ministry of Foreign Affairs, Hanoi, 1979

Vinarov, Ivan, *Boytsi na Tikhiya Front* (Fighters on the Secret Front), Izd. na BKP, Sofia, 1969

VKP(b), Komintern i Kitay: Dokumentyi (The A-UCP(b), the Comintern and China: Documents), Titarenko, M. L., et al., eds, 4 vols (1920–37) to date, Moscow, 1994–2003

Vladimirov, O. & Ryazantsev, V., *Mao Tse-tung: A Political Portrait*, Progress, Moscow, 1976

Vladimirov, P. P., *Osobyi Rayon Kitaya* (The Special Region of China), Novosti, Moscow, 1973 [ORK]

Vladimirov, Peter, *The Vladimirov Diaries: Yenan, China: 1942–1945*, Hale, London, 1976

Vladimirov, Y., "The Question of Soviet-Chinese Economic Relations in 1950–1966," *Chinese Economic Studies*, vol. 3, no. 1 (1969)

Vlasov, Yuri, "The Story of My Father," *FEA*, nos 1 & 2, 1991

Volkogonov, Dmitri, *Stalin*, Grove Weidenfeld, New York, 1991

Volkogonov, Dmitri, *The Rise and Fall of the Soviet Empire*, HarperCollins, London, 1998

Volokhova, Alena, "Armistice Talks in Korea (1951–1953)," *FEA*, no. 2, 2000

Waack, William, *Camaradas*, Companhia das Letras, São Paulo, 1993

Wada, Haruki, "The Korean War, Stalin's Policy, and Japan," *Social Science Japan Journal*, vol. 1, no. 1 (1998)

Walder, Andrew G., *Communist Neo-traditionalism: Work and Authority in Chinese Industry*, University of California Press, Berkeley et al., 1988

Walder, Andrew G., & Su, Yang, "The Cultural Revolution in the Countryside: Scope, Timing and Human Impact," *CQ*, no. 173 (2003)

Walters, Vernon A., *Silent Missions*, Doubleday, Garden City, 1978

Wang, Anna, *Ich kämpfte für Mao*, C. Wegner, Hamburg, 1964

Wang Fan-hsi, *Chinese Revolutionary* (translated & introduced by Gregor Benton), Oxford University Press, Oxford, 1980

Wang Li, "An Insider's Account of the Cultural Revolution" (Schoenhals, Michael, ed.), *CLG*, vol. 27, no. 6 (1994)

Wang Li, "The First Year of the 'Cultural Revolution' " (Schoenhals, Michael, ed.), *CLG*, vol. 32, no. 4 (1999)

Wang Ming, *Mao's Betrayal*, Progress, Moscow, 1979

Watt, George, *China "Spy,"* Johnson, London, 1972

Weathersby, Kathryn, *"Should We Fear This?" Stalin and the Danger of War with America*, Cold War International History Project, Working Paper no. 39, Washington, DC, 2002

Wedemeyer, Albert C., *Wedemeyer Reports!*, Henry Holt, New York, 1958

Wei Jingsheng, *The Courage to Stand Alone*, Viking, New York, 1997

Wei Kouo-lou, *Chou En-lai durant la Longue Marche*, Foreign Languages Press, Peking, 1979

Werner, Ruth, *Sonya's Report*, Chatto & Windus, London, 1991

Westad, Odd Arne, *Cold War & Revolution: Soviet-American Rivalry and the Origins of the Chinese Civil War*, Columbia University Press, New York, 1993

Westad, Odd Arne, ed., *Brothers in Arms: The Rise and Fall of the Sino-Soviet Alliance*, Stanford University Press, Stanford, 1998

Westad, Odd Arne, et al., eds, *77 Conversations Between Chinese and Foreign Leaders on the Wars in Indochina, 1964–1977*, Cold War International History Project, Working Paper no. 22, Washington, DC, 1998

Westad, Odd Arne, *Decisive Encounters: The Chinese Civil War, 1946–1950*, Stanford University Press, Stanford, 2003

White, Theodore H., *In Search of History*, Harper & Row, New York, 1978

Whiting, Allen S., and Sheng Shih-ts'ai, *Sinkiang: Pawn or Pivot?*, Michigan State University Press, East Lansing, 1958

Whitlam, Gough, *The Whitlam Government 1972–1975*, Viking, Ringwood, 1985

Wilbur, C. Martin, & How, Julie Lien-ying, *Missionaries of Revolution: Soviet Advisers and Nationalist China, 1920–1927*, Harvard University Press, Harvard, 1989

Willeke, Bernward H., "Franciscan Mission Work in Northern Shensi: Mission of Yenanfu," MS, Franciscan Archives, Rome, 1984

Wingrove, Paul, "Mao in Moscow, 1949–50: Some New Archival Evidence," *Journal of Communist Studies & Transition Politics*, vol. 11, no. 4 (1995)

Wingrove, Paul, "Gao Gang and the Moscow Connection: Some Evidence from Russian Sources," *Journal of Communist Studies & Transition Politics*, vol. 16, no. 4 (2000)

Wishnick, Elizabeth, *Mending Fences: The Evolution of Moscow's China Policy from Brezhnev to Yeltsin*, University of Washington Press, Seattle et al., 2001

Witke, Roxane, *Comrade Chiang Ching*, Weidenfeld & Nicolson, London, 1977

Witke, Roxane, "The Last Days of Madame Mao," *Vanity Fair*, Dec. 1991

Wolf, Markus, *Memoirs of a Spymaster*, Pimlico, London, 1998

Wolff, David, *"One Finger's Worth of Historical Events": New Russian and Chinese Evidence on the Sino-Soviet Alliance and Split, 1948–1959*, Cold War International History Project, Working Paper no. 30, Washington, D.C., 2000

Wood, Frances, *Hand-Grenade Practice in Peking*, J. Murray, London, 2000

Woody, W. (Schoenhals, Michael, ed.), *The Cultural Revolution in Inner Mongolia*, Centre for Pacific Asia Studies, Stockholm University, Stockholm, 1993

Wu Xiuquan, *Eight Years in the Ministry of Foreign Affairs*, New World Press, Beijing, 1985

Xiang, Lanxin, *Mao's Generals: Chen Yi and the New Fourth Army*, University of America Press, Lanham, 1998

Xu Xiangqian, "The Purchase of Arms from Moscow," in Li, X., et al., 2001

Yan Jiaqi & Gao Gao, *Turbulent Decade: A History of the Cultural Revolution*, University of Hawai'i Press, Honolulu, 1996

Yang, Benjamin, "The Zunyi Conference as One Step in Mao's Rise to Power," CQ, no. 106 (1986)

Yang, Benjamin, *From Revolution to Politics: Chinese Communists on the Long March*, Westview, Boulder, 1990

Yang, Dali L., *Calamity and Reform in China*, Stanford University Press, Stanford, 1996

Yang Kuisong, "The Sino-Soviet Border Clash of 1969," CWH, vol. 1, no. 1 (2000)

Yang Kuisong, "Changes in Mao Zedong's Attitude toward the Indochina War, 1949–1973," Cold War International History Project, Working Paper no. 34, Washington, DC, 2002

Ybañez, Celestino, *Episodios Misioneros*, Franciscan Procuration, Shanghai, 1949

Yeh, K. C., "Soviet and Communist Chinese Industrialization Strategies," in Treadgold, Donald W., ed., *Soviet and Chinese Communism: Similarities and Differences*, University of Washington Press, Seattle, 1967

Yick, Joseph K. S., "Communist Puppet Collaboration in Japanese-Occupied China," *Intelligence & National Security*, vol. 16, no. 4 (2001)

Young, Édouard, "La Mission de Nananfu du 18 au 27 janvier 1929," *Annales de la Congrégation de la Mission*, vol. 94, no. 4 (1929)

Yu, Chen Liang, & Buckwell, Allan, *Chinese Grain Economy and Policy*, CAB International, Oxford, 1991

Yu, Maochun, *OSS in China: Prelude to Cold War*, Yale University Press, New Haven et al., 1996

Yu Miin-ling, "A reassessment of Chiang Kaishek and the policy of alliance with the Soviet Union, 1923–1927," in Leutner

Yu-Ang-Li, "The Communist International and the Foundation of the C.P. of China," *Communist International*, vol. 6. nos. 9–10 (1929)

Zagoria, Donald S., *The Sino-Soviet Conflict 1956–1961*, Atheneum, New York, 1967

Zakharov, M. V., ed., *Finale*, Progress, Moscow, 1972

Zazerskaya, Tatiana, "URSS–Chine populaire, 'l'aide fraternelle'," *Communisme*, nos. 49–50 (1997)

Zazerskaya, T. G., *Sovietskiye Spetsialistyi i Formirovaniye Voyenno-Promyishlennogo Kompleksa Kitaya* (Soviet Specialists and the Formation of China's Military-Industrial Complex), St. Petersburg State University, St. Petersburg, 2000

Zhai, Qiang, *China and the Vietnam Wars, 1950–1975*, University of North Carolina Press, Chapel Hill et al., 2000

Zhang, Shu Guang, *Economic Cold War: America's Embargo against China and the Sino-Soviet Alliance, 1949–1963*, Stanford University Press, Stanford, 2001

Zhang, Shu Guang, *Deterrence and Strategic Culture: Chinese-American Confrontations, 1949–1958*, Cornell University Press, Ithaca, 1992

Zhang, Shu Guang, *Mao's Military Romanticism: China and the Korean War*, University Press of Kansas, Lawrence, Kansas, 1995

Zhang, Shuguang, & Chen, Jian, eds, *Chinese Communist Foreign Policy and the Cold War in Asia: New Documentary Evidence, 1944–1950*, Imprint, Chicago, 1996

Zhang Songshan, "On the 'He Long Case Group' " (in Schoenhals, Michael, ed., "Mao's Great Inquisition"), *CLG*, vol. 29, no. 3 (1996)

Zhang, Xiaoming, *Red Wings Over the Yalu: China, the Soviet Union, and the Air War in Korea*, Texas A&M University Press, College Station, 2002

Zhang Yufeng, "Anecdotes of Mao Zedong and Zhou Enlai in Their Later Years" (Part 1), *FBIS-CHI-89-017* (27 Jan. 1989)

Zhang Yunsheng, "True Account of *Maojiawan*: Reminiscences of Lin Biao's Secretary" (Sullivan, Lawrence R., & Liu, Nancy, eds), *CLG*, vol. 26, no. 2 (1993)

Zheng Chaolin, *An Oppositionist for Life: Memoirs of the Chinese Revolutionary Zheng Chaolin* (edited and translated by Gregor Benton), Humanities Press, Atlantic Highlands, 1997

Zheng Yi, *Scarlet Memorial: Tales of Cannibalism in Modern China*, Boulder, Westview, 1996

Zhivkov, Todor, *Memoari* (Memoirs), "SIV" AD—"ABAGAR" EOOD, Sofia, 1997

Zhou Enlai, *Selected Works*, vol. 2, Foreign Languages Press, Beijing, 1989

Zhu, Fang, *Gun Barrel Politics: Party–Army Relations in Mao's China*, Westview, Boulder, 1998

Zimonin, Viacheslav, "The Soviet-Japanese War of 1945," *FEA*, no. 4, 1995

Zubok, Vladislav, " 'Look What Chaos in the Beautiful Socialist Camp!': Deng Xiaoping and the Sino-Soviet Split, 1956–1963," *CWB*, no. 10 (1998)

Zubok, Vladislav, & Pleshakov, Constantine, *Inside the Kremlin's Cold War*, Harvard University Press, Cambridge, Mass., 1996

Since we completed our book, all the cables we cited (from Russian archives) between Mao and Stalin in the years 1947–1949, plus the reports of Anastas Mikoyan from China to Stalin in January-February 1949, and many other previously unpublished documents have become available in Tikhvinsky, S. L., et al., eds., *Russko-kitayskiye otnosheniya v XX veke: sovietsko-kitayskiye otnosheniya: Materialyi i dokumentyi*, vol. V (1946-fevral [February] 1950); book 1: 1946–1948; book 2: 1949–fevral 1950 (Russo-Chinese Relations in the 20th Century . . . Materials & Documents) (Moscow, Pamyatnik Istoricheskoy Myisli, 2005) [Tikhvinsky 2005].

WEB REFERENCES
Web/Dimitrov
http://www.marxists.org/reference/archive/dimitrov/works/1937/china1.htm
http://www.revolutionarydemocracy.org/rdv2n2/dimitrov.htm
http://www.revolutionarydemocracy.org/rdv5n2/dimitrov.htm
Web/JPRS
http://e-asia.uoregon.edu
http://www.marxists.org/reference/archive/mao/works/collected-works/index.htm
Web/NSA
http://www2.gwu.edu/~nsarchiv/NSAEBB/
http://www2.gwu.edu/~nsarchiv/nsa/publications/china-us/index.html
Web/PHP
http://www.isn.ethz.ch/php/

Diaries (Dimitrov; P. P. Vladimirov) are referenced by date entry only. References to the names "Dimitrov" and "Vladimirov" alone are to their diaries.

PHOTOGRAPHIC CREDITS

Photograph no. 10, by Auguste François, is reproduced by
permission of Réunion des Musées Nationaux; no. 14, by Cecil
Beaton, by permission of the Beaton Estate; no. 16, by permission of Getty Images; no. 19, by permission of Wang Danzhi;
nos. 29 and 39, by permission of the Rossiiskii Gosudarstvennyi
Arkhiv Kinofotodokumentov (the Russian State Archive of
Photodocuments); no. 34, by Henri Cartier-Bresson, by
permission of Magnum Photos; no. 45, by Du Xiuxian; no. 53,
by Lu Houmin; nos. 61, 63, 64 and 65, by Li Zhensheng; nos.
67, 72, 76 and 77, by Du Xiuxian.

THE CHINA READER
The Reform Era
edited by Orville Schell and David Shambaugh

Perhaps no nation in recent history has undergone as total a transformation as China has in the past twenty-five years. *The China Reader* is a fascinating compilation of the most important documents, articles, and statements on China from 1972 to the present. Here are the voices of the experts and the artifacts of an era from Chinese analyses of the fall of Soviet Communism to regulations to control Chinese cyberspace. Authoritative and comprehensive, *The China Reader* is a timely guide to understanding a nation in the throes of change.

Current Affairs/Asian Studies/0-679-76387-2

CHINA WAKES
The Struggle for the Soul of a Rising Power
by Nicholas D. Kristof and Sheryl WuDunn

"When China wakes, it will shake the world," Napoleon predicted, and at last China is waking. And in the twenty-first century, its economy is rapidly outstripping those of the United States and Japan. Yet China is a nation where women are sold on the open market and crooked factories peddle "antibiotics" made from talcum powder. In this heroically researched book, two Pulitzer Prize–winning *New York Times* reporters travel from the highlands of Tibet to the bloody environs of Tiananmen Square and produce a canvas that is insightful, affecting, and bursting with color on every page.

Asian Studies/0-679-76393-7

DRAGON LADY
The Life and Legend of the Last Empress of China
by Sterling Seagrave

The Last Empress has been remembered as one of history's most monstrous women—a ruthless Manchu concubine who seduced and murdered her way to the throne in 1861 to rule China through perversion, corruption, and intrigue for half a century. Yet Sterling Seagrave's magnificent biography of the Dowager Empress Tzu Hsi is both a timely reassessment of the myth and an unsparing account of the imperialism from which it arose.

Biography/0-679-73369-8

RED AZALEA
by Anchee Min

Red Azalea is Anchee Min's celebrated memoir of growing up in the last years of Mao's China. As a child, she was asked to publicly humiliate a teacher; at seventeen, Min was sent to work at a labor collective. Forbidden to speak, dress, read, write, or love as she pleased, she found a lifeline in a secret love affair with another woman. Miraculously selected for the film version of one of Madame Mao's political operas, Min's life changed overnight. Then Chairman Mao suddenly died, taking with him an entire world. A revelatory and disturbing portrait of China, *Red Azalea* is exceptional for its candor, poignancy, courage, and for its delicate and evocative prose.

Memoir/1-4000-9698-7

RED CHINA BLUES
My Long March From Mao to Now
by Jan Wong

Jan Wong, a Canadian of Chinese descent, went to China as a starry-eyed Maoist at the height of the Cultural Revolution. A true believer—and one of only two Westerners permitted to enroll at Beijing University—she renounced rock and roll, hauled pig manure in the paddy fields, and turned in a fellow student who sought her help in getting to the United States. And through the individuals and events she encounters during her years as a correspondent in China, Wong reveals long-hidden dimensions of the world's most populous nation, and comes to terms with the legacy of her ancestral homeland.

Memoir/0-385-48232-9

RED DUST
A Path Through China
by Ma Jian

In 1983, at the age of thirty, dissident artist Ma Jian finds himself divorced by his wife, separated from his daughter, betrayed by his girlfriend, facing arrest for "Spiritual Pollution," and severely disillusioned with the confines of life in Beijing. So with little more than a change of clothes and two bars of soap, Ma took off to immerse himself in the remotest parts of China. His journey would last three years and take him through smog-choked cities and mountain villages, from scenes of barbarity to havens of tranquility. Remarkably written and subtly moving, the result is an insight into the teeming contradictions of China.

Travel/Asia/0-385-72023-8

SON OF THE REVOLUTION
by Liang Heng and Judith Shapiro

Liang Heng was born in 1954 in Changsha, a large city in Central China. His parents were intellectuals—his father a reporter on a major provincial newspaper, his mother a ranking cadre in the local police. This is Liang Heng's own story of growing up in the turmoil of the Great Cultural Revolution. His story is unique, but at the same time it is in many ways typical of those millions of young Chinese who have been tested almost beyond endurance in recent years. In his words we hear an entire generation speaking.

Memoir/0-394-72274-4

WILD GRASS
Three Stories of Change in Modern China
by Ian Johnson

In *Wild Grass*, Pulitzer Prize–winning journalist Ian Johnson tells the stories of three ordinary Chinese citizens moved to extraordinary acts of courage: a peasant legal clerk who filed a class-action suit on behalf of overtaxed farmers, a young architect who defended the rights of dispossessed homeowners, and a bereaved woman who tried to find out why her elderly mother had been beaten to death in police custody. Representing the first cracks in the otherwise seamless façade of Communist Party control, these small acts of resistance demonstrate the unconquerable power of the human conscience and prophesy an increasingly open political future for China.

Current Affairs/Asia/0-375-71919-9

VINTAGE AND ANCHOR BOOKS
Available at your local bookstore, or call toll-free to order:
1-800-793-2665 (credit cards only).